Encyclopedia of the Third World

Third Edition

Volume III
(Philippines to Zimbabwe)

by George Thomas Kurian

Facts On File, Inc.
New York, New York • Oxford, England

Encyclopedia of the Third World
Third Edition

Copyright © 1978, 1982, 1987 by Facts On File, Inc.

Library of Congress Cataloging in Publication Data

Kurian, George Thomas
  The encyclopedia of the Third World.

  Bibliography: p.
  Includes index.
  1. Developing countries—Dictionaries. I. Title.
HC59.7.K87   1986   909'.09724   84-10129
ISBN 0-8160-1118-4 3 Vol. Set
ISBN 0-8160-1119-2 Vol. 1
ISBN 0-8160-1120-6 Vol. 2
ISBN 0-8160-1121-4 Vol. 3

9 8 7 6 5 4 3 2 1

PRINTED IN THE UNITED STATES OF AMERICA

Volume III
(Philippines to Zimbabwe)

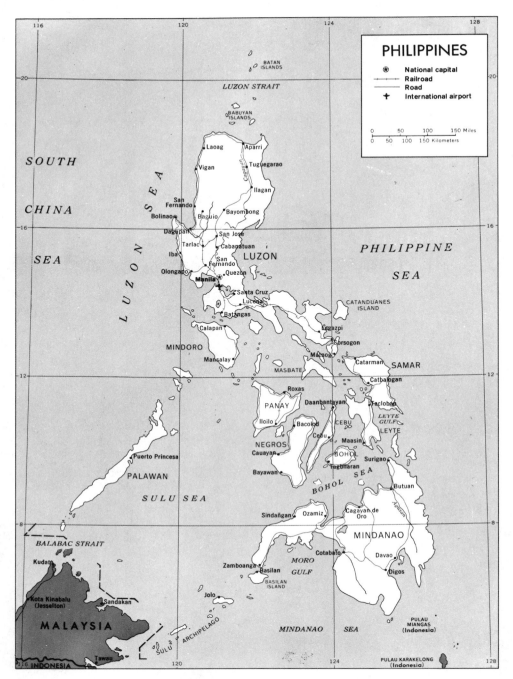

PHILIPPINES

- ⊛ National capital
- ┼┼┼ Railroad
- ─── Road
- ✈ International airport

0   50   100   150 Miles
0 50 100 150 Kilometers

SOUTH

CHINA

SEA

LUZON SEA

LUZON STRAIT

BATAN
ISLANDS

BABUYAN
ISLANDS

Laoag   Aparri

Vigan   Tuguegarao

Ilagan

San
Fernando   Bayombong

Bolinao   Baguio

Dagupan   San Jose

Tarlac   Cabanatuan   LUZON

Iba   San
Fernando

Olongapo   Quezon

Manila

Santa Cruz

Lucena

Batangas

Calapan

MINDORO

Mansalay

PHILIPPINE

SEA

CATANDUANES
ISLAND

Legazpi

Sorsogon

Masbate

MASBATE   Catarman   SAMAR

Catbalogan

Roxas

PANAY   Daanbantayan   Tacloban

Iloilo   Bacolod

CEBU   *LEYTE
GULF*   LEYTE

Cebu

NEGROS   Maasin

Puerto Princesa   Cauayan   BOHOL

Tagbilaran   Surigao

Bayawan

PALAWAN   *BOHOL   SEA*   Butuan

SULU SEA

Sindangan   Ozamiz   Cagayan de
Oro

BALABAC STRAIT   MINDANAO

Kudat   Cotabato   Davao

Zamboanga   Basilan   *MORO
GULF*   Digos

BASILAN
ISLAND

Kota Kinabalu
(Jesselton)   Sandakan

Jolo

MALAYSIA   *SULU   ARCHIPELAGO*

Tawau

INDONESIA   *MINDANAO   SEA*

PULAU
MIANGAS
(Indonesia)

PULAU KARAKELONG
(Indonesia)

PHILIPPINES

BASIC FACT SHEET

OFFICIAL NAME: Republic of the Philippines (Republika ng Pilipina) (*Note:* The 1973 constitution calls for a change in the name of the country to Maharlika [Pilipino for noble] but the change has not yet been implemented.)

ABBREVIATION: PH

CAPITAL: Manila

HEAD OF STATE & HEAD OF GOVERNMENT: President Corazon Aquino (from 1986).

NATURE OF GOVERNMENT: Partial Democracy

POPULATION: 56,808,000 (1985)

AREA: 299,404 sq km (115,600 sq mi)

ETHNIC MAJORITY: Filipino

LANGUAGES: Pilipino (also known as Tagalog) and English

RELIGION: Roman Catholicism

UNIT OF CURRENCY: Peso ($1 =P18.666, August 1985)

NATIONAL FLAG: A white equilateral triangle at the hoist with a blue stripe extending from its upper side and a red stripe from its lower side. In the middle of the triangle is a bright yellow sunburst with eight rays (representing the eight provinces to rise in revolt against Spain in 1896). There is a star on each cor-ner of the triangle representing Luzon, Visayas and Mindanao.

NATIONAL EMBLEM: A shield with a central oval (or cartouche) on which appears the eight-rayed sunburst found also in the national flag. The shield outside the cartouche is divided into three sections: three gold stars appear on a white background in the upper segment; a gold lion on a red field and a gold eagle on a blue field appear on the lower segments.

NATIONAL ANTHEM: "Land of the Morning"

NATIONAL HOLIDAYS: June 12 (National Day, Independence Day); January 1 (New Year's Day); April 9 (Bataan Day); May 1 (Labor Day); July 4 (Philippine American Friendship Day); November 30 (National Heroes' Day); December 30 (Rizal Day); All major Catholic festivals.

NATIONAL CALENDAR: Gregorian

PHYSICAL QUALITY OF LIFE INDEX: 75 (up from 73 in 1976) (On an ascending scale in which 100 is the maximum. U.S., 95)

DATE OF INDEPENDENCE: June 12, 1946

DATE OF CONSTITUTION: January 17, 1973 (Suspended, March 1986)

WEIGHTS & MEASURES: The metric system is in force but some traditional units are used.

LOCATION & AREA

The Philippine archipelago is located along the southeastern rim of Asia forming a land chain between the Pacific Ocean on the east and the South China Sea on the west. The archipelago consists of some 7,100 islands and islets, of which only 700 are inhabited; 154 have areas exceeding 13 sq km (5 sq mi); 11 have areas exceeding 2,590 sq km (1,000 sq mi). These 11 are: Luzon (105,708 sq km, 40,814 sq mi); Mindanao (95,586 sq km, 36,906 sq mi); Samar (13,079 sq km, 5,050 sq mi); Negros (12,704 sq km, 4,905 sq mi); Palawan (11,784 sq km, 4,550 sq mi); Panay (11,515 sq km, 4,446 sq mi); Mindoro (9,736 sq km, 3,759 sq mi); Leyte (7,213 sq km, 2,785 sq mi); Cebu (4,411 sq km, 1,703 sq mi); Bohol (3,864 sq km, 1,492 sq mi); and Masbate (3,269 sq km, 1,262 sq mi). These islands account for 95% of the land area, and Luzon and Mindanao together account for 65%. The smaller islands include Catanduanes, Basilan, Jolo, Culion, Dinagat, Dumaran, Siargao, Tablas, Tawi Tawi and the legendary Corregidor, where 10,000 U.S. and Filipino troops fought heroically against the Japanese in 1942. (Corregidor is now a national shrine). The total land area is 299,404 sq km (115,600 sq mi) extending 1,851 km (1,150 mi) SSE to NNW and 1,062 km (660 mi) ENE to WSW. The Palawan and the Sulu Archipelago extending southwest toward Borneo are separated from Malaysia by the Balabac Strait and the Sibutu Passage, respectively, while the Bataan Islands and the Babuyan Islands extending northwest from Luzon are separated from Taiwan by the Bashi Channel. The total length of the coastline is 12,958 km (8,052 mi), slightly exceeding that of the United States.

The capital is Manila, whose position as capital was restored in 1976 when Quezon, the former capital, and 15 other smaller towns were merged with Manila to form a new metropolis of Metropolitan Manila with a population of 4.5 million.

Except for the two large islands of Luzon and Mindanao, the islands of the archipelago are the crests of submerged mountain ranges, separated by shallow waters except for the deeper Sulu Sea. Most of the is-

OTHER MAJOR URBAN CENTERS

Manila	1,630,485	Quezon City	1,165,865
Davao	610,375	Angeles	188,834
Cebu	490,281	Olongapo	156,430
Caloocan	467,816	Batuan	172,489
Zamboanga	343,722	Batangas	143,570
Iloilo	244,827	Cadiz	129,632
Bacolod	262,415	Iligan	167,358
Pasay	287,770	San Pablo	131,655
Cagayan de Oro	227,312	Cabanatuan	138,298

lands have a simple north to south structural alignment. Another feature of the topography is its vulcanism. The country has over 47 volcanoes, of which a dozen are still active. The highest, Mount Apo (2,953 meters, 9,690 ft), has three peaks, and Mount Mayon, the most famous, has a perfect cone rising 2,421 meters (7,943 ft) above the Albay Gulf in southern Luzon. It has erupted 30 times since 1615. The mountain range culminates in Mount Pulog (2,931 meters, 9,613 ft) in northern Luzon.

Luzon, Mindanao and the Visayas Islands are generally considered as three separate geographical regions. Luzon, like Mindanao, is a series of peninsulas joined together by plateaus and lowland strips. It accounts for over one-third of the national territory and is 400 km (250 mi) in length and between 120 and 160 km (75 and 100 mi) in width, being 222 km (138 mi) at its widest. The island has three north to south mountain ranges, the Sierra Madre, running close to the eastern shore, the Cordillera Central and the Zambales Mountains. Between the Sierra Madre and the Cordillera Central is the Cagayan Valley, a rich agricultural region. West of the Cordillera Central lies the Central Luzon Plain, the country's largest single stretch of lowland. Mindanao has five major mountain systems and three great alluvial plains: the Agusan, Davao and Cotabato valleys. The Cotabato lowlands, the scene of bloody conflicts between Moros and government forces, has extensive marshlands. The central mountain complex in Mindanao terminates in the northwest in the Bukidnon-Lanao Highlands. The Visayan Group contains seven large islands—Samar, Masbate, Bohol, Cebu, Leyte, Panay and Negros—and over 3,000 islands, accounting for over 19% of the national territory. The major lowland areas in this group are the Leyte Valley, the Iloilo Plain on Panay, and the western and northern plains on Negros. Southwest of the Zamboanga Peninsula on Mindanao is the Sulu Archipelago, a chain of over 800 islands including 500 unnamed ones.

Rivers are generally short and seasonal in flow, subject to frequent floods. The more important ones are the Rio Grande de Cagayan, the Agno, the Abra, the Bicol, the Pampanga and the Pasig (at the mouth of which Manila is located) on Luzon and the Mindanao and the Agusan on Mindanao.

There are a number of fine lakes, including Lake Sultan Alonto (formerly Lake Lanao), Lake Mainit and Lake Buluan, all on Mindanao, Lake Taal on Luzon and Lake Naujan on Mindoro.

WEATHER

The Philippine Archipelago lies entirely in the tropical zone. Most of the country, except along the east coast, has a summer season during April, May and June and a season of heavy rains from June to October, although September and October are essentially transition months. The hottest months are April and May, but the seasonal variation between the hottest and coolest months is generally 4.4.C (8°F). Temperatures are exceptionally uniform with the annual average ranging from about 26°C to 28°C (79°F to 82°F). The only significant temperature variations are those that result from differences in altitude.

On the other hand, rainfall varies markedly as a result of varying exposures to the two major wind systems: the northeast monsoon in the winter and the southwest monsoon in the summer. The western sections of the country are generally the wettest, receiving from 203 cm to 355 cm (80 to 140 in.) in the summer, while the east coast may receive up to 305 cm (120 in.). Less rain, between 102 cm and 203 cm (40 in. and 80 in.), is received in the Cagayan Valley in northern Luzon, the Cotabato Valley and the Davao-Agusan Valleys on Mindanao and the Central Visayan Islands. In general about 10% of the national territory receives less than 178 cm (70 in.) while 30% receives rainfall in excess of 305 cm (120 in.). The world's heaviest 24-hour rainfall was recorded in Baguio, in the mountains of northern Luzon, in 1911 (127 cm, 50 in.).

The Philippines lies in the world's severest tropical cyclone belt. From 1900 until 1972 the Manila Weather Bureau recorded 1,533 typhoons, an average of 21 per year. They generally occur during the months of June to November, although they have been reported during every month of the year. A particularly violent one in 1972 brought rains and storms that lasted a month resulting in widespread damage.

POPULATION

The population of the Philippines was estimated in 1985 at 56,808,000 on the basis of the last official census held in 1980, when the population was 48,098,460. The population is expected to reach 77.7 million by 2000 and 101.5 million by 2020.

The annual growth rate is estimated at 2.49% on the basis of an estimated birth rate of 32.3 per 1,000 per year.

The population density ranges from 15.9 per sq km (41.1 per sq mi) on Palawan to 1,529 per sq km (3,960 per sq mi) in Rizal Province east of Manila. Manila itself has a density of 34,570 per sq km (89,536 per sq mi). Density of population is 182 per sq km (471 per sq mi) overall and 442 per sq km (1,145 per sq mi) in agricultural areas. The highest population densities are found on Cebu and Luzon.

Despite sustained internal migration toward the cities, fully 61% of all Filipinos live in rural areas. The census of 1980 defined as urban all towns having at

DEMOGRAPHIC INDICATORS (1984)	
Population, total (in 1,000)	56,808
Population ages (% of total)	
0-14	38.6
15-64	58.3
65+	3.1
Youth 15-24 (000)	11,553
Women ages 15-49 (000)	13,721
Dependency ratios	71.5
Child-woman ratios	607
Sex ratios (per 100 females)	102.0
Median ages (years)	20.1
Marriage Rate (per 1,000)	7.7
Average size of Household	5.6
Decline in birthrate (%, 1965-83)	-32.6
Proportion of urban (%)	39.63
Population density (per sq. km.)	182
per hectare of arable land	3.27
Rates of growth (%)	2.49
urban	3.7
rural	1.7
Natural increase rates (per 1,000)	25.4
Crude birth rates (per 1,000)	32.3
Crude death rates (per 1,000)	6.9
Gross reproduction rates	2.05
Net reproduction rates	1.85
Total fertility rates	4.20
General fertility rates (per 1,000)	130
Life expectancy, males (years)	62.8
Life expectancy, females (years)	66.3
Life expectancy, total (years)	64.5
Population doubling time in years at current rate	28
% Illegitimate births	4.8

least 1,000 inhabitants per sq km (2,590 per sq mi), poblaciones, or seats of government, with at least 500 inhabitants per sq km (1,295 per sq mi), and all settlements with a parallel or right-angle street network, at least six business establishments, and any three of the following, a church, town hall, public plaza, park, cemetery, marketplace, school, hospital or library. Nearly 30% of the population live in such centers, and their annual growth rate is 3.7%. The most popular destination of rural migrants is Greater Manila, which accounts for 10% of the national population. Nearly 35% of the population of Manila live in slums and squatter settlements. There are 17 other cities with over 100,000 inhabitants. The rural areas experiencing the worst population loss through internal migration are the Visayas and the Bicol Peninsula.

The age profile shows 38.6% of the population under 14, 58.3% between 15 and 64, and 3.1% over 65. The 1980 census showed a sex ratio of 50.2 males to every 49.8 females, as contrasted with a 1960 sex ratio of 50.9 males to every 49.1 females.

Since the relaxation of immigration controls in the United States in 1968, the Philippines has become a major contributor of emigrants estimated at 35,000 in 1984. During the early 1970s, 20,000 immigrant visas were granted to Filipinos every year, the maximum permissible under the new law. Another 13,000 Filipinos emigrate every year to Canada, Australia and Spain. An estimated one-third of the emigrants are engineers, physicians and nurses.

Women enjoy full voting privileges and have the right to own and inherit property. They are prominent in Philippine society and represented in large numbers in business and in professions such as law, medicine, education and journalism. They are also active in politics, being well represented in both national and local governments and within the political opposition. In addition to the president, there are two women members of the cabinet and 10 in the current National Assembly, and numerous posts within the judicial and executive branches of the government are held by women.

The Philippines has both a high birth rate and a large family size (averaging 5.6 members). The consequent pressures on available resources compelled the government to embark on a population moderation program in the early 1970s, but it has yet to make an impact on the overall birth rate. In 1971 the government established the National Population Commission (POPCOM), which has issued a Four-Year Plan, 1974-77, targeting a reduction in birth rate from 43.2 per 1,000 to 35.9 by 1978. The strategies include information, incentives and training. An existing ban on the importation of contraceptives was lifted, although abortion continues to be illegal unless required to save the life of the mother. Efforts to stimulate acceptance of government-sponsored programs include limitation of maternity benefits to the first four deliveries, provision of free family planning services for employees in all establishments employing 300 or more workers, and the awarding of incentive bonuses. The program involves 2,465 physicians, 1,667 integrated clinics and 826 family planning clinics. In 1984 there were an estimated 5,148,000 users of all types of contraceptives, representing 36% of married women of child-bearing age.

ETHNIC COMPOSITION

The Philippines, in one sense, is a deeply fractionated and pluralistic society with over 50 ethnic groups; yet, in a more profound sense, the Filipinos are imbued with a strong sense of national unity, stemming from a common cultural and racial history, a common religious faith and a common language. Except for the Moros, a separate identity is only an expression of group pride and does not form the basis for racial hostility and conflict. The result has been cultural variety in the midst of national homogeneity. Although each group has a recognized core region, there is a fair amount of interspersion as a result of internal migrations. Furthermore, there are no exclusive ethnic neighborhoods, and there is a readiness to adapt to the prevailing local language and social patterns. Intermarriages among groups are frequent and unremarkable.

The racial homogeneity of the islands is rooted in the descent of the Filipinos from a small group of migrants from Southeast Asia, both Proto-Malay (Indonesian) and Deutero-Malay (Southern Mongoloid), who pushed out earlier Negrito settlers, short, dark-skinned and kinky-haired stragglers who had found their way into the archipelago across the Borneo land bridge. Later Indonesian, Chinese, Arab and Spanish colonists added some variety to the racial stock but did not basically alter its composition. Today, ethnic Filipinos constitute 95.5% of the population (Christian Malays 91.5% and Muslim Malays 4%). Ethnic minorities make up only 4.5% of the population, of which the Chinese, the largest minority group, constitute one-third.

MAJOR ETHNIC GROUPS OF THE PHILIPPINES

Group	Religion	Number
Aklanon	Christian	304,800
Apayo	Pagan	33,000
Badjao	Pagan & Muslim	12,600
Bagobo	Pagan	31,700
Banton	Christian	14,000
Bikol	Christian	2,108,800
Bilaan	Pagan	94,700
Bontok	Pagan	78,100
Bukidnon	Pagan	26,000
Callagan-Caragan	Pagan	134,000
Cagayanes	Christian	71,600
Cebuano	Christian	6,529,000
Gaddang	Pagan and Christian	13,800
Hantik	Christian	268,000
Hanunoo	Pagan	6,000
Hiligaynon	Christian	2,813,300
Ibaloi	Pagan	63,000
Ibanag	Christian	314,300
Ilagnum	Muslim	268,100
Ifugao	Pagan	74,900
Ilocano	Christian	3,158,500
Jama Mapun	Muslim	6,000
Isinai	Christian	11,500
Ivatan	Christian	11,800
Kalamian	Christian	6,500
Kankanai	Pagan	71,300
Kalinga	Pagan	46,600
Magindanao	Muslim	550,000
Mangyan	Pagan	20,000
Manobo	Pagan	46,800
Maranao	Muslim	15,000
Palawan	Muslim & Pagan	18,900
Pampangan	Christian	875,500
Pangasinan	Christian	666,000
Samal	Muslim	126,100
Subanon	Pagan	81,800
Tagakaola	Pagan	11,000
Tagalog	Christian	5,694,000
Tagbanua	Pagan	5,500
Tagabili	Pagan	8,700
Tawsug	Muslim	325,000
Tasaday	Pagan	N.A.
Tinggian	Christian & Pagan	6,300
Tiruray	Pagan	26,300
Waray-Waray	Christian	1,488,600
Yakan	Muslim	58,100
Zambal	Christian	72,800

The lowland Christians, constituting over 91.5% of the population and bound together by common adherence to the Roman Catholic faith, form the core of Filipino society. Muslim Filipinos, commonly known as Moros, constitute the largest unassimilated minority group. Racially and linguistically indistinguishable from other Filipinos, they inhabit the coastal lowlands of Mindanao, the Sulu Archipelago and southern Palawan. Enmity between Christian Filipinos and Moros dates back to the Spanish conquest, and the Moros have resisted both Spanish and later Filipino attempts to subjugate them. The most serious source of conflict is the growing influx of Christian migrants to Mindanao, which the Moros consider as their national territory. Moro separatist sentiments, always smoldering under Spanish and American rule, erupted into armed guerrilla warfare after 1972 with the help of coreligionists in Malaysia and, farther afield, in Libya. Moros are divided into at least 10 groups on the basis of language and degree of Muslim orthodoxy. But despite local differences, they display considerable solidarity against their Christian foes.

Also cut off from the mainstream of Filipino society are the pagan tribes of the interior, collectively known as the Igorots, or mountaineers. They are the descendants of the Negritos, who are believed to have been the earliest inhabitants of the islands. Included among the Igorots are the Tasaday, whose very existence was not known until recently and who are believed to lead a stone-age existence without even agriculture or livestock. Recently a government agency, called the Commission on National Integration and the Presidential Arm for National Minorities (PANAMIN), was established to protect these people from being exploited by more advanced groups.

The Chinese are considered as aliens, and they occupy an ambivalent position in society. While assimilated Chinese who have intermarried with Filipinos have been accepted into the national society, ethnic Chinese without Philippine citizenship have been subjected to discrimination and restrictive legislation. Numbering 114,185 in 1973—only slightly over the estimated Chinese population of Manila in 1896—the Chinese community's cultural isolation and conspicuous economic success have been resented by the majority community. A presidential decree of 1974 requiring the registration of all aliens was directed against them. By 1975 nearly 19,000 Chinese had filed applications for citizenship.

Americans form the second largest foreign community. Other foreign groups include Spanish (1,020), Indian (1,556), British (933), German (531), Belgian (299) and other nationalities (2,907).

In terms of ethnic and linguistic homogeneity, the Philippines ranks 21st in the world with 26% homogeneity (on an ascending scale in which North and South Korea rank 135th with 100% homogeneity and Tanzania ranks first with 7% homogeneity).

LANGUAGES

The official languages of the Philippines are Pilipino and English. English, introduced by the U.S. administration (against the wishes of President William McKinley), is the universal language of government, mass communication, commerce and higher education. For all practical purposes, the Philippines can be considered as an English-speaking country with close to 45% of the population literate in it. In several provinces the number of English speakers exceeds that of

Pilipino speakers. Debates in Congress are usually conducted in English and are only later translated into Pilipino by the Institute of National Language. Seven of the eight Manila daily newspapers are published in English or in English and another language.

Since 1939 in an effort to promote national unity, the government has made the use of the national language Pilipino mandatory in all schools. Pilipino is derived from Tagalog and any distinction between them is purely academic, although the former is often considered a more formal or purer version and latter a vernacular. Tagalog, as the national language was called until 1959, has a rich literature, and its development and spread are entrusted to the Institute of National Language. Today more than 55% of the population speak Pilipino compared to 25.4% in 1937.

Spanish was spoken according to the last 1975 census by 1,331,769 persons, and its use is declining.

Some 87 languages and dialects, all belonging to the Malayo-Polynesian family, are spoken on the islands. Of these, eight are spoken by over 86% of the population: Cebuano (24.1%), Tagalog (21%), Ilocano (11.7%), Hiligaynon (10.4%), Bikol (7.8%), Waray-Waray (5.5%), Pampangan (3.2%) and Pangasinan (2.5%). While the relationships between these languages and dialect groups have not been determined precisely, they are broadly divided into three or four subgroups: Northern Luzon (including Ilocano, Ifugao, Bontok and Kalinga), Central Philippines (including Tagalog, Cebuano, Hiligaynon, Waray-Waray and Bikol; sometimes Cebuano, Hiligaynon and Waray-Waray are grouped together as Bisayan languages) and Southern Mindanao (including Tiruray, Bilaan, Tagabili and Magindanao). Each of these languages has a number of dialects, Bikol having as many as 10 and Cebuano eight. Several pidgins have also evolved, such as Chabakano (Spanish and Cebuano) and Caviteno (Spanish and Tagalog).

RELIGIONS

The Philippines is the only Asian country with a predominantly Christian population. In mid-1980s 43,922,700 persons, or 84.1%, declared themselves as Roman Catholics; other Christians numbered 5,279,000, including 3,236,000 indigenous Christians and 1,827,000 Protestants. The largest religious minority, the Muslims, constituted less than 4.3% of the population with 2,210,000 adherents. Animists, generally described as pagans, constitute about 0.7% and Buddhists less than 1%.

Roman Catholicism, introduced in the 17th Century, was accepted by the Filipinos with remarkable rapidity and soon became the national faith and an important element in the cohesiveness, continuity and unity of Filipino culture. However, it suffered a brief decline in the late 19th and early 20th Centuries because of its association with the Spanish colonial rule. It was forced to retreat further as it faced the onslaught of the nationalist Aglipayan movement and the Protestant missions following the disestablish-ment of the Church by the U.S. administration in 1902. By the 1930s, through a process of internal renewal, the Church had regained most of its organizational strength and membership. Roman Catholicism also became identified with Filipino nationalism against both the United States and Japan. The Church continues to exert a strong social and political influence. Although the separation of church and state is reaffirmed in the 1973 constitution, it does permit religious instruction in public schools.

Although the hierarchy is, by and large, conservative it has not been immune to pressures from the younger clergy and laity for an active involvement in social reform and a firmer stand against violations of human rights by the Marcos regime. The Catholic liberals, called the Christian left by the government, were a thorn on the side of President Marcos, and there were a number of expulsions and arrests of priests and closures of Catholic publications that were critical of official abuses. President Aquino is reported to be a devout Catholic and is close to the Catholic hierarchy, led by Jaime Cardinal Sin, the Archbishop of Manila. Among her advisers are a number of Jesuit priests on whose spiritual as well as political counsel she relies heavily.

Ecclesiastically, the country is divided into 10 archdioceses, 30 dioceses, 12 prelatures nullius, four apostolic vicariates, four apostolic prefectures and 1,633 parishes. The church is faced with a severe shortage of priests, reflected in the estimated clergy-laity ratio of 1:7,000. There are also over 1,600 church-run schools and colleges.

The highly syncretic nature of the Philippine religious mind has produced a number of indigenous cults verging on heresy but incorporating some insidiously appealing elements of the Christian faith. These cults include the Aglipayan church, officially called the Philippine Independent Church, which has its roots in the anti-Catholic and nationalist agitations of the early decades of the 20th Century. Aglipayanism is now split into numerous factions, some of which are unitarian, while the official faction has returned to trinitarian orthodoxy. Another indigenous politico-religious movement is the virulently anti-Catholic Iglesia ni Kristo. Protestants are divided into over 200 denominations and are troubled by schisms resulting at least in part from nationalist sentiments.

Philippine Muslims, particularly the Tawsugs, are devoted to Islam to the point of fanaticism. The focal point of their faith is hostility to Christians, and they believe that any one who kills a Christian will enter "heaven" on a white horse. The reported Moro trait of running amok with the purpose of killing Christians is called juramentado.

COLONIAL EXPERIENCE

The Philippines has been under three colonial rulers: the Spanish from the 1570s to the end of the Spanish-American War in 1898, the Americans from 1898 to 1942 and from 1945 to 1946, and the Japanese from

1942 to 1945. The islands were also briefly under British rule from 1762 to 1763.

The Spanish rule was the longest and the most productive of changes. The success the Spanish achieved in Hispanizing Filipino society was paralleled only by the rapidity with which the Filipinos were converted to the Christian faith. Among the most significant and enduring results of Spanish rule were the introduction of the concept of private property (replacing the traditional communal ownership of land), the creation of a judicial organization and legal processes based on Spanish law, and the establishment of an administrative organization that retained traditional units at the local level. U.S. colonial policy, on the other hand, recognized the need to prepare the Filipinos for self-government and therefore addressed itself to a wide range of political, administrative, social and economic reforms. Some 440 laws were adopted to initiate and hasten the process of modernizing the country. The temporal power of the Church was greatly reduced and the Philippines became a secular state. Government administration was strengthened and centralized, roads and public services were improved, educational facilities were expanded, the judicial system was reorganized (although Spanish civil law was retained), a constabulary was created as the national law enforcement agency, English was introduced as the language of education and administration, and Filipino participation was secured in the political and legislative process by authorizing an elected assembly. The stability and durability of these reforms have resulted partly from the favorable response of Filipinos to these innovations, helped by an acute perception of their own self-interest.

CONSTITUTION & GOVERNMENT

The political and governmental system of the Philippines entered a new era with the ouster of Ferdinand Marcos and the inauguration of Mrs. Corazon Aquino as president in February 1986. Within a month, Mrs. Aquino abolished the National Assembly that had been dominated by Marcos supporters, abrogated the 1973 constitution, and claimed all legislative powers for herself. She announced a new "freedom constitution" under which she would hold power until a new charter was written and submitted to a referendum and legislative elections were held. Under the proclamation, the government's aims were described as reorganizing the government, restoring democracy, reviving the economy, recovering the ill-gotten wealth of Marcos and his allies, protecting basic rights, wiping out corruption, restoring peace and order and affirming civilian supremacy over the military. The proclamation retained most provisions of the 1973 constitution including the Bill of Rights. Aquino also abolished the post of prime minister.

The constitution of 1973 provided for a symbolic or titular president as head of state. He was elected for a six-year term by a majority of the National Assembly. On the other hand, the constitution vested an array of broad powers in the office of the prime minister, who controlled executive departments and local governments, functioned as commander in chief of the armed forces and concluded treaties. He could also place the nation or any part of it under martial law. He was elected, and removed, by the Assembly by a simple majority vote. The transitory provisions authorized Ferdinand Marcos to hold the posts of prime minister and president for an unspecified term until the emergency was lifted. The provisions also legitimized the acts and decrees of the incumbent president.

Freed from all constitutional restraints, the presidency became, under Marcos, the most powerful institution in the nation's history. Radiating from it are a number of executive agencies, all of which are only instruments of presidential authority. The principal advisory body is the cabinet, composed of the president, the vice president, the heads or secretaries of all executive departments, the budget commissioner, the chairmen of the National Science Development Board, the Civil Service Commission and the National Economic and Development Authority, the governor of the Central Bank, the presidential press secretary, and the presidential executive assistant. The chief executive is also assisted by a number of staff units, the most important of which is the Office of the President. Within this office there are a cabinet-rank executive assistant and five presidential assistants. There are also a number of committees, commissions, and boards. It has also been reported that there is an executive cabinet committee, but its membership has not been divulged.

CABINET LIST (1986)	
President	*Mrs.* Corazon Aquino
Vice President	Salvador Laurel
Minister of Defense Minister	Juan Ponce Enrile
Minister of Finance	Jaime Ongpin
Minister of Trade & Industry	Jose Concepcion, Jr.
Minister of Agriculture	Ramon Mitra
Minister of Local Government	Aquilino Pimental
Minister of Natural Resources	Ernesto Maceda
Minister of Information	Teodoro Locsin, Jr.
Minister of Education	Lourdes Quisumbing
Minister of Public Works	Rogaciano Mercado
Minister of Tourism	Jose Antonio Gonzales
Minister of Budget	Alberto Romulo
Minister of Justice	Neptali Gonzales
Executive Secretary	Joker Arroyo
Presidential Commission on Good Government	Jovito Salonga
Presidential Commission on Government Reorganization	Luis Villafuerte
Presidential Spokesperson	Rene Saguisag
Central Bank Governor	Jose Fernandez

Suffrage is universal. The voting age under the 1973 constitution is 18 (as compared to 21 under the 1935 constitution), but the proclamation establishing

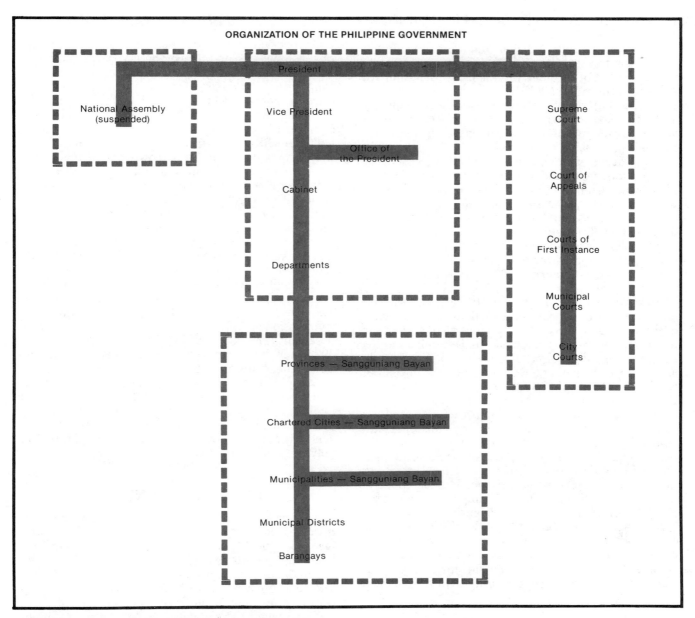

ORGANIZATION OF THE PHILIPPINE GOVERNMENT

President

National Assembly (suspended)

Vice President

Supreme Court

Office of the President

Cabinet

Court of Appeals

Courts of First Instance

Departments

Municipal Courts

City Courts

Provinces — Sangguniang Bayan

Chartered Cities — Sangguniang Bayan

Municipalities — Sangguniang Bayan

Municipal Districts

Barangays

RULERS OF THE PHILIPPINES
(from 1945)

1945 (April) to 1946 (May) Sergio Osmena
1946 (May) to 1948 (April) Manuel Roxas
1948 (April) to 1953 (November) Elpidio Quirino
1953 (November) to 1957 (March) Ramon Magsaysay
1957 (March) to 1961 (December) Carlos P. Garcia
1961 (December) to 1965 (December) Diosdado Macapagal
1965 (December) to 1986 (February) Ferdinando Edralin Marcos
1986 (February) —
    Mrs. Corazon Aquino

---

the barangays, or local citizens' assemblies, lowered the voting age to 15. Voting is compulsory and absence from the polling place is a punishable offense. The last national election was held in 1986.

Because of the tendency of Filipino voters to sell their votes for money or rewards, election expenses had soared to scandalous amounts. The elections of 1961, described as one of the most expensive in Philippine history, cost the country a sum equal to 8% of the annual national budget. The bulk of the expenses was for dispensation of pork barrel favors and outright vote buying. Most election expenses traditionally have been recovered by the successful candidate through flagrant graft. The high cost of elections also favored wealthy candidates and thus perpetuated the power of the oligarchy.

All elections are conducted by the Election Commission (COMELEC). A nationally organized civic group, the National Citizens' Movement for Free Elections (NAMFREL), was accredited in 1984 by the Commission on Elections as the commission's official citizens' arm. NAMFREL received substantial support from the business community, several church groups, students, workers, professionals and ordinary citizens.

Its organizers successfully lobbied the National Assembly for reforms in the election law, and actively solicited and obtained 300,000 volunteers on a nationwide basis to assist its poll-watching and vote count monitoring effort. Under the auspices of its "operation quick count," NAMFREL conducted its own canvass of a majority of electoral seats in the country, and published its own results and projections, often well in advance of the announcement of official results by the Commission on Elections.

The Marcos regime, clothed under such labels as the New Society and Constitutional Authoritarianism, was essentially an unabashed dictatorship. It was described by Marcos himself as a transitory process designed to halt the development of traditional democratic politics and to reconstruct political values emphasizing order and discipline rather than freedom and personal initiative. More significantly, the military emerged as the principal instrument of power in the New Society.

In November 1985 President Marcos, with the concurrence of the opposition, called for a presidential election in early 1986, slightly more than a year earlier than had been scheduled. In December, active campaigning began by both President Marcos, the candidate of the ruling KBL Party, and the opposition candidate, Corazon Aquino, widow of the murdered Benigno Aquino. Mrs. Aquino's candidacy was encouraged by broad popular support as indicated, for example, by a petition urging her to run reportedly signed by more than 1.2 million Filipinos. Her "unity ticket" with vice presidential candidate Salvador Laurel was created under the banner of his United Nationalist Democratic Organization. Marcos chose as his running mate National Assembly member and former foreign minister Arturo Tolentino.

Although one of the stated goals of President Marcos was to dislodge the oligarchs, they have shown a remarkable capacity for survival and continue to dominate Filipino society. Thus, the Marcos regime introduced new evils without getting rid of the old ones.

FREEDOM & HUMAN RIGHTS

In terms of political and civil rights, the Philippines is classified as a free country with a rating of 3 in civil rights and 3 in political rights (on a descending scale in which 1 is the highest and 7 the lowest in rights).

With the fall of Marcos, the Philippines has entered what may be termed a "Manila Spring," in terms of human rights. Habeus corpus was restored by Aquino in one of her first acts and all political detainees were released despite objections from the military. There are no reports of Marcos' supporters being muzzled or of any large-scale reprisals against the "New Society" power bases. The basic rights in the constitution of 1973 have been retained in the so-called "freedom constitution" which will govern the transitionary period until a new constitution is ratified.

CIVIL SERVICE

Civil servants are classified into two main categories: competitive and noncompetitive. Approximately one-third is competitive, that is recruited through competitive examinations, and the remaining two-thirds are appointed by the president at his discretion or by the heads of local government. These latter appointees are generally proteges of local and national politicians. Relatives are commonly appointed, and though nepotism is officially frowned upon it is considered normal in the context of Filipino social values.

In an effort to improve morale, integrity and efficiency, President Marcos created in 1972 a special cadre known as Career Executive Service comprising the positions of secretary, under secretary, assistant secretary, chief of department services and equivalent ranks. These officers are trained through the Career Executive Service Development Program.

The civil service is supervised by a constitutional commission known as the civil service commission. The commission is composed of a chairman and two commissioners appointed for seven-year terms by the president. The commission's powers, as expanded in 1975, include approval of all appointments and promotions other than those of presidential appointees, conducting civil service examinations, promulgating standards, policies and guidelines, inspecting and auditing personnel work and reviewing official actions and decisions, conducting investigation of official misconduct, and advising the president on all matters involving public administration.

LOCAL GOVERNMENT

For purpose of local government, the Philippines is divided into six types of units: 12 regions, 72 provinces, 61 cities, 1,438 municipalities, 21 municipal districts and 35,000 barangays.

Provinces are governed by appointed officials known as governors. Legislative bodies at the provincial, city and municipal levels are all named Sangguniang bayan. The membership of the sangguniang bayans consists at the provincial level of one representative each from the municipalities and barangays under its jurisdiction. Municipal and city sangguniang bayans consist of barangay captains and so-called sector representatives representing the professions, labor, business and agriculture, appointed by the president. Local chief executives report to the Department of Local Government and Community Development, while subordinate officials report directly to their respective departments in the capital.

Intermediate-level local governments comprise chartered cities, municipalities, and municipal districts. Chartered cities, each headed by a mayor, are independent of provincial governments. They have broader taxing powers, and their mayors have also certain appointive powers. Municipalities, also administered by mayors, have less autonomy than chartered cities and are under the control of the provincial

PROVINCES OF THE PHILIPPINES

Province	Capital	Province	Capital
Batanes	Basco	Cagayan	Tuguegarao
Ilocos Norte	Laoag	Abra	Bangued
Kalinga-Apayao	Tabuk	Marinduque	Boac
Ilocos Sur	Vigan	Albay	Legazpi
Mountain	Bontoc	Romblon	Romblon
Isabela	Ilagan	Sorsogon	Sorsogon
Ifugao	Lagawe	Masbate	Masbate
La Union	San Fernando	Northern Samar	Catarman
Benguet	La Trinidad	Aklan	Kalibo
Nueva Vizcaya	Bayombong	Samar	Catbalogan
Quirino	Cabarroquis	Eastern Samar	Borongan
Pangasinan	Lingayen	Capiz	Roxas
Nueva Ecija	Palayan	Antique	San Jose de Buenavista
Quezon	Lucena	Iloilo	Iloilo
Zambales	Iba	Leyte	Tacloban
Tarlac	Tarlac	Cebu	Cebu
Pampanga	San Fernando	Southern Leyte	Maasin
Bulacan	Malolos	Negros Occidental	Bacolod
Bataan	Balanga	Bohol	Tagbilaran
Rizal	Pasig	Surigao del Norte	Surigao
Cavite	Trece Matires	Palawan	Puerto Princesa
Laguna	Santa Cruz	Negros Oriental	Demaguete
Camarines Norte	Daet	Siquijor	Siquijor
Batangas	Batangas	Agusan del Norte	Butuan
Camarines Sur	Naga	Camiguin	Mambajao
Catanduanes	Virac	Surigao del Sur	Tandag
Mindoro Occidental	Mamburao	Misamis Oriental	Cagayan de Oro
Mindoro Oriental	Calapan	Zamboanga del Norte	Dipolog
Misamis Occidental	Oro Quita	North Cotabato	Kidapawan
Bukidnon	Malaybalay	Basilan	Isabela
Agusan del Sur	Prosperidad	Sultan Kudarat	Isulan
Zamboanga del Sur	Pagadian	Davao del Sur	Digos
Lanao del Norte	Iligan	Davao Oriental	Mati
Lanao del Sur	Marawi	South Cotabato	Koronadal
Davao	Tagum	Sulu	Jolo
Maguindanao	Magonoy	Tawitawi	Balimbing

government. Municipal districts are territorial units in areas inhabited by non-Christians.

The lowest and the most numerous territorial units are the barangays also known as barrios until 1974. The term barangay is derived from the name of the boats which brought the Malay immigrants from mainland Asia and Indonesia. In pre-Spanish times it was a group of extended families who lived along a waterway. The structure was preserved intact as the basic unit of local administration during the Spanish period. Barangays are located in wards and divisions of cities, municipalities, municipal districts and chartered cities. Each barangay is run by a council headed by a captain. The primary functions of the council are to maintain law and order and to participate in community development projects by providing labor and materials. Councils are elected by eligible voters 15 years of age or older. Barangays, like other local units, have some limited powers of taxation but depend heavily on subsidies from the national treasury.

FOREIGN POLICY

Even after independence, economic needs and perceived military threats kept the Philippines well within the U.S. sphere of influence. U.S. ties necessarily circumscribed the scope and thrust of foreign policy. Particularly at the height of the cold war in the 1950s and 1960s, Manila hewed closely to the anti-Communist policies of the U.S. and isolated itself from most of its neighbors through identification with SEATO and related alliances. Relations between the U.S. and the Philippines were governed by the Mutual Defense Treaty of 1951, the Military Bases Agreement of 1947 and the Laurel-Langley Agreement of 1955 (which expired in 1974).

With the fall of Vietnam and growing uncertainty about the direction of Washington's policy toward Asia, Manila decided to strike out on its own and rearrange its diplomatic goals and priorities. Deepening involvement in Southeast Asian affairs through ASEAN, a growing sense of identification with the Third World and rapprochement with Communist countries, particularly Vietnam and China, have been accompanied by a hard-nosed reassessment of the traditional "special relations" with the United States. The most dramatic aspect of this new diplomacy was the state visit of President Marcos to Beijing in 1975. A Vietnamese embassy was set up in Manila in 1976 and a Philippine embassy in Hanoi in 1977. Formal diplomatic relations with the Soviet Union are also scheduled to be established, but there has been only slow progress in this direction and Moscow's first prospective ambassador to Manila was turned down because he was a KGB agent.

The subject of military bases is at the heart of Philippine nationalist agitations for a new framework of relations with the United States. The bases in question are the huge Clark Airbase and the Subic Bay naval station. The 16,000 U.S. military personnel based in the Philippines are the last U.S. forces in Southeast Asia. While Manila welcomes the $200 million a year these bases generate in foreign exchange and additional spin-off employment, the bases are an embarrassment in the context of the new Third World image that the Philippines is trying to build. Talks between the two countries began in 1976 when Secretary of State Henry Kissinger offered $1 billion in economic aid over a five-year period in return for the continued use of the bases. In 1983 the United States and the Philippines signed a new military bases agreement. The U.S. agreed to pay $900 million in compensation for the use of the two bases, the Subic Bay Naval

Base and the Clark Air Base, both on the island of Luzon. The $900 million represented in increase of $400 million over the compensation paid to the Philippines in 1979, the last time the agreement was renewed. The figure included $475 million in economic aid, $300 million in military sales credits and $125 million in military aid grants. The renewed agreement amended the 1979 pact by giving Filipino commanders a greater say in the running of the bases and including new provisions covering criminal jurisdiction over the 14,000 U.S. personnel at the bases. It obliged the U.S. to inform the Philippines of personnel and equipment changes and to consult with Manila if it wanted to store long-range missiles at the bases. The five-year period covered by the pact began in October 1984.

In addition to this agreement the Philippines achieved a number of positive advances in its so-called "diplomacy of many options," including a strengthening of relations with China, the holding of UNCTAD V conference in Manila, and the acceptance of the Philippines as an observer at the Havana conference of nonaligned nations.

The Philippines and the United States are parties to 96 agreements and treaties covering agricultural commodities, atomic energy, aviation, claims, consuls, copyright, customs, defense, economic and technical cooperation, education, finance, general relations, health, informational media guaranties, investment guaranties, maritime matters, meteorological research, military cemeteries and monuments, mutual security, patents, Peace Corps, postal matters, publications, relief supplies and packages, social security, telecommunications, trade and commerce, visas.

The anchor of the new Philippine foreign policy is the five-nation group known as Association of Southeast Asian Nations (ASEAN), which is being developed as an Asian forum. To demonstrate his interest in ASEAN harmony, President Marcos dropped his country's territorial claim over the East Malaysian state of Sabah.

Relations with Japan, which now rivals the United States as the country's biggest trading partner, were finally normalized in 1973 with the ratification of the Treaty of Amity, Commerce and Navigation. The Muslim conflict in the south has emerged as the most serious issue in foreign relations as a result of its impact on relations with Muslim Malaysia, Libya and other Arab countries. A patch-up accord signed between Imelda Marcos, the then first lady, and Col. Muammar Qaddhafi of Libya lasted for only a few months and served only to demonstrate the intractability of the bitter conflict.

The Philippines joined the U.N. in 1945; its share of the U.N. budget is 0.18%. It is a member of 15 U.N. organizations and 18 other international organizations.
U.S. Ambassador in Manila: Stephen W. Bosworth
U.K. Ambassador in Manila: Robin McLaren
Philippine Ambassador in Washington, D.C.: Benjamin T. Romualdez
Philippine Ambassador in London: Jose V. Cruz

PARLIAMENT

The 1973 constitution provided for a unicameral legislature known as National Assembly (Batsang Pambansa) elected by universal suffrage for six-year terms. Regular elections were held on the second Monday in May, and the Assembly convened annually on the fourth Monday in July. The Assembly elected the prime minister, and it could withdraw its confidence in the prime minister by a simple majority vote and override a prime-ministerial veto by a two-thirds majority vote. An election code signed by the president on February 7, 1978, provided that the *Balasang Pambansa* should have 200 members, 165 directly elected, 21 appointed by the president from the Cabinet (including himself) and 14 members elected by youth, agriculture and labour organizations. The National Assembly, elected in January 1986, was dissolved by President Aquino in March 1986.

POLITICAL PARTIES

Before 1972 the Philippine political system was dominated by two political parties: the Nacionalistas and the Liberals. Both were mass parties, virtually identical in ideologies and mode of operations. There were a number of minor parties, all of them short-lived. Both the major parties were essentially patronage parties—less instruments of sociopolitical change than vehicles through which maximum personal benefits could be obtained. They functioned as mutual-aid groups cemented by patron-client relationships at every level and expectations of pork-barrel benefits. Both leaders and followers readily switched from one party to another, and no stigma was attached to turncoats.

The present Nacionalista Party, to which President Marcos belonged at the time of his election, represents the right-wing element and the Liberal Party the left-wing element of the former Partido Nacionalista. In 1978 Marcos' party was renamed the New Society Movement and the opposition coalition the People's Force Party. A cautious return to politics was permitted during the 1978 legislative elections and also after the end of martial law in 1981. In February 1980 representatives of eight opposition groups formed a loose coalition, the United Democratic Organization (UNIDO) which was reorganized in April 1982 as the United Nationalist Democratic Organization, a 12-party alignment that retained the former acronym. With the murder of opposition leader, Benigno Aquino, anti-Marcos forces began to coalesce under the UNIDO banner. Components of UNIDO are:
• Nacionalista Party, essentially the conservative wing of the former Nationalist Party. It is led by Jose B. Laurel, vice president of the republic.
• Liberal Party. Composed of the center-liberal elements of the old Nationalist Party and led by former president of the republic, Diosdado Macapagal.

• People's Power Movement — Fight. A splinter of the Liberal Party, it was nominally headed by Benigno Aquino prior to his assassination.

• Philippine Democratic Party, ideologically descended from the Christian Social Movement founded by Raul Manglapus.

• National Union for Liberation, also led by former president of the republic, Diosdado Macapagal.

• Pusyon Visaya, a regional Visaya group, one faction of which calls for a reannexation of the Philippines by the United States.

• Mindanao Alliance, a regional Mindanao group.

The Coalition for the Restoration of Democracy, founded in 1983, is a leftist coalition comprising National Alliance for Freedom, Justice and Democracy and Movement for Philippine Sovereignty and Democracy.

Minor political parties include the Labor Party, founded in 1983; Alliance of Metropolitan Associations, founded in 1983; and the Social Democratic Party, founded in 1982.

At least two proscribed parties are in armed opposition to the government: the New People's Army (NPA), the military arm of the outlawed Communist Party, and the Moro National Liberation Front, a radical Muslim group whose military arm is known as the Bangsa Moro Army. Although the NPA threat has diminished in recent years, it still controls 33 of the 37 municipalities in Isabela Province and it has a secondary foothold in the Bicol Peninsula. There are also scattered pockets of militancy in the Visayan Islands, Mindanao and the Sulu Archipelago. The rebels reportedly receive arms and training from China.

In military terms the more serious struggle is with the Bangsa Moro Army, which has a reported strength of 8,000 with 30,000 active supporters and up to 400,000 sympathizers. The Moros receive arms and equipment from Libya, Malaysian Sabah and other Muslim countries. Fighting reached a peak in 1974 with the destruction of the city of Jolo. Since then both sides have moved in the direction of a political settlement but without any tangible results.

ECONOMY

The Philippines is one of the 39 lower-middle income countries of the world with a free-market economy dominated by the private sector.

National economic planning began in 1936 with the creation of the National Economic Council, which evolved through a series of agencies, such as the Program Implementation Agency, the Presidential Economic Staff and the Congressional Economic Planning Office, into the National Economic Development Authority. The first long-range development plan following the imposition of martial law in 1972 was the 1974-77 plan calling for a total investment of P21.5 billion, of which the foreign exchange component was 42%. Of the total outlay, 35% was expended on transportation, 33% on energy and power, 20% on water resources, 10% on education, health and welfare and 2%

PRINCIPAL ECONOMIC INDICATORS

Gross National Product: $39.420 billion (1983)
  GNP Annual Growth Rate: 5.8% (1973-82)
  Per Capita GNP: $760 (1983)
  Per Capita GNP Annual Growth Rate: 2.9% (1973-82)

Gross Domestic Product: P548.47 billion (1984)
  GDP at 1980 Prices: P267.62 billion
  GDP Deflator (1980=100): 200.8
  GDP Annual Growth Rate: 5.4% (1973-83)
  Per Capita GDP: P10,280 (1984)
  Per Capita GDP Annual Growth Rate: 3.4% (1970-81)

Income Distribution: 21.4% of the national income is received by the bottom 60%; 42% of the national income is received by the top 10%.

Percentage of Population in Absolute Poverty: rural 41%; urban 32%

Consumer Price Index (1970=100):
  All Items: 351.3 (June 1985)
  Food: 330.4 (June 1985)

Wholesale Price Index (1980=100): General: 210.0 (April 1984)

Average Annual Rate of Inflation: 11.7% (1973-83)

Money Supply: P29.098 billion (May 1985)
  Reserve Money: P32.501 billion (May 1985)

Currency in Circulation: P21.80 billion (1984)

International Reserves: $602 million, of which foreign exchange reserves were $574.0 million (1984)

BALANCE OF PAYMENTS (1984)
(million $)

Current Account Balance	−1,251
Merchandise Exports	5,391
Merchandise Imports	−6,070
Trade Balance	−679
Other Goods, Services & Income	+ 2,626
Other Goods, Services & Income	− 3,584
Other Goods, Services & Income Net	−958
Private Unrequited Transfers	118
Official Unrequited Transfers	268
Capital Other Than Reserves	1,397
Net Errors & Omissions	97
Total (Lines 1,10 and 11)	243
Counterpart Items	148
Total (Lines 12 and 13)	391
Liabilities Constituting Foreign Authorities Reserves	—
Total Change in Reserves	−391

---

on telecommunications. The 1976-79 plan envisioned a total outlay of P38 billion, of which the foreign exchange component was 42%. Energy and power led all the sectors, accounting for 34% of expenditures, followed by transportation 30%, water resources 23% and social programs 7%. On the whole, the plan's basic strategy of balanced growth of all sectors represented a departure from the earlier policy of emphasizing the industrial to the neglect of the rural and agricultural sectors. Within the framework of this strategy greater stress was also placed on income distribution and social development.

The Five-Year Plan 1978-82 called for rural development, agrarian reform, expansion of industry, irrigation, water supply, power, transport, communications, education and improved housing. The plan identified income inequality, unemployment, underemployment, population growth price instability, and energy constraints as the nation's most critical problems. Industrial growth was defined as the engine of development and within this sector, heavy manufacturing was favored. The plan also envisaged a shift in trade flow from the USA and Japan toward ASEAN, Middle East and EEC. The plan's projections included a population growth of 2.0%, a labor force growth rate of 3.0%, creation of 350,000 jobs annually between 1985 and 2000, increase in arable land by 20% and electrification of the entire country by 1990.

The 1983-87 Five-Year Plan, which aimed for an annual growth rate of 6.5%, has been made largely redundant by the economic crisis. Following IMF recommendations, an amended plan will put increased emphasis on agriculture, rather than import-substitution industries. As a result, agriculture's share of budget expenditure rose from 18% in 1984 to about 25% in 1985. Public investment has been reduced, and labor-intensive and small-scale projects will receive more encouragement.

GROSS DOMESTIC PRODUCT BY ECONOMIC ACTIVITY (1970-81)

	%	Rate of Change %
Agriculture	25.9	4.9
Mining	2.4	6.4
Manufacturing	24.6	6.9
Construction	7.0	16.4
Electricity, Gas & Water	1.0	8.7
Transport & Communications	5.3	9.3
Trade & Finance	22.8	4.6
Public Administration & Defense	—	—
Other Branches	10.9	5.1

The Philippines was the recipient of substantial economic assistance from the United States during the 1940s and 1950s, but since then sources of aid have diversified.

FOREIGN ECONOMIC ASSISTANCE

Sources	Period	Amount (million $)
United States Loans	1946-83	676.6
United States Grants	1946-83	1,727.8
International Organizations	1946-83	5,908.4
(Of which World Bank)	1946-83	3,871.6
All Sources	1979-81	648.2

During 1979-81 the Philippines received $13.50 per capita in foreign aid.

BUDGET

The Philippine fiscal year is the calendar year. The national budget is issued annually by presidential decree. Despite an improved tax structure and fiscal restraints, the budgets have shown chronic deficits.

BUDGET (million pesos)

Revenue	1983	1984
Taxes	36,581	40,036
Income and profits	8,700	9,500
Property	280	295
Domestic goods and services	13,520	14,911
Foreign trade and transactions	13,263	14,497
Others	818	833
Other receipts	4,699	5,324
Recently approved measures	2,190	2,140
TOTAL	43,470	47,500

Expenditure	1984	1985
Agriculture	2,821	5,143
Natural resources	773	633
Industry	940	942
Power and energy	1,352	1,246
Water	2,790	4,161
Transport and communications	6,155	8,288
Other economic services	425	436
Education and culture	8,928	10,719
Health and population	2,822	3,411
Housing	1,035	857
Other social services	2,231	2,262
Defense	5,586	6,342
General public services	6,591	4,005
Public order	2,085	2,502
International development aid	189	210
Administration and research	199	181
Debt service	13,908	15,987
TOTAL	58,830	67,325*

*The total was reduced to 66,100 million pesos, according to the terms of an IMF agreement.

Of current government revenues, 21.8% comes from taxes on income, profit and capital gain, 40.9% from domestic taxes on goods and services, 23.9% from taxes on international trade and transactions, 3.1% from other taxes and 10.4% from non-tax revenues. Current taxes represent 11.2% of GNP. Of current expenditures 13.6% goes to defense, 16.0% to education, 5.3% to health, 4.2% to housing, social security and welfare, 53.7% to economic services and 7.2% to other functions. Current expenditures represent 12.2% of GNP and overall deficit 4.3% of GNP.

In 1983, public consumption was P 33.98 billion and private consumption P 404.70 billion. During 1973-83 public consumption grew by 3.7% and private consumption by 4.6%.

In 1983 total outstanding disbursed external debt was $13.659 billion of which $10.385 billion was publicly guaranteed and $3.274 billion was private and nonguaranteed. Of the publicly guaranteed debt, $4.824 billion was owed to official creditors and $5.561 billion was owed to private creditors. The total debt service was $1.251 billion of which $601.5 million was repayment of principal and $650.3 million was interest. Total external debt represented 127.7% of export revenues and 30.6% of GNP. Debt service represented 15.4% of export revenues and 3.7% of GNP.

FINANCE

The Philippine unit of currency is the peso divided into 100 centavos. Coins are issued in denominations of 5, 10, 25 and 50 centavos and 1 and 5 pesos; notes are issued in denominations of 1, 2, 5, 10, 20, 50 and 100 pesos.

From 1962 to 1970 on the peso's value was determined in a free market. In 1970 the peso was floated downward and the average market rate has been adjusted from month to month. In 1985 the exchange value against the dollar was $1=P18.666. The sterling exchange rate on this basis was £1=P22.901.

The government had planned to fix the peso against a "basket" of currencies which would initially include the U.S. dollar, the yen and the deutsche mark. In the interim there was an informal link with the U.S. dollar, with the central bank intervening in the foreign exchange market to keep the peso in line with the dollar within a narrow band (1% either way in the late 1970s). The planned arrangement would more adequately reflect the importance of Japan as a source of imports and foreign investment and would make the exchange rate a more flexible instrument of policy. However, this strategy was overtaken by events and, on the IMF's insistence, periodic devaluations occurred in 1983, culminating in June 1984 with a devaluation of the peso by 22.2%.

The banking system is supervised by the Central Bank. Its governor is also the chairman of the Monetary Board. Special development finance institutions include the Philippine National Bank, Private Development Corporation, the National Investment Development Corporation, the Development Bank of the Philippines and the Land Bank of the Philippines. The commercial bank system consists of 34 banks. Other institutions in this sector include about 600 rural banks, 45 private development banks, 13 investment banks and eight savings banks. The largest commercial bank is the state-owned Philippine National Bank with over 100 provincial branches and agencies. Only four foreign banks are permitted by law to operate full branches. Legislation passed in September 1976 permitted the establishment of offshore banks in the Philippines. By mid-1982 25 foreign banks had been authorized to operate offshore banking units. In August 1984 the commercial banks had reserves of P11.65 billion, demand deposits of P11.84 billion and time and savings deposits of P76.40 billion. The discount rate in 1979 was 11%.

AGRICULTURE

Of the total land area of 29,940,400 hectares (73,982,728 acres), 37% is classified as agricultural area, or 0.2 hectare (0.5 acre) per capita. Based on 1974-76=100, the index of agricultural production in 1982 was 130, the index of food production was 129 and the index of per capita food production was 113. Agriculture employs 46% of the labor force. Agriculture contributes 22% of the GDP, and its annual

GROWTH PROFILE Annual Growth Rates (%)	
Population 1980-2000	2.1
Birthrate 1965-83	-32.6
Deathrate 1965-83	-43.7
Urban Population 1973-83	3.8
Labor Force 1980-2000	2.5
GNP 1973-82	5.8
GNP per capita 1973-82	2.9
GDP 1973-83	5.4
GDP per capita 1970-81	3.4
Consumer Prices 1970-81	13.1
Wholesale Prices 1970-81	15.3
Inflation 1973-83	11.7
Agriculture 1973-83	4.3
Manufacturing 1973-83	5.0
Industry 1973-83	6.4
Services 1973-83	5.2
Mining 1970-81	6.4
Construction 1970-81	16.4
Electricity 1970-81	8.7
Transportation 1970-81	9.3
Trade 1970-81	4.6
Public Administration & Defense	—
Export Price Index 1975-81	11.0
Import Price Index 1975-81	16.5
Terms of Trade 1975-81	-4.8
Exports 1970-78	7.5
Imports 1970-78	1.3
Public Consumption 1973-83	3.7
Private Consumption 1973-83	4.6
Gross Domestic Investment 1973-83	7.3
Energy Consumption 1973-83	2.3
Energy Production 1973-83	20.8

growth rate during 1973-83 was 4.3%. Agricultural products account for nearly 70% of exports by value. The value added in agriculture in 1983 was $8.609 billion.

The Philippines is one of the many countries in Asia that are reaching the limits of arable land. Since the 1950s agricultural expansion has taken place on marginal lands and on steep slopes susceptible to erosion. Although favored with a year-round rainy season and a high rainfall, poor drainage, typhoons and soil erosion seriously reduce agricultural productivity.

The future development of agricultural resources is therefore dependent on the expansion of intensive forms of cultivation including the sustained application of fertilizers, mechanization, introduction of high-yield varieties, use of pesticides and conservation of soil. In 1982 there were 17,500 tractors and 460 harvester-threshers in use. Annual consumption of fertilizers was 321,800 tons, or 28.8 kg (63.5 lb) per hectare of agricultural land. In 1974, 1,351,000 hectares (3,338,000 acres) were under irrigation.

The three major crops are rice, corn and coconut, taking up about 34, 25, and 23% of cultivated acreage, respectively. Fruits, nuts and sugarcane account for another 9%. The bulk of the rice production comes from central Luzon, which is described as the nation's rice bowl. Other regions of surplus production are the Cagayan Valley, the Bicol Peninsula, the Visayan Islands and the southern and western regions of Mindanao. The area devoted to commercial crops has been growing at the expense of food crops because of export needs.

The Philippines is the world's largest producer and exporter of coconuts and coconut products, which in 1982 provided 12% of total export earnings. The country supplies more than 70% of world trade in coconut oil. Exports of this commodity declined in value by 24.8% in 1982, owing to depressed prices and a temporary export levy on coconuts, but increased by 28.6% in 1983. Coconut oil is being used increasingly in domestic chemical production and for fuel, in combination with diesel oil, thus reducing the volume available for export. Exports of copra from the Philippines were temporarily banned in 1982 to preserve domestic supply; production was badly hit by drought and typhoons in 1983, and export volume fell dramatically, from 190,000 metric tons in 1982 to 12,000 tons in 1983, causing steep price rises. The country achieved a small exportable surplus of rice between 1978 and 1982 but, following a long drought in 1982/83, rice imports were again necessary in 1984. In 1983 1,343,000 tons of cereals were imported.

Agrarian reform has a long history in the Philippines, beginning in 1904 when the U.S. administration purchased lands from the Roman Catholic Church for redistribution to peasants. Since independence there have been 19 acts and decrees directed at alleviating tenant misery and rationalizing land ownership patterns. But many of these measures were only cosmetic and were never seriously enforced. The most meaningful effort to date has been the presidential decree of 1972 that undertook to transfer ownership to about half of the country's 900,000 landless peasants and tenants. Under the plan tenants on farms of seven hectares (17.2 acres) or more are entitled to purchase lands from their owners; the payment was limited to 2.5 times the average harvest to be paid in 15 amortization payments together with 6% interest. By 1976 certificates for land purchase had been issued to 210,054 tenants covering 369,054 hectares (911,932 acres). But the continuing increase in the number of landless peasants suggests that even this reform has not made much headway. The average size of a farm is 3.27 hectares (8 acres), and over half of the farms are less than 2 hectares (4.8 acres).

Livestock generates 20% of the gross value of agricultural production, but it plays only a minor role in the national economy. Meat consumption is low, and cattle are used principally as draft animals. In 1983 the livestock population consisted of 1,938,000 cattle, 7,980,000 pigs, 2,946,000 buffaloes, 300,000 horses, 1,859,000 goats, 30,000 sheep, 62,000,000 chickens and 5,000,000 ducks.

Forests cover about 44% of the national territory with 98% of these forests owned by the government and managed through the forestry and land bureaus. Commercial hardwoods, known only by their native names, include narra, tindalo, camagong, molave, ipil, yakal, banuyo, akbe and guijo. Mahoganies, such as lauan, tanguile, almon, bagtkan, mayapis and tianong, make up the bulk of the lumber exports. Forest

PRINCIPAL CROP PRODUCTION (1983)		
	Area (000 hectares)	Production (000 metric tons)
Rice	3,758	8,150
Corn	3,474	3,385
Sweet potatoes	222	1,050
Cassava	178	2,300
Other roots & tubers	55	3,587
Pulses	71	45
Groundnuts	64	50
Coconuts	n.a.	9,200
Copra	n.a.	1,930
Vegetables	n.a.	2,114
Sugar cane	503	21,467
Mangoes	n.a.	550
Pineapples	n.a.	1,300
Bananas	n.a.	4,200
Plaintains	n.a.	280
Coffee	77	160
Cocoa beans	7	5
Tobacco	79	45
Natural rubber	n.a.	80

products rank among the country's top four categories in export value. Roundwood removals in 1982 totaled 34.967 million cubic meters (1.235 billion cubic ft).

Although the Philippines lies in a fertile fishing belt, the domestic fishing industry has remained underdeveloped. Obsolescent techniques, inadequate refrigeration and marketing facilities, and lack of investment capital have handicapped the industry so that production does not meet even domestic needs. The annual fish catch in 1982 totaled 1,787,700 metric tons, mostly anchovies, mackerels, sea bass, sardines, tuna, bonito and shark.

Agricultural credit is provided by the Agricultural Credit Administration, which provides credit without collateral up to P1,200 per hectare at low interest.

INDUSTRY

Manufacturing is the second most important economic sector, employing 10.2% of the labor force and contributing 24.6% of the GDP, but its rate of growth at 6.9% during 1970-78 was twice that of agriculture. Based on 1975=100, the index of industrial production in 1982 was 252. In 1980 there were 85,236 establishments (each employing five or more workers) employing 1,178,000 workers and generating an output valued at P137.529 billion. The value added in manufacturing in 1982 was $5.510 billion of which agro-based products accounted for 39%, textiles 13%, machinery and transport equipment 9%, and chemicals 9%. During the period immediately following World War II, industrial production was geared to the domestic market. Export industries are a more recent development stimulated by the floating of the peso and by the Export Incentives Act of 1970, which made Philippine products more competitive in international markets.

Manufacturing is dominated by the private sector and is generally concentrated in large-scale, vertically integrated and capital-intensive units. Firms employing over 100 workers together contribute 70.1% of the value added in manufacturing. Concentration is most pronounced in beverages, tobacco, cosmetics, paper and paper products, and household appliances and somewhat less so in textiles and food processing.

Food and beverages constitute the largest manufacturing sector, followed by chemicals and textiles. Over 65% of the manufacturing establishments are concentrated in the Manila area and the southern Luzon region. The government's industrial strategy places high priority on the dispersal of manufacturing capacity outside the capital.

The Philippine government embarked on the Export Processing Zone project in 1972, and since then, the concept has assumed a more important role in national development. These zones are designed to promote the processing of goods for export, thereby earning foreign exchange, generating employment, and broadening the industrial base. There are at present five such zones. The program is to develop a total of 15 zones in various parts of the country. Development of these zones follows the requirements of a modern industrial area, where aside from the basic utilities, the amenities of community life also are provided. The industry mix in the zones gives significant weight to labor-intensive operations. As a matter of policy, however, all categories of manufacturing activity are evaluated on their overall contribution to the attainment of zone objectives. A large number of companies now operate in the zones, and they represent investments from the United States, the United Kingdom, Australia, Canada, Austria, Germany, France, Japan, Italy, Korea, Malaysia, Taiwan, Norway, Singapore, Indonesia and Hong Kong. U.S. companies now located in the zones include Texas Instruments, Timex, Ford Motor Co. and many others. The organization mandated to develop and manage the zones is the Export Processing Zone Authority (EPZA), created in 1972 as a government corporation.

The most dynamic component of the industrial sector has been the performance of non-traditional manufactured exports. Within the category garments and electronics have led the way, but furniture, wood products, shoes and leather goods have also shown increasing export potential. Most of these industries also tend to be labor intensive and some of the fastest growing, such as ready-made garments and transistorized electronics, depend on imported raw materials that are assembled or fashioned in the Philippines—often in the Bataan Free Trade Zone or one of the two new equivalents in Baguio or Cebu—for shipment abroad. A public-private sector dialogue was also opened with 40 leading domestic market companies to motivate expansion of their export efforts and to encourage 12 leading business groups to organize international trading networks.

In line with reshaping the manufacturing sector to meet international competition the decision was also made to dismantle protective measures that sheltered domestic industries from foreign competition but stymied growth. Such changes will entail, among other things, a gradual but significant tariff reduction, scaling down the "list of overcrowded industries" in order to permit new entrants into the market, emphasis on larger and more internationally competitive plant units, and decentralization outside the metropolitan Manila area.

In September 1983, Marcos announced a stepped up industrialization program that would include some 11 major projects at a total cost of about $6 billion. Most of these projects, such as a copper smelter, a phosphate fertilizer plant, an aluminum smelter, an integrated steel mill, a diesel engine plant, a downstream petrochemical project, rationalization of the concrete and coconut industries, and an integrated pulp and paper mill have been under discussion for several years and have suffered from mounting cost inflation. It is now planned that as many of the projects as possible should be put into place in the next decade to reduce plant costs and move the country ahead into heavy industry. A key element in implementation will be the attraction of maximum foreign investment, as well as the utilization of export credits with extended grace periods.

Foreign investments are governed by the Investment Incentives Act of 1973, which created the Board of Investments (BOI). The BOI annually issues an export priorities plan indicating product areas that qualify for export incentives. BOI's annual investment priorities plan divides qualifying investments into preferred non-pioneer and preferred pioneer categories. Only in a pioneer industry may the equity share of foreign investors go up to 100%. BOI also considers the ratio of capital to employment and balanced regional development.

The United States remains the main source of foreign investment but with a lesser share of the total than formerly. U.S. investment in the Philippines is mostly direct investment. The book value of U.S. direct investment in the Philippines in 1981 was $1.3 billion, up from $644 million in 1972. Current asset value is well over $2 billion. Until 1970, U.S. firms accounted for 80% of all foreign investment. From February 1970 to December 1981, of the $1.6 billion of Central Bank (CB) approved investment, the United States accounted for 54% compared with Japan's 15%. Japanese investment, as of March 1982, totaled $687 million or 20% of all foreign investment in the Philippines. While the value of U.S. investment has risen, the trend in percentage of U.S. share of total foreign investment has been downward in recent years. Of those investments approved by the Board of Investments (BOI), the U.S. share was 25% of the 1981 total of $252 million, compared with 44% of $15 million in 1970. Filipino majority control is required for industries exploiting natural resources. The pace of foreign investment increased following the declaration of martial law, because the Marcos regime allowed repatriation of new foreign capital and unrestricted remittance of profits. Net direct private investment in 1983 totaled $104 million.

ENERGY

In 1982 the Philippines produced energy equivalent to 1.952 million metric tons of coal and consumed energy equivalent to 16.830 million metric tons of coal, or 331 kg (730 lb) per capita. The national energy deficit is equivalent to 14.878 million metric tons of coal. Annual refinery capacity is 286,000 barrels per day.

Philippine petroleum production in 1983 was 5 million barrels from the Nido field near Palawan Island with proved reserves of 16 million barrels. Two more fields opened in 1980 at Cadlao and Matinloc. All sources of domestic energy contribute only 18% of the country's energy needs.

The annual growth rates during 1973-83 were 20.8% for energy production and 2.3% energy consumption. Energy imports account for 44% of all merchandise imports. Apparent per capita consumption of gasoline is 45 gallons per year.

Electric power production in 1984 was 23 billion kwh, or 414 kwh per capita.

LABOR

The economically active population is estimated at 19.085 million, of which women constitute 35.7%. Half the work force is employed in agriculture, 11.6% in trade, 10.2% in manufacturing, 4.2% in transport and communications, 3.2% in construction and 2.1% in finance. Wage and salary workers constitute 41.3% of the labor force, self-employed persons 40.4% and unpaid family workers the remainder. The range of open unemployment ranges between 8 and 10%, although only 4.0% is admitted in official records. With 600,000 new entrants each year, the average annual growth rate of the work force is 3.4%.

Children under 15 may not legally be employed except when working directly under the sole responsibility of parents or guardians. However, with parental assent and under the rules laid down by the Ministry of Labor and Employment (MOLE), apprentice programs are allowed for children 14 years and over. The Labor Code also places responsibility on the minister of labor for conditions of employment of all persons aged 15 to 18 but prohibits employment in hazardous occupations of those younger than 18. There are credible reports of many violations of these provisions of the Labor Code.

The 8-hour day, 48-hour week and a rest day after each 6 working days are mandated by law. With exceptions, women are prohibited from working between 10 p.m. and 6 a.m. The Labor Ministry plays a key role in the setting of legislated minimum daily wages rates. The minimum daily rate for nonagricultural workers in Metro Manila was $57.08 per day as of November 1, 1984. Outside of Metro Manila the rate was $56.00. In the agricultural sector, and for nonplantation workers, it is $35.67. The Ministry of Labor conducts inspections to ensure compliance with minimum wage standards and working conditions but admits that it faces a difficult task. It cites a study claiming that of the Manila sweatshops it surveyed half paid substandard wages. The ministry concludes that the 8-hour day requirement is more apt to be respected but notes that firms in the Bataan export processing zone usually report considerable overtime. There are reports of compulsory overtime. All workplace laws apply equally to export zones. Inspections between January-October 1984 of 923 establishments revealed 1,980 violations of wage rules involving cost of living allowances, 13th-month payments, overtime, and related matters.

The Philippine government reports that wages in the Philippines are the second lowest in Southeast Asia; only Indonesia ranks lower. Working conditions are governed by the Labor Code of 1974, which prohibits unfair labor practices and regulates industrial health and safety, private employment agencies and wage payments, and ensures speedy disposal of claims.

Effective March 22, 1981, the current legal effective daily minimum wages (legal minimum wage plus mandatory cost-of-living allowance plus daily portion of mandatory 13th month pay) range from P37.63 for large establishments in Metro Manila to a low of P18.53 for agricultural workers employed by small firms. Minimum wages vary according to nonagricultural and agricultural firms, whether located in Metro Manila or outside Metro Manila, and capitalization of enterprise. The Department of Labor, however, may require higher wages than these in certain industries to maintain the employee's health and well-being. Most foreign companies in the Philippines pay wages substantially above the legal minimum. Workers on piecework basis are guaranteed wages not below the applicable minimum wage rates. The minimum wage law does not apply to farm tenants, domestic servants and persons working at home in needlework or in any cottage industry registered under the National Cottage Industry Act.

The right of labor to strike is guaranteed by the Industrial Peace Act. Until recently however, Presidential Decree No. 823, which was enacted in November 1975, prohibited the staging of strikes and picketing in vital industries. A new law, known as National Assembly Bill 130, removed the ban on strikes in a long list of industries which had embraced virtually the entire economy. The law provides for the right to strike or lockout in the private sector, except over issues involving inter-union or intra-union disputes. Thirty-day notice of strike or lockout must be filed in cases of collective bargaining impasses, and 15 days in case of an alleged unfair labor practice. The decision to strike must be approved by two-thirds of the members. In granting the right to strike the new law removed the prior clearance employers had to obtain from Ministry of Labor and Employment before they could terminate an employee. Employers, however, must introduce due process procedures under which workers may appeal unfair dismissals. A provision of the Peaceful Picketing Law permits companies to freely take into and out of the company premises company products.

Several thousand Filipino workers are currently working abroad, many of them on construction projects.

EMPLOYMENT
('000 persons aged 15 years and over, October–December 1983)

Agriculture, hunting, forestry and fishing	10,250
Mining and quarrying	188
Manufacturing	1,795
Electricity, gas and water	88
Construction	626
Trade, restaurants and hotels	2,257
Transport, storage and communication	901
Financing, insurance, real estate and business services	313
Community, social and personal services	3,246
Activities not adequately defined	8
Total employed	19,672
Males	12,004
Females	7,668

A variety of trade unions claim slightly more than two million workers out of a total labor force of 20 million. There are also about 2.7 million workers in the National Congress of Farmers Organizations. Union membership in the Philippines tends to be nominal, rather than being composed of active, dues-paying members. However, there are no government restrictions on the right to organize and to affiliate with federations, confederations, or international organizations, or on the right to strike, except for public servants and employees of certain government corporations. National labor organizations are affiliated to the International Confederation of Free Trade Unions (ICFTU), and to the Communist-dominated World Federation of Trade Unions (WFTU). The nation has 1,954 registered labor groups; none has been canceled or "deregistered" during 1983-85. Union certification elections are generally considered to be fairly run. Unions continue to negotiate collective bargaining agreements and to strike. In October 1984, the Ministry of Labor and Employment (MOLE) reported 2,007 collective bargaining agreements covering 266,000 workers as "active".

Compulsory arbitration was exercised in 12 of 937 strike notice instances in 1984, and in 7 of 275 instances through August 1985. The incidence of strikes in the garment industry, in semi-conductor firms, and at export processing zones increased in 1985. Even some public sectors "exempted" from strikes have experienced stoppages. Although a penalty of 6 months' imprisonment for illegal acts by strikers exists, the Labor Ministry asserts that there have been no convictions. However, a Presidential Letter of Instruction was issued in 1985 allowing police to serve injunctions on the picket line in order to halt strikes which the ministry has not authorized. The use of violence is endemic in the Philippines among management and labor. There have been numerous assassinations of labor leaders and trade union members. The military charges that some leftist labor leaders have engaged in assassination.

The Trade Union Congress of the Philippines (TUCP), established in 1975, claims 1.3 million non-agricultural workers and is the only officially recognized trade union umbrella organization in the country. As a result of this official status, TUCP officials are appointed as representatives of labor on tripartite boards such as the Social Security Commission and the National Council on Wages. Because of these links, the TUCP is often criticized by non-TUCP union leaders as being government controlled. However, the TUCP frequently criticizes the government about poor wages and bad working conditions as well as on issues affecting trade union autonomy from government controls.

Most government-owned and controlled organizations (a different category from public servants), are unionized and negotiate collective bargaining agreements. Public service associations, such as public school teachers, cannot legally form recognized unions nor can they legally go on strike. Nonetheless, the Manila Public School Teachers Association struck several times in 1984. The government is considering a bill to permit public sector employees to organize and bargain but with limitations on their right to strike.

The ILO has communicated with the government to criticize aspects of the Filipino labor situation, including the requirement of approval by 30% of the work force before union recognition is granted; restrictions on the right to establish federations; compulsory arbitration in certain instances; a 1982 law banning strikes in industries that affect the national interest (including export-oriented ones in export processing zones); advance approval of strikes by two-thirds of union members; decrees threatening imprisonment of picketers propagandizing against the government; and denial of the right to organize unions for teachers, public health personnel and other public servants. The government has replied in some detail to ILO criticisms; its reply appeared in the report of the Committee on the Application of Conventions and Recommendations. The ILO has noted that a review of labor legislation is under way and that a draft bill is before the National Assembly incorporating some of the provisions referred to by ILO supervisory bodies.

FOREIGN COMMERCE

The foreign commerce of the Philippines consisted in 1984 of exports of $5.342 billion and imports of $6.262 billion, leaving an unfavorable trade balance of $919.5 million.

Of the imports, crude petroleum constituted 25.3%, nonelectrical machinery 11.1%, chemicals 9.9%, electrical machinery 4.8%, petroleum products 4.2%, iron and steel 4.1%, motor vehicles 3.4%, cereals 3.2%, textiles 1.9% and dairy products 1.7%. Of the exports, clothing constituted 10.8%, sugar 9.9%, coconut oil 9.3%, copper concentrates 7.5%, fruits and vegetables

6.6%, gold 3.8%, logs 3.6%, veneers and plywood 2.7%, fish 2.5% and electrical machinery 2.1%.

The major import sources are: the United States 22.5%, Saudi Arabia 13.1%, Kuwait 5.2% and West Germany 4.0%. The major export destinations are: the United States 30.4%, Japan 21.9%, the Netherlands 5.6%, West Germany 4.2% and Hong Kong 3.9%.

FOREIGN TRADE INDICATORS (1984)	
Annual Growth Rate, Imports:	7.5% (1973-83)
Annual Growth Rate, Exports:	1.3% (1973-83)
Ratio of Exports to Imports:	46:54
Exports per capita:	$94
Imports per capita:	$110
Balance of Trade:	–$919.5 million
Ratio of International Reserves to Imports (in months)	0.9
Exports as % of GDP:	19.2
Imports as % of GDP:	23.6
Value of Manufactured Exports:	$2.492 billion
Commodity Concentration:	26.4%

Direction of Trade (%)	Imports	Exports
EEC	10.3	16.2
U.S.	22.6	30.9
Industrialized Market Economies	57.2	75.3
East European Economies	0.1	1.1
High Income Oil Exporters	15.2	1.2
Developing Economies	39.7	21.8

Composition of Trade (%)	Imports	Exports
Food	8.5	34.6
Agricultural Raw Materials	2.2	4.8
Fuels	30.1	0.7
Ores & Minerals	5.6	15.7
Manufactured Goods	40.7	22.8
of which Chemicals	9.9	1.9
of which Machinery	22.6	2.7

Based on 1975=100, the import price index in 1981 was 229, the export price index was 156.0 and the terms of trade (export prices divided by import prices x 100) 68.0.

TRANSPORTATION & COMMUNICATIONS

The rail system consists of 1,144 km (710 mi) of track, of which the Philippine National Railways owns 1,028 km (638 mi). Industrial railroads are also operated by sugar mills, known as centrals, and logging companies. The northern line runs from Manila to San Fernando and the southern line from Manila to Legaspi. On Panay, the capital city, Iloilo, is linked with Roxas. Rail traffic in 1982 consisted of 204 million passenger-km and 24 million net-ton-km. The length of oil pipelines is 251 km (156 mi). The inland waterways are navigable for 3,219 km (2,000 mi) by shallow draft vessels.

Of the 350 ports, only 20 are ports of entry for vessels engaged in foreign trade. The largest is Manila, which handles 70% of the national imports and 5% of its exports. Other ports handling a substantial

volume of shipping are Iloilo, Batangas, Catbalogan, Tacloban, Butuan, Cebu, Cagayan de Oro, Iligan, Oramiz, Damaguete, Zamboanga, Jolo, Davao, Pulupandan and Gen. Santos. The Philippine national merchant marine consists of over 884 vessels with a total GRT of 4,719,300, of which 577,000 GRT are accounted by oil tankers and 961,000 GRT by ore and bulk carriers. In 1982 Philippine ports handled 30,816,000 tons of cargo.

The road system is 152,800 km (94,888 mi) long, of which 27,800 km (17,264 mi) are paved. About half of the total length is in Luzon and one-third in the Visayan Islands. Roads are divided into four categories: National, National Aid, Provincial and City, and Municipal. The principal artery is the Pan-Philippine Highway which runs from Aparri in northern Luzon through Samar and Leyte to Davao in southern Mindanao. It has two major inter-island crossings served by ferries. In 1982 these roads were used by 318,085 passenger cars and 485,667 commercial vehicles. Per capita passenger car ownership is 5.6 per 1,000 inhabitants. City transportation is handled by buses as well as jeepneys, colorfully painted and decorated taxis that hold up to 10 passengers.

The national airline is Philippine Air Lines (PAL), which operates a fleet of 53 aircraft on internal services as well as international services to Australia, Hawaii, Hong Kong, Japan, Pakistan, Taiwan, Thailand, the U.S.A., West Germany, Italy and the Netherlands. In 1982 the airline flew 45.7 million km (12.97 million mi) and carried 3,867,000 passengers. There are 338 airfields in the country, of which 289 are usable, 68 have permanent-surface runways and nine have runways over 2,500 meters (8,000 ft).

In 1984, 707,000 telephones were in use, or 1.28 per 100 inhabitants.

The Philippines has 2,038 post offices. No information is available on mail traffic. There are 8,637 telex subscriber lines.

In 1982, 878,000 tourists visited the Philippines. Of these, 174,300 were from the United States, 22,400 from the United Kingdom, 193,100 from Japan, 20,500 from Canada, 63,900 from Australia and 32,100 from West Germany. In 1982 tourism generated revenues of $450 million while expenditures by tourists abroad totaled $127 million. There are 25,000 hotel beds and the average length of stay was 5.3 days.

MINING

Mining contributes only 2% to the GDP, but the Philippines has rich mineral resources. The total mineral base has not been precisely determined because only 10% of the national territory has been geologically surveyed. The principal minerals currently being produced are copper, gold, iron, coal, manganese and chromite. Copper is mined in northern Luzon, Cebu, Negros and Samar, gold in northern Luzon and Cebu, iron ore in southeastern Luzon and southern and northern Mindanao, and chromite in western Luzon.

MINERAL PRODUCTION (1983) (000 tons)			
Coal	1,020	Iron	3
Chromium	155	Copper	271
Gold (000 troy oz)	817	Nickel (metric tons)	13,900
Silver (000 troy oz)	1,182		

DEFENSE

The defense structure is headed by the president, as the commander in chief of the armed forces. The chain of command runs through the minister of national defense to the chief of staff, who presides over the General Military Council. The bulk of the army is now deployed in two recently established commands, CENCOM (Cotabato and Lanao provinces in Mindanao) and SOWESCOM (Zamboanga province on Mindanao and Sulu). The Moro rebels are most active in Jolo Island in Sulu.

Military manpower is obtained through voluntary enlistment. But all Filipino males are required to register for conscription on reaching the age of 20. Certain inducted men are mobilized in special units called Kamagong (after a native hardwood) available for active service at short notice.

The total strength of the armed forces is 114,800 or 2.9 armed persons for every 1,000 civilians.

ARMY:

Personnel: 70,000

Organization: 5 infantry divisions; 1 ranger regiment; 2 engineer brigades; 1 light armored regiment; 4 artillery regiments; 1 military police brigade

Equipment: 28 tanks; 45 armored vehicles; 200 armored personnel carriers; 212 howitzers; mortars; rocket launchers

NAVY:

Personnel: 28,000

Units: 7 frigates; 10 corvettes; 12 large patrol craft; 3 support ships; 99 amphibious craft; 1 search and rescue squadron; 1 presidential yacht; 3 repair ships; 2 tankers

Marines: 3 brigades

Major Naval Base: Sangley Point

AIR FORCE:

Personnel: 16,800

Organization: 64 aircraft; 17 helicopters; 1 fighter squadron; 1 air defense squadron; 3 counterinsurgency squadrons; 1 presidential transport squadron; 5 transport squadrons; 1 liaison squadron; 3 training squadrons; 1 weather squadron

Major Air Bases: Clark (Angeles), Pampanga, Basa (Florida Blanca), Fermando (Lipa), Batangas, Sangley, Cavite, Mactan (Lapu), Edwin Andrew (Zamboanga) and Nichols (Manila)

The defense budget in 1985 totaled $422.078 million, representing 15.1% of the national budget, 1.9% of the GNP, $13 per capita, $8,558 per soldier and $3,223 per sq km of national territory.

Until the 1970s defense policy was based on the principle of limiting the size of the standing military forces while maintaining a large body of reserves, a principle first enunciated by Gen. Douglas MacArthur in the belief that any conventional attack could be turned back with U.S. assistance. Defense policy also stressed basic weaponry in preference to sophisticated equipment. With the fall of Saigon the central assumptions of this policy underwent a reappraisal. The potential threat to national security is perceived now as arising from domestic subversion and not external aggression. The new strategy therefore calls for a people's army capable of coping with externally supported subversion without relying on outside assistance.

From 1946 through 1983 the Philippines received $1.207 billion in military grants and loans from the United States. Arms purchases abroad during 1973-83 totaled $540 million, of which $200 million was supplied by the United States.

Small arms and aerospace system components are produced domestically.

EDUCATION

The national literacy rate is 83% (84.6% for males and 82.2% for females). Of the population over 25, 19.8% have had no schooling, 56.4% have entered and/or completed first level, 14.2% have entered and/or completed second level, and 9.6% have some kind of post-graduate training.

Schooling is free, universal and compulsory, in principle, for six years from the ages of seven to 13. The net school enrollment ratios are 90% at the first level (7 to 12) and 45% at the second level (13 to 16), for a combined gross enrollment ratio of 90%. The third level enrollment ratio is 26.6%. Girls constitute 49% of primary school enrollment, 51% of secondary school enrollment and 54% of post-secondary enrollment.

Schooling lasts for 10 years (among the shortest in the world in duration), divided into six years of primary school and four years of secondary school. Both primary and secondary education are deficient in several respects. Only one out of four (one out of 17 in rural areas) students can afford to buy text books. The curriculum is heavily oriented toward rote learning. Standardized tests and audiovisual materials are in short supply. There is a dropout rate of 25% at the secondary level. In 1982 there were 32,304 primary schools, 2,445 secondary schools and 558 institutions of higher learning in the educational system.

The school year runs from June to March. The medium of instruction is Pilipino until the third year and English thereafter.

There is a surplus of teachers in both primary and secondary schools. About 94% of the teachers are believed to be fully qualified. The national teacher-pupil ratio is 1:32 in primary schools, 1:34 in secondary schools and 1:29 in post-secondary institutions.

Vocational schools generally provide terminal programs enabling students to join the work force on completion. Private schools, many of them run by the Catholic Church account for 5% of primary and 38% of secondary enrollment.

The administration and financing of education are the responsibility of the Ministry of Education and Culture assisted by the National Board of Education and the Board of Higher Education. In 1982 the ministry's budget totaled P6,581,205,000, representing 13.3% of the national budget, 2.0% of the GNP and $15.0 per capita.

EDUCATIONAL ENROLLMENT (1983)			
	Schools	Teachers	Students
First Level	32,304	272,134	8,591,267
Second Level	2,445	90,226	3,092,128
Third Level	N.A.	44,506	1,335,889

Higher education is provided in 41 universities and over 600 other institutions with a total enrollment in 1983 of 1,335,889. Enrollment in higher education is at a ratio of 3,680 per 100,000 inhabitants. About 86% of the institutions are privately operated and just under 50% are located in Manila.

MAJOR UNIVERSITIES OF THE PHILIPPINES	
University	Location
Adamson University	Manila
Araneta University	Manila
Bicol University	Legazpi
University of the East	Manila
Far Eastern University	Manila
Feati University	Manila
University of Mindanao	Davao
University of Nueva Caceres	Naga
University of Pangasinan	Dagupan
Manuel L. Quezon University	Manila
Saint Louis University	Baguio
University of San Carlos	Cebu
University of Santo Tomas	Manila
University of the Visayas	Cebu

In 1980, 208,767 students were graduated from Philippine universities. Of these, 20,416 were awarded degrees in medicine, 20,833 in engineering, 11,445 in natural sciences, 52,320 in commercial and business administration, 2,339 in law, 11,229 in education and 7,252 in agriculture.

In 1982, 3,778 Philippine students were enrolled in institutions of higher learning abroad. Of these, 2,727 were in the United States, 110 in Canada, 48 in the United Kingdom, 339 in Saudi Arabia, 109 in Australia, 107 in Japan, 127 at the Vatican, 31 in Belgium and 84 in West Germany. In 1981 5,901 foreign students were enrolled in the Philippines.

In 1982, 5,146 scientists were reported engaged in research and development. Expenditures on scientific research in the same year totaled P522,970,000. The Philippines ranks 38th in the world in contribution to world scientific authorship with a share of 0.25% (U.S., 42%). One hundred and ten scientific journals are published in the country.

LEGAL SYSTEM

The legal system is based on Spanish law as modified by Anglo-American law.

The judiciary is headed by the Supreme Court, comprising a chief justice and 14 associates. Most appellate cases other than those reserved for the Supreme Court are heard by the 18-member court of appeals, which sits either en banc or in six divisions of three justices each.

Below the court of appeals, the country is divided into 16 judicial districts with 212 courts of first instance, with each court having one or more judges of first instance. There is a municipal court for each city and a justice of the peace for each municipality.

If a defendant cannot afford counsel, the court will appoint a lawyer. Private and government legal assistance is available to indigents, and there are lawyers' organizations which provide assistance to alleged national security offenders. Because of case backlogs, a shortage of judges, and the practice of hearing cases concurrently, trials in civilian courts often take two or three years. Subversion and rebellion trials have frequently lasted longer. Trial by jury is not a part of Philippine jurisprudence. Questions of law and fact, including determinations of guilt or innocence, are all resolved by the presiding judge.

The national penitentiary is the Bilibid prison at Manila. There are four penal colonies in the provinces of Davao (Davao Penal Colony), Zamboanga (San Ramon Prison Farm), Mindoro (Sablayon Penal Colony) and Palawan (Iwahig Penal Colony). There is also a correctional institution for women at Rizal. Each municipality and province has its own place of detention, often consisting of a few rooms at the police headquarters.

LAW ENFORCEMENT

The principal law enforcement agencies are the National Police Commission, the National Bureau of Investigation, the Integrated National Police, the Philippine Constabulary and the National Intelligence Coordinating Agency. The total strength of the police force in the mid-1970s was 38,059, or one policeman for every 1,025 inhabitants.

The National Police Commission is the main administrative body charged with the supervision and control of all law enforcement agencies. Each province and city has at least one Board of Investigators representing the commission. The National Bureau of Investigation is modeled on the Federal Bureau of Investigation in the United States. It functions as an investigative, training and technical agency under a director with 10 regional offices and numerous suboffices. In 1975 all municipal, police, fire and jail organizations were consolidated into one force called the Integrated National Police under the control of a director general. The Integrated National Police functions directly under the department of national defense and is thus subject to the immediate command of the president as commander in chief of the armed forces. The force comprises 64 former city forces and 1,447 former municipal forces. The core of the force is the Philippine Constabulary, whose chief is concurrently director general of the Integrated National Police. The constabulary is divided into five zone commands, eight battalions and 134 companies, including a dog company and a company of horse cavalry. Each provincial detachment operates under a provincial commander, and there are 187 posts and stations manned by units of varying size. There are also a number of specialized units, such as the anti-narcotics unit, the offshore anticrime battalion and the presidential security command. The unnamed secret police are known simply as internal security units.

Crime statistics are published regularly. Of an estimated total of 216,472 crimes committed in 1972 (down from 298,991 in the pre-martial law year of 1971), 26.3% were crimes against persons, 41.7% were crimes against property, 2.1% against chastity, 16.8% against morals and order and 13.1% fell in other categories. The national crime rate is 554 per 100,000 persons with sharp regional variations. The provinces with the highest crime rates (per 100,000 population) are Manila (1,928), Nueva Ecija (7,521), Benguet (1,596) and Rizal (1,367). The province with the lowest crime rate is Occidental Mindoro with a reported rate of 84 per 100,000.

HEALTH

Expenditures for health services accounted for 3.5% of the national budget and $3.70 per capita. Private and public health services reach about two-thirds of the population. Major health problems include pneumonia and tuberculosis. Malaria is prevalent in Luzon and Mindanao. Only 43% of the population have access to safe water.

```
PRINCIPAL HEALTH INDICATORS (1984)
Crude Death Rate: 6.9 per 1,000
Decline in Death Rate: -43.7% (1965-83)
Life Expectancy at Birth: 62.8 (Males); 66.3 (Females)
Infant Mortality Rate: 50.0 per 1,000 Live Births
Child Death Rate (Ages 1-4) per 1,000: 4
```

In 1980 there were 1,416 hospitals in the country with 93,474 beds, or one bed per 518 inhabitants. In 1975 there were 7,378 physicians, or one physician per 6,713 inhabitants, 1,090 dentists, and 9,614 nursing personnel. Of the hospitals 25.1% are state-run, and 74.9% are run by private nonprofit agencies.

FOOD

The staple food is rice supplemented by a variety of vegetables. The main source of protein is fish. Most meals are simply prepared except on festive occasions when more elaborate dishes, such as lechon (pig stuffed with rice and vegetables), are prepared. The common alcoholic beverages are tuba (fermented coconut juice), basi (fermented sugarcane juice) and lambanog (fermented rice juice).

The daily per capita intake of food is 2,315 calories, 51.7 grams of protein, 28 grams of fats and 378 grams of carbohydrates.

MEDIA & CULTURE

In 1982, 22 daily newspapers were published in the country with a total circulation of 1,972,000, or 35 per 1,000. One newspaper is published in Pilipino and one in Chinese and English. The rest are published in English. The best-selling daily is *People's Journal* with a circulation of 508,000. In addition, there are 84 nondailies, of which 73 are issued from once to three times a week. The periodical press consists of some 143 titles with an aggregate circulation of 6 million copies. Of these, the largest circulate up to 170,000 copies per issue. The annual consumption of newsprint in 1981 was 81,900 tons, or 1,621 kg (3.5 lb) per 1,000 inhabitants.

The Philippines had a vigorous and diverse press before the imposition of martial law in 1972 when all newspaper and radio stations were shut down. The president claimed that he had silenced the media because some were giving aid and comfort to the Communists. A number of editors, publishers and reporters were arrested. Resumption of publication required the authorization of the Mass Media Council, whose real function was the suppression of the media. These strict controls were gradually relaxed, and the Mass Media Council was replaced in 1973 by the Media Advisory Council, which, in turn, was replaced by the Philippine Council for Print Media, an all-civilian body. Newspapers are expected to publish only news of "positive national value." Since the end of martial law in 1981, the media have moved cautiously but steadily toward a more candid coverage and commentary. Censorship of foreign publications has virtually ceased.

The national news agency is the Philippines News Agency founded in 1973. Foreign news bureaus represented in Manila include AFP, AP, CNA, Hsinhua, Reuters, Tass and UPI.

There are two large, 28 medium-sized and 58 small publishers in Manila and 13 in the provinces with a total annual output in 1981 of 431 titles. Although the Philippines adheres to the Universal Copyright, Berne and Florence Conventions, piracy is widespread and is tolerated under certain specious provisions of the Stockholm Agreement.

Broadcasting is carried out, under the supervision of the Broadcast Media Council, by over 70 networks operating 270 radio stations, of which 40 are in the Greater Manila area. The largest network is operated by the Philippine Broadcasting Service under the Office of the President with three medium-wave and 13 short-wave stations. Other stations belong to one of three categories: commercial, religious or educational. Most of the private religious networks have programs for overseas listeners; the Far East Broadcasting Company, a Protestant missionary outreach, broadcasts in 46 languages beamed to seven regions including the Soviet Union. Of the 3,949,560 radio program hours, 254,140 hours are devoted to information, 789,912 hours to education, 671,426 hours to culture, 118,488 hours to religion, 535,772 hours to commercials and 1,382,344 hours to entertainment. In 1982 there were 2,180,000 radio receivers in the country, or 43 per 1,000 inhabitants.

Television, introduced in 1953, is operated by five major networks with 19 carrying and 7 relay stations, of which seven are in Greater Manila. Broadcasting hours are governed by the type of license and vary from 10 to 19 hours per day. Of the total 376,246 television program hours, 26,338 hours are devoted to information, 75,250 hours to education, 63,961 hours to culture 11,286 hours to religion, 48,911 to commercials and 131,687 hours to entertainment. In 1982 there were 1,250,000 television sets in the country, or 25 per 1,000 inhabitants.

There are over 45 domestic motion picture producers with an annual output of 143 full-length feature films in 1975. In 1980 there were 716 fixed cinemas with 569,800 seats, or 13.5 seats per 1,000 inhabitants. Annual movie attendance is 315 million, or 7.5 per capita. In 1981 589 full length foreign films were imported, 206 of these from the United States.

The Philippines has 449 public libraries, of which the largest is the National Library with 129,000 volumes. Per capita there are 19 volumes and five registered borrowers per 1,000 inhabitants.

There are 79 museums, of which 22 are national museums and 36 private museums. Annual museum attendance is close to 2 million. There are nine nature preservation sites.

There are 10 theaters in Manila serving three professional companies and 16 amateur troupes.

SOCIAL WELFARE

The Social Security System, introduced in 1957, provides mandatory coverage for all wage and salary workers. Public servants are covered by the Philippine Government Service Insurance System. Benefits include compensation for work-related injuries, pensions, death benefits for widows and orphans. All covered workers also participate in the Philippine Medicare System, which pays hospitalization and surgical expenses.

Public welfare programs are administered by the Social Welfare Administration which cooperates with private relief agencies in providing services for the needy in a variety of situations.

GLOSSARY

barangay: a citizens' assembly established by the 1973 constitution as the lowest unit of local self-government.

barrio: until 1974, the lowest political subdivision of the municipality consisting of one core hamlet and a number of satellite hamlets.

datu: a local leader of the Muslim Moros.

Igorot; literally mountaineer. Member of any one of numerous pagan communities of the interior.

poblacion: the government seat of a municipality.

samahong nayon: an agricultural cooperative created as part of the 1973 agrarian reform.

sandiganbayan: court with special jurisdiction over civil and criminal cases involving graft and corruption.

sangguniang bayan: a municipal, city, or provincial council.

sitio: a hamlet, as an administrative unit of a barrio.

tanodbayan: (In the 1973 constitution) office of the ombudsman who receives and investigates complaints against public officials and policies.

CHRONOLOGY (from 1946)

1946— The Philippines becomes an independent republic with Manuel Roxas as president.

1947— The Philippines signs the Military Bases Agreement with the United States.

1948— President Roxas dies and is succeeded in office by Elpidio Quirino.

1950— The Communist Hukbalahap movement collapses as their leadership is captured.

1953— Ramon Magsaysay is elected to the presidency on the Nationalist Party ticket.

1954— The Philippines joins SEATO.

1955— The Laurel-Langley Agreement is signed with the United States providing for certain tariff preferences.

1957— Magsaysay dies in an air crash and is succeeded in office by Vice President Carlos P. Garcia.

1961— Diosdado Macapagal is elected president over incumbent Garcia.

1965— Ferdinand E. Marcos is elected president defeating incumbent Macapagal.

1969— Marcos is reelected president and becomes the first president ever to be sworn in for a second time.

1972— Marcos imposes martial law citing internal and external dangers; all opposition leaders are arrested; the media are shut down; the constitution is suspended and the Assembly is dissolved.

1973— A new constitution is approved in national referendum proposing a return to parliamentary form of government. . . . Moro insurgency in the south intensifies.

1976— Pact is signed with Libya granting partial autonomy to southern areas with Moro majority.

1977— The Philippines drops its claims on Sabah.

1978— In national election Marcos' New Society Movement claims to have won all 200 seats in the Interim National Assembly, while the opposition People's Force Party charges electoral fraud.... Philippines occupies Spratley Islands.... Marcos sworn in as prime minister as the new assembly convenes.

1979— In a partial relaxation of martial law, 1,602 prisoners are released and the power of military courts is curtailed.

1980— Marcos party wins local elections but the results are clouded by charges of fraud, some of them acknowledged by Marcos; Beningo Aquino, the government's principal opponent, is released from prison; Government attempts to patch up differences with the Catholic clergy.

1981— Marcos lifts martial law but retains martial law decrees.... Marcos is reelected to another six years in office.

1982— Opposition parties merge into the United National Democratic Organization (UNIDO) under Salvador Laurel.

1983— Opposition leader Benigno Aquino is shot dead in Manila Airport on return from exile in the United States and his assassin is shot dead by the military... Commission of Inquiry concludes that the assassination was masterminded by the army... Chief of Staff Gen. Fabian Ver is relieved of his position and is indicted for the crime.... United States and Philippines sign accord renewing U.S. rights to naval bases until 1988.

1984— In parliamentary elections, opposition parties win 59 out of 183 elective seats... Over 100 people are believed to have been killed in election-related clashes.

1985— Growing domestic unrest and international pressure force Marcos to call an early presidential election in 1986.

1986— In presidential elections, marred by fraud and violence, President Marcos declares himself winner and Assembly ratifies his election... Opposition presidential candidate Mrs. Corazon Aquino, contests the decision and declares herself winner... Defense minister and long time ally Juan Ponce Enrile and Chief of Staff Fidel Ramos defect to the Aquino forces... International and domestic outrage over election fraud force Marcos to flee to the United States hours after his formal inauguration... Mrs. Aquino is sworn in as president with Salvador Laurel, her running mate, as vice president... President Aquino dissolves the National Assembly and the constitution until a new constitution is drafted and ratified... Philippine government launches effort to uncover and reclaim hidden Marcos millions abroad.

BIBLIOGRAPHY (from 1970)

Averch. H.A., *The Matrix Policy in the Philippines* (Princeton, N.J., 1971).

—, F.H. Denton and J. E. Koehler, *A Crisis of Ambiguity: Political and Economic Development in the Philippines* (Santa Monica, Calif., 1970).

Baldwin, Robert, *The Philippines* (New York, 1975).

Bello, Walden and David Kinley, *Development Debacle: The World Bank in the Philippines* (San Francisco, Calif., 1982).

Buss, Claude A., *The United States and the Philippines: Background for Policy* (Stanford, Calif., 1977).

Carlson, Sevinc and Robert A. Kilmarx, *United States-Philippines Economic Relations* (Washington, D.C., 1971).

Cebu: City of Legend. B&W film, 11 min. Producer: not available.

Cultural Policy in the Philippines (Paris, 1974).

Day, Beth, *The Philippines: Shattered Showcase of Democracy in Asia* (New York, 1974).

Del Mar Pernia, Ernesto, *Urbanization, Population Growth and Economic Development in the Philippines* (Westport, Conn., 1977).

Fernando, Enrique M., *The Constitution of the Philippines* (Dobbs Ferry, N.Y., 1975).

Golay, Frank H., *The Philippines: Problems and Prospects* (New York, 1971).

George T.J., *Revolt in Mindanao: The Rise of Islam in Philippine Politics* (New York, 1980).

Hawkins, Edward K., *The Philippines: Priorities and Prospects for Development* (Washington, D.C., 1976).

Hicks, George L. and Geoffrey McNicoll, *Trade and Growth in the Philippines: An Open Dual Economy* (Ithaca, N.Y., 1971).

Hill, Gerald N. and Kathleen Thompson Hill, *The Aquino Assassination: The True Story and Analysis* (Sarver, Pa., 1983).

Infante, Jaime, T., *The Political, Economic and Labor Climate in the Philippines* (Philadelphia, Pa., 1980).

Jocano, F. L., *Social Work in the Philippines A Historical Overview* (Detroit, Mich., 1980).

Kaul, Man M., *The Philippines and Southeast Asia* (New York, 1978).

Kerkvliet, Benedict J., *Political Change in the Philippines* (Honolulu, Hawaii, 1974).

——, *The Huk Rebellion: A Study of Peasant Revolt in the Philippines* (Berkeley, Calif., 1982).

Lawson, Don, *Marcos and the Philippines* (New York, 1984).

Lightfoot, Keith, *The Philippines* (New York, 1973).

Loveday, Douglas F., *The Role of Military Bases in the Philippines Economy* (Santa Monica, Calif., 1971).

Lupdag, Anselmo, *In Search of Filipino Leadership* (Manila, 1984).

Mahajani, Usha, *Philippine Nationalism: External Challenge and Filipino Response* (St. Lucia, Australia, 1971).

Majul, Cesar A., *The Political and Constitutional Ideas of the Philippine Revolution of 1896* (New York, 1973).

Manglapus, Raul S., *Philippines: The Silenced Democracy* (Maryknoll, N.Y., 1976).

Maring, Ester G. and Joel Maring, *Historical and Cultural Dictionary of the Philippines* (Metuchen, N.J., 1973).

May, R.J. and Francisco Nemenzo, *The Philippines After Marcos* (New York, 1985).

McCoy, Alfred W. and Ed. C., De Jesus, Philippine Social History (Honolulu, 1982).

Pasqual, Crisolito, *The Philippines* (Sydney, Australia, 1970).

———, *Philippines Yearbook* (Manila, Annual).

Philippine Republic. B&W film, 15 min. March of Time.

Philippines: Gateway to the Far East. Color/B&W film, 11 min. Coronet.

Philippines: Nation of Islands. Color film, 15 min. Dudly Pictures.

Pomeroy, William J., *American-Made Tragedy: Neo-Colonialism and Dictatorship in the Philippines* (New York, 1973).

Poole, Fred and Max Vanzi, *Revolution in the Philippines: The U.S. in Hall of Cracked Mirrors* (New York, 1984).

Pringle, Robert, *Indonesia & the Philippines* (New York, 1980).

Rosenbert, David A., *Marcos & Martial Law in the Philippines* (Ithaca, N.Y., 1979).

San Juan E., *Crisis in the Philippines: The Making of a Revolution* (South Hadley, Mass., 1985).

Stanley, Peter W., *A Nation in the Making: The Philippines and the United States, 1899-1921* (Cambridge, Mass., 1974).

Steinberg, David J., *Philippines: A Singular and a Plural Place* (Boulder, Colo., 1982).

Sturtevant, David R., *Popular Uprisings in the Philippines* (Ithaca, N.Y., 1976).

The Philippines. B&W film, 10 min. Encyclopaedia Britannica.

The Philippines: Eastern Neighbors. Color film, 11 min. Dudly Pictures.

The Philippines: Island Republic. Color film, 16 min. Contemporary.

The Philippines: Land and People. Color/B&W film, 14 min. Encyclopaedia Britannica.

The Republic of the Philippines. Color film, 18 min. Dudly Pictures.

Thompson, W.S., *Unequal Partners: Philippine and Thai Relations with the United States* (Lexington, Mass., 1975).

Vries, Barend A., *Philippines: Industrial Development Policy and Strategies* (Washington, D.C., 1980).

Wolters, William, *Politics, Patronage and Class Conflict in Central Luzon* (Manila, 1984).

World Bank, *The Philippines: Priorities & Prospects for Development* (Baltimore, Md., 1976).

OFFICIAL PUBLICATIONS

Audit Commision, *Annual Consolidated Financial Report of the Government.*

———, *report of the Auditor General to the President and the National Assembly of the Philippines on the National Government.*

Budget Commission, *Republic of the Philippines Budget.*

Philippines Central Bank, *Annual Report.*

———, *Philippine Financial Statistics* (quarterly).

Treasury Bureau, *Annual Report of the Treasurer of the Philippines.*

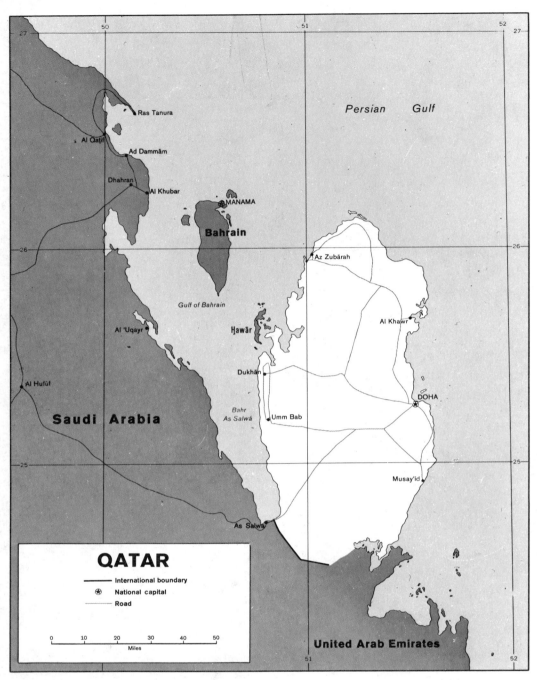

Persian Gulf

Ras Tanura

Al Qaṭif

Ad Dammām

Dhahran

Al Khubar

⊕MANAMA

Bahrain

Az Zubārah

26

Al Khawr

Gulf of Bahrain

Al 'Uqayr

Ḥawār

Dukhān

Al Hufūf

Saudi Arabia

Bahr
As Salwá

Umm Bab

DOHA

25

Musay'id

As Salwá

United Arab Emirates

QATAR

▬▬▬ International boundary

⊛ National capital

─── Road

0   10   20   30   40   50
Miles

QATAR

BASIC FACT SHEET

OFFICIAL NAME: State of Qatar (Dawlat Qatar)

ABBREVIATION: QA

CAPITAL: Doha (Al Dawhah)

HEAD OF STATE & HEAD OF GOVERNMENT: Emir and Prime Minister Sheikh Khalifa bin Hamad Al Thani (Prime Minister from 1970; Emir from 1972)

NATURE OF GOVERNMENT: Absolute monarchy

POPULATION: 301,000 (1985)

AREA: 11,000 sq km (4,247 sq mi)

ETHNIC MAJORITY: Arab

LANGUAGE: Arabic

RELIGION: Wahhabi Islam

UNIT OF CURRENCY: Qatar Rial ($1 = QR3.64, August 1985)

NATIONAL FLAG: Maroon field covering three-fourths of the flag, separated by a vertical serrated line from a white vertical stripe at the hoist

NATIONAL EMBLEM: A design in oval shape consisting of two silver scimitars joined at blade-tip by a silver shell. The device is surrounded by palm branches and superimposed on it is the state's name in Arabic.

NATIONAL ANTHEM: "Qatar National Anthem"

NATIONAL HOLIDAYS: September 3 (National Day, Independence Day); January 1 (New Year's Day); December 25 and 26 (Christmas and Boxing Day); Also variable Islamic festivals

NATIONAL CALENDAR: Islamic and Gregorian

PHYSICAL QUALITY OF LIFE INDEX: 53 (unchanged since 1976) (On an ascending scale with 100 as the maximum. U.S., 95)

DATE OF INDEPENDENCE: September 3, 1971

DATE OF CONSTITUTION: 1970 (Basic Law serving as a constitution)

WEIGHTS & MEASURES: Both Imperial and metric systems are used; full conversion to the metric system is planned.

LOCATION & AREA

Qatar is located on a peninsula projecting northward into the Persian Gulf from the Arabian mainland. It comprises an area of 11,000 sq km (4,247 sq mi) and extends 161 km (100 mi) N to S and 89 km (55 mi) E to W. Its landward frontiers are 112 km (69 mi) in length, of which 67 km (42 mi) are with Saudi Arabia and 45 km (28 mi) with the United Arab Emirates. The total length the Persian Gulf coastline is 378 km (235 mi). The state also has sovereignty over a number of islands, of which Hawar and Halalu are the most important.

The capital is Doha (also known as Al Dawhah) with a 1985 population of 190,000. Umm Said, the onshore oil terminal and industrial zone, has a population of 40,000. The only other urban center is Dukhan.

Qatar has border disputes with all its neighbors: with Saudi Arabia over a small territory north of Khor al-Udayd, with Abu Dhabi over territory south of Khor al-Udayd, and with Bahrain over certain islands in the Gulf of Salwa. These disputes have been quiescent for some time.

The terrain is flat, barren, stony and sandy. The land rises from the east to a low plateau in the center and north pitted with scores of shallow depressions. The southern base of the peninsula is covered by extensive salt flats.

WEATHER

Temperatures range from 6°C (42.8°F) in January to 48°C (118.4°F) in July. Humidity is oppressive along the coast. Annual rainfall ranges between 25 mm (1 in.) and 212.4 mm (8.5 in.).

POPULATION

The population of Qatar is estimated at 301,000 in 1985 on the basis of the nation's first census held in 1981 when the population was 244,534. The population is expected to reach 500,000 by 2000 and 700,000 by 2020.

The urban component of the population is estimated at 86%. Over 77% of the total population of the country lives in the capital city of Doha.

As in other Gulf states, migration is a significant demographic factor providing a constant stream of foreign workers. By 1975 non-natives, both Arabs and non-Arabs, constituted 50% of the population.

In this conservative society, women remain in a subordinate position, largely relegated to roles as mothers and homemakers, although some are now finding jobs in education, medicine, and the news media. Their activities are still bound by a number of social customs and quasi-legal restrictions, such as

```
          DEMOGRAPHIC INDICATORS (1985)
Population (000)                                    301
Density per sq km                                  24.2
% Urban                                            86.1
Sex distribution
  Male %                                          63.62
  Female %                                        36.38
Age Profile: (%)
  0-15                                             32.3
  15-29                                            31.8
  30-44                                            25.8
  45-59                                             7.8
  Over 60                                           2.3
Population doubling time in years at current rate    19
Crude birthrate 1/1000                             29.4
Crude deathrate                                     2.2
Natural increase rate 1/1000                       27.2
Total fertility rate                                6.8
Divorce rate                                        5.3
Average household size                              2.9
Average annual population growth rate               3.4
Life expectancy at birth: (years)
  Males                                            54.8
  Females                                          58.3
```

veiling and prohibitions against the issuance of driver's licenses, and they continue to face widespread discrimination. For example, women do not regularly receive the overseas university scholarships available for males, and their employment, while tolerated, is discouraged beyond such fields as nursing, teaching and home economics. Public life is a male sphere. Expatriate women find it easier to get jobs or to own and manage a business than their Qatari counterparts. On the other hand, mandatory schooling for girls and the opening of employment opportunities for women in medicine and education represent a shift in attitude, as does the slowly expanding number of women allowed to go abroad for university studies. There are signs that as more Qatari women receive education, they will press for a relaxation of some of the restrictions from their country's tribal past.

Qatar has no birth control policy or programs.

ETHNIC COMPOSITION

The ethnic mix is less varied in Qatar than in the other Gulf states. Native Qataris, who are of Northern Arab stock, constitute a bare majority, while another 20% is comprised of immigrants from Egypt, Palestine, Iraq and Oman, who are racially indistinguishable from the natives. Iranians form the largest ethnic minority, with 23% of the population, followed by Indians and Pakistanis, who form roughly 7%.

As strict Wahhabis, Qataris are more conservative than neighboring Bahrainis or Abu Dhabians, and Qatari attitudes toward foreigners are, accordingly, warped by traditional attitudes of distrust. The presence of a large European community (now numbering over 1,000) in Doha has, however, led to a growing tolerance, and even acceptance, of non-Muslim standards and customs. In 1976 there were 182 U.S. citizens in Qatar, of whom 165 were private residents.

LANGUAGE

The official language is Arabic, and the spoken dialect is Gulf Arabic influenced by Farsi.

English is widely understood, especially in the business community and among the bureaucrats. It is taught as a second language in secondary schools.

RELIGION

Islam is the official religion, and most Qataris belong to the puritanical Wahhabi sect of Islam. The smaller Shia community is of Iranian origin. Christians are tolerated, and private Christian worship is permitted.

COLONIAL EXPERIENCE

Although Qatar was a British Protectorate from 1868 to 1872 and from 1916 to 1971, it was never a formal colony of the United Kingdom. Qatar declared its independence only after the United Kingdom announced its decision to withdraw its forces from the Persian Gulf States. A new Treaty of Friendship and Cooperation was signed between the two countries in 1971.

CONSTITUTION & GOVERNMENT

Qatar is an absolute emirate in the medieval sense of the term. An effort to clothe this absolutism in constitutional forms was made in the Basic Law of 1970, which created for the first time a Council of Ministers and a 23-member Advisory Council. However, there are no elective posts in government. No electoral system has been created, and no suffrage has been granted. The emir, who also holds the portfolios of prime minister and defense minister, dominates the cabinet, which merely carries out his decrees. Of the fourteen members of the cabinet, eight belong to the ruling Al Thani family.

Qatar's political institutions blend the characteristics of a traditional Bedouin tribal state and of a modern bureaucracy. There are no political parties, elections, or organized opposition to the government, and the Emir exercises all executive and legislative powers. His autocratic rule, however, is checked to some extent by entrenched local customs. Interlocking family networks and the recognized right of citizens to submit appeals or petitions personally to their Emir provide effective, if informal, avenues for redress of grievances and also serve to limit abuses. The custom of rule by consensus leads to extensive consultations between the Emir, leading merchants, religious leaders, and other notables on important policies. Women for the most part play no role in public life. Under Qatar's Basic Law of 1970, the Emir must be chosen from among and by the adult males of the Al Thani family. The current Emir, Khalifa bin Hamad, has designated his son Hamad as heir apparent. This took

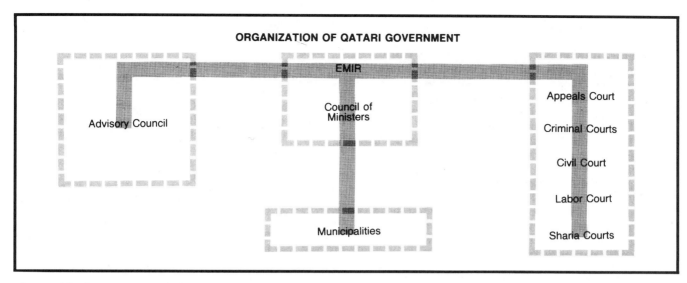

ORGANIZATION OF QATARI GOVERNMENT

EMIR

Advisory Council

Council of Ministers

Municipalities

Appeals Court

Criminal Courts

Civil Court

Labor Court

Sharia Courts

place with the consent of the notables and religious leaders according to established custom. There are no serious challenges to this arrangement, and in the foreseeable future effective political power will remain in the hands of the Emir, his family and the local notables.

CABINET LIST (1985)

Emir	Khalifa bin Hamad Al Thani
Prime Minister	Khalifa bin Hamad Al Thani
Minister of Agriculture & Industry	Faysal bin Thani Al Thani
Minister of Commerce & Economy	Nasir bin Khalid Al Thani
Minister of Defense	Hamad bin Khalifa Al Thani
Minister of Education	Muhammad bin Hamad Al Thani
Minister of Electricity & Water Resources	Jasim bin Muhammad Al Thani
Minister of Finance & Petroleum	'Abd al-'Aziz bin Khalifa Al Thani
Minister of Information	'Isa Ghanim al- Kawari
Minister of Interior	Khalid bin Hamad Al Thani
Minister of Labor & Social Affairs	'Ali bin Ahmad al- Ansari
Minister of Public Health	Khalid bin Muhammad al- Mani
Minister of Public Works	Khalid bin 'Abdallah al- 'Atiya
Minister of Transportation & Communications	'Abdallah bin Nasir al- Suwaydi
Minister of State for Foreign Affairs	Ahmad bin Sayf Al Thani

of freedom in all areas of public life; yet the lack of freedom does not create a climate of oppression nor do the people yearn for a different order of things. Because the whole political and tribal structure is sanctioned by Islam, there is an immutability about it. Indeed, within the context of Arab culture authority seems to flow smoothly through the traditional channels and new fangled concepts such as elections, constitution, and suffrage seem foreign and irrelevant. Within the limitations of a conservative society, people enjoy many of the freedoms associated with constitutional democracies: there is no torture or any inhuman, cruel and degrading punishments. The courts provide free and public trials. There is no pre-publication censorship and the few publications that exist accept government guidelines voluntarily. There are no restraints on freedom of movement or travel outside the country. On the other hand, there is no organized labor movement and strikes are not permitted. The predominant alien community is excluded from all political rights.

CIVIL SERVICE

No current information is available on the Qatari civil service.

FREEDOM & HUMAN RIGHTS

In terms of civil and plitical rights Qatar is classified as a partly free country with a negative rating of five in political rights and five in civil rights (on a descending scale on which 1 is the highest and 7 the lowest). It is difficult to apply the modern standards of human rights to a traditional and authoritarian emirate as Qatar where political and social values are still bound by medieval paternalism. There is an absence

LOCAL GOVERNMENT

Local government is the responsibility of the Ministry of Municipal Affairs. Each of the six larger towns—Doha, Wakrah, Khor, Takhira, Rayan and Umm Salal—has its own municipal council with its own planning and development programs. The Doha municipal council has 15 elected members and 4 appointed members, with a similar composition in other municipalities.

FOREIGN POLICY

The principal features of Qatar's recent foreign relations have been the Anglo-Qatar Treaty of Friendship of 1971 and the failure of postindependence efforts at federation with the other Persian Gulf states. Qatar has played a relatively minor role in the politics of the region and has not used any of its wealth in aid programs to less developed Arab countries. Qatar has supported Iraq in the Gulf War. In 1981 Qatar joined the Gulf Cooperation Council. It joined the U.N. in 1971 and is also a member of 12 other U.N. organizations. Its share of the U.N. budget is 0.02%. It is an active member of OPEC and OAPEC.

U.S. Ambassador in Doha: (Vacant)
U.K. Ambassador in Doha: Julian F. Walker
Qatari Ambassador in Washington, D.C.: Abdelkader Braik Al-Ameri
Qatari Ambassador in London: Sherida Sa'ad Jubran Al- Ka'abi

PARLIAMENT

The Qatari legislature is the Majlis esh-Shura, or the National Advisory Council, with 23 members. Under the Basic Law of 1970, 20 of the 23 members are to be elected while three are to be appointed by the emir, but in practice all 23 are appointed by the emir. There is no constitutional apparatus for election. The advisory council has little effective power or influence.

POLITICAL PARTIES

Political parties are not permitted to operate legally in Qatar. Qatari society is too tradition-bound to accept modern political groups or ideologies.

ECONOMY

Qatar is one of the 37 high-income countries of the world with an economy based 90% on oil revenues. The private sector predominates in Qatar's free market economy.

Qatar has no central planning organization, but developmental allocations are shown as capital expenditures in the annual budget.

From 1974 Qatar ceased to be in need of foreign capital aid for development although it still needs foreign technical aid and still has not become a donor country. During the period 1979-81 Qatar received $800,000 in foreign aid, or $3.3 per capita.

BUDGET

The Qatari fiscal year runs from February 1 through January 31. There is no personal tax liability for resident foreigners or nationals. Locally registered companies are liable to a corporation tax of up to 50%. Oil income provides 90% of the revenues. Qatar has no external debt.

PRINCIPAL ECONOMIC INDICATORS

Gross National Product: $5.960 billion (1983)
  GNP Annual Growth Rate: –2.0% (1973-82)
  Per Capita GNP: $21,060 (1983)
  Per Capita GNP Annual Growth Rate: –8.7% (1973-82)
Gross Domestic Product: QR23.365 billion (1983)
  GDP Annual Growth Rate: –15.5% (1983)
  GDP Per Capita: QR3,446 (1983)
  GDP Per Capita Annual Growth Rate: N.A.
  All Items: 103.8 (1982)
  Food: 105.6 (1982)
Price Indices: 1970=100
Money Supply: QR3.654 billion (March 1984)
Reserve Money: QR1.350 billion (December 1984)
Currency in Circulation: QR1.068 billion (1983)
International Reserves: $380 million of which foreign exchange reserves were $326.5 million (1984)
  *Note: Despite its immense wealth the government of Qatar does not have a statistics office. Most data in this section are estimates derived from various sources.

BALANCE OF PAYMENTS (1983)
(QR million)

Exports	12,202
Imports	–5,299
Trade Balance	6,703
Services & Private Transfers	–5,212
Current Balance	1,491
Capital Movements (net)	–3,660
Total	–2,169

GROSS DOMESTIC PRODUCT BY ECONOMIC ACTIVITY
(1983) (QR million)

Agriculture	200
Mining	10,714
Manufacturing	1,389
Public Utilities	108
Construction	1,666
Trade	1,559
Transport & Communications	499
Finance	211
Other	5,119
Total	23,365

NATIONAL BUDGET (1984/85)
(QR million)

Revenues	11,970
Expenditures	16,951

The revenues are almost entirely derived from petroleum. Of the expenditures, 5.9% goes to housing, 4.9% to industry and agriculture, 4.3% to electricity and water, 3.2% to education, 3.1% to transport and communications, 1.7% to social services and 0.8% to health.

FINANCE

The Qatari unit of currency is the Qatar rial divided into 100 dirhams. Coins are issued in denominations of 1, 5, 10, 25 and 50 dirhams; notes are issued in denominations of 1, 5, 10, 100 and 500 rials.

Before 1966 the Qatari unit of currency was the Persian Gulf Indian rupee. In 1966 Qatar briefly adopted the Saudi Arabian rial before introducing the Qatar/Dubai rial which became the common currency in the Trucial Oman states and Qatar. When the United Arab Emirates adopted a national currency in 1973, the Q/D rial was superseded by the Qatar rial. Since 1975 the rial has been linked to the IMF Special Drawing Right with a value determined by a weighted basket of the currencies of Qatar's 16 major trading partners. In August 1985 the average market rate in dollars was $1 = QR3.64, and the average market rate in sterling was £1=QR4.219.

Qatar's banking system consists of the Qatar Monetary Agency and 13 commercial banks, of which the Qatar National Bank and the Commercial Bank of Qatar are the only Qatari-owned banks. The foreign holdings of the commercial banks totaled QR3.855 billion in 1984. In the same year bank reserves totaled QR278.0 million, demand deposits QR2.556 billion and time and savings deposits QR4.863 billion.

AGRICULTURE

Of the total land area of 1,099,973 hectares (2,718,090 acres), only around 5% is considered arable, or 0.6 hectares (1.4 acres) per capita. Of these only about 11,000 hectares (27,180 acres) are cultivated. Agriculture employs 12% of the working force.

In spite of the low agricultural potential, Qatar manages to be self-sufficient in vegetables and even exports tomatoes. The average size of the 450 farms and holdings in the country is three hectares (7 acres) and all the farms are irrigated with the help of 1,400 natural wells. In 1983 production totaled 42,000 tons of fodder, 17,900 tons of vegetables, 9,500 tons of fruits and dates and 1,400 tons of cereals.

In 1982 livestock totaled 10,000 head of cattle, 51,000 sheep, 57,000 goats, 10,000 camels and 3,000 horses. In 1976 the government established a sheep-rearing station with 13,000 stock and a dairy farm with 500 cows.

There are no forests in Qatar.

The Qatar National Fishing Company, owned jointly by the government and British interests, dominates the fishing industry. The annual fish catch in 1982 was 2,315 tons.

The Central Trials and Research Station at Rodait al-Khail provides extension services. The government provides free tractor ploughing, seeds, insecticides and pesticides.

INDUSTRY

The government is committed to a program of developing heavy industry based on the Umm Said industrial zone. The main large-scale industrial plants are:
• The Qatar National Cement Company at Umm Bab with a present production capacity of 600,000 tons a day.
• A refrigeration and fish processing plant near Doha with a daily capacity of seven tons of shrimps.
• An ammonia and urea fertilizer plant at Umm Said with a planned output of 430,000 tons per annum.
• The privately owned Qatar Flour Mills that can process 100 tons of flour a day.
• A $2-billion liquefied natural gas plant constructed by the Qatar Gas Company.

No surprisingly, virtually all heavy industrial projects that have been initiated thus far rely on Qatar's petroleum reserves for either fuel or feedstock. The total capital cost of these projects is over $4 billion. For the execution of most industrial projects, the government has formed joint venture companies with foreign partners.

The private sector has played a limited role in industrial development. The government plans to place more emphasis on light and medium industries financed by private enterprise.

Planned projects include an $800-million iron and steel complex to be built in conjunction with two Japanese firms at Umm Said with a first-stage production capacity of 400,000 tons, a petrochemicals complex at Umm Said to be built by the Qatar Petrochemical Company in association with French interests with an annual production capacity of 200,000 tons of ethylene and 145,000 tons of polyethylene, and a second cement plant.

Steel, cement and construction have also become important activities, although all suffered in 1983 from the relative recession affecting the Gulf region. A primary objective in development was to diversify the country's economic base against dependence on petroleum. The non-oil sector contributed 54.9% of GDP in 1983, compared with 45.7% in 1982, but this increase in significance was seen to result more from inactivity in the petroleum sector than from growth elsewhere.

All industries are registered and licensed by the Commercial Registry Office. Government regulations require at least 51% local participation in all undertakings and 100% local participation in construction contracting firms. All foreign investments are coordinated by the Qatar Investment Board.

ENERGY

Qatar ranks first in the world in per capita energy production. In 1982 total production was equivalent to 31.430 million metric tons of coal. Consumption was equivalent to 8.148 million metric tons. Per capita consumption was 30,178 kg (66,542 lb) of coal equivalent. In 1984 electric power production was 4.149 billion kwh and per capita production 14.250 kwh per year. Since electricity is free to Qataris and heavily subsidized to non-Qataris, peak demand has been increasing at an astonishing rate. Department of Electricity experts predict that there will be an energy crunch in the mid-1980's if Qatar does not soon begin construction of new generating facilities.

Qatar is the 16th largest oil producer in the world with reserves estimated at 3.330 billion barrels (enough to last 34 years at current rates of extraction), and production in 1983 of 107.3 million barrels (less than 2% of OPEC oil production); 60,100,000 barrels onshore and 47,200,000 barrels offshore. Qatar's first and largest producing field is Dukhan on the western side of the peninsula, operated by the Qatar Petroleum Company. Crude oil from Dukhan is transported first to the deep-water terminal and refinery at Umm Said south of Doha on the eastern coast. Since 1962 the Shell Oil Company has operated an offshore concession near Halul Island, east of Doha. Shell's offshore commercial fields, Idd al-Sharqi and Maydan Mahzam, produce an average of 150,000 barrels a day. The Qatar Oil Company (Japan) began production in the waters between Qatar and Abu Dhabi in 1976 with the proceeds split between Qatar and Abu Dhabi.

In 1974 the government acquired a 60% interest in both the Qatar Petroleum Company and Shell Company of Qatar and in 1975 began negotiations with both companies for a complete takeover in line with OPEC policy. To hasten the process of achieving full ownership, the government in 1974 formed the Qatar General Petroleum Corporation (QGPC) as a holding company and as the operational arm of the Ministry of Petroleum. In addition to its interests in oil production, QGPC controls the Arab Maritime Company for Oil Transport, the Arab Company of Petrol Pipes, the National Oil Distribution Company and the Arab Company for Shipbuilding and Repairs.

A new offshore gasfield being developed is estimated to contain reserves of 1.756 trillion cubic meters (62 trillion cubic ft), ranked among the world's largest with Hassi R'Mel in Algeria and Groningen in the Netherlands. The Qatar Gas Company has been formed to exploit the reserves. The emirate holds a 70% interest in the company. Production of natural gas in 1982 was 2.478 billion cubic meters (87.5 billion cubic ft).

The Qatar Oil Refinery at Umm Said has a capacity of 485,000 tons of crude a day. A new refinery with a capacity of 50,000 barrels per day was inaugurated in 1983.

LABOR

The emirate has never had a census of its economically active population, but it is believed that over 88% of that population, estimated at 103,000 in 1983, is engaged in industry and services and the remaining 12% in agriculture. More than half the labor force is of foreign origin with Pakistanis and Indians constituting 7%, Palestinians 20% and Iranians 23%. There is also a small contingent of South Korean workers. Labor immigration is, however, strictly controlled and work permits are issued by the Department of Labor and Immigration for limited periods.

Qatar has launched a program of Qatarization. All joint-venture industries and government offices have been urged to move Qatari citizens into positions of authority. Foreign-educated Qataris are returning to Qatar and taking responsible positions that normally have been held by expatriates.

The shortage of labor and expansion of economic activity have increased wage levels by an estimated 30-50% per year since 1973. Unskilled construction workers in the private sector receive $20-25 per day, and trained clerical staff are now getting starting salaries of $600 per month.

Conditions of work are governed by legislation ratified in 1972. The laws provide for a 48-hour week and other benefits, such as annual leave, sickness leave, paid holidays and dismissal notice. Labor unions are not permitted, but consultative bodies of workers have been set up in the oil companies. The minimum working age is 18 years, but expatriate children frequently work at younger ages in small businesses and shops. Some regulations concerning worker safety and health exist, but enforcement is spotty. There is no minimum wage in Qatar and most workers spend less than 48 hours per week on the job. Strikes are banned.

FOREIGN COMMERCE

The foreign commerce of Qatar consisted in 1984 of exports of $4.579 billion and imports of $1.144 billion, leaving a favorable trade balance of $3.435 billion. Petroleum constitutes 99% of the exports. Of the imports, machinery and transport equipment constituted 42.5%, food and live animals 11.4% and chemicals 4.8%. The major import sources are: Japan 20.4%, the United Kingdom 16.5%, the United States 11.5%, West Germany 7.2%, France 5.9% and Italy 4.8%. The major export destinations are: Japan 18.3%, the United Kingdom 17.7%, the United States 11.3%, West Germany 6.1%, France 5.4% and Italy 5.3%.

Import licenses are not required except for liquor, firearms and ammunition, and dangerous drugs. There is a duty on goods in transit.

TRANSPORTATION & COMMUNICATIONS

Qatar has no railways or inland waterways. The chief port is Doha, a four-berth, deep-water port with five additional berths being built. Umm Said, the country's main oil terminal, can accommodate tankers up to 60,000 d.w.t. In 1982, 18,120,000 metric tons of cargo were handled at Doha and Umm Said. The merchant marine consists of 63 vessels with a GRT of 474,100.

There are 840 km (522 mi) of roads, of which 490 km (304 mi) are asphalted, radiating from Doha and connecting the oil centers of Dukhan and Umm Said with the northern end of the peninsula. Roads also link Qatar with Saudi Arabia and the United Arab Emirates.

Oil is transported by a 235-km (146-mi) pipeline from the oilfield at Dukhanto the loading terminal at Umm Said. Natural gas is brought by a 360-km (223-mi) pipeline from Dukhan to Doha.

Qatar has a part interest in Gulfair owned jointly with Bahrain, the UAE and Oman but has no national airline. The international airport is Doha with a runway of 4,572 meters (15,000 feet). There are only three airports, two of them usable and with permanent-surface runways.

In 1982 Qatar had 70,000 telephones, or 26.1 per 100 inhabitants.

No statistics are available on the volume of mail traffic. There are 1,068 telex subscriber lines.

In 1982 126,000 tourists visited Qatar. There are 3,000 hotel beds and the average length of stay was 3.9 days.

MINING

Qatar has no known deposits of minerals other than oil.

DEFENSE

The defense structure is headed by the emir who is also the defense minister. The defense establishment is commanded almost exclusively by the members of the Al Thani royal family. As the supreme commander, the emir is assisted by the Defense Council and the commander of the Internal Security Organizations.

The total strength of the armed forces, whose manpower is provided by voluntary enlistment, is 6,000 or 20.00 armed persons for every 1,000 civilians.

ARMY:

Personnel: 5,000

Organization: 1 royal guard regiment; 1 tank battalion; 3 infantry battalions; 1 artillery battery; 1 SAM battery

Equipment: 24 tanks; 10 armored vehicles; 30 mechanized combat infantry vehicles; 169 armored personnel carriers; 6 howitzers; mortars

NAVY:

Personnel: 700

Units: 3 fast attack craft; 6 patrol craft; 3 coastal defense craft

AIR FORCE:

Personnel: 300

Organization: 17 combat aircraft; 2 armored helicopters 5 fighters; 2 transports, 11 helicopters; 5 SAM

Air Base: Doha

The annual military budget in 1983/84 was $165.939 million. The 1980 military budget was 20.1% of the national budget, 9.1% of the GNP, $3,519 per capita, $100,000 per soldier and $54,546 per sq km of national territory.

The combat readiness of the Qatari armed forces has not been tested. The army evolved from the security force of the public security department, and its functions are still oriented to internal peacekeeping and counter-subversion.

By treaty obligations Britain has been the traditional supplier of military hardware to Qatar. British supplies include combat aircraft and coastal patrol boats. Arms purchases abroad during 1973-83 totaled $830 million.

EDUCATION

The national literacy rate is 40%.

Schooling is free but neither universal nor compulsory. The state also provides students with free books, stationery, clothing, food, pocket money and transportation.

Schooling consists of six years of primary school, three years of intermediate school and three years of secondary school for a total of 12 years. The net school enrollment ratio is 91% in the primary age group (6 to 11) and 59% in the secondary age group (12 to 17) for a combined gross ratio of 96%. The third level enrollment ratio is 16.5%. Girls constitute 48% of the primary school enrollment 49% of the secondary school enrollment and 56% of post-secondary enrollment. The academic year runs from September to June. The medium of instruction is Arabic, but English is taught as a second language from secondary grades.

Increasing attention is being paid to the training of teachers. The teacher-pupil ratio is 1:14 at the primary level and 1:9 at the secondary level.

All of the children at the preprimary level and 7% of the children at the primary level are enrolled in private schools, including kuttabs, or traditional Muslim schools. Curricula in public and private schools conform to the Arab League standards. Adult education is conducted at 52 centers. Nearly 4% of the secondary school students are enrolled in the vocational stream. The UNDP Regional Training Center at Doha has 500 artisan and technical students.

The Ministry of Education has overall control of the school system. In 1982 the educational budget was QR1,640,997,000, of which 73.7% was current expenditure. This amount was 4.2% of the national budget, 3.1% of the GNP and $1,015 per capita.

In 1976 the teacher-training college established with the help of UNESCO was upgraded into the University of the Lower Gulf, with additional faculties for civil aviation, science, engineering and administration. All Qatari students who qualify are provided with state scholarships for higher education abroad. In 1982, 984 Qatari students were enrolled in institutions of higher learning abroad. Of these 569 were in

EDUCATIONAL ENROLLMENT (1982)		
	Teachers	Students
First Level	2,508	34,805
Second Level	2,139	18,864
Vocational	87	518
Third Level	215	4,016

the United States, 26 in the United Kingdom, 56 in Saudi Arabia and 286 in Egypt. In the same year, 1,430 foreign students were enrolled in Qatar.

LEGAL SYSTEM

The foundations of the legal system are the Sharia and the Basic Law of 1970. The latter provides for an independent judiciary with five secular courts (two criminal courts, one civil court, one labor court, one appeals court) and religious courts. Except for security cases, most disputes are judged before either a civil or Shari'a court. Most commercial litigation involving expatriates takes place before the civil courts. The Shari'a courts administer criminal and family law and may, if one party requests, take jurisdiction in business cases. Although the judiciary is nominally independent, most judges are expatriates holding residence permits granted by the civil authorities and thus hold their positions at the government's pleasure. Many expatriates find proceedings in the Shari'a courts bewildering. Only the disputing parties, their relatives and associates, and witnesses are allowed in the courtroom. Lawyers may not play any formal role save that of preparing litigants for their cases. Although non-Arabic speakers are provided with translators, foreigners report being at a considerable disadvantage, especially in cases involving the nonperformance of contracts. Shari'a trials are normally brief. After both parties have stated their cases, and examined witnesses, the judge is likely to deliver a verdict with only a short delay. Criminal cases are normally tried two to three months after suspects are detained. No information is available on the penal system.

LAW ENFORCEMENT

The national police is a small force of 1,300 with responsibility for internal security, traffic, marine patrol and guarding the palace.

HEALTH

Free health services are provided for all residents of the emirate. Qatar has four large hospitals with 733 beds, or 1 bed per 338 inhabitants. In 1981 there were 186 doctors in the country or 1 doctor per 1,333 inhabitants, 24 dentists and 437 nurses. In addition the Qatar Petroleum Company maintains its own hospitals. The 640-bed Hamad Hospital was completed in 1980. Per 10,000 inhabitants the admissions/discharge rate was 1,328.

PRINCIPAL HEALTH INDICATORS (1984)
Crude Death Rate: 2.2 per 1,000
Infant Mortality Rate per 1,000 Live Births: 57
Life Expectancy at Birth: Males 54.8; Females 58.3

Great strides have been made in Qatar in the fight against traditional endemic scourges of southeastern Arabia, such as tuberculosis, malaria and trachoma.

FOOD

No information is available on the daily calorie or protein intake of the average Qatari.

MEDIA & CULTURE

Qatar has five dailies, three weekly magazines and six monthlies. Of the dailies, three are published in Arabic, one — the *Daily News Bulletin,* — in English and Arabic, and one — *Gulf Times* — in English. Total daily circulation is around 50,000. All weeklies and monthlies are published in Arabic. The national news agency is Qatar News Agency founded in 1975.

Although both expatriates and Qataris are free to say what they wish privately, public criticism of the ruling family and its policies is not tolerated. The government strongly discourages attacks on other Arab governments as well. This policy applies to the electronic media, which are government-owned and controlled, and to the press. The journalists, particularly expatriates, generally avoid pressing against these restrictions because of the risk of having residence permits canceled. The authorities routinely screen all video cassettes, audio tapes, books, and periodicals for objectionable political sentiments and pornography.

Qatar has a small book publishing industry, which produced 337 books, all in Arabic, in 1982. Qatar does not adhere to any copyright convention.

The Qatar Broadcasting Service, a service of the Ministry of Information, operates two medium-wave transmitters (10 and 50 kw) and two short-wave transmitters (each 100 kw), all located at Doha. The stations are on the air for 104 hours a week, of which one hour daily is in English and the rest in Arabic. In 1975 a 750-kw medium-wave transmitter began operation at Al-Arish. In 1982 there were 120,000 radio sets, or 465 per 1,000 inhabitants.

The Qatar Television Service, which began operation in 1970, has two transmitters at Doha; its color programs can be received not only throughout Qatar but also in much of the Gulf area and in lower Iran. Programs are broadcast in Arabic for 36 hours a week. Of the 1,339 annual program-hours, 1,177 program hours are locally produced. In 1982 there were 125,000 television sets in the country or 484 per 1,000 inhabitants.

In 1981 there were four cinemas in the country with 4,000 seats, or 16.1 seats per 1,000 inhabitants. Annual movie attendance in the same year was 800,000, or 3.2 per inhabitant. Annual box office receipts were QR6.9 million.

The largest public library in the country is the public library of Doha with 53,000 volumes, or 596 volumes per 1,000 inhabitants. Per capita, there are seven registered borrowers per 1,000 inhabitants.

The national museum at Doha reported 60,000 visitors in 1980.

There is one theater serving four amateur troupes.

SOCIAL WELFARE

The Ministry of Labor and Social Affairs provides a comprehensive system of social welfare to the needy, disabled and destitute. Public health services and education are also provided free to all resident aliens and citizens. Under a home ownership scheme, generous subsidies and long-term loans are extended to nationals without houses of their own.

GLOSSARY

emir: properly, prince; title of the rulers of Qatar; also, **amir.**
Basic Law: constitution of Qatar, adopted in 1970.
majlis esh-shura: advisory council of the emir of Qatar, serving as a national deliberative body without legislative powers.
Wahhabi: member of a puritanical Sunni sect of Islam advocating a return to the teachings of the Koran in their literal sense.

CHRONOLOGY (from 1971)

1971— Qatar declares independence as United Kingdom withdraws from the Persian Gulf region, ending treaty obligations to the Trucial states. . . . Anglo-Qatari Treaty of Friendship and Co-operation is signed.
1972— In a bloodless coup Emir Sheikh Ahmad bin Ali bin Abdullah Al Thani is overthrown by his cousin and prime minister, Sheikh Khalifa bin Hamad Al Thani.
1973— Qatar rial replaces Qatar/Dubai rial as the national currency; Qatar Monetary Agency is established as the central bank.
1974— In line with OPEC policy Qatar acquires 60% of the assets of Qatar Petroleum Company and Shell Company of Qatar and begins negotiations for total takeover of both companies.
1976— Qatar joins fund to aid Egypt, following visit by President Sadat.
1978— Qatar's economic development plans are reported to be slowing down as a result of shortages of skilled manpower and transportation bottlenecks.
1979— Qatar breaks with Egypt over the Peace Treaty with Israel.
1983— Qatar joins the Gulf Cooperation Council.

BIBLIOGRAPHY (from 1970)

Anthony, John Duke, *Arab States of the Lower Gulf* (Washington, D.C., 1975).
————, *Historical and Cultural Dictionary of the Sultanate of Oman and the Emirates of Eastern Arabia* (Metuchen, N.J., 1976).
Mallakh, Raggaei E., *Qatar: Energy and Development* (London, 1985).
Middle East Economic Digest, *Qatar* (Boulder, Colo., 1984).
Nafi, Zuhair A., *Economic and Social Development in Qatar* (Dover, N.H., 1983).
Qatar (Doha, Qatar, 1970).
Qatar into the Seventies (Doha, Qatar, 1973).
Unwin, P.T., *Qatar* [World Bibliographical Series] (Santa Barbara, Calif., 1982).
Zahlan, Rosemarie Said, *The Creation of Qatar* (New York, 1979).

Rwanda

- International boundary
- ⊛ National capital
- Surfaced road
- Unsurfaced road
- ✚ International airport

0 10 20 30 Kilometers
0 10 20 30 Miles

BOUNDARY REPRESENTATION IS
NOT NECESSARILY AUTHORITATIVE

RÉPUBLIQUE RWANDAISE
LIBERTÉ · COOPÉRATION · PROGRÈS

RWANDA

BASIC FACT SHEET

OFFICIAL NAME: Republic of Rwanda (Republique Rwandaise; Republika Y'U Rwanda)

ABBREVIATION: RW

CAPITAL: Kigali

HEAD OF STATE & HEAD OF GOVERNMENT: President Maj. Gen. Juvenal Habyarimana (from 1973)

NATURE OF GOVERNMENT: Military dictatorship

POPULATION: 6,246,000 (1985)

AREA: 26,388 sq km (10,188 sq mi)

ETHNIC MAJORITY: Hutu

LANGUAGES: French and Kinyarwanda

RELIGION: Animism and Christianity

UNIT OF CURRENCY: Rwandan Franc ($1=RF99.520, August 1985)

NATIONAL FLAG: Tricolor of red, yellow, and green vertical stripes (from left to right) with the letter "R" in black in the central yellow stripe

NATIONAL EMBLEM: A shield displaying a black bow tensed to shoot an arrow within a triangle. Superimposed on the bow and arrow are a hoe and a sickle. The shield is crested by a white dove and flanked by two crossed flags with the legend Republique Française and the national motto in French: "Liberte, Cooperation, Progres"

NATIONAL ANTHEM: "Our Rwanda"

NATIONAL HOLIDAYS: July 1 (Independence Day, National Day); January 28 (Proclamation of the Republic); October 26 (Inauguration of the Legislative Assembly in 1961); December 10 (Human Rights Day); May 1 (Labor Day); August 15 (National Peace and Unity Day); September 25 (Kamparampaka Day); October 26 (Armed Forces Day); Christian festivals include All Saints' Day, Christmas, Whit Monday, Assumption, Ascension and Pentecost Monday.

NATIONAL CALENDAR: Gregorian

PHYSICAL QUALITY OF LIFE INDEX: 45 (up from 27 in 1976) (On an ascending scale with 100 as the maximum. U.S., 95)

DATE OF INDEPENDENCE: July 1, 1962

DATE OF CONSTITUTION: November 24, 1962 (partially suspended in 1973)

WEIGHTS & MEASURES: The metric system is in force.

LOCATION & AREA

Rwanda is a landlocked country located in east-central Africa with an area of 26,388 sq km (10,188 sq mi) extending 248 km (154 mi) NE to SW and 166 km (103 mi) SE to NW. The total length of the international borders is 893 km (555 mi) shared by four countries: Uganda (169 km, 105 mi); Tanzania (217 km, 135 mi); Burundi (290 km, 180 mi); and Zaire (217 km, 135 mi).

The northern and western boundaries were defined by an agreement among the colonial powers in 1910 and have remained essentially unchanged since then. The Rwanda-Tanzania and the Rwanda-Burundi borders originally marked internal administrative divisions in German East Africa. There are no current border disputes between Rwanda and its neighbors.

The capital is Kigali with a 1982 population of 117,749, up from 15,000 in 1969. The other large towns are: Butare (21,691), Ruhengeri (16,025) and Gisenyi (12,436).

Rwanda is divided into six topographical regions from west to east: the narrow Great Rift Valley, sloping sharply to Lake Kivu; the volcanic Virunga Mountains with their highest peak, snow-capped Mt. Karisimbi (4,532 meters, 14,870 ft) towering over the high lava plains of northwestern Rwanda; the steep north-south slopes of the Congo-Nile Divide, averaging 40 km (25 mi) in width; the ridgeline of the Congo-Nile Divide with an average elevation of 2,750 meters (9,000 ft); the central plateaus east of the mountains, covered by rolling hills; and the savannas and swamps of the of the eastern and southeastern border areas, including the vast Kagera National Park, which covers one-tenth of the nation's land area. Most of Rwanda is 900 meters (3,000 ft) above sea level; the central plains have an average elevation of 1,932 meters (4,700 ft). Southeastern Rwanda has a desert appearance.

Rwanda's eastern border is formed by the Kagera River's path to Lake Victoria. Lake Kivu drains into Lake Tanganyika through the swift and sharply descending Ruzizi River. The central uplands are drained by the Nyabarongo River and its main tributaries: the Lukarara, Mwogo, Biruruma, Mukungwa, Base, Nyabugogo and Akanyaru Rivers.

Of the nation's nine large lakes six are entirely within the national territory—Ruhondo, Muhazi,

Mugasera, Ihema, Rwanye and Burera—while three—Rugwero, Cyohoha and Kivu—are shared with its neighbors.

WEATHER

Although located only two degrees south of the equator, Rwanda has a relatively pleasant tropical highland climate. The country has two dry seasons: the short season in January and February and the long season lasting from June through September; there are two wet seasons, from October to December and from March through May. The capital, Kigali, has an average temperature of 19°C (66°F) during the wet months with slightly higher averages during the dry months. Westward, toward Lake Kivu, the weather is much cooler with night temperatures dropping to freezing levels at higher elevations. Eastward, temperatures increase to an average of 32.2°C (90°F).

The highest rainfall, over 177 cm (70 in.), is received in the west, decreasing to 102 to 140 cm (40 to 55 in.) in the central uplands and 76 cm (30 in.) in the northeast and east.

POPULATION

The population of Rwanda was estimated in 1985 at 6,246,000, on the basis of the last official census held in 1978, when the population was 4,830,984. The population is expected to reach 10.7 million by 2000 and 20.3 million by 2020. The annual rate of population growth is estimated at 3.46%. The annual birth rate is 51.1 per 1,000.

Rwanda is one of the most densely populated areas in Africa apart from the Nile Delta. The average density of population is estimated at 232 per sq km (601 per sq mi) nationwide and 357 per sq km (925 per sq mi) in agricultural areas.

At the 1980 census males numbered 2,363,177 and females 2,468,350, yielding a male/female ratio of 48.9:51.1. The median age of the population is 15.6 years. The largest age group is that between 15 and 64 years of age, constituting 48.8% of the population. Some 48.8% are below 14 years of age and 2.5% over 65.

The general settlement pattern is one of dispersion in extended family groups throughout the country with no concentration in large villages or towns. The urban component of the population is estimated at only 5.07% growing annually by 6.8%. The only sizable town is Kigali, the capital, with a 1982 population of 117,749.

As in most countries with high population densities, Rwanda has witnessed migrations on a massive scale in times of famine, chronic unemployment and ethnic conflict. During the Hutu-Tutsi conflicts from 1959 through 1964, over 150,000 Tutsi refugees fled their homeland. In the mid-1960s nearly 400,000 Rwandans were listed as permanent residents in Uganda, and 50,000 were listed as residents of Tanzania. Offset-

DEMOGRAPHIC INDICATORS (1984)	
Population, total (in 1,000)	6,246.0
Population ages (% of total)	
0-14	48.8
15-64	48.8
65+	2.5
Youth 15-24 (000)	1,152
Women ages 15-49 (000)	1,315
Dependency ratios	105.0
Child-woman ratios	921
Sex ratios (per 100 females)	97.4
Median ages (years)	15.6
Marriage Rate (per 1,000)	3.3
Divorce Rate (per 1,000)	0.0
Proportion of urban (%)	5.07
Population density (per sq. km.)	232
per hectare of arable land	5.86
Rates of growth (%)	3.46
urban	6.8
rural	3.3
Natural increase rates (per 1,000)	34.5
Crude birth rates (per 1,000)	51.1
Crude death rates (per 1,000)	16.6
Gross reproduction rates	3.60
Net reproduction rates	2.63
Total fertility rates	7.30
General fertility rates (per 1,000)	236
Life expectancy, males (years)	47.8
Life expectancy, females (years)	51.2
Life expectancy, total (years)	49.5
Population doubling time in years at current rate	19
Average household size	6.0
Change in birth rate 1965-83:	0.8

ting this emigration was an inflow of 15,000 Zaireans and 6,000 Burundians into Rwanda during the same period.

Women perform most of the agricultural labor and have benefited less than men from social development. Despite the language in the constitution, women's rights to property are limited, and women are not treated equally in divorce proceedings. Moreover, women have fewer chances for education, employment, and promotion, often because men prefer them to remain in uneducated traditional roles at home. Family planning services are still inadequate but are improving. There are virtually no day care services for children of mothers who wish to work. There are few organizations promoting women's interests, and efforts to establish a national union of Rwandan women within the political movement have been unsuccessful to date. However, in 1985, the Ministry of Public Health and Social Affairs held a three-day seminar to examine the problems of women working in urban areas, possibly indicating increased attention to this subject by the government.

Women play a marginal role in political life. Nevertheless, there is one woman in the party's 21-member central committee, nine of 70 legislative deputies are women, and there are a good number of women council members at the local level.

Despite being one of the most densely populated countries in Africa, Rwanda has no official birth control programs or policies.

ETHNIC COMPOSITION

The African population is relatively homogeneous, with the Hutu comprising about 88% of the population. The only other major ethnic group is the Tutsi whose numbers have markedly declined since the massacres of 1959-61 and 1964 and who are believed to constitute 9 to 11% of the population. The Twa, a tribe of Pygmy hunters and perhaps the descendants of the earliest known inhabitants of the region, complete the ethnic makeup and account for 1% of the population.

Though differing markedly in physical features, the Hutu and the Tutsi share a common language, kinship and clan systems and religious values. Until independence in 1962, the Tutsi were the feudal masters of the country, organized under a mwami, or king. Racially, the Hutu belong to the Bantu family, while the Tutsi are Nilotics. Further, the Tutsi are warriors and herdsmen while the Hutu are farmers. The Hutu outnumber the Tutsi in all regions. Approximately 45% of all Tutsi reside in the central region of the country near Nyanza, the former capital of the Tutsi kings or bami.

Ethnic aliens include some 3,000 Asians, of whom Indians, Pakistanis and Arabs form the major groups. Almost all aliens are engaged exclusively in trade. In general they have not suffered the kind of discrimination which Asians have been subjected to in other African countries. The European population has never numbered more than 2,000 in recent years, and Belgians constitute 60% of this number.

In terms of ethnic and linguistic homogeneity, Rwanda is ranked 96th among nations of the world with 86% homogeneity on an ascending scale in which North and South Korea are ranked 135th with 100% homogeneity and Tanzania ranks 1st with 7% homogeneity.

Although Rwandans display very little animosity toward foreigners and are generally free of anti-Western sentiments, the Western presence in the country is negligible because of its limited economic potential.

LANGUAGES

The official languages of Rwanda are French and Kinyarwanda. The latter is a Bantu language spoken by all Rwandans, both Hutu and Tutsi. French is spoken by an increasing number of educated Rwandans. The country's major periodical are published in French, and the main language of broadcasting is also French. In some border areas Swahili is also spoken.

RELIGIONS

The majority of Rwandans follow traditional religions built around the concept of a supreme spirit called Imana. Christianity, introduced by Catholic missionaries in the 19th century, spread rapidly and now claims over 40% of the population. Though Christianity was accepted with relative ease, adherence to Church dogmas is flexible and in some cases combined with simultaneous elements of traditional practice. According to official figures, there are nearly 2 million Catholics in the country organized into one archdiocese and four dioceses. The number of Protestants is estimated at 400,000, divided among a number of denominations. Protestant influence and activities have never been significant and during recent years have suffered a decline.

The government does not openly favor one religion over another, although the Catholic Archbishop of Kigali is a member of the party's central committee, and all but one or two members of the National Development Council are Catholic. The government depends upon church-sponsored schools for a considerable portion of education in Rwanda (over 85% of secondary schools are church sponsored).

Muslims are mainly limited to the Asian and Arab communities.

COLONIAL EXPERIENCE

Rwanda, together with Urundi, now Burundi, was a German colony from 1885 when it was designated as a German sphere of interest at the Congress of Berlin. But it was not until nine years after that conference that the first European official reached Rwanda—Count G. A. von Gotzen, who later became governor of German East Africa. Rwanda was in fact one of the last regions of Africa to be penetrated by Europeans. German rule was indirect, exercised through the mwami, or Tutsi king, who in turn used the German presence to strengthen his own authority and extend it throughout the territory. At its height, the German administration consisted of only five officials and about 166 soldiers.

Rwanda fell to Belgian troops in 1916 and in 1923 became a mandated territory of the League of Nations under Belgian supervision. Belgian administration followed the German pattern of relying on the mwami and the Tutsi aristocracy. In 1925 Rwanda and Burundi were joined in an administrative union with the Belgian Congo. In 1946 Rwanda-Burundi was made a Trust Territory under the United Nations. Under pressure from the U.N. Trusteeship Council, the first popular representative institutions were introduced in the country in 1952.

The main legacy of Belgian rule was the restoration of the Hutu majority to their rightful role in national life. The administrative, educational and legal machinery has survived the transfer of power almost intact. French remains the official language of Rwanda along with Kinyarwanda.

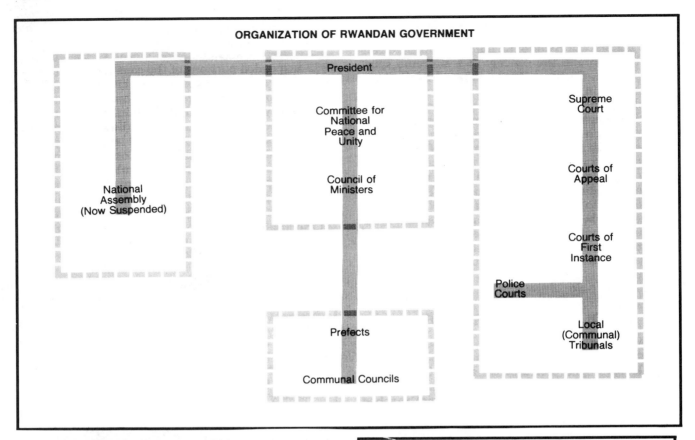

ORGANIZATION OF RWANDAN GOVERNMENT

CONSTITUTION & GOVERNMENT

The constitutional basis of the government of Rwanda is the constitution of 1962, some of whose provisions were suspended in 1973. The constitution provided for a unitary republic in which the executive, headed by a president, shared power with a unicameral legislature, the National Assembly. The new government that seized power in the coup of 1973 suspended portions of the constitution and dissolved the National Assembly. A civil-military government comprised largely of technocrats has been in power ever since, and the administrative system has been centralized. Under the military regime the president is the sole executive and legislative power. He is assisted by a 11-member Committee for National Peace and Unity, whose members are all army officers appointed by the president. The council of ministers is headed by the president, and its members are responsible only to the president. The military-dominated cabinet is characterized by the ascendancy of northern elements: key cabinet posts are held by northern officers, and nine majors out of 12 are from the north.

Until 1973 the President of the republic, deputies of the National Assembly and the mayor and councilors of communes (see below, Local Government) were elected by direct universal suffrage by Rwandan citizens 18 years of age or older. Participation in elections and referendums was mandatory.

Habyarimana's military regime created a number of conditions favorable to internal stability. Foremost among these is the reconciliation of Hutus and Tutsis.

COUNCIL OF MINISTERS (1985)

President . . . . *Maj. Gen.* Juvénal Habyarimana
Minister of Agriculture, Livestock
& Forests . . . . Anastase Nteziryayo
Minister of Civil Service & Labor . . . . François Habiyakare
Minister of Finance . . . . Jean-Damascene Hategekimana
Minister of Foreign Affairs
& Cooperation . . . . .François Ngarukiyintwali
Minister of Health & Social Affairs . . . . .François Muganza
Minister of Higher Education
& Scientific Research . . . . .Charles Nyandwi
Minister of Industry, Mines & Handicrafts . . Mathieu Ngirira
Minister of Interior . . . . Thomas Habanabakize
Minister of Justice . . . . . . Jean Marie Vianney Mugemana
Minister of Natl. Defense . *Maj. Gen.* Juvénal Habyarimana
Minister of Planning . . . . .Ambroise Mulindangabo
Minister of Posts, Communications
& Transport . . . . André Ntagerura
Minister of Primary & Secondary
Education . . . .*Col.* Aloys Nsekalije
Minister of Public Works
& Equipment . . . . .Joseph Nzirorera
Minister of Youth, Sports & Cooperative
Societies . . . . *Maj.* Augustin Ndindiliyimana
Minister at the Presidency in Charge
of the Economy . . . . Simeon Nteziryayo
Minister at the Presidency in Charge
of Institutional Relations . . . . Edouard Karemera

The government appears to be firmly in power, and there are no visible external or internal threats.

```
RULERS OF RWANDA
1962 (July) to 1973 (July) Gregoire Kayibanda
1973 (July) —    Juvenal Habyarimana
```

FREEDOM & HUMAN RIGHTS

In terms of civil and political rights Rwanda is classified as a not-free country, with a negative rating of 6 in political rights and 6 in civil rights (on a descending scale in which 1 is the highest and 7 is the lowest in civil and political rights).

Although Rwanda, along with Burundi, has acquired a certain degree of notoriety as the scene of some of the worst ethnic conflicts in African history, it has recently emerged into the forefront of the human rights movement. Kigali was the location of the 1978 colloquium on human rights and economic development and it was part of a five-nation fact-finding team that investigated human rights violations in Central African Republic. Nevertheless, there are certain residual violations of human rights, such as detention for long periods without being formally arraigned and occasional torture against prisoners. A more lenient penal code that became effective in January 1980 is designed to lessen the incidence of such violations. In 1979 the president also granted amnesty to some prisoners and halved the sentence of others, but high officials of the previous regime were not among them.

In 1984, a cabinet reshuffle brought into office a new minister of justice, one of whose tasks has been to implement the commitment to human rights enunciated by the president in his inaugural address. Measures included a general amnesty of several thousand "common law" prisoners, a tightening up of precharging detention regulations, removal of the security officers responsible for abuses in 1983, and a program of prison reform.

Rwandans are subject to some interference in their private lives, following practices inherited from the former monarchy which ruled the country for several hundred years. Police are normally required to have warrants before entering a private residence. Using the pretext of checking required documentation, police authorities can gain unwarranted entry into homes. A person can move out of his home commune only with the permission of the mayor of the commune into which he wishes to move; the government can bar a person from specific employment, but not all employment; and people must carry identification cards.

There are few channels of public expression, but limited criticism is tolerated and sometimes even encouraged. Freedom of religion and assembly also are generally respected so long as they are exercised cautiously to avoid government disapproval. Internal freedom of movement is restricted to discourage rural emigration to the cities. Rwandans have the right to vote, but they have no choice of candidates outside of the ruling National Revolutionary Development Movement. The right to unionize and the right to strike are granted in the constitution, but there is no national union and no strikes have been reported.

CIVIL SERVICE

No current information is available on Rwandan civil service.

LOCAL GOVERNMENT

Rwanda is divided for purpose of local government into 10 prefectures: Byumba, Butare, Cyangugu, Gikongoro, Gisenyi, Gitarama, Kibungo, Kibuye, Kigali and Ruhengeri.

Each prefecture is headed by a prefect appointed by the president. The former tribal divisions are reorganized into 141 communes that function as the basic political and administrative units. Each commune is administered by an elected communal council and an elected mayor who may be dismissed by the prefect if the directions of the central government are ignored or disobeyed.

FOREIGN POLICY

The Habyarimana regime has in many ways reversed the generally pro-Western, anti-Communist foreign policy of former President Kayibanda. Rwanda was the first African nation to break relations with Israel as a result of the October War of 1973. Relations with Burundi, the most crucial area of Rwandan foreign relations, have improved following a state visit by President Micombero of Burundi and the adoption of more moderate (i.e. less openly anti-Tutsi) racial policies by the Habyarimana regime. However, the overthrow of the Micombero regime a few months after the visit cast a shadow on these better relations. Since 1973 relations with Zaire and Uganda have also improved. However, the hijacking of Rwanda-bound tanker trucks from Kenya in 1976 by Ugandan troops introduced a new element of discord into Rwanda-Uganda relations. They grew worse in 1982 when Uganda ordered 45,000 Tutsi refugees out of the country.

Rwanda continues to maintain close relations with the former colonial power, Belgium. Belgium continues to be the major source of aid, and Belgian advisers and consultants hold important positions in the Rwandan army and government.

Rwanda joined the U.N. in 1962; its contribution to the U.N. budget is 0.02%. It is a member of 13 U.N. organizations and 13 other international organizations including the Joint Economic Community of the Great Lakes, whose other members are Burundi, Tanzania, Zaire and Zambia.

Rwanda and the United States are parties to six treaties and agreements covering investment guaranties, Peace Corps, taxation, and economic and technical cooperation.

U.S. Ambassador in Kigali: Vacant

Rwandan Ambassador in Washington, D.C.: Simon Insonere

PARLIAMENT

The national legislature is the unicameral National Development Council (Conseil pour le Developpement National) founded in 1982 as successor to the former National Assembly. The National Development Council has a membership of 70 elected by voters from 140 candidates nominated by MNRD. The National Development Council has shown a keen interest in financial questions, suggested modifications to some proposed legislation, and developed specialized committees to facilitate its work, but it has not ventured to initiate legislation on its own. However, when a member of the legislature and former minister of social affairs, Felicien Gatabazi, was accused in 1984 of misappropriation of refugee funds, the council defeated a government motion to lift his parliamentary immunity. The action became moot at the end of the legislative session, when the immunity lapsed in any case, but the vote showed that some parliamentary freedom of action is possible.

POLITICAL PARTIES

At the time of independence there were four political parties in the country: Parti du Mouvement de l'Emanicipation Hutu (PARMEHUTU) and Association pour la Promotion Sociale de la Masse (APROSOMA), representing the Hutu majority; Union Nationale Ruandaise (UNAR), representing the Tutsi governing elite; and Rassemblement Democratique Ruandaise (RADER), representing pro-Belgian political opinion. In the 1960 elections PARMEHUTU obtained 70.4% of the votes, and the two Hutu parties together obtained 83.8% of the votes. By late 1960s PARMEHUTU was the sole political party.

All political parties were abolished by the military government in 1973. In 1975 Habyarimana launched Mouvement Revolutionnaire National pour le Developpement (MRND) as a sole national political party embracing all military and civilian elements with himself as president. MRND's most important ideological plank is ethnic unity. There is no active illegal opposition within or without the country.

ECONOMY

Rwanda is one of the poorest countries of the world; it is one of the 49 low-income countries, one of the 29 least developed (LLDC) countries and one of the 45 countries considered by the U.N. to be most seriously affected (MSA) by recent adverse economic conditions. The private sector predominates in Rwanda's free-market economy.

PRINCIPAL ECONOMIC INDICATORS

Gross National Product: $1.540 billion (1983)
  GNP Annual Growth Rate: 5.9% (1973-82)
  Per Capita GNP: $270 (1983)
  Per Capita GNP Annual Growth Rate: 2.3% (1973-82)

Gross Domestic Product: RF141.9 billion (1983)
  GDP Deflator (1980=100): 114.9
  GDP Annual Growth Rate: 5.6% (1973-83)
  Per Capita GDP: RF24,895 (1983)
  Per Capita GDP Annual Growth Rate: 1.8% (1970-81)

Income Distribution: Information not available

Percentage of Population in Absolute Poverty: 30% urban; 90% rural

Consumer Price Index (1980=100):
  All Items: 128.9 (1984)

Average Annual Rate of Inflation: 11.2% (1973-83)

Money Supply: RF13.582 billion (May 1985)
  Reserve Money: RF8.322 billion (May 1985)

Currency in Circulation: RF7.030 billion (1984)

International Reserves: $106.86 million of which $89.26 million were foreign exchange reserves (1984)

BALANCE OF PAYMENTS (1983)
(million $)

Current Account Balance	−48.7
Merchandise Exports	124.1
Merchandise Imports	−197.6
Trade Balance	−73.6
Other Goods, Services & Income	+36.5
Other Goods, Services & Income	−129.4
Other Goods, Services & Income Net	—
Private Unrequited Transfers	5.5
Official Unrequited Transfers	112.3
Direct Investment	11.1
Portfolio Investment	—
Other Long-term Capital	25.4
Other Short-term Capital	−5.2
Net Errors & Omissions	1.8
Counterpart Items	−7.1
Exceptional Financing	—
Liabilities Constituting Foreign Authorities' Reserves	—
Total Change in Reserves	22.6

Development planning began under Belgian rule with the 10-Year Development Plan (1952-61). Following independence, a development plan was outlined for 1962-71 with the aid of a U.N. survey mission. The 1972-76 Development Plan stressed agriculture and called for a modest increase of 15% in food-crop production. The 1977-1981 Five-Year Plan was designed to encourage a liberal investment climate and provide a base for long-term economic growth.

Most public sector investment after independence was financed by foreign aid in the form of grants. Belgium continues to be the major source of external financing, furnishing approximately one-third of all foreign aid. A considerable portion of Belgian aid consists of annual maintenance support of technical assistance personnel, including teachers. Major areas to which Belgian aid has been directed are agriculture, telecommunications and health care. The second major source of foreign aid is the EEC (European Economic Community) through its European Develop-

GROSS DOMESTIC PRODUCT BY ECONOMIC ACTIVITY (1982)		
	%	**Rate of Change % 1970-81**
Agriculture	44.6	5.3
Mining	2.1	6.8
Manufacturing	15.1	9.1
Construction	5.4	8.2
Electricity, Gas & Water	0.3	2.3
Transport & Communications	—	9.1
Trade & Finance	—	7.4
Public Administration & Defense	—	47
Other Branches	32.5	1.2

ment Fund (FED), again directed toward agricultural diversification. Other sources of foreign aid in the West include the United States, the U.N. Development Program, France, West Germany, Switzerland and Canada. Aid from the Communist Bloc amounted to $23 million during 1954-76, all supplied by China. In 1974 the Arab Fund entered the rank of donors with RF 82.9 million. During 1979-81 Rwanda received $151.7 million in foreign aid, or $30.0 per capita.

BUDGET

The Rwandan fiscal year runs from January 1 through December 31. The national budget consists of two parts: the budget ordinaire, or the recurrent budget, and the budget extraordinaire, or the development budget, which is financed entirely by foreign aid. All direct taxes are collected by the communes.

Of current revenues, import and export duties provide 42.4%, income tax 24.7% (of which profits and capital gain 17.8%, and individual 6.9%) and excise taxes 19.2%. Of the expenditures, economic services claim 41.4%, of which roads and waterways 12.4%, education 18.8%, defense 13.1% and health 7.5%.

In 1983, total outstanding disbursed external debt was $219.7 million all of which was owed to official creditors. Debt service was $4.2 million of which $1.9 million was repayment of principal and $2.3 million interest. External debt represented 136.8% of export revenues and 13.9% of GNP. Debt service represented 2.6% of export revenues and 0.3% of GNP.

FINANCE

The unit of Rwandan currency is the Franc Rwandais (or Rwanda Franc), divided into 100 centimes. Coins are issued in denominations of 50 centimes, and 1, 2, 5 and 10 francs. Notes are issued in denominations of 20, 50, 100, 500 and 1,000 francs.

The Rwanda franc was introduced in 1964, replacing the Rwanda-Burundi franc. In 1966 the franc was devalued by 50%. The 1985 dollar exchange value of the Rwanda franc was $1=RF99.520. The sterling exchange rate was £1=RF121.45.

The National Bank of Rwanda, founded in 1964, took over the functions of a central bank from the for-

BUDGET (million Rwanda francs)			
Revenue	**1981**	**1982**	**1983***
Taxes on income and profits	4,222.6	3,114.7	2,921.3
Taxes on property	156.6	274.2	235.8
Taxes on goods and services	3,294.9	3,996.7	4,416.6
Import duties	3,484.6	3,998.8	3,849.8
Export duties	1,028.4	1,155.5	1,333.5
Other receipts	1,699.2	1,523.6	1,559.2
TOTAL REVENUE	13,885.4	14,063.5	14,316.1
Expenditure	**1981**	**1982**	**1983***
Presidency	517.7	718.2	745.0
National Development Council	—	88.9	94.6
National defense	2,499.4	2,622.4	2,692.7
Interior	360.9	285.4	427.8
Foreign affairs and co-operation	971.9	1,030.6	1,141.4
Economy and finance	2,214.1	2,624.6	2,005.8
Justice and the Supreme Court	679.2	738.1	749.2
Education	4,677.3	4,481.9	4,491.3
Planning	99.5	85.3	89.2
Public service and employment	103.8	105.9	71.6
Posts and communications	383.0	400.4	379.8
Public health	785.5	841.9	862.0
Agriculture and livestock	702.8	824.6	821.9
Social affairs and the Co-operative Movement	209.1	279.4	241.3
Public works	1,015.1	1,164.8	1,162.1
Youth and sport	142.6	175.3	141.9
Economy and commerce	69.3	79.5	77.5
Natural resources, mines and quarries	168.1	152.9	173.2
TOTAL EXPENDITURE	15,599.3	16,700.1	16,368.3

*Provisional.

Development budget (million Rwanda francs): 2,113.2 in 1980; 3,500 in 1982; 3,450 in 1984.

mer Issuing Bank of Rwanda and Burundi (BERB). Full commercial bank services are offered by two private banks: the Commercial Bank of Rwanda and the Bank of Kigali. In 1984 these two banks had reserves of RF966 million and demand deposits of RF5.743 billion and time and savings deposits of RF6.154 billion. The country's only specialized credit institution is the Development Bank of Rwanda.

AGRICULTURE

The economy of Rwanda is almost exclusively based on agriculture. Nearly 91% of the economically active population derives its livelihood from the production of food crops or from industrial activities involving their processing. Of the total land area of 2,638,800 hectares (6,520,474 acres) almost 62% is cultivable, but because of the high population density arable land per capita is less than 0.40 hectares (1 acre). Based on 1974-76=100, the index of agriculture production in 1982 was 130, the index of food production was 129, and the index of per capita food production was 114. Agriculture contributes 50% to the GDP, and its annual rate of growth during 1970-81 was 5.3%. Agriculture also accounts for approximately 80% of total export revenues.

GROWTH PROFILE Annual Growth Rates (%)	
Population 1980-2000	3.4
Birthrate 1965-83	0.8
Deathrate 1965-83	11.8
Urban Population 1973-83	6.6
Labor Force 1980-2000	3.2
GNP 1973-82	5.9
GNP per capita 1973-82	2.3
GDP 1973-83	5.6
GDP per capita 1970-81	1.8
Consumer Prices 1970-81	14.2
Wholesale Prices 1970-81	15.1
Inflation 1973-83	11.2
Agriculture 1970-81	5.3
Manufacturing 1970-81	9.1
Industry	—
Services	—
Mining 1970-81	6.8
Construction 1970-81	8.2
Electricity 1970-81	2.3
Transportation 1970-81	9.1
Trade 1970-81	7.4
Public Administration & Defense 1970-81	4.7
Export Price Index 1975-81	11.4
Import Price Index 1975-81	11.5
Terms of Trade 1975-81	−0.1
Exports 1973-83	2.6
Imports 1973-83	12.9
Public Consumption	—
Private Consumption	—
Gross Domestic Investment	—
Energy Consumption 1973-83	13.0
Energy Production 1973-83	2.0

Of the 718,900 hectares (1,776,402 acres) under cultivation, 95% is under food crops. The basic agricultural unit is the family subsistence farm; only 18% of the total crop is brought to the market. Rwanda is generally self-sufficient in food, but output has failed to keep pace with the explosive population growth. Moreover, agriculture is subject to periodic crop failures, leading to widespread famines. The main factor affecting land use is the location of most farms on slopes of up to 50°. The intensely cultivated areas of the country are subject to soil erosion and depletion of fertility. Erosion control work was largely discontinued after independence, and the use of fertilizers has been negligible; less than 300 tons annually or 1 kg per arable hectare. The hilly terrain and the fragmentation of holdings also make mechanization impossible; there were only 86 tractors in the country in 1982.

The average size of a farmholding is estimated at 1.32 hectares (3.26 acres) of arable land and 1.33 hectares (3.29 acres) of grazing land. Farmholdings are in some cases deliberately fragmented to minimize the risk of complete crop failure in any one area. The land tenure system has not been clearly defined in law. Tutsi feudal land rights have been replaced in most areas by customary rules of tenure under which groups of elders hold cultivation and grazing rights to all local lands. Customary tenure has been replaced by individual titles to land only on the paysannats, planned agricultural settlements originally introduced by the Belgian administration in under-developed areas. Over 50,000 families were resettled on paysannats by the early 1970s, all of them financed by the EEC or the Belgian government.

The two most fertile agricultural regions in the country are the mountains forming the Congo-Nile watershed and the central plateau, where it is normally possible to grow two crops a year. The principal food crops are bananas, sweet potatoes, cassava, sorghum and beans. The bananas are used mainly to make beer, the national drink. The principal export crops are coffee, tea, pyrethrum, cotton and cinchona.

PRINCIPAL CROP PRODUCTION (1983) (000 metric tons)	
Corn	95
Sorghum	235
Potatoes	273
Sweet potatoes	723
Cassava	490
Dry Beans	242
Dry Peas	44
Groundnuts	14
Plaintains	2,277
Coffee	27
Tea	7.1

Cattle played an important political and social role in the country under the Tutsi, whose dominance was based on the ubuhake (or a feudal patron-client relationship based on the use of cattle). Much of the Kinyarwanda language is built around pastoral metaphors and idioms. Most farmers have some livestock though animal husbandry is considered only a supplemental means of income. Livestock productivity is limited by the incidence of parasitic diseases, undernourishment, overstocking and poor range management. The livestock population in 1983 consisted of 647,000 cattle, 352,000 sheep, 1,016,000 goats, 139,000 pigs and 1,223,000 chickens.

Forests cover approximately 1,502 sq km (580 sq mi), concentrated along the top of the Nile-Congo Divide, on the volcanic mountains of the northwest and on Wahu Island in Lake Kivu. Erosion and clearcutting have seriously depleted Rwanda's original forest wealth. An afforestation program undertaken by the Belgian authorities was continued on a smaller scale after independence. Production of roundwood in 1982 amounted to 6.186 million cubic meters (218 million cubic ft), worth $400,000 in export-revenues.

Rwanda's nine major lakes, covering nearly 1,243 sq km (480 sq mi), are potentially rich fishing grounds, but fishing remains underdeveloped, restricted to small farmers living near the lake shores. The number of professional fishermen is believed not to exceed 500. The annual fish catch in 1982 was 1,210 tons.

INDUSTRY

Manufacturing is a relatively minor activity employing less than 2% of the labor force and contributing only 13.1% to the GDP. Most manufacturing takes place at the artisan level. The limited supply of skilled labor and the small size of the domestic market have acted as further constraints on expansion of the industrial base. In 1979 there were 47 industrial units with a capital of over one million Rwanda francs, employing 4,600 workers and producing goods valued at RF15.969 billion. The value added in manufacturing in 1983 was $107 million.

The industrial sector expanded rapidly after 1962 and received considerable impetus from the breakup of the economic union with Burundi in 1964. The major areas of expansion were food processing and textiles, but some new industries were also established in wood, paper, printing, chemicals, rubber and metals. Most manufacturing firms are located at Kigali, but small-scale consumer goods establishments are scattered throughout the country.

Rwanda has a liberal investment code designed to stimulate industrial activity, create investor confidence and promote import substitution. However, the resulting investments have not been large or significant, even in enterprises with favored-status benefits such as tourism, mining, transportation and construction. The net direct private investment in 1983 was $11 million. Most manufacturing firms are owned by Europeans or Asians, while many of the processing firms and workshops are run as cooperatives.

ENERGY

The total production of energy in Rwanda in 1982 was equivalent to 20,000 metric tons of coal and total consumption to 117,000 metric tons of coal, or 21 kg (46 lbs) per capita. The annual growth rates during 1973-83 were 2.0% for energy production and 13.0% energy consumption. Energy imports account for 12.4% of all merchandise imports. Apparent per capita consumption of gasoline is 2 gallons per year.

Rwanda's total electric power production in 1984 was 132 million kwh and per capita production 22 kwh per year.

LABOR

In 1983 the total labor force was estimated at 2.7 million, of whom 88.6% were engaged in agriculture, 3% in industry and commerce, 3% in government and 1% in services. Women constituted 48% of the economically active population.

A significant characteristic of the Rwandan labor force is its fluidity and mobility. The fluidity results partly from the high proportion of temporary workers in all occupations and partly from the constant flow of internal and external migrations. A large but undetermined number of workers migrate annually to Zaire, Uganda, Congo and Tanzania. There is a high rate of turnover and voluntary absenteeism combined with low productivity. Only about 9% of workers are considered to be skilled. Most supervisory positions requiring skills are filled by either Europeans or Asians. This is particularly true of private indus-try, because all trained Africans are readily absorbed by public service.

Working conditions and wages are regulated by the Labor Code of 1967. Minimum wage legislation was first introduced in 1949. Outside the urban centers, ordinary laborers are paid just 90 cents per day, and in Kigali—the economic as well as government center—most households have incomes between $40 and $100 per month. The legal workweek is 48 hours with a compulsory rest day and 50% additional wages for overtime over two hours. The Labor Code also governs labor contracts and conditions of recruitment and dismissal. Fringe benefits include subsidized housing, pension rights and medical or health services. Pensions and employment injury benefits are covered by social security legislation enacted in 1962 and administered by the Social Fund.

Children under 18 are not permitted to work without their guardian's authorization, and they may not work at night except under exceptional circumstances on a temporary basis. The minister responsible for labor affairs may grant work permission to a child under 14. This minister also sets the minimum wage and overtime rates. Hours of work and occupational health and safety are controlled by law and enforced by labor inspectors.

Though statistics are lacking, unemployment is a growing problem aggravated by a high population growth rate. There is also a permanent pool of underemployed workers in the agricultural sector.

The Rwandan Labor Code grants workers the right to organize "professional organizations." If such organizations establish a collective bargaining agreement with the employer, they may negotiate salaries and terms of employment. No unions currently exist in Rwanda, but the government is in the process of forming a labor confederation. This confederation is expected to begin functioning in early 1987. It is organized under the guidance of the party, which must approve its choice of officers, and hence will be limited in its independence. All member unions will have the right to strike, but only with the approval of the confederation executive bureau. In meetings prefatory to the confederation's creation, the responsibility of labor to contribute to the development of the nation and to transcend the parochial interests of individual workers and trades were recurrent themes. The government has permitted seminars on labor issues, organized by unofficial local labor bodies, which receive some support from foreign labor confederations and the International Labor Organization.

FOREIGN COMMERCE

The foreign commerce of Rwanda consisted in 1984 of imports of $202.84 million and exports of $142.64 million, leaving an unfavorable trade balance of $60.2 million. Of the imports, transport equipment constituted 12.8%, machinery and tools 12.8%, fuels and lubricants 12.4%, clothing 11.5%, food 9.7 % and construction materials 8.7%. Of the exports, coffee accounted for 58.6%, tea for 17.2% and tin for 7.9%. The major import sources are: Belgium-Luxembourg 14.8%, Japan 11.4%, France 10.9%, Kenya 9.4%, West Germany 8.9% and Iran 8.4%. The major export destinations are: Kenya 13.4%, Belgium-Luxembourg 9.5%, Italy 2.3% and West Germany 1.7%.

Based on 1975=100, the import price index in 1981 was 174, the export price index 186, and the terms of trade (export price divided by imprice price × 100) 117.

FOREIGN TRADE INDICATORS (1984)

Annual Growth Rate, Imports:	12.9% (1973-83)
Annual Growth Rate, Exports:	2.6% (1973-83)
Ratio of Exports to Imports:	41:59
Exports per capita:	$23
Imports per capita:	$32
Balance of Trade:	−$60.2 million
Ratio of International Reserves to Imports (in months)	4.1
Exports as % of GDP:	15.0
Imports as % of GDP:	25.4
Value of Manufactured Exports:	—
Commodity Concentration:	100%

Direction of Trade (%)

	Imports	Exports
EEC	45.2	10.4
U.S.	8.3	0.5
Industrialized Market Economies	54.0	81.2
East European Economies	—	—
High Income Oil Exporters	—	—
Developing Economies	44.5	16.2

Composition of Trade (%)

	Imports	Exports
Food	9.8	72.7
Agricultural Raw Materials	12.4	72.7
Fuels	12.4	72.7
Ores & Minerals	12.4	23.4
Manufactured Goods	45.7	—
of which Chemicals	—	—
of which Machinery	25.6	—

TRANSPORTATION & COMMUNICATIONS

Rwanda has no railways. None of Rwanda's many rivers is navigable for commercial purposes, and there is only limited freight traffic on Lake Kivu.

Roads are virtually the only means of commercial transportation. In 1983 there were about 5,688 km (3,532 mi) of roads, most of which are unsurfaced and cannot be used during the rainy seasons. Five main roads connect Kigali with Kagitumba, Kibungo, Gisenyi, Gatuna and Cyangugu. Internal public road transport is undertaken by private carriers and a state transport company.

The country's external trade is directed toward the Indian Ocean, using two main routes. The 2,131 km (1,325-mi) southern route runs from Kigali by road, steamer and rail to the Tanzanian port of Dar es Salaam through Burundi. The 1,866-km (1,160-mi) northern route runs from Kigali by road and rail to the Kenyan port of Mombasa through Uganda. International trade traffic is handled by two transport companies on a monopoly basis.

In 1982 there were 6,188 passenger vehicles and 8,297 commercial vehicles in the country. Per capita vehicle ownership was 1 per 1,000.

The national airline is Air Rwanda which acquired a Boeing 707 in 1979. Rwanda is also regularly served by Sabena, Air Zaire, Air France, East Africa Airways and Ethiopian Airlines. Internal service is provided by two charter companies. There are eight airfields and airstrips in the country, all of them are usable, two with permanent surface runways and one with a runway over 2,500 meters (8,000 ft). There are international airports at Kigali-Kanombe and at Kamembe, outside Cyangugu.

In 1984 there were 4,600 telephones in the country or 0.1 per 100 inhabitants.

In 1982 the postal service handled 15,964,000 pieces of mail and 35,000 telegrams. The volume of postal traffic per capita was 2.5 pieces. There are 79 telex subscriber lines.

Despite government efforts to expand tourist facilities and despite the scenic beauty of the Kagera National Park, tourism is an underdeveloped activity. No statistics are available on the number of tourists who visit the country.

MINING

Mining plays a comparatively minor role in the economy, accounting for only 2% of the GDP. However, it contributes 30% to 40% of the total value of exports. The main export minerals are tin, tungsten, beryl, amblygonite and columbium-tantalum. The country produces 1.1% of the world's tin concentrates. Because of economic difficulties, including lack of capital and low-grade ores, some mines have been closed while others are operating at far less than optimum capacity. The mining sector as a whole is controlled by four2Belgian companies, and most exports are destined for the Benelux countries and the U.S.A..

DEFENSE

The defense structure is headed by the president who is also the defense minister and the commander-in-chief. Military manpower is provided by voluntary enlistment. The total strength of the armed forces is 5,150, or 0.92 armed persons per 1,000 civilians.

ARMY:
Personnel: 5,000
Organization: 8 infantry companies; 1 engineer company; 1 commando battalion; 1 reconnaissance squadron
Equipment: 12 armored cars; 6 field guns; 8 mortars; 16 armored personnel carriers

AIR FORCE:

Personnel: 150

Organization: 4 combat aircraft; 3 transports; 8 helicopters; 1 trainer; 2 counterinsurgency aircraft

There is no navy.

The annual military budget in 1984 was $29.949 million, which was 1.4% of GNP, 10.1% of the national budget, $3 per capita, $5,200 per soldier and $1,000 per sq km of national territory.

The Rwandan Army is almost entirely Hutu in ethnic composition, and this homogeneity as well as its historic success in repelling a number of invasion attempts by Tutsi forces armed with Chinese equipment have increased its prestige and credibility. Though staffed almost entirely by Rwandans, Belgian advisers are attached to most units. But the deterrent capability of the armed forces is undermined by a number of geo-economic factors, including the country's landlocked position and faltering economy.

Apart from military equipment and training, Belgian military aid continues at the rate of about $250,000 annually.

EDUCATION

The national literacy rate is 49.7% (61.0% for males and 39.0% for females).

In principle, education is free, universal and compulsory for eight years from age 7 to age 15. Only about one-fifth of all primary schools and a few secondary schools belong to the public school system; the rest are government-approved Roman Catholic or Protestant mission schools.

School enrollment ratios are 70% for the primary age group (7 to 14) and 2% for the secondary age group (15 to 20), for a combined enrollment ratio of 45%. At the third level (20 to 24) the enrollment ratio falls to 0.4%. Girls constitute 48% in the first level, 36% in the second level and 10% in the third level.

Schooling consists of 14 years divided into eight years of primary school and six years of secondary school. Primary education is divided into two cycles: a premier cycle of four years, known as the literacy cycle, in which subjects are taught in Kinyarwanda, and the deuxieme cycle of two years in which subjects are taught in French. Attrition is heavy at the primary level, and only 25% of students advance as far as the fourth grade. Fewer still reach the secondary system, which is divided into two cycles: a three-year tronc commun d'orientation, structured as a general orientation course, and a three-year sections moyennes generales leading to the university. Some 30% of all boys study in private religious institutions, known as seminaries, where the courses are based on Greek and Latin.

The academic year runs from September to July. The medium of instruction, except in the first cycle of primary school, is French. The curricula are based on the National Catholic Federation of Intermediate Education of Belgium, though some Africanization of school texts has occurred.

Almost 63% of primary school teachers are insufficiently qualified. At the secondary level the country relies heavily on Belgian, Canadian and French teachers. There are three types of teacher training institutions: Ecoles de Moniteurs Auxiliaires for boys and Ecoles de Monitrices Auxiliaires for girls, both offering two-year courses; Ecoles Normales Inferieures which offer five-year courses; and Ecoles Normales Moyennes which offer seven-year courses. Teacher trainees account for 38% of secondary school enrollments. The teacher-pupil ratio is 1:55 at the primary level, 1:14 at the secondary level and 1:4 at the tertiary level.

Technical and vocational students account for about 25% of the secondary school enrollment. Two-year and four-year programs are offered in technical and vocational subjects at the postprimary level.

The educational system is under the control of the Ministry of National Education. In 1981 the educational budget was RF5,471,735,000, which was 4.6% of GNP, 28.6% of the national budget and $1,200 per capita.

EDUCATIONAL ENROLLMENT (1982)		
	Teachers	Students
First Level	13,590	747,172
Second Level	1,037	14,230
Third Level	290	1,212

The National University of Rwanda at Butare was established in 1963 by the government and the Roman Catholic Dominican Order of Canada as an autonomous, public institution. About two-thirds of the university staff are Belgian or Canadian. Its total enrollment in 1982 was 1,212, or 19 per 100,000 inhabitants. In 1981, 324 students graduated from the National University. Of these 48 were awarded degrees in medicine, 43 in natural sciences, 59 in social sciences, 28 in law, 37 in agriculture and 19 in education. In 1982, 403 Rwandan students were enrolled in institutions of higher learning abroad. Of these 15 were in the United States, 106 in Belgium, 41 in West Germany, 61 in Switzerland and 44 in Canada. In the same year, 66 foreign students were enrolled in Rwanda.

LEGAL SYSTEM

Rwandan jurisprudence is based on Belgian procedures and precedents and is largely codified. Uncodified customary law is administered in certain jurisdictions.

The judicial structure is headed by a supreme court with a president and five departments, each headed by a vice president. Sitting together, the six justices act as both the constitutional court and the appellate court. The supreme court's department of courts and tribunals supervises the work of all lower courts, while the court of accounts acts as an audit review and accounting office. The supreme court sits in the ancient Tutsi capital of Nyabisindu.

The three lower jurisdictions are 10 courts of first instance (one in each prefecture), courts of appeal in Kigali, Nyabisindu and Ruhengeri, and cantonal, or communal courts, which dispense justice according to traditional law. In addition, there are a number of police courts. Both cantonal and police courts try only minor cases and do not maintain records of cases tried.

The judiciary is statutorily independent and expected to apply the penal code impartially, but the president names and dismisses magistrates. New laws in January 1982 strengthened the independence of the judiciary somewhat by improving the nomination process and more closely defining the functions of judicial personnel. Rwanda has three separate court systems for criminal/civil, military, and state security cases. All but security cases may ultimately be appealed to the court of appeals. The state security court has jurisdiction over national security charges such as treason. Some cases tried before this court have resulted in innocent verdicts. Although all defendants are constitutionally entitled to representation, a shortage of lawyers makes it difficult for the accused to prepare an adequate defense. Family and other nonprofessional counsel is permitted. Trials which arouse extensive public interest are often broadcast to the street, so that persons who cannot be seated in the courtroom may still follow the proceedings.

No information is available on the nature of the penal system or the number of prisons.

LAW ENFORCEMENT

The National Police functions under a director general who oversees discipline, training, promotion and policy. Most of the police are assigned to the 10 prefectures or communes. Each communal force is under the operational command of a brigadier and under the administrative control of the prefect. The police force is assisted by Belgian advisers and equipped with Belgian weapons. The total strength of the force is estimated at 1,200.

Data concerning crime are not available, but law enforcement problems are believed to be minor.

HEALTH

In 1982 there were 232 hospitals in the country with 7,882 beds, or 1 bed per 648 inhabitants. In the same year there were 182 physicians in the country, or 1 physician per 26,071 inhabitants, 1 dentist and 97 nursing personnel. Of the hospitals 43.1% are state-run, and 56.9% are run by private nonprofit agencies. Per 10,000 inhabitants, the admissions/discharge rate is 75, the bed occupancy rate is 80.8% and the average length of stay is 11 days.

```
PRINCIPAL HEALTH INDICATORS (1984)
Crude Death Rate: 16.6 per 1,000
Change in Death Rate: 11.8 (1965-83)
Infant Mortality Rate: 111.9 per 1,000 Live Births
Child Death Rate (Ages 1-4) per 1,000: 26
Life Expectancy at Birth: 47.8 (males); 51.2 (females)
```

The government expenditures on national health services represents 4.8% of the national budget, and $1.40 per capita. The principal health problems are kwashiorkor, infectious hepatitis, dysentery, malaria and tuberculosis. Only 35% of the population have access to safe water.

FOOD

The average Rwandan diet is inadequate and nutritionally unbalanced. The staple foods are sweet potatoes and beans. Beer is drunk on all occasions. Consumption of meat and fish is rare. The per capita intake of food is 2,201 calories per day (as against a WHO recommendation of 2,600 calories per day), 55.7 grams of protein, 13 grams of fats and 443 grams of carbohydrates.

MEDIA & CULTURE

No daily newspapers are published in the country but there are 13 non-daily newspapers, with a total circulation of 21,000 and 16 periodicals. Official news and announcements appear in a French-language monthly. One monthly in Kinywarwanda claims a circulation of over 60,000. Censorship is generally informal and light and is exercised through the Ministry of Information. The national news agency is Agence Rwandaise de Presse (ARP); AFP and Reuters are represented in the capital.

Kigali has five book publishers with a very limited annual output, mostly in French. Rwanda does not adhere to any copyright convention.

Radio Kigali, operated by Radiodiffusion de la Republique Rwandaise, broadcasts 95 program hours a week in Kinyarwanda, French and Swahili. Deutsche Welle of the Federal Republic of Germany has two relay stations in the country. In 1982 there were 158,000 radio receivers in the country, or 30 per 1,000 inhabitants. Rwanda has no television service.

In 1981 there were two cinemas in the country with 3,600 seats, or 0.7 seats per 1,000 inhabitants. Annual movie attendance was 300,000 or 0.1 per inhabitant. Annual box office receipts in 1981 were RF61.5 million.

The largest library is the National University Library at Kigali with 60,000 volumes. Per capita, there are 16 volumes and one registered borrowers per 1,000 inhabitants.

There are three museums reporting an annual attendance of 33,000.

SOCIAL WELFARE

State social welfare programs are channeled through 659 rural aid centers and the Social Fund, which administers pension and employment injury benefits. Missionaries are also active providers of welfare services.

GLOSSARY

commune: administrative subdivision of a prefecture.

mwami: (plural, bami) title of the Tutsi kings of Rwanda.

paysannat: a planned agricultural settlement introduced by Belgian rulers.

prefecture: the principal unit of regional administration.

ubuhake: a feudal relationship between the Tutsi masters and Hutu serfs, abolished at the time of independence.

umusozi: a hill as a social and economic unit.

CHRONOLOGY (from 1962)

1962— Rwanda becomes independent with Gregoire Kayibanda, leader of PARMEHUTU, as president.... New constitution is promulgated.

1963— Tutsi malcontents launch an invasion of Rwanda but are repelled; in retaliation over 12,000 Tutsis are massacred by the Hutu, while uncounted Tutsis flee the country.

1964— The economic union of Rwanda and Burundi is terminated; Rwanda introduces its own national unit of currency, the Rwanda franc.

1969— Kayibanda is reelected to a second four-year term.

1973— As a fresh wave of Hutu-Tutsi conflict threatens to engulf the country, Kayibanda is toppled in a swift and bloodless coup led by Maj. Gen. Habyarimana; the 1962 constitution is partially suspended and the National Assembly is dissolved.

1974— At the Bujumbura Conference the heads of Zaire, Burundi and Rwanda agree to concerted action in defense and eonomic affairs.

1975— Habyarimana launches Mouvement Revolutionnaire National pour le Developpement as the sole political party.

1979— Rwanda hosts Franco-African summit meeting.

1982— Uganda expels over 45,000 Rwandan Tutsis.

1983— The National Development Council is established as the national legislature with limited powers. Habyarimana is reelected to another term as president.

BIBLIOGRAPHY (from 1970)

Kagame, Alexis, *Un Abrege de l'Ethno-Histoire du Rwanda* (Butare, Rwanda, 1972).

Lemarchand, Rene, *Rwanda and Burundi* (New York, 1970).

Levesque, Albert, *Contribution to the National Bibliography of Rwanda* (Boston, 1979).

Linden, Ian, *Church and Revolution in Rwanda* (New York, 1977).

OFFICIAL PUBLICATIONS

Finance and Economy Ministry, *Livres de Caisse des Comptables Publics* (Accounts of Government Accountants) (monthly).

———, *Rapport Annuel.*

———, *Resultats d'Execution du Budget General et des Comptes hors Budget* (Budgetary and Special Treasury Final Accounts) (annual).

———, *Situation du Caissier de l'Etat* (Statement of Government Cashier) (monthly).

Planning Ministry, *Bulletin de Statistique*, Ministere du Plan (quarterly).

Central Bank, *Bulletin Trimestriel* (quarterly).

———, *Etats des Encaissements et Decaissements* (Statements of cash receipts and Payments) (daily and monthly).

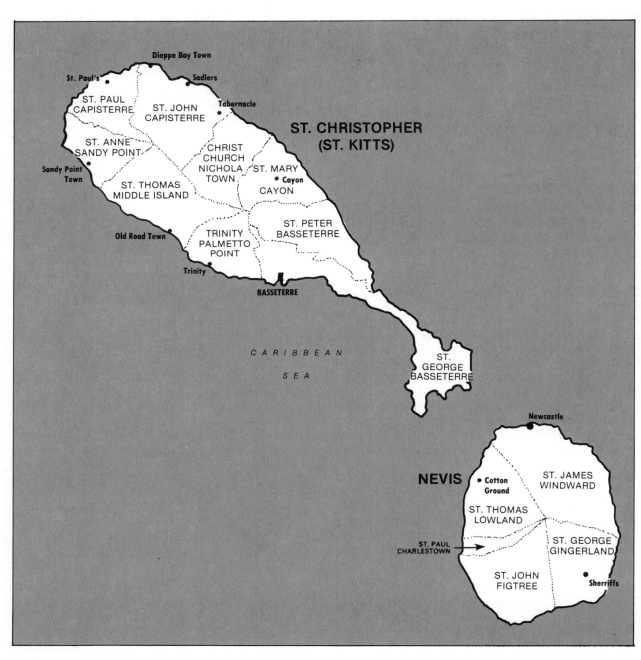

Dieppe Bay Town

St. Paul's

Sadlers

ST. PAUL
CAPISTERRE

ST. JOHN
CAPISTERRE

Tabernacle

ST. CHRISTOPHER
(ST. KITTS)

ST. ANNE
SANDY POINT

CHRIST
CHURCH
NICHOLA
TOWN

ST. MARY

Sandy Point
Town

Cayon

CAYON

ST. THOMAS
MIDDLE ISLAND

Old Road Town

TRINITY
PALMETTO
POINT

ST. PETER
BASSETERRE

Trinity

BASSETERRE

CARIBBEAN

SEA

ST.
GEORGE
BASSETERRE

Newcastle

NEVIS

Cotton
Ground

ST. JAMES
WINDWARD

ST. THOMAS
LOWLAND

ST. PAUL
CHARLESTOWN

ST. GEORGE
GINGERLAND

ST. JOHN
FIGTREE

Sherriffs

ST. KITTS-NEVIS

BASIC FACT SHEET

OFFICIAL NAME: Federation of St. Christopher and Nevis

ABBREVIATION: CN

CAPITAL: Basseterre

HEAD OF STATE: Queen Elizabeth II represented by Governor General Clement Athelston Arrindell (from 1981)

HEAD OF GOVERNMENT: Prime Minister Kennedy Alphonse Simmonds (from 1980)

NATURE OF GOVERNMENT: Parliamentary Democracy

POPULATION: 44,000 (1985)

AREA: 261 sq km (101 sq mi)

ETHNIC MAJORITY: African Negro

LANGUAGE: English

RELIGION: Christianity

UNIT OF CURRENCY: East Caribbean Dollar ($1=EC$2.70, 1985)

NATIONAL FLAG: Two triangles, one of green (with its base at the hoist and apex at the upper fly) and the other of red (with its base in the fly and its apex in the lower hoist) separated by a broad yellow-edged black diagonal stripe (from the lower hoist to the upper fly) bearing two five-pointed white stars.

NATIONAL EMBLEM: A shield flanked by two seabirds and displaying a ship at the lower end. The national motto appears on a scroll at the bottom: "Country Above Self."

NATIONAL ANTHEM: "O Land of Beauty"

NATIONAL HOLIDAYS: Labour Day; Whit Monday; Queen's Official Birthday; August Monday; Independence Day (September 19); Prince of Wales's Birthday; Christmas; Carnival Day

NATIONAL CALENDAR: Gregorian

PHYSICAL QUALITY OF LIFE INDEX: 84 (On an ascending scale in which 100 is the maximum. U.S. 95)

DATE OF INDEPENDENCE: September 19, 1983

DATE OF CONSTITUTION: September 19, 1983

WEIGHTS & MEASURES: Metric system is in force

LOCATION & AREA

Shaped like an exclamation mark, St. Kitts and Nevis lie in the northern part of the Leeward Islands in the Eastern Caribbean, with Saba and St. Eustatius in the northwest, Barbuda in the northeast, and Antigua to the southeast. They are volcanic islands separated by a channel known as the Narrows some two miles wide. St. Kitts is roughly oval, some 37 km (23 mi) long and 176 sq mi (68 sq mi) in area. It is centered on a mountain range, the highest point of which is Mount Lianuiga (1,156 meters; 3,792 ft). Nevis is 93 sq km (36 sq mi) in area rising to a central peak of 985 meters (3,232 ft).

WEATHER

Because the islands are set in the path of the North East trade winds, the climate is remarkably equitable even by Caribbean standards. There is a steady cooling breeze for most of the year. The highest recorded temperature in this century is 92°F and the lowest 62°F. Humidity is low; there is no rainy season as such, the average annual rainfall being 55 inches on St. Kitts and 48 inches on Nevis.

POPULATION

The population of St. Kitts and Nevis was 44,000 in 1985 on the basis of the last census held in 1980 when it was 43,309. The population is expected to reach 50,000 by 2020. Some 36,000 people live on St. Kitts and 8,000 on Nevis. Basseterre, the capital of the nation, has a population of some 14,283, while Charlestown, capital of Nevis, has a population of 1,243.

St. Kitts and Nevis had a negative growth rate of −1.2% in 1985 because of a low birthrate, high infant mortality rate, and high migration. Women play an active role in society and there is a minister of women's affairs.

ETHNIC COMPOSITION

The population is almost entirely of African Negro descent.

LANGUAGES

English is the official language.

DEMOGRAPHIC INDICATORS (1985)	
Population (000)	44
Sex distribution (%)	
Males	48.12
Females	51.88
Density per sq km	169.3
Age breakdown: (%)	
0-15	37.2
15-29	30.4
30-44	9.5
45-59	9.4
60-74	10.0
Over 75	3.5
Population doubling time in years at current rate	39
Birthrate 1/1000	29
Death rate 1/1000	11.2
% Illegitimate births	81.4
Natural increase rate 1/1000	17.8
Total fertility rate	3.4
Marriage rate 1/1000	2.6
Divorce rate 1/1000	0.1
Annual growth rate	1.35
Gross reproduction rate	1.40
Net reproduction rate	1.34
Life expectancy at birth (years)	
Males	68.5
Females	72.9

RELIGIONS

The bulk of the population belongs to the Anglican communion, but six other Protestant denominations and the Roman Catholic confession are also represented.

COLONIAL EXPERIENCE

St. Kitts (the Carib name of which was Lianuiga, "the Fertile Isle,") was the first of the British West Indian islands to be settled. Sir Thomas Warner and his followers landed at the Old Roadstead in 1623; in course of time they sent expeditions to other nearby islands. It was thus that St. Kitts acquired the title of "Mother Colony of the West Indies." At one time there were French settlements at the two ends of the island but the whole island was ceded to Great Britain by the Treaty of Versailles in 1783. Nevis was settled by the British in 1628 and although it came under French and Spanish attacks in the 17th and 18th centuries, it remained one of the most prosperous islands in the Antilles until the mid-19th century. In 1816 St. Christopher, Nevis, Anguilla, and the British Virgin Islands were united under the administration of a captain general and a governor in chief. The first three territories formed the Leeward Islands Federation in 1871 and a member of the West Indies Federation from 1958 to 1962. In 1960 each member of the British Leeward Islands received a new constitution. Following the abortive East Caribbean Federation, St. Christopher-Nevis-Anguilla attained Associated Statehood in 1967. The Legislative Council was replaced by a House of Assembly, the administrator became governor, and the chief minister and leader of the Labour Party, Robert Bradshaw, became the first premier. Anguilla rebelled against this arrangement and was

formally separated from the group in 1980. The 30-year rule of the Labour Party was broken in 1980 when the People's Action Movement (PAM) and the Nevis Reformation Party formed a coalition government after winning five out of nine seats in the Assembly. The coalition government under Kenneth A. Simmonds, the PAM leader, led the nation to independence under a federal constitution on September 19, 1983.

CONSTITUTION & GOVERNMENT

St. Kitts and Nevis is a constitutional federation with the British monarch represented by a governor general as head of state, and a prime minister as head of government and the cabinet of ministers. Nevis has a deputy governor general. The constitution also accords Nevis the right of secession from St. Kitts if a bill to that effect is approved by two-thirds of the elected legislators and endorsed by two-thirds of the voters in a national referendum. St. Kitts has a premier and deputy premier in the cabinet. Suffrage is universal over 18.

CABINET LIST 1985	
Governor General	Clement Athelston Arrindell
Prime Minister	Kennedy Alphonse Simmonds
Deputy Prime Minister	Michael Oliver Powell
Premier of Nevis	Simeon Daniel
Deputy Premier of Nevis	Ivor Stevens
Minister of Agriculture, Lands, Housing, Labor & Development	Hugh Heyliger
Minister of Communications, Works & Public Utilities	Ivor Stevens
Minister of Education, Health & Community Affairs	Sydney Earl Morris
Minister of External Affairs	Kennedy Alphonse Simmonds
Minister of Finance	Kennedy Alphonse Simmonds
Minister of Labor & Tourism	Michael Oliver Powell
Minister of Natural Resources & Environment	Simeon Daniel
Minister of Trade & Industry	Roy Jones
Minister of Women's Affairs	Constance Mitcham
Minister Without Portfolio	Uhral Swanston
Minister in the Ministry of Finance	Richard Caines
Attorney General	Tapley Seaton

FREEDOM & HUMAN RIGHTS

St. Kitts and Nevis has a good human rights record. British legacies in law, freedom of speech, religion, and the exercise of political rights are carefully maintained.

CIVIL SERVICE

No information is available on the Kittisian civil service.

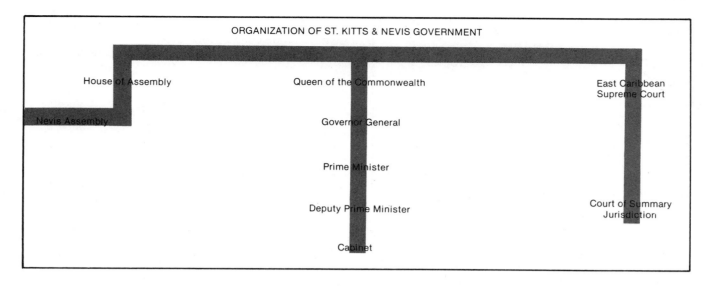

ORGANIZATION OF ST. KITTS & NEVIS GOVERNMENT

House of Assembly

Nevis Assembly

Queen of the Commonwealth

Governor General

Prime Minister

Deputy Prime Minister

Cabinet

East Caribbean Supreme Court

Court of Summary Jurisdiction

LOCAL GOVERNMENT

St. Kitts is divided into 10 parishes and Nevis into five parishes for the purpose of local administration. The parishes are as follows:

St. Kitts:

St. Christopher, Christ Church, Saint Ann, Saint George Basseterre, Saint John, Saint Mary, Saint Paul, Saint Peter, Saint Thomas, Trinity.

Nevis:

St. George, St. James, St. John, St. Paul Charlestown, St. Thomas.

FOREIGN POLICY

St. Kitts & Nevis is a member of the Commonwealth, OAS, CARICOM, and OECS (Organization of Eastern Caribbean States). It was part of the U.S.-backed force that invaded Grenada in 1983.

PARLIAMENT

The unicameral House of Assembly consists of 11 elected representatives (eight from St. Kitts and three from Nevis), plus a maximum of seven nominated members (styled senators) two-thirds of whom are nominated by the government and one-third by the opposition. At the 1984 balloting, voters elected six PAM members, three NRP members, and two Labour Party members.

Constitutional changes require the approval of a two-thirds majority of elected representatives, while certain other entrenched provisions must receive approval of two-thirds of the valid votes in a national referendum in order to be changed.

Nevis has an island Assembly consisting of five elected and three nominated members (the number of the latter is not allowed to exceed two-thirds of the former). In addition, the governor general appoints a premier and two other members of the Nevis Assembly to serve as the Nevis administration.

POLITICAL PARTIES

The ruling government coalition consists of the People's Action Movement (PAM) and the Nevis Reformation Party (NRP). PAM is a moderate left-of-center party and NRP is an exclusively Nevisian party. The opposition Labour Party had been in power for close to 30 years when it was ousted in 1980. There are two other Nevis parties with no electoral seats: the People's Democratic Party and the United National Movement.

ECONOMY

The Kittisian economy is in a transitional stage, moving from an economy dominated by the cultivation and production of sugar to one based on tourism and small manufactures.

PRINCIPAL ECONOMIC INDICATORS

Gross National Product: $40 million (1983)
  GNP Average Annual Growth Rate: 1.9% (1973-82)
  GNP per Capita: $820 (1983)
  GNP per Capita Average Annual Growth Rate: 1.0% (1973-82)

Gross Domestic Product: $48.1 million (1980)
  GDP Average Annual Growth Rate: 4.4% (1977-82)
  GDP per Capita: $1,083 (1980)

Consumer Price Index (1978=100): 157.6 (1983)

No information is available on money supply, currency in circulation, reserve money and international reserves, or on the balance of payments.

Bilateral commitments from Western non-U.S. countries during 1970-81 totaled $15 million. A major donor is the United Kingdom which, on independence, provided a special grant-loan package of £10 million.

GROSS DOMESTIC PRODUCT BY ECONOMIC SECTORS 1981 (%)	
Agriculture	15.6
Mining	0.2
Manufacturing	14.2
Construction	8.4
Trade	15.2
Public Utilities	0.9
Transportation & Communications	11.9
Finance	4.6
Public Administration & Defense	20.8
Services	5.2
Other	3.0

BUDGET

The 1984 national budget consisted of revenues of EC$65.8 million and expenditures of EC$54.6 million leaving an overall surplus of EC$11.2 million. Of the revenues, inland revenues provided 51.1%, customs and excises 19.7%, and others 29.2%. Of the expenditures, 21.5% went to meet financial obligations, 15.9% to education, 14.8% to public utilities, and 10.9% to health. Outstanding external public debt in 1980 was $7 million.

FINANCE

The national unit of currency is the East Caribbean Dollar (EC$) divided into 100 cents. Coins are issued in denominations of 1, 2, 5, 10, 25, and 50 cents and notes in denominations of 1, 5, 20, and 100 dollars. In 1980 the exchange rates were $1 = EC$2.70 and E1 = EC$3.129.

The central bank is the Eastern Caribbean Central Bank located in Basseterre. It serves as the bank of issue for Anguilla, Antigua and Barbuda, Dominica, Grenada, Montserrat, Saint Christopher and Nevis, St. Lucia, and St. Vincent and the Grenadines. There are three local banks, including the government-owned National Bank, and three foreign banks, including two Canadian ones.

AGRICULTURE

Agriculture is dominated by sugar which accounts for 20% of the GDP and 65% of export revenues. It employs 25% of the working population. The sugar industry was nationalized in 1975 when the St. Kitts Sugar Manufacturing Corporation was taken over. In an effort to reduce dependence on sugar, the government has encouraged the growth of other crops, such as peanuts, coffee, seacotton, and coconuts, especially on smallholdings. Only about 30% of domestic food requirements are being met locally. As a result, food imports cost EC$26 million in 1983, equivalent to 41% of total earnings from domestic exports. The sugar production in 1983 was 368,000 tons; the production of other crops was negligible.

There are several large privately owned livestock farms on the islands. Livestock population in 1983 was 8,000 cattle, 20,000 pigs, 24,000 sheep, 15,000 goats, and 80,000 poultry.

Total fish catch was 1,880 tons in 1982, mostly from local waters.

INDUSTRY

Manufacturing activity is presently small and mostly centered on processing sugar, cotton, and copra. In recent years, several garment, shoe, and electronic plants have been established. There are three industrial estates, two on St. Kitts and one on Nevis.

ENERGY

St. Kitts and Nevis does not produce any form of energy. In 1984 it produced 30 million kwh of electricity or 682 kwh per capita.

LABOR

St. Kitts and Nevis has a work force estimated at 22,800 distributed as follows:

	(%)
Agriculture	50.9
Mining	0.4
Manufacturing	7.9
Construction	2.6
Trade	16.7
Public Utilities	0.9
Transportation & Communications	2.2
Finance	0.9
Services	17.5

Minimum wage rates exist only for domestics and retail employees and average $0.67 an hour in textiles and somewhat higher in electronics. The typical work-week is 44 hours with double-time on Sundays and holidays and time-and-a-half for other days' overtime. There are 12 holidays on St. Kitts and 13 on Nevis. Workers normally earn 14 days of paid vacation during one year.

There are four unions on the islands: the St. Kitts and Nevis Trades and Labor Union, the United Workers Union, the Waterfront and Allied Workers Union, and the General Workers Union.

FOREIGN COMMERCE

The foreign commerce of St. Kitts and Nevis consisted in 1983 of exports of $30.6 million and imports of $47.3 million leaving a trade deficit of $16.7 million. Of the imports, machinery and transport equipment constituted 20.5%, manufactured goods 20.1%, food 19.5%, fuels 10.9%, and chemicals 8.9%. Of the exports, food constituted 63.4%, machinery and transport equipment 12.3%, manufactured goods 2.7%, and crude materials except fuels 2.0%. The major import sources are: the United States 30.1%, the United

Kingdom 17.3%, Trinidad and Tobago 11.9%, and Puerto Rico 6.7%. The major export destinations are: the United States 42.2%, the United Kingdom 29.4%, Trinidad and Tobago 8.3%, and Puerto Rico 6.3%.

TRANSPORTATION & COMMUNICATIONS

A 58-km (36-mi) narrow gauge light railway on St. Kitts serves the sugar industry. A state-run motor boat service links the two islands. There are two major ports, Basseterre on St. Kitts and Charlestown on Nevis, both of which handled 99,000 tons of cargo in 1983.

Of the 300 km (186 mi) of roads, 125 km (77 mi) are paved. In 1983 there were 2,329 passenger cars and 263 commercial vehicles on the islands, or 53 per 1,000 inhabitants.

There is no national airline, but the islands are served by a number of smaller inter-island airlines. Golden Rock Airport, 4 km (2.5 mi) from Basseterre, is equipped to serve jets. Newcastle airfield on Nevis can serve only light aircraft.

There are 2,400 telephones, or 5.0 per 100 inhabitants. The islands' nine post offices handled 6,381,000 pieces of mail and 16,000 telegrams. The volume of mail was 145 pieces per capita. There are 34 telex subscriber lines.

Following the introduction of regular air services between the United States and St. Kitts and Nevis, the number of tourists rose to 57,108 (including 19,195 cruise passengers) in 1983.

MINING

There is no significant mining activity on the islands.

DEFENSE

A small army was disbanded by the government in 1981 and its functions were absorbed by the Volunteer Defense Force and a special tactical unit of the police.

EDUCATION

The national literacy rate is 97.6%, and the rate is the same for males and females.

Education is free, universal, and compulsory for nine years between the ages of five and 14. Schooling lasts for 13 years, divided into seven years of primary, four years of lower-secondary, and two years of upper-secondary school. Girls constitute 49% of primary enrollment, 49% of secondary enrollment, and 70% of third-level enrollment. There are 34 government, 14 private, and six denominational schools. The teacher-pupil ratios are 1:23 at the first level, 1:16 at the second level, 1:10 at the vocational level, and 1:7 at the post-secondary level.

In 1980 the educational budget was EC$7.137 million of which 88.6% was current expenditures. This amount represented 6.5% of GNP and 10.2% of the national budget.

EDUCATIONAL ENROLLMENT 1983-84			
Level	Schools	Teachers	Students
First	31	334	7,569
Second	8	296	4,615
Vocational	1	18	182
Higher	1	9	67

LEGAL SYSTEM

Justice is administered by the Eastern Caribbean Supreme Court based in St. Lucia which consists of a Court of Appeal and a High Court. One of the seven puisne judges of the High Court presides over the Court of Summary Jurisdiction in St. Kitts. District magistrate courts deal with petty offenses and minor civil actions involving sums of not more than EC$5,000. Certain types of appeal can be brought before the British Privy Council. The judiciary is highly regarded and trials are fair, speedy, and efficient.

LAW ENFORCEMENT

The St. Kitts and Nevis police is limited to general duties although a paramilitary tactical unit is now operational at Springfield. A police training center has been established at Pond's Pasture. Personnel strength is about 150.

HEALTH

In 1980 there were seven hospitals with 379 beds (or 1 bed per 114 inhabitants) and 16 physicians (1 per 2,706 persons). There were five dentists and 227 nurses. The admissions/discharge rate per 10,000 persons was 701, the bed occupancy rate was 58.9%, and the average length of hospital stay was 10 days.

PRINCIPAL HEALTH INDICATORS (1984)
Crude Death Rate 1/1000: 11.2
Infant Mortality Rate per 1,000 Live Births: 45.7
Life Expectancy at Birth (Years): 68.5 (Males); 72.9 (Females)

FOOD

The reported daily per capita consumption of calories and proteins is 2,147 and 56.5 grams respectively.

MEDIA & CULTURE

St. Kitts and Nevis does not have a daily newspaper, but the major political parties and labor unions publish weekly or biweekly newspapers. The largest of these, the *Labour Spokesman,* published by the Trades and Labour Union, has a circulation of 6,000.

There are commercial radio and television stations and a religious radio station. The government owns and operates a television station. In 1983 there were 21,000 radio receivers and 8,100 television sets in use, or 477 and 184 per 1,000 respectively.

No information is available on film media or cinemas.

SOCIAL WELFARE

No information is available on social welfare programs.

CHRONOLOGY

1983— St. Kitts and Nevis becomes an independent federal state.

1984— St. Kitts and Nevis becomes a member of the Commonwealth and of the OAS.

1984— In House of Assembly elections, the ruling PAM-NRP coalition is returned to power with a decisive majority.

BIBLIOGRAPHY

Hamshere, Cyril, *The British in the Caribbean* (Cambridge, Mass., 1972).

Lowenthal, David, *West Indian Societies* (Oxford, England, 1972).

Merrill, Gordon, *Historical Geography of St. Kitts-Nevis* (Mexico, 1958).

Sherlock, Sir Philip M., *West Indian Nations: A New History* (New York, 1973).

Tooley, Ronald V., *The Printed Maps of St. Kitts-Nevis* (London, 1958).

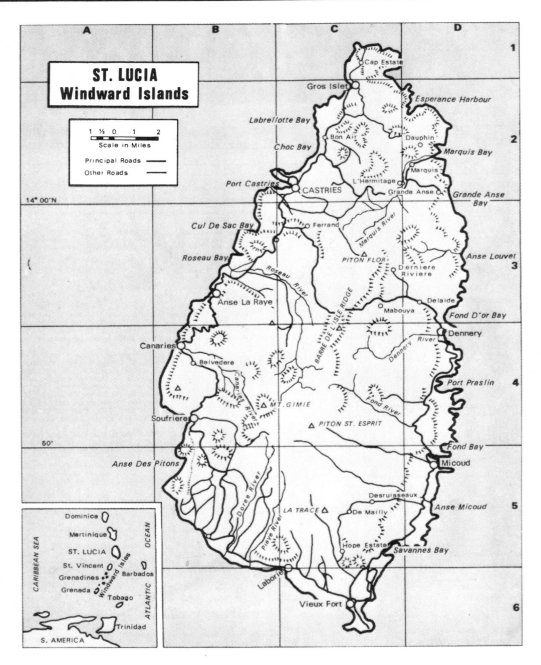

ST. LUCIA
Windward Islands

1½ 0 1 2
Scale in Miles

Principal Roads ——
Other Roads ——

14° 00'N

50'

A   B   C   D

1
2
3
4
5
6

Cap Estate
Gros Islet
Esperance Harbour
Labrellotte Bay
Choc Bay
Bon Air
Dauphin
Marquis Bay
Marquis
Port Castries
CASTRIES
L'Hermitage
Grande Anse
Grande Anse Bay
Cul De Sac Bay
Ferrand
Marquis River
Roseau Bay
PITON FLOR
Derniere Riviere
Anse Louvet
Roseau River
Anse La Raye
Mabouya
Delaide
Fond D'or Bay
BARRE DE L'ISLE RIDGE
Dennery
Canaries
Belvedere
Canaries River
Dennery River
Port Praslin
MT. GIMIE
Fond River
Soufriere
PITON ST. ESPRIT
Fond Bay
Anse Des Pitons
Micoud
Doree River
Desruisseaux
Anse Micoud
LA TRACE
De Mailly
Piaye River
Hope Estate
Savannes Bay
Laborie
Vieux Fort

Dominica
Martinique
ST. LUCIA
St. Vincent
Grenadines
Grenada
Tobago
Trinidad
CARIBBEAN SEA
ATLANTIC OCEAN
Windward Isles
Barbados
S. AMERICA

The LAND The LIGHT
The PEOPLE
St LUCIA

ST. LUCIA

BASIC FACT SHEET

OFFICIAL NAME: Saint Lucia

ABBREVIATION: XK

CAPITAL: Castries

HEAD OF STATE: Governor General Allen Montgomery Lewis (from 1982)

HEAD OF GOVERNMENT: Prime Minister John George Melvin Compton (from 1982)

NATURE OF GOVERNMENT: Parliamentary Democracy

POPULATION: 122,000 (1985)

AREA: 616 sq km (238 sq mi)

ETHNIC MAJORITY: African Negro

LANGUAGE: English: Also, a French-Based Patois

RELIGION: Christianity

UNIT OF CURRENCY: East Caribbean Dollar ($1=EC$2.70 1985)

NATIONAL FLAG: Blue field bearing in its center an isosceles triangle inside which a gold equilateral triangle rises from the common base. The remaining portion of the triangle is black, edged with white.

NATIONAL EMBLEM: A shield with four quarters flanked by two eagles with outstretched wings. Underneath are the national motto, "The Land, The People, The Light," and the name "St. Lucia."

NATIONAL ANTHEM: "Sons and daughters of St. Lucia"

NATIONAL HOLIDAYS: January 1 and 2 (New Year); February 22 (Independence day); May 1 (Labor Day); June 14 (Official Birthday of the Queen of England); August 4 (Bank Holiday); December 13 (St. Lucia Day); also, Christmas, Easter, Whit Monday, Corpus Christi, and Thanksgiving

NATIONAL CALENDAR: Gregorian

PHYSICAL QUALITY OF LIFE INDEX: 86 (On an ascending scale with 100 as the maximum; U.S., 95).

DATE OF INDEPENDENCE: February 22, 1979

DATE OF CONSTITUTION: February 12, 1979

WEIGHTS & MEASURES: The metric system is in force

LOCATION & AREA

The island of St. Lucia lies in the Windward Islands group in the Caribbean between Martinique and St. Vincent. The land area is 616 sq km (238 sq mi) extending 43 (km (27 mi) long and 22 km (15 mi) wide. The total length of the coastline is 158 km (98 mi).

The island is of volcanic formation and is relatively hilly, the highest peak, Morne Gimie, being 958 meters (3,145 ft).

The capital is Castries with a population of around 48,782, or 37% of the entire population; the other principal towns are Vieux Fort (6,981) and Soufriere (7,325).

A number of small rivers flow outward from the central highlands; the principal ones being Dennery, Fond, Piaye, Doree, Canaries, Roseau, and Marquis.

WEATHER

St. Lucia has a tropical climate tempered by the sea winds. The mean temperature is 28°C (79°F) with a dry season lasting from January to April and a rainy season from May to August. Annual rainfall is between 1,500 and 3,500 mm (60 to 138 inches) depending upon the altitude.

POPULATION

The population of St. Lucia was estimated in 1985 at 122,000 based on the last census held in 1981 when the population was 120,300, composed of 47,763 males and 53,130 females. The population is expected to reach 200,000 in 2020.

The annual growth rate is estimated at 1.2% based on a birthrate of 30.4 per 1,000.

Family planning is not a serious issue in the island.

There are no legal restrictions on the role of women is St. Lucia. Although the more traditional household role is the predominant one for St. Lucian women, they are well-represented in government and the professions. As more women take advantage of public schooling and other government programs, the participation of women in other sectors of society is expected to increase.

ETHNIC COMPOSITION

St. Lucians are mainly of African Negro descent. Few Caribs, the original inhabitants of the island, have survived.

```
DEMOGRAPHIC INDICATORS (1985)
Population (1985) ......................     122,000
Annual Rate of Growth .................        1.21
Crude Birthrate 1/1000 ................        30.4
Crude Death Rate 1/1000 ..............         6.2
Gross Reproduction Rate ...............        1.75
Net Reproduction Rate .................        1.66
Life Expectancy (Years)
    Males ............................         66.8
    Females ..........................         71.4
Density per sq km ....................        201.3
Urban % ..............................         52.1
Sex Distribution: (%)
    Males ............................        47.23
    Females ..........................        52.77
Age Profile: (%)
    0-14 .............................         49.6
    15-29 ............................         21.3
    30-44 ............................         11.6
    45-59 ............................          9.8
    60-74 ............................          5.5
    Over 75 .........................           2.2
Marriage Rate (per 1,000) ............         3.5
Divorce Rate (per 1,000) .............         0.2
Natural Increase Rate 1/1000 .........        24.8
Fertility Rate ......................          3.57
% Illegitimate births ................          87
Average Household size ...............         1.9
Population doubling time in years at current rate    28
```

LANGUAGE

The official language is English. However, a large proportion of the population speak only a French-based patois.

RELIGION

St. Lucia is predominantly Roman Catholic. Castries is an archbishopric with a native St. Lucian as an archbishop. The government gives an annual grant to the three leading denominations: Catholic, Anglican and Methodist.

COLONIAL EXPERIENCE

The first known settlement of St. Lucia was by 67 Englishmen in 1624, but the attempt is believed to have failed. In 1639 Sir Thomas Warner was granted a commission for colonization of the island, but after a few months the entire colony of some 400 people was wiped out in 1640. The French established a colony in 1651 and their occupancy was not seriously challenged until 1664 when 1,000 Barbadians and Caribs invaded the island and took it without any resistance. This event marked the beginning of a struggle between the French and the British for possession of the island which lasted for over a century with the British finally winning out.

Representative government was introduced in the dependency in 1924. Until 1959 the colony was a member of the Windward Islands. It joined the West Indies Federation in 1958 and remained a member until the dissolution of the Federation in 1962. In 1967 it became one of the West Indies Associated States with a governor, prime minister and House Assembly replacing the administrator, chief minister and legislative council respectively. In 1975 the Associated States agreed that they would seek independence individually. Following a constitutional conference at London in 1978, St. Lucia proclaimed its independence in 1979.

CONSTITUTION & GOVERNMENT

Under the 1979 constitution, St. Lucia is a parliamentary democracy which the queen of England as the titular head of state represented locally by a governor general. The emergency powers of the governor general are subject to legislative review. The governor general is appointed by the queen on the advice of the prime minister. The governor general, in turn, has the right to appoint the prime minister and other ministers. The governor general may remove a prime minister from office if a resolution of no-confidence is passed in the House and the prime minister does not resign within three days or advise the dissolution of parliament. The cabinet consists of the prime minister, other ministers and the attorney general as an ex officio member.

```
CABINET LIST (1985)
Governor General .................. Sir Allen Lewis
Prime Minister ..................... John Compton
Minister of Agriculture & Lands .......... Ira Dauvergne
Minister of Communications,
    Works & Transport ............... Allen Bousquet
Minister of Community
    Development .................. Romanus Lansiquot
Minister of Education & Culture ..... Margarita Alexander
Minister of Finance ............... John Compton
Minister of Foreign Affairs .......... John Compton
Minister of Health & Housing ........ Wilendon Mason
Minister of Information ........... Romanus Lanisquot
Minister of Labor
    & National Insurance ............. Wilendon Mason
Minister of Legal Affairs ............ Leonard Riviere
Minister of Trade, Industry & Tourism ..... George Mallet
Attorney General .................. Leonard Riviere
Minister of State in the Office
    of the Prime Minister ................ John Bristol
Minister of State for Agriculture
    & Lands .................... Clarence Rambally
Minister of State for Communications,
    Works & Transport ................. Peter Phillip
Minister of State for Health,
    Housing & Labor ................ Ferdinand Henry
Minister of State for Tourism ........... Brian Charles
```

The constitution provides for universal adult suffrage, the age of eligibility being 21. The ninth general election was held in 1982.

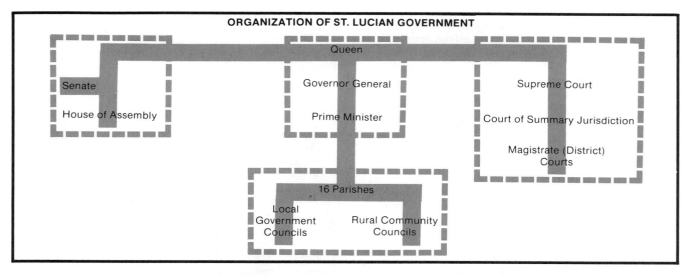

ORGANIZATION OF ST. LUCIAN GOVERNMENT

Queen — Senate, House of Assembly — Governor General, Prime Minister — Supreme Court, Court of Summary Jurisdiction, Magistrate (District) Courts — 16 Parishes, Local Government Councils, Rural Community Councils

FREEDOM & HUMAN RIGHTS

In terms of political and civil rights St. Lucia is classified as free, with a rating 2 in political rights and 3 in civil rights (on a descending scale in which 1 is the highest and 7 the lowest)

There have been no allegations of denials of any human rights in St. Lucia either before or after independence. The constitutional guarantees of these rights are effectively safeguarded by the fact that the West Indies court of appeal has a reputation for impartiality. There is no censorship and no restrictions on the rights of speech, assembly and press. Long years of experience with English common law has left an open political system that permits change and voter participation in the political process.

CIVIL SERVICE

No information is available on the civil service of St. Lucia.

LOCAL GOVERNMENT

St. Lucia is divided into 16 parishes; with a few exceptions, each parish represents a town or village. There are local government councils in Anse La raye, Canaries, Castries, Choiseul, Dennery, Gros Islet, Laborie, Micoud, Soufriere, and Vieux Port. Rural Community Councils are being formed in the country areas and 10 such councils are now in existence. The Castries Town Council, raised to the status of mayoralty in 1966, enjoys almost full autonomy.

With the exception of the Castries Town Council, which has been a wholly elected body since 1836, all local government bodies have both elected and nominated members. Elected members are elected for three-year terms while the nominated members are appointed by the governor general on the advice of the minister of community development.

FOREIGN POLICY

Given the small size of the island, foreign affairs are not an important consideration. However, the post-independence government of Prime Minister Louisy moved closer to Cuba, the Third World and the non-aligned movement. This trend was reversed on the return of the United Workers' Party to office in 1982. St. Lucia joined the Organization of East Caribbean States (OECS) in 1981 and participated in the invasion of Grenada. The historic links of the island with the United Kingdom continue to be maintained at pre-independence levels.

St. Lucia and the United States are parties to 22 treaties and agreements covering aviation, consuls, economic and tehnical cooperation, extradition, investment guaranties, mutual security, Peace Corps, postal matters, property, taxation, telecommunications, trademarks and visas.

St. Lucia is a member of the United Nations as well as seven non-UN organizations, including OAS and CARICOM and the Commonwealth.

The United States has no diplomatic representation at the ambassadorial level in Castries.

U. K. High Commissioner in Castries: J.S. Arthur (1980)

St. Lucian Ambassador in Washington D.C.: Joseph Edsel Edmunds

St. Lucian High Commissioner in London: Claudius C. Thomas

PARLIAMENT

The national legislature consists of an appointed senate and an elected House of Assembly, both with a normal term of five years, subject to dissolution.

The senate comprises 11 members, six appointed on the advice of the prime minister, 3 on the advice of the leader of the opposition, and two after consultation with religious, economic and social groups.

The House of Assembly consists of 17 members. Following the 1982 election, the party position in the lower house was as follows: United Workers Party

14, St. Lucia Labour Party 2 and Progressive Labour Party 1. Only the House may introduce money bills and the power of the senate to delay legislation is restricted.

The leader of the opposition is appointed by the governor general and appointments to various public bodies (such as the Public Service Commission, Integrity Commission, Teaching Commission) as well as the designation of a parliamentary ombudsman, require consultation with the leader of the opposition.

POLITICAL PARTIES

There are two traditional political parties. The ruling party is the United Workers' Party in opposition from 1979 until 1982 when it won a landslide victory. It is led by John Compton, prime minister.

The opposition is the St. Lucia Labour Party (SLP) which was in power for three years from 1979 to 1982. Led by former prime minister, Allan Louisy and Julian Hunte, it has been moving to the right after its electoral reverse in 1982. A faction of SLP, Progressive Labour Party, is led by George Odlum.

ECONOMY

St. Lucia is one of the 39 lower-income countries in the world with a free-market economy in which the private sector is dominant.

PRINCIPAL ECONOMIC INDICATORS

Gross National Product: $130 million (1983)
  GNP Annual Growth Rate (1973-82) 5.5%
  GNP per capita: $1,060 (1983)
  Per capita GNP Annual Growth rate: 3.9% (1973-82)
Gross Domestic Product: EC$377.5 million (1983)
  GDP at 1980 Prices: EC$325.9 million
  GDP Deflator (1980=100) 115.8
  GDP per capita: EC$2,904 (1983)
  GDP Annual Growth Rate 3.1% (1982)
Consumer Price Index (1970=100);
  All Items: 443.1 (1983)
  Food: 492.9 (1983)
  Money supply: EC$71.935 million (March 1985)
  Reserve Money: EC$46.70 million (1984)
  Currency outside Banks: EC$34.17 million (1984)
  International Reserves: $12.38 million of which foreign exchange $12.38 million (1984)

St. Lucia receives aid principally from the United Kingdom, Canada and the EEC. During 1970-81 bilateral aid totaled $34 million.

BUDGET

The fiscal year is the calendar year.

Sources of government revenue include import and export duties, excise duty, income tax, succession duty and land and house tax.

The 1982/83 budget consisted of revenues of EC$137.280 million and expenditures of EC$153.090

GROSS DOMESTIC PRODUCT BY ECONOMIC ACTIVITY (1980)

	%
Agriculture	12.8
Mining	1.3
Manufacturing	6.7
Electricity, Gas & Water	2.1
Construction	10.7
Trade	14.9
Transportation & Communications	7.1
Finance & Real Estate	15.4
Public Administration & Defense	16.0
Other	13.0

BALANCE OF PAYMENTS (1982) (million $)

Current Account Balance	−28.51
Merchandise Exports	41.60
Merchandise Imports	−110.67
Trade Balance	−69.07
Other Goods, Services & Income	+51.76
Other Goods, Services & Income	−31.34
Other Goods, Services & Income Net	—
Private Unrequited Transfers	13.36
Official Unrequited Transfers	6.78
Direct Investment	20.00
Portfolio Investment	4.39
Other Long-term Capital	1.30
Other Short-term Capital	−0.73
Net Errors & Omissions	5.86
Counterpart Items	0.29
Exceptional Financing	—
Liabilities Constituting Foreign Authorities Reserves	—
Total Change in Reserves	−2.60

million leaving a deficit of EC$15.81 million. Of the current revenues, 26.9% comes from income taxes, 23.0% from customs duties, 15.4% from aid grants, 15.1% from taxes on goods and services and 11.3% from non-tax revenues. Of the expenditures, 76.4% goes to current charges, 23.0% to capital charges and 0.6% to public debt repayment.

In 1983 total outstanding external debt was $17 million.

No information is available on the national debt.

FINANCE

The St.Lucian unit of currency is the East Caribbean dollar divided into 100 cents. Coins are issued in denominations of 1, 2, 5, 10, 25, and 50 cents and notes in denominations of 1, 5, 20, and 100 dollars.

The East Caribbean dollar was introduced in 1965 replacing at par the West Indian dollar. It was linked to the sterling until July 1976 when the exchange rate was fixed at $1 = EC$2.70 / EC$1 = $0.3704. This rate remained in force in 1985. The sterling exchange rate is £1 = EC$3.129.

The banking system comprises five commercial banks and one cooperative bank as well as the Agricultural and Industrial Development Bank, the Caribbean Investment Corporation, Government Savings Bank, and the Housing Development Bank. Commercial banks are required to have an authorized capital of at least EC$500,000 and overseas banks, in addition, must have a principal office in the state. In 1984 commercial banks had reserves of EC$12.53 million, demand deposits of EC$33.02 million and time and savings deposits of EC$210.93 million.

AGRICULTURE

Of the total land area of 61,645 hectares (152,320 acres) 50% of arable land, 35 pasture, 19% forest, 5% unused but potentially productive and 23% wasteland and built-on. Some 10,036 hectares (24,800 acres) are owned by the government leaving $1,477 hectares (127,200 acres) in private ownership. Farms occupy 33,209 hectares (82,060 acres).

Saint Lucia lies within the hurricane belt and consequently suffers frequent devastations of its crops and infrastructure. Hurricane Allen, in August 1980, wiped out the entire banana crop. The production of coconuts, cocoa and local food crops was also severely affected. Banana production, however, has made a good recovery, with exports increasing steadily in 1981 and 1982. Exports of bananas were considerably higher in 1983, with shipments of 54,320 metric tons, valued at EC$52.8 million. This was the highest figure for 14 years, despite crop damage from strong winds in January and September 1983. Production in 1984 increased substantially to a total of 64,583 tons.

The types of land tenure are freehold, leasehold and multiple tenancy, commonly known as family land. Because inherited land is divided among heirs, four fifths of the island's farms are of less than 2 hectares (5 acres). Certain restrictions are imposed on the purchase of land by aliens. In 1982 there were 38 tractors and the annual consumption of fertilizers was 1,000 tons.

Agriculture is the largest economic sector in terms of employment (32.1%) and it is also the largest export earner (22.9%). It contributes 12.8% to the GDP. The principal crop is bananas, of which St. Lucia is the largest exporter in the Windward Island. The other major crops are coconuts and cocoa. Considerable efforts are being made to diversify agricultural production and to reduce the substantial bill for food imports.

AGRICULTURAL PRODUCTION (1982) (000 tons)	
Bananas	59
Mangoes	44
Coconuts	34
Copra	6

There has been a steady increase in the number of cattle of both beef and dairy types. Graded Holsteins and Guernseys are the main breeds raised by dairy farmers. Pigs are raised mainly by peasant farmers. Livestock population in 1982 consisted of 11,000 cattle, 10,000 pigs, 14,000 sheep, and 10,000 goats. For-

ests cover approximately 8,100 hectares (20,000 acres) in the mountainous interior, with 40 hectares (100 acres) being replanted every year.

Fishermen's cooperatives account for most of the annual catch of 2,404 tons in 1982. A modern fishing complex with cold storage facilities is planned for Castries.

Agricultural credit is provided by the St. Lucia Agricultural Bank.

INDUSTRY

Manufacturing contributes 6.7% to GDP and employs 4.4% of the labor force.

A vigorous industrial program, initiated in the early 1970's, has resulted in the establishment of a number of large manufacturing plants, including those producing textiles, batteries, plastics, industrial gases, beer and electronic components. By the late 1970's exports of manufactured goods represented 48% of total exports as compared to 25% in 1974. The Caribbean Development bank has financed the construction of two industrial estates, one at Castries and the other at Vieux Fort, both of them free trade zones. A U.S. company is constructing a giant petroleum transshipment terminal costing $150 million at Cul de Sac, within the free zone. There are also plans for an oil terminal. The industrialization program is being coordinated by the National Development Corporation. An agreement was signed with Taiwan in 1984 for technical assistance and investment.

ENERGY

St. Lucia does not produce any form of energy but consumes 84,000 tons of coal equivalent, or 683 kg (1506 lb). Production of electric power in 1984 was 56 million kwh, or 467 kwh per capita.

LABOR

The labor force was estimated in the early 1980s at 49,451, of which women constituted 55.2%. Over 32% of the economically active population is engaged in agriculture, 4.4% in manufacturing, 5.1% in construction, 8.8% in trade, 22.6% in services and 27% in other sectors. In 1984 the unemployment rate was estimated at 22%.

Industrial relations are governed by legislation and supervised by the Labor Department. The minimum legal working age in St. Lucia is 14. The work week is 40 hours in five days and workers are guaranteed a minimum annual vacation of two weeks. Some of the provisions of an occupational safety law passed in 1985 are being disputed by labor unions. Although no minimum wage is established by law, a government-established Wage Council reviews wage rates in different sectors and makes recommendations which are generally accepted as having the force of law. The wages set by this procedure are arguably less than that on which a person can be reasonably expected to live.

There are 14 labor unions representing 20% of the labor force. The largest are the National Workers' Union and the Farmers and Farm Workers Union. A trade union council has been established to remedy the lack of unity among these unions.

FOREIGN COMMERCE

The foreign commerce in St. Lucia consisted in 1982 of exports of $42.07 million and imports of $119 million leaving a trade deficit of $76.9 million. Of the imports, petroleum constituted 10.0%, electrical machinery 9.5%, chemicals 8.8%, nonelectrical machinery 7.7%, transport equipment 6.6%, wood and paper products 6.5%, metal manufactures 5.1%, meat and meat products 4.1% and cereals and cereal products 3.8%. Of the exports, bananas constituted 22.9%, excavating machinery 9.6%, iron sheets 9.2%, electrical switches 8.5%, beverages 6.8%, coconut oil 6.4%, clothing 6.3%, and cardboard boxes 5.6%.

The main import sources are: the United States 31.8%, the United Kingdom 15.6%, Trinidad & Tobago 12.3%, Japan 5.7%, Canada 4.2% and Venezuela 3.7%. The major export destinations are: the United States 27.6%, the United Kingdom 25.1%, U.S. Virgin Islands 10.7%, Jamaica 9.2%, and Trinidad & Tobago 6.1%.

TRANSPORTATION & COMMUNICATIONS

There are no railways on the island.

The main port is Castries which has anchorage for all but the largest vessels. Ships also are accommodated at Vieux Fort. Total cargo handled in 1982 was 288,000 tons.

The island is well served by roads with a circular highway passing through all major towns and villages. The total length of the road system is 760 km (466 mi) of which 500 km (280 mi) are paved. In 1982 there were 4,479 passenger cars (37 per 1,000 inhabitants) and 1,171 trucks and buses.

The main airfield is at Vigie, near Castries. A second airport, the Hewanorra International Airport (formerly Beave Field, a deactivated U.S. Air Force field) at Vieux Fort, can handle long-range jets. There is no national airline, but the island is served by 11 airlines including the St. Lucia Airways.

In 1984 there were 9,500 telephones, or 8.0 per 100 inhabitants.

In 1982 the postal service handled 3,679,000 pieces of mail and 19,000 telegrams. Mail per capita was 30 pieces. There are 76 telex subscriber lines.

St. Lucia is one of the favorite resorts of European and U.S. tourists in the Caribbean, drawn by its spectacular scenery, white sand beaches and balmy climate. Including cruise ship passengers, over 70,000 tourists visited the island in 1982 generating $30 million in tourist revenues.

MINING

There is virtually no mining activity on the island.

DEFENSE

St. Lucia has no internal defense force but receives the protection of U.K. military guarantees.

EDUCATION

The national literacy rate is about 82% (80.8% for males and 82.4% for females).

Primary education is free and compulsory for 10 years from age 5 to 15 and is provided in over 90 state-aided schools. Schooling lasts for 12 years divided into seven years of primary school, three years of the first secondary cycle and two years of the second cycle. There are six junior secondary schools and five secondary schools, including one built by the Canadian government. An educational complex at Morne Fortune provides industrial, technical and teacher training while also serving as a branch of the University of the West Indies. Girls constitute 50% of primary enrollment, 56% of secondary enrollment and 47% of post-secondary enrollment. The teacher-pupil ratio is 1:31 at the primary level and 1:20 at the secondary level.

Educational expenditures in 1982 totaled EC$27,466,000, of which 83.9% was current expenditure. This amount represents 7.8% of GNP (as compared to a UNESCO recommendation of 4%) and 16.8% of the national budget.

EDUCATIONAL ENROLLMENT (1982/83)			
	Schools	Teachers	Students
First Level (5-14)	79	957	31,785
Second Level (11-19)	12	229	4,582
Vocational	1	25	131
Higher	1	51	199

In 1982, 95 St. Lucian students were enrolled in higher education institutions abroad. Of these 25 were in the United States, 15 in the United Kingdom and 29 in Canada. In the same year 57 foreign students were enrolled in third-level institutions in St. Lucia.

LEGAL SYSTEM

The judicial system comprises the Supreme Court, courts of summary jurisdiction and district courts. Appeals lie with the Privy Council in London under certain circumstances. The island is divided into two judicial districts with nine magistrate courts. The Judicial and Legal services Commission oversees the judiciary and advises on appointments to the bench. The attorney general also serves as the director of public prosecutions.

Prisons are administered by the superintendent of prisons.

LAW ENFORCEMENT

The police force is administered by a commissioner of police who is responsible to the premier. Its total strength is 516, including 11 officers and 11 inspectors.

HEALTH

There are seven hospitals including the 233-bed Victoria Hospital at Castries and 24 health centers, with a total of 525 beds, or 1 bed per 236 inhabitants. In 1983 there were 36 physicians, or 1 physician for 3,444 inhabitants, 5 dentists, and 112 nursing personnel. Of the hospitals, 85.7% are state-run and 14.3% are run by private nonprofit agencies. Per 10,000 inhabitants the admissions/discharge rate is 1,289. The bed occupancy rate is 74.3% and the average length of stay is 7 days.

PRINCIPAL HEALTH INDICATORS (1984)
Crude Death rate per 1,000: 6.2
Life Expectancy at Birth: (Males) 66.8 (Females) 71.4
Infant Mortality rate per 1,000: 24.1

FOOD

Although much of the food is imported St. Lucians enjoy a varied diet. The per capita daily availability of energy, protein, fats and carbohydrates is 2,388 calories, 64.4 grams, 64 grams and 341 grams respectively.

MEDIA & CULTURE

The St. Lucian press consists of seven non-dailies, of which *The Voice of St. Lucia* appears twice weekly, with a circulation of 5,000. The press is privately owned and free of official censorship. There is no national news agency.

The island's book publishing output is limited to telephone directories.

The official radio station is Radio St. Lucia (RSL) which broadcasts in English, French and Creole. The Radio Caribbean International is a private station owned by the French CIRTES. In 1982 there were 91,000 radio receivers and 1,900 television sets, or 746 and 16 per 1,000 inhabitants respectively. Television is provided by St. Lucia Television Service, a private commercial station.

No information is available on the number of cinemas, movie attendance and the production and import of films.

There is a free public library service administered by the Central Library at Castries. Per capita, these libraries have 433 volumes and 89 registered borrowers per 1,000 inhabitants. The island's only museum has an annual attendance of 7,000.

SOCIAL WELFARE

A National Provident Fund covering all workers between the ages of 16 and 60 was introduced in 1970.

CHRONOLOGY (from 1979)

1979— St. Lucia becomes an independent member of the Commonwealth with John Compton as prime minister. . . . In general election, St. Lucia Labor Party wins upset victory; Allan Louisy is named prime minister.

1981— Prime Minister Allan Louisy is forced to resign when George Odlum and 12 other SLP members vote against the government. . . Winston Cenac, the attorney general, is named prime minister with a parliamentary majority of one. . . Odlum and two others form a new party, the Progressive Labour Party.

1982— Cenac resigns and Michael Pilgrim of PLP forms an all-party caretaker government pending elections. . . In general elections UWP wins 14 out of 17 seats. . . John Compton takes office as prime minister. . . Sir Allen Lewis is reappointed governor general following the dismissal of Boswell Williams.

1983— St. Lucia, as member of the Organization of East Caribbean States, participates in U.S.-led invasion of Grenada.

1984— Prime Minister Compton leads trade mission to the Far East.

BIBLIOGRAPHY

Eggleston, Hazel, *Saint Lucia Diary* (Greenwich, Conn., 1977).

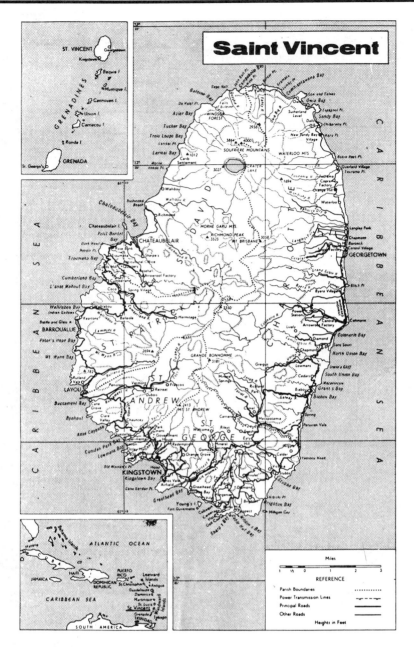

Saint Vincent

PAX · ET · JUSTITIA

ST. VINCENT

BASIC FACT SHEET

OFFICIAL NAME: Saint Vincent and the Grenadines

ABBREVIATION: XM

CAPITAL: Kingstown

HEAD OF STATE: Governor General Joseph Lambert Eustace(from 1985)

HEAD OF GOVERNMENT: Premier James F. Mitchell (from 1984)

NATURE OF GOVERNMENT: Parliamentary Democracy

POPULATION: 102,000 (1985)

AREA: 389 sq km (150 sq mi)

ETHNIC MAJORITY: Negroes of African Descent; also, East Indians and Carib Indians

LANGUAGE: English

RELIGION: Christianity

UNIT OF CURRENCY: East Caribbean Dollar ($1 = EC$2.70, 1985)

NATIONAL FLAG: Three equal vertical bands of blue, gold and green with the national emblem superimposed on a breadfruit leaf in the center

NATIONAL EMBLEM: A field of Green with fire burning on an ancient altar between two female figures dressed in azure, the figure onthe right holding its hand an olive branch and the figure on the left kneeling on the right knee to make sacrifices on the altar; on the crest a sprig of the cotton plant and below the motto: "Pax et Justita."

NATIONAL ANTHEM:"St. Vincent so beautiful"

NATIONAL HOLIDAYS: Independence Day (October 27); January 22 (Discovery Day); July 7 (Caricom day); also, Christmas, New Year's Day, Labor day and Thanksgiving Day

NATIONAL CALENDAR: Gregorian

PHYSICAL QUALITY OF LIFE INDEX: 83 (On an ascending scale in which 100 is the maximum, U.S., 95)

DATE OF INDEPENDENCE: October 27, 1979

DATE OF CONSTITUTION: October 27, 1979

WEIGHTS & MEASURES: The metric system is in force.

LOCATION & AREA

St. Vincent lies at the lower end of the Caribbean chain of Windward Islands some 96 km (60 mi) north of Grenada and 160 km (100 mi) west of Barbados. It is a small green island, only 29 km (18 mi) long and 18 km (11 mi) wide with a total land area of 389 sq km (150 sq mi). The length of the coastline is 84 km (52 mi).

Down its whole length the island is dominated by a volcanic range of mountains with four peaks at almost equal distance from each other: Soufriere, Richmond, Grand Bonhomme, and St. Andrew. The land slopes gently to the coast on the east in contrast to the rugged terrain on the west. There are many fast flowing rivers.

The capital is Kingstown with a 1982 population of 24,764. Other principal towns are Chateaubelair, Barrouallie, and Layou in the west and Georgetown in the east.

The Grenadines are a chain of islets between St. Vincent and Grenada. All of them have white beaches noted for their intense beauty and coral reefs with enclosed bays that are ideal for underwater sports. The larger of the Grenadines are Bequia, Canouan, Mustique, and Unionwhile among the smaller are Mayreau, Palm or Prune, Baliceaux, Battawia, and Isle de Quatre. Many of the islets are privately owned and some of them are uninhabited.

WEATHER

The climate is tropical with average temperatures between 18°C and 32°C (64°F and 90°F). From January to June the northeast tradewinds predominate and temperatures are equable. The rainy season is from May to November when the rainfall ranges from 1,500 mm (60 in) to 3,750 mm (150 in). The central mountains experience the heaviest rainfall. St. Vincent lies just inside the hurricane belt but seldom suffered much damage.

POPULATION

The population of St. Vincent was estimated in 1985 at 102,000, based on the last census held in 1970 when the population was 87,305 composed of 41,325 males and 45,980 females. The population is expected to reach 200,000 by 2020.

The annual rate of population growth during 1980-85 was 1.20%, based on a crude birth rate of 30.4 per 1,000 and a natural increase of 19.6 per 1,000. The population density is 338.4 per sq km (876 per sq mi), almost evenly distributed throughout the island. Because of the smallness of the island, the distinctions between urban and rural settlements are not demographically significant.

From 1971 through 1975 the island had a net gain through migration in three years and a net loss in two years.

The role of women in society is not restricted by law, but custom dictates that most Vincentian women center their lives around the home. As women take greater advantage of public education programs, health facilities, and family planning, many observers expect the women of St. Vincent and the Grenadines to participate in larger numbers in the nation's economic, professional and political life.

DEMOGRAPHIC INDICATORS (1985)	
Population (1985)	102,000
Annual Rate of Growth (1980-85)(5)	1.20
Crude Birth Rate (per 1,000) (1976-80)	30.4
Gross Reproduction Rate per Woman (1975-80)	1.75
Marriage Rate (per 1,000)	3.2
Divorce Rate (per 1,000)	0.2
Crude Death Rate 1/1000	6.2
Total Fertility Rate	3.57
Net Reproduction Rate	1.66
Life Expectancy Rate (Years)	
Males	66.8
Females	71.4
Density per sq km	338.4
% Urban	26.3
Sex Distribution %	
Male	47.0
Female	53.0
Age Distribution (%)	
0-14	44.9
15-29	29.8
30-44	10.3
45-59	8.2
60-74	5.0
Over 75	1.8
Population Doubling Time in Years at Current Rate	27
Natural Increase 1/1000	19.6

Population planning has had little impact on the island.

ETHNIC COMPOSITION

The original inhabitants of the island were the fierce Caribs who have disappeared through natural disasters, forced expulsion, and intermarriage with Negroes. After the abolition of slavery in 1838, Portuguese workers from Madeira and indentured laborers from India were imported adding some variety to the ethnic composition. The ethnic breakdown of the population is as follows:

ETHNIC COMPOSITION	
African Negro	65.5%
Mixed	19.0
White	3.5
East Indian	5.5
Amerindian	2.0
Others	4.5

LANGUAGE

The official language is English which is spoken with varying levels of fluency by almost all St. Vincentians.

RELIGION

Anglican, Methodist and Roman Catholic Churches are represented on the island in addition to a host of smaller groups and cults. The Anglican bishop of the Windward Island is resident in St. Vincent.

COLONIAL EXPERIENCE

St. Vincent was discovered by Columbus in 1498, but remained in the possession of the Carib Indians until 1627 when the king of England granted it to the Earl of Carlisle, who did not occupy it and allowed the grant to lapse. In 1779 it was captured by the French, but was finally restored to the United Kingdom under the terms of the Treaty of Versailles in 1783. For the next 13 years, the French and their Carib allies tried to wrest the possession from the British without success, although in 1795, they overran the island and murdered all the British colonists. In 1797 the Caribs were expelled to the island of Ruatan in the Bay of Honduras. With other nearby British territories St. Vincent was administered by the govenor of the Windward Islands until 1959. From 1958 to 1962 it was a member of the West Indian Federation. Upon the failure of negotiations to form the East Caribbean Federation, St. Vincent, along with other British colonies in the region, became an associated state with full internal self-government in 1967. The Legislative Council was renamed the House of Assembly, the administrator became governor and the chief minister was restyled premier. Following the constitutional conference of 1978, the island was granted full independence as St. Vincent and the Grenadines on October 27, 1979. The governor became governor general and the premier prime minister as a result of this transition. St. Vincent remains a "special member" of the Commonwealth not represented at summit meetings.

CONSTITUTION & GOVERNMENT

St. Vincent is a constitutional monarchy with the queen of England as sovereign, represented on the island by the governor general and an elected member of the House of Assembly who commands the support

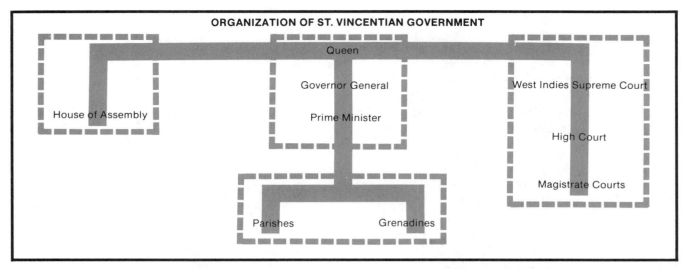

ORGANIZATION OF ST. VINCENTIAN GOVERNMENT

of the majority as prime minister and head of government. The governor general is appointed on the advice of the prime minister and the latter, in turn, is appointed by the governor general. As in the tradition in countries following the Westminster system, the governor general is empowered to remove the prime minister from office if a resolution of no confidence is passed by the House and the prime minister does not resign within three days or advise the governor general to dissolve the House. The cabinet consists of the prime minister, six other ministers and the attorney general as an ex officio member.

CABINET LIST (1985)	
Governor General	Joseph Lambert Eustace
Prime Minister	James F. Mitchell
Minister of Communications & Works	Burton B. Williams
Minister of Education	Allan C. Cruickshank
Minister of Foreign Affairs & Finance	James F. Mitchell
Minister of Health	Edward G. Griffith
Minister of Housing, Labor & Community Development	David E. Jack
Minister of Information, Tourism & Culture	John C.A. Horne
Minister of Legal Affairs	Emery Robertson
Minister of Trade, Industry & Agriculture	Marcus P.W. Defreitas
Minister of State in the Ministry of Housing, Labor & Community Development	Jeremiah C. Scott
Minister of State in the Ministry of Trade, Industry & Agriculture	Herbert G. Young
Minister of Attorney General	Emery Robertson

Elections are held every five years on the basis of universal adult suffrage. The last elections were held in 1984 when the New Democratic Party gained 9 seats and control of the government.

FREEDOM & HUMAN RIGHTS

In terms of civil and political rights St. Vincent is classified as a free country with a rating of 2 in civil rights and 2 in political rights on a scale in which 1 is the highest and 7 the lowest.

The British rule has left a deep impression on the political and legal systems which specifically respect the integrity of the person, and guarantee fair trial, due process, freedom from arbitrary arrest, and other civilized practices. While there is unfettered participation in the political processes, political parties function actively only during elections and at other times, the government tends to neglect opposition viewpoints. There is no form of censorship or government interference in media activities.

CIVIL SERVICE

No information is available on the Vincentian civil service.

LOCAL GOVERNMENT

For purpose of local government, the island of Saint Vincent is divided into five local parishes: Charlotte, St. George, St. Andrew, St. David and St. Patrick. The Grenadines are under the control of the prime minister's office.

FOREIGN POLICY

St. Vincent's international contacts are limited to its immediate neighbors, the United Kingdom, and to a lesser extent, the United States and Canada, who are among the principal donors of aid.

One of the moderate Caribbean states, St. Vincent and the Grenadines followed a generally conservative foreign policy under former prime minister Robert Cato. The Mitchell government has adopted a less conservative posture and has been unwilling to join regional military alliances.

St. Vincent and the United States are parties to three treaties and agreements covering investment guaranties, Peace Corps and postal matters.

St. Vincent and the United States have not exchanged ambassadors. St. Vincent has not yet applied for membership inthe United Nations.

PARLIAMENT

The national legislature is the House of Assembly consisting of 13 elected representatives and six senators. The senators are appointed by the governor general—four on the advice of the prime minister and two on the advice of the leader of the opposition. The term of the house is five years.

The leader of the opposition is appointed by the governor general and his position and responsibilities are set forth in the constitution.

Following the 1984 elections, the party position in the house was as follows: New Democratic Party 9 seats and St Vincent Labour Party 4.

POLITICAL PARTIES

There are eight political parties, of which the ruling party is the New Democratic Party led by the prime minister James F. Mitchell. It is essentially a Grenadine Party. The only parliamentary opposition is the St Vincent Labour Party that led the nation to independence under Robert Milton Cato. The ruling party until 1967 was the People's Progressive Party, but it did not gain any seat in the 1979 elections. The other parties are the United People's Movement, a coalition of left-wing groups; St. Vincent and Grenadines National Movement; Movement for National Unity led by veteran Marxist, Ralph Gonsalver; People's Democratic Movement; and People's Political Party.

ECONOMY

St. Vincent is one of the 39 lower middle-income countries of the world with a free-market economy in which the private sector is dominant.

PRINCIPAL ECONOMIC INDICATORS

Gross National Product: $90 million (1983)
  GNP Annual Growth Rate 3.8% (1973-82)
  GNP per capita: $860 (1983)
  GNP Per Capita Annual Growth Rate: 3.0% (1973-82)
Gross Domestic Product EC$248.2 million (1983)
  GDP Annual Growth Rate –2.5% (1982)
Consumer Price Index (1980=100) 130 (1984)
Money Supply EC$49.757 million (March 1985)
  Reserve Money EC$44.50 million (1984)
Currency in Circulation EC25.04 million (1984)
International Reserves: $12.82 million
  of which foreign exchange $12.82 million (1984)

Bilateral external aid commitments (ODA and OOF) during 1970-81 totaled $25 million.

BALANCE OF PAYMENTS (1983)
(million $)

Current Account Balance	–3.00
Merchandise Exports	42.00
Merchandise Imports	–64.91
Trade Balance	–22.91
Other Goods, Services & Income	+21.70
Other Goods, Services & Income	–21.19
Other Goods, Services & Income Net	—
Private Unrequited Transfers	16.00
Official Unrequited Transfers	3.40
Direct Investment	3.00
Portfolio Investment	—
Other Long-term Capital	2.60
Other Short-term Capital	–1.30
Net Errors & Omissions	–0.19
Counterpart Items	–0.09
Exceptional Financing	—
Liabilities Constituting Foreign Authorities Reserves	—
Total Change in Reserves	–1.20

GROSS DOMESTIC PRODUCT BY ECONOMIC SECTOR
(1981)

	%
Agriculture	16.7
Mining	0.3
Manufacturing	10.9
Construction	12.5
Trade	12.7
Public Utilities	2.6
Transportation & Communications	14.8
Finance	13.7
Public Administration & Defense	17.7
Services	3.2
Other	–5.3

BUDGET

The fiscal year is the calendar year.

The 1982 national budget consisted of revenues of EC$65.954 million and expenditures of EC$72.486 million. Of the revenues, 26.9% came from income taxes, 19.5% from import duties, 9.7% from stamp duties, 9.4% from consumption duties and 2.8% from licenses. Of the expenditures, 19.0% went to education, 17.4% to public works, 11.4% to health, 7.6% to police, 4.4% to pensions and 2.7% to agriculture.

In 1978-79 outstanding external debt was $7.8 million.

FINANCE

The Vincentian unit of currency is the East Caribbean dollar divided into 100 cents. Coins are issued in denominations of 1, 2, 5, 10, 25, and 50 cents and notes are issued in denominations of 1, 5, 20, and 100 dollars.

In 1976 the link between the sterling and the East Caribbean dollar was discontinued and the exchange rate was fixed at $1=EC$2.70/EC$1 =0.3703. This rate remained in effect in 1985. The sterling exchange rate is £1 = EC$3.129.

The banking system comprises four national banks and four overseas banks. The national banks are the Agricultural and Cooperative Bank of St. Vincent, the National Commercial Bank, the St. Vincent Agricultural Credit and loan bank, and the St. Vincent Cooperative Bank. In 1984 commercial banks had reserves of EC$19.46 million, demand deposits of EC$25.32 million and time and savings deposits of EC$123.53 million.

AGRICULTURE

Of the total land area of 38,900 hectares (96,122 acres), 50% is classified as arable, 44% as forest, 3% as pasture and 3% as wasteland and built-on. Agriculture is the basis of the economy and providing 29% of total employment, 16.7% of GDP and 80% of the exports.

Tree crops occupy 3,920 hectares (9,687 acres). The chief agricultural products are bananas, arrowroot and coconuts. Secondary products include nutmegs, mace and cocoa. The island is the world's leading producer of arrowroot, used in making starches. Banana production suffered as a result of the eruption of the volcano at Soufriere in 1979 submerging thousands of acres of banana plantations.

In terms of land ownership, the state owns 15,378 hectares (38,000 acres), planters 6,880 hectares (17,000 acres), small farmers 10,320 hectares (25,500 acres), and settlements 2,428 hectares (6,000 acres).

PRINCIPAL CROP PRODUCTION (1982) (000 lb)	
Bananas	70,000
Arrowroot	2,106
Nutmeg & Mace	142
Sweet Potatoes	3,197
Plantains	4,383
Ginger	286
Ground nuts	400

In 1982 there were 75 tractors in the islands and the consumption of fertilizers was 3,900 tons.

State owned plantations are managed by the St. Vincent Agricultural Development Corporation.

Livestock raising is limited to small farmers. The livestock population in 1983 consisted of 8,000 cattle, 13,000 sheep, 7,000 pigs and 4,000 goats.

The greater part of the central highlands is covered with forests owned by the state. Of these, some 6,070 hectares (15,000 acres) are designated as forest reserves. The stands contain few species of high economic value.

Although fishing is encouraged, the island is a net importer of fish. Fish marketing and cold storage are handled by the St. Vincent Marketing Board. Total catch in 1983 was 547 tons.

INDUSTRY

Manufacturing contributes 10.9% to GDP.

Apart from food processing, there was very little manufacturing until the 1970's. Expansion of this sector was primarily the work of the St. Vincent Development Corporation established in 1971 to promote joint ventures. Two industrial estates have been established and the government is offering tax exemptions and other incentives to foreign investors. Industrial products include flour, sugar, concrete and furniture.

ENERGY

St. Vincent produces 2,000 metric tons of energy and consumes 21,000 metric tons or 208 kg (459 lb) per capita.

Electric power production in 1984 was 22 million kwh, or 220 kwh per capita.

LABOR

The labor force in 1980 was 32,617, of whom 34.5% were women. The sectoral breakdown showed 29% in agriculture, 0.2% in mining, 7.8% in manufacturing, 12.1% in construction, 12.1% in trade, 0.9% in public utilities, 4.5% in transportation and communications, 30.3% in services and 3.1% in other. Unemployment is estimated in certain seasons as high as 25%.

The minimum working age is 15. The work week is 40 hours in five days, and workers are guaranteed a minimum annual vacation of two weeks. The government is currently endeavoring to convert loose arrangements covering occupational safety and health into statutes. The minimum wage established by law is arguably not enough on which a person can be reasonably expected to live.

Nearly 10% of the work force is unionized in a number of trade unions, including The Civil Service Association, Commercial, Technical and Allied Workers' Union, Federal Industrial and Agricultural Workers' Union and the Teachers' Union.

FOREIGN COMMERCE

The foreign commerce of St. Vincent consisted in 1984 of imports of $26.93 million and exports of $19.26 million, leaving a trade deficit of $7.67 million. Of the imports, food and food products constituted 27.5%, manufactured articles 13.4%, machinery 13%, chemicals 11.8%, petroleum products 8.8%, textiles and shoes 4.5%, lumber 3.9%, tobacco 2.7%, cement 1.9%, beverages 1.7% and motor vehicles 1.6%. Of the exports, bananas constituted 42.8%, flour 13.8%, taro 8.7%, miscellaneous manufactures 7.0%, chemicals 4.5%, arrowroot 4.4%, machinery and transport equipment 3.7% and plantains 3.2%.

The major import sources are: the United States 32.5%, the United Kingdom 17.2%, Trinidad and Tobago 13.5%, Canada 5.8%, Barbados 4.4% and

Guyana 3.7%. The major export destinations are: the United Kingdom 45.9%, Trinidad and Tobago 23.9%, the United States 6.9% and Barbados 4.8%.

TRANSPORTATION & COMMUNICATIONS

All transport moves by road as there is no rail system. The length of the highways total 1,000 km (621 mi), of which roughly 300 km (186 mi) are paved. The principal road encircles the island running from Chateaubelair on the west coat, through Kingstown and Calliaqua in the south, to Georgetown on the east coast. Feeder roads link the villages in the valleys, but no road as yet crosses the central mountains. Registered automobiles total 4,482 (44 per 1,000 inhabitants) and trucks and buses 1,306.

The main port of entry is Kingstown which can accommodate two ocean-going vessels and about five motor vessels. In 1982 it handled 61,000 tons of cargo. Other points, such as Bequia and Union Island, are served by motor launches and open boats which ply daily between Kingstown and the islands on the Leeward coast, and tri-weekly between the Grenadines and the mainland. The island has 44 registered ships with a GRT of 80,331.

The principal airport at Arnos Vale, southeast of Kingstown, is served by the Caribbean Airways of Barbados, LIAT of Antigua and Air Martinique. There are five other usable airfields, three of them with permanent-surface runways.

The postal system comprises a general post office at Kingstown and 39 district post offices. The telephone system has 6,050 subscribers (4.6 per 100 inhabitants). There are 53 telex subscriber lines.

St. Vincent and the Grenadines are among the finest tourist attractions in the Caribbean and with well-developed yachting facilities. In 1983 86,350 tourists visited the islands generating revenues of EC$89.8 million.

MINING

St. Vincent has no mineral resources.

DEFENSE

St. Vincent has no standing army, but is currently developing a joint coastguard service with Barbados and Trinidad & Tobago as partners. The United Kingdom provides adequate military guarantees against external attack.

EDUCATION

The national literacy rate is about 85%.

Primary education is free and compulsory for 10 years from the age of five to 15, and is provided in 39 government, 11 Methodist, 9 Anglican and 2 Roman Catholic schools. Secondary education is provided in 2 government and 11 denominational schools in addition to four junior secondary schools.

The duration of schooling is 14 years divided into seven years of primary school, five years of lower secondary and two years of upper secondary. The school year runs from September through July. The medium of instruction is English throughout. Girls constitute 49% of primary enrollment, 59% of secondary enrollment and 88% of higher education enrollment. The teacher-pupil ratio is 1:20 at the primary level, 1:18 at the secondary level and 1:6 in post-secondary institutions. Post-secondary institutions include one teacher training college and one technical collage.

The educational system is subject to the supervision of the Board of Education, headed by the chief education officer. The annual current expenditures on education in 1978 were EC$5.931 million. The educational budget represented 4.9% of GNP.

EDUCATIONAL ENROLLMENT (1983)			
	Institutions	Teachers	Students
First Level	62	1,251	24,551
Second Level	19	292	5,170
Vocational	5	48	275
Third level	1	19	105

LEGAL SYSTEM

The legal system is headed by the West Indies Supreme Court which includes a Court of Appeal and a High Court, one of whose judges is resident on St. Vincent and presides over a Court of Summary Jurisdiction. The islands are divided into three magisterial districts, the first at Kingstown, the second covering Georgetown, Biabou, Mesopotamia and Colonarie, and the third covering Layou, Chateaubelair, Calliaqua and the Grenadines.

The islands' only prison is at Kingstown with accommodation for 100 prisoners.

LAW ENFORCEMENT

The law enforcement force comprises one commissioner of police, one deputy commissioner, one assistant commissioner, two superintendents, five assistant superintendents, and nine inspectors. The total strength of the force is 489 men and eight women. The headquarters are in Kingstown with subpolice stations in all towns and inhabited Grenadine Islands.

HEALTH

St. Vincent has a good standard of health marred only by a high infant mortality rate. The principal hospital is the Kingstown General Hospital with 210 beds. In addition there are three rural hospitals, three specialist hospitals and 33 clinics. There is a resident doctor in each of the six medical districts, and 16 other physicians and two dentists. Per 10,000 inhabitants the admissions/discharge rate is 649, the bed occupancy rate is 68.3% and the average length of stay is 9 days. Public health expenditures constitute 11.8% of the national budget and $17.30 per capita.

PRINCIPAL HEALTH INDICATORS (1984)
Crude Death rate per 1,000: 6.2
Life expectancy at Birth: (Males) 66.8 (Females) 71.4
Infant Mortality Rate per 1,000 live births: 60.2

Per capita there are 316 inhabitants for each hospital bed and 4,318 inhabitants for each physician.

FOOD

The staple articles of diet are sweet potatoes, yams, tannias, dasheen, eddoes and maize. The daily per capita availability of energy, protein, fats and carbohydrates is estimated at 2,208 calories, 48.5 grams, 54 grams and 414 grams respectively.

MEDIA & CULTURE

Three non-daily newspapers are published in the island: *The Star,* the organ of the St. Vincent Labour Party, *The New Times,* organ of NDP, and *The Vincentian,* an independent weekly. The latter sells 3,000 copies. In addition there are two government publications. The press is not subject to any form of censorship. There is no national news agency or foreign news bureau in Kingstown.

There is no book publishing activity on the islands.

The national radio station is Radio St.Vincent which provides local programming in addition to transmitting BBC news. There is no television service, but programs from Barbados are received on the island. In 1983 the number of radio sets was 55,000 (539 per 1,000) and the number of television sets 8,000 (78 per 1,000).

There are three cinemas with 2,400 seats, or 34 per 1,000 inhabitants. Annual attendance is estimated at 0.6 per inhabitant.

The library service consists of the central library at Kingstown, with 59,640 books and 15 branch libraries, with 10,600 registered borrowers. Per capita, there are 589 volumes and 167 registered borrowers per 1,000 inhabitants.

SOCIAL WELFARE

A National Provident Fund Scheme was introduced in 1970 and covers all workers between the ages of 16 and 60. Employees contribute 5% of their earnings matched by an equal amount by employers.

CHRONOLOGY

1979— St. Vincent and the Grenadines becomes fully independent as a special member of the Commonwealth. . . . In House of Assembly elections Prime Minister Milton Cato's St. Vincent Labor Party wins 11 out of 13 seats. . . . Government quells uprising on Union Island organized by the Rastafarian cult, a cult that, among other things, worships the former Emperor Haile Selassie of Ethiopia.

1984— In general elections, the New Democratic Party led by James Mitchell wins nine out of 13 Assembly seats while the St. Vincent Labour Party wins only four... Cato steps down and Mitchell takes office as prime minister.

BIBLIOGRAPHY

Shepard, Charles, *Historical Account of the Island of St. Vincent* (Totowa, N.J., 1971).
Young, William, *Account of the Black Caribs in the Island of St. Vincents* (Totowa, N.J., 1971).

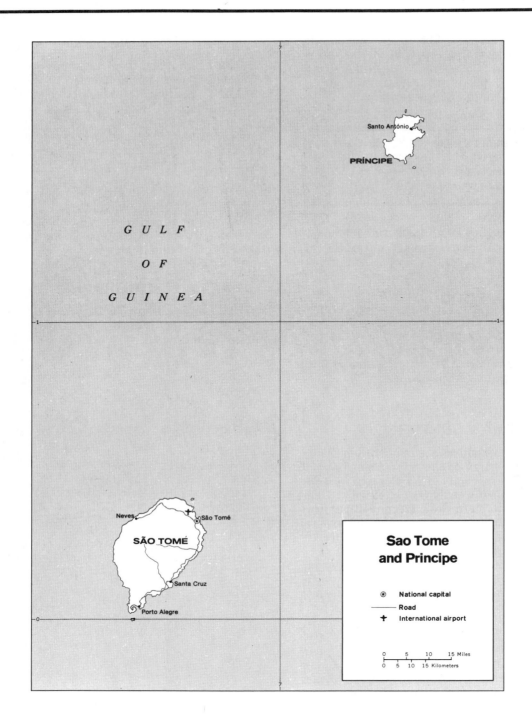

GULF

OF

GUINEA

Santo António

PRÍNCIPE

Neves   ✛ São Tomé

SÃO TOMÉ

Santa Cruz

Porto Alegre

Sao Tome
and Principe

⊛   National capital

——   Road

✛   International airport

0   5   10   15 Miles

0   5   10   15 Kilometers

SAO TOME & PRINCIPE

BASIC FACT SHEET

OFFICIAL NAME: Democratic Republic of Sao Tome and Principe (Republica Democratica Sao Tome e Principe)

ABBREVIATION: SF

CAPITAL: Sao Tome

HEAD OF STATE: President Manuel Pinto de Costa (from 1975)

NATURE OF GOVERNMENT: Modified democracy

POPULATION: 88,000 (1985)

AREA: 963 sq km (372 sq mi)

ETHNIC MAJORITY: Negro

LANGUAGE: Portuguese

RELIGION: Roman Catholicism

UNIT OF CURRENCY: Dobra $1=D 43.620 (August 1985)

NATIONAL FLAG: A red triangle at the hoist from which three equal horizontal stripes of green, yellow and green run to the fly. On the yellow middle stripe are two black stars.

NATIONAL EMBLEM: Two parrots holding a tear-drop shaped shield on which appears a cocoa tree; the shield is surmounted by a star.

NATIONAL ANTHEM: An instrumental with no words.

NATIONAL HOLIDAYS: July 12 (National Day, Independence Day); also variable Christian festivals.

NATIONAL CALENDAR: Gregorian

PHYSICAL QUALITY OF LIFE INDEX: Not available

DATE OF INDEPENDENCE: July 12, 1975

DATE OF CONSTITUTION: December 12, 1975

WEIGHTS & MEASURES: The metric system is in force

LOCATION & AREA

Sao Tome & Principe is located in the Gulf of Guinea off the northern coast of Gabon. It has an area of 963 sq km (372 sq mi), of which Sao Tome accounts for 862 sq km (333 sq mi) and Principe for 101 sq km (39 sq mi). Sao Tome, located about 201 km (125 mi) off the northern coast of Gabon, extends 49 km (30 mi) NNE to SSW and 29 km (18 mi) ESE to WNW. Principe, located about 442 km (275 mi) off the northern coast of Gabon, extends 21 km (13 mi) SSE to NNW and 15 km (9 mi) ENE to WSW. Sao Tome has a coastline of 141 km (88 mi) and Principe a coastline of 79 km (49 mi). In addition, there are two small islets, Rolas, crossed by the equator, and Pedras Tinhosas.

The capital is Sao Tome with a 1980 population of 25,000. The largest town on Principe is Santo Antonio. Other urban centers include Ribeira Alfonso, Neves and Porto Alegre on Sao Tome and Infante Don Henrique on Principe.

Both islands are active volcanoes and have many craters and lava flows. The highest point in Sao Tome rises 2,024 meters (6,640 ft); there are 10 peaks over 1,067 meters (3,500 ft). Principe, with a larger plateau area than Sao Tome, rises 948 meters (3,110 ft).

WEATHER

The islands have a tropical climate moderated by altitude and the cold Benguela Current. The dry season lasts from June to September and the wet season from October to May. Thera are four climatic zones on both islands: the hot and humid northeast lowlands, with about 100 cm (40 in.) annual rainfall; the plateau above 400 meters (1,300 ft), where the temperature is lower and the rainfall ranges from 380 cm to 500 cm (150 in. to 200 in.); over 600 meters (2,000 ft), where the temperature is still lower and the nights are cold and mist is common; and the southeast lowlands, where there is no dry season. Temperatures average around 26.6°C (80°F) on the coast and 20°C (68°F) on the plateau.

POPULATION

The population of Sao Tome & Principe was estimated in 1985 at 88,000 on the basis of the last official census held in 1981 when the population was 95,000. The population is expected to reach 100,000 by 2020.

The annual growth rate is estimated at 2.68% on the basis of an annual birth rate of 38.7 per 1,000. The overall population density is 103.7 per sq km (268 per sq mi). Nearly one-fifth of the population lives in the capital city and the remainder in the small quasi-urban centers that dot the southern western coasts. No information is available on the median age of the population. The sex ratio conforms to the general African pattern, with males forming a slight majority.

DEMOGRAPHIC INDICATORS (1984)	
Population 1985 (000)	88
Density per sq km	103.7
Annual Growth Rate %	2.68
Urban %	15
Sex Distribution (%)	
Male	51.47
Female	48.43
Age Profile (%)	
0-14	37.3
15-24	17.3
25-60	38.0
Over 60	7.4
Population Doubling Time in Years at Current Rate	50
Birthrate 1/1000	38.7
Death Rate 1/1000	10.2
Natural Increase 1/1000	28.5
Total Fertility Rate	5.2
Life Expectancy (Years)	
Males	47.1
Females	50.0
% Illegitimate Births	91.2

Virtually all Sao Tomeans are descendants of migrants from Angola, Cape Verde and Mozambique. Since independence, the European population has dropped significantly.

Women have constitutional guarantees of equality, and several are active in public life. One senior official, the minister of education and culture, is a woman, as is the president of the Popular Assembly. There are at least two female members of the central committee of the party. Cultural factors, rather than legal or political restraints, limit the actual participation of women in government.

There are no official birth control programs or policies.

ETHNIC COMPOSITION

The population is predominantly African, although there are scattered traces of racial admixture. The islands were probably inhabited by fishermen from West Africa long before the first Europeans set foot on them in the second half of the 15th century. Genoese, Spanish and French immigrants settled on the islands around 1485, and in the late 15th century the Portuguese settled convicts and exiled Jews here. Along the southeast coast of Sao Tome live a group called Angolares, believed to be descendants of Angolan slaves. Within the African groups there are no visible tribal divisions; such divisions, if they existed, were obliterated during the centuries of Portuguese rule.

With the departure of the Portuguese, there are no permanent Western communities. No U.S. citizens are reported to be permanently resident in the country.

LANGUAGES

The official language is Portuguese, spoken in a heavy creole accent.

RELIGIONS

The dominant religion is Roman Catholicism. Sao Tome is the seat of a suffragan see under the archdiocese of Luanda in Angola.

COLONIAL EXPERIENCE

Sao Tome & Principe's colonial history begins in 1485 as a concession or donatario of a Portuguese adventurer named Joao de Paiva. For many years the islands served as slave stations between the Congo and Portugal. By the 16th century, flourishing sugarcane plantations had been established on the islands with the help of plantation slaves "recruited" from other Portuguese colonies. By the early 1900s, Sao Tome had become the largest producer of cocoa in Africa, but it was not until 1906 when Henry Nevinson described the inhuman conditions on the cocoa plantations in *A Modern Slavery* that there was a call for reform. But despite these oppressive conditions, Sao Tome & Principe did not witness a guerrilla struggle against the Portuguese on the scale of the other colonies. Even when independence came in 1975, it did so as the logical culmination of a change of regime in Lisbon, and it was granted voluntarily and through an orderly transfer of power.

CONSTITUTION & GOVERNMENT

The constitution of 1975 describes Sao Tome & Principe as a "unitary and democratic state," but at the same time it declares the Movimento de Libertacao de Sao Tome e Principe (MLSTP) as the "leading force" of the nation and the sole political organization. The general principles of the constitution calls for the destruction of the old colonial economic structure and the establishment of a public sector that will control the entire national economy.

The head of state is the president, elected for a term of four years by the People's Assembly from a list of candidates presented by MLSTP.

Government policy is determined by President Da Costa, in consultation with his key cabinet and security officials. The leadership uses the single political party to consolidate its rule at the local levels and to assist in selecting candidates for the Popular Assembly. In the 1985 elections to the Popular Assembly, persons at local levels were allowed, even encouraged, to speak out and to give their opinions on various government policies. In many districts, the

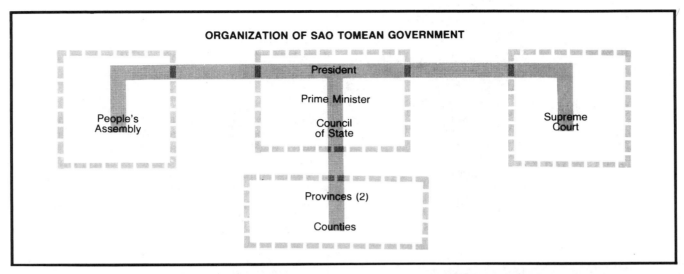

ORGANIZATION OF SAO TOMEAN GOVERNMENT

- President
- Prime Minister
- Council of State
- People's Assembly
- Supreme Court
- Provinces (2)
- Counties

voters rejected the official party candidate in favor of another candidate. There are small exile groups in Portugal and Gabon. Internal security is reinforced by Angolan troops.

CABINET LIST (1985)

President . . . . Manuel Pinto da Costa

Minister of Agriculture
& Ranching . . . . Tome Dias da Costa

Minister of Commerce
& Fisheries . . . . Celestino Rocha da Costa

Minister of Cooperation . . . . Carlos Alberto Pires Tiny

Minister of Defense, National Security,
Transport &
Communications . . . . Oscar Aguiar Sacramento e Sousa

Minister of Education
& Culture . . . . Ligia Silva Graça do Espirito Santo Costa

Minister of Foreign Affairs
& Planning . . . . Manuel Pinto da Costa

Minister of Health & Sports . . . . . Frederico José Henrique Sequeira

Minister of Industry, Construction
& Housing . . . . Jose Fret Lau Chong

Minister of Information . . . . Manual Vaz Afonso Fernandes

Minister of Justice . . . . Francisco Fortunado Pires

Minister of Labor
& Social Affairs . . . . Armindo Vaz de Almeida

Sec. of State for
Foreign Affairs . . . . Guilherme Posser da Costa

Sec. of State for Planning . . . . . Agostinho da Silveira Rita

Secretary, Council
of Ministers . . . . Manuel Vaz Afonso Fernandes

Suffrage is universal over age 18. No elections have been held since 1975.

Sao Tome & Principe faces a bleak economic future that is bound to have political repercussions. The decline in cocoa prices, the departure of the Portuguese plantation managers, chronic trade deficits and a high unemployment rate are only a few of the problems with which the nation is confronted. The islands have no strategic importance, and they have few natural resources.

FREEDOM & HUMAN RIGHTS

In terms of civil and political rights, Sao Tome & Principe is classified as a not-free country with a rating of 6 in civil and political rights (on a descending scale in which 1 is the highest and 7 the lowest in rights).

Although characterized as a not-free country, there are few reports of serious violations of human rights in this country. Its smallness of size and population seems to preclude the establishment of a full-fledged apparatus of oppression. Nevertheless, because of its one-party governmental system, charges of plotting against the state are often levied indiscriminately against those opposed to the party policies. The former prime minister, Miguel Trovoada, was himself arrested on charges of connivance in attempted coups. A number of other opponents of President Pinto da Costa, are in exile. The press is state-controlled as also the labor movement.

CIVIL SERVICE

No current information is available on the Sao Tomean civil service.

LOCAL GOVERNMENT

Administratively, Sao Tome & Principe is divided into two provinces (co-terminous with the two main islands) and 12 counties, of which 11 are on Sao Tome.

FOREIGN POLICY

Sao Tome & Principe is perhaps the only former Portuguese colony that maintains cordial ties with Portugal. Although diplomatic relations are maintained with 14 nations, only Portugal has an embassy in Sao Tome; most of the other ambassadors accredited to Sao Tome & Principe are resident in Libreville, Gabon. Neither the United States nor the United Kingdom are represented in the country.

The country's foreign policy has been free of ideological rigidity, and has sought to maximize aid and assistance from overseas. Thus, regular visits by President da Costa to Communist countries in the early years (to China in December 1975, to the USSR in 1976 and to Cuba in 1978) have been balanced by membership of the IMF (1977), accession to the Lomé Convention (1978) and the cultivation of good relations with France, which is probably the most generous supplier of aid to the country (Sao Tome frequently attends the Franco-African summits).

Sao Tome & Principe joined the U.N. in 1975; its share of the U.N. budget is 0.02%. It is a member of two U.N. organizations and the OAU.

PARLIAMENT

The national legislature is the unicameral Popular Assembly (Assembleia Popular), consisting of 33 members, of whom 13 are members of the Area Committees, two are representatives of the Women's Organization, two are representatives of the Youth Organizations, five are "suitable" citizens and the remainder are members of the Political Bureau of the MLSTP. The Assembly is "elected" for four years (in practice it is nominated by the MLSTP) and meets in ordinary session twice a year. Among its powers are the election or the dismissal of the president of the republic. The Assembly may delegate some of its legislative powers to the Council of Ministers. Between the ordinary sessions of the Assembly, its powers and functions are assumed by an 11-member Permanent Commission.

POLITICAL PARTIES

The country's only legally recognized political group is the Movimento de Libertacao de Sao Tome e Principe (MLSTP, Movement for the Liberation of Sao Tome & Principe) founded in 1972 by Manuel Pinto da Costa, currently the president of the republic and the secretary general of the party. The party's supreme organ is a nine-member political bureau. The party's ideology favors a moderate form of socialism, far removed from the strident Marxism of the other former Portuguese colonies.

ECONOMY

Sao Tome & Principe is one of the 39 lower middle-income countries of the world with a free-market economy dominated by the public sector.

Beyond frequent statements of intention, the government has not moved into the more complex area of hard development planning. As foreign investments and aid have dried up, the government has directed its meager resources to the primary sectors, such as agriculture.

Aid received from Western countries excluding the United States during 1970-81 was $583 million. U.S.

PRINCIPAL ECONOMIC INDICATORS
Gross National Product: $30 million (1983)
GNP Annual Growth Rate: 3.5% (1973-82)
Per Capita GNP: $310 (1983)
Per Capita GNP Annual Growth Rate: 1.4% (1973-82)
Gross Domestic Product at Market Prices: D1.105 billion (1981)
GDP Annual Growth Rate: 1.2% (1970-81)
GDP per Capita: D9,609 (1981)
GDP per Capita Annual Growth Rate: –0.6% (1970-81)
Currency in Circulation: D380.3 million
Income Distribution: Information not available
Consumer Price Index: Information not available
International Reserves: Information not available

BALANCE OF PAYMENTS (1983) (million SDR)	
Merchandise Exports	8.1
Merchandise Imports	–14.1
Trade Balance	–6.0
Services and Transfers Net	–5.1
Current Balance	–11.1
Long-Term Capital Net	–3.0
Short-Term Capital (Including Net Errors & Omissions)	9.2
Total (Net Monetary Movements)	–4.9

GROSS DOMESTIC PRODUCT BY ECONOMIC SECTORS (1981)	%	Annual Growth Rate (%) 1970-81
Agriculture	31.3	0.9
Mining	...	1.9
Manufacturing	4.3	3.2
Construction	2.0	–1.7
Trade	16.3	3.6
Public Utilities	0.5	–2.1
Transportation & Communications	3.7	6.2
Public Administration & Defense	17.0	0.7
Other	24.9	...

aid during 1977-83 was $2.7 million. Aid received from Communist countries during 1970-83 was $23 million.

BUDGET

The Sao Tomean fiscal year is the calendar year. The 1983 budget consisted of revenues of D 949.6 million and expenditures of D1.010 billion.

No information is available on the public debt.

FINANCE

The Sao Tomean unit of currency is the dobra (introduced in 1977) divided into 100 centavos. Coins are issued in denominations of 10, 20 and 50 centavos and 1, 2 ½, 5, 10, 20 and 50 dobras; notes are issued in denominations of 20, 50, 100, 500 and 1,000 dobras.

In August 1985 the dollar exchange value of the dobra was $1=D43.620. The sterling exchange rate on this basis was £1=D53.504.

The bank of issue is the Banco Nacional de Sao Tome e Principe. The only source of development finance is the Caixa Popular, a government savings and loan institution for housing.

AGRICULTURE

Of the total land area of 96,300 hectares (237,957 acres), less than half is suited for agriculture. Nevertheless, commercial agriculture is the mainstay of the economy, and the islands have been described as two large plantations. In fact, there are 110 plantations in the country, known as *rocas*, formerly owned by the Portuguese but abandoned after independence. These plantations have been nationalized and are run as cooperatives, each under the supervision of a managerial team consisting of one technician, one worker and one MLSTP member. The principal crop is cocoa, of which the islands were the world's leading producers at the turn of the century. Cocoa still provides 80% to 90% of export earnings. However, severe drought reduced production in 1982 and 1983 to 4,081 and 4,451 tons respectively. The concentration of agriculture on export commodities has forced Sao Tome to import about 90% of its food requirements. Lack of adequate rain since 1983 has further reduced all agricultural crops, resulting in serious food shortages and the need for food assistance from the United States and other Western countries. Exhaustion of soil fertility, archaic agricultural techniques, plant diseases, labor problems and a slump in world prices have depressed production levels.

There are 123 tractors in use in the *rocas*. Agriculture contributes 31.3% of GDP and employs 51.3% of the labor force.

```
PRINCIPAL CROP PRODUCTION (1981) (tons)
Cocoa . . . . . . . . . . . . . . . . . . . . . . . . .      8,000
Copra . . . . . . . . . . . . . . . . . . . . . . . . .      5,000
Palm kernels . . . . . . . . . . . . . . . . . . . . .      5,000
Bananas . . . . . . . . . . . . . . . . . . . . . . . .      3,000
Coconuts . . . . . . . . . . . . . . . . . . . . . . .     42,000
```

Secondary crops include copra palm kernels, bananas and coffee.

The livestock population in 1982 consisted of 3,000 cattle, 2,000 sheep, 4,000 goats, 3,000 pigs and 100,000 chickens. The annual fish catch in 1983 was 3,600 tons. In 1983 the government signed a fishing agreement with the EEC, which permitted French ships to operate off the islands in return for $154,000 annually in compensation. Similar agreements have also been signed with Portugal, Angola and the USSR. Most of the mountain forests have been heavily cut because of population pressures. Roundwood removals are estimated at 5,000 cubic meters (176,575 cubic ft) annually.

INDUSTRY

There is virtually no manufacturing industry other than the production of soap, soft drinks, tiles and vegetable oils, which generate 4% of GDP and employ 13.6% of the labor force.

ENERGY

Sao Tome & Principe does not produce any form of mineral energy. Its consumption of energy in 1982 was equivalent to 17,000 metric tons of coal, or 191 kg (421 lbs) per capita. In 1984 electric power production totaled 7 million kwh, or 78 kwh per capita.

LABOR

The Sao Tomean labor force consisted in 1981 of 29,378 workers of whom 51.3% were employed in agriculture, 13.6% in manufacturing and 35.1% in other sectors.

Laborers for the plantations come from Cape Verde, Angola and Nigeria on a contract basis. Nearly 10,000 workers are estimated to be employed in the plantation sector. Paradoxically, while labor is being imported the islands suffer from a high unemployment rate.

Legislation requires that a minimum wage of approximately $65 per month be paid to workers. A legal minimum employment age of 18 years is apparently observed in practice. Basic occupational health and safety standards are established in the Social Security Law of 1979. Members of the island's small educated class appear to enjoy advantages in government employment possibilities.

FOREIGN COMMERCE

Sao Tome & Principe's foreign commerce consisted in 1981 of exports of $8.8 million and imports of $20.0 million, leaving an unfavorable trade balance of $11.2 million. The major exports are cocoa 90.3% and copra 8.7%. The major imports are food, textiles and motor vehicles. The main suppliers are: Portugal 61.2%, Angola 13.1%, the Netherlands 3.9%, France 3.3%, the United Kingdom 2.2%, Mozambique 2.1% and Nigeria 1.8%. The main customers are the Netherlands 51.8%, Portugal 32.9%, West Germany 7.7%, Belgium-Luxembourg 2.2%, Angola 0.9% and Italy 0.9%.

During 1970-81 exports declined by 3.5% while imports grew by 4.3%. Imports constituted 56.8% of GDP and exports 51.7%. In 1981 the commodity concentration was 49.4%.

TRANSPORTATION & COMMUNICATIONS

The road network of 288 km (179 mi) links plantations with export towns. The two main ports of Sao Tome and Santo Antonio handled 27,000 tons of cargo in 1982. In 1975 there were 1,774 passenger cars and 265 commercial vehicles on the islands. Per capita passenger car ownership is 20 per 1,000. The national airline is Linhas Aereos de Sao Tome, with a fleet of light aircraft, operating regular services to Principe, Cabinda (in Angola), Brazil and Gabon. There are two usable airfields in the country with permanent surfaces; their runways are less than 2,500 meters (8,000 ft).

In 1984 there were 1,500 telephones in use, or 1.7 per 100 inhabitants. In 1982 the postal service handled 334,000 pieces of mail and 18,000 telegrams.

Tourism is being developed following the modernization of Sao Tome Airport.

MINING

There are no known mineral deposits on the islands.

DEFENSE

The fledgling army consists of some 150 men equipped with surplus arms transferred from the former Portuguese garrison. About 1,500 Angolan troops are reported to have been stationed on the islands since 1977, and some 2,000 Cuban and Soviet troops are also reported to have been based on Sao Tome since 1984.

EDUCATION

The national literacy rate is 10%. Schooling is universal, free and compulsory in principle for six years between the ages of 6 and 12. Girls constitute 49% of primary school enrollment and 45% of general secondary school enrollment. Schooling lasts for 11 years divided into four years of primary school, two years of lower secondary school and five years of upper secondary school. In 1980 there were 64 primary schools and three secondary schools.

In 1982 educational expenditures came to D91,169,000 representing 7.0% of the GNP.

In 1982, 16,132 students were enrolled in primary schools and 6,303 students in secondary schools. The single technical school had an enrollment of 143 students. With 628 primary school teachers and 268 secondary school teachers, the teacher-pupil ratio is 1:26 at the first level, and 1:23 at the second level.

There are no institutions of higher learning on the islands. In 1982 110 Sao Tomese students are reported enrolled in overseas universities. Of these four are in the United States, 69 in Portugal and 36 in Cuba.

LEGAL SYSTEM

The legal system is based on Portuguese and customary law. The judiciary is headed by the Supreme Court whose members are appointed by the People's Assembly on the recommendation of MLSTP. The constitution does not address the right to a public trial, but there have been instances of public trials of persons accused of common crimes in recent years. Criminal trials are occasionally reported by the local media. In most cases, however, common criminals are given a hearing and sentenced by a judge. No information is available on the penal system.

LAW ENFORCEMENT

No information is available on law enforcement in the country.

HEALTH

In 1981, there were 16 hospitals in the country with 665 beds, or one bed per 120 inhabitants. There were 38 physicians during the same period, or one physician per 2,263 inhabitants. Per 10,000 inhabitants the admissions/discharge rate is 1,733, the bed occupancy rate is 68.7% and the average length of stay is 12 days.

PRINCIPAL HEALTH INDICATORS (1984)

Crude Death Rate: 11.2 per 1,000

Life Expectancy at Birth: Males 47.1; Females 50.0

Infant Mortality Rate: 69.5 per 1,000 Live Births

*No information available since 1975

Most tropical diseases have been eliminated as a result of Portuguese efforts. However, malaria is still prevalent.

FOOD

Nearly all food products are imported. Daily per capita availability of energy, proteins, fats and carbohydrates is 2,324 calories, 50.1 grams, 66 grams and 338 grams respectively.

MEDIA & CULTURE

One weekly general interest newspaper and one weekly official bulletin, both in Portuguese, are published in Sao Tome. There is no national news agency. No books are published locally.

The government-owned Radio Nacional operates three transmitters, one medium-wave, one short-wave and one FM, broadcasting in Portuguese for over 18 hours a day. In 1982 there were 25,000 radio receivers in the country, or 291 per 1,000 inhabitants. There is no television service.

There is one fixed cinema in Sao Tome city, with 1,000 seats, or 14 seats per 1,000 inhabitants. Annual movie attendance is 105,000, or 1.3 per capita.

The largest library is the Henriques da Silva Municipal Library with over 4,000 volumes. Per capita, there are 62 volumes per 1,000 inhabitants.

SOCIAL WELFARE

Social welfare programs are handled by private agencies, Catholic missions, and plantations.

GLOSSARY

gravana: dry season from June to September.

filhos de terra: literally, sons of the soil. The native-born Sao Tomeans, as distinguished from imported contract workers.

roca: a cocoa or coffee plantation, formerly owned by Portuguese companies.

roceiros: plantation owners or managers.

CHRONOLOGY (from 1975)

1975— Sao Tome & Principe achieves full independence with Manuel Pinto da Costa as president.... Constituent Assembly approves new constitution.

1978— The government puts down a "coup" by former health minister, carlos de Graca

1979— Angolan troops are called in to support the government against agitators; Prime minister, Miguel Trovoada is arrested for backing coups.

1982— Defense minister Daniel Daio is arrested... President takes over defense portfolio.

BIBLIOGRAPHY (from 1967)

Abshire, David M. and Michael A. Samuels, *Portuguese Africa: A Handbook* (New York, 1969).

Chilcote, Ronald H., *Portuguese Africa* (Englewood Cliffs, N.J., 1967).

Saudi Arabia

— International boundary
⊛ National capital
+—+ Railroad
—— Road
+ International airport

0   100   200 Kilometers
0   100   200 Miles

Israel Haifa Damascus **Syria**
Tel Aviv Amman **Jordan**
Iraq Baghdad
Iran Eṣfahān
Dezfūl
Al Ţurayf
Eilat Al 'Aqaba
Haql
Tabūk
Hā'il
Al Baṣrah Ābādān
Kuwait Kuwait
Neutral Zone
Bandar-e Shāhpūr
Shīrāz
Būshehr
Persian
Buraydah
Ad Dammām Bahrain
Dhahran Manama
Bandar 'Abbās
Strait of Hormuz
Yanbu' al Baḥr
Medina
Riyadh
Al Hufūf
Gulf
Qatar
Doha
Ash Shāriqah
Dubayy
Oman
Red
Sea
Harad
Abu Dhabi
United Arab Emirates
Buraymi Ṣuḥār
Gulf of Oman
Muscat
Jiddah
Mecca
As Sulayyil
Oman
Sudan
Port Sudan
Al Qunfudhah
Abhā
Salālah
Jīzān
Administrative line
Ethiopia
Āsmera
Massawa
Al Hudaydah
Yemen (Sana) Sana
Yemen (Aden)
Sayḥūt
Al Mukallā
Arabian Sea
T'ana
Mocha
Taʻizz
Āseb
Bab el Mandeb
Aden
Gulf of Aden
Socotra
Yemen (Aden)
Djibouti Djibouti
Zeila
Somalia

NAMES AND BOUNDARY REPRESENTATION
ARE NOT NECESSARILY AUTHORITATIVE

SAUDI ARABIA

BASIC FACT SHEET

OFFICIAL NAME: Kingdom of Saudi Arabia (Al-Mamlaka al'Arabiyya es-Sa'oudiyya)

ABBREVIATION: SU

CAPITAL: Riyadh (royal capital); Jidda (diplomatic capital)

HEAD OF STATE & HEAD OF GOVERNMENT: King Fahd bin Abd al-Aziz Al Sa'ud (from 1982)

NATURE OF GOVERNMENT: Absolute monarchy

POPULATION: 11,152,000 (1985)

AREA: 2,149,690 sq km (829,997 sq mi)

ETHNIC MAJORITY: Arabs

LANGUAGE: Arabic

RELIGION: Sunni Islam

UNIT OF CURRENCY: Rial ($1=R3.645) (August 1985)

NATIONAL FLAG: Green and white with the creed of Islam, "There is no god but Allah; Muhammad is the messenger of Allah," in white Arabic script; beneath the script is a white sabre.

NATIONAL EMBLEM: Two gold-hilted silver scimitars crossed below the base of a tall palm tree

NATIONAL ANTHEM: Royal anthem, an instrumental piece without words. (All songs are banned in the country under Muslim law. The unnamed anthem is a small concession to modernity).

NATIONAL HOLIDAYS: September 23 (National Day, Unification of the Kingdom Day); also variable Islamic festivals.

NATIONAL CALENDAR: Islamic calendar (354 days long and based on the lunar year). The Muslim day begins at sunset and is reckoned in two 12-hour periods.

PHYSICAL QUALITY OF LIFE INDEX: 45 (up from 29 in 1976) (On an ascending scale with 100 as the maximum. U.S., 95)

DATE OF INDEPENDENCE: September 23, 1932 (Unification of the Kingdom)

DATE OF CONSTITUTION: None

WEIGHTS & MEASURES: The metric system prevails

LOCATION & AREA

Saudi Arabia occupies about four fifths of the Arabian peninsula and covers an area of 2,149,690 sq km (829,997 sq mi). Saudi Arabia shares its total international boundary of 4,589 km (2,850 mi) with eight neighbors: Jordan (744 km, 462 mi), Iraq (895 km, 556 mi), Kuwait (163 km, 101 mi), Qatar (67 km, 42 mi), United Arab Emirates (586 km, 364 mi), Oman (676 km, 420 mi), People's Democratic Republic of Yemen (830 km, 516 mi), and Yemen Arab Republic (628 km, 390 mi). Few of the land boundaries have been precisely determined or measured. The frontier with Iraq was delimited in the Treaty of Mohammara in 1922, and the diamond-shaped zone between the two countries was divided with the border following a straight line through the zone. A convention at Uqair in 1922 fixed the boundary with Kuwait and established a Neutral Zone in which Saudi Arabia and Kuwait hold equal rights. The greatest distance ESE to WNW is 2,295 km (1,420 mi) and NNE to SSW is 1,423 km (884 mi). The total length of the coastline is 2,510 km (1,560 mi).

The capital is Riyadh (1984 pop. 1,308,000). Jidda (1,500,000) serves as the administrative and diplomatic capital. The other major urban centers are Mecca (366,801), At-Taif (204,857), Medina (198,186), Dammam (127,844) and Al Khubar (48,817). There are four main geographic regions. The Red Sea escarpment consists of Hejaz in the north and Asir in the south. The central plateau, the Nejd, extends to the Tuwaiq mountains and beyond. The sand desert Dahana separates the Nejd from eastern Arabia, and the sand desert Nafud separates the Nejd from northern Arabia. South of the Nejd is the largest sand desert in the world, the forbidding Rub al-Khali. The four regions constitute four provinces: Nejd, 1,683,492 sq km (650,000 sq mi); Hejaz, 379,648 sq km (135,000 sq mi); Hasa or Eastern Province, 106,189 sq km (41,000 sq mi); and Asir, 103,600 sq km (40,000 sq mi).

Saudi Arabia has no permanent rivers or even bodies of water.

WEATHER

Saudi Arabia is one of the hottest regions of the world. In the interior the summer temperature averages 44.4°C (112°F). Frosts and freezing weather occur in winter. Coastal areas have high humidity. The country suffers from severe duststorms, the southerly kauf and the northwesterly shamal. Rainfall is infrequent and erratic averaging 101 mm (4 in.) a year except in Asir where 30.4 mm (12 in.) fall on the average every year. Rain generally occurs in sudden torrential cloudbursts. Several years may pass in some areas between rains.

POPULATION

Having rejected the findings of an earlier census carried out in 1962-63 the Saudi government held another census in 1974 giving a total population figure of 7,012,592. In the light of this census, which invalidated earlier U.N. figures, a much lower estimate has now been accepted in 1985 at 11,152,000. The populaton is expected to reach 18.9 million by 2000 and 30.6 million by 2020. Of this population total, nomads constitute 27%. The provinces of Mecca and Riyadh account for 43.1% of the total.

Saudi Arabia's annual growth rate was 3.94% during 1980-85 based on a birthrate of 43.0 per 1,000. The average density of five per sq km (13 per sq mi) is misleading because only 1% of the land is suited for habitation. The density of population per square kilometer of agricultural land is 10.4 (27 per sq mi). More than half the population is under 20 years of age. The age distribution is as follows: under 15, 43.1%; 15-64, 54.1%; 65 and over, 2.7%. The male-female ratio is 1.023:1; the surplus men being found among immigrants. Nearly 73% of the population live in urban areas and 41% of the urban population live in cities with over 5,000 inhabitants. The annual urban growth rate during 1980-85 was 5.7%.

DEMOGRAPHIC INDICATORS (1985)	
Population, total (in 1,000)	11,152
Population ages (% of total)	
0-14	43.1
15-64	54.1
65+	2.7
Youth 15-24 (000)	2,042
Women ages 15-49 (000)	2,219
Dependency ratios	84.7
Child-woman ratios	896
Sex ratios (per 100 females)	120.2
Median ages (years)	18.6
Average size of Household	5.2
Decline in birthrate (%, 1965-83)	−11.1
Proportion of urban (%)	72.99
Population density (per sq. km.)	5
per hectare of arable land	4.74
Rates of growth (%)	3.94
urban	5.7
rural	−0.2
Natural increase rates (per 1,000)	30.9
Crude birth rates (per 1,000)	43.0
Crude death rates (per 1,000)	12.1
Gross reproduction rates	3.45
Net reproduction rates	2.75
Total fertility rates	7.07
General fertility rates (per 1,000)	217
Life expectancy, males (years)	54.5
Life expectancy, females (years)	57.6
Life expectancy, total (years)	56.0
Population doubling time in years at current rate	23

There is virtually no permanent emigration. There is a growing immigration of professionals, technicians and others from neighboring Arab countries attracted by the oil wealth. The number of such immigrants, estimated at 3.5 million in 1985, is not restricted as long as they are Muslims.

Due to orthodox religious beliefs and traditional social practices, women do not enjoy equality with men. By Koranic precept, a daughter's share of an inheritance is less than that of a male offspring. Women are obliged to demonstrate legally specified grounds for divorce, whereas men may divorce without such grounds. In Shari'a court the testimony of one man equates to that of two women. Women may not drive motor vehicles, and there are restrictions on their use of public facilities when men are present. They do not by custom travel alone. They are restricted to reserved women's sections on urban buses. Women may travel abroad only with the written permission of their nearest male relative. Employment opportunities for Saudi women either in the civil service or with public corporations are extremely limited. In practice their employment is largely restricted to the teaching and health care professions. In public, women are required to dress with extreme modesty. Free but segregated education through the university level is now available to Saudi women locally. The number of civil service jobs available to women (in segregated offices) has increased somewhat. Polygamy is becoming less common, particularly among younger Saudis. This may be due in part to economic factors.

As a strict Muslim country, Saudi Arabia discourages birth control.

ETHNIC COMPOSITION

The population is virtually all Arab. There are, however, two ethnic zones: a northern, central and western area with a relatively unmixed racial composition and the coastlands of the south, southwest and east with a mixed population.

Ethnic aliens include Negro immigrants from Africa, estimated at 500,000, Javanese, Indians, Pakistanis and Egyptians, all of them Muslims. The non-Saudis are concentrated in the cities: 15-20% of Mecca, Medina and Taif, 35% of Jidda and 23% of Riyadh are non-Saudis. Christians are only nominally tolerated outside the cities of Mecca and Medina.

Foreigners living in Saudi Arabia, except for Yemenis, are required to carry identification cards. They are not permitted to travel outside the city of their employment or to change their workplace without their sponsor's permission, nor are they permitted to travel abroad without their sponsor's permission since sponsors hold foreign national employees' passports and are responsible for obtaining exit visas for them. Foreigners involved in or often merely incidental to commercial disputes or criminal investigations are usually not allowed to leave the country until the problem has been resolved. Sponsors have taken advantage of this arrangement at times to exert unfair pressure to resolve commercial disputes in their favor and occasionally have been able to prevent foreign nationals from departing Saudi Arabia for long periods. The official Saudi practice of seizing passports of all potential suspects and witnesses in criminal cases has sometimes forced foreign nationals to remain in Saudi Arabia for lengthy periods.

In terms of ethnic and linguistic homogeneity, Saudi Arabia is ranked 112th among the nations of the world with 94% homogeneity (on an ascending scale in which North and South Korea are ranked 135th with 100% homogeneity and Tanzania 1st with 7% homogeneity).

LANGUAGE

Arabic is the native tongue of the entire indigenous population. It exists in two forms: the classical and the colloquial. The former is the language of the Koran and the standard means of communication between all parts of the Arab world.

English is the principal foreign language taught in the secondary schools.

RELIGION

The national religion of Saudi Arabia is Islam in its Wahhabi version of the Hanbalite school. Wahhabism has been closely identified with the power of the House of Saud. Declaration of oneself as a Muslim is a prerequisite for citizenship.

The Shi'ite Muslims of the Eastern Province, usually estimated at 500,000 persons, constitute a religious minority subject to social and economic discrimination. In the wake of the Iranian revolution, they have been periodically subjected to surveillance and limitations on travel abroad. Certain of their members have been arrested without charge and detained, sometimes for many months. For security reasons, the government does not permit Shi'a public processions to mark Ashura, the holiest of the exclusively Shi'a holidays. The Shi'a are free to adjudicate exclusively intra-Shi'ite disputes within their own legal tradition, but Shi'ite judges receive no stipend or salary from the government. Likewise, the government provides no financial support for the Shi'ite religious establishment and does not permit the costruction of Shi'ite mosques. In recent years the authorities have made efforts to redress the Shi'a's complaints about the economic underdevelopment of their areas. Nevertheless, most Shi'a continue to live under conditions notably poorer than those of their Sunni compatriots.

Non-Muslim religious services are not permitted. Saudi customs officials prevent the importation of non-Islamic religious materials. Foreign nationals practice their religions only in discreet, private gatherings. Large gatherings or elaborate organizational structures are likely to attract official attention and may lead to the deportation of leaders. Islam exer-

cises a pervasive influence on the lives of all Saudi Arabians. All public and private acts are judged in terms of their appropriateness or inappropriateness in light of Islamic precepts. It also colors all national policies. Prince Faisal declared in 1962 that the government would adopt every means necessary to spread, strengthen, and promote Islam by word and by deed.

COLONIAL EXPERIENCE

Parts of Saudi Arabia were under Ottoman rule from 1818 to 1840 although the Hijaz and the Asir remained as provinces of the Ottoman Empire until World War I. The Turkish interlude left no permanent impress on Saudi Arabia.

CONSTITUTION & GOVERNMENT

Saudi Arabia has no formal constitution. Law is the expression of the will of the monarch as limited by tribal customs and religious laws embodied in the Sharia. All power is vested in the king who combines religious political powers as imam and king and tribal and military power as sheikh of sheikhs and commander in chief. This power is modified only by the requirement that his acts conform to the Sharia and that he retain the consensus of the royal family, the ulema and the sheikhs. Legislation is by royal decree or, in minor matters, by ministerial regulations. The chief mufti and the other muftis, interpreters of religious laws, are constantly consulted on all political and social issues and have power to impose a number of restrictions. Certain noble families, as for example the Jiluwis, also wield considerable influence on the conduct of government.

By convention, the king is chosen from among the sons of Abd al Aziz, who themselves have preponderant influence in the choice. Senior religious scholars and other princes also have a voice. The king serves concurrently as prime minister. Officials from the highest levels on down maintain contact with citizens by holding open-door audiences regularly. There are no elected assemblies or political parties, and nonreligious public assembly and demonstrations are not permitted. There are no known organized opposition groups. The legitimacy of the regime rests upon its perceived adherence to the defense of Islam, particularly the austere Hanbali school of Islamic jurisprudence. Rulers and ruled share a respect for laws believed to be divinely inspired and ancient customs which call for authority based on consensus in government, internal social cohesion, and economic private enterprise. Social custom mandates separation of the sexes.

The king rules the country in matters secular and religious, within limits established by religious law, tradition, and the need to maintain consensus among the ruling family and religious leaders. The king's legitimacy is based upon his descent, his selection by

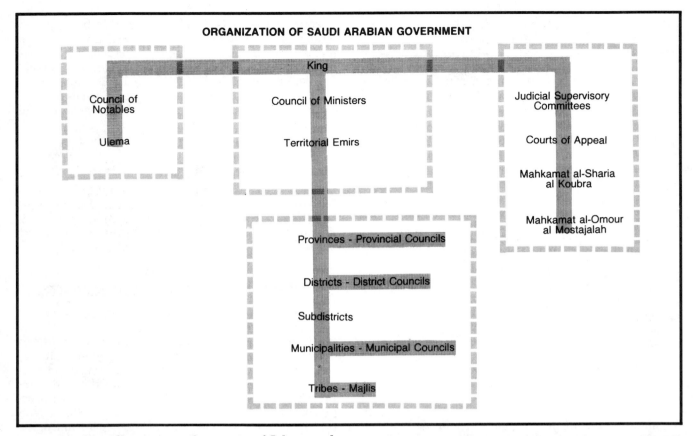

ORGANIZATION OF SAUDI ARABIAN GOVERNMENT

King

Council of Notables

Ulema

Council of Ministers

Territorial Emirs

Judicial Supervisory Committees

Courts of Appeal

Mahkamat al-Sharia al Koubra

Mahkamat al-Omour al Mostajalah

Provinces - Provincial Councils

Districts - District Councils

Subdistricts

Municipalities - Municipal Councils

Tribes - Majlis

consensus, his adherence to the tenets of Islam, and his perceived concern for the welfare of the nation. With the consent of other senior princes, the king appoints the crown prince, who is the first deputy prime minister. All other ministers are appointed by the king. They, in turn, appoint subordinate officials with cabinet concurrence. There are no elected officials in Saudi Arabia. (The only elections in Saudi Arabia appear to be businessmen's elections of two-thirds or more of the board members of the quasi-official Saudi Chambers of Commerce and Industry.)

Traditionally, public opinion has been expressed through client-patron relationships and interest groups such as tribes, families, and professional hierarchies. The open-door audience (majlis) remains the primary forum for expression of opinion or grievance. Subjects typically raised at a majlis are complaints about bureaucratic dilatoriness or insensitivity, requests for redress or assistance, or criticism of particular acts of government affecting personal or family welfare. Broader "political" concerns — Saudi social, security, economic, or foreign policy — are not considered appropriate and are seldom raised. The king meets on a weekly basis with religious leaders. This informal consultative means of ascertaining public opinion has limitations. Participation by women in the process is severely restricted. Rural-urban migration has weakened tribal and familial links. Citizens are not directly able to change policies or officials through the majlis system, which is largely a forum in which grievances are aired and favors sought.

RULERS OF SAUDI ARABIA
(from 1945)

1926 (May) to 1953 (November) Abdul Aziz III ibn Saud
1953 (November) to 1964 (November) Saud
1964 (November) to 1975 (March) Faisal
1975 (March) to 1982 (June) Khaled ibn Abdul Aziz
1982 (June) — Fahd bin Abd al-Aziz Al Sa'ud

Assisting the king as head of state and prime minister is the royal cabinet, which was formally established in 1958. Eight members of the cabinet in 1982 were members of the royal family of Saud.

Saudi Arabia has had a fairly stable government during the past 30 years. Transitions of power from King Saud to King Faisal and from King Faisal to King Khalid and from King Khalid to King Fahd were smooth. During the period from 1948 to 1967 the kingdom did not suffer a single reported riot or significant instance of domestic violence. (The assassination of King Faisal was the personal act of a disgruntled member of the royal family and had no political significance.)

FREEDOM & HUMAN RIGHTS

In terms of civil and political rights, Saudi Arabia is classified as a not-free country with a negative rating of 6 in political rights and 6 in civil rights (on a descending scale where 1 denotes the highest and 7 the lowest in civil and political rights).

CABINET LIST (1985)

King	Fahd bin 'Abd al-'Aziz Al Sa'ud
Prime Minister	Fahd bin 'Abd al-'Aziz Al Sa'ud
Deputy Prime Minister	'Abdallah bin 'Abd al-'Aziz Al Sa'ud
Second Dep. Prime Minister	Sultan bin 'Abd al-'Aziz Al Sa'ud
Minister of Agriculture & Water	'Abd al-Rahman 'Abd al-'Aziz Al al-Shaykh
Minister of Commerce	Soliman Abdulaziz Solaim
Minister of Communications	Husayn Ibrahim al- Mansuri
Minister of Defense & Aviation	Sultan bin 'Abd al-'Aziz Al Sa'ud
Minister of Education	'Abd al-'Aziz 'Abdallah al- Khuwaytir
Minister of Finance & Natl. Economy	Muhammad 'Ali Aba al-Khayl
Minister of Foreign Affairs	Sa'ud al-Faysal Al Sa'ud
Minister of Health	Faysal 'Abd al-'Aziz Alhegelan
Minister of Higher Education	Hasan ibn 'Abdallah Al al-Shaykh
Minister of Industry & Electricity	'Abd al-'Aziz ibn 'Abdallah al- Zamil
Minister of Information	Ali Hasan al- Sha'ir
Minister of Interior	Nayif bin 'Abd al-'Aziz Al Sa'ud
Minister of Justice	Ibrahim ibn Muhammad ibn Ibrahim Al al-Shaykh
Minister of Labor & Social Affairs	Muhammad 'Ali al Fayiz
Minister of Municipal & Rural Affairs	Ibrahim ibn 'Abdallah al- Angari
Minister of Petroleum & Mineral Resources	Ahmad Zaki Yamani
Minister of Pilgrimage Affairs & Religious Trusts	'Abd al-Wahab 'Abd al-Wasi
Minister of Planning	Hisham Muhyi al-Din Nazir
Minister of Post, Telephone & Telegraph	'Alawi Darwish Kayyal
Minister of Public Works & Housing	Mit'ib bin 'Abd al-'Aziz Al Sa'ud
Minister of State	Muhammad Ibrahim Mas'ud
Minister of State	Muhammad 'Abd al-Latif al- Milhim

While not a free country by any means in the strict sense of the term, Saudi Arabia is a good example of a country that, within the context of a traditional value system, adheres to many of the standards of a free society. Saudi justice may appear harsh by Western standards, but it is neither capricious nor cruel. On the other hand, the Saudi sense of justice and fairness is extremely intense and the occasional instances of torture, amputation of hands, capital punishment for adultery, and public flogging are regarded not as inhumane, but as divinely ordained. In all cases, the law follows the Sharia closely; people can be imprisoned for non-payment of debts; there is no habeas corpus and arrestees are held pending trial for weeks. So long as it is in the Sharia, nothing is regarded as draconian or uncivilized. Most trials are open and defenders are assisted by counsellors, or, sometimes, in the case of non-Arabic speaking persons, interpreters. People have the right to appeal even to the king. Indeed, as in other tribal societies, the king is expected to receive any petition or listen to any complaint that a subject may wish to present. But political activities and organizations as such are banned as subversive. The press is not formally censored, but it manages to keep within safe bounds by exercising sound journalistic instincts. When a newspaper oversteps these bounds occasionally, it simply fails to appear for a period of time. Criticism does appear in newspaper pages, but it is respectful and even deferential and is smothered in ornate and adulatory prose that Arabs love so much. Pictures are regarded as anti-Islamic so that some papers appear as sheets of unrelieved text. Not only is Islam the established religion, but the only religion for Saudis. Foreigners are expected to hold only discreet and private religious services and non-Muslim clergymen may not use their clerical garb in public. The status of women continues to be deplorable. They cannot drive cars, and they need the permission of a male (husband, guardian, father) to travel abroad and a male escort for domestic travels. Emigration requires official permission. The regulations regarding travel and emigration are so complex that it provides unscrupulous employers the means to extract concessions from their employees recruited from abroad.

CIVIL SERVICE

Saudi Arabia has a unified civil service open to all Saudis. There are nine grades below minister. Appointments to grades 1 to 3 are made by ministers and grades 4 to 9 through qualifying examinations.

LOCAL GOVERNMENT

By the provincial regulations of 1963 the kingdom was divided into five provinces, or mokatas, subdivided into districts, or mantikas, further subdivided into raiz, or markez or subdistricts. The five provinces are Nejd, Al-Hasa, Hejaz, Asir and the Northern Frontier Province. Each province is administered by a governor general, or hakem, each district by a governor, and each subdistrict by a headman. Provincial councils composed of not more than 30 members are elected for two-year terms by tribal chiefs. In municipalities local councils assist the chief administrative officers. Authority over the tribes is indirect and is exercised through sheikhs, some of whom are semiautonomous. The tribal government is conducted through the majlis. The central government's control over local government is maintained through territorial emirs. Tribal loyalty is reinforced through a system of subsidies.

FOREIGN POLICY

Saudi Arabia is the leading conservative power in the Arab world. The basic determinants of its foreign policy are the security of the Arabian peninsula, Arab and Islamic solidarity, and anti-Communism. It has no diplomatic relations with any Communist state and opposes encroachment by Communist influences in the Middle East. It has supported with men and money the governments of Yemen and Oman against radical subversion from the People's Democratic Republic of Yemen. As a charter member of the Arab League, it has consistently pursued an anti-Israeli course and provided financial backing to Arab states engaged in conflict with Israel. Its financial clout was also used to persuade Muslim states in Central and West Africa to sever relations with Israel. It has been a prime mover behind pan-Islamic conferences, and Jidda is the headquarters of the Islamic secretariat. As the world's leading oil exporter, it is a member of the Organization of Petroleum Exporting Countries (OPEC) and the Organization of Arab Petroleum Exporting Countries (OAPEC) but has tended to be a restraining influence in both these bodies. In 1974 it established a $2.8-billion fund to extend loans to underdeveloped nations.

In the rapidly shifting kaleidoscope of Mid-East alignments, Saudi Arabia found itself in the late 1970's drifting away from the United States. Saudi apprehensions were based on diplomatic and military reverses that the United States has suffered; the revolution in Iran, the break in relations with Taiwan despite solemn obligations, the withdrawal from Vietnam, and inaction over the Soviet invasion of Afghanistan. According to the Saudi Minister of State Fayez Badr, "The United States has abandoned its role as world leader for that of spectator. . . . It has no Middle East policy." These disappointments crystallized over the Egyptian-Israeli peace treaty which Washington was determined to push and which the Saudis opposed bitterly. At the same time, Saudi Arabia affirmed its policy of not making oil a weapon against the United States. It also stated that disagreement on the peace process in no way affected the relations between the two countries. The United States, on its part, tried to allay Saudi fears by offering more military hardware; by 1980 Saudi Arabia had become the largest buyer of U.S. military hardware, its purchases totaling $5.1 billion.

Because of its increasing financial clout, Saudi Arabis is playing an active role as an arbiter in small Mid-East conflicts. It played a key role in mediating the Lebanese conflict in 1976 and in bolstering North Yemen when it was attacked by the Marxist government of South Yemen in 1979.

Saudi Arabia along with other Arab Gulf states, is a strong supporter of Iraq in its war with Iran. In 1981 the Saudis concluded a treaty with Iraq partitioning the Neutral Zone, established in 1922. At the signing of the treaty, Riyadh called on all Arab nations to lend material and moral support for Iraq. Since then, Saudi Arabia has upgraded its military capabilities by massive arms purchases, including four Airborne Warning and Control Systems (AWACS), M-1 Abrahms tanks, and missile batteries from the United States, and mobile anti-aircraft missile systems from France. The Saudis also have conducted joint military exer-

cises with Kuwait and concluded a military cooperation agreement with Trukey.

In December 1982, an Arab League peace delegation visited Moscow. The delegation included the Saudi foreign minister Prince Saud al-Faysal, the first Saudi envoy to visit Moscow. Saudi Arabia is also in the forefront of peace initiatives in the Middle East, particularly in Lebanon.

Saudi Arabia and the United States are parties to 37 treaties and agreements covering cultural relations, defense, desalination, economic and technical cooperation, investment guaranties, military missions, and trade and commerce.

U.S. interests in Saudi Arabia are extensive. The value of U.S. investments in Saudi Arabia, including 40% ownership of ARAMCO, is about $1.5 billion, and Saudi Arabia is the largest customer of American goods and services in the Middle East. Saudi investment in the United States is estimated at $14 billion. In addition to military hardware, the United States has provided technical assistance in geological mapping, seawater desalination and public administration. A joint U.S.-Saudi Economic Commission has been set up in Riyadh. According to a study published in The New York Times, 30,000 U.S. citizens are working in Saudi Arabia, of whom 3,400 were in the defense sector. The U.S. Army Corps of Engineers is supervising the execution of military projects estimated to cost $15 billion including the $10 billion al-Assad military complex, a new defense military complex at Riyadh, and four new naval bases.

Saudi Arabia is a member of 13 U.N. organizations and eight other international organizations. It joined the U.N. in 1946; its contribution to the U.N. budget is 0.06%.

U.S. Ambassador in Jidda: Walter L. Cutler
U.K. Ambassador in Jidda: Sir Patrick Wright
Saudi Ambassador in Washington, D.C.: Prince Bandar bin Sultan
Saudi Ambassador in London: Sheikh Nasser Almanqour

PARLIAMENT

Saudi Arabia has no parliament. There is a 24-member consultative, or advisory council, which plays no decisive role. The only other power group is the ulema, or council, of Muslim theologians who serve as the guardians of orthodoxy and who express approval or disapproval by using a fetwa. The real power of the ulema, however, has waned in recent years, and it has been overruled on some occasions.

POLITICAL PARTIES

No political parties are permitted to function in the country.

ECONOMY

Saudi Arabia is one of the richest countries of the world and is on the United Nations' official list of 37 high-income countries. The private sector predominates in Saudi Arabia's free-market economy.

```
PRINCIPAL ECONOMIC INDICATORS
```

Gross National Product: $127.080 billion (1983)
 GNP Annual Growth Rate: 11.3% (1973-82)
 Per Capita GNP: $12,180 (1983)
 Per Capital GNP Annual Growth Rate: 6.2% (1973-82)

Gross Domestic Product: R381.5 billion (1984)
 GDP at 1980 Prices: R381.30 billion
 GDP Deflator (1980=100): 100.1
 GDP Annual Growth Rate: 6.9% (1973-82)
 Per Capita GDP: R35,332 (1984)
 Per Capita GDP Annual Growth Rate: 5.5% (1976-81)

Income Distribution: Information not available

Consumer Price Index: All Items: 370.6 (March 1984)

Food: 288.6 (March 1986)

Average Annual Rate of Inflation: 16.5% (1973-83)

Money Supply: R81.920 billion (February 1985)
 Reserve Money: R42.350 billion (February 1985)

Currency in Circulation: R35.11 billion (1984)

International Reserves: $24.748 billion, of which foreign exchange reserves were $14.188 billion (1984)

Planning is under the Central Planning Organization. The Second Development Plan (1975-80) provides for the expenditure of $142 billion and plans to raise the GDP by 114% and to reduce the proportion of GDP accounted for by oil from about 86% to 82%. Allocations were as follows: Economic and social development, 63%; defense, 18%; administration, 8%; and other items including foreign aid, 11%.

The Third Development Plan (1980-85) aimed to achieve major industrial development, in order to shift the balance of the economy away from a heavy dependence on sales of crude petroleum. The foundation of the industrialization program lay in the construction of refineries and processing industries, to exploit reserves of petroleum and natural gas. Other heavy industry, notably the manufacture of iron and steel, fertilizers, methanol, industrial gases and petrochemicals, was under rapid development during 1983 and 1984. These projects were controlled by the Saudi Arabian Basic Industries Corporation (SABIC) and most were established as joint ventures with foreign companies. Plans for the future included the development of a petrochemical manufacturing concern with Italy and Finland, and the establishment of a pharmaceuticals company.

A primary objective of the 1985-90 Development Plan was to encourage the involvement of the private sector in industry; initial steps towards this end included the sale, in 1984, of 30% of SABICs capital to the public. In order to sustain and encourage local and secondary industries, a 1984 law stipulated that at least 30% of work undertaken on major projects by foreign companies should be sub-contracted, where possible, to local firms.

FIVE-YEAR PLAN — 1980-85 (proposed expenditure in million riyals)	
Education	101,171.0
Health and social services	42,405.7
Transport and communications	143,018.1
Desalination	39,602.0
Petromin	27,684.8
Saudi Basic Industries Corp	25,564.0
Electricity	52,585.2
Agriculture	7,974.5
Public works	21,204.4
Other	320,790.3
Total	**782,000.0**

The infrastructure, put in place during the past five years, has eliminated the physical limits on the economy's absorptive capacity and soaring oil revenues (backed up by a huge government portfolio of foreign assets) have lifted financial constraints on development. However, this does not herald unbridled economic expansion. While the government can be expected to set budgets at the levels required to promote its goals for national development, policymakers clearly perceive the potential social and political drawbacks of overly rapid modernization. Overall growth targets for the Plan will therefore synthesize desired economic development and the maintenance of the valued religious, cultural and social traditions of the kingdom.

Within overall spending targets, Ministry of Planning officials have indicated that the new Plan will emphasize the development of social rather than physical infrastructure, concentrating on manpower training. The Minister has emphasized the importance of training and the need to reduce reliance on foreign workers. Development of the "productive sectors" of industry and agriculture also rank high on the priority list. The next plan should also provide for greater decentralization both in terms of projects and in terms of greater provision of social services and in infrastructure to outlying areas. The Jubail and Yanbu projects are perhaps the best examples of new poles of development outside the traditional Jidda-Riyadh-Dhahran axis.

A relatively small amount is spent by Saudi Arabia as aid to poorer countries; most goes to frontline Arab states and other Muslim states such as Pakistan. Saudi Arabia is the biggest contributor to Arab funds set up to help poorer Arab and African Muslim states. The Saudi Development Fund lends to Muslim countries farther afield. The value of Saudi Arabian aid reached an annual average of about U.S. $5,000 million between 1979 and 1983.

The country's vast foreign holdings are managed by the Saudi Arabian Monetary Agency. Most of the funds are held as short-term deposits by the big banks in London, New York and Hamburg. Saudi Arabia has moved into long-term investments only recently and, compared to Kuwait, has only a small proportion of its funds in equity and real estate. Of the $22 billion believed to be invested in the United States about $6 billion are in government bonds, some $1.5

BALANCE OF PAYMENTS (1983)
(million $)

Current Account Balance	−18,433
Merchandise Exports	45,379
Merchandise Imports	−33,453
Trade Balance	11,926
Other Goods, Services & Income	+21,070
Other Goods, Services & Income	−46,193
Other Goods, Services & Income Net	—
Private Unrequited Transfers	−5,236
Official Unrequited Transfers	—
Direct Investment	3,653
Portfolio Investment	14,331
Other Long-term Capital	—
Other Short-term Capital	−1,060
Net Errors & Omissions	—
Counterpart Items	−753
Exceptional Financing	—
Liabilities Constituting Foreign Authorities' Reserves	—
Total Change in Reserves	2,262

BUDGET ALLOCATIONS
(million riyals, year ending 30 June)

	1982/83	1983/84	1984/85
Defense and security	92,889	75,733	79,900
Transport and communications	32,532	24,950	23,630
Human resources	31,864	27,791	30,460
Municipal facilities	26,224	19,070	17,460
Internal credits	23,382	20,000	16,000
Economic resources	22,045	13,209	17,560
Public administration	9,480	n.a.*	n.a.
Health and social services	17,010	13,591	18,080
Infrastructure	11,705	9,583	9,830
Local subsidies	11,162	9,020	10,525
Miscellaneous	35,107	47,053*	36,555*
Total expenditure	313,400	260,000	260,000
Actual expenditure	243,652	223,000	n.a.
Total revenue	313,400	225,000	214,100
Actual revenue	246,200	190,800	n.a.

*Figure for public administration amalgamated with all miscellaneous items.

GROSS DOMESTIC PRODUCT BY ECONOMIC ACTIVITY
(1982-83)

	%	Rate of Change % 1970-81
Agriculture	2.1	5.5
Mining	46.6	8.4
Manufacturing	5.7	6.6
Construction	13.1	20.7
Electricity, Gas & Water	0.2	12.0
Transport & Communications	5.1	8.3
Trade	6.7	18.4
Finance	7.2	18.4
Public Administration & Defense	11.1	7.6
Service and Other	2.0	14.0

PROJECTS BUDGET
(planned expenditure in million riyals)

	1979/80	1980/81	1981/82
Council of ministers	13,964.0	18,983.7	37,208.7
Municipal and rural affairs	9,789.8	16,597.2	22,703.5
Public works and housing	3,022.5	5,573.8	6,308.4
Information	634.3	878.1	965.3
Civil aviation	6,804.6	10,644.6	11,044.5
Interior	4,131.9	5,507.2	7,551.1
Labor and social affairs	2,126.5	3,491.9	2,626.0
Health	1,822.0	2,420.0	2,793.0
Education	5,771.5	7,863.3	9,869.4
Communications	9,811.3	14,835.5	17,760.6
Finance and national economy	7,868.3	10,638.7	13,904.9
Industry, electricity and commerce	3,450.5*	3,027.3*	1,086.5
Agriculture and water resources	3,112.0	3,470.3	3,185.1
Public investment fund	4,250.0	7,500.0	10,000.0
Other	49,379.4	63,305.8	58,918.3
Less: Earmarked expenditure	−20,258.6	—	—
Total	105,680.0	174,737.4	205,925.3

*Including gathering and liquefaction of gas.

billion in corporate bonds and stocks, and the balance in liquid capital.

BUDGET

The Saudi fiscal year runs from October 1 through September 30. Oil revenues provide over 90% of the state's budget revenues. The Islamic charity tax, the zakat, is the only tax levied on Saudi nationals.

Oil provides 63.3% of the revenues. Of the expenditures, 30.7% goes to defense and security, 14.1% to public administration, 11.7% to human resources and 9.1% to transport and communications.

In 1983 government consumption was R119.45 billion and private consumption R138.99 billion. During 1973-83 public and private consumption grew by 21.2%.

General government consumption represents 17.4% of GDP.

Saudi Arabia has no external public debt.

FINANCE

The Saudi unit of currency is the rial (or riyal) divided into five qurushes and 100 halalahs. Coins are issued in denominations of 1, 5, 10, 25 and 50 halalahs and 1, 2 and 4 qurushes; notes are issued in denominations of 1, 5, 10, 50 and 100 rials. The official exchange rate in 1985 was /$1=R3.645. The sterling exchange rate on this basis was £1=R4.143.

The Saudi Arabian banking system consists of the Saudi Arabian Monetary Agency, or SAMA (established in 1952 as the central bank, note issuing and regulatory body, and administrator of monetary reserves), two specialist banks, two national commercial banks and 10 foreign banks. SAMA administers gold, foreign exchange and investments amounting to R421.52 billion rials (U.S. $120.28 billion). Other institutions in the capital market include the Saudi Industrial Development Fund (managed by the Chase Manhattan Bank), the Saudi Arabian Investment Company, the Saudi Capital Corporation, the Saudi Credit Bank, the Real Estate Development Fund, the Saudi International Bank (a full-fledged merchant bank in London, managed by the Morgan Guaranty

Trust Company), and the Saudi Arabian Investment Bank with Chase Manhattan Bank as a partner. In 1984 commercial banks had reserves of R 11.04 billion, demand deposits of R 47.86 billion, foreign assets of R 67.24 billion and quasi-monetary deposits of R41.79 billion.

Interest is officially prohibited, in accordance with Islamic law, but in practice is charged.

GROWTH PROFILE Annual Growth Rates (%)	
Population 1980-2000	3.6
Birthrate 1965-83	-11.1
Deathrate 1965-83	-41.4
Urban Population 1973-83	7.4
Labor Force 1980-2000	3.2
GNP 1973-82	11.3
GNP per capita 1973-82	6.2
GDP 1973-83	6.9
GDP per capita 1970-81	5.5
Consumer Prices 1970-81	13.7
Wholesale Prices	—
Inflation 1973-83	16.5
Agriculture 1973-83	6.6
Manufacturing 1973-83	8.0
Industry 1973-83	3.9
Services 1973-83	12.9
Mining 1970-81	8.4
Construction 1970-81	20.7
Electricity 1970-81	12.0
Transportation 1970-81	8.3
Trade 1970-81	18.4
Public Administration & Defense 1970-77	7.6
Export Price Index 1975-81	22.5
Import Price Index 1975-81	9.6
Terms of Trade 1975-81	11.9
Exports 1973-83	-4.5
Imports 1973-83	27.6
Public Consumption	—
Private Consumption 1973-83	21.2
Gross Domestic Investment 1973-83	27.1
Energy Consumption 1973-83	6.8
Energy Production 1973-83	-1.2

AGRICULTURE

Of the total land area of 214,969,000 hectares (531,188,390 acres) agriculture takes place on less than 1%. Of the cultivated area, only 20% in the coastal Asir and the southern Hejaz receives enough rainfall to permit cultivation without irrigation. The remaining 80% consists of oases. Some 93.8 million hectares (230.7 million acres) are used for low-grade grazing; 1,497,000 hectares (3.7 million acres) are forests; and 130 million hectares (321.6 million acres) are wastelands. Based on 1974-76 = 100 the index of food per capita production in 1983 was 34. Agriculture contributed only 2% to the GDP in 1983, although it employed 61% of the population. The annual rate of agricultural growth during the 1973-83 period was 6.6%. The value added in agriculture in 1983 was $1.713 billion.

Most farms are subsistence units, and basic foodstuffs have to be imported to meet demand. In 1983 3,482,000 tons of cereals were imported. Determined efforts were made to increase wheat production in 1983, including a system of large subsidies, whereby the government was prepared to pay up to 10 times the price of imported grain for locally produced wheat. As a result of these efforts, the 1984 wheat harvest reached 1.3 million metric tons, exceeding domestic demand. By 1983 Saudi Arabia was self-sufficient in milk (which it exported to neighboring countries in 1984), and had reached near self-sufficiency in eggs and broiler chickens. Self sufficiency in food is a major priority in the development programs; budgetary allocations for agriculture have increased from $39.77 million (140 million rials) in 1964/65 to over R7.974 billion in 1980-85, in addition to allocations for water resources and desalination plants. Four important agricultural projects undertaken by the government include the al-Hasa irrigation scheme, the Faisal model settlement, the Wadi Jizam dam, and the Abha dam. Twenty-seven desalination plants have increased the daily capacity to 549 million liters (145 million gal). Mechanization has been introduced in some areas; 1,300 tractors were in use in 1982. Annual consumption of fertilizer in 1982 was 67,200 tons, or 83.2 kg (183 lb) per arable hectare.

The average size of farms is 2.02 hectares to 5 hectares (5-12.5 acres) in Asir and the Eastern Province, 5 to 20 hectares (12.5 to 50 acres) in Nejd and 10 to 30 hectares (25 to 75 acres) in Hejaz. Sharecropping is the prevailing form of tenancy covering over 50% of the total cultivated area; 40% is cultivated by individual owners and 10% by tenants, who pay rent in cash. There are four types of land ownership; Miri lands are technically owned by the state but held in fief or by tenants; mulk lands are held by extended families or tribes; mushaa lands are collectively owned by groups; and waqf lands are held by religious and charitable institutions.

Some 1,497,340 hectares (3,749,600 acres) are officially listed as forests and woodlands, but only 9,740 hectares (24,700 acres) are used for the production of timber. Date palms are the major source of timber.

Fishing in the Red Sea and Persian Gulf is an underdeveloped activity limited by small demand and inadequate marketing facilities. The 1982 production was 26,400 metric tons.

Agricultural credit is provided by the Agricultural Bank, which offers interest-free loans to farmers. The state also offers subsidies for machinery and pumps, and chemical fertilizer is distributed at half price.

The camel still provides livelihood for 300,000 Bedouin. Sheep and goats provide the bulk of the meat supply. (The most noted animal of Saudi Arabia is the Arabian horse, famous for its speed and beauty.)

INDUSTRY

The contribution of manufacturing to the GDP is 6%, and it employs 3.3% of the labor force. Most of the manufacturing is geared to the local market, especially construction. Consumer industries include cot-

PRINCIPAL CROP PRODUCTION (1982)

Wheat	400
Barley	12
Millet	12
Sorghum	110
Sesame seed	1
Tomatoes	200
Onions	60
Grapes	60
Dates	400
Lemons & limes	300

LIVESTOCK POPULATION (1982)(000)

Cattle	450
Sheep	3,000
Goats	2,300
Asses	110
Camels	160
Chickens	6,000

ton textiles and carpet mills, shoe factories and food processing. The annual growth rate in manufacturing during 1973-83 was 8.0%. The value added in manufacturing in 1983 was $3.817 billion.

The chief agent of industrial development has been Petromin, the state-owned General Petroleum and Mineral Organization, set up in 1962 to diversify the economy through the establishment of industries based on hydrocarbons and other minerals. Petromin's projects include a steel rolling mill in Jidda, the Saudi Arabian Fertilizer Company, three petrochemical complexes, three oil refineries and an aluminum plant. Industrial development has been concentrated in the Dammam-Dhahran complex on the Persian Gulf and in Jidda on the Red Sea.

INDUSTRIAL PRODUCTS (1982)

Nitrogenous fertilizers	'000 metric tons	157.5
Liquefied petroleum gas	'000 barrels	57,243
Gasoline Naphtha	'000 barrels	66,853
Kerosene	'000 barrels	10,244
Jet fuel	'000 barrels	1,670
Fuel oil	'000 barrels	93,748
Petroleum bitumen (asphalt)	'000 barrels	14,125
Cement	'000 metric tons	5,262.7
Electric energy	million kWh	26,630

The government has adopted a liberal policy toward foreign collaboration and private enterprise. Under the foreign investment regulations companies must be 51% Saudi-owned, not less than 75% of all employees must be Saudis, the accounts must be in Arabic, the headquarters must be in Saudi Arabia and Muslim laws must be honored. Net direct private investment in 1983 was $3.653 billion. The Saudi Arabian Basic Industries Corporation (SABIC), the Saudi government entity responsible for development of the petrochemical industry, has signed a number of final contracts with foreign joint venture partners for the key installations at the two new industrial cities of Jubail and Yanbu. These projects are at the heart of the Saudi drive to industralize and modernize the economy. One of the major goals of the Second Development Plan (1975-1980) was to provide the infrastructure for these two new cities. The actual construction of these industrial installations will be a primary goal of the Third Plan (1980-1985) which is to be unveiled soon. For Jubail, joint venture agreements for projects have been signed with a Japanese consortium for a methanol plant, with Korf Steel for a steel mill, when Exxon for a low-density polyethylene petrochemical complex, with Pecten for a petrochemical complex, with Dow Chemicals for a petrochemical complex, with Mitsubishi for a ethylene unit at Jubail, and with Mobil for an ethylene complex.

ENERGY

Saudi Arabia's energy production in 1982 was the equivalent of 490.621 million metric tons of coal and consumption was equal to 30.335 million metric tons of coal. The per capita consumption was 3,026 kg (6,672 lb). The annual growth rates during 1973-83 were –1.2% for energy production and 6.8% energy consumption. Apparent per capita consumption of gasoline is 127 gallons per year. Electricity production was 52.702 billion kwh in 1984, and per capita electric power consumption was 4,882 kwh.

The Saudi oil industry is the genie that sustains the entire economy. It generates 96% of state revenues and an equal proportion of export revenues. It claims the largest onshore oil field in the world at Ghawar and the largest offshore oil field as well at Safaniyah. Between 1978 and 1982 Saudi Arabia's production of crude petroleum was more than one-third of the total output of all OPEC countries, and about 14% of the world total. In 1981 the value of Saudi Arabia's total exports, almost all in the form of petroleum, reached a record US $120,000 million. In that year Saudi Arabia ranked fourth in the world among exporting countries, behind only the USA, the Federal Republic of Germany and Japan. At the beginning of 1984 Saudi Arabia's proven reserves of crude petroleum were estimated to be 166,000 million barrels, or about 25% of the world total. At 1983 levels of production, the country's petroleum reserves will not be exhausted for a further 93 years. Exports amount to 95% of the country's exports by value and 90% of state revenues.

Over 90% of the oil is produced by the Arabian-American Oil Company (ARAMCO), in which the Saudi government has a 60% interest. Of the remaining 40%, Standard Oil Company of California owns 30%, the Texas Oil Company 30%, Standard Oil of New Jersey 30% and Socony 10%. ARAMCO is the industrial giant of Saudi Arabia, providing over 96% of the state revenues. Its working concessions, originally granted in 1933, cover an area of 220,149 sq km (85,000 sq mi). The Saudi government acquired its 60% equity in the company in 1974, and negotiations in 1976 called for eventual nationalization. The Japanese-owned Arabian Oil Company and the Getty Oil

Company hold concessions in the former Saudi-Kuwait Neutral Zone. Petromin does not yet have any oil production of its own but is a partner in several French and U.S. exploration projects.

Offshore explorations are conducted in the Red Sea by the French company Auxerap and the American companies Sun Oil and Natomas, acting as contractors for Petromin, which holds legal title to the concessions.

The main oil refineries are at Jidda, Ras Tanura, Riyadh, Jubail and Yenbo.

OIL PRODUCTION & REVENUES		
	Production (million barrels)	Revenues ($ million)
1939	0.5	3.2
1946	59.9	10.4
1955	356.6	340.8
1971	1,740.8	1,884.9
1972	2,201.7	2,744.6
1973	2,772.7	4,340.0
1974	3,095.1	22,573.5
1975	2,582.5	25,676.2
1976	3,139.5	30,747.5
1977	3,358.0	36,540.1
1978	3,046.9	32,233.4
1981	3,585.8	101,813.0
1982	2,367.0	70,478.8
1983	1,865.7	37,120.0

As part of the government's overall plan to industrialize, Petromin has been active in establishing refinery and lubricating oil plants. There are three 250,000 barrel/day export refineries, each a joint venture with a different foreign partner — Shell in Jubail, Mobil in Yanbu, and Petrola in Rabigh. To serve the domestic market, there are a 170,000 barrel/day refinery at Yanbu and a 250,000 barrel per day refinery at Ju'aymah near Ras Tanura. The Mobil/Petromin lube plant in Jidda was recently expanded sufficiently. An Ashland/Petromin lube project in Rabigh was recently announced and a Texaco/Socal/Petromin lube plant for Jubailis under study. Total oil refinery capacity in 1982 was 860 million barrels per day.

In 1982 oil production was 1.851 billion barrels. With proved reserves of 3.426 trillion cubic meters (121 trillion cubic ft) natural gas production in 1982 was 10.803 billion cubic meters (381.5 billion cubic ft).

LABOR

The labor force is estimated at roughly 2.331 million, of which only 2.2% are women. In 1981 61% of the labor force was in agriculture, 14% in industry, including mining, and 25% in services. Foreigners working in Saudi Arabia number between 1 and 1.5 million concentrated primarily in the cities.

Saudi Arabia is the only country in the Middle East where slavery is officially countenanced. Though slavery was officially abolished in 1962, the demand for slaves is sufficient to enable slave traders to continue operating profitably, although perhaps with more circumspection. Private auctions are common. Africa and Baluchistan are the main sources of slaves.

Each workday is broken by a two-or-three-hour lunch period as well as breaks for prayer. In the month of Ramadan workdays are reduced and work is severely disrupted during the annual pilgrimage season. The minimum age of employment is 10. Labor unions and strikes are banned. The Supreme Labor Committee is the highest labor tribunal.

The 1969 Saudi Labor and Workmen Law requires the employer to take necessary precautions for the protection of workmen from hazards and diseases resulting from the work and the machinery used, and for the protection and safety of the work. Labor Ministry inspectors and the labor courts seek with some success to enforce the labor code, but foreign nationals report frequent failures to enforce health and safety standards. Saudi authorities have reportedly enjoyed greater success in enforcing contract terms and working hours. There have been press reports that some foreign workers are living and working under poor conditions, and there are indications that the authorities may take corrective measures. Saudi labor law establishes maximum hours at regular pay at 48 per week and allows employers to require up to 12 additional hours of overtime at time-and-a-half. Employees may volunteer for additional overtime. There is no legal minimum wage. The labor law provides, however, that minimum wages may be set by the Council of Ministers on the recommendation of the minister of labor. The market minimum is in effect the amount required to induce foreign laborers to work in Saudi Arabia.

There is no minimum age for those employed in agriculture, family enterprises, private homes, or repair of agricultural machinery. Adolescents (ages 15-18), juveniles (under 15), and women may not be employed in hazardous or harmful industries, such as mines or industries employing power-operated machinery. In other cases the labor law provides for a minimum age of 13, which may be waived by the Ministry of Labor in certain areas and with the consent of the juvenile's guardian. Child labor does not appear to be a significant problem in Saudi Arabia.

Saudi Arabia has a generous social security program. The large expatriate work force does not, for the most part, receive the same economic and social benefits available to native Saudis and must abide by considerable restrictions on its life-style. The poorest of these expatriates, almost two million Yemenis, Africans and Asians, live under conditions significantly worse than those of the Saudi urban classes. Labor Ministry inspectors and the labor courts seek with considerable success to enforce a generous labor code which regulates hours and working conditions, but not wages. Some foreign workers, particularly those in unskilled positions such as housemaids, are exploited due to their ignorance of the labor code, inability to understand Arabic, and/or lack of written contracts.

FOREIGN COMMERCE

The foreign commerce of Saudi Arabia consisted in 1984 of exports of $42.654 billion and imports of $33.368 billion leaving a favorable balance of trade of $9.286 billion. Based on 1975=100, the import price index in 1981 was 156, the export price index 318 and the terms of trade (export prices divided by import prices × 100) 205. Of the imports, machinery and equipment constituted 25.5%, transport equipment 17.4%, textiles 5.9%, vegetables 5.9%, live animals and animal products 3.6%, pearls, precious and semiprecious stones 2.7%. Of the exports, crude and refined petroleum products constituted 100%.

The major import sources are: the United States 21.0%, Japan 19.6%, West Germany 11.0%, the United Kingdom 6.6%, Italy 6.1%, France 5.3% and South Korea 2.7%. The major export destinations are: Japan 23.8%, France 9.0%, the United States 7.8%, Singapore 5.3%, Italy 5.0%, the Netherlands 4.8% and West Germany 4.3%.

FOREIGN TRADE INDICATORS (1984)

Annual Growth Rate, Imports:	27.6 (1973-83)
Annual Growth Rate, Exports:	−4.5 (1973-83)
Ratio of Exports to Imports:	56:44
Exports per capita:	$3,877
Imports per capita:	$3,033
Balance of Trade:	$9.286 billion
Ratio of International Reserves to Imports (in months)	4.4
Exports as % of GDP:	69.0
Imports as % of GDP:	31.7
Value of Manufactured Exports:	$824 million
Commodity Concentration:	88.4%

Direction of Trade (%)

	Imports	Exports
EEC	33.9	34.5
U.S.	21.6	13.4
Industrialized Market Economies	79.4	59.3
East European Economies	—	—
High Income Oil Exporters	—	—
Developing Economies	17.4	36.4

Composition of Trade (%)

	Imports	Exports
Food	14.4	0.1
Agricultural Raw Materials	1.1	—
Fuels	0.7	99.3
Ores & Minerals	7.6	—
Manufactured Goods	76.0	0.6
of which Chemicals	3.9	0.1
of which Machinery	40.4	0.4

Trade restrictions are minimal. Imports contrary to Islam, such as liquor, pork, films, musical instruments and records, are either entirely banned or permitted to be imported only by non-nationals.

TRANSPORTATION & COMMUNICATIONS

The Saudi Arabian rail system consists of one 575-km (350-mi) single track connecting Dammam with Riyadh. It is operated by the Saudi Government Railroad Organization. In 1982 rail traffic consisted of 88 million passenger-km and 458 million net ton-km of freight.

In 1984 there were 63,000 km (39,123 mi) of roads of which 28,000 km (17,388 mi) were asphalted. The most important road is the Trans-Arabian Highway linking Dammam, Riyadh, Taif, Mecca and Jidda. In 1982 there were 757,395 passenger cars and 661,290 other commercial vehicles. Per capita automobile ownership was 68 per 1,000 inhabitants.

The main ports are Dammam, Jubail and Ras Tanura on the Persian Gulf and Jidda, Yanbu and Gizan on the Red Sea. The total seaborne traffic at these ports in 1982 was 329,257,000 metric tons, of which oil constituted over 95%. The Saudi Lines and the Nashar Saudi Line operate regular passenger and cargo services. The Saudi merchant fleet of 435 vessels has a GRT of 9.312 million of which oil tankers account for 2.893 million, and ore and bulk carriers 312,000.

The international flag airline is Saudia (Saudi Arabian Airlines), which operates all internal services and international services to 25 cities abroad with a fleet of 162 aircraft, principally Boeings and Tristars. There are a total of 184 airfields: 156 usable, 59 with permanent-surface runways, nine with runways over 2,500 m (8,000 ft). The major international airports are at Dhahran, Jidda and Riyadh. In 1982 Saudia carried 10.152 million passengers and flew 99.4 million km (61.7 million mi).

Crude oil is piped through a 6,000-km (1070-mi) pipeline from Abqaiq to Sidon in Lebanon known as the Trans-Arabian Pipeline (TAP). The refined products pipeline is 150-km (93 mi) and the natural gas pipeline 2,200 km (1,366 mi). The length of the natural gas liquid pipeline is 1,600 km (993 mi).

In 1984 Saudi Arabia had 790,000 telephones, or 8.0 per 100 inhabitants.

There were 437 post offices in 1982. Mail traffic in 1982 was 223,632,000 pieces of mail and 3,219 telegrams. Domestic letter mail per capita was 20 pieces. There are 575 telex subscriber lines.

In 1983-84 900,000 tourists visited Saudi Arabia generating receipts of $1.809 billion. Pilgrims to Mecca accounted for almost all the tourists. Expenditures by nationals abroad totaled $2.761 billion. There are 22,000 hotel beds and the average length of stay is 1.7 days.

MINING

The only minerals other than hydrocarbons being developed at present are limestone, gypsum, marble, clay and salt. Known deposits of iron, copper, gold, silver and lead exist.

DEFENSE

The defense structure is headed by the King who is also commander in chief. The King is also the commander in chief of the National Guard (White Army).

Armed forces service is voluntary, and recruits enlist for a three-year term. Recruiting for the regular armed forces is done nationally, while recruitment for the National Guard is done on a tribal basis.

The strength of the armed forces is 62,500 (including 10,000 National Guard), or 5.3 armed persons for every 1,000 civilians.

ARMY:

Personnel: 35,000
Organization: 3 armored brigades; 3 mechanized brigades; 1 infantry brigade; 1 airborne brigade; 1 royal guard regiment; 5 artillery battalions; 18 AA artillery battalions; 14 SAM batteries
Equipment: 450 tanks; 550 armored vehicles; 1,300 armored personnel carriers; 502 howitzers; mortars; antitank rocket launchers; antitank guided weapons; 248 air defense guns; SAMs

NAVY:

Personnel: 3,500; 24 combat helicopters
Naval Bases: Al Qatif/Jubail, Jidda, Ras Tanura, Dammam, Yenbo, Ras al-Mishab and three coast-guard bases.
Equipment: 2 Fleet HQ (Western and Eastern); 4 frigates; 4 corvettes; 9 fast attack craft; 1 large patrol craft; 4 mine countermeasures vessels; 19 amphibious vessels; 2 support ships;

AIR FORCE:

Personnel: 14,000
Organization: 205 combat aircraft; 3 fighter squadrons; 4 interceptor squadrons; 4 AWACS; 2 operational conversion units; 3 transport squadrons; 2 helicopter squadrons; 39 trainers; air-to-air missiles; air-to-surface missiles.
Air Defense Command
Air Bases: Jidda, Dhahran, Abha, Tebuk, Riyadh, Taif, Medina, Yenbo and Khamis Mushait.
Foreign Contract Military Personnel: 10,000
National Guard: 10,000 regular; 15,000 reserve. HQ Brigade; 4 all-arms, 16 regular infantry and 24 irregular infantry battalions; 1 ceremonial cavalry squadron; support units; 240 armored personnel carriers; howitzers; mortars; AA guns; antitank guided weapons

Annual military expenditures in 1985/86 were $17.777 billion, or 29.6% of the GNP, 24.3% of the national budget, $2,508 per capita, $500,865 per soldier and $12,114 per sq km of national territory.

The Saudis have been building up their defense capability in recent years buying sophisticated equipment, armaments, and other military hardware, most of which may not be in operation for many years to come because of a lack of skilled manpower. It is not clear whether this build-up is designed to be used against the Israelis or against potential dissidents at home. If the present pace of arms purchases continues it is to be expected that the Saudi armed forces will rank with those of Israel and Iran as among the most effective in the Middle East by the 1990s. Arms purchases from 1973 through 1983 totaled $15.585 billion.

The National Guard, or the White Army, consists of 10,000 tribal levies equipped with antitank weapons and armored cars. It is distinguished by its special loyalty to the Saud royal family. Military officers are trained at the Royal Military College at Riyadh. Advanced training is provided in war colleges in the United Kingdom and the United States.

Saudi Arabia is a major recipient of U.S. military aid, amounting to $292.4 million from 1946 to 1983, in addition to $589,000 in excess stocks of defense materials. The United States maintains a military mission in the country.

Saudi Arabia has formed a multinational arms consortium with Egypt, the United Arab Emirates and Qatar for defense production. Ammunition, small arms, and rockets are currently manufactured at El Kharj arsenal staffed by U.S. and West German experts.

EDUCATION

The estimated literacy rate in Saudi Arabia is 24.6% (34.5% for males and 12.2% for females).

Public education is free but not compulsory at all levels and grants are provided for poorer children. Schooling consists of 12 years of which the first or elementary level lasts six years, the intermediate level three years and the secondary level three years. Islamic emphasis is strong at all levels. In a few schools the first two or three years are coeducational, but after the age of nine girls attend segregated schools and wear veils in public. Girls constituted 40% of students in primary schools, 39% in secondary schools, and 30% in higher education. Primary school classes have a teacher-pupil ratio of 1:18. The shortage of qualified teachers has been a limiting factor in the expansion of education and has led to the importation of teachers, mostly Egyptians, Palestinians and Lebanese. The teacher-pupil ratio is 1:15 at the secondary level and 1:9 at the post-secondary level. Over 67% of eligible children are enrolled at the elementary level and 32% at the secondary level for an adjusted combined ration of 51%. The third-level enrollment ratio is 8.7%.

Vocational schooling is organized in two cycles of three years each, intermediate and secondary. Vocational students constituted 1.5% of secondary enrollment in 1981.

The academic year runs from September to May. The language of instruction is Arabic. English is the most commonly taught second language.

The three government bodies that administer education are the Ministry of Education, the office of the Grand Mufti, which oversees female education, and the Supreme Educational Council, which formulates educational policy and administers the educational budget. The country is divided into 23 educational districts for purpose of administration. Educational expenditure in the 1982 national budget was R31.404 billion or 10.0% of all public expenditures, 5.8% of GNP and $924 per capita.

EDUCATIONAL ENROLLMENT (1982)			
	Schools	**Teachers**	**Students**
First Level	6,287	55,015	998,307
Second Level	2,364	25,163	390,092
Vocational	186	3,174	27,444
Third Level	17	6,906	63,563

Higher education in Saudi Arabia is provided by six universities, the Imam Mohammed bin Saud Islamic University at Riyadh, the Islamic University at Medina, the King Abdel-Aziz University at Jidda, the King Faisal University at Dammam, the University of Petroleum and Minerals at Dhahran, and Riyadh University. Nearly 570 students are enrolled in institutions of higher learning per 100,000 inhabitants. A total of 9,585 Saudi students were enrolled in institutions of higher learning abroad in 1982 including 8,175 in the United States, 289 in the United Kingdom and 503 in Egypt. In the same year, 16,469 foreign students were enrolled in Saudi Arabia.

Saudi Arabia's contribution to world scientific authorship is 0.0080 (U.S.=42%). No scientific journals are published within the country.

LEGAL SYSTEM

Justice is administered in accordance with the Koran and the Sharia supplemented by decree law. Some of the penalties specified in the Sharia are extremely severe and include stoning, mutilation and lashing. The beheading in 1977 of a princess of the Saudi royal house for adultery illustrated vividly both the severity of the Sharia as interpreted by the Wahhabis and its application to all citizens without discrimination. The right of habeas corpus is not recognized.

At the apex of the judicial system is the Judicial Supervisory Committee consisting of a president and three members. Below it are three tiers of courts: the Courts of Appeal or the Courts of Cassation, the Mahkamat al-Sharia al-Koubra, and the Mahkamat al-Omour al Mostajalah. The Grievance Board of the Council of Ministers functions as the final arbiter in cases of decree law.

In accordance with Shari'a law, Saudi Arabia imposes capital punishment for the crimes of premeditated murder, adultery, apostasy from Islam, and, depending upon the circumstances, rape and armed robbery. The interior minister and Cassation Courts review all cases in which capital punishment has been imposed. During 1985, the number of death sentences increased sharply (34 executions in the first nine months of the year) from the low levels (five or fewer)

in most recent years. Furthermore, death sentences have been handed down for crimes that are not normally considered capital. Four Saudis were beheaded for crimes in which no one was hurt: two for armed robbery and two policemen for burglary, drug dealing and other offenses. Beheading is the usual method of execution. Execution by firing squad or stoning may be imposed for adultery. Severe social disapproval discourages adultery, and the requirement of confession or testimony by four eyewitnesses renders conviction for adultery rare. A recidivist thief may suffer severance of a hand. For less severe crimes, such as drunkenness, or publicly infringing Islamic precepts, flogging with a cane is often imposed. Public flogging is intended to humiliate the criminal and serve as a deterrent to others. The skin is not to be broken, but floggings are painful and leave welts. Government policy prohibits torture, but some punishments meted out under Islamic Shari'a law involve amputation. There have been reports during 1985 of police beatings of detainees to elicit confessions, which in the absence of witnesses are usually required for conviction in Shari'a courts.

Among the most fundamental of Islamic precepts are the sanctity of family life and the inviolability of the home. The police generally must demonstrate reasonable cause and obtain permission from the provincial governor before searching a private home, but warrants are not required. The Mutawwi'in assert the right to enter homes to search for evidence of un-Islamic behavior when they have "grounds for suspicion," but instances of this appear to be exceedingly rare. Wiretapping and mail surveillance can be carried out on the authority of officials of the Interior Ministry or the Directorate of Intelligence. A wide network of informants is believed to be employed.

Some social norms and structures affecting personal life are matters of law and are enforced by the government. Saudi women may not marry non-Saudis without government permission. Saudi men must seek approval to marry women from countries other than the six members of the Gulf Cooperation Council. During Ramadan, the prohibition against public eating, drinking, or smoking during daylight hours is enforced on Muslims and non-Muslims alike. Prohibitions against alcohol and pornography are strictly enforced. Members of the officially supported Committee for the Propagation of Virtue and the Supression of Vice patrol the streets and markets to assure Islamic decorum in dress and demeanor and the closing of shops during the daily prayer periods.

The Board of Grievances arbitrates claims against the state. The president and vice president of the board are experienced jurists. They are aided by board members expert in administrative, contract, corruption, civil service, and forgery legislation. The president is responsible directly to the king, and the members of the board are guaranteed considerable independence. The board has vigorously wielded new powers, granted by a 1983 decree, to call erring officials to account.

LAW ENFORCEMENT

The principal law enforcement agency is the National Guard, a highly mobile and lightly armed force chosen from the so-called noble tribes. The National Police number 15,000 to 20,000. The regional emirs have considerable autonomy in matters relating to public security.

The Public Morality Committees under the Grand Mufti enforce public observance of Muslim religious laws, such as fasting during Ramadan, the seclusion of women, and the ban against alcohol, the display of images, smoking, and dancing. Statistics on crime are not available, but it is believed that offenses against property and persons are less common than infractions of the strict Wahhabi code of conduct, such as absence from public prayers, adultery and drunkenness.

HEALTH

In 1981 there were 95 hospitals with 14,451 beds, or 1 bed per 666 inhabitants. In the same year, there were 3,576 physicians, or 1 physician per 2,693 inhabitants, 217 dentists and 6,706 nursing personnel. The King Faisal Medical City on the outskirts of Riyadh claims to be the most technically advanced medical unit in the world. Health expenditures account for 1.4% of the national budget and $132.70 per capita. Of the hospitals 72.6% are state-run and 27.4% are run by private agencies.

```
PRINCIPAL HEALTH INDICATORS (1984)
Crude Death Rate: 12.1 per 1,000
Decline in Death Rate: –41.4% (1965-83)
Life Expectancy at Birth: 54.5 (Males); 57.6 (Females)
Infant Mortality Rate: 121.1 per 1,000 Live Births
Child Death Rate (Ages 1-4) per 1,000: 13
```

The principal health problems are trachoma, tuberculosis, night blindness, dysentery and typhoid. Over 84% of the population have access to safe water.

FOOD

The staple food of the settled Arab is millet supplemented by rice, barley or wheat. The main source of meat is lamb. Fruits, especially dates, are eaten regularly. Per capita food intake is 78.8 grams of protein 2,889 calories, 43 grams of fats, and 445 grams of carbohydrates per day.

MEDIA & CULTURE

Saudi Arabia has 10 daily newspapers with a total circulation of 500,000 and seven non-dailies with a total circulation of 30,000. Newspaper circulation per 1,000 inhabitants is 45. Seven newspapers are published in Arabic and three in English by officially approved, but independent, organizations as required by the Press Law of 1964. The principal dailies are: *Arab News* (60,000), *al Madina al-Munawara* (55,000), *al-Bilad* (30,000) and *al-Riyadh* (140,000). The periodical press consists of 80 titles with a total circulation of 43,000 copies. The largest weekly is the Ministry of Information's English-language bulletin, which has a circulation of 22,000 copies. Most newspapers depend on state subsidies in the form of duty-free newsprint and advertising. Newsprint consumption in 1982 was 6,400 tons, or 687 kg (427 lb) per 1,000 inhabitants.

There is no official censorship, but any publication that offends the state or Islam or praises or even mentions Israel is immediately suspended. Under the Press Law of 1964 all newspapers are required to have a minimum number of professional staff and a capital base of at least R100,000.

The national news agency is Saudi News Agency founded in 1970. Foreign agencies whose services are recieved in the country include UPI, AP, AFP, MENA and Reuters.

In 1980, 218 books were published in Saudi Arabia. Saudi Arabia does not adhere to any copyright convention.

Broadcasting is a state monopoly under the direction of the Saudi Arabian Broadcasting Service, a department of the Ministry of Information. It broadcasts a total of 822 hours a week. Its foreign service is beamed to five world areas in Arabic, English, French, Indonesian, Persian, Swahili and Urdu. The service has three medium-wave transmitters (1200, 100 and 50 kw) and two short-wave transmitters (100 and 50 kw). Of total 36,865 annual radio broadcasting hours, 5,161 hours are devoted to information, 738 to education, 12,534 to culture, 11,059 to religion and 7,373 to entertainment. The number of radio receivers in 1982 was 3,025,000, or 312 per 1,000 inhabitants. No receiver license fee is required.

The Saudi Arabian Government Television Service, which began operations in 1965, now has five transmitters at Riyadh, Jidda, Medina, Dammam and Qassim, broadcasting for 38 hours a week. ARAMCO Television, based at Dhahran, is a non-commercial station that broadcasts for 4½ hours a day. The opposition of conservative religious leaders has proved an obstacle to the expansion of television. Of the 2,920 annual television broadcasting hours, 426 hours are devoted to information, 162 to education, 182 to culture, 365 to religion, and 1,156 to entertainment. The number of television receivers in 1982 was 2,541,000, or 262 per 1,000 inhabitants. No receiver license is required. Films are prohibited throughout the kingdom in the context of Muslim religious laws.

In 1982 there were eight public libraries in Saudi Arabia, of which the most important were the National Library at Riyadh and the Saudi Library at Riyadh. Per capita, there are five volumes per 1,000 inhabitants.

There are 76 theaters of which three are in the capital.

The national museum reported 27,000 visitors in 1982.

SOCIAL WELFARE

Public welfare programs are coordinated by the Ministry of Labor and Social Affairs and are administered through the directorate general of social affairs, the Red Crescent Society (the Muslim Red Cross) and the Social Security Administration. The zakat, or the alms tax enjoined by Islam, is the main source of social welfare, but since the government began receiving larger oil revenues the zakat has not been regularly collected. Free medicine and medical care are provided for all citizens and foreign nationals. The social security program provides a minimum of 360 rials a year to indigent heads of families.

GLOSSARY

alim: Plural: **ulema.** a religious scholar or jurist.

Bedouin: nomadic Arabs considered to be of pure Semitic stock. They are a pastoral people who herd camels, sheep and goats.

dunum: a measure of land area equal to 1,000 sq m (10,764 sq ft).

emir: an Arabic title meaning commander, now used to designate a provincial viceroy.

fetwa: a canonical ruling by the ulema or council of Islamic jurists.

Grand Mufti: head of the ulema and chief expounder of Islamic law.

hakem: governor of a province.

haj: the pilgrimage to Mecca enjoined on every Muslim by the Koran.

id al fitr: the feast that ends the fast of the Ramadan; one of the national religious holidays in Saudi Arabia.

imam: title of the person who leads the faithful in daily prayers.

majlis: a popular assembly or tribal council.

mantika: a district or subdivision of a province.

markez: a subdistrict.

mokata: a province.

qadi: a religious judge.

Ramadan: the ninth month of the Islamic year in which all Muslims are required to fast from dawn to dusk.

Sharia: literally, the way. The law of Islam as revealed in the Koran that forms the basis of Muslim jurisprudence.

sherif: a noble descended from Prophet Muhammad in the line of Hassan, son of Ali and Fatima.

Wahhabism: a reform sect of the Hanbali school of Sunni jurisprudence founded by Muhammad ibn Abdul Wahhab in the 1730s, distinguished by strict, literal adherence to the Koran.

zakat: an obligatory tax imposed on Muslims for charitable purposes.

CHRONOLOGY (from 1945)

1945— Saudi Arabia joins the Arab League.

1949— United States establishes embassy in Jidda.

1951— Saudi Government Railroad connecting Dammam and Riyadh is completed. . . . Ministry of Interior is established. . . . Saudi Arabia is included in the Military Assistance Act and Point-Four Program in return for granting the United States usage rights at the Dhahran airfield for five years.

1952— Saudi Arabian Monetary Agency (SAMA) is established.

1953— Council of Ministers is established. . . . King Saud dies; his son Ibn Abdel-Aziz al-Saud succeeds him as king.

1955— Clashes with United Kingdom occur over Buraimi Oasis.

1956— Diplomatic relations with United Kingdom and France are broken over British and French invasion of Egypt and the Buraimi dispute.

1957— "Kings' Alliance" is formed with Jordan's Hussein and Iraq's Faisal. . . . University of Riyadh is founded.

1958— Crown Prince Faisal is appointed prime minister and virtual ruler. . . . Cabinet is established on modern lines.

1960— Faisal is ousted from post as prime minister; King Saud reassumes reins of power. . . . Saudi Arabia becomes founding member of Organization of Petroleum Exporting Countries (OPEC). . . . Saudi rial is devalued.

1961— University of Medina is founded. . . . Supreme Planning Council is established.

1962— In major cabinet reshuffle, Faisal returns to power as deputy prime minister; Faisal proposes a basic constitutional law. . . . Saudi Arabia sides with royalists in the Yemeni civil war, and breaks with United Arab Republic over Egyptian military aid to the Yemeni republican regime, forming a joint defense council with Jordan against Egypt (Taif Pact). . . . Slavery is officially abolished. . . . Red Crescent Society is founded. . . . General Petroleum and Mineral Organization (Petromin) is founded. . . . Dhahran Air Base is taken over from United States. . . . Social Security Administration is established.

1963— Provincial regulations are promulgated. . . . Saudis and Egyptians reach agreement calling for disengagement in Yemen. . . . Ties with United Kingdom are resumed.

1964— King Saud is deposed and replaced as king by Faisal. . . . The joint Saudi-Kuwait Neutral Zone is partitioned.

1965— Khaled is named crown prince. . . . Border with Qatar is delimited. . . . Saudi Television Service is launched.

1967— Abdel Aziz University is founded at Jidda.

1968— Continental shelf agreement is concluded with Iran.

1969— Saudi Arabia sponsors Islamic summit meeting at Rabat, Morocco, following a fire in the Al Aqsa mosque at Jerusalem.

1970— Islamic secretariat is established at Jidda. . . . Saudi Arabia signs pact ending Yemeni civil war and recognizes Yemen.

1973— In retaliation against U.S. military aid to Israel, Saudi Arabia joins other OPEC members in hiking the price and cutting the production of oil.

1974— Saudi Arabia increases its share of the concessions and assets of ARAMCO to 60% under an interim agreement.

1975— King Faisal is assassinated; Crown Prince Khaled succeeds him as king, and Prince Fahd is named crown prince.

1978— President Carter announces plans to sell Saudi Arabia 60 F15 fighter bombers.

1979— A fanatical sect, known as the Safiyeen Salfiyeen (advocates of a return to the origin), of between 250 and 600 members, take over the Grand Mosque at Mecca and barricade themselves in its vast cellars; most of the attackers are killed or taken alive after two weeks of fighting; army shakeup is reported following the incident.

1981— Saudi Arabia concludes treaty with Iraq partitioning the Neutral Zone.

1982— King Khaled dies, and is succeeded as monarch by Prince Fahd.

BIBLIOGRAPHY

Abdrabboh, Bob, *Saudi Arabia: Forces of Modernization* (Brattleboro, Vt., 1985).

Abdullah, Al-Mani Muhammad and Abdulrahman Sbit As-Sbit, *Cultural Policy in the Kingdom of Saudi Arabia* (Paris, 1981).

Al-Bashir, Faisal S., *A Structural Econometric Model of the Saudi Arabian Economy* (New York, 1977)

Alireza, Marianne, *At the Drop of a Veil* (Boston, 1971).

Al-Yassini, Ayman, *Religion and State in the Kingdom of Saudi Arabia* (Boulder, Colo., 1985).

American University, *Area Handbook for Saudi Arabia* (Washington D.C., 1971).

Beling, Willard, A., *King Faisal & the Modernization of Saudi Arabia* (Boulder, Col., 1979).

Bingdagji, Hussein H., *Atlas of Saudi Arabia* (New York, 1978).

Bligh, Alexander, *From Prince to King: Royal Succession in the House of Saud in the 20th Century* (New York, 1984).

Cleron, Jean P., *Saudi Arabia Two Thousand: A Strategy for Growth* (New York, 1978).

Crane, Robert D., *Planning the Future of Saudi Arabia; A Model for Achieving National Priorities* (New York, 1978).

El Mallakh, Ragaei, *Saudi Arabia: Rush to Development* (Baltimore, Md., 1982).

——, and Dorothea H. El Mallakh, *Saudi Arabia: Energy, Development Planning and industrialization* (Lexington, Mass., 1982).

Grayson, Benson L., *Saudi American Relations:* (Lanham, Md., 1982).

Hallam, Harry M., *Saudi Arabia and the Political and Economic Control of the World* (Albuquerque, N.M., 1983).

Heller, Mark and Nadav Safran, *The New Middle Class and Regime Stability in Saudi Arabia* (Cambridge, Mass., 1985).

Helms, Christine M., *The Cohesion of Saudi Arabia: Evolution of Political Identity* (Baltimore, Md., 1981).

Hobday, Peter, *Saudi Arabia Today* (New York, 1978).

Islami, A., Reza and Rostam M. Kavoussi, *The Political Economy of Saudi Arabia* (Seattle, Wash., 1984).

Katakura, Motoko, *Bedouin Village: A Study of a Saudi Arabian People in Transition* (Tokyo, 1977).

Kay, Shirley, *Saudi Arabia: Past & Present*, New York, 1979).

Knauerhase, Ramon, *The Saudi Arabian Economy* (New York, 1975).

Koury, Enver M., *The Saudi Decision-Making Body: The House of Saud* (Hyattsville, Md., 1978).

Lee, Eve, *An American in Saudi Arabia* (Chicago, 1980).

Long, David E. *Saudi Arabia* (Beverly Hills, Calif., 1976).

Looney, Robert E., *Saudi Arabia's Development Potential: Potential Applications of an Islamic Growth Model* (Lexington, Mass., 1981).

Middle East Economic Digest, *Saudi Arabia* (Boulder, Colo., 1983).

Nakhleh, Emile A., *The United States and Saudi Arabia* (Washington, 1975).

Niblock, Tim, *State, Economy and Society in Saudi Arabia* (New York, 1981).

Quandt, William B., *Saudi Arabia in the 1980s: Foreign Policy Security and Oil* (Washington D.C., 1981).

Riley, Carroll L., *Historical and Cultural Dictionary of Saudi Arabia* (Metuchen, N.J., 1972).

Safran, Nadav, *Saudi Arabia: The Ceaseless Quest for Security* (Cambridge, Mass., 1985).

Sidebotham, William C., *The Hell & Truth about Saudi Arabia* (New York, 1977).

Sparrow, Judge Gerald, *Modern Saudi Arabia* (London, 1970).

Tahtinen, Dale R., *National Security Challenges to Saudi Arabia* (Washington, D.C. 1978).

Troeller, Gary C., *The Birth of Saudi Arabia* (London, 1976).

Wells, Donald A., *Saudi Arabian Revenues and Expenditures: The Potential for Foreign Exchange Savings* (Baltimore, Md., 1974).

Young, Arthur N., *Saudi Arabia: The Making of a Financial Giant* (New York, 1983).

OFFICIAL PUBLICATIONS

Saudi Arabian Monetary Agency, *Annual Report.*
——, *Statistical Summary.*

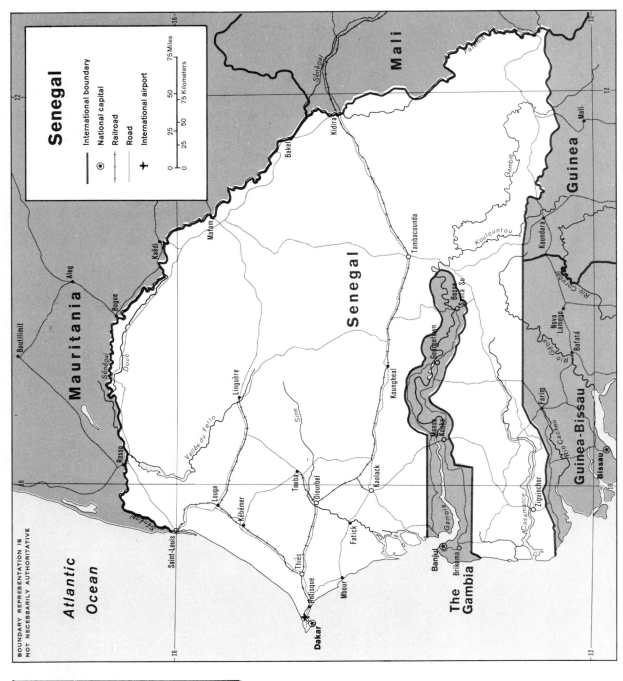

Senegal

Legend:
- International boundary
- ⊛ National capital
- Railroad
- Road
- ✈ International airport

75 Miles
75 Kilometers

Mauritania

Mali

Guinea

Guinea-Bissau

The Gambia

Atlantic Ocean

Senegal

BOUNDARY REPRESENTATION IS
NOT NECESSARILY AUTHORITATIVE

Boutilimit
Aleg
Bogué
Kaédi
Matam
Bakel
Kidira
Sénégal
Falémé
Rosso
Vallée du Ferlo
Doué
Sénégal
Linguère
Sine
Tambacounda
Koulountou
Gambie
Koundara
Saint-Louis
Louga
Kébémer
Touba
Diourbel
Kaolack
Koungheal
Georgetown
Basse
Santa Su
Nova Lamego
Balaté
Farim
Rio Géba
Rio Cacheu
Rio Corubal
Mali
Thiès
Fatick
Mbour
Rufisque
Dakar
Banjul
Brikama
Mansa Konko
Gambie
Casamance
Ziguinchor
Bissau

SENEGAL

BASIC FACT SHEET

OFFICIAL NAME: Republic of Senegal (Republique du Senegal)

ABBREVIATION: SG

CAPITAL: Dakar

HEAD OF STATE & HEAD OF GOVERNMENT: President Abdou Diouf (from 1981)

NATURE OF GOVERNMENT: Modified democracy

POPULATION: 6,755,000 (1985)

AREA: 197,161 sq km (76,124 sq mi)

ETHNIC MAJORITY: Wolof, Fula, Serer, Tukulor and Dyola

LANGUAGE: French (official)

RELIGIONS: Islam and Christianity

UNIT OF CURRENCY: CFA (Communaute Financiere Africaine) Franc ($1=CFA Franc 424.980, August 1985)

NATIONAL FLAG: A tricolor of green, yellow and red vertical stripes with a green star at the center of the yellow stripe

NATIONAL EMBLEM: A shield divided into vertical halves, one side in red displaying a gold lion and the other side in yellow displaying a green baobab tree.

Below the tree is a wavy green line representing the Senegal River. The shield is enclosed within black and white palm branches opening at the top to frame a green star. From the wreath is suspended the white jeweled National Order of the Republic and a white ribbon entwined among the branches bearing the motto "Un Peuple—Un But—Une Foi" ("One People, One Goal, One Faith")

NATIONAL ANTHEM: "Pluck Your Koras, Strike the Balafons"

NATIONAL HOLIDAYS: April 4 (National Day); January 1 (New Year's Day); May 1 (Labor Day); Christian holidays include Christmas, Assumption, All Saints' Day, Ascension, Whitsun, Easter Monday; also, four Islamic holidays.

NATIONAL CALENDAR: Gregorian

PHYSICAL QUALITY OF LIFE INDEX: 23 (up from 22 in 1976) (On an ascending scale with 100 as the maximum. U.S., 95).

DATE OF INDEPENDENCE: April 4, 1960

DATE OF CONSTITUTION: March 3, 1963

WEIGHTS & MEASURES: The metric system is in force.

LOCATION & AREA

Senegal is the westernmost country in Africa, situated on the western bulge with a total land area of 197,161 sq km (76,124 sq mi), extending 690 km (429 mi) SE to NW and 406 km (252 mi) NE to SW. Its Atlantic coastline stretches 446 km (277 mi).

Senegal shares its total international boundary of 2,655 km (1,649 mi) with five countries: Mauritania (813 km, 505 mi), Mali (418 km, 260 mi), Guinea (330 km, 205 mi), Guinea-Bissau (338 km, 210 mi) and Gambia (756 km, 470 mi). The borders with Mauritania, Mali and Guinea follow lines that originally divided internal administrative divisions of French West Africa. The northern border with Mauritania follows the Senegal River for 804 km (500 mi) to its confluence with the Faleme River. The borders with Guinea and Mali have little or no relation to natural features. The border with Guinea-Bissau was settled by a Franco-Portuguese Treaty in 1886. Gambia forms an enclave within Senegal and partially separates Senegal's southern region from the central and northern regions. The western sections of the Senegal-Gambia border are artificially drawn straight lines, but in the east they conform to the course of the Gambia River. There are no current border disputes.

The capital is Dakar with a 1981 population of 978,553. Other major urban centers are Kaolack (115,679), Theis (126,886) and Saint-Louis (96,594).

Senegal is a western segment of the broad savanna that extends across Africa at the southern edge of the Sahara. Variations in elevations are minor, and contrasts between the six primary geographical regions are not sharp. These six regions are the Senegal River Valley, the Coastal Belt, the Western Plains, the Ferlo, Casamance and the East.

The floodplain of the Senegal River is broken by many marshes and branching channels. Where the river approaches the sea its various channels form an extensive network in a wide area resembling a delta. In the middle reach of the valley above Dagana is the Ile a Morfil, a narrow island between channels, several hundred kilometers long. The coastal belt north of Cap Vert Peninsula is covered by small swamps or pools separated by dunes, often as high as 30 meters (100 ft). This coastal belt extending 24 km (15 mi) inland is known as Cayor. Between the dunes are fresh-water swamps that are transformed into green oases in the summer. South of Dakar the coastal belt narrows into a maze of meandering creeks, channels and flats. The Western Plains extend southeastward from Thies to Kaolack and consist of dry, barren land in the summer that springs to life with the rains, turning into green farmlands. The Ferlo is an inland continuation of the Western Plains and is semidesert. Casamance, separated from the rest of Senegal by the Gambia, is different in terms of natural features, vegetation and rainfall. The East is a plain extending southeastward from the Ferlo to the borders of Mali and Guinea and consists of poor, seasonal pastureland.

Senegal shares the Senegal River with Mauritania. Over 4,023 km (2,500 mi) long, the Senegal rises in Guinea and is known as the Bafing until it is joined in eastern Mali by the Bakoy. As it enters Senegalese territory, it is joined by the Faleme. Near Saint-Louis, the river breaks into a network of distributaries. During the annual flood the crests reach a maximum of 13.7 meters (45 ft) above the minimum at the Senegal-Mali border. During low water tides reach nearly 483 km (300 mi) upstream, and the river is normally salty for half that distance. During the flood the salt water encroachment is reversed. A number of dikes have been built to retain fresh water and bar the advance of salt water. The largest of these dikes controls a shallow freshwater lake known as Lac de Guiers.

The Gambia River rises in the Guinean Highlands and receives the Koulountou near the Gambian border. The Casamance River in southern Senegal drains a narrow basin between the Gambia and the border with Portuguese Guinea. Its main tributary is the Songrougrou River. North of the Gambia the Saloum River and its affluent, the Sine River, flow into an extensive tidal swamp.

WEATHER

Senegal has a varied climate. The northern coast is cooled by the prevailing northeasterly trade winds and the Canaries current. Casamance in the south lies on the fringe of the tropical monsoon area. The rest of the country has a pre-desert Sudanese climate, with the northern part having semi-desert Sahelian conditions. There are two well-defined dry and humid seasons: the rainy season from June to October in the Sahelian Zone, from May to October in the Sudanese Zone, and from May to December in the Casamance. Dakar on the coast has a mean maximum temperature of 27°C (87°F) in January and 33°C (91°F) in August and a mean minimum temperature of 18°C (64°F) in January and 25°C (77°F) in August. Temperatures rise rapidly inland, reaching over 37.8°C (100°F).

Rainfall is subject to wide seasonal variations. Average annual precipitation varies from 101 cm (40 in.) in the north to 152 cm (60 in.) in the south and 51 cm (20 in.) in the east. Senegal, along with other Sahelian countries, is periodically affected by serious drought. The cumulative effects of these droughts made the

early 1970s, particularly 1973, a period of unprecedented disaster, damaging its ecology irreparably.

Winds of gale strength occur at the beginning and end of the rainy season. Known as tornades, they are accompanied by thunder, lightning and squalls.

POPULATION

The population of Senegal was estimated in 1985 at 6,755,000, based on the last official census held in 1976 when the population was 4,907,507. The population is expected to reach 10.5 million by 2000 and 17.9 million by 2020. The annual growth rate is 2.6%, based on an annual birth rate of 47.6 per 1,000.

The highest population densities are recorded in the Cap Vert and Thies region, the westernmost of Senegal's six natural regions. Nearly one-third of the national population lives in this area, which accounts for less than 4% of the national territory. The densities decrease in direct ratio to the distance from the Atlantic coast. Most of the eastern regions, particularly Senegal Oriental and Fleuve, have average densities of less than 4.2 per sq km (11 per sq mi). The overall density is 33 per sq km (85 per sq mi), rising to 52.2 per sq km (135 per sq mi) in agricultural areas.

DEMOGRAPHIC INDICATORS (1985)	
Population, total (in 1,000)	6,755.0
Population ages (% of total)	
0-14	45.0
15-64	52.1
65+	2.9
Youth 15-24 (000)	1,211
Women ages 15-49 (000)	1,476
Dependency ratios	92.1
Child-woman ratios	813
Sex ratios (per 100 females)	98.0
Median ages (years)	17.5
Percentage change in Birthrate (%, 1960-78)	1.7
Proportion of urban (%)	42.38
Population density (per sq. km.)	33
per hectare of arable land	0.80
Rates of growth (%)	2.66
urban	4.9
rural	1.2
Natural increase rates (per 1,000)	26.6
Crude birth rates (per 1,000)	47.7
Crude death rates (per 1,000)	21.2
Gross reproduction rates	3.20
Net reproduction rates	2.10
Total fertility rates	6.50
General fertility rates (per 1,000)	210
Life expectancy, males (years)	41.7
Life expectancy, females (years)	44.9
Life expectancy, total (years)	43.3
Population doubling time in years at current rate	22
Average household size	4.2

In 1984 42.38% lived in towns with over 10,000 inhabitants, up from 30% in 1970. The urban growth rate of 4.9% is nearly 50% above the national growth rate. There are 25 towns of over 10,000 in population, and 10 of these towns—Dakar, Kaolack, Thies, Saint-Louis, Ziguinchor, Rufisque, Diourbel, Louga, Mbour and Tambacounda—have populations of over 25,000.

All except Louga, Rufisque and Mbour are regional capitals. Dakar, the only true urban complex, is one of the great seaports and industrial centers in West Africa. More than 15% of the national population live in the metropolitan area of Dakar, which has an annual growth rate of 6%. Over 60% of the population of Dakar live in slums and squatter settlements.

The age profile shows 45% in the under-14 age group, 52.1% in the 15-to-64 age group and 2.9% in the over-65 age group. At the time of the 1976 census, the male/female ratio was 49.5:50.5. The reasons for this female predominance are not known.

As one of the most industrialized countries in West Africa, Senegal has attracted migrant workers from Mali, Gambia, Guinea, Upper Volta and Guinea-Bissau. Some of these migrants return home while others become permanent residents. The numbers involved in permanent or seasonal migrations have not been statistically determined, but in the early 1970s the government referred to the presence of 800,000 non-Senegalese in the country, accounting for nearly 20% of the population. The migration appears to increase in times of famine and drought in the interior countries. Relative to immigration, emigration is not significant. Some 20,000 Senegalese are believed to be domiciled in France. Some 10,000 to 12,000 Senegalese go to Gambia for the harvest season, but few of them leave Senegal permanently.

Women are active participants in the political process, and several parties, including the dominant Socialist Party, have sections promoting women's rights. Twelve women are deputies in the National Assembly and there are four women in President Diouf's cabinet. In addition, a number of government ministries employ women in key positions, i.e., the political director in the Ministry of Foreign Affairs. In other ministries key agronomists, statisticians, and economists are women. Traditional values, both societal and religious (chiefly Islamic), have limited women's access to certain types of employment and higher education. There are, however, no legal hindrances to advancement for women and, as noted, they are present in respectable numbers in the governmental and private sectors. Women, including several professors at the University of Dakar, are prominent among Senegal's intellectual elite. Senegal also has several active organizations promoting women's rights, including the Federation of Women's Rights which held a two-week conference in March 1984. The federation has ties to a number of women's groups in Africa and, since 1979, has been a sister organization of the National Council of Negro Women in the United States.

There is no official family planning program. Very few Senegalese have any interest in limiting the size of their families.

ETHNIC COMPOSITION

As in other African countries, the ethnic configuration of Senegal is diverse.

ETHNIC GROUPS IN SENEGAL		
Group	Number	Percentage
Wolof (Ouolof)	1,375,000	36.2
Serer	722,000	19.0
Fulani (Fulbe, Peul) & Toucouleur	817,000	21.5
Diola (Djola, Jola)	266,000	7.0
Mandingo (Malinke, Mandinka) & Bambara (Bamana)	243,000	6.4
Sarakole (Soninke) & Diankhanke	79,800	2.1
Lebou	68,400	1.8
Bassari, Balante, Mandjaque, Mancagne, & Other	83,000	2.2
Maures	57,000	1.5
Cape Verdeans	30,000	0.8
Europeans	40,000	1.0
Lebanese	18,000	0.5

The Wolof, Serer and Diola are primarily Senegalese tribes, while other African groups are branches of larger communities based outside Senegal. The Wolof are concentrated in the northwestern quarter of the country, but they are also more evenly dispersed. As the largest group they dominate the political and economic life of the country. They represent 43% of the population of Dakar and the majority in most other cities. Through a long process of assimilation they have incorporated many of the cultural traits of their neighbors and, in turn, have influenced others. The Serer are the largest non-Muslim group and are traditionally divided into Serer-Sine and Serer-Non. Most Serer are cultivators in the Sine-Saloum region, but a few of the better educated, like President Leopold-Sedar Senghor, have made significant contributions to national life. The Fulani and the related Toucouleur are mostly stockraisers and cultivators, but because of their dispersion, Islamic fanaticism and resistance to modernization, participate less than others in national politics or economy. The Diola are the people of the Casamance, divided into at least seven linguistic subgroups. The Mandingo and the Bambara are ethnically related, but the former are Muslims, while the latter are mainly animists. The Lebou who live along the coast have a number of cultural and social traits in common with the Wolof and Serer.

Despite such heterogeneity, there is no visible ethnic strife. Many economic and social relationships cut across ethnic lines, and urbanization and education have helped the process of adaptation and mutual interaction. Although ethnic boundaries are rigid, there is a growing sense of nationalism that transcends ethnic distinctions. Significantly, no group has sought autonomy on ethnic grounds, although many national leaders are considered specific representatives of ethnic interests. Favoring the growth of a Senegalese nationalism are a number of factors such as the predominance of Islam, the universal use of Wolof as a lingua franca, common patterns of diet and dress and historical similarities in social organization. However, urbanization, education and receptivity to Western influences have favored the Wolof, Serer and, to some degree, the Lebou, in participating effectively in modern political and economic activities, while other tribes, such as the Fulani, Mandingo and Diola, are more lightly represented in the modern sector relative to their numbers.

The largest single non-African group is the French; their continuing presence is aided by Senegal's being one of the most francophile nations in Africa. The number of Frenchmen has decreased by only 26% since independence in 1960. The second largest alien group is the Lebanese, most of whom are small-scale commercial middlemen. Relations between the Senegalese and the French are amicable and in some cases warm, and the Senegalization of the economy has not been seen by the French as a threat. On the other hand, the Lebanese have been often accused of economic exploitation, and they have been subjected to periodic outbursts of animosity.

In terms of ethnic and linguistic homogeneity, Senegal ranks 25th in the world with 28% homogeneity (on an ascending scale in which North and South Korea are ranked 135th with 100% homogeneity and Tanzania is ranked first with 7% homogeneity).

LANGUAGES

The official language is French, although only a small minority, estimated at no more than 12%, is literate in it.

The major indigenous languages are Wolof, Serer, Pulaar (the mother tongue of the Fulani and Toucouleur), Diola, Manding and Sarakole. All these languages are members of the Niger-Congo linguistic family; Mande, Sarakole and Bambara belong to the western branch of the Mande subfamily, while the others belong to the western branch of the West Atlantic sub-family. Most of these languages have no script, and it was only in 1971 that the government began a major program to transcribe the country's six main languages into a modified Latin alphabet.

The national lingua franca is Wolof, spoken by over 80% of the population either as their mother tongue or as an acquired language. Competing with Wolof in the south are the two dialects of Diola, Fogny and Casa. About 2% of the population, including the Maures, speak Arabic, and Pulaar is sometimes written with an Arabic script.

RELIGIONS

Senegal has no state religion, but it is one of the most Islamized nations in West Africa, with 80% of the population adhering to one of two sects of Islam, Sunni and Shia. In addition, most Senegalese Muslims belong to one of three Islamic brotherhoods, with 57% belonging to the Tidjaniya, 26% to the Muridiya and 16% to the Qadiriya. These brotherhoods are not sepa-

rated by doctrinal differences, but share a common Sufi-type mystical approach to religious activity and emphasize various spiritual disciplines. They are organized hierarchically around some holy man, or marabout, who is said to possess baraka, or charismatic power, and they have considerable economic power through ownership of farms, transport and other enterprises. Membership in these brotherhoods requires little more than loyalty to its founder and his successors. The Tidjaniya is known to be tolerant, flexible and individualistic, while the Muridiya is rigid, disciplined and centralized. The Qadiriya is considered relatively staid and legalistic.

Christianity, introduced around 1845, is followed by only 5% of the population, mainly the Serer and the Diola, but Christians are found in almost every ethnic group. The European and Lebanese minorities are almost entirely Christian. Most Christians are Roman Catholics, who number 250,000 distributed among five dioceses. There are also a few thousand Protestants. Although outnumbered by Muslims in the general population, Christians are heavily represented in the government, commerce and education and occupy many important public positions.

Animists constitute about 10% of the population. Most of the smaller ethnic groups and, among the larger ethnic groups, the Serer and the Diola follow traditional religions. Common elements in indigenous religions include beliefs in intermediary spirits, sacrifices, witches, fertility rites and magic.

COLONIAL EXPERIENCE

Senegal's contacts with Europeans began with the Portuguese in the middle of the 15th Century. The French arrived in the 17th Century; Saint-Louis was established as a fortified trading post in 1659. French rule was largely confined to trading posts until its expansion under the Second Empire during the governorship of Gen. Louis Faidherbe. French control was consolidated and extended under the Third Republic. From 1871 on, Senegal regularly sent a deputy to the French parliament, and municipalities were established in Saint-Louis, Dakar, Goree and Rufisque. In 1895 Dakar became the administrative capital of the newly created Federation of French West Africa (Afrique Occidentale Francaise—AOF),

Senegal was the only French colony where the policy of assimilation was applied to a relatively large segment of the population; it was also the only African colony in which the French made a determined effort to educate the natives. In addition, the French also introduced social institutions that brought about fundamental changes in the Senegalese way of life.

Senegal's first tentative step toward self-government was the establishment in 1919 of a Colonial Council, part of whose membership was elected. In 1946 the franchise was extended, and a Territorial Assembly was set up. Universal suffrage was granted in 1957. In 1958 Senegal accepted the new French constitution and became an autonomous republic within the

French Community. From 1959 until 1960, Senegal was a member of the short-lived Mali Federation.

Among the French-speaking African states, Senegal is regarded as closest to France politically, militarily, and culturally. The strength of Franco-Senegalese links is partly attributable to the personality of former President Leopold-Sedar Senghor and his remarkable success in reconciling French values and institutions with his own concept of Negritude, which is in his terms a search for African identity.

CONSTITUTION & GOVERNMENT

The legal basis of the government of Senegal is the constitution of 1963, as amended subsequently, most recently in 1976. The constitution establishes a strong presidential form of government with a prime minister as head of government. Although the Parti Socialiste Senegalais (PSS), the country's sole legal party (until 1974), is not named in the constitution, Senegal is for all practical purposes a one-party state. The constitution provides explicit guarantees for a broad range of civil liberties and human freedoms.

The president is elected by universal direct suffrage for five years and is eligible for reelection to a second term. (This provision applied to President Senghor only for the 1978 election). Among the president's extraordinary powers are the proclamation of an emergency, during which he may rule by decree and submit draft laws to referendum, with the consent of the president of the National Assembly and of the Supreme Court. The president may not veto legislation, but he may ask the National Assembly to reconsider an act it has passed, in which case it must be passed again by a three-fifths majority before it becomes law. The Secretariat General attached to the presidency emerged during the years of presidential rule as a major organ of government. The Secretariat General includes the High Council of the Judiciary, the High Council for National Defense, the Inspectorate General and the Fiscal Control Office.

The post of prime minister was abolished in 1983. The Council of Ministers comprises ministers and state secretaries. Each minster is assisted by a personal cabinet of five civil servants. The ministries are divided into departments or services and these into divisions or bureaus.

Suffrage is universal for all adults. Elections are usually uncontested.

During the first 18 years as an independent nation, Senegal suffered less from internal violence and insurgency than the majority of African nations. There is no record of inter-ethnic conflicts. A solitary attempt to unseat President Senghor, by Prime Minister Mamadou Dia in 1962, was soon halted. There have been displays of opposition by students, but these were sporadic and unorganized. A number of factors have helped to create Senegalese stability. The first was the personal influence and standing of President Senghor among both peasants and the urban classes. The second is the uninterest among educated Senegalese in political participation. The third is the stabilizing influence of the Islamic brotherhoods, with their basically conservative orientation. The last is the acceptance of the one-party state in Senegalese political thought. Political opposition simply does not perform any useful function, according to Senghor. In 1981 Senghor became the first West African head of state to step down voluntarily when he yielded the presidency to former Prime Minister Abdou Diouf.

CABINET LIST (1985)

President	Abdou Diouf
Minister of State for Foreign Affairs	Ibrahima Fall
Minister of Armed Forces	Médoune Fall
Minister of Civil Sevice, Employment & Labor	André Sonko
Minister of Commerce	Abdourahmane Touré
Minister of Culture	Abdel Kader Fall
Minister of Economy & Finance	Mamadou Touré
Minister of Emigration	*Mrs.* Fambaye Fall Diop
Minister of Environment	Cheikh A. Khadre Cissoko
Minister of Equipment	Robert Sagna
Minister of Housing & Urban Affairs	Hamidou Sakho
Minister of Industrial Development & Crafts	Serigne Lamine Diop
Minister of Information, Telecommunications & Relations with Parliament	Djibo Laity Ka
Minister of Interior	Ibrahima Wone
Minister of Justice, Guardian of the Seals	Doudou N'Doye
Minister of National Education	Iba Der Thiam
Minister of Plan & Cooperation	Cheikh Amidou Kane
Minister of Public Health	Thierno Ba
Minister of Rural Development	Bator Diop
Minister of Scientific & Technical Research	Moussa Daffe
Minister of Social Development	*Mrs.* Maimouna Kane
Minister of Tourism	Momar Talla Cisse
Minister of Universities	Iba Der Thiam
Minister of Water Resources	Samba Yella Diop
Minister of Youth & Sports	Landing Sane
Minister Without Portfolio in Prime Minister's Office	*Mrs.* Caroline Diop
Secretary of State for Decentralization	Moussa N'Doye
Secretary of State for Employment	Alioune N'Diaye
Secretary of State for Rural Development & Fisheries	Bocar Dialla
Secretary of State for Technical & Professional Training	*Mrs.* Marie Sarr M'Bodj

FREEDOM & HUMAN RIGHTS

In terms of civil and political rights, Senegal is classified as a partly free country, with a rating of 4 in political rights and 4 in civil rights (on a descending scale in which 1 is the highest and 7 the lowest in rights).

Senegal is a model African state for human rights practices although theoretically it is only a partial democracy. Partly because of President Senghor's

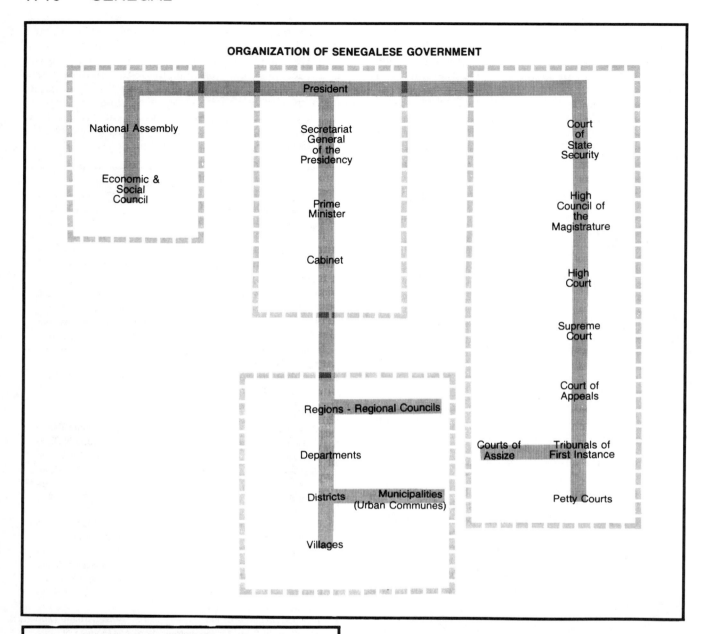

ORGANIZATION OF SENEGALESE GOVERNMENT

President

National Assembly

Economic & Social Council

Secretariat General of the Presidency

Prime Minister

Cabinet

Court of State Security

High Council of the Magistrature

High Court

Supreme Court

Court of Appeals

Regions - Regional Councils

Departments

Districts   Municipalities (Urban Communes)

Villages

Courts of Assize   Tribunals of First Instance

Petty Courts

SENEGAMBIA, CONFEDERATION OF

(On 1 February 1982 the Confederation of Senegambia came into existence, two months after the agreement was signed by the heads of state of Senegal and the Gambia. The treaty calls for the integration of the security services, the armed forces, and the economic and monetary systems of both countries. The presidents of Senegal and the Gambia serve as president and vice president respectively of Senegambia. The cabinets of Senegal and the Gambia continue to function.)

President . . . . Abdou Diouf
Vice President . . . . *Sir* Dawda Kairaba Jawara
Minister of Defense (Senegal) . . . . Médoune Fall
Minister of Economic
  Affairs (Gambia) . . . . Abdoulie Alieu N'Jie
Minister of Finance (Gambia) . . . . . . Sheriff Saikula Sisay
Minister of Foreign Affairs (Senegal) . . . . . . .Ibrahima Fall
Minister of Information (Senegal) . . . . .Djibo Laity Ka
Minister of Security (Senegal) . . . . Ibrahima Wone
Minister of Transportation (Senegal) . . . . . . Robert Sagna
Deputy Minister of Foreign Affairs
  (Gambia) . . . . Lamin Kiti Jabang
Deputy Minister of Security (Gambia) . . . . Alieu Badji

guiding hand and intellectual stature, and partly because of strong Francophone influences, Senegal has not been subjected to the ordeals of dictatorship as many of its sister republics in Africa have been. It has at the same time achieved a record of political stability unequalled at least in West Africa. Constitutional freedoms not only exist on paper but are respected in practice. A lively press flourishes even while it attacks government programs and policies. In the National Assembly, the opposition is vehement and courageous. The judiciary has demonstrated its independence by overturning government decrees. In openly contested local elections, opposition is able to unseat government candidates. The income tax structure is progressive and does not favor the entrenched rich and privileged. There is no discrimination based on race, ethnic origin or religion and the fact that a member of a minority community, Leopold Senghor, was able to rule Muslim-dominated Senegal for 20 years is a testimony to the religious tolerance that prevails in the country. In 1979 the National Assembly passed a series of constitutional measures permitting a minority of legislators to challenge the constitutionality of laws before the Supreme Court. The major political limitation is that which puts a ceiling of four on the number of political parties and also defines their ideological orientation. Even this restriction is being currently challenged. The status of women, while unsatisfactory by Western standards, is among the best in Africa. Senegal is one of the few countries with a full-fledged Ministry for Women's Affairs. The smooth transfer of power from Senghor to Diouf in 1981 demonstrated the political maturity of the Sengalese and offered an example to their troubled neighbors. Further, Senegal has taken an active role in human rights in Africa. In 1979 Senghor submitted a proposal for the creation of a human rights commission as part of OAU. Africa's first Institute for Human Rights Education began work in Dakar in 1979 and Sengalese lawyers are trying to establish an All-African Bar Association.

CIVIL SERVICE

The civil service is regulated by the Supreme Council of the Public Service. It is divided into two major groups: functionaries with permanent tenure and agents, mostly contractual or temporary employees. The growth of the civil service has been modest, increasing from about 30,000 at the time of independence in 1960 to around 40,000 in the mid-1970s. Almost 42% of civil servants are concentrated in the capital region. All civil servants are required to be Senegalese citizens (although exceptions are made in positions requiring specialized technical competence), and to reach the highest ranks they must be graduates of the National School of Administration. All civil servants are appointed by the president. They have the right to organize and strike within certain limits and also to hold elective office.

LOCAL GOVERNMENT

For purposes of local government the country is divided into four levels of units — regions, departments, arrondissements (or districts) and villages, with parallel units, municipalities, in urban areas. Cap Vert region containing the capital district is considered as a separate unit.

The seven regions are (with their capitals in parentheses): Cap Vert (Dakar), Diourbel (Diourbel), Thies (Thies), Casamance (Ziguinchor), Senegal Oriental (Tambacounda), Fleuve (Saint-Louis) and Sine-Saloum (Kaolack). Each region is headed by a governor, assisted by two deputy governors, one for administration and the other for coordination of economic development. The regions are subdivided into 27 departments, each headed by a prefect. Almost all ad-

ministrative activities take place at the departmental level or lower. The prefect is also responsible for maintaining law and order and has plenary police powers. Departments are divided into 95 arrondissements or districts, each headed by a chief or subprefect. Like the prefect, the subprefect has investigative and police powers. Each arrondissement is made up of from 100 to 600 villages under the nominal authority of a village chief.

Municipalities, properly called urban communes, number 34 and have separate administrative structures. Dakar has a special status as both a region and a municipality. Cap Vert region and the Dakar urban commune are divided into six arrondissements, each of which has its own council and mayor. The six arrondissement councils together constitute the Greater Dakar Council with an elected mayor.

Representative institutions exist in only rudimentary form at the local level. The former regional assemblies were abolished in 1972 and replaced by purely advisory regional councils. Similar councils function in the newly created rural communes. Two-thirds of the rural council members are chosen by popular election. The municipal councils are elected by universal suffrage for six-year terms. They consist of between 13 and 37 members, depending on the population represented. These councils have no police or financial powers.

FOREIGN POLICY

Senegalese foreign policy bears the impress of the personal philosophy of President Leopold-Sedar Senghor, Senegal's only decision maker until 1981. Senghor's concepts blend his unique ideology of Negritude with his deep francophilism. Senghor's own Catholicism, a national aversion to extremism and pressures from the Islamic or Arabic bloc combine in the formulation of foreign policy.

Relations with France are so close that they can hardly be termed "foreign relations." The French presence includes nearly 30,000 Frenchmen, 1,500 French troops and numerous technical missions. Under the Accord on Cooperation in Matters of Defense, France is permitted to use the naval base and airfields at Dakar. A number of Frenchmen remain in positions of leadership in government.

Next to France, ties are closest with Gambia, to which Senegal is bound by geography and common ethnic traditions as well as the formal Senegambian Federation established in 1982. The Confederation was based on the following principles: The Confederation shall be based on the integration of the armed and security forces of the Gambia and Senegal; economic and monetary union; co-ordination of policy in the fields of external relations and communications, and in all other fields where the confederal state may agree to exercise joint jurisdiction. The institutions shall be the president and the vice president of the Confederation; the confederal Council of Ministers; and the confederal Assembly. The president of Senegal shall be president of the Confederation; the president of the Gambia shall be vice president of the Confederation. Each of the confederal states shall maintain its independence and sovereignty. The official languages are to be the African languages chosen by the confederal president and vice president, along with English and French; the confederal president is to be in charge of the armed and security forces of the Confederation, the Gambian president remaining commander-in-chief of the Gambian armed forces. The confederal Assembly consists of 60 members, of whom one-third are chosen by the Gambian House of Representatives and two-thirds by the Senegalese National Assembly. The Assembly meets twice a year.

President Senghor had long been committed to a federation of West African states, especially those that share French language and culture. He was in the forefront of efforts to form a semi-political association of the francophone states of the world. He has also been instrumental in the creation of a West African Economic Community and the Organization for the Development of the Senegal River. There is some rivalry with the Ivory Coast for leadership of former French West African states. But both President Felix Houphouet-Boigny of the Ivory Coast and Senghor share a deep commitment to French values and have muted their rivalries for the sake of larger interests. A treaty between the two countries was signed in 1971. Relations with Guinea, however, were strained for a long time and were further aggravated by President Sekou-Toure's charges that Senegal was backing anti-Toure plots. The independence of Guinea-Bissau has relieved much of the tension that existed when the territory was under Portuguese control.

Because of the dominance of France in foreign relations, Senegalese relations with the United States have been limited. In accordance with the general framework of non-alignment, Senegal has relations with the Soviet Union and China, but those with the former are strained. Senghor took a strong stand against Soviet and Cuban interference in African affairs in 1978.

Senegal has stong religious ties to the Arab world, especially with Morocco, where the mother lodge of the Tidjaniya Brotherhood, to which the majority of Senegalese Muslims belong, is maintained. These links proved strong enough to cause Senghor to sever relations with Israel in 1973.

The major event in Sengalese foreign affairs in the late 1970s was the Summit of Reconciliation at Monrovia, Libera, in 1978 that ended five years of friction with both Guinea and the Ivory Coast. Following the meeting, a Guinean-Sengalese Cooperation was established and President Sekou Toure of Guinea visited Dakar in 1979.

Senegal and the United States are parties to seven treaties and agreements covering agricultural commodities, Peace Corps, Investment Guaranties, defense, aviation, and economic and technical cooperation.

Senegal joined the U.N. in 1960, and its share of the U.N. budget is 0.02%. It is a member of 16 U.N. organizations and 27 other international organizations, including the OAU and OCAM.

U.S. Ambassador in Dakar: Lannon Walker
U.K. Ambassador in Dakar: Peter O'Keefe
Senegalese Ambassador in Washington, D.C.: Falilou Kane
Senegalese Ambassador in London: Ousmane Camara

PARLIAMENT

The National Assembly is a unicameral body consisting of 120 members elected for five-year terms by direct universal suffrage; following the 1983 elections 111 seats are held by the Parti Socialiste Senegalais, eight by the Parti Democratique Senegalais, and one by Rassemblement National Democratique.

The Assembly holds two regular sessions a year. The budget is debated in the first session. No ordinary session lasts longer than two months. Legislation may be initiated either by the president or by the National Assembly. Draft legislation is reviewed by standing committees and there is an executive committee known as the Bureau, headed by the president of the Assembly. Both bills introduced by members (called propositions de loi) and bills introduced by the executive (called projets de loi) are referred to standing committees before being debated on the floor. Technically, bills introduced by the government may be defeated, but they rarely are. There are nine standing committees, such as foreign affairs and defense. The president of the republic is required to sign into law or return to the Assembly all bills within two weeks of receiving them. In the latter case the Assembly is required to re-open the debate, and a three-fifths majority of the full membership is required for passage a second time. Certain types of laws, called organic laws, dealing with the judiciary, elections and similar subjects require the vote of an absolute majority for passage and can only be passed after the Supreme Court, at the request of the president has declared them to be in conformity with the constitution. The legislative powers of the Assembly may be delegated to the president or suspended only during states of siege, states of emergency or when the independence and territorial integrity of the nation are threatened.

The constitution also provides for an Economic and Social Council, an advisory body of 45 members, sitting for six-year terms. Of these members, nine are nominated by labor unions, 18 by professional bodies, nine by rural economic interests and nine by the president. The Council holds two sessions a year, but a permanent bureau functions under the chairman.

POLITICAL PARTIES

The ruling party, the Parti Socialiste Senegalais (PSS), formerly the Union Progressiste Senegalais (UPS), has been continuously in power since independence in 1960. PSS is a moderate Francophile party founded by President Senghor in 1949. From 1963 to 1974 it was the only legal party in the country. It was formed through a series of coalitions by which opposition parties were absorbed rather than proscribed.

At various times PSS espoused forms of socialism, but the emphasis was always on organization rather than ideology. As a mass-based party, PSS operates down to the village level and represents a fusion of powerful religious and tribal interests. The core of PSS strength is in the regions of Thies, Diourbel and Kaolack, among the small farmers and the Muridiya Brotherhood. At the base are 2,500 village or neighborhood committees representing occupational, ethnic and other groups. These committees elect 400 subsections which in turn form sections at the geographic departmental level. There are seven regional unions at the regional level. At the apex is the National Council, consisting of ministers, deputies, members of the Youth Movement and delegates from the departments. The total strength of the National Council is about 300. The Council elects the Executive Bureau, consisting of 38 members, including four delegates from the Youth Movement. The party national congress is held every two years. The election of party officials at all levels is strictly controlled by the national leadership.

In 1974 the government freed all political prisoners and permitted the first legal opposition in the country in 11 years, the Parti Democratique Senegalais (PDS). With an estimated 100,000 members, it is described by its secretary general, Abdoulaye Wade, as a left-wing party, although it is required by the constitution to be right-wing. In 1976 a constitutional amendment authorized the formation of three political parties, each espousing a specific ideology: rightwing, centrist and Marxist. PSS assumed the role of the centrist, or democratic socialist, party; PDS was assigned the rightwing, or liberal democratic role; and Parti Africain de l'Independance (PAI) the role of the leftwing Marxist party. A conservative party, the Senegalese Republican Movement, was added in 1977.

The process of political liberalization under President Diouf culminated in the removal of all restrictions on party activities. As a result, nine more parties entered the political scene. These are:

- The Independence and Labor Party, a pro-Moscow Communist Party.
- Senegalese People's Party, with no clear-cut ideology but with some ties to the Casamance separatists.
- Revolutionary Movement for the New Democracy, a populist party of the extreme left that includes socialists and Maoists.
- Union for People's Democracy, a pro-Albanian Marxist group.
- People's Democratic Movement, led by former prime minister and Senghor opponent, Mamadou Dia.
- Democratic League-Labor Party Movement, a Marxist group affiliated to the Teachers' Union.
- National Democratic Rally, self-described as a "party of the masses." It gained one seat in the 1983 election.
- Party for the Liberation of the People, a splinter group that broke away from the New Democratic Rally in 1983.
- African Party for the Independence of the People, a Marxist-Leninist group.

ECONOMY

Senegal is one of the 39 lower middle-income countries of the world; it is also one of the 45 countries designated by the U.N. as Most Seriously Affected by recent adverse economic conditions. It has a free-market economy in which the dominant sector is private.

The Sengalese economy has not yet recovered from the disastrous drought of 1977. During the next year, the GDP dropped nearly 20%, the balance of payments deficit reached a record low, forcing the government to design a three-year austerity program. industrial production was off in almost every sector and unemployment continued at a high rate. In 1979 the GDP rebounded by over 10% although the balance of payments deficits persisted.

PRINCIPAL ECONOMIC INDICATORS

Gross National Product: $2.730 billion (1983)
  GNP Annual Growth Rate: 2.0% (1973-82)
  Per Capita GNP: $440 (1983)
  Per Capita GNP Annual Growth Rate: –0.7% (1973-82)

Gross Domestic Product: CFAF 977.7 billion (1983)
  GDP at 1980 prices: CFAF640.8 billion (1981)
  GDP Deflator (1980=100): 104.5
  GDP Annual Growth Rate: 2.6% (1973-83)
  Per Capita GDP: CFAF 154,700 (1984)
  Per Capita GDP Annual Growth Rate: –0.7% (1970-81)

Income Distribution: 3.2% of the national income is received by bottom 20%; 36.8% of the national income is received by top 5%.

Percentage of Population in Absolute Poverty: 36

Consumer Price Index (1970=100):
  All Items: 460.7 (May 1985)
  Food: 456.8 (December 1984)

Average Annual Rate of Inflation: 8.9% (1973-83)

Money Supply: CFAF 186 billion (March 1985)
  Reserve Money: CFAF 87 billion (March 1985)

Currency in Circulation: CFAF 77.53 billion (1984)

International Reserves: $3.7 million, of which foreign exchange reserves were $2.6 million (1984)

Centralized development planning was introduced by France soon after World War II. These plans were designed to promote the development of French West Africa as a single integrated unit in relation to the

BALANCE OF PAYMENTS (1982) (million $)	
Current Account Balance	−399.5
Merchandise Exports	458.0
Merchandise Imports	−857.6
Trade Balance	−399.6
Other Goods, Services & Income	—
Other Goods, Services & Income	—
Other Goods, Services & Income Net	—
Private Unrequited Transfers	—
Official Unrequited Transfers	—
Direct Investment	—
Portfolio Investment	—
Other Long-term Capital	—
Other Short-term Capital	—
Net Errors & Omissions	358.7
Counterpart Items	7.3
Exceptional Financing	—
Liabilities Constituting Foreign Authorities Reserves	—
Total Change in Reserves	33.5

needs of the French economy. The two development plans (1947-53, 1954-59) invested CFAF 25.8 billion in Senegal, representing one-third of French investment in all seven French West African colonies. After independence, the planning momentum was continued through a series of four-year development plans (1961-64, 1965/66-1968/69, 1969/70, 1972/73, 1973-77). The fourth plan (1973-77) projected an overall investment target of CFAF 181 billion; its official objective was to attain an overall annual growth rate of 5.7%. Of the total investment CFAF 40 billion was allotted to agriculture, CFAF 27 billion to industry, CFAF 21 billion to tourism and CFAF 11 billion to water supplies. Three-fourths of the financing came from foreign sources.

The 1977-81 Fifth Five-Year Plan projected a capital spending of CFAF410 billion, which was later cut to CFAF390 billion as part of an austerity program. The Sixth Development Plan (1981-85) envisaged that the annual growth rate in GDP would not exceed 4% (compared with 3% in 1980). The plan was revised in 1983, with total proposed investment increased from CFAF464,000 million to CFAF667,000 million. A Seventh Five-Year Plan was lauched in July 1985.

GROSS DOMESTIC PRODUCT BY ECONOMIC ACTIVITY (1970-81)		
	%	Rate of Change %
Agriculture	24.6	2.6
Mining	—	—
Manufacturing	18.5	3.2
Construction	5.0	7.4
Electricity, Gas & Water	—	—
Transport & Communications	6.7	−1.0
Trade & Finance	22.8	−1.8
Public Administration & Defense	12.9	6.0
Other Branches	9.5	1.6

Foreign aid is the most important source of development financing. France remains the largest single donor, but aid has also been forthcoming from West

SIXTH DEVELOPMENT PLAN, 1981-85 (proposed expenditure in million CFAF)	
Investment	
Primary	106,652
Agriculture	55,169
Livestock	10,977
Fisheries	11,414
Forestry and nature conservancy	10,665
Rural water supply	10,703
Irrigation	7,724
Secondary	151,851
Energy	25,044
Industry and mining	123,562
Crafts	3,245
Tertiary	99,281
Trade	2,000
Tourism	12,396
Transport and telecommunications	84,885
Quaternary	89,620
Urban development	700
Housing	16,000
Urban water supply and sanitation	14,973
Health and social welfare	7,715
Education	22,449
Reform schools	451
Human development	6,800
Culture	406
Youth and sports	3,000
Information	1,626
Study and research	10,000
Administrative facilities	5,500
Total for national projects	447,404
Total for local projects	16,443
Grand Total	463,847

Germany, the EEC, the United States and Arab countries.

FOREIGN ECONOMIC ASSISTANCE TO SENEGAL		
Sources	Period	Amount (million $)
United States Loans	1946-83	1.6
United States Grants	1946-83	221.5
International Organizations	1946-83	780.3
(Of which World Bank)	1946-83	158.9
All Sources	1979-81	323.7

Per capita aid received during 1979-81 was $56.80.

BUDGET

The Senegalese fiscal year runs from July 1 to June 30. Because Senegal has a meager tax base and many elements of government expenditures are not susceptible to government restraints, the use of public finance as an instrument of economic or social policy is limited. In general, the government has followed a conservative fiscal policy, financing development partly from surplus revenues. It also relies heavily on indirect taxes and income from state monopolies in agricultural marketing.

NATIONAL BUDGET

1980/81 budget: balanced at CFAF193,092 million.

1981/82 budget: balanced at CFAF220,169 million (recurrent budget CFAF125,493 million, capital budget CFAF55,602 million, special treasury expenses CFAF39,074 million).

1982/83: budget balanced at CFAF230,200 million (investment budget CFAF23,000 million).

1983/84: draft budget balanced at CFAF273,984 million (investment budget CFAF20,000 million).

1984/85: draft budget balanced at CFAF301,875 million.

Of current central government revenues, 22.8% comes from taxes on income, profit and capital gain, 3.5% from social security contributions, 25.8% from domestic taxes on goods and services, 35.0% from taxes on international trade and transactions, 5.3% from other taxes and 7.4% from non-tax revenues. Current revenues represent 20.1% of GNP. Of current expenditures, 9.1% goes to defense, 15.8% to education, 3.6% to health, 7.0% to housing and social security, 20.4% to economic services and 44.1% to other functions. Total expenditures represent 30.9% of GNP and overall deficit 9.8% of GNP.

In 1983 government consumption was CFAF 185.8 billion and private consumption CFAF 764.5 billion. During 1973-83 public consumption grew by 6.6% and private consumption by 3.3%.

In 1983 total outstanding disbursed external debt was $1.504 billion of which $1.496 billion was publicly guaranteed. Of the publicly guaranteed debt, $1.182 billion was owed to official creditors and $313.6 million was owed to private creditors. The debt service was $47.5 million of which $16.7 million was repayment of principal and $30.9 million was interest. Total external debt represented 61.2% of GNP and total debt service 1.9% of GNP.

Agreement to reschedule part of Senegal's debt was reached with the Paris Club of creditors in January 1985, following the announcement of an 18-month IMF stand-by arrangement worth SDR 76.6 million. The 1983/84 economic and financial program, supported by the IMF, succeeded in reducing the country's fiscal deficit to 4.7% of GDP, compared with 8.2% of GDP in 1982/83. As part of the program, austerity measures were imposed, which included a reduction in state subsidies on imported staple foods, increased import taxation, and a restriction on wage increases. Further increases in the price of basic commodities, including petrol and rice, were implemented in 1984, in response to IMF pressure. An austerity plan, launched in 1984, aimed to reduce the external current account deficit to around 9.2% of GDP in 1984/85, and to 6.9% of GDP in 1985/86. State intervention in the agricultural sector was to be reduced as part of the government's plan, and in January 1985 two state agricultural agencies were dissolved.

FINANCE

The Senegalese unit of currency is the CFA (Communaute Financiere Africaine) franc, divided into 100 centimes. Coins are issued in denominations of 1, 2, 5, 10, 25, 50 and 100 francs; notes are issued in denominations of 50, 100, 500, 1,000 and 5,000 francs. In 1985 the dollar exchange rate of CFA franc was $1= CFAF424.980. On this basis, the sterling exchange rate was £1=CFAF 558.5.

The central bank and bank of issue is the Banque Centrale des Etats de l'Afrique de l'Ouest, the common central bank for all six African states that use the CFAF as their unit of currency—Benin, Ivory Coast, Senegal, Niger, Togo and Burkina. The bank is headquartered in Dakar.

The commercial banking system consists of six banks, including the Senegal Kuwait Bank and the International Bank for West Africa. The largest source of development finance is the National Bank of Development. In 1984 the commercial banking sector had reserves of CFAF 24.19 billion, demand deposits of CFAF 109.58 billion and time deposits of CFAF 95.47 billion. In 1984 the ruling rate of interest was 10.50%.

GROWTH PROFILE Annual Growth Rates (%)	
Population 1980-2000	2.9
Birthrate 1965-83	1.7
Deathrate 1965-83	−19.2
Urban Population 1973-83	3.8
Labor Force 1980-2000	2.6
GNP 1973-82	2.0
GNP per capita 1973-82	−0.7
GDP 1973-83	2.6
GDP per capita 1970-81	−0.7
Consumer Prices 1970-81	10.7
Wholesale Prices	—
Inflation 1973-83	8.9
Agriculture 1973-83	0.3
Manufacturing 1970-81	3.2
Industry 1973-83	6.1
Services 1973-83	2.2
Mining	—
Construction 1970-81	7.4
Electricity	—
Transportation 1970-81	−1.0
Trade 1970-81	−1.8
Public Administration & Defense 1970-81	6.0
Export Price Index 1975-81	5.0
Import Price Index 1975-81	13.9
Terms of Trade 1975-81	−7.8
Exports 1973-83	−0.9
Imports 1973-83	−1.2
Public Consumption 1973-83	6.6
Private Consumption 1973-83	3.3
Gross Domestic Investment 1973-83	−0.7
Energy Consumption 1973-83	−2.8
Energy Production	—

AGRICULTURE

Of the total land area of 19,716,100 hectares (48,718,236 acres), nearly 57% is agricultural land, or 2.83 hectares (7 acres) per capita. Based on 1974-76=100, the index of agricultural production in 1982 was 86, the index of food production 87 and the index of per capita food production 71. Agriculture employs 77% of the labor force, generates 21% of the

GDP and contributes 50% to export earnings. Its annual growth rate during 1973-83 was 0.3%. The value added in agriculture in 1983 was $702 million.

Although the area under cultivation has been progressively extended, it still accounts for only 15% of the total land area. Most of the cultivated land is the so-called Groundnut Basin or Triangle, extending from between Saint-Louis and Louga in the north to Kaolack in the sourth and including the regions of Thies, Diourbel and Sine-Saloum. As a result of excessive concentration on the groundnut crop, soil fertility in these regions has been depleted. Furthermore, because of recurrent failures of rainfall, average crop yields are low.

Each Senegalese tribe has its own system of cultivation and agricultural techniques. In general, most of them follow the shifting cultivation and slash-and-burn agriculture found in every African country south of the Sahara. The main features of this form of cultivation are burning of the vegetation, the use of wood ash as fertilizer and long fallow periods. The Wolof and the Serer specialize in rain-fed cultivation in the plains, while the Diola and the Toucouleur are river valley cultivators. The Serer particularly use relatively advanced agricultural means and techniques, such as animal manure, crop rotation and arrangement of plots in a checkerboard fashion around the village, with fields of cassava, cotton and vegetables alternating with millet, groundnuts and fallow fields. The Wolof practice a more traditional form of slash-and-burn, with longer years of fallow and less rotation of crops and application of manure. The Diola practice one of the most intensive systems of river valley rice cultivation in tropical Africa. They grow different strains of rice under both the river flood irrigation and dry land slash-and-burn method. The Diola use animal manure, nursery seedbeds for growing rice seedlings and an intricate system of irrigation, employing dikes with hollowed logs. Among the Toucouleur, who practice a less intensive form of cultivation, farms are divided into dieri (rain-fed) and oualo (river-flooded). The latter lands are cultivated during the dry season and the former during the rainy season. Fertilizer consumption is relatively common among all classes of farmers. During 1981/82, 24,300 tons of fertilizer were used, or 3.5 kg (7.7 lb) per hectare. On the other hand, mechanization has made little headway. In 1982 there were only 470 tractors and 145 harvester-threshers in the country.

Senegal's land tenure systems reflect both the country's ethnic diversity and successive migrations. The tenure systems of the dominant Wolof and Serer resemble those of feudal Europe, under which eminent domain vests with royal lineages, chiefs and nobles who may grant and distribute land. Although some rights may be acquired by virtue of occupation, they may not be sold or disposed of. In many cases an annual tribute is due to an Islamic leader or local noble in the form of crop, cash or labor. As a result, a minority of former noble families control the bulk of the farmland in the older settlements. In the newer settlements these inequalities persist in different forms as wealthy marabouts and capitalists with financial backing have appropriated large tracts of land. The average farm size among the Wolof is between 1 and 4 hectares (2½ and 10 acres); over 35% of the holdings are between 4 and 10 hectares (10 and 25 acres).

The Diola adhere to the communal tenure prevalent among most non-Muslim tribes in Africa. Under this system individual members of a tribe make use of the land and enjoy rights of inheritance, but land may not be sold. The inalienability of tribal land protects farmers from being deprived of their land by creditors or new settlers and also fosters communal cohesiveness.

During the colonial period the French made numerous attempts to modify tenure systems and to introduce registration of titles. Since independence the government has worked to eliminate feudal rights such as tribute, develop of pioneer zones of planned resettlements, expropriate idle and insufficiently developed lands and grant ownership to tenants. Because there are no large foreign-owned plantations in Senegal, nationalization has not been a major issue.

Senegalese agriculture has not yet recovered from the catastrophic drought period beginning in 1966 when droughts of increasing severity occurred every other year until 1972. The cumulative effect of these years proved particularly disastrous in 1972 when the rains nearly failed, and the Senegal River reached a high water mark of only 4.8 meters (16 ft) instead of its usual 9.1 meters (30 ft) in flood season. As the water table fell, the wells and streams dried up, the natural vegetation cover withered and the national herd was virtually wiped out by thirst and starvation. The drought affected nearly 85% to 90% of the population, with some areas in Thies and Diourbel reporting losses of up to 100%. The resulting exodus to the towns placed the country's scanty resources under further strain until short-term relief supplies arrived from international agencies. Efforts, under the auspices of the Organization for the Development of the Senegal River, are being made to conserve existing water resources and prevent a similar calamity in the future. The 1983 Sahel drought severely affected agricultural production in Senegal and the government launched an urgent appeal for international food aid to help to alleviate the shortfall in cereal needs, estimated at 300,000 tons. In 1983 591,000 tons of cereals were imported.

Because of the nation's dependence on agriculture, the government is engaged in constant efforts to improve productivity. Proclaimed by president Senghor "the priority of priorities," agriculture and livestock projects received CFAF 55.169 billion in investment under the 1981-85 development plan. Primary goals are to diversify productionto reduce dependency on grounduts, develop irrigation systems to stabilize production, and eventually to attain self-sufficiency in foodgrains. Agricultural projects include the Groundnut-Millet Productivity Project, the Terres Neuves Resettlement Pilot Project, the Casamance Agricultural Development Project, the Delta Rice Project, the Cotton Project, the Sine-Saloum Project and the Louga-Kebemer Agricultural Development Project. The government is also involved in research and marketing through 2,153 cooperatives. The former National Cooperation and Development Assistance Office (Office Nationale de Cooperation et d'Assistance pour le Developpement, ONCAD) which had a monopoly over the marketing of peanuts, millet and sorghum, was abolished by President Diouf.

A scheme to develop the Senegal River basin (in a joint project with Mali and Mauritania) was begun in 1981. The scheme aims to control seasonal flooding and to irrigate 375,000 hectares (962,625 acres) of land, of which 240,000 hectares (593,090 acres) are in Senegal. The project includes construction of the Diarra dam, near St-Louis, which was scheduled for completion in 1985, and will allow 120,000 hectares (296,520 acres) of land to be irrigated.

The major cash crop is peanuts, grown in 45% of the cultivated area. Senegal ranks fifth in the world in peanut production and first in export of peanut oil. Peanut production generated 14% of the GDP, 35% of export earnings and 66% of the money income of the rural population. The other major cash crop is cotton, produced and marketed under the direction of Compagnie Francaise pour le Developpement des Fibres Textiles, a company of mixed private and government ownership, but backed by French expertise and finance. The prices of both cotton and peanuts are fixed by the government. The chief food crops are millet and sorghum, followed by cassava, rice and maize. Millet and sorghum are drought-resistant crops, suited to the country's low rainfall and poor soil conditions.

PRINCIPAL CROP PRODUCTION (1982) (000 metric tons)	
Rice	100
Corn	55
Millet & Sorghum	600
Potatoes	6
Sweet potatoes	8
Cassava	28
Pulses	30
Groundnuts	700
Cottonseed	21
Cotton (lint)	8
Palm kernels	6.2
Tomatoes	25
Dry onions	32
Other vegetables	40
Mangoes	33
Oranges	20
Bananas	6
Other fruit	23
Coconuts	4
Sugar cane	60

The national herd was almost entirely wiped out in 1972, The livestock population in 1982 consisted of 2,300,000 cattle, 2,100,000 sheep, 1,050,000 goats, 150,000 pigs, 220,000 horses, 240,000 asses, 6,000 camels and 9,000,000 chickens. Livestock raising is concentrated in the northern third of the country, along the Senegal River Valley and among the Fulani, who derive their livelihood almost entirely from herding. The prevalence of tsetse fly limits cattle raising in the south. Because of the low productivity rate and the low numbers slaughtered, the country relies heavily on imports of live animals and meat. Senegal has 809,400 hectares (2 million acres) of forest lands, mainly in the Casamance. Exploitation is regulated by the government. In 1982 roundwood removals totaled 3.806 million cubic meters (134 million cubic ft). A national reafforestation campaign was begun in 1984, and aims to reverse the desertification process by replanting 140,000 hectares (345,940 acres) per year for the next 25 years.

The country's abundant fish resources sustain a flourishing fishing industry, divided into a traditional fleet of dugout canoes and an industrial fleet with modern boats and trawlers. There are nearly 30,000 fishermen and 32 fishery cooperatives in the traditional sector. The industrial fleet consists of five sardine boats, 48 tuna boats and 92 trawlers. Only 33 of these boats fly the national flag, and 87 are owned by the French. The annual catch in 1982 was 212,900 tons. Exports in 1982 were worth $158.881 million, mostly in tuna exported to France, and shrimp and sole exported to the United States and Japan. National consumption of fish is high for an African country and is estimated at between 34 and 41 kg (75 and 90 lb) per year. In 1972 Senegal extended its fishing limits to 177 km (110 mi) off its coast. An industrial fisheries complex, with an annual capacity of 36,000 metric tons, has been constructed in Casamance, and began production in 1982.

Agricultural credit is provided by the National Bank of Development.

INDUSTRY

Senegal is one of the most industrialized nations of former French West Africa, and its industry is heavily export-oriented. Manufacturing employs 10% of the labor force and generates 18% of the GDP in 1980, but its growth rate was seriously depressed as a result of the drought conditions of 1968-1973, 1977-78 and 1983/84. Despite these setbacks industrial growth rate was a respectable 3.2% during 1973-83. Based on 1975=100, the index of industrial production was 115 in 1982.

Manufacturing is concentrated around Dakar, which accounted for 80% of gross output in this activity. Another 8% was accounted for by Sine-Saloum, 6% by Thies, 3.4% by Casamance, 1.8% by Diourbel, 1.4% by Fleuve and 0.9% by Senegal Oriental. The largest subsector is food processing and beverages (39%) followed by textiles (22%) and chemicals (13%). The value added in manufacturing in 1983 was $443 million and the output per capita $65.

The Investment Code of 1962 (as amended in 1965 and 1972) encourages private foreign investment and provides guidelines to investors. Special incentives in the form of tax holidays are available to encourage firms in export-oriented industry and, in a move to encourage decentralization, for enterprises locating outside the Dakar region. A revision of the investment code in 1978 extended these incentives to include small enterprises. In addition, Senegal has established an industrial free zone designed to attract foreign investment in export industries. American investment in Senegal is approximately $24 million.

With the aim of attracting foreign companies and providing employment, an industrial free zone was established near Dakar, but with limited success. Foreign firms operating there are free of taxes, duties and bureaucratic controls. A new bonus system was introduced in 1981, in an attempt to stimulate investment.

The Senegalese government is a shareholder in over 140 companies. This represented an initial investment of nearly $100 million concentrated in banking, industry, tourism, utilities and agriculture. Annual government contributions to mixed companies in forms of loans and subsidies have run about $50 million in recent years. The government has undertaken a program, with World Bank assistance, to streamline the para-public system, which has proved to be a serious drain on government resources. One encouraging step in this direction was taken in 1978 with a decision by the cabinet to suspend government participation in newly created enterprises. Over the past year, one of the largest state enterprises underwent an extensive audit by an American auditing firm, and plans call for the entire sector to adopt modern management techniques. Private French investment in the country is substantial and is estimated at CFAF 24.3 billion.

ENERGY

In 1982 Senegal produced no energy but consumed 1.169 million metric tons of coal equivalent, or 194 kg (427 lb) per capita. The annual growth rate during 1973-83 was −2.8% for energy consumption. Energy imports account for 58% of all merchandise imports. Apparent per capita consumption of gasoline is 26 gallons per year. The petroleum refinery capacity is 18,000 barrels per day.

In 1984 production of electric power was 725 million kwh, or 110 kwh per capita.

LABOR

The economically active population was estimated in 1980 at 2.068 million, of which 41% were women. By occupational sectors, 76% were employed in agriculture (including fishing and livestock raising), 10% in manufacturing, and 14% in services. Wage earners numbered 175,000, including 105,000 in government service and 70,000 in private employment. The unemployment rate is estimated at 20% to 30%.

A major issue is Senegalization, to which the government is firmly committed. Although the proportion of foreign employees is only 7% in industry and 10% in commerce, more than three-fourths of the technical and managerial positions are occupied by Europeans who enjoy high salary scales. Non-Africans make up only 4% of the country's total wage earning labor force, but account for 34% of the wage bill. There is therefore considerable pressure on private employers to hire, train and promote Africans. Potential foreign investors are required to make written commitments to hire African personnel where possible and to train other Africans where qualified Senegalese are not available. An estimated 20,000 Senegalese are working in France, mostly in menial occupations.

Wages and working conditions are governed by the Labor Code of 1952. The workweek is 40 hours, except in the case of unskilled agricultural workers for whom the annual maximum is 2,400 hours. The code also provides for paid annual leave and child allowances. While there are industry-wide statutes on the minimum age for employment of children, the economic situation in Senegal has created an environment wherein a substantial number of underage workers are employed, particularly in cottage industry. Through collective bargaining, principally by the National Confederation of Senegalese Workers, there are legal guidelines for occupational safety and health, minimum wages and limits on working hours.

The official labor union affiliated to the PSS is Confederation Nationale des Travailleurs Senegalais (CNTS). Other labor federations include the Union of Confederated Trade Unions and the National Confederation of Christian Workers. No information is available on the incidence of strikes in the country.

FOREIGN COMMERCE

The foreign commerce of Senegal consisted in 1984 of imports of $1.111 billion and exports of $586.93 million, leaving an unfavorable trade balance of $524.35 million. Of the imports, food, beverages and tobacco accounted for 22.7%, machinery and transport equipment for 21.8%, basic manufactures for 14.9%, crude petroleum for 12.8% and chemicals for 9.5%. Of the exports, peanuts accounted for 24.8%, fish for 21.5%, phosphates for 13.8%, basic manufactures for 9.7%, chemicals for 6.1% and peanut oil for 6.0%. The major import sources are: France 36.8%, the United States 5.7%, West Germany 4.0%, the Ivory Coast 4.0% and Algeria 3.7%. The major export destinations are: France 24.9%, the Ivory Coast 8.2%, Mali 7.5%, Mauritania 7.4% and the United Kingdom 6.0%.

Based on 1975=100, the import price index in 1981 was 199, the export price index was 135 and the terms of trade (export prices divided by import prices × 100) 68.0.

Senegal is a member of the West African Economic Community (Communaute Economique de l'Afrique de l'Ouest). An annual international trade fair is held at Dakar.

FOREIGN TRADE INDICATORS (1984)

Annual Growth Rate, Imports:	–1.2 (1973-83)
Annual Growth Rate, Exports:	–0.9 (1973-83)
Ratio of Exports to Imports:	34:66
Exports per capita:	$88
Imports per capita:	$166
Balance of Trade:	–$524.35 million
Ratio of International Reserves to Imports (in months)	—
Exports as % of GDP:	33.6
Imports as % of GDP:	45.2
Value of Manufactured Exports:	$110 million
Commodity Concentration:	20.8%

Direction of Trade (%)

	Imports	Exports
EEC	51.9	35.9
U.S.	5.7	6.0
Industrialized Market Economies	59.9	53.1
East European Economies	—	—
High Income Oil Exporters	—	—
Developing Economies	36.4	22.6

Composition of Trade (%)

	Imports	Exports
Food	28.3	33.2
Agricultural Raw Materials	0.9	2.7
Fuels	19.0	24.4
Ores & Minerals	3.6	16.5
Manufactured Goods	47.7	23.2
of which Chemicals	9.5	6.1
of which Machinery	22.4	5.2

TRANSPORTATION & COMMUNICATIONS

The state-owned railroad operates 1,034 km (643 mi) of track. The main lines run from Dakar to Kidira on the Mali border and from Dakar to Saint-Louis. There are also branch lines from Guinguineo to Kaolack, Louga to Linguere, and Diourbel to Touba. Rail traffic in 1982 consisted of 133 million passenger-km and 309 million net-ton-km.

Senegal has three navigable rivers. The Senegal, navigable for three months in the year as far as Kayes in Mali, for six months as far as Kaedi in Mauritania and all year as far as Rosso and Podor, is closed to foreign ships. The Saloum is navigable by ocean-going ships to the peanut port of Kaolack. The Casamance is navigable up to Ziguinchor. The total navigable length of these rivers is 1,505 km (935 mi).

Dakar is one of the major seaports in Africa and a port of call for freight and passenger ships between the North and South Atlantic and Indian Ocean ports. The port can accommodate supertankers and ships with drafts of up to 10 meters (33 ft). Secondary ports include Saint-Louis and the river ports of Kaolack and Ziguinchor. In 1982 these ports handled 3.570 million tons of cargo.

The length of the road system is 13,898 km (8,630 mi), of which 3,461 km (2,149 mi) are paved. The roads are poorly maintained except in the heavily populated northwest. In 1982 there were 50,875 passenger cars and 27,767 commercial vehicles. Per capita passenger car ownership was 7.5 per 1,000 inhabitants.

The national airline is SONATRA-Air Senegal, in which 50% interest is owned by the Senegal government and 40% interest is held by Air Afrique, in which Senegal has a 7% share. With three DC-3s and seven light planes, SONATRA-Air Senegal serves all domestic routes, while Air Afrique serves international air routes. In 1982 the former flew 3.0 million km (1.8 million mi) and carried 121,000 passengers. Dakar's Yoff International Airport can handle jumbo jets. There are 25 other airfields of which 22 are usable and 10 have permanent-surface runways.

In 1984 there were 40,200 telephones in the country, or 0.8 per 100 inhabitants.

In 1982 the postal service handled 12,961,000 pieces of mail, and 225,000 telegrams. Per capita volume of mail was 1.9 pieces. There are 737 telex subscriber lines.

In 1982, 216,000 tourist arrivals were reported in the country. Of these 8,300 were from the United States, 3,200 from the United Kingdom, 9,100 from Switzerland, 85,800 from France, 2,200 from Canada, 17,900 from West Germany, 9,800 from Italy and 7,100 from Belgium. Tourist revenues in 1982 totaled $62 million and expenditures by nationals abroad $42 million. There are 9,000 hotel beds and the average length of stay was 4.5 days.

MINING

The principal mineral resource is phosphate, production of which in 1982 was 1.792 million tons. Senegal exploits deposits of lime phosphate and aluminium phosphate, both near Thiès, and the government has a 50% share in each of the two operations. A chemical complex, built by Industries Chimiques du Sénégal, was opened in 1984, comprising a phosphatic fertilizer plant at Mbao and two factories for the production of sulphuric and phosphoric acids at Darou Khoudou. The complex processes phosphates mined at Thaiba, and has an annual capacity of 580,000 tons of sulphuric acid and 220,000 tons of phosphoric acid. Further phosphate deposits, estimated at 40 million tons, were discovered in 1984 at Matam in north-east Senegal. There are plans to exploit the extensive deposits of iron ore at Falémé, and work on a new rail link to Tambacounda and a port at Bargny is scheduled to begin in 1987. Proven reserves total 371 million tons, and production is expected to begin in 1990 with proposed annual output of 6 million tons of ore.

DEFENSE

The defense structure is headed by the president as the commander in chief of the armed forces. He is assisted by a Supreme Defense Council whose other members include the secretary general of the office of the president, the prime minister, the minister of state for the armed forces, the chief of staff of the armed forces, and ministers of foreign affairs, interior and finance.

Military manpower is obtained through voluntary enlistment. Although a conscript service period of two years is provided for by law, in practice it has not been implemented.

The total strength of the armed forces is 9,700, or 2.9 armed persons for every 1,000 civilians.

ARMY:
Personnel: 8,500

Organization: 4 military zone HQ; 5 infantry battalions; 1 engineer battalion; 1 training battalion; 1 presidential guard; 1 reconnaissance squadron; 1 artillery group; 1 AA artillery group; 2 parachute companies; 3 construction companies

Equipment: 71 armored vehicles; 65 armored personnel carriers; 12 howitzers; 16 mortars; 21 guns; rocket launchers; antitank guided weapons

NAVY:
Personnel: 700

Units: 8 patrol craft; 3 amphibious craft

Naval Base: Dakar

AIR FORCE:
Personnel: 500

Organization: 2 combat aircraft; 2 maritime reconnaissance and search and rescue planes; 1 transport squadron; 6 trainers; 4 helicopters

Air Bases: Yoff (Dakar); Saint-Louis, Tambacounda, Ziguinchor, Thies and Kedougou

The annual military budget in 1985/86 totaled $59.932 billion, representing 9.1% of the national budget, 2.3% of the GNP, $9 per capita, $6,100 per soldier and $311 per sq km of national territory.

During World War II Senegalese troops earned a reputation as fierce and dependable fighters. They have not seen action since independence, but most of the officer corps has been thoroughly trained in tactics and strategy by French advisers. Arms purchases abroad during 1973-83 totaled $85 million.

Under the Accord on Cooperation in Matters of Defense, France is accorded base rights and transit and overflight privileges, while Senegal receives military training and equipment grants. Dakar is the headquarters for French Zone d'Outre-Mer 1, and a permanent French garrison of 1,500 men remains there, guarding the airfield and certain key installations. This force is said to be ready for deployment anywhere in Africa. It is also available to assist the government in maintaining internal security. The naval units of this force are two coastal escorts; the Air Force units have six transports.

EDUCATION

The national literacy rate is 47.7% (60.4% for males and 32.3% for females).

Education is free, universal and compulsory for five years between the ages of 6 and 12. The national school enrollment ratios are 48% at the first level (6 to 11) and 12% at the second level (12 to 18), for a combined enrollment ratio of 30%. Girls constitute 40% of the primary enrollment, 34% of secondary enrollment and 19% of postsecondary enrollment.

Schooling lasts for 13 years, divided into six years of elementary education, four years of middle school and three years of upper secondary school. Middle school is called the short cycle (enseignement court), while the full secondary course is called the long cycle (enseignement long). Grading is based on a 20-point system, with 10 as the passing score. Students completing the secondary course receive the baccalaureat. The curriculum is based on the French model with African elements added.

The school year runs from October to June. The language of instruction is French, but secondary students are required to learn either English or Arabic as a second language. Elementary school teachers are trained at normal schools, secondary teachers at the Higher Teacher Training School.

The teacher-pupil ratio is 1:43 at the primary level, 1:24 at the secondary level and 1:13 at the postsecondary level. There are two types of vocational training schools. The first, called training centers (centres de formation), offer a three-year program leading to a certificate and the second, called technical agents schools (ecoles d'agents techniques), offer a four-year program leading to a diploma. Shorter programs are offered by the National Center of Professional Courses. Nearly 10% of secondary school goers are enrolled in the vocational stream. The Ministry of Popular Education offers a number of adult education programs through regional centers as well as through radio and television. Private schools account for 12% of primary and 22% for secondary enrollment.

The educational system is administered by four government departments, the Ministry of National Education, the Ministry of Technical Education and Vocational Training, the Ministry of Popular Education and the Ministry of Youth and Sports. In 1980 the current educational budget was CFAF 27,485,411,000. This amount represented 23.5% of the national budget, 4.4% of the GNP (compared to a UNESCO recommendation of 4%) and $22 per capita.

EDUCATIONAL ENROLLMENT (1982)			
	Schools	Teachers	Pupils
Primary	1,795	10,586	452,079
Secondary	N.A.	4,384	103,821
Vocational	N.A.	N.A.	10,820
Post secondary	N.A.	925	12,522

Higher education is provided by the University of Dakar and the university of St-Louis with an enrollment of 12,522 students in 1982. Per capita enrollment is 554 per 100,000 inhabitants. A second national university was established recently at Saint-Louis, with France meeting half the cost. The University of

Dakar witnessed considerable student unrest during the early 1970s.

In 1981, 2,666 students graduated from the University of Dakar. By fields of study, 114 received degrees in medicine, 372 in education, 142 in natural sciences, 610 in social sciences, 389 in law and 73 in agriculture.

In 1982, 2,906 Senegalese students were enrolled in institutions of higher learning abroad. Of these, 110 were in the United States, 2,188 in France, 45 in West Germany, 12 in the United Kingdom, 88 in Belgium, 65 in Ivory Coast and 83 in Morocco. In the same year, 2,880 foreign students were enrolled in Senegal.

LEGAL SYSTEM

The legal system is based on French civil law. Senegal has an active, independent, and well-trained judiciary, which is constitutionally independent of the executive, the legislature and the military. Court officials are trained lawyers who have completed a number of years of required apprenticeship. Trials are open to the public, and defendants have the right to a defense counsel, many of whom are very skilled and aggressive in the protection of their clients. Ordinary courts hold hearings which are presided over by a panel of judges and, in the case of criminal charges, include a jury. There are three categories of courts: the High Court of Justice, the security ("political") court and the military courts. There are four superior courts: the High Council of the Magistrature, which determines the constitutionality of civil laws and international agreements, a 16-member High Court of Justice elected by the National Assembly from among its own members, a Supreme Court and a Court of State Security.

The full bench of the Supreme Court consists of the chief justice, three presiding justices (for the three sections of the court: civil and criminal; jurisdictional; and auditing of state financial transactions), six associate justices, known as conseillers. Ten civil servants, known as auditeurs, assist in preparing and hearing cases. The High Court of Justice has only one function—the trial of high government officials for treason or malfeasance.

Below the Supreme Court there are three levels of courts: the Court of Appeal; tribunals of first instance located in each of the regional capitals and four courts of assize trying major criminal offenses; and petty courts in each department and district presided over by justices of the peace.

There are 26 prisons scattered throughout the country with an annual prison population of over 6,000.

LAW ENFORCEMENT

There are two law enforcement agencies: the 1,600-man National Gendarmerie, controlled by the minister of state for armed forces, and the National Police Force (Surete Nationale, SN), controlled by the minister of interior.

The National Gendarmerie is essentially a rural police force, but it is also used for guarding the presidential palace, government buildings, airports, harbors and key border points. Its members are generally well trained and skilled in anti-insurgency and anti-riot techniques. Units of the Gendarmerie, known as Legions, are stationed in each of the country's seven administrative regions. Legions are divided into smaller units called brigades.

The 3,600-man National Police Force is essentially an urban police force, generally concerned with traffic duties, enforcement of crime and vice laws and protection of the railroads. The force includes three mobile companies. Per capita strength of law enforcement agencies is one policeman for every 769 inhabitants.

Dakar and Cap Vert Region account for half of all crimes committed in the country. A detailed breakdown of crimes is not available.

HEALTH

In 1977 there were 44 hospitals in the country with 7,092 beds, or one bed per 760 inhabitants. In 1981 there were 449 physicians in the country, or one physician per 13,000 inhabitants, 70 dentists and 1,766 nursing personnel. Per 10,000 inhabitants the admissions/discharge rate was 324; the bed occupancy rate was 77.2% and the average length of stay was 10 days.

PRINCIPAL HEALTH INDICATORS (1984)
Crude Death Rate: 21.2 per 1,000
Decline in Death Rate: −19.2 (1965-83)
Infant Mortality Rate: 152.6 per 1,000 Live Births
Child Death Rate (Ages 1-4) per 1,000: 28
Life Expectancy at Birth: 41.7 (Males); 44.9 (Females)

The major health problems are malaria, tuberculosis, schistosomiasis, gastroenteric infections, encephalomyelitis, hepatitis, venereal infections, tetanus and leprosy. Health expenditures in 1982 represented 5.9% of the national budget, and $4.20 per capita. Only 37% of the population have access to safe water.

FOOD

Millet is the traditional dietary staple, but it is being increasingly supplanted by rice. Supplementary items of diet include corn, sorghum, potatoes, cassava (manioc) and peanuts. Consumption of fish is high, but meat and dairy products are used in limited quantities. One feature of Senegalese food habits is the recurring period of near-famine, known as soudure, during the pre-harvest season.

Daily per capita intake of food is 2,389 calories, 71.4 grams of protein, 53 grams of fats and 363 grams of carbohydrates.

MEDIA & CULTURE

One daily newspaper *Le Solieil* owned by the PSS—is published in Dakar with a circulation of 40,000, or six per 1,000 inhabitants. *Le Democrat* is a new monthly published by the opposition PDS. However, major French dailies, such as *Le Monde, Le Figaro* and *France-Soir* are available in Dakar on the day of publication. The 22 periodicals and non-daily general interest newspapers include four weeklies. Annual consumption of newsprint in 1982 was 5,000 tons, or 860 kg (1,896 lb) per 1,000 inhabitants.

Senegal enjoys freedom of speech and press in theory and in practice. The constitution guarantees the right of each person to express and disseminate opinions freely. There are several regularly published newspapers and magazines and a number of publications which appear sporadically, reflecting a broad range of opinion from conservative to Marxist. The country's most professional and informative newspaper is controlled by, and supports, the majority Socialist Party. However, articles critical of government policies and officials regularly appear even in this newspaper.

In August 1985, the editor of an opposition publication was arrested and charged with defamation of the chief of state and the government after his magazine published an article accusing members of the president's family and entourage of corruption. Opposition leaders described this as an attempt to muzzle the media. Other publications, representing other viewpoints, are sometimes vociferously critical of the government.

An independent press has failed to evolve in Senegal because of the historical circumstances of PSS ascendancy. However, even PSS owned newspapers are less timid than similar African newspapers when it comes to commenting on official policies and programs. Senegal ranks 74th in the world in press freedom with a rating of –1.98 (on a scale in which +4 is the highest and –4 is the lowest).

The national news agencies are Agence de Presse Senegalais (APS), and Pan-African News Agency. Foreign agencies represented in Dakar include AFP, Reuters, UPI, AP, Tass, Novosti, ANSA and DPA.

There are 12 book publishing houses, all located in Dakar producing 64 titles in 1982. In 1972 Senegal, Ivory Coast and French publishing interests combined to found an imprint called Les Nouvelles Editions Africaines. The University of Dakar's Institut Fondamental d'Afrique Noire is also active.

The Office de Radiodiffusion-Television du Senegal (ORTS) operates both radio and television broadcasting as an autonomous public body. ORTS' two medium-wave transmitters and five short-wave transmitters in Dakar are on the air for 18 hours a day in French. There are four regional stations, at Saint-Louis, Tambacounda, Kaolack (each with one medium-wave transmitter) and Ziguinchor (with two short-wave transmitters), each of which is on the air for eight to nine hours daily in six vernaculars: Wolof, Toucouleur, Sarakole, Serere, Diola, and Manding. Of the 7,616 annual radio broadcasting hours, 2,208 hours are devoted to information, 442 hours to education, 286 hours to culture, 702 hours to religion, 520 hours to commercials, and 2,678 hours to entertainment. In 1982 there were 370,000 radio receivers in the country, or 62 per 1,000 inhabitants.

Television, introduced in 1965, discontinued in 1969, and resumed in 1972, operates for only 3½ hours daily. There are two transmitters, at Dakar and Thies. Of the 1,602 annual television broadcasting hours, 455 hours are devoted to information, 391 hours to education, 143 hours to culture, 12 hours to religion, and 463 hours to entertainment. In 1982 there were 5,000 television sets in the country, or 0.8 per 1,000 inhabitants.

Senegal is the fourth major producer of full-length feature films in Africa and has noted film producers and directors. A state-owned film company oversees the import and production of films. In 1976, 248 films were imported, 96 films from the United States. In 1980 there were 60 fixed cinemas in the country with 33,500 seats, or 7.8 per 1,000 inhabitants. Annual movie attendance was 3.6 million, or 0.7 per capita.

The largest library in the country is at the University of Dakar, with 185,000 volumes. The Archives of Senegal has a valuable collection of 16,000 volumes on Senegalese history.

There are four museums in the country reporting an annual attendance of 55,000. There are 16 nature preservation sites.

SOCIAL WELFARE

There is no official social security program. The government offers certain benefits to wage earners, such as grants at the birth of each of their first three children and family allowances for each child under 14 years of age.

GLOSSARY

auditeur: a civil servant attached to the Supreme Court to assist in preparing and hearing cases.

conseiller: an associate justice of the Supreme Court

dieri: rain-fed land suitable for peanut cultivation.

marabout: a teacher of the Koran or a leader of one of the Islamic brotherhoods.

Negritude: literally, blackness. Ideology developed by President Leopold Senghor defining African culture in universal terms.

projet de loi: a bill introduced in the National Assembly by the executive

proposition de loi: a bill introduced in the National Assembly by a private member.

oualo: river-flooded land suitable for rice cultivation.

soudure: chronic near-famine prevailing in rural areas during the pre-harvest season.

CHRONOLOGY (from 1960)

1960— Senegal withdraws from the Mali Federation and declares its independence. . . . Leopold Senghor is elected president and Mamadou Dia prime minister.

1962— Dia leads abortive coup against Senghor; with the help of the army Senghor arrests Dia; office of prime minister is abolished.

1963— New constitution is promulgated.

1968— Senghor declares emergency in the wake of student riots.

1970— Electorate approves new constitutional amendment by overwhelming vote; Abdou Diouf is named to the recreated post of prime minister.

1973— Catastrophic drought strikes Sahel. . . . Senegal breaks diplomatic relations with Guinea and Israel. . . . Senegalization of employment is adopted as official policy.

1974— Parti Democratique Senegalais is formed as the first legal opposition since 1964.

1975— All political prisoners are released under a general amnesty; three political parties are authorized, representing the right, center and left, respectively.

1978— Leopold Senghor is reelected president with 82% of the national vote; opposition Parti Democratique Senegalais gains 17 seats out of 100 in the National Assembly. . . . President Senghor attends the summit of Reconciliation at Monrovia with Guinea and Liberia.

1981— President Sanghor steps down and names Prime Minister Abdou Diouf as his successor. . . . On the request of President Sir Dawda Jawara of Gambia, Senegal sends its troops to Bathurst to quell a military coup. . . Gambia and Senegal agree on a Confederation of the two states, known as Senegambia, with a common president, military forces and monetary institutions. . . . In major cabinet reshuffle, Diouf drops two cabinet ministers: Adrien Senghor, the ex-president's nephew, and Louis Alexandrenne, the powerful planning minister.

1983— The Senegambia Federation comes into effect. . . . In his first presidential election, Diouf wins an easy victory and carries his Socialist Party to a dominant position in the National Assembly with 111 out of 120 seats. . . . Prime Minister Habib Thiam is demoted to president of National Assembly and is later forced to vacate that post as well.

1984— Casamance separatists battle police claiming 24 lives in one of the most violent civil disturbances in the country's history.

BIBLIOGRAPHY (from 1970)

Bachmann, Heinz B., *Senegal: Tradition, Diversification, & Economic Development* (Baltimore, Md., 1974).

Behrman, Lucy C., *Muslim Brotherhood and Politics in Senegal* (Cambridge, Mass., 1970).

Colvin, Lucie G., *Historical Dictionary of Senegal* (Metuchen, N.J., 1981).

Crowder, Michael, *Senegal: A Study in French Assimilation Policy* (New York, 1967).

Cruise O'Brion, Rita, *White Society in Black Africa: The French of Senegal* (Evanston, Ill., 1972).

——, *The Political Economy of Underdevelopment: Dependence in Senegal* (Beverly Hills, Calif., 1979).

Gellar, Sheldon, *Senegal* (Boulder, Col., 1981).

Johnson, G. Wesley, *Emergence of Black Politics in Senegal* (Stanford, Calif., 1971).

Markovitz, Irving Leonard, *Leopold-Sedar Senghor and the Politics of Negritude* (New York, 1969).

M'Bengue, Mamdou S., *Cultural Policy in Senegal* (Paris, 1974).

Middleton, Toni, *Senegal: France in West Africa* (London, 1975).

PUDOC, *Two Studies in Ethnic Group Relations in Africa* (New York, 1978).

Remy, Mylene, *Senegal Today* (New York, 1974).

Samb, M. *Spotlight on Senegal* (Dakar, 1972).

Schumacher, Edward J., *Politics, Bureaucracy, and Rural Development in Senegal* (Berkeley, Calif., 1975).

Skurnik, W.A., *The Foreign Policy of Senegal* (Evanston, Ill., 1972).

Venema, L.B., *The Wolof of Saloum: Social Structure and Rural Development in Senegal* (New York, 1978).

OFFICIAL PUBLICATIONS

Public Establishments Center, *Bilan et comptes d'exploitation de chaque unite* (balance sheet and operating account of each unit), *Centre des Etablissements Publics* (annual).

Treasury, *Balance Definitive Mensuelle* (Final Monthly Balance.

——, *Budget General* (annual).

——, *Depenses Budgetaires* (Budgetary Expenditures),, Centre Comptable A. Peytavin (A. Peytavin dAccounting Center) (monthly).

——, *Situation Commulee de l'Execution des Operations de Recette* (Cumulative Statement of Revenue Operations). Service Central de la Recette (Central Reserve Service) (monthly).

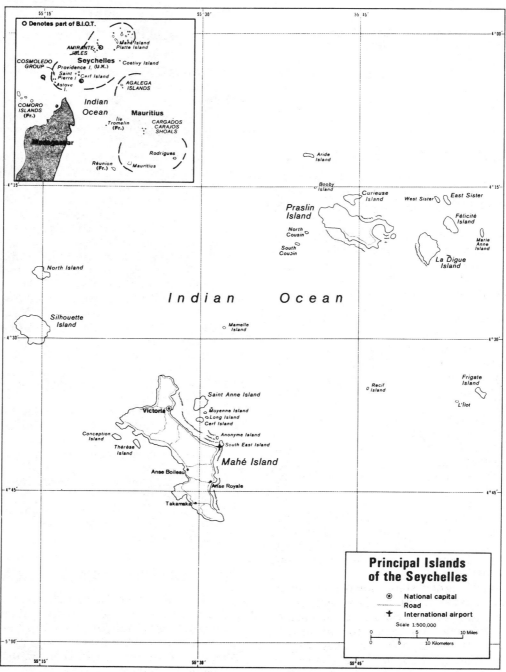

AMIRANTE ISLES

Mahé Island
Platte Island

COSMOLEDO GROUP
Seychelles (U.K.)
Providence I.
Coetivy Island
Saint Pierre I.
Cerf Island
Astove I.
AGALEGA ISLANDS

COMORO ISLANDS (Fr.)

Indian Ocean

Mauritius

Madagascar

Ile Tromelin (Fr.)

CARGADOS CARAJOS SHOALS

Rodrigues

Réunion (Fr.)
Mauritius

Aride Island

Booby Island

Curieuse Island

West Sister
East Sister

Praslin Island

Félicité Island

North Cousin

Marie Anne Island

South Cousin

La Digue Island

North Island

Indian   Ocean

Silhouette Island

Mamelle Island

Recif Island

Frigate Island

L'Îlot

Saint Anne Island

Moyenne Island
Long Island
Cerf Island

Victoria

Anonyme Island

Conception Island

South East Island

Thérèse Island

Mahé Island

Anse Boileau

Anse Royale

Takamaka

Principal Islands of the Seychelles

⊛   National capital
- - -   Road
✛   International airport

Scale 1:500,000

0   5   10 Miles
0   5   10 Kilometers

FINIS·CORONAT·OPUS

SEYCHELLES

BASIC FACT SHEET

OFFICIAL NAME: Republic of the Seychelles

ABBREVIATION: SE

CAPITAL: Victoria

HEAD OF STATE: President France Albert Rene (from 1977)

HEAD OF GOVERNMENT: (None formally designated after former Prime Minister France Albert Rene became president following a coup in 1977)

NATURE OF GOVERNMENT: Civilian dictatorship

POPULATION: 66,000 (1985)

AREA: 285 sq km (110 sq mi)

ETHNIC MAJORITY: Creole

LANGUAGES: English (official) and Creole

RELIGION: Christianity

UNIT OF CURRENCY: Seychelles Rupee ($1=SR7.010, August 1985)

NATIONAL FLAG: Four triangles demarcated by a thin white cross; the east-west triangles are red and the north-south triangles are blue

NATIONAL EMBLEM: A shield in which the principal element is the cinnamon tree with a ship and a mountain in the background and a giant tortoise in the foreground. The shield is flanked by two sharks.

NATIONAL ANTHEM: Lime National RepiblicSeychelles

NATIONAL HOLIDAYS: June 29 (National Day, Independence Day); January 1 and 2 (New Year's Days); May 1 (Labor Day); Christian festivals include Easter, Corpus Christi, Assumption, All Saints' Day, Immaculate Conception and Christmas.

NATIONAL CALENDAR: Gregorian

PHYSICAL QUALITY OF LIFE INDEX: 74 (On an ascending scale in which 100 is the maximum: U.S.A. 95)

DATE OF INDEPENDENCE: June 29, 1976

DATE OF CONSTITUTION: March 26, 1979

WEIGHTS & MEASURES: The metric system is in force

LOCATION & AREA

Seychelles consists of the Seychelles archipelago, a group of over 100 islands widely scattered in the western Indian Ocean, and a number of other island groups, the southernmost of which is 209 km (130 mi) north of Madagascar. Of these islands 83 have geographical names, and 46 are permanently inhabited. The total land area of the country is 285 sq km (110 sq mi). Mahe, the principal island, is located 1,600 km (1,000 mi) off the coast of Kenya and extends 27 km (17 mi) N to S and 11 km (7 mi) E to W, with a coastline of 127 km (79 mi). The length of the coastline of all the islands is 491 km (305 mi).

The capital and principal city is Victoria with a 1982 population of 57,000.

The Seychelles islands are generally divided into two groups, of which the granitic islands number 32 and the coralline islands over 60. The granitic islands rise above the sea, forming a peak or ridge, while the coralline islands are low-lying, rising only a few feet above the surface of the sea. Beside Mahe which, with a land area of 142 sq km (55 sq mi), accounts for half the national territory, the other islands form two principal groups: Praslin with La Digue, Felicite, East Silver, West Silver, Curieuse and Aride form the first group, while Silhouette and North Island form the second group. The most easterly island is Frigate, the most southerly is Platte, and the most northerly are Bird and Denis.

Most of Mahe is mountainous; in general the hills rise abruptly from the sea. The highest peaks are Morne Seychellois (912 meters; 2,993 ft) and Trois Freres (728 meters; 2,390 ft). Towering and rugged crests, cliffs and boulders contribute to the great natural beauty of the island. Many waterfalls descend from the heights to the white, sandy beaches, which are fronting flats of coral and shell known locally as plateaus. After Mahe, the three largest islands are Praslin, with a maximum elevation of 384 meters (1,260 ft); La Digue, with a maximum elevation of 358 meters (1,175 ft); and Silhouette, with a maximum elevation of 754 meters (2,473 ft). From Mahe to the outlying island farthest from the main group is 1,014 km (630 mi).

WEATHER

Although the Seychelles lies close to the equator, the climate is equable and healthy because of the maritime influence. The hot season lasts from October to April, and the cool season from May to September. Temperatures at sea level are fairly constant, about 26.6°C (80°F) throughout the year, and rarely exceed 29.4°C (85°F). At higher elevations, temperatures are proportionally lower, falling to 16°C (61°F) at night.

The south-east monsoon blows from May to October, the dry season, and the west-north-west monsoon from December to March, bringing with it frequent and heavy rains. The average rainfall on the coast is 228 cm (90 in.); it increases to about 304 cm (120 in.) at elevations of up to 183 meters (660 ft) and 381 cm (150 in.) at higher levels.

The Seychelles lies outside the cyclone belt; thus storms are rarely encountered.

POPULATION

The population of the Seychelles was estimated in 1985 at 66,000, on the basis of the last official census held in 1977 when the population was 61,898. The annual growth rate is 0.6%, on the basis of an annual birth rate of 25.8 per 1,000. The population is expected to reach 100,000 by 2020.

DEMOGRAPHIC INDICATORS	
Population 1985	66,000
Density per sq km	142.8
Sex distribution (%)	
Male	50.64
Female	49.36
Urban %	37.2
Age breakdown (%)	
0-14	37.1
15-29	30.0
30-44	13.1
45-64	13.4
Over 65	6.4
Population doubling time in years at current rate	37
Birthrate 1/1000	25.8
Death Rate 1/1000	7.0
%Births illegitimate	66.6
Natural increase 1/1000	18.8
Total fertility rate	3.4
Marriage rate 1/1000	4.8
Life expectancy at birth: years	
Male	64.6
Female	71.1
Annual Growth Rate 1980-83 (%)	0.6
Average household size	4.6

Nearly 80% of the Seychellois live on Mahe and another 18% on Praslin and La Digue. The coralline Seychelles are largely undeveloped and unpopulated. The overall density of population is 142.8 per sq km (370 per sq mi). The only town is the capital, Victoria, within whose environs live a quarter of the country's total population. In 1983 nearly 37.1% was under 14, whereas the corresponding percentage in 1960 was 39%. Those between 15 and 64 constituted 56.5% and those over 65, 6.4%. Since 1921, when an influenza epidemic selectively decimated the males, women have been in a numerical majority. But this imbalance has been progressively reversed until the 1980s when males were in the majority again.

Because of overpopulation, immigration is strictly controlled; work permits for aliens are issued for only a maximum of five years. Immigrants include retired British civil servants attracted by the islands' famed natural beauty. No reliable figures exist for emigrants, but emigration is generally encouraged as a solution to the population problem. It is believed that there are over 28,000 Seychellois in the United Kingdom and Australia.

Family planning services were introduced in 1965 but have made little headway because of the prevalent religious values.

Women enjoy high status in this essentially matriarchal society. Women have the same legal, political, economic and social rights as men. Although there are no women currently serving in the Council of Ministers, two women are serving as Central Committee members of the party. Many senior government officials, up to and including the rank of principal secretary, are women.

ETHNIC COMPOSITION

The Seychelles has a relatively homogeneous population, in which persons of mixed African and European origin, called Creoles, comprise the majority. There is a small white group claiming pure French ancestry, and there are more recent white arrivals, most of whom are retired British colonial administrators.

Alien minorities include Indians and Chinese, both of whom number only a few hundred. The Indians have resisted assimilation, but the Chinese have married freely with the Creoles.

LANGUAGES

The official language is English, but it is spoken by only a small minority. The mother tongue of 94% of the Seychellois is Creole, a picturesque language based on a simplified French syntax and enriched by many African loan words. There are five times more speakers of French than of English, and French is the language of the social elite. Many newspapers and magazines are published alternately in French and English.

RELIGIONS

Almost all native Seychellois are Christians, some 90% Roman Catholic and the remainder Protestant. Hinduism, Islam and Buddhism are practiced mainly by Asian immigrants, and each claims less than 200 adherents.

The cathedral of the Seychelles Catholic diocese is at Victoria on Mahe. Most of the Catholic clergy are still foreign. The church has considerable social influence and a virtual monopoly over education. Despite the Rene regime's Socialist bent, there is complete freedom of religion.

COLONIAL EXPERIENCE

The French first claimed the Seychelles (then uninhabited) in 1756 and named it after their finance minister, the Vicomte de Sechelles. Colonization began in 1768 when a party of 22 Frenchmen arrived with slaves. Between 1793 and 1813 the French and the British fought for the control of the islands and twice—in 1794 and 1804—the French were forced to yield. The islands were eventually ceded to Great Britain under the terms of the Treaty of Paris of 1814. Henceforth the islands were administered from Mauritius as a dependent colony. With the abolition of slavery in 1883, many of the French landowners departed, taking their slaves with them. This loss was offset by the arrival of thousands of liberated slaves as well as Indian and Chinese indentured laborers. In 1903 the islands became a British crown colony no longer subordinate to Mauritius. However, the British presence in the island never consisted of more than a handful of civil servants, and the Seychellois continued to remain more French than English in their culture.

The progress of Seychelles toward self government began in 1888 when a Legislative Council and an Executive Council were created. The first popular elections were held in 1948, universal adult suffrage was introduced in 1967, and a House Assembly, a cabinet and a prime minister were named in 1975. Independence was achieved in 1976 when Seychelles became a republic within the Commonwealth of Nations. At that time the United Kingdom transferred the islands of Aldabra, Farquhar and Desroches from its Indian Ocean Territory to the Seychelles. Control of the Chagos atoll of Diego Garcia, the site of a controversial U.S. base in the Indian Ocean, remains in the hands of the United Kingdom and the United States.

Relations between the United Kingdom and the Seychelles have remained untroubled by any major issues, except perhaps that of Diego Garcia.

CONSTITUTION & GOVERNMENT

The independence constitution of 1976 was abrogated in 1977 and a new constitution was promulgated by a constitutional council. Under its provisions, the president is elected by popular vote simultaneously with the elections for the National Assembly. The presidential term of office is five years and he may be elected for a maximum of three consecutive terms. All candidates standing for the National Assembly are required to be members of the Seychelles People's Progressive Front and elections are on a constituency basis.

Suffrage is universal. The island's first elections were held in 1979 when 55 candidates all belonging to the Seychelles People's Progressive Front contested 23 seats. Apparently 50% of the electorate of 35,000 voted in the elections. The second general elections were held in 1983. In 1984 President Rene was reelected by a reported 92.8% of the vote after a new or-

CABINET LIST (1985)	
President	France Albert René
Minister for Administration	France Albert René
Minister for Agriculture	France Albert René
Minister for Education & Information	James Michel
Minister for External Relations	France Albert René
Minister for Finance	France Albert René
Minister for Health	Esme Jumeau
Minister for Industry	France Albert René
Minister for Labor & Social Services	Joseph Belmont
Minister for Natl. Development	Jacques Hodoul
Minister for Tourism	France Albert René
Minister for Transportation	France Albert René
Minister for Youth & Defense	Ogilvie Berlouis

dinance under which those who failed to vote lost their right to public assistance.

Seychelles had its first military coup within its first year of independence, reflecting deep-seated instability within the political system. The coup was denounced by former President Mancham as Soviet-inspired, but there was no evidence of Soviet involvement, nor has there been any dramatic change in the domestic and foreign policies of the government.

The government has faced security threats in the past from its opponents living in Australia, the United Kingdom and South Africa. Government forces repulsed a group of mercenaries who attacked Seychelles in November 1981. An internal mutiny by some members of the armed forces in 1982 was also put down with the assistance of Tanzanian troops then in Seychelles. In 1984 all Tanzanian troops were removed by mutual agreement, but there are an estimated 100 North Korean military advisers stationed in Seychelles.

FREEDOM & HUMAN RIGHTS

In terms of political and civil rights, Seychelles was classified in 1980 as a not free nation (it was classified as free in 1977) with a rating of 6 in political rights and 6 in civil rights (on a descending scale in which 1 is the highest and 7 the lowest in rights).

The 1979 constitution does not include a bill of rights and there are no legal safeguards against arbitary executive actions. In practice, however, a considerable degree of freedom is enjoyed by the people. Even though a number of persons opposed to the Rene regime were incarcerated for different periods of time, there are no reports of torture or degrading and cruel treatment. Because Rene is constantly apprehensive of a possible counter-coup, he has expanded the government's authority to detain suspects without filing charges and to control the movements of designated individuals. The judiciary lacks the power to protect individuals against abuses by the state. Political prisoners are denied legal representation and were held without being formally arraigned or tried. Some who were arrested in 1979 were held

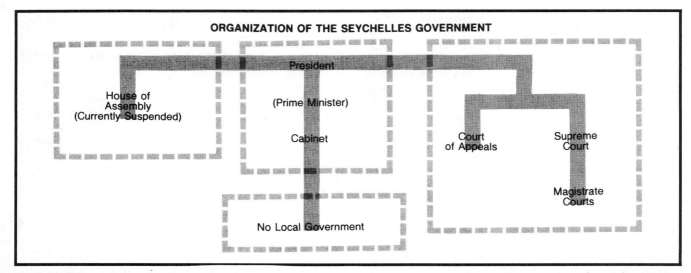

ORGANIZATION OF THE SEYCHELLES GOVERNMENT

President

House of Assembly (Currently Suspended)

(Prime Minister)

Cabinet

No Local Government

Court of Appeals

Supreme Court

Magistrate Courts

for seven to 13 months in jail and when released were asked to leave the country. Emergency powers permit detention without trial if the president signs a detention order. The police have broad powers of search, seizure and arrest without warrant. These powers, however, have been used very sparingly. Released political prisoners have complained of intimidating surveillance of their homes. For the Seychellois, anti-government statements can result in imprisonment. For expatriates, it would mean expulsion on a 24-hour notice without explanation. No organized opposition to the government is allowed. The SPPF controls the National Workers Union, the only labor union.

CIVIL SERVICE

No current information is available on the civil service in Seychelles.

LOCAL GOVERNMENT

Until 1968 there were district-level governments on the islands of Mahe, Praslin, La Digue and Silhouette. Local government was abolished in 1971, and the functions of the district councils were taken over by the national government.

FOREIGN POLICY

Seychelles was admitted to the Commonwealth and the U.N. in 1976. It is also a member of the Organization of African Unity (OAU) and the Common African and Mauritian Organization. The only issue in foreign affairs relates to the sovereignty over the Chagos Archipelago, including the Diego Garcia atoll on which the United States maintains a military and communications base. The Seychelles has expressed itself in favor of the Indian Ocean Zone of Peace concept. The United States maintains cordial relations with the Seychelles and, along with the United Kingdom, ex-

tended speedy recognition to the new government after the 1977 coup.

In 1979 President Rene imposed restrictions on foreign naval vessels visiting the islands, especially those carrying nuclear arms. In 1983 this restriction was quietly dropped after a substantial aid agreement was concluded with the United States. Relations with South Africa have been considerably strained since the Pretoria-backed coup attempt. Some 45 of the mercenaries in the invading force commandeered an Air India Boeing and flew to Durban where they surrendered to the South African police. Although formally tried, most were released after a modest four-week jail sentence.

In 1983 Seychelles agreed with Madagascar and Mauritius on the terms of a constitution for the Indian Ocean Commission which aims to increase cooperation in the region, particularly in the field of trade.
U.S. Ambassador in Victoria: Irwin Hicks
U.K. High Commissioner in Victoria: Colin Mays
Seychelles Ambassador in Washington, D.C.: Mrs. Giovinella Gonthier
Seychelles High Commissioner in London: Mrs. Danielle de St. Jorre

PARLIAMENT

The unicameral National Assembly consists of 23 elected members and two nominated members who represent small islands without fixed populations. The members are elected for four-year-terms. All members belong to the Seychelles People's Progressive Front.

POLITICAL PARTIES

Prior to 1977 there were two major political parties in the Seychelles: the Seychelles Democratic Party (SDP), a centrist party long opposed to independence, and the Seychelles People's United Party (SPUP), with an ill-defined leftist ideology, although it is closely identified with the Catholic clergy in its approach to social issues. With the fall of Mancham, the Democratic Party leader, the SDP has apparently been proscribed. In 1978 SPUP transformed itself into the Seychelles People's Progressive Front (SPPF). The constitution specifies that SPPF will be the sole legal political party in the country.

ECONOMY

Seychelles is one of the lower middle income countries of the world with a free-market economy, in which the dominant sector is private.

PRINCIPAL ECONOMIC INDICATORS

Gross National Product: $160 million (1983)
   GNP Annual Growth Rate: 5.1% (1973-82)
   Per Capita GNP: $2,400 (1983)
   Per Capita GNP Annual Growth Rate: 3.7% (1973-82)
Gross Domestic Product: SR993.4 million (1983)
   GDP Annual Growth Rate: Not available
   Per Capita GDP: SR15,522 (1983)
   Per Capita GDP Annual Growth Rate: Not available
Income Distribution: Not available
Consumer Price Index (1970=100):
   All items: 174.9 (May 1985)
   Food: 160 (May 1985)
Money Supply: R154 million (April 1985)
   Reserve Money: R87 million (April 1985)
Currency in Circulation: R69.9 million (1985)
International Reserves: $5.40 million, of which foreign exchange reserves were $5.38 million (1985)

BALANCE OF PAYMENTS (1983)
(million $)

Current Account Balance	−25.8
Merchandise Exports	5.1
Merchandise Imports	−74.5
Trade Balance	−69.4
Other Goods, Services & Income	+65.1
Other Goods, Services & Income	−32.9
Other Goods, Services & Income Net	—
Private Unrequited Transfers	−2.8
Official Unrequited Transfers	14.1
Direct Investment	4.4
Portfolio Investment	—
Other Long-term Capital	10.4
Other Short-term Capital	−0.4
Net Errors & Omissions	8.9
Counterpart Items	−0.6
Exceptional Financing	—
Liabilities Constituting Foreign Authorities' Reserves	—
Total Change in Reserves	3.1

The visible trade deficit is offset by earnings from tourism and by capital inflows in the form of aid and private investment. The U.S. pays annual rent of R12.7 million for land leased for its satellite tracking station in Seychelles.

Just before his ouster in 1977, President Mancham announced a five-year development plan, the fate of which after the coup is not known. In June 1978 the government announced a five-year development plan,

subject to annual revision: in 1982 total investment for 1982-86 was set at SR2,320 million, of which 19% was allocated to agriculture and fishing, 24% to infrastructural development, 21% to public utilities and 27% to social services and housing. A new five-year national development plan, launched in 1985, projected expenditure of US $380 million. The Development Bank of Seychelles was formed in 1978, and in 1983 it was reported that, since its foundation, the bank had invested some SR40 million in 985 ventures. Almost 40% of the loans had financed trade operations, 33% had been invested in tourism schemes, and 15% in fisheries development projects, with the remainder financing agricultural projects. The Seychelles National Investment Corporation was founded in 1979 as a holding company covering important sectors of the economy.

GROSS DOMESTIC PRODUCT BY ECONOMIC ACTIVITY (1982)

	%
Agriculture	5.7
Manufacturing	14.8
Construction	14.8
Tourism & Trade	11.3
Public Administration	19.5
Transport	36.3
Services & Finance	12.3
Other	—

At independence in 1976, the United Kingdom agreed to provide £10 million as capital aid for the first two years, budgetary aid of £1.7 million during 1976-79, as well as £750,000 annually until 1980 when the program ended. The Seychelles has also received $9.1 million from the United States as grants and loans. During 1979-81 the Seychelles received $21.8 million in aid from all sources, or $363.3 per capita.

BUDGET

The fiscal year of the Seychelles is the calendar year.

The 1982 national budget consisted of revenues of SR 384.3 million and expenditures of $410 million. Of the revenues 33.3% came from import duties, 27.0% from income taxes, 6.5% from excise duties, 5.7% from rents and royalties, 5.0% from turnover taxes and 3.8% from airport landing fees. Of the expenditures, 28.4% went to general administration (of which 11.8% went to defense, police and prisons), 19.2% to education and information, 10.1% to health, 9.3% to economic services and 6.5% to national youth services.

The total outstanding disbursed external debt in 1983 was $41.7 million of which $36.3 million was owed to official creditors and $5.4 million to private creditors. The total debt service was $2.7 million of which $1.5 million was repayment of principal and $1.2 million interest. Total external debt was 59.3% of export revenues and 27.9% of GNP. Total debt service was 3.9% of export revenues and 1.8% of GNP.

FINANCE

The Seychelles unit of currency is the Seychelles rupee, divided into 100 cents. Coins are issued in denominations of 1, 5, 25 and 50 cents and 1, 5 and 10 rupees; notes are issued in denominations of 5, 10, 20, 50 and 100 rupees.

The Seychelles rupee was tied to the pound sterling. After 1972 it floated in line with the sterling. Since 1979, it has been linked to the SDR (IMF Special Drawing Right). In 1981 it was revalued by 15% as part of a program to curb inflation. In August 1985, the dollar exchange rate was $1=SR7.010. The sterling exchange rate is pegged at £1=SR14.62/SR1= £0.0684.

On January 1, 1983 the Central Bank of Seychelles was established to take over the functions of the Seychelles Monetary Authority. There are three government-owned banking institutions: the Government Savings Bank, the Post Office Savings Bank and the Development Bank of Seychelles. The commercial banking system includes two British banks, Barclays and Standard and Chartered Banks. In 1984 commercial banks had reserves of R16.5 million, demand deposits of R55.1 million, and time and savings deposits of R187.9 million.

AGRICULTURE

Of the total land area of 28,500 hectares (70,423 acres), 4,000 hectares (9,884 acres) are under permanent crops, 1,000 hectares (2,471 acres) are arable, 5,000 hectares (12,355 acres) are covered by forests and 18,500 hectares (45,713 acres) are either wasteland or used for other purposes. Agriculture employs 10.3% of the labor force, contributes 5.7% to the GDP and 85% to the export earnings.

Although per capita farmland is only a low 0.06 hectare (0.1 acre) and although agricultural employment and contribution to the GDP are also relatively low, the Seychelles economy is still described as basically agricultural. The coralline islands are unsuitable for agriculture, but the remaining land is devoted primarily to export crops; staple foods, such as rice and cereals, are imported. In 1982, 32 tractors were in use.

New land is being opened on the outlying islands managed by the Islands Development Company. The Seychelles Agricultural Development Company manages four of the larger farms, while half of the small holdings are run by part-time farmers. The marketing of agricultural produce is handled by Seychelles Commodity Company. One of its subsidiaries, the National Agro Industries, operates a dairy products unit, a poultry unit and a vegetable and fruit canning unit. Nevertheless, food imports, especially of rice, continue to be a severe drain on the treasury. It con-

stituted 20% of total imports in 1981, 18% in 1982 and 16% in 1983.

The largest acreage is in coconuts, followed by cinnamon and vanilla. Tea is being developed as a secondary crop. The major food crops include breadfruit, cassava, yams, sweet potatoes and plantains.

PRINCIPAL CROP PRODUCTION (1982) (metric tons)	
Coconuts	29,000
Copra	2,176
Tea	−146
Bananas	1,000
Cinnamon bark	810

Small numbers of livestock are raised. In 1982 the number of livestock was estimated at 11,000 pigs, 2,000 cattle, 4,000 goats and 134,000 chickens. Of the forested area, only one-fourth is used for commercial timber exploitation. Agricultural credit is provided by the Agricultural Loans Board.

Seychelles has one of the highest per capita fish consumption rates in the world at 90 kg (198 lb), and fishing is emerging as one of the major revenue earners. In an attempt to diversify the economy away from tourism, the fishing industry is being modernized and expanded. In December 1978 the government unilaterally declared an economic zone extending for 200 nautical miles (370 km) around the islands to protect Seychelles' waters from unlicensed foreign fishing vessels. Studies on the zone's fisheries potential have been carried out by Norwegian and French companies, and in 1983 and 1984 the government signed separate agreements allowing Spanish and EEC tuna-fishing vessels to operate in the economic zone, in return for license fees and financial aid. License fees from fishing were expected to bring in at least US $4 million in 1984. A joint fishing company is to be established with Spain, and talks have also been held with France with a view to establishing a similar company. In 1984 a major port and fisheries development project was launched. New unloading and fish-processing facilities are to be constructed at Victoria port to handle the anticipated increase in catch. The total annual catch was about 5,200 metric tons in 1981 but is expected to rise to 14,000 tons when development is completed.

INDUSTRY

There are few industries in the modern sector. There are small establishments using simple technology for processing copra, vanilla and other agricultural products, extracting patchouli and cinnamon oil, and making coir rope and mattress fibers.

Although the government has taken over a majority share-holding in certain key sectors, through the Seychelles National Investment Corporation set up in 1979, there is no overall nationalization policy and it is continuing actively to encourage foreign investment, both public and private, particularly in tourism, farming, fisheries and small-scale manufacturing, although joint ventures are preferred where foreign investors are concerned. Taxed profits can be freely repatriated. A number of parastatal bodies have been created to take over functions such as utilities and commodity marketing, formerly carried out by ministries.

ENERGY

In 1982 the Seychelles produced no form of mineral energy but consumed 46,000 metric tons of coal equivalent, or 667 kg (1,470 lb) per capita. In 1984 electric power production was 52 million kwh, or 787 kwh per capita.

LABOR

The economically active population is estimated at 29,250, of which wage earners number 15,000. Women constitute around 40% of the labor force. By occupational sectors, agriculture employs 10.3%; mining, manufacturing and construction 21.4%; trade and tourism 11.3%; transportation and communications 3.4%; finance and services 39%; and other sectors 14.7%. Less than 40% of workers have skills of any kind, and apprenticeship programs are few and limited.

Minimum wage legislation was passed in 1957, and wage levels are periodically revised upward. The work week is 45 hours.

Unemployment is estimated at 8%. As a result of limited job opportunities in the islands, there is a constant outflow of workers. Thousands of Seychellois work in the United Kingdom and Australia as waiters and as seamen in the British naval auxiliary.

There is one legal union (the National Workers Union) which is under direct control of the ruling party. It does not function as a free trade union, although it has some limited powers to negotiate wage increases and better working conditions for its members. Legislation was passed in 1983 which restricts an employer from dismissing workers. There has been no official strike in Seychelles since 1977, although 1984 saw a work stoppage by stevedores who protested a change in their contract. The issues were handled peacefully and without publicity in meetings between the union, workers and government. All associations, clubs and other groups require government permission to organize. The National Workers Union is a member of the Ghana-based, continent-wide Organization of African Trade Union Unity (OATUU).

Labor laws have not yet been promulgated, but written guidelines published in 1980 establish the minimum working age at 14. The guidelines cover leave, dismissal, overtime, minimum wages, reports of service injury or death, and salary deductions. According to officials of the National Workers Union, occupational safety and health conditions are a part of the union's inspection program. Wages are determined by the union in conjunction with the government. The government, which maintains a register of vacancies, determine which candidates will be sent to employers for interviews. Third country nationals need work permits which are issued only when qualified Seychellois are unavailable.

FOREIGN COMMERCE

The foreign commerce of the Seychelles consisted in 1984 of exports of $21.8 million and imports of $86.2 million, leaving an unfavorable trade balance of $64.4 million. Of the imports, petroleum constituted 24.8%, machinery and transport equipment 22.9%, chemicals 5.6%, mineral manufactures 4.1%, cereals 4.0% and textiles 2.6%. Of the exports, copra constituted 8.3%, fish 6.7% and cinnamon bark 2.4%.

The major import sources are: Bahrain 14.2%, the United Kingdom 13.2%, Italy 9.8%, South Africa 9.2%, Singapore 8.4%, Japan 6.0% and France 4.7%. The major export destinations are: Pakistan 51.8%, Reunion 18.1%, Japan 13.9%, Algeria 3.7%, France 2.9% and the United Kingdom 1.5%.

TRANSPORTATION & COMMUNICATIONS

The Seychelles has no railroads or inland waterways. Victoria, the only port, handled 106,000 tons of cargo in 1982. A thrice-weekly inter-island ferry is operated by the Port and Marine Department.

There are 215 km (133 mi) of roads in all the islands, of which 145 km (90 mi) are asphalted. In 1982 these roads were used by 3,520 passenger cars and 1,056 commercial vehicles. Per capita vehicle ownership is 16 per 1,000 inhabitants.

Air transport is provided by Air Seychelles in which the government holds 60% interest and British Airways 40%. There are seven usable airports on Mahe, Bird, Praslin and Astove Islands. The Mahe airport, known as Seychelles International Airport, has a permanent-surface runway between 2,500 and 3,700 meters (8,000 and 12,000 ft). There are direct flights to London via Nairobi.

In 1984 there were 8,300 telephones in the country, or 11.9 per 100 inhabitants. In 1982 the postal service handled 1,618,000 pieces of mail and 12,000 telegrams. Per capita volume of mail was 24 pieces. There are 136 telex subscriber lines.

Tourism is the mainstay of the economy. In 1975 tourism overtook agriculture as the major contributor to GDP and its present share is 20% versus 10% for agriculture. Tourism employs about one-third of the working population and supplies 90% of the foreign exchange earnings. The number of visitors rose to 55,867 in 1983 compared to 1,622 in 1970. In 1984 a long-term joint tourism promotion project was agreed with Kenya to be financed by the European Development Fund. Tourist revenues in 1983 were estimated at $34.417 million. Of the 60,400 arrivals reported in 1981, 2,800 were from the United States, 7,900 from the United Kingdom, 3,400 from South Africa, 9,400 from France, 6,400 from West Germany, 8,600 from Italy, 1,600 from Switzerland, 3,400 from Japan, 1,100 from Denmark and 1,100 from Austria.

MINING

The Seychelles has no known mineral reserves except small quantities of guano on Assumption Island.

DEFENSE

The Seychelles has no formal defense force.

EDUCATION

The national literacy rate is 62% (males 54.9% and females 59.6%). Of the population over 25, 28.3% have had no schooling, 34.5% have entered but not completed first level, 21.5% have completed first level, 7.3% have entered but not completed second level, 5.9% have completed second level, and 2.6% have completed some kind of post-secondary training program. Schooling is compulsory and free for nine years from age 6 to 15. Girls constitute 49% of primary school enrollment, 53% of secondary school enrollment and 89% of post secondary education (for the teaching profession which is almost exclusively female).

Schooling lasts for 13 years, divided into nine years of primary school, two years of lower secondary or middle school and two years of upper secondary school. The school system consists of 27 primary schools, 3 secondary schools, one vocational and technical school and one teacher-training school. Of the primary schools, all but two are private, 19 are run by the Roman Catholic Church, seven by the Church of England and one by Seventh Day Adventists. All private schools receive state aid. In 1982, 210 students were enrolled in the teacher-training college and 754 in the vocational schools. The teacher-pupil ratio is 1:21 at the primary level, 1:18 at the secondary level and 1:9 at the post-secondary level. A voluntary National Youth Service, launched in February 1981, now caters for the secondary education of most children between 15 and 17 years of age.

The school year runs from January through December. The language of instruction is English in the upper grades, French in the middle grades and Creole in the lower grades.

The educational budget in 1982 was R88,086,000, of which 90.2% was current expenditure. This amount represented 21.1% of the national budget, 7.0% of the GNP and $190 per capita.

Seychellois pursuing higher studies in fields other than education have to go abroad. The government provides scholarships for higher studies in Commonwealth countries.

EDUCATIONAL ENROLLMENT (1984)			
	Schools	Teachers	Students
First Level	27	695	14,333
Second Level	2	147	2,605
Vocational	1	143	1,284
Third Level	N.A.	28	144

In 1982, 66 Seychellois attended institutions of higher education abroad, including 7 in the United States, 41 in the United Kingdom and 4 in Canada.

LEGAL SYSTEM

The Seychelles legal system is a blend of French and English codes. The civil and commercial codes are French. The criminal law was French until 1952 when the British system was introduced.

There are three courts: the Court of Appeal, the Supreme Court and the Magistrate Courts. The Court of Appeal hears appeals from the Supreme Court in both civil and criminal cases, and the Supreme Court from the Magistrate Courts. The president of the court of appeal and the chief justice of the Supreme Court are appointed by the president on the advice of the Public Service Commission. Nonpolitical prisoners are granted fair public trials. Most judges are aliens, mostly British, on short-term contracts. The appellate judges come once a year from Britain.

Defendants in nonpolitical cases (both civil and criminal) have access to counsel and have enjoyed speedy and fair trials. Right to trial is patterned in large measure on English common law, although there is also a heavy influence of Napoleonic customary law. Judges are provided under arrangements with the Commonwealth and, except for security cases, they have exhibited considerable independence from both the executive and legislative branches of the government.

No information is available on penal or correctional facilities in the Seychelles.

LAW ENFORCEMENT

The national police force consists of 450 policemen and 87 officers under a commissioner of police. There is a special posse of security guards at the U.S. Air Force Tracking Station in Mahe. In addition to the regular force, there is a Special Force for riot duty and a special Intelligence Branch. All British officers in the force were expelled after the coup of 1977. The police are well equipped with shotguns and rifles; communication with outislands is maintained by radio. No information is available on the nature or incidence of crime on the islands.

HEALTH

In 1982 there were seven hospitals in the country with 352 beds, or 1 bed per 183 inhabitants. In the same year there were 35 physicians, or 1 physician per 1,838 inhabitants, 5 dentists and 169 nursing personnel.

```
PRINCIPAL HEALTH INDICATORS (1984)
Crude Death Rate: 7.0 per 1,000
Life Expectancy at Birth: 64.6 (Males); 71.1 (Females)
Infant Mortality Rate: 14.4 per 1,000 Live Births
```

The government abolished private medical practice in 1979 and several doctors and dentists left Seychelles. Under a new health plan, each of the districts is to provide a medical/dental clinic for treatment of all citizens regardless of their means. There are few health problems because of the salubrious climate. Public health expenditures constitute 8.7% of the national budget and $23.20 per capita.

The major health problems are tuberculosis, venereal diseases and parasitic intestinal infections.

FOOD

The staple food is rice, eaten with lentil or vegetable and often fish. The meat and eggs of giant tortoises are consumed as delicacies. Breadfruit is eaten as a supplement to rice or as a substitute when rice is scarce. The national drink is bacca, a beer made from sugarcane juice. No information is available on the daily per capita protein and calorie intake.

MEDIA & CULTURE

In 1982 two daily newspapers and three non-daily newspapers with aggregate circulations of 3,400 and 5,700 respectively were published in the country. Per capita circulations were 51 for daily newspapers and 86 for non-dailies per 1,000 inhabitants. The periodical press consists of 22 titles.

Although theoretically protected under the constitution of 1979, freedom of speech is curtailed in practice. Legislation provides for up to three years detention for anyone "who with intent to bring the President into hatred, ridicule or contempt, publishes any defamatory or insulting matter whether in writing, print or word of mouth or in any other manner." Apparently no charges have been brought under this legislation. This same legislation allows a two-year sentence for anyone who "prints, makes, imports, sells, supplies, offers for sale or supply, distributes, reproduces, or has in his possession or control" any publication banned by the government for security reasons, but again there has been no prosecution under it. The government has sought to curtail the importation of pamphlets printed by its opposition abroad. The government controls the major newspaper in the country, as well as all radio and television broadcasting. The Catholic church publishes an increasingly lively paper, *Echo Des Isles*, which is not subject to government control or censorship. Since the president promised not to interfere with religious

expression in September 1984, that paper has published hard-hitting articles which obliquely criticize the government. The two largest religious denominations in the country, the Roman Catholic and Anglican churches, are each provided two free hours of uncensored broadcasting each month. Again, in late 1984 both churches have used these broadcasts to comment on social and political issues. Foreign broadcasts are widely listened to and are uncensored. Except for opposition material, foreign publications, including those critical of the government, have been imported and sold without hindrance.

There is no national news agency. News is obtained by the press from the government information department. Two books were published in the country in 1982.

The government-owned Radio Television Seychelles operates two medium-wave transmitters and broadcasts 60 hours a week in English, French and Creole. The Far East Broadcasting Association, a Christian missionary outreach, operates FEBA Seychelles with a 30-km short-wave transmitter, broadcasting in 12 languages and on nine frequencies beamed to southern Asia, India, the Middle East and eastern and southern Africa. Of the 4,200 annual radio broadcasting hours, 800 are devoted to information, 600 to education, 100 to culture, 80 to religion, 40 to commercials and 2,580 to entertainment. In 1982 there were 22,000 radio receivers in the country, or 344 per 1,000 inhabitants. Television introduced in 1983 is operated by RTS Television. In 1984 there were 3,500 television sets or 53 per 1,000 inhabitants.

In 1982 there were two fixed cinemas in the country with 1,000 seats, or 15.5 seats per 1,000 inhabitants. Annual movie attendance was 80,000, or 13.6 per capita.

There are seven public libraries, of which the largest is at Victoria.

There are two museums reporting an annual attendence of 21,000.

There are two theaters serving three amateur troupes.

SOCIAL WELFARE

The Poor Relief Ordinance provides for children and mothers in need. A number of homes for the elderly are maintained by the Catholic Church.

GLOSSARY

coco-de-mer: a type of huge coconut peculiar to the Seychelles, often weighing up to 18 kg (40 lbs).

CHRONOLOGY (from 1976)

1976— Following the London Constitutional Conference, Seychelles is granted independence as a republic within the Commonwealth with James R. Mancham as president; the United Kingdom transfers Aldabra, Desroches and Farquhar Islands of the British Indian Ocean Territory (BIOT) to the Seychelles.

1977— President James R. Mancham is ousted in a coup led by Prime Minister France Albert Rene, who assumes the presidency.

1979— New constitution is promulgated. Albert Rene is elected president along with a new National Assembly. . . .Violent demonstrations against a proposed compulsory national youth service force the government to revise the scheme.

1981— South African mercenaries attempt unsuccessful coup.

1983— Legislative elections are held for the National Assembly. . . . Seychelles joins Madagascar and Mauritius in setting up an Indian Ocean Commission.

1984— In presidential elections, sole candidate France Rene is reelected.

BIBLIOGRAPHY (from 1965)

Benedict, Burton, *People of the Seychelles* (London, 1970).

———, and Marion Benedict, *Men, Women and Money in Seychelles* (Berkeley, Calif., 1982).

Franda, Marcus, *Seychelles: The Unquiet Islands* (Boulder, Colo., 1982).

Lionnot, Guy, *The Seychelles* (Harrisburg, Pa., 1972).

Maubouche, Robert and Naimeh Hadjitarkhani, *Seychelles: Economic Memorandum* (Washington, D.C. 1980).

Pavard, Claude, *Seychelles: From One Island to Another* (New York, 1983).

Sauer, Jonathan D., *Plants and Man on the Seychelles Coast* (Madison, Wis., 1967).

Thomas, Athol, *Forgotten Eden* (London, 1968).

Webb, W. T., *Story of Seychelles* (Victoria, Seychelles, 1966).

OFFICIAL PUBLICATIONS

Seychelles Monetary Authority, *Quarterly Review.*
Government Statistics Division, *Statistical Abstract.*

Fria

Mamou

GUINEA

Niger

Kindia

Faranah

Konkouré

Koba

Forécariah

Kabala

Rokel

Bagbe

Kambia

Great Scarcies

Little Scarcies

Makeni

Meli

Mabole

Pampana

Lunsar Marampa

Magburaka

Sefadu

Rokel

Kainkordu

Lungi

Pepel

Sierra Leone R.

Yonibana

FREETOWN

Beudu

BANANA ISLANDS

YAWRI BAY

Moyamba

Mano

Bo

Segbwema

Pendembu

Shenge

Sewa

Kenema

ATLANTIC

OCEAN

Jong

TURTLE ISLANDS

Sherbro River

Waanje

Mano

SHERBRO ISLAND

Bonthe

Gbundapi

Pujehun

Moa

Zimi

Lofa

LIBERIA

Juring

Bomi Hills

SIERRA LEONE

- ▬▬ International boundary
- ⊛ National capital
- ┼┼┼ Railroad
- ─── Road
- ✠ International airport

0 10 20 30 40 50 Miles

0 10 20 30 40 50 Kilometers

BOUNDARY REPRESENTATION IS
NOT NECESSARILY AUTHORITATIVE

UNITY FREEDOM JUSTICE

SIERRA LEONE

BASIC FACT SHEET

OFFICIAL NAME: Republic of Sierra Leone

ABBREVIATION: SL

CAPITAL: Freetown

HEAD OF STATE: President Joseph Saidu Momoh (from 1985)

NATURE OF GOVERNMENT: One-party modified democracy

POPULATION: 3,883,000 (1985)

AREA: 71,740 sq km (27,699 sq mi)

ETHNIC MAJORITY: Mende and Temne

LANGUAGE: English

RELIGIONS: Animism, Christianity and Islam

UNIT OF CURRENCY: Leone (Le) ($1=Le5.531, August 1985)

NATIONAL FLAG: Tricolor of green, white and blue horizontal bars

NATIONAL EMBLEM: A shield held by erect gold lions with red tongues and claws standing on a grassy green mound bearing on a white scroll the national motto: "Unity, Freedom, Justice." On the shield, flanked by two palm trees, a lion crouches beneath a serrated border and between the notches of the border three torches burn against a white background.

NATIONAL ANTHEM: "High We Exalt Thee, Realm of the Free"

NATIONAL HOLIDAYS: April 19 (Republic Day, National Day); January 1 (New Year's Day); April 27 (Independence Day). Also variable Christian and Islamic festivals.

NATIONAL CALENDAR: Gregorian

PHYSICAL QUALITY OF LIFE INDEX: 26 (down from 29 in 1976) (On an ascending scale in which 100 is the maximum. U.S. 95)

DATE OF INDEPENDENCE: April 27, 1961

DATE OF CONSTITUTION: June 1978

WEIGHTS & MEASURES: Both metric and Imperial systems are in use.

LOCATION & AREA

Sierra Leone is a circular-shaped country located in the southwestern part of West Africa with an area of 71,740 sq km (27,699 sq mi). Its greatest distance N to S is 338 km (210 mi), and its greatest distance E to W is 304 km (189 mi). The total length of the Atlantic coastline is 406 km (252 mi).

Sierra Leone's total international border of 958 km (595 mi) is shared with two countries: Guinea (652 km, 405 mi) and Liberia (306 km, 190 mi). The border with Guinea was demarcated by the two former colonial powers, France and Great Britain, and reflects the final agreement made in 1911. The border with Liberia was determined by agreements between independent Liberia and Great Britain in 1885 and by adjustments made in 1903, 1911 and 1930. Natural boundaries, such as rivers and watersheds, constitute most of the borders. There are no current border disputes.

The capital is Freetown with a 1984 population of 500,000. The other major urban centers are Bo (45,000), Koidu (75,846), Kenema (31,458) and Makeni (30,000).

Sierra Leone is divided topographically into four regions: the interior plateaus and mountains, the interior low plains, the coastal swamplands, and the Sierra Leone peninsula.

In the east and northeast plateaus rise sharply in a flight of steps to mountains such as the Tingi Hills and the Loma Mountains, which reach 1,948 meters (6,390 ft), one of the highest points in West Africa. Below them are the Nimini and Sula Mountains and the Gola, Gori and Jojina Hills. The plateaus and the mountains encompass nearly half the country. Between the highlands and the coastal swamps there is a rolling lowland area up to 96 km (60 mi) broad, covered in its northeastern part by a swampy grassland, known as bolilands. The coastal swamplands are on a plain with an average width of 32 km (20 mi) that stretches along the coastline marked by numerous estuaries and peninsulas. The Sierra Leone peninsula, on which Freetown, the capital, is situated, is a central mountainous area with a maximum elevation of nearly 900 meters (3,000 ft) with a strip of flat land running around the base of the mountains.

All these four topographical regions are collectively known as the mainland, as distinguished from the islands offshore, the largest of which are the Bananas, Plantains and Sherbro.

The country is drained by nine roughly parallel rivers: the Rokel, Gbangbar, Jong, Sewa, Waanje, Great Scarcies, Little Scarcies, Moa and the Mano, all of which flow into the Atlantic. All these rivers are navigable only for short distances.

WEATHER

The climate is marked, as in all tropical countries, by sharp alternations of wet and dry seasons. The wet season lasts from May to October and the dry season from November to April. The coastal regions receive the highest rainfall of over 508 cm (200 in.), and Freetown receives an average 381 cm (150 in.) annually. Rainfall decreases inland toward the north with Kabala averaging 216 cm (86 in.). The rainiest months are July, August and September.

Both temperature and humidity are consistently high throughout the country with maximum diurnal variations of up to 16.6°C (30°F) in the interior. The mean temperature in the interior and coastal lowland plains is 26.6°C (80°F), while the eastern plateau region has a mean of 25°C (77°F).

The prevailing wind systems are the southwest monsoon (in the wet season) and the hot and dry harmattan that blows from the northeast Sahara regions.

POPULATION

The population of Sierra Leone was 3,883,000 in 1985 based on U.N. estimates and the last census held in 1974 when the population was 2,729,479. The population is expected to reach 4.9 million by 2000 and 7.3 million by 2020. The annual rate of population growth is estimated at 1.77% nationwide and 4.6% in urban areas, based on an annual birthrate of 47.4 per 1,000.

The heaviest concentration of population is found in the western area where Freetown is located. A second region of dense population lies north and east of this area. The southeast has a moderate concentration. The least populated areas are in the north and northeast. Nationwide the average density of population is estimated at 50 per sq km (130 per sq mi), but since there are few areas without human settlements of some sort the average density in arable areas is not significantly higher.

Those between 15 and 64 constitute 55.6% of the population and the largest age group. Those below 14 years of age constitute 41.4% and those over 65, 3%. However, in view of the high rate of population growth, the median age is being gradually lowered. The male/female ratio favors females by 100:96.1, though there are ethnic and regional variations in the sex ratios.

The population is predominantly rural, distributed widely over 19,000 settlements with names and countless others without names. There are only 160 localities with over 1,000 inhabitants. Of these, only five had populations of over 10,000 and only Freetown could be considered a true metropolitan city with a population close to 200,000. However, the prevailing trend is toward urbanization and the movement of population toward cities has continued unchecked during the 1980s. In some cities and towns the pace of urbanization has been phenomenal. Lunsar has grown from 78 people in 1927 to 12,000, Koidu from 96 people in 1927 to 12,000, and Kenema from 1,200 people in 1927 to 13,000. The urban component of the population is estimated at 28.26%.

DEMOGRAPHIC INDICATORS (1984)	
Population, total (in 1,000)	3,883.0
Population ages (% of total)	
0-14	41.4
15-64	55.6
65+	3.0
Youth 15-24 (000)	668
Women ages 15-49 (000)	867
Dependency ratios	79.7
Child-woman ratios	689
Sex ratios (per 100 females)	96.1
Median ages (years)	19.4
Average size of Household	4.9
Change in birthrate (%, 1965-83)	2.3
Proportion of urban (%)	28.26
Population density (per sq. km.)	50
per hectare of arable land	1:38
Rates of growth (%)	1.77
urban	4.6
rural	0.8
Natural increase rates (per 1,000)	17.7
Crude birth rates (per 1,000)	47.4
Crude death rates (per 1,000)	29.7
Gross reproduction rates	3.02
Net reproduction rates	1.63
Total fertility rates	6.13
General fertility rates (per 1,000)	196
Life expectancy, males (years)	32.5
Life expectancy, females (years)	34.5
Life expectancy, total (years)	34.0
Population doubling time in years at current rate	41

There is considerable internal migration in search of jobs and better educational and physical facilities. Permanent out-migration is insignificant. Immigration into the country is controlled and limited under the Non-Citizen Act of 1965.

Women in Sierra Leone are guaranteed equal rights by the constitution. In practice access to education for women remains more limited than it is for men. For example, only 39% of the children enrolled in primary school are female (1977 figure). Yet this figure indicates gradual improvement has been made since independence. The status of women varies substantially in different parts of the country and depends upon cultural values of various tribal groups. In some areas of Sierra Leone women have been elected to the prestigious position of paramount chief. In other areas, this would not happen. In the modern sector, women are prominent in the professions and one woman is a Supreme Court justice. The political sphere continues to be overwhelmingly male-dominated.

Official policy toward family planning is ambivalent, dictated in part by political and in part by religious considerations. The major programs in this field are conducted by the Sierra Leone Planned Parenthood Association, a private organization, which operates four clinics. Contraceptive materials are permitted to be freely imported. Most of the opposition to family planning comes from women in rural areas, where only one out of 10 women seems to favor it.

ETHNIC COMPOSITION

Sierra Leone is an ethnic mosaic of 18 groups of whom three —the Mende, Temne and Limba—account for 69% of the population. The major ethnic groups also have their ecological zones in which they have established their dominance.

ETHNIC GROUPS OF SIERRA LEONE		
Ethnic Group	Percentage of Total Population	Region
Mende	30.9	Southeast
Temne	29.8	Southwest
Limba	8.4	Northcentral
Kono	4.8	Northeast
Koranko	3.7	Northeast
Sherbro	3.4	West coastal
Susu	3.1	Northwest border
Fullah	3.1	North and East
Lokko	3.0	Northcentral
Madingo	2.3	East
Kissi	2.2	Eastern border
Creole	1.9	Peninsula
Yalunka	0.7	Northern border
Krim	0.4	South coastal
Vai	0.3	East
Gola	0.2	East border
Kroo	0.2	East border
Gallinas	0.1	East border
Others	1.2	Various

The Mendes, who are the largest single group, form the majority in four districts of the southern province and two districts of the eastern province. On the basis of cultural and linguistic peculiarities, there are three distinct Mende subgroups: Kpa-Mende, the warrior class, the Sewa-Mende, and the Ko-Mende. The Temne constitute the majority in four districts of the southwestern province and in Freetown. The Creoles are descendants of African slaves later returned to the continent at different periods, particularly after the outlawing of the slave trade. The term Creole is also sometimes applied to anyone who has adopted the Western way of life. At one time Creoles were a Westernized elite who dominated commerce and administration but they have been displaced in many professional areas by other groups since independence. Creoles form the second largest ethnic group in Freetown, the Sierra Leone Peninsula, and the Sherbro and Bananas Islands.

The dominant factor in interethnic relations is the competition between the northern and southern peoples, focused on the Temne and the Mende. The historic division and rivalry between the Creoles and non-Creoles have lost much of their edge as the influence of the Creoles has declined. Despite economic tensions, interethnic relations are characterized by a lack of the virulence common in other African countries. Politically, the Sierra Leone People's Party is a Mende organ, while the ruling All People's Congress is a Temne-Creole-Limba alliance.

Ethnic alien groups include both Africans and non-Africans. Among African aliens the largest community is Guinean, comprising between 300,000 and 400,000 refugees from Sekou Toure's regime. There are also 8,000 Liberians and 6,000 Hausa Nigerians.

Among non-Africans the most important are the Lebanese, who began emigrating to Sierra Leone in the 1890s and by the 1920s virtually monopolized commerce and trade. Although subject to periodic official harassment, the Lebanese control rural marketing and agricultural credit, motor transport, hotels, tourism, motion picture distribution and the diamond trade. Nearly 7,000 Lebanese were registered as aliens in 1971. There are also a few hundred Indians.

The Western presence consists mainly of British businessmen, although French, German and Swiss nationals are also represented.

Sierra Leone is one of the most Westernized of African countries, and there is little or no organized anti-Western sentiment in politics, society or commerce.

In terms of ethnic and linguistic homogeneity, Sierra Leone ranks 15th among the nations of the world with 23% homogeneity (on an ascending scale in which North and South Korea rank 135th with 100% homogeneity and Tanzania ranks 1st with 7% homogeneity).

LANGUAGES

The official language of Sierra Leone is English, though its use is restricted to administrative, business and technical communications.

The most widespread lingua franca is Krio, the mother tongue of the Creoles. Krio is based on a Pidgin English core with an essentially African syntax and words borrowed from English, Portuguese and African languages. It has, however, no standardized orthography.

The African languages may be classified as either Mande or West Atlantic, also called Mel, both belonging to the Niger-Congo stock. The Mande languages spoken in Sierra Leone include Mende, Kono, Koranko, Susu, Lokko, Madingo, Yalunka and Vai. Of these, the most important is Mende, which is spoken in the southern half of the country and used as a first language by the tribe of that name as well as by the Sherbro, Krim and Vai and as a lingua franca by the Gola, Kissi and Kono.

West Atlantic languages include Temne, Fula, Limba, Bullom, Kissi and Gola. Of these, the most important is Temne, which is spoken by over 30% of the population and is used as a second language by the Lokko, Susu and Limba and as a lingua franca in central and northern Sierra Leone. Of the African languages, only Mende, Temne and Vai exist in written form. Mende and Temne are written in the Roman alphabet with the addition of a few specially devised letters to accommodate African sound patterns.

RELIGIONS

The fluid nature of African religious beliefs makes a statistical count of religious adherents subject to wide margins of error. Generally speaking, over 70% of Sierra Leoneans follow traditional religious beliefs, 25% adhere to Islam, and 5% are Christians. Islam is strongest in the north among the Madingo, Fullah and the Vai, while Christianity is strongest in coastal areas among the Creoles, Sherbro and Mende.

Christianity was introduced into Sierra Leone by white missionaries and freed slaves in the late 18th century. Missionaries, however, made relatively fewer converts because Christianity assailed entrenched social institutions, such as polygamy, ancestor worship and secret societies. Even converted Sierra Leoneans retained some forms of traditional beliefs or broke away from mission churches to form syncretist movements. But Christian influence in Sierra Leone transcends religion and extends to politics, education and health services. Both the Anglicans and the Roman Catholics have archbishoprics in Freetown.

Most Sierra Leonean Muslims are Sunnites. The Ahmadiyya, a militant Muslim sect of Pakistani origin, is active in the country.

COLONIAL EXPERIENCE

The colony of Sierra Leone was founded by British philanthropists in the late 18th century as a home for freed African slaves. From 1791 to 1808 it was administered by the Sierra Leone Company; it was transferred to the British Crown in 1808. In 1896 a British Protectorate was declared over the hinterland or mainland. Sierra Leone became independent in 1961.

Sierra Leone is among the few countries of Africa that have retained Western traditions in their political and economic systems. The major legacies of British rule—the English language, legal system, educational and administrative structures—have been preserved almost intact. Relations with Great Britain continue to be friendly, and Great Britain continues to be the principal source of economic aid and assistance.

CONSTITUTION & GOVERNMENT

The constitutional basis of Sierra Leonean government is the constitution of 1978, which established a one-party state with a presidential form of government. The constitution is basically the same as the constitutions of 1961 and 1971 except for the provisions creating the posts of two vice presidents, a 16-member Defense Council, and extending the presidential term to seven years. In 1985 the constitution was amended to permit Gen. Joseph Momoh, the president-elect, to hold his military rank as head of state.

RULERS OF SIERRA LEONE

PRESIDENTS
1971 (April) to 1985 (November) Siaka Probyn Stevens
1985 (November) — Joseph Saidu Momoh
PRIME MINISTERS
1961 (April) to 1964 (April) Sir Milton Margai
1964 (April) to 1967 (March) Sir Albert Michael Margai
1967 (March)   Siaka Probyn Stevens
1967 (March)   David Lansana
1967 (March)   Ambrose Genda
1967 (March) to 1968 (April) Andrew Juxon Smith
1968 (April)   John Bangura
1968 (April) to 1971 (April) Siaka Probyn Stevens
1971 (April) to 1975 (July) Sorie Ibrahim Koroma
1975 (July) to 1984 (May) Christian A. Kamara-Taylor
Post of prime minister abolished.

CABINET LIST (1986)

President	Joseph Momoh
1st Vice President	Francis Misheck Minah
2nd Vice President	Abu Bakar Kamara
Minister of Agriculture, Natural Resources & Forestry	Soufian Kargbo
Minister of Defense	Joseph Momoh
Minister of Education	Aloysius Joe-Jackson
Minister of Finance, Development & Economic Planning	Joe Amara-Bangali
Minister of Foreign Affairs	Abdul Karim Koroma
Minister of Health	Salia Jusu Sheriff
Minister of Information, Broadcasting, Tourism & Cultural Affairs	A. G. Sembu-Forna
Minister of Internal Affairs	*Dr.* S. B. Kawusu-Conteh
Minister of Justice	Francis MisheckMinah
Minister of Lands, Housing & Country Planning	Abu Bakar Kamara
Minister of Mines & Labor	Sanie Sesay
Minister of Social Welfare & Rural Development	Tom Michael Smith
Minister of State Enterprises	Joseph Momoh
Minister of Trade & Industry	*Brig.* Michael Abdulai
Minister of Transport & Communications	Sheku R. Deen Sesay
Minister of Works, Energy & Power	Hassan G. Kanu
Minister of State for Party Affairs	*Dr.* E. T. Kamara
Minister of State in Ministry of Foreign Affairs	A. K. Stevens
Minister of State, Inspector General of Police	Patrick M. Johnson
Minister of State, RSLMF Force Commander	*Maj. Gen.* Sheku Mohamed Tarawalli
Leader of the House	Harry Williams
Attorney General	Francis Misheck Minah

Executive authority is vested in the president, who is elected by the House of Representatives for a seven-year term. The president may not hold office for more than two consecutive terms. The president appoints two vice presidents, members of the cabinet and deputy ministers, all of whom are responsible to and may be dismissed by him.

The cabinet, headed by the president, consists of nine ministers of state, 19 ministers, and an attorney general. The defense portfolio is usually held by the president himself. Assisting the cabinet are 17 deputy ministers.

The constitution grants universal adult suffrage over age 21. However, Sierra Leone has a history of rigged elections, and the 1973 elections were boycotted by the main opposition party, because of fraudulent practices by the ruling party.

Between 1964 and 1975 Sierra Leone was torn by severe political instability. Three changes of government followed successful military coups, and there were an equal number of abortive coups. Widespread violence and rioting occurred in 1968 and 1970. Much of this instability had its roots in the polarization of the country along ethnic and regional lines and consequent rivalry between the major ethnic groups: the Mende on the one hand, and the Temne, Limba and Creoles on the other. Although the army has not been politicized, it is still sensitive to ethnic issues and its ethnic composition has varied in accordance with that of the dominant political party. Though the challenge from Sierra Leone People's Party-oriented factions has weakened in recent years, the government faces threats from newer and more radical forces in society.

FREEDOM & HUMAN RIGHTS

In terms of political and civil rights, Sierra Leone is classified as a partly free country with a negative rating of 5 in political rights and 5 in civil rights (on a descending scale in which 7 is the lowest and 1 is the highest in civil and political rights).

Sierra Leone was once hailed as a model African democracy, but it has since developed into a one-party state where no opposition exists. The constitutions of 1961, 1971, and 1978 each represents a step in the direction of a controlled democracy where the interests of the ruling party are supreme. However, this transformation has not been accompanied by actual repression. There are no reports of arbitrary arrests, torture, cruel and degrading punishment and disappearances of opposition figures. Trials are reasonably free and British procedures are still followed ensuring defendants at least a fair hearing and counsel of their choice. The government has not made any efforts to impose an ideological straitjacket or to restrict intellectual inquiry.

It is widely believed in Sierra Leone legal circles that as a form of harassment persons are picked up by the police and held for short periods without charge before being released. Under the constitution, the president may take measures to detain any person who is, or is reasonably suspected to be, dangerous to the well-being of the republic. Writs of habeas corpus granted by the court during a state of emergency would not extend to suspects detained pursuant to an order under the Public Emergency Act. A state of emergency must come into force within 28 days after the detention, or a detainee not charged with an of-

fense must be released. There is no one currently detained under Public Emergency regulations.

Following violence in the Pujehun district in late 1983, the army detained from 100 to 150 persons in its efforts to restore order. While a state of emergency was not declared, some detainees were held for considerable periods before criminal charges were filed. In mid-1984, most of those originally detained were released or charged with various criminal offenses. However, press reports in 1984 and 1985 have suggested that between 10 and 20 of those detained ultimately died of malnutrition while still in prison. Several individuals originally detained in the Pujehun incident and charged with serious criminal offenses, including murder, still have not been brought to trial. While some in legal circles contend that the complexity of the legal cases and the overburdened legal system account for the delay, other observers claim that political pressure from the government is responsible for the judicial lethargy.

CIVIL SERVICE

The civil service is controlled by the Public Service Commission, one of the two independent agencies under the constitution. The commission has power to appoint all but about 100 of the most senior administrators holding politically sensitive positions. Recruitment and training of civil servants are supervised by the establishment secretary.

With the exception of legal, customs, post office and railroad departments, all civil service positions are filled from a single list. Personnel move freely from one department or ministry to another. There are eight classes of civil servants, the first four classes constituting the senior civil service and the other four the junior civil service. All civil service positions were completely Africanized by 1963.

LOCAL GOVERNMENT

The historical differences between the local administrative structures of the Colony, or the Western Area, and the mainland Protectorate have continued after independence. The mainland is divided into three provinces: Northern, Eastern and Southern, each headed by a minister of state with cabinet rank. The provinces are divided into 12 districts where the unit of administration was the district council until 1972; since 1972 it has been the interim committee, an advisory committee of mixed local and central government representatives.

Below the districts, in descending order of importance, are the chiefdoms, sections (or extended villages) and villages. There are 147 chiefdoms, each under the control of a paramount chief and a council of elders known as the Tribal Authority. Of these chiefdoms, 143 have the power to raise and disburse funds, maintain law, order and public health, operate local courts and the local police force, and allocate land.

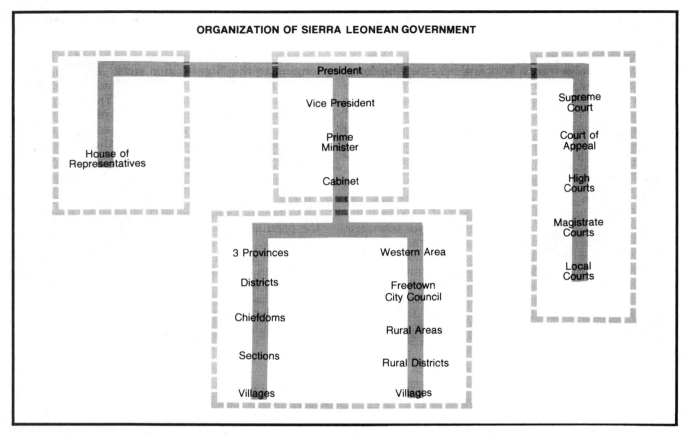

ORGANIZATION OF SIERRA LEONEAN GOVERNMENT

The Western Area has a slightly different regional administrative setup. Freetown has a city government with an elected city council, aldermen for each of the city's wards, permanent committees and an elected mayor. Outside the city the Western Area is administered by Rural Area Councils, Rural District Councils and Village Committees, in descending order.

The 12 mainland districts are: Kambia, Koinadugu, Port Loko, Bombali, Moyamba, Tonkolili, Bo, Bonthe, Pujehun, Kenema, Kono and Kailahun.

FOREIGN POLICY

Sierra Leone's foreign policy is limited in scope and objectives. Historically, it consistently has pursued a conservative and generally pro-Western policy under the numerous military and civilian regimes. The only major development was a gradual shift toward nonalignment and diversification of the country's foreign ties in the mid-1960s. Because Sierra Leone always has been at peace with its two neighbors, national security has not been a major consideration in the formulation of foreign policy. On the other hand, pragmatic economic considerations always have loomed important and Sierra Leone, like many other small countries, has tended to use foreign policy as an instrument for securing economic aid from all quarters. The only ideological content of foreign policy is an opposition to racial discrimination and a desire to elimi-

nate the remnants of colonialism and racialism from Africa.

Among African nations, Sierra Leone maintains closest relations—in descending order of importance—with Guinea, Liberia, Gambia, Nigeria and Ghana. A defense agreement was concluded with Guinea in 1971 providing for the stationing of Guinean troops in Sierra Leone. In 1973 relations with Liberia assumed a broader dimension when Sierra Leone joined the Mano River Union. This agreement calls for a customs union of the two countries in two phases and joint efforts in such areas as forestry, fisheries, ports and telecommunications.

Relations with neighboring Liberia and Guinea have been strained in recent years after military coups in those countries. In 1983, it came close to war with Liberia as Liberian troops massed at the border following a false report in a Freetown weekly that Gen. Doe had shot and killed his wife. The two governments clashed publicly over the arrival in Liberia of refugees fleeing political violence in Sierra Leone's Pujehun district. The situation eased following a state visit to Freetown by Gen. Doe.

Among Western nations, relations with Great Britain continue to be the closest. Both the United States and West Germany have close diplomatic links with Sierra Leone. Sierra Leone opened its first embassy in Moscow in 1967 and since then has expanded its contacts with the Communist world with embassies in Peking, Havana, Belgrade and most East European capitals.

Sierra Leone and the United States are parties to 22 agreements and treaties covering agricultural commodities, aviation, consuls, economic and technical cooperation, extradition, investment guaranties, judicial procedure, mutual security, Peace Corps, postal matters, property, taxation, telecommunications, and trademarks.

Sierra Leone joined the U.N. in 1961; its share of the U.N. budget is 0.02%. It is a member of 15 U. N. organizations and 17 other international and regional organizations, including the Economic Community of West African States.

U.S. Ambassador in Freetown: Arthur W. Lewis
U. K. High Commissioner in Freetown: Richard Dennis Clift
Sierra Leonean Ambassador in Washington, D.C.: Dauda S. Kamara
Sierra Leonean High Commissioner in London: Victor E. Sumner

PARLIAMENT

Under the 1978 constitution, the national legislature is the House of Representatives which consists of not less than 104 members, of whom 85 are ordinary members whose nomination must be approved by the central committee of the All People's Congress, 12 are paramount chiefs and seven are presidential nominations. Constitutional amendments must be approved through referenda and not by parliament.

Candidates for Parliament are chosen in each constituency by the party's local executive committee. The executive committee chooses three candidates from the list of citizens who seek nomination. The central committee of the party has the power to disapprove the nomination of any candidate selected by the local executive committees if it believes that candidacy would be inimical to the state. In addition to the national political system, there is also a traditional system which operates in the provinces outside of the urban area. Paramount chiefs are elected for life by the member of the chiefdom council. They have considerable authority in local affairs and in resolving traditional disputes.

POLITICAL PARTIES

Sierra Leone is a one-party state where opposition parties are illegal. Power now rests with the All People's Congress (APC), founded in 1960 by Siaka Stevens. APC, which is moderately leftist, represents an ethnic coalition of Temne, Creole and Limba elements, but in economic terms its main constituency is the wage-earning lower middle class. In an effort to establish a broader and national base, APC has begun to shed some of its tribal character. More recently, fissures have begun to appear in the party between radicals and conservatives.

The former opposition party, The Sierra Leone People's Party (SLPP), was founded in 1951 as Sierra Leone's first political party by Milton Margai and his half brother, Albert Margai, the country's first and second prime ministers, respectively. SLPP controlled Sierra Leone's legislatures for 16 years from 1951 to 1967, while remaining all the time a southern, Mende-based party espousing a deeply conservative and elitist ideology. It was overwhelmed by APC's populism and divisive strategies in the late 1960s and entered the political wilderness after boycotting the 1973 elections.

ECONOMY

Sierra Leone is one of the 49 low-income countries and one of the 45 countries considered by the U.N. as most seriously affected (MSA) by recent adverse economic conditions. The private sector is predominant in Sierra Leone's free-market economy.

PRINCIPAL ECONOMIC INDICATORS

Gross National Product: $1.290 billion (1983)
  GNP Annual Growth Rate: 1.8% (1973-82)
  Per Capita GNP: $380 (1983)
  Per Capita GNP Annual Growth Rate:−0.3% (1973-82)
Gross Domestic Product: Le2.762 billion (1984)
  GDP Annual Growth Rate: 1.9% (1973-83)
  GDP Per Capita: Le789 (1984)
  GDP Per Capita Annual Growth Rate: −0.8% (1970-81)
Income Distribution: 4.5% of national income is received by the lowest 20%; 33.8% of national income is received by the top 5%.
Percentage of Population in Absolute Poverty: 39; 65% rural
Consumer Price Index (1970=100): All items: 1,776.1 (March 1985) Food: 1,651.7 (March 1985)
Average Annual Rate of Inflation: 14.7% (1973-83)
Money Supply: Le618 million (May 1985)
  Reserve Money: Le518 million (May 1985)
Currency in Circulation: Le260.1 million (1984)
International Reserves: $7.7 million of which foreign exchange reserves were $7.7 million (1984)

BALANCE OF PAYMENTS (1983)
(million $)

Current Account Balance	−32.8
Merchandise Exports	107.0
Merchandise Imports	−133.0
Trade Balance	−25.9
Other Goods, Services & Income	+28.0
Other Goods, Services & Income	−71.7
Other Goods, Services & Income Net	−43.7
Private Unrequited Transfers	3.6
Official Unrequited Transfers	33.2
Capital Other Than Reserves	8.6
Net Errors & Omissions	17.4
Total (Lines 1,10 and 11)	−6.8
Counterpart Items	−2.3
Total (Lines 12 and 13)	−9.2
Liabilities Constituting Foreign Authorities' Reserves	—
Total Change in Reserves	9.2

Development planning began in 1962 with a 10-year development plan that was revised in 1965 as a five-year plan (1965-70). The National Planning Council, established in 1962, issued a five-year National Development Plan (1974-79). The plan called for a total investment of Le623 million and envisaged a growth rate of 6.5% a year. The priority was agricultural expansion, especially self-sufficiency in rice and increased production of palm oil, coffee, cocoa, sugar, groundnuts (peanuts) and rubber. Industrial development was stimulated by a National Industrial Development Corporation. A projected fall in diamond production was offset by increased production of iron ore, bauxite and rutile.

The 1981-84 investment program projected total expenditure of Le 560.8 million, of which Le 136.5 million was allocated to production of staple foods, Le 280.7 million to infrastructure development and Le 44 million to increasing mineral production.

GROSS DOMESTIC PRODUCT BY ECONOMIC ACTIVITY (1970-81)		
	%	**Rate of Change %**
Agriculture	33.6	2.4
Mining	12.8	-9.7
Manufacturing	5.7	3.7
Construction	3.7	3.8
Electricity, Gas & Water	0.5	4.2
Transport & Communications	13.2	5.0
Trade & Finance	22.4	2.3
Public Administration & Defense	6.8	10.1
Other Branches	1.4	-1.4

The large deficits of recent years have been financed mainly by the banking system, and the inflation in consumer prices has been brisk — averaging about 15% annually since 1975. On this and other grounds, the Sierra Leone Labour Congress mounted in mid-1981 a campaign of criticism of government economic policies which led to a general strike in August, an increase in the rice subsidy, and finally the declaration of a state of emergency in September.

The IMF stand-by arrangement in 1980 was followed by a three-year plan of public investment, costed at Le 561 million, for the years 1981-84. Major items in the plan are a hydroelectric project at Bumbuna (Le 185 million) and further development of rice production (Le 136 million); other emphases are on road-building and additional mineral exploitation. The bulk of the finance is being sought externally and the IMF has undertaken to provide SDR 186 million (Le 256 million) in balance-of-payments support — subject to conditions concerning credit creation and external debt which the government has had difficulty in meeting. Confidence in the ability of the government to execute this or any other program has been weakened by charges of large-scale embezzlement of public funds, brought in early 1981 against three ministers and several of the most senior civil servants, and by a further financial scandal at the end of the year.

During the years 1964 through 1973 between one-half and three-fourths of the financing for gross fixed capital formation was obtained from external sources; during the period 1964 through 1971 two-thirds of government expenditure on development also came from abroad. The major sources of aid are the United Kingdom and the United States. From 1946 through 1983 U.S. aid alone amounted to $110.6 million, including Peace Corps, Food for Peace and other programs. In the mid-1970s Sierra Leone began receiving aid from the U.N. Special Emergency Fund for "Most Seriously Affected Countries." Aid from the Communist bloc countries amounted to $58 million from 1954 through 1976, of which China's share was $30 million. During 1979-81 Sierra Leone received $67.7 million in foreign aid, of which $39.7 million was bilateral aid and $28.0 million multilateral aid. Per capita aid received was $19.50.

BUDGET

The Sierra Leonean fiscal year runs from July 1 through June 30. The national budget is divided into a current budget and a development budget. The current budget embraces the entire public sector including central government, local governments, and the parastatal sector of 30 or more agencies, including the Marketing Board and the National Commercial Bank.

Of current government revenues, 24.1% comes from taxes on income, profit and capital gain, 23.5% from domestic taxes on goods and services, 49.5% from taxes on international trade and transactions, 1.1% from other taxes and 1.8% from non-tax revenues. Current revenues represent 11.6% of GNP.

Of current government expenditures, 14.28% goes to general public services, 4.21% to defense, 14.76% to education, 6.20% to health, 1.15% to social security and welfare, 0.38% to housing, 2.64% to other community and social services, 32.13% to economic services, 10.17% to agriculture, 4.64% to roads, 0.77% to other transportation and communications and 9.11% to other functions. Total expenditures represent 22.7% of GNP and overall deficit 10.7% of GNP.

In 1984 government consumption was Le 189 million and private consumption Le 2.812 billion. During 1973-83 public consumption declined by 2.1% and private consumption grew by 3.2%.

In 1983, total outstanding disbursed external debt was $359.4 million of which $271.6 million was owed to official creditors and $87.8 million to private creditors. Total debt service was $9.7 million of which $6.9 million was repayment of principal and $2.8 million interest. Total external debt represented 34.5% of GNP and debt service 0.9% of GNP.

FINANCE

The Sierra Leonean unit of currency is the leone (Le) divided into 100 cents. Coins are issued in denomi-

BUDGET ESTIMATES (Le million, year ending 30 June)			
Revenue	1981/82	1982/83	1983/84
Direct taxes	43.8	43.3	49.6
Import duties	40.3	45.7	58.1
Export duties	14.0	10.6	31.4
Excise duties	42.0	45.6	49.3
Other sources*	44.5	32.8	40.0
TOTAL	184.6	200.6	253.5

*Including licenses, duties, fees and receipts for departmental services, receipts from posts and telecommunications royalties, and revenue from government lands, contributions from government corporations and companies, interest and loan repayments, etc.

Expenditure	1981/82	1982/83	1983/84*
Current budget	237.8	—	—
Education and social welfare	49.9	61.0	63.2
Health	18.0	22.1	25.9
General administration	51.7	48.7	98.4
Transport and communications	6.9	5.3	6.0
Police and justice	15.9	14.0	13.4
Defense	14.8	17.5	24.0
Agriculture and natural resources	14.0	14.1	19.6
Tourism and cultural affairs	0.8	0.6	0.7
Pensions and gratuities	6.6	6.8	7.4
Trade and industry	1.4	0.9	1.0
Construction and development	20.4	18.3	20.2
Housing and country planning	1.9	1.6	1.6
Other	35.5	7.9	9.0
Public debt charges	73.0	52.5	146.2
TOTAL	310.8	271.3	436.6

*Estimates.

GROWTH PROFILE Annual Growth Rates (%)	
Population 1980-2000	2.3
Birthrate 1965-83	2.3
Deathrate 1965-83	−19.2
Urban Population 1973-83	3.3
Labor Force 1980-2000	1.7
GNP 1973-82	1.8
GNP per capita 1973-82	−0.3
GDP 1973-83	1.9
GDP per capita 1970-81	−0.8
Consumer Prices 1970-81	12.8
Wholesale Prices	—
Inflation 1973-83	14.7
Agriculture 1973-83	2.2
Manufacturing 1973-83	2.5
Industry 1973-83	−2.9
Services 1973-83	4.1
Mining 1970-81	−9.7
Construction 1970-81	3.8
Electricity 1970-81	4.2
Transportation 1970-81	5.0
Trade 1970-81	2.3
Public Administration & Defense 1970-81	10.1
Export Price Index 1975-81	8.2
Import Price Index 1975-81	14.2
Terms of Trade 1975-81	−5.1
Exports 1973-83	−5.3
Imports 1973-83	−5.0
Public Consumption 1973-83	−2.1
Private Consumption 1973-83	3.2
Gross Domestic Investment 1973-83	1.1
Energy Consumption 1973-83	6.9
Energy Production	—

clude the National Development Bank and the National Cooperative Development Bank. In addition, there is a Post Office Savings Bank with 41 branches. About 85% of bank lending is to a small group of foreign traders.

nations of ½, 1, 5, 10, 20 and 50 cents; notes are issued in denominations of 50 cents and 1, 2, and 5 leones.

The leone was introduced in August 1964 to replace the West African pound. The leone has always maintained its exchange rate with sterling at the rate of £1=2 leones. Since 1972 it has been floating with the British pound. In 1978 the leone's link with the British pound was broken and the leone was revalued in terms of IMF's SDR (based on a weighted basket of 16 currencies). This link was severed in December 1982, when a dual exchange system was introduced to conserve foreign exchange and to curb trading on the black market. However, this two-tier exchange rate proved largely unsuccessful, and was abandoned in July 1983 in favor of a new fixed exchange rate. A further devaluation, of around 58%, was implemented in February 1985. In 1984 the leone's exchange value against the pound was *L1=Le 2.909. The August 1985 dollar exchange rate was $1=Le5.531.

The central bank is the Bank of Sierra Leone, established in 1963. Of the three commercial banks, two are foreign-owned and one, the Sierra Leone Commercial Bank, is owned by the government. In 1984 commercial banks held a total of Le185.6 million in reserves, Le221.7 million in demand deposits and Le222.6 million in time deposits. Specialized credit institutions in-

AGRICULTURE

Agriculture is the largest economic sector in terms of its contribution to GDP (32%). It contributes 16 to 20% of exports by value, and its growth rate during 1973-83 was 2.2%. Agriculture employs 65% of the labor force. The value added in agriculture in 1983 was $312 million.

Of the total land area of 7,174,000 hectares (17,726,954 acres), some 82% is regarded as arable, or 2.02 hectares (5 acres) per capita. Land under actual cultivation is estimated at 528,133 hectares (1,305,000 acres), of which 203,159 hectares (502,000 acres) are in the Eastern Province, 183,733 hectares (454,000 acres) in the Northern Province, 137,598 hectares (340,000 acres) in the Southern Province, and 3,642 hectares (9,000 acres) in the Western Area. Based on 1974-76=100, the index of agricultural production in 1982 was 111, the index of food production was 109 and the index of per capita food production was 98.

The prevailing land tenure system, as in most other African countries, is communal ownership, officially sanctioned by the Protectorate Ordinance of 1927, which vested all land rights in the tribal authorities who held the land on behalf of the community. The individual landholder has no right to sell or mortgage the land or convey such rights of disposal to his heirs, though, in principle, usufructary rights are passed down within the same family. The only ways in which the mortmain could be modified were through pledging and leasing, but both arrangements are temporary and do not affect the communality of tenure. The average size of a farmholding is estimated at 1.8 hectares (4.5 acres).

The prevailing system of cultivation is described as shifting cultivation, or rotational bush fallow, or slash-and-burn agriculture. Under this system fields are cleared in rotation within walking distance of a village, cultivated for a season, and then left fallow for a number of years. The planting calendar varies from year to year depending on the time and duration of rains. Over 98% of holdings are cultivated by hand and only 3% use fertilizers. The number of tractors in the country was 330 in 1982. The annual consumption of fertilizers in 1982 was 3,300 tons, or 0.6 kg (1.3 lb) per arable hectare.

Sierra Leone's farmlands are divided into two broad classes: low-lying, inundated swamplands, known in other countries as wet or irrigated lands, and uplands, known elsewhere as dry or rain-fed lands. Swamplands constitute only 25% of the acreage under crops but provide 56% of the output. In 1970 84,083 hectares (207,766 acres) were under swampland rice and 262,815 hectares (649,408 acres) were under upland rice. Of the 56% of annual rice tonnage produced by swamplands, 27% was produced by inland freshwater mangrove swamps, 10% from tidal mangrove swamps, 15% from inland valley swamplands, 2% from southern grasslands, and 2% from seasonally flooded inland grasslands in the north, known as bolilands. The average rice yield on inland valley swamplands is 1,593 kg per hectare (645 lbs per acre), the highest in West Africa.

Agricultural development has been given top priority in the five-year plans. Among the integrated agricultural development projects (IADP) undertaken by the government and funded by the International Development Association, are the Eastern Area Project, the Northern Area Project, the World Food Program inland swamp project in Kambia and Port Loko districts, and the oil palm plantation project at Daru. Government control over agricultural marketing and production is exerted through the Sierra Leone Produce Marketing Board (SLPMB). The SLPMB was set up in 1949 with a statutory monopoly in the export of the major cash crops, and this has facilitated export taxation in a range of 30% – 60% of gross receipts. The SLPMB's high administrative costs, as well as trading surpluses, may be considered as hidden taxation on the farmers. An attempt by the SLPMB to establish plantations and processing plants in the early to mid-1960s was a financial disaster, and partly accounted for the national financial crisis which brought in the first IMF-sponsored stabili-

zation program. The low prices that were offered to farmers by the SLPMB (for example, in 1979/80 cocoa producers received 61% of the export price, whereas coffee and palm kernel producers were paid only 45% and 43% respectively) have tended to encourage the smuggling of produce to neighboring countries, especially Liberia, where «hard» currency can be earned.

Of the 60 different food crops grown in the country rice accounts for 40% of the value of output and other food crops for 25%. Over 65% of the land under cultivation is planted with rice, and 80% of cultivators are engaged in rice growing. Sierra Leone is normally self-sufficient in rice but imports rice in poor years. In 1983, 119,000 tons of cereals were imported. The import of rice is controlled by two or three powerful businesses. Other food crops include cassava, yams, peanuts, corn, pineapples, coconuts, tomatoes and peppers. Export crops include palm kernels, coffee, cocoa, pissava (a raffia palm fiber) and bananas.

PRINCIPAL CROP PRODUCTION (1982) (000 metric tons)	
Corn	13
Millet	11
Sorghum	11
Rice	550
Sweet potatoes	13
Cassava	97
Tomatoes	16
Dry broad beans	1
Citrus fruit	62
Mangoes	4
Palm kernels	30
Palm oil	48
Groundnuts	15
Coconuts	3
Coffee	11
Cocoa beans	10

Stockraising is an important activity only among the Fullah and Kissi tribes, and over 90% of the cattle herd is raised in the Northern Province. The national cattle herd consists mostly of the small N'dama breed, whose low yield is offset by its hardiness. The livestock population in 1982 consisted of 350,000 cattle, 40,000 pigs, 275,000 sheep, 158,000 goats and 4,000,000 chickens.

In 1982 forests covered 320,117 hectares (791,000 acres), mostly in government reserves in the mountainous east and western hills. Annual roundwood production in 1982 was 7.946 million cubic meters (281 million cubic ft). About 41,000 cubic meters (1.448 million cubic ft) of sawn timber are produced annually by four sawmills. Some timber is imported.

Fishing employs over 10,000 fishermen, and the fishing fleet consists of 2,500 canoes. Annual catch in 1982 was 65,500 tons, of which Bonga fish and sardines constituted 78%. As in Ghana, most of fish marketing is in the hands of women traders called mammies who also act as moneylenders to the trade. Offshore fishing is conducted mostly by foreign fishermen. The annual per capita consumption of fish is 17.5 kg (38.8 lbs).

Agricultural credit is available only through non-institutional channels, such as moneylenders, who lend money at rates often in excess of 150% per year. Many smallholders are perpetually in debt, and average rural indebtedness is estimated at Le39 per farmholder.

sumption. Energy imports account for 10% of all merchandise imports. Apparent per capita consumption of gasoline is 15 gallons per year.

Total electric power production in 1984 was 210 million kwh, or 55 kwh per capita.

An oil refinery using Nigerian crude has been operating since 1969 producing about 10,000 barrels per day.

INDUSTRY

Sierra Leone's earliest industries in the modern sector were directed toward import substitution. In a reordering of priorities in the 1975-79 plan, the emphasis was shifted to export-oriented industries based on domestic raw materials and agricultural products. There was also a move away from large-scale, capital-intensive enterprises to labor-intensive, small-scale industries and handicrafts.

Most of the industries established under the Development of Industries Act of 1960 are foreign-owned. Under this act the government also built the Wellington Industrial Estate in the suburbs of Freetown. The act was revised in 1975, eliminating loopholes, discouraging repatriation of funds, and reducing the broad nature of fiscal and tax incentives.

In the early 1980s there were 46,948 establishments employing fewer than 50 workers and 28 establishments employing more than 50 workers, of which only six employed more than 100 workers. Of the total value added of $38 million in this sector, 80.5% was derived from food, beverage and tobacco products and 8.1% from the manufacture of chemicals and related products. Manufacturing employs 11% of the labor force and contributes 5.1% to the GDP; its growth rate during the 1973-83 was 2.5%.

Official industrial policy envisages a mixed role for the public and private sectors. The poor performance of public industries in the 1960s has discouraged the government from expanding its share of the manufacturing sector. Private industrial development is favored by the current government. In 1982 the government called for the privatization of some public enterprises, and sold one-half of its shares in the petroleum refinery to five foreign oil companies. The government also encourages foreign investment through generous provisions permitting repatriation of capital and profits and through guarantees against nationalization. Net direct private investment in 1983 was $2 million. Industrial credit and development are coordinated by the Sierra Leone Investment Corporation and the Development of Industries Board.

ENERGY

Sierra Leone does not produce any form of energy other than electric power. Its total consumption of energy in 1982 was 310,000 million metric tons of coal equivalent, or 91 kg (201 lbs) per capita. The annual growth rate during 1973-83 was 6.9% for energy con-

LABOR

Of the total estimated economically active population of 1.353 million in 1982, 65% was engaged in agriculture, 19% in industry and 16% in services. Women constituted 36% of those economically active. Of the 70,541 wage earners 8.2% were employed in agriculture, 8.2% in mining, 11% in manufacturing, 11.1% in construction, 9.8% in trade, 2.6% in public utilities, 10.2% in transportation and communications and 38.6% in public administration and defense.

Wages, conditions of work and collective bargaining are regulated by the National Negotiating Board and 14 trade group councils. In 1981 the average workweek was 44 hours and the average wage Le19.20 per week.

There is no minimum age for the employment of children. The work week is defined as 7 hours for five weekdays plus three and a half hours on Saturday. There is an established code outlining acceptable conditions of work, but in actual practice in the very limited manufacturing sector of Sierra Leone, maintenance of machinery, safety procedures, and sanitary conditions probably do not conform to the code.

The number of unemployed workers is steadily rising. The 8,380 workers registered with employment exchanges in 1981 represent only a fraction of those actually unemployed.

There are 27 registered labor unions, representing 35% of wage earners. Twelve are affiliated with the powerful Sierra Leone Labour Congress, which claims 18,000 members.

FOREIGN COMMERCE

The foreign commerce of Sierra Leone consisted in 1984 of imports of $171.59 million and exports of $225.39 million, leaving a favorable trade balance of $53.8 million. Of the imports food constituted 30.5%, fuels 22.4%, machinery and transport equipment 17.5%, manufactured goods 15.3% and chemicals 5.3%. Of the exports, diamonds constituted 45.4%, cacao 13.2%, coffee 13.1%, rutile 9.9, bauxite 9.8%, gold 2.8% and palm kernels 1.4%.

The major import sources are: the United kingdom 23.0%, Japan 10.0%, the United States 9.0%, and West Germany 8.0%. The major export destinations are: the United Kingdom 45.0%, the United States 20.0%, the Netherlands 9.0% and West Germany 8.6%.

Based on 1975=100, the import price index in 1981 was 202, the export price index was 146 and the terms

of trade (export price divided by import price × 100) 73.

FOREIGN TRADE INDICATORS (1984)	
Annual Growth Rate, Imports:	–5.0 (1973-83)
Annual Growth Rate, Exports:	–5.3 (1973-83)
Ratio of Exports to Imports:	56:44
Exports per capita:	$58
Imports per capita:	$44
Balance of Trade:	$53.8 million
Ratio of International Reserves to Imports (in months)	1.0
Exports as % of GDP:	23.3
Imports as % of GDP:	33.1
Value of Manufactured Exports:	—
Commodity Concentration:	18.4%

Direction of Trade (%)		
	Imports	Exports
EEC	35.5	63.7
U.S.	8.7	17.8
Industrialized Market Economies	71.1	71.1
East European Economies	—	—
High Income Oil Exporters	—	—
Developing Economies	15.7	11.2

Composition of Trade (%)		
	Imports	Exports
Food	22.1	30.1
Agricultural Raw Materials	2.8	0.7
Fuels	17.3	—
Ores & Minerals	1.7	69.1
Manufactured Goods	55.4	—
of which Chemicals	7.4	—
of which Machinery	24.6	—

In 1973 the government entered the import trade through the state-owned National Trading Company. Sierra Leone, Liberia and Guinea are members of a customs union under the Marro River Agreement.

TRANSPORTATION & COMMUNICATIONS

Sierra Leone's former 499-km (310-mi) rail system from Freetown to Pendembu and Makeni ceased operation in 1973; the line was dismantled and shipped as scrap to Japan. It is being reactivated in the mid-1980s with the reopening of the iron ore mines of Marampa.

Sierra Leone's inland waterways total close to 800 km (497 mi). Some of the upper reaches of the rivers are only navigable for three months of the year, and many have rapids or falls where only canoes can be used. Most of the river traffic is handled by private launches.

Freetown has one of the best natural harbors in the world with a channel more than 11 meters (36 ft) deep and 6 km (4 mi) wide, free from silting. The port has berth facilities for six to eight ships with 58,000 sq meters (625,000 sq ft) of storage space. Pepel, on the Sierra Leone River, is a special port for the export of iron ore. The port of Point Sam is used for bauxite and rutile. The only other major ports are Bonthe and Sulima which, together with Freetown, are managed by the Sierra Leone Ports Authority. In 1982 these ports handled 687,000 metric tons of cargo. The National Shipping Company is partly government owned and partly owned by the Norwegian Ocean Transport.

There are 7,460 km (4,633 mi) of main roads maintained by the Public Works Department and 3,480 km (2,161 mi) of roads maintained by local authorities. The main highways run from Freetown to Sefadu, from Freetown to Kenema, and from Freetown to Wellington. Some 1,225 km (761 mi) are paved. Road development has received high priority in the five-year plans. New routes constructed in the mid-1970s included one linking Bo and Kenema and another linking Liberia and Sierra Leone. Motor vehicles registered in the country include 16,009 passenger cars and 4,826 commercial vehicles. Per capita vehicle ownership is 4.1 per 1,000 inhabitants. The Sierra Leone Road Transport Corporation operates transport services throughout the country, with a fleet of 60 buses and 16 trucks.

The national airline is Sierra Leone Airways, in which the government holds 51% interest, British Caledonian Airways 43%, and Mining General Services 6%. It operates weekly flights to London, daily flights to Accra, Monrovia and Lagos, and domestic flights. Of the 11 usable airfields in the country, five have permanent-surface runways, one with a runway over 2,500 meters (8,000 ft). The largest international airport is Lungi, across the bay from Freetown. The largest domestic airport is Hastings, near Freetown.

In 1984 there were 16,000 telephones in the country, or 0.5 per 100 inhabitants.

Sierra Leone's 137 post offices handled 151,584,000 pieces of mail and 93,000 telegrams in 1982. The volume of mail per capita was 39 pieces. There are 224 telex subscriber lines.

In 1982, 53,000 tourists visited the country. Total tourist receipts were $7 million and expenditures by nationals abroad $10 million. There are 1,000 hotel beds and the average length of stay was 4.4 days. Sierra Leone's main tourist attraction is Lumley Beach, said to be among the world's best.

MINING

Sierra Leone's known mineral resources include diamonds, iron ore, rutile and bauxite. Minerals accounted for 69% of export earnings in 1982.

Sierra Leone is the fourth largest producer of gem diamonds in the world, and its stones are highly prized in the market. Diamonds are scattered over a very large area, particularly along the upper Sewa Riva. Until 1955 diamond mining was a monopoly of the Sierra Leone Selection Trust. In 1955 SLST's monopoly was restricted to two areas in Kono and Kenema. An Alluvial Diamond Mining Scheme was introduced in 1956 by which native Sierra Leoneans were issued licenses to dig in declared areas. A Government Diamond Office was set up as the sole legal exporter in agreement with the Central Selling Organization of the De Beers group. In 1962 the government ordered the SLST to sell its diamonds only through the GDO. In 1970 the government acquired a 51% interest in SLST, whose name was changed to the National Diamond Mining Company. Both production and exports of diamonds are variable from year to year; in 1982 production was 303,000 metric carats. On average about one-third is produced by the National Diamond Mining Company, one-third by licensed diggers, and one-third by illicit diggers. The number of legal diggers is estimated at 16,000 and that of illegal diggers at 20,000. Between 1968 and 1973 some 4.2 million carats of diamonds (equal to the legal production) are believed to have been smuggled out of the country. The official production of diamonds has been declining in volume since 1970, and it is believed that the reserves will be exhausted in the not-too-distant future.

Sierra Leone is the world's second largest producer of rutile, a form of titanium oxide. Major deposits are found near Gbangbama and in Rotifunk. The Gbangbama deposits are being exploited by Sierra Rutile, in which Nord Resources holds an 85% interest. Proven reserves are estimated at over 3.5 million tons. Production in 1984 was 91,000 tons.

The main iron ore deposits of 64% pure iron are near Marampa in Port Loko district and between Sokoya and Waka Hills in Tonkolili district. Until 1975 these deposits were mined by the Sierra Leone Development Company (DELCO). Beset by labor problems, the slump in iron ore prices and heavy debts, DELCO went into voluntary liquidation in 1975. The mines were reactivated in 1982. Production of iron ore in 1984 was 147,000 metric tons.

Bauxite, discovered in 1928, is mined in the Mokanji Hills in Moyamba district by the Sierra Leone Ore and Metal Company (SIEROMCO), a subsidiary of the Swiss Alusuisse. Production was 1 million tons in 1984. New deposits discovered near Port Loko are estimated at 100 million tons with a 47% aluminum content. The government will have a majority interest in the Port Loko operations. A new plant is being constructed at Port Loko to process the bauxite into alumina.

DEFENSE

The defense structure is headed by the president, who is also the commander in chief and the minister of defense. The Armed Forces Council consists of the prime minister, the forces commander and the defense secretary. The forces commander is also a member of the House of Representatives. Military manpower is provided by voluntary enlistment.

The total strength of the armed forces is 3,100, or 1.6 armed persons per 1,000 civilians.

ARMY:
Personnel: 3,000

Organization: 2 infantry battalions; 2 artillery batteries; 1 engineer squadron

Equipment: 14 armored cars; 10 guns/howitzers; mortars; rocket launchers; SAM

NAVY:
Personnel: 100

Naval Base: Freetown

Units: 1 fast attack craft

AIR FORCE:
Personnel: 4

Organization & Equipment: 1 helicopter

Air Base: Hastings

The military budget in 1983/84 was $9.562 million, which was 6.2% of the national budget, 0.9% of the GNP, $3 per capita, $4,000 per soldier and $167 per sq km of national territory.

Sierra Leone has no pressing strategic or territorial defense needs. Defense spending, therefore, has become a means of containing the military's political ambitions. There is also a correlation, demonstrated in 1967, between internal security and ethnic loyalties in the army. The army remains small and untried in field combat, and the likelihood of its being called upon to defend the nation against external aggression is very slim.

Upon independence British military equipment was turned over to Sierra Leone, and Great Britain continued to supply arms and to train Sierra Leonean army personnel. In the 1960s British disbursements provided 25% of the total defense budget. Military training assistance has also been provided by Israel, Nigeria, Sweden and China. Arms purchases abroad during 1973-83 totaled $10 million.

EDUCATION

The national literacy rate is 15% (13.4% for males and 17.0% for females). Of the population over 25, 94.4% have had no schooling, 0.4% have attended but not completed first level, 2.9% have completed first level, 1.1% have attended but not completed second level, 0.9% have completed second level and 0.3% have completed post-secondary education. Sierra Leone has not yet introduced free, universal and compulsory education. Schooling consists of 14 years divided into seven years of primary school and five years of lower secondary school and two years of upper secondary school, the latter for those who wish to pursue higher studies. In the mid-1980s there were a total of 1,182 primary schools and 165 secondary schools in the country.

The school enrollment ratio is 40% in the primary grades (5 to 11) and 13% in the secondary grades (12 to 18), for a combined enrollment ratio of 28%. The third level enrollment ratio is 0.6%. Girls constitute 40% of primary school enrollment, 32% of secondary school enrollment and 16% of post-secondary enrollment.

The academic year runs from September to July. The medium of instruction at all levels is English.

Christian missionary schools account for a significant percentage of enrollment: 78% at primary and 87% at secondary levels. The Muslim Ahmadiyya movement also runs secondary schools.

Only 47% of primary school teachers and 52% of secondary school teachers are qualified. In relation to other countries, women make up a comparatively smaller proportion of Sierra Leone's total stock of teachers. They constitute about 30% of the teaching staff in secondary schools and 23% of total enrollment in primary teachers training colleges. The teaching staff has been completely Sierra Leoneanized at the primary level, but non-Sierra Leoneans constitute 10 to 15% of teachers in secondary schools and over 36% of university teachers. Non-Sierra Leonean teachers include volunteers from Britain and Canada and members of the U.S. Peace Corps. The teacher-pupil ratio is 1:32 at the primary level, 1:22 at the secondary level and 1:10 at the tertiary level.

Adult education programs are coordinated by the National Committee for Literacy Development and the non-governmental Provincial Literacy Bureau, but the main efforts in this field are conducted by voluntary groups.

Less than 2% of secondary school students are enrolled in the vocational stream. The Freetown Technical Institute offers both secondary and post-secondary courses, while three trade centers at Kissy, Kenema and Magburaka offer three-year vocational programs at the secondary level.

Educational policy is formulated by the Ministry of Education. Both primary and secondary school systems are supervised by principal education officers. Primary education is controlled by local authorities, and secondary schools are managed by government-appointed boards of governors. The University of Sierra Leone is an autonomous institution governed by a court and senate. Fees are collected at all levels of education, but almost all students in the university and in the teachers colleges receive loans or scholarships. The education budget in 1980 was Le42,734,000, which constituted 3.9% of the GNP, 14.76% of the national budget and $13 per capita.

EDUCATIONAL ENROLLMENT (1981)

	Schools	Teachers	Students
First Level	1,182	8,472	263,724
Second Level	165	2,828	63,299
Vocational	10	301	3,007
Third Level	1	270	1,809

The University of Sierra Leone, established in 1966, comprises two campuses: the Fourah Bay College at Freetown and the Njala University College at Njala, with a combined enrollment of 1,809 in 1981. Close to one-fifth of the student body came from foreign countries, including Nigeria, Cameroon, Zimbabwe and The Gambia. University enrollment is 205 per 100,000 inhabitants.

In 1982, 857 students from Sierra Leone were enrolled in institutions of higher learning abroad. Of these 504 were in the United States, 165 in the United Kingdom, 42 in West Germany and 27 in Canada.

Sierra Leone's contribution to world scientific authorship is 0.0030% (U.S.=42%), and its rank in the world in this respect is 106th.

LEGAL SYSTEM

Sierra Leone has retained the English legal system, which it inherited from colonial days. Most of the judges and lawyers are trained in England.

The court system consists of five levels: the Supreme Court, the Court of Appeal, and the High Courts in Freetown and in the Provinces constitute the superior courts. Below this level the country is divided into 12 judicial districts, one for each province and nine for the Western Area. At least one magistrate's court is located in each district. Local courts, formerly called native courts, are located at the chieftaincy level.

The independence of the judiciary is guaranteed by the constitution. All judges have tenure and may be removed only by a two-thirds vote of parliament. All judges are appointed by the president on the advice of the prime minister, but magistrates and other court officers are appointed on the advice of the Judicial Service Commission.

The judiciary has generally maintained its independence from the government, although some critics charge that the legal system is increasingly subject to political manipulation, often before cases reach the courts. The 1978 constitution gives the president power to retire judges after age 55. This controversial provision was used most recently by President Stevens in mid-November to retire Chief Justice Ebenezer Livesey Luke. Luke's predecessor was retired by the same provision. This surprise move against Luke provoked considerable public criticism, particularly among the local legal community. Sierra Leone's courts have a reputation for providing fair public trials. Defendants are allowed counsel of their choice, and convictions may be appealed. However, many poor defendants cannot afford counsel, and a public defender is provided only in capital offense cases. Persons detained under the Public Emergency Act are not guaranteed a hearing unless charged with a capital offense. There are no political prisoners, although informed observers suspect that some of the individuals sentenced for criminal activity in the 1983 Pujehun incident were originally held for political reasons.

In 1976 there were 16 prisons in the country, of which the largest is the Freetown Central Prison.

LAW ENFORCEMENT

The national police force has an authorized strength of 82 police officers, 211 junior police officers and 3,833 other ranks, including 382 women. Sierra Leone ranks 103rd in the world in per capita strength of internal security forces.

The force is organized into five geographic divisions under a police commissioner, who is also a member of the House of Representatives and a minister of state without portfolio. Each regional division is subdivided into a number of formations, including the Criminal Investigation Department, which is also concerned with counterinsurgency and countersubversive activities. The diamond mines form a special police region. Each chiefdom keeps an additional force known as the chiefdom police.

There are two other special groups concerned with law enforcement: ISU-1 and ISU-2. Their composition and functions are not precisely known, but ISU-2 was formerly known as the militia or Active Security Unit. Its strength is reported to be 550, and its members are believed to have been trained by Cuban instructors.

The most important law enforcement problems, in descending order of incidence, are armed robbery with violence, illegal trafficking in djamba (a form of cannabis) and ritual murder by secret societies. Sexual offenses are relatively uncommon. Available statistics also indicate that offenses by juveniles are increasing in relation to other age groups. The growing threat of armed gangs has led to a gradual enlargement of the type of crimes to which the death penalty is applicable.

HEALTH

In 1980 there were 112 hospitals in the country with 3,752 beds, or 1 bed per 952 inhabitants. In 1981 there were 220 physicians in the country, or 1 physician per 16,232 inhabitants, 18 dentists and 708 nursing personnel. Of the hospitals 76.8% are state-run, 15.2% are run by private nonprofit agencies and 8.0% by private for-profit agencies. Per 10,000 inhabitants, the admissions/discharge rate is 13, the bed occupancy rate is 77.1% and the average length of stay is 18 days.

PRINCIPAL HEALTH INDICATORS (1984)

Crude Death Rate: 29.7 per 1,000

Decline in Death Rate: −19.2% (1965-83)

Infant Mortality Rate: 136.3 per 1,000 Live Births

Child Death Rate (Ages 1-4) per 1,000: 54

Life Expectancy at Birth: 32.5 (Males); 34.5 (Females)

In 1982 health expenditures constituted 4.1% of the national budget, and $3.50 per capita. Major health problems include parasitic and infectious diseases, schistosomiasis, gastroenteritis, helminthiasis, goiter and leprosy. Only 12% of the population have access to safe water.

FOOD

The staple diet of Sierra Leone consists of rice and vegetables. Meat and fish are consumed mainly in towns. Per capita food intake per day is 2,106 calories, 44.8 grams of protein, 54 grams of fats and 392 grams of carbohydrates.

MEDIA & CULTURE

The daily press consists of one government-owned newspaper, *Daily Mail*, published in Freetown with a circulation of 12,000, or 4 per 1,000 inhabitants. Nondailies include nine papers, of which all but two are published in Freetown. Twenty-six periodicals are also published. In 1982 newsprint consumption was 200 metric tons, or 56 kg (123 lb) per 1,000 inhabitants.

Sierra Leone's long-standing tradition of press freedom is being increasingly eroded under APC rule. Newspapers that stray from the government line are harassed and their editors occasionally jailed. The political opposition currently has no major press outlet.

There is in practice considerable press freedom and no prior press censorship in Sierra Leone. Newspapers report on sensitive political topics such as misuse of government funds, bribery, and bureaucratic indiscipline. The government, in the person of the president or minister of information, regularly issues press releases stating that there is no press censorship, but usually adds that critics should be fair and place events in the context of the development process. President-elect Joseph Saidu Momoh met the press the day after his nomination and, while reaffirming his support for freedom of the press, warned that press freedom must not lead to excessive criticism of the country. The government thus expects journalists to exercise some self-censorship. Most editors avoid publishing articles portraying the country in a critical light or attacking the personality of the head of state. This approach is embedded in the Newspaper Act of 1983, which set qualification standards for editors and a fee for registration of newspapers.

The national news agency is Sierra Leone News Agency. Tass, UPI, Hsinhua, and AFP are the only news agencies with bureaus in Freetown.

Sierra Leone has a modest book publishing industry with a 1982 output of 17 titles. The largest title output comes from the Government Printer. The Njala University Publishing Center and the Sierra Leone University Press began a limited scholarly book publishing program in the mid-1970s. The Provincial Literature Bureau produces literacy texts in African languages.

The Sierra Leone Broadcasting Service operates Radio Sierra Leone (RSL), broadcasting for 108 hours a week on two short-wave lengths and one medium-wave length. Over 60% of the programs are in English, and the rest are in Mende, Temne, Krio and Limba. RSL regularly carries commercial advertising. Of the 9,125 annual radio broadcasting hours, 4,800 are devoted to information, 165 to education, 15 to culture, 225 to religion, 3,300 to commercials and 650 to entertainment. In 1982 the number of radio receivers in the country was estimated at 650,000, or 177 per 1,000 inhabitants.

Television broadcasting is part of the Sierra Leone Broadcasting Service and serves the Freetown area with one channel. A nationwide television service is planned with a new transmitter located outside Freetown. The service is on the air for 35 hours a week, but only one-third of the programs are of domestic origin. Of the 1,267 annual television broadcasting hours, 331 are devoted to information, 128 to education, 25 to culture, 104 to religion, 99 to commercials and 580 to entertainment. In 1982 there were 22,000 television receivers in the country, or 6.0 per 1,000 inhabitants.

In 1980 there were 15 cinemas in the country with 5,500 seats or 2 per 1,000 inhabitants. Annual movie attendance was 1,020,000, or 0.3 per inhabitant. Over 600 films are imported annually.

The largest library is that at the University of Sierra Leone with over 85,000 volumes. Main libraries are located in Freetown and in each of the provincial capitals under the auspices of the Sierra Leone Library Board. Per capita, there are 144 volumes and 32 registered borrowers per 1,000 inhabitants.

The national museum at Freetown reports an annual attendance of 63,000.

SOCIAL WELFARE

Sierra Leone does not have a comprehensive social security system. Welfare assistance provided by missions and voluntary organizations is coordinated by the National Council of Social Services. The Ministry of Social Welfare handles family casework, probation work with juvenile delinquents, and programs for the care of the aged, the blind and the mentally deficient. Activities of different ministries engaged in community development are integrated by the Coordinating Committee.

GLOSSARY

bolilands: seasonally flooded low-lying grasslands in the north.
mainland: the hinterland of Sierra Leone as distinct from the Peninsula and the Islands.

CHRONOLOGY (from 1961)

1961— Sierra Leone becomes an independent country within the Commonwealth of Nations with Milton Margai as prime minister.
1962— In first national elections, Margai's Sierra Leone People's Party (SLPP) wins a plurality and forms a government with independents' support.

1964— Milton Margai dies and is succeeded as prime minister by his half brother, Albert Margai.
1967— In second national elections the opposition All People's Congress, led by Siaka Stevens, wins a plurality; Stevens is sworn in as new prime minister; Brig. David Lansana declares martial law and prevents Stevens from taking office; Lansana is ousted within two days by a group of officers opposed to both Margai and Stevens; Col. A. Juxon-Smith is named leader of the new junta, which names itself the National Reformation Council
1968— Soldiers' revolt led by Private Morlai Kamara and Warrant Officer Alex Conteh restores John Bangura as army head and Siaka Stevens as prime minister.
1969— SLPP leaders are arrested in the wake of widespread riots.
1970— The newly formed United Democratic Party is banned and its leaders are arrested in the wake of widespread riots in the north.
1971— Under new constitution Sierra Leone becomes a republic within the Commonwealth with Stevens as president. . . . Army units attempt to kill Stevens; Commander Bangura is tried and executed after loyal army units suppress coup.
1973— Sierra Leone and Liberia join in the Mano River Union. . . . SLPP boycotts national elections citing APC's terror tactics.
1975— Christian A. Kamara-Taylor is named prime minister. . . . National Assembly passes motion calling for a one-party state.
1976— Stevens is reelected president.
1977— In elections to the House of Representatives APC wins 74 seats and SLPP 15 seats.
1978— Constitutional referendum approves new constitution under which APC became the sole legal political party; President Stevens is re-elected for another seven-year term; Christian A. Kamara-Taylor becomes first vice-president.
1980— Sierra Leone hosts OAU summit conference at Freetown at a cost of Le123 million.
1982— Elections are held for the House of Representatives.
1983— Tribal violence erupts in Pujehan district leading to the arrests of hundreds.
1984— First vice president, Christian Kamara-Taylor, resigns.
1985— President Stevens steps down and nominates Gen. Joseph Momoh as his successor; Momoh is installed as president.

BIBLIOGRAPHY (from 1970)

Abraham, Arthur, *Mende Government & Politics Under Colonial Rule: A Historical Study of Political Change in Sierra Leone 1890-1973* (New York, 1979)
Barrows, Walter, *Grassroot Politics in an African State: Integration and Development in Sierra Leone* (New York, 1976).

Cartwright, John R., *Politics in Sierra Leone, 1947-67* (Toronto, 1970).

——, *Political Leadership in Sierra Leone* (Toronto, 1978).

Clapham, C., *Liberia and Sierra Leone* (New York, 1976).

Clarke, J. I., *Sierra Leone in Maps* (New York, 1972).

Collier, Gershon B., *Sierra Leone: Experiment in Democracy in an African Nation* (New York, 1970).

Cox, Thomas S., *Civil-Military Relations in Sierra Leone: A Case Study of African Soldiers in Politics* (Cambridge, Mass., 1976),

Crooks, J.J., *A History of the Colony of Sierra Leone* (London, 1971).

Foray, Cyril P., *Historical Dictionary of Sierra Leone* (Metuchen, N.J., 1977).

Fyfe, Christopher, *A Short History of Sierra Leone* (New York, 1979).

International Monetary Fund, *Surveys of African Economies*, Vol. 6 (Washington, D.C., 1975).

Kup, A. P., *Sierra Leone: A Concise History* (New York, 1975).

Riddell, Barry J., *Spatial Dynamics of Modernization in Sierra Leone* (Evanston, Ill., 1970).

Roberts, George O., *The Anguish of Third World Independence: The Sierra Leone Experience* (Lanham, Md., 1982).

Sibthorpe, A. B., *History of Sierra Leone* (New York, 1970).

Spitzer, Leo, *The Creoles of Sierra Leone: Responses to Colonialism, 1870-1945* (Madison, Wis., 1974).

Steady, F. C., *Female Power in African Politics: The National Congress of Sierra Leone* (Pasadena, Calif., 1975).

UNESCO, *Cultural Policy in Sierra Leone* (Paris, 1979).

Van Der Laan, H. L., *The Lebanese Traders in Sierra Leone* (New York, 1976).

West, Richard, *Back to Africa: History of Sierra Leone and Liberia* (New York, 1971).

Wylie, Kenneth, *The Political Kingdoms of the Temne* (New York, 1977).

Williams, Geoffrey J., *A Bibliography of Sierra Leone, 1925-67* (New York, 1971).

OFFICIAL PUBLICATIONS

Auditor General, *Audit Report*.

Finance Ministry, *Financial Report*.

——, *Government Gazette* (monthly).

——, *Public Accounts Committee Report*.

Sierra Leone Bank, *Annual Report and Statement of Accounts*.

——, *Economic Review* (quarterly).

——, *Economic Trends* (quarterly).

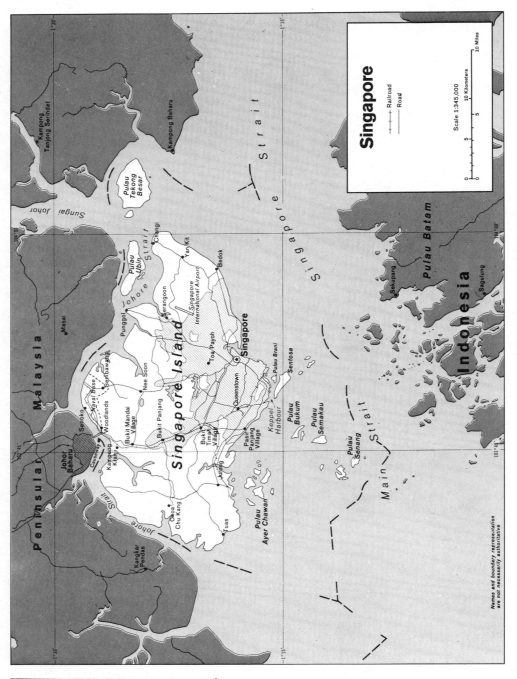

Singapore

Scale 1:345,000

Railroad
Road

Names and boundary representation
are not necessarily authoritative

MAJULAH SINGAPURA

SINGAPORE

BASIC FACT SHEET

OFFICIAL NAME: Republic of Singapore (Sing-ka-poh Kung-woh-kwok in Cantonese; Republik Singapura in Malay)

ABBREVIATION: SI

CAPITAL: Singapore

HEAD OF STATE: President Wee Kim Wee (from 1985)

HEAD OF GOVERNMENT: Prime Minister Lee Kuan Yew (from 1963)

NATURE OF GOVERNMENT: One-party modified democracy

POPULATION: 2,562,000 (1985)

AREA: 581.4 sq km (224.5 sq mi)

ETHNIC MAJORITY: Chinese

LANGUAGES: English, Chinese Cantonese, Tamil and Malay

RELIGIONS: Buddhism, Taoism, Confucianism, Islam, Hinduism and Christianity

UNIT OF CURRENCY: Singapore Dollar ($1=SD2.188, 1985)

NATIONAL FLAG: Two stripes, red at the top and white at the bottom. On the red stripe, near the hoist, are a white crescent opening to the fly and five white stars.

NATIONAL EMBLEM: A shield with five stars arranged in a circle over an upturned crescent moon.

The shield is flanked by a lion (the name Singapore means in Sanskrit, the lion-city) and a black-striped gold tiger. Beneath the device is a blue scroll with gold letters proclaiming the national motto: "Majulah, Singapura" ("Advance, Singapore").

NATIONAL ANTHEM: "Long Live Singapore"

NATIONAL HOLIDAYS: August 9 (National Day, Independence Day); January 1 (New Year's Day); May 1 (Labor Day); Also Buddhist, Chinese, Hindu, Muslim and Christian festivals.

NATIONAL CALENDARS: Gregorian and Chinese

PHYSICAL QUALITY OF LIFE INDEX: 89 (up from 85 in 1976) (On an ascending scale in which 100 is the maximum. U.S. 95)

DATE OF INDEPENDENCE: August 9, 1965

DATE OF CONSTITUTION: June 3, 1959 (as amended in 1965)

WEIGHTS & MEASURES: The metric system is to be adopted universally by 1980. Meanwhile many traditional measures and units are used in domestic commerce. These include: chupak=0.94 liter (0.249 gallon); gantang=3.785 liters (1 gallon); tahil=37.7 grams (1.3 oz); kati=0.6kg (1.3 lb); picul=60 kg (133 lb); koyan=2.419 kg (5,333 lb); ela=0.609 meters (2 ft); depa=1.8 meters (6 ft); sq jemba= 13.3776 sq meters (144 sq ft); and sq orlong=0.6 hectare (1.5 acres)

LOCATION & AREA

Singapore is located in SE Asia off the southern tip of the Malay Peninsula. It consists of the island of Singapore and several smaller adjacent islets, with a total land area of 581 sq km (224.5 sq mi), of which Singapore Island comprises 542.6 sq km (209.5 sq mi), extending 50.7 km (31.5 mi) ENE to WSW and 31.4 km (19.5 mi) SSE to NNW. Singapore has a total coastline of 193 km (120 mi) and is connected to the southern tip of Malaysia by a causeway 1.2 km (0.75 mi) in length across the narrow Johore Strait. The island is separated from Indonesia by the Strait of Malacca and the Singapore Strait, among the busiest sea passages in the world. The land area of Singapore is being constantly expanded by an ambitious program of land reclamation. The original area has already been increased by 5%, or about 30 sq km (11.5 sq mi) at a cost of about SD1 billion. A further SD1 billion is to be spent over the next decade recovering a further 20 sq km (7.7 sq mi).

The capital is Singapore. The city of Singapore is officially an area of 60 sq km (37.6 sq mi), but this is a purely academic distinction because the entire republic is one large metropolis.

The islands are generally flat and low. The highest point, Bukit Timah (Tin Hill), is less than 177 meters (581 ft) above sea level. The topography is relieved only by a few low cliffs and shallow valleys toward the southwest. The smaller islands account for 6% of the national territory. Only about 26 of these islands are inhabited, and the largest Pulau Tekong Besar is only 18 sq km (7 sq mi) in extent.

The main island is drained by a number of short streams, such as the Singapore, Jurong, Kalang, Kranji, Seletar and Serangoon.

WEATHER

Located less than 2° north of the equator, Singapore has a hot, humid tropical climate. As in most equatorial countries, the range of temperature variations is slight; the average annual daily maximum is 30.6°C (87°F) and the average minimum 24°C (75°F). The effects of high temperatures are moderated by sea breezes. Rainfall, averaging about 241 cm (95 in.) annually, is distributed fairly evenly throughout the year with rain falling on at least 180 days in a given year. Serious floods are common during the northeast monsoon.

The southwest monsoon is usually accompanied by violent squalls called sumatras.

POPULATION

The population of Singapore was estimated in 1985 at 2,562,000 on the basis of the last official census held in 1980, when the population was 2,413,945. The population is expected to reach 3.0 million by 2000 and 3.2 million by 2020.

The annual growth rate is estimated at 1.27% on the basis of an annual birth rate of 18.0 per 1,000.

With an average nationwide density of 4,427 per sq km (11,466 per sq mi), Singapore ranks second most-crowded nation in the world, after Hong Kong. As a result of the declining birth rate, the median age has been rising. In 1984 proportion in the lowest age bracket, those under 14, had dropped to 24.8% from 39% in the early 1970s. The other two age cohorts have registered proportionate gains, that between 15 and 64 rising from 58% to 70.1% and that over 65 rising from 3% to 5.1%. The sex ratio has almost reached equilibrium, 1.05 males to every 1 female. The percentage of population living in slums and squatter settlements is estimated at 15%.

Singapore is a nation of immigrants, but since independence immigration has been restricted in an effort to stabilize the population levels. All non-citizens are required to obtain work permits and have to establish residence for several years to qualify for citizenship. In an average year in the mid-1970s, nearly 4,000 entry permits for permanent residence were issued by the government, in addition to 65,000 employment passes.

Women generally enjoy equal rights, primarily under the 1969 Women's Charter and the constitution. Muslim women's rights are protected by the provisions of the 1957 Administration of Muslim Law, which permits Muslim women to apply for divorce and provides for women to hold and dispose of property. Women have voting rights and the right of equality of economic opportunity under the law. There are few women in the top ranks of the civil service or business. As a result of the 1984 election, however, there are now three PAP female members of Parliament. In 1983 the median gross monthly income of female workers was 64% of that for male workers. A shortage of workers has led the government to en-

DEMOGRAPHIC INDICATORS (1984)	
Population, total (in 1,000)	2,562
Population ages (% of total)	
0-14	24.8
15-64	70.1
65+	5.1
Youth 15-24 (000)LD]	522
Women ages 15-49 (000)	755
Dependency ratios	42.7
Child-woman ratios	279
Sex ratios (per 100 females)	103.6
Median ages (years)	27.1
Marriage rate (per 1,000)	8.8
Divorce rate (per 1,000)	0.7
Average size of Household	4.7
Decline in birthrate (%, 1960-78)	−44.6
Proportion of urban (%)	74.21
Population density (per sq. km.)	4,427
per hectare of arable land	28.00
Rates of growth (%)	1.27
urban	1.3
rural	1.1
Natural increase rates (per 1,000)	12.7
Crude birth rates (per 1,000)	18.0
Crude death rates (per 1,000)	5.3
Gross reproduction rates	0.84
Net reproduction rates	0.82
Total fertility rates	1.74
General fertility rates (per 1,000)	62
Life expectancy, males (years)	69.1
Life expectancy, females (years)	75.5
Life expectancy, total (years)	72.2
Population doubling time in years at current rate	64

courage women to work. Singaporean women do not have equal rights with men in the transmission of citizenship to their children. A Singapore woman married to a foreigner can not pass citizenship to children born outside the country, although a Singaporean man can. Additionally, the wife of a Singaporean male can receive permanent resident status and citizenship based on the marriage while the husband of a Singaporean woman cannot.

Singapore is the first Asian country to bring its population growth under control and also the first country in Asia where a zero growth rate is a realizable goal within the next few decades. The official family planning programs are administered by the Family Planning and Population Board operating 38 clinics, of which 36 are maternal and child health centers. Abortions were legalized in 1970, and the government also instituted a number of disincentives to parents of large families, such as maternity fees. The measurable results of this program are the 38,300 acceptors of government family planning services and 212,300 users of contraceptive methods, constituting 77.1% of married women of childbearing age.

ETHNIC COMPOSITION

Singaporeans belong to one of three major ethnic groups—Chinese, Malay and Indian—who together made up 98% of the population in 1978. The racial proportions of 76% Chinese, 15% Malay and 7% Indian have remained fairly stable over the years, with the

Chinese and the Indians decreasing by 2% each over the last 30 years while the Malays, reproducing somewhat more rapidly, gained slightly. In 1984 the Chinese numbered 1,935,000, Malays 374,400, Indians 162,600 and others 57,100. None of the three main communities is entirely homogeneous. The majority of the Chinese belong to the Hokkien, Teochew and Cantonese descent groups. The Malays are divided into those from the Malay Peninsula and those from Indonesia, while those called Indians actually include not only Tamils, Malayalis, Punjabis and other groups from India but also Pakistanis and Sri Lankans. While ethnic differences persist, relations between the three major groups are fairly harmonious and the government has successfully managed to keep the lid on divisive forces. Multiracialism has been stressed as a national value and a Singaporean national idenity has evolved that has no ethnic frame of reference.

In 1984 there were an estimated 57,100 residents outside of these three groups, including sizable British and U.S. communities.

In terms of ethnic and linguistic homogeneity, Singapore is ranked 62nd in the world with 58% homogeneity (on an ascending scale in which North and South Korea are ranked 135th with 100% homogeneity and Tanzania is ranked first with 7% homogeneity).

LANGUAGES

The official language is English but it is facing increasing competition from Chinese (Cantonese). The government has recently begun stressing the need for developing bilingualism. Significantly, in 1977, the *Straits Times* began publishing a regular bilingual section designed to instruct its English-language readers in Chinese.

Both Tamil and Malay have a semiofficial standing as the mother tongues of the two largest national minorities.

RELIGIONS

Singapore is a completely secular state and religious affiliations are not recorded in the census. Nevertheless, it may be safely assumed that most of the Chinese are Buddhists, Confucianists or Taoists. The Indians are Hindus and the Malays, Pakistanis and Bangladeshis are Muslims. There is a sprinkling of Christians in the Chinese and Indian communities, while the Eurasians and Europeans are overwhelmingly Christian. Singapore is the seat of an Anglican diocese and a Roman Catholic archdiocese.

Unlike in neighboring Malaysia and Indonesia, religion is not a major force in national life and its influence is purely parochial. However, the government launched a program in 1982 to spread Confucianism, whose ideals of good government happened to coincide with its own.

COLONIAL EXPERIENCE

Singapore was an almost uninhabited island when Sir Stamford Raffles established a trading station of the British East India Company there in 1819. Five years later the island was ceded outright to the company by the Sultan of Johore and was incorporated with Malacca and Penang to form the Straits Settlements. With its excellent harbor and and strategic location, the city became a flourishing commercial center. In 1938 the British constructed a large naval station on the island. It was captured by the Japanese in 1942 and recaptured by the British in 1945. In 1946 Singapore was detached from the Straits Settlements to become a separate crown colony. In 1959 Singapore became a self-governing state, and in 1963 it joined the new Federation of Malaysia. The federation was an uneasy one, and Singapore and Malaysia terminated the union in 1965 when the Republic of Singapore was proclaimed. Despite the Chinese majority in the population, the city is more British than Chinese and its prosperity is dependent on its cosmopolitan character. Anti-colonial sentiments are weaker in Singapore than in any other country in Asia.

CONSTITUTION & GOVERNMENT

The legal basis of government is the charter called the Singapore (Constitution) Order in Council, 1958, under which Singapore became a self-governing colony. With some modifications, this document became the constitution of the state of Singapore when it joined the Federation of Malaysia in 1963. Later, when Singapore left the federation and declared its independence in 1965, it served as framework of the new republic. The transition to a republic was accomplished through two amendments: the Republic of Singapore Independence Act of 1965 and the Constitution (Amendment) Act of 1965. The former provides for the continuance of certain provisions of the Malaysian constitution subject to modifications, adaptations, qualifications and exceptions. The resulting constitution is divided into seven main sections; the first deals with the presidency and the cabinet, the second with the legislature, the third with the judiciary, the fourth with citizenship, the fifth with public service, the sixth with finances, and the seventh with general and transitional provisions.

In form, the structure of government established by the constitution is parliamentary, but in substance and practice Singapore is an authoritarian and paternalistic state in which opposition is barely tolerated and in which the People's Action Party has assumed a preemptive role. Because of the country's small size, the national government exercises a direct and powerful influence on every aspect of political, economic and social life and nothing escapes its vigilant attention. The government's overriding concern is with efficiency and uninterrupted economic growth; the successful pursuit of these goals has resulted in a concentration of power in the bureaucracy and in an

ORGANIZATION OF SINGAPORE GOVERNMENT

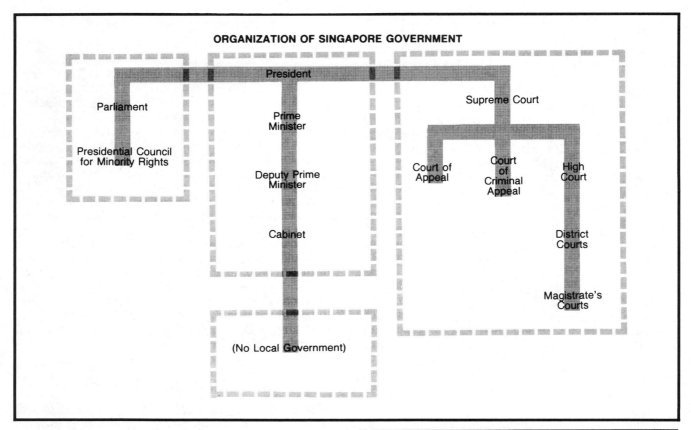

attrition of legislative powers and competitive politics.

The head of state is the president elected by parliament for a term of four years. The presidency is only a ceremonial office, although the president is vested with power to appoint the prime minister and dissolve parliament. By convention the prime minister is the leader of the majority party in parliament, and he, as well as all cabinet ministers, are collectively responsible to the parliament. The second most powerful office in the government is that of deputy prime minister, who, in 1985, was also the minister of defense.

A constitutional body whose influence has grown in recent years is the 21-member Presidential Council chaired by the chief justice. The Council examines material of racial or religious significance, including legislation, to see whether it differentiates between racial or religious minorities or contains provisions inconsistent with the fundamental liberties guaranteed by the constitution.

Elections are held every five years. Suffrage is universal over 20.

Singapore has been described as a bureaucratic state under one-party rule. Its ultimate legitimacy is its success in providing an efficient and incorruptible government, stability and economic prosperity along with minor elements of participatory democracy. It has also created a new national image and a new set of national values that emphasizes austerity, discipline and unity. Lee Kuan Yew's strategy has been to speed up the orderly march of progress through the elimination of divisive and unproductive partisan poli-

CABINET LIST (1985)

President	Wee Kim Wee
Prime Minister	Lee Kuan Yew
First Deputy Prime Minister	Goh Chok Tong
Second Deputy Prime Minister	Ong Teng Cheong
Senior Minister (PM's Office)	Sinnathamby Rajaratnam
Minister of Communications & Information	Yeo Ning Hong
Minister of Community Development	S. Dhanabalan
First Minister of Defense	Goh Chok Tong
Second Minister of Defense	Yeo Ning Hong
Minister of Education	Tony Tan
Minister of Environment	Ahmad Mattar
Minister of Finance	Richard Hu
Minister of Foreign Affairs	S. Dhanabalan
Minister of Health	Richard Hu
Minister of Home Affairs	S. Jayakumar
Minister of Labor (Acting)	Lee Yock Suan
Minister of Law	E.W. Barker
Second Minister of Law	S. Jayakumar
Minister of National Development	Teh Cheong Wan
Minister of Trade & Industry	Tony Tan
Minister Without Portfolio	Ong Teng Cheong
Minister Without Portfolio	Wan Soon Bee

tics and other forms of dissent. In doing so Lee has built up an efficient and pragmatic administration manned by a corps of loyal and devoted technocrats numbering no more than about 300. The inner core of leaders has been notably cohesive and stable, and there are no reports of internal rifts or power struggles common in many smaller nations. Lee also controls with an iron hand all areas of national life: the mass media, labor unions, schools and colleges, and the defense and police establishments. Organized labor cooperates closely with government; students are quiet if only because those who do not pass security clearance are not admitted to colleges; the press, intimidated by the government's awesome powers, exercises self-censorship; and the armed forces have no tradition of political intervention. What opposition exists is unable to provide an alternative in the face of Lee's organizational skills and responsive government. Lee's grip on the country and his party is stronger than ever before, and a stable Singapore has become an assured political reality in Southeast Asia.

In 1984, the Parliament approved a constitutional amendment creating three "non-constituency" legislative seats for opposition members. Because they were ineligible to vote on major bills, including financial bills, they were dubbed as "toothless MPs."

In 1984 Lee announced that his government was considering the introduction of a constitutional amendment that would establish a directly elected executive president. Since he had already announced that he planned to retire in 1988 when he reached the age of 65, there is speculation that Lee might himself stand for president in 1988.

FREEDOM & HUMAN RIGHTS

In terms of civil and political rights, Singapore is classified as a partly free country with a rating of 5 in civil rights and 5 in political rights (on a descending scale in which 1 is the highest and 7 the lowest in rights).

Singapore is governed under a parliamentary system modeled on British lines, but political power is concentrated in one party. The government, therefore, exhibits the characteristics of both democracy and authoritarianism. But in terms of freedom from widespread corruption, efficiency of civil service, and emphasis on quality of life, Singapore has a track record not equalled in Asia.

Although there have been no terrorist incidents in recent years, the government cites the threat of insurgency and the possibility of renewed communal conflict to justify preventive detention. Amnesty International claims that 21 of these detainees have been subjected to psychological duress and physical abuse. A government panel rebutted the charge, but acknowledged that the process of interrogation involved psychological stress. Under the Internal Security Act (ISA), a person may be held for an initial 30-day period of investigation and interrogation. After that, a person may be held only under an order of detention recommended by the Ministry of Home Affairs and the Cabinet and signed by the president. The detained person has the right of appeal to an independent advisory board.

Article Nine of the constitution recognizes the right of habeas corpus. However, the government makes use of detention without trial in not only cases involving internal security but also criminal law. Naturalized citizens may be stripped of their citizenship under the Banishment Act and deported as undesirable aliens. The Internal Security Act (ISA) is sometimes extended to those journalists who portray Singapore as undemocratic, totalitarian, autocratic and oppressive. The government declared in 1983 that only one person was held in detention under the terms of the ISA. However, 1,000 persons, approximately 70 of whom are believed to be narcotics traffickers, are detained under the Criminal Law Act which is primarily directed against organized crime. Under the Misuse of Drugs Act, the Central Narcotics Bureau may summarily force any person to submit to a urinalysis in order to detect drug use. If the test is positive, the Bureau is empowered, without further process, to commit the user to a six-month term in a drug rehabilitation center. Even upon release, the former detainee is required to remain under Bureau supervision for a period of two years. As as result, Singapore has one of the lowest recidivist rates in the world.

The right to a fair public trial is one of the strongest features of the island's human rights picture. The judicial system operates in accordance with the basic tenets, practices, and precedents of British jurisprudence. The rights of the defendants are ensured at every stage. The courts are independent of the executive and the military and appeals lie to the Judicial Committee of the Privy Council.

The rights of racial and religious minorities are monitored and upheld by the Presidential Council for Minority Rights. On the other hand, freedoms of press, speech and assembly are circumscribed in several areas. While there is no formal censorship, the press is unduly timid, being mindful of the need for annual renewal of publishing licenses. Opposition viewpoints are only occasionally published. There is also a ban on reporting on ethnically sensitive issues that might arouse communal tensions. Assemblies of more than five persons in a public place are required to have a police permit. Societies and clubs with over 10 members must be registered with the government and such registration is denied to secret societies.

All residents are required to register with the government and receive an identity card.

Although there are 17 registered opposition political parties, only seven parties ran candidates in the 1980 general election and opposition members were elected for the first time in 1981. The activities of the opposition are closely monitored by the government and campaign speeches are tape-recorded by the Internal Security Department. The successful prosecution of at least eight libel and defamation suits against the opposition parties in 1972 and 1976 have bankrupted several opposition politicians and removed them from the political scene. (Bankrupts are barred from political activities by law).

Ninety-five per cent of the unionized workers belong to 51 unions' controlled by the ruling party. Because of this tie, strikes are rare, with none since 1977.

Singapore is extremely sensitive to international criticisms of its handling of human rights issues. It denounced the ILO convention on forced labor because ILO asserted that prisoners in preventive detention were subject to forced labor and it withdrew from the Socialist International because of criticisms directed at the Internal Security Act.

CIVIL SERVICE

Singapore is an administrative state in which civil servants constitute the true ruling class. The central agency for public personnel administration is the Public Service Commission, which is a constitutional body with some autonomous powers. The commission is composed of a chairman and from five to nine members. Under the commission's jurisdiction are about 56,500 civil servants, of whom almost 50% work for the ministries of education and health. Temporary employees, numbering about 15,000, are recruited through the Employment Service of the Ministry of Labor and are excluded from the Commission's purview as are also employees of public corporations and statutory bodies. Recruitment is through competitive examination. Nepotism, so common in many other countries, and racial quotas, currently being introduced in even advanced countries, do not influence access to the civil service. In the mid-1980s women constituted 37% of all civil servants.

Administrative irregularities and minor abuses of power by public officials are investigated by the Central Complaints Bureau, while more serious charges of corruption are handled by the Corrupt Practices Investigation Bureau of the Prime Minister's Office.

LOCAL GOVERNMENT

Singapore has no local government. There are two intermediary institutions at the local level that serve as pipelines between the masses and the government: the citizens' cunsultative committees in each district and the 172 management committees of the community centers run by the People's Association, a statutory body headed by Prime Minister Lee. Each citizens' consulative committee is headed by a civil servant who reports to the Prime Minister's Office.

FOREIGN POLICY

Singapore is one of those growing number of nations for whom foreign relations are an instrument of economic policy and are geared to ensuring the continued flow of technology and investments from abroad. Diplomatic relations are only extensions of trade relations. The only area where ideology impinges on the conduct of foreign affairs is in Singapore's relations with China, with which Singapore has been long hesitant to exchange diplomatic missions. The Lee regime has stated that a Chinese embassy will not be allowed in Singapore until the Chinese majority firmly identifies itself as Singaporean. The government fears that otherwise China would exert a growing influence on the nation's Chinese population and that such influence would tend to erode the delicate multiracial balance of Singaporean society. Nevertheless, Lee was hosted and feted in Beijing in 1976, and trade relations between the two countries continue to grow with a series of business deals.

The other focal point of Singapore foreign relations is the Association of South-East Asian Nations (ASEAN), which provides the framework for the conduct of regional diplomacy. Singapore is perhaps the most ardent advocate of expanded economic cooperation within the region. Its ability to separate trade and political ideology were again underscored when it advocated developing productive relations with Vietnam, Cambodia (Kampuchea) and Laos. In 1977 a Singapore trade mission visited Hanoi and a Cambodian delegation led by Deputy Prime Minister, Ieng Sary, visited Singapore. Trade and investment issues dominate relations with Japan, which has assumed the role of a senior partner in Asian economic development. The climax of Singaporean foreign policy in 1977 was Lee's visit to the United States, where he met with President Jimmy Carter and made an eloquent plea against a precipitate U.S. withdrawal from Southeast Asia. Since the withdrawal of British defense forces from east of Suez, Singapore has been a member of the five-power defense arrangement (along with the United Kingdom, Malaysia, Australia and New Zealand), a regional security system that calls for the maintenance of Commonwealth forces in Singapore. Relations with Malaysia reverberate periodically with alarums of plots, but there has been no serious rift between the two countries. In 1979, Singapore took the toughest stand against Vietnam's aggression in Cambodia, attacking Hanoi for seeking hegemony over South East Asia. In general, it seems to articulate Asean causes more forcefully than other members.

Singapore and the United States are parties to 17 agreements and treaties covering aviation, consuls, defense, economic and technical cooperation, extradition, investment guaranties, postal matters, property, social security, trade and commerce, trademarks, and visas.

Singapore joined the U.N. in 1965; its share of the U.N. budget is 0.04%. Singapore is a member of 14 U.N. organizations and four regional groupings including the Commonwealth, ASEAN and Colombo Plan.

U.S. Ambassador in Singapore: J. Stapleton Roy
U.K. High Commissioner in Singapore: Hamilton Whyte
Singaporean Ambassador in Washington, D.C.: Tommy T.B. Koh
Singaporean High Commissioner in London: Ho Guan Lim

PARLIAMENT

The parliament is a unicameral 79-member body elected by direct universal suffrage for five-year terms. Parliament convenes at least once a year and discussions are conducted in any of the four languages: English, Chinese (Mandarin), Tamil and Malay. All bills passed by parliament require the immediate assent of the president. The parliament also elects the president of the republic.

In the last elections in 1984 People's Action Party (PAP) won 77 seats, and the Workers' Party and Singapore Democratic Party one each.

POLITICAL PARTIES

The ruling party is the People's Action Party founded in 1955 by Lee Kuan Yew. Originally a radical socialist party, it has become since 1961 (when a radical faction split off to form the Socialist Front) a moderate anti-Communist party espousing a socialist program of accelerated economic development and social welfare. Since the separation from Malaysia in 1965, the party has downplayed competitive pluralistic politics and emphasized controlled consensus under an efficient and disciplined bureaucracy. Called the "Politics of Survival", PAP ideology was oriented toward two principal goals: political stability and economic prosperity. To ensure political stability the party has worked to stamp out all opposition forces and to rally the entire population behind it.

PAP organization reflects its authoritarian philosophy. Power is concentrated within the party in the Central Executive Committee comprising the 20 most powerful men in the republic. Members of the Committee are elected—nominally—by party activists called party cadres or cadre members, who, in turn, are appointed by the Committee. The Committee is under the direction of the secretary general, a post that has been held by Lee since 1955. The Committee has eight special sections, of which one deals with political training and indoctrination. The basic units of party organization are branches established in the 65 electoral constituencies. These branches are controlled by local executive committees headed in most instances by the member of parliament representing that district. The local executive committees meet at least once a month when comments and opinions, but not criticisms, are heard from the party faithful.

The strength of the party is estimated between 15,000 and 30,000 members, more than two-thirds of them Chinese. In its early days nearly one-fourth of the membership were identified as labor unionists, but since the defection of the radical faction in 1961 this ratio has declined. However, the party is still active in the labor field through its affiliate the National Trades Union Congress. Some 2% of the party members constitute the party cadre, but a list of cadres has never been published, and the operation of the cadre system is itself shrouded in secrecy. The entire party organization comes alive at election times, although the party's electoral victories are always assured.

In 1981 the victory of the opposition Workers' Party in gaining the first seat in a hitherto all-PAP Parliament came as a shock to the PAP leadership. Although one lone opposition member posed no serious practical threat to the government, it shook the ruling party's complacency. At the party's next conference in 1982, power was further concentrated in the hands of the central executive committee and the party sought to refurbish its image as an above-politics national movement. Lee also sought to bring in new blood, a prominent example being Goh Chok Tong, chief architect of the industrial program, who was made first deputy prime minister. For the first time in 1982, second generation leaders outnumbered the Old Guard in the Central Committee.

Lee continually expresses the hope that a responsible and loyal opposition will emerge in Singapore, but that prospect has grown dimmer every year. Part of the reason lies in the government's intolerance of dissent, let alone opposition, and the methodical way in which PAP has sought to emasculate all rival institutions, through means such as detention of opposition leaders, deregistration of opposition organizations, denial of permits to hold outdoor rallies and the exclusion of the opposition from the media. Nevertheless, at least five legal and numerous illegal organizations maintain a precarious existence. The best-known of these is the Barisan Sosialis, popularly known as Barisan. The party has been torn by internal dissensions, resulting in one wing of the party going underground. Barisan is led by the veteran pro-Beijing labor unionist Lee Siew Choh. The Workers' Party, founded in 1971, led by J. B. Jeyaretnam, advocates closer relations with Malaysia and China. Closer Malay links are also the main plank of the United People's Front and the Singapore Malays National Organization. The Singapore Democratic Party, founded in 1980 as a liberal alternative to PAP, won its first parliamentary seat in 1984.

The illegal opposition comprises the Malayan Communist Party, proscribed since 1948, and the Peking-based Malaya National Liberation Front. The strength of these organizations may not exceed a few hundred.

ECONOMY

Singapore is one of the 37 high-income countries of the world with a free-market economy in which the private sector is predominant.

Ironically, the action of the International Monetary Fund (IMF) in 1977 upgrading the status of Singapore to that of a high-income developed country was protested by the government. The action threatened to deprive Singapore of the benefits and concessions that go with the status of a developing or less-developed country, including the Generalized Scheme of Preferences (GSP) and profits from the IMF gold auctions. Singapore claims that much of its wealth is based on entrepot trade and multinational and expatriate capital.

As Singapore moves into the 1980's, it is embarking on a "second industrial revolution" (which is referred to by a variety of names). It was launched in June 1979, when the National Wages Council (NWC—a tripartite organization that announces wage guidelines each year), set the 1979 wage increase guideline so as to increase employers' wage bills by an average 20% and wages by an average 14%. The high-wage policy is one of the key measures to restructure Singapore's economy for reducing the labor intensity of production and conversely increasing labor productivity in all sectors. The wage bill for workers at the low end of the pay scale will increase proportionately more than those of workers at the high end.

The move was prompted by several factors. One was the extremely tight labor market, which results from previous wage restraint, a low birth rate, the government's reluctance to allow permanent and large inflows of unskilled foreign workers, and the high economic growth rates of the 1970's. Increased labor productivity also will permit the standard of living to rise at the high rates to which Singaporeans have become accustomed. Another factor was the belief that capital-intensive and technologically sophisticated products are apt to encounter less protectionist pressures than labor-intensive ones.

Other elements of the new policy are incentives and an increased emphasis on manpower training. The government has added to and expanded the already impressive incentives available for capital expenditure and research and development, and has made it clear it will use the leverage of its new and existing incentives afford it to influence the character of new investments. The Economic Growth Board (EDB), the government's investment promotion and chief economic planning organ, has blessed 11 industries as primary targets for promotion: automotive components; machine tools and machinery; medical and surgical apparatus and instruments; specialty chemicals and pharmaceuticals; computers, computer peripheral equipment and software; electronic instrumentation; optical instruments and equipment; precision engineering products; advanced electronic components; hydraulic and pneumatic central systems; and supporting industries for the preceding industries.

Manpower training is viewed as one of the keys to increased labor productivity, along with increased capital investment and technological innovation. A Skills Development Fund financed by a payroll tax has been established to fund a wide range of training programs. In addition, local technical training institutions are being upgraded.

In 1981 Singapore achieved the high watermark of its economy, recording its highest growth rate in eight years, the third highest per capita income in Asia (outside the Middle East), and after Japan and Brunei, and the highest among ASEAN countries. Of the newly industrializing countries in Asia, only South Korea experienced a higher growth rate, but

none could beat Singapore's low inflation rate. The nation's economic strategy rested on diversification, upgrading industry and labor forces to higher skill levels, and developing the island into a regional service and international financial center. Higher productivity in skill-intensive and hi-tech industries was encouraged through investment credit and investment allowance schemes. Research and development were encouraged through a number of tax incentives given in 1980. The Asian Dollar market has resulted in the complete removal of foreign exchange controls. Although entrepot trade continues to be maintained, export promotion has become the major economic policy objective.

PRINCIPAL ECONOMIC INDICATORS

Gross National Product: $16.560 billion (1983)
  GNP Annual Growth Rate: 7.9% (1973-82)
  Per Capita GNP: $6,620 (1983)
  Per Capita GNP Annual Growth Rate: 6.5% (1973-82)
Gross Domestic Product: SD35.171 billion (1983)
  GDP at 1980 prices S$30.647 billion
  GDP Deflator (1980=100) 114.8
  GDP Annual Growth Rate: 8.2% (1973-83)
  Per Capita GDP: SD14,068 (1983)
  Per Capita GDP Annual Growth Rate: 6.9% (1970-81)
Income Distribution: Information not available
Percentage of Population in Absolute Poverty: 6
Consumer Price Index (1970=100):
  All Items: 219.9 (June 1985)
  Food: 237.0 (June 1985)
Wholesale Price Index (1975=100):
  General: 95 (April 1985)
  Manufactured Goods: 90 (February 1985)
Average Annual Rate of Inflation: 4.5% (1973-83)
Money Supply: S$8.663 billion (March 1985)
  Reserve Money: S$6.805 billion (March 1985)
Currency in Circulation: S$4.619 billion (1984)
International Reserves: $10.416 billion, of which foreign exchange were $10.291 billion (1984)

Singapore's balance of payments clearly reflects its small trade-oriented service economy; merchandise trade has regularly shown a deficit, with sizeable earnings from services. The widening trade deficit was plainly the consequence of rapid industrialization which generated an urgent and greater need to import capital goods and raw materials in a period of rising prices.

Singapore has not adopted national development planning because the economy is too sensitive to external influences and is not susceptible to long-range manipulations. Singapore's present economic prosperity, however, is based on the single conscious economic policy decision made by the government in the early 1960s: to deemphasize its role as an entrepot and to industrialize rapidly. This strategy continues to dominate economic thinking on the island with some minor changes.

Singapore is now officially classified as a donor country rather than a donee, but until recently it continued to receive some economic and technical aid from more advanced countries. U.S. aid from 1946

BALANCE OF PAYMENTS (1984)
(million $)

Current Account Balance	−1,001
Merchandise Exports	22,344
Merchandise Imports	−26,733
Trade Balance	−4,389
Other Goods, Services & Income	+9,429
Other Goods, Services & Income	−5,834
Other Goods, Services & Income Net	3,594
Private Unrequited Transfers	−193
Official Unrequited Transfers	−13
Capital Other Than Reserves	2,123
Net Errors & Omissions	392
Total (Lines 1,10 and 11)	1,514
Counterpart Items	−363
Total (Lines 12 and 13)	1,152
Liabilities Constituting Foreign Authorities' Reserves	—
Total Change in Reserves	−1,152

GROSS DOMESTIC PRODUCT BY ECONOMIC ACTIVITY
(1983)

	%	Rate of Change % 1970-81
Agriculture	1.0	1.7
Mining	0.4	8.8
Manufacturing	24.1	9.7
Construction	11.0	5.8
Electricity, Gas & Water	1.9	10.0
Transport & Communications	13.0	14.0
Trade	20.6	10.1
Finance	22.4	10.1
Public Administration & Defense	—	—
Services	11.6	8.6
Other Branches	6.0	8.6

through 1983 amounted to $2.8 million in grants, and aid from international organizations $385.9 million including $179.4 million from World Bank. During 1979-81 Singapore received $11.4 million in bilateral and multilateral assistance, or $4.70 per capita.

BUDGET

The Singaporean fiscal year runs from April 1 through March 31.

Several features mark Singapore's budget each year. A high percentage of the consolidated public sector budget, averaging about 36%, is devoted to development expenditure, which reflects both prudent management of current expenditure and the importance the government attaches to development of infrastructures. Another feature is that there is always a surplus of current expenditure over current revenue. Borrowing is usually almost entirely from domestic sources (primarily placements with the Central Provident Fund and the Post Office Savings Bank).

Following the 1974 recession, expansionary budgetary policies of the major statutory boards helped to sustain economic growth. This has been the distinctive feature of public sector financing in Singapore.

To enable the government to carry out long-term economic and social development projects with the minimum of administrative delay, the government created various statutory bodies and provided the capital funds for their expansion and operation. The seven major statutory boards are the Housing and Development Board, the Jurong Town Corporation, the Public Utilities Board, the Port of Singapore Authority, Telecoms, the Urban Redevelopment Authority and the Sentosa Development Corporation. The deficit incurred by these boards in 1983 was S$2,048 million. Thus, although the government sector had a surplus of S$1,999 million in 1983, the overall public sector deficit was S$49 million.

ORDINARY BUDGET
(S$ million — estimates for year ending 31 March)

Revenue	1984/85
Direct taxes	4,598.2
Indirect taxes and taxes on outlay	2,226.9
Reimbursements and sales on goods and services	1,114.5
Income from investments and property	1,035.4
Others	994.3
TOTAL	9,969.3

Expenditure	1984/85
General services	588.1
Defense and justice	2,442.0
Social and community services	2,218.2
Economic services	369.7
Public debt	1,853.7
Unallocable	94.7
Add: Transfer to development fund	2,402.9
TOTAL	9,969.3

Of current government revenues, 37.6% comes from taxes on income, profit and capital gain, 14.5% from domestic taxes on goods and services, 5.5% from taxes on international trade and transactions, 15.0% from other taxes and 27.4% from non-tax revenues. Current revenues represent 28.5% of GNP. Of current expenditures, 22.9% goes to defense, 19.2% to education, 6.4% to health, 8.2% to housing, social security and welfare, 14.2% to economic services and 29.1% to other functions. Current expenditures represent 22.6% of GNP and overall surplus 2.7% of GNP.

In 1983 public consumption was S$3.984 billion and private consumption S$16.622 billion. During 1973-83 public consumption grew by 6.4% and private consumption by 6.1%.

In 1983 external debt, representing 10% of total public debt, was $1.243 billion. Of this amount, $425.6 million was owed to official creditors and $818.0 million to private creditors. Total debt service was $394.3 million of which $277.9 million was repayment of principal and $116.4 million was interest. Total external debt represented 4.1% of export revenues and 7.6% of GNP. Debt service represented 1.3% of export revenues and 2.4% of GNP.

DEVELOPMENT BUDGET (S$ million — estimates for year ending 31 March)			
Expenditure	1982/83	1983/84	1984/85
General services	424.9	441.4	524.4
General administration	380.0	393.5	453.5
Fiscal administration	11.6	11.7	12.5
General economic regulation	7.5	11.5	8.9
Conduct of foreign affairs	12.0	14.0	14.0
Others	13.8	10.7	35.5
Defense and justice	164.9	181.7	179.5
Defense	150.0	150.0	150.0
Justice and police	14.7	27.7	25.7
Others	0.2	4.0	3.8
Social and community services	3,201.9	4,188.5	5,094.2
Community	59.6	64.0	43.6
Environment	266.1	307.1	310.1
Education	500.2	577.1	630.0
Health	96.1	111.6	88.7
Housing	2,253.0	3,102.0	4,000.0
Others	26.9	26.7	21.8
Economic services	3,057.7	2,977.0	3,196.1
Land development	445.2	499.1	512.8
Agricultural and non-mineral resources	9.0	11.1	17.6
Industrial and commercial development	2,197.0	1,673.6	1,442.4
Tourism	4.5	—	1.2
Transport and communications	354.2	670.4	1,194.1
Public utilities	—	80.0	—
Others	47.8	42.8	28.0
TOTAL	6,849.4	7,788.6	8,994.2

FINANCE

The Singaporean unit of currency is the Singapore dollar divided into 100 cents. Coins are issued in denominations of 1, 5, 10, 20 and 50 cents and 1 dollar; notes are issued in denominations of 1, 5, 10, 25, 50, 100, 500, 1,000 and 10,000 dollars.

The Singapore dollar was introduced in 1967 replacing at par the Malayasian dollar, but the formal link with the Malayasian dollar was ended only in 1973, when the Singapore dollar was allowed to float. In 1985 the dollar exchange value was $1= SD2.188 and the sterling exchange value was £1= SD2.891. The Singapore dollar was made freely convertible in 1978.

The Singapore monetary system is coordinated by the Monetary Authority of Singapore (MAS), which performs all the functions of a central bank except the issuance of currency which has been delegated to the Board of Commissioners of Currency. Singapore has emerged in recent years as a major banking center, providing a varied range of financial services in South-East Asia and outside the region.

The financial sector averaged an annual growth of 14% in the 1970s, making it one of the fastest growing sectors. Total assets/liabilities of commercial banks, however, grew at a reduced rate of 9% in 1982, compared with 34% in 1981, owing to the contraction of interbank activities. The number of commercial banks operating in Singapore was 124 at May 1984. Of the 1984 total, 13 were local and the rest foreign. Three types of banking licenses are issued for commercial

banks: full licensed (37 in 1984), restricted (14 in 1984) and offshore (73 in 1984). The number of representative banking offices increased from eight in 1970 to the present total of 57.

The focal point of Singapore's development as an international financial center has been the Asian Dollar market. The market was launched in 1968 when the local branch of the U.S.-based Bank of America secured government approval to borrow deposits of nonresidents, mainly in foreign currencies, and to use them to finance corporate activities in Asia. At that time, expanding economic development in South-East Asia was rapidly increasing the demand for foreign funds and the desirability of a regional center able to carry out the necessary middleman functions was apparent. Singapore offered the ideal location. It also enjoyed a special advantage over Hong Kong and Tokyo with respect to time zones in that the European and Far East money markets remained open while the Singapore market was still operating. The impetus to the creation of the Asian Dollar market in Singapore was provided when the government decided to abolish the withholding tax on interest on foreign currency deposits earned by nonresidents.

The market functions through Asian Currency Units (ACU), which are separate divisions of participating banks or other financial institutions licensed by the MAS to accept deposits in foreign currencies and to process international investment loans in such currencies. The number of ACU increased to 150 in 1982 from 19 in 1971. Although the size of the Asian Dollar market is about 6% the size of the Eurodollar market, its growth has been phenomenal. After Japan, the market is the largest external currency in Asia. Assets grew from U.S. $30.5 million in 1968 to surpass the U.S. $100,000 million mark in August 1982. The growth averaged 77.5% annually between 1969 and 1979. U.S. dollars constitute more than 90% of all funds dealt with in the market although some 20 different currencies are dealt with. The market is characterized by interbank activities. Interbank deposits constitute the main source of funds for ACU. More than 90% of the interbank deposits are from banks abroad or from the ACU themselves. Deposits from non-bank customers form about 16% of total liabilities. Interbank lending constitutes about 67% of total assets while loans to non-bank customers constitute about 27%.

The participants in the Asian Dollar market come from a wide geographical region covering Asia, the Middle East, Europe, the USA and Australia. Generally, the net suppliers of funds are from the UK, the EEC, the Middle East and the U.S., while net users include the ASEAN countries, Hong Kong and Japan. Approximately 60% of the total deposits placed with ACU originate from outside Asia, but on the users' side, Asian countries, excluding Singapore, absorb about 62% of the funds.

To promote further the growth of Singapore as a financial center, several measures were implemented in 1977. These included the extension of the 10%

concessionary tax on income from Asian Dollar loans to nonresidents to cover all offshore income other than foreign exchange profits and transactions with domestic banking units and residents. In 1978 the U.S. dollar negotiable certificate of deposit (CD) was introduced to add greater depth to the Asian Dollar market. In June 1978 all foreign exchange controls were abolished. ACU were also to be allowed to open savings accounts and underwrite offshore debt-security issues. In 1979 and 1980 more fiscal incentives were given to stimulate further the offshore market. For 1980, the concessionary tax rate of 10% was extended to offshore gold transactions by the ACU. Stamp duty on documents for offshore loans and on Asian dollar bonds was also abolished. The Singapore Gold Exchange, launched in 1978, was renamed the Singapore International Monetary Exchange (SIMEX) in 1983 and opened a market for trading in currency "futures" in 1984.

In August 1984 commercial banks had reserves of SD2.060 billion, demand deposits of SD4.247 billion and time and savings deposits of SD18.254 billion.

GROWTH PROFILE Annual Growth Rates (%)	
Population 1980-2000	1.4
Birthrate 1965-83	−44.6
Deathrate 1965-83	−9.1
Urban Population 1973-83	1.3
Labor Force 1980-2000	1.1
GNP 1973-82	7.9
GNP per capita 1973-82	6.5
GDP 1973-83	8.2
GDP per capita 1970-81	6.9
Consumer Prices 1970-81	7.2
Wholesale Prices 1970-81	7.4
Inflation 1973-83	4.5
Agriculture 1973-83	1.5
Manufacturing 1973-83	7.9
Industry 1973-83	8.5
Services 1973-83	8.1
Mining 1970-81	8.8
Construction 1970-81	5.8
Electricity 1970-81	10.0
Transportation 1970-81	14.0
Trade 1970-81	10.1
Public Administration & Defense	—
Export Price Index 1975-81	7.4
Import Price Index 1975-81	7.4
Terms of Trade 1975-81	−0.1
Exports	—
Imports	—
Public Consumption 1970-78	6.4
Private Consumption 1970-78	6.1
Gross Domestic Investment 1970-78	9.2
Energy Consumption 1970-78	4.9
Energy Production	—

AGRICULTURE

Of the total land area of 58,140 hectares (143,663 acres), 16% is classified as agricultural land, or 0.004 hectare (0.01 acre) per capita. Based on 1974-76=100, the index of agricultural production in 1982 was 244, the index of food production was 249 and the index of per capita food production was 107. Agricultural employs less than 2% of the labor force. Its contribution to the GDP in 1982 was 1%, and its rate of growth during 1973-83, 1.5%. The value added in agriculture in 1983 was $143 million.

Cultivation on the island is described as the most intensive in all of Southeast Asia. In 1982 there were 46 tractors in use and the annual consumption of fertilizers was 4,700 tons or 783 kg (1,726 lb) per arable hectare. Nevertheless, the island is not self-sufficient in food except for vegetables. In 1983, 1,455,000 tons of cereals were imported. Agricultural production in 1978 consisted of 8,070 tons of fruits, and 35,326 tons of mixed vegetables. Two major agricultural exports are orchids and aquarium fish.

Poultry farming is Singapore's largest traditional industry and meets 80% of poultry meat requirements. In 1978 there were 1,110,000 pigs on the island but hog farms are being phased out because of pollution costs. There are no natural forests left on the island. Fishing is relatively more developed than other traditional pursuits and accounted for an annual fish catch of 19,549 tons in 1983.

INDUSTRY

Manufacturing is the pacesetter of the economy, generating 26% of the GDP, experiencing an annual growth rate of 7.9% during 1973-83, and employing 27.8% of the labor force. Manufacturing has not only expanded its share of GDP over the years to 24% in 1983, it has also changed its complexion to include relatively more sophisticated and higher value-added operations even in advance of the formal launching of the new economic policy. These hi-tech industries employ 55% of the industrial work force and contribute 72% to total value added in manufacturing. The largest manufacturing subsector measured by value of production is petroleum refining (40% in 1983), which reflects the high price of crude oil more than the importance of the sector to the economy. By value-added, the largest manufacturing sector is machinery and appliances, which includes the large electronics industry. The fast growing manufacturing subsector is metal engineering and precision equipment which grew by 32%. Sixty percent of the sector's output was exported. The value added in manufacturing in 1982 was $2.431 billion.

The modern industrial history of Singapore began in 1961 with the creation of the Economic Development Board. The earliest industries were oriented toward import-substitution but circumstances soon led the government to embark on a soundly conceived and boldly implemented policy of rapid industrialization concentrating on high-technology and high value-added industries, such as metals and engineering, shipbuilding and repairing, electronics and electrical products, petroleum, chemicals and plastics, and precision equipment and optical products. Most of the heavy industries are concentrated in the Jurong Town

Corporation established in 1968 as an industrial estate. The electronics sector, particularly, provided much of the impetus behind economic growth, although it was hurt by the duty levied by the EEC on imports of Singapore-made electronic calculators above a certain quota. In 1977 Japan announced the largest single industrial venture ever undertaken in Singapore: a SD2 billion ethylene complex completed in 1981 on the island of Pulau Ayer Merbau. This project changed the industrial map of the island enabling it to move into the production of petrochemical intermediates.

An important feature of Singapore's investment incentives is the so-called "pioneer" status. The Minister of Finance may accord an industry "pioneer" status when, although not operating on a scale adequate to Singapore's economic needs, it nevertheless shows favorable growth prospects. Such status entitles the industry to a wide range of benefits which may include: Full exemption from the 40% corporation tax for 5 to 10 years, a lower tax on export profits, an accelerated depreciation allowance, lower tax rates for offshore income, government equity participation, labor training programs, government purchases of local products, and technical advisory services.

Based on 1975=100, the index of industrial production in 1982 was 95. In 1981 there were 3,451 establishments employing 10 or more workers employing a total of 283,500 workers and generating an output valued at SD37.561 billion.

Foreign investments are governed by the most generous legislation in Southeast Asia, especially the Export Expansion Incentives (Relief from Income Tax) Act of 1967. The act grants exemption from taxation for a five-year period to investors and guaranteed repatriation of profits and capital. Overseas investment promotion offices have been set up in New York, Chicago, San Francisco, London, Paris, Frankfurt, Zurich, Tokyo, Hong Kong, Stockholm and Melbourne. The Capital Participation Scheme of 1973 permits high-technology industries to set up branches in Singapore with 50% equity participation by the government.

Investment commitments in manufacturing continued to be dominated by foreign investors, who in 1983 committed S$1.795 billion. Investment in fixed assets by foreigners stood at S$10.1 billion at mid-1983. While precise statistics are not available, it appears Americans are the largest foreign investors in fixed assets in Singapore, with the Japanese gaining rapidly. U.S. investments in 1983 represented one-third of the total, most of it in electronics and computers. The Census of Industrial Production in 1980 listed 451 foreign firms accounting for 26% of the manufacturing establishments, contributing 66% to the value added in manufacturing, 69% to the gross value of output, and employing 55% of the work force. Net direct private investment in 1983 was $1.389 billion.

ENERGY

Singapore does not produce any from of mineral energy. In 1976 it consumed energy equivalent to 11.070 million metric tons of coal, or 4,471 kg (9,858 lb) per capita. The annual growth rate for energy consumption during 1973-83 was 4.9%. Energy imports account for 40% of all merchandise imports. Apparent per capita consumption of gasoline is 133 gallons per year.

Singapore's petroleum refining capacity, estimated at 1.1 million barrels per year, is the world's third largest.

In 1984 production of electric power totaled 8.6 billion kwh, or 3,400 kwh per capita.

LABOR

The economically active population in 1983 was estimated at 1,208,800.

The percentage of women in the workforce is 35.6% (72% for the 20 to 24 age group). Among able-bodied males, the participation rate in the workforce was 79%. A trend toward a better educated workforce is evident. In 1974, 40% of employed persons had not completed grammar school. In 1977 this had dropped to 29%.

Persons making up Singapore's 1983 unemployment rate of 3.2% are found disproportionately among the young, the less-educated, and minority or disadvantaged groups. The rate for females was 5%; for males 3.4%. Unemployment among Malay and Indian minorities was at a somewhat higher rate than their percentages of the population. Much of the unemployment was of short-term duration.

DISTRIBUTION OF LABOR FORCE BY INDUSTRY
(at June 1983)*

		%
Agriculture, forestry, hunting and fishing	11,800	1.0
Mining and quarrying	2,400	0.2
Manufacturing	324,900	27.8
Construction	84,100	7.2
Electricity, gas, water and sanitary services	8,500	0.7
Commerce	266,000	22.8
Transport, storage and communications	131,900	11.3
Services	338,400	28.9
Activities not adequately defined	1,600	0.1
Total	1,169,600	

*Employed persons aged 10 years and over.

No accurate statistics exist on the number of foreign workers in Singapore. Estimates range between 80,000 and 120,000. A modest labor shortage exists. The government conducts active recruiting for qualified workers in neighboring countries, notably, Malaysia, although it went further afield in mid-1978 when it hired 200 Gurkhas to serve as prison guards, and about the same number of factory workers from

Thailand. Nearly 677,400 were wage-earners, 34,200 were employers, 89,200 were self-employed and the remainder were unpaid domestic workers.

The Employment Act of 1968 effectively ended labor unrest, reduced fringe benefits, and provided for generally stable wages through three-year minimum collective bargaining agreements under compulsory arbitration. Throughout the 1980s Singapore has enjoyed remarkable industrial peace. At the same time provisions for workers' welfare were enlarged and strictly enforced. The Industrial Arbitration Court and the Labor Court play a major role in the reduction of labor-management disputes. The National Wages Council sets guidelines for increases in wages and fringe benefits commensurate with productivity. A retrenchment unit within the Employment Service helps workers to find alternative jobs.

Singapore enforces child labor laws which protect young people from exploitation and hazardous working conditions. Employment below the age of 12 is prohibited, as is employment of young people during the night. Relatively high wage rates and working conditions consistent with accepted international standards are features of the Singapore labor market which, despite the economic downturn, still provided jobs for some 50,000 foreign workers. The unemployment rate in late 1985 stood at 4.1%, and the government has predicted that this will rise to between 5 and 6% in 1986. Singapore has no minimum wage legislation.

Singapore enforces comprehensive occupational safety and health laws. Enforcement procedures, coupled with the promotion of educational and training programs, have reduced the frequency rate of job-related accidents from 7.0 accidents per million man hours worked in the early 1970s to 4.7 during a comparable 3-year period in the 1980s. The severity rate of accidents has been reduced commensurately.

Productivity increases are zealously sought after, given the zero population growth policy and the policy to minimize the economic and social pressures of a large imported work force. The high-wage policy to induce economic upgrading has resulted in the average earnings of workers growing, which in August 1982 was 15.3% higher than the year before, falling to 9% in 1983. In 1979 the NWC also recommended a 2% levy on employers, based on their employees' salaries, as an economic tax to be paid into a Skills Development Fund (SDF). The SDF was to provide funds for training of workers and complemented the wage correction policy in encouraging employers to utilize labor more efficiently and restructure their workers' skills. In 1980 the levy was raised to 4% and the usage of the SDF was extended to subsidize interest payments on the purchase of new machinery and equipment required to increase labor productivity and the use of skilled workers. All in all, the wage correction policy appeared to be having its greatest impact on the manufacturing sector whose workers enjoyed the sharpest wage increase in 1981. In 1983 the improvement in productivity of the manufacturing sector was most impressive, as it grew by 8.8%, reversing the decline (–2.9%) of the previous year. Wages in Singapore remain the highest in South-East Asia.

Except for the brief recession in 1974-75, Singapore had experienced near full or full employment coupled with labor productivity growth at an average rate of 4% in the 1970s (as measured by real value-added per worker). Since 1972 the National Wages Council (NWC), formed as a tripartite body comprising equal representation from the government, employers and workers, has been formulating wage policies and guiding wage increases. While such NWC recommendations were not mandatory, they have been accepted in full by the public sector (which, as the largest single employer, employed 11.2% of all workers in 1983), and widely followed by the private sector. From 1983 government would withdraw from active participation, leaving the unions and employers to work out wage settlements themselves. Thus wage levels would reflect more accurately the diversity in the productivity performance of the various industries. The 1983 NWC recommendation of a single-digit wage increase guideline of S$10 plus 2% to 6% was equivalent to an average increase of 5.7% based on an average salary of S$600 per month.

Unions are legally allowed in Singapore. However, the Trades Union Act places restrictions on workers' rights. Unions are organized under an umbrella organization, the National Trades Union Congress (NTUC), which has a deputy prime minister as its secretary general and members of Parliament on the board of directors. The NTUC has about 191,000 members in a national work force of about 1.2 million. The NTUC's campaign to encourage the formation of house unions, criticized by traditionalists in the labor sector as a government effort to co-opt the union movement, abated markedly in 1985. A government proposal in 1985 to limit the role of the National Wages Council in establishing wage guidelines could significantly alter the environment for collective bargaining, providing unions a more direct role in negotiating wage agreements with management. Although workers have the legal right to strike, there have been no strikes in Singapore for over seven years. The NTUC remains a member of the International Confederation of Free Trade Unions (ICFTU) and Singapore continues its membership in the International Labor Organization (ILO).

FOREIGN COMMERCE

The foreign commerce of Singapore consisted in 1984 of exports of $24.070 billion and imports of $28.667 billion, leaving an unfavorable trade balance of $4.597 billion. Of the imports, machinery and transport equipment constituted 30.3%, crude petroleum 24.0%, manufactured goods 20.2%, food 5.9%, chemicals 5.0% and crude materials 4.4% (of which crude rubber 2.7%). Of the imports, machinery and transport equipment constituted 30.3%, crude petroleum 24.0%, manufactured goods 20.2%, food 5.9%, chemicals 5.0% and crude materials 4.4% (of which crude rubber 2.7%). Of the exports, machinery and transport equipment constituted 31.8% (of which office machines 10.9%, and ships and boats 2.9%), petroleum products 27.2% and manufactured goods and articles 14.7%.

The major import sources are: Japan 18.0%, the United States 15.1%, Malaysia 14.5%, China 2.9%, the United Kingdom 2.8%, West Germany 2.7% and Hong Kong 2.1%. The major export destinations are: the United States 18.1%, Malaysia 17.6%, Japan 9.2%, Hong Kong 6.8%, Thailand 4.3%, Australia 2.9% and West Germany 2.3%.

FOREIGN TRADE INDICATORS (1984)

Annual Growth Rate, Imports:	—
Annual Growth Rate, Exports:	—
Ratio of Exports to Imports:	46:54
Exports per capita:	$9,395
Imports per capita:	$11,189
Balance of Trade:	−$4.597 billion
Ratio of International Reserves to Imports (in months)	3.5
Exports as % of GDP:	166.7
Imports as % of GDP:	176.2
Value of Manufactured Exports:	$11.834 billion
Commodity Concentration:	3.3%

Direction of Trade (%)

	Imports	Exports
EEC	9.8	10.5
U.S.	12.6	13.2
Industrialized Market Economies	48.4	44.7
East European Economies	0.4	1.7
High Income Oil Exporters	18.2	6.9
Developing Economies	47.9	51.9

Composition of Trade (%)

	Imports	Exports
Food	7.8	7.7
Agricultural Raw Materials	3.2	5.6
Fuels	33.6	27.5
Ores & Minerals	5.5	3.8
Manufactured Goods	48.9	46.9
of which Chemicals	5.0	9.2
of which Machinery	28.0	25.5

Based on 1975=100, the import price index in 1980 was 147.0, the export price index was 146.0 and the terms of trade (export prices divided by import prices × 100) 99.0.

Entrepot trade (as measured by re-exports) accounts for 40% of Singapore's total trade, emphasizing the precarious base of the economy. This trade is sensitive to swings in the international economy. Singapore is therefore trying to develop new markets in ASEAN countries and in West Asia.

TRANSPORTATION & COMMUNICATIONS

Singapore's 26-km (16-mi) meter-gauge railway links with the Malaysian rail system. The main line crosses the Johore causeway and terminates near Keppel Harbor.

Singapore is the fourth largest port in the world handling, in 1983, 100,128,000 tons of cargo. The container port facilities comprise three main berths totaling 914 meters (2,176 ft), a feeder service berth of 213 meters (699 ft) and a cross berth of 213 meters (699 ft). Two additional berths totaling 640 meters (2,100 ft) were completed in 1978. Ships of some 250 shipping lines call regularly, about 200 of them arriving each day of the year. Singapore's merchant marine consists of 855 ships with a total GRT of 12,027,600, of which oil tankers account for 2,583,000 tons and ore and bulk carriers for 1,866,000 tons.

The road system is 2,314 km (1,437 mi) long, of which 2,006 km (1,246 mi) are paved. These roads are used by 216,933 passenger cars and 113,075 commercial vehicles. The per capita passenger car ownership is 84.6 per 1,000 inhabitants.

The national airlines is Singapore Airlines (SIA), which operates 30 aircraft (including two Concordes, 10 Boeing 707s, five Boeing 737s and four Boeing 747s) on international routes serving 21 countries. In 1982 the airline flew 68.5 million km (42.5 million mi) and carried 4,592,000 passengers. The principal international airport is Payar Lebar and a new international airport is being built at Changi. There are six usable airports, with permanent-surface runways and two with runways over 2,500 meters (8,000 ft).

In 1982 there were 700,000 telephones in use, or 26.5 per 100 inhabitants.

Singapore's 72 post offices handled 218,389,000 pieces of mail, and 93,000 telegrams in 1982. Per capita volume of mail was 85 pieces.

Singapore is also an attractive regional and international convention center and a convenient stop-over for visitors bound for the East and South-East Asian region. The restaurant and hotel industry has thus become a major service industry.

In 1983, 2.85 million tourists visited Singapore generating revenues of $1.916 billion. Of these tourists, 143,600 were from the United States, 145,000 from the United Kingdom, 477,700 from Malaysia, 354,800 from Japan, 439,500 from Indonesia, 258,600 from Australia, 24,200 from Canada, 44,600 from France, 79,800 from West Germany, 116,900 from India, 58,000 from New Zealand, 53,600 from the Philippines and 108,700 from Thailand. Expenditures by nationals abroad totaled $438 million. There are 28,000 hotel beds and the average length of stay was 2.3 days.

MINING

Singapore has no mineral activity.

DEFENSE

The defense structure is headed by the president. The line of command runs through the minister of defense (who is a civilian) to the senior officer of the armed forces who holds the rank of a brigadier and who heads the General Staff division. Military policy is determined by the Armed Forces Council, a civilian body.

Military manpower is obtained through compulsory national service in effect since 1967. All male citizens are called up for 24 to 36 months' full time military service at age 18.

The strength of the armed forces totals 55,500, or 24.0 armed persons per 1,000 civilians.

ARMY:

Personnel: 45,000

Organization: 1 division HQ; 1 armored brigade; 3 infantry brigades; 6 artillery battalions; 1 commando battalion; 6 engineer and 3 signals companies

Equipment: 270 light tanks; 1,000 armored personnel carriers; 60 howitzers; some 50 mortars; rocket launchers; air defense guns

NAVY:

Personnel: 6,000

Units: 6 fast attack craft with guns; 6 fast attack craft; 12 patrol craft; 2 minesweepers; 6 amphibious craft; 8 landing craft; 1 training ship

AIR FORCE:

Personnel: 4,500

Organization: 164 combat aircraft; 3 fighter squadrons; 1 air defense squadron; 1 reconnaissance squadron; 3 counterinsurgency squadrons; 1 transport/search and rescue squadron; 11 trainers; 2 helicopter squadrons; 4 SAM squadrons; air-to-air missiles

In 1985/86 the defense budget amounted to $970 million, representing 17.1% of the national budget, 5.8% of the GNP, $366 per capita, $19,595 per soldier and $1,371,667 per sq km of national territory.

Singapore ranks among the most highly militarized nations of the world in per capita strength of the armed forces and defense expenditures. The nation's concern with the development and maintenance of such an unusually large defense establishment is directly related to what has been described as its siege mentality, threatened as Lee described it by "an ocean of 100 million Malays." None of the three major ethnic communities has a martial tradition and the fighting qualities of the Singaporean soldier have never been tested in the field. However the defense forces have been built up on the Israeli model, and some 40 Israeli advisers helped to develop the first training program for the officer corps.

Singapore is a member of the Five-Power Defense Arrangement along with the United Kingdom, Australia, Malaysia and New Zealand. Within this arrangement, the Integrated Air Defense System is a sophisticated scheme for the air defense of Malaysia and Singapore.

There is a growing defense production program, whose output consists of small arms and armaments (including M-16 rifles), fast patrol boats and aerospace systems components. Arms purchases abroad during 1973-83 totaled $690 million, of which $300 million was supplied by the United States and $30 million by the United Kingdom.

EDUCATION

The national literacy rate is 84.2% (92.1% for males and 78.1% for females). Of the population over 25, 47.6% have had no schooling, 29.6% have completed the first level, 20.9% have completed the second level, and 2.0% have completed post-secondary studies.

Primary education is free but not compulsory. The gross school enrollment ratios are 108% at the first level (6-11) and 66% at the second level (12-17), for a combined enrollment ratio of 86%. The third level enrollment ratio is 10.7%. Girls constitute 47% of primary school enrollment, 49% of secondary school enrollment and 40% of post-secondary enrollment.

Schooling lasts for 12 years divided into six years of primary school, four years of lower secondary school and two years of upper secondary school. In 1982 the school system consisted of 321 primary schools and 147 secondary schools. Private schools account for 35% of primary enrollment, and 1% of secondary enrollment.

The medium of primary education is English or any of the three major vernaculars: Chinese (Cantonese), Tamil and Malay. The medium of secondary and post-secondary education is English. The school year runs from January to December.

The national teacher-pupil ratio is 1:30 at the primary level, 1:22 at the secondary level and 1:10 at the post-secondary level. Vocational training is provided by seven technical institutes with a total enrollment of 10,303 students, or 5.5% of the total secondary enrollment in 1982.

In 1982 the Ministry of Education's budget totaled SD1,358,429,000, of which 72.4% was current expenditures. This amount represented 4.5% of the GNP, 9.6% of the national budget and $262 per capita.

EDUCATIONAL ENROLLMENT (1983)			
Level	Schools	Teachers	Students
First Level	321	10,286	289,092
Second Level	147	10,231	187,148
Vocational	16	1,060	15,610
Third Level	5	3,052	30,966

Higher education is provided by two universities—the University of Singapore and the Nanyang University—with a combined enrollment of 30,966 in 1983. University enrollment is 1,739 per 100,000 inhabitants.

In 1982, 7,671 students graduated from Singapore's universities. Of these, 254 were awarded degrees in medicine, 2,516 in engineering, 634 in natural sciences, 80 in law and 597 in education.

In 1982, 4,873 Singaporean students were enrolled in institutions of higher learning abroad. Of the these, 1,470 were in the United States, 1,132 in the United Kingdom, 1,204 in Canada, 658 in Australia, 66 in Japan, 208 in New Zealand and 61 in West Germany. In the same year, 3,241 foreign students were enrolled in Singapore.

In 1980 there were 38,259 scientists and engineers in the country, of whom 724 were engaged in basic research. In the same year expenditures on scientific research totaled SD81.895 million.

LEGAL SYSTEM

The Singaporean legal system is based on English common law.

At the apex of the judiciary is the Supreme Court with three chambers: the High Court, the Court of Appeal and the Court of Criminal Appeal. The High Court exercises original civil and criminal jurisdiction in appeals from the subordinate courts. An appeal from the High Court lies to the Court of Criminal Appeal or the Court of Appeal, and, in certain cases, an appeal lies to the Judicial Committee of the Privy Council in the United Kingdom.

The subordinate courts comprise Magistrate's and District Courts with limited civil and criminal jurisdictions. There are 10 magistrate's courts and six district courts.

Judges of the High Court are appointed by the president on the advice of the prime minister and may not be removed from office except on the recommendation of an independent tribunal of judges. Subordinate judges are appointed by the president on the recommendation of the chief justice.

Arrest without a warrant and detention without charge for periods of one to 30 days are authorized under some specific provisions of the law. The Ministry of Home Affairs can issue an order under the Internal Security Act (ISA), a British measure used by Singapore extensively during the 1965-74 postindependence period when Communist-led disturbances and communal violence were widespread, or the Criminal Law (Temporary Provisions) Act to authorize a longer period of detention of a 'suspected person". The director of the Central Narcotics Bureau in cases of a positive urinalysis can commit suspected drug users to a six-month term in a drug rehabilitation center. Habeas corpus exists in the law, but in ISA cases the government can extend detention indefinitely. In others, such as those involving the Criminal Law (Temporary Provisions) Act, which is used primarily to detain drug traffickers and members of secret societies, the government can detain people for periods of up to one year. People who are detained are arrested openly. There is a functioning system of bail, and detainees are entitled to legal counsel.

The Misuse of Drugs Act allows Central Narcotics Bureau officers and customs officials to arrest without warrant any person suspected of manufacturing, importing, exporting, possessing, consuming or trafficking in controlled drugs. Such persons actually arrested are tried in court. A few individuals have maintained that they were not drug users and were improperly detained but, thus far, have failed to substantiate their allegations in court. The government has maintained that adequate safeguards exist to prevent innocent persons being detained.

The Criminal Procedures Code provides that a charge against a defendant must be read and explained to him as soon as it is framed by the magistrate. The accused has the right to be defended by an attorney (advocate). Individuals are tried by a magistrate or judge and do not have the right to trial by jury. Defendants may appeal their verdicts in most cases to higher courts. Singapore is a member of the British Commonwealth and allows for further appeal to the Judicial Committee of the Privy Council in London.

Judges are appointed by the president on the recommendation of the prime minister and the cabinet. Four of the seven High Court judges hold what amount to contract appointments, most frequently for one year. Subordinate court judges (magistrates) and public prosecutors are civil servants and can be transferred by the Ministry of Law.

There are six major penal institutions under the control of a director of prisons: three maximum-security prisons, one at Queenstown and two at Changi, two medium-security institutions, the Moon Crescent and the Khasa Crescent, and a Female Prison. Annual prison population is estimated at around 3,000. There is also a pre-release camp serving as a half-way house for long-term prisoners to smooth their reentry into society.

LAW ENFORCEMENT

The national law enforcement agency is the Police of the Republic of Singapore commanded by a commissioner. The authorized strength of the force is approximately 7,300. Per capita strength of the force is one policeman for every 452 inhabitants.

The operational units of the police force are designated serially from A to E. Department A is in charge of patrolling in the streets and housing areas. Department B deals with traffic, marine surveillance, riots, and other emergencies; it also has a canine unit and controls the radio and communications systems. Department C is in charge of criminal investigation, secret societies, criminal records, organized crime, vice, and gambling. Department D is responsible for training. Department E, also known as Internal Security Department, is in charge of intelligence gathering and counter-subversion.

Singapore does not have a serious crime problem compared to other large metropolitan areas. The majority of the offenses are against property, and housebreaking and theft are the most frequently reported crimes. However, law enforcement concern is directed against two problems that have proved difficult to control: drug abuse and organized crime. Despite some of the toughest laws in Asia, drug addiction, especially heroin addiction, has shown an alarming increase. The laws provide for the death penalty for trafficking in more than 15 grams of heroin or 30 grams of morphine and 10 years in jail for mere possession of drugs. There were 5,682 arrests in 1976 for heroin offenses out of a total of 6,534 drug-related offenses. The majority of those arrested are committed to one of three drug rehabilitation centers for a period of six months' detoxification followed by two years of compulsory aftercare. According to the Central Narcotics Bureau, there are over 30,000 known drug addicts, most of whom are between 17 and 29 years of age.

Another intractable problem relates to organized crime, an offshoot of the notorious Chinese secret societies (tongs), which have infiltrated gambling, vice and other vulnerable areas.

HEALTH

Singapore enjoys one of the highest levels of health care in Southeast Asia, as a result of modern housing, environmental sanitation and a clean water supply. The health budget in 1982 constituted 6.9% of the national budget, and $69.10 per capita. As in other developed countries, cancer and circulatory diseases remain the most frequent causes of death. In 1983 there were 25 hospitals with 9,807 beds, or one bed per 255 inhabitants. In the same year there were 2,361 physicians on the island, or one physician per 1,060 inhabitants, 370 dentists and 5,024 nursing personnel. Of the hospitals 48% are state-run and 52% are run by private nonprofit agencies. The admissions/discharge rate per 10,000 inhabitants is 1,091, the bed occupancy rate is 73% and the average length of stay is 10 days.

PRINCIPAL HEALTH INDICATORS (1984)
Crude Death Rate: 5.3 per 1,000
Decline in Death Rate: –9.1% (1965-83)
Life Expectancy at Birth: 69.1 (Males); 75.5 (Females)
Infant Mortality Rate: 9.2 per 1,000 Live Births
Child Death Rate (Ages 1-4) per 1,000: 1

FOOD

Rice is the staple food of the Chinese, Indians, and Malays, but it is being supplemented, according to the level of income of each household, by various modern convenience foods. The per capita daily intake of food is 3,094 calories and 80.8 grams of protein (both below the recommended minimums of 2,600 calories and 65 grams of protein), 66 grams of fats and 482 grams of carbohydrates.

MEDIA & CULTURE

In 1983, 11 daily newspapers and five non-dailies were published on the island with aggregate circulations of 706,000 and 327,000, respectively. Per capita circulations are 286 daily copies per 1,000 inhabitants and 132 non-dailies per 1,000 inhabitants. The oldest and the most widely circulated daily is the *Straits Times* with a circulation of 240,000. By language of publication, four titles are published in Chinese, four in English, one in romanized Malay, one in Tamil and one in Malayalam. The periodical press consists of over 1,506 titles. Annual consumption of newsprint is 78,700 tons, or 32,571 kg (71,819 lb) per 1,000 inhabitants.

The absence of a free press is generally acknowledged by Singapore's leaders, but they claim this intolerance toward the press is only part of a broad philosophy that places self-discipline and civil order above freedom. The Newspapers and Printing Press Act of 1974 provides that all directors of a newspaper should be Singapore citizens. In an amendment to this act passed in 1977, the government required that no individual own more than 3% of the ordinary shares in any newspaper. Two major Chinese-language newspapers have been subjected to forced change of ownership under this provision. Newspapers operate as independent companies but under close governmental supervision. The government required the reorganization and merger of Chinese language newspapers in 1983, stating that such mergers were needed for the newspapers to remain viable. In 1984 the boards of directors of the companies which publish Singapore's major newspapers announced their intention to merge into one holding company. The move, which was approved by the government, could reduce the level of press competition. The merger plan was devised ostensibly to avoid the expense and waste of an anticipated circulation war. Singapore ranks 30th in the world in press freedom with a rating of +1.81 (on a scale in which +4 is the highest and –4 is the lowest).

Singapore has no national news agency. Foreign news agencies with local bureaus include AAP, UPI, AP, Kyodo, PANA and Tass.

Singapore has an active book publishing industry with over 14 major publishers, of whom five are British and two are American. Annual title output in 1982 was 1,530. Singapore adheres to the Florence Ageeement. Singapore holds an annual book fair regularly attended by Asian publishers.

Radio and television broadcasting is operated by Singapore Broadcasting Corporation with five medium-wave transmitters, seven short-wave transmitters, and four FM transmitters. There are four programs, one in Malay, Chinese and Tamil (each for 133 hours a week), one in English language (for 126 hours a week), one multilingual service (for eight hours a day) and one English and Chinese stereo service (for eight hours a day). Total program-hours per year are 31,165 of which 4,450 hours are devoted to information, 2,484 hours to education, 744 hours to culture, 684 hours to religion, 505 hours to commercials and 22,298 hours to entertainment. In addition, a commercial station, Radiodiffusion, operates four simultaneous wired networks, and the Far East Broadcasting Association operates a Christian radio ministry. In 1982 there were 497,000 radio receivers on the island, or 201 per 1,000 inhabitants.

Television, introduced in 1963, is now broadcast on two channels in all four national languages for around 133 hours a week. Of the total 5,455 program-hours a year, 35% are nationally produced. Of the 5,455 annual television broadcasting hours, 950 hours are devoted to information, 241 hours to education, 112 hours to culture and 4,152 hours to entertainment. In 1982 there were 424,000 television sets in the country, or 172 per 1,000 inhabitants.

Domestic film production is on the decline; the number of long films produced in 1977 was only one compared to 11 in 1965. In 1981 there were 73 fixed cinemas in the country with 74,000 seats, or 31.8 seats per 1,000 inhabitants. Annual movie attendance was 36.5 million, or 15.2 per capita. In 1981, 868 long films were imported including 192 from the United States. Annual box office receipts were S$84 million.

The largest library is the National Library of Singapore with 702,696 volumes. Per capita there are seven volumes and one registered borrower per 1,000 inhabitants.

There are 10 museums reporting an annual attendance of nearly 4.3 a million.

There are three theaters serving three professional companies and 48 amateur groupes.

SOCIAL WELFARE

Public social welfare programs are coordinated by the Social Welfare Department and the Singapore Council of Social Service. The Department runs 13 homes for boys and girls, destitute persons and the aged and also provides public assistance to persons 55 years of age and older. The Chinese community has numerous mutual-aid societies. The principal form of social security is the Central Provident Fund, a compulsory retirement benefit scheme.

GLOSSARY

Straits Chinese: Westernized Chinese who identify themselves with Singapore.

CHRONOLOGY (from 1955)

1955— Under the Sir George Rendel constitution, David Marshall, leader of the Labor Front, is sworn in as chief minister.

1956— Marshall resigns following failure of London constitutional talks in which he pleads for complete independence; Lim Yew Hock is named chief minister.

1959— United Kingdom grants complete self-government to Singapore.... In first elections under home rule People's Action Party led by Lee Kuan Yew wins 43 of 51 seats in the National Assembly; Lee is sworn in as prime minister.

1961— The moderate wing of the People's Action Party under Lee expels the radical wing, which thereupon forms an opposition party named Barisan Sosialis.

1963— Singapore joins the Malaysian Federation.

1965— Singapore leaves the Federation and declares its independence by passing two constitutional amendments.

1968— United Kingdom announces withdrawal of all British forces east of Suez.... In national elections PAP gains 51 out of 68 seats in the assembly.

1969— Racial riots erupt but the government acts swiftly to contain the conflict.

1971— Benjamin Henry Sheares is elected president of the republic.... Singapore joins the five-power defense arrangement.

1975— Lee attends ASEAN summit meeting at Denpasar, Bali, Indonesia.

1976— Lee visits Peking and receives a warm welcome.... European social democrats expel Singapore from the Socialist International, citing jailing of opposition leaders and violation of human rights.

1977— IMF promotes Singapore to the status of a developed nation.

1979— Singapore denounces Vietnamese expansionist moves in S.E. Asia.

1981— First opposition member is elected to Parliament... C.V. Devan Nair is named president.

1982— People's Action Party is restyled as a national movement rather than a "political party" and 11 of the 12 seats on its executive committee go to younger members.

1984— PAP loses two seats in legislative elections... Constitutional amendment is passed assigning three non-voting nonelective seats to the opposition in Parliament.... President Nair, plagued by alcoholism, resigns and Wee Kim Wee is installed in his place.

BIBLIOGRAPHY (from 1970)

Alfrendras, Evangelos and Eddie C. Kuo, *Language and Society in Singapore* (Singapore, 1986).

Arasaratnam, S., *Indians in Malaysia and Singapore* (Kuala Lumpur, 1970).

Bedlington, Stanley, S., *Malaysia & Singapore: The Building of New States* (Ithaca, N.Y., 1978).

Bellows, Thomas J., *The People's Action Party of Singapore* (New Haven, Conn., 1970).

Buchanan, Iain, *Singapore in Southeast Asia: An Economic and Political Appraisal* (London, 1972).

Brailey, Nigel, *Thailand and the Fall of Singapore* (Boulder, Colo., 1985).

Chan, Heng Chee, *Singapore: The Politics of Survival, 1965-67* (Singapore, 1971).

Chen, Peter S., *Singapore: Development Policies and Trends* (New York, 1983).

———, & James T. Fawcett, *Public Policy & Population Change in Singapore* (New York, 1979).

Chong, Peng-Khuan, *Problems in Political Development: Singapore* (Berkeley, Calif., 1970).

Chua, Peng Chye, *Planning in Singapore* (Singapore, 1973).

Clutterback, Richard L., *Riot and Revolution in Singapore and Malaysia, 1945-63* (London, 1973).

Deyo, Fredric C., *Political Consolidation & Economic Growth in Singapore* (New York, 1980).

Gamer, Robert E., *The Politics of Urban Development in Singapore* (Ithaca, N.Y., 1972).

Geiger, Theodore, & Francis M. Geiger, *Tales of Two City-States: The Development Progress of Hong Kong & Singapore* (Washington, D.C., 1979).

George, T.J.S., *Lee Kuan Yew's Singapore* (London, 1973).

Goh, K.S., *The Economics of Modernization* (Singapore, 1972).

Hassan, Riaz, *Singapore: Society in Transition* (New York, 1977).

Josey, Alex, *The Singapore General Elections, 1972* (Singapore, 1972).

Kuo, Eddie and Peter S. Chen, *Communication Policies and Planning in Singapore* (London, 1984).

Lee Sheng-yi, *The Monetary and Banking Development of Malaysia and Singapore* (Singapore, 1974).

Lee Soo, Ann, *Industrialization in Singapore* (New York, 1974).

Leifer, M., *Malacca, Singapore & Indonesia* (The Hague, The Netherlands, 1978).

Pang, Cheng Lian, *Singapore's People's Action Party* (New York, 1971).

Quah, Jon S., *Government and Politics of Singapore* (New York, 1985).

Saw, Swee-hock, *Singapore: Population in Transition* (Philadelphia, 1970).

Seah, Chee Meow, *Community Centres in Singapore: Their Political Involvement* (Singapore, 1973).

Siddique, Sharon and Nirmala P. Shotam, *Singapore's Little India: Past, Present and Future* (London, 1984).

Singapore Year Book (Singapore, Annual)

Singapore: Facts and Figures (Singapore, Annual).

Turnbull, C.M., *A History of Singapore* (New York, 1977).

———, *A Short History of Malaysia, Singapore and Brunei* (Singapore, 1981).

Wilson, Richard S., *The Future Role of Singapore* (London, 1972).

Wong, Francis Hoy Kee, *Perspectives: The Development of Education in Malaysia and Singapore* (Singapore, 1972).

Wong, Kum Poh, *Singapore in the International Economy* (Singapore, 1972).

Wu, Yuan-Li, *Strategic Significance of Singapore* (Washington, D.C., 1972).

Yeo, Kim Wah, *Political Development in Singapore, 1945-55* (Singapore, 1973).

Yue-Man Yeung, *National Development Policy and Urban Transformation in Singapore* (Chicago, 1973).

You, P.S. and Lim, C.Y., *The Singapore Economy* (Singapore, 1971).

OFFICIAL PUBLICATIONS

Finance Minstry, *Financial Statements*, Accountant General.

———, *Main Development Estimates*.

Singapore Monetary Authority, *Annual Report*.

———, *Quarterly Bulletin*.

Statistics Department, *Yearbook of Statistics*.

———, *Monthly Digest of Statistics*.

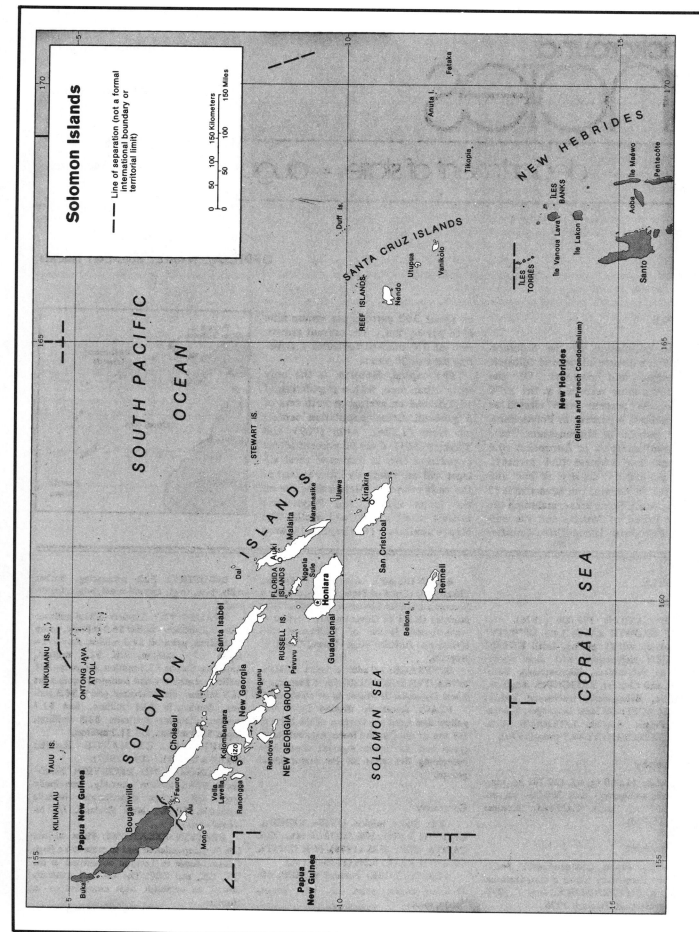

Solomon Islands

— Line of separation (not a formal
international boundary or
territorial limit)

150 Kilometers

150 Miles

SOUTH PACIFIC

OCEAN

Fataka

Anuta I.

Tikopia

NEW HEBRIDES

Duff Is.

SANTA CRUZ ISLANDS

REEF ISLANDS

Nendo

Utupua

Vanikolo

ÎLES
BANKS

Île Vanoua Lava

Île Lakon

Île Maéwo

Pentecôte

Aoba

Santo

New Hebrides
(British and French Condominium)

STEWART IS.

ISLANDS

Ulawa

Kirakira

Maramasike

Malaita

Auki

Dai

FLORIDA
ISLANDS

Nggela
Sule

Honiara

San Cristobal

Rennell

Bellona I.

CORAL

SEA

NUKUMANU IS.

ONTONG JAVA
ATOLL

SOLOMON

Santa Isabel

New Georgia

Vanunu

RUSSELL IS.

Pavuvu

Guadalcanal

SOLOMON SEA

KILINAILAU

TAUU IS.

Papua New Guinea

Bougainville

Choiseul

Kolombangara

Gizo

New Georgia
GROUP

Rendova

Fauro

Vella
Lavella

Ranongga

NEW GEORGIA GROUP

Alu

Mono

Buka

Papua
New Guinea

Emblem not available

SOLOMON ISLANDS

BASIC FACT SHEET

OFFICIAL NAME: Solomon Islands

ABBREVIATION: SN

CAPITAL: Honiara

HEAD OF STATE: Governor General Baddeley Devesi (from 1978)

HEAD OF GOVERNMENT: Prime Minister Peter Kenilorea (from 1984)

NATURE OF GOVERNMENT: Parliamentary Democracy

POPULATION: 273,000 (1985)

AREA: 28,530 sq km (11,015 sq mi)

ETHNIC MAJORITY: Melanesian

LANGUAGE: English (in its pidgin form)

RELIGION: Christianity

UNIT OF CURRENCY: Solomon Dollar ($1=SI$1.520, 1985)

NATIONAL FLAG: Light blue and green field divided diagonally by a narrow yellow stripe from the lower left to upper right; five white stars in the upper hoist

NATIONAL EMBLEM: A shield with four quarters occupying the lower two thirds and a lion couchant in the upper one third. The four quarters represent two birds, a tortoise and a fruit.

NATIONAL ANTHEM: "God Save the Queen"

NATIONAL HOLIDAYS: July 7, (Independence Day); New Year's Day; Christmas and most Christian festivals

NATIONAL CALENDAR: Gregorian

PHYSICAL QUALITY OF LIFE INDEX: 70 (On an ascending scale in which 100 is the maximum. U.S. 95)

DATE OF INDEPENDENCE: July 7, 1978

DATE OF CONSTITUTION: July 7, 1978

WEIGHTS & MEASURES: The metric system is in force

LOCATION & AREA

The Solomon Islands comprise a double chain of high continental islands formed from the exposed peaks of the submerged mountain chain that extends from Bougainville to northern Vanuatu about 485 km (11,015 sq mi) extending 1,688 km (1,049 mi) ESE to WNW and 468 km (292 mi) NNE to SSW. The total coastline is about 5,313 km (3,300 mi).

The largest island in the group is Guadalcanal, the fabled site of one of the fiercest battles in World War II, which has an area of 6,475 sq km (2,500 sq mi). Only five other islands are large enough to be named on most maps: Choiseul, New Georgia, Santa Isabel, Malaita, and San Cristobal. Smaller islands are Bellona, Duff, Florida Islands, Gizo, Kolombangara, Ndeni, Ontong Java, Reef Islands, Rennell, Santa Cruz Islands (including Anuta, Fetaka, Santa Cruz, Tevai, Tikopia, Utupua, and Vanikoro), Savo, Shortland, Sikaiana, Tulagi, Vella Lavella.

The capital is Honiara (21,170 in 1981) on the island of Guadalcanal.

Almost all of the larger islands are volcanic in origin and are covered with steaming jungles and mountain ranges intersected by narrow valleys. The highest peak is the 2,320 meter (7,647 ft) Mt. Popomanishu on Guadalcanal. Guadalcanal also contains the nation's only extensive alluvial plains. Most rivers are short and narrow and impassable except by canoe. Most of the smaller islands are raised, coral or low atolls.

WEATHER

Solomon Islands lie wholly within the tropics and as a result its climate is uniformly hot and humid, tempered by continuous breezes from the sea. Temperatures rarely exceed 29.4°C (85°F) or drop below 21.1°C (70°F). The variation may be only a degree or two all year long. There are no true changes of season; rather, the year is divided into seasons of greater and lesser rainfall, the former occurring between November and March and the latter from April to November. During the drier season the islands are cooled by the southwest trade winds. Annual mean rainfall is about 3.0480 meters (120 in.) although Honiara receives only 228.6 CM (90 in.). During the rainy seasons the islands are subject to cyclones and hurricanes that bring much destruction.

POPULATION

The population of the Solomon Islands is estimated in 1985 at 273,000 on the basis of the last census held in 1976 when the population was 192,823. The population is expected to reach 400,000 by 2000 and 700,000 by 2020.

The annual growth rate is estimated at 3.78% on the basis of a crude birth rate of 39.9 per 1,000, and a natural increase of 32.9 per 1.000.

The national population density is 9 persons per sq km (23 per sq mi) but the density varies from island to island. The most populous island is Malaita with about 60,000 inhabitants. Honiara, the capital, had a population of around 21,000. The interiors of most islands are inhabited sparsely, if at all.

As in other Pacific Islands, Solomon Islands have a large surplus of males. At the time of the 1976 census, males constituted 52.2% of the population. Nearly 50% of the population is under the age of 20.

DEMOGRAPHIC INDICATORS (1985)	
Population 1985 (000)	273
Annual rate of growth (%)	3.78
Density per sq km	9.0
Urban (%)	25.2
Sex distribution (%)	
Male	52.23
Female	47.77
Age profile (%)	
0-14	49.0
15-29	25.9
30-49	17.1
50-59	4.5
Over 60	3.5
Population doubling time in years at current rate	22
Crude birthrate 1/1000	39.9
Crude death rate 1/1000	6.6
Total fertility rate	5.98
Gross reproduction rate	2.90
Net reproduction rate	2.70
Natural increase rate 1/1000	32.9
Life expectancy at birth (Years)	
Male	64.7
Female	69.1
Average household size	5.6

Women have equal legal rights, but traditional culture has hampered their moving into leadership roles. There are no women in senior governmental positions or in Parliament but women are involved in politics and have run for national office.

The government is committed to the promotion of family planning and a gradual reduction in the rate of population growth. The National Development Plan 1975-79, envisages a reduction in the rate of population growth to 2% by the nearly 1980's. A voluntary Planned Parenthood Association has been funded with government approval.

ETHNIC COMPOSITION

Melanesians constitute 93% of the population. Other groups making up the rest of the population include Polynesians (4%), Micronesians (1.5%), Chinese (0.3%), Europeans (0.8%), and others (0.4%). Generally, the inhabitants of the high islands are Melanesians while the outliers are predominantly Polynesian.

LANGUAGES

The official language of Solomon Islands is English but the lingua franca of the market place is pidgin. Neither have quite displaced the over 60 Melanesian languages and dialects spoken by the various islanders. All of them are derived from the Austronesian linguistic family. In the interior regions, however, Melanesian gives way to earlier and more primitive Papuan languages.

RELIGIONS

Over 95% of the population is Christian with the Anglican, Roman Catholic and Methodist Churches more dominant. In certain parts, particularly in the interior, the people have retained varying degrees of adherence to the traditional religions.

Because Christian missionaries were responsible for introducing literacy, medicine, crafts and technology and other avenues of civilization to the islands, the Christian influence is pervasive and deeply interwoven with every facet of national life.

COLONIAL EXPERIENCE

The northern Solomon Islands became a German protectorate in 1885 while the Southern Solomon Islands came under the hegemony of the United Kingdom in 1893. Germany ceded most of its possessions in this region to the United Kingdom between 1898 and 1900 and the whole territory, now called British Solomon Islands Protectorate (BSIP), was placed under the jurisdiction of the Western Pacific High Commission with headquarters at Fiji and represented locally by a resident commissioner. World War II brought the islands into contact with both Japan and the United States, locked in mortal combat in the fields of Guadalcanal. The widespread destruction caused by the war created a strong anti-European sentiment which led to the development of pro-independence political movements, such as the "Marching Rule" in Malaita.

The territory's first step toward self government was the establishment of executive and legislative councils in 1960. A new constitution was promulgated in 1970 and the nation's first general elections were held in the same year. A second constitution adopted in 1974 created a single Legislative Assembly of 24 members whose chose a chief minister with the right to appoint his own council of ministers. In 1975 the country's name was officially changed from British Solomon Islands Protectorate to Solomon Islands. A year later the country achieved internal self-government followed by full independence in 1978. Solomon Islands remains a member of the Commonwealth and retains the Queen of England as the titular head of state.

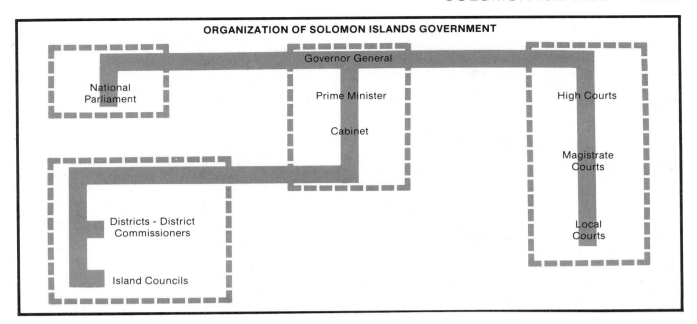

ORGANIZATION OF SOLOMON ISLANDS GOVERNMENT

Governor General

National Parliament

Prime Minister

Cabinet

High Courts

Magistrate Courts

Districts - District Commissioners

Island Councils

Local Courts

CONSTITUTION & GOVERNMENT

Under the 1978 constitution, which took effect upon independence, Solomon Islands is a constitutional monarchy with the British sovereign as titular head of state represented on the islands by the governor general who is required to be a citizen of the country. The head of government is the prime minister, who presides over the cabinet. The governor general is appointed for a term of five years on the advice of parliament and he, in turn, appoints the prime minister and other members of the cabinet.

One of the provisions of the constitution provides for the devolution of power to proposed provincial governments and the incorporation of traditional leadership structures within the government. The details of such a decentralization have not yet been worked out.

Suffrage is universal for all Solomon Islanders over the age of 21. The first post-independence elections were held in 1980. An electoral commission oversees electoral rolls and ensures free elections.

FREEDOM & HUMAN RIGHTS

In terms of civil and political rights Solomon Islands is classified as a free country with a rating of 2 in civil rights and 2 in political rights on a scale in which 1 is the highest and 7 the lowest.

No violations of human rights have been reported in the country. Democratic institutions and practices seem to have struck firm roots and there are no restrictions on freedom of speech, press, religion and assembly. Preventive detention does not exist and habeas corpus is honored in practice.

CIVIL SERVICE

The civil service is currently almost entirely native in composition. The constitution provides for a public service commission charged with recruitment, pay scales and conditions of service.

LOCAL GOVERNMENT

For purposes of local government, the country is divided into four administrative districts, each under a district commissioner, who is assisted by one or more district officers. The larger islands are divided into subdistricts. The Malaita District includes the island of Malaita, and the Polynesian islands of Rennell and Bellona. At the village level, headmen and assistant headmen are responsible for carrying out the orders of the district commissioners.

All areas except Tikopia, Anuta and the small outlying islands of Reef Islands are under the authority of

---

CABINET LIST (1985)

Governor General	*Sir* Baddeley Devesi
Prime Minister	*Sir* Peter Kenilorea
Minister for Agriculture & Lands	Sethuel Kelly
Minister for Education & Training	Danny Philip
Minister for Energy, Public Works & Utilities	John Tepaika
Minister for Finance	George Kejoa
Minister for Foreign Affairs	Paul Tovua
Minister for Home Affairs & Provincial Government	Ezekiel Alebua
Minister for Immigration & Labor	Jason Dorovolomo
Minister for National Economic Planning & Development	Tony Harihiru
Minister for Natural Resources	Daniel Sande
Minister for Police & Justice	Swanson C. Konofilia
Minister for Public Service	Seth Lekelalu
Minister for Trade, Commerce & Industry	Robert Bera
Minister for Transport & Communications	John Maetia

their own local councils. Choiseul, Santa Isabel, Malaita, San Cristobal and Guadalcanal have island-wide councils while others administer subdistricts. Members of these councils are elected by universal adult suffrage. Malaita and Honiara have town councils with a wider range of powers and responsibilities.

FOREIGN POLICY

The cornerstone of Solomon Islands' foreign policy is the close link with the United Kingdom. The country was admitted to the United Nations in 1978.

Solomon Islands and the United States are parties to six treaties and agreements covering consuls, economic and technical cooperation, extradition, mutual security, Peace Corps and telecommunications. There is no U.S. embassy in Honiara.
United Kingdom High Commissioner in Honiara: George N. Starsfield
Solomon Islands' Ambassador in Washington D.C., Francis Saemala

PARLIAMENT

The unicameral National Parliament is a 38-member body elected by universal adult suffrage for four-year terms. In the parliament elected in 1976, independents formed the majority but in the bitterly contested 1984 elections, the United Solomon Islands Party won 13 seats, the People's Alliance Party 12, the Solomone Agu Sogu Fenua 4, the National Democratic Party 1, Independents 7.

POLITICAL PARTIES

The ruling party is the United Solomon Islands Party, led by Prime Minister Peter Kenilorea, which led the nation into independence. An outgrowth of the Civil Servants' Association, it advocates retention of the links to the British crown.

The National Democratic Party, led by Bartholomew Ulufalu, campaigns vigorously for repulic status and for greater autonomy for districts.

The People's Alliance Party, led by former chief minister Solomon Mamaloni, has been described sometimes as a radical group, but follows in many respects policies to the right of the United Solomon Islands Party.

Solomone Agu Sogu Fenua (My Land) is a party allied with United Solomon Islands Party. It was founded in 1984.

ECONOMY

Solomon Islands is one of the 39 lower middle income countries of the world with a free-market economy in which the private sector is dominant.
Development Budget: 1980, SI$'000: Development sector 25,200 (Natural resources 6,500, Commerce

---

> **PRINCIPAL ECONOMIC INDICATORS**
> *Gross National Product*: $160 million (1983)
>   GNP Annual Growth Rate: 5.5% (1973-82)
>   GNP per capita: $640 (1983)
>   Per capita GNP Annual Growth Rate: 2% (1973-82)
> *Consumer Price Index* (1970=100)
>   All Items: 206.4 (March 1980)
>   Food: 219.4 (March 1980)
> *Average Annual Inflation Rate*: 13% (1982)
> *Gross Domestic Product*: SI$155.5 million (1982)
>   GDP per Capita: SI$622 (1982)
> *Money Supply*: SI$29 million (December 1984)
>   Reserve Money SI$29 million (December 1984)
> *Currency in Circulation*: SI$12.75 million (1984)
> *International Reserves*: $60.60 million of which foreign exchange $58.82 million.

and industry 4,500, Economic infrastructure 14,200), Social sector 20,000 (Education 5,100, Health 4,100, Culture and welfare 900, Administrative sector 9,900), Total 45,200.

Under a 1977 agreement the United Kingdom agreed to provide $43 million in nonrepayable financial assistance during 1978-82. During 1979-81 Solomon Islands received $34.0 million in bilateral and multilateral aid or $147.8 per capita.

BUDGET

The financial year is the calendar year.

The national budget in 1981 consisted of revenues of SI$150.480 million and expenditures of SI$150.963 million. Of the recurrent revenues of SI$136.059 million, 26.6% came from income taxes, 25.8% from import duties and 11.3% from export duties. Of the recurrent expenditures of SI$134.667 million, 43.5% went to administration, 23.7% to economic services, 14.3% to health and 8.8% to education.

The total external public debt was $20.4 million, all of it owed to official creditors. Total debt service was $200,000 of which $100,000 was repayment of principal and $100,000 interest. Total external debt represented 26.8% of export revenues and 14.2% of GNP. Total debt service represented 0.3% of export revenues and 0.2% of GNP.

FINANCE

The Solomon Islands' unit of currency is the Solomon Islands Dollar divided into 100 cents. Coins are issued in denominations of 1, 2, 5, 10 and 20 cents and 1 dollar and notes are issued in denominations of 2, 5, and 10 dollars.

The Solomon Islands dollar was introduced in 1977 replacing at par the Australian dollar. The direct link with the latter was ended in 1979 and since then the value of the Solomon Islands dollar has been determined in relation to a weighted basket of currencies of the country's principal trading partners.

In 1985 the exchange value of the Solomon Islands dollar was as follows: $1=SI$1.520 and £1=SI$1.55.

BALANCE OF PAYMENTS (1983) $ million	
Current Account Balance	–6
Merchandise Exports	62
Merchandise Imports	–61
Trade Balance	1
Other Goods, Services & Income	+23
Other Goods, Services & Income	–42
Other Goods, Services & Income Net	–19
Private Unrequited Transfers	–3
Official Unrequited Transfers	15
Capital Other Than Reserves	14
Net Errors & Omissions	7
Total (Lines 1, 10 and 11)	15
Counterpart Items	–6
Total (Lines 12 and 13)	9
Liabilities Constituting Foreign Authorities' Reserves	—
Total Change in Reserves	–9

PRINCIPAL CROPS (1982) (metric tons)	
Copra	32,172
Cocoa	668
Rice (paddy)	10,538
Palm oil	19,238

The national banking system is supervised by the Central Bank of Solomon Islands, which is also the issuer of currency. The only national banks are the Development Bank of Solomon Islands and the National Bank of Solomon Islands. Two British and Australian banks have offices in Honiara. In 1984 these banks had reserves of SI$16.01 million, demand deposits of SI$15.98 million and time and savings deposits of SI$35.43 million.

AGRICULTURE

Of the total land area of 2,853,000 hectares (7,049,763 acres) 96% is held by the natives, classified into three types: bush, garden and village land. Bushlands produce wild crops, garden lands are planted with food crops and village lands are plots close to houses planted with vegetables and related crops. Most native land is held by kinship groups. Title to land is a recent phenomenon dating back only to 1959. Agriculture employs 33.2% of the labor force. Based on 1974-76, the index of agricultural production in 1982 was 166 and the index of food production was 166.

Copra is the mainstay of Solomon Islands agriculture and also the dominant export product. The development of copra plantations was mainly the work of Lever Pacific and Burns Philp Company. Cocoa is also produced commercially and exported. The principal food crops are taro, yams, sweet potatoes, cassava, and green vegetables. In 1967 largescale dry rice cultivation was initiated on the Guadalcanal plains combined with the production of soybeans.

On May 19, 1986, one of the worst typhoons in the islands' history, Typhoon Namu, struck Solomons. The 115-mph winds lashed the islands for 17 hours, virtually wiping out coconut, rice and copra plantations in the Guadalcanal plains. At least 97 people were believed killed and hundreds were reported missing. A third of the population were left homeless. A government official said that it will take years to recover from the devastation.

Production of livestock is mostly on a small scale except on the Guadalcanal plains project and on Lever Pacific plantations. In 1982 the cattle population was estimated at 23,671.

Fishing is a subsistence activity but small scale commercial fishing is carried on Honiara, Aiku (on Malaita) and Gizo (on the New Georgia Islands). Total catch in 1982 was 33,000 tons, providing 38% of export revenues.

Most forestry is centered on the Shortlands, Gizo and Santa Isabel and roundwood production in 1982 totaled 512,000 cubic meters (18 million cubic ft), providing 28% of export revenues. A mill at Honiara provides lumber for local use. Kuari, balsa and teak are the major timbers.

INDUSTRY

Manufacturing activities are rudimentary and (apart from facilities for processing copra and cocoa) are mainly intended for local use.

ENERGY

Solomon Islands does not produce any form of energy but consumes 55,000 metric tons of coal equivalent or 221 kg (487 lb).

In 1984 production of electric power was 30 million kwh or 114 kwh per capita.

LABOR

Of the economically active population, the vast majority is engaged in subsistence farming and only 21,132 were in the employed work force. Because of the shortage of skilled labor, the islands depended on expatriates for senior positions in government and industry. Special emphasis has been placed since independence in training natives to take over these positions. Some 34% of the wage earners are employed by the government, 33.2% in agriculture, 8.7% in manufacturing, 9.9% in trade, 1.3% in public utilities, 2% in finance, 29.5% in services, 6.3% in construction and 9.1% in transportation.

Wages and conditions of service are set forth in the Labor Ordinance of 1960 administered by the Department of Labor. Solomon Islands has comprehensive laws on workers' rights. Child labor is forbidden for children under the age of 12 except in the company of parents in light agricultural or domestic work. Children under 15 are barred from work in industry of on ships; those under 18 cannot work underground or in mines. The standard workweek is 45 hours and is limited to six days. Power to set minimum wages has been devolved to the provincial governments. In Honiara, the capital, the minimum wage is about 30 cents per hour. There are provisions for premium pay for overtime and holiday work. Both a strong labor movement and an independent judiciary ensure widespread enforcement of labor laws in major state and private enterprises. The extent to which the law is enforced in smaller establishments and in the subsistence sector is problematic. No information is available on occupational safety and health legislation.

Labor unions are required to registered with the registrar of trade unions. In 1980 there was only one union registered: the Solomon Islands General Workers Union.

FOREIGN COMMERCE

In 1984 Solomon Islands' foreign trade consisted of exports of $83.040 million and imports of $65.485 million, leaving a surplus of $17.555 million. Of the imports, machinery and transport equipment constituted 26.2%, fuels 25.3%, manufactured goods 17.8%, food 11.6%, chemicals 6.0% and beverages and tobacco 3.9%. Of the exports, fish constituted 41%, timber 28.1%, copra 11.8%, palm oil 10.9%, cocoa 3.2% and gold 0.7%.

The major import sources are: Australia 33.0%, Japan 19.5%, Singapore 18.7%, New Zealand 6.9%, the United States 4.1% and the United Kingdom 3.1%. The major export destinations are: Japan 43.5%, Puerto Rico 11%, the United Kingdom 11.4%, South Korea 5.1%, Denmark 4.5% and West Germany 4.3%.

TRANSPORTATION & COMMUNICATIONS

In the absence of a rail system roads handle all transportation within each island. What roads there are are mostly feeder roads, except on Guadalcanal and Malaita, which have main roads. The total length of the highways is 834 km (518 mi), including 241 km (150 mi) of all-weather roads. In 1983 there were 974 passenger cars (3.5 per 1,000 inhabitants) and 1,040 commercial vehicles (3.8 per 1,000 inhabitants).

The two main ports are at Honiara and Gizo but a new deep-sea harbor is being built at Noro on New Georgia to replace the port at Gizo. There are three minor ports serving other islands. A fleet of 138 vessels provided interisland service; of these 32 are government owned. There are regular shipping services between Honiara and Australia, New Zealand, Hong Kong, Japan, Papua New Guinea, Singapore, Europe and other Pacific islands. Annual freight traffic at Solomon Islands ports average 394,000 tons.

The national flag line is the Solomon Islands Airways Ltd. (SOLAIR), which provides scheduled and chartered services to Papua New Guinea and Vanuatu with a fleet of seven small aircraft. Honiara

has two airports: Henderson and Kukum; there are 23 other airfields.

There are 2,000 telephones in use, or 7.5 per 1,000 inhabitants. In 1982 the mail traffic consisted of 3,820,000 pieces of mail. Telecommunication facilities include one ground satellite station.

An average of about 11,000 tourists, including 5,000 cruise ship passengers, visit the islands annually.

MINING

Solomon Islands are known to have considerable mineral resources; 25 million tons of high-grade bauxite deposits on Rennell Island, 10 million tons of phosphates on Bellona and asbestos on Choiseul. But exploitation of these minerals has presented difficulties and at present none are being mined.

DEFENSE

Solomon Islands has no defense force and is under the protection of the U.K. military guarantees.

EDUCATION

The national literacy rate is 54.1% (62.4% for males and 44.9% for females).

Education is not compulsory and most schools charge nominal fees. Schooling lasts for 11 years divided into six years of primary, three years of middle and two years of secondary education. Primary education is provided mostly by Christian missions and government role is confined to the secondary schools. Provincial secondary schools (formerly New Secondary Schools) provide practical education, mainly in agriculture. The national teacher-pupil ratio is 1:25 at the primary level and 1:14 at the secondary level. Girls constitute 42% of primary enrollment and 25% of secondary enrollment. There is one teacher training school and a technical school.

The school year runs from January through December. The language of instruction is English.

EDUCATION ENROLLMENT (1981)			
	Schools	Teachers	Students
First Level	383	1,199	30,316
Second Level	18	299	4,262
Vocational	2	62	664

No information is available on educational expenditures since 1979, when they were A$3,959,000 or 10.6% of the national budget, and 3.6% of GNP.

Scholarships are provided by the government for higher education overseas. In 1977 the University of the Pacific opened a center in Honiara.

LEGAL SYSTEM

The judicial system is a three-tier one with the High Court at the top, the magistrate courts and the local courts. Magistrate courts have both civil and criminal jurisdictions. Local courts, composed of a president and a panel of judges drawn from the village or subdistrict deal with native customs and litigation concerning customary right to land.

The chief of police is also the superintendent of prisons and in his latter capacity runs the islands' four prisons. The largest is the central prison at Honiara; smaller prisons, called district prisons, are established at the headquarters of the other police divisions. Penal policies are oriented toward rehabilitation rather than punishment and emphasize adult and vocational training. The average prison population rarely exceeds a few hundred.

LAW ENFORCEMENT

The Solomon Islands Police Force is a relatively small establishment considering that in addition to the maintenance of law and order it is responsible for fire fighting, administration of prisons and control of immigration. Its total strength is 333 (1 policeman for every 642 inhabitants) including 10 officers and seven inspectors. The islands are divided into four police districts (corresponding to the political divisions) each commanded by a senior inspector. Training is provided for new recruits at the Police Training School at Honiara, but officers and men requiring advanced training are sent abroad. Members of the force have two uniforms, one for duty and the other for ceremonial occasions. The former consists of khaki shirt and shorts, a blue beret and black sandals and the latter has a white tunic, a blue sulu or short sarong and black sandals.

The incidence of crime is relatively low. Although published figures are not available since independence, it is estimated that 68% of reported crimes are against the person.

HEALTH

There are 130 health establishments in Solomon Islands with 1,351 beds (or 1 bed per 181 inhabitants) including the government-operated 171-bed Central Hospital at Honiara, six district and rural hospitals, a leprosarium, and three mission hospitals. In 1982 there were 38 physicians, or 1 per 6,447 inhabitants, three dentists, and 392 nursing personnel.

The standards of hygiene and sanitation are generally poor leading to the continuing prevalence of yaws and malaria.

FOOD

As in other parts of Oceania, the diet relies heavily on vegetarian foods, especially foods high in starch

---

PRINCIPAL HEALTH INDICATORS (1984)
Crude Death Rate (per 1,000): 6.6
Life Expectancy at Birth (Males): 64.7 (Females): 69.1
Infant Mortality Rate (per 1,000) Live Births: 48.0
Public health expenditures represent 11.2% of the national budget and $14.00 per capita.

---

content, such as yams, sweet potatoes, taro, and maniota (also called cassava, manior or tapioca), the pith of sago palm trees, and bananas.

Much use is made of coconut cream or milk. Daily protein is obtained from seafood and rarely, from small game or fowl. The flesh of mammals, especially pigs and sea turtles, is almost exclusively festival food. Solomon Islanders have a noted preference for the harder liquors unlike other Pacific-Islanders. The daily per capita availability of energy, proteins, fats and carbohydrates is estimated at 2,134 calories, 44.1 grams, 51 grams and 358 grams respectively.

MEDIA & CULTURE

No daily newspapers are published in the country. The Government Information Service publishes a weekly entitled *Solomon Star* with a circulation of 4,000; the only other weekly is the *Solomon Toktok* with a circulation of 2,000.

There is no book publishing activity on the islands.

The Solomon Islands Broadcasting Corporation provides daily radio service mainly in pidgin with some broadcasts in English to 24,000 radio receivers. The station is on the air for 119 hours every week. There is no television service.

There are two cinemas with 1,000 seats. The annual movie attendance is 100,000 or 3 per 10 inhabitants.

There are two libraries including the national library at Honiara.

SOCIAL WELFARE

A social security system known as National Provident Fund was established in 1976 covering all wage-earners.

CHRONOLOGY

1978— Solomon Islands becomes an independent state within the Commonwealth; the Legislative assembly becomes the National Parliament and the chief minister, Peter Kenilorea, is named the nation's first prime minister.

1980— Solomon Islands holds its first-post independence elections to the National Parliament.

1981— Solomon Mamaloni is chosen to succeed Peter Kenilorea as prime minister because of a realignment of independent members.

1983— East Kwaio Council of Chiefs declare the Malaita Island independent.

1984— Peter Kenilorea forms a new coalition government on the fall of Mamaloni government.

BIBLIOGRAPHY

Hogbin, H., Ian., *Experiments in Civilization: The Effects of European Culture on a Native Community on the Solomon Islands* (New York, 1970)

Kent, Janet, *The Solomon Islands* (Harrisburg, Pa., 1973).

Maka'a, Julian, *Solomon: A Portrait of Traditional and Contemporary Culture of the Solomon Islands* (Wellington, New Zealand, 1985).

Oliver, Douglas L., *Solomon Island Society* (Boston, 1980)

Ross, Harold M., *Baegu: Social & Ecological Organization in Malaita, Solomon Islands* (Urbana, Ill., 1973).

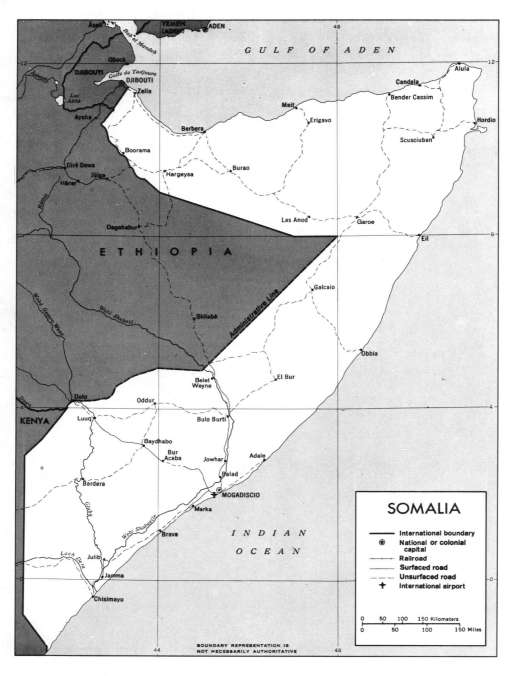

GULF OF ADEN

YEMEN (ADEN)

ADEN

Bab el Mandeb

Assab

Obock

DJIBOUTI

Golfe de Tadjoura

DJIBOUTI

Zeila

Awash

Lac Abbé

Aysha

Dirē Dawa

Jijiga

Harer

Ramis

Boorama

Hargeysa

Berbera

Burao

Mait

Erigavo

Candala

Bender Cassim

Alula

Hordio

Scusciuban

Dagahabur

E T H I O P I A

Wabe Gestro Wenz

Wabi Shabelē

Shilabē

Administrative Line

Las Anod

Garoe

Eil

Galcaio

Obbia

Belet Weyne

El Bur

Dolo

Dawa

Oddur

KENYA

Luuq

Bulo Burti

Baydhabo

Bur Acaba

Jowhar

Adale

Balad

Ciuba

Bardera

MOGADISCIO

Marka

Webi Shabeelle

Brava

INDIAN OCEAN

Lach Dera

Julib

Jamma

Chisimayu

SOMALIA

International boundary

⊛ National or colonial capital

Railroad

Surfaced road

Unsurfaced road

✦ International airport

0   50   100   150 Kilometers
0   50   100   150 Miles

BOUNDARY REPRESENTATION IS
NOT NECESSARILY AUTHORITATIVE

SOMALIA

BASIC FACT SHEET

OFFICIAL NAME: Somali Democratic Republic (Jamhurriyadda Dimoqradiga Soomaliya, or Al-Jumhouriyya es-Somaliyya ed-Democratiyya)

ABBREVIATION: SO

CAPITAL: Mogadishu (Official spelling: Muqdisho; also, Mogadiscio)

HEAD OF STATE & HEAD OF GOVERNMENT: President Maj. Gen. Muhammad Siad Barre (from 1969)

NATURE OF GOVERNMENT: Military dictatorship

POPULATION: 7,595,000 (1985)

AREA: 637,140 sq km (246,000 sq mi)

ETHNIC MAJORITY: Somali

LANGUAGE: Somali

RELIGION: Sunni Islam

UNIT OF CURRENCY: Somali Shilling (or Somalio) ($1=S40.608, August 1985)

NATIONAL FLAG: A light blue field with a five-pointed white star in the center

NATIONAL EMBLEM: A light blue shield with gold border displays a large white five-pointed star in the center; black-spotted African gold leopards poised on a design of gold crossed spears and palm branches paw the sides of the shield.

NATIONAL ANTHEM: "Long Live Somalia"

NATIONAL HOLIDAYS: October 21 (National Day, Anniversary of the 1969 Revolution); April 15 (African Solidarity Day); May 1 (Labor Day); June 21 (Independence Day); July 1 (Foundation of the Republic); October 12 (Flag Day); October 24 (U.N. Day); also, variable Islamic festivals.

NATIONAL CALENDARS: Gregorian and Islamic

PHYSICAL QUALITY OF LIFE INDEX: 17 (down from 19 in 1976) (On an ascending scale in which 100 is the maximum. U.S. 95)

DATE OF INDEPENDENCE: October 21, 1969

DATE OF CONSTITUTION: None at present

WEIGHTS & MEASURES: The metric system is in force; some Imperial units are in force in former British Somaliland areas

LOCATION & AREA

Somalia is located on the Horn of Africa in East Africa with an area of 637,140 sq km (246,000 sq mi), extending 1,847 km (1,148 mi) NNE to SSW and 835 km (519 mi) ESE to WNW. The coastline on the Gulf of Aden stretches 1,046 km (650 mi) and that on the Indian Ocean 2,173 km (1,350 mi).

Somalia shares its international border of 2,388 km (1,483 mi) with three neighbors: Kenya (682 km, 424 mi); Ethiopia (1,645 km, 1,022 mi); and Djibouti (61 km, 38 mi). All borders are arbitrary lines drawn during colonial times that ignore ethnic boundaries. The border with Djibouti is based on the Anglo-French Agreement of 1888, that with Kenya on the Anglo-Italian Agreement of 1925 and that with Ethiopia on agreements among Italy, the United Kingdom and Ethiopia in 1897 and 1908, as modified by the Anglo-Ethiopian Protocol of 1948 returning the Ogaden area to Ethiopia. None of these borders has been formally accepted by Somalia, which continues to press irredentist claims against all its neighbors, but so far without success.

The capital is Mogadishu with an estimated population, in the mid-1980s, of 450,000. The other major urban centers are Merca (70,000), Hargeysa, the former capital of British Somaliland(50,000), Berbera (45,000) and Jowhar (20,000).

Topographically, there are four natural divisions: the Guban, the northern highlands, the Ogo, including the Mudug Plain, and the Somali Plateau, including the Haud. In general, there is only limited contrast among these regions.

The northern coastal plains, which stretch from the Gulf of Tadjoura along the Gulf of Aden into Mijirtein region, are known as Guban (burned land) from its semi-arid and parched condition. Inland this coastal strip gives way to the rugged mountain ranges that extend from Ethiopia to the tip of the Horn at Cape Guardafui, the easternmost point of Africa. This range contains the country's highest point, Surud Ad (2,408 meters, 7,900 ft). The mountains descend to the south through a region, known as the Ogo, consisting of shallow plateau valleys, dry watercourses and broken mountains. This region merges into an elevated plateau and then continues into Central Somalia as the Mudug Plain, whose eastern section is known as the Nugaal Valley. This region merges imperceptibly into the vast tilting Haud Plateau, with an average elevation of 900 meters (3,000 ft) in the center, itself a part of the larger Somali Plateau. The region between the Juba and Shebeli Rivers is low agricultural land; southwest of the Juba River to the Kenyan border is low pasture land.

The country has only two permanent rivers, the Juba and Shebeli, both originating in the Ethiopian Highlands and flowing into the Indian Ocean. The Shebeli, with a total length of 2,000 km (1,250 mi), runs parallel to and north of the Juba through southern Ogaden to Balad, about 30 km (20 mi) from the Indian Ocean, where it turns southwest and after a further 270 km (170 mi) disappears in a series of marshes and sandflats. During exceptionally heavy rains it breaks through to the Juba farther south and thus enters the sea. The largest seasonal streams in the north are the Daror and the Nogal.

WEATHER

Somalia has a generally arid and tropical climate, determined principally by the northeast and southwest monsoonal winds and transitional periods known as tangambilis. There are two wet seasons: the gu, beginning in March and extending into May and sometimes June, and the dayr, the shorter wet season in October and November. Alternating with these wet seasons are two dry seasons, the jilal from December or January to March, dominated by hot, dry dusty winds, and the hagaa, from the June to August, the hottest season of the year when temperatures may soar to 48.9°C (120°F). The temperatures are moderated along the coast by cooling sea breezes. The average mean temperatures are 29.4°C to 40.6°C (85°F to 105°F) in the north and 18.3°C to 40.6°C (65°F to 105°F) in the south.

Most of the country receives less than 50 cm (20 in.) of rain annually, but some of the northern parts receive less than 5 cm (2 in.). Severe droughts are common, such as that which devastated the economy in 1974 and 1975. The inland plains, particularly the Haud, have little surface water except in seasonally filled basins.

POPULATION

The population of Somalia was estimated at 7,595,000 in 1985. The first nation-wide census was held in 1975, when the population count was 3,722,000. The population is expected to reach 9.1 million by 2000 and 14.1 million by 2020. Because two-fifths of the population are nomadic and a further one-third semi-nomadic, estimates tend to vary widely. The annual growth rate is estimated at 3.71%, based on an annual birth rate of 46.5 per 1,000.

The population is largely concentrated in two pockets: in the southwest and in the northwest on the plateau around Hargeysa; elsewhere the density is less than 1 person per sq km (2.5 persons per sq mi). Overall, the density is 9 per sq km (23 per sq mi).

Urbanization is estimated at 34.08%. There are some 60 settlements officially designated as municipal centers; of these, 25 have 5,000 or more inhabitants,

DEMOGRAPHIC INDICATORS (1984)	
Population, total (in 1,000)	7,595.0
Population ages (% of total)	
0-14	43.7
15-64	52.3
65+	4.0
Youth 15-24 (000)	1,036
Women ages 15-49 (000)	1,332
Dependency ratios	91.2
Child-woman ratios	748
Sex ratios (per 100 females)	84.4
Median ages (years)	18.1
Decline in birthrate (%, 1965-83)	−0.4
Proportion of urban (%)	34.08
Population density (per sq. km.)	9
per hectare of arable land	2.72
Rates of growth (%)	3.71
urban	6.2
rural	2.6
Natural increase rates (per 1,000)	25.2
Crude birth rates (per 1,000)	46.5
Crude death rates (per 1,000)	21.3
Gross reproduction rates	3.0
Net reproduction rates	1.96
Total fertility rates	6.09
General fertility rates (per 1,000)	192
Life expectancy, males (years)	41.3
Life expectancy, females (years)	44.5
Life expectancy, total (years)	42.9
Population doubling time in years at current rate	27
Average household size	4.9

and nine have populations over 10,000. Mogadishu itself accounts for 20% of the urban population. Most of the migration from rural areas is directed to Mogadishu, which has registered a 231% gain in population since 1967. Part of this migration is due to the recurrent droughts in the northeast. Nearly 77% of the population of Mogadishu live in slums and squatter settlements.

The age profile shows 43.7% in the under-14 age group, 52.3% in the 15 to 64 age group and 4.0% over 65. The sex ratio is estimated at 84 males to 100 females.

Migration is a way of life for Somalis, who treat all the country's international borders with disdain. The result is a constant and substantial movement back and forth across the frontiers, posing political problems at official levels.

President Siad has long been an advocate of greater rights for women, despite Muslim opposition to this policy. In this respect, Somali culture remains overwhelmingly traditional, based around extended clan families. Long-established practices, such as female circumcision, remain prevalent despite government opposition. The Somali government has improved the legal and political status of women in recent years. For example, in 1975 women were given equal rights in several respects, including equal inheritance rights. The government also promotes universal coeducational schooling, to the extent resources allow, which is mostly limited to urban centers. Women and minorities participate in politics and government. The Somali Women's Democratic Organization, though subordinate to the party, has advocated greater political participation and mobilization for women. A number of women are members of Parliament. Other women occupy important positions within the party and in various ministries. Several vice ministers and one ambassador are women.

Somalia has no official birth control programs or policies.

ETHNIC COMPOSITION

Somalia has one of the most homogeneous populations in Africa with 85% of its people beloning to Hamitic stock and 14% to the Bantu stock. As a result of intermixture, 98% of the people are described as Somalis. The Somalis are united by language, culture and religion as well as common descent. All Somalis trace their origin to two brothers, Samaal and Saab, said to have been members of the Arabian tribe of Quraysh, to which Muhammad belonged. The descendants of these two brothers constitute six clan-families or tribes. The Dir, the Darod, the Isaq, and the Hawiyahmake up an estimated 75% of the population and belong to the Samaal line. The Rahanweyn and the Digil belong to the Saab line. The Samaal are nomadic or seminomadic pastoralists, while the Saab are farmers and sedentary herders.

Relationship among clans and subclans is based on the principle of contracts (or heers). Clans are usually associated with a given territory defined by the circuit of nomadic migration; the territories of neighboring clans tend to overlap, resulting in occasional conflicts. Clans have ceremonial heads known as soldaans (or sultans) or bokors, but their internal affairs are managed by informally constituted councils known as shirs, of which all adult males are members. Interlineage or inter-clan alliances are known as diapaying groups, or groups that accept the burden of paying blood compensation (dia) for homicide. Traditionally, every Somali belongs to a dia-paying group, and there are over 1,000 such groups in the republic. These groups are also important social and economic units and function as mutual-aid associations and political blocs. Saab clans are subdivided into three subclans, each called a gember (or stool), whose affairs are managed by leading elders called gobweins. The Saab are also more heterogeneous than the Samaal and have assimilated some non-Somali elements.

There are also a number of despised groups who are believed to have inhabited the country before the arrival of the Somalis. Known as Sab among the Samaal and as Bon among the Saab, they follow so-called inferior occupations such as hunting, blacksmithing, weaving, tanning and shoemaking. The most numerous of these groups are the Midgaan, the Yibir, the Tumal, the Dardown, the Gaggab and the Madarrala.

Along the Indian Ocean coast and in the valleys of the Juba and Shebeli Rivers are groups known as habasho, believed to be descendants of Negro slaves. Many of these groups, such as the Gobawein, the Helai, the Tunni Torre, the Shidle, the Rer Issa, the Kabole, the Makanne and the Gosha have been partially Somalized. Also along the coast live the Bajun, who display Indonesian traits, the Swahili-speaking Amarani and the primitive Boni and Eile.

Over 500,000 refugees from Ethiopia, most of whom are ethnic Somalis, live in Somalia. The Somali government purports to encourage repatriation of these refugees, but many unofficial obstacles are placed in the path of those who wish to return to their native regions. There has been considerable controversy over the number of refugees, with many living in camps suspected of being local Somalis seeking food assistance. Conditions in the camps are often better than conditions among the local inhabitants. There have been reports that some ethnic Somalis with ties to the Ogaden region have agitated to receive preferential treatment in third-country resettlement programs.

Ethnic aliens include some 35,000 Arabs, 3,000 Europeans (including 1,000 Italians) and 800 Indians and Pakistanis.

In terms of ethnic and linguistic homogeneity, Somalia ranks 107th in the world with 92% homogeneity (on an ascending scale in which North and South Korea are ranked 135th with 100% homogeneity and Tanzania is ranked first with 7% homogeneity).

LANGUAGES

The national and official language is Somali, a Cushitic language with dialectal differences that follow clan divisions. Of the several dialects, the most widely used is Common Somali, spoken by Somalis not only within Somalia but also in Ethiopia, Kenya and Djibouti. The other dialects are regional, such as Central Somali and Coastal Somali, but all dialects are mutually intelligible.

Until the 1970s, Somali was a purely oral language with no script of its own. In 1972 a written form of Somali with a script based on the Latin alphabet was adopted as the official language. This script has 31 letters; long Somali vowels are usually shown by doubling the letter. A language committee has been established to prepare textbooks, a national grammar and a new dictionary based on the official orthography.

Most Somalis have some knowledge of Arabic, and educated Somalis have some familiarity with Italian and English. Newspapers in both Italian and English are published in the country.

RELIGIONS

The state religion is Islam in its Sunni form, adhered to by nearly 99.9% of the population. Although freedom of religion is the state policy, Christian schools have been closed and Christians are not permitted to proselytize. Mogadishu is a Roman Catholic bishopric.

Most Somalis belong to one or the other of four brotherhoods, or religious orders (called in Arabic tariga, from tariq, way or path): Qadiriyyah, Salihiyyah, Ahmadiyyah and Rifaiyyah. Pre-Islamic traditions are still preserved in religious practices outside the centers of orthodoxy. Since 1969, the nation's new military leaders have attempted to reduce, or at least modify, the political influence of religion by vigorously propagating a secular ideology called scientific socialism. The government has adopted the line that scientific socialism is an extension of Koranic principles and is therefore not at odds with Islam. Although the government is anxious to avoid conflict with organized religion, it has not hesitated to suppress opposition from religious leaders. When in 1975 23 religious leaders protested a new religious law that gave equal inheritance rights to women, they were arrested within hours and 10 were publicly executed.

COLONIAL EXPERIENCE

British authority in Somalia dates from the period 1884-86 when the British signed a number of protectorate treaties with Somali chiefs in the northern areas. From 1899 to 1920, British rule was constantly challenged by the jihad or holy war waged by Muhammad Abdallah bin Hasan (better known in the West as the Mad Mullah). Italian entry into Somalia began in 1889 when the Somali sultans of Obbya on the Indian Ocean coast and Alula on the Gulf of Aden accepted the protection of Italy in return for annual payments. In the same year, Italy leased the ports of the Benadir Coast (from Adale to Brava) partly on a sublease from the Imperial British East Africa Company and partly on a direct 25-year lease from the owner of the coast, the Sultan of Zanzibar. Direct administrative control of the territory known as Italian Somaliland was not established until 1908. The Italian colony was enlarged as a result of the treaty of 1925 that transferred the region between the Juba River and the Kenyan frontier to Italy.

Italian Somaliland came under British control in 1941 and remained so until 1950 when it became a U. N. trust territory. In 1960 both British and Italian Somalilands became independent thus enabling the two territories to join in a united Somali Republic. Very few colonial legacies remain, but relations with both Italy and the United Kingdom have been notably free of friction.

CONSTITUTION & GOVERNMENT

Until 1969 Somalia was a parliamentary democracy governed by the constitution of 1960. In 1969 the constitution was suspended by the military, which had seized power, and executive and legislative powers were vested in the Supreme Revolutionary Council, a 25-member body headed by Maj. Gen. Mohamed Siad Barre. The legal bases of the military government are to be found in the First and Second Charters of the

Revolution, which served as both provisional constitutions and revolutionary manifestos. Subordinate to the Supreme Revolutionary Council was the Council of Secretaries of States, which functioned as a cabinet, but there was interlocking membership with members of the former council who headed the key ministries.

```
┌─────────────────────────────────────────┐
│            RULERS OF SOMALIA             │
│ PRESIDENTS:                              │
│ 1960 (July) to 1967 (June) Aden Abdullah │
│   Osman Daar                             │
│ 1967 (July) to 1969 (October) Abdi Rashid│
│   Ali Shermarke                          │
│ 1969 (October) to—Siad Barre             │
└─────────────────────────────────────────┘
```

CABINET LIST (1985)

President	*Maj. Gen.* Mohamed Barre Siad
1st Vice President	*Lt. Gen.* Mohamed Ali Samantar
2nd Vice President	*Maj. Gen.* Hussein Afrah Kulmie
Minister of Agriculture	Rafle Gulaid Bile
Minister of Air and Land Transport	Jama Ma-Awiye Gas
Minister of Culture & Higher Education	Sheikh Hussein Abdisalam
Minister of Defense	*Lt. Gen.* Mohamed Ali Samantar
Minister of Education	Abdulle Osman Abdurahman
Minister of Finance	Mohamed Sheikh Osman
Minister of Fisheries	Mohamed Ali Aden
Minister of Foreign Affairs	Abdurahman Jama Barre
Minister of Health	Dakhare Yusuf Hassan
Minister of Industry & Commerce	*Maj. Gen.* Abdullah Mohamed Fadil
Minister of Information & National Guidance	*Col.* Mohamed Omar Jess
Minister of Interior	Abdalla Ahmed Suleiman
Minister of Juba Valley Development	Ahmed Ahmed Habib
Minister of Justice & Religious Affairs	Sheik Hassan Abdalle Farah
Minister of Labor, Youth & Sports	*Col.* Jama Mireh Aware
Minister of Livestock, Forestry & Range	Mussa Ghod Rabile
Minister of Mineral & Water Resources	*Col.* Ahmed Mohamud Farah
Minister of Natl. Planning	*Maj. Gen.* Hussein Afrah Kulmie
Minister of Ports & Sea Transport	Mohamoud Yusuf Ghelle
Minister of Posts & Telecommunications	Abdullahi Siad Ossoble
Minister of Public Works	Salad Hussein Abdikasim
Minister of Tourism & Natl. Parks	Mohamed Mohamoud Saeed
Minister of Treasury	Abdullahi Warsame Nur
Minister in the President's Office for Economic & Political Affairs	Abdullahi Ahmed Addou
Minister in the President's Office for Labor & Social Affairs	Jama Abdulle Ahmed

In 1976, with the creation of the Somali Socialist Revolutionary Party (SSRP), the structure of government was radically altered. The 74-member Central Committee of the SSRP took over the aministration of

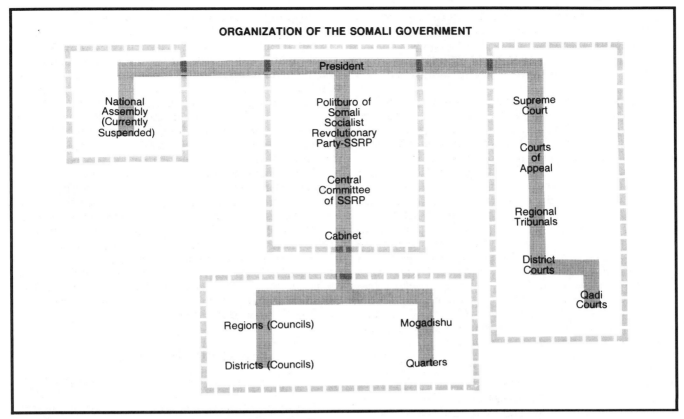

ORGANIZATION OF THE SOMALI GOVERNMENT

President

National Assembly (Currently Suspended)

Politburo of Somali Socialist Revolutionary Party-SSRP

Central Committee of SSRP

Cabinet

Regions (Councils)

Districts (Councils)

Mogadishu

Quarters

Supreme Court

Courts of Appeal

Regional Tribunals

District Courts

Qadi Courts

the country from the SRC, which was dissolved. The Council of Secretaries of State was replaced by the Council of Ministers. However, decision-making power lies with the five-member Politburo consisting of President Siad Barre, Vice President and Defense Minister Mohamed Ali Samantar, the two other vice presidents, and the head of the National Security Service. Twelve of the 23 members of the Council of Ministers are military men.

A new Constitution was approved by a referendum in August 1979 and received presidential assent the following month. Its main provisions are summarized below.

The Somali Democratic Republic is a socialist state led by the working class. Islam is the state religion. All citizens, regardless of sex, creed, origin and language, have equal rights and duties before the law. The Republic upholds the principle of self-determination of peoples and, through peaceful and legal means, shall support the liberation of Somali territories under colonial occupation, and shall encourage the unity of the Somali people through their own free will. The Somali Revolutionary Socialist Party (SRSP) shall have supreme political and economic authority; no other political party or organization may be established.

The president shall be Head of State and Commander-in-Chief of the Armed Forces. Political leadership of party and state are indivisible. The candidate for the presidency shall be proposed by the Central Committee of the SRSP and shall be elected by a majority of at least two-thirds of the deputies of

the People's Assembly. His term of office shall be six years. The president is empowered to appoint and dismiss ministers and deputy ministers and is chairman of joint meetings of party and state institutions. He may initiate referenda concerning decisions of national importance and may, after consultations with the National Defence Council, declare a state of emergency.

The first People's Assembly elections were held in 1979 and the second in 1984.

In 1978 the Barre regime, still licking its wounds and reeling from the shocks of the Ogaden debacle, immediately instituted measures to protect itself against possible internal threats. (See section below on "FOREIGN POLICY.") Although information is limited, the government appears stable and the military basically united under the pressures of defeat. The government's ability to survive the crisis testified to its success in eliminating all organized internal opposition through a carrot-and-stick policy, the stick being the dramatic public executions of its enemies. The most serious threat to the regime after the Ogaden War was the reported coup by army officers, in which 20 were killed in April 1978. Because of the tight control of the army and the police over the media, it is not possible to assess the extent of dissent within the country. All contacts with foreigners are suspect, and active support for the old order is considered as treason. The Victory Pioneers and the National Security Service search out and arrest those who criticize scientific socialism, and heavy penalties are imposed for rumor-mongering. At the same time, the government has successfully undermined the two traditional sources of authority in Somali society: religious and clan leadership. Whether the government's hold on the country is permanent will depend on its ability to rebuild the shattered army and to refill the empty treasury.

In October 1980 the president declared a state of emergency and reinstated the Supreme Revolutionary Council. In 1982, when the refugee position had improved, the SRC was dissolved. During 1983 Siad faced considerable opposition in the northern region, where a mutiny occurred in February and riots later in the year. In November 1984, the hijacking of a Somali plane by dissidents attracted international attention to growing domestic opposition to Siad.

Although the country is ethnically and linguistically homogeneous, clan divisions exert a major impact on domestic politics. President Siad recognizes the continuing strength of the traditional, clan-based political coalitions, and government officials frequently hold formal and informal consultations with various clan leaders. President Siad has used clan politics to maintain his rule by placing members of his own clan, the Marehan, in key positions. He is conscious of clan constituencies, and members of other clans also occupy important positions. Clan identification is very strong, and for many Somalis, the traditional clan system is the accepted vehicle of political expression. Clan politics and clan rivalries occasionally erupt into violence.

FREEDOM & HUMAN RIGHTS

In terms of civil and political rights, Somalia is classified as a not-free country with the maximum negative rating of 7 in political rights and 7 in civil rights (on a descending scale in which 1 is the highest and 7 the lowest in rights).

In 1980, Somalia began its first year under the new constitution, but within months a state of emergency was declared. The newly elected People's Assembly was also suspended. In the spring of 1980 as many as several dozen military officers were executed for allegedly having supported the Somali Salvation Front, an anti-government guerrilla movement. Amnesty International reports that at least 100 people are believed to be held on political grounds, without charge or trial. Some officials of the previous government overthrown in 1969, including a former prime minister, remain in detention. The national security court operates outside the court system and has jurisdiction over a broad range of crimes. Amnesty International characterizes trials before the national security court as "unfair."

Freedoms of the press, speech, and assembly are seriously circumscribed. The press is entirely government controlled and foreign publications are subject to censorship before they can be sold to the public.

No opposition groups exist. Citizen participation in the political process outside of the ruling party is virtually nil.

Despite a constitutional provision that accords Somali citizens the right to formal charges and a speedy trial, the government frequently makes arrests without warrants and detains indefinitely persons whom it views as a threat to national security. Habeas corpus or its equivalent does not exist in national security cases. In some instances, political prisoners are held incommunicado and denied access to lawyers prior to being formally charged. Delays in bringing charges can be lengthy in criminal cases as well as political cases.

At least 200 of the 350-500 political prisoners are being held without charge, including six high government officials arrested in June 1982. A seventh ranking official arrested at the same time died in prison. Seven youths were arrested in the autumn of 1984 for antiregime activities and later sentenced to death, although their death sentences have not been carried out. In 1985, the government arrested and detained without charge 22 members of the Muslim Brotherhood. It has released only two of them, and they departed Somalia upon their release.

CIVIL SERVICE

The national civil service, with a personnel strength of 77,500 in 1975, includes all members of the national and local governments, employees of public corporations, as well as temporary employees. The civil service is administered by the Social and Political Committee of the Central Committee of the Somali Socialist Revolutionary Party. Recruitment of public as well as private employees is the responsibility of the National Recruiting Board. Most public employees are transferred frequently and are also subject to indoctrination programs by the Somali Institute of Administration and Management and the Halane Revolutionary Training School. Civil servants are expected to be politically committed to the ideology of scientific socialism, and "morally corrupt" anti-revolutionaries are barred from their ranks.

LOCAL GOVERNMENT

For purposes of local government, Somalia is divided into 16 regions.

REGIONS OF SOMALIA			
Region	**Capital**	**Region**	**Capital**
Jubada Hoose	Kismayo	Galgduud	Dusa Mareb
Dijuuma	Dijuuma	Hiraan	Belet Weyn
Gedo	Garbaharay	Mudug	Galkayo
Baydhaba	Baydhaba	Nugaal	Garowe
Bakool	Xuddur	Bari	Bosaso
Shabelle Hoose	Marka	Sanaag	Erigavo
Shabelle Dhexe	Jowhar	Togdheer	Burao
Mogadishu	Mogadishu	Waqooyi Galbeed	Hargeysa

The 16 regions are divided into 78 districts. Each of the regions contains from three to seven districts, except the capital region, which is subdivided into 14 quarters. Both the regions and districts are headed by commissioners.

The local government reform law of 1972 created three levels of representative institutions. The regional councils consist of heads of regional units of the government ministries, chairmen of the subordinate district councils and a citizen from each district. The district councils are grouped into three categories of nine, 13 and 17 community representatives appointed for two-year renewable terms. The village councils, each with seven members chosen annually by the local residents, are the only elected bodies in the country. In the towns, village council-level units are elected at the ward level; each quarter in Mogadishu, the only city with a separate municipal status, has a district council-level unit, called a quarter committee, consisting of six ex-officio and 20 nominated members. Mogadishu is governed by a mayor and a city council. Regional and district councils have six committees: economic development, social affairs, public security, finance, political orientation and mediation and conciliation. All councils have borrowing and taxing powers.

FOREIGN POLICY

Somalia is one of the few nations in the world where irredentism is still an overriding national issue. About one-third of the Somalis in the Horn of Africa live outside the national borders: about one million in Ethiopia, about 250,000 in Kenya and a sizeable number in Djibouti. Italian colonial policy was directed toward encouraging Somali irredentism in order to bolster Italian imperialistic ambitions. The Italians are credited with coining the phrase Greater Somalia, which would bring under Somali control one-fifth of Kenya, one-quarter of Ethiopia, and about one-half of Djibouti. Greater Somalia would be double the size and population of the present Somali Republic. It would not necessarily mean additional national wealth because most of the contested areas are either desert or semi-desert.

Pan-Somalism has brought Somalia into conflict with all its neighbors and has also influenced its relations with the great powers. Between 1963 and 1964, there were sporadic clashes along the Ethiopian border and in the northeastern region of Kenya. By 1967 the republic was faced with a crisis along all its international borders without prospect of immediate solution. Defense expenditures were draining the treasury, and Somalia was unable to obtain diplomatic support for its claims becuase President Jomo Kenyatta of Kenya and Emperor Haile Selassie of Ethiopia, who opposed them, were two of the most respected elder statesmen in Africa. Without therefore renouncing its claims, Somalia decided in 1967 to end open hostilities and seek an improvement in relations with her neighbors. The detente did not last long and was ended when the military seized power in 1969.

By the mid-1970s several factors seemed to favor a renewal of conflict and to give Somalia a significantly greater chance of success: the growth in the size and capability of the Somali armed forces, substantial military aid from the Soviet Union and the civil turmoil in Ethiopia following the deposition of Haile Selassie. In 1977 Somalia decided to risk everything on a desperate gamble to conquer the Ogaden region. After gaining initial successes, Somalia found herself deserted by the Soviet Union and deprived of all her sources of supplies. By 1978 the numerically superior Ethiopian forces, supported by Soviet arms and Cuban troops, launched a successful counteroffensive, regaining all the lost territory and expelling the invaders. For Somalia the war was a national disaster. The Somali Army, considered by observers at the beginning of the conflict as one of the finest in Africa, suffered such serious losses that it might not be able to recover its former strength. It lost many thousands of its 32,000 troops and most of its combat planes and tanks. The end of the war also found Somalia without a friend or patron among the big powers. In 1978 President Siad Barre made a trip to China to explore possible assistance from Peking, but the results were not encouraging.

Somalia's closest ties are with the Arab world, with which it is linked by history, culture and religion. As a member of the Arab League, Somalia received some assistance from Arab countries during the Ogaden conflict. However, Somalia's socialism conflicts with the conservatism of many of the wealthier Arab states, while its anti-Soviet stance has brought it into conflict with radical states such as Southern Yemen, Libya and Syria. Nevertheless, because Somalia desperately needs the moneraty benefits of the Arab association, its pan-Arabism is likely to grow at the expense of its pan-Africanism.

Of the Western countries, Italy and West Germany remain the most significant sources of aid. Italians dominate much of the country's economy, even under the socialist regime, and ties between Italy and her former colony have remained close.

In 1980 Somalia agreed to make port facilities at Mogadishu and Berbera available to a U.S. Rapid Deployment Force in return for credits to American arms. Somalia also promised not to support external irredentists. However, the United States has been slow in extending further military and technical aid, causing relations to become strained, and in 1984 Said called for a renormalization of relations with the Soviet Union. Although relations with the Arab world continued to improve (following a nationwide campaign to promote the teaching of Arabic) those with Libya were severed in 1981 on account of Libyan support for Ethiopian-backed Somali rebels. Rapprochement with Kenya, a traditional enemy, was at least partially achieved as a result of a state visit to Mogadishu by Kenya's President Arap Moi during which Siad asserted that "Somalia has no longer any claim to Kenyan territory." The two leaders thereupon reached agreement on a series of border and technical cooperation issues.

Somalia and the United States are parties to five agreements and treaties covering agricultural commodities, defense, economic and technical cooperation, investment guaranties and Peace Corps.

Somalia joined the U.N. in 1960; its share of the U.N. budget is 0.02%. It is a member of 13 U.N. organizations and seven other international organizations.
U.S. Ambassador in Mogadishu: Peter S. Bridges
U.K. Ambassador in Mogadishu: William Fullerton
Somali Ambassador in Washington, D.C.: Mohamud Haji Nur
Somali Ambassador in London: Mohamed Jama Elmi

PARLIAMENT

The former National Assembly (Aljamiahtol Wadaniyah) was dissolved in 1969. Under the new Constitution of 1979 the People's Assembly shall be a legislative body consisting of 177 deputies, 171 elected by the people through direct secret ballot and an additional six presidential nominees. The normal life of the Assembly is five years. The People's Assembly shall elect the president and is also empowered to relieve him of office. A two-thirds majority of the Assembly may amend the constitution. No amendments to the constitution may affect the republican system of the country, the adoption of the principle of socialism, territorial unity or the fundamental rights and freedoms of the citizen.

POLITICAL PARTIES

In 1976 the Somali Socialist Revolutionary Party (SSRP) was formally constituted as the country's only legal party. Its governing bodies are the 74-member Central Committe (which took over from the Supreme Revolutionary Council as the nation's highest legislative and executive body) and the five-member Politburo.

The SSRP's ideology is defined as "scientific socialism," a form of Islamized Marxism which, according to President Siad Barre, consists of three elements: community development, socialism and Islam. The president defines socialism as the sharing of work and wealth to ensure "justice, equality and a life free of expoliters." The Somali version of socialism differs from the Soviet model in its willingness to permit organized religion a role in national life, a tolerance of some degree of private enterprise and an emphasis on diversity within a broad framework.

Since 1980 a number of opposition groups have emerged; backed by Ethiopia, most of their members are drawn from the Mijarteyn and other dissident tribes. The umbrella organization of these groups is the Somali Democratic Salvation Front (SDSF), founded in 1982. SDSF consists of the Somali Salvation Front, Democratic Front for the Liberation of Somalia, Somali Workers' Party, and the Somali Na-

tional Movement. SDSF has been credited with the hijacking of a Somali plane in 1984, and guerrilla attacks on military installations in border areas.

Another opposition group, the Somali National Movement (SNM), launched in London in 1981, moved to Ethiopia in 1982, from where it helped to orchestrate a series of small-scale attacks on military targets in the north. SNM draws its members from the Isaq clan, large numbers of whom are found in the Gulf States. In 1983, it scored its first major success with an attack on Mandera prison in which hundreds of prisoners escaped.

ECONOMY

Somalia is one of the 49 low-income countries (within this classification it is among the 10 lowest), one of the 29 least-developed countries and one of the 45 countries considered by the U.N. as most seriously affected by recent adverse economic conditions. It has a centrally planned economy in which the dominant sector is public. It was declared a socialist state in 1970.

PRINCIPAL ECONOMIC INDICATORS
Gross National Product: $1.140 billion (1983)
  GNP Annual Growth Rate: 4.7% (1973-82)
  Per Capita GNP: $250 (1983)
  Per Capita GNP Annual Growth Rate: 1.9% (1973-82)
Gross Domestic Product: $1.540 billion (1983)
  GDP Average Annual Growth Rate: 2.8% (1973-83)
  GDP per Capita: $203 (1983)
  GDP per Capita Average Annual Growth Rate: 1.0% (1970-81)
Income Distribution: Information not available
Percentage of Population in Absolute Poverty: 40% Urban; 70% Rural
Consumer Price Index: Information not available
Average Annual Rate of Inflation: 20.1% (1973-83)
Money Supply: S5.752 billion (March 1985)
  Reserve Money: S3.516 billion (March 1985)
Currency in Circulation: S1.9 billion (1984)
International Reserves: $1.0 million, of which foreign exchange reserves were $1.0 million (1984)

Development planning began with the First Five-Year Plan, 1963-67, acknowledged to be a failure. It was replaced by a second short-term plan, 1968-70, which carried on unfinished projects of the first plan. After seizing power in 1970, the new military regime issued its first plan, the Development Program, 1974-78, an ambitious projection that is given little chance of meeting its goals because of the intervention of the Ogaden War. Of the total investment of S3,863,354,000, 32.6% was to be covered by domestic financing and 67.4% by foreign financing. Included in the plan were such projects as the Northwest Region Development Project, the Mogadishu Port Project and the completion of the Kismayo airport.

About one-half of the expenditure of S7,104 million envisaged in the 1979-81 Development Plan was to fi-

```
    BALANCE OF PAYMENTS (1983)
          (million $)
Merchandise Exports ...................         90.1
Merchandise Imports ...................       -362.1
Trade Balance .......................         -272.0
Exports of Services ...................         78.8
Imports of Services ...................       -124.0
Balance on Goods and Services ..........      -317.2
Private Unrequited Transfers Net ..........     19.1
Government Unrequited Transfers Net .......    148.2
Current Balance .....................         -149.9
Long-term Capital Net .................         76.6
Short-term Capital Net
Net Errors and Omissions ...............        -4.4
Total (Net Monetary Movements) ..........      -77.7
Valuation Changes ....................           4.7
Changes in Reserves ..................         -73.0
```

nance projects carried forward from the previous Five-Year Plan. Of this budget, 35.4% was allocated to agriculture and fisheries, 18% to economic infrastructure and 7.4% to education. There was a new emphasis on the needs of small producers rather than large-scale schemes. A target of 4% annual growth was announced in the 1982-86 Development Plan, which had projected spending of S16,000 million. However, this, like previous plans, was unlikely to realize its objectives.

GROSS DOMESTIC PRODUCT BY ECONOMIC ACTIVITY (1970-81)		
	%	Rate of Change %
Agriculture	59.2	3.0
Mining	0.7	—
Manufacturing	7.4	-3.8
Construction	4.8	-3.6
Electricity, Gas & Water	0.6	19.9
Transport & Communications	5.6	3.0
Trade & Finance	11.7	8.6
Public Administration & Defense	8.0	7.8
Other Branches	2.1	4.0

As a least developed country, Somalia is entitled to concessional development aid from international agencies. In addition, it has received bilateral and multilateral aid from Arab countries and the Soviet Union. Until the 1970s, U.S. aid was also significant.

FOREIGN ECONOMIC ASSISTANCE		
Source	Period	Amount (million $)
United States Loans	1946-83	98.9
United States Grants	1946-83	285.1
International Organizations	1946-83	401
(Of which World Bank)	1946-83	—
Soviet Union	1954-76	154.0
East European Countries	1954-76	5.0
China	1954-76	133.0
OPEC	1981-82	33.2
Kuwait	1981-82	35.0
All Sources	1979-81	261.0

During 1979-81 Somalia received $56.20 in per capita foreign aid.

BUDGET

The Somali fiscal year is the calendar year. The national budget is a consolidated budget covering central government, local governments and autonomous agencies. Public finances are limited by a low tax base, a partially monetized economy and the absence of conventional yardsticks of fiscal performance.

Of the current revenues, 51.1% comes from income from government property, 23.2% from import duties and 1.0% from income tax. Of current expenditures, 39.2% goes to financial and central services, 28.4% to defense, 7.4% to education, 3.8% to foreign affairs, 3.2% to transportation, 2.8% to health and 2.1% to agriculture.

In 1983, total outstanding disbursed external debt amounted to $1.149 billion of which $986.3 million was owed to official creditors and $162.8 million to private creditors. The total debt service was $22.1 million of which $12.6 million was repayment of principal and $9.5 million was interest. Total external debt represented 680.4% of export revenues and 127.5% of GNP. Debt service represented 13.1% of export revenues and 2.5% of GNP.

FINANCE

The Somali unit of currency is the Somali shilling (or the Somalo) divided into 100 centisemi. Coins are issued in denominations of 1, 5, 10 and 50 centisemi and 1 shilling; notes are issued in denominations of 5, 10 20 and 100 shillings. The shilling was devalued by 48% in 1984 and by 29% in 1985.

In 1985 the dollar exchange rate was $1=S40.608 and the 1984 sterling exchange rate was £1=S25.32.

All banks were nationalized in 1970. The bank of issue is the Somali Central Bank; the Commercial and Savings Bank serves as the only commercial bank in the country; development finance is provided by the Somali Development Bank. In 1984 the commercial bank had reserves of S1.048 billion, demand deposits of S2.898 billion and time and savings deposits of S1.595 billion.

AGRICULTURE

Of the total land area of 63,714,000 hectares (157,437,290 acres), 34% is classified as agricultural land, or 6.8 hectares (17 acres) per capita. Agriculture employs 82% of the labor force, contributes 50% of GDP, and (including livestock, forestry and fisheries) accounts for 100% of exports by value. Its annual growth rate during 1973-83 was 3.5%. The value added in agriculture in 1983 was $570 million. Based on 1974-76 = 100 the index of agricultural production in 1982 was 113, the index of food production was 113, and the index of per capita food production was 72.

CURRENT BUDGET (million Somali shillings)

Revenue	1981	1982	1983*
Taxes on income and profits:	145.8	85.5	90.0
Income tax	59.3	44.4	50.0
Development levy	53.9	11.2	—
Profit tax	32.6	29.9	40.0
Taxes on production, consumption and domestic transactions	716.4	824.2	652.0
Taxes on international transactions:	1,206.4	1,312.6	1,634.9
Import duties	922.4	1,039.1	1,200.0
Total tax revenue	2,068.6	2,222.3	2,376.0
Fees and service charges	59.2	22.4	86.3
Income from government property	132.7	256.0	68.5
Other revenue	86.8	57.6	2,643.2
Total non-tax revenue	278.7	336.0	2,798.0
TOTAL	2,347.3	2,558.3	5,174.0

Expenditure†	1981	1982	1983*
Defense	843.4	902.0	1,324.8
Interior and police	177.4	147.4	204.5
Finance and central services	1,015.2	1,518.5	1,827.8
Foreign affairs	59.6	177.7	178.0
Justice and religious affairs	91.6	112.1	118.5
Presidency and general administration	34.7	41.6	59.6
Planning	3.7	10.0	5.6
National Assembly	7.0	8.4	10.1
Total general services	2,232.6	2,917.7	3,728.9
Transportation	56.9	66.3	67.4
Posts and telecommunications	28.7	39.7	50.0
Public works	26.1	33.0	26.3
Agriculture	31.1	50.8	96.5
Livestock and forestry	32.3	41.7	55.1
Mineral and water resources	17.2	22.5	49.6
Industry and commerce	5.6	8.4	8.7
Fisheries	3.9	4.8	30.1
Total economic services	201.8	267.7	383.7
Education	224.9	280.5	344.0
Health	98.4	102.1	130.0
Information	25.8	43.3	48.2
Labor, sports and tourism	11.7	24.0	29.4
Total social services	360.8	449.9	551.6
TOTAL	2,795.2	3,634.8	4,664.2

* Estimates.
† Excluding development expenditure (million Somali shillings): 285.8 in 1981; 345.6 in 1982.
1984: Draft budget expenditure (million Somali shillings): 6,492 (Development projects 3,192, Defense 2,601, Social services 698).

GROWTH PROFILE
Annual Growth Rates (%)

Population 1980-2000	3.0
Birthrate 1965-1983	−0.4
Deathrate 1965-1983	−27.0
Urban Population 1973-83	5.5
Labor Force 1980-2000	1.7
GNP 1973-82	4.7
GNP per capita 1973-82	1.9
GDP 1973-83	2.8
GDP per capita 1970-81	1.0
Consumer Prices 1970-81	16.2
Wholesale Prices	—
Inflation 1973-83	20.1
Agriculture 1973-83	3.5
Manufacturing 1970-81	−3.8
Industry 1973-83	1.1
Services 1973-83	2.6
Mining	—
Construction 1970-81	−3.6
Electricity 1970-81	19.9
Transportation 1970-81	3.0
Trade 1970-81	8.6
Public Administration & Defense 1970-81	7.8
Export Price Index 1975-81	10.9
Import Price Index 1975-81	11.1
Terms of Trade 1975-81	−1.0
Exports 1973-83	7.3
Imports 1973-83	0.0
Public Consumption 1973-83	1.5
Private Consumption 1973-83	7.9
Gross Domestic Investment 1973-83	−8.2
Energy Consumption 1973-83	16.8
Energy Production	—

Although the constitution of 1960 had stated that all lands belonged to the state, both arable and pasture land were traditionally under the control of the numerous clans or tribes, and the right of cultivation or pasturage was restricted to clan members. The average holding was 13.7 hectares (34 acres), but there was considerable variation, with 60% averaging 2 hectares (5 acres) and 40% averaging 22.6 hectares (50 acres). The modern sector includes about 138 banana plantations (of which 50 are Italian-held leaseholds), each with an average area of 300 hectares (740 acres). Under the land tenure law of 1975, arable land may be held only for 10-year concessions, and these are not to exceed 100 hectares (247 acres) in the case of corporations and 60 hectares (148 acres) of rain-fed land and 30 hectares (75 acres) of irrigated land in the case of family holdings. Mortgage, sale, lease or other transfer is prohibited, but land may be inherited. Among the nomads there is no individual land tenure system, no system of registration of land and no general land tax.

The country's most fertile area is the Juba-Shebeli area. It is believed that three-fourths of the suitable land is already under cultivation. Estimates of irrigated farmlands vary, but some 150,000 hectares (247,000 acres) are under some form of controlled irrigation. The planned Bardera Dam, due for completion in 1989, would add another 250,000 hectares (617,750 acres) to this total. Most of the country's farms are without access to irrigation and must depend on the two annual rainy seasons, which together provide only, in the best years, less than 50 cm (20 in.) of rain. In an average five-year cycle, three are drought years, one is a flood year and one is a bumper crop year. Since 1970 the government has launched a series of agricultural development programs, the most successful of which were the Agricultural Crash Program, the North West Region Development Project and the Rural Development Project. An important element of these programs was the state-owned sector, covering 13,776 hectares (34,040 acres). A major objective of the Development Program, 1974-78, was a massive effort to establish agricultural cooperatives. Over 68% of development spending was allocated to 14 irrigation projects. The Juba-Shebeli Emergency Settlement Scheme called for the relocation of up to 110,000 nomads at three agricultural settlement projects, at Dijuuma, Sablale and Kurtun Warey. In 1982, 1,750 tractors were in use and annual consumption of fertilizers was 1,300 tons or 0.9 kg.

Bananas constitute the nation's major crop, accounting for about 20% of the exports in 1973. Sugar is cultivated at Jowhar by the state-owned National Company for Agriculture and Industry. Somalia has achieved occasional self-sufficiency in foodgrains.

PRINCIPAL CROP PRODUCTION (1983) (000 tons)	
Corn	120
Sorghum	235
Rice	2.8
Cassava	34
Dry beans	20.8
Grapefruit	6
Bananas	98.9
Groundnuts	6.0
Cotton	4
Sesame seed	59.5
Coconuts	1
Sugar Cane	449.7

Somalia has one of the highest livestock-to-man ratios in the world, with 4.0 million cattle and 10.3 million sheep in 1982. Before the 1974 drought, it was estimated that nearly 80% of the population depended primarily on livestock, of which 35 to 40% were nomads and 25 to 30% semi-nomads. An average nomadic family had 5.75 people, 110 goats and sheep, 20 camels and eight head of cattle. Camels are usually in the care of boys and unmarried men, while sheep and goats are tended by women. About 83% of the national cattle herd is in the southern region, about 79% of the national flock of sheep and goats is in the north, while the camel herd is about equally divided between north and south. The annual offtake for slaughter is about 7 to 10%. The 1974 drought is estimated to have decimated about 60% of the livestock population and led to the introduction of range management and grazing control programs under the auspices of the Livestock Development Agency and the U.N.-sponsored Ecological Management of Arid and Semi-Arid Rangelands. The five main national cattle breeds are derived from the hardy but low-yielding zebu. In 1982 livestock population was estimated at 4 million cattle, 10.3 million sheep, 16.7 million goats, 10,000 pigs, 24,000 asses, 22,000 mules, 5.6 million camels and 3.084 million chickens. Livestock export statistics indicate that this sector is recovering from the disastrous effects of the 1974-75 drought. The increase of livestock exports is affected by the Ethiopian government's decision to nationalize all livestock holdings over five head throughout the Ogaden and the rest of Ethiopia. This policy forced Somali herders and nomads to transfer their stock from the superior rangelands in the Ogaden to Somalia proper for export. However, grazing land in Somalia is not sufficient to handle any permanent, large-scale transfer from the Ogaden. Arab countries, especially Saudi Arabia, formerly the sole importer of Somali livestock, imposed an embargo in 1983 following an outbreak of rinderpest.

There are no large forests; wood and wood products are imported. Government forest plantations have been established near Berbera and Gcanlibax. Roundwood removals in 1982 totaled 4.9 million cubic meters (173 million cubic ft).

Fishing is regarded as a despised occupation and is conducted principally by people living along the shore. In 1983 about 4,000 full-time and 10,000 part-time fishermen manned about 2,500 small boats, while on the north coast about 1,680 traditional fishermen, using about 500 dugout canoes and 215 motorized boats, fish for tuna. The fishing season extends from October to March. The annual catch is 6,580 tons of tuna, mackerel, sardines and lobster, about 80% of which is exported, accounting for 4% of total exports. However, a recent survey has suggested a potential of 100,000 tons a year. There is one tuna-freezing plant at Ras Filuch, near Alula, and another at Kismayo. With Soviet aid, the government has set up more than 21 fishing cooperatives with a fleet of 70 vessels. A UNDP-FAO project assists in boatbuilding, training and marketing.

Originally organized with Soviet assistance, the industry suffered a setback in 1977 when Soviet advisers were expelled and withdrew their trawlers from the projects. The industry is being revitalized with the help of the EEC and other Western aid. In February 1979 Somalia helped to found a joint Arab fisheries company, created under the auspices of the Arab League. Agreement was reached with Italy in May 1980 on a joint fishing venture in which the Italians were to provide four trawlers as well as training and technology. The FAO has identified the Hafuna region as one of excellent potential for sardine fishing, and is expanding its training and technical assistance. The development of Hafuna is an important part of the 1982-86 Five-Year Plan, which proposes to settle 3,000 people to operate a fishing port and revitalize the export market which collapsed after Soviet withdrawal.

INDUSTRY

The manufacturing sector, small even by African standards, consists of a few relatively large government-owned plants and about 255 small private establishments, each employing over five workers. The sector employs 7% of the work force, and contributes 7% of the GDP. Its annual rate of growth during 1973-83 was −3.8%. Artisan establishments employing fewer than five workers each are not included in official statistics. Some 89% of the value added in manufacturing of $53 million is accounted for by the public sector and 79% by the food processing sector.

The largest industrial plant is the state-owned sugar plant at Jowhar, which accounts for approximately half of the gross value of industrial output and about a third of total industrial employment. Also state-owned is the Somaltex textile mills, which supply virtually the entire domestic market. Newer industries include cement and pharmaceuticals.

Since declaring itself a socialist state in 1970, Somalia has nationalized a number of industries and companies, but compensation was offered in all cases. In 1975 the United States declared that Somalia was no longer eligible for special tariff concessions because of unresolved investment disputes with U.S. firms. Within a socialist framework, the government is not averse to private foreign investment and provides favorable tax terms for foreign investors, protection of investments and repatriation of profits and capital.

ENERGY

In 1982 Somalia produced no form of mineral energy and consumed 524,000 metric tons of coal equivalent, or 103 kg (227 lb) per capita. In the same year, Somalia produced 62 million kwh, or 9 kwh per capita of electric power. The annual growth rate during 1973-83 was 16.8% for energy consumption. Energy imports account for 31% of all merchandise imports. Apparent per capita consumption of gasoline is 5 gallons per year. A petroleum refinery which began operation in 1979 had to close in late 1980 when its source of crude oil was cut off by the Iran-Iraq War, but supplies were obtained from Saudi Arabia during 1982, enabling the refinery to start up again.

LABOR

The economically active population is estimated at 2.2 million, of which 30% are women. Agriculture employs 84% of the labor force, industry 8%, and services 8%. Nearly 61% of all industrial workers are employed by the 14 state-owned corporations. Unemployment is an urban phenomenon and is most serious in the capital, Mogadishu. The annual growth rate of the labor force during 1973-83 was 2.0%.

Wages and working conditions are established by decree. After the 1969 revolution, the military regime dissolved all labor unions and organized workers' committees in every establishment. It appears that only a few of the committees are actively functioning.

Even though child labor is prohibited, children often find odd jobs such as selling cigarettes on the street corner or watching and cleaning parked cars to support themselves or supplement family income. The work day is eight hours or a total of 48 hours a week with stipulations on the amount of overtime that can be worked. Workers are entitled to paid holidays, annual leave and holiday bonuses. However, the salary scale is extremely low, especially for civil servants. Workers resort to second jobs, bribes, misuse of public funds, assistance from other family members, and remittances from abroad to support themselves and their families.

FOREIGN COMMERCE

The foreign commerce of Somalia in 1984 consisted of exports of $122.96 million and imports of $413.46 million, leaving a trade deficit of $290.5 million. Of the imports, food and live animals constituted 23.8% (of which cereals 17.4%), motor vehicles 21.1%, electrical machinery 7.5%, oils and fats 6.9%, cement 4.4% and iron and steel 3.3%. Of the exports, live animals constituted 76.6%, fruits and vegetables 8.4%, livestock products 5.0% and distillate fuels 4.7%.

The major import sources are: Italy 34.5%, the United States 9.2%, the United Kingdom 7.9%, France 7.5% and Saudi Arabia 5.5%. The major export destinations are: Saudi Arabia 69.9%, Italy 12.9%, UAE 5.4%, Iraq 3.8% and Yemen Arab Republic 2.3%.

Based on 1975=100, the import price index in 1981 was 170, the export price index 167, and the terms of trade index (export prices divided by import prices × 100) 98.

FOREIGN TRADE INDICATORS (1984)	
Annual Growth Rate, Imports:	0.0% (1973-83)
Annual Growth Rate, Exports:	7.3% (1973-83)
Ratio of Exports to Imports:	23:77
Exports per capita:	$16
Imports per capita:	$54
Balance of Trade:	−$290.5 million
Ratio of International Reserves to Imports (in months)	0.4
Exports as % of GDP:	13.5
Imports as % of GDP:	26.0
Value of Manufactured Exports:	$1 million
Commodity Concentration:	73.7%

Direction of Trade (%)	Imports	Exports
EEC	45.0	18.0
U.S.	8.3	7.0
Industrialized Market Economies	66.7	9.8
East European Economies	0.4	—
High Income Oil Exporters	18.5	81.7
Developing Economies	32.7	90.1

Composition of Trade (%)	Imports	Exports
Food	32.5	16.2
Agricultural Raw Materials	4.2	7.0
Fuels	0.7	7.2
Ores & Minerals	3.5	29.3
Manufactured Goods	58.8	30.3
of which Chemicals	4.7	5.0
of which Machinery	35.3	4.6

TRANSPORTATION & COMMUNICATIONS

Somalia has no railways or navigable inland waterways. There are three major ports: Mogadishu, Berbera and Chisimaio, which together handled 1,064,000 tons of cargo in 1982. Berbera serves the northern region and handles about 90% of all exports of livestock on the hoof. Bananas are exported through Marka or Kismayo. Mogadishu handles two-thirds of all imports. Until 1975 the Somalian flag was one of the major flags of convenience, used by over 250 foreign ships, but in 1975 this practice was abolished.

The road system consists of 17,215 km (10,692 mi), of which 2,335 km (1,450 mi) are paved. In 1982 these roads were used by 17,200 passenger cars and 8,050 commercial vehicles. Per capita passenger car ownership was 2.3 per 1,000 inhabitants.

The national flag carrier is Somali Airlines, owned 51% by the government and 49% by Alitalia, the Italian airline. With a fleet of five aircraft, Somali Airlines flies to six countries, including Italy. In 1982 it flew 0.5 million km (0.3 million mi) and carried 16,000 passengers. There are 59 airports and airfields in the country, of which 47 are usable, six have permanent-surface runways and five have runways over 2,500 meters (8,000 ft).

In 1984 there were 6,000 telephones in use, or 0.2 per 100 inhabitants.

In 1982 the postal service handled 3,820,000 pieces of mail. Per capita volume of mail traffic was 0.5 pieces.

In 1982 tourist revenues totaled $9 million, but no information is available on the number and nationalities of the tourists.

MINING

Known mineral deposits in the country include uranium, tin, iron, quartz and columbite. Currently, only tin is being exploited, at Majayahan.

DEFENSE

The defense structure is headed by the president. The chain of command runs through the minister of defense, who is also the commander of the National Army, to which the navy and air force are subordinate. Although a conscription law is on the statute books, enlistment is voluntary.

The Somali armed forces were virtually wiped out in the Ogaden conflict, and their personnel and equipment were totally shattered. No information has been published on the actual losses suffered by the armed forces. The following statistics relate to the armed forces on the eve of the war, when the total strength was 62,700, or 7.7 armed persons per 1,000 civilians. Somalia ranked 74th in the world in per capita military manpower.

ARMY:
Personnel: 60,000
Organization: 3 corps; 8 divisions HQ; 3 tank/mechanized brigades; 20 infantry brigades; 1 commando brigade; 1 SAM brigade; 30 field, 1 AA artillery battalions
Equipment: 215 tanks; 50 armored combat vehicles; 489 armored personnel carriers; 130 guns/howitzers; 50 mortars; 300 antitank rocket launchers; 100 antitank guided weapons; 40 SAMs; air defense guns

NAVY:
Personnel: 700
Units: fast attack craft; 5 patrol craft; 1 amphibious craft
Naval Bases: Berbera and Mogadishu

AIR FORCE:
Personnel 2,000
Organization: 64 combat aircraft; 3 fighter squadrons; 3 fighter ground attack squadrons; 1 counterinsurgency squadron; 1 transport squadron; 1 helicopter squadron; 6 trainers; air-to-air missiles
Major Air Bases: Hargeysa, Mogadishu and Berbera

In 1984 the defense budget totaled $129.927 million, representing 22.7% of the national budget, 9.1% of the GNP, $17 per capita, $1,921 per soldier and $190 per sq km of national territory.

Before the Ogaden War, Somali armed forces were considered among the strongest in sub-Saharan Africa, but they have always been inferior to the Ethiopian armed forces. One notable feature of the Somalian army was its large tank force, which made it the largest armored force in black Africa. However, since the end of the war that force is plagued by problems of servicing and spare parts. The air force is considered part of the army, and its role is primarily ground support. The size of the military establishment and budget in such a poor country as Somalia is a reflection of national policy and the determination to unite Somali ethnic areas in neighboring countries within a Greater Somalia. It is not known how far this determination has been affected by the recent disaster. But it may take years, even decades, to rebuild the armed forces to their pre-war levels.

Somalia has received no military assistance from the United States; aid received from the Soviet Union until 1977 has not been divulged. From 1973 to 1983 arms purchases abroad totaled $1.2 billion including $410 million from Italy.

EDUCATION

The national literacy rate is 5% (10% for males and 0.2% for females).

Primary and intermediate education is free and compulsory for eight years from the age of 6 to 14. The gross school enrollment ratios are 30% at the first level (6 to 13) and 11% at the second level (14 to 17) for a combined enrollment ratio of 24%. Girls constitute 36% of primary grade enrollment, 27% of secondary grade enrollment and and 11% of post-secondary enrollment.

Schooling lasts for 12 years, divided into eight years of primary school, and intermediate school and four years of secondary school. Education is free at all levels, but secondary education facilities are limited to the areas of Mogadishu, Hargeysa and Burao. The curriculum is radically modified to reflect the new socialist ideology of the military regime. All private schools were nationalized in 1970.

The school year runs from November to July. The language of instruction is Somali, but both Arabic and Italian are taught in the intermediate and secondary grades.

Primary school teachers are trained at the National Teachers Education Center. There is a serious shortage of teachers at all levels. The national teacher-pupil ratios are 1:35 in primary grades, 1:18 in secondary grades and 1:9 in post-secondary classes.

In 1974 the government launched the Rural Development Campaign, which was designed among other things to extend literacy among the nomads. An estimated 22,000 teachers, including 11,000 students from the last two grades of intermediate school and the first two grades of secondary school (whose classes were closed during a whole school year), were directed to teach the nomads to read and write Somali. The results of this campaign are reportedly encouraging.

Vocational education is provided by three technical institutes at the secondary level and a technical college at the post-secondary level. The two institutes had a total enrollment in 1980 of 7,704, representing 16% of the secondary enrollment.

Educational administration is centralized in the Ministry of Education. In 1980 the ministry's budget was S169,384,000, of which 91.1% was current expenditure. This amount represented 1.8% of the GNP (compared to a UNESCO recommendation of 4%), 8.7% of the national budget and $5.00 per capita.

EDUCATIONAL ENROLLMENT (1982)			
Level	Schools	Teachers	Students
First Level	1408	12,007	418,935
Second Level	N.A.	925	17,020
Vocational & Teachers Training	N.A.	2,920	25,966
Third Level	9	—	2,899

Higher education is provided by the Somali National University at Mogadishu, with 2,899 students in 1982. The university has branches at Afgoi, Hargeysa and Kismayo. A new university, financed by the EEC, was opened in 1978. Per capita university enrollment is 38 per 100,000 inhabitants.

In 1982, 1,162 Somali students were enrolled in institutions of higher learning abroad. Of these, 314 were in the United States, 192 in Italy, 10 in Canada, 115 in India, 62 in West Germany and 57 in the United Kingdom.

LEGAL SYSTEM

Somali jurisprudence is a composite of four disparate legal traditions: English common law, Italian law, the Sharia and Somali customary law. The basis of Somali customary law is the dia (or compensation), payable by the dia-paying group to which the offending party belongs to the group to which the victim belongs.

At the summit of the judicial system is the Supreme Court, composed of a chief justice with the title of president, a vice president, nine surrogate justices and four laymen. At the next level are the regional courts of appeal comprising two sections, one of which hears appeals from the district tribunals and from the ordinary sections of the regional tribunals, and the other, which hears appeals from the regional assize sections. Both sections are presided over by single judges assisted by laymen. Courts of appeal sit in Mogadishu and Hargeysa. The subordinate courts consist of regional tribunals and district courts. There are eight regional tribunals, each with two sections: assize and general. The district courts, numbering 78, are divided into civil and criminal sections. Civil matters such as marriage and divorce are handled by the district qadis under the Sharia. The Military Supreme Court tries members of the armed forces.

The Somali judicial system, in both criminal and political cases, is subject to review and control by the executive branch of government. Since 1970, the Supreme Revolutionary Council has nominated all judges, and council members occupy all positions on the Higher Judicial Council, the highest body of judicial review. The 1979 constitution designated the president as chairman of the Higher Judicial Council and added amnesty matters to its jurisdiction.

The National Security Court, established in 1969, has authority over cases involving crimes against the state, the government, or public order and is subject to control by the government. There is no right of appeal in these cases. The court's deliberations are secret.

The nation's central prisons are located at Mogadishu and Manderia. Because these prisons are overcrowded, new ones have been built at Gelib and Jamama. All prisoners are required to participate in compulsory labor programs.

LAW ENFORCEMENT

The Somali National Police (SNP), formed in 1960, operates under the authority of the Ministry of the Interior. The SNP has a mobile unit, the Darawishta Poliska, which operates in remote areas and along the frontier, and a riot unit; the Birmadka Poliska, which maintains order in urban areas. In addition, there is a Criminal Investigation Division and a small unit of policewomen. The police air wing is equipped with two aircraft. The total strength of the police force is estimated at 6,000, or one policeman for every 500 inhabitants. Somalia ranks 53rd in the world in this respect.

Each region has a regional commandant and each district force is commanded by a commissioned officer. The smallest police units are the station commands and the police posts, both manned by noncommissioned officers and askaris.

Serious crimes such as murder or rape are not common, and the increase in the crime rate, especially in urban areas, has been manageable. A traditional law enforcement problem is the inter-tribal fighting over grazing and water rights. Drunkenness has assumed national proportions. The largest category of reported and verified crimes is burglary, including theft of animals. On a different level, organized smuggling has proved to be virtually immune to official interference because of the alleged complicity of public officials.

The national intelligence agency is the National Security Service (NSS), which was organized in the early 1970s on the lines of the Soviet KGB. It is headed by President Siad Barre's son-in-law, Col. Ahmed Suleiman Abdulle.

HEALTH

In 1980 there were 61 hospitals with 5,232 beds, or one bed per 714 inhabitants. In 1980 there were 262 physicians in the country, or one physician per 14,290 inhabitants, two dentists and 1,365 nurses.

PRINCIPAL HEALTH INDICATORS (1984)

Crude Death Rate: 21.3 per 1,000
Decline in Death Rate: −27.00 (1965-73)
Life Expectancy at Birth: 41.3 (Males); 44.5 (Females)
Infant Mortality Rate: 150 per 1,000 Live Births
Child Death Rate (Ages 1-4) per 1,000: 30

All health services and facilities were nationalized in 1972. Somalia has a high incidence of tuberculosis, bilharziasis, malaria, yaws and parasitic and venereal infections. Only 37% of the population have access to safe water. Health expenditure accounts for 3.5% of the national budget and $4.20 per capita.

FOOD

Millet, rice and corn are the staple foods. Millet and corn are usually boiled in water to make a porridge. Meat is not a staple and is eaten only on ritual or festive occasions. On the other hand, milk, especially camel milk, is regularly consumed, and it is the sole food of camel herders for months on end. The national drinks are coffee and tea.

The daily per capita intake of food is 2,131 calories and 72.4 grams of protein (both below the recommended minimums of 2,600 calories and 65 grams of protein), 52 grams of fats and 304 grams of carbohydrates.

MEDIA & CULTURE

In 1982 one daily newspaper and two non-dailies were published, with circulations of 4,000 and 5,000 respectively. Per capita circulation is 1.3 dailies and 1.6 non-dailies per 1,000 inhabitants. All newspapers are published under government auspices. The daily newspaper, *Xiddigta Oktobar*, is published in Somali, while the non-dailies are published in Arabic, Italian and English. Annual consumption of newsprint in 1982 was 200 tons, or 41 kg (90 lb) per 1,000 inhabitants.

Immediately after the 1969 coup, a Board of Censorship was established in the Ministry of Information and National Guidance. Its functions include screening of materials from abroad and surveillance of domestic publications.

The national news agency is Somalia National News Agency (SONNA). Foreign news agencies represented in Mogadishu include ANSA.

The country's book publishing industry is completely in government hands, under the administrative control of the State Printing Agency. Most of the output consists of textbooks and books for neo-literates.

The National Broadcasting Service operates two stations: Radio Mogadishu, broadcasting in Somali, English, Arabic, Swahili, Amharic and Qoti, and Radio Hargeysa, located in Hargeysa. The two stations with five transmitters are on the air for 52 hours a week. In 1984 there were 95,000 radio receivers in the country, or 13 per 1,000 inhabitants. Somalia's first television service, financed by Kuwait and UAE was launched in 1983.

Domestic film production consists almost entirely of documentaries. In the mid-1970s, there were 26 fixed cinemas in the country with 23,000 seats, or 8.2 seats per 1,000 inhabitants. Annual movie attendance was 8.0 million, or 1.3 per capita.

The largest library is that of the National Museum at Mogadishu. There is one museum in the capital with a reported annual attendance of 20,000.

SOCIAL WELFARE

No comprehensive social security scheme exists, but under various programs certain classes of workers receive work injury benefits, pensions and funeral grants. Social welfare and community development programs have been initiated through self-help groups, such as Victory Pioneers.

GLOSSARY

Aljamiahtol Wadaniyah: the former National Assembly.

birmadka poliska: the riot police, operating in urban areas.

darawishta poliska: the mobile police, operating in frontier and rural areas.

dia: compensation in kind, as the basis for settlement of conflicts between groups. A dia-paying group is one bound by contract to pay blood or similar compensation on behalf of an offending member and to collect it on behalf of an aggrieved member.

Gulwaadayal: the Somali youth organization that propagates socialist ideology.

jalle: comrade; term of address used in public and official context since the 1969 revolution.

shir: council of elders of a lineage or tribe.

tariqa: an Islamic religious order or brotherhood.

CHRONOLOGY (from 1960)

1960— British Somaliland attains independence and merges with the U.N. Trust Territory of Somaliland (former Italian Somaliland) to form the Republic of Somalia; Aden Abdullah Osman is president and Abderashid Ali Shermarke premier.

1961— The electorate ratifies new constitution in referendum; northern dissatisfaction with the southern domination of the government culminates in a mutiny of junior army officers, which is easily suppressed.

1963— Diplomatic relations with the United Kingdom are suspended over British refusal to cede Somali-populated areas in Kenya.

1964— President Osman names Abdirazak Haji Hussein premier as clan rivalries with the government and the ruling Somali Youth League intensify.

1965— Military incidents and border hostilities between Kenya and Ethiopia on the one hand and Somalia on the other lead to OAS intervention.

1967— Shermarke is elected president; new president names Mohamed Ibrahim Egal premier.... Egal reverses policy of confrontation with Ethiopia and Kenya and seeks detente.

1968— Diplomatic relations with the United Kingdom are resumed.

1969— President Shermarke is assassinated; as Egal tries to manipulate the election of a new president, the army takes over under Maj. Gen. Mohamed Siad Barre.... The constitution is suspended along with the National Assembly; the Supreme Revolutionary Council is created as the nation's top executive and legislative body; the country is renamed Somali Democratic Republic.

1970— Somalia is proclaimed a socialist state; banks and foreign enterprises are nationalized.... First Vice President Maj. Gen. Jamal Ali Korshel, head of the police force, is arrested as leader of an abortive coup.... U.S. aid is suspended in retaliation for continuing Somali defiance of a U.S. embargo against trade with North Vietnam.

1971— Second Vice President Maj. Gen. Mohamed Ainanshe Guleid and others are arrested and charged with plotting against the state and executed.

1972— New Somali script based on the Latin alphabet is introduced.

1974— Severe drought hits Somalia and decimates the national herd.

1975— The United States accuses Somalia of permitting Soviet missile-handling facilities at Berbera on the Gulf of Aden.

1976— The Somali Socialist Revolutionary Party is created as the nation's sole legal political party; the Supreme Revolutionary Council is replaced by the Central Committee and politburo of the SSRP.

1977— After years of preparation, Somalia launches full-scale war against Ethiopia, gains impressive initial victories in the Ogaden region and captures Jijiga, breaks with the Soviet Union following suspension of Soviet aid.... Cuba and the Soviet Union rebuild the Ethiopian forces and back an Ethiopian counter-offensive.

1978— Ethiopia retakes conquered territories and expels the invaders; Somali forces suffer heavy losses in men and materiel.... President Siad Barre survives a reported coup attempt.... Several army officers are reported executed following the aborted coup.

1979— New constitution is promulgated... Somalia holds first elections in nation's history to the People's Assembly.

1980— New constitution is suspended along with People's Assembly as Barre imposes martial state of emergency... The United States obtains right to military bases in Somalia.

1981— Relations with Libya are severed.

1982— State of emergency is ended.

1984— Kenya's President Moi visits Mogadishu and agreement is reached on border issues; Somalia renounces territorial claims on Kenya.... Elections are held for the People's Assembly.... Siad offers amnesty to rebels and dissidents.

BIBLIOGRAPHY (from 1965)

Cahill, Kevin M., *Somalia: A Perspective* (Albany, N.Y., 1980).

Cassanelli, Lee V., *The Shaping of Somali Society* (Philadelphia, Pa., 1982).

Castagno, Margaret, *Historical Dictionary of Somalia* (Metuchen, N.J., 1975).

Contini, Paolo, *The Somali Republic* (London, 1969).

Laitin, David D. and Said S. Samatar, *Somalia* (Boulder, Colo., 1985).

Legum, Colon, *Horn of Africa in Continuing Crisis* (New York, 1979).

Lewis, I.M. *The Modern History of Somaliland* (New York, 1965).

Pestalozza, Luigi, *The Somali Revolution* (Paris, 1974).

OFFICIAL PUBLICATIONS

Finance Ministry, *Annual Financial Statements.*
——, *Monthly Abstract of Accounts.*
Planning and Coordination Commission, *Statistical Abstracts* (annual).

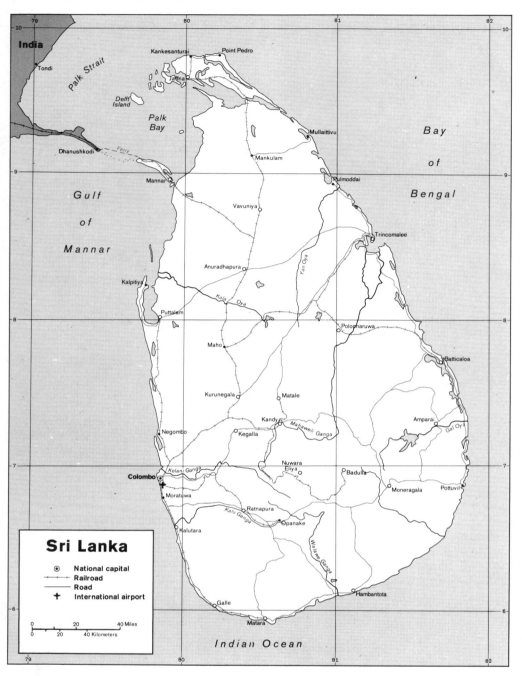

India

Tondi

Palk Strait

Kankesanturai   Point Pedro

Jaffna

Delft
Island

Palk
Bay

Mullaittivu

Dhanushkodi   Ferry

Mannar   Mankulam

Gulf

of

Mannar

Vavuniya

Pulmoddai

Bay

of

Bengal

Trincomalee

Anuradhapura

Yan Oya

Kalpitiya

Kala Oya

Puttalam

Polonnaruwa

Maho

Batticaloa

Kurunegala   Matale

Negombo   Kandy

Kegalla   Mahaweli Ganga

Amparai

Gal Oya

Colombo   Kelani Ganga

Nuwara
Eliya

Badulla

Moratuwa

Moneragala

Pottuvil

Ratnapura   Kalu Ganga

Opanake

Kalutara

Walawe Ganga

Sri Lanka

- ⊛ National capital
- ┼┼┼ Railroad
- —— Road
- ✦ International airport

0   20   40 Miles

0   20   40 Kilometers

Galle

Hambantota

Matara

Indian Ocean

SRI LANKA

BASIC FACT SHEET

OFFICIAL NAME: Democratic Socialist Republic of Sri Lanka (Sri Lanka Drajatantrika Samajawadi Janarajya) (formerly Ceylon)

ABBREVIATION: SK

CAPITAL: Colombo

HEAD OF STATE: President Junius Richard Jayewardene (from 1977)

HEAD OF GOVERNMENT: Prime Minister Ranasinghe Premadasa (from 1978)

NATURE OF GOVERNMENT: Parliamentary democracy

POPULATION: 16,206,000 (1985)

AREA: 65,610 km (25,332 sq mi)

ETHNIC MAJORITY: Sinhalese

LANGUAGE: Sinhala

RELIGION: Buddhism

UNIT OF CURRENCY: Rupee ($1 = R27.250, August 1985)

NATIONAL FLAG: Two narrow green and orange vertical stripes on left side with a yellow lion carrying a sword in one upraised paw against a red background occupying the rest of the flag. The flag is bordered by a yellow band with a vertical yellow band separating the green and orange stripes from the red background. A gold bo leaf is in each corner.

NATIONAL EMBLEM: The main symbols in the national emblem are the punkalasa (a filled vessel), a heraldic lion within the palapeti vataya (a lotus petal border), and the dhammachakka (the wheel of the Buddhist doctrine.) The sun and the moon and two ears of corn appear on both sides of the filled vessel signifying prosperity, discipline, righteousness, eternity and self-sufficiency.

NATIONAL ANTHEM: "Hail, Hail, Motherland"

NATIONAL HOLIDAYS: May 22 (National Day, Republic Day); April 11 and 12 (Sinhala and Tamil New Years Days); May 1 (May Day); January 1 (New Year); Christmas, Good Friday, Easter; full moon poya holidays every lunar month on the day of the full moon; Maha Sivarathri, Tamil Thai Pongal, Deepavali, Ramadan, Id-ul-fitr, Milad-un-nabi and Id-ul-Azha.

NATIONAL CALENDAR: Gregorian as well as a lunar calendar used for religious festivals. The day of rest is the Poya Day which is set according to the phases of the moon.

PHYSICAL QUALITY OF LIFE INDEX: 85 (down from 83 in 1976) (On an ascending scale with 100 as the maximum; U.S. 95)

DATE OF INDEPENDENCE: February 4, 1948

DATE OF CONSTITUTION: September 7, 1978

WEIGHTS & MEASURES: The metric system, adopted in 1974, prevails.

LOCATION & AREA

Sri Lanka is a pear-shaped island in the Indian Ocean, 804 km (500 miles) north of the equator, separated from the Indian mainland by 29 km (18 miles) at the closest point. It is often called the Resplendent Isle and the Isle of Delight. It has a total area of 65,610 sq km (25,332 sq mi) and a total coastline of 1,204 km (748 mi). The longest distance north-south is 435 km (270 mi) and east-west 225 km (140 mi).

Colombo is the capital with a 1981 population of 586,000. The other major urban centers are Dehiwala (174,000), Jaffna (118,000), Moratuwa (136,000), Kotte (102,000), Kandy (107,000), Galle (82,000) and Negombo (60,000).

Sri Lanka has two geographical regions. A flat or gently rolling plain, occupying four-fifths of the country, makes up the entire northern half of the island and continues around the coast of the southern half. The south-central part is hilly and mountainous, ranging from 900-2,100 meters (3,000-7,000 ft) above sea level, with two abruptly ascending platforms flanking the Uva Basin, Hatton Plateau, the Kandy Plateau, Knuckles Group and Piduru Ridges.

There are 16 significant rivers of which the longest are the Mahaweli Ganga 332 km (206 mi) and the Aruvi Aru 167 km (104 mi).

WEATHER

Sri Lanka has a generally uniform tropical climate with little variation in daily or seasonal temperature. Humidity is high throughout the year, frequently 90%. The average annual temperature for the whole country ranges from 26.7°C to 28.3°C (80°F to 83°F). The highest temperature recorded is 36.7°C (98°F) in the region around Trincomalee. The island receives two monsoons, from the southwest in May and the northeast in November. The dry zone in the north, central plain, and SE plain receives from 127 to 190 cm (50 to 75 in.) of rainfall, and the wet zone in the SW plain and SW uplands receives 254 to 508 cm (100 to 200 in.) a year. Two small arid zones stretching from Puttalam to Jaffna and from Tangalla to Pottuvil receive some 63 to 126 cm (25 to 50 in.) a year.

POPULATION

The population of Sri Lanka was estimated at 16,206,000 in 1985 based on the last official census held in 1981 when the population was 14,848,364. The population is expected to reach 20.8 million by 2000 and 25.4 million by 2020.

The annual rate of growth is 2.03%. The annual birth rate is 27 per 1,000.

The average density was 250 per sq km (647.5 per sq mi) in 1983 and 570 per sq km (1,538 per sq mi) of arable land. The density is greatest in the southwest quarter of the island. About 22% of the population lives in the Colombo district.

The national male/female ratio is 104 males to 100 females; the ratio is higher in urban areas at 108 males to 100 females and lower in rural areas at 102 males to 100 females. The population is young with 34.2% of the population under 14 years of age. 61.4% is between 15 and 64 years of age and 4.4% over 65.

The urban component of the population is estimated at 21%, with an annual growth rate of 1.6%. There were four cities with populations of over 100,000, four cities between 50,000 and 99,000 and nine cities between 25,000 and 49,000. Nearly 44% of the population of Colombo lives in slums and squatter settlements.

Since 1950 the net flow of migration has been outward. Following an agreement with the government of India, 525,000 Indian Tamils were repatriated. Legal immigration has been stopped but some illegal immigration still takes place.

Birth control has been accepted as official policy since 1954. The Family Planning Association is a voluntary organization but receives a state subsidy. Some 270 clinics have been established throughout the country with the help of the Swedish government. The stated goal is to reduce the birth rate to 25 per 1,000. About 7% of married women of child bearing age are believed to practice contraception.

Since 1977 the government has had a stronger commitment to population control than any previous government. Population policy has been assigned to the Ministry of Plan Implementation which functions directly under the president.

Family Planning services have for some years been integrated with maternal and child care services into the national family health system. The government has now gone further and allocated the subject of Family Health within the Ministry of Health to a separate Minister to enable more attention to be devoted to these services. The government's tax policies are being reoriented to favor small families. There will be no special child allowance as in the past. This measure

DEMOGRAPHIC INDICATORS (1984)	
Population, total (in 1,000)	16,206.0
Population ages (% of total)	
0-14	34.2
15-64	61.4
65+	4.4
Youth (15-24) (000)	3,504.0
Women ages 15-49 (000)	4,218
Dependency ratios	62.8
Child-woman ratios	507
Sex ratios (per 100 females)	103.7
Median ages (years)	22.2
Marriage Rate (per 1,000)	8.1
Divorce Rate (per 1,000)	0.2
Average size of Household	5.2
Decline in birthrate (%, 1965-83)	−20.2
Proportion of urban (%)	21.10
Population density (per sq. km.)	250
per hectare of arable land	7.77
Rates of growth (%)	2.03
urban	1.6
rural	2.2
Natural increase rates (per 1,000)	20.3
Crude birth rates (per 1,000)	27.0
Crude death rates (per 1,000)	6.7
Gross reproduction rates	1.65
Net reproduction rates	1.53
Total fertility rates	3.37
General fertility rates (per 1,000)	107
Life expectancy, males (years)	66.0
Life expectancy, females (years)	69.0
Life expectancy, total (years)	67.5
Population doubling time in years at current rate	33
% Illegitimate births	7.5

was introduced as a disincentive to large families; further measures will be introduced later. The legal age for marriage has been raised to 18 for women and 21 for men.

Women have equal rights under the law, including equal property and inheritance rights. The various ethnic and religious groups have their own "personal" laws, which place some limitations on women. Some Tamil families believe their women members should not be seen working in public. Some Muslim women are discouraged from seeking higher education or employment. One important result of the plantation workers' strike in 1984 was obtaining equal wages for men and women in that sector. The Labor Ministry reportedly is considering equalizing wages in all organized sectors of the economy. Women fill important posts in the civil service, the professions, and business, but the majority are found in manual and semiskilled jobs. Women vote in large numbers, but otherwise play a more limited role than men in the political process. There presently are eight women members of Parliament, and Sri Lankans are proud of the fact that they had the world's first woman prime minister, Mrs. Sirimavo Bandaranaike. In 1983 the president created a Ministry of Women's Affairs and Teaching Hospitals and gave the minister, a woman, cabinet rank.

ETHNIC COMPOSITION

Sinhalese, the ethnic majority, form a fairly homogeneous group, though they are sometimes divided on the basis of geography and culture into the low country Sinhalese and the Kandyan Sinhalese. The next most numerous group is the Ceylon Tamils, who have never been fully assimilated into the social or cultural mainstream. Moors, Burghers and Malays form smaller ethnic groups.

ETHNIC COMPOSITION	
	(%)
Low-Country Sinhalese	42.8
Kandyan Sinhalese	29.1
Sri Lankan Tamils	11.1
Indian Tamils	9.4
Sri Lanka Moors	6.5
Indian Moors	0.2
Burghers and Eurasian	0.3
Malays	0.3
Others	0.1

Throughout the 50s and 60s relations between the various ethnic groups were characterized by rivalry and, at times, open hostility. Contributing to the ethnic disequilibrium was the high correlation between race, language and religion. Ninety percent of the Sinhalese are Buddhists and speak Sinhala, while about the same percentage of Tamils are Hindus speaking Tamil, and the Burghers are Christian and English-speaking.

The Sri Lankan Tamils, who are concentrated in the northern and eastern coastal regions, are the descendants of the inhabitants of the ancient Tamil kingdoms of Ceylon. The Indian Tamils are more recent immigrants and are primarily plantation workers in the Kandyan highlands. Long regarded by the Sinhala as aliens, they were disenfranchised in 1948. Under the terms of the 1964 agreement with India, 600,000 Indian Tamils were to be repatriated while 375,000 were to be granted Sri Lankan citizenship. By October 31, 1981, when the two countries were to have settled this issue, India had taken more than 300,000 persons as repatriates. Sri Lanka had granted citizenship to over 185,000 plus over 62,000 post-1964 offspring. Over 207,000 Indian Tamils in Sri Lanka before 1964, plus nearly 45,000 offspring, were granted Indian citizenship but still awaited repatriation. In the wake of the July 1983 anti-Tamil violence, some in this latter group are being processed for repatriation or have migrated to India.

With the lapse of the 1964 agreement India declined to consider any more applications for citizenship. The government of Sri Lanka believes that the 1964 pact remains in force until the citizenship cases and permanent residence of all Indian Tamils covered by the pact have been settled. The All-Party Conference has agreed that the government should grant Sri Lankan citizenship to stateless Indian Tamils who did not apply for Indian citizenship and were not granted Sri Lankan citizenship under the 1964 agreement.

Some thousands of Veddahs, the original inhabitants of Sri Lanka, still survive in the Uva and north-central provinces.

In terms of ethnic and linguistic homogeneity, Sri Lanka is ranked 57th among nations of the world with 53% homogeneity (on an ascending scale in which North and South Korea are ranked 135th with 100% homogeneity and Tanzania 1st with 7% homogeneity).

The caste system is reportedly breaking down among Buddhists, but it remains important when marriages are arranged, and it continues to be widely observed among Hindu Tamils. Members of virtually all of Sri Lanka's ethnic minorities occupy prominent positions in all walks of public and private life, but since independence the Sinhalese majority has steadily strengthened its relative position of influence in most sectors of society. The minuscule Veddah population in 1985 became even more thoroughly assimilated into larger Sri Lankan society. A number of hunting and gathering Veddah communities were provided with land on which to begin settled agriculture, and a few former hunters were offered jobs in national parks and reserves.

LANGUAGES

Sinhala is the official language but the "reasonable" use of Tamil is permitted in northern and eastern provinces where Tamils predominate. English was replaced by Sinhala and Tamil as the media of administration and education, but it is still the lingua franca and the second language in all schools. About 10% of the population can speak or understand English while 58.9% can speak Sinhala only and 21.6% Tamil only.

The Department of Official Language Affairs carries out programs necessary to implement the government's language policy and promote Sinhala.

RELIGION

Buddhism in its Theravada form is the religion of most of the Sinhalese, Hinduism that of the Tamils, and Islam that of the Moors and Malays. Christianity cuts across ethnic lines with about 900,000 followers, most of them descendants of converts to Roman Catholicism during the Portuguese era. The constitution makes no reference to an official religion. However, Buddhism is generally identified with Sinhalese nationalism and the Sinhala language. In 1971 Buddhists formed 67.4% of the population with 9 million members, Hindus 17.6% with 2.2 million members, Christians 7.7% with 987,000 members, and Muslims 7.1% with 910,000 members.

Sri Lankan Buddhist society is distinguished by a social structure based on caste. Though distinctions of caste are not officially recognized they permeate social life in rural areas. Embedded within its matrix are social status, occupational levels and a ritualized pecking order. Each caste group forms a separate subcommunity in each village; in some cases whole villages contain only one caste. The Hindu Tamils also follow the caste system based more closely on religious sanctions, but with a modified hierarchical structure. Over 50 castes and subcastes are found in the Jaffna region of which the high-caste Vellalas are the most numerous.

Though Sri Lanka is officially secular, there has been, since the advent of the Sri Lanka Freedom Party, an increasing Buddhization of public life. Buddhist observances and activities are promoted through official participation and, in some cases, receive public funds. The Buddhist clergy is also becoming increasingly politicized. There is no discrimination against religious minorities, but a number of recent reforms have worked against the Christian minority such as the abolition of Sundays as weekly rest days and the nationalization of Christian missionary schools.

COLONIAL EXPERIENCE

Sri Lanka was under three major Western colonial powers from the mid-16th century to the mid-20th: The Portuguese were in control of coastal Sri Lanka for nearly 150 years from 1505. The Dutch supplanted them, beginning in 1658, and were, in turn, supplanted by the British who were successful in bringing the entire country under their control. The British rule was relatively benevolent compared to that of the Dutch and the Portuguese; by permitting native participation in the governmental process, through the Donoughmore Constitution of 1931 and the Soulbury Constitution of 1946, the British prepared Sri Lankans for eventual self-government. The greatest legacy of Dutch rule was the civil law and that of British rule the English language and the British-oriented educational system. The British departure was entirely peaceful, and Sri Lankans have no deep-rooted anti-colonial sentiments.

CONSTITUTION & GOVERNMENT

The constitution of May 22, 1972 was amended by Parliament on October 4, 1977, and promulgated on September 7, 1978. Under the constitution, sovereignty is vested entirely in the National State Assembly, which is the supreme instrument of legislative, executive, and judicial powers. Laws passed by the National State Assembly are not subject to judicial review, although there is a provision for a Constitutional Court to determine whether a provision in a bill is inconsistent with the constitution. The constitution incorporates a chapter dealing with fundamental rights and a chapter on principles of state policy. These principles include the establishment of Buddhism as the "foremost" religion and Sinhala as the official language, the progressive advancement of so-

cialist democracy, and the abolition of social and economic privileges.

CABINET LIST (1985)	
President	J.R. Jayewardene
Prime Minister	R. Premadasa
Minister of Agricultural Development & Research	Gamini Jayasuriya
Minister of Cultural Affairs	E.L.B. Hurulle
Minister of Defense	J.R. Jayewardene
Minister of Education	Ranil Wickremasinghe
Minister of Emergency Civil Administration	R. Premadasa
Minister of Energy	J.R. Jayewardene
Minister of Finance & Planning	R.J.G. De Mel
Minister of Fisheries	Festus Perera
Minister of Food & Cooperatives	Gamini Jayasuriya
Minister of Foreign Affairs	A.C.S. Hameed
Minister of Health	*Dr.* Ranjit Atapattu
Minister of Higher Education	J.R. Jayewardene
Minister of Highways	R. Premadasa
Minister of Home Affairs	K.W. Devanayagam
Minister of Industries & Scientific Affairs	N. Denzil Fernando
Minister of Janatha (People's) Estate Development	J.R. Jayewardene
Minister of Justice	Nissanka Wijeratne
Minister of Labor	Prema Chandra Imbulana
Minister of Land, Land Development & Mahaweli Development	Gamini Dissanayake
Minister of Local Government, Housing & Construction	R. Premadasa
Minister of Manpower Mobilization & National Service	Ranil Wickremasinghe
Minister of National Security	Lalith Athulathmudali
Minister of Parliamentary Affairs	Vincent Perera
Minister of Plan Implementation	J.R. Jayewardene
Minister of Plantation Industries	W.G. Montague Jayewickreme
Minister of Posts & Telecommunications	D.B. Wijetunga
Minister of Power	J.R. Jayewardene
Minister of Private Omnibus Transport	M.H. Mohamed
Minister of Public Administration	W.G. Montague Jayewickreme
Minister of Regional Development	Chelliah Rajadurai
Minister of Rural Development	*Mrs.* Wimala Kannangara
Minister of Rural Industrial Development	S. Thondaman
Minister of Security for Commercial & Industrial Establishments	M.H. Mohamed
Minister of Social Services	Asoka Karunaratne
Minister of State Plantations	J.R. Jayewardene
Minister of Textile Industries	T. Wijepala Mendis
Minister of Trade & Shipping	M.S. Amarasiri
Minister of Transport	M.H. Mohamed
Minister of Women's Affairs & Teaching Hospitals	*Mrs.* Sunethra Ranasinghe
Minister of Youth Affairs & Employment	Ranil Wickremasinghe
Minister Without Portfolio	Bakeer Markar
Minister of State for Information, Broadcasting & Tourism	Anandatissa De Alwis

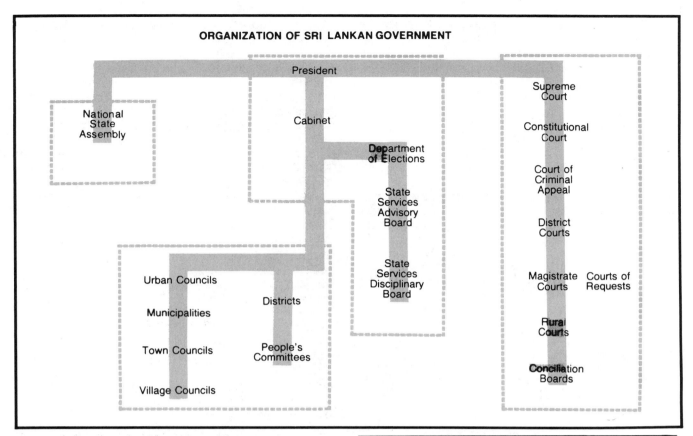

ORGANIZATION OF SRI LANKAN GOVERNMENT

The amended constitution of 1978 established a strong presidential form of government on the U.S. model. The presidential term of office is seven years.

Sri Lanka was the first country in Asia to adopt universal franchise for men and women over age 21 (later reduced to 18). There are two types of electoral districts: one based on population and the other based on area. Multimember constituencies have been created to assure adequate representation to minorities. Both local and parliamentary elections are administered by the Department of Elections, an independent statutory body headed by a commissioner. An electoral register is maintained in both Sinhala and Tamil, and recognized political parties are provided with symbols for the benefit of illiterate voters. The country is divided into 145 electoral districts. Of the population eligible to vote, 90% went to the polls in 1977. The Constitution has established a new system of proportional representation for future elections in an effort to reduce the large swings in Parliamentary majorities experienced in 1970 and 1977 by having distribution of seats in Parliament more accurately reflect the popular vote.

The head of government is the prime minister, who is the leader of the majority party in the National State Assembly. The prime minister and the cabinet of ministers are collectively responsible to the National State Assembly and hold office only as long as they enjoy its confidence. The president holds the portfolios of defense and plan implementation in the cabinet.

RULERS OF SRI LANKA
PRIME MINISTERS:
1947 (August) to 1952 (March)
  Don Stephen Senanayake
1952 (March) to 1953 (October)
  Dudley Senanayake
1953 (October) to 1956 (April)
  Sir John Lionel Kotelawala
1956 (April) to 1959 (September)
  Solomon West Ridgway Dias Bandaranaike
1959 (September) to 1960 (March)
  Wijayananda Dahanayake
1960 (March) to (July)
  Dudley Senanayake
1960 (July) to 1965 (March)
  Sirimavo Bandaranaike
1965 (March) to 1970 (May)
  Dudley Senanaike
1970 (May) to 1977 (July)
  Sirimavo Bandaranaike
1977 (July) to 1978 (February)
  Junius Richard Jayewardene
PRESIDENTS:
1978 (February) to—
  Junius Richard Jayewardene

Sri Lanka has a strong democratic tradition with six peaceful elections and no violent change of government in its history. Jayewardene became the first president under the 1978 constitution and was returned to office in the presidential election of October 1982, gaining 53% of the popular vote. General elections to Parliament due in 1983 were not held. Instead, citizens went to the polls in a referendum held in December 1982 to vote on a constitutional amendment to extend the term of the 1977 Parliament from 6 to 12 years. Restrictions were imposed on the activities of opposition parties during the referendum campaign, and some voting irregularities were reported. The amendment was approved with 54.5% of the votes and Parliament's term now runs until August 1989. UNP candidates have won most of the by-elections held since 1977, including the two held in 1985. President Jayewardene's United National Party now holds 140 out of 153 occupied seats in Sri Lanka's unicameral legislature.

Sri Lanka's political parties represent a variety of political views. Most opposition parties function freely, several operate their own newspapers, and the activities of their leaders are covered by the media. One party, however, the extreme leftist Janatha Vimukti Peramuna (JVP), has been proscribed since July 1983 for alleged involvement in communal riots during the last week of that month. In addition, the civic rights of the leader of the SLFP, Mrs. Sirimavo Bandaranaike, were suspended in 1980 for a period of seven years on the grounds that she exceeded her authority during her tenure as prime minister from 1970-77. Until her pardon on January 1, 1986, the suspension of her civic rights prevented her from serving in Parliament and campaigning on behalf of her party's candidates in elections.

FREEDOM & HUMAN RIGHTS

In terms of civil and political rights, Sri Lanka is classified as a partially free country with a positive rating of 2 in political rights and 3 in civil rights (on a descending scale where 1 denotes the highest and 7 the lowest in civil and political rights).

Sri Lanka has been continuously under democratic governments since independence, but pressures on the political systems have been more intense than those in neighboring India. An extremely militant minority of Tamils, a well-directed leftist alliance, and an entrenched Buddhist right-wing have brought Sri Lanka to the brink of totalitarianism a number of times in recent years.

Some Sri Lankan Tamils are pressing for the creation of a separate Tamil state, "Tamil Eelam." Most Sinhalese, Muslims, and Indian Tamils oppose this objective, however. Representatives elected by Sri Lankan Tamils in Tamil-majority areas call for an independent state, but also have negotiated with the government over proposals which would permit Tamils in those areas to have more control over their local affairs. Although the larger part of all Sri Lankan Tamils live outside Tamil-majority areas, some of these also support the separatist goal.

Since the mid-1970s young Tamil militants have engaged in acts of terrorism. They claim that peaceful political means have failed to achieve autonomy or to satisfy other Tamil demands concerning language, education, employment and fair treatment under the law and by security forces. Loosely organized into several groups, some of which pursue intense rivalries with one another, the terrorists are generally referred to as Tamil Tigers. The government claims that these groups receive substantial financial assistance from expatriate Tamils and that many terrorists have received paramilitary training and arms abroad, particularly in India's state of Tamil Nadu. In 1984 the conflict between the Tigers and the security forces in the north and east escalated significantly. The government responded to attacks against security forces in the north, which had resulted in considerable damage and loss of life. It established a surveillance zone around the northern coastline to prevent the alleged flow of arms and terrorists from India.

Tamil political leaders renamed their party the Tamil United Liberation Front (TULF) and contested the 1977 elections on a platform of independence, winning all 14 seats in the heavily Tamil Northern Province and two seats in the Eastern Province, which has a sizable Tamil minority. Many militant Tamil youths turned to armed struggle and to terrorism as their way of attaining Eelam. Their targets have been government security forces, officials, Sinhalese civilians and Tamils who do not support their cause. Government security forces have not succeeded in their efforts to end separatist violence. Poorly prepared for the task, they have sometimes retaliated against innocent Tamil civilians. Despite the TULF's advocacy of separatism, from 1977 onwards it sought to negotiate with the government a political resolution of Tamil grievances. TULF members lost their seats in Parliament in 1983 after they refused to swear allegiance to the Sri Lankan unitary state, as required by a constitutional amendment enacted that year. By-elections to fill these seats have been postponed because of the unsettled security situation in the north and east, and as a result Tamils living in those constituencies are currently without representatives in Parliament. There are currently three Tamil United National Party members of Parliament and three Tamils in the cabinet, including the leader of the Ceylon Workers Congress (CWC), a labor union-cum-political party which represents the interests of Sri Lanka's Indian Tamil community.

Throughout 1984 an All-Party Conference sought to develop a political compromise based on the devolution of certain powers to local government bodies. The process ended in stalemate in December 1984 when the TULF rejected the government's proposals for devolution, and the government subsequently withdrew them. During early 1985, both sides stepped up their attacks, with the government mounting a series of military operations in the north and east in an effort to locate the Tamil separatists and their facilities and to eliminate them. The murder by Tamil militants of 146 mostly Sinhalese civilians in an attack on the Buddhist sacred city of Anuradhapura in May shocked the nation and led to renewed efforts to find a negotiated settlement to the communal problem. With India's help, a "cessation of hostilities" between the major militant groups and the government was arranged, and face-to-face talks were begun in Bhutan; these broke down in August in the face of mounting ceasefire violations by both sides. The talks revealed a wide gap between Tamil demands and the concessions that the government was prepared to make. Indirect exchanges between the government and representatives of the Tamil separatists continued sporadically through the end of the year, but violence resumed at previous levels as intercommunal fighting spread to the multiethnic Eastern Province. The cessation of hostilities remained in effect only nominally, while a multiethnic ceasefire monitoring committee endeavored to investigate reports of violations by both sides.

Due to concern that Tamil terrorists were frequently crossing from southern India to northern Sri Lanka via the Palk Straits, the government adopted a series of measures beginning in April 1984 which progressively restricted freedom of movement in that area. Expanding on the maritime surveillance zone imposed in April 1984, in November of that year the government announced a prohibited zone along some 200 miles of Sri Lanka's northern coastline. It also imposed a security zone in the entire Jaffna Peninsula. These measures restricted free movement in the area to a considerable extent and made it virtually impossible for the large number of fishermen resident in that area to earn their livelihood. These restrictions as well as nightly curfews in the north were gradually relaxed during the late spring of 1985. The curfew was terminated in July, but the restrictive zones remain technically in effect under the emergency regulations. As a result of these various restrictions as well as the threat or fear of becoming involved in the spreading communal violence, large numbers of Sri Lankans were displaced from their homes in 1985. According to some estimates, during the period 1983-1985 more than 100,000 Sri Lankan Tamils sought refuge in the Indian state of Tamil Nadu. The government estimates that as of year's end some 46,000 persons were housed in refugee camps in Sri Lanka with another 94,000 having sought refuge elsewhere in the country (with friends or relatives). Of the total estimated 140,000 displaced persons, 88,000 are Tamils, 49,000 are Sinhalese, and the remainder Muslim. The continued unsettled security situation has made it difficult for these people to return to their homes.

The death toll, mostly in the north and east, from politically motivated violence arising from the communal conflict rose again in 1985. The government estimated that 1,078 persons were killed due to ethnic violence. Of these, 885 were civilians, 75 police and 118 members of the armed forces. Continuing violence throughout the year was punctuated by a number of particularly serious incidents of violence by both sides.

The constitution stipulates that no person "shall be arrested except according to procedure established by law" and that an arrested person must be informed of the reason for his arrest. Within 24 hours, an arrested person must be brought before a magistrate who may authorize bail or, for serious crimes, continued detention. A suspect may be detained up to three months without bail, or longer if a court so rules. Persons convicted of criminal offenses may be sentenced to "rigorous imprisonment" (hard labor) under which they are compelled to work.

There are exceptions to the normal rules for a person detained under the emergency regulations or under the Prevention of Terrorism Act. Under the state of emergency, first declared in May 1983 and renewed monthly by Parliament since then, the president reissues each month the emergency regulations by gazette notification. The regulations give extraordinary powers to the police to use preventive detention on persons suspected of planning to commit offenses or to arrest individuals suspected of having committed a wide variety of crimes. Detainees under these emergency regulations can be held for up to 90 days on orders of the attorney general, after which time the suspect must be produced before a magistrate. The magistrate is not empowered to investigate the case, but under the regulations he "shall" remand the detainee to a prison, where he can be held indefinitely. Bail may be granted at the discretion of the government.

The Prevention of Terrorism Act (PTA) provides that any person arrested under this law must be produced bofore a magistrate within three days unless the minister of national security orders the suspect to be detained for a period of three months. Such an order may be renewed for a period of up to 18 months. The terms of detention are set out in this order; detainees do not have the same rights as other prisoners regarding visits by family, access to lawyers, food, and other conditions of incarceration. The PTA and emergency regulations were used extensively in 1985 to detain large numbers of persons, mostly Tamil youths, especially in the north and east. The government has reported it arrested 1,878 persons under the PTA. Of those, 880 had been released at year's end. According to local human rights activists, there were 55 detainees, as of November, who had been held without charges under the PTA for more than the legally permissible 18 months. In five cases, the government chose to redetain them under the emergency regulations. The others were to be released, but at year's end only 8 of the 50 had been released and 1 charged under the PTA; the other 41 remained in custody. Several observers reported that a common practice of the security forces is to round up all young men between the ages of 16 and 35 within about a square mile radius of the site of a terrorist incident.

CIVIL SERVICE

The civil service, officially known as Sri Lanka Administrative Service, was enlarged and reorganized in 1963. The civil service is regulated by the State Services Advisory Board and the State Services Disciplinary Board, which have taken the place of the Public Service Commission, abolished in 1972.

LOCAL GOVERNMENT

The basic unit of local administration is the district, under a government agent from the Sri Lanka Administrative Service appointed by the central government. Subunits in a district are under the charge of district revenue officers. At the base of the field administration are the grama sevakas, called headmen until 1961, who are locally recruited government officials in each village. Popular local government in 1972 consisted of 12 municipal councils, 39 urban councils, 85 town councils, and 542 village councils. The chief executive officer of the municipal council is called the mayor and he is assisted by a commissioner. Nearly 90% of the country's total area is administered by village councils. Only 5 to 6% of local government finances is derived from taxation; the balance is made up of central government grants.

FOREIGN POLICY

Sri Lanka has consistently maintained a nonaligned position in world politics and is one of the few Third World countries to attend every nonaligned summit conference since 1961. Other than two problems in its relations with India—the repatriation of Tamil laborers and a territorial dispute regarding the Island of Kachchativu in the Palk Strait, both now resolved—it has not had bilateral disputes with other countries.

Sri Lanka's relations with the United States have gone through some bad patches. In 1962 the expropriation of Esso Standard Eastern and Caltex oil distribution facilities led to a suspension of U.S. aid under the Hickenlooper Amendment. In 1970 the Peace Corps and the Asia Foundation programs were terminated. Relations with the People's Republic of China are reinforced by a barter agreement first negotiated in 1953 and renewed periodically.

Sri Lanka was chairman of the Nonaligned Nations Conference for three years, from 1976 through 1979, and in this position achieved great international visibility. Some Western analysts had speculated that Jayewardene would initiate a rightward direction in foreign affairs. Such a change in direction has not been apparent during the past three years. However, Jayewardene was the first leader to create a separate ministry of foreign affairs in the Sri Lankan government and to appoint a minister to handle that portfolio. In the past the ministry was part of the prime minister's office. Sri Lankan foreign policy also began placing greater emphasis on personal contacts with foreign leaders and on personal diplomacy.

Traditionally cordial relations with the Arab world were threatened in late 1983 by the establishment of an Israeli-interests section in the U.S. embassy in Colombo, primarily to provide the Jayewardene government with access to Israeli anti-terrorism expertise.

Despite the intensification of Tamil separatist violence within the country, relations with New Delhi have not suffered. Sri Lanka joined India and other nations in the Indian subcontinent in founding the South Asian Regional Conference in 1985. At the conference's inaugural meeting Jayewardene praised Rajiv Gandhi's leadership unstintingly.

Sri Lanka and the United States are parties to 24 treaties and agreements covering agricultural commodities, aviation, consuls, defense, economic and technical cooperation, education, extradition, finance, investment guaranties, postal matters, property, publications, telecommunications, trade and commerce, trademarks, and visas.

Sri Lanka continues to be a member of the Commonwealth. It is a member of 15 U.N. agencies and 20 other international agencies. It joined the U.N. in 1955, and its contribution to the U.N. budget is 0.03%.
U.S. Ambassador in Colombo: John H. Reed
U.K. High Commissioner in Colombo: John A.B. Stewart
Sri Lankan Ambassador in Washington, D.C.: Ernest Corea
Sri Lankan High Commissioner in London: Chandra Monerawela

PARLIAMENT

The legislature of Sri Lanka is the unicameral Parliament, with 196 (168 at present) members, of which 160 members are elected by universal suffrage for a maximum six-year term. The powers of the Assembly are absolute and unlimited. The party position in the Parliament in 1980 was as follows: United National Party, 143; Tamil United Liberation Front, 16; Sri Lanka Freedom Party, 8.

The Sixth Amendment to the constitution, passed in August 1983, requires all members of Parliament to take an oath disavowing separatism. The 15 TULF members refused to take the oath and were deemed to have relinquished their seats, which represent Tamil-majority areas. By-elections to fill their seats have been postponed under the state of emergency on the grounds that campaigns in those troubled areas will lead to breaches of the peace. The TULF also is opposed to holding these by-elections in current circumstances. Following the withdrawal of TULF members the party position in 1983 was: UNP 140, SLFP 9, and CWC, SLCP and MEP one each.

By-elections to fill the seats in Sinhalese-majority areas of two members who died were held in October 1983 after the government rushed a bill through Parliament to enable parties founded since 1981 to register and thus participate in elections. The act also gives wide powers to the election commissioner to decide, in the event of disturbances at a polling station, whether to count the ballots from that station or to call for a fresh poll.

The 1978 constitution provides for proportional representation. The system will not come into use until the next general election, not required until 1989. Politicians of all parties, however, are having doubts about this system, and a parliamentary committee was appointed in July 1983 to review the 1978 constitution and all voting laws.

POLITICAL PARTIES

Since 1947 political power has alternated between the two principal parties, the Sri Lanka Freedom Party and the United National Party. By 1977 each had held power for a total of exactly 15 years. The government party is the United National Party, a right-of-center party, with a strong appeal to the upper middle class and non-communal groups. It is conservative in economic policies and Western-oriented in foreign policy. Its president is J. R. Jayewardene.

There are seven legal opposition parties of which the Sri Lanka Freedom Party founded by S. W. R. D. Bandaranaike is the largest. It is a left-of-center, non-Marxist party with special appeal to Buddhist groups, Sinhalese intellectuals and professionals, and the lower middle class. It supports a nonaligned, Afro-Asian-oriented foreign policy, Sinhala and Sinhalese supremacy, and nationalization of banks, publishing, heavy industry, import trade, and plantations. Until 1977 the party ruled in alliance with the Sri Lanka Sama Samaja and Communist Parties. Its present leader is Sirimavo Bandaranaike. It is currently in disarray largely because the civic rights of its leader, former Prime Minister Mrs. Sirimavo Bandaranaike, were suspended in 1980 for seven years on the grounds that she had exceeded her powers during her tenure as prime minister, 1970-77. In January radical members of the SLFP, including Mrs. Bandaranaike's daughter and son-in-law, broke away and formed the Sri Lanka Mahajana (Peoples) Party. In the two by-elections in October 1983 this new party lost decisively. The last few years have witnessed a decline in electoral support for parties of the extreme left, although the JVP retains a small following among students and other youths. The political wing of the Ceylon Workers Congress represents most Indian Tamils. Its leader is a member of the cabinet. The Tamil United Liberation Front's (TULF) constituency is primarily among Sri Lankan Tamils in the north and east. One of the TULF's avowed objectives is partition of the island and the creation of a separate Tamil State in the northern and eastern districts where Sri Lankan Tamils either form the majority or represent substantial minorities.

The minor parties are almost all leftist. The best organized of these parties is the Sri Lanka Communist Party which had been for a time a SLFP partner in the Sirimavo Bandaranaike era. The others include Ceylon Equal Society Party, a Trotskyite group, also a former SLFP partner which lost all its seats in the 1979 elections; the New Equal Society Party, a splinter of the Ceylon Equal Society Party; People's United Front, strongly Sinhalese, Buddhist and leftist; the Democratic Workers' Congress; the People's Democratic Party organized in 1977 by SLFP dissidents; and the Maoist People's Liberation Front.

Tamil guerrilla groups have burgeoned since 1980. They include the Liberation Tigers, People's Liberation Tigers, Tamil Eelam Army, Tamil Eelam Liberation Army, and the Tamil People's Revolutionary Liberation Front.

On July 30, 1983, the government proscribed three political parties under emergency regulations because it believed these parties fomented or sought to take advantage of the July 1983 communal violence. The ban on one party was lifted in October 1983 and on another in September 1984. The Marxist Janatha Vimukthi Peramuna (JVP) still is proscribed, but one of its members has begun legal proceedings challenging the proscription.

ECONOMY

Sri Lanka is one of the 49 low-income countries of the world, and it is also one of the 45 countries considered by the U.N. to be most seriously affected (MSA) by recent adverse economic conditions. It has a free-market economy in which the dominant sector is private.

PRINCIPAL ECONOMIC INDICATORS

Gross National Product: $5.140 billion (1983)
  GNP Annual Growth Rate: 4.9% (1973-82)
  Per Capita GNP: $330 (1983)
  Per Capita GNP Annual Growth Rate: 3.2% (1973-82)
Gross Domestic Product: R152.615 billion (1984)
  GDP at 1980 prices R81.581 billion (1984)
  GDP Deflator (1980=100) 187.1
  GDP Annual Growth Rate: 5.2% (1973-82)
  GDP Per Capita: R9,783 (1984)
  GDP Per Capita Annual Growth Rate: 3.0% (1970-81)
Wholesale Price Index: (1980=100) (April 1980)
  General: 168
  Domestic Products: 180
Income Distribution: 12% of the national income is received by the lowest 40%; 54% of the national income is received by the top 20%.
Percentage of Population in Absolute Poverty: 22
Consumer Price Index (1970=100):
  All Items: 410.6 (June 1985)
  Food: 446.0 (June 1985)
Average Annual Rate of Inflation: 14.5% (1973-82)
Money Supply: R17.031 billion (May 1985)
  Reserve Money: R15.286 billion (April 1985)
Currency in Circulation: R8.561 billion (July 1980)
International Reserves: $510 million (of which $504 million were foreign exchange reserves in 1984)

Development planning is the responsibility of the National Planning Council under the Ministry of Planning. The Five-Year Plan, put into effect in 1972, emphasized employment, import substitution, and export industries. But because of continuing adverse terms of trade and commitments to high welfare pro-

BALANCE OF PAYMENTS (1984)
(million $)

Current Account Balance	6.5
Merchandise Exports	1,461.6
Merchandise Imports	−1,698.7
Trade Balance	−237.1
Other Goods, Services & Income	+334.3
Other Goods, Services & Income	−569.9
Other Goods, Services & Income Net	−235.6
Private Unrequited Transfers	276.5
Official Unrequited Transfers	202.6
Capital Other Than Reserves	349.5
Net Errors & Omissions	−45.3
Total (Lines 1,10 and 11)	310.7
Counterpart Items	9
Total (Lines 12 and 13)	311.6
Liabilities Constituting Foreign Authorities' Reserves	−73.3
Total Change in Reserves	238.3

grams the government has experienced difficulty in mustering domestic resources to implement the plan.

In June 1984 the government announced the 1984-89 Development Plan, envisaging a total outlay of R202,000 million, of which R106,000 million will be spent on public sector investment and R96,000 million on private sector investment. Average annual growth in GDP of 5.5% was forecast for the period.

The state has a monopoly position in the economy and intervenes in most areas of economic life. Sri Lankanization and socialism are the directive principles of economic regulation. The state-controlled industrial corporations produce or process 19 foodstuffs and other consumer goods with a monopoly in half of them. Half the total value of industrial production is earned by state agencies and corporations. The government also controls communications, transportation, insurance, banking and plantations. Exports and imports are subject to government licensing, and food importation is a state monopoly. The government also influences the economy through subsidies and price supports.

GROSS DOMESTIC PRODUCT BY ECONOMIC ACTIVITY
(1982)

	%	Rate of Change % 1970-81
Agriculture	25.4	30
Mining	1.0	21.7
Manufacturing	16.1	2.1
Construction	8.9	3.8
Electricity, Gas & Water	1.6	8.7
Transport & Communications	10.0	4.0
Trade	20.0	5.1
Finance	3.5	5.1
Public Administration & Defense	5.0	6.2
Services	2.6	5.2
Other Branches	5.7	5.2

Since Independence Sri Lanka has received over $2 billion in foreign aid, of which the United States has provided $725.2 million, the People's Republic of China $110 million and the Soviet Union $30 million. The International Bank for Reconstruction and De-

velopment and the International Monetary Fund organized an aid effort by a group of countries including Australia, Canada, Denmark, France, West Germany, India, Italy, Japan, Sweden, the United Kingdom and the United States. Since its formation in 1965 this group has provided over $1.221 billion in aid commitments. The Asian Development Bank has been another source of aid. During 1979-81 Sri Lanka received $355.4 million in bilateral and multilateral aid, or $24.1 per capita.

BUDGET

The Sri Lankan fiscal year is the calendar year. In 1973 direct taxes provided 18.6% of government revenues, indirect taxes 70.2%, and non-tax revenues 11.2%. Direct taxes include the income tax, which begins at 7 ½% and runs through 12 brackets to a top rate of 65% on taxable income over 48,000 rupees, wealth, gift and estate taxes, and a rice subsidy tax. Indirect taxes include export and import duties, excise, and liquor license fees.

Huge increases in investment spending by government ministries led to a doubling of the total budget deficit to more than 21% of GDP in 1980. After the IMF temporarily suspended disbursement of a $335 million loan, drastic cuts in government spending were imposed in the 1981, 1982 and 1983 budgets, and it was agreed that no new projects would be sanctioned.

The total budget deficit fell to 13% of GDP in 1983, and to an estimated 10% in 1984, but government expenditure was still about twice as much as revenue. Foreign aid accounted for around 60% of government expenditure, which led to an increasingly high level of foreign borrowing. The government forecast a surplus of R1,700 million for the 1985 budget, which provided incentives to boost exports, more protection for efficient local industries and some personal tax relief.

Of current revenues, 17.4% comes from taxes on income, profit, and capital gain, 34.1% from domestic taxes on goods and services, 39.8% from taxes on international trade and transactions, 1.9% from other taxes and 6.8% from non-tax revenues. Total current revenues represent 17.2% of GNP. Of current expenditures, 1.4% goes to defense, 7.4% to education, 3.3% to health, 12.8% to housing, social security and welfare, 13.1% to economic services and 62.0% to other functions. Current expenditures represent 34.4% of GNP and overall deficit 14.4% of GNP.

In 1983 government consumption was R11.935 billion and private consumption R111.235 billion. During 1973-83 public consumption grew by 1.6% and private consumption by 4.3%.

In 1983 total outstanding disbursed external debt was $2.207 billion of which $2.205 billion was publicly guaranteed. Of the publicly guaranteed debt, $1.615 billion was owed to official creditors and $589.3 million was owed to private creditors. The total debt service was $166.9 million of which $80.7 million was repayment of principal and $86.2 million was interest. Total

BUDGET (million rupees)			
Revenue	1981	1982	1983*
General sales and turnover taxes	2,828.6	4,051.4	6,224.4
Selective sales taxes	2,027.5	2,273.1	3,230.1
Import levies	3,225.5	3,222.4	4,835.8
Export levies	3,685.0	2,483.5	2,458.6
Receipts from foreign exchange entitlement certificates	22.5	—	—
Income taxes	2,028.9	2,922.8	3,366.8
Gross receipts from government trading enterprises	1,131.0	1,247.0	1,456.8
Interest, profits & dividends	239.9	378.0	657.0
Sales & charges	268.3	458.0	349.8
TOTAL (incl. others)	16,227.8	17,808.6	25,210.0
Expenditure	1981	1982	1983*
President, prime minister, Supreme Court judges, etc.	140.0	165.0	261.1
Defense	1,050.9	1,117.0	1,758.2
Foreign affairs	167.5	196.9	240.3
Plan implementation	728.0	426.6	533.6
Lands & land development	875.5	1,016.0	1,361.7
Education	1,789.3	2,187.7	2,461.6
Higher education	285.4	395.2	489.3
Power	903.7	523.2	539.1
Public administration	915.9	1,183.9	1,664.5
Local government, housing & construction	2,237.5	1,933.9	2,426.5
Industries & scientific affairs	204.3	151.4	92.9
Finance & planning	7,132.6	10,521.8	12,772.3
Transport	1,070.8	1,068.4	1,248.3
Agricultural development & research	929.7	658.9	841.2
Mahaveli development	3,852.3	7,505.4	7,253.2
Rural industries development	145.8	143.4	117.7
Posts & telecommunications	772.5	830.3	970.7
Health	953.7	926.5	1,735.0
Food & cooperatives	1,717.7	1,683.5	1,760.2
Highways	350.5	433.5	337.1
TOTAL (incl. others)	27,769.4	36,166.1	40,670.0

*Provisional.

external debt represented 157.0% of export revenues and 43.5% of GNP. Debt service represented 11.9% of export revenues and 3.3% of GNP.

FINANCE

The Sri Lankan unit of currency is the rupee divided into 100 cents. Coins are issued in denominations of 1, 2, 5, 10, 25 and 50 cents; notes are issued in denominations of 2, 5, 10, 50 and 100 rupees. The official rate of exchange in 1985 was $1= R27.250. The sterling exchange rate in 1984 was £1= R30.57.

In his budget presentation on November 15, 1977, Finance Minister Ronnie de Mel announced the abolishment of the old two-tier exchange rate system and the institution of a unified, floating rate initially set at 16 rupees per U.S. dollar. This represented a devaluation of 46% against the old official exchange rate and 11.2% against the previous premium rate.

The Foreign Exchange Entitlement Certificate applies to most imports, tourists, and non-traditional exports. In 1976 the rupee's link with the pound sterling was ended and the rupee's value has fluctuated in relation to a weighted basket of currencies of Sri Lanka's trading partners.

The Sri Lankan banking system consists of the Central Bank, nationalized indigenous banks, state development banks and foreign banks. The Central Bank, founded in 1949, has the sole right to issue currency. It is also the fiscal agent of the government, manager of the public debt and warden of the banking system. The largest of the commercial banks are the People's Bank, an amalgam of cooperative banks, and the Bank of Sri Lanka, which together have over 75% of commercial bank deposits.

In 1979 there were two important developments in domestic banking. One was the decision to allow foreign banks to open branches in Sri Lanka with a view to attracting foreign investment. By the end of 1983, 21 foreign banks had opened branch offices in Colombo. The second was the establishment of the Foreign Currency Banking Units (FCBU) in commercial banks, as a prelude to the development of an offshore banking center in Sri Lanka. FCBU were allowed to deal in foreign currency with nonresidents, "approved residents" and firms affiliated to the GCEC. By the end of 1983, 24 such banking units, with total assets amounting to U.S. $818 million, were in operation.

In 1984 the commercial banks had reserves of R5.384 billion, demand deposits of R8.002 billion and time and savings deposits of R27.674 billion. Specialized credit institutions include the State Mortgage Bank, the Agricultural and Industrial Credit Corporation, the Development Finance Corporation and the National Housing Fund. Over 25 to 30% of credit needs are supplied by professional moneylenders and commission agents.

The prime rate of interest in 1984 was 13%.

AGRICULTURE

Of the total land area of 6,561,000 hectares (16,212,231 acres), about 55% or 3,642,170 hectares (8.9 million acres) are under cultivation, or 0.15 hectares (0.4 acres) per capita. In 1982 agricultural production index (based on 1974-76= 100) was 143, the index of food production was 163 and the per capita food production index 127. Agriculture contributes 27% of the GDP, and its annual rate of growth during 1973-83 was 4.1%. The agricultural sector employs 54% of labor force. The value added in agriculture in 1983 was $1.199 billion.

There are few sections of the island that will not support cultivation of some sort. Of the 3,642,170 hectares under cultivation, 1,011,800 hectares (2,500,157 acres) are under chena, or slash-and-burn cultivation. Of the land under permanent cultivation, 572,574 hectares (1.4 million acres) are under paddy or other crops and about 809,400 hectares (2 million acres) are under tree crops. About 23% of the cultivated area is in the wet zone, 63% in the dry zone and 14% in the intermediate zone. About 356,000 hectares (880,000

GROWTH PROFILE
Annual Growth Rates (%)

Population 1980-2000	1.8
Birthrate 1965-83	−20.2
Deathrate 1965-83	−26.8
Urban Population 1973-83	2.9
Labor Force 1980-2000	2.2
GNP 1973-82	4.9
GNP per capita 1973-82	3.2
GDP 1973-83	5.2
GDP per capita 1970-81	3.0
Consumer Prices 1970-81	8.6
Wholesale Prices 1970-81	15.8
Inflation 1973-83	14.5
Agriculture 1973-83	4.1
Manufacturing 1973-83	3.4
Industry 1973-83	4.8
Services 1973-83	6.0
Mining 1970-81	21.7
Construction 1970-81	3.8
Electricity 1970-81	8.7
Transportation 1970-81	4.0
Trade 1970-81	5.1
Public Administration & Defense 1970-81	6.2
Export Price Index 1975-81	10.7
Import Price Index 1975-81	15.0
Terms of Trade 1975-81	−3.8
Exports 1973-83	2.6
Imports 1973-83	4.7
Public Consumption 1973-83	1.6
Private Consumption 1973-83	4.3
Gross Domestic Investment 1973-83	15.7
Energy Consumption 1973-83	3.4
Energy Production 1973-83	6.0

acres) are under irrigation, of which major storage reservoirs provide for half. Large-scale multipurpose projects like the Mahaweli Ganga Development Project, the Gal-Oya Project and the Uda-Walawe Project are expected to double the area under irrigation. Some 24,985 tractors were in use in 1982. Annual consumption of fertilizers was 165,800 tons or 71.3 kg per arable hectare.

The land utilization census of 1962 showed a steady decline over the years in both agricultural land per capita from 0.258 hectares (0.64 acres) to 0.182 hectares (0.45 acres) and the average size of agricultural holdings from 1.3 hectares to 1.09 hectares (3.3 to 2.7 acres) during 1946 to 1962. Small holdings dominate the agricultural sector with 1,163,929 units of 1,629,265 hectares (4,025,913 acres) as against 5,872 estates of 623,447 hectares (1,540,572 acres). About 8% of the total number of holdings contained less than 0.101 hectares (¼ acre); 35% less than 0.404 hectares (1 acre); 95% less than 4.04 hectares (10 acres); and 99.5% less than 20.23 hectares (50 acres). The census also established that of the 1,861,512 hectares (4.6 million acres) surveyed 1,286,945 hectares (3.18 million acres) were owner-cultivated, 113,312 hectares (280,000 acres) were farmed by sharecroppers, 246,858 hectares (610,000 acres) by state land tenants, 93,078 hectares (230,000 acres) by leasees, and 101,172 hectares (250,000 acres) by squatters. Under the Land Reform Act of 1972 a ceiling of 10.11 hectares (25 acres) of paddy land or 20.23 hectares (50 acres) of other land was placed on all holdings. A

Land Reform Commission was set up to take over all land above these limits. During the next two years nearly 222,577 hectares (550,000 acres) of land were taken over and converted into cooperative settlements. During the second phase of the land reform all plantations were nationalized. By the end of 1975 the nationalizations had been completed; the government now controls 63% of all tea lands, 32% of rubber lands, and 10% of the coconut producing areas.

The small size of the typical paddy unit reflects the severe pressure on existing land, especially in the densely populated wet zone of the country. The settlement of farming families on undeveloped state-owned land in the dry zone (land colonization) has been the government's answer to this problem. This program, which began in the mid-1930s, has received a major boost under the Accelerated Mahaweli Diversion Program (AMDP). When completed, this is expected to provide irrigation for about 130,000 hectares (321,230 acres) of new land and a further 100,000 hectares (247,100 acres) of land already under cultivation. Under its original plan, the program was to be completed in 30 years (1969-98). However, the present government has accelerated its implementation with the help of large amounts of foreign aid — the total estimated cost at 1977 prices was R22,400 million or 65% of that year's GNP — from the World Bank and other Western donors, and hopes to complete the program before 1989.

The R8,500 million Victoria Dam project, started in March 1980, aims to provide irrigation for some 100,000 acres (40,470 hectares) of land. It was inaugurated in April 1985. The Maduru Oya reservoir project was completed in October 1984 and will irrigate 1,400 hectares (3,459 acres) of land.

Food subsidies have been an important feature of the Sri Lankan economy since World War II. Various governments have tried to reduce the subsidy program without lasting success. At the time of the 1977 elections, nearly all Sri Lankans received a weekly ration of one free pound of rice and three additional pounds at a subsidized price. Sugar, wheat flour, and infant milk foods were also subsidized. The total cost of these subsidies accounted for about one-fifth of the government's current expenditures. In an effort to shift resources from consumption to investment, the UNP government undertook a major revision of the ration program in early 1978. After an island-wide survey of incomes, the new government effectively limited the rice ration to the poorer half of the population (i.e., about 7 million people). The sugar ration was taken away from everyone but children under 12 years of age of families still eligible for the rice ration. Other foods, particularly wheat flour (which must all be imported), continue to be subsidized.

Agricultural production falls into four categories: major export crops, minor export crops, rice and supplementary food crops. The annual food crops are broken down further into maha, big monsoon (July to November), and yala, small monsoon (February to June). Tea, rubber and coconuts are the major export crops, accounting for 90% of foreign exchange and 30% of GNP beside providing employment for 20% of labor force. Since independence, paddy output has shown impressive growth. It has quadrupled from 450,000 tons in the 1950s to 2 million tons in the early 1980s as a result of both expansion in area and a rise in productivity because of the Green Revolution. This has made Sri Lanka not only self-sufficient in rice but by 1985 also a net exporter.

PRINCIPAL CROP PRODUCTION (1982)	Area (000 hectares)	Production (000 metric tons)
Rice	839	2,150
Corn	24	23
Millet	34	16
Potatoes	2	52
Sweet potatoes	20	127
Cassava	74	355
Dry beans	4	7
Sesame seed	26	13
Coconuts	451	1,716
Copra	n.a.	385
Chillies	50	38
Onions	8	9
Sugar cane	12	372
Cashew nuts	7	917
Coffee	7	8
Cocoa beans	8	190
Tea	242	244
Tobacco	13	8
Natural rubber	226	135

LIVESTOCK POPULATION (1982) (000)	
Buffaloes	920
Cattle	1,726
Sheep	30
Goats	512
Pigs	94
Chickens	6,296
Ducks	25

Though forests covered 44.2% of the land, only 3.3% produced commercially valuable timber, such as satinwood, ebony, palu (a species of ironwood), and milla. The mahna grass, from which citronella oil is obtained, is native to Sri Lanka. The total roundwood production in 1982 was 8.149 million cubic meters (288 million cubic ft).

The total fish catch was 221,900 metric tons in 1982.

Agricultural credit is provided through multipurpose rural cooperative societies.

INDUSTRY

Manufacturing contributes 16.1% to the GNP and employs 9.4% of the labor force. Its annual growth rate from 1970-77 was 3.4%. The industrial production index in 1980 was 151 (based on 1975=100). The value added in manufacturing in 1982 was $748 million, of which agro based products accounted for 45%, textiles for 13% and chemicals for 9%.

The pattern of industrialization has been marked by an increasing government role in investment and production, a rapid shift from consumer to strategic and basic industries, and growing export orientation.

In terms of production, the industrial sector comprises four components. The first is the traditional and unorganized sector made up of over 100,000 small-scale manually worked units engaged in handicrafts and cottage industries. They account for 15% of the value of industrial output. The second is the private sector consisting of over 2,000 light and intermediate consumer industries. They account for 45% of the value of industrial output. The third is the public sector with industries operated as corporations and numbering nearly 30 in all. Among them are cement, sugar, chemicals, paper, textiles, tires, flour, plywood, leather, fertilizer, ceramics, steel, petroleum, pharmaceuticals and rubber. In addition to these a number of research and servicing institutes are run as state boards and corporations. The public sector accounts for 40% of the industrial output. Fourth is the industrial cooperatives sector. There are over 500 such units engaged in mineral, agricultural and light engineering industries.

The goal of the government's industrial policy is to strengthen and enlarge the public sector as the primary instrument of economic development. Large and intermediate investment-oriented industries are identified as falling exclusively within the public sector. The Business Undertaking Acquisition Act of 1971 also empowers the government to acquire any existing business for the state.

All large-scale manufacturing units are run by state industrial corporations of which there are 22. The private sector produces a wide range of light consumer goods and a few producer goods industries such as machine tools. The government continues to control the establishment of new industrial units throuth the Local Investments Approval Committee (LIAC), Foreign Investments Approvals Committee (FIAC), and the Greater Colombo Economic Commission (GCEC), but the policies of the UNP government are generally favorable to private enterprise.

The Bandaranaike administrations pursued a vigorous policy of nationalization. Among the sectors brought under state control were oil distribution, heavy industry, plantations and communications. The dominant position of British capital in Sri Lankan economy was ended with the nationalization of the powerful British-Ceylon Corporation.

U.S. direct investment in Sri Lanka is presently estimated at approximately $3 million. Because of the nationalization of tea estates and other foreign-owned companies, total foreign direct investment has declined over the past twenty years. With the notable exception of Japanese joint ventures in the local production of ceramics and textiles for export and foreign participation in tourist hotels, there was virtually no new foreign investment in Sri Lanka during the 1970-77 period. The Jayewardene government, however, has established an Investment Promotion

Zone (IPZ) north of Colombo to encourage foreign investment in export-oriented industries. Tax holidays of seven to 10 years and other concessions are being offered for industrial, commercial, and banking enterprises with up to 100% foreign ownership. Sri Lanka's large supply of low-cost, relatively well-educated labor makes the country a natural successor to such export centers as Singapore and Hong Kong where labor costs are rising rapidly. By 1983 IPZ had approved 165 projects with an investment totaling $130 million, and generated gross export earnings of R2.420 billion. A second IPZ is being planned to accommodate heavy industry.

Industrial credit is provided by the Agricultural and Industrial Credit Corporation and the Development Finance Corporation.

ENERGY

Sri Lanka's total energy production in 1982 was the equivalent to 198,000 million tons of coal and total consumption 2.107 million tons of coal equivalent. Per capita consumption was 137 kg (302 lb). Electric power production in 1984 was 2.1 billion kwh, and the per capita output was 132 kwh. The annual growth rates during 1973-83 were 6.0% for energy production and 3.4% energy consumption. Energy imports account for 40% of all merchandise imports. Apparent per capita consumption of gasoline is 6 gallons per year.

Sri Lanka has no oil or natural gas reserves. There is a major refinery at Colombo with a capacity of 50,000 barrels per day.

LABOR

The economically active population in 1981 was 5,697,946 million, of whom 27.4% were women; 5.2% were professional and managerial workers; 9.7% were urban workers; 90% were rural workers; 2% were juveniles; and 12.9% were clerical and sales workers. Agricultural workers formed the largest occupational group and civil servants the second. Self-employed and unpaid family workers accounted for over 30% of the total.

DISTRIBUTION OF LABOR FORCE BY INDUSTRY (1981)

	%
Agriculture, forestry, hunting & fishing	41.7
Mining & quarrying	1.1
Manufacturing	9.4
Construction	3.9
Electricity, gas, water & sanitary services	0.3
Wholesale and retail trade, restaurants & hotels	8.8
Transport, storage & communications	3.6
Community, social & personal services	11.4
Finance, insurance, real estate & business services	0.9
Other	18.9

Under Sri Lankan labor laws, employment of children under age 12 is prohibited. Those between age 12 and 14 called child workers and may not be employed in industry or dangerous occupations; employment of young persons between 15 and 18 is subject to certain restrictions. Employees under age 18 cannot be required to work outside of specified hours. In addition, employers are required to provide annual leave, rest periods and meal breaks. In practice, however, there is a child work force, probably numbering at least several thousand, who work illegally in Sri Lanka, mostly at jobs in rice cultivation, as domestics or as street peddlers. Efforts to address this problem have been hampered by the fact that, in some cases, child workers are a major source of family income.

There is no minimum wage, but wage boards for 34 different trades set minimum wages and working conditions. Actual wages and working conditions generally exceed these minimums. Most permanent, full-time workers are covered by laws which provide that they shall work no more than 45 hours per week, no more than nine hours per day or more than five and a half days per week, and that they will receive a 14-day paid holiday annually. Workers in the unorganized agricultural sector are not covered by these or any labor laws, although the government may investigate individual complaints.

Worker rights are recognized and protected by law. Any seven workers may form a union, draw up their own procedures, elect their own representatives and formulate programs. Workers are expressly granted the right to bargain collectively. When workers and employers are not able to resolve a dispute, there is an arbitration system which involves Labor Department officers. These officers are stationed throughout the country to assure that employers fulfill their legal and contractual obligations to workers and to be available for arbitration in minor local disputes.

Excepting public service employees, workers are free to strike in Sri Lanka and have done so frequently. Under the emergency regulations, the president may declare any business to be an essential service, making a strike illegal. During 1985, the government used this power to terminate strikes or other job actions several times. In the case of public service employees as well as workers in "essential services," the government generally agreed to discuss grievances with a labor representative. A group of the 8,000 workers who were fired during a strike in 1980 brought a complaint against the government in 1983 before the International Labor Organization Committee on Freedom of Association. In its session of May-June 1985, the committee urged the Sri Lankan government to do its utmost to reinstate those workers who had been without employment since 1980 and to conclude as rapidly as possible the trials of five trade union leaders who had been charged in connection with the 1980 strike. The total number of unemployed in 1981 was 767,601. The government conducts 23 employment exchanges.

Although more than 1.5 million workers are members of labor unions, organized labor is fragmented into 1,592 labor unions. Plantation workers comprise nearly half of organized labor. The largest unions are the Sri Lanka Workers Congress (no political affiliations), the Democratic Workers Congress (no political affiliations), the Sri Lanka Federation of Labor (affiliated with the Lanka Sama Samaja Party), the Sri Lanka Trade Union Federation (affiliated with the Communist Party), the Central Council of Sri Lanka Trade Unions (affiliated with the Mahajana Eksath Peramuna), and the Sri Lanka Trade Union Federation (affiliated with the Freedom Party). There are also two major federations of government employees, the Government Workers Trade Union Federation and the Public Service Workers Trade Union Federation, both of which claim membership of over 100,000. Because of the conflicting interests of the numerous trade unions, collective bargaining virtually does not exist. Industrial disputes are generally settled by compulsory arbitration, wage boards, labor tribunals and industrial courts.

FOREIGN COMMERCE

The foreign commerce of Sri Lanka consisted in 1984 of exports of $1.435 billion and imports of $1.845 billion, producing an unfavorable trade balance of $410 million. In 1981, the export price index (based on 1975=100) was 169, the import price index was 211 and the terms of trade (export price divided by import price x 100) was 80.0.

Of the imports, petroleum accounts for 51.6%, machinery 27.6%, food and beverages 8.5% and textiles 5.2%. Of the exports, tea accounts for 30%, rubber 11%, coconut products 4.9% and precious and semiprecious stones 3.2%.

The major import sources are: Japan 15.2%, Iran 11.7%, the United Kingdom 6.6% and the United States 6.3%. The major export destinations are: the United States 14.4%, the United Kingdom 6.6%, West Germany 5.6% and Japan 5.0%.

All imports and exports are handled by the State Trading Corporation.

TRANSPORTATION AND COMMUNICATIONS

The Sri Lanka Government Railway operates a network of 1,496 km (929 mi) of broad gauge and narrow gauge track. Railway traffic in 1982 consisted of 3,194 billion passenger-km and 215 million net-ton km of freight.

Inland navigation is made possible by 430 km (267 mi) of canals. International sea-borne traffic in 1982 consisted of 4,872,000 metric tons. Colombo is one of the most important ports in Asia. Other major ports include Trincomalee, Galle and Jaffna. The merchant marine consists of 68 vessels with a GRT of 586,700.

FOREIGN TRADE INDICATORS (1984)	
Annual Growth Rate, Imports:	4.7% (1973-83)
Annual Growth Rate, Exports:	2.6% (1973-83)
Ratio of Exports to Imports:	44:56
Exports per capita:	$88
Imports per capita:	$114
Balance of Trade:	$410 million
Ratio of International Reserves to Imports (in months)	1.7
Exports as % of GDP:	30.4
Imports as % of GDP:	40.2
Value of Manufactured Exports:	$277 million
Commodity Concentration:	50.6%

Direction of Trade (%)

	Imports	Exports
EEC	16.3	19.5
U.S.	7.2	14.0
Industrialized Market Economies	46.2	43.9
East European Economies	0.6	5.9
High Income Oil Exporters	22.7	28.0
Developing Economies	50.4	42.7

Composition of Trade (%)

	Imports	Exports
Food	19.4	47.5
Agricultural Raw Materials	1.6	17.1
Fuels	25.0	12.9
Ores & Minerals	4.8	0.8
Manufactured Goods	48.9	21.5
of which Chemicals	8.3	1.8
of which Machinery	22.8	0.5

The road system consists of 66,176 km (41,095 mi) of which about 24,000 km (14,904 mi) are paved. In 1982 the total number of passenger cars in the country was 128,256 and the number of commercial vehicles 91,519. Per capita vehicle ownership was 7.9 cars per 1,000 inhabitants.

The state-owned Sri Lanka Transport Corporation has a monopoly of road and bus transport. The Corporation operates 7,194 vehicles.

The national airline is Air Lanka which is associated with British Airways and had a fleet of eight aircraft in 1983. Air Lanka carried 573,000 passengers and flew 10.1 million km (6.2 million mi) in 1982. The major airports are at Colombo (Ratmalana), Katunayake (Bandaranaike), Trincomalee, Jaffna, Gal Oya and Batticaloa. The country has a total of 14 airfields, of which 10 are usable, 10 have permanent-surface runways, and one (Ratmalana) has a runway over 2,500 meters (8,000 ft.).

In 1984 Sri Lanka had 75,000 telephones, or 0.5 telephones per 100 inhabitants.

In 1982 there were 422 post offices and sub post offices and 1,503 telegraph offices. These handled 670.3 million pieces of mail, and 2.1 million telegrams. Per capita volume of mail was 41 pieces. There are 976 telex subscriber lines.

In 1982, 322,000 tourists visited Sri Lanka, of whom 12,800 were from the United States, 36,400 from the United Kingdom, 85,500 from West Germany, 37,600 from France, 48,500 from India, 19,200 from Switzerland, 12,300 from Sweden, 8,100 from Australia and

4,600 from the Soviet Union. The total tourist receipts were $147 million. Expenditures by nationals abroad totaled $79 million. There are 17,000 hotel beds and the average length of stay was 7.4 days.

MINING

The island is rich in industrial rocks and minerals, such as graphite, gemstones, mica and mineral sands. Forty-four varieties of gems occur, including zircon, garnet, moonstone, sapphire, ruby, topaz, spinel and chrysoberyl. Ilmenite reserves are estimated at over 20 million metric tons. Sri Lanka is the world's largest producer of graphite. Production of graphite in 1983 was 5,870 metric tons. Mining contributed 1% to the GDP in 1982.

DEFENSE

The defense structure is headed by the President and the line of command runs through the minister of defense. Volunteers provide the main source of manpower. The strength of the armed forces is 37,660, or 1.2 armed persons per 1,000 civilians.

ARMY:
Personnel: 30,000
Organization: 5 task forces (5 regular infantry brigades); 2 reconnaissance regiments; 2 field artillery; 1 AA regiments; 1 field engineer regiment; 1 signals battalion; 1 special forces battalion
Equipment: 45 combat vehicles; 10 armored personnel carriers; 46 guns; 24 mortars; 48 air defense guns; rocket launchers

NAVY:
Personnel: 3,960
Naval Bases: Trincomalee, Karainagar, Colombo, Welsara, Tangala.
Units: 2 large patrol craft; 28 coastal patrol craft; 7 fast attack craft

AIR FORCE:
Personnel: 3,700 (Reserves: 900).
Organization & Equipment: 2 combat helicopters; 1 transport squadron; 1 helicopter squadron; 14 trainers
Air Bases: Ratmalana (Colombo), Katunayake; 8 small fields.
Annual military expenditures in 1985 were $131.396 million or 1.5% of the GNP and 3.9% of the national budget, $4 per capita, $4,688 per soldier and $1,136 per sq km of national territory. Sri Lanka has no defense production. Arms purchases abroad during 1973-83 totaled $35 million.

EDUCATION

Sri Lanka has the seventh highest literacy rate in Asia at 86.5% (90.5% for males and 82.4% for females).

Of the population over 15, 38.4% have had no schooling, 53.9% have completed primary level, 7.2% have completed second level, and 0.5% have completed post-secondary level.

In theory schooling is free, universal and compulsory for 10 years from ages 5 to 15. In 1983 enrollment in the 5-10 age group was 103% and in 11-17 age group 54% for a combined enrollment ratio of 76%. Third level enrollment ratio is 3.6%. Girls constitute 48% of primary school enrollment, 52% of secondary school enrollment and 43% of postsecondary enrollment.

The educational system was restructured in 1968 to provide six years of elementary education, five years of middle and two years of higher secondary for a total of 13 years. In 1982 there were 9,209 primary schools of which 8,571 were operated by the government, 45 by private agencies and 774 by plantations. About 55% of the teachers in these schools are trained. There are 27 training colleges. The teacher-pupil ratio was 1:32 at the primary level, 1:21 at the secondary level, and 1:6 at the tertiary level.

The academic year begins in January and is divided into three terms. The medium of instruction is Sinhala or Tamil, depending on the region, but English is a compulsory language from the third primary grade on.

In 1960 the government nationalized most of the private denominational schools and made them part of the state school system. The schools most affected by this act were the 1,117 Catholic and Protestantschools, which charged tuition and had high teaching standards, 224 Buddhist pirivenas, or religious schools, were also nationalized. Private schools account for 6% of the enrollment in primary schools. Only 1% of secondary school pupils is enrolled in the vocational stream.

Control of education is centralized in the Ministry of Education and is exercised through 25 education districts under 17 directors of education. Textbooks are prepared by the publications section of the Ministry of Education, which took over this function in 1964. The education budget in 1981 was R2,485,499,000 of which 95% was current expenditure. This expenditure was 3.0% of the GNP and 8.7% of the national budget. Per capita expenditure on education was $10.

EDUCATIONAL ENROLLMENT (1981)			
	Schools	Teachers	Students
First Level	9,209	133,658	2,153,595
Second Level	5,948	75,174	1,560,923
Vocational	25	488	9,235
Third Level	8	1,609	10,040

In 1972 all four universities in Sri Lanka and the College of Technology at Katubedde were amalgamated as the University of Sri Lanka. The university now has six campuses, at Colombo, Jaffna, Katubedde, Peradeniya, Vidyalankara and Vidyodaya, with a total student strength of 10,040 in 1981. University enrollment was 257 students per 100,000 inhabitants. In 1982, 2,453 Sri Lankan students were enrolled in institutions of higher learning abroad. Of these 677 were in the United Kingdom, 675 in the United States, 390 in India, 166 in Australia, and 150 in Canada.

Over 20 scientific journals are published in the country, and the Sri Lankan contribution to scientific authorship was 0.0150% (U.S.=42%). Sri Lanka's world rank in this respect is 58th. Scientific research is coordinated by the Sri Lanka Institute of Scientific and Industrial Research and the Sri Lanka Association for the Advancement of Science.

LEGAL SYSTEM

The administration of justice is based on Roman-Dutch law and three customary codes —Sinhalese, Tamil and Muslim. The Sinhalese law is also known as Kandyan law and the Tamil law as Desawalamai.

At the apex of the court system is the Supreme Court with a chief justice, 10 puisne judges, and a commissioner of assizes who enjoys the same rights and powers as a supreme court judge. For judicial administration the country is divided into five judicial circuits, and each circuit is subdivided into districts and divisions, the former with district courts and the latter with magistrate's courts. Lower courts include courts of requests, municipal courts and rural courts. At the lowest level are conciliation boards that try minor civil and criminal cases. Court systems and court procedures were simplified and standardized by the Administration of Justice Law of 1973.

Sri Lankan law derives from the British common law tradition. The constitution guarantees the independence of the judiciary, and lawyers and judges are held in high esteem. An accused person is entitled by the constitution to — and under normal circumstances receives — a fair trial in open court, is represented by counsel of his choice, and is apprised of the charges and the evidence against him. Although trial by jury is the custom, juries are not provided in trials under the Prevention of Terrorism Act on the grounds that jury members could be intimidated. The chief justice and all judges of the Supreme Court, Court of Appeal, and High Court are appointed by the president. The chief justice and two Supreme Court judges comprise a Judicial Service Commission which appoints, transfers and dismisses all lower court judges and magistrates. Prior to February 1984, it also appointed all senior attorneys. In February, however, Parliament passed the Eighth Amendment to the constitution giving the president power to appoint senior attorneys, which many lawyers regard as a threat to the independence of the judiciary.

The judicial system in the northern Jaffna Peninsula has virtually ceased functioning due to intimidation by the Tamil militants. For most of 1985, police in the area have not performed their normal law enforcement activities and judges have tried only a few cases.

The constitution provides for three judicial organizations outside of this structure. The first is the Constitutional Court that determines the constitutionality of bills placed before the National State Assembly. The second is the Judicial Commission that tries offenses in connection with a rebellion or insurrection. The third is the Judicial Services Advisory Board that has taken over some of the functions of the old Judicial Service Commission.

The corrections system consists of 14 prisons, four open prison camps and two training schools for youthful offenders, with a daily average population of 6,350, of whom convicted inmates account for 70%. Only 1% of convicts are sentenced for over 10 years; 62% are first offenders.

LAW ENFORCEMENT

The police are headed by an inspector general under the prime minister. The force consisted in 1974 of 16,116 men posted at 260 stations throughout the country—except in certain unpoliced areas where police functions were performed by grama sevakas and divisional revenue officers. There are three territorial units called ranges (Central, Northern and Southern) divided into divisions, districts and stations. Colombo is a special division. Emergency duties are undertaken by the Depot Police. An auxiliary force called the Special Police Reserve is maintained to assist the regular force if needed. The per capita strength of internal security forces is 4.00 per 1,000 working inhabitants.

Crimes against property account for 63% of the crimes; 37% are against persons. Juvenile delinquency is the most serious law enforcement problem. The city of Colombo accounts for 34% of all crimes.

Secret police duties are performed by a Criminal Investigation Department, divided into a special branch and an investigation branch.

HEALTH

In 1981 there were 488 hospitals with 42,257 beds, or 1 bed per 470 inhabitants. In the same year there were 2,035 physicians, or one physician per 9,763 inhabitants, 269 dentists and 7,040 nursing personnel. The admissions/discharge rate is 1,519 per 10,000 inhabitants. The bed occupancy rate is 68.9% and the average length of stay 15 days. Medical training is provided by two colleges, a dental institute, and a college of ayurvedic medicine. Health expenditures in 1982 represented 3.3% of the national budget, and $3.80 per capita.

Compared to other Asians, Sri Lankans are relatively healthy and free from major endemic and infectious diseases. According to WHO, the major causes of death are, in order, gastritis, pneumonia, malignant neoplasms, heart diseases and anaemia. Only 20% of the population have access to safe water.

FOOD

The staple diet consists of rice and curry. Coconuts are used with almost every dish. The principal drinks are tea and pol-hodi, a coconut milk soup. Per capita food intake is 50 grams of protein and 2,251 calories per day, which falls below the minimum 2,600 calories recommended by WHO, 44.3 grams of fats and 379 grams of carbohydrates.

MEDIA & CULTURE

Sixteen daily newspapers are published in Sri Lanka with a combined circulation of 1,681,000, or 111 per 1,000 inhabitants. Six dailies are published in Sinhala, five in Tamil, and five in English. All of them except one are published in Colombo. Annual consumption of newsprint in 1982 was 10,400 tons, or 688 kg (1,517 lb) per 1,000 inhabitants.

There are five main publishing groups: Associated Newspapers, The Times of Sri Lanka, Express Newspapers, Independent Newspapers and Upali Newspapers. The first two have been subjected to a number of restrictive controls because of their anti-government stance since 1970. In 1973 the ownership of the Associated Newspapers was transferred by legislation, and 75% of its shares were sold to labor unions and the public. In the same year legislation was passed setting up a Press Council and imposing additional controls on newspapers.

In addition, 108 non-dailies are published in Sri Lanka with a total circulation of 1,058,000. Over 405 periodicals are published with a circulation exceeding 1.565 million, or 106 per 1,000 inhabitants.

The Bandaranaike regime had been strenuous in its efforts to mute criticism in the media and to establish a press more sympathetic to its socialist ideology. The offices of the Independent Newspapers were closed down in 1974. Partial censorship is imposed during elections and emergencies. Though prepublication censorship does not exist, a copy of every newspaper and book and periodical published in Sri Lanka has to be deposited with the Registrar of Newspapers, while film, concert and theater productions require official permits. Sri Lanka ranks 43rd among nations of the world in press freedom in which it is scaled at +1.14 (on an index with +4 as the maximum and –4 as the minimum).

Sri Lankans are generally free to express their views in private but may be prosecuted under the emergency regulations for making certain kinds of remarks in public. Press censorship was in effect for five months in 1985 on articles relating to terrorist activities, security operations, and communal matters. After formal censorship was ended on July 18, the government asked the media to exercise restraint in publishing information on security-related subjects, and a measure of self-censorship was apparently practiced. In November, restrictions were placed on the publication of press reports on the activities of the Ceasefire Monitoring Committee.

The government adopted a more restrictive policy regarding issuance of press credentials to foreign correspondents. Sri Lankan diplomatic missions were authorized to review a correspondent's past reporting or that of his journal for fairness and accuracy before a visa and press credentials were issued. In practice, however, many foreign journalists entered the country in 1985 on tourist visas. At the request of four opposition parties the government lifted restrictions on the publication of speeches and distribution of leaflets during two parliamentary by-elections. On October 12, the government removed all censorship except on the All-Party Conference's proceedings, but required editors to apply "self-censorship" on reports of terrorist activities and security operations.

One publication, however, has been subject to special censorship. *The Saturday Review*, an English-language weekly published in Jaffna which has advocated the creation of a separate Tamil state, was ordered closed on July 1, 1983. It was permitted to resume publication in February 1984, but all items intended for publication, including sports reports, must be submitted to the government censor in Jaffna.

The national news agency is the Press Trust of Sri Lanka (Newstrust), a private company founded in 1951, in association with Reuters. Other news agencies are Lankapuvath, Cesmos Economic News Agency and Sandesa News Agency. Major foreign news bureaus include DPA, Tass, Hsinhua, Tanjug and Prensa Latina (Cuba).

Sri Lanka has a modest book publishing industry, with about 20 major imprints. In 1981, 2,352 books were published, of which 584 were in English. Sri Lanka adheres to the Berne and Florence Copyright Agreements.

The Sri Lanka Broadcasting Corporation controls all broadcasting in the country and functions under the Ministry of Information and Broadcasting. The corporation operates 9 medium-wave transmitters, 8 FM transmitters and 12 short-wave transmitters, all at Ekala, and broadcasts two services: National and Commercial. The two services are on the air for a total of 630 hours a week, of which the National Service accounts for 359 and the Commercial Service for 192. Broadcast time in Sinhala is 170 hours, in English 161 hours, in Tamil 140 hours and in Hindi 58 hours. An overseas service beamed to SE Asia broadcasts for 116 hours a week in Hindi, English and Tamil. In 1982 there were 1,700,000 radio receivers in the country, or 112 per 1,000 inhabitants and 50,000 television sets or 3.3 per 1,000 inhabitants.

Of the total 32,799 radio broadcasting hours, 3,343 hours are devoted to information, 2,096 hours to education, 1,873 hours to culture, 1,620 hours to religion, 1,476 hours to commercials and 18,602 hours to entertainment. Experimental television, broadcasting within a 50-km radius of Colombo, began in April 1979 and was taken over by the government in June 1979. A national television network was constructed, with stations at Mount Pidurutalagala, Kokavil and Kandy, and boardcasting bagan in December 1982.

Forty-two feature films were produced in 1981. A national film institute was set up in 1970 to control film production, imports and distribution. All films are subject to Government censorship. In 1981 there were 357 cinemas with 202,000 seats, or 13.5 seats per 100 persons. Annual attendance was 63.8 million, or 4.3 per person. In 1981 135 films were imported, of which 50% came from the United States. Box office receipts in 1981 totaled R169.4 million.

In 1982 there were 44 university libraries, 67 special libraries and 381 public libraries in the country. The national depository library is the Colombo Museum. The oldest and perhaps the largest library is the Colombo Public Library with over 100,000 volumes. Per capita, there are 48 volumes and eight registered borrowers per 1,000 inhabitants.

There are 15 museums reporting an annual attendance of over 1.4 million. There are 35 nature preservation facilities.

SOCIAL WELFARE

The Department of Social Services provides a wide range of social services, including monthly allowances to disabled, sick and old persons, relief to persons affected by natural disasters, state-run homes for the aged and the very young, service for the handicapped, full cost of maternity to indigent mothers and workmen's compensation.

GLOSSARY

aswaddumized: relating to rice grown on flooded flatland.

bhikku: Buddhist monk; also used as a term of address and title.

chena: slash-and-burn agriculture practiced in hill districts. Forest or shrub undergrowth is cleared by cutting and burning and the land is farmed until its productivity falls, when a new area is cleared.

grama sevaka: the chief administrative officer in a village; in some areas, also a law enforcement agent.

kachcherie: a government official.

maha: crop sown during the SW or Big Monsoon.

pansala: a Buddhist school, often attached to a temple.

pattu: a group of villages.

pirivena: a Buddhist institution of higher learning.

pol hodi: a coconut milk soup.

sambal: national dish made with ground chilies onions, fish and coconuts.

sangha: the community of bhikkus or monks, especially as forming the core of Buddhist church.

yala: crop sown during the NE monsoon, or the lesser monsoon.

CHRONOLOGY (from 1947)

1947— United National Party wins country's first election; Don Stephen Senanayake becomes first prime minister.... Ceylon Independence Act is passed.

1948— The Ceylon Independence Act comes into force; Ceylon becomes a dominion within the Commonwealth.... Soulbury Constitution of 1946 is adopted as the constitution of Ceylon.

1949— Indian Tamils are disenfranchised.... The Royal Ceylon Army is organized.... Rupee is devalued.... Central Bank is established.

1950— Colombo Plan for Cooperative Economic Development in South and Southeast Asia is launched.... Royal Ceylon Navy and Royal Ceylon Air Force are organized.

1951— S. W. R. D. Bandaranaike founds Sri Lanka Freedom Party.

1952— Premier D. S. Senanayake dies and is succeeded in office by Dudley Senanayake.

1953— Dudley Senanayake retires; John Kotelawala becomes premier and leader of UNP.

1955— UNP loses general elections; Sri Lanka Freedom Party forms coalition government under S. W. R. D. Bandaranaike.... Ceylon is admitted to the U.N.

1956— Sinhala is proclaimed official language of Ceylon.

1957— Great Britain begins phased withdrawal from naval base at Trincomalee.

1958— Tamil-Sinhalese language riots occur; reasonable use of Tamil is permitted in administration and education.

1959— Coalition government is dissolved.... Bandaranaike is assassinated by a Buddhist monk; Wijeyanada Dahanayake forms a new cabinet.

1960— Dahanayake dissolves parliament; UNP wins 50 elections in general elections and, as largest parliamentary group, forms new government under Dudley Senanayake.... Senanayake's government falls; in fresh elections the SLFP is returned to power under Sirimavo Bandaranaike.... All private schools are nationalized.

1961— Sinhala is made sole official language.

1962— William Gopallawa is named new governor general.... Expropriation of U.S. oil companies' distribution facilities leads to suspension of U.S. aid under Hickenlooper Amendment.

1963— Barter agreement is reached with People's Republic of China.

1964— Agreement is reached with India (Sirimavo-Shastri Accord) over status of Indian Tamils in Ceylon.

1965— In general elections UNP is returned to power under Dudley Senanayake.

1966— Use of Tamil for official purposes is permitted in Tamil-speaking areas.... Army chief, Richard Udugama, is arrested in coup attempt.

1967— Rupee is devalued.

1970— SLFP wins landslide victory in general elections; Sirimavo Bandaranaike heads coalition cabinet with Trotskyite and Communist support.... U.S. Peace Corps and Asia Foundation programs are terminated.

1971— A Maoist group, Jonatha Vimukthi Peramuna, leads nationwide uprising, but is suppressed within weeks.

1972— Nation adopts a new constitution and is proclaimed a republic within the Commonwealth.... Ceylon is renamed Sri Lanka.... All existing universities are amalgamated as the University of Sri Lanka.... A ceiling of 50 acres is set on land holdings under new Land Reform Act.... Tamil United Front is formed to counter rising Sinhala nationalism.

1973— Press Council is established as a statutory body; public body takes over majority ownership in Associated Newspapers group.

1974— Accord is reached with India over Kachchativu Isle in Palk Strait; India agrees to take back more Indian Tamils.

1975— All plantations and domestic banks are nationalized.... Trotskyites leave cabinet.

1977— Increasing defections erode SLFP strength in Assembly.... New Leftist Front is formed by Trotskyites and Communists.... Prime Minister Bandaranaike and her Freedom Party are swept out of power in general elections for the National State Assembly; Junius Richard Jayewardene, leader of the United National Party, which wins 139 of the 166 seats, is sworn in as prime minister.... Fifty-four die in post election Tamil-Sinhalese riots; nearly 15,000 Tamils flee homes under attacks by Sinhalese.... Constitution is amended to establish a strong presidential form of government.

1978— Under new constitutional amendment, promulgated on January 1, Junius Jayewardene becomes president; R. Premadasa is named prime minister.

1979— State of emergency is declared in Jaffna as Tamil violence escalates.

1980— Commission probing abuse of power under Mrs. Bandaranaike bars her from parliament.

1981— As Sinhala – Tamil relations worsen, the government declares a state of emergency for five days.

1982— Jayewardene calls for early presidential elections after Parliament amends the constitution permitting him to do so... Jayewardene is reelected with 53% of the vote... A new state of emergency is declared as armed Tamil insurrection leads to breakdown of law and order in the north.

1983— Term of Parliament is extended for another six years, i.e. until 1989, under a national referendum... In by-elections UNP wins 14 out of 18 contested seats... Leftist parties are banned.... TULF members boycott Parliament and they are ousted.... Parliament passes no-separatism amendment to constitution under which those who espouse a breakup of Sri Lanka will lose their civil rights... The state of emergency is ended.

1984— An All-Party Conference convenes to resolve the Tamil separatist demands, but is abandoned in December after failing to reach any agreement... Government imposes restricted zone between Munnar and Mulaitivu for restricting movement of illegal Tamils across the Palk Straits.

1985— Sri Lanka joins the South Asian Regional Conference.

1986— Tamils blow up plane in Colombo airport.

BIBLIOGRAPHY (from 1970)

Bandara, H.H., *Cultural Policy in Sri Lanka* (New York, 1973).

Ceylon and Bali: Southeast Asian Islands. Color film, 17 min. Universal.

Ceylon: Eastern Neighbors. Color film, 11 min. Dudly Pictures.

Ceylon: Pearl of the Orient. Color film, 13 min. Films of the Nations.

Ceylon: The New Dominion. B&W film, 20 min. This Modern Age.

Ceylon: The Resplendent Land. Color film, 12 min. Russell Bailey Productions.

Coomaraswamy, Radhika, *Sri Lanka: The Crisis of the Anglo-American Constitutional Tradition in a Developing Society* (New York, 1983).

De Silva, K.M., *Lanka* (Boulder, Colo., 1976).

———, *A History of Sri Lanka* (Berkeley, Calif., 1981).

Fernando, Tissa and Robert N. Kearney, *Modern Sri Lanka: A Society in Transition* (Philadelphia, Pa., 1979)

———, *Sri Lanka: Profile of an Island Republic* (Boulder, Colo., 1986).

Gems from a Rice Paddy. Color film, 12 min. Producer: not available.

Gold, Martin E., *Law and Social Change: A Study of Land Reform in Sri Lanka* (New York, 1984).

Grossholtz, Jean, *Forging Colonial Patriarchy: The Economic and Social Transformation of Feudal Sri Lanka and its Impact on Women* (Durham, N.C., 1984).

Gunatilleke, Godfrey, *Participatory Development & Dependence: The Case of Sri Lanka* (Washington, D.C., 1980).

Horowitz, Donald L., *Coup Theories & Officer's Motives: Sri Lanka in Comparative Perspective* (Princeton, N.J., 1980).

Jacob, L.M., *Sri Lanka: From Dominion to Republic* (Mystic, Conn., 1974).

Jayewardena, Kumari V., *The Rise of the Labor Movement in Ceylon* (Durham N.C., 1972).

Jiggins, Janice, *Caste & Family in the Politics of the Sinhalese* (New York, 1979).

Jupp, James, *Sri Lanka: Third World Democracy* (Totowa, N.J., 1978).

Karunatilake, H.N., *Central Banking and Monetary Policy in Sri Lanka* (Mystic, Conn., 1975)

Kearney, Robert N., *The Politics of Ceylon* (Ithaca, N.Y., 1973).

Kodikari, S., *Foreign Policy of Sri Lanka* (Atlantic Highlands, N.J., 1982).

Leary, Virginia A., *Ethnic Conflict and Violence in Sri Lanka* (New York, 1981).

Manor, James, *Sri Lanka in Change and Crisis* (New York, 1984).

Moore, Mick, *The State and Peasant Politics in Rural Sri Lanka* (New York, 1986).

Nissanka, H.S., *Sri Lanka's Foreign Policy: A Study in Non-Alignment* (New York, 1984).

Oberst, Robert, *Legislators, Development and Representation in Sri Lanka* (Boulder, Colo., 1985).

Phadnis, Urmilla, *Religion and Politics in Sri Lanka* (Columbia, Mo., 1976).

Ponnambalam, Satchi, *Dependent Capitalism in Crisis: The Sri Lankan Economy*, 1948-78, (Iotowa, N.J., 1981).

———, *Sri Lanka: National Conflict and the Tamil Liberation Struggle* (London, 1983).

Peebles, Patrick, *Sri Lanka: A Handbook of Historical Statistics* (Boston, Mass., 1982).

Prasad, Dhirendra M., *Ceylon's Foreign Policy under the Bandaranaikes* (New York, 1974).

Raby, Namika, *Katcheri Bureaucracy in Sri Lanka: The Culture and Politics of Accessibility* (Syracuse, N.Y., 1985).

Richards, Peter, and Wilbert Gooneratne, *Basic Needs, Poverty & Government Policies in Sri Lanka* (Geneva, 1983).

Robinson, M., *Political Structure in a Changing Sinhalese Village* (New York 1975).

Singer, Marshall R., *Emerging Elite: A Study of Political Leadership in Ceylon* (Cambridge. Mass., 1964).

Song of Ceylon. B&W film, 37 min. Contemporary Films.

Sri Lanka: Jewel of the Orient. Color film, 24 min. Centron Educational Films.

United Nations University, *Needs: Their Perception & Expression-Sri Lanka Experience* (Tokyo, 1980).

Visaria, Pravin, *Some Aspects of Relative Poverty in Sri Lanka* (Washington, D.C., 1981).

Wilson, A.J., *Politics in Sri Lanka, 1945-1973* (New York, 1974).

———, *A Gaullist System in Asia: The Constitution of Sri Lanka* (London, 1981).

Zeylanicus, *Ceylon: Between Orient and Occident* (New York, 1970).

OFFICIAL PUBLICATIONS

Ceylon Central Bank, *Annual Report.*

———, *Bulletin* (monthly).

General Treasury, *Estimates of the Revenue and Expenditure of the Government of the Republic of Sri Lanka.*

———, *State Accounts of the Republic of Sri Lanka.*

LIBYA

EGYPT

LAKE NASSER

SAUDI ARABIA

RED SEA

Wadi Halfa

LAKE NUBIA

Halā'ib

Karmah

Abū Ḥamad

Port Sudan

Dunqulah

Sawākin

CHAD

Kuraymah

Kūrtī

Barbar

Ṭawkar

Al 'Aṭrūn

Wadi Howar

'Aṭbarah
Ad Dāmir

NILE

Nahr 'Aṭbarah

Omdurman   *Khartoum North*

Halfā'al Jadīdah

Ak'ordat

KHARTOUM

Kassalā

Asmera

Takazē

Al Junaynah

Al Fāshir

Bārah

Wad Madanī

Al Qaḍārif

Adré

Al Ubayyiḍ

Kūstī

Sannār

T'ana

An Nuhūd

Blue Nile

Nyala

Ar Rank

Ar Ruṣayriṣ

Rahad al Bardī

Babanūsah

Kāduqlī

White Nile

Buram

Malūṭ

ETHIOPIA

ADDIS ABABA ✪

Umm Rawq

Bahr al 'Arab

Birao

Malakāl

Sobat

Gambēlā

Uwayl

Jur

Bahr al Jebel

Omo

CENTRAL AFRICAN EMPIRE

Wāw

Rumbek

Bor

Sue

SUDAN

——— International boundary
✪ National capital
┼┼┼ Railroad
——— Road
✛ International Airport

0 50 100 150 Kilometers
0   50   100   150 Miles

Tambura

Jūbā

Yei

LAKE RUDOLF

ZAIRE

KENYA

UGANDA

Isiro

BOUNDARY REPRESENTATION IS NOT NECESSARILY AUTHORITATIVE

SUDAN

BASIC FACT SHEET

OFFICIAL NAME: The Democratic Republic of the Sudan (Jumhouriyyat es-Sudan ad-Democratiyya)

ABBREVIATION: SJ

CAPITAL: Khartoum

HEAD OF STATE: Gen. Abdel Rahman Mohamed El Hassan Suwar El Dahab as head of five-man supreme council (from 1986)

HEAD OF GOVERNMENT: Prime Minister Sadiq al-Mahdi (from 1986)

NATURE OF GOVERNMENT: Military dictatorship

POPULATION: 21,761,000 (1985)

AREA: 2,505,813 sq km (967,500 sq mi)

ETHNIC MAJORITY: Arabs and Negroes

LANGUAGES: Arabic in the north and Arabic and English in the South

RELIGIONS: Sunni Islam and Animism

UNIT OF CURRENCY: Sudanese pound ($1 = S £2.5, July 1985)

NATIONAL FLAG: Horizontal white, red, and black stripes with a green triangle extending from the staff to one-third of the flag's length

NATIONAL EMBLEM: A lammergeier, or desert hawk, with stylized wings shown between two scrolls both in Arabic; the upper scroll reads "Victory to our Cause" and the lower the state's official name.

NATIONAL ANTHEM: "Soldiers of God"

NATIONAL HOLIDAYS: January 1 (National Day, Independence Day); March 3 (Unity Day); May 25 (Anniversary of the Revolution); October 12 (Republic Day); Muslim New Year (variable); Christmas. Also, variable Islamic festivals.

NATIONAL CALENDAR: Gregorian and Islamic

PHYSICAL QUALITY OF LIFE INDEX: 39 (up from 33 in 1976) (On an ascending scale with 100 as the maximum. U.S. 95)

DATE OF INDEPENDENCE: January 1, 1956

DATE OF CONSTITUTION: May 8, 1973

WEIGHTS & MEASURES: Metric system prevails

LOCATION & AREA

Sudan is the largest country in Africa and lies across the middle reaches of the River Nile stretching 2,192 km (1,362 mi) SSE to NNW and 1,880 km (1,168 mi) ENE to WSW. With an area of 2,505,813 million sq km (967,497 sq mi), it is one-third as large as the United States. It has a coastline of 716 km (445 mi).

Sudan shares its total international boundary of 7,820 km (4,856 mi) with eight neighbors as follows: Egypt (official: 1,275 km, 792 mi; administrative: 357 km, 222 mi), Ethiopia (2,266 km, 1,408 mi), Kenya (306 km, 190 mi), Uganda (435 km, 270 mi), Zaire (628 km, 390 mi), Central African Republic (1,167 km, 725 mi), Chad (1,360 km, 845 mi) and Libya (383 km, 238 mi). There are no current border disputes.

The capital is Khartoum with a 1983 population of 476,218. With Omdurman (526,287) and Khartoum North (341,146), the capital city forms an urban complex and the main industrial, commercial, and communications center. There are only 10 cities of over 20,000 population of which the most important are Port Sudan (206,727), Wadi Medani (141,065), El Obeid (140,024), Atbara (73,009), and Juba (57,000).

Sudan has three distinct physical regions. Most of the country is made up of a flat plain extending some 804 to 965 km (500 to 600 mi) east to west and more than 1,600 km (1,000 mi) north to south. The heart of this region is the confluence of the Blue and the White Nile, especially the broad wedge of land between the two rivers south of Khartoum. In the southern part of this region permanent swamplands, known as the Sudd, cover an area of 80,450 km (50,000 sq mi). The northern quarter of the country is covered by the Libyan and Nubian Deserts. Four mountain zones comprise the third region: the Red Sea hills to the northeast, the Jabal Marrah to the west, the Nuba Mountains in the center, and the Immatong and Dongotona ranges to the south.

The country's vast areas of contrasting terrain are linked together by the Nile River. The White Nile enters the Sudan from Uganda and is fed by a number of tributaries draining the southwest. The Blue Nile rises in the Ethiopian Highlands and joins the White Nile at Khartoum. The two rivers are different in their seasonal volume of flow. In August the Blue Nile is in flood and makes up nearly 90% of the discharge at the confluence while at other times the more regularly flowing White Nile makes up nearly 83%.

WEATHER

Sudan has a wide range of tropical continental climates. The dry season ranges from three months in the humid south to nine months in Khartoum. In the north high temperatures are common throughout the year. The mean daily maximum reaches about 40°C (104°F) in Khartoum in May and June with a high of 47.8°C (118°F). In the south mean maximums are only slightly lower in the hot months of February and March. January, the coolest month, has a mean maximum of 32.2°C (90°F) in the north. In the south the rainy season produces over 127 cm (50 in.) of rainfall. This is reduced to between 38 and 76 cm (15 and 30 in.) in the central area and between 13 and 25 cm (5 and 10 in.) in the Khartoum region. Much of the northern desert area receives only a few scattered showers each year and northern border areas may not receive any rain at all during some years.

POPULATION

The population of Sudan was estimated at 21,761,000 in 1985, based on the last official census held in 1983 when the population was 20,564,364. The population is expected to reach 33.2 million by 2000 and 51.3 million by 2020. The annual rate of population growth is 2.86% for the country as a whole and 6.3% for the urban areas. The annual birth rate is 45.9 per 1,000.

Sudan is one of the least densely populated countries of the world with an average density of 9.0 per sq km (23 per sq mi). Half of the population lives on 15% of the land surface. The Northern Desert and and the Dindar Game Reserve near the Ethiopian border are uninhabited. The average density on arable land is 27.3 per sq km (71 per sq mi).

The national male/female ratio is 100.7 males to 100 females. Reflecting the pattern of male migration to urban areas, the ratio is 118 males to 100 females in Khartoum, while it is reversed to 91 males to 100 females in the rural Darfur Province. The population is young with 45% under 14 years of age; 52% are in the 15 to 64 age bracket while 3% are over 65.

The urban component of the population is estimated at 29.40% with only 2.7% living in cities over 100,000. Over 55% of the population of Port Sudan live in slums and squatter settlements.

The borders are not well guarded and nomads cross freely between Sudan and Ethiopia, Kenya, Uganda, the Central African Republic and Chad. The main direction of emigration is into Egypt where thousands of Sudanese work as domestic workers and laborers. In recent years many have moved into Libya to share in its oil wealth. During the North-South civil war many southerners fled to neighboring black countries, and, although some have been repatriated, some 45,000 are still residing in Uganda, 20,000 in Zaire, 5,000 in Ethiopia and 3,000 in Kenya. On the other hand, the civil war in Eritrea has displaced thousands of Muslim Eritreans, some 7,000 of whom have

DEMOGRAPHIC INDICATORS (1984)	
Population, total (in 1,000)	21,761.0
Population ages (% of total)	
0-14	45.1
15-64	52.1
65+	2.8
Youth 15-24 (000)	4,049
Women ages 15-49 (000)	4,848
Dependency ratios	92.0
Child-woman ratios	815
Sex ratios (per 100 females)	100.7
Median ages (years)	17.4
Decline in birthrate (%, 1965-83)	—2.1
Proportion of urban (%)	29.40
Population density (per sq. km.)	9
per hectare of arable land	1.13
Rates of growth (%)	2.86
urban %	6.3
rural %	1.6
Natural increase rates (per 1,000)	28.5
Crude birth rates (per 1,000)	45.9
Crude death rates (per 1,000)	17.4
Gross reproduction rates	3.22
Net reproduction rates	2.25
Total fertility rates	6.58
General fertility rates (per 1,000)	203
Life expectancy, males (years)	46.6
Life expectancy, females (years)	49.0
Life expectancy, total (years)	47.7
Population doubling time in years at current rate	24
Average household size	5.1

sought refuge in the Sudan. Because of the Sudan's relatively large and unused area it has served as a magnet for the overpopulated countries in North and West Africa. The number of foreign immigrants in the population is estimated at 420,000, of whom the majority are from Nigeria, Chad and other countries and the minority are from Egypt. Former immigration from Southern Europe and India has now ceased.

Sudan currently hosts approximately 1.4 million refugees and other displaced persons from Ethiopia, Uganda and Chad. The government, in cooperation with the United Nations High Commissioner for Refugees (UNHCR) and other international bodies, strives to meet their needs. Private voluntary organizations, including American groups, have contributed substantially to improved health and sanitation. Refugees and displaced persons live in reception centers, camps, and settlements. Despite the burdens of hosting these people, Sudan has not impeded or discouraged their movement into Sudan. The government prefers, however, that they remain in refugee centers rather than move to urban areas. The new government has tried former Numayri officials for permitting Ethiopian Jewish refugees to resettle in Israel. During 1985, about 50,000 Tigreans returned to Ethiopia after the onset of rains, but their departure was more than offset by a new influx of Eritreans. The 120,000 displaced persons along the Chadian border interact with their compatriots on both sides of the frontier. Sudan hosts about 250,000 Ugandan displaced persons; this group remains generally stable. Refugees in Sudan must possess valid refugee documentation or risk detention, especially in Khartoum.

While men and women retain traditional roles within Sudanese society, women play an active role in the professions and in higher education. In urban areas, they drive automobiles and work in offices with men. Separate educational facilities for men and women, however, are the rule. Sudanese women dress as they please. In urban parts of the north, they often wear the Sudanese female wrapping over Western clothing. Sudanese women participate in both national and international forums. A recent example was the women's conference held in 1985 in Nairobi. Their writings and interviews appear in newspapers and periodicals. In the rural milieu, men and women also work side-by-side, although a division of labor does exist. Grandparents and other relatives often care for children, thus facilitating female employment outside the home. Female circumcision, though illegal, is widely practiced throughout much of Sudan. Efforts to eradicate it have failed so far, despite significant concern among educated women. The drive to Islamize Sudanese society has not had a dramatic impact upon women's rights thus far. While more conservative attire has been encouraged, the veil has not become mandatory. As a result of the rash of arrests for "attempted adultery" during the early months of the state of emergency, relations between unmarried persons have become more circumspect.

Family planning has not yet been accepted as official policy and has made little impact on population dynamics.

ETHNIC COMPOSITION

Ethnically Sudan is fragmented into 56 ethnic groups and 597 subgroups, but the basic division of the country is into the Arab north and the black African south. About one-third of the people of Sudan are Arabs, but the term Arab is used, as indeed it is throughout the Middle East, loosely to cover Arabized inhabitants who may only speak Arabic. Their historical position as the conquerors and their concentration in the more developed regions have made the Arabs the dominant group in national affairs, and Sudan is officially considered as an Arab country. Arabs constitute 73.7% of the Blue Nile Province, 66% of the Northern Province, 60% of the Khartoum Province, 56% of Kordofan Province, and 28% of Darfur Province. Almost all the pure Arabs claim descent, through ingeniously constructed genealogical trees, from ancestors in Arabia, and tribes are ranked by the purity and nobility of their blood.

The Nubians, who constitute the next major ethnic element, are the oldest settlers of the land. They include the northern Maha, the Danagla, the Gerkid and the Midob. They formed 3.2% of the population in the 1955-56 census. The nomadic Beja, who formed 6.3% of the population in the 1955/56 are concen- trated in the Red Sea hills of Kassala Province. The majority of the Beja belong to one of three Bedawiye-speaking groups: the Bisharin, Amarar, and Hadendowa. The next group, the Nuba, who formed 5.5% of the population in the 1955-56 census, are sedentary people who live mainly in scattered communities in the southern Kordofan Province. Minor groups in the north include the Fur, after whom Darfur Province is named, the Daju of the western Nuba Mountains, and the Zaghawa. To the east in the Blue Nile Province live the Fung peoples, though the term Darfung is used to designate all the heterogeneous peoples living in the region. Most people of the southern Sudan are called Nilotes because of their association with the Nile. The Dinka are the largest Nilotic group constituting 11.5% of the population in the 1955-56 census. They formed 41% of the southern regional population. The Nuer are closely associated with the Dinka in language, culture, and territory. Other groups in the Nilotic family are the Shilluk, Bari, Lotuko, Toposa, Anuak, Luo, Didinga, Beir, and Murle. The peoples of Equatoria and Western Bahr al Ghazal are grouped under the term Sudanic, of whom the Azande are the most numerous. There are also a number of groups, such as the Moru and Madi, whose ethnic affiliations have not been established.

Interethnic relations are colored by the historic conflict between Arabs and blacks. The southern Sudan was one of the principal catchment areas of the Arab slave trade and memories of Arab indignities and slave raids still linger in the south. Islam with its strong assimilationist tendencies poses a continuing threat to the fragile social structure of the black tribes.

Ethnic aliens constitute an important element of the population. West African Muslims have increased in numbers in the recent past and now form 5.8% of the population. The majority are settled in agricultural areas in Al Jazirah between the Blue and White Nile. There are also smaller numbers of Greeks and Armenians, who until the late 60s held a high proportion of skilled jobs and managerial positions in Khartoum, Egyptians and Maltese.

In terms of ethnic and linguistic homogeneity the Sudan ranks 23rd in the world with 27% homogeneity (on an ascending scale in which North and South Korea rank 135th with 100% homogeneity and Tanzania ranks first with 7% homogeneity).

LANGUAGES

Over 115 languages are spoken in the Sudan including 26 major ones. No single language is understood by all Sudanese. Arabic is the language of slightly more than half the population and the official language since 1956, though it is spoken by less than 1% of the southern region. But the use of Arabic is spreading among the non-Arabic northerners, and the native dialects are slowly giving way. The adoption of Islam has introduced a number of Arabic terms into common use and personal names have been arabicized.

By the accord that ended the civil war in 1972, English is recognized as a working language in the south. The major vernaculars in the south are Dinka, Nuer, Lango, Zande and Moru-Madi.

RELIGION

Sunni Islam, introduced in the 14th century, is the official religion and is followed by 70% of the population. But, except among the Arabs, Islam has not totally displaced vestiges and observances of earlier traditional forms. The roughly 4 million people of the southern provinces adhere mainly to indigenous, animistic beliefs, and they have long resisted the call of Islam. Christianity is followed by approximately 5% of the population, most of them concentrated among the Dinka in the south.

From 1957 the state launched an official policy of Islamicization. Over 350 Christian mission schools were nationalized and the missionaries expelled. Arabic and the Koran were made compulsory subjects in schools, and Sunday was replaced as a day of rest by Friday. From 1971 these rules against Christian churches were relaxed, and Christian priests were allowed to return provided they were not Westerners. The Ministry of Religious Affairs and Religious Trusts was set up in 1972 to supervise Christian churches and to promote Africanization.

The Sudanese government supports mosques and Muslim educational projects; government schools include both Muslim and Christian religious education. Muslims, Christians and Jews maintain centralized offices in Khartoum for administration and keeping records such as birth certificates. Both Muslim and Christian missionaries are active in Sudan. Christian education, health and welfare projects operate freely, especially in the south. Christians are free to maintain strong ties with coreligionists outside Sudan.

The Umma, Democratic Unionist Party, and National Islamic Front reflect the memberships of the Ansar, Khatmiyya, and conservative Muslims, respectively. Anti-Christian tensions which existed in parts of south Kordofan in 1984 appear to have abated, and no harassment of Christian institutions has occurred recently. That area includes adherents of all major religious groups in Sudan.

Christian-Muslim relations in the Nuban areas of South Kordofan have always been uneasy and tensions have reached a new level of confrontation recently. Authorities ordered 16 Christian churches in the Nuba-inhabited area of Heiban in South Kordofan to be closed. A number of local residents and churchmen were arrested for disobeying the order. An Italian priest in Kadugli was arrested, charged with "inciting the people against the government" and two clinics in Kadugli operated by Italian priests and nuns were closed. When Heiban area residents protested, the chairman of the Higher Council for Religious Affairs and the deputy governor of Kordofan ordered the commissioner of South Kordofan to allow the oldest of the churches to reopen. He has not complied; and two churches in Heiban remain closed. The churches in the surrounding area remain open, except four which were burned down by persons unknown.

COLONIAL EXPERIENCE

The Sudan was under effective British rule (although technically an Anglo-Egyptian condominium) from 1899 to 1956. But it was not until 1916, when the last stronghold of Mahdism was taken, that the country was completely pacified. The "colony" was administered by a governor general appointed by the Khedive of Egypt on the recommendation of the British government; the fiction of Egyptian participation in the government was maintained until the end for diplomatic and political convenience. However, the British nature of the rule became more obvious after 1924 when all Egyptian civil servants were evacuated. British colonial policy had three objectives: to encourage tribalism as an alternative to nationalism, to detach the southerners from the Arabic and northern influences, and to prevent a link-up of Egyptian and Sudanese nationalists. The British were successful in only the last; Sudan decisively rejected union with Egypt and unilaterally declared its independence in 1955.

CONSTITUTION & GOVERNMENT

Following the 1985 coup, the 1973 constitution was suspended, along with the Presidential Council and the National and People's Regional Assemblies. Following the 1986 elections, the National Assembly was reconvened, and a civilian government was permitted to function under the aegis of the military.

The constitution of 1973 provided for a strong presidential form of government. The president was nominated by the Sudanese Socialist Union for a six-year term. Legislative authority was vested in the unicameral People's Assembly, which was partly elected and partly appointed.

The Southern Sudan Regional Constitution created the three southern provinces, forming an autonomous region with Juba as its capital. The region was administered by a regional executive, the High Executive Council for the Southern Region, whose chairman was also vice president of the republic. His responsibilities included all regional matters but exclude national defense, external affairs, communications, currency and foreign trade. The regional government included a Regional People's Assembly and a cabinet.

Central government control over the administrative structure was decentralized since 1974 by breaking up six northern provinces into 12, by conferring greater autonomy on provincial governors, and by establishing local people's councils at the grass-roots level. These councils now number 4,500. A decentralization plan introduced in February 1980 provided for regional government in the five northern regions.

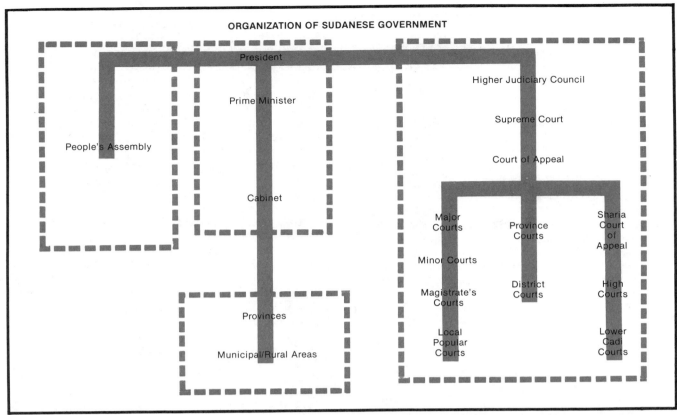

ORGANIZATION OF SUDANESE GOVERNMENT

President

Prime Minister

People's Assembly

Cabinet

Higher Judiciary Council

Supreme Court

Court of Appeal

Major Courts

Minor Courts

Magistrate's Courts

Local Popular Courts

Province Courts

District Courts

Sharia Court of Appeal

High Courts

Lower Cadi Courts

Provinces

Municipal/Rural Areas

An amendment to the constitution needed a two-thirds vote of the People's Assembly; an amendment of the Regional Constitution required a four-fifths vote of the People's Assembly and the president's assent for ratification.

The president was nominated by the Sudan Socialist Union and was elected by public referendum for a period of six years. The cabinet was responsible to him and not to the People's Assembly. He was also the supreme commander of the People's Armed Forces and Security Forces. The president could declare a state of emergency and take any measure he regards as "suitable," including suspension of all freedoms and rights. In his role as chief executive the president was assisted by a cabinet.

Sudan is in transition. An era ended on April 6, 1985, when professional elites and senior military officers combined to overthrow the 16-year government of President Jaafar Numayri. The beginning of the end came with the public hanging on January 18 of a 76-year old religious thinker on charges of apostasy. Many Sudanese deemed the hanging an outrageous violation of Sudan's traditional tolerance. In subsequent months, unresolved civil war in the south, arguments over Shari'a law, a worsening economy, revelations about drought and starvation, and finally price increases on staples led to public demonstrations that triggered Numayri's fall. Military leaders set up a 15-member Transitional Military Council (TMC) chaired by Lt. General Abdel Rahman Suwer el Dahab. In consultation with Sudan's leading political parties, unions, and professional associations, the TMC chose a civilian cabinet headed by Prime Minister Dr. el Gizouli Dafalla. The TMC, however, retained executive power. On October 10, 1985, the TMC approved a transitional constitution providing for decentralization of government and observance of basic human rights, e.g., freedom of speech. Almost 40 political parties, representing all ideological and regional viewpoints, contested the April 1986 elections when the transitional state ended.

Following the 1986 April elections and the convening of the Assembly on April 26, Suwar el-Dahab and his civilian prime minister al-Gazouli Dafalla formally turned over power to a civilian coalition government of the Umma and Democratic Unionist Party who together commanded 165 seats out of a total of 301. Umma leader Sadiq al-Mahdi was named prime minister and a five-man supreme council was chosen to act as collective head of state in lieu of a president.

The High Executive Council for the Southern Region consisted of a president and 11 members.

Members of the People's Assembly and the Regional People's Assembly are elected by direct, secret ballot. Suffrage is universal. The most recent election was that for the National People's Assembly in 1985.

During its first 25 years of independence, Sudan underwent three military coups d'etat, a 17-year civil war, and two abortive coups.

FREEDOM & HUMAN RIGHTS

In terms of civil and political rights Sudan is classified as a partly free country, with a negative rating of

CABINET LIST (1985)

Chmn., Transitional Military Council . . *Gen.* Abdel Rahman Mohamed El Hassan Suwar El Dahab

Prime Minister . . . . *Dr.* El Gizouli Dafalla

Deputy Prime Minister . . . . Samuel Aru Bol

Minister of Agriculture & Natural Resources . . . . Siddig Abdeen

Minister of Cabinet Affairs . . . . Abu Bakr Osman Mohamed Salih

Minister of Commerce, Cooperation & Supply . . . . Sid Ahmed El Sayed

Minister of Construction & Housing . . . . *Dr.* Amin Makki Medani

Minister of Culture and Information . . . . Mohamed Bashir Hamid

Minister of Defense . *Maj. Gen.* Osman Abdalla Mohamed

Minister of Education & Instruction . . . . Bashir Haj El Tom

Minister of Energy, Industry & Mining . . . . Abdel Aziz Osman Musa

Minister of Foreign Affairs . . . . Ibrahim Taha Ayoub

Minister of Health & Social Welfare . . . . *Dr.* Hussein Abu Salih

Minister of Interior . . . . *Gen.* Abbas Medani

Minister of Irrigation & Hydro-Electric Power . . . . Samuel Aru Bol

Minister of Public Service & Labor . . . . Stanley James Wango

Minister of Transport & Communications . . . . Peter Gatkuoth Gwal

Attorney General . . . . Omer Abdel Atti Omer

RULERS OF SUDAN

1958 (November) to 1964 (November)
        Ibrahim Abboud
1964 (November) to 1965 (July)
        Five Man Council of Sovereignty
1965 (July) to 1969 (May)
        Ismail el-Azhari
1969 (May) to April (1985)
        Jafar Muhammad Numayri
April (1985) to April (1986)
        Abdel Rahman Mohamed El Hassan Suwar El Dahab

PRIME MINISTERS

1986 (April)— Sadiq al-Mahdi

5 in political rights and 5 in civil rights (on a descending scale where 1 denotes the highest and 7 the lowest in civil and political rights).

There were positive human rights developments in 1985. Since Nimeiri's overthrow, Sudan's leaders have advocated democracy and moved cautiously toward pluralism. The TMC dismantled the secret police, freed about 1,000 political prisoners, repealed laws banning strikes, and removed press restrictions. However, the government imposed a state of emergency soon after taking power and banned marches after ethnic clashes in September. The Shari'a laws introduced in 1983 remain on the statute books.

The new government did not rush into a series of quick trials of former government officials. Many of those detained following the revolution were soon released. Lengthy investigations preceded the formulation of charges against those now being tried. Both the Idris and al Tayyeb trials have been televised. Cross-examination of both prosecution and defense witnesses has taken place. During the Idris trial, however, the defense was refused the opportunity of cross-examination of a prosecution witness on at least one occasion. The case is now on appeal. The other four potential defendants in the Tayyeb case have turned state's evidence in exchange for a pardon. The government will also try former President Numayri in absentia.

Despite the new government's expressed desire for national reconciliation and unity, it has been unable to end the southern insurgency that resumed in 1983 after Numayri breached southern autonomy and imposed Islamic laws (Shari'a). In April 1985, the TMC called on Col. John Garang de Mabior, leader of the Sudan People's Liberation Army/Movement (SPLA/SPLM), to negotiate, but he refused, claiming distrust of the TMC. The SPLM has, however, maintained contacts with the civilian Council of Ministers (CM), southerners, and other Sudanese. In October, Garang declared a cease-fire and hinted at sending a delegation to talk with civilians. In the south, many innocent civilians continue to suffer from the fighting and breakdown in law and order.

Well-informed and reliable sources estimate the number of political detainees at about 264, most of them interned after the revelation in September of an alleged antigovernment plot involving mainly Nubans and southerners. The constitution guarantees habeas corpus and requires a court-issued warrant to arrest a citizen. The State Security Act of 1975 authorizes arrest without a warrant and detention without charges for renewable 90-day periods on security grounds. Many persons have been detained for short periods of time under the Security Act, then either released or tried. About 80 people, mainly from the Ansar sect and the Republican Brothers, were taken into custody in mid-1983. In December, Ansar leader Sadiq al Mahdi and his chief lieutenants were released after 15 months detention, as were Republican Brother leader Mahmoud Taha and several followers. In January 1985, Taha and four other Republican Brothers were rearrested for distributing anti-Shari'a literature and executed.

CIVIL SERVICE

No current information is available on the Sudanese Civil Service.

LOCAL GOVERNMENT

Under the constitution Sudan is divided into 18 provinces, 12 in the north and six in the southern region, as follows: Northern, Gezira, Kassala, Khartoum, Nile, Northern Darfur, Northern Kordofan, Red Sea, Southern Darfur, Southern Kordofan, Upper Nile, White Nile, Lakes, Jonglei, Bahr el Ghazal, Eastern Equatoria, Western Equatoria, and Blue Nile.

The provincial administration is composed of the commissioner, the province council, and the province authority. The province councils are composed of ex-officio members, members elected by and from local government authority panels, and members appointed by the government. The province authority is composed of the head representatives of of the central government ministries in the province. A local government council is two-thirds elected and one-third appointed by the government.

FOREIGN POLICY

The foreign policy of Sudan has shifted in tune with the internal policies of the regime in power from pro-Communist to pro-Western and from pro-Arab and pro-Egyptian to pro-African. Relations with the West deteriorated after the Arab-Israeli War of 1967 and diplomatic relations with the United States were suspended from 1967 to 1972. U.S.-Sudanese relations came under further strain after the murder of the U.S. ambassador, Cleo A. Noel, and his deputy, Curtis G. Moore, by Palestinian terrorists in Khartoum in 1973 and after the release of their convicted murderers in 1974. Cooperation between the two countries remained circumscribed until 1977 when there was a marked improvement. Relations with the USSR deteriorated after the abortive Communist coup of 1971 and led to a recall of ambassadors, but formal relations have since been reestablished.

Relations with Egypt were strained after the coup attempts of 1969 and 1971 and the elimination of pro-Egyptian elements in the government. Tension between the two countries was eased by the visit of President Numayri to Egypt in 1974 and an agreement on mutual cooperation leading to the creation of a joint defense command. Hostility toward Libya stems from Libyan involvement in a number of antigovernment conspiracies. But Numayri has good relations with the conservative regimes in Saudi Arabia, Kuwait and the United Arab Emirates, all of whom supply financial assistance. Initially the concept of nonalignment provided a frame of reference for foreign relations, but the Sudanese have since separated the economic and political aspects of foreign policy. Since 1970 there has been a reorientation of attitude away from nonalignment and toward conservative Arab regimes as well as toward the West.

Relations with the Communist-dominated regime in Ethiopia have steadily deteriorated and there have been a number of border incidents. Sudan has been accused by Ethiopia of aiding Eritrean secessionists who have a strong claim on Sudanese sympathies on account of both religion and race.

During 1978 Numayri supported Sadat on the latter's peace treaty with Israel. Although this support was qualified in 1979 as a result of continued Arab opposition to Camp David Accords, Egypt and Sudan agreed in the same year to integrate the two countries in the social, economic and cultural spheres.

During its first year in office, the Suwar el-Dahab regime has followed a generally pro-Libyan and anti-American line, although in both respects it has maintained a low profile. Libya was one of the first countries to grant recognition to the Dahab coup and the Soviet Union sent a message applauding the military takeover and the fall of Numayri. Reactions from conservative Arab and Western nations, although less enthusiastic, were not negative. Because Libyan terrorists have unrestricted access to Khartoum, the United States has placed the city on a list of potentially dangerous places for its citizens. The new regime is also more anti-Israel than its predecessor, and has placed a former member of the Numayri cabinet on trial for his complicity in providing an airlift for Falasha Jews from Ethiopia to Israel. Sudan and the United States are parties to 13 agreements and treaties covering agricultural commodities, defense, economic and technical cooperation, investment guaranties, and judicial assistance.

Sudan is a member of the Arab League and the Organization of African Unity. It joined the U.N. in 1956 and is a member of 14 U.N. organizations and 19 other international organizations. Its share of the U.N. budget is 0.02%.

U.S. Ambassador in Khartoum: Hume A. Horan
U.K. Ambassador in Khartoum: *Sir* Alexander Stirling (1980)
Sudanese Ambassador in Washington, D.C.: Salah Ahmed
Sudanese Ambassador in London: Abdullahi El-Hassan

PARLIAMENT

When it was dissolved in 1985 by the Transitional Military Committee (TMC) the unicameral People's Assembly had 151 members, including 52 representatives from the geographical constituencies elected directly by universal suffrage; 16 southern representatives; 70 seats elected by sectoral organizations such as women's, youth, and village associations, peasants, military, workers, intellectuals and administrative workers; and 13 nominated by the president. Only members of the Sudanese Socialist Union, or those approved by the party could be members of the People's Assembly. The Regional People's Assembly of the Southern Region had 60 members with the same proportions. Elections were held for a new 301-member Assembly in April 1986. Voting in 37 southern districts was postponed because of the civil war, making the contest for the remaining 264 seats in the 301-member assembly largely an exercise of the Moslem north. The voting was spread out over 12 days due to Sudan's huge size and poor communications and transportation network. While there were some reports of ballot rigging, the election appeared to be one of the freest seen in Africa in recent years, with as many as 30 political parties fielding candidates.

Initial results were announced April 20. Leading the field were the Umma Party, which won a plurality of 99 seats, and the Democratic Unionist Party (DUP), which won 63. The two parties, which were variously described in the U.S. and British press as being centrist or right-wing, were the same ones that had dominated Sudanese electoral politics in the 1960s, before Numayri's 16-year dictatorial rule. The fundamentalist National Islamic Front (NIF), previously known as the Moslem Brotherhood, won 51 seats in what was considered a surprisingly strong showing. The Sudan National Party (SNP), led by a Christian deemed to be the northern politician most sympathetic to the southern rebels, took eight seats. The Communist Party won two, while the remainder were taken by independent and minor parties.

POLITICAL PARTIES

Numayri's Sudanese Socialist Union, the country's sole legal political party, collapsed with his ouster, and when political activity was relegitimized under Dahab more than 30 groups entered the lists. The more important ones bore names familiar in Sudan's modern political history: the Umma Party, led by the legendary heir to the Mahdi, Sadiq al-Mahdi, and the Democratic Unionist Party, both centrist or right-wing; the fundamentalist National Islamic Front, previously known as the Moslem Brotherhood; the Sudan National Party, led by a Christian, representing non-Muslim interests; and the Communist Party.

The southern guerrillas control large areas of the south and have refused to participate in northern electoral activities.

Commonly referred to as Anya Nya II, the rebel groups are organized into political and military wings, known as the Sudanese People's Liberation Front (SPLF) and the Sudanese People's Liberation Army (SPLA) respectively. Reportedly assisted by several thousand deserters from the armed forces in the South, Anya Nya II is led by Col. John Garang, a highly-trained military officer who also holds a post-graduate degree in economics from a U.S. university.

ECONOMY

Sudan is one of the 49 low-income countries of the world, one of the 29 least developed countries and one of the 45 countries most seriously affected by recent adverse economic conditions. It has a free-market economy dominated by the private sector.

The imposition of Sharia law in September 1983 had serious repercussions on the economy; the 1984 Civil Transactions Act was designed to bring existing company, investment and taxation law into line with Islamic principles. In 1984 the first Islamic budget, like previous budgets, placed emphasis on agriculture, energy and transport, with priority given to rehabilitating existing projects, but, under the new zakat (alms) system, 20 taxes were abolished, while the official ban

on alcohol removed a major source of revenue. Sudan's already overwhelming financial problems were compounded by the effects of drought and famine in 1983-84; huge numbers of refugees, mainly from Ethiopia, added to the strain on the Sudanese economy, and in November 1984 the government appealed for 160,000 tons of emergency food aid, as it seemed probable that the disaster in Sudan might become comparable to that in neighboring Ethiopia.

PRINCIPAL ECONOMIC INDICATORS

Gross National Product: $8.420 billion (1983)
  GNP Annual Growth Rate: 6.7% (1973-82)
  Per Capita GNP: $400 (1983)
  Per Capita GNP Annual Growth Rate: 3.5% (1973-82)

Gross Domestic Product: S £6.218 billion (1982)
  GDP Annual Growth Rate: 6.3% (1973-83)
  Per Capita GDP: S £314 (1982)
  Per Capita GDP Annual Growth Rate: –3.0% (1970-81)

Income Distribution: 4.0% of the national income is received by the lowest 20%; 34.5% of the national income is received by the top 10%.

Percentage of Population in Absolute Poverty: 43; Rural 85%

Consumer Price Index (1970=100):
  All Items: 1,497.8 (September 1984)
  Food: 1,672.1 (September 1984)
  Average Annual Rate of Inflation: 18.0% (1973-83)

Money Supply: S £2.741 billion (January 1985)
  Reserve Money: S £2.298 billion (January 1985)

Currency in Circulation: S £1.247 billion (1984)

International Reserves: $17.2 million, of which $17.2 million were foreign exchange reserves (1984)

BALANCE OF PAYMENTS (1984)
(million $)

Current Account Balance	89.3
Merchandise Exports	519.0
Merchandise Imports	–558.8
Trade Balance	–36.8
Other Goods, Services & Income	+268.8
Other Goods, Services & Income	–412.9
Other Goods, Services & Income Net	–144.2
Private Unrequited Transfers	248.5
Official Unrequited Transfers	21.7
Capital Other Than Reserves	–107.7
Net Errors & Omissions	0.6
Total (Lines 1, 10 and 11)	–17.8
Counterpart Items	40.9
Total (Lines 12 and 13)	23.1
Liabilities ConstitutingForeign Authorities' Reserves	3.7
Total Change in Reserves	–26.8

The First 10-Year Plan 1961/62-1971/72 targeted a total development expenditure of S £565.4 million. A Second Five-Year Plan 1971-75, which was later extended to 1977, had a total investment of 666.3 million pounds Sudanese. In general terms it sought full employment, increased industrial activity, expansion of public services and the raising of annual GNP growth rate to 7.6%. Agricultural output was to be increased by 60.8%, investment in education and culture by 60%, health by 82%, public utilities by 58% and livestock production by 75.5%. The number of projects in the plan for the public sector was 276, of which 239 have actually been started.

A six-year plan (1977-83) for social and economic development, which followed the 1970-75 plan, was announced in July 1977. Investment expenditure of £S2,670 million was proposed, with highest priority given to agricultural and agro-industrial development and to mining and manufacturing industry. An average annual GNP increase of 7.5% was predicted, raising per capita income by 180% to £S307 in 1983, compared with £S110 in 1975/76. The plan allowed for a wider spread of private and mixed investment than previously, with foreign investment capital accounting for 52% of financing requirements. However, increased fuel costs and the growing burden of Sudan's short-term debt led to the formualtion of a three-year interim development program by the Ministry of Planning in conjunction with the World Bank, with revised production and financial targets.

The latest in the series, the 1982/83-1984/85 three-year public investment program, was announced in October 1982. Backed by the World Bank and the IMF, its central emphasis is the rehabilitation of existing production units and the removal of transport and energy bottlenecks. It is described by the World Bank as a "minimal program," since the envisaged expenditure, totaling £S1,656.2 million, over the three years, is the minimum amount which, it is judged, will be necessary to achieve the program's objectives. These include a 3%–3.5% average annual growth rate in GDP to 1984/85, accelerating to 5.6% in the five years to 1991/92. Agriculture is allocated the largest share of proposed spending, with 32.2% of the total. Most of this will go to irrigated agriculture, the sector which generates the majority of export earnings. Transport and communications are next, with 21.1%, followed by power, with 10.9%, and education and health, with 10.1%.

GROSS DOMESTIC PRODUCT BY ECONOMIC ACTIVITY (1970-81)		
	%	Rate of Change %
Agriculture	38.8	4.3
Mining	0.2	−7.5
Manufacturing	6.4	4.1
Construction	5.2	11.2
Electricity, Gas & Water	1.9	3.8
Transport & Communications	9.9	11.0
Trade & Finance	23.0	12.4
Public Administration & Defense	11.9	5.2
Other Branches	2.7	0.2

Until 1971 the main source of foreign aid was the Eastern Bloc, mainly from the USSR, Rumania and Yugoslavia. From 1971 more aid has been received from Western countries and the People's Republic of China, most of it tied to specific development projects. From 1976 Sudan begun to benefit from Arab aid channeled through the Arab Fund for Economic and Social Development, which drew up a 10-year plan calling for a massive investment of $6 billion, aimed at converting Sudan into the breadbasket of the Arab world. Saudi Arabia and Kuwait have emerged since 1974 as the largest donors of investment aid, particularly for the Rahad project, the Triad Naft oil refinery and sugar refineries. The Arab Authority for Agricultural Investment and Development, with a capital of over $500 million, prepared a $5.7 billion ten year investment program for Sudan with productive investments of $3.9 billion and infrastructure investments on concessionary terms of $1.8 billion. The United Kingdom, Norway, the Netherlands and West Germany have also contributed substantial foreign aid. The World Bank has contributed loans of $245 million under generous terms since 1958, financing such vital projects as the Roseires Dam, the Managil Extension, and the dieselization of Sudan Railways. Total U.S. aid received from 1946 to 1983 was $636.6 million, and total aid from international organizations during the same period was $1.176 billion. During 1979-81 bilateral and multilateral aid amounted to $434.9 million, or $23.30 per capita.

BUDGET

The Sudanese fiscal year runs from July 1 through June 30.

The Sudanese national budget is drawn up in two parts: the first an ordinary or current one and the second a capital or development one. Like many other developing countries, Sudan depends heavily on indirect taxes, which contributed 44.3% of government revenues in 1981. Direct taxes contributed 36% (compared to 2.7% in 1963/64) and non-tax revenues 19.7%.

The direct taxes of Sudan were income taxes, stamp duty and consumption and development taxes introduced since 1979. All these taxes were replaced by Islamic taxation in September 1984, following the passing of the Alms and Taxation Act. Under this, Muslims will pay alms and non-Muslims taxes at equivalent rates. Official estimates put taxation under the new system at £S500 million for 1984/85, compared with original estimates for the year of £S217 million.

Of current revenues, 15.8% comes from taxes on income, profit and capital gain, 14.1% from domestic taxes on goods and services, 49.7% from taxes on international trade and transactions, 0.7% from other taxes and 19.7% from non-tax revenues. Current revenues represented 11.8% of GNP. Of current expenditures, 9.5% goes to defense, 6.1% to education, 1.3% to health, 2.3% to housing, social security and welfare, 23.5% to economic services and 57.3% to other functions. Current expenditures represented 16.9% of GNP and overall deficit 4.6%.

In 1983 total outstanding disbursed external debt was $5.664 billion of which $4.203 billion was owed to official creditors and $1.460 billion to private creditors. Total debt service was $144.4 million of which $73.5 million was repayment of principal and $70.9 million interest. Total external debt represented

BUDGET (£S million, year ending 30 June)*			
Revenue†	1978/79	1979/80	1981/82
Tax revenue	405.1	459.9	673.3
Tax on income, etc.	55.3	79.3	132.2
Excises	117.9	116.9	118.4
Profits of fiscal monopolies	3.0	26.2	—
Import duties	167.9	224.1	383.6
Customs duties	148.1	175.8	318.3
Defense tax	2.4	28.8	65.3
Export duties and royalties	15.0	9.7	33.3
Exchange taxes	42.6	—	—
Non-tax current revenue†+	139.1	89.5	165.5
Capital revenue	3.0	9.2	0.7
TOTAL	547.2	558.6	839.5
Expenditure§	1978/79	1979/80	1981/82
General public services	180.4	255.5	215.8
Defense	66.4	102.9	113.9
Education	58.6	76.6	72.7
Health	10.0	10.9	16.0
Social security and welfare	9.0	5.3	26.8
Other community and social services	2.8	2.1	17.5
Economic services	145.4	154.7	281.0
Agriculture, forestry and fishing	77.2	73.6	101.9
Mining, manufacturing and construction	31.3	28.4	49.3
Transport and communications	32.5	41.1	41.9
Other services	227.2	198.8	465.0
Adjustment to cash basis	−17.2	−27.1	−10.5
TOTAL	682.6	779.7	1,198.2

* Figures represent consolidated cash transactions covered in the Central Budget and the Development Budget. Figures for 1980/81 are not available.

† Revenue excludes capital grants from abroad (£S107.2 million in 1979/80; £S194.0 million in 1981/82).

†+ Including adjustments to a cash basis (£S million): −17.7 in 1978/79; −26.8 in 1979/80; −13.3 in 1981/82.

§ Expenditure excludes net lending (£S million): 0.5 in 1978/79; 16.0 in 1979/80; 161.7 in 1981/82.

1982/83 (estimates, £S million): revenue 1,343; expenditure 1,910; development 502.

1983/84 (estimates, £S million): revenue 1,599; expenditure 2,463; development 610.

1984/85 (estimates, £S million): revenue 1,640 (tax revenue 1,315, non-tax revenue 325); expenditure 2,663; development 658.

698.8% of export revenues and 81.4% of GNP. Total debt service represented 17.8% of export revenues and 2.1% of GNP.

FINANCE

The Sudanese unit of currency is the pound divided into 100 piastres and 1,000 milliemes. Coins are issued in denominations of 1, 2, 5 and 10 milliemes and 2, 5, 10 piastres, while notes are issued in denominations of 25 and 50 piastres and 1, 5 and 10 pounds. The official rate of exchange in 1985 was $1 = S £2.5. The sterling exchange rate in 1984 was £1= £1.507. In June 1978 the Sudanese pound was devalued by 25%. In September 1979 a dual exchange market system was introduced; the parallel rate applied to about 5% of exports, 40% of imports, and private transactions.

The Sudanese banking system was nationalized in 1970 when seven banks and their 62 branches were nationalized. The Bank of Sudan acts as the central bank with the sole right of issue of Sudanese banknotes. Under the terms of the 1984 Civil Transactions Act, payment of interest was unenforceable in the courts. In November 1984 the Bank of Sudan instructed all non-Islamic banks, including foreign-owned banks, to cease charging interest. Specialized banks include the Agriculture Bank, the Industrial Bank and the Estates Bank. In 1984 commercial bank reserves totaled S£936.7 million, demand deposits S£1.315 billion and time and saving deposits S£723.4 million.

GROWTH PROFILE Annual Growth Rates (%)	
Population 1980-2000	2.8
Birth Rate 1965-83	−2.1
Death Rate 1965-83	−27.2
Urban Population 1973-83	5.5
Labor Force 1980-2000	2.9
GNP 1973-82	6.7
GNP per capita 1973-82	3.5
GDP 1973-83	6.3
GDP per capita 1970-81	3.0
Consumer Prices 1970-81	17.3
Wholesale Prices	—
Inflation 1973-83	18.0
Agriculture 1973-83	3.5
Manufacturing 1970-81	4.1
Industry 1973-83	6.7
Services 1973-83	8.6
Mining 1970-81	−7.5
Construction 1970-81	11.2
Electricity 1970-81	3.8
Transportation 1970-81	11.0
Trade 1970-81	12.4
Public Administration & Defense 1970-81	5.2
Export Price Index 1975-81	7.2
Import Price Index 1975-81	10.5
Terms of Trade 1975-81	−2.9
Exports 1973-83	−1.5
Imports 1973-83	1.3
Public Consumption 1973-83	4.5
Private Consumption 1973-83	7.6
Gross Domestic Investment 1973-83	5.6
Energy Consumption 1973-83	−3.3
Energy Production 1973-83	9.0

AGRICULTURE

Of the total land area of 250,581,300 hectares (619,186,390 acres) about 12% or 39.2 million hectares (97 million acres) was prime agricultural land or 1.6 hectares (4 acres) per capita. Of this 5.4 million hectares (13.5 million acres) were under crops, and the balance was unused but potentially productive land. The agricultural production index was 106, the index of food production was 111, and the per capita food index 94 (based on 1974-76) in 1982. The agricultural sector employs 78% of the labor force, and Sudan ranked sixth among world nations in percentage of agricultural manpower relative to total manpower. Agriculture contributed 34% of GDP in 1983, and its growth rate during 1973-83 was 3.5%. Agricultural products account for 86% of export earnings. Value added in agriculture in 1983 was $2.318 billion.

Land is abundant, but the desert is gradually encroaching on the savanna. By the late 1980s it is estimated that half of Sudan will be covered by sand. In most regions the main limiting factor is water rather than land, and irrigation plays a significant role in agricultural development. The total area under irrigation reached 1.82 million hectares (4.5 million acres) in 1975. Sudan is now entitled to draw 20.5 billion cubic meters of water at the Aswan High Dam, opening the way for considerable expansion of irrigated agriculture. Major developments under way include the Rahad scheme, the Kenana project, the Jonglei Canal, the Sukki project and the Mangalla extension, all of which are expected to bring another 809,400 hectares (2 million acres) under irrigation. Egypt is cooperating with Sudan in constructing the 360-km (223 mi.) Jonglei Canal project, to increase the flow of water in the White Nile, to shorten the river from north to south, and to aid Southern Sudan through the reclamation of 3.7 million acres (1.49 million hectares) of potential agricultural land. However, work on the canal was halted in 1984 as the security situation in the south deteriorated.

Agriculture consists of both traditional and modern sectors. The heart of the modern sector is at the junction of the White and Blue Nile where state development programs are concentrated. The region is divided into large plots managed by producers' cooperatives. The largest, the Gezirah scheme, is regarded as one of the world's greatest agricultural undertakings. It produces 60% of the country's cotton, 50% of its wheat, 12% of its durra, and 30% of its lubia, a forage bean. The traditional sector produces a greater proportion of Sudan's foodstuffs. Depending on the quantity, timing, and distribution of rainfall, the output of this sector varies widely. About 75% of the population is still occupied in the traditional sector, but, nevertheless, there are recurring labor shortages. Though notably inefficient, this sector furnishes all of the country's food supply. In fact, Sudan is self-sufficient in all its essential food crops. In 1982 there were 11,600 tractors and 1,200 harvester-threshers in use in the country. Annual consumption of fertilizers in 1982 was 75,200 tons, (down from 95,100 in 1975) or 4.4 kg (9.7 lb) per arable hectare.

The heavy dependence of the agricultural economy on the cotton crop, which is subject to annual fluctuations in price, has a retarding effect on the growth of the sector. Cotton remains the main generator of national income with an average share of 58% of exports. The cotton is of two types: the long-stapled, Skallarides and its derivatives (Sakel), and the short-staple varieties. Cotton marketing was nationalized in 1970 and vested in the Cotton Marketing Board, which controls both production and export. Until 1971, when peanuts displaced it, gum arabic was the second most important export; Sudan accounts for about 92% of the world production. Gum arabic is now handled by a company in which the state has a 30% holding. The Kenana Sugar Estate (in which Kuwait holds a 33% interest and Saudi Arabia 22.8% interest) is the biggest sugar estate in the world employing 20,000 workers and producing 300,000 tons of refined sugar a year.

The pattern of Sudan's agricultural production is changing. Historically, cotton has been the principal export and will remain an important export crop despite diversification into oilseeds and sugar. For a variety of reasons, Sudan has decided to reduce its dependence on cotton. It has restricted long staple cotton acreages while encouraging cultivation of medium staple cotton. Sudan should maintain its position as the world's second largest producer of long staple cotton. However, increases in production will be of medium and short staples, partially because harvesting can be mechanized. One of the most important development projects of recent years is the Rahad scheme. Located on the Blue Nile, and served by the Roseires Dam, Rahad is the first project in Sudan to use long-furrow irrigation on a large scale. The first 126,000 hectares (311,346 acres) were brought into cultivation in 1978 at a cost of $364 million. Finance was provided by the World Bank, the USA and Kuwait. About one-half of the irrigated area is given to medium-staple cotton, and the remainder to groundnuts and vegetables. Production is organized under a tenancy system similar to that operating in the Gezira, with management provided by the state Rahad Corporation. The second stage, now being implemented, will bring a further 210,000 hectares (518,910 acres) into production.

The growth of oilseed production has been phenomenal. The area under present cultivation has more than doubled in the last six years to about 2 million acres. Sudan has become the world's second leading exporter of peanuts behind the United States. Oilseed exports now exceed $100 million per year and should continue to grow.

Sudan's main cereal crop is sorghum (durra). It is the most important staple food in Sudan and is mainly grown in the rainlands. Sudan produces about 1.5 million tons of durra annually, which is usually sufficient for domestic consumption. Excellent yields of over 2 million tons in 1981 and 1982 have encouraged the development of durra into an increasingly important export crop.

In 1981 livestock herding provided about 10% of the GDP and 6% of exports in skins and hides. In 1982 the livestock population consisted of 19,234,000 cattle, 18,547,000 sheep, 13,174,000 goats, 8,000 pigs, 20,000 horses, 701,000 asses, 2,570,000 camels and 28,021,000 chickens.

In 1982 the country's 3.5 million acres of forest lands, which are completely government-owned, produced 37.073 million cubic meters (1.309 billion cubic ft) of roundwood.

Sudan is also rich in its aquatic resources. More than 20,000 sq km (7,700 sq mi) are fished on inland waters, and the Red Sea produced a catch of 29,710 metric tons in 1982.

PRINCIPAL CROP PRODUCTION (1982) (000 metric tons)	
Wheat	150
Corn	52
Millet	230
Sorghum	2,100
Rice	8
Sugar cane	2,529
Potatoes	26
Sweet potatoes	44
Cassava	122
Other roots & tubers	113
Onions	40
Water melons	96
Dry beans	4
Dry broad beans	22
Chick-peas	3
Other pulses	57
Oranges & tangerines	54
Lemons & limes	39
Grapefruits	59
Mangoes	71
Dates	115
Bananas	93
Groundnuts	800
Seed cotton	460
Cottonseed	300
Sesame seed	200
Castor beans	10
Cotton lint	160
Tomatoes	152
Pumpkins	61
Aubergines	80
Melons	10

Agricultural credit is provided by the Agricultural Bank of Sudan, with a paid-up capital of £S7 million.

INDUSTRY

Manufacturing and handicrafts account for 6.4% of the GDP and employ 9% of the labor force. Most of the industrial units are concentrated in the Khartoum area. Manufacturing growth, estimated at 4.1% during 1970-81, has been halting, uneven and beset with the usual problems of developing countries: dearth of manpower, capital, managerial talent and inadequate transportation. The value added in manufacturing in 1982 was $433 million, of which agro based products accounted for 41%, textiles for 36%, machinery and transport equipment for 3% and chemicals for 11%.

Until 1970 most of the industries were privately owned. State participation in industrial activity began with the establishment of the Industrial Development Corporation in 1962. After 1970 the government began establishing a dominant role in the industrial sector by nationalizing all the banks and confiscating 16 large Sudanese and foreign firms, including a British cement factory and a Canadian shoe factory. The government is the chief investor in public utilities and the main promoter of such diverse industries as sugar refining, cotton-ginning, food processing, tanning, printing and the hotel trade. Since 1971, however, the government has reversed many of its earlier economic policies. The process started with the denationalization of a number of companies, including the Bata Shoe Co. and the Belgravia Dairies. In 1980 trading monopolies were removed from most of the state marketing corporations while a number of nonessential industrial companies, including confectionery firms, were put up for sale. This policy was taken a stage further in November 1983, with the announcement that the national carrier, Sudan Airways, was to be privatized. Some of the nationalized businesses have been returned to their owners, and compensation settlements have been made with foreign firms that had been confiscated. Fiscal guarantees have been provided against future nationalization to encourage investment. Legislation was introduced in 1972 to provide generous concessions to investors including tax holidays for the first five years. A new Encouragement of Investment Act was introduced at the end of 1980, repealing the previous investment laws. Like its predecessors, it offered tax incentives, guaranteed repatriation of foreign capital and profits, facilitated land acquisition, customs exemption and favorable freight and electricity rates. It set up a Secretariat-General for Investment, which took over administration of the investment regulations from several ministries and government departments, thus simplifying procedures. The situation has been thrown into confusion, however, by the introduction of Islamic law in September 1983, and by the subsequent Civils Transaction Act, which became law in March 1984. The act, with the parallel Alms and Taxation Act, is designed to bring existing company, investment and taxation laws into line with Islamic principles. The actual implications of both acts, and which of the preceeding ones they replaced, are still unclear, however, as is how far they will, in practice, be implemented. The Civils Transaction Act appeared to make joint ventures illegal, but new ones were being formed after March 1984.

Industrial credit is provided by the Industrial Development Bank, which finances private industrial enterprises with up to two-thirds of the capital required.

ENERGY

Sudan's total energy production in 1982 was the equivalent of 63,000 metric tons of coal. Consumption was equal to 1.697 million tons of coal, or 86 kg (190 lb) per capita. Refinery capacity in 1982 was 24,000 barrels per day. The annual growth rates during 1973-83 were 9.0% for energy production and −3.3% energy consumption. Energy imports account for 57% of all merchandise imports. Apparent per capita consumption of gasoline is 13 gallons per year. Total electric power production was 1.419 billion kwh, and per capita consumption 67 kwh per year in 1984.

Petroleum has been discovered in commercial quantities in south-western Sudan, and this, with an ultimate potential capacity of 190,000 barrels per day and potential annual revenue of $136 million, provides the country's main hope of overcoming its chronic balance-of-payments difficulties. However, Sudan's hopes of becoming an oil exporter by 1986 were dashed when U.S. companies working on the oilfields suspended all operations in 1984, as attacks by rebel groups on foreign installations increased.

LABOR

The economically active population in 1981 was 8.6 million, of which 79% were employed in agriculture, 10% in industry and 12% in services. Of the total labor force, 56% were adult males, 24.7% were adult females, and 19.3% were children. The labor force includes over 400,000 Africans from neighboring countries; a number of Sudanese work in Egypt and Libya as domestics and laborers.

Sudanese labor law and practice embrace international standards. The workweek is limited to 48 hours, with a full 24-hour rest period. Sudanese labor custom grants an extra month's pay for each year's labor, as well as allowances for transportation and sometimes housing. A new salary scale introduced in August 1985 prescribed a minimum wage of about $15 per month, but particular skills are rewarded with legally mandated supplements. Annual raises must be a minimum of 5% of annual salary. The salary scale for industries sets a higher minimum wage (about $16 per month) than that for government workers. Under Sudanese law, the minimum age for workers is 16. All workers, even domestic servants, enjoy paid annual holidays prescribed by law. Sudanese labor law also prescribes health and safety standards, but in a country where the general standards are so low, conditions are poorer than those found in the industrialized West. Many young people in Sudan are self-employed or employed in family enterprises.

Among the government's first acts was to abolish legislation that prohibited strikes. The primary labor organizations are the Sudanese Workers Trade Union Federation (SWTUF), the Sudanese Federation of Employees Trade Unions (SFETU), and the Trade Unions Alliance (TUA), representing respectively blue collar, nonprofessional white collar, and professional white collar unions. The SWTUF and SFETU existed before the April 1985 change of government, but the TUA arose from an alliance of those professional unions that former President Numayri had abolished following the doctors' strike of March-April 1984. The TUA has joined with all major political parties (excluding the National Islamic Front) to form the National Alliance for the Salvation of the Country (NASC). Because the civilian Cabinet was drawn from among NASC supporters and was chosen in cooperation with them, the NASC maintains close ties to it. The SWTUF has complained periodically to the attorney general about his interference in trade union law,

arrests of trade union leaders connected with the former regime, and support for the NASC which it views as a political rather than a labor organization. The National Islamic Front, excluded from the NASC, joined with others involved in the September 1985 "security march" to form a new "security alliance" to rival the NASC. Unlike the NASC, which favors negotiations with the SPLA, the new group tends to advocate a military solution if Col. Garang rejects present government overtures for dialogue. Trade unions from all parts of Sudan are represented in these federations.

FOREIGN COMMERCE

The foreign commerce of Sudan in 1982 consisted of exports of $633.1 million and imports of $1.417 billion, producing a trade deficit of $783.9 million.

On the basis of 1975=100, the import price index in 1981 was 164, the export price index was 144, and the terms of trade (export prices divided by import prices × 100) 88.

FOREIGN TRADE INDICATORS (1982)

Annual Growth Rate, Imports:	1.3% (1973-83)
Annual Growth Rate, Exports:	−1.5% (1973-83)
Ratio of Exports to Imports:	31:69
Exports per capita:	$29
Imports per capita:	$65
Balance of Trade:	$783.9 million
Ratio of International Reserves to Imports (in months)	0.2
Exports as % of GDP:	11.3
Imports as % of GDP:	19.8
Value of Manufactured Exports:	$10 million
Commodity Concentration:	43%

Direction of Trade (%)

	Imports	Exports
EEC	43.4	31.8
U.S.	7.7	—
Industrialized Market Economies	55.8	40.3
East European Economies	1.5	7.6
High Income Oil Exporters	23.4	24.1
Developing Economies	40.8	51.6

Composition of Trade (%)

	Imports	Exports
Food	19.3	58.8
Agricultural Raw Materials	2.1	35.4
Fuels	19.1	4.4
Ores & Minerals	5.0	0.4
Manufactured Goods	54.1	0.8
of which Chemicals	11.9	—
of which Machinery	22.0	—

Of the imports, machinery constituted 28.3%, petroleum 27.1% and chemicals 8.2%. Of the exports, cotton constituted 25.1%, cereals 23.3% and animals 12.3%.

The major import sources are: Saudi Arabia 16.2%, the United Kingdom 12% and the United States 9.6%. The major export destinations are: Saudi Arabia 36.6%, Italy 7.5% and Japan 6.6%.

TRANSPORTATION & COMMUNICATIONS

Sudan depends chiefly on its rail system for transport, and with 5,516 km (3,425 mi) of line it has the longest trackage in Africa. The railways carry 40% of the freight and 60% of the passenger traffic. But only 6% of trains run on time, and in holiday seasons they are so overcrowed that people have to ride on the roofs. The main line runs from Wadi Halfa on the Egyptian border to El Obeid via Khartoum. Another line runs from Atbara and Sennar to Port Sudan. The railways are administered by the Sudan Railways Corporation. In 1982 rail traffic consisted of 1.167 billion passenger-km and 2.620 billion net-ton-km. of freight.

The total length of navigable river routes is 5,310 km (3,297 mi) of which 1,723 km (1,070 mi) are open all year round. River transport is chiefly used between Kosti and Juba and between Dongola and Kareima. The first river steamer line between the Port of Aswan High Dam and Wadi Halfa in Sudan went into operation in 1975. The river fleet comprises 380 old steamers of various types, supplemented by new vessels purchased in 1982 with West German and Dutch aid. Steamer services are controlled by the Sudan River Transport Corporation. The length of the pipeline from Port Sudan to Khartoum is 815 km (506 mi).

Port Sudan is the country's main port but there are seven other minor ports. The state-owned Sudan Shipping Line owns 22 dry cargo ships with a gross registered tonnage of 124,300. Over 3,200 vessels called at Port Sudan in 1982 and the total freight handled was 3,558,000 metric tons.

Roads are the least developed means of transport in Sudan. Of the total 20,000 km (12,420 mi) only about 2,000 km (1,242 mi) are asphalted. The rest are cleared tracks covered with gravel, which become impassable after every rain. In the south motor traffic is limited to the months between January and May. A highway between Khartoum and Port Sudan has been completed recently. As a result, between 1980 and 1983, roads carried over 60% of freight. Registered motor vehicles in 1982 included 150,000 passenger cars and 22,000 commercial vehicles. Per capita vehicle ownership was 7 cars per 1,000 inhabitants.

The national airline is Sudan Air Transport Company, which became a private enterprise in 1983. It operates 13 aircraft on internal and international services to over 20 cities. Kuwaiti interests hold a 49% share in the international service. The airline carried 478,000 passengers and flew 8.0 million km (4.9 million mi) in 1982. Khartoum is the main international airport. The country has a total of 89 airfields, 79 usable, nine with permanent surface runways, two with runways over 2,500 meters (8,000 ft).

In 1984 Sudan had 68,500 telephones, or 0.4 per 100 inhabitants.

In 1982 there were 231 permanent post and telegraph offices, 24 mobile post and telegraph offices, and 372 agencies. These handled 52,529,000 pieces of mail, and 1,453,000 telegrams. Per capita volume of mail was 2.4 pieces. There are 416 telex subscriber lines.

In 1982, 25,000 tourists visited Sudan. Of these 1,800 were from the United States, 3,900 from the United Kingdom, 1,000 from Italy, 1,900 from West Germany and 6,000 from Egypt. In the same year tourism generated revenues of $5.8 million and expenditures by nationals abroad totaled $75 million. There are 3,000 hotel beds and the average length of stay was 2.3 days.

MINING

Sudan is believed to possess a long list of useful minerals, but none have been exploited in commercial quantities. Small concessions for mining copper, iron, gold, mica and manganese are being operated. Reserves of iron are estimated at 250 million metric tons and those of copper at 10 million. Mining activity contributed only 0.2% of GDP.

DEFENSE

The defense structure is headed by the president of the republic who is also the prime minister, defense minister and commander in chief. Under the Defense Ministry are the six regional commands: northern, eastern, central, western, and southern and the Khartoum garrison.

Manpower is provided by a system of conscription established in 1971 with 18 as the age of enlistment.

The total strength of the armed forces is 56,600, or 4.3 per 1,000 inhabitants.

ARMY:
Personnel: 53,000
Organization: 6 regional commands; 4 division HQ consisting of: 1 Republican Guard brigade; 2 armored brigades; 7 infantry brigades; 1 parachute brigade; 3 artillery regiments; 1 engineer regiment; 2 AA artillery brigades; 1 SAM brigade
Equipment: 170 tanks; 183 light tanks; 109 combat vehicles; 145 armored personnel carriers; 157 guns; 82 howitzers; 30 mortars; rocket launchers; antitank guns; antitank guided weapons; 180 air defense guns; 20 SAM

NAVY:
Personnel: 600
Naval Base: Port Sudan
Units: 13 patrol craft; 3 landing craft

AIR FORCE
Personnel: 3,000
Organization & Equipment: 45 combat aircraft; 1 fighter squadron; 1 fighter ground attack squadron; 1 counterinsurgency squadron; 2 maritime reconnaissance aircraft; 1 transport squadron; 1 helicopter squadron; 12 trainers; air-to-air missiles

The opposition Southern People's Liberation Army has a reported strength of 5,000 troops.

Air Bases: Khartoum, Malakal, Juba, Atbara, Geneina, El Obeid, El Fashir, Wad Medani, Dongola, Merowe, Waw, Port Sudan

The annual military budget was $269.231 million in 1984/85 or 1.7% of the GNP, 9.0% of the national budget, $8 per capita, $5,155 per soldier and $119 per sq km of national territory.

Sudan's armed forces have only modest capabilities compared to the size of the country and the length of its international borders. The military inadequacy has been highlighted in encounters with the well-trained and equipped Ethiopian forces. The forces are deployed almost entirely along the Ethiopian border.

From 1946 through 1983 the United States provided $210.9 million in military aid to the Sudanese armed forces. British army and air training missions continued until 1966. Until 1967 the principal suppliers of military equipment were Britain, West Germany and the United States. Since 1967 Sudan has accepted substantial military hardware from the Soviet Union, Czechoslovakia, Yugoslavia and, since 1971, from the People's Republic of China. The Soviet military program was of the order of $150 million. U.S. military aid programs resumed in 1977 and ended in 1985. Arms purchases abroad during 1973-83 totaled $950 million, of which $110 million came from the United States, $270 from West Germany and $70 from China.

EDUCATION

The national literacy rate is 31% (45% for males and 18% for females). Of the population over 25, 91.2% have had no schooling, 6.1% have attended first level, 1.9% have completed first level, 0.5% have attended second level, and 0.3% have completed second level and/or have some kind of post-secondary training.

Sudan provides free, universal and compulsory education for six years from 7 to 13. Only 52% of children in the 7-12 age group attend primary school, and less than 18% of the 13-18 group attend secondary schools, for a combined enrollment ratio of 36%. The third level enrollment ratio is 2.0%. The percentage of girls was 40% in the elementary grades, 41% in the secondary grades, and 28% in the intermediate grades. Nearly 82% of schools are in the public sector. Private schools account only for 2% of primary enrollment and 13% of secondary enrollment.

The academic year runs from July to mid-March or April. The medium of instruction in the primary and intermediate grades is Arabic, but English is a compulsory subject from the intermediate grades on and is the medium of instruction in secondary grades. The medium of instruction in the South is English. The school system is organized in three levels: primary (six years), general (three years), and high secondary (three years) with academic and vocational tracks. Islamic instruction is actively promoted and subsidized, while Christian instruction is banned even in the South.

The shortage of teachers is a limiting factor in the expansion of education. A major institution for training teachers was founded at Omdurman in the 60s with assistance from the United Nations Special Fund. The national teacher-pupil ratio is 1:35 in primary grades, 1:23 in secondary grades and 1:14 in post-secondary classes.

Control of public education is centralized in the Ministry of Education at Khartoum, with one subdivision for each province. The 1980 educational budget was £S187,005,000 of which 92.2% was current expenditure. This expenditure was 4.7% of the GNP, 9.1% of the national budget and $21 per capita.

EDUCATIONAL ENROLLMENT (1983)			
	Schools	Teachers	Students
First Level	6,176	46,437	1,524,381
Second Level	1,477	18,689	426,932
Vocational & Teachers	60	1,369	17,954
Third Level	17	1,934	26,883

In 1984 Khartoum University had 10 faculties, the Khartoum branch of the University had four faculties and the Islamic University of Omdurman had three faculties. University enrollment was 243 per 100,000 inhabitants.

In 1981, 4,643 students graduated from the two Sudanese universities. By fields of study 297 were awarded degrees in medicine, 489 in engineering, 95 in natural sciences, 409 in social sciences, 361 in law, 245 in education and 540 in agriculture.

In 1982, 10,522 Sudanese students were enrolled in institutions of higher learning abroad. Of these, 658 were in the United States, 785 in the United Kingdom, 7,117 in Egypt, 883 in Saudi Arabia, 83 in West Germany, 260 in Morocco and 122 in Yugoslavia. In the same year 247 foreign students were enrolled in Sudan.

Sudan's contribution to world scientific authorship was .0250% (U.S.=42%), and it ranks 106th among the nations of the world in this respect.

LEGAL SYSTEM

The legal system is based on the Sharia, the Commercial Code of Egypt, and Roman law.

The control of the judiciary is vested in the Higher Judiciary Council headed by the president of the republic. Civil justice is administered by the courts constituted under the 1973 Judiciary Act, namely the Supreme Court, the Court of Appeal, and the province courts consisting of courts of provinces and districts. The Supreme Court is the custodian of the constitution. Criminal justice is administered by the courts constituted under the Code of Criminal Procedure, namely major courts, minor courts, and magistrates' courts. Serious crimes are tried by the major courts, which have the right to pass death sentence. Local "Popular Courts" try lesser criminal and civil cases. Justice in personal matters for Muslims is administered by a parallel system of Islamic or Sharia courts with a court of appeal under a grand cadi, high courts, and lower cadi courts. Where there is no special enactment the law is administered on the basis of equity, justice, and good conscience.

The criminal code introduced in 1983 contains penalties based on traditional Islamic laws. Public lashing for both men and women is now a common punishment for many minor crimes. For example, those found guilty of drinking/possessing liquor, blasphemy, gambling, or illegal possession of commodities usually receive lashes (often with a fine and/or imprisonment). The maximum lashing sentence is 100 lashes. The new code made right-hand amputation the standard sentence for theft of anything valued at over $40. Aggravated theft and many other offenses carry a maximum penalty of cross-limb amputation, i.e., of the right hand and left foot. As of December 31, 1984, there had been 54 hand and 16 cross-limb amputations. In the same period there were eight public hangings. The first man hanged under the new penal code, in June 1984, was convicted of armed robbery. All of the others executed were convicted of murder. Three were sentenced to posthumous crucifixion after hanging, but the crucifixion was not carried out. No women have been sentenced to amputation or hanging. The exact proportion of non-Muslims and Muslims subjected to these punishments is not available, because neither prison records nor official announcements record the religion or ethnic background of those sentenced. Amputations and hangings continued after the state of emergency was lifted in October 1985. Under the Islam-based criminal code, persons injured by someone committing a criminal act have the option to invoke the right of retribution. (The victim would otherwise accept monetary compensation from the defendant.) For example, in one case, a woman found to have started a fight in which another woman's arm was broken was sentenced to have her arm broken as punishment. There were three reported instances of such punishment in 1984; the others involved two tooth extractions and a stabbing.

Adultery by Muslims and recurrent homosexuality are capital offenses. No capital sentences have been executed owing to the onerous standard of proof required. (For adultery, the testimony of four male eyewitnesses is required before a sentence of death can be imposed.) More circumstantial evidence of adultery or homosexuality has resulted in conviction for "shameful acts." Evidence of adultery has also sometimes resulted in conviction for "attempted adultery." Many people have been convicted of and lashed for these offenses.

Southerners have opposed the Islam-based criminal code on the grounds that it infringes upon the rights of non-Muslims. Most southerners, as non-Muslims, believe that Sudan's legal codes, based in part on traditional Islamic laws and containing Islamic punishment for certain crimes, intrinsically make non-Muslims second-class citizens. While insisting that the new laws are fair because they treat Muslims and non-Muslims equally, the government has not implemented them in the three southern regions. However, the laws have been enforced on non-Muslims, including southerners, living in the north.

Theoretically, defendants may choose their own lawyers. In the Baha al Din Idris case, however, the attorney general called on attorneys to refuse to serve as defense counsel. Persons charged with minor crimes often go without counsel; the government sometimes provides legal aid to those charged with serious crimes if they cannot afford a lawyer. Khartoum university students maintain a legal aid service. A new legal aid society, formed by practicing lawyers, has found office space but has not yet begun to function. Limited appeal rights reappeared with the establishment of a Decisive Justice Court of Appeal. Appeals had to be submitted within three days of sentencing. The Appeals Court generally limited its scope to the question of whether sentence was appropriate. The judge who originally passed sentence also sat on the Court of Appeal, and most sentences were upheld. In two instances, the Appeals Court added hand amputation to a lesser sentence. Once it lowered a death sentence to 40 lashes when the accused changed his confession.

Under the former government, the president appointed judges. Although the judicial structure remains in place, a panel of qualified persons now selects magistrates. This panel also administers preventive detention. The law still mandates use of tangible property as bail. Financial disputes require bond until settlement. Traffic injury or death cases may require bonds of up to $1,000. Bond may also be required for nonphysical charges such as defamation.

The corrections system consists of three central prisons (Khartoum North, Port Sudan, and Sawakin), 68 local prisons and 50 detention camps.

LAW ENFORCEMENT

The national police force is the Sudan Police Force under the command of the president and the administrative control of the Minister of Interior. The total strength of the force was 11,000 in 1970. Within each province the police are under the control of the commandant of police. The provincial police have both mounted and foot branches; the mounted police is mainly motorized but still retains camels, mules, and horses for special assignments. Training is provided by the Sudan Police College near Khartoum. Per capita strength of the police force is 1.5 per 1,000 working inhabitants, and Sudan's world rank is 103rd in this respect.

The most common crime was theft of animals followed by tribal fights.

In 1971 a new Office of State Security was established charged with evaluation of information gathered by various agencies relating to state security and "protection of the Socialist Revolution." The central files of this agency are maintained under the direct custody of the president of the republic.

HEALTH

Most public health and hospital services are free. Only 46% of the population have access to safe water. Health expenditures account for 1.6% of national budget, 0.9% of GNP and $2 per capita.

```
PRINCIPAL HEALTH INDICATORS (1984)
Crude Death Rate: 17.4 per 1,000
Decline in Death Rate: −27.2% (1965-83)
Infant Mortality Rate: 131 per 1,000 Live Births
Child Death Rate (Ages 1-4) per 1,000: 19
Life Expectancy at Birth: Males 46.6; Females 49.0
```

In 1982 there were 160 hospitals in the country with 17,328 beds, or 1 bed per 1,110 inhabitants. In the same year the number of physicians was 2,169, or 1 physician per 8,870 inhabitants, 207 dentists and 12,826 nursing personnel. Per 10,000 inhabitants the admissions/discharge rate was 81.

FOOD

The diet of the average Sudanese is limited to a few staple foods. Semi-starvation and short periods of famine are common. The food of the nomads and herders is derived from animal products supplemented by grain and is low in vitamins, minerals and carbohydrates. Nearly all the protein is obtained from milk and fish. The usual diet of the sedentary population is sorghum or millet, supplemented by cassava and peanuts, and is seriously deficient in proteins. Per capita food intake is 69.9 grams of protein and 2,371 calories per day in 1976, as against WHO's recommendation of 2,600 calories, 59 grams of fats and 323 grams of carbohydrates.

MEDIA & CULTURE

In 1970 the government nationalized all privately owned Sudanese newspapers and periodicals and established the General Corporation for Press, Printing, and Publishing with a monopoly over all types of publications. The two principal Arabic dailies are *El-Ayam* and *El-Sahafa*. An English-language weekly, *Nile Mirror*, is published at Juba. The periodical press consisted of 20 titles. The total newspaper circulation was 120,000 in 1982, or 5.5 per 1,000 inhabitants. The total non-daily circulation was 63,000. Newsprint consumption in 1982 was 1,600 tons or 85 kg (187 lb) per 1,000 inhabitants.

There is no need for censorship as the media are totally state-owned.

The national news agency is the Sudan National News Agency (SUNA), but a number of foreign news agencies are represented in Khartoum, including Tass, MENA, AP and Hsinhua.

Book publishing is entirely under the control of the state. The most active imprints are the El-Ayam Press Company and the Government Printing Press. The Khartoum University Press, set up in 1967, has published a few titles with the technical support of UNESCO. Sudan does not adhere to any copyright convention. In 1982, 138 books were published in the country.

The state-owned Sudan Broadcasting Service operates three medium-wave transmitters of 50 and 100 kw and five short-wave transmitters of 20, 50, and 120 kw with stations at Khartoum, Omdurman, Malakal, Kassala and Nyala. Total broadcasting time is 149 ½ hours weekly, of which 124 hours are in Arabic. In 1982 there were an estimated 1,450,000 radio sets in the country or 75 per 1,000 inhabitants. Of the total 6,787 annual radio broadcasting hours, 30 hours are devoted to information, 945 hours to culture, 24 hours to religion, 4 hours to commercials and 4,239 hours to entertainment.

An earth satellite station operated on 36 channels at Umm Haraz has much improved Sudan's telecommunication links. A nationwide satellite network is being established with 14 earth stations in the provinces. A microwave network of television transmission covered 90% of inhabited areas in 1983. There are regional stations at Gezira (Central Region) and Atbara (Northern Region).

The first television station in the Sudan was established in 1963. Sudan Television has one transmitter at Omdurman serving Khartoum, Omdurman, and Khartoum North with a new microwave link to Wad Medani. New stations are planned at Atbara and Port Sudan. Total weekly program time is 45 hours, and over 60% of the programs are produced locally; imported shows are subtitled in Arabic. Commercials are accepted on both radio and television. There were 108,000 television sets in 1982, or 6 per 1,000 inhabitants. Of the total 2,374 annual television broadcasting hours 442 hours are devoted to information, 154 hours to culture, 385 hours to religion, 16 hours to commercials and 1,130 hours to entertainment.

Motion picture theaters were originally included in the government's nationalization plans, but they were left out during actual implementation. Sudan does not produce any feature films. In 1979, 189 films were imported from abroad, of which 96 were from the United States. In 1981 there were 56 cinemas in the country with 107,800 seats, or 5.7 seats per 1,000 inhabitants. The annual attendance was 2.8 million, or 0.2 per inhabitant.

In 1970 there were 10 major library facilities in the country, the largest of which was the University of Khartoum Library with 90,000 volumes. Per capita there are six volumes and four registered borrowers per 1,000 inhabitants.

There are five museums reporting an annual attendance of over 157,000. There are 17 nature preservation sites.

SOCIAL WELFARE

No comprehensive national social security system exists in Sudan. Old-age pensions, workers' compensation and other welfare programs are limited to government workers. Christian welfare work ceased when the missionaries were expelled in 1964. Muslim awqaf or charitable institutions provide charity on a very limited scale.

GLOSSARY

cadi: Muslim judge administering the Sharia or religious laws of Islam.

feddan (pl. feddan): unit of area equal to 0.42 hectare (1.038 acres).

ferik: commander in chief of the Sudanese Army.

hariq: a slash-and- burn type of cultivation practiced in the Sudan.
A thick, coarse mat of grass is allowed to grow for two to four years and then burned to enrich the soil.

khalwa: a small Islamic school where the Koran is taught. In Sudan the term is used to designate village schools.

omadiya: a tribe or large ethnic group among nomads, headed by an omda or chief.

qoz: a belt of sandy soil.

semn: clarified butter.

CHRONOLOGY (from 1956)

1956— Sudan becomes an independent republic on New Year's Day with Ismail al Azhari as first premier; interim constitution is promulgated.... Sudan joins U.N.... University of Khartoum is founded.... Abdullah Khalil replaces Azhari as premier.

1958— Ummah Party wins majority in first national elections; Khalil is elected premier; Gen. Ibrahim Abboud seizes power in military coup; Abboud is sworn in as premier.

1959— Abboud assumes supreme power.

1962— All Christian missionaries are expelled from the country.

1963— Television is introduced.

1964— Abboud yields power in the wake of mass riots in Khartoum; El Khatib el-Khalifa is named premier; Abboud leaves country.

1965— National elections are held for the Constituent Assembly; Ummah Party wins largest number of seats; Muhammad Ahmed Mahgoub is elected premier.

1966— Mahgoub loses vote of confidence in Assembly; Sadik al Mahdi becomes new premier.

1967— Mahgoub is premier again as party loyalties shift in Assembly.... Relations with the United States are suspended following Arab-Israeli War.

1968— Parliament is dissolved; new elections are held; Mahgoub returns as premier.... Gen. Ja'far

Muhammad Numayri leads army back into power in coup d'etat; Babikir Awadullah becomes premier.

1969— All political parties are outlawed.

1970— Rebellion by the Ansar, a religious sect, is put down and their leader, the Mahdi, is killed.... Banks, press, foreign commercial firms and domestic industries are nationalized.... Communist ministers are dismissed.

1971— Abortive Communist coup displaces Numayri for a few days; Numayri wins back power in counter coup; Communist Party is outlawed and conspirators in the coup attempt are excuted.... The Sudan Socialist Union is founded as the country's sole political party.... Numayri is elected president in referendum.... Labor unions are nationalized.

1972— Addis Ababa accord ends 17-year-old civil war in the southern region; southern region is granted autonomy.... Sudan resumes diplomatic relations with the United States.

1973— U.S. Ambassador Cleo A. Noel and his deputy Curtis G. Moore are assassinated by Black September group of Palestinian terrorists.... New constitution is promulgated.

1974— United States recalls ambassador following release of the assassins of Noel and Moore.

1975— Abortive coup is led by Hassan Hussein Usman; Numayri accuses Libya of masterminding plots against regime.

1977— Numayri grants general amnesty to political prisoners; Sadik al-Mahdi, former prime minister, returns to Khartoum from exile in London.

1978— In first parliamentary elections since Numayri's rise to power in 1969, opposition parties win almost half the seats.... The Sudanese pound is devalued to ease massive debt arrears.

1979— In the wake of student riots Numayri dismisses his vice president, Abdel Kassim Mohammed Ibrahim and replaces him with defense minister Abel Magid Hamid Khali.

1980— Sudan protests Egyptian-Israeli exchange of ambassadors.

1981— The National People's Assembly is dissolved.... The High Executive Council for Southern Sudan is dissolved.

1982— New elections are held for the Southern Region People's Assembly.... Charter of Integration with Egypt is signed.

1983— Numayri is reelected for the third term... Southern province is redivided into three smaller regions... The Islamic Sharia is introduced as the basis of the nation's legal system.... The Nile Valley Parliament, the joint Egyptian-Sudanese legislative organ, meets.

1984— Numayri declares indefinite state of emergency... Special emergency "decisive justice" courts are set up.

1985— Mahmoud Mohamed Taha, leader of the outlawed Republican Brothers, is executed amidst popular indignation.... The Council of Ministers is replaced with a 64-member Presidential Council. . . . National People's Assembly rejects Numayri's proposal to make Sudan an Islamic state. . . . State of emergency is lifted. . . . Southern People's Liberation Front emerges as dominant power in the south and conducts armed insurrection against the Khartoum government. . . . Public riots break out in northern cities against rise in food prices. . . . Numayri is deposed in bloodless coup by junta headed by Gen. Abdel Rahman Suwar el-Dahab who sets up a Transitional Military Council (TMC). . . . TMC names a civilian cabinet headed by prime minister El Gizouli Dafalla.

1986— In general elections held under TMC auspices, the Umma Party and the Democratic Unionist Party gain majority of seats in the Assembly. TMC hands over power to a civilian government headed by Umma Party's Sadiq al-Mahdi.

BIBLIOGRAPHY (from 1970)

Abdel Hai, Mohamed, *Cultural Policy in the Sudan* (Paris, 1982).

Albino, Oliver, *Sudan: A Southern Viewpoint* (New York, 1970).

Barnett, Tony, *The Gezira Scheme: An Illusion of Development* (Totowa N.J. 1977).

Bechtold, Peter K., *Politics in the Sudan: Parliamentary and Military Rule in an Emerging African Nation* (New York, 1976).

Beshir, M.O., *The Southern Sudan: From Conflict to Peace* (New York, 1975).

———, *Revolution and Nationalism in the Sudan* (New York, 1974).

Collins, Robert, *The South Sudan in Historical Perspective* (New Brunswick, N.J., 1976).

———, *Land Beyond the Rivers: The Southern Sudan, 1898-1918* (New Haven, Conn., 1971).

———, *Shadows in the Grass: Britain in the Southern Sudan* (New Haven, Conn., 1981).

———, and Francis Deng, *The British in the Sudan, 1898-1956* (Stanford, Calif., 1985).

Daly, M.W., *Sudan* [World Bibliographical Series] (Santa Barbara, Calif., 1983).

———, *Modernization in the Sudan* (New York, 1985).

Deng, Francis M., *Dinka of the Sudan* (New York, 1972).

Eprile, Cecil, *War and Peace in the Sudan, 1955-1972.* (London, 1974).

Land and Water Resources Survey in the Jebel Marra Area of the Sudan (New York, 1971).

Lees, Francis and Hugh C. Brooks, *The Economic & Political Development of Sudan* (Boulder, Co., 1978).

Mahmoud, Fatima B., *The Sudanese Bourgeoisie: Vanguard of Development?* (London, 1984).

Malwal, Bona, *Sudan: A Second Challenge to Nationhood* (New York, 1985).

———, *People and Power in Sudan: The Struggle for National Stability* (London, 1981).

Morrison, Godfrey, *The Southern Sudan & Eritrea: Aspects of Wider African Problems* (London, 1973).

Nachtigal, Gustav, *Sahara & Sudan* (Berkeley, Calif., 1971).

O'Fahey, R.S., *State & Society in Dar Fur* (New York, 1980).

Sanderson, Lillian P. and Neville Sanderson, *Education, Religion and Politics in Southern Sudan* (London, 1981).

University Press of Africa, *Sudan Today* (New York, 1971).

Voll, John, *Historical Dictionary of the Sudan* (Metuchen, NJ., 1978).

———, and Sarah P. Voll, *Sudan* (Boulder, Colo., 1985).

Wai, Dunstan M., *The Southern Sudan and the Problem of National Integration* (London, 1973).

———, *The African-Arab Conflict in the Sudan* (New York, 1981).

Warburg, Gabriel, *Islam, Nationalism, & Communism in a Traditional Society: The Case of Sudan* (Totowa N.J., 1978).

Whiteman, A.J., *Geology of the Sudan Republic* (New York, 1971).

Woodward, Peter, *Condominium & Sudanese Nationalism* (New York, 1980).

Worrall, Nick, *Sudan* (London, 1984).

OFFICIAL PUBLICATIONS

Auditor General, *Southern Region Accounts* (annual, unpublished).

Finance & National Economy Ministry, *Estimates of Revenue and Expenditure* (annual).

———, *Liquidity Position Reviews* (monthly and quarterly, unpublished).

———, *Public Accounts and Accounts of the Funds* (monthly and annual, unpublished).

National Planning Commission, *Economic Survey,* (annual).

———, *Statistical Yearbook* (annual).

Sudan Bank, *Annual report.*

———, *Economic and Financial Bulletin* (quarterly).

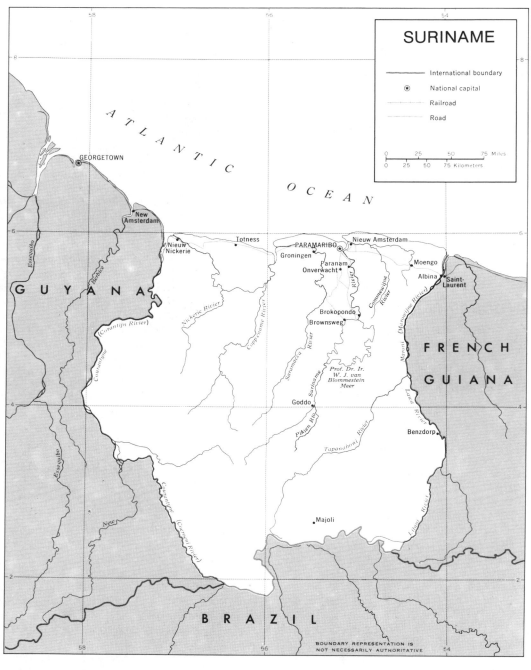

SURINAME

International boundary
National capital
Railroad
Road

0   25   50   75 Miles
0 25 50 75 Kilometers

ATLANTIC

OCEAN

GEORGETOWN

New
Amsterdam

GUYANA

Totness

Nieuw
Nickerie

Essequibo

Berbice

(Corantijn Rivier)

Corantijne

Nickerie Rivier

Coppename Rivier

PARAMARIBO

Groningen

Paranam
Onverwacht

Suriname Rivier

Saramacca Rivier

Commewijne Rivier

Nieuw Amsterdam

Moengo

Albina
Saint-
Laurent

FRENCH

GUIANA

Brokopondo

Brownsweg

Prof. Dr. Ir.
W. J. van
Blommestein
Meer

Goddo

Pikien Rio

Tapanahoni Rivier

Maroni (Marowijne Rivier)

Lawa Rivier

Benzdorp

Essequibo

New

Courantyne (Cotoroni Rivier)

Litani Rivier

Majoli

BRAZIL

BOUNDARY REPRESENTATION IS
NOT NECESSARILY AUTHORITATIVE

JUSTITIA   PIETAS   FIDES

SURINAME

BASIC FACT SHEET

OFFICIAL NAME: Republic of Suriname (Republiek Suriname); Formerly, Dutch Guiana
Note: In 1978 the name of the country was changed from Surinam to Suriname

ABBREVIATION: SR

CAPITAL: Paramaribo

CHIEF OF STATE: Lt. Col. Desire Delano Bouterse (from 1980)

PRESIDENT: Lachmipersad Frederick Ramdat Misier (from 1982)

HEAD OF GOVERNMENT: Prime Minister Willem Alfred Udenhout (from 1984)

NATURE OF GOVERNMENT: Military Dictatorship

POPULATION: 377,000 (1985)

AREA: 163,265 sq km (63,037 sq mi)

ETHNIC MAJORITY: East Indian and Creole

LANGUAGES: Dutch, English, Hindi, Javanese and Sranan Tongo (Taki-Taki); a government announcement has called for adoption of Spanish as the official language.

RELIGIONS: Christianity, Hinduism and Islam

UNIT OF CURRENCY: Suriname guilder (81=SG1.785, August 1985)

NATIONAL FLAG: Five horizontal stripes, green, white, red, white, and green, in that order with the middle red stripe being of double width; in the center of the middle red stripe there is a five-pointed yellow star.

NATIONAL EMBLEM: Two Indian warriors flanking a circular shield divided vertically into two halves. In one half appears a sailing ship on an ocean and in the other a palm tree. In a diamond in the center of the shield is displayed a five-pointed star. The shield as well as the two Indians stand on a scroll proclaiming the national motto: "Justitia, Pietas, Fides."

NATIONAL ANTHEM: "God be with our Surinam"

NATIONAL HOLIDAYS: November 25 (National Day, Independence Day); January 1 (New Year's Day); May 1 (Labor Day); July 1 (Emanicipation Day); Also, Christian, Hindu and Islamic festivals.

NATIONAL CALENDAR: Gregorian

PHYSICAL QUALITY OF LIFE INDEX: 78 (down from 85 in 1976) (On an ascending scale with 100 as the maximum. U.S. 95)

DATE OF INDEPENDENCE: November 25, 1975

DATE OF CONSTITUTION: November 20, 1975 (currently suspended)

WEIGHTS & MEASURES: The metric system is in force

LOCATION & AREA

Suriname is located on the NE coast of South America. With a total land area of 163,265 sq km (63,037 sq mi), it is the smallest independent nation on the continent. It extends 662 km (411 mi) NE to SW and 487 km (303 mi) SE to NW. The Atlantic coastline stretches 364 km (226 mi).

Suriname shares its total international land border of 1,786 km (1,109 mi) with three countries: French Guiana (467 km, 290 mi); Brazil (593 km, 368 mi); and Guyana (726 km, 451 mi). Nearly 17,000 sq km (6,564 sq mi) of national territory is disputed; Guyana claims 15,540 sq km (6,000 sq mi) of a tract reputed to be rich in bauxite and France claims 1,460 sq km (564 sq mi) of a tract believed to contain deposits of gold. An effort has been made to resolve these disputes by the formation of a National Council of Borders, but the results of its deliberations are not known.

The capital is Paramaribo with a 1980 population of 67,718. The next largest urban center is Nieuw Nickerie (6,078).

The land is divided into four distinct natural regions: a coastal belt, an intermediate plain, a region of high mountains and a high savanna in the southwest. The coastal plain, beyond which the early settlers seldom penetrated, covers about 16% of the national territory. It is approximately 15 km (10 mi) wide on the eastern border widening to about 80 km (50 mi) in the west. Most of the region is at sea level and diking is necessary to utilize the land. The intermediate plain runs to the edge of the vast rain forest and is about 50 km to 65 km (30 mi to 40 mi) wide. The mountainous rain forest region, rising gradually to an elevation of 1,256 meters (4,120 ft) in the Wilhelmina Mountains, makes up about 75% of the national territory but has been only partially explored. The central chain of the Van Asch Van Wijk range runs south to the Tumac-Humac mountains on the Brazilian border with the

Wilhelmina and Kayser ranges on the west and the Orange mountains on the east.

Numerous rivers dissect the land, all interconnected by a remarkable system of channels. The principal rivers are the Corantyne, the Nickerie, the Coppename, the Saramacca, the Surinam, the Commewijne and the Marowijne. The largest lake is the Prof. Dr. Ir. W. J. van Blommestein Meer lake.

WEATHER

Suriname has a tropical climate characterized by high rainfall and equable temperatures, with a narrow seasonal range moderated by the NE trade winds on the coast and the high altitudes in the interior. There are four seasons, but none of them is completely wet or dry. The main dry seasons are August to November and February to April, and the main wet seasons are April to August and November to February.

The daytime temperature range is between 23°C (73°F) and 31°C (88°F) with an annual mean of 27°C (81°F). The diurnal variation is slight, about 4°C (8°F).

Rainfall is heaviest between April and August and between November and Febuary. The rainfall varies from east to west with an annual average of 220 cm (86.6 in.) in Paramaribo, 197 cm (77.6 in.) in Nickerie, 223 cm (87.8 in.) in Commewijne, 216 cm (85 in.) in Saramacca, 222 cm (87 in.) in the Surinam River region and 164 cm (64.6 in.) in Coronie.

Suriname lies outside the Caribbean hurricane zone and does not experience destructive wind systems.

POPULATION

The population of Suriname was estimated in 1985 at 377,000 on the basis of the last official census held in 1980 when the population was 354,860. The population is expected to reach 500,000 by 2000 and 600,000 by 2020.

The annual growth rate is estimated at 0.06% on the basis of an annual birth rate of 29.5 per 1,000.

Traditionally the population has been concentrated on the coastal belt with only the aboriginal Amerindians and the bush Negroes inhabiting the interior regions "beyond the falls." The overall density of population is 2 per sq km (5.2 per sq mi). Only 3% of the national territory is settled.

Paramaribo, the capital, accounts for one-fourth of the national population and another one-fourth lives in its vicinity. There are no other urban centers with over 10,000 inhabitants. Overall some 45% of the population is urbanized.

Until independence migration to the Netherlands outstripped natural population increase. The number of Surinamers living in the Netherlands is variously estimated from 90,000 to 120,000, most of them skilled laborers and professionals.

Suriname has no official family planning programs or policies.

DEMOGRAPHIC INDICATORS (1984)	
Population, total (in 1,000)	377.0
Population ages (% of total)	
0-14	42.6
15-64	53.0
65+	4.5
Youth 15-24 (000)	98
Women ages 15-49 (000)	82
Dependency ratios	88.8
Child-woman ratios	635
Sex ratios (per 100 females)	97.5
Median ages (years)	17.4
Marriage Rate (per 1,000)	6.7
Divorce Rate (per 1,000)	1.1
Average size of Household	3.9
Proportion of urban (%)	45.59
Population density (per sq. km.)	2
per hectare of arable land	1.87
Rates of growth (%)	0.06
urban %	0.4
rural %	−0.2
Natural increase rates (per 1,000)	23.3
Crude birth rates (per 1,000)	29.5
Crude death rates (per 1,000)	6.1
Gross reproduction rates	2.0
Net reproduction rates	1.91
Total fertility rates	4.10
General fertility rates (per 1,000)	131
Life expectancy, males (years)	67.0
Life expectancy, females (years)	71.9
Life expectancy, total (years)	69.4
Population Doubling Time in Years at Current Rate	34

ETHNIC COMPOSITION

Suriname has one of the most varied ethnic configurations in the Western Hemisphere with at least eight groups (including autochthonous Amerindians) represented in the population.

ETHNIC GROUPS OF SURINAME	
Group	Percentage
Creoles	30.8
East Indians	36.95
Indonesian	15.3
Bush Negroes	10.25
Amerindians	2.65
Europeans	1.05
Chinese	1.65
Others	1.35

Creoles are persons of European and African or of other mixed descent, while East Indians and Indonesians are descendants of indentured estate laborers. All bush Negroes are of unmixed African descent. The shrinking Amerindian community includes the Arawak, Carib and Warrau tribes along the river banks and in the coastal plains and the Trios, Akurios and Wyanas along the upper reaches of the rivers. The East Indians, with their pheonomenal fertility rates, have been increasing their proportion in the population and have replaced the Creoles as the largest group.

Despite this ethnic crazy quilt, interethnic relations are fairly harmonious. Although East Indians have the numerical advantage they constitute a minority in the political sense. Their rights are protected in the constitution, which also provides for equal representation in the army for all ethnic groups.

LANGUAGES

The official language is Dutch, although it is to be replaced gradually by Spanish in order to facilitate closer contacts with other Latin American countries. The lingua franca is a pidgin English known as Sranang Tongo, or Taki-Taki. English is widely spoken by the educated elite. The East Indian, Indonesian and Chinese groups have retained their own vernaculars.

RELIGIONS

Religious affiliations reflect the ethnic diversity. Creoles are either Roman Catholic or Protestant; East Indians are either Hindus or Muslims; and Indonesians are Muslim. The majority of the bush Negroes follow traditional religions.

Both the Roman Catholic and Moravian Churches have bishoprics in Paramaribo.

COLONIAL EXPERIENCE

The first effective European settlements were made in Suriname between 1651 and 1657, when some 500 plantations had been established under the auspices of Francis, Lord Willoughby of Parham who was the governor of Barbados. Charles II granted land in the country in 1662 to Lord Willoughby and Lawrence Hyde. The country was ceded to the United Netherlands in 1667, and 15 years later the States of Zeeland sold the colony to the West Indies Company. Nearly a century later, in 1779, the English took back the country and kept it until 1802 when it was returned under the Peace of Amiens to the Batavian Republic. The English took it back again in 1804 and kept it for 12 years before restoring it to the Kingdom of Holland under the Treaty of Amiens in 1816. As a Dutch territory, the country advanced in status from a group of unorganized settlements to a colony and, finally in 1954, to the status of an equal partner in the Kingdom of the Netherlands. After full independence in 1975, historic ties with the Netherlands have been maintained and even strengthened.

CONSTITUTION & GOVERNMENT

Suriname has been governed by the military since the 1980 coup which overthrew its elected government and suspended the constitution. Since the coup, political power has been exercised or delegated by Leader of the Revolution and Commander of the Armed Forces, Lt. Col. Desire D. Bouterse and by other members of the military authority. In 1985, Suriname continued to operate under an official state of emergency.

In January 1985, a new Cabinet consisting of nominees of the military, labor and business was installed under Prime Minister Wim Udenhout and given a mandate by the military to govern until March 31, 1987, the end of the announced transitional period to "democracy." The military, organized labor and organized business also nominated members to a new National Assembly whose main tasks include the writing of a constitution, approving a budget, and legislating. In August, the Assembly approved a decree formalizing the de facto role of the military in the government by naming Commander Bouterse as Head of Government and by identifying the five-member Military Authority as a component of the government. However, the military has said that, when the constitution is completed and has received popular approval, it will hand over governing power to new constitutional authorities.

Until 1980, the legal basis of government was the constitution of 1975, which provided for a parliamentary form of government. The presidency was a largely ceremonial office and the head of government was the prime minister who was constitutionally responsible to the Staten, or the legislature. Both the president and the vice president were elected by parliament. The prime minister was the head of the majority party in the Staten, and he presided over the cabinet whose members were appointed by ordinance. The only other constitutional bodies were the Constitutional Court and the Advisory Council. The latter was a body consisting of between five and nine members whose opinions were sought on matters of national importance.

Just prior to the March 1980 election, a long-festering problem over unionization in the military led to a coup by army NCO's in February 1980. What had started as a labor dispute soon became a political revolt and government ministers were dismissed and in some cases arrested as the army took control. While the president remained in office the army suspended political activity and replaced the elected government with an appointed interim civilian government.

In August a new crisis occurred when the president resigned and a plot by leftist NCO's was uncovered. The army suspended the constitution and parliament and declared a state of emergency.

Suffrage is universal over 21. Elections are held every four years. The last elections were held in 1977.

Suriname emerged as an independent nation with well defined democratic traditions and a moderate foreign policy. The army coup of 1980, however, has jolted the stability of the country and may permanently alter the democratic basis of the government.

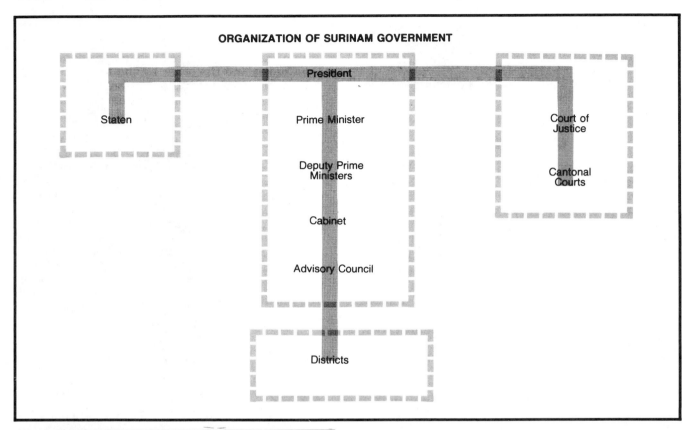

ORGANIZATION OF SURINAM GOVERNMENT

President

Staten

Prime Minister

Court of Justice

Deputy Prime Ministers

Cantonal Courts

Cabinet

Advisory Council

Districts

CABINET LIST (1985)

Chief of State . . . . *Lt. Col.* Desire Delano Bouterse
Acting President . . .Lachmipersad Frederick Ramdat-Misier
Prime Minister . . . . .Willem Alfred Udenhout
Minister of Agriculture,
  Animal Husbandry,
  Fisheries & Forestry . . . . Radjkoemar Randjietsing
Minister of Army & Police . . . . .Wilfred Paul Maynard
Minister of Education, Science
  & Culture . . . . Allan Li Foe Sjoe
Minister of Finance & Planning . . . . Norman Kleine
Minister of Foreign Affairs . . . . . Erik Leopold Tjon Kie Sim
Minister of General Affairs . . . . . .Willem Alfred Udenhout
Minister of Internal Administration . . . . Jules Wijdenbosch
Minister of Justice . . . . Soebhas Punwasi
Minister of Labor . . . . .Edmund Dankerlui
Minister of Natural Resources
  & Energy . . . . .Kenneth Renne Koole
Minister of Public Health . . . . *Dr.* Robert E. Van Trikt
Minister of Public Works,
  Telecommunications
  & Construction . . . . Cyrill Bisoedad Ramkisoor
Minister of Social Affairs . . . . Reuben Setrowidjojo
Minister of Transport,
  Trade & Industry . . . . Imro Etienne Fong Poen

FREEDOM & HUMAN RIGHTS

In terms of civil and political rights, Suriname is classified as a not-free country with a rating of 7 in civil and 5 in political rights (on a descending scale in which 1 is the highest and 7 the lowest in rights).

Government officials in Suriname maintain that the country is still being administered in accordance with the civil and human rights guarantees of the former (pre-1980) constitution. However, those guarantees have no longer any legal force and abuses have been reported, particularly during the period immediately following the coup. Persons arrested on criminal charges were severely beaten or held naked for several days exposed to insects in unscreened cells. Although the civil police operate under the same legal restraints as before the coup, the military police enter and search homes at will. Due process is not abandoned but has been abbreviated where political crimes are involved.

Freedoms of speech, press and assembly have suffered most since the coup. Since then, the assembly of more than three persons without permission from the military police is forbidden. The press has received sharp reprimands from the military leaders. While there is no formal censorship, formal guidelines have been issued on certain subjects and the army commander in chief. Bouterse, has advised it to say nothing that "harms the revolution." A five-man communications policy board has been set up to advise the government on all matters relating to the media. Trade unions, strong and active in public affairs before the coup, are considerably hampered in the exercise of their normal rights.

For the most part, Surinamers have been intimidated by the regime. The people have not forgotten the events of December 9, 1982, when 15 prominent opposition leaders (all but one of whom were civilians) were killed while in government custody. Activities by the military police, whose growing power was demonstrated by a continuous intrusion into areas formerly reserved to the civilian police during 1984, further intimidate the general population. Nonetheless, certain rights are respected by the military government. Trade union and business organizations, service clubs and fraternal orders carry out their normal functions. There is complete freedom of religion. The People's Militia, the "Anti-intervention Committies" and the February 25 Movement are organizations which have the potential to monitor what people say and to act as informers to the authorities. However, the People's Militia and the Youth Militia, once so visible on guard at various government buildings and other sites, virtually disappeared from sight. In February 1984, the government decreed a revision in Suriname's criminal code. Some of the more significant changes involved increased penalties for crimes against the state. The following examples from the revised code were reported in the press: "Attacks against the Highest Military Authority or Head of State are punishable by imprisonment for 10-20 years or life; threats or use of violence to break up government sponsored meetings can result in a prison sentence of 10-20 years; and the rendering of assistance to foreigners who engage in anti-state activities will be punishable by a 10-20 year jail sentence, with such assistance defined to include assisting in the import of items to be used against the State." Formerly such crimes stipulated a maximum penalty of five years imprisonment or a monetary fine.

CIVIL SERVICE

No current information is available on the Surinamese civil service.

LOCAL GOVERNMENT

For purpose of local government Suriname is divided into nine districts, each governed by a district commissioner. These nine districts are the urban district of Paramaribo and the districts of Suriname, Commewijne, Saramacca, Nickerie, Coronie, Marowijne, Brokopondo and Para. The administration is centralized and there are no popular representative institutions at the local level. The Paramaribo district is administered by the Ministry of Home Affairs and the rural districts by the Ministry of Local Government and Decentralization under the first deputy prime minister.

FOREIGN POLICY

The main issues in Suriname's foreign relations are the long-standing border disputes with French Guiana and Guyana and economic and political ties with the Netherlands. The Netherlands offered a $1-billion aid loan to Suriname in three stages over a period of 10 to 15 years. One of the conditions to which the loan is tied is the suspension of the right of Surinamers to emigrate to the Netherlands. This aid has been suspended in 1982 following the execution of opposition leaders.

The largely unplanned 1980 coup took a leftward course in foreign policy within the first year. The increasingly dominant Bouterse faction within the National Military Council adopted a pro-Cuban posture, leading to a flight of moderate Surinamese to the Netherlands and the withdrawal of the Dutch ambassador. The suspension of Dutch aid in 1982 was a serious blow to the economy and the regime drew closer to Libya and Cuba in the hope of getting new sources of aid. However, following reports that Brazil would invade Suriname if the Cuban influence was not curbed, Bouterse dismissed Badressein Sital, the most pro-Cuban member of the ruling junta. Later, Bouterse visited Washington, and following the Grenada action, asked Havana to withdraw its ambassador in Paramaribo. Since then, Suriname has once again become persona grata in the Western community, although relations with the Netherlands remain suspended.

Suriname and the United States are parties to 13 agreements and treaties covering aviation, consuls, economic and technical cooperation, extradition, judicial assistance, mutual security, postal matters, telecommunications, trade and commerce, and visas.

Suriname joined the U.N. in 1975; its share of the U.N. budget is 0.02%. It is a member of nine U.N. organizations and also the International Bauxite Association, the Group of 77 and the OAS.

U.S. Ambassador in Paramaribo: Robert E. Barbour
Surinamese Ambassador in Washington, D.C.: Donald A. McLeod
Surinamese Ambassador in London: (Vacant) (1980)

PARLIAMENT

The unicameral Parliament, or Staten, was a 39-member legislature elected every four years by universal suffrage. Following the 1977 elections, the ruling National Partij Komibnate (NPK) obtained a clear majority of 22 seats with the opposition United Democratic Parties holding 17 seats. The Staten was suspended in 1980.

A 31-member National Assembly was appointed in January 1985. Fourteen members were nominated by the military. Labor unions and a business association nominated the other 17 members. The principal task of the Assembly is the drafting of a new constitution. The Assembly also has certain legislative powers. During 1985, leaders of Suriname's traditional political parties began a series of discussions with the Military Authority regarding future democratic political structures, which led to a signed agreement on November 23 between the military and the political leaders to continue the discussions, the goal of which is restoration of democracy. As a result of this agreement, each of the three parties nominated two members to participate in discussions on questions of a political or administrative nature in the Supreme Council, the top policy-making body of the government.

POLITICAL PARTIES

Suriname's political parties were polarized along ethnic lines into two broad groups: one dominated by the Creoles and the other by the East Indians. The Nationale Partij Komibnatie (NPK) was a Creole-dominated alliance, of which the core party was the Suriname National Party led by Henck Arron, the former prime minister. The other members of the alliance were the Nationalist Republic Party, the Progressive Suriname People's Party and the Indonesia Farmers' Party. The leading opposition party was the East-Indian dominated Progressive Reformed Party led by Jaggernath Lachmon, which originally opposed independence because of fears of Creole dominance. The other opposition parties included the Indonesian People's Party, the Surinamese Democratic Party, the Surinamese People's Party, the Progressive National Party, the Suriname Communist Party, the Progressive Socialist Party and the Suriname Socialist Party.

All political parties were suspended following the 1980 coup. In 1985 Bouterse founded a political "movement" known as February 25 United Movement, styled "stanvaste', or "steadfast." The movement was designed to provide the junta with a mass organization when constitutional government is restored to the country. Two leftist parties also function, although without formal government sanction. They are the pro-Cuban Revolutionary People's Party and the Communist Party. In 1983 a Movement for the Liberation of Suriname was formed in exile in the Netherlands under the leadership of former prime minister Chin and former deputy prime minister, Andre Haakmat.

ECONOMY

Suriname is one of the 35 upper middle-income countries with an economy based on bauxite. It has a free-market economy in which the private sector is dominant.

The Suriname Planning Bureau (Stichting Planbureau Suriname) is responsible for drawing up annual and four-year plans in close cooperation with the departments concerned. It also receives input from the Netherlands Mission for a 10-year plan. The Bureau's plans comprise a number of sub-plans or schemes aimed at improving the infrastructure and streamlining marketing.

Until 1982 Suriname was a relatively prosperous country, on account of its bauxite exports and generous aid from the Netherlands which amounted to SG1.7 billion between 1975 and 1982. When the Dutch aid was halted in 1982, the economy went into a tail-

---

PRINCIPAL ECONOMIC INDICATORS

Gross National Product: $1.280 million (1983)
  GNP Annual Growth Rate: 4.4% (1973-82)
  Per Capita GNP: $3,520 (1983)
  Per Capita GNP Annual Growth Rate: 5.1% (1973-82)
Gross Domestic Product: SG2.293 billion (1983)
  GDP Average Annual Growth Rate: 3.9% (1970-81)
  Per Capita GDP: SG6,180 (1983)
  Per Capita GDP Average Annual Growth Rate: 4.7% (1970-81)
Income Distribution: Information not available
Consumer Price Index (1970=100):
  All Items: 287.0 (1983)
  Food: 272.3 (1983)
Money Supply: SG662 million (May 1985)
  Reserve Money: SG740 million (May 1985)
Currency in Circulation: SG305.19 million (1984)
International Reserves: $24.87 million, of which foreign exchange reserves were $23.62 million (1984)

BALANCE OF PAYMENTS (1984)
(million $)

Current Account Balance	−43.0
Merchandise Exports	355.7
Merchandise Imports	−345.8
Trade Balance	9.9
Other Goods, Services & Income	+69.1
Other Goods, Services & Income	−116.6
Other Goods, Services & Income Net	—
Private Unrequited Transfers	−7.4
Official Unrequited Transfers	2.0
Direct Investment	−39.7
Portfolio Investment	—
Other Long-term Capital	30.9
Other Short-term Capital	−2
Net Errors & Omissions	−5
Counterpart Items	−2.5
Exceptional Financing	—
Liabilities Constituting Foreign Authorities' Reserves	—
Total Change in Reserves	55.1

---

spin from which it never recovered. In 1983 it was forced to draw on its foreign reserves in order to finance an escalating budget deficit and costly capital expenditure programs. By 1984 the country's total non-gold reserves, which had stood at $207 million in 1981 had slumped to $18.7 million. An IMF loan of $300 million was withdrawn in February 1984 after the government rescinded proposed tax increases that were built into the IMF package. The decline in bauxite exports accounted for a trade deficit in 1981, and later years, as well as budget deficits, equal to 13.2% of GDP in 1983. The five-week strike by bauxite workers in 1985 caused an estimated loss of $70 million. The economic decline has been accelerated by an outward flight of capital, following the political unrest.

During 1979-81 Suriname received $233.80 per capita in foreign aid.

GROSS DOMESTIC PRODUCT BY ECONOMIC ACTIVITY (1970-81)

	%	Rate of Change %
Agriculture	10.6	4.6
Mining	22.9	-7.0
Manufacturing	6.9	10.7
Construction	4.5	21.2
Electricity, Gas & Water	2.2	6.3
Transport & Communications	4.2	11.1
Trade & Finance	20.8	10.0
Public Administration & Defense	21.3	11.9
Other Branches	6.4	3.5

FOREIGN ECONOMIC ASSISTANCE

Sources	Period	Amount (million $)
United States Loans	1946-83	1.0
United States Grants	1946-83	5.4
International Organizations	1946-83	58.5
ODA & OOF	1970-82	1.400.0
(Of which EEC)	1946-83	47.8
Netherlands	1946-76	123.4
All Sources	1979-81	91.2

BUDGET

The Surinamese fiscal year is the calendar year.

The national budget in 1983 consisted of revenues of SG468.78 million and expenditures of SG801.26 million. Of current revenues 90% was tax revenues and 10% non-tax revenues. Of the tax revenues, 23.9% came from taxes on income, profit and capital gain, 31.6% from domestic taxes on goods and services, 33.1% from taxes on international trade and transactions and 1.3% from other. Of the non-tax revenues, 8.1% came from public enterprises. Of current expenditures, 15.9% went to education, 8.6% to health, 6.9% to social security and welfare, 3.7% to housing and community services, 23.1% to economic services and 41.7% to other. Of the economic services, 1.9% went to agriculture, 5.1% to industry, 2.2% to public utilities, 6.7% to transport and communications and 7.2% to other.

In 1983 external public debt totaled $15 million.

FINANCE

The Surinamese unit of currency is the Suriname guilder (also called gulden or florin) divided into 100 cents. Coins are issued in denominations of 1, 5, 10 and 25 cents; notes are issued in denominations of 1, 2½, 5, 10, 25, 100 and 1,000 guilders.

In 1971 a central market rate of $1=SG1.785 was established, and this rate has remained in effect despite two devaluations of the U.S. dollar. The sterling exchange rate in 1984 was £1=SG2.069 /SG1= £0.2422.

The banking system is headed by the Central Bank van Suriname, which also functions as the bank of is-

sue and supervises all commercial banks and credit institutions. Other government-owned financial institutions include the Suriname People's Credit Bank, Suriname Postal Savings Bank, the Suriname Mortgage Bank, the Suriname Investment Bank, the Agency for the National Redevelopment Finance Company, the National Development Bank and the Agrarian Bank. There are three commercial banks owned in varying degrees by Dutch interests. In 1984 commercial banks had reserves of SG316.2 million and demand deposits of SG266.57 million.

AGRICULTURE

Of the total land area of 16,326,500 hectares (40,342,781 acres), 0.3% is classified as agricultural area, or 0.12 hectare (0.3 acre) per capita. Agriculture contributes 10.6% to the GDP and employs nearly 7.8% of the economically active population. Its annual growth rate during 1970-81 was 4.6%. Although the country has achieved self-sufficiency in sugar, rice, citrus fruits, coffee and bananas, it is still a net importer of food. Based on 1974-76=100, the agricultural production index and the food production index were 166 in 1982.

The bulk of the land is crown land, but there is a growing proportion of private ownership in the coastal belt. Some 52% of the farms are rented from private owners or from the government on short leases; only 17% is owned by the farmers themselves. Most of the larger landlords are absentee owners using tenants.

Of the total cultivated area, 26,574 hectares (65,664 acres) are under annual crops, 2,982 hectares (7,146 acres) under biennial crops, 6,843 hectares (16,909 acres) under perennial crops and 6,292 hectares (15,547 acres) under pasture. Smallholders predominate in the agricultural sector as shown in the table below.

FARM OWNERSHIP PATTERN

Size (in hectares)	Number of Farms	Area (in hectares)	Average Area (in hectares)
0 to 2	7,636	7,943	1.04
2.01 to 4	4,418	12,091	2.74
4.01 to 10	3,056	17,799	5.82
10.01 to 50	990	16,429	16.59
Over 50	139	51,568	371.00

A number of smallholders supplement their income by holding other jobs. By racial distribution, nearly half the farms (occupying 45% of the farmland) are cultivated by East Indians, 38% of the farms (occupying 14% of the farmland) are owned by Indonesians and the remainder is in the hands of Creoles, who show a preference for tree crops.

Because water is overabundant, irrigation is less of a problem than is flood control, particularly in coastal areas, which are just above sea level and are subject to both tides and flood waters. To overcome this problem polders have been constructed on the Dutch model. The Commission for the Application of Mechanized Techniques to Agriculture is in charge of modernization programs and reclamation. In 1982 there were 1,450 tractors and 114 harvester-threshers in use. Annual consumption of fertilizers was 6,000 tons.

Rice occupies 75% of the total area under cultivation, although it accounts for only 56% of the value of agricultural production. Nickerie in the western coastal area is the principal rice district. The Wageningen rice-growing project is believed to be the largest in the world. Over the long term, rice production, centering around the highly mechanized Stichting Machinale Landbouw rice farm in northwestern Suriname, should increase sharply as the result of an aid-financed water storage and irrigation scheme, the Corantijn Canal project, which would permit the doubling of land under rice culture. The Canal was completed in 1982. Oil palm is the second most important crop. Cultivation began in 1976, and by 1982 covered 2,800 hectares (69,188 acres). A palm oil refinery at Victoria, in the Brokopondo area, began operating in 1977, and produced 3,300 liters (6,974 pints) of edible oil in 1981, virtually satisfying local demand. There were plans to cultivate another 5,000 hectares (12,355 acres) near Moengo. Sugar, once the principal commodity, is grown only on two heavily mechanized plantations. Coffee is the third highest money-earner, 90% of which is exported to Europe. Cocoa is concentrated in the Suriname, Commewijne and Saramacca districts. Oranges and grapefruits are grown on the coastal plain.

```
┌─────────────────────────────────────────────────┐
│           PRINCIPAL CROP PRODUCTION (1982)        │
│                   (000 tons)                      │
│ Rice . . . . . . . . . . . . . . . . . . .  280   │
│ Root vegetables . . . . . . . . . . . . . .   1   │
│ Cabbages . . . . . . . . . . . . . . . . .    1   │
│ Sugar cane . . . . . . . . . . . . . . . .  140   │
│ Bananas . . . . . . . . . . . . . . . . . .  39   │
│ Oranges ('000 units) . . . . . . . . . . .    8   │
│ Grapefruits ('000 units) . . . . . . . . .    1   │
│ Coconuts ('000 units) . . . . . . . . . . .   1   │
└─────────────────────────────────────────────────┘
```

Livestock raising is a relatively minor sector, although the government has undertaken a number of stock improvement measures including the importation of Santo Gertrudis bulls, Friesian Holstein cattle and Landrace pigs. In 1982 the livestock population consisted of 51,000 beef cattle, 18,000 hogs, and 9,000 goats and 4,000 sheep.

About 85% of the country is covered by forests, but they have never been fully exploited. The forestry industry is dominated by the Dutch company Bruynzeel. The principal hardwoods are bolletrie, bruinhart, geelhart, tonka, purpuurhart and the kankan, or kapok. A modern lumbermill began operation in 1975. Roundwood removals totaled 266,000 cubic meters (939,379 cubic ft) in 1982.

Fishing is carried on in coastal waters and the numerous rivers. The chief commercial catch is shrimp, which is exported. Annual catch in 1982 totaled 6,377 tons.

Agricultural credit is provided by the People's Bank and the Agricultural Credit Bank.

INDUSTRY

Manufacturing is a relatively recent phenomenon, employing 7.4% of the labor force, and contributing 6.9% to the GDP, but its growth of 10.7% during 1970-81 was stimulated by the large scale production of bauxite. The largest industrial undertakings in the country are the bauxite plants at Paranam, Onverdacht and Moengo, the aluminum works in the Paramaribo Industrial Park, the aluminum smelter near Paranam and the woodworking factory at Bruynzeel. A large aluminum complex is being built in West Surinam as a joint venture with Reynolds Metals Company. Two projects are planned, one in the Bakhuis Mountains and the other in the area of the Coppename River. The Bakhuis factory will have an initial capacity of 200,000 tons expandable to 400,000 tons.

In order to attract foreign investors and encourage industrial development, the government has established an industrial development agency, which manages the Paramaribo Industrial Park and makes technical and economic surveys. Since 1973 the government has pursued a policy of joint or mixed capital ventures, offering as incentives public lands, concessionary rights and tax write-offs.

ENERGY

In 1982 Suriname's total production of energy was equivalent to 197,000 metric tons of coal. Consumption was equivalent to 1.219 million metric tons of coal, or 3,483 kg (7,680 lb) per capita.

Production of electric power in 1984 totaled 1.4 billion kwh, or 3,784 kwh per capita.

LABOR

The economically active population in 1982 was estimated at 83,461, of whom 7.8% are in agriculture, 5.7% in mining, 7.4% in manufacturing, 4.1% in construction, 11.6% in trade, 1.3% in public utilities, 3.0% in transport and communications, 2.1% in finance and 38.9% in services.

The unemployment rate was 18% in 1982 nationwide. The unemployment rate is also reflected in the generally depressed wage levels, benefits and working conditions. Approximately half of the work force is organized. The unions are usually able to monitor working conditions and to enforce conditions of labor acceptable to national standards. Wages generally provide for an adequate standard of living for workers. The workweek in most companies is between 39 and 45 hours long. The legal minimum age for employment of children is 14 except in the fisheries industry where it is 15. The government is concerned that worsening economic conditions are encouraging the spread of child labor, and established a commission to study the problem. The commission did not examine the extent, form or causes of child labor, but concluded that economic decline contributed to an increase in child labor. The commission noted that economic growth would cause child labor to decline. The commission recommended that the legal minimum age for employment be raised from 12 to 15, that the government begin a study of the extent, form and causes of child labor and improve surveillance and enforcement of existing laws. In areas in which unions are organized, such as in industry and retail establishments, child labor does not exist. There is little effective government supervision of labor conditions. The government has few inspectors and many conditions are not covered by regulation or law. For instance, there is no legal minimum wage in Suriname. On the other hand, the country enjoys a highly-developed labor movement with a tradition of effective bargaining over wages.

Heavy migration from Suriname to the Netherlands, where job opportunities and social benefits are better, stripped the country of much of its skilled and semiskilled labor force and of professional people. Government offices are operating with less than optimum staffs, and many business firms, including Suralco, have lost a number of skilled workers trained at their expense. It is estimated that over 120,000 people of Suriname origin now reside in the Netherlands. One of the most remarkable phenomena in Suriname in recent years has been the rise of the organized labor movement. Today, the five militant and politically conscious labor federations are a major factor in the economy.

About 33% of the labor force is unionized in four main unions: the Suriname General Trade Union Federation with 13,000 members; the predominantly Roman Catholic Progressive Trade Union; Centrale 47, which is affiliated to the ruling party; and the Association of Civil Service Organizations.

FOREIGN COMMERCE

The foreign commerce of Suriname consisted in 1984 of exports of $324.71 million and imports of $326.94 million, leaving a favorable trade balance of $2.23 million. Of the imports, raw materials and semimanufactures constituted 39%, machinery and equipment 28.7%, and petroleum 19.9%. Of the exports, alumina constituted 55.9%, bauxite 13.3%, aluminum 10.3%, shrimp 7.6%, rice 7.5%, bananas 1.4% and plywood 1.2%. The major import sources are: Caribbean countries 29.0%, the United States 28% and the Netherlands 9.0%. The major export destinations are: the United States 35.0%, the Netherlands 14.0%, Norway 13.0% and the United Kingdom 7.0%. Based on 1975=100 the export price index was 187, the import price index 199, and the terms of trade index 94, in 1981.

FOREIGN TRADE INDICATORS (1984)	
Annual Growth Rate, Imports:	—
Annual Growth Rate, Exports:	—
Ratio of Exports to Imports:	50:50
Exports per capita:	$861.0
Imports per capita:	$867.20
Balance of Trade:	$2.23 million
Ratio of International Reserves to Imports (in months)	—
Exports as % of GDP:	59.1
Imports as % of GDP:	57.0
Value of Manufactured Exports:	
Commodity Concentration:	70.8%

Direction of Trade (%)	Imports	Exports
EEC	27.9	21.1
U.S.	32.5	32.6
Industrialized Market Economies	63.6	88.8
East European Economies	—	—
High Income Oil Exporters	—	—
Developing Economies	34.3	11.0

Composition of Trade (%)	Imports	Exports
Food	15.0	18.0
Agricultural Raw Materials	1.0	18.0
Fuels	30.4	18.0
Ores & Minerals	—	76.8
Manufactured Goods	50.2	5.2
of which Chemicals	—	—
of which Machinery	21.4	—

TRANSPORTATION & COMMUNICATIONS

The Suriname Government Railroad is a 166-km (103-mi) single track line running from Paramaribo via Republiek to Zandery and from there to Brownsweg.

The inland waterways, 1,200 km (745 mi) long, are the most important means of transport. The Suriname River is navigable by oceangoing freighters. The Suriname Shipping Company operates regular service to Nieuw Nickerie, Moengo, and Albina as well as ferry service on the large rivers.

Paramaribo, located on the western bank of the Suriname River about 22 km (14 mi) upstream, is the chief port, handling almost all exports with the exception of bauxite, which is loaded at the specially constructed ports of Paranam, Rorac and Moengo. Paramaribo and six other minor ports handled 7,597,000 tons of cargo in 1982.

The road system consists of 8,800 km (1,552 mi) of roads, of which 1,000 km (621 mi) are paved. The main east-west road links the town of Albina on the eastern border with Nieuw Nickerie on the western border. The other main road runs along the banks of the Suriname and Commewijne Rivers, linking Meerzorg, Nieuw Amsterdam and Spieringshoek. In 1982 these roads were used by 26,500 passenger cars and 11,000 commercial vehicles. Per capita passenger car ownership is 75 per 1,000 inhabitants.

The national airline is SLM (Suriname Airways Ltd), which operates a fleet of four aircraft (including one DC-8) on domestic routes as well as external thrice-weekly flights to Amsterdam, the Caribbean and Guyana. Zanderij International Airport near Paramaribo can handle jet aircraft. There are 39 airfields in the country, of which 38 are usable, four have permanent-surface runways and one has a runway over 2,500 meters (8,000 ft). There is also a seaplane station.

In 1984 there were 27,500 telephones in use, or 6.3 per 100 inhabitants. There are 192 telex subscriber lines.

Tourist revenues totaled $17 million and expenditures by nationals abroad $29 million in 1981. In the same year 46,000 tourists visited Suriname. The average length of stay is 1.6 days.

MINING

Suriname ranks third (behind Australia and Jamaica) in world production of bauxite, and is the fourth largest exporter, supplying 10% of the total. Total production in 1983 was 3 million tons. The sites of the two major bauxite deposits—Moengo and Paranam—are accessible to navigable rivers, thus reducing production and transportation costs. The industry, controlled by two giants: SURALCO, a subsidiary of the U.S. company ALCOA, and Billiton, a subsidiary of the Royal Dutch Shell group, accounts for 80% of Suriname's exports, approximately 40% of government's tax revenues, and about 18% of the Gross Domestic Product. In 1974 the government became a minority partner in these companies, thus increasing state revenues by more than $20 million annually. New bauxite reserves have been discovered in the Bakhuis Mountains in the northern Nickerie area, and these are being exploited in collaboration with Reynolds Metals Company. Prospects for the sector are not encouraging. Exports of metal-grade bauxite have been halted. In March 1984 Billiton and Suralco announced plans to reorganize their mining and refining activities because of poor market prospects. Production was then running at only 60%-70% of capacity. The loss of production, due to strikes within the bauxite industry, and the low international price for aluminium further depressed the industry during 1984. Plans for the development of bauxite reserves in the Backhuis mountains have been abandoned because of the poor quality of the ore. Suriname's other mineral resources include iron ore (with an estimated 6 billion ton deposits), manganese, copper, nickel, platinum and gold.

DEFENSE

Suriname's armed forces have grown in size and importance since their takeover of the government in 1980. They are headed by the National Military Council (Nationale Militaire Radd) and the commander-in-chief is styled as the chief of state as distinguished from the civilian president.

The total strength of the armed forces is 2,020 or 5 per 1,000 inhabitants.

ARMY:
Personnel: 1,800
Organization: 1 infantry battalion; 30 armored personnel carriers; 6 mortars

NAVY:
Personnel: 160
Equipment: 9 patrol craft

AIR FORCE:
Personnel: 60
Equipment: 4 aircraft

The defense budget in 1984 was $43.305 million representing 2.2% of GNP and $68 per capita. Arms purchases abroad during 1973-83 totaled $15 million.

EDUCATION

The national literacy rate is 65% (68.4% for males and 62.9% for females). Education is free, universal and compulsory in principle, for six years between the ages of six and 12. The gross school enrollment ratios are 100% at the first level (6 to 11) and 48% at the second level (12 to 17), for a combined ratio of 78%. The third level enrollment ratio is 2.7%. Girls constitute 48% of primary school, 52% of secondary school, and 36% of post secondary enrollments.

Schooling lasts for 11 or 12 years divided into six years of primary school and six years of general academic secondary school leading to the university or five years of secondary school offering specialized programs leading to a certificate. In 1981 there were 385 schools in the educational system in addition to three technical schools and five teacher-training institutions. Private schools account for 65% of primary school enrollment and 52% of secondary school enrollments.

The school year runs from September to August. The language of instruction is Dutch. The national teacher-pupil ratio is 1:27 in primary schools, 1:16 in middle schools, and 1:15 in post-secondary classes.

In 1980 the national education expenditure was SG146,116,000 of which 72.5% was current. This amount represented 8.3% of GNP and 25.0% of the national budget. Of current expenditures 41.8% goes to teachers' salaries and 23.3% to administration.

EDUCATIONAL ENROLLMENT (1981)			
	Schools	Teachers	Students
First Level	285	2,803	75,139
Second Level	96	1,854	29,790
Vocational	4	148	1,275
Third Level	2	155	2,353

Higher education is provided by the Universiteit van Suriname with an enrollment of 2,353 students in 1981. Per capita university enrollment is 624 per 100,000 inhabitants.

No information is available on the number of Surinamers attending overseas universities.

LEGAL SYSTEM

The legal system is based on Dutch civil law. The judiciary is headed by the Court of Justice (High Court), with six judges who are nominated for life. There are three subordinate courts known as cantonal courts.

No information is available on the penal system and institutions.

LAW ENFORCEMENT

The police force is under the jurisdiction of the attorney general, and its strength is estimated at a few hundred.

HEALTH

By tropical standards the health conditions are good. Health and medical facilities are under the control of the Public Health Bureau. Tuberculosis, malaria and syphilis, once the major causes of death, have been controlled and leprosy is almost unknown. Public health expenditures represent 8.6% of the national budget and $47.30 per capita.

PRINCIPAL HEALTH INDICATORS (1984)
Crude Death Rate: 6.1 per 1,000
Life Expectancy at Birth: 67.0 (Males); 71.9 (Females)
Infant Mortality Rate: 30.4 per 1,000 Live Births

In 1980 there were 17 hospitals in the country with 2,250 beds, or one bed per 160 inhabitants. In the same year there were 214 physicians, or one physician per 1,729 inhabitants, 21 dentists and 600 nursing personnel. Of the hospitals 58.8% are state-run, 29.4% are run by private nonprofit organization and 11.8% by private for-profit agencies. Per 10,000 inhabitants there are 820 admissions/discharges. The bed occupancy rate is 41.6% and the average length of stay is 15 days.

FOOD

The staple food is rice. Beef consumption levels are low. The national drink is coffee.

The daily per capita intake of food is 2,468 calories, 58.1 grams of proteins, 57 grams of fats and 412 grams of carbohydrates.

MEDIA & CULTURE

Six daily newspapers and seven non-dailies are published in the country with circulations of 30,000 and 14,000, respectively. Per capita circulation is 84 for dailies and 51 for non-dailies. Three of the daily newspapers are published in Dutch, one in Dutch and Taki-Taki and one in Chinese. The periodical press consists of 24 titles. Annual consumption of newsprint is 1,500 tons, or 3,769 kg (8,311 lb) per 1,000 inhabitants.

The press is not free of government restrictions and a vigorous opposition press has not developed. (See Freedom & Human Rights.) In April 1985, a new, privately owned radio station was opened; there are now three privately owned radio stations and one public radio station. There is one government-owned television station. There are two private daily newspapers and one private weekly newspaper. In addition, the Catholic and Moravian churches each publish a small weekly newspaper which often carry articles critical of the government. The Lutheran and Reformed churches publish a combined monthly journal.

The national news agency is Surinaame Nieuws Agentschap (SNA). Informa, the Suriname News Service, issues news bulletins. Foreign news bureaus represented in Paramaribo include CANA.

Less than 10 books are published locally per year by some three active publishers.

The government-owned Stichting Radio Omroep Suriname operates a medium-wave transmitter and an FM transmitter at Paramaribo, which are on the air for 18 hours every day broadcasting in Dutch, Hindi, Indonesian and English. Threre are six private commercial stations, of which the largest are the Radio A.B.C., Radio Apintie and Radio Paramaribo. In 1982 there were 215,000 radio receivers in the country, or 528 per 1,000 inhabitants.

Television, introduced in 1968, is operated by Surinaamse Televisie Stichting, which operates a main transmitter at Paramaribo with relay stations at Moengo and Brokopondo broadcasting for about 30 hours per week. In 1982 there were 42,000 television sets in the country, or 103 per 1,000 inhabitants.

There is no local film production. There are 26 fixed cinemas showing imported films. Annual movie attendance is 1,700,000, or 4 per capita.

The only public library is the Suriname Cultural Center in Paramaribo with 21,000 volumes.

SOCIAL WELFARE

There are no organized public social welfare or social security programs.

GLOSSARY

Staten: national legislature of Suriname.

CHRONOLOGY (from 1975)

1975— Suriname becomes an independent republic under a new constitution; Henck Arron is named as minister president (prime minister) until elections are held.

1977— In national elections Arron's Nationale Partij Komibnatie (NPK) wins 22 out of 39 seats in Staten.

1980— Following a dispute over unionization, army NCO's stage a successful coup and depose Prime Minister Arron; President Ferrier is retained but an interim civilian cabinet is named by the military council, led by Lt. Michel van Rey; A force of 300 mercenaries that crossed into Suriname from French Guiana with the plan of overthrowing the new government is captured and its leader is executed; President Ferrier is ousted and replaced by Premier Henk R. Chin A. Sen; a state of emergency is declared; The chairman of the ruling military council, Sgt. Chas Mijnals is arrested and replaced by Sgt. Desi Bouterse; Legislature is dissolved and a state of emergency is declared.

1981— An East Indian coup led by Wilfred Hawker is foiled and Hawker is executed.

1982— President Chin is ousted and Justice L. Fred Ramdat Misier is named interim president while Desi Bouterse, leader of the military council is effective chief of state... State of siege is declared along with martial law... Henry Neyhorst is named premier.... Arrest of Cyril Daal, leader of the powerful labor union, De Moederbond, prompts general strike... Government responds by executing Daal and 14 others... Action provokes international indignation.... Netherlands breaks diplomatic relations and suspends aid and United States suspends aid; Cabinet resigns; schools are closed; borders are closed.

1983— Following the sixth coup against the Bouterse regime, two-thirds of the officer corps are dismissed... Errol Alibux is named prime minister; Bauxite workers strike paralyzes the industry.... Illegal Guyanese are expelled.... Chastened by the Grenada action, Suriname breaks relations with Cuba.

1984— Alibux cabinet is dismissed and Wm. Udenhout is named prime minister.

1985— Bouterse unveils plans to form a 25 February Movement as a political party base for his regime.

BIBLIOGRAPHY (from 1971)

Goslinga, Cornelis C., *A Short History of the Netherlands Antilles & Surinam* (Boston, 1978).

Kloos, Peter, *Maroni River Caribs of Suriname* (New York, 1971).

Price, Richard, *Maroon Societies* (New York, 1973).

———, *The Guiana Maroons* (Baltimore, Md., 1976).

Voorhoeve, Jan and Ursy M. Lichtveld, *Creole Drum* (New Haven, Conn., 1975).

Swaziland

- International boundary
- ⊙ National capital
- Railroad
- Road

0   10   20 Miles
0 10 20 Kilometers

South Africa

Mozambique

Komatipoort
Resano Garcia
Rio Incomati
Moamba

Krokodilrivier
Barberton

Havelock
Piggs Peak
Tshaneni
Namaacha
Boane

Komati
Umbuluzi
Goba

Little Usutu
Ka Dake Station
Black Umbuluzi
White Umbuluzi

Mbabane

Manzini
Siteki

Great Usutu
Bhunya

Amsterdam

Mankayene
Siphofaneni

Mkonda
Big Bend
Great Usutu
Catuane

Ndhlozane
Assegaairivier
Piet Retief
Hlatikulu

South Africa

Mkonda
Nhlangano

Pongola
Lavumisa
Golela

Paulpietersburg
Pongola
Pongola

J. G. Strijdom Dam

SIYINQABA

SWAZILAND

BASIC FACT SHEET

OFFICIAL NAME: Kingdom of Swaziland

ABBREVIATION: SQ

CAPITAL: Mbabane

HEAD OF STATE: King Mswati III (from 1986)

HEAD OF GOVERNMENT: Prime Minister Prince Bhekimpi Dlamini (from 1983)

NATURE OF GOVERNMENT: Constitutional monarchy

POPULATION: 671,000 (1985)

AREA: 17,364 sq km (6,704 sq mi)

ETHNIC MAJORITY: Swazi (properly AmaSwazi or Bantu Bakwa Ngwane)

LANGUAGES: SiSwati and English

RELIGIONS: Christianity and Animism

UNIT OF CURRENCY: Lilangeni (pl., Emalangeni) ($1=L2.176, August 1985)

NATIONAL FLAG: Five horizontal stripes—blue, yellow, crimson, yellow and blue—with shield, two spears and staff superimposed on the crimson stripe.

NATIONAL EMBLEM: A bright blue shield displaying the insignia of the Masotja Regiment: an oval, black and white inner shield with pointed ends, silver-tipped gold spears and a tasseled staff. The shield is flanked by a lion (representing the king, the Ngwenyama) and an elephant (representing the queen mother, the Ndlovukazi). The emblem is crested by a Masotja headdress made of otter skin adorned with the green tail feathers of the lisakabuli bird. The national motto, "Siyinqaba" ("We are the Fortress"), is engraved on a scroll at the base.

NATIONAL ANTHEM: "O God, Bestower of the Blessings of the Swazi"

NATIONAL HOLIDAYS: September 6 (National Day, Somhlolo or Independence Day); January 1 (New Year's Day); April 25 (National Flag Day); Second Monday in June (Commonwealth Day); Second Monday in July (Umhlanga or Reed Dance Day); July 22 (King's Birthday); Also Christmas, Boxing Day, Ascension, and variable Christian festivals such as Good Friday, Holy Saturday and Easter Monday. Incwala Day, an annual ceremony roughly translated as the Feast of the First Fruits, is held in December or January. It is the most important of the tribal festivals.

NATIONAL CALENDAR: Gregorian

PHYSICAL QUALITY OF LIFE INDEX: 55 (up from 36 in 1976) (On an ascending scale in which 100 is the maximum. U.S. 95)

DATE OF INDEPENDENCE: September 6, 1968

DATE OF CONSTITUTION: None in force

WEIGHTS & MEASURES: The metric system is in force, but some traditional units are still used such as the morgan (0.85 hectares, 2.11 acres).

LOCATION & AREA

Landlocked Swaziland is located in Southern Africa with an area of 17,364 sq km (6,704 sq mi) extending 176 sq km (109 mi) N to S and 135 km (84 mi) East to West.

Swaziland shares its international boundary of 554 km (344 mi) with two neighbors: South Africa (446 km, 277 mi) and Mozambique (108 km, 67 mi). There are no current border disputes.

The capital is Mbabane with a 1982 population of 33,000. King Mswati III, however, resides at Lozithehlezi (also called Lozitha), which therefore functions as the administrative and military capital. The other major urban centers are Manzini (14,000), Havelock Mine (4,500), Siteki (3,600), Big Bend (2,900), Mhlume (2,200), Mhlangano (1,700) and Pigg's Peak (3,000).

Swaziland is topographically part of the South African Plateau and is generally divided into four well-defined regions of nearly equal breadth. From the High Veld in the west, averaging 1,050 to 1,200 meters (3,500 ft to 3,900 ft) in elevation, there is a step-like descent eastward through the Middle Veld (450 to 600 meters, 1,475 to 1,970 ft) to the Low Veld (150 to 300 meters, 490 to 980 ft). To the east of the Low Veld is the Lebombo Range (450 to 825 meters, 1,475 to 2,700 ft), which separates the country from the Mozambique coastal plain.

Swaziland is well-watered with four large rivers flowing eastward across it into the Indian Ocean. These are the Komati and the Umbeluzi Rivers in the north, the Great Usutu River in the center and the Ngwavuma River in the south.

WEATHER

Swaziland is a subtropical country, but the climate varies sharply from region to region. The High Veld has a humid, near temperate climate with an annual average rainfall of 100 cm to 230 cm (40 in. to 90 in.), while the Middle Veld and the Lubombo Plateau are subtropical and somewhat drier with 90 cm to 115 cm (35 in. to 45 in.) and the Low Veld is tropical and semiarid with 50 cm to 90 cm (20 in. to 35 in.). Mean annual temperatures range from 15.6°C (60°F) in the High Veld to 22.2°C (72°F) in the Low Veld. There are frequent frosts during the cool season (June to August) and occasional snow on the high peaks.

POPULATION

The population of Swaziland was estimated in 1985 at 671,000 on the basis of the last official census held in 1976, when the population was 496,835. The population is expected to reach 1 million by 2000 and 1.8 million by 2020.

The annual growth rate is estimated at 3.03% on the basis of an annual birth rate of 47.5 per 1,000.

Nearly 42% of the Africans live in the Middle Veld. The overall density of population is 37 per sq km (96 per sq mi). The Swazi are overwhelmingly rural with only 26.34% living in urban areas. The annual urban growth rate is 8.8%. The age profile shows 46% in the under-14 age group, 51% between 15 and 64 and 3% over 65.

DEMOGRAPHIC INDICATORS (1984)	
Population, total (in 1,000)	671.0
Population ages (% of total)	
0-14	46.0
15-64	51.0
65+	3.0
Youth 15-24 (000)	121
Women ages 15-49 (000)	146
Dependency ratios	95.9
Child-woman ratios	825
Sex ratios (per 100 females)	95.5
Median ages (years)	17.0
Proportion of urban (%)	26.34
Population density (per sq. km.)	37
per hectare of arable land	2.65
Rates of growth (%)	3.03
Urban %	8.8
Rural %	1.3
Natural increase rates (per 1,000)	30.2
Crude birth rates (per 1,000)	47.5
Crude death rates (per 1,000)	17.2
Gross reproduction rates	3.20
Net reproduction rates	2.37
Total fertility rates	6.50
General fertility rates (per 1,000)	211
Life expectancy, males (years)	45.3
Life expectancy, females (years)	51.9
Life expectancy, total (years)	48.6
Population doubling time in years at current rate	22
Average household size	5.7

Swaziland is within the catchment area of South African manpower recruitment and an estimated 30,000 Swazi are living in South Africa. Offsetting this emigration is the steady immigration of refugees from South Africa, all of them blacks, causing political problems between the two countries.

The ability of Swazi women to deal with the problems of a developing society is hampered by both legal and cultural constraints. Traditional values are a major influence on the role of women in Swazi society. Since men are away from their homesteads much of the time, women perform most agricultural tasks and have virtually all responsibility for child rearing and domestic chores. However, they are not given authority to make necessary decisions, to make expenditures to acquire additional capital, or to try new approaches. Women are, in some cases, not legally equal to men, and a married woman is virtually a minor. She is not responsible for contracts she signs, and she cannot own real property or inherit property under normal circumstances. She must obtain her husband's permission to borrow money, to leave the country, and often to take a job. A divorced woman has no right to the custody of her children, although she may have to care for them with no support from their father. A small and growing number of women are beginning to participate in social, economic and political life outside their traditional fields of teaching, nursing and clerical work. Women have equal access to schools and constitute around half the student body in nearly all institutions.

Swaziland has no official birth control programs or policies.

ETHNIC COMPOSITION

The population is less heterogeneous than that of other countries in Sub-Saharan Africa. Of the African population, which makes up 96% of the total population, over half is Swazi while the other half belongs to the Zulu, Tonga and Shangaan tribes.

The Swazis call themselves Bantu Bakwa Ngwane (or Bantfu Ba Kwa Ngwane), or People of Ngwane. Originally the Swazis belonged to the Dlamini clan of the Nguni people who were led by the clan's founder, Dlamini, into southern Africa during the 16th Century, settling south and west of Delagao Bay in Mozambique. Two hundred years later they were led by Ngwane III across the Lubombo Mountains into what is now Swaziland. The clans of Swaziland are divided into three groups: Bemdzabuko, or the true Swazis; the Emakhandzambili, or the forerunners; and Emafikem Amuva, or the latecomers. The Bemdzabuko consist of 13 clans and claim the royal house as their own. The Emakhandzambili consist of 23 clans who predated the arrival of King Sobhuza I with his followers. The Emafik Amuva consist of 10 tribes who arrived in the country late in the 19th Century as refugees from Zulu persecutions.

Ethnic minorities include 10,695 Europeans (Afrikaaners, Britons and Portuguese), 6,010 other non-Africans, and about 5,000 Euraficans (as mulattoes are called in the country). In 1976 there were 638 U.S. citizens in the country, of whom 450 were private citizens.

LANGUAGES

The official and national language is SiSwati, a Nguni language related to Zulu, but English is a co-official language and the effective and working language of administration, commerce and education.

RELIGIONS

About 57% of the population describe themselves as Christians and 43% as animists, but there is considerable mixing of beliefs and practices. The traditional religions ascribe a special spiritual role to the king. Tribal festivals such as Umhlanga, the reed dance, and Incwala are celebrated throughout the country.

The Swaziland Conference of Christian Churches represents 24 church denominations and three Christian organizations. Both the Roman Catholic and Anglican Churches have bishoprics in the country, the former located at Manzini and the latter at Mbabane.

COLONIAL EXPERIENCE

The earliest contacts between Swaziland and a Western power took place in the 1840s, when King Mswati appealed to the British for help against the Zulus. In 1877, after the United Kingdom temporarily annexed Transvaal, the kingdom's northern, eastern and western borders were demarcated. In 1894 as a result of the Anglo-Transvaal Agreement, Swaziland came under Boer protection. But after the Boer War of 1899-1902 Swaziland returned to the British fold as a High Commission territory. The relationship between the British crown and Swaziland was defined by the order in council of 1903. The first constitutional talks on self government were held in London in 1964 and four years later, in 1968, Swaziland became an independent nation within the Commonwealth. Relations between the two countries have continued to be cordial since independence.

CONSTITUTION & GOVERNMENT

Swaziland is a constitutional monarchy without a constitution. King Sobhuza II (called Ngwenyama in Siswati), who at the time of his death in 1982 was the longest reigning constitutional monarch in the world (he ascended the throne in 1921), suspended the constitution of 1964 in 1973 and then ruled through an array of traditional institutions and councils. These include the Libandla Laka Ngwane (Council of the Ngwane, i.e. Swazi Nation), the Standing Committee of the Libandla, and a third organ known as the Liqoqo, or advisory council. The Libandla consists of all the chiefs (or the bantfanenkosi) and other notables chosen for their wisdom. When the king approves a decision of the Libandla it becomes law. The Libandla meets regularly once a year, during the winter, sitting for about a month. The Liqoqo, on the other hand, is a more informal body with no fixed

membership. It is headed by the king's chief uncle and includes a number of counsellors known as Tindvuna (singular: indvuna) who represent the king in an official capacity in any of the royal villages. The king also consults the Standing Committee of the Libandla, called Libandla Ncane (or little council), which consists of the treasurer, the secretary of the nation and representatives of the country's administrative districts. The committee meets weekly or more often if necessary. While political power is not confined to the royal family, it is concentrated there. This system is essentially a version of the traditional Swazi government as modified during the reign of King Sobhuza II. It provides for extensive consultation and depends on consensus-building. The people are encouraged to bring their views to their local chiefs in private or in meetings held to discuss various topics. The formation of opposition groups is discouraged.

Since the death of King Sobhuza the effective power was in the hands of the Liqoqo and the "Authorized Person". King Mswati III, the youngest Sobhuza's 70 sons, ascended the throne in April 1986, ending the regency of his mother Ntombi Thwala. The King's first act was to abolish The Liqoqo.

CABINET LIST (1985)

Queen Regent	Ntombi Thwala
Prime Minister	*Prince* Bhekimpi Dlamini
Minister of Agriculture & Cooperatives	Sipho Hezekiel Mamba
Minister of Commerce, Industry, Mines & Tourism	Derick Von Wissel
Minister of Defense & Youth	*Col.* Fonono Dube
Minister of Education	Dabulumjiva Nhlabatsi
Minister of Finance	Sibusiso Barnabas Dlamini
Minister of Foreign Affairs	Mhambi Moses Mnisi
Minister of Health	*Prince* Phiwokwakhe Dlamini
Minister of Interior & Immigration	King Mtetwa
Minister of Justice	David Matse
Minister of Labor & Public Service	Mhlangano Matsebula
Minister of Natural Resources, Land Utilization & Energy	*Prince* Khuzulwandle Dlamini
Minister of Works & Communication	*Chief* Sipho Shongwe

Suffrage is universal for adults. The last elections were held in 1979.

Swaziland is one of the most stable countries in Africa and faces no internal or external threats. The political underdevelopment of the population is a major factor contributing to this stability.

FREEDOM & HUMAN RIGHTS

In terms of political and civil rights, Swaziland is classified as a partly free country with a rating of 5 in political rights and 5 in civil rights (on a descending scale in which 1 is the highest and 7 the lowest in rights).

Swaziland is a constitutionless state (the 1968 constitution having been repealed in 1973) but the king's

ORGANIZATION OF SWAZI GOVERNMENT

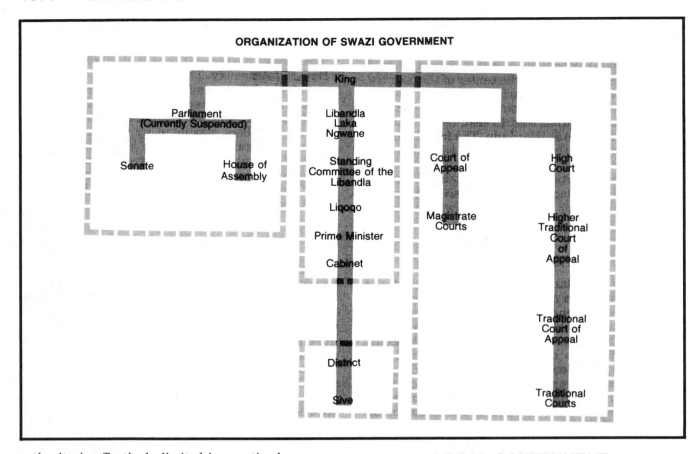

authority is effectively limited in practice by a complex system of traditional Swazi custom and rights. A further step was made toward a responsible administration with the reopening of the parliament in 1979. The judiciary is reasonably independent, and there have been no attempts by the government to systematically disregard or subvert human rights. A 1978 law permits the government to detain any citizen for a renewable period of 60 days without formal charges. Such detention is not appealable in the courts, but may be appealed directly to the king. The right to a fair public trial is provided for in law and is generally honored in practice. The courts are independent of executive or military control and there are no special courts to deal with security or political offenses. Freedom of speech is not guaranteed by law but criticism is permitted in the parliament, and in the traditional Swazi councils and to a more limited extent in the media, which exercises self-censorship to avoid direct confrontation with the government. There is no organized opposition. The concept of such an opposition runs counter to traditional Swazi ideas of monarchical rule.

CIVIL SERVICE

No current information is available on the Swazi civil service.

LOCAL GOVERNMENT

For purpose of local government Swaziland is divided into four districts. Hhohho (also Hoho and Horo) is the northernmost and smallest of these districts with its administrative headquarters in the national capital, Mbabane. Manzini district extends from the western border to the center of the country, its administrative headquarters is at the town of Manzini. Shiselweni is the southernmost district and spans the country from west to east; its administrative headquarters is at Hlatikulu. The fourth district of Lubombo is on the east with its administrative headquarters at Siteki.

Under the traditional tribal system of government, the lowest local unit is the sive headed by either a sikulu (or chief) or umtfwanenkosi (or prince).

FOREIGN POLICY

Although Swaziland is generally considered as a conservative nation on the basis of its repeated condemnation of violence against South Africa, it has vigorously opposed South Africa on a number of key issues: on Namibia, on the sale of arms to South Africa by Western countries, and the creation of Bantustans. Relations are also complicated by economic issues between the two countries, such as the unfavorable and unfair terms of the monetary agreements under which Swaziland is a member of the rand area. As an expression of its independence, Swaziland issued its own currency in 1974. Swaziland has no diplomatic relations with South Africa, but its interests are represented in Pretoria by an official without formal title. The question of South African refugees from South Africa has also remained unresolved. On several occasions South African security forces have pursued and captured refugees inside Swaziland.

Swaziland also attaches considerable importance to its image in black Africa and therefore fosters relations even with countries like Mozambique, whose socialist policies are anathema to Swaziland's conservative monarchy. The need to keep open its export routes through Maputo makes good relations with Mozambique absolutely essential for Swaziland. Relations with Botswana have been strengthened since the two countries decided to continue operating a joint university after Lesotho's unilateral withdrawal in 1975. Trade agreements have been signed with Ghana, Nigeria, Kenya, Tanzania and Zambia.

In foreign affairs, Swaziland has moved recently to stabilize its borders. In March 1984, it was revealed that a non-aggression pact had secretly been concluded with South Africa in February 1982, and, on August 10, 1984, a security accord was concluded with Mozambique. In the wake of the latter a series of deportations and armed altercations between ANC rebels and Swazi police were reported.

Swaziland and the United States are parties to six treaties and agreements covering development assistance, economic and technical cooperation, extradition, investment guaranties, and Peace Corps.

Swaziland joined the U.N. in 1968; its share of the U.N. budget is 0.02%. It is a member of 12 U.N. organizations as well as the OAU and the Commonwealth.
U.S. Ambassador in Mbabane: Harvey F. Nelson, Jr.
U.K. High Commissioner in Mbabane: Martin Reith
Swazi Ambassador in Washington, D.C.: Peter H. Mtetwa
Swazi High Commissioner in London: George Mbikwakhe Mamba

PARLIAMENT

The former parliament consisted of a Senate and a House of Assembly. The Senate was a 12-member body, of which six members were appointed by the king and six were elected by the House of Assembly. The House of Assembly consisted of 24 elected members, six members appointed by the king and the attorney general, who had no vote. In 1972 the House of Assembly had only three opposition members, who belonged to the Ngwane National Liberatory Congress, while 21 belonged to the official Imbokodvo National Movement.

In 1979 the king allowed the parliament to reconvene after an interregnum of six years. The new parliament consists of 10 senate members and 40 members of a new House of Assembly, both elected by an 80-member electoral college drawn from tribal councils. In addition, 10 members were appointed to each house by the king.

POLITICAL PARTIES

Until 1973, when all political parties were banned by royal proclamation, there were five political parties of which the Imbokodvo ("Grindstone") National Movement was the strongest. The Imbokodvo National Movement was formed in 1964 by King Sobhuza and was dedicated to the preservation of the monarchy and Swazi traditions. There are no legal opposition parties. Illegal parties include the Swazi Liberation Movement and the Swaziland United Front, both of which are inactive.

ECONOMY

Swaziland is one of the 39 lower middle-income countries of the world with a free-market economy dominated by the private sector.

```
┌─────────────────────────────────────────────────┐
│          PRINCIPAL ECONOMIC INDICATORS          │
│ Gross National Product: $610 million (1983)     │
│   GNP Annual Growth Rate: 3.5% (1973-82)        │
│   Per Capita GNP: $890 (1983)                   │
│   Per Capita GNP Annual Growth Rate: 0.0%       │
│     (1973-82)                                    │
│ Gross Domestic Product: E650.6 million (1983)   │
│   GDP Annual Growth Rate: 6.1% (1970-81)        │
│   Per Capita GDP: E970 (1983)                   │
│   Per Capita GDP Annual Growth Rate: 2.8%       │
│     (1970-81)                                    │
│ Income Distribution: Information not available  │
│ Percentage of Population in Absolute Poverty: 46│
│ Consumer Price Index (1970=100):                │
│   All Items: 543.8 (January 1985)               │
│   Food: 580 (January 1985)                      │
│ Money Supply: E79 million (June 1985)           │
│   Reserve Money: E118.0 million (June 1985)     │
│ Currency in circulation: E16.77 million (1984)  │
│ International Reserves: $80.10 million of which  │
│   foreign Exchange Reserves are $76.16 million  │
│   (1984)                                         │
└─────────────────────────────────────────────────┘
```

Swaziland has long had a visible trade surplus, but this surplus is usually more than offset by a net deficit on invisibles despite the positive contribution of tourism. Net official transfers from South Africa under the new monetary arrangements are substantial positive items as are government capital inflows, but in recent years the overall positive balance on the current and long-term capital accounts had depended largely on private transfers such as remittances of migrant labor, which are poorly recorded and highly volatile.

The Second National Development Plan, 1973-77, had a total investment target of E42.7 million of which E11 million was to come from external sources. Swaziland's third National Development Plan, introduced in 1977 and revised in 1980, forecast average annual growth of 6.5% in the agricultural sector and 7% in the manufacturing and processing sectors. Public sector investment in construction was also set at an annual 7% growth rate by the end of 1983. Growth rates fell far short of these targets, however, and reached an average of only 2.2% annually in 1978-81, dropping still further to 1% in 1982. Government estimates forecast an annual average of 2.1% growth in

GDP over the 1984-89 period; however, this projected growth is insufficient to offset the country's estimated 3.4% annual increase in population.

```
              BALANCE OF PAYMENTS (1984)
                      (million $)
Current Account Balance ................       -11.3
Merchandise Exports ..................        271.8
Merchandise Imports ..................       -350.6
Trade Balance ........................        -78.8
Other Goods, Services & Income ..........    +101.8
Other Goods, Services & Income ..........     -95.0
Other Goods, Services & Income Net .......       —
Private Unrequited Transfers .............        1
Official Unrequited Transfers ............     60.7
Direct Investment ....................         -7
Portfolio Investment ..................         -1
Other Long-term Capital ...............       17.4
Other Short-term Capital ..............        2.2
Net Errors & Omissions ...............        13.9
Counterpart Items ...................        -31.4
Exceptional Financing
Liabilities Constituting Foreign Authorities'
    Reserves .......................          -1.7
Total Change in Reserves ..............       11.7
```

```
   GROSS DOMESTIC PRODUCT BY ECONOMIC ACTIVITY
                     (1970-81)
                                           Rate of
                            %            Change %
Agriculture                33.3              3.1
Mining                       —              -7.8
Manufacturing              26.0              4.0
Construction                 —              10.3
Electricity, Gas & Water     —               8.2
Transport & Communications   —              -7.9
Trade & Finance              —               9.4
Public Administration &
    Defense                  —               —
Other Branches             40.7              6.2
```

```
          FOREIGN ECONOMIC ASSISTANCE
Source              Period          Amount
                                  (million $)
United States       1946-83            73.2
International
   Organizations    1946-83           142.1
   (Of which World Bank) 1946-83       65.6
ODA and OOF         1970-82           280.0
All Sources         1979-81            64.1
```

During 1979-81 Swaziland received $116.50 per capita in foreign aid.

BUDGET

The Swazi fiscal year runs from April 1 through March 31. The government has followed since independence sound fiscal policies resulting in budgetary surpluses in most years and a stable tax base, two key elements of which are the sugar levy and revenues from the South African Customs Union.

```
            NATIONAL BUDGET (1983)
                (000 Emalangeni)
Revenues
Customs and Excise ...................      117,000
Income Tax .........................        40,000
Other Taxes & Duties .................       11,545
Earnings of Departments .............       17,100
TOTAL (Including Others) ..............     190,000
Expenditures
Public Debt .........................       24,892
Prime Minister's Office ..............        5,710
Police & Defense ....................       16,544
Home Affairs ........................        4,311
Education ..........................        21,062
Health .............................        9,755
Works Power Communications .........        9,177
Agriculture ........................       10,147
Judiciary ..........................        3,725
Foreign Affairs ....................        2,586
Total (Including Others) ............      118,797
1984/85 Budget: Revenues ...........      208,780
    Expenditures ....................      210,840
```

Of current revenues, 32.06% comes from taxes on net income and profit, 16.35% from individual taxes, 13.73% from corporate taxes, 0.27% from taxes on property, 2.01% from domestic taxes on goods and services, 57.18% from taxes on international trade and transactions, 0.63% from other taxes, 7.81% form non-tax revenues and 4.66% from property income. Of current expenditures, 20.67% goes to general public services, 6.09% to defense, 21.18% to education, 5.41% to health, 10.52% to housing and community services, 25.27% to economic services, 10.67% to agriculture, 5.15% to roads, 7.49% to other transportation and communications and 5.65% to other purposes.

In 1983, total outstanding disbursed external debt was $182.7 million of which $174.6 million was owed to official creditors and $8.2 million to private creditors. Total debt service was $18.7 million of which $10.3 million was repayment of principal.

FINANCE

The Swazi unit of currency is the lilangeni (plural: emalangeni) divided into 100 cents. Coins are issued in denominations of 1, 2, 5, 10, 20 and 50 cents and 1 lilangeni; notes are issued in denominations of 1 lilangeni and 2, 5, 10 and 20 emalangeni.

The lilangeni was introduced in 1974 at par with the rand, which circulates freely inside the country as legal tender. In 1985 the dollar and sterling exchange rates were the same as the exchange rates of the rand: $1= L2.176 and £2.2985.

The emalangeni circulate interchangeably (and at par) with the rand, and the currency issue is wholly backed by rand, held in a special interest-earning account with the South African Reserve Bank. Under a bilateral agreement between the governments of Swaziland and South Africa, Swaziland receives interest payments on the estimated rand currency in circulation in the country.

Although a member of the South African Monetary Union, Swaziland's fiscal policies are determined by the Central Bank of Swaziland. Two commercial banks, Barclays Bank and Standard Bank, each owned 40% by the state, operate in the country. Development finance is provided by the Swaziland Development and Savings Bank. In 1984 commercial bank reserves totaled E86.47 million, demand deposits E48.74 million and time and savings deposits E161.15 million.

AGRICULTURE

Of the total land area of 1,736,400 hectares (4,290,644 acres), 82% is classified as agricultural land, or 2.8 hectares (7 acres) per capita. Agriculture employs 39.9% of the labor force and contributes 20% of the GDP. Based on 1974-76=100, the index of agricultural production in 1982 was 135 and the index of food production was 131.

As a result of lavish concessions to foreigners in the 1880s, about 44% of the land is held on freehold terms by whites, who make only up 2.3% of the population. The remainder of the land is held by the king as a trust for the Swazi nation. Most of the non-Swazi-owned land is held by large companies and includes highly successful estates producing sugar and citrus fruits and commercial forests and ranches. This modern sector also accounts for the bulk of the 2,710 tractors in use in 1981 and the annual consumption of 19,400 tons of fertilizers. Communal tenure Swazi Nation Land (SNL), though covering 56% of the total land area, contributes only 12% of total crop production. Including cattle, SNL production is 23% of GDP (at factor cost). On the other hand, freehold Individual Tenure Farms (ITF), in conjunction with agro-based industries, accounted for about 43% of GDP and three-quarters of total exports, while employing one-half of the country's wage-earners. Though most of Swaziland's agricultural production in the modern sector is owned or controlled by foreign interests, the Tibiyo Taka Ngwane Fund of the Swazi Nation has, over the past few years, acquired substantial shareholdings in all three of the sugar mills, as well as the outright purchase of farms and other commercial enterprises. Yields remain low and techniques primitive in the traditional sector farmed by Swazis. Of the cash crops, sugar accounts for 75% of the total value of agricultural production.

```
┌─────────────────────────────────────────────┐
│        PRINCIPAL CROP PRODUCTION (1982)       │
│                  (000 tons)                   │
│  Rice . . . . . . . . . . . . . . . .     5   │
│  Corn . . . . . . . . . . . . . . .      63   │
│  Potatoes . . . . . . . . . . . . .       6   │
│  Sweet potatoes . . . . . . . . . .       2   │
│  Cottonseed . . . . . . . . . . . .      21   │
│  Citrus fruit . . . . . . . . . . .       5   │
│  Sugar cane . . . . . . . . . . . . 3,300     │
│  Cotton lint . . . . . . . . . . . .     11   │
└─────────────────────────────────────────────┘
```

The livestock population in 1982 consisted of 675,000 cattle, 330,000 goats, 40,000 sheep, 2,000 horses, 620,000 chickens and 22,000 pigs. Most of the national herd consists of indigenous breeds. The off-take rate for slaughter is 11% per year.

Forests cover 99,592 hectares (246,091 acres). In 1982 roundwood removals totaled 2.223 million cubic meters (78.5 million cubic ft).

Fishing, limited to rivers and fish farms, is a negligible activity.

INDUSTRY

For a small undeveloped country Swaziland has a relatively well developed manufacturing sector contributing 23% of the GDP and employing 12.3% of the work force. The sector expanded at a healthy average annual rate of 7.4% during 1977-82. Originally limited to processing of agricultural produce—still a major element—it has progressively diversified into wood-pulp, cement, confectionary, brewing, textiles, agricultural machinery, fertilizers and color television assembly. In 1980 there were 113 establishments employing over 10 workers each producing an output valued at E296.2 million. Sugar, wood pulp and fruit canning provide about 80% of the income from manufacturing.

Outside the agro-forestry industries, manufacturing is highly centralized; of the 77 firms with more than 10 employees, the majority are based at the Matsapha industrial estate.

Two state-owned organizations have been instrumental in stimulating and sustaining this development: the Industrial Development Corporation and the Small Enterprise Development Corporation. The latter runs seven different estates in which 100 small companies are in operation. Although Africanization has been pursued as a national goal since 1973, foreign capital is actively welcomed. The largest foreign investments have been made by the Commonwealth Development Corporation.

Perhaps the most serious impediments to the future growth of small industries in Swaziland, most being heavily dependent on the South African market, are the highly subsidized inducements which are offered by the South African government and its Homelands in their efforts to attract and decentralize industry. Recently, Swaziland has lost a number of small firms (including garment and textile manufacturers and a copperware producer) which have relocated in Transkei.

ENERGY

No information is available on the total production or consumption of energy in Swaziland. In 1984, 150 million kwh of electric power were produced in the country, or 230 kwh per capita.

LABOR

The economically active population was estimated in the mid-1980s at 266,000; 60,000 are engaged in subsistence agriculture; the balance are mostly wage-earners with 36% in agriculture, 20% in community and social services, 9% in construction, 11% in government, 14% in manufacturing, and 10% in mining and other. Women make up 45.6% of the labor force. In 1976 the average earnings in manufacturing were E607 for skilled workers and E127 for unskilled workers per month. The Employment Act of 1980 forbids employers to discriminate among employees based on race, religion, sex, marital status or political affiliation. It requires equal pay for equal work. There are provisions covering the employment of children, maternity leave, and domestic employees. Legally, women are not discriminated against in the job market but, in practice, discrimination occurs frequently. Around three-fourths of the wage-paying jobs are held by men; their average wage rate by skill category is higher than for females. An element in the income tax law, which taxed married women more than married men, was partially removed in 1982. Nearly 12,000 Swazis, representing one-sixth of the total labor force, are employed in South Africa. Wages and working conditions are governed by law. Nearly 15% of the labor force is unionized. The largest of these unions are the Railway Workers' Union and the Mineworkers' Trade Union.

FOREIGN COMMERCE

The foreign commerce of Swaziland consisted in 1983 of exports of $330 million and imports of $464 million, leaving a trade deficit of $134 million. Of the imports, machinery and transport equipment constituted 23.1%, manufactured goods 22.1%, fuels 17.7%, food and live animals 7.5% and chemicals 6.7%. Of the exports, sugar constituted 31.7%, chemicals 19.4%, wood pulp 14.1%, canned fruits 5.5%, citrus fruits 4.7%, electronic equipment 4.7% and asbestos 4.5%.

The major import source is South Africa (94%). The major export destinations are South Africa 30% and the United Kingdom 20%.

During 1970-81 the annual export growth rate was 2.8% and the annual import growth rate was 5.7%. During the same period exports constituted 68.8% of the GDP and imports 75.8% of the GDP.

Swaziland belongs to the South African Customs Unions, whose other members are South Africa, Botswana and Lesotho.

TRANSPORTATION & COMMUNICATIONS

The 224-km (138-mi) Swaziland Railway links Bomvu Ridge near Mbabane to the Mozambique border. The main traffic is iron ore, which is being exported to Japan through Maputo. Another 100-km (62-mi) links with the South African rail network providing Swaziland with direct access through Lavusima to the port of Richards Bay and Durban.

The road system has a total length of 2,853 km (1,772 mi), of which 510 km (317 mi) are paved, and links the country with both South Africa and Mozambique. In 1982 these roads were used by 13,308 passenger cars and 5,406 commercial vehicles. Per capita passenger car ownership is 20 per 1,000 inhabitants.

The national airline is Royal Swazi National Airways Corporation with only one plane flying to Lusaka, Durban and Johannesburg. There are 27 airports and airfields in the country, of which all are usable and all have runways under 2,500 meters (8,000 ft). The principal international airport is at Manzini.

In 1984 there were 15,400 telephones in use, or 2.3 per 100 inhabitants.

In 1982 the country's 55 post offices and 16 postal agencies handled 9,316,000 pieces of mail and 51,000 telegrams. Per capita volume of mail was 14 pieces. A telecommunication satellite facility was established at Ezulwini valley in 1983. There are 242 telex subscriber lines.

In 1982, 88,000 tourists visited Swaziland generating $12 million in revenues. Expenditures by nationals abroad totaled $28 million. There are 2,000 hotel beds and the average length of stay was 3.4 days.

MINING

Swaziland is a major coal-producing country with reserves of five billion tons and annual production in 1982 of 115,000 tons.

Mining, however, is a relatively declining sector, contributing only 3% to the GDP (as against 10% in the 1960s) and 6% to export revenues (as against 17% in 1977). The Hayelock asbestos mine is closed in 1986 and the Ngwenya iron ore mine closed in 1978. Coal is the only major mineral resource in the 1980s.

DEFENSE

The defense structure is headed by the king as the commander of the Royal Defense Forces, which consist of emabutfo (singular: libutfo), or regiments organized according to tribal—not modern—lines. Members of the emabutfo serve as royal warriors and their loyalty is to the king as a person. The total strength of the emabutfo is 2,657 (5 per 1,000 inhabitants), but 500 of these warriors are being reportedly organized as a modern military unit. Annual estimated defense expenditures average about $18 million, or 11.5% of the national budget, 3.1% of GNP, $29 per capita, $12,000 per soldier and $706 per sq km of national territory.

EDUCATION

The national literacy rate is estimated at 56% (57.9% for males and 54.5% for females). Of the population over 25, 73.1% have had no schooling, 20.9% have attended and/or completed first level, 5.6% have attended and/or completed the second level, and 0.4% have some kind of post-secondary training.

Swaziland has not yet introduced universal, free and compulsory education. The gross school enrollment ratios are 111% at the first level (6 to 12) and 42% at the second level (13 to 17), for a combined enrollment ratio of 86%. Third-level enrollment ratio is 3.5%. Girls constitute 50% of primary school enrollment, 49% of secondary school enrollment and 41% of post-secondary enrollment.

Schooling lasts for 12 years divided into seven years of primary school, three years of middle school and two years of secondary school. The majority of the primary and secondary schools are run by missions with grants from the government. In 1982 there were 470 primary schools, 86 secondary schools, two teacher training institutions and three industrial training institutes in the school system. Nearly 80% of primary students are enrolled in private schools, and 2.4% of secondary students are enrolled in vocational schools.

The school year runs from January to December. The language of instruction is SiSwati in lower primary grades and English from middle primary grades on.

The annual output of the two teacher-training institutions is less than 100. The national teacher-pupil ratios are 1:33 at the primary level, 1:17 at the secondary level and 1:9 at the tertiary level.

The annual education budget in 1981 was E28,193,000, of which 80% was current expenditure. This amount represented 14.1% of the national budget, 5.2% of the GNP and $52.0 per capita.

EDUCATIONAL ENROLLMENT (1983)			
Level	Schools	Teachers	Students
First Level	470	3,586	119,913
Second Level	86	1,433	24,826
Vocational	3	224	1,162
Third Level	1	108	979

Higher education is provided by the Joint University of Botswana and Swaziland (formerly the Joint University of Lesotho, Botswana and Swaziland) located at Kwaluseni in Botswana. Per capita university enrollment is 264 per 100,000 inhabitants.

In 1982 342 students graduated from the Joint University, of these 118 received degrees in agriculture, 19 in law, and 12 in education.

In 1982, 177 Swazi students were enrolled in institutions of higher learning abroad. Of these, 87 were in the United States, 74 in the United Kingdom and 10 in Canada.

LEGAL SYSTEM

The Swazi legal system is an amalgam of Roman-Dutch law (introduced by the Boers) and Swazi traditional law.

The right to a fair public trial is provided for by law and is generally honored in practice. The judiciary consists of a Court of Appeals, a High Court, and various subordinate magistrates' courts. The head of state appoints members of the Court of Appeals and the High Court. Parallel to this modern government structure is a traditional structure consisting of traditional courts and 40 regional councils.

In magistrates' courts, a defendant is entitled to counsel at his own expense. Court-appointed defense counsel is provided in capital cases. Defendants are made fully aware of the charges against them. They and their lawyers are generally able to inform themselves of the evidence on which the charges are based. The courts are independent of executive and military control. Appeals from the magistrates' courts may be heard by the High Court, and all final appeals are heard by the Court of Appeals which is the highest judiciary body. These rights are not guaranteed to persons held under the 1978 detention law or charged with sedition. In traditional courts, where ethnic Swazis may be brought for relatively minor offenses and violations of Swazi traditional laws or customs, legal counsel is not allowed, but defendants are usually heard on their own behalf. Swazi traditional law has not been formally codified, but both offenses and punishments are limited and findings are subject to a review system and appeal to the High Court and Court of Appeals.

In 1983, the Swazi Parliament passed an amendment to the Sedition and Subversive Activities bill which increased the maximum penalty for sedition from two years to 20 and permitted the appointment of a special tribunal to hear such cases. It was left to the prime minister to appoint the members of the tribunal and determine their qualifications. Proceedings of such a tribunal are held in camera if the prosecution so requests. There is no provision for appealing the tribunal's decision to the courts. It is not clear if the amendment is, in fact, in force and there are no known cases of persons being tried under these new provisions.

There are 17 traditional courts dispensing customary law including two courts of appeal and a higher court of appeal. There are subordinate courts presided over by magistrates, one in each of the four administrative districts. All judges are nominated by the king.

No information is available on the nature of the penal system or the number and location of penal institutions.

LAW ENFORCEMENT

The Swaziland Police Force, first formed in 1907, has a strength of about 700, or one policeman for every 714 inhabitants. The national headquarters are at Mbabane, and there are district headquarters at Manzini, Siteki, and Mhlangano. The district units are linked to the capital by a radio network.

HEALTH

In 1980 there were 33 hospitals in the country with 1,470 beds, or one bed per 372 inhabitants. In the same year there were 100 physicians, or one physician per 5,790 inhabitants, 7 dentists and 84 nursing personnel. The main health problem is tuberculosis. Of the hospitals 21.2% are state-run, 57.6% are run by private nonprofit agencies and 21.2% are run by private for-profit agencies. The admissions/discharge rate is 456 per 10,000 inhabitants. Public health expenditures represent 7.2% of the national budget and $19.70 per capita.

PRINCIPAL HEALTH INDICATORS (1984)

Crude Death Rate: 17.2 per 1,000
Life Expectancy at Birth: 45.3 (Males); 51.9 (Females)
Infant Mortality Rate: 140.1 per 1,000 Live Births

FOOD

The staple food is corn, also called mealies. The daily per capita availability of energy, protein, fats and carbohydrates is estimated at 2,499 calories, 63.8 grams of proteins, (144% of requirements), 43 grams of fats, and 376 grams of carbohydrates.

MEDIA & CULTURE

Three daily newspapers, *The Times of Swaziland*, *Swaziland Observer*, and *Tikhatsi Temaswati*, are published in the country, with a circulation of 22,000, or 33 per 1,000 inhabitants. However, South African newspapers circulate widely. Two English-language weeklies appear in the capital with a combined circulation of around 12,000. The periodical press consists of 20 titles. The government information services publish a weekly and a fortnightly.

There is no national news service and no foreign news agencies are represented in the capital. No books are published locally.

The government-owned Swaziland Broadcasting Service operates one medium-wave transmitter and one FM transmitter broadcasting mainly in SiSwati with some programs in English for 62 hours a week. In 1985 there were 85,000 radio receivers in the country, or 131 per 1,000 inhabitants. Television service, inaugurated in 1978, is run by the state-owned Swaziland Television Broadcasting Corporation. There are 7,000 television sets in use (or 11 per 1,000 inhabitants).

In 1980 there were four fixed cinemas in the country with 1,300 seats, or 2.7 seats per 1,000 inhabitants.

Annual movie attendance was 0.1 million, or 0.2 per capita.

The Swaziland National Library Service has 10 branches throughout the country. Per capita there are 66 volumes and 1 registered borrower per 1,000 inhabitants.

SOCIAL WELFARE

There are no organized social security or social welfare programs.

GLOSSARY

indvuna (plural: tindvuna): variously translated as counsellor, governor or representative.

libandla: also, **libandla laka ngwane.** Advisory royal council consisting of all the chiefs and other elders.

libutfo (plural: emabutfo): a class or regiment of royal warriors

mtfanenkosi (plural: bantfanenkosi): a prince, especially as a royal representative.

ndlovukazi: literally, lady elephant. Title of the queen mother.

ngwenyama: literally, lion. Title of the Swazi king.

liqoqo: national council headed by the king's uncle and consisting of the tindvuna.

sikulu: chief of a sive.

sive: the lowest unit of tribal territorial organization.

tinkundla: (sing: nkundla): rural district councils.

CHRONOLOGY (from 1968)

1968— Swaziland gains independence following successful talks in London.

1972— Nation holds first parliamentary elections; the royalist Imbokodvo Party wins but the opposition gains three seats.

1973— King Sobhuza declares constitution unworkable and voids it. . . . Royal Defense Force is reactivated.

1974— Royal Constitutional Commission concludes study for a new constitution. . . . Swaziland introduces new national currency, the lilangweni.

1976— Prince Maphevu Dlamini is named premier replacing Prince Makhosini Dlamini. . . . Swaziland establishes diplomatic relations with Mozambique.

1979— Prime Minister Maphevu Dlamini dies and is succeeded of office by Mabendl Dlamini.

1982— King Sobhuza dies. . . Power of head of state is transferred to Queen Mother Dzeliwe who is named regent. . . In power struggle in the *Liqoqo*, the traditionalists gain upper hand. . . Prime Minister Prince Mabandla Dlamini, head of the liberal faction, is dismissed and replaced by conservative Prince Bhekimpi Dlamini. . . Queen regent is presented with document transferring most of her power to the Liqoqo and the ''Authorized Person''. . . On her refusal to sign, she is ousted in favor of Ntombi, mother of the heir apparent. . .

Prince Gabeni who championed the cause of Dzeliwe is dismissed from his post as minister of home affairs... Ntombi is installed as regent.

1984— Prime Minister Bhekimpi arrests the "Gang of Four," the ministers of foreign affairs and finance and the chiefs of the army and police, for plotting against the state... Prince Sozisa Dlamini, the "Authorized Person" and head of the Liqoqo, is dismissed.... Agreement is reached with South Africa on trade representation for Swaziland at Pretoria.

1986— Prince Makhosetive is installed as King Mswati III.

BIBLIOGRAPHY (from 1965)

Booth, Alan R., *Swaziland: Tradition and Change in a South African Kingdom* (Boulder, Colo., 1984).

Fair, T. J. O., G. Murdoch and H.M. Jones, *Development in Swaziland* (Johannesburg,1969).

Grotpeter, John J., *Historical Dictionary of Swaziland* (Metuchen,N.J.,1975).

Halpern, Jack, *South Africa's Hostages* (Baltimore, Md., 1965).

Kuper, Hilda, *Sobhuza II; Ngwenyama & King of Swaziland* (New York, 1978).

Matsebula, J. S. M., *A History of Swaziland* (London, 1972).

Nyeko, Balan, *Swaziland* [World Bibliographical Series] (Santa Barbara, Calif., 1982).

Potholm, Christian P., *Swaziland: The Dynamics of Political Modernization* (Berkeley, Calif., 1972).

Stevens, Richard P., *Lesotho, Botswana and Swaziland* (New York, 1967).

OFFICIAL PUBLICATIONS

Central Bank, *Annual Report.*
———, *Quarterly Review.*
Central Statistical Office, *Annual Statistical Bulletin.*
———, *Digest of Statistics.*
Swaziland Monetary Authority, *Annual Report.*
———, *Quarterly Review.*
Treasury, *Capital Fund Estimates.*
———, *Estimates of Revenue and Recurrent Expenditures.*
———, *Treasury Department Annual Report.*

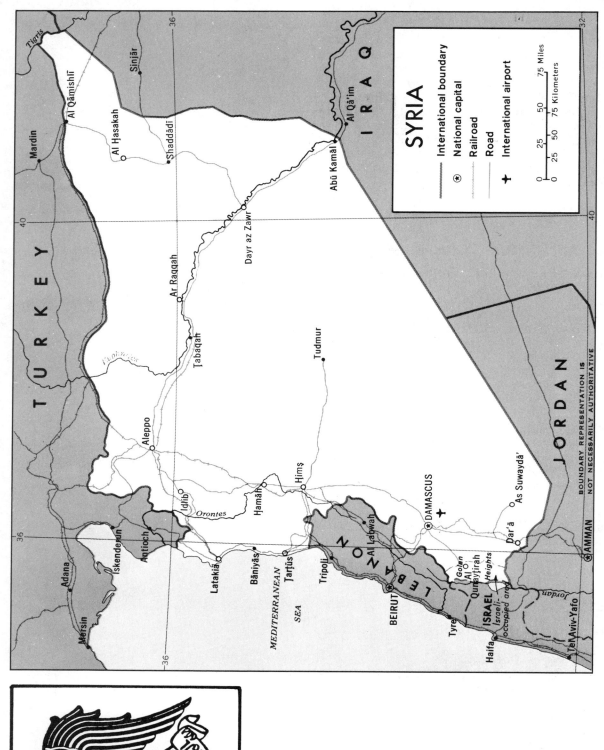

SYRIA

International boundary
⊛ National capital
Railroad
Road
✈ International airport

75 Miles
75 Kilometers
0 25 50
0 25 50

BOUNDARY REPRESENTATION IS
NOT NECESSARILY AUTHORITATIVE

TURKEY

Tigris
Sinjār
Al Qāmishlī
Mardin
Al Hasakah
Shaddādī

IRAQ

Al Qā'im
Abū Kamāl

Dayr az Zawr

Ar Raqqah

Euphrates
Ṭabaqah

Tudmur

Aleppo

Idlib
Orontes
Hamāh
Hims

Adana
Mersin
Iskenderun
Antioch

Latakia
Bāniyās
Ṭarṭūs
Tripoli

MEDITERRANEAN
SEA

LEBANON

BEIRUT
Tyre

Al Labwah
Golan
Al
Qunayṭirah
Heights

ISRAEL
Israeli-
occupied area

Haifa
Tel Aviv-Yafo

Jordan

DAMASCUS ✈

As Suwaydā'
Dar'ā

JORDAN

⊛ AMMAN

SYRIA

BASIC FACT SHEET

OFFICIAL NAME: Syrian Arab Republic (Al Jumhouriyya al-Arabiyya as-Souriyya)

ABBREVIATION: SY

CAPITAL: Damascus

HEAD OF STATE: President Lt. Gen. Hafez al-Assad (from 1971)

HEAD OF GOVERNMENT: Prime Minister Abdul Rauf Kassem(from 1980)

NATURE OF GOVERNMENT: Military dictatorship

POPULATION: 10,535,000 (1985)

AREA: 185,180 sq km (71,498 sq mi)

ETHNIC MAJORITY: Arabs

LANGUAGE: Arabic

RELIGION: Sunni Muslim

UNIT OF CURRENCY: Syrian Pound ($1=S £3.925, August 1985)

NATIONAL FLAG: Three horizontal stripes of red, white and black with a golden eagle in the center of the middle white stripe

NATIONAL EMBLEM: An erect falcon with outstretched wings, its head and beak facing to its left. Its body is represented as a shield on which the three-pointed Syrian stars are displayed in a vertical line. At the feet of the eagle are crossed stalks of grain, beneath which is a scroll reading, in Arabic, "The Syrian Arab Republic."

NATIONAL ANTHEM: "Protectors of the Homeland, Peace Be Upon You"

NATIONAL HOLIDAYS: April 17 (National Day, Independence Day); January 1 (New Year's Day); February 22 (Unity Day); March 8 (1963 Revolution Day); April 17 (Evacuation Day); Also variable Islamic festivals and Easter and Christmas according to Western and Eastern Orthodox reckoning

NATIONAL CALENDAR: Islamic and Gregorian

PHYSICAL QUALITY OF LIFE INDEX: 71 (up from 52 in 1976) (On an ascending scale with 100 as the maximum. U.S. 95)

DATE OF INDEPENDENCE: April 17, 1946

DATE OF CONSTITUTION: March 12, 1973

WEIGHTS & MEASURES: The metric system is in force. Traditional units are still used in rural areas. These include: 1 okiya=225 grams, 7.9 oz; 6 okiyas=1 oke (1.5 kg, 3.3 lb); 2 okes=1 rottol (3 kg, 6.6 lb); 200 okes=1 kantar (300 kg, 660 lb).

LOCATION & AREA

Syria is located in SW Asia and is bounded by Turkey on the north, Lebanon and the Mediterranean Sea on the west, Israel and Jordan on the south and Iraq on the east. The greatest distance is 793 km (493 mi) ENE to WSW and 431 km (268 mi) SSE to NNW. The total land area is 185,180 sq km (71,498 sq mi) of which around 20% has been properly surveyed. The length of the Mediterranean coastline is 183 km (114 mi).

The frontiers of Syria are largely artificial. The 845-km (525-mi) border with Turkey is defined by a railway line, while the 76 km (47 mi) border with Israel includes the demilitarized zone and the Israeli-occupied Golan Heights. The border with Lebanon runs 359 km (223 mi), that with Jordan 356 km (221 mi) and that with Iraq 596 km (370 mi).

The capital is Damascus with a 1984 population of 1,178,000. It is also the country's largest city and cultural center. Aleppo, the second largest city, is the industrial and commercial center, famous for its suq, or bazaar, considered the largest in the world. Its population was 1,109,100. The other major urban centers are Homs (406,300) Hama (190,000), Latakia (222,500) and Deir-ez-Zor (66,000).

Geographically, Syria consists of four main zones. A narrow coastal plain stretches from the Turkish border to Lebanon. Its maximum width is 32 km (20 mi) but in some places it practically disappears where the mountains meet the sea. The second zone is a series of mountains opening out fanlike from the southwest: Jabal Ansariyeh (the Anti-Lebanon range) with Mount Hermon, the highest peak in Syria at 2,743 meters (9,000 ft), and the Jabal al Shaykh which descends to the Hawran Plateau. To the southeast of this plateau lies the Jabal Druze range, home of the Druze. Third, east of the mountain ranges is a high plateau, sloping south-east and containing the fertile regions of Aleppo, Homs, Hama, the valley of the Buqaa, the Ghab depression and the Jazirah district between the Tigris and the Euphrates. Fourth, south of this region and separated from it by a low chain of mountains is the barren desert region known as the Hamad, covering one-third of the country's total land area.

Syria's most important waterway is the Euphrates River, flowing diagonally across the country for some

644 km (400 mi) and providing more than 80% of the water resources. The Orontes is the next major river, though shallow, unnavigable and subject to destructive flash floods, it is a valuable source of irrigation. Other rivers used for irrigation are the Balikh, Khabur and Barada.

WEATHER

On the coastal strip winters are mild, but humidity is high in the summer. The temperature ranges from 0.5°C (33°F) to 34.8°C (95°F). The mountain regions have moderate summers with temperatures ranging from 3.5°C (38°F) to 38°C (100°F). The interior plateaus have very hot summers with temperature ranging up to 42.2°C (108°F), though the winters are cold, with frost on many nights. The Hamad region has true desert climate with temperatures in July exceeding 43.3°C (110°F) and severe sandstorms during February and May. The coolest month in all regions is January, and the hottest are July and August. The average annual rainfall is 304.80 cm (10 in.) with great variations between regions. In general, rain is heaviest in the west and the north with the mountains receiving an annual precipitation of up to 101 cm (40 in.), mainly between November and May. The interior plateau receives less than 203 mm (8 in.) of rain annually. The southeastern desert receives only half of that amount; in some years it receives no rain at all.

POPULATION

The population of Syria was estimated at 10,535,000 in 1985 on the basis of the last official census held in 1981 when the population was 9,053,000. The population is expected to reach 18.1 million by 2000 and 29.5 million by 2020. The annual rate of population growth is 3.69% for the population as a whole and 4.5% for the urban population. The annual birth rate during 1970-83 was 46.5 per 1,000.

Syria is one of the most densely populated countries in the Middle East with an average density of 57 persons per sq km (148 persons per sq mi) going up to 64 persons per sq km (166 persons per sq mi) in arable areas. The population is concentrated in a fairly wide belt along the western borders and in the Aleppo-Homs region where the density is nearly double the national average. The greatest population increases are recorded in the northwestern and southwestern provinces, notably Damascus and Aleppo, which together account for 44% of all population. In the barren eastern desert regions the density falls to 3 persons per sq km (8 per sq mi).

The urban population grew by 4.7% annually between 1970 and 1980. Damascus alone accounts for 37.7% of the urban population and 13.3% of the entire population. The urban component of the population is 50%, with 27% living in the five cities with populations of over 100,000.

DEMOGRAPHIC INDICATORS (1984)	
Population, total (in 1,000)	10,535.0
Population ages (% of total)	
0-14	48.1
15-64	49.0
65+	2.9
Youth 15-24 (000)	2,110
Women ages 15-49 (000)	2,214
Dependency ratios	104.1
Child-woman ratios	922
Sex ratios (per 100 females)	103.4
Median ages (years)	15.9
Marriage Rate (per 1,000)	8.0
Divorce Rate (per 1,000)	0.6
Average size of Household	4.2
Decline in birthrate (%, 1965-83)	−3.4
Proportion of urban (%)	49.45
Population density (per sq. km.)	57
per hectare of arable land	0.77
Rates of growth (%)	3.69
Urban %	4.5
Rural %	2.9
Natural increase rates (per 1,000)	39.2
Crude birth rates (per 1,000)	46.5
Crude death rates (per 1,000)	7.2
Gross reproduction rates	3.50
Net reproduction rates	3.14
Total fertility rates	7.17
General fertility rates (per 1,000)	222
Life expectancy, males (years)	65.6
Life expectancy, females (years)	68.5
Life expectancy, total (years)	67.0
Population doubling time in years at current rate	18

At the 1970 census, males numbered 4,622,546 and females 4,427,658, producing a male/female ratio of 105 to 100. The ratio of males is highest in the heavily urbanized Damascus, Latakia, and Al Raqqah provinces to which male migration in search of employment is directed. The ratio may be distorted by the usual under-reporting of females in Islamic societies.

The population is young, with 48.1% of the population under 14 years of age, 49.0% between 15 and 64, and 2.9% over 65.

A significant factor affecting Syrian demographic trends is the influx of Palestinian refugees into Syria. No separate figures were given for these refugees in the 1970 census, but in 1971 their number was estimated at nearly 300,000. The size of the nomadic population is also undetermined but is unofficially estimated at 450,000. Offsetting this immigration was an exodus during the 1960s and early 1970s of some 10,000 urban business, managerial and professional persons, mostly Christians and non-Arabs, to Western countries. Government efforts to encourage these emigres to return have been uniformly unsuccessful.

The equality of women is guaranteed by the constitution. Women participate extensively in the work force, particularly in Damascus, and the women's union works to expand the participation of women in all sectors of society, utilizing the media and a network of chapters throughout Syria to convey its message. At the same time, traditional religious law continues to apply in matters of personal status. Particularly among the majority Muslim population, this continues to limit women's rights in matters such as marriage, divorce and inheritance.

Syria has no officially sponsored population planning programs.

ETHNIC COMPOSITION

The Syrian government does not officially recognize ethnic communities. Census reports enumerate only religious groups and ethnic groups are not identified as such in the press. Nevertheless ethnicity is the most important factor in Syrian political and social life. Although about more than 90% of the people are Arabs, they do not constitute a unified or monolithic force because of internal divisions. Distinctions of language, religion, region and race cut across Syrian society producing a large number of separate communities, each with its own system of shared values and loyalties. There is also a further division into villagers and townsmen and into settled people and nomads. Though there is a vague commitment to the general idea of Arab unity, the primary loyalty is to the family, clan, tribe and sect. The ethnic minorities, none of whom forms more than 10% of the population, derive their strength from their concentration in certain regions or domination of certain occupations. Over 90% of non-Arabs are clustered in the Halab Province north of Aleppo or in the Jazirah region in the northeast. Non-Arabs also live in partial isolation either in their own village or cluster of villages or in ethnic quarters in towns and cities.

Though the vast majority of Syrian Arabs are Sunni Muslim, the term Arab may be loosely applied to Christians, Ismailis, Druzes, Alawaites, Shiites, Palestinian refugees and Bedouins. The government's policy of Arabization has tended to reinforce the broader identification of all these communities as a single group.

The Kurds, who constitute roughly 6% of the population, are a fiercely independent people, most of whom arrived as refugees from Turkey between 1924 and 1938. Although they are now entirely settled, they retain some tribal features in their social organization. They live mainly as farmers and herdsmen in the foothills of the Taurus Mountains, in the Jazirah, in the Jarabulus area and in Damascus. They are being rapidly assimilated into Arab society and increasing numbers have adopted Arabic speech and dress.

The Armenians, estimated to number around 225,000, form the largest unassimilated group in Syria. Adamantly dedicated to the maintenance of Armenian identity, they have found themselves threatened by the Arabism of Syrian rulers and have emigrated in large numbers to foreign countries. About 75% of the Armenians live in Aleppo where, as traders and craftsmen, they have achieved a strong economic position.

Minor ethnic groups include 60,000 Turkomans, 50,000 Circassians, 20,000 Assyrians and 4,000 Jews. Both the Turkomans and Circassians, being Sunni Muslim, are being gradually assimilated and may eventually cease to be distinct groups. The Assyrians, on the other hand, are Nestorian Christians, who fled persecution in Iraq in 1933 and were settled near the Khabur River with the assistance of the French government and the League of Nations. The once prosperous Jewish community of Aleppo and Damascus has dwindled in numbers and influence. Syrian Jews publicly dissociate themselves from Zionism and Israel but are nevertheless looked upon with suspicion as possible traitors.

There is a Palestinian community of over 240,000, predominantly refugees from the 1948 and 1967 Arab-Israeli wars. Several thousand Lebanese and Palestinians entered Syria in 1982, fleeing Israel's invasion of Lebanon. Many participate fully in the Syrian economy, although Palestinians claim that procedures for the purchase of real property are cumbersome and they are allowed to own only one building or plot of land. Palestinians are free to choose their place of residence and occupation, and they occupy several senior positions in the Syrian bureaucracy. They are issued special Palestinian travel documents by the government in lieu of Syrian passports. They may not acquire citizenship or vote in Syrian elections.

Syrians are traditionally xenophobic and are particularly hostile toward Americans, whom they consider pro-Zionist. Russians and East Europeans form the largest and most influential foreign community in Damascus.

In terms of ethnic and linguistic homogeneity, Syria ranks 81st in the world with 78% homogeneity (on an ascending scale in which Tanzania is ranked 1st with 7% homogeneity and South and North Korea are ranked 135th with 100% homogeneity).

LANGUAGE

The official language of Syria is Modern Standard Arabic, a literary language derived from Classical Arabic. Dialects of spoken Arabic vary widely throughout the Arab world. The Syrians speak one, known as Syrian Arabic, which is common to Syria, Lebanon and parts of Jordan and Iraq. The majority of the Kurds speak Kurdish, an Indo-European language, written in both Arabic and Latin alphabets; the majority of the Armenians speak Armenian, an Indo-European language with a highly developed literature; and the majority of the Assyrians speak Syriac, a form of the ancient Aramaic language. In the 1970 census the breakdown of the population by language was as follows: Arabic, 85%; Kurdish, 8.2%; Armenian, 2%; Turkic, 3%; and Syriac, 1.8%.

Most Syrians speak a Western language in addition to Arabic. French is the most common; most educated are as fluent in it as in Arabic and it is taught as a compulsory second language in all schools from the intermediate level. However, English is coming into increasing use.

RELIGION

Unlike most Arab states, Syria has no official religion, though the 1973 constitution prescribes Islamic law as the source of Syrian jurisprudence and requires that the president be a Muslim. The constitution of 1950 guaranteed freedom of belief for all theistic religions. In matters of personal status, minority religions are allowed to follow their own legal systems. Although all religions enjoy, in theory, equal status before the law, Islam is the most favored. The condition of non-Muslim minorities, particularly Christians and Jews, has steadily deteriorated. Over 30,000 Christians are believed to have emigrated to Western countries since 1960. In 1967 all Christian schools were nationalized.

Muslims constitute 85% of the population and this percentage is growing as a result of their higher birth rate. Of the Muslims, 85% are members of the Sunni sect, 13 to 15% are Alawaites and the Ismailis and other Shiites form the rest. Druzes account for 3% of the total population, and Christians, divided among a number of denominations, are variously estimated at between 8 and 12%. Two tiny minorities, the Yazidis and the Jews, together make up less than 0.5%.

The numerically dominant Sunnis are dispersed throughout the country, but they have been declining in importance. About 90% of the Sunnis are Arabs, and the remainder are Kurds, Circassians and Turkomans. The Alawaites, or Nusayris, form the largest religious minority and the dominant group in Al Ladhiqiyah Province. The religion of the Alawaites is a Shiite form of Islam with Christian and pagan elements. Alawaites differ from Shiites in their belief in the divinity of Ali, the son-in-law of the Prophet Muhammad, and in a system of reincarnation. They do not have houses of worship and only a chosen few learn the tenets of their esoteric faith. Though they consider themselves as Muslims, they are not recognized as such by conservative Sunnis. As settled cultivators they occupy a social and economic position generally below that of Sunnis but with the rise of President Assad, an Alawaite, they have achieved considerable power and prestige in the army and government.

The Shiite group, numbering around 40,000, live in the Aleppo and Homs area. Shiism, which proclaims the imamate of Ali, is itself split into a number of sub-religions each recognizing its own line of imams who are, for the Shiites, chosen companions of God. The main body of Shiism is the Twelvers who accept a succession of 12 imams, the last of whom disappeared in 878. The major offshoot of Shiism, the Ismailis, or the Seveners, recognize only seven imams. They are represented in Syria by a few thousand followers living in Al Ladhiqiyah Province. The Druzes, Syria's third largest religious minority, number over 100,000 concentrated in the Jabal Druze and Dimasq Province. The Druze religion is a form of Shiism but differs from it in the exaltation of Abu Ali Mansur al Hakim, the tenth Fatimid caliph of Egypt, as an incarnation of the deity.

The Christian community is composed of three religious traditions: the Western Roman Catholic and Protestant churches; the Eastern Churches, including the autonomous Greek Orthodox churches, the Nestorian Church, and the monophysite Syrian Jacobite and Armenian churches; and the Uniate churches in communion with Rome. The largest denomination is the Greek Orthodox Church, also known as the Melkite Church; the second largest is the Armenian Orthodox, or Gregorian, Church. With the exception of the Armenians, most Christians are Arabs and they have participated in the nationalist movements out of proportion to their actual numbers. Syrian Christians are also more urbanized, educated and prosperous than the Muslims. The number of Christians is estimated at around 700,000.

The Jews, numbering a few thousand, are officially described as musawiyin (followers of Moses) rather than as yahudin (Jews), since the latter is a pejorative term applied to Israelis. Syrian Jews speak Arabic and are considerably Arabized. Nevertheless, they remain objects of suspicion and hostility and are under constant surveillance.

There are also about 12,000 Yazidis, also known as devil-worshipers, in the Jazirah and Aleppo regions.

COLONIAL EXPERIENCE

From 1920 to 1946, Syria was under French rule, which was considered oppressive. The franc became the base of Syrian economy, which was managed by French bankers. The French language became compulsory in schools, and the French controlled nearly every feature of Syrian life. Twenty-five years of such rule left politically minded Syrians with a strong antagonism to France. In 1948 Syria left the franc bloc, and French influence declined steadily thereafter. Hostility toward France became more marked as France became a major supplier of military equipment to Israel and later joined Great Britain in the invasion of Egypt in 1956. Relations between the two countries improved following De Gaulle's tilt to the Arab side in 1967. The principal legacy of French rule is the French language, which is spoken fluently by most educated Syrians and remains the major channel of communication between Syria and the West.

CONSTITUTION & GOVERNMENT

The present constitution of Syria was approved by a referendum in 1973. The 157-article constitution defines Syria as a "Socialist Popular Democracy," with a planned socialist economy. Under the constitution the head of state is the president who is also the commander in chief, the secretary general of the Baath Socialist Party and the president of the National Socialist Front. The constitution also provides for a People's Council and a Council of Ministers. The princi-

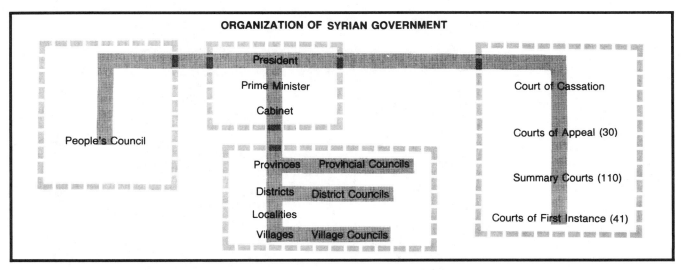

ORGANIZATION OF SYRIAN GOVERNMENT

President
Prime Minister
Cabinet
People's Council

Provinces — Provincial Councils
Districts — District Councils
Localities
Villages — Village Councils

Court of Cassation
Courts of Appeal (30)
Summary Courts (110)
Courts of First Instance (41)

ples of the Baath party are written into the constitution which, however, contains two concessions to the religious, establishment: the president of the republic is required to be a Muslim, and Islamic law is recognized as the principal source of legislation.

The constitution vests supreme power in the president who is elected for a seven-year term by universal suffrage. He has the right to appoint or dismiss the vice president, the prime minister and state officials, to declare war and states of emergency, and to amend the constitution. He also has the right to convene and dissolve the People's Council, to issue laws and ordinances when the Council is not in session and to veto legislation, although the veto may be overridden by the Council during a second review. The constitution requires that the president be a member of the Regional Command of the Baath Party and that presidential acts conform to Baath principles.

The prime minister and his cabinet serve at the president's discretion and may be dismissed by him at any time. In 1976 there were 29 ministries, of which 17 were headed by Baathists, six by independents, four by members of the Arab Socialist Union and one each by a Communist and a member of the Socialist Union.

The constitution provides for popular and direct elections to the People's Council on the basis of universal suffrage over age 18. The first general election to the Council under the constitution was held in 1973.

Syria has a tradition of unstable governments, coups and countercoups. Since 1946 there have been 47 cabinets and 11 violent transitions of power. The country has, however, enjoyed an unprecedented period of stability and economic prosperity since the rise of President Assad in 1970.

FREEDOM & HUMAN RIGHTS

In terms of civil and political rights, Syria is ranked as a not-free nation with a negative rating of 5 in political rights and 6 in civil rights (on a descending scale in which 1 is the highest and 7 the lowest in civil and political rights). > ..05

Under Hafez al-Assad Syria has enjoyed its longest period of stable rule since independence. But, despite this stability, Syria has experienced considerable internal strife which culminated in serious domestic violence during 1979-80. Internal unrest reached its height in early 1980 when the major cities of northern Syria were virtually closed down as a result of general strikes. Initially, the Syrian government attempted to strike a balance between applying harsh measures and satisfying broader demands for liberalization. Finally, it swung to the former extreme by moving troops to Hama, Aleppo and Homs to put down all opposition. During this period numerous violations of human rights and civil liberties occurred. Large numbers of people were detained under martial law. There were credible reports of torture being used on a wide scale primarily during interrogation. According to reliable observers (quoted by Amnesty International) detainees were beaten with rifle butts and clubs by military personnel, sometimes to elicit information and sometimes to intimidate the general opposition. During house-to-house searches people were dragged from their residences and brutally beaten. The military also carried out summary executions of persons considered to be terrorists. Following an unsuccessful assassination attempt against President Assad in June 1980, the security forces reportedly killed between 250 and 300 prisoners; according to Amnesty International, they were released and then strafed by helicopter gunships to make it appear as a mass escape. In July, the Syrian Parliament enacted a law decreeing the death penalty for membership in the Muslim Brotherhood. Besides an unknown number of Muslim Brotherhood members several hundred Lebanese and Palestinians are also believed to be in Syrian jails. No international organization, such as the Red Cross, is allowed access to detention facilities. Under the state of emergency currently in force, detainees may be held indefinitely. One private legal organization estimates the number of those under detention as close to 5,000. This num-

```
┌─────────────────────────────────────────────┐
│              CABINET LIST (1985)              │
│                                               │
│ President . . . . . . . . . . . . . . . . Gen. Hafez al- Assad │
│ Vice President . . . . . . . . . . . . . 'Abd al-Halim Khaddam │
│ Vice President . . . . . . . . . . . . . Dr. Rif 'at al- Assad │
│ Vice President . . . . . . . . Muhammad Zuhayr Mashariqa │
│ Prime Minister . . . . . . . . . . . . Dr. 'Abd al-Ra'uf al- Kasm │
│ Deputy Prime Minister . . . . . . . . Lt. Gen. Mustafa Talas │
│ Deputy Prime Minister                          │
│    for Economic Affairs . . . . . . . . . . . . . Dr. Salim Yasin │
│ Deputy Prime Minister                          │
│    for Services Affairs . . . . . . . . . . . . . Mahmud Qaddur │
│ Minister of Agriculture                        │
│    & Agrarian Reform . . . . . . . . . . . Dr. Mahmud al- Kurdi │
│ Minister of Communications . . . . . . . . Eng. Murad Quwatli │
│ Minister of Construction . . . . . . . . . . . . . Riyad Baghdadi │
│ Minister of Culture and Natl. Guidance   Dr. Najah al- 'Attar │
│ Minister of Defense . . . . . . . . . . Lt. Gen. Mustafa Talas │
│ Minister of Economy                            │
│    & Foreign Trade . . . . . . . . . . Dr. Muhammad al- 'Imadi │
│ Minister of Education . . Muhammad Najib al-Sayyid Ahmad │
│ Minister of Electricity . . . . . . . . . . . . Eng. Kamil al- Baba │
│ Minister of Finance . . . . . . . . . . . . Dr. Qahtan al- Suyufi │
│ Minister of Foreign Affairs . . . . . . . . . . Farouk al- Shara' │
│ Minister of Health . . . . . . . . . . . . . . Dr. Ghasub al- Rifa'i │
│ Minister of Higher Education . . . . . . . . . Dr. Kamal Sharaf │
│ Minister of Housing & Utilities . . . . . . . . . . . . 'Adnan Quli │
│ Minister of Industry . . . . . . . . . . . . . . . . 'Ali al- Tarabulsi │
│ Minister of Information . . . . . . . . . . . . . . . Yasin Rajjuh │
│ Minister of Interior . . . . . . . . . . . . Muhammad Ghabbash │
│ Minister of Irrigation . . . . . . . Eng. 'Abd al-Rahman Madani │
│ Minister of Justice . . . . . . . . . . . . . . . . Sha'ban Shahin │
│ Minister of Local Administration . . . Dr. Muhammad Harba │
│ Minister of Oil & Mineral Wealth . . . . . Dr. Ghazi al- Durubi │
│ Minister of Religious                          │
│    Trusts . . . . . . . . . . . . Muhammad Muhammad al- Khatib │
│ Minister of Social Affairs                     │
│    & Labor (Acting) . . . . . . . . . . . . . . . . . Antoine Jubran │
│ Minister of Supply & Internal Trade . . . . Riyad al-Haj Khalil │
│ Minister of Tourism . . . . . . . . . . . . . . Dr. Nawras al- Daqr │
│ Minister of Transportation . . . . . . . . Eng. Yusuf al- Ahmad │
│ Minister of State . . . . . . . . . . . . . . Dr. Muhammad Jum'a │
│ Minister of State . . . . . . . . . . . . . 'Abd al-Hamid Munajjid │
│ Minister of State . . . . . . . . . . . . . . . . . . . Ghazi Mustafa │
│ Minister of State for                          │
│    Cabinet Affairs . . . . . . . . . . . . . 'Abd al-Mun'im Hamawi │
│ Minister of State for Foreign Affairs . . . . . . . 'Isam al- Na'ib │
│ Minister of State for People's                 │
│    Assembly Affairs . . . . . . . . . . . . . . . . . Antoine Jubran │
│ Minister of State for Planning Affairs . . . . Dr. Saba Baqjaji │
│ Minister of State for Presidential Affairs . . . . . Wahib Fadil │
└─────────────────────────────────────────────┘
```

```
┌─────────────────────────────────────────────┐
│                RULERS OF SYRIA                │
│                 (from 1946)                   │
│ 1943 (July) to 1949 (March)                   │
│              Shukri al Quwwatli               │
│ 1949 (March) to 1949 (August)                 │
│              Husni az- Zaim                   │
│ 1949 (December) to 1951 (December)            │
│              Hashim al- Atasi                 │
│ 1951 (December) to 1954 (February)            │
│              Adib Shishaqli                   │
│ 1954 (February) to 1955 (September)           │
│              Hashim al- Atasi                 │
│ 1955 (September) to 1958 (February)           │
│              Shukri al- Quwwatli              │
│ From 1958 (February) to 1961 (September) Syria was part │
│ of the United Arab Republic                   │
│ 1961 (December) to 1962 (March)               │
│              Nazim Kudsi                       │
│ 1962 (April) to 1963 (March)                  │
│              Nazim Kudsi (2nd time)           │
│ 1963 (March) to 1963 (July)                   │
│              Luai al- Atassi (Chairman of Revolutionary │
│              Council)                          │
│ 1963 (July) to 1966 (February)                │
│              Amin Hafez (Chairman of Revolutionary │
│              Council)                          │
│ 1966 (February) to 1970 (November)            │
│              Nureddin Atassi                  │
│ 1970 (November) to 1971 (February)            │
│              Ahmad Khatib                     │
│ 1971 (Feb) —  Hafez al- Assad                 │
└─────────────────────────────────────────────┘
```

1980 the Lawyers' Association and the League for the Defense of Human Rights solicited the Syrian government to end the state of emergency and to abolish the state security court. The organizers of this appeal were arrested for their efforts on behalf of human rights.

The Syrian press functions as a mouthpiece of the government. On foreign issues and matters relating to domestic security the media adhere to guidelines from the government. Foreign language publications are not generally censored, but Arabic language publications from outside the country are banned when they present viewpoints opposed to those of the government. During 1980, the government was particularly sensitive to international reporting. Foreign correspondents were not allowed to enter Syria during the height of the disturbances. Even the clandestine distribution of opposition leaflets was suppressed.

The government interferes with the private lives of its citizens in a number of ways. Electronic surveillance is believed to be widespread. Intelligence organizations maintain a network of guards to protect officials and important buildings, as well as to monitor the activity of people living in those neighborhoods. The postal system censors the mail but does not check every letter or package. Private schools are carefully inspected by the government and follow the governmental curriculum. Although the legal system provides safeguards, including a requirement of arrest and search warrant before police are allowed to enter private homes, regulations under the state of emergency currently in effect suspend these safeguards in security-related cases. During security operations,

ber includes 20 Baath Party officials and members of former governments who have been under detention since 1970 as well as a number of professionals who were arrested when the Syrian government dissolved the executive councils of the nation's professional associations.

Persons charged with security or political offenses fall under the jurisdiction of the military courts or the state security court. Under this system the accused has no recourse to habeas corpus and may not choose his lawyer. All court sessions are closed. In 1979 and especially in 1979-1982, there have been warrantless house-to-house searches by security personnel.

Membership in the Ba'ath Party is politically expedient but not forced; indeed, membership is only achieved through recommendation and invitation.

Emigration and foreign travel are discouraged. Exit visas are difficult to obtain and are often subject to the posting of large bonds.

The government of Syria does not generally cooperate with international investigations of human rights in the country.

CIVIL SERVICE

All government positions below the ministry level are filled from the ranks of the civil service. Entry and promotion, are based upon a system of examinations. Until the rise of the Baath Party, the civil service generally remained outside politics. The upper ranks of the civil service were depleted during the 1960s as a result of an emigration of trained managers and administrators to Western countries. The effectiveness of the service was also reduced as the Baath regimes began appointing civil servants on the basis of party loyalty.

LOCAL GOVERNMENT

Syria is divided into 13 provinces or muhaafazat (sing.: muhaafaza): Tartous, Daraa, Al Suwayda, Hims, Dayr al Zawr, Al Hasakah, Al Raqqah, Halab, Idlib, Al Ladhiqiyah, Hamah, Al Qunaytirah and Dimashq. The city of Damascus is an independent municipality with the status of a province. Each province is divided into administrative districts known as manatik (sing.: mantika), and they in turn are divided into localities known as nawahi (sing.: nahia). The smallest unit of local administration is the village headed by a mukhtar (pl.: mukhtaara). Each province is ruled by a governor, or muhaafez, each mantika by a mudir al-mantika, or district officer, and each nahia by a mudir al-nahia, or sub-district officer.

Popular government at the provincial level is vested in the Provincial Assembly, three-fourths of whose members are elected and one-fourth appointed by the Ministry of Interior and the governor. There are also district councils and village councils with limited popular participation. Municipal councils govern towns with an elected mayor, and each quarter of the town has its own mukhtar. Nomadic tribes usually govern themselves with the shaykh or chief acting as the government's principal representative in fiscal and legal matters.

FOREIGN POLICY

The key determinants of Syrian foreign policy are an ideological commitment to Arab unity and an unremitting hostility to Israel. Its principal goals are the liberation of Palestine, the recovery of the Golan Heights, replacement of Arab monarchies by socialist regimes through revolutionary means and nonalignment in the East-West conflict.

Syria is a member of the radical bloc of Arab nations noted for strident opposition to Western imperialism and dogmatic intransigence toward moderate or conservative Arab regimes. As a result of its radical policies, Syria was by 1970 in open conflict with Iraq, Lebanon, Jordan, Saudi Arabia, Morocco and Tunisia. One of President Assad's earliest initiatives in the field of foreign policy was to bring Syria out of its isolation and to introduce some measure of flexibility in its relations with other countries. Relations were normalized with Lebanon, Jordan, Saudi Arabia, Tunisia, Morocco and Egypt. Relations with Iraq, however, have remained strained and the tensions have been heightened by a rivalry between the Syrian and Iraqi factions of the Baath Party and by a dispute over the utilization of the waters of the Euphrates River.

Syrian nationalism has always been characterized by a strong element of antagonism toward the West, particularly the United States. The government and public opinion are more hostile to the West in Syria than in any other Arab nation. Diplomatic relations with Great Britain and the United States were broken off in 1967 following the Arab-Israeli War and were not resumed until 1973 and 1975, respectively. Significant economic agreements were signed with the United States in 1975 and 1976.

The Soviet Union has long been Syria's principal source of military equipment and economic aid. "Development of relations with the socialist camp, particularly with the friendly Soviet Union" was declared as the primary objective of Syria's foreign policy by the Baath Party meeting soon after Assad's coup in 1970. But Soviet influence is not absolute, and Syria has diversified its contacts with the Communist world by establishing relations with the People's Republic of China.

Syrian intervention in the civil war in Lebanon in 1975-76 has introduced new factors into the complex Middle Eastern scene. At the outbreak of that civil war, Syria wanted to protect the position of the Palestinians in Lebanon and sent in 2,000 Saiqa (the Syrian-controlled wing of the Palestine Liberation Army) soldiers to secure a ceasefire. But by June 1976 the fighting was so fierce that Syria was compelled to intervene in strength. This intervention was welcomed by the Christian Right and condemned by the Palestinians and the Muslim Left. Syria's action was opposed by other confrontation regimes (particularly Iraq and Libya). A meeting of Arab League foreign ministers later agreed to establish an Arab peace-keeping force in Lebanon.

Faced with Sadat's peace moves and unilateral initiatives for direct negotiations with Israel in 1977, Syrian positions in the foreign policy field have hardened. Assad personally toured the Middle Eastern oil states to marshal support for the radical Arab groups opposed to any negotiated settlement with Israel. Relations between Cairo and Damascus were broken again in late 1977. In the continuing Muslim-Christian conflict in Lebanon Syria has moved toward the Muslim guerrillas, reflecting perhaps a growing Libyan influence in Syrian councils. Libya has extended $1 billion to Syria for arms purchases from abroad.

By 1980 Syria found itself embroiled in hostilities in the east, west and south. The rivalry with Iraq degenerated into a bitter feud between Assad and the new Iraqi strongman, Saddam Husayn al-Tikriti, with both accusing each other of fomenting coups and plots. Naturally, Assad sided with Iran in the Iran-Iraq war of 1980. Even a stranger alliance was formed with Libya, although very few took the Libyan proposals for a merger between Libya and Syria seriously. In Lebanon, Syria found its own Vietnam, unable to extricate itself from its self-ordained role of a mediator. To the south, it came to the brink of war with Jordan, an ardent ally of Iraq. With so many enemies around him, Assad found little time to devote to his traditional antagonists: Israel, Egypt and the United States. The only noticeable improvement was in Syrian relations with the Soviet Union. After resisting for many years Soviet demands to sign a treaty of peace and friendship, Assad finally gave in and signed such a treaty in 1980.

Syria and the United States are parties to 13 treaties and agreements covering agricultural commodities, aviation, cultural relations, customs, economic and technical cooperation, investment guaranties and telecommunications.

Syria joined the U.N. in 1945 but lost its membership in 1958 when it joined with Egypt to form the United Arab Republic. It rejoined the U.N. in 1961 when it became independent again. Its contribution to the U.N. budget is 0.02%. It is a member of 15 U.N. organizations and 11 other international and regional organizations including the Arab League.

U.S. Ambassador in Damascus: William L. Eagleton, Jr.

U.K. Ambassador in Damascus: Roger Tomkys

Syrian Ambassador in Washington, D.C.: Rafiq Jouejati

Syrian Ambassador in London: Loutouf Allah Haydar

PARLIAMENT

The legislature of Syria is the People's Council, a directly elected unicameral body consisting of 195 members serving four-year terms. Among the powers delegated to it by constitution are the right to monitor the actions of cabinet ministers and to withdraw its confidence from an individual minister or from the cabinet as a whole. In the current People's Council the Progressive Front of National Union holds all 195 seats, with the Baath Party alone holding 117.

Candidates for Parliament are selected by the ruling Baath Party and, in theory, by four other parties which comprise the Progressive National Front. Personal loyalty to the regime and the president is a necessary qualification. Opposition lists of independents are offered but rarely prevail, probably because of the Front's far greater resources and organization and because of restrictions on freedom of expression. No independents were elected in the most recent elections, in 1981.

POLITICAL PARTIES

All political parties are included in the governing Progressive Front of National Union founded by Assad in 1972. The Front is composed of five parties:

The Baath Party, formally known as the Regional Command of the Arab Socialist Renaissance Party, is the Syrian branch of an international Arab movement founded in 1953 through the merger of Akram Al-Hourani's Syrian Socialist Party and the Arab Resurrection Party of Michael Aflaq and Salah al-Din al-Bitar. The party set forth a pan-Arab, Marxist and secular ideology based on the motto, "Unity, Freedom, Socialism." The Baathism of Assad, however, differs in methodology and attitude from that of Aflaq and Bitar and emphasizes democratic centralism and pragmatism. Never a mass popular movement, Baathists infiltrated and indoctrinated the armed forces and seized full power in 1963. The party has dominated the political system since then. President Hafez al-Assad is the party leader.

The Arab Socialist Union is a pro-Egyptian, Nasserist group led by Jamal Atasi.

The Socialist Unionist Movement is another pro-Egyptian, Nasseristgroup led by Sami Soufan.

The Arab Socialist Party is an anti-Egyptian and democratic party led by Abdul Ghani Kannout.

The Communist Party of Syria is illegal but is, nevertheless, permitted to operate openly and has had a representative in the cabinet since 1966. It is headed by Khaled Baqdash, one of the leading Communists in the Arab world.

ECONOMY

Syria is one of the 39 lower middle-income countries with a planned socialist economy, in which the dominant sector is public.

Development planning was begun in the 1950s, and the first Five-Year Plan was launched in 1961 under the stimulus of Egyptian programming concepts and the guidance of international agencies. The planning apparatus consisted of the Supreme Planning Council, the State Planning Organization and the Central Statistical Office, the latter two attached to the prime minister's office. Although exposed to serious disruptions as a result of the Arab-Israeli wars of 1967 and 1973, both the Second and Third Five-Year Plans achieved reasonable success. The Fourth Development Plan began in 1976 with an overall investment target of S £70 billion. It called for an 11.9% annual increase in national income. The major investment sectors are railways and roads, electricity and cotton textiles.

```
╔══════════════════════════════════════════╗
            PRINCIPAL ECONOMIC INDICATORS
  Gross National Product: $16.510 billion (1983)
    GNP Annual Growth Rate: 8.6% (1973-82)
    Per Capita GNP: $1,680 (1983)
    Per Capita GNP Growth Rate: 4.9% (1973-82)
  Gross Domestic Product: S£77.5 billion (1983)
    GDP at 1980 Prices: S£77.5 billion
    GDP Deflator (1980=100): 127.5
    GDP Annual Growth Rate: 8.0% (1973-83)
    GDP Per Capita: S£8,064 (1983)
    GDP Per Capita Growth Rate: 5.5% (1970-81)
  Percentage of Population in Absolute Poverty: 10%
  Consumer Price Index (1970=100): All Items: 507 (March
    1985) Food: 556 (March 1985)
  Average Annual Rate of Inflation: 12.7% (1973-83)
  Money Supply: S£34.429 billion (December 1983)
    Reserve Money: S£29.737 billion (December 1983)
  Currency in Circulation: S£17.348 billion (1984)
  International Reserves: $52 million, of which foreign ex-
    change reserves were $43 million (1984)
╚══════════════════════════════════════════╝
```

The Fifth Five-Year Plan (1981-85) projected a total investment of SL101.493 billion of which agriculture received SL17.2 billion. A major project is the Euphrates Dam which will eventually irrigate 640,000 hectares (158,440 acres), although only 64,000 hectares (158,144 acres) had been irrigated by 1984.

GROSS DOMESTIC PRODUCT BY ECONOMIC ACTIVITY (1982)

	%	Rate of Change % 1970-81
Agriculture	16.6	8.2
Mining	16.6	—
Manufacturing	16.6	8.2
Public Utilities	16.6	—
Construction	6.4	14.9
Transport & Communications	7.0	2.3
Trade	26.2	10.7
Finance	6.0	10.7
Public Administration & Defense	21.3	18.2
Other Branches	—	15.9

BALANCE OF PAYMENTS (1983)
(million $)

Current Account Balance	−815
Merchandise Exports	1,928
Merchandise Imports	−4,152
Trade Balance	−2,224
Other Goods, Services & Income	+781
Other Goods, Services & Income	−1,111
Other Goods, Services & Income Net	−330
Private Unrequited Transfers	461
Official Unrequited Transfers	1,278
Capital Other Than Reserves	644
Net Errors & Omissions	40
Total (Lines 1, 10 and 11)	−131
Counterpart Items	−15
Total (Lines 12 and 13)	−146
Liabilities Constituting Foreign Authorities' Reserves	—
Total Change in Reserves	146

The success of Syria's ambitious economic development program depends on a number of factors: the absence of war, continued internal stability, development of a trained cadre capable of executing and administering the economic projects, and a continued inflow of foreign money to help pay for the necessary goods and services until such time as the Syrian economy generates enough production to take off on its own. Dependent to a large extent at this stage for its economic development upon foreign largess, the Syrian economy is vulnerable to outside political pressures.

Arab aid continues to flow generously. A massive increase occurred in 1979 as a result of the November 1978 Baghdad Conference. The U.S. economic assistance program continued through 1979 at a level of $100 million annually.

Other major aid donors to Syria are the Federal Republic of Germany, the IBRD, and the Soviet Union, bringing total aid to Syria in 1979 and 1980 to an estimated $1.5 billion. Although still relatively insignificant, a number of steps have been taken by Damascus to encourage foreign private investment. Most important has been the signing of investment guarantee agreements with the United States (OPIC), France, West Germany, and Switzerland. During 1979-81 Syria received a total of $162.7 million in bilateral and multilateral aid or $16.10 per capita.

BUDGET

The Syrian fiscal year is the calendar year. Under the Organic Public Finance Law of 1967, a single, consolidated, centralized annual budget was introduced to cover all expenditures and receipts of central ministries, the public ministries, the public sector agencies and enterprises, and local municipal and religious administrative units. Expenditures and receipts of ministries and agencies are included in the budget in full while in the case of other units only the net total surplus and deficit of their respective budgets are included. Under the law each budgeted outlay is to be matched by funds required to finance it.

Of total current government revenues, 12.5% comes from taxes on income, profit and capital gain, 6.2% from domestic taxes on goods and services, 14.6% from taxes on international trade and transactions, 6.1% from other taxes and 60.7% from non-tax revenues. Current revenues represented 22.1% of GNP. Of current expenditures, 37.7% goes to defense, 7.1% to education, 1.1% to health, 11.4% to housing, social security and welfare, 30.9% to economic services and 11.8% to other functions. Total expenditures represented 37.8% of GNP and overall deficit 6.2% of GNP.

In 1983 public consumption totaled SL16.027 billion and private consumption SL53.532 billion. During 1973-83 public consumption grew by 10.7% and private consumption by 9.2%.

In 1983 total outstanding disbursed external debt was $2.660 billion of which $2.600 billion was owed to

ORDINARY BUDGET
(£S million)

Expenditure	1984
Community, social and personal services	21,071
Agriculture, forestry and fishing	123
Mining and quarrying	9
Manufacturing	50
Electricity, gas and water	4
Construction and building	28
Trade	31
Transport, communications and storage	123
Finance, insurance and real estate	n.a.
Others	2,000
TOTAL	23,439

CONSOLIDATED BUDGET
(£S million, incorporating both ordinary and development budgets)

Expenditure	1984
Community, social and public services	26,860
Agriculture, forestry and fishing	3,211
Mining and quarrying	1,161
Manufacturing	1,697
Electricity, gas and water	1,672
Construction and building	555
Trade	1,030
Transport, communications and storage	2,577
Finance, insurance and real estate	477
Others	2,049
TOTAL	41,289

official creditors and $60.7 million to private creditors. Total debt service was $396.4 million of which $294.4 million was repayment of principal and $102.0 million interest. Total external debt represented 98.2% of export revenues and 13.6% of GNP. Total debt service represented 14.6% of export revenues and 2.0% of GNP.

FINANCE

The Syrian unit of currency is the Syrian pound divided into 100 piastres. Coins are issued in denominations of 2½, 5, 10, 25 and 50 piastres and 1 pound; notes are issued in denominations of 1, 5, 10, 25, 50, 100 and 500 pounds. The monetary system is based on a managed, non-convertible currency.

The official exchange rate in August 1985 was $1 = S£3.925. The official exchange rate in 1984 with British pound was £1 Sterling=S£4.549. A parallel free market in Syrian pounds existed until 1973. Foreign exchange transactions are rigorously controlled.

The Syrian banking system consists of a Central Bank, the state-owned Commercial Bank and four specialized banks, also state-owned. The Central Bank is responsible for the issue of currency and the control of money supply. It also acts as the fiscal agent to the government and the lender of last resort to the state banks. The Central Bank itself is controlled and directed by the Council of Money and Credit, which monitors the country's financial and economic health. The commercial banking system was completely nationalized in 1963, and all the banks were merged into the Commercial Bank which, in 1976, had 25 branches and resources of S£3.398 bil-

lion. Specialized banks include the Agricultural Bank, Industrial Bank, Popular Credit Bank and Real Estate Bank. The credit system also includes the nationalized Societe d'Assurances Syrienne. In 1984 the commercial banks had reserves of S£9.816 billion, demand deposits of S £15.174 billion and time and savings deposits of S£5.204 billion. Outside the banking system are professional moneylenders who advance loans at usurious rates as high as 50 to 100%. The maximum legal rate of interest is 9%.

GROWTH PROFILE
Annual Growth Rates (%)

Population 1980-2000	3.4
Birthrate 1965-83	−3.4
Deathrate 1965-83	−56.3
Urban Population 1973-83	4.2
Labor Force 1980-2000	4.0
GNP 1973-82	8.6
GNP per capita 1973-82	4.9
GDP 1973-83	8.0
GDP per capita 1970-81	5.5
Consumer Prices 1970-81	11.6
Wholesale Prices 1970-81	12.4
Inflation 1973-83	12.7
Agriculture 1973-83	8.2
Manufacturing 1970-81	8.2
Industry 1973-83	5.9
Services 1973-83	8.9
Mining	—
Construction 1970-81	14.9
Electricity	—
Transportation 1970-81	2.3
Trade 1970-81	10.7
Public Administration & Defense 1970-81	18.2
Export Price Index 1965-71	15.1
Import Price Index 1965-71	11.7
Terms of Trade 1965-71	3.2
Exports 1973-83	−3.3
Imports 1973-83	9.1
Public Consumption 1973-83	10.7
Private Consumption 1973-83	9.2
Gross Domestic Investment 1973-83	11.3
Energy Consumption 1973-83	13.3
Energy Production 1973-83	3.6

AGRICULTURE

Agriculture remains the mainstay of the Syrian economy. Of the total land area of 18,568,000 hectares (45,881,528 acres), 3,337,914 hectares (8,221,003 acres) are under crops. Agricultural land constitutes 67% of the total land area, or 1.62 hectares (4 acres) per capita. The index of agricultural production in 1982 was 158, the index of food production was 166, and the per capita index of food production 129 (both indices based on 1974-76=100). Agriculture employs 33% of the labor force.

Agriculture contributes 19% to the GDP and its growth rate during 1973-83 was 8.2%. The share of the agricultural sector in the economy has been declining since 1956 when its contribution to the GDP was 39%. Agricultural products, however, still contribute two-thirds to three-fourths of exports by value. The value added in agriculture in 1983 was $2.751 billion.

Agricultural production is concentrated in four main regions: the narrow coastal strip along the Mediterranean; the valley of the Orontes River; the 160-km (100-mi) wide steppe-plain running north from the Jordan border to the Euphrates valley; and the Jazirah region between the Tigris and the Euphrates.

The chief characteristic of Syrian agriculture is the annual fluctuation in output resulting from variations in rainfall. Rainfall exceeds 50.8 cm (20 in.) a year in only 10% of the land, while 59% received 25.4 cm (10 in.) or less. Irrigation has therefore assumed great importance for increasing, stabilizing and diversifying the output. The most ambitious of the irrigation projects is the Euphrates Dam begun in 1968 and completed in 1975. The dam is designed to irrigate 640,000 hectares (1,581,473 acres) and produce 2 billion kwh annually. A number of smaller irrigation projects irrigate a further 538,000 hectares (1,354,136 acres). These include the Al-Ghab-Acharne project, the Yarmuk River project, the Barada River project, the Homs-Hamah project, the Matkh project, the Sinn project, the Ruj project, the Tall Maghas project, the Rastan Dam, the Mahardah Dam, the Asharinah Dam and the Al Murayah Dam.

The small-scale family holding is the basic unit of agricultural production, and most farmer-owners and sharecroppers are engaged in subsistence farming. The main crops grown in winter are wheat and barley; the major summer crop is cotton. In 1976 private holdings constituted 81% of agricultural units, cooperatives 15% and state farms 4%.

Until the agrarian reforms of 1969, land was very unequally distributed. Most of the rural population owned no land at all but worked as sharecroppers and laborers, while large estates, some of them exceeding 101,000 hectares (250,000 acres), constituted 29% of cultivable area. The land reform program introduced by the government after the merger with Egypt in 1958 broke up the large estates and modified the tenancy system in favor of the sharecroppers. Some of the provisions of the Agrarian Reform Law were rescinded by the Maruf Dawalibi government in 1961 but were reinstated by the Baathists with further radical modifications. Individual landholdings of irrigated land vary from 15 hectares (37 acres) to 57 hectares (136 acres), and those of rain-fed land vary from 80 hectares (198 acres) to 300 hectares (741 acres). The price of redistributed land was reduced to one-fourth of the compensation for expropriation. By 1969 some 1,497,338 hectares (3,700,000 acres) had been expropriated, 566,557 hectares (1,400,000 acres) had been distributed to 40,000 farm families, and 8,188 hectares (20,234 acres) had been organized into state farms. Undistributed land was rented to farmers at low cost. State-domain lands were distributed to farmers on similar terms. Over 400 agrarian cooperatives were organized, covering 561 villages.

An important state program in the agricultural sector is the regulation of prices of agricultural commodities. The state has monopoly pricing powers and preemptive purchasing rights in cotton, tobacco, and to a lesser extent sugar. The government also sets fixed prices for other agricultural products, notably fruits and vegetables.

In most regions agriculture is extensive rather than intensive, although the actual extent of rain-fed cultivated area has been declining since 1963. Mechanization is widespread in Jazirah region. In 1982, 31,387 tractors were in use and 2,659 harvester-threshers. Annual consumption of fertilizers was 133,600 tons, or 27 kg (60 lb) per arable hectare.

The country's main food crops are wheat and barley. In normal years the country is self-sufficient in food and has a surplus for export. Cotton is the main cash crop and commodity export, earning S £1.008 billion in 1983. Sugar beets and tobacco are the two most important cash crops after cotton.

PRINCIPAL CROP PRODUCTION (1983)		
	Area (hectares)	Production (000 metric tons)
Wheat	1,555,376	1,612
Barley	1,032,565	1,043
Corn	26,597	70
Millet	18,573	18
Lentils	136,116	61
Seed Cotton	n.a.	521
Tobacco	n.a.	13
Sesame	35,723	20
Grapes	93,835	450
Olives	234,424	235
Figs	20,647	51
Apricots	12,318	65
Apples	21,015	150
Sugar beet	13,682	1,200
Pomegranates	5,227	57
Onion	8,429	188
Tomatoes	30,755	750
Potatoes	14,587	300

Most of the livestock are sheep and goats raised by the bedouins. The livestock population in 1983 consisted of 800,000 cattle, 1,100,000 goats, 11,000,000 sheep, 7,000 camels, 56,000 horses, 242,000 asses and 15,000,000 chickens.

Over 404,000 hectares (1 million acres) are listed as forests, but only 60,000 hectares (150,000 acres) are productive forests. Production of roundwood is insignificant. Fishing, similarly, contributes little to the economy. Annual fish catch in 1983 was only 3,800 tons.

Agricultural credit is provided by the Agricultural Bank.

INDUSTRY

The industrial sector, including mining, has replaced agriculture as the main contributor to the GDP, accounting for 25%, though it employs only 31% of the labor force. Its rate of growth was also significantly higher 5.9% during 1973-83. In 1980 there were 34,542 industrial units employing 194,600 workers producing S£13.217 billion in goods and services. The value added in manufacturing in 1982 was $1.510 billion, of which agro-based products accounted for 27%, textiles 32%, chemicals 4% and machinery and transport equipment 4%.

The principal industrial centers are around the towns of Homs, Damascus, Aleppo and Latakia. Damascus, Aleppo, Latakia and Tartous are also the sites of Syria's free zones set up to encourage foreign investment in light industry and assembly plants. In 1978, 80.6% of industrial enterprises, or 34,355 establishments in the manufacturing, electricity and water and mining and quarrying branches of industry, were still concentrated in the country's traditional economic centers: 14,211 in Damascus and its district (33.4%), 10,066 in Aleppo (26%), 3,893 in Homs (9.1%), 2,742 in Hama (6.4%) and 2,443 in Latakia (5.7%).

The comparatively steady industrial expansion of the 1960s and early 1970s was primarily attributable to government intervention following the nationalization of all large- and medium-sized firms in 1965. By 1970 the state gained direct control of 108 such firms. Public investment in industry increased from S£300 million in 1963 to S £4.646 billion in 1976. Nationalized enterprises were reorganized into four broad federations: textiles, food processing, engineering and chemicals. The state-owned sector provides 75% of the value of industrial production. The private sector, employing two-thirds of the industrial labor force, is confined to handicrafts and other small-scale enterprises.

Textile manufacturing is the largest industrial branch accounting for about 40% of industrial production. Food processing, including sugar refineries and grain mills, is the second largest, accounting for about 20% of output. Other established industries include chemicals and fertilizers, cement, rubber, paper, iron and steel, and assembly of tractors, refrigerators and television sets.

Between 1970 and 1977 the total number of industrial enterprises grew by 37.4%. The private sector recorded a growth rate of 33.9% during the period while the public sector grew at a rate of 5.5%. In 1977, 99.7% of all enterprises employing less than four workers were privately owned. Only 2.3% of private sector enterprises employed more than nine workers. In certain strategic industries the public sector has a virtual monopoly.

Industrial credit is provided by the Industrial Bank.

ENERGY

In 1982 Syria's total energy production was equivalent to 12.302 million metric tons of coal and consumption to 9.377 million metric tons. Per capita energy consumption was 991 kg (2,185 lbs). The annual growth rates during 1973-83 were 3.6% for energy production and 13.3% energy consumption. Apparent per capita consumption of gasoline is 47 gallons per year.

Oil was first discovered in Syria in 1956 at Karachuk and was followed by further discoveries at Suweidiya and Rumelan. Syria was the first Arab country to nationalize its oil industry, in 1964, and for the next 10 years oil exploration and production was conducted solely by the state-owned General Petroleum Authority and the Syrian Petroleum Company with Soviet assistance. In 1975 Syria granted its first concession to a Western company, a United States group, and later offered a dozen onshore concessions for international bidding. Two new fields were opened, Jbeisseh in 1975 and Habari in 1976, producing better quality oil. Syria's oil reserves are estimated at 1.490 billion barrels, sufficient to last 25 years at current rate of extraction. In 1976 Syria was formally admitted to the OPEC and OAPEC.

The country's principal oilfields are located in northeastern Syria. The five largest fields are Karatchuk, Suweidiya, Rumelan, Jubaisseh, and Alayane.

Natural gas in commercial but limited quantities exists north of Tudmur. Total oil production in 1983 was 60 million barrels. Production of natural gas was 238 million cubic meters (8.404 billion cubic ft) in 1983. Reserves of natural gas are estimated at 37 billion cubic meters (1.306 trillion cubic ft).

Syria has two refineries: one at Homs with a capacity of 5.2 million tons per year and the other at Banias built with Rumanian cooperation with a capacity of 6 million tons per year. Total refinery capacity is 229,000 barrels per day. A number of problems have beset petroleum production in Syria: the cost of extraction is high, and the crude oil itself was uniformly of poor quality (until the Deir-ez-Zor discovery of 1984), having a high sulphur content, so that it had to be mixed with lighter imported oil to be marketable. Since the closure of the pipeline from Iraq in 1982, of the 11 million tons of light crude oil which it has imported for domestic refining, Syria has received the bulk, an estimated 44 million barrels (including 7.3 million barrels at no cost), from Iran at a substantial discount. In return, Syria has acted as a conduit for arms deliveries to Iran. Iran is treating Syrian debts of about $1,000 million, which it is currently unable to pay (owing to a shortage of foreign exchange), as long-term loans. In addition to oil, Iran is the dominant supplier of goods to Syria, its total exports to that country reaching more than $1,000 million in 1983, or 26% of Syria's total merchandise imports (more than three times the value of imports from the second largest supplier, Federal Germany).

Electric power production in 1984 was 5.93 billion kwh and per capita consumption 588 kwh. Generation and distribution of electricity is a monopoly of the state-owned Syrian Electricity Public Organization. The new Euphrates Dam at Taqba has an installed capacity of 1,200 megawatts and is expected to produce 2 billon kwh annually.

LABOR

In 1983 the labor force numbered 2,112,708, equivalent to 22.4% of the population. Women accounted for only 12.2% of this figure. Agriculture was the largest sector, employing 31.5%.

ECONOMICALLY ACTIVE POPULATION (sample survey, January 1983)			
	Males	Females	Total
Agriculture, hunting, forestry and fishing	506,105	99,648	605,753
Mining and quarrying	249,194	29,140	278,334
Manufacturing	249,194	29,140	278,334
Electricity, gas and water	20,130	731	20,861
Construction	321,129	3,238	324,367
Trade, restaurants and hotels	203,414	6,280	209,694
Transport, storage and communications	123,663	3,688	127,351
Financing, insurance, real estate and business services	15,166	2,729	17,895
Community, social and personal services	387,245	91,580	478,825
Activities not adequately defined	—	6	6
Total labor force	1,826,046	237,040	2,063,086
* Figures exclude persons seeking work for the first time, totaling 49,674 (males 29,278; females 20,396).			

The labor force is composed predominantly of unskilled and illiterate workers, and there is a critical shortage of trained managerial and technical personnel. Only 3.3% of the labor force is classified as professional and managerial, which has resulted in the employment of a large number of foreigners, mostly Russians, in technical and executive positions in industry.

Minimum wages are fixed in each province by wage commissions subject to the approval of the Ministry of Social Affairs and Labor. Wages are supplemented by profit-sharing programs, by which one-fourth of annual profits is distributed to employees. The state social insurance system includes retirement pensions, disability benefits and unemployment compensation.

Syrian labor statutes provide for comprehensive working standards. The minimum age in the predominant public sector is 18. In the private sector it is more variable: the absolute minimum age in the private sector is 12, while parental permission is required for children to work below the age of 16. The Labor Ministry has an enforcement mechanism, but the number of labor investigators is small, and violations of minimum-age laws may be extensive. Labor statutes provide for a 48-hour work week (six 8-hour days), though in certain fields in which workers are not continuously busy a 9-hour day is permitted. In actual practice, government employees rarely put in more than a five-to-six hour day. The statutes also stipulate a full 24-hour rest day per week and a minimum of one hour of rest per day; 14 days per year of annual leave (which rises to 21 days per year after 10 years' service); 70% of wages during the first 90 days of illness,

then 80% for the next 90 days; and overtime pay (25% for daytime overtime, 50% for night, 100% for holiday). Employers are required to provide limited medical care, and if there are more than 100 employees, a nurse must be hired and the service of a physician provided as necessary. Minimum wages are prescribed in all sectors. Typically, a government employee earns no more than $150-200 per month. However, many of them have second jobs. Rent controls and price subsidies allow such employees to enjoy a moderately comfortable existence despite nominally low wages.

The rate of unemployment is high, but is variously estimated at 5.1% to 11.4%. The true figure is probably closer to the higher end of the range. Official estimates cover only unemployed persons registered at state employment offices and make no provision for those seasonally unemployed.

Labor unions are officially encouraged and supported by the government and the ruling Baath Party, but, at the same time, are closely supervised. In 1968 the state established a pyramidal structure for labor unions with provincial occupational unions at the base. Provincial workers' unions are federations of all workers, irrespective of occupation, within a province. All unions representing the same occupation are affiliated to national labor unions, of which there are nine, all headquartered in Damascus. At the top of the pyramid is the General Federation of Workers' Unions, which represents the labor movement as a whole. There is a parallel structure for agricultural workers, with the Peasants' Federation at the top. About 36% of employed nonagricultural wage earners are believed to be unionized.

FOREIGN COMMERCE

Syria's foreign commerce in 1984 consisted of exports of $1.914 billion and imports of $3.516 billion, leaving an unfavorable trade balance of $1.602 billion. Of the imports, fuels constituted 26.5%, machinery and transport equipment 25.2%, food, beverages and tobacco 15.5%, chemicals 14.3% and metals and metal manufactures 5.9%. Of the exports, petroleum constituted 70.5%, textiles and leather 20.4%, cereals 5.3% and sand and stone 1.4%. The major import sources are: Iran 26.1%, West Germany 8.5%, Belgium 7.6%, Italy 7.3% and Japan 6.7%. The major export destinations are: Romania 29.7%, Italy 16.1%, the Soviet Union 10.7%, France 10.2% and Iran 5.3%. In 1981 the import price index was 242, the export price index was 361 and the terms of trade (export price divided by import price x 100) was 149 (based on 1970=100).

The import and export trade was nationalized in 1965. The State Import Export Company (SIMEX) has a monopoly over the import and distribution of 23 basic commodities, which are distributed through public consumption organizations.

The Damascus International Trade Fair is held annually at Damascus in July/August. There are seven

```
┌──────────────────────────────────────────────────────┐
│              FOREIGN TRADE INDICATORS (1984)            │
│  Annual Growth Rate, Imports:       9.1% (1973-83)     │
│  Annual Growth Rate, Exports:      –3.3% (1973-83)     │
│  Ratio of Exports to Imports:             35:65        │
│  Exports per capita:                       $182        │
│  Imports per capita:                       $335        │
│  Balance of Trade:                –$1.602 billion      │
│  Ratio of International                                 │
│    Reserves to Imports                                 │
│    (in months)                             0.7         │
│  Exports as % of GDP:                     68.8         │
│  Imports as % of GDP:                     75.8         │
│  Value of Manufactured Exports:             —          │
│  Commodity Concentration:                69.8%         │
│              Direction of Trade (%)                     │
│                          Imports      Exports          │
│  EEC                      35.11        63.3            │
│  U.S.                      5.3          —              │
│  Industrialized Market Economies  31.9  41.2          │
│  East European Economies  12.1        13.2            │
│  High Income Oil Exporters 38.3        7.7            │
│  Developing Economies     52.7        44.7            │
│            Composition of Trade (%)                    │
│                          Imports      Exports          │
│  Food                     13.7         6.1            │
│  Agricultural Raw Materials 3.1        7.3            │
│  Fuels                    37.6        69.6            │
│  Ores & Minerals           0.1          —             │
│  Manufactured Goods       45.3        10.0            │
│    of which Chemicals      8.8         1.0            │
│    of which Machinery     15.6         0.5            │
└──────────────────────────────────────────────────────┘
```

free trade zones at Damascus, Adra, Damascus International Airport, Tartus, Latakia, Aleppo, and Deraa.

TRANSPORTATION & COMMUNICATIONS

The Syrian rail system consists of 1,281 km (795 mi) of standard gauge and 262 km (163 miles) of narrow-gauge track. The northern line, one of the oldest in the Middle East, connects Aleppo with Turkey and Iraq, while the southern line connects Homs, Aleppo, Damascus, Latakia and Lebanon. The narrow-gauge track is mostly the historic Hejaz Railway, running south through Jordan to Medina in Saudi Arabia. In 1983 rail traffic consisted of 413 million passenger-km and 708 million net-ton-km of freight.

Two pipelines carried oil from Kirkuk in Iraqthrough Syria; one to Tripoli and the second to Banias. Both have been closed since the outbreak of the Iran-Iraq Gulf War. A third pipeline, owned by the Trans-Arabian Pipeline Company (TAPLINE), carries Saudi Arabian crude to Sidon in Lebanon, crossing about 160 km (100 mi) of Syrian territory. Oil transit fee income is a substantial item in the Syrian national budget.

Latakia is the oldest and principal seaport, but Banias and Tartous have developed into the main points of oil export. The three ports handled 24,500,000 metric tons of cargo in 1983. The Syrian merchant marine consists of 52 vessels with a GRT of 70,300.

Syria has 16,939 km (10,519 mi) of roads of which 12,051 km (7,484 mi) are paved. Roads are more nu-merous and better maintained in the western part where the main trunklines run north to south. The total number of passenger cars in 1982 was 79,141 and the number of commercial vehicles 113,440. Per capita vehicle ownership was 7.5 per 1,000 inhabitants.

The national airline is Syrian Arab Airlines, which as a fleet of 11 aircraft serving domestic and international routes. It flew 9.6 million km (5.96 million mi) in 1982 and carried 466,000 passengers. Damascus is the principal international airport. Besides Damascus there are 76 airfields, 70 usable, 26 with permanent surface runways, and 20 with runways over 2,500 meters (8,000 feet).

In 1984 there were 472,000 telephones, or 4.7 per 100 inhabitants.

In 1981 the postal service's 500 post offices handled 35,690,000 pieces of mail, and 337,000 telegrams. The per capita volume of mail was 3.3 pieces. There are 1,430 telex subscriber lines.

In 1982, 831,000 tourists visited Syria, of whom 6,700 were from the United States, 7,500 from the United Kingdom, 119,700 from Turkey, 53,500 from Saudi Arabia, 8,400 from Romania, 346,800 from Lebanon, 288,700 from Jordan, 19,300 from Iraq, 11,300 from Iran, 10,800 from West Germany, 39,900 from Egypt, 11,200 from Bulgaria, 4,900 from the Soviet Union and 9,700 from France. Total tourist receipts were $150 million. There are 22,000 hotel beds and the average length of stay was 1.4 days.

MINING

Phosphate is the only mineral found in significant quantities. Phosphate reserves are estimated at 600 million tons of high chlorine (0.15-0.25%) ore. Production began in 1971 with 20,000 tons and attained 857,000 tons in 1975 before falling back to 425,000 tons in 1977. Responding to improved prices, Syrian production staged a comeback in 1978, with confirmed production of 747,000 tons rising to 1,461,000 tons in 1982. Existing production is concentrated at three points, built with Romanian, Polish, and Bulgarian assistance, near Palmyra in central Syria.

DEFENSE

The defense structure is headed by the president of the republic who is also the commander in chief. The general staff organization is based on the Soviet model. Military service is compulsory and is required of every Syrian citizen by the constitution. Upon completion of the mandatory conscript service of 30 months, every soldier joins the reserve for 18 years.

The total strength of the active armed forces is 402,500 or 22.7 armed persons per 1,000 civilians.

ARMY

Personnel: 270,000 (Reserves: 100,000)

Organization: HQ 2 corps; 5 armored divisions; 3 mechanized divisions; 1 special forces division; 2 independent mechanized brigades; 6 artillery brigades; 8 parachute commando regiments; 3 surface-to-surface missile regiments; 30 SAM battalions

Equipment: 4,200 tanks; 800 combat vehicles; 600 mechanized infantry combat vehicles; 1600 armored personnel carriers

Artillery: 40,000 guns; howitzers; mortars; rocket launchers; surface-to-surface missiles; antitank guns; 1,300 antitank guided weapons; 1,000 air defense guns

Air Defense Command: 22 air defense brigades

NAVY:

Personnel: 2,500 (Reserves: 2,000)

Fleet: 2 frigates; 22 fast attack craft; 7 patrol craft; 4 mine countermeasures vessels; 2 landing craft

Naval Bases: Latakia and Banias.

AIR FORCE:

Personnel: 70,000 (Reserves: 8,000)

Organization: 500 combat aircraft; 9 fighter squadrons; 10 reconnaissance MiG-25R; 15 interceptor squadrons; 2 transport squadrons; 90 trainers; 40 attack helicopters; 100 transports

Air Bases: Damascus, Hamah, Dumayr, Palmyra, Sahles, Sahra, Aleppo, Rasafa, Blay, Sayqat, Khalkhalah and Masiriyah.

Forces Abroad: 30,000 in Lebanon

The annual military budget in 1985 was $3.312 billion, 29.8% of the national budget, 13.0% of GNP, $209 per capita, $9,802 per soldier and $11,762 per sq km of national territory.

The bulk of the Syrian army is stationed on the three hostile borders; Israel, Iraq and Jordan; in addition, 35,000 troops, ironically named the Arab Deterrent Force, are stationed in Lebanon.

Outside the normal command structure of the army stand the 15,000-strong Special Forces and the division-strength Detachments for the Defense of the Regime commanded by the president's brother Rifat Assad. Both these formations are recruited exclusively from Alawite areas and are fanatical in their personal loyalty to President Assad. The Detachments for the Defense of the Regime are permanently kept in Damascus to protect the presidential palace and no other unit of the army is permitted to enter the capital.

The Syrian army is almost entirely equipped by the Soviet Union. It is believed that there are over 3,000 Soviet military and technical advisers serving with Syrian combat units. Soviet military aid to Syria since 1954 is estimated at over $1 billion. In 1978 Syria obtained additional aid from the Soviet Union to replace equipment lost in military engagements in recent years. In addition, Syria has received $1 billion from Libya for arms purchases. Some of the Syrian arms and equipment have been transferred to the Somalis, the Eritrean rebels and the Palestinians. The Syrian-controlled wing of the Palestine Liberation Army (known as the Saiqa) has been fully integrated within the Syrian Army.

Syria has no internal defense production. Arms purchases abroad during 1973-83 totaled $15.180 billion, of which the Soviet Union accounted for $9.2 billion.

EDUCATION

The national literacy rate is 65.7% (80.0% for males and 50.8% for females). There are striking differences between urban and rural literacy and between male and female literacy. Nearly 63% of Damascenes are literate, while only 15% of the inhabitants of Al Raqqah province are literate. Illiteracy among women ranges from 50 to 70%, while only 20% of the men are illiterate. Of the population over 25, 68.6% have had no schooling, 25.9% have completed first level, 4.3% have completed second level, and 1.3% have completed post-secondary courses.

Schooling is universal, compulsory and free from 6 to 11, and textbooks are free in primary schools. In 1982 the primary school enrollment ratio, covering the 6-to-11 age group, was 101% and at the secondary level, covering the 12-to-17 age group, 51%. The adjusted school enrollment ratio at both levels was 79%. The third level enrollment ratio is 16.1%.

Schooling consists of six years of primary school, three years of intermediate school, both general and vocational, and three years of secondary school, both general and vocational. Girls constituted 44% of the enrollment at the primary level, 38% at the secondary level, 10% in vocational schools, 32% in post-secondary classes and 31% in teacher training schools.

The academic year runs from September to May. The medium of instruction is Arabic, but both French and English are taught as second languages.

The primary school curriculum emphasizes religion, Arabic, arithmetic, history, geography and civics. Foreign languages, science, political studies and agricultural training are introduced at the intermediate stage. At the secondary level students can choose either a humanities or a science program. During the senior year humanities students are required to take some science courses and science students some courses in humanities. Military training is compulsory.

Classrooms are crowded and many classes must be taught in both morning and afternoon shifts. The teacher-pupil ratio in 1982 was 1:27 in primary schools and 1:18 in secondary schools. Because of an acute teacher shortage, many teaching positions are filled by unqualified persons.

Most private and Christian schools were nationalized in 1967. There are 295 private primary schools, 66 operated by UNRWA (U.N. Relief and Works Agency) and 297 private secondary schools, including 29 operated by UNRWA. All private schools are administered by Ministry of Education officials to ensure conformity with official standards.

Despite government efforts to channel more student into vocational schools, only 6.3% of secondary school students are in the vocational stream. Because of Syrians' dislike of manual occupations, there is a persisting shortage of technical personnel and skilled workers.

Literacy courses are offered in special classes run by the government. There are also 24 adult education schools offering courses in basic subjects.

Education administration is highly centralized in the Ministry of Education and the Ministry of Higher Education. Curricula and teaching methods are supervised by a central inspectorate. There is also a director of education for each province and a School Building Authority in charge of school construction and maintenance. In 1982 the educational budget was S£4,058,679,000, of which 54.7% was current expenditure. This budget was 6.0% of GNP and 12.2% of the national budget. Per capita educational expenditure was $108.

EDUCATIONAL ENROLLMENT (1982)			
	Schools	Teachers	Students
First Level	8,003	58,244	1,610,548
Second Level	1,395	32,274	587,047
Vocational	148	5,424	46,193
Third Level	24	N.A.	119,341

Higher education is provided by three universities, the University of Damascus (also known as the Syrian University), the University of Aleppo and the University of Latakia, with a combined enrollment of 119,341 in 1982. University enrollment was 1,136 per 100,000 inhabitants. In 1981, 14,469 Syrian students graduated from the three national universities. Of these, 1,766 received degrees in medicine, 3,704 in engineering, 1,261 in natural sciences, 501 in law, 295 in education and 1,437 in agriculture. In 1982, 13,725 Syrian students were enrolled in institutions of higher learning abroad. Of these, 1,036 were in the United States, 1,486 in France, 317 in Spain, 249 in Italy, 491 in West Germany and 139 in the United Kingdom. Many of these students fail to return to Syria on completion of their studies. In 1975, 7,032 foreign students were enrolled in Syria.

The Syrian contribution to world scientific authorship is .0010% and Syria's world rank in this area is 106th. No scientific journal is published in Syria.

LEGAL SYSTEM

The constitution specifies that the source of Syrian jurisprudence is the Sharia, or Muslim law, but in many areas the Sharia has been superseded by secular law based on European civil, commercial and criminal codes. Under the constitution the judiciary is theoretically independent of other branches of government, and the appointment, transfer and dismissal of judges are in the hands of the High Judicial Council.

The court system is headed by the Court of Cassation under which there are 30 courts of appeal in 30 prefectures, each presided over by three judges. On the next lower level are 110 summary courts presided over by judges of the peace. At the base of the system are 41 first instance courts, each consisting of one judge. There are also juvenile courts and personal status courts for Muslims, Druzes and non-Muslim communities, such as Catholics, Armenians and Jews. Outside the regular court system are the emergency courts or military courts set up on an ad hoc basis to try alleged enemies of the state.

Criminal cases with no political implications are conducted according to a French-based legal code. The defendant is detained provisionally upon the accusation of the public prosecutor, then remanded to a judge of arraignment, who may either free him on the basis of insufficient evidence or refer the case to a criminal court. Defendants are entitled to legal representation of their choice; if they cannot afford an attorney, the court appoints and pays for a lawyer. Civilian courts impose no restrictions on lawyers in representing clients and allow the right of appeal. In noncontroversial criminal cases, the civilian courts are typically free from governmental interference; nevertheless, pressure from the party, state security forces, or other special units affects the course of the trials or the verdicts if there is high-level interest in a case.

The penal system is a department of the national police under a director of prisons. Every major city and town has a detention facility. The main maximum security penitentiary is located at Tudmur. Damascus has two major prisons, the Mezza and the the Citadel. Most prisons are old and crowded, and political prisoners are often brutally treated.

LAW ENFORCEMENT

The Syrian police force is patterned after the French Surete and functions under a police commander and director of internal security with headquarters at Damascus. The total strength of internal security forces is 9,500, including 1,500 desert guards. This is equivalent to 38 law enforcement agents per 1,000 working inhabitants. Syria ranks 44th in the world in per capita strength of law enforcement forces. The central headquarters at Damascus exercises strict control over policy, operations and administration. In each province the police are nominally under the jurisdiction of the governor, but effectively operations are supervised by the centrally appointed director of police.

The Syrian secret police is the Political Security Section (PSS) of the police department, which is charged with sensitive police activities involving national security, countersubversion and surveillance. PSS agents are located in most towns and public places: markets, airfields, universities, hotels and mosques, and they also work as barbers, taxidrivers and waiters. Their functions also include control of smuggling and narcotics.

No reliable crime statistics are available for Syria.

HEALTH

In 1982 there were 151 hospitals with 10,770 beds, or 1 bed per 863 persons. The number of physicians in the country was 4,633, or one physician per 2,006 persons, 1,404 dentists and 5,910 nursing personnel. Of the hospitals 25.2% are state-run, 2.0% are run by private nonprofit agencies and 72.8% by private for-profit agencies. The admissions/discharge rate per 10,000 inhabitants was 240, the bed occupancy rate was 53.0% and the average length of stay was 5 days.

Health expenditures represent 0.9% of the national budget, and $4.90 per capita.

```
PRINCIPAL HEALTH INDICATORS (1984)
Crude Death Rate: 7.2 per 1,000
Decline in Death Rate: −56.3% (1965-83)
Life Expectancy at Birth: 65.6 (Males); 68.5 (Females)
Infant Mortality Rate: 67.2 per 1,000 Live Births
Child Death Rate (Ages 1-4) per 1,000: 4
```

Gastrointestinal and parasitic ailments and trachoma are the most prevalent diseases in the country, especially in rural areas. Incidence of trachoma is highest where dust storms are common. Bejel, a non-venereal form of syphilis, is endemic among Bedouins. Over 75% of the population has access to safe water.

FOOD

Wheat bread is the staple food supplemented by vegetables and fruits. Meat is consumed only occasionally. Per capita food intake in 1982 was 78.1 grams of protein and 2,863 calories per day, slightly higher than the recommended WHO minimum of 2,600 calories per day 56 grams of fats and 441 grams of carbohydrates.

MEDIA & CULTURE

The Syrian press consists of nine dailies, with a total circulation of 186,000, and six non-dailies. Per capita circulation is 17.6 per 1,000 persons. Consumption of newsprint in 1982 was 3,500 tons, or 375 kg (827 lb) per 1,000 inhabitants.

The largest selling daily is *Al-Baath*, the organ of the ruling Baath Socialist Party. Almost all newspapers are published in Arabic. Periodicals number 35 titles, most of them published by religious organizations, associations and state ministries. The Press Organization for Printing, Publishing and Distribution is one of the largest publishers in the country, producing all official publications.

Imported foreign printed matter and films generally are not censored, although articles are occasionally deleted from magazines and newspapers before distribution. This news material, along with fictional and non-fictional literature on the Middle East, is banned when considered critical of Syria. Control is much stricter on materials in Arabic. Censorship is exercised through offices in the Ministries of Information and of Culture and National Guidance. During the November 1983 assault by Syrian-surrogate Palestinian organizations against pro-Arafat Palestinian forces in Tripoli, television news from neighboring Jordan was jammed and Beirut periodicals were often withheld from the market.

Both the domestic and foreign press are strictly controlled and censored by the Ministry of Information. Censorship regulations were somewhat eased after the accession to power of Assad in 1970 but are still severe enough for Syria to be ranked 75th in press freedom among the nations of the world with a minus rating of −1.99 (on a scale with +4 as the maximum and −4 as the minimum. Norway = +3.06; U.S., +2.72). Further control over the press is exercised through allocation of newsprint and licensing of publications. In 1978, 10 journalists, including Adnan Baghajati, editor of al-Baath, were barred from press activity, bringing to 120 the number of journalists purged since 1976.

The national news agency is Syrian Arab News Agency (SANA) with 10 foreign bureaus. Foreign agencies represented in Damascus include Tass, UPI, DPA, Reuters and ANSA.

Book publishing is relatively limited and is either owned or controlled by the state. In 1980, 95 titles were published. Most of the imports came from the Soviet Union. Commercial advertising and promotional materials are also controlled by the state through the Arab Advertising Organization. Syria does not adhere to any copyright convention.

Radio broadcasting and television services are operated by the General Directorate of Broadcasting and Television. The home service of the radio network, with eight medium-wave and three short-wave transmitters ranging in power from 10 to 600 kw, is on the air for 140 hours a week, broadcasting from Damascus, Aleppo, Deit-ez-Zor, Sabburah, Homs and Tartous. A foreign service is broadcast for 30 hours a week. No license fee is required for radio receivers. Of the total 2,363 radio broadcasting hours annually, 602 hours are devoted to information, 317 to culture, 164 to religion and 1,255 hours to entertainment. Television, introduced in 1960, has been extended to cover 75% of the population. There are five transmitters, at Damascus, Aleppo, Homs, Slenfe and Sarankhiyah, broadcasting for 54½ hours a week. An annual license fee is payable for television receivers. In 1982 there were 1,850,000 radio receivers, or 192 per 1,000 persons and 430,000 television receivers, or 45 per 1,000 persons. Of the 863 annual television broadcasting hours, 110 hours are devoted to information, 114 hours to education, 40 hours to religion and 249 hours to entertainment.

The Public Institution for the Cinema was established in 1963 to promote the domestic film industry. Production, however, is restricted to short films and documentaries. In 1981, 201 full-length films were imported including 88 from the Soviet Union. All films are censored by the Censorship Commission for their political content as well as conformity to current morals. In 1981 there were 92 cinemas with 53,200 seats, or 5.7 per 1,000 inhabitants. Annual movie attendance was 14.5 million, or 1.6 per capita. Annual box office receipts are S£22.2 million.

There are 49 public libraries and 14 college and university libraries in the country. The national library is Al Zahiriah in Damascus with 64,000 volumes. The University of Damascus Library has over 100,000 volumes as well as an extensive collection of Arabic manuscripts. Per capita there are 49 volumes and 146 registered borrowers per 1,000 inhabitants.

There are 27 museums reporting an annual attendance of over 600,000.

SOCIAL WELFARE

A contributory social security scheme for illness, maternity, disability and old age was introduced in 1963. The Social Security Institute also provides low-cost loans to urban workers. Community Development Centers provide a wide range of social services in rural areas.

GLOSSARY

fellah (pl. fellahin): a peasant or cultivator.
kuttab: Muslim elementary school, often attached to a mosque.
mantika (pl. manatik): administrative district, subdivision of a province.
mudir: local official, especially head of a district or subdistrict.
muhaafaza (pl. muhaafazat): province.
mukhtar (pl. mukhtaara): headman of a village.
nahia (pl. nawahi): a locality, subdivision of a district.
shaykh: tribal chief.

CHRONOLOGY (from 1946)

1946— French evacuate Syria. . . . Independent Syrian Republic is proclaimed with Shukri Al Kuwatly as president and Khalid Al Azm as premier.
1948— Syrian troops invade Israel and share Arab defeat. . . . Syria leaves the franc zone.
1949— Husni Al Zaim seizes power in the first of a series of army coups. . . . Zaim is overthrown after 4½ months by another army coup under Sami Hinnawa who is turn is unseated by Adib Shishakli. . . . Civilian government is allowed to continue under Hashim Al Atassi as president. . . . Women vote for the first time in national elections.
1950— New constitution is promulgated by constituent assembly.
1951— Conflict between the army and the civilian government leads to a showdown in which Shishakli seizes absolute power, abolishes all political parties and dissolves the chamber of deputies. . . . Fawzi Silu is appointed by Shishakli as premier.
1952— Arab Liberation Movement is founded by Shishakli as the nation's sole political party.
1953— Syrians approve new constitution by referendum making Syria a presidential republic with Shishakli as president. . . . Martial law is imposed as Druzes revolt against the government. . . . Baath Socialist Party is founded.
1954— Shishakli is ousted in country's fourth coup. . . . 1950 constitution is restored; new civilian government is formed with Hashim Al Atassi as president
1955— Syria and Egypt agree to the creation of a joint military command with headquarters at Damascus. . . . Shukri Al Kuwatly succeeds Atassi as president.
1956— Anglo-French invasion of Suez swings Syria into the Soviet camp; Syrian troops put oil pipelines out of order; Syria breaks off relations with Britain and France. . . . Oil is found at Karachuk field. . . . USSR offers to supply arms.
1957— Baathists and Communists win elections. . . . Syria sides with leftwing forces in political crisis in Jordan. . . . United States Sixth Fleet is ordered to the Eastern Mediterranean to avert possible Syrian military intervention in Jordan; Syria withdraws forces from Amman.
1958— Syria and Egypt announce the creation of the United Arab Republic through a union of the two countries; union is confirmed by a plebiscite; Nasser is elected first president of UAR. . . . Akram Howrani and, later, Abdul Hamid Sarraj become chairmen of the executive council for the Syrian Province.
1960— Syrian opposition to the union grows as Nasser attempts complete integration of the two countries
1961— Union with Egypt is dissolved following coup in Damascus. . . . Syria rejoins U.N. . . . Conservatives win elections; Nazim Al Qudsi is elected president with Maruf Dawalibi as prime minister.
1962— Brief army coup succeeds in holding power for twelve days; Qudsi regime is restored.
1963— The government, weakened and demoralized by internal and external dissensions, is swept out of power by Baathist coup; a National Revolutionary Command Council is formed as the supreme ruling body with a Baathist-dominated cabinet headed by Silah Al Bitar. . . . Pro-Nasserists are expelled from the cabinet and the army; attempted Nasserist revolt is crushed. . . . Amin Al Hafiz emerges as the strong man and president of the National Council of the Revolution.

1964— Provisional constitution is announced, making Syria a Socialist People's Democratic Republic.... Banks and industrial enterprises are nationalized.... Hafiz is elected head of state.

1966— Extremist wing of the Baath Party, led by Salah Al Jadid and Nur-ud-din Atassi, topples Hafiz.... Yusuf Zeayen is appointed prime minister.

1967— Arab-Israeli war breaks out; Israel overruns the Golan Heights and occupies the town of Quneitra; Syria breaks off diplomatic relations with the United States and the United Kingdom.

1970— Moderate wing of the Baath Party led by Lt. Gen. Hafez al Assad seizes power and ousts Jadid and Atassi; Assad assumes post of premier with Ahmad al Khatib as president.... TAPLINE is sabotaged.

1971— Under a provisional constitution, Assad is elected president for a seven-year term with Abdul Rahman Khulayfawi as premier.... People's Council is established as the national legislature.... Federation of Arab Republics is formed with Syria, Egypt and Libya as members.... Syria accedes to the Tripoli Charter States Alliance.

1972— Assad forms the Progressive Front of National Union, an alliance of left-wing political parties dominated by the Baath Party.... Mahmoud Al Ayyoubi is named new premier.

1973— New constitution is promulgated.... The Progressive Front gains absolute majority in People's Council in new elections.

1975— Diplomatic relations with United States and United Kingdom are restored.

1976— Ayyoubi resigns as premier and is replaced by Khulayfawi.... Syria intervenes in force in the Lebanese civil war.

1977— President Assad denounces President Sadat's visit to Jerusalem and declares a national day of mourning; Egypt breaks relations with Syria and recalls ambassador.

1978— Running as the only candidate Assad is reelected president for a second seven-year term by 99.9% of the electorate; Premier Abdul Rahman Khulayfawi is replaced by Mohommed Ali al-Halabi.

1978— Assad is reelected president.... Prime Minister Abdel Rahman Khleifawi steps down and is replaced by Mohammed Ali al—Halabi.... Soviet Union agrees to step up arms flow.... Egypt cuts diplomatic ties.

1979— Sixty Alawite army cadets are gunned down by Sunni fanatics; Alawite-Sunni clashes erupt in major cities.... Assad vows to suppress the Muslim Brotherhood.... Army moves into northern Syria to quell mass violence.

1980— Relations with Iraq worsen as the personal animosity between President Assad and President Saddam Husayn of Iraq intensifies; Iraq cuts diplomatic ties; Syria moves to the brink of war with Jordan but yields to Saudi mediation.... Syria and the Soviet Union sign 20-year treaty of friendship calling for stronger military as well as political and economic ties.... Libya proposes merger with Syria.... Syria and Libya rally behind Iran in its war with Iraq.... Abdul Rauf Kassem is named premier replacing al-Halabi.

1981— Elections are held to the People's Assembly in which the National Front wins all seats.

1982— A Muslim Brotherhood uprising in Hama is brutally suppressed.

1983— Syria helps anti-Yasir Arafat faction in PLO to oust him from Syria.... Assad suffers a heart attack and is hospitalized for months.

1984— President Mitterand of France visits Syria.

1985— Assad is reelected for a third seven-year term in office.

BIBLIOGRAPHY (from 1970)

Akhras, Safouh al-, *Revolutionary Change and Modernization in the Arab World: A Case from Syria* (Damascus, 1972).

Bar-Siman-Tov, Yaacov, *Linkage Politics in the Middle East: Syria Between Domestic and External Conflicts* (Boulder, Colo., 1983).

Dawisha, Adeed I., *Syria and the Lebanese Crisis* (New York, 1980).

Devlin, John F., *A History of the Ba'ath Party from its Origins to 1966* (Stanford, Calif., 1976).

——, *Syria: Modern State in an Ancient Land* (Boulder, Colo., 1982).

Haddad, Robert M., *Syrian Christians in Muslim Society* (Princeton, N.J., 1971).

Kanovsky, Eliahu, *The Economy of Syria* (Portland, Ore., 1979).

Longrigg, Stephen H. *Syria and Lebanon under the French Mandate* (New York, 1972).

McLaurin, R.D., *Foreign Policy Making in the Middle East: Domestic Influences on Policy in Egypt, Iraq, Israel and Syria* (New York, 1977).

Maos, Moshe and Avner Yaniv, *Syria Under Assad* (New York, 1986).

Olson, Robert W., *The Ba'ath and Syria, 1947-82* (Princeton, N.J., 1982).

Petran, Tabitha, *Syria* (New York, 1972).

Rabinovitch, Itamar, *Syria under the Ba'ath, 1963-1966* (New Brunswick, N.J., 1972).

Seeleye, Talcott, *U.S.-Arab Relations: The Syrian Dimension* (Washington, D.C., 1985).

Tibawi, A.L., *A Modern History of Syria* (New York, 1970).

OFFICIAL PUBLICATIONS

Finance Ministry, *La Statistique* (Annual, French).

Syria Central Bank, *Bilan Annuel* (Annual Balance Sheet) (French).

——, *Quarterly Bulletin* (Arabic and English).

————, *Revue Financiere et Bancaire* (Financing and Banking Journal) (quarterly, Arabic and French).

TANZANIA

- ▬▬▬ International boundary
- ⊛ National capital
- ┼─┼ Railroad
- ─── Road

| 0 | 50 | 100 Miles |
| 0 | 50 | 100 Kilometers |

CONGO
Lake Edward
UGANDA
Kabale
Bukoba
Musoma
Nyeri
Lake Naivasha
NAIROBI
KENYA
Lac Kivu
KIGALI
LAKE VICTORIA
Magadi
RWANDA
UKEREWE I.
Biharamulo
Mwanza
Lake Eyasi
Lake Natron
Lake Manyara
Moshi
Kagera
BUJUMBURA
BURUNDI
Shinyanga
Arusha
Mombasa
Malagarasi
Nzega
Wembere
Pangani
Kigoma
Tabora
Singida
Korogwe
Wete
Tanga
PEMBA I.
Ugalla
Mkokotoni
Koani
LAKE TANGANYIKA
Kalemi
Dodoma
Wami
Zanzibar
ZANZIBAR I.
Mpanda
Kisigo
DAR ES SALAAM
Kilosa
Morogoro
Ruvu
INDIAN OCEAN
ZAIRE
Great Ruaha
Mikumi
Kidatu
MAFIA I.
Sumbawanga
Lake Rukwa
Iringa
Ifakara
Rufiji
Lake Mweru
Kilombero
Kilwa Kivinje
Mbeya
Luwegu
Njombe
Tunduma
ZAMBIA
Kasama
Chambeshi
LAKE NYASA
Lindi
Lake Bangweulu
MALAWI
Songea
Masasi
Mtwara
Mzimba
BOUNDARY REPRESENTATION IS NOT NECESSARILY AUTHORITATIVE
MOZAMBIQUE (Port.)
Ruvuma

UHURU · NA · UMOJA

TANZANIA

BASIC FACT SHEET

OFFICIAL NAME: United Republic of Tanzania (Jamhuri Ya Muungano Wa Tanzania)

ABBREVIATION: TZ

CAPITAL: Dar es Salaam

HEAD OF STATE: President Ali Hassan Mwinyi (from 1985)

HEAD OF GOVERNMENT: Prime Minister Joseph Warioba (from 1985)

NATURE OF GOVERNMENT: One-party modified democracy

POPULATION: 21,733,000 (1985)

AREA: 939,361 sq km (362,688 sq mi)

ETHNIC MAJORITY: Bantu

LANGUAGE: Swahili

RELIGIONS: Animism, Christianity and Islam

UNIT OF CURRENCY: Shilling ($1=Sh16.975, 1985)

NATIONAL FLAG: Diagonal black band running from the lower corner of the hoist to the upper corner of the fly, flanked by thin yellow bands, separating a green triangular field at the upper left and a blue triangular field at the lower right

NATIONAL EMBLEM: A native shield divided horizontally into four parts: a flashing red torch on a yellow field, the national flag, crossed war axes and spears in gold on a red background and wavy blue and white lines. The shield is flanked by a barefoot youth and a girl, wearing an orange head scarf supporting two elephant tusks, standing on a mound representing Mount Kilimanjaro. The national motto, "Uhuru Na Umoja" ("Freedom and Unity"), appears below on a white ribbon in red-gold letters.

NATIONAL ANTHEM: "God Bless Africa"

NATIONAL HOLIDAYS: April 26 (National Day, Union Day); January 1 (New Year's Day); January 12 (Zanzibar Revolution Day); February 5 (Chama Cha Mapinduzi Day); May 1 (Labor Day); July 7 (Saba Saba Day, i.e. Foundation of the Independence Movement Day); December 9 (Republic Day); also Christmas, Good Friday, Easter Monday, Boxing Day and three Islamic festivals.

NATIONAL CALENDAR: Gregorian

PHYSICAL QUALITY OF LIFE INDEX: 61 (up from 28 in 1976) (On an ascending scale with 100 as the maximum. U.S. 95)

DATE OF INDEPENDENCE: December 9, 1961 (Tanganyika); December 10, 1963 (Zanzibar); Union of Tanganyika and Zanzibar (April 26, 1964)

DATE OF CONSTITUTION: June 1965; revised 1985

WEIGHTS & MEASURES: Both imperial and metric systems are used. One common traditional weight is the frasla=15.8 kg (35 lb).

LOCATION & AREA

Tanzania is located in East Africa, south of the Equator, and includes the islands of Mafia, Pemba and Zanzibar. It occupies an area of 939,361 sq km (362,688 sq mi), extending 1,223 km (760 mi) N to S and 1,191 km (740 mi) E to W. Zanzibar is separated from the mainland by a channel 36 km (22 ½ mi) across at its narrowest point and has an area of 1,658 sq km (640 sq mi). To the northeast, some 40 km (25 mi) away is the island of Pemba with an area of 984 sq km (380 sq mi). The total length of the coastline is 1,424 km (884 mi), of which that of Zanzibar is 212 km (132 mi), that of Pemba 177 km (110 mi) and that of Mafia 113 km (70 mi).

Tanzania shares its international land boundary of 3,843 km (2,386 mi) with eight countries: Uganda (418 km, 260 mi), Kenya (769 km, 478 mi), Mozambique (756 km, 470 mi), Malawi (451 km, 280 mi), Zambia (322 km, 200 mi), Zaire (459 km, 285 mi), Burundi (451 km, 280 mi) and Rwanda (217 km, 135 mi). The only boundary dispute is recent times has been with Malawi. The boundary with Kenya was established by an agreement between the United Kingdom and Germany in 1886 and confirmed in 1890, the boundary with Uganda by the Anglo-German Agreement of 1890, those with Rwanda and Burundi by the Anglo-Belgian Protocol of 1924, that with Zaire at the Berlin Conference of 1885, those with Zambia and Malawi by the Anglo-German Agreement of 1890, and that with Mozambique by the Portuguese-German Agreement of 1866. With the exception of the border with Kenya, boundaries follow natural features.

The capital is Dar es Salaam, with a 1980 population of 870,020. The future capital, Dodoma, on the rim of the Eastern Rift, has a population of 23,440. Other major urban centers are Tanga (143,878), Mwanza (170,823), Arusha (88,155), Moshi (52,223), Iringa

(51,000), Morogoro (44,000) Tabora (29,000), Musoma (33,000), Ujji/Kigoma (28,000) and Mtwara (27,000).

The topography of the country is determined by the Great Rift Valley that runs through the middle of the country from north to south. As defined by this valley, the major physical regions are the Western Rift, the central plateau, Lake Victoria basin, the Eastern Rift and mountains, the eastern plateau and the coastal belt and islands. The greater part of the country consists of the central plateau with an elevation of between 1,000 and 1,400 meters (3,500 and 4,500 ft). The nation's mountain systems are grouped mainly along the Eastern Rift. Its western wall comprises the Kondoa and Mbulu ranges, the Gogoland Hills, the Mpwapwa Mountains and the southern highlands. The northern part of the Eastern Rift contains the Winter Highlands, including the volcanic region comprising Mount Loolmalasin, Ngorongoro Crater and Mount Lengai, one of the most famous game reserves in the world. Within the lower part of the Rift lies the Olduvai Gorge where, according to the paleontologist L. S. B. Leakey, the earliest forms of man originated. In the northern highlands are two of the highest peaks in Africa, Mount Kilimanjaro (5,922 meters, 19,430 ft) and Mount Meru (4,566 meters, 14,980 ft). Toward the south is a dry steppe merging into the Masai Steppe, a part of the eastern plateau. The northeast of the Masai Steppe is bounded by the Pare and Usambara Mountains, cut by deep, broad valleys. In the south are the Livingstone Mountains, the Kipengere Range, the Poroto Mountains, Mount Rugwe and, further west, the Ufipa Highlands and the isolated Uluguru Mountains. In the Songea district lies another range, the Matengo Highlands.

The coastal belt is 15 to 65 km (10 to 40 mi) wide, broader in the center and narrower in the north and south. The coast contains numerous coral reefs and shifting sandbars.

Zanzibar is a low-lying coral country covered by bush and grass plains. The highest point in the island is Masingini Ridge (104 meters, 340 ft). Siniongoni, the highest point on Pemba, is 95 meters (311 ft).

The main rivers flowing into the Indian Ocean are the Pangani, rising in the snows of Kilimanjaro, the Wami and its tributary the Mkondoa, the Ruvu or the Kingani, the Rufiji with its tributaries the Ruaha, the Kilombero and the Mbaragandu, and farther south the Matandu, the Mbemkuru, the Lewugu, the Lukuledi and the Ruvuma, the last forming the southern boundary with Mozambique. The basin of the Rufiji covers one-fourth of the national territory, and it is navigable for 97 km (60 mi). The Mkomazi flows through the Masai Steppe. A number of rivers discharge into the country's lakes: the Grummeti, the Kagera, the Mori and the Mara into Lake Victoria, the Rungwe into Lake Rukwa; the Malagarasi into Lake Tanganyika; the Songwe and the Ruhuhu into Lake Nyasa; and the Wembere, the Manyonga and the Sibiti into Lake Eyasi. Of these, only the Kagera is navigable, for 145 km (90 mi). Although there are no large rivers in Tanzania, the country is the divide for the three great river systems of the African continent: the Nile, the Zaire and the Zambezi.

On the borders are three large lakes: Victoria, the second largest fresh-water lake in the world; Lake Tanganyika, the second deepest lake in the world; and Lake Nyasa. Entirely within the country are Lakes Natron, Eyasi, Manyara and Rukwa.

WEATHER

Tanzania has a tropical equatorial climate modified by altitude. Broadly, the country is divided into three climatic zones: the northern coastal belt, from Dar es Salaam to the Kenya border; the lake region around Lake Victoria; and the interior plateau and the southern coastal belt. In general, the nationwide temperatures are lower than those of countries in similar latitudes. The mean daily maximums range between 22.2°C and 32.2°C (72°F and 90°F). The north has two distinct wet seasons: the longer one from March to May and the shorter one from November to December. The rest of the country has only one rainy season, from November to April or May. The overall rainfall is not great. About half the country receives 76 cm (30 in.) annually, the maximum being recorded at Lake Nyasa (254 cm, 100 in.) and the minimum in parts of the central plateau and the Masai Steppe (51 cm, 20 in.).

The northern coastal belt has two wet seasons and two dry seasons. The long rains occur from March to May and the short rains from November to December, alternating with dry seasons from June to October and January to February. Rainfall is slightly greater in the area of the Rufiji Basin, with an annual mean of 127 to 152 cm (50 to 60 in.); elsewhere it is 102 to 127 cm (40 to 50 in.). The temperature ranges from 22°C (72°F) to 30°C (85°F). February is the hottest month.

The lake region also has two wet seasons and two periods each of warm and cool weather. The rainy seasons are from November to December and from April to mid-June, while the warm periods are in October and February or March, and cool seasons are in January and from July to September. Temperatures range from 28°C (82°F) during the warm season to 17°C (63°F) during the cool season. Areas to the east receive 77 to 101 cm (30 to 40 in.), while those to the west receive from 203 to 228 cm (80 to 90 in.) of rainfall.

The interior plateau receives rain during only one season. Precipitation is highest in the Lake Nyasa region, which receives 254 cm (100 in.); the rest of the plateau receives from 77 to 101 cm (30 to 40 in.). The climate is healthy and bracing in the highland areas. The temperatures vary from 15°C (60°F) in the cool season to 28°C (83°F) in the hot season.

The offshore islands have a more tropical climate with higher rainfall and temperatures than the mainland, but the heat is tempered by sea breezes. There are three well-defined seasons: the rainy season from April to May and from November to December, the hot season from December to March and the cool season from June to October. Pemba receives 234 cm (80 in.) of rainfall, while Mafia and Zanzibar receive from 152 cm to 234 cm (60 in. to 80 in.)

The prevailing winds are the southeast trade winds from November to March and the northeast trade winds from April through October.

POPULATION

The population of Tanzania was estimated in 1985 at 21,733,000 on the basis of the last official census held in 1978 when the population was 17,512,611. The population is expected to reach 37.3 million in 2000 and 70.7 million by 2020. The annual growth rate is 3.52%, based on an annual birth rate of 50.4 per 1,000.

Over one half of the population is concentrated on a little more than one-sixth of the land area, mainly in the highlands. The area around Lake Victoria contains over one-fourth of the total population. Density is lower in the steppe lands and on the central plateau and lowest in the lowland bush. The average population density of the islands is not only higher than that of the mainland but also above that of all countries south of the Sahara. Pemba, with a density higher than that of Zanzibar, has a fairly evenly distributed population. Nationwide the density is 24 per sq km (62 per sq mi), rising to 46.2 per sq km (120 per sq mi) in agricultural areas.

Tanzania ranks lowest in the world in urbanization with only 14.84% of its population living in towns of any size, up from 4.1% in 1957. While the annual urban growth rate is a healthy 8.1%, net urbanization is small relative to the whole population. Dar es Salaam accounts for 30% of the urban total and Tonga for another 10%. Nearly 50% of the population Dar es Salaam live in slums and squatter settlements. The slum population has an annual growth rate of 35.7%. There are 12 other towns with populations of over 10,000. By the end of 1974 about 3 million lived in ujamaa (a form of cooperative) villages, 2 million in other new villages, 1.5 million in older villages and another 3.5 million in scattered homesteads.

The age profile shows 48.8% in the under-14 age group, 48.9% in the 15-to-64 age group and 2.3% in the over-65 age group. Zanzibar taken alone had 1,112 males to every 1,000 females, while on the mainland the ratio was reversed: 926 males to every 1,000 females.

Traditionally, tribal migration across land borders has always been free and unrestricted; there are no statistics on such population movements. During the 1960s and early 1970s Tanzania was the destination of refugees from Portuguese Mozambique and African countries such as Uganda, Rwanda and Burundi. Statistics for Asian and European migration show a continuing trend toward an excess of emigrants over immigrants. Entry of non-citizens is controlled by entry permits, liable to cancellation at any time.

In 1983, President Nyerere was awarded the Nansen Prize of the United Nations High Commissioner for Refugees for his outstanding assistance to refu-

DEMOGRAPHIC INDICATORS (1984)	
Population, total (in 1,000)	21,733.0
Population ages (% of total)	
0-14	48.8
15-64	48.9
65+	2.3
Youth 15-24 (000)	4,232
Women ages 15-49 (000)	4,900
Dependency ratios	104.6
Child-woman ratios	918
Sex ratios (per 100 females)	97.3
Median ages (years)	15.6
Percentage change in Birthrate (1965-83)	2.5
Proportion of urban (%)	14.84
Population density (per sq. km.)	24
per hectare of arable land	3.45
Rates of growth (%)	3.02
urban %	8.1
rural %	2.8
Natural increase rates (per 1,000)	35.1
Crude birth rates (per 1,000)	50.4
Crude death rates (per 1,000)	15.3
Marriage rate 1/1000	9.8
Gross reproduction rates	3.50
Net reproduction rates	2.62
Total fertility rates	7.10
General fertility rates (per 1,000)	231
Life expectancy, males (years)	49.3
Life expectancy, females (years)	52.7
Life expectancy, total (years)	51.0
Population doubling time in years at current rate	20
Average household size	3.6

gees. There is a refugee population of about 100,000 of whom approximately 80% are from Burundi, the rest mainly from Uganda and Zaire. Some 30,000 Rwandans were offered naturalization in 1980, although only a few have so far acquired Tanzanian citizenship. The same offer of citizenship is expected to be made to the Burundians when they become self-sufficient. In general, the same services and rights available to citizens are offered to refugees insofar as local resources permit. Tanzania's refugee acceptance is largely limited to persons from contiguous countries. Refugees from other countries are required to find resettlement elsewhere.

For most of Tanzania's ethnic groups, women's traditional role has been that of mother and field laborer, and women are still underrepresented in government, the professions and in skilled occupations. Social limitations on the roles women play are generally more pervasive on Zanzibar than on the mainland. Women in many parts of the country continue to suffer discriminatory restrictions on inheritance and ownership of property because of concessions to custom and Islamic law. These laws dictate in many areas that daughters receive smaller shares of their father's property than do sons. Although the practice is declining, female circumcision is still performed by a minority within approximately 20 of the country's 120 mainland ethnic groups. Despite the obstacles, the government has made progress in its efforts to ensure equality for women, especially in urban areas where traditional values have a weaker hold on the population. The Union of Tanzanian Women, a wing of the party, is dedicated to the eradication of inequality for women in all spheres of society. Women have been encouraged to take an active role in politics. Using its powers of direct appointment, the government has ensured that about 20% of the membership of village councils is female. In late 1985, there were two women cabinet ministers, one woman on the 18-member Central Committee of the party, and 13 women on the National Executive Committee. Under the new 1984 Union and Zanzibar constitutions, 15 seats are reserved for women in the 244-member National Assembly and five seats in the 75-member Zanzibari House of Representatives. This reform was instituted in recognition of the traditional obstacles women face in popular elections for constituency seats in Parliament.

Tanzania has no official population policy, but the government encourages the activities of the private Family Planning Association headed by the Minister of Labor and Social Welfare. Known in Swahili as UMATI (for Chama Cha Uzazi Na Malezi Bora Cha Tanzania), it has 54 branches and 50,000 members.

ETHNIC COMPOSITION

Tanzania is the least homogeneous nation in the world with 7% homogeneity (on an ascending scale in which North and South Korea and ranked 135th with 100% homogeneity). Africans, who form 99% of the population, are divided into over 130 groups, each with its own physical and social characteristics and languages. These tribes have been broadly categorized into five ethnic families: Bantu, Nilotic, Nilo-Hamitic, Khoisan and the unclassified Iraqw comprising Iraqw, Gorowa, Burungi and others. About 95% of Tanzanians are classified as Bantu, a blend of Hamitic and Negroid stocks. Bantu tribes range in membership from a few thousand to the Sukuma, which numbers over one million. The Nyamwezi (4.13%), Ha (3.30%), Makonde (3.80%), Gogo (3.41%), Haya (3.70%), Chagga (3.62%) and Hehe (2.86%) each number more than 250,000. (Figures in parenthesis are percentages of total population.) The only tribe of Nilotic origin is the Luo. The Nilo-Hamites are generally grouped into two clusters: the Masai and the Tatog. Scattered throughout the north-central region of the country are small groups of Bushmen-like people.

The population of the offshore islands is equally heterogeneous. The African population is composed of the indigenous Watumbatu, Wahadimu, Wapemba and others belonging to 50 mainland tribes. Non-Africans belong primarily to a group called the Shirazi who consider themselves descendants of immigrants from Shiraz in Persia, although they show evidence of mixed descent.

Ethnic aliens belong to one of three groups: Asians from the Indian subcontinent, Arabs and Europeans. The cultural and economic influence of these groups far exceeds their numbers, although their position is increasingly insecure in a nation that has adopted Africanization as an official ideology. In the mid-1970s Asians numbered 88,000, Arabs 85,000 and Euro-

MAJOR ETHNIC GROUPS OF TANZANIA			
Arusha	Kaguru	Mbunga	Safwa
Bahima	Kahe	Mepa	Sagara
Barabang	Kara	Meru	Sandawe
Baraguyu	Kerewe	Mpepo	Sangu
Bena	Kimbu	Mwera	Segeju
Bende	Kindiga	Ndali	Shambala
Bondei	Kinga	Ndamba	Sigua
Burungi	Konongo	Ndendeuli	Sonjo
Chagga	Kuria	Ndengereko	Suba
Digo	Kutu	Ngindo	Subi
Doe	Kwavi	Ngoni	Sukuma
Dorobo	Kwaya	Nguruimi	Sumbwa
Fipa	Kwere	Ngulu	Tatog
Gogo	Lambia	Nyakusa	Tongwe
Gorowa	Luguru	Nyamwanga	Tumbatu
Ha	Luo	Nyamwezi	Turu
Hadimu	Machinga	Nyasa	Vidunda
Hadzapi	Makonde	Nyiha	Vinza
Haya	Makua	Nyika	Wanda
Hehe	Malila	Pangwa	Wanji
Holoholo	Mambwe	Pare	Wungu
Ikiza	Masai	Pimbwe	Yao
Ikomo	Matambe	Pogoro	Zanaki
Iramba	Matengo	Rangi	Zaramo
Iraqw	Matumbi	Rufiji	Zigua
Isanzu	Mawia	Rundi	Zinza
Jiji	Mbugu	Rungu	
Jita	Mbugwe	Rungwa	

peans 15,000. Apart from some ill-will toward Asians for their exclusivity, there is no discrimination against any foreign group.

LANGUAGES

More than 100 African languages are spoken in the country. These languages belong to four groups: Bantu, Nilo-Hamitic, Nilotic and Khoisan. The Bantu languages belong to the Congo-Kordofanian language family, the Nilo-Hamitic and Nilotic languages to the Nilo-Saharan language family, and the Khoisan languages to the Khoisan language family that includes languages spoken by the Bushman and Hottentot peoples of southern and southwestern Africa. All these languages are mutually unintelligible, but dialects within the same language may be intelligible to a degree. In general, Bantu languages are agglutinative, their syntax being formed by adding prefixes and suffixes to various roots. The languages of the Iraqw, Gorowa and Burungi tribes have not been classified.

The official language and the lingua franca is Swahili (also known as Kiswahili), spoken as a mother tongue by a large number of inhabitants. Swahili is basically a Bantu language in structure and origin, but its vocabulary is drawn from a variety of sources, particularly Arabic and English. The form of Swahili spoken in Zanzibar is known as Kiunguja. English enjoys the status of a co-official language, but its use is restricted to the educated elite.

Within the Asian community a number of languages are spoken, including Hindi, Punjabi and Urdu. Most Asians also speak English and Swahili.

RELIGIONS

About one-half of Tanzanians adhere to tribal religions, and the rest are about equally divided between Christianity and Islam.

Tribal religions have their strongest hold in rural Tanzania. Although each tribe has its own set of practices, there are certain common denominators such as belief in a high god whose common name, Mulungu, is also often used interchangeably for sky or sun. Most religious activities center on ancestral spirits, rites of passage, witchcraft and sorcery. While there is no priesthood as such, there are religious specialists in all tribes who are concerned with the performance of rituals and with divination.

Christianity is the most recent religion, first introduced by French Catholic missionaries in the 1860s. Lutherans followed in the 1880s, the Moravians in the 1890s, and the Mennonites and Seventh Day Adventists after World War I. By informal agreement, the Catholics and the Protestants concentrated their activities in different areas. The Catholic Church has two archdioceses, 19 dioceses, one apostolic prefecture and one apostolic administration. Both archdioceses, the Eastern Province at Dar es Salaam and the Western Province at Tabora, are headed by native Africans. The church runs 26 general hospitals, schools, adult education centers, five newspapers, book publishing houses and radio programs. More than seven Protestant denominations are represented in the country, of which the largest are the Lutherans, the Baptists, the Moravians and the Presbyterians. The Christian Council of Tanzania is composed of 17 member bodies. Ecumenism appears to be on the increase, with both Catholics and Protestants cooperating in a number of areas of mutual concern. Although Africanization of the clergy has made considerable progress, there are no independent African churches or messianic movements as in other countries of the continent. Many Tanzanian Christians practice a form of Christianity in which residual elements of their former religious traditions persist, and there is an unorthodox flexibility in beliefs and practices, particularly in the area of charms and taboos.

Muslims are concentrated on the offshore islands, the coastal region, and around the towns of Kondoa, Singida, Tabora and Kigoma and along the Ruvuma River. There are three distinct ethnic groups among Muslims: Arabs, Indo-Pakistanis and Africans. The nature of religious beliefs among these groups varies from the strict and exclusive Islam of Arabs and Indo-Pakistanis to the blend of Islam and tribalism practiced by Africans. With few exceptions, both Arabs and African Muslims are Sunnites. Two elements that make Islam compatible with African traditions are its approval of polygamy and its belief in the existence of spirits.

Hinduism, Sikhism and Buddhism are represented by small groups of Indians.

COLONIAL EXPERIENCE

Tanzania's earliest contacts with Europeans date only from the 19th Century. In 1857 Richard F. Burton and John Hanning Speke crossed the country to discover the source of the White Nile. Tanganyika (as mainland Tanzania came to be known) came under German influence in 1884-85 after Karl Peters concluded treaties with the chiefs of the interior on behalf of the German East Africa Company. In 1890 Germany and the United Kingdom partitioned the territory, establishing a British zone of influence in the Upper Nile, Zanzibar and Pemba, while Tanganyika and Rwanda-Urundi together became German East Africa. The British took over Tanganyika during World War I and administered it after the end of the war as a mandate of the League of Nations. The main goals of colonial administration were to develop political institutions and to promote inter-tribal cooperation. The first organized nationalist movement appeared in Tanganyika in 1954. It took only seven more years for Tanganyika to receive its independence and one additional year to become a republic. Zanzibar became independent in 1963. Perhaps because the nation was spared the usual birth pangs of independence, anti-colonialist sentiments are not strong. Tanzania remains a member of the Commonwealth, and current relations with the United Kingdom are good.

CONSTITUTION & GOVERNMENT

The constitution of the United Republic of Tanzania was adopted in 1965 following the union of Zanzibar and Tanganyika. The constitution officially incorporated the fundamental principles of socialism and gave legal status to the Tanganyika African National Union (TANU), now Chama Cha Mapinduzi (CCM, Revolutionary Party of Tanzania). All political activities and functions of the state became the responsibility of the party. As the constitution defines the relationship between the party and the state, every citizen is eligible for party membership, the sole presidential candidate is nominated by the Electoral Conference of the party, and ministers and civil servants are required to be active party members. The party's national executive committee also approves the nomination of both elected and institutionally sponsored members of the National Assembly.

In 1979 a new constitution was prolmugated for Zanzibar by its Revolutionary Council after having been approved by the ruling CCM. Under the new constitution, designed to provide more democracy for Zanzibar within the union's framework, the president of the island is to be nominated by CCM but directly elected for a five-year term with a maximum of three successive terms. There is also to a be a directly elected council of representatives to replace the existing revolutionary council, which will be renamed high executive council with members appointed by the president.

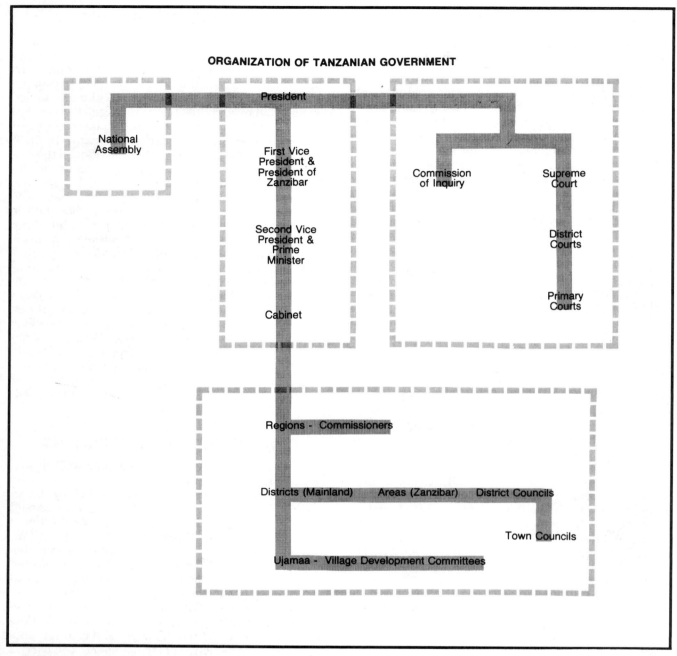

ORGANIZATION OF TANZANIAN GOVERNMENT

Executive power is vested in the president, who is nominated by the CCM and elected by universal adult suffrage for a five-year term. The president has no legislative powers; if any bill from which he has withheld his assent should be passed again by the National Assembly by a two-thirds majority, he is required to give his assent within 21 days or dissolve the Assembly, in which latter case he must also stand for reelection. The president is assisted by two vice presidents. The second vice president is chosen from among the elected members of the National Assembly and is also the prime minister and official leader of the Assembly. The first vice president is concurrently the president of Zanzibar. The cabinet is composed of the president, the two vice presidents and ministers.

All ministers must be members of the National Assembly, and the president often uses his right to appoint Assembly members to ensure compliance with this provision.

The constitution was amended in 1984-85 in several respects. The post of a second vice president (concurrently prime minister) was revived. The number of presidential terms was limited to two. Major changes were also made in the electoral procedures (see *Parliament*). Collateral changes were also made in the Zanzibar constitution in 1985.

Following the constitutional changes, President Nyerere voluntarily stepped down and turned over the presidency to his handpicked successor, Ali Hassan Mwinyi, who had been serving as president of

Zanzibar and vice president of Tanzania. Mwinyi, running as the sole candidate for the office, received 92% of the vote in a national election held on October 27, 1985. Although he relinquished the presidency, Nyerere continues to wield great influence as chairman of CCM, a post he plans to retain until 1987. Mwinyi, a devout Muslim and committed Socialist, was described as unassuming and lacking the charisma of Nyerere. One of Mwinyi's first acts was to name former justice minister Joseph Warioba as prime minister. Mwinyi began his administration as CCM began revising some of the basic tenets of Nyerere's "African Socialism." The country's sisal plantations are being returned to private ownership, and the ban on private ownership of houses for rent was being dropped.

```
┌─────────────────────────────────────────────┐
│             CABINET LIST (1986)             │
│ President ..................... Ali Hassan Mwinyi │
│ First Vice President ............. Joseph S. Warioba │
│ Second Vice President ............ Idris Abdul Wakil │
│ President, Zanzibar & Chaiman,              │
│   Revolutionary Council ........... Idris Abdul Wakil │
│ Prime Minister ................. Joseph S. Warioba │
│ Deputy Prime Minister .......... Salim Ahmed Salim │
│ Minister of Agriculture & Livestock         │
│   Development ..................... Paul Bomani │
│ Minister of Communications                  │
│   & Works ..................... Mustafa Nyang'anyi │
│ Minister of Community Development,          │
│   Culture, Youth & Sports ........... Fatuma Said Ali │
│ Minister of Defense                         │
│   & Natl. Service ............... Salim Ahmed Salim │
│ Minister of Finance, Planning               │
│   & Economic Affairs .......... Cleopa David Msuya │
│ Minister of Foreign Affairs ........... Benjamin Mkapa │
│ Minister of Health                          │
│   & Social Welfare ............. Dr. Aaron D. Chiduo │
│ Minister of Home Affairs ...... Brig. Muhiddin M. Kimario │
│ Minister of Industries & Trade ........ Basil P. Mramba │
│ Minister of Justice ................. Damian Lubuva │
│ Minister of Labor & Manpower                │
│   Development ............... Daudi N. Mwakawago │
│ Minister of Lands, Water, Housing           │
│   & Urban Development ............. Pius Ng'wandu │
│ Minister of Local Government                │
│   & Cooperative Unions ..... Kingunge Ngombale-Mwiru │
│ Minister of National Education ....... Jackson Makweta │
│ Minister of Natural Resources               │
│   & Tourism .................... Getrude Mongella │
│ Minister of Water, Energy & Minerals .... Al-Noor Kassum │
│ Minister of State, President's Office ... Kighoma Ali Malima │
│ Minister of State, President's Office ..... Samuel J. Sitta │
│ Minister of State, Vice President's Office ... Charles Kileo │
│ Minister of State, Prime Minister's Office ... Anna Makinda │
│ Minister of State for Finance,              │
│   Economic Affairs & Planning ....... Damas Mbogoro │
│ Minister Without Portfolio ...... Rashidi Mfaume Kawawa │
└─────────────────────────────────────────────┘
```

Suffrage is universal for all adults. The CCM nominates two candidates for each constituency from whom the electorate chooses its representative. In

```
┌─────────────────────────────────────────────┐
│              RULERS OF TANZANIA             │
│ 1962 to 1985 (November)                     │
│         Julius K. Nyerere                   │
│ 1985 (November) —                           │
│         Ali Hassan Mwinyi                   │
└─────────────────────────────────────────────┘
```

1975 there were 5 million registered voters in the country.

Tanzania is one of the most stable nations in Africa, having had only two presidents since independence and having suffered no internal turmoil or external invasion. Despite one of the most heterogeneous populations in the world, there are no separatist movements. The CCM dominates politics so completely that there is no room for opposition movements to thrive.

FREEDOM & HUMAN RIGHTS

In terms of political and civil rights, Tanzania ranks as a not-free country with a negative rating of 6 in civil rights and 6 in political rights (on a descending scale in which 1 is the highest and 7 the lowest in rights).

Although Tanzania is a one-party state, it is in many respects an open society committed to fair, equal and humane treatment for all citizens.

During 1985, the government took steps to improve its human rights record. It added a Bill of Rights to the constitution, amended the 1962 Preventive Detention Act to limit abuses, and adopted a new criminal code which grants detainees more rights. These and other trends, including constitutional reforms which require that a majority of members of the Zanzibari and Union Parliaments be directly elected by popular vote, indicate that Tanzania is moving toward greater liberalization. Nevertheless, legal rights embedded in the national and Zanzibar constitutions have not always been observed, particularly freedom of speech. Both on the mainland and in Zanzibar, religion, custom, and rigid tradition, especially in rural areas, often work against the exercise of these rights, particularly with regard to the treatment and equality of women. Freedom of the press is severely restricted. Government policy prohibits the use of torture, but it occasionally occurs. Police officials have been sentenced to stiff terms of imprisonment for torture, abuse and killing of prisoners.

In January 1985, the National Assembly amended the 1962 Preventive Detention Act under which police and security officers could, with a written order from the president, arrest and detain indefinitely any person considered dangerous to the public order or national security. Previously, detainees had no recourse to the judicial system. Under the amended act, the government is now required to inform detainees within 15 days of the reasons for their detention. Otherwise, they must be released immediately. In addition, the order must be reviewed by an advisory committee within 90 days, and the names of the detainees are to be published in the government *Gazette*. Detainees can also challenge the legality of the detention order in the High Court. The amendment also extends applicability of the law to Zanzibar for the first time. Approximately 15-20 people were held under the Preventive Detention Act in 1985, most of whom were accused of participating in a 1983 plot to overthrow the government.

Approximately 1,000 people were detained in 1984 under presidential decree for alleged violations of the Economic Sabotage Act of 1983, such as hoarding and exchange control violations. However, new legislation adopted in September 1984 placed persons newly accused of economic crimes within the normal judicial process. Persons already charged under the previous law were tried by special tribunals which did not always provide full procedural safeguards. The 1983 Human Resources Deployment Act required local governments to ensure that every resident be engaged in productive or other lawful employment. Those persons not so engaged were subject to transfer to another area where they would be required to engage in gainful employment. In 1983 and 1984 there were large-scale roundups of unemployed in Dar es Salaam who were then repatriated to their home villages or other areas for agricultural work. The roundups were ended in mid-1984 because they were ineffective, and the government is no longer compelling individuals to return to the rural areas. In late 1983, the Dar es Salaam regional authorities launched a series of sweeps designed to net the unemployed. Thousands were arrested and hundreds were sent out from Dar es Salaam to work on national coffee, tea, cashew nut, sugar cane or sisal plantations. In January 1984, 1,623 people were rounded up in Dar es Salaam, 225 of whom were detained for further questioning as unemployed. While large-scale roundups ceased in January, on May 26, 157 people were arrested in Dar es Salaam for loitering and being unemployed.

Implementation of the Human Resources Deployment Act has been delayed while municipal authorities search for ways of enforcing it without the abuses that marked the October 1983 sweeps. In an effort to revive the act, the Dar es Salaam City Council conducted a house-by-house survey of all urban residents on December 2-3, 1984. Plans call for other city governments to conduct similar surveys. After the surveys, those who are unemployed or unproductively employed could be repatriated to their home villages or sent to yet-to-be-established centers where they will be engaged, presumably, in agriculture or in small craft workshops.

During the height of the campaign against "economic saboteurs" in 1983, roadblocks were ubiquitous. During 1984 the number of roadblocks declined significantly in the country as a whole, but in areas where surplus crops were produced, roadblocks reappeared to prevent the private movement of food within the country. On November 1 the government instructed regional governments to end all roadblocks aimed at stopping the free flow of food in Tanzania. The only other roadblocks are in border areas and in areas where disease or poaching are a problem.

CIVIL SERVICE

The Civil Service is regulated by the Civil Service Commission, headed by the principal secretary to the first vice president. The commission conducts examinations, determines salary scales and regulates promotion. The Central Recruiting Section of the Commission recruits not only from within the country but also from abroad, and many technical and professional positions are filled through external recruitment. At the time of independence, the proportion of Africans in the civil service was only 14%, but it had risen to nearly 90% by the mid-1970s. Civil servants are not forbidden to participate in politics; but are even required to become members of the CCM. However, there is little overt interference with the civil service by the party leadership. Training programs for civil servants are conducted at the Civil Service Training Center and the Institute of Public Administration.

In 1976 public employees numbered 45,000. As a result of the severe fiscal crisis of that year, 9,000 civil servants were discharged in a move designed to save the government 86.3 million.

LOCAL GOVERNMENT

For purposes of local government, mainland Tanzania is divided into 20 regions and Zanzibar and Pemba into four regions. The mainland regions are as follows (with capitals of the same name unless shown within parentheses): Arusha; Dar es Salaam; Iringa; Kigoma; Kilimanjaro (Moshi); Mara (Musoma); Mbeya; Morogoro; Mtwara; Mwanza; Rukwa; Ruvuma (Songea); Shinyanga; Singida; Tabora; Tanga; West Lake and Lindi. The regions of Zanzibar are: Pemba (Wete); Zanzibar Mjini (Zanzibar); Zanzibar Shambini North (Mkokotoni); and Zanzibar Shambini South (Mkoami).

Each region is administered by a regional commissioner appointed by the central government. These commissioners are concurrently members of the National Assembly. The regions are subdivided into 60 districts on the mainland and nine areas in Zanzibar, each under an area commissioner. Representative institutions at the local level are the four types of councils, of which 58 are district councils, 13 town councils, one municipal council and one city council. These councils have a primarily elected membership, but up to 10 members may be appointed by the president. The district chairman of the CCM also serves as the ex officio chairman of the council in his locality, and elected councilors are also nominated by the party. The local Village Development Committees are composed of local party leaders. The town councils are responsible to the Ministry of Local Government, and the district councils to the regional commissioners.

FOREIGN POLICY

Under President Nyerere's leadership, Tanzania pursued a foreign policy directed toward the elimination of neo-colonialism in Africa; yet, at the same time, it has been instrumental in enlarging the Chinese sphere of influence in East Africa. Various African liberation groups are headquartered at Dar es Salaam, and Tanzania serves as the pipeline for the transmission of men and material from China to these groups. Its closest relations in the continent are with Zambia, with which it is linked by the TamZam rail line, built with Chinese aid. Tanzania's active support of the Mozambique Liberation Front bore fruit when, after Mozambique achieved its independence, the two countries began to cooperate closely, based on their common socialist ideology. In 1976 a joint commission was established to improve their political, economic and cultural ties.

Relations with Uganda became strained after the downfall in 1971 of that country's president, Milton Obote, when a military coup brought Gen. Idi Amin to power. President Nyerere gave sanctuary to Obote, a longtime personal friend, and denounced Amin's regime. In 1972 an armed force of Obote supporters invaded Uganda from Tanzania but were repulsed. In 1979, Tanzania earned the gratitude of the civilized world by helping to overthrow the Idi Amin regime in Uganda. In January 1979, a force consisting of Tanzanian regular troops and members of the Ugandan National Liberation Front entered Uganda. In April Kampala was taken and Amin's forces capitulated in spite of military reinforcements from Libya. By the end of June, all pockets of resistance had been wiped out. The invasion, which was criticized by OAU, cost Tanzania over $500 million and virtually depleted the treasury.

Relations with the other member of the East African Community, Kenya, continue to be strained. In 1977 the border between the two countries was closed following Kenya's decision to dissociate itself from the Community's common transportation programs and to form its own national airline and rail system. Relations with Kenya improved in 1983 upon the conclusion of an accord on the distribution of EAC assets. On November 17 the border between Tanzania and Kenya was reopened and both countries reached agreement on a series of technical cooperation issues. On December 12, all of the three former EAC members exchanged high commissioners. Relations with Malawi were impaired because of Malawi's reluctance to actively oppose South Africa's racial policies and also Malawi's territorial claims on Tanzania. The flight to Tanzania of Hutu refugees pursued by Burundian soldiers in the early 1970s caused a number of incidents that have permanently embittered relations between Burundi and Tanzania.

Although Tanzania is an active member of the Commonwealth, relations with the United Kingdom were severed from 1965 to 1968 in protest against the latter's Rhodesian policy. The United States is concerned over Chinese influence in Tanzania, and President Nyerere has often been openly critical of American policies in Africa and Asia. Nevertheless, there are no outstanding issues between the two countries, and the United States continues to administer a low-level economic aid program.

Tanzania and the United States are parties to 10 treaties and agreements covering agricultural commodities, consuls, economic and technical cooperation, extradition, investment guaranties, Peace Corps, postal matters, and treaty obligations.

Tanzania joined the U. N. in 1961; its share of the U.N. budget is 0.02%. It is a member of 14 U.N. organizations and 23 other international organizations.

U.S. Ambassador in Dar es Salaam: John W. Shirley
U.K. High Commissioner in Dar es Salaam: John A. Sankey
Tanzanian Ambassador in Washington, D.C.: Asterius M. Hyera
Tanzanian High Commissioner in London: Anthony B. Nyakyi

PARLIAMENT

Until 1985 the National Assembly (Bunge) comprised 239 members, including 111 elected members (including 10 from Zanzibar), 25 regional commissioners, 15 national members elected by statutory bodies, up to 32 members of the Zanzibar Revolutionary Council, and up to 23 other Zanzibar members appointed by the president in consultation with the first vice president, 30 presidential appointees, representatives of 25 regional organizations, and the president ex officio. The National Assembly has a term of five years, subject to dissolution.

In addition to the smooth transition in the presidency, voters on October 27, 1985 chose 169 elected members of the 244-seat Parliament. Under the new constitution, which went into effect in 1985, the proportion of representatives chosen by popular vote in those elections increased from approximately 50 to 75%. The remaining 25% is composed of members appointed by the government and the various "mass organizations" associated with the party. All candidates for Parliament must be party members. The national executive committee of the party chooses at least two candidates from a list provided by each constituency to compete in the general election. Within this one-party system voters have registered dissatisfaction by sending incumbent members of Parliament to defeat. This happened again in the 1985 elections. In past years, there were reports of election fixing and intimidation of village leaders both on the mainland and on Zanzibar. In 1985 23 petitions were filed, primarily by individual voters, challenging the results of the elections on both the mainland and Zanzibar. The petitions alleged a variety of voting irregularities. Party membership and, hence, active participation in the political process, is not open to anyone engaged in private business, which traditionally consists largely of Asians, but is slowly being joined by more and more Africans.

Zanzibar has its own House of Representatives. In 1985, for the first time, the majority of Zanzibar's representatives were elected directly, albeit within the one-party structure. This is a sharp break from the past in which all but 10 of the members were elected through district and regional "revolutionary committees" or directly or indirectly appointed by the Zanzibar president. Under the terms of the new constitution, the House of Representatives consists of 50 directly elected members, 10 members nominated by the president of Zanzibar, 5 regional commissioners, 5 seats reserved for women, and 1 representative from each of the party's 5 mass organizations.

Julius Nyerere ran unopposed in the four presidential elections since independence. While voters have the option of voting "no" by secret ballot or staying home, local party officials bring pressure to bear in elections to ensure a high turnout. In an effort to break down ethnic and linguistic distinctions, the election code requires that campaigns be conducted only in Swahili and prohibits references to ethnic and regional origin. An appeal process is available to candidates who feel that the code has been violated, and a number of appeals have been successful.

The constitution stipulates the legislative supremacy of the National Assembly. It states that the president has no power to legislate without recourse to parliament. Should the president dissolve the Assembly for overriding his veto, he himself is obliged to stand for reelection. In practice, however, the Assembly is subservient to the president, who can get passed any bill he wants. The Assembly has six standing committees: Finance and Economic, Political Affairs, Public Accounts, Social Services, Standing Orders and General.

POLITICAL PARTIES

The sole legal political party is the Chama Cha Mapinduzi (CCM), formed in 1977 through the amalgamation of the Tanganyika African National Union (TANU), the sole political party on the mainland, and the Afro-Shirazi Party, the sole political party on Zanzibar and Pemba. The National Conference of the party elects 40 delegates to the National Executive Council, which in turn elects 30 members to the Central Committee. The chairman and the vice chairman of the party are elected by the national conference. The CCM has four principal affiliates: the Youth League, the Workers' Organization, the Union of Cooperative Societies and the United Women of Tanzania.

The CCM is generally characterized as a socialist party, but its ideology as formulated by President Nyerere emphasizes the purely African elements of socialism, such as mutual help. The main goals of

TANU were outlined by the president in a policy statement, known as the Arusha Declaration in 1967. It called for self-reliance, using local resources, gradual de-emphasis of foreign aid, ujamaa (a Swahili word meaning literally brotherhood and implying the socialist ideals of mutual help), common ownership and sharing, popular participation in the process of nation building, the removal of all distinctions based on class, wealth and status and control by the people of all major sources of wealth and production. The declaration was incorporated within the interim constitution. Another important goal of the party was Africanization of the civil service and the creation of a party organization that will permit some competition within a one-party framework. Over the years, CCM and the government merged into a single administrative system, and there is considerable overlapping of CCM and local government councils, cooperative societies and labor unions in both leadership and functions. The over-7,000 village development committees are headed by the local CCM chairmen; the district councils are headed by the district CCM chairmen; regional commissioners are ex officio regional chairmen of CCM. On Zanzibar and Pemba, the Afro-Shirazi Party occupied a similar position and had a similar organizational structure. At least initially, ASP was oriented toward Cuban and Chinese revolutionary ideologies.

The costs of public elections are borne both by the party and the government. The party nominates two candidates for each constituency; one is assigned the hoe as his symbol and the other a hut, and voters are instructed to vote for the one or the other symbol. Candidates are forbidden to discuss race, tribe or religion and are required to use only Swahili in public speeches. Three election supervisors supervise elections in each constituency. Despite the single-party monopoly, campaigns are often hard fought, press coverage is impartial and there are surprising upsets in which favorites and incumbents are defeated.

Through the party structure, the government intervenes in the private lives of people. The Chama Cha Mapinduzi has party cadres covering the smallest units of society. The "ten-cell" leader is the party official responsible for monitoring events and resolving problems at the grass-roots level. Ten-cell leaders receive an introductory session of evening classes on political indoctrination. Individual cells vary in size from single-family homes to large apartment buildings. Hence, individual ten-cells may have anywhere from 20 to several hundred individuals. Ten-cell leaders, who are unpaid, act as intermediaries between individuals and the government and are required to resolve problems which the people in their area may have. They also monitor store rationing to ensure "equitable" distribution and report to government or party authorities any suspicious behavior or events within their neighborhood.

The party permits exceptions to be made for police to search without a warrant for unemployed persons and under other special circumstances. There also have been numerous instances of forced entry, search, and harassment of persons suspected of economic crimes. There is evidence that mail is sometimes opened and read by authorities, although the opening of mail is exceptional. Those who are not considered productively employed are not allowed to remain in urban areas. Some have returned voluntarily to their home regions; others have been returned under escort or sent to other rural areas selected by the government and forced to work.

ECONOMY

Tanzania is one of the 49 low-income countries of the world. It is also one of the 29 countries considered by the U.N. to be among the least developed (LLDC) and one of the 45 countries considered to be most seriously affected by recent adverse economic conditions. Tanzania has a free-market economy in which the dominant sector is public.

PRINCIPAL ECONOMIC INDICATORS

Gross National Product: $4.880 billion (1983)
  GNP Annual Growth Rate: 3.4% (1973-82)
  GNP Per Capita: $240 (1983)
  Per Capita GNP Annual Growth Rate: 0.1% (1973-82)

Gross Domestic Product: Sh51.675 billion (1983)
  GDP at 1980 Prices: Sh38.718 billion (1982)
  GDP Deflator (1980=100): 123.6 (1982)
  GDP Annual Growth Rate: 3.6% (1973-83)
  Per Capita GDP: Sh2,532 (1984)
  Per Capita GDP Annual Growth Rate: 0.8% (1970-81)

Income Distribution: 2.3% of the national income is received by the bottom 20%; 33.5% of the national income is received by the top 5%.

Percentage of Population in Absolute Poverty: 10% urban; 60% rural

Consumer Price Index (1970=100):
  All Items: 7,604 (1983)
  Food: 887.2 (1983)

Average Annual Rate of Inflation (1973-83): 11.5%

Money Supply: Sh20.541 billion (1983)
  Reserve Money: Sh9.951 billion (1983)

Currency in Circulation: Sh8.194 billion (1984)

International Reserves: $26.9 million, of which $26.8 million were foreign exchange reserves (October 1980)

Development planning began in Tanzania even before independence. In 1947 a 10-year plan was initiated when Tanganyika became a U.N. Trust Territory. It was followed by a second plan (1955-60) and a three-year plan (1961-64), based upon the recommendations of a World Bank mission. In 1964 the government issued the first of a series of three five-year plans covering the period until 1980. The last of this series began in 1976 after a year's postponement because of economic problems. This plan targeted an investment of Sh13.889 billion spread out among 11 sectors.

The Fourth Five-Year Plan (1981–86) was launched in July 1981 and provided for total spending of Sh. 40,200 million. Industry was allocated nearly one-

---

BALANCE OF PAYMENTS (1981)
(million $)

Current Account Balance	−278.0
Merchandise Exports	688.3
Merchandise Imports	−1,037.9
Trade Balance	−349.7
Other Goods, Services & Income	+220.3
Other Goods, Services & Income	−288.5
Other Goods, Services & Income Net	−68.3
Private Unrequited Transfers	27.4
Official Unrequited Transfers	112.5
Capital Other Than Reserves	199.5
Net Errors & Omissions	82.0
Total (Lines 1, 10 and 11)	3.5
Counterpart Items	15.6
Total (Lines 12 and 13)	19.1
Liabilities Constituting Foreign Authorities' Reserves	—
Total Change in Reserves	−19.1

---

quarter of total expenditure, while agriculture took second place. However, the country's economic situation worsened drastically between 1979 and 1982 and, almost as soon as the plan was launched, it seemed likely it would be virtually abandoned. In March 1981 the government announced the National Economic Survival Program (NESP). NESP 1982 originally envisaged total export earnings of Sh. 8,130 million, but this was subsequently revised downwards to Sh. 6,985 million. Even so, this was only 50.6% achieved. Agricultural and mineral exports earned 70% of their target, industry only 25%. Total target export earnings under NESP 1983 were Sh. 5,265 million.

GROSS DOMESTIC PRODUCT BY ECONOMIC ACTIVITY
(1982)

	%	Rate of Change % (1970-81)
Agriculture	45.4	3.2
Mining	0.3	−4.9
Manufacturing	8.2	1.4
Construction	3.6	1.7
Electricity, Gas & Water	1.1	8.4
Transport & Communications	4.4	5.3
Trade & Finance	6.6	2.0
Public Administration & Defense	—	10.1
Services	30.4	—
Other Branches	—	0.5

Tanzania received $36.30 per capita during the period 1979-81. The major source of aid is China, which regards Tanzania as a prime showcase of its aid programs in Africa. Tanzania is one of the Third World countries whose debts were generously written off by Sweden in 1978.

BUDGET

The Tanzanian fiscal year runs from July 1 through June 30. The national budget covers cash expenditures and receipts (including development expenditures) for the mainland only and does not include Zanzibar's revenues and expenditures.

FOREIGN ECONOMIC ASSISTANCE TO TANZANIA

Sources	Period	Amount (in million $)
United States Loans	1946-83	93.5
United States Grants	1946-83	243.1
International Organizations	1946-83	1,304.6
(Of Which World Bank)	1946-83	318.2
China	1954-79	360.0
Soviet Union	1954-79	40.0
West European (ODA & OOF) Countries	1970-79	100.0
All Sources	1979-81	651.5

BUDGET
(million shillings, year ending 30 June)*

Revenue	1978/79	1979/80	1980/81
Tax revenue	5,835	6,831	8,151
Personal tax	212	865	1,012
Other taxes on income	1,344	1,542	1,718
Sales tax	2,512	2,930	4,335
Excises	216	12	8
Import duties	950	819	656
Export duties	452	465	215
Non-tax revenue	858	577	632
Parastatal dividends and interest	217	213	150
Royalties and rents	—	53	18
Administratives fees, charges, etc.	140	220	210
Miscellaneous receipts	501	91	254
TOTAL	6,693	7,408	8,783

Expenditure	1978/79	1979/80	1980/81
General public services	2,589	2,126	3,080
Defense	3,298	1,110	1,612
Education	1,574	1,613	1,738
Health	724	721	789
Economic services	4,337	5,196	5,388
General administration, regulation and research	962	721	724
Agriculture, forestry and fishing	944	1,319	1,450
Mining, manufacturing and construction	861	1,404	1,264
Electricity and water	588	639	597
Roads	493	636	807
Other transport and communications	482	467	542
TOTAL (incl. others)	13,463	12,433	14,419

* Figures refer to the Tanzania government, excluding the revenue and expenditure of the separate Zanzibar government.

1981/82 Budget Estimates (million shillings): Recurrent revenue 12,445; Recurrent expenditure 12,205; Development expenditure 6,622.

1982/83 Budget Estimates (million shillings): Revenue from taxation 8,749; Recurrent expenditure 14,144; Development expenditure 4,816.

1983/84 Budget Estimates (million shillings): Recurrent revenue 12,500; Recurrent expenditure 15,620; Development expenditure, 5,830.

1984/85 Budget Estimates (million shillings): Recurrent revenue 16,465.1; Recurrent expenditure 18,119.7; Development expenditure 6,560.4.

Of current government revenues, 31.1% comes from taxes on income, profit and capital gain, 50.6% from domestic taxes on goods and services, 10.2% from taxes on international trade and transactions, 0.9% from other taxes and 7.2% from non-tax revenues. Current revenues represented 19.6% of GNP. Of current expenditures, 11.2% goes to defense, 12.1% to education, 5.5% to health, 2.4% to housing, social security and welfare, 37.4% to economic services and 31.5% to other functions. Current expenditures represent 32.2% of GNP.

In 1983, public consumption totaled Sh8.781 billion and private consumption Sh37.992 billion. During 1973-83, public and private consumption grew by 3.0%.

In 1983 total outstanding disbursed external debt was $1.819 billion of which $1.705 billion was owed to official creditors and $1,114.7 million was owed to private creditors. The total debt service was $77.8 million of which $39.7 million was repayment of principal and $38.1 million was interest. Total external debt represented 41.5% of GNP and total debt service 1.8% of GNP.

FINANCE

The Tanzanian unit of currency is the shilling, divided into 100 cents. Coins are issued in denominations of 5, 20 and 50 cents and 1 and 5 shillings; notes are issued in denominations of 5, 10, 20 and 100 shillings.

The Tanzanian shilling was introduced in 1966, replacing at par the East African shilling, which until 1973 was equivalent to 80.14; this rate was restored in 1974. Until 1975, the Tanzanian shilling remained tied to the U.S. dollar, but in that year the link was broken and the shilling tied to the SDR (Special Drawing Right) based on a weighted basket of 16 national currencies. The exchange rate against the U.S. dollar is adjusted from month to month. The shilling was devalued by 10% in 1982 and by an additional 20% in June 1983. In August 1985 the rate was $1=Sh16.975. On this basis, the exchange rate with sterling was £1=Sh20.984.

The central bank and the bank of issue is the Bank of Tanzania, founded in 1966. The entire banking system was nationalized in 1967 in accordance with the Arusha Declaration, and all banks are now state owned. These include the National Bank of Commerce, the People's Bank of Zanzibar, the Tanzania Housing Bank, the Tanzania Post Office Savings Bank, the Tanzania Investment Bank and the Tanzania Rural Development Bank. Together they had reserves in 1982 of Sh622 million, demand deposits of Sh10.334 billion and time and savings deposits of Sh6.405 billion. Development finance is provided by the National Development Corporation and the Tanganyika Development Finance Company.

```
                  GROWTH PROFILE
              Annual Growth Rates (%)
Population 1980-2000                          3.4
Birthrate 1965-83                             2.5
Deathrate 1965-83                           -27.3
Urban Population 1973-83                      8.6
Labor Force 1980-2000                         3.1
GNP 1973-82                                   3.4
GNP per capita 1973-82                        0.1
GDP 1973-83                                   3.6
GDP per capita 1970-81                        0.8
Consumer Prices 1970-76                      14.8
Wholesale Prices                               —
Inflation 1973-83                            11.5
Agriculture 1973-83                           2.6
Manufacturing 1970-81                         1.4
Industry 1973-83                              0.2
Services 1973-83                              5.4
Mining 1970-81                               -4.9
Construction 1970-81                          1.7
Electricity 1970-81                           8.4
Transportation 1970-81                        5.3
Trade 1970-81                                 2.0
Public Administration & Defense 1970-81      10.1
Export Price Index 1975-81                   12.6
Import Price Index 1975-81                   13.6
Terms of Trade 1975-81                       -0.9
Exports 1973-83                              -4.6
Imports 1973-83                              -2.7
Public Consumption                             —
Private Consumption 1973-83                   3.0
Gross Domestic Investment 1973-83             4.4
Energy Consumption 1973-83                   -2.6
Energy Production 1973-83                     5.9
```

AGRICULTURE

Of the total land area of 93,936,100 hectares (232,178,100 acres), 60% is arable; 40% is actually cultivated in Zanzibar and 15% on the mainland. Overall, 11,150,000 hectares (27,551,880 acres) are arable, and 1,180,000 hectares (2,918,880 acres) are cultivated. Per capita agricultural land is 0.7 hectare (0.2 acre). Based on 1974-76=100, the index of agricultural production in 1982 was 109, the index of food production was 117 and the index of per capita food production was 103. Agriculture employs 83% of the labor force. It contributes 51% to the GDP and 66% to export earnings. Its rate of growth during 1973-78 was 2.6%. The value added in the agricultural sector in 1983 was $1.886 billion.

Land use is severely restricted by the presence of the tsetse fly, which infests over 60% of the land area and the lack of adequate rainfall in over half the land area. In general, the eastern and central plateau regions are not suitable for intensive forms of cultivation. Areas under the bush fallow system are often cultivated for three or four years and then left to return to bush for 10 years or longer, with resulting loss in fertility. Conditions are most favorable for farming around Mounts Kilimanjaro and Meru, Lake Victoria, in the Mbeya region and in the northeast.

On the mainland, approximately 80% of the land is held by individuals or groups under customary rules of tenure, and about 10% is held by plantation farmers under leasehold. Customary tribal tenure patterns vary from one tribe or one area to another, but these systems are being gradually modified under pressures of population, the expansion of monetary economy, the construction of permanent homes on tribal lands and government regulations encouraging individual ownership of land. The concept of individual proprietary rights has gained increasing acceptance among tribes living in the fertile lake and mountain areas. Lands held by plantation farmers under leasehold from the government are governed by strict regulations concerning their use. The farmer is expected to cultivate fully five-eighths of the area, and he is also expected to reside on the land.

Most of the tribes practice subsistence farming, although in the more fertile areas cash crops are becoming popular. The principal food crops are corn, millet, rice, cassava, wheat, sorghum and pulses. The chief cash crops are tea, cashew nuts, coffee, cotton and sisal. Tanzania is the world's leading producer of sisal, accounting for 40% of world production. Zanzibar is also noted for its cloves (producing two-thirds of the world's supplies), nutmeg, mace and cardamom.

Mechanization has made little headway. In 1982 there were only 18,720 tractors in use in the country. Annual consumption of fertilizers in the same year was 29,100 tons, or 4.4 kg (9.7 lb) per cultivated hectare.

In 1970 the government began an extensive rural resettlement scheme by forming communal ujamaa villages designed to raise rural standards of living and agricultural production. The ensuing disruption of traditional agriculture, coupled with serious drought in 1971, 1973 and 1974, has meant a steady decline in food production and an increase in food imports that is considered alarming. The drought conditions intensified during 1979-83 and, in addition, a ground borer beetle pest destroyed 20% of the corn crop in the same period. Food imports rose to 214,000 tons in 1983. In mid-1983 the food shortage was so serious that food rationing cards had to be introduced in Dar es Salaam.

Cattle are raised mainly by the Masai, primarily for the social prestige conferred by their ownership. Cattle also serve as partial marriage payments made on behalf of the young men of the family. Other constraints on commercial livestock raising include the prevalence of the tsetse fly in the coastal belt, eastern plateau and central plateau and communal ownership and grazing practices. Government attempts to modernize livestock raising have included the establishment of ranches under the National Development Corporation, the extension of veterinary services and the building of abattoirs. In 1982 the livestock population included 13,150,000 cattle, 3,937,000 sheep, 166,000 asses, 5,906,000 goats, 170,000 pigs and 25,000,000 chickens.

Forests cover some 246,050 sq km (95,000 sq mi), of which forest reserves account for 33%. Vast tracts of miombo woodland cover one-third of the country in the south and west-central areas. The main timber ex-

PRINCIPAL CROP PRODUCTION (1982) (000 metric tons)	
Wheat	75
Rice	200
Corn	800
Millet	150
Sorghum	220
Potatoes	145
Sweet potatoes	332
Cassava	4,900
Dry beans	152
Chick-peas	8
Groundnuts	58
Castor beans	5
Sunflower seed	43
Sesame seed	18
Cottonseed	83
Coconuts	330
Copra	32
Onions	45
Other vegetables	930
Sugar cane	1,511
Citrus fruit	28
Mangoes	180
Pineapples	49
Bananas	800
Plaintains	800
Other fruit	222
Cashew nuts	45
Coffee	55
Tea	16
Tobacco	16
Sisal	80
Cotton	43

ports consist of woods known as podo, mvule, mninga and Grevillae Robusta. Roundwood removals in 1982 totaled 38.747 million cubic meters (1.368 billion cubic ft).

Most of the annual fish catch of 226,000 (1982) tons is obtained from the major inland lakes. Tanzanian fish exports were valued at $767,000.

Agricultural credit is provided mainly through the National Cooperative Bank, the National Development Credit Agency and the National Bank of Commerce.

INDUSTRY

Manufacturing, which contributed 8.2% of the GDP in 1982, is restricted to the processing of agricultural products for both export and domestic markets and production of import substitutes and consumer goods. Manufacturing employs only 6% of the total economically active population, but 17.4% of all wage earners. During 1970-81, the rate of manufacturing growth was 1.4%. The average annual growth rate of industrial production was about 10% during the First Five-Year Plan and declined to 4.2% in 1974-77. Since then, overall production has been falling in real terms. Many factories have closed down, or suspended operations for long periods, since early 1980. Most factories which are operating do so at less than 30% of capacity. One of the main reasons for poor performance in the industrial sector is the frequent interruptions of electricity and water supply. In addition, all industries have suffered from the rising cost of fuel and other imports and the severe lack of foreign exchange to pay for raw materials, machinery, equipment and spares. The value added in manufacturing in 1982 was $151 million. Most of the manufacturing units are small, and the average work force in an establishment numbers only around 20. Nearly 40% of the manufacturing capacity is concentrated in Dar es Salaam, but newer industries are being established in the Moshi-Arusha areas, in the Tanga region and near Lake Victoria. There are, overall, 503 establishments employing 10 or more workers. Next to food processing, the most important industries are textiles, brewing, cigarette manufacture, sugar, tanneries and cement. Small rural industries are being developed by the Small Industries Development Organization, created in 1974 as part of the ujamaa program.

It is often difficult to distinguish between the public and private sectors because the National Development Corporation participates in industrial promotion even in the private sector. Following the Arusha Declaration of 1967, the government began a phased program of acquiring a controlling interest in all key services and industries. Transport, oil, sisal, banking and insurance were affected by these measures. Industry (including mining) receives the largest sectoral allotment in the current five-year plan.

Ownership of the private sector is almost entirely in the hands of Europeans or Asians. Lack of experience, financing and technical expertise inhibited the emergence of an African entrepreneurial class. In terms of the number of companies in Zanzibar and the mainland, 71% are privately owned, 3.1% are publicly owned and 25% are foreign-owned. However, in terms of net processing and manufacturing output, firms in the public sector account for between 45% and 50%; this share is expected to increase in time.

The government, however, is not enamored of foreign investment as a matter of principle and is likely to remain very selective in the types of investment proposals it will consider. Investment terms are worked out carefully on a case-by-case basis, although it is possible that government guidelines covering foreign investments will be issued in the near future. At present, there is very little U.S. investment in Tanzania. Most of the private foreign capital is invested in plantations.

Industrial credit is provided by the National Development Corporation, the Commonwealth Development Corporation, and the Tanganyika Development Finance Company.

ENERGY

In 1982 Tanzania produced 70,000 metric tons of coal equivalent and consumed 901,000 metric tons of coal equivalent, or 45 kg (99 lb) per capita. The national energy deficit is 831,000 metric tons of coal equivalent. The annual growth rates during 1973-83 were 5.9% for energy production and −2.6% energy consumption. Energy imports account for 26.5% of all merchandise imports. Apparent per capita consumption of gasoline is 9 gallons per year. Annual petroleum refinery capacity is 17,000 barrels per day.

In 1984 Tanzania produced 1.127 billion kwh of electric power, or 53 kwh per capita.

LABOR

Based on the last official census, the economically active population in 1982 is estimated at 7.704 million, reflecting a participation rate (percentage of economically active persons in the whole population) of 40.3%. About 9% of the economically active population are wage earners, and about 29% are women.

Nearly 60% of the labor force is totally unskilled, and 34% is semiskilled. Of the remaining 6%, a large proportion consists of either Asians or Europeans. Africanization is a high priority in the government's manpower development programs. At the time of independence, Africans occupied only 380 of the over 4,000 top- and middle-level jobs. There were only 13 African physicians, no African judges or magistrates, and only 17 Africans among 685 secondary school teachers.

The occupational distribution of the labor force is lopsided toward agriculture, which engages 83% of the labor force. Industry employs 6% and services 11%.

The minimum wage is fixed by law, but regional differentials are permitted, and minimum wages may be reduced when housing is provided or rations given to workers. In industries such as non-plantation agriculture, tea and gold mining, which are excluded from these statutory minimums, wages are negotiated by the wage boards. All such negotiated wage rates are higher than the minimum wage rates. In many cases, wage increases are limited to 5% of the total wage bill, and they are tied to productivity. In 1980 the average monthly remuneration in non-agricultural sectors was Sh883.

Workers in Tanzania perform a 40-hour, six-day workweek. Section 77 of the employment ordinance prohibits children under the age of 15 from working. This provision applies to the formal wage sector in both urban and rural areas only and not to children working on family farms or herding domestic livestock. A young person between the ages of 15 and 18 may be employed provided the work is "safe and not injurious to health." There is no legal discrimination in wages on the basis of sex, but in practice discrimination occurs. In general, women cannot be employed between 10 p.m. and 6 a.m., and young people are not allowed to work between 6 p.m and 6 a.m. Several laws regulate safety in the workplace, including the Factories Ordinance, the Accidental and Occupational Diseases Notification Ordinance, and the Workman's Compensation Ordinance.

Under the Trades Disputes (Settlement) Act, strikes and lockouts are illegal unless the statutory conciliation procedure has been followed. In 1964 the existing 13 trade unions were dissolved and merged into the National Union of Tanganyika Workers (NUTA) which later became the National Union of Tanzania Workers (JUWATA). The general secretary of the union is appointed by the president and he is simultaneously the minister of labor, thus making NUTA a part of the ministry of labor. NUTA has closed shop facilities whenever more than 50% of the workers in an establishment are members. All business and government offices with more than a few employees are required to have a JUWATA chapter. JUWATA represents about 60% of the workers in the modern, industrial and government sectors. At the local level, it is charged with promoting employee welfare. As the workers' representative, JUWATA can file grievances against employers. Those cases which cannot be settled at the workplace are referred to the Permanent Labor Tribunal, whose decisions are final. While strikes are not prohibited by law, they do not take place because the decisions of the Labor Tribunal are binding. The government sets wages and JUWATA, as an organ of the party, acts as an adviser to the government on wages but does not engage in collective bargaining on behalf of the workers.

FOREIGN COMMERCE

The foreign commerce of Tanzania in 1984 consisted of imports of $914 million and exports of $456.2 million, leaving an unfavorable trade balance of $458 million. Of the imports machinery constituted 28.9%, fuel 26.5%, transport equipment 12.4%, food, beverages and tobacco 10.2% and metals 7.7%. Of the exports, coffee beans constituted 31.0%, cotton 14.7%, manufactured goods 9.8%, cloves 9.2%, cashew nuts 7.3%, sisal 6.2% and diamonds 5.4%.

The major import sources are: the United Kingdom 17.5%, West Germany 9.8%, Japan 8.6%, the Netherlands 6.3%, the United States 6.1% and Italy 4.9%. The major export destinations are: the United Kingdom 17.5%, West Germany 13.2%, Indonesia 9.9%, Italy 4.9% and the Netherlands 4.8%.

Based on 1975=100, the import price index in 1981 was 196, the export price index was 221 and the terms of trade (export prices divided by import prices × 100) 113.

Foreign trade is one of the key areas of the economy over which the government has exercised increasing control. The various government regulations have been directed toward ending Asian and foreign domination over the export-import trade. Tanzania is a formal member of the East African Community, but the Community has not been functioning for some years now.

TRANSPORTATION & COMMUNICATIONS

Until 1977 Tanzania was a member of the East African Railway Corporation, along with Kenya and Uganda. Following the dissolution of this organiza-

FOREIGN TRADE INDICATORS (1984)	
Annual Growth Rate, Imports:	-2.7% (1973-83)
Annual Growth Rate, Exports:	-4.6% (1973-83)
Ratio of Exports to Imports:	33:67
Exports per capita:	$21.0
Imports per capita:	$42.0
Balance of Trade:	-$458 million
Ratio of International Reserves to Imports (in months)	—
Exports as % of GDP:	15.7
Imports as % of GDP:	25.7
Value of Manufactured Exports:	$71 million
Commodity Concentration:	47.3%

Direction of Trade (%)	Imports	Exports
EEC	46.8	41.1
U.S.	6.2	3.9
Industrialized Market Economies	63.2	60.7
East European Economies	1.5	3.5
High Income Oil Exporters	5.5	1.5
Developing Economies	32.1	32.2

Composition of Trade (%)	Imports	Exports
Food	13.3	58.1
Agricultural Raw Materials	0.8	17.5
Fuels	21.0	4.7
Ores & Minerals	5.4	5.6
Manufactured Goods	59.5	14.0
of which Chemicals	10.8	0.7
of which Machinery	35.4	0.6

tion, Tanzania nationalized its domestic rail system, which had a length of 3,555 km (2,207 mi). The central line runs from Dar es Salaam to Kigoma, with branch lines from Tabora to Mwanza and from Kaliua to Mpanda. The Tanga line extends from Tanga to Arusha. The 1,860-km (1,154-mi) Tazara Railroad, linking Dar es Salaam with Kpiri Mposhi in Zambia, was completed in 1975. In 1982 rail traffic consisted of 1.015 billion ton-km of freight. The length of the domestic refined oil pipeline is 982 km (610 mi).

Interruptions of transportation routes supplying Tanzania's landlocked neighbors have demonstrated repeatedly the importance and also the limitations of the present transit facilities. The washout of a major section of the Chinese-built Tanzania-Zambia railway (TAZARA) in the first half of 1979, serious equipment problems, and the destruction of the TAZARA bridge at Chambeshi in Zambia severely hampered the movement of goods to and from Zambia and Dar es Salaam ports.

The length of the inland waterways is 1,168 km (725 mi). Lake marine services operate on Lakes Tanganyika and Victoria.

The three major ports are Dar es Salaam with eight deep-water berths and one oil jetty for super oil tankers, Mtwara with two deep-water berths and Tanga with lighterage facilities. In 1983 these ports handled 3,158,000 metric tons of cargo. Mwanza is the main port on Lake Victoria.

Tanzania has 34,260 km (21,275 mi) of roads, of which 3,620 km (2,248 mi) are paved. A "unity bridge" was completed in 1977 linking Mozambique and Tanzania. There are three main east-west routes and

three main north-south routes. In 1982 these roads were used by 48,752 passenger cars and 31,390 commercial vehicles. Per capita passenger car ownership is 2.2 per 1,000 inhabitants.

The national airline is Air Tanzania Corporation, founded in 1977 upon the dissolution of the East African Community common air services. It carried 402,000 passengers and flew 4.6 million km (2.8 million mi) in 1982. There are three international airports, at Dar es Salaam, Zanzibar and Kilimanjaro; that at Dar es Salaam has a runway of over 2,500 meters (8,000 ft). There are 101 airfields, of which 94 are usable and 11 have permanent-surface runways.

In 1984 there were 96,600 telephones in use in the country, or 0.6 per 100 inhabitants.

In 1982 the postal service handled 83,232,000 pieces of mail, and 1,070,000 telegrams. Per capita volume of mail was 3.8 pieces. There are 1,650 telex subscriber lines.

Tanzania's major tourist attractions are its world-famous game parks and reserves (Serengeti, Manyara and Ngorongoro in the north and Ruaha and Mikumi in the south). In 1982, 71,000 tourist arrivals were reported, down from 178,000 in 1974. Tourist revenues in 1982 totaled $15 million. There are 6,000 hotel beds and the average length of stay is 1.3 days.

MINING

The contribution of mining to the GDP has remained relatively unchanged at 0.3% to 1% since 1965. Of the country's many known mineral resources, only diamond mining is of economic importance. Diamonds are mined at Williamson field in Mwadui, Shinyanga Province; the deposits are owned jointly by the Tanzanian government and the DeBeers Corporation. Production in 1981 totaled 237,000 metric carats. Coal reserves are estimated at over 370 million tons, but their exploitation is impeded by technical difficulties.

DEFENSE

The defense structure is headed by the president, who also exercises operational control over the armed forces. The entire military establishment is commanded nominally by the chief of staff, but in practice his authority is limited to the mainland; the Zanzibar forces are commanded by a senior colonel in Zanzibar.

Military manpower is provided by voluntary enlistment for two-year terms. The total strength of the armed forces is 40,350. This figure represents 2.1 armed persons for every 1,000 civilians.

ARMY:
Personnel: 38,500
Organization: 2 divisional HQ; 8 infantry brigades; 1 tank battalion; 2 field artillery battalions; 2 AA artillery battalions; 2 mortar battalions; 1 SAM battalion; 2 antitank battalions; 2 signals battalions

Equipment: 30 heavy tanks; 66 light tanks; 20 combat vehicles; 50 armored personnel carriers; 240 guns; 50 rocket launchers; 350 mortars; antitank recoilless launchers; 400 air defense guns; 61 SAMs

NAVY:

Personnel: 850
Units: 7 fast attack craft; 12 patrol craft

AIR FORCE:

Personnel: 1,000
Organization: 29 combat aircraft; 3 fighter squadrons; 1 transport squadron; 2 training squadrons; 2 helicopter squadrons
Air Bases: Dar es Salaam, Morogoro, Tabora and Zanzibar
Forces Abroad: Mozambique 200; Uganda 500

In 1982/83 the military budget totaled $307.31 million, representing 6.3% of the national budget, 2.5% of the GNP, $5 per capita, $8,125 per soldier and $344 per sq km of national territory.

The Tanzanian armed forces had their finest moment in the successful invasion of Uganda in 1979 and the overthrow of Idi Amin. As the first such military operation in modern African history, it helped to establish the superiority of the Tanzanian armed forces in relation to that of its East African neighbors. The army has improved its firepower and logistical reach and also acquired the capability to perform sustained operations. Tanzanian sailors, officers and pilots are trained in China.

Initially, military aid was received exclusively from the United Kingdom. When Tanzania broke diplomatic relations with the United Kingdom over Rhodesia in 1965, China and the Soviet Union stepped in. Chinese arms transfers include 24 aircraft, light and medium tanks, AA guns, howitzers and light arms. The Chinese also built a naval base at Dar es Salaam and a military airfield near Morogoro. There is no internal defense production. Arms purchases abroad during 1973-83 totaled $615 million, including $270 million from the Soviet Union and $40 million from China.

EDUCATION

The national literacy rate is 73.5% (77.7% for males and 69.6% for females).

Education is theoretically free, universal and compulsory for seven years from the ages of seven to 14. The gross school enrollment ratios are 98% at the first level (7 to 13) and 3% at the second level (14 to 19), for a combined enrollment ratio of 63%. Girls constitute 48% of primary enrollment, 34% of secondary school enrollment and 21% of post-secondary enrollment.

Schooling lasts for 13 years divided into seven years of primary school, four years of middle school and two years of secondary school. The primary grades are called standards; the middle and secondary grades are called forms. The dropout rates are high, as reflected in the disparity in the enrollment rates at the first and second levels. The curriculum has been diversified, through a growing emphasis on non-academic subjects, and also Africanized, through incorporation of purely African materials. In 1982 there were 9,980 primary schools and 145 secondary schools in the country.

The school year runs from November to September. The language of instruction is Swahili, except in 12 schools for foreign children. English is taught as a subject beginning from standard one (first grade).

Because there were so few Tanzanian teachers in the school system at independence, much attention has been paid to programs for training them. There are 22 teacher-training institutions, with a total enrollment of 7,449 primary teacher trainees. Teachers fall into five categories, depending on their level of training. The national teacher-pupil ratios are 1:40 in primary grades, 1:21 in secondary grades and 1:4 in post-secondary classes.

Adult education programs are conducted by voluntary agencies as well as by the Directorate of Adult Education. According to official sources, more than 5 million are enrolled in these classes, but this figure seems unrealistically high given the current literacy rates. Vocational education is provided in five technical and commercial institutes. Nearly 4% of primary school children and 29% of secondary school children are enrolled in private schools.

Secondary, vocational and teacher-training schools are administered directly by the Ministry of Education; primary schools are administered by local authorities. Primary education was nationalized in 1969, but private secondary schools continue to function subject to government supervision. In 1981 the Education Ministry's budget totaled Sh1.738 billion, of which 82.5% was current expenditure. This figure represented 5.9% of the GNP, 10.7% of the national budget and $14 per capita.

EDUCATIONAL ENROLLMENT (1981/82)			
	Schools	Teachers	Students
First Level	9,980	88,370	3,512,799
Second Level	145	3,362	69,145
Vocational	34	627	8,101
Third Level	1	719	2,984

Higher education is provided at University College in Dar es Salaam. Per capita university enrollment is 14 per 100,000 inhabitants.

In 1979, 853 students graduated from University College. By field of study, 92 were awarded degrees in medicine, 60 in natural sciences, 57 in law, 92 in engineering, 181 in education and 66 in agriculture.

In 1982, 1,825 Tanzanian students were enrolled in institutions of higher learning abroad. Of these, 483 were in the United States, 525 in the United Kingdom, 169 in Canada, 231 in India, 82 in West Germany, 18 in Hungary and 35 at the Vatican. In 1981, 85 foreign students were enrolled in Tanzania.

LEGAL SYSTEM

The legal system is a blend of English common law, Islamic law, African customary law and German civil law. In Zanzibar, the Islamic element predominates, but on the mainland it has only limited juridical status.

The judicial system is headed by the high court, consisting of a chief justice and 14 judges. District courts are situated in each district and are presided over by either a resident magistrate or district magistrate. The subordinate courts are the primary courts presided over by primary court magistrates. These courts number around 900.

The president appoints all judges: the judges of the high court in consultation with the chief justice and subordinate judges upon the recommendation of the Judicial Service Commission, a body generally concerned with judicial integrity and discipline. In addition, there is a commission of inquiry to which citizens may apply for redress of grievances resulting from abuse of office by public servants.

The mainland legal system is based on the British model with modifications to accommodate customary and Islamic law in civil cases. Criminal trials are open to the public and the more sensational are covered by the press. While an independent judiciary is constitutionally mandated, some members of the legal community, including judicial officers, have complained that the legal system is being corrupted through bribery. Although the allegations remain largely undocumented, there is at least one confirmed report of a magistrate demanding a bribe to issue a court order. There has been no suggestion that the Court of Appeals and the High Court are corrupt. Judges are appointed by the executive with the advice of the chief justice.

The court system on Zanzibar, which has considerable autonomy, was revised by the Zanzibar constitution promulgated in late 1984. Under the system used throughout 1984, defendants could not be represented by attorneys, but could request a relative or neighbor to represent them as long as no fee was paid. With the exception of High Court judges, no members of the Zanzibar judiciary were required to have any training in the law. The Supreme Council, which could review decisions made by the High Court, was attached to the Revolutionary Council and accountable to its president. There existed, therefore, considerable possibility of political interference in the judiciary in Zanzibar. Under the new Zanzibar constitution, implemented in 1985, People's Courts, which did not provide defendants with normal legal procedures, were abolished. The court system was integrated into the legal system of the United Republic of Tanzania for the first time. High Court judges are required to have both a degree in law and several years' practice prior to appointment to the bench. Defendants are allowed the right to legal representation. The new constitution retains Islamic, or Kadhi, courts to deal with marriage, divorce, inheritance and childcare cases involving only Muslims. Cases concerning constitutional issues and Islamic law are appealable only within the Zanzibar courts; for the first time, all other cases may be appealed to the Court of Appeal of the United Republic of Tanzania.

The passage of the new law on economic sabotage in 1984, which replaced the Economic Sabotage Act of 1983, appears to have ended a period in which many perceived that the government sought to circumvent its inability to obtain convictions within the regular court system. However, the special tribunals, established under the Economic Sabotage Act of 1983, which will remain active until cases entered before September 24, 1984, are completed, bypass normal legal procedures by suspending rules of evidence, the right of representation, and the appeal process.

Tanzanian law requires that a person arrested for crimes, other than security violations under the Preventive Detention Act, must be brought within 24 hours before a magistrate to be charged. Under the new criminal procedure code, enacted in 1985, the accused person is guaranteed bail either by the police or by the court. Also under the new code, the accused has the right to challenge the order for his arrest, his name must be published in the government *Gazette*, and his case must be referred to a board of review within three months. If it is not referred within this time, he is entitled to be released. Although the new system has been in effect only a short time, it appears that it is being respected by legal authorities.

The Prisons Service is an agency of the police force and is headed by the commissioner of prisons. There are about 50 prisons of four types on the mainland: remand prisons, minimum security prison farms, prison farms, a prison for the mentally ill and a maximum security prison. In addition, there are temporary detention facilities adjoining major police stations at regional capitals. Women prisoners are not segregated, but juveniles are. Most prisons offer vocational courses.

LAW ENFORCEMENT

Tanzania has a very small police force in relation to its population, numbering around 10,800, or one policeman for every 1,500 inhabitants. In addition, a small constabulary of 2,000 helps the police in auxiliary duties such as traffic regulation. Tanzania ranks lowest in the world in per capita strength of internal peacekeeping forces.

The police are commanded by an inspector general who is a member of the CCM Central Committee. He heads the three operational divisions in the headquarters and 24 regional subdivisions corresponding to the 20 local government divisions on the mainland and the four regions on the offshore islands. A regional police commander is in charge of each region. Each regional district has at least one police station commanded by a district police commander and temporary police stations called police posts. Apart from the regular force, a marine police patrols the coastline and the inland lakes; there is also a field force and an elite paramilitary force trained in riot control and emergencies. Policemen are generally armed with batons, but officers carry pistols.

Traditional defense groups in Central Tanzania called Sungu Sungu or Wasalama, encouraged by both government and party officials in 1983 and 1984 to help eliminate theft in some areas, often used extreme tactics and occasionally took on the appearance of vigilante groups.

Intelligence gathering, countersubversion and investigation of political offenses are the functions of the 700-man Criminal Investigation Division (CID). The CID also maintains criminal records and statistics relating to crime throughout the nation.

Although many crimes go unreported, recorded offenses indicate a low level of criminal activity. The most common offenses are thefts, assaults, burglary and cattle rustling.

HEALTH

In 1980 there were 2,407 hospitals in the country with 33,714 beds, or one bed per 501 inhabitants. In the same year, there were 900 physicians, or one physician per 20,590 inhabitants, 18 dentists and 5,658 nursing personnel.

PRINCIPAL HEALTH INDICATORS (1984)

Crude Death Rate: 15.3 per 1,000
Decline in Death Rate: -27.3% (1965-83)
Infant Mortality Rate: 107.4 per 1,000 Live Births
Child Death Rate (Ages1-4) per 1,000: 18
Life Expectancy at Birth: 49.3 (males); 52.7 (females)

Health services are administered by the Ministry of Health with an annual budget, in 1982 equal to 5.4% of the national budget, and $4.90 per capita. The major health problems are malaria, sleeping sickness, tuberculosis, pneumonia, venereal diseases and various parasitic diseases. Only 39% of the population have access to safe water.

FOOD

The staple foods are cereals (corn, sorghum or millet) or cassava supplemented by vegetables and bananas, legumes and rice. Little meat, fish or poultry is consumed. Some tribal members drink blood taken from the jugular vein of cattle.

The daily per capita intake of food is 2,028 calories and 48.1 grams of protein (compared to a recommended minimum of 2,600 calories and 65 grams of protein), 30 grams of fats and 376 grams of carbohydrates.

MEDIA & CULTURE

In 1984 three daily newspapers were published in the country with a total circulation of 200,000, or 9 copies per 1,000 inhabitants. Two are published in Dar es Salaam; the *Daily News* is the government organ with a circulation of 55,000 and *Uhuru* the CCM party organ with a circulation of 100,000. One daily, *Kipanga*, is published in Zanzibar. The periodical press includes 17 titles. Annual newsprint consumption in 1982 was 3,200 metric tons, or 173 kg (0.2 lb) per 1,000 inhabitants.

The press is under either CCM party or government control, and no news or opinions contrary to the party line or ideology are ever published. There is, however, no formal or prepublication censorship, and criticisms of poor middle-level administrators or policies often appear in print.

The national news agency is Shihata, founded in 1976. ADN, AFP, CTK, KCNA, Hsinhua, Novosti, Reuters and Tass are represented in Dar es Salaam.

A domestic book publishing industry exists, but its growth has been inhibited by the concentration in Kenya of East African book publishing, especially that in English. The government-owned Tanzania Publishing House is the largest imprint. The East African Literature Bureau has a branch in Dar es Salaam. In 1982 annual title output was 246. Tanzania adheres to the Florence Agreement.

On the mainland, Radio Tanzania, owned by the government, operates five short-wave transmitters broadcasting three programs simultaneously for a total of 165 hours a week. Both the national and the commercial programs are in Swahili; the external program is in English. Radio Tanzania Zanzibar broadcasts from Zanzibar in Swahili for about 50 hours a week. In 1982 there were 530,000 radio receivers in the country, or 28 per 1,000 inhabitants. Of the total 9,191 annual radio broadcasting hours, 3,038 hours are devoted to information, 1,054 to education, 234 hours to culture, 178 hours to religion, 455 hours to commercials and 4,232 hours to entertainment. There is no television service on the mainland but in January 1973 a color television service, the first in black Africa, began on Zanzibar. There are 8,000 television sets in use or 0.4 per 1,000 inhabitants.

No full-length commercial feature films have been produced in the country. In 1981, 162 films were imported, of which 53 came from the United States. There are 34 fixed cinemas in the country with 14,700 seats, or 0.9 seat per 1,000 inhabitants. Annual movie attendance totals 4.0 million or 0.2 per capita. Box office receipts totaled Sh.72 million.

The largest library is the University Library at Dar es Salaam, with 120,000 volumes. The Tanzania Library Service maintains the National Central Library and 13 public libraries, with an aggregate holding of 900,000 volumes.

There are 51 museums reporting an annual attendance of 127,000. There are 20 nature preservation sites.

There are five theaters (three in the capital) serving four professional companies and two amateur troupes. In 1977 these groups performed in seven dramas, and 14 traditional dances.

SOCIAL WELFARE

There is no official social welfare or social security program. In most tribes welfare is a function of the extended family or lineage. A number of private and missionary social service organizations operate in both urban and rural areas.

GLOSSARY

baraza: a traditional village meeting serving as a forum for the exchange of news and opinions among members of a tribe.

Bunge: the National Assembly

uhuru: literally, freedom, the national motto of Tanzania

ujamaa: literally, brotherhood; the ideal of a socialist society in which members share available resources and work.

CHRONOLOGY (from 1961)

1961— Tanganyika gains full internal self-government with Julius Nyerere as prime minister; the former National Legislative Council becomes the National Assembly. Tanganyika becomes a fully independent republic.

1962— Nyerere takes office as president, defeating his only rival, Zuheir Mtemwu, by an overwhelming majority in the first elections to be held on the basis of universal adult suffrage.... Regional commissioners are appointed

1963— Zanzibar gains full independence

1964— Some 600 armed insurgents overthrow the government of Zanzibar and install in its place a revolutionary council headed by Abeid Karume.... Tanganyika and Zanzibar unite to form Tanzania.... The Tanganyika Rifles First Battalion rises in mutiny and seizes Dar es Salaam; the mutiny is quelled with the help of British troops.

1965— An interim constitution is proclaimed for the United Republic of Tanzania; the constitution establishes the Tanganyika African National Union as the sole legal political party and an integral part of government.

1966— The Tanzania shilling is introduced as the new national currency replacing the East African shilling.... Diplomatic relations with Britain are broken over the Rhodesia issue.

1967— The East African Community is formed as a common market with Uganda, Kenya and Tanzania as members.... Nyerere issues the Arusha Declaration defining ujamaa-type socialism as the national goal.

1968— Swahili becomes the sole official language and the medium of instruction in primary schools.... Relations with Britain are restored.

1970— All schools are nationalized; the University of Dar es Salaam is founded.... Nyerere is reelected president.

1972— Vice President Karume is assassinated.... Armed followers of Milton Obote, deposed president of Uganda, invade Uganda from Tanzania but are repulsed.

1975— TanZam Railway, built with Chinese aid, is opened for traffic.

1977— TANU and ASP merge to form the Chama Cha Mapinduzi (Tanzania Revolutionary Party).... Edward Sokoine is named prime minister.... Border with Kenya is closed as the East African Community disintegrates in a welter of recriminations.

1978— Ugandan forces occupy the Kagera salient advancing south as far as the Kagera River; Tanzania counterattacks with 40,000 troops including Ugandan dissidents; after a six-month campaign the invaders rout Idi Amin's forces and occupy Kampala; Amin flees Uganda.

1980— Nyerere is re-elected president in national elections.... Zanzibar is granted a new constitution under which it will elect its own president.

1981— Tanzanian troops are withdrawn from Uganda.

1983— The Human Resources Deployment Act authorizes government to round up vagrants and unemployed people and resettle them forcibly in productive sectors.... Kenya and Tanzania reach accord on distribution of EAC assets and border issues.

1984— Prime Minister Edward Sokoine is killed in auto accident; Salim Ahmed Salim is named prime minister.... Vice President Aboud Jumbe, president of Zanzibar, resigns and is replaced by Ali Hassan Mwinyi.

1984— Constitution is amended reducing the number of presidential terms for Nyerere's successors to two and creating two vice presidents.

1985— The National Assembly amends the 1962 Preventive Detention Act removing many potential abuses.... Julius Nyerere steps down from the presidency and Ali Hassan Mwinyi is elected to the office by an overwhelming 92% vote in national election; Mwinyi names Joseph S. Warioba as prime minister.

BIBLIOGRAPHY (from 1968)

Africa Changes: A Young Leader in a Young Nation. Color film, 14 min. CBS.

African Quest. Color film, 23 min. Anglo American Corp.

An African Community: The Masai. Color film, 16 min. CBS.

Ayany, S. G., *A History of Zanzibar* (Nairobi, 1970).

Bailey, Martin, *The Union of Tanganyika and Zanzibar* (Syracuse, N.Y., 1973).

Barkan, Joel D., and John J. Okumu, *Politics and Public Policy in Kenya & Tanzania* (New York, 1984).

Bolton, Dianne, *Nationalization: A Road to Socialism? The Case of Tanzania* (London, 1985).

Central Africa. Color film, 20 min. ABC.

Chiteji, Frank M., *The Development & Socio-Economic Impact of Transportation in Tanzania* (Washington, D.C., 1980).

Clark, W. Edmund, *Socialist Development & Public Investment in Tanzania* (Toronto, 1978).

Coulson, Andrew, *Tanzania: A Political Economy* (New York, 1982).

Darch, Colin, *Tanzania* [World Bibliographical Series] (Santa Barbara, Calif., 1985).

Dryden, Stanley, *Local Administration in Tanzania* (New York, 1968).

Due, Jean M., *Costs, Return & Repayment Experience of Ujamaa Villages in Tanzania* (Washington, D.C., 1980).

Duggan, William and John R. Civille, *Tanzania and Nyerere: A Study of Ujamaa and Nationhood* (Maryknoll, N.Y., 1976).

East Africa. Color film, 23 min. Paul Hoefler.

East Africa: Kenya, Tanganyika, Uganda. Color film, 21 min. Encyclopaedia Britannica.

East Africa: Two Lifestyles. Color film, 19 min. CBS.

El-Namaki, M.S., *Problems of Management in a Developing Environment: The Case of Tanzania* (New York, 1979).

Fortmann, Louise, *Peasants, Officials and Participation in Rural Tanzania: Experiences with Villagization and Decentralization* (Ithaca, N.Y., 1980).

Freedom Railway. Color film, 45 min. Supreme Film Service.

Hatch, John, *Tanzania: A Profile* (New York, 1972).

Hyden, Goran, *Beyond Ujamaa in Tanzania* (Berkeley, Calif., 1980).

Hopkins, Raymond, *Political Roles in a New State: Tanzania's First Decade* (New Haven, Conn., 1971).

Inge, Clyde R., *From Village to State in Tanzania: The Politics of Rural Development* (Ithaca, N.Y., 1972).

Kim K., *Papers on the Political Economy of Tanzania* (London, 1980).

Kimambo, I. M. and A. J. Temu, *A History of Tanzania* (Dar es Salaam, 1970).

Kurtz, Laura S., *A Historical Dictionary of Tanzania* (Metuchen, N.J., 1978).

Lappe, Frances, M., *Mozambique & Tanzania* (San Francisco, Calif., 1980).

Masai In Tanzania. Color film, 13 min. Producer: not available.

McHenry, Dean E., *Tanzania's Ujamaa Villages: The Implementation of a Rural Development Strategy* (Berkeley Calif., 1979).

Mittelman, James H., *Underdevelopment and the Transition to Socialism: Mozambique and Tanzania* (Orlando, Fla., 1981).

Mwansasu, Bismarck and C. Pratt, *Towards Socialism in Tanzania* (Toronto, 1979).

Nellis, John R., *A Theory of Ideology: The Tanzanian Example* (New York, 1972).

Nnoli, Okwudiba, *Self Reliance and Foreign Policy in Tanzania* (New York, 1977).

Nyerere, Julius, *Freedom and Development* (New York, 1976).

Polome, Edgar C., and C. P. Hill, *Language in Tanzania* (New York, 1980).

Pratt, C., *The Critical Phase in Tanzania, 1945-1968* (New York, 1976).

Profile of Tanganyika. Color film, 31 min. USIS.

Resnick, Idrian, *The Long Transition: Building Socialism in Tanzania* (New York, 1982).

Sabot, R.H., *Economic Development & Urgan Migration: Tanzania 1900-1971* (New York, 1979).

Samoff, Joel, *Tanzania: Local Politics and the Structure of Power* (Madison, Wisc., 1974).

Smith, William, *We Must Run While They Walk: A Portrait of Africa's Julius Nyerere* (New York, 1971).

Starting from Scratch. Color film, 27 min. United Nations.

Tanzania: Progress through Self-Reliance. Color film, 21 min. Minerva Films.

Tanzania – The Quiet Revolution. B&W film, 60 min. National Educational Television.

This is Tanganyika. B&W film, 14 min. British Information Services.

UNESCO, *Two Studies in Ethnic Group Relations in Africa* (Paris, 1980).

Van Freyhold, Michaela, *Ujamaa Villages in Tanzania: Analysis of a Social Experiment* (New York, 1981).

Yeager, Rodger, *Tanzania: An African Experiment* (Boulder, Colo., 1982).

Youth Builds a Nation in Tanzania. Color film, 18 min. Encyclopaedia Britannica.

Yu, George T., *China's African Policy: A Study of Tanzania* (New York, 1975).

Zanzibar. B&W film, 17 min. Gateway Films.

OFFICIAL PUBLICATIONS

Auditor General, *Appropriations Accounts Revenue Statements. Accounts of the Funds and Other Public Accounts of Tanzania.*

Finance Ministry, *Estimates of Public Expenditures, Consolidated Fund Sources, Supply Votes and Development Expenditures* (Vol. II).

———, *Financial Statements and Revenue Estimates* (Vol. I).

Tanzania Bank, *Economic Bulletin* (quarterly).

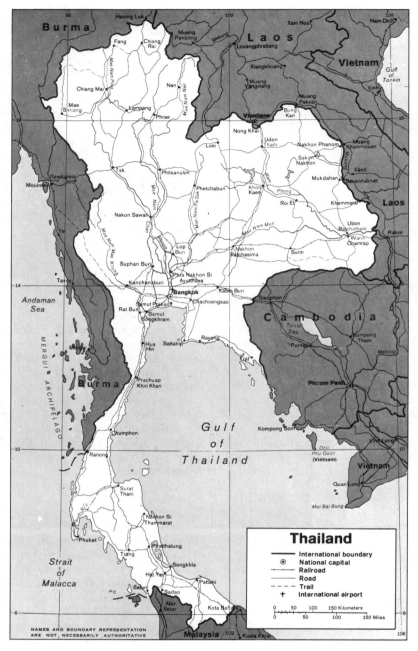

Thailand

- International boundary
- ⊛ National capital
- ┼┼┼┼ Railroad
- Road
- - - - - Trail
- ✛ International airport

0 50 100 150 Kilometers
0 50 100 150 Miles

NAMES AND BOUNDARY REPRESENTATION
ARE NOT NECESSARILY AUTHORITATIVE

THAILAND

BASIC FACT SHEET

OFFICIAL NAME: Kingdom of Thailand (Prades Thai or Muang Thai); also known as Siam, from 1850 to 1936 and from 1945 to 1949.

ABBREVIATION: TH

CAPITAL: Bangkok

HEAD OF STATE: King Bhumibol Adulyadej Rama IX (from 1946)

HEAD OF GOVERNMENT: Prime Minister Gen. Prem Tinsulanonda (from 1980)

NATURE OF GOVERNMENT: Constitutional monarchy (de jure); military dictatorship (de facto)

POPULATION: 52,700,000 (1985)

AREA: 514,000 sq km (198,456 sq mi)

ETHNIC MAJORITY: Thai

LANGUAGE: Thai

RELIGION: Theravada Buddhism

UNIT OF CURRENCY: Baht ($1=B26.75, August 1985)

NATIONAL FLAG: A wide blue horizontal center stripe flanked by two white and red stripes at the top and at the bottom.

NATIONAL EMBLEM: Known as the Krut, the national emblem represents Garuda, the winged creature of Hindu mythology, used as a mount by Vishnu, one of the gods in the Hindu pantheon. The bird appears with a human torso wearing a gold headdress and the ritual mask of Asian demons.

NATIONAL ANTHEM: "Thailand is the Unity of Thai Blood and Body." The royal anthem, known as Sanrasorn Phra Barami ("Anthem Eulogizing His Majesty") is also sung at all public functions.

NATIONAL HOLIDAYS: December 5 (King's Birthday, National Day); January 1 (New Year's Day) ; April 6 (Chakri Day); April 13 (Songkran or Thai New Year's Day by the Maha Sakaraj Calendar); May 5 (Coronation Day); August 12 (Queen's Birthday); October 23 (King Chulalongkorn Memorial Day); November 18 (Loy Krathong); December 10 (Constitution Day)

NATIONAL CALENDAR: Both the lunar, or the Maha Sakaraj, calendar and the solar, or Gregorian, calendar are used. By legislation passed in 1940, the year 2484 of the Buddhist Era, according to the former calendar, began on January 1, 1941. Thus 1978=2521 B.E.

PHYSICAL QUALITY OF LIFE INDEX: 79 (up from 70 in 1976) (On an ascending scale with 100 is the maximum. U.S. 95).

DATE OF INDEPENDENCE: Never under foreign rule in modern times.

DATE OF CONSTITUTION: December 1978

WEIGHTS & MEASURES: The metric system is the legal standard but traditional units are used. These include: the pikul (or hap)=60 kg (132.3 lb); the kwian=2,000 liters (440 gallons); the thang=20 liters (4.4 gallons); the rai=0.16 hectare (0.4 acre); the catty=0.6 kg (1.3 lb); the baht=14.9 grams (0.529 oz); the ban=757 liters (220 gallons); the sat=16.6 liters (4.4 gallons); the sen= 40 meters (43.774 yards); the wa=2 meters (2.187 yards); the sok=50 cm (19.685 in); the khup=2.5 cm (9.84 in); the ngan=400 sq meters (478.4 sq yards); the tarang wa=4 sq meters (4.784 sq yards).

LOCATION & AREA

Thailand is located in the middle of mainland SE Asia with a total land area of 514,000 sq km (198,456 sq mi), extending 1,555 km (966 mi) N to S and 790 km (491 mi) E to W. Its coastline on the Gulf of Siam extends 1,875 km (1,165 mi) and that on the Andaman Sea 740 km (460 mi). The land area includes numerous offshore islands, the largest of which is Phuket at the northern end of the Strait of Malacca.

Thailand shares its international boundary of 4,932 km (3,062 mi) with four neighbors: Burma (1,799 km, 1,118 mi); Malaysia (576 km, 358 mi); Cambodia (803 km, 499 mi); Laos (1,754 km, 1,090 mi). There are no current border disputes with any neighbor except Cambodia. The two nations have a long-standing dispute over a ruined temple in the Phanom Dongrak mountain range.

The capital is Bangkok, the country's only metropolitan center. Together with Thon Buri, a major suburb on the west bank of the Chao Phraya River, Bangkok forms a special administrative unit known as Krungthep Mahanakhon with a 1980 population of 4,967,071. The other cities are Chiang Mai (101,595), Hat Yai (93,519), Khon Kaen (85,863) and Nakhon Ratchasima (78,246).

On the basis of natural terrain, there are five distinct topographical regions: the southeast coast, the northeastern region, the central lowland region, the northern and western mountain region and the southern peninsular region.

The heart of Thailand is the central valley, dominated by the Chao Phraya River and watered by an extensive network of canals. It stretches from the foothills of northern mountains at Uttaradit to the Gulf of Siam and is flanked on the west by the Bilaukthang Range and in the east by the Khorat Plateau. The valley, which comprises 22% of the national territory, is about 482 km (300 mi) from north to south, with an average width of 160 to 240 km (100 to 150 mi).

The north-eastern Khorat Plateau region, comprising one-third of the national territory, is an undulating tableland about 122 meters to 213 meters (400 to 700 ft) above sea level in the north and 61 meters (200 ft) in the south. It is rimmed on the south by the Phanom Dongrak mountain range along the Cambodian border and on the west by the Phetchabun Mountains. Much of the land is poor and consists of sandstone and saline soil.

The northern and western mountain region is a series of parallel mountain ranges separated by deep and narrow alluvial valleys. These ranges have an average elevation of 1,585 meters (5,200 ft) and contain the highest peak in the country, Doi Intharnon (2,590 meters, 8,500 ft). The notorious Death Railway, built by the Japanese during World War II, ran through the Three Pagodas Pass, one of the few natural gaps through this region.

The small southeast coast region on the Gulf of Siam is a lush, fertile plain separated by low mountains from the central valley.

The southern region is a long sliver of land extending from Thailand to Malaysia, no wider than 19 km (12 mi) in some places near the Isthmus of Kra. South of the Isthmus, Thailand widens to include the full width of the peninsula facing both the Andaman Sea on the west and the Gulf of Siam on the east. A series of north-to-south parallel ridges divides the peninsula into a narrow, swampy indented west coastal plain and a broad and smooth east coast plain.

The northern lowlands are drained by three rivers, the Ping, the Yom and the Nan, which unite to form the country's principal river, the Chao Phraya. Further downstream, the Chao Phraya is joined by the Pa Sak. Because it flows through a flat plain, the Chao Phraya is a slow river indented with backwaters. The largest rivers in the north-eastern Khorat Plateau are the Mun and its principal tributary, the Chi. Although not strictly a Thai river, the Mekong forms the nation's eastern and northern boundaries for 804 km (500 mi).

WEATHER

Thailand has a tropical climate dominated by the monsoons. In most regions there are four distinct seasons: the dry season, from January through February; the hot season, from March through May; the rainy season, from June through October; and the cool season, from November through December.

For most of Thailand, the temperature rarely falls below 13°C (55°F) or goes above 35°C (95°F) although there are occasional recordings above 37.8 °C (100°F). The mean temperature is considerably lower in the dry season. The temperature variations are much greater in the northern and northeastern regions, but it is more or less constant in the southern peninsula. Bangkok has a mean annual temperature of 28.4°C (83 °F), with a low of 25 °C (77 °F) in December and a high of 30 °C (86 °F) in April.

About 90% of the rainfall falls during the wet monsoon, from June to October. But some parts of peninsular Thailand receive rain during all seasons. The amount of precipitation varies from 102 cm (40 in.) to 152 cm (60 in.) in the northern highlands, central lowlands and the Khorat Plateau to 203 cm (80 in.) to 305 cm (120 in.) in the western mountains and the southern peninsula.

Twice a year, toward the end of the dry and rainy seasons, Thailand experiences typhoons of considerable violence. Thunderstorms are common between May and October in the north and between March and November in the south.

POPULATION

The population of Thailand was estimated in 1985 at 52,700,000 on the basis of the last official census, held in 1980, when the population was 46,961,338. The population is expected to reach 67.6 million by 2000 and 85 million by 2020. The annual growth rate is 2.09%, based on an annual birth rate of 28.6 per 1,000.

Overall population density is 100 per sq km (259 per sq mi). The lowest density is in the northern highlands, where it does not exceed 32 per sq km (83 per sq mi) and highest in the central lowlands where, in the agricultural areas, it approaches 234 per sq km (606 per sq mi), and where nearly 40% of the national population is concentrated. In some sections of the southern peninsula, the density approaches 1,158 per sq km (3,000 per sq mi).

Thailand is predominantly a rural nation, with 85% of its population living in three types of villages: strip villages, along both sides of a river or canal; cluster villages, in river valleys and around farmlands; and dispersed villages, in the delta regions. About one half of the country's urban dwellers live in and around Bangkok. Only 8-15% of Bangkok's inhabitants live in slums and squatter settlements. No other Thai city approaches Bangkok in size or importance, and only one other has a population exceeding 100,000: Chiang Mai. There are 19 cities with over 20,000 inhabitants. The annual urban growth rate is less than 3.8%. The rural population has remained stable for a number of decades, and urban migration is demographically insignificant.

The age profile shows 36.7% in the under-14 age group, 60% in the 15-64 age group and 3.3% in the over-65 age group. The sex ratio is uniformly well bal-

```
               DEMOGRAPHIC INDICATORS (1984)
Population, total (in 1,000) . . . . . . . . . . . . . .   52,700.0
Population ages (% of total)
    0-14 . . . . . . . . . . . . . . . . . . . . . . . . . . .       36.7
    15-64 . . . . . . . . . . . . . . . . . . . . . . . . . .       60.0
    65+ . . . . . . . . . . . . . . . . . . . . . . . . . . .        3.3
Youth 15-24 (000) . . . . . . . . . . . . . . . . . . .     11,363
Women ages 15-49 (000) . . . . . . . . . . . . . . .     13,284
Dependency ratios . . . . . . . . . . . . . . . . . . . .       66.6
Child-woman ratios . . . . . . . . . . . . . . . . . . .         564
Sex ratios (per 100 females) . . . . . . . . . . . .       101.0
Median ages (years) . . . . . . . . . . . . . . . . . .       20.7
Marriage Rate (per 1,000) . . . . . . . . . . . . . .        7.2
Divorce Rate (per 1,000) . . . . . . . . . . . . . . .        0.5
Average size of Household . . . . . . . . . . . . . .        5.3
Decline in birthrate (%, 1965-83) . . . . . . . . . .      -37.2
Proportion of urban (%) . . . . . . . . . . . . . . . .      15.63
Population density (per sq. km.) . . . . . . . . . .         100
    per hectare of arable land . . . . . . . . . . . .       2.17
Rates of growth (%) . . . . . . . . . . . . . . . . . .       2.09
    urban % . . . . . . . . . . . . . . . . . . . . . . . .        3.8
    rural % . . . . . . . . . . . . . . . . . . . . . . . .        1.8
Natural increase rates (per 1,000) . . . . . . . . .       20.9
Crude birth rates (per 1,000) . . . . . . . . . . . .       28.6
Crude death rates (per 1,000) . . . . . . . . . . . .        7.7
Gross reproduction rates . . . . . . . . . . . . . . .       1.75
Net reproduction rates . . . . . . . . . . . . . . . . .      1.56
Total fertility rates . . . . . . . . . . . . . . . . . . .      3.59
General fertility rates (per 1,000) . . . . . . . . . .       114
Life expectancy, males (years) . . . . . . . . . . .       60.8
Life expectancy, females (years) . . . . . . . . . .       64.8
Life expectancy, total (years) . . . . . . . . . . . .       62.7
Population doubling time in years at current rate       36
```

anced in all regions. In 1980 there were 22,308,607 males and 22,495,933 females, yielding a male-female ratio of 50.3:49.7.

The Thais are an extremely settled people, and there is little internal migration, much less emigration to other countries. Nearly 87% of the population live and die in the province in which they are born. Strict immigration regulations have stemmed the flow of Chinese into the country, which was a major problem until the 1920s. The recent upheavals in Laos and Cambodia have prompted the flight of refugees from these countries into Thailand, forcing a reluctant Thai government to relax its regulations regarding the entry of immigrants. Since 1975, almost 650,000 persons from Vietnam, Laos and Cambodia have fled to Thailand. Thai policy has generally been to allow U.N. assistance to them until such time as they can be repatriated or resettled in third countries. The Thai afford first asylum to bona fide Lao refugees arriving by land and to Vietnamese boat refugees, and promote voluntary repatriation along with third-country-resettlement, particularly of the Khmer and Lao, who comprise 95% of Thailand's refugee population. In 1985 the refugee population on Thai territory was about 130,000. In addition, about 50,000 Vietnamese who arrived before 1954 remain in Thailand with limited rights, along with about 10,000 Chinese who were Kuomintang supporters and about 17,000 Karen hill tribe refugees from Burma.

With few exceptions, the government has not granted long-term asylum to new arrivals from Cambodia since early 1980, but it has provided temporary safe haven to about 245,000 Cambodians at evacuation sites on the Thai side of the border. Thailand has assisted international voluntary agencies to provide food and medical care to Khmer in camps along the border. The Thai government permitted these displaced Khmer to move temporarily into Thailand in the wake of attacks by forces of Vietnam and the Heng Samrin regime in Cambodia in 1984 and early 1985. Since early 1980, small groups of Khmer caught trying to move illegally from border camps into refugee camps inside Thailand have generally been returned by Thai authorities to the border region, though several thousand have managed to remain in the camps. There have been reports that would-be Lao refugees have been turned back to Laos by Thai officials. The government has instituted a system of screening of Lao with the United Nations High Commissioner for Refugees (UNHCR) as observer and this has improved the fair treatment of these displaced persons. To date none of those screened out have been returned to Laos. Vietnamese coming overland via Cambodia after April 1981 have had to remain at the border for lengthy periods until they were allowed to be considered for third country resettlement. About 4,000 overland Vietnamese refugees were on the border at the end of 1985. Since 1979, nearly 67,500 Vietnamese refugees have arrived in Thailand after perilous journeys, often in small, unseaworthy boats, across international waters. Although less than in the peak years of 1979-81, the number of arrivals in 1985 showed no significant decrease from the previous two years.

The UNHCR and the major resettlement countries have supported the Thai policy of promoting voluntary repatriation. About 2,800 Lao have returned to their homeland under UNHCR supervision following successful bilateral Thai/Lao negotiations in September 1980. UNHCR negotiations with the Heng Samrin regime concerning the repatriation of Khmer refugees remain stalled. The government of Vietnam has been unwilling to discuss repatriation of Vietnamese refugees in Thailand. Most Indochinese refugees are not willing to return to their home country.

The status and role of women has continued to progress at a moderate but noticeable pace over the past several years. For the most part, women have equal legal rights in Thailand, with specific guarantees of property and divorce rights; and there are no allegations that these rights are denied. Women are not, however, permitted to participate fully in Buddhist religious institutions or to become monks. They are well represented in the labor force, and are becoming increasingly well represented in professional positions, particularly those in the commercial sector. In general, women are not legally barred from positions traditionally held by men. Thailand does, however, have limitations on women serving in the armed forces. In rural areas, sex stereotypes exist with respect to occupational and social roles. These barriers are being modified as mass communications bring modern role models to even the most remote communities. In 1980, a group called the Friends of Women was founded to advance the cause of women's rights in Thailand. Their efforts are aided by other groups such as the CGRS which follows certains issues such as exploitation of women as prostitutes.

Women vote in numbers equal to men and participate fully in the political process. There are several female members of the national legislature. However, women are underrepresented in national politics and in high government positions.

In 1974 the government appointed a special committee to advise the cabinet on population policy. Official policy is to reduce the population growth rate to 2% by 1981. To expand family planning services in rural areas, an Accelerated Development of Maternal and Child Health and Family Planning Services is under way with assistance from the U.N. Fund for Population Activities. In 1975 government expenditures on family planning services were $935,000, representing 0.04% of the national budget and 1.2% of the health budget. Expenditures on family planning by private and public bodies totaled $3.686 million, or $0.8 per capita. In the same year, there were 513,000 acceptors of government-supported family planning programs and 1,731,000 users of contraceptives, representing 32% of married women of childbearing age.

ETHNIC COMPOSITION

Thailand is one of the most cohesive and integrated societies in SE Asia with over 75% belonging to the Thai stock. The Central Thai, or Thai Bhak Klang, formerly known as the Siamese, form the largest component of this majority. Their cultural and social patterns form the standard for other Thai groups. There are three other major Thai groups: the Thai Isan or Thai Lao of the northeastern region, who are distinguished from the Central Thai by food habits and use of the Lao language; the Thai Yuan (also known as Lana Thai or Yonock) of the northern region, who have been independent of Central Thai control for centuries; and the Thai Pak Tai of the southern region along the Isthmus of Kra, whose physical features reveal Malay influences. There are three minor Thai groups: the Phu Thai, an agricultural people of the Northeast; the Lu or Lue, whose ancestors are believed to have emigrated from Yunnan in China; and the Shan (also called Ngiaw, Thai Yai, Thai Long or Great Thai), who are also ethnically related to the Shans of Burma.

The Chinese are the largest ethnic minority, constituting 14% of the population as a whole and 33% of the population of Bangkok. For hundreds of years, the Chinese moved into Thailand in large numbers until immigration quotas were enforced in 1948. Concentrated in the Bangkok and the Isthmus of Kra regions, the Chinese dominate finance and industry, operate 80% of the rice trade, and run most of the export, import, wholesale and retail trade establish-

ments. They are far from homogeneous and are divided by differences of dialect and province of origin. The average Chinese often considers himself as a Teochiu, a Cantonese, a Hakka, a Hainanese, a Hokkien or a Taiwanese. As a result of the pressures of Thai nationalism, they have become well integrated into Thai society.

The second largest minority are the Thai Malay or Thai Islam, a Malayo-Polynesian group separated from the Thai by both religion and race, and, to some extent, language. They reside for the most part in the four provinces of the southern region: Pattani, Yala, Narathiwat and Satun. They have proved highly resistant to assimilation and have been sometimes implicated in secessionist movements. In the mid-1970s they were estimated to number around one million.

Under the general category of hill tribes, there are over eight major groups and nearly 20 minor ones. The best-known of these tribes is the Meo (H'Moong of Mong), an opium-growing tribe in the northern region, numbering about 50,000, divided into Blue Meo, White Meo and Gua M'Ba Meo. They revolted unsuccessfully against the government in 1967. The other hill tribes are the Soai or Kui (120,000), the Mon (100,000), the Lawa (9,000), the Yao (10,000), the Akha (28,000), the Lahu (17,000) and the Lisu (20,000). Also included in this category sometimes are the Karens, a Tibeto-Burmese people, numbering about 75,000.

Even before the present influx of refugees from the Indochinese Peninsula, there were large Laotian, Cambodian and Vietnamese communities in Thailand. The Khmer, or Cambodian, minority lives in provinces east and southeast of Bangkok and in the southern Khorat Plateau, a territory once Cambodian. Estimates of their size range up to 400,000. The Vietnamese in north and northeast Thailand are a much smaller group, not exceeding 90,000 in number. More recent ethnic alien groups include the Indians and the Pakistanis, numbering together 60,000, who have no fixed niche in Thai society.

There is a large Western community in Bangkok, numbering over 50,000 in the early 1980s.

Thailand is one of the countries most affected by refugees. Since 1975 more than half a million people from Vietnam, Laos and Cambodia have fled into the country, including 60,000 Vietnamese, 210,000 Khmer, and 250,000 Lao; about a quarter million have been resettled in third countries. As of 1983, some 265,000 people were still in Thai camps awaiting permanent resettlement.

In terms of ethnic and linguistic homogeneity, Thailand is ranked 37th in the world with 34% homogeneity (on an ascending scale in which North and South Korea are ranked 135th with 100% homogeneity and Tanzania is ranked first with 7% homogeneity).

LANGUAGES

The official language of Thailand is Thai or Siamese, which in its various dialects is the mother tongue of 90% of Thai peoples. Its linguistic affinities have not been established. But most linguists assign it to the Chinese-Tai branch of the Sino-Tibetan family of languages.

Thai has four dialectal forms, of which Central Thai is the official standard and the language of the media. Central Thai and Lao are mutually intelligible. The other dialects of Thai are Kham Muang and Southern Thai, also called Tamprue.

Thai, also called Tai, is a monosyllabic, tonal, uninflected language. Its alphabet is of Sanskritic origin with borrowings from Khmer and Pali. There are 44 consonants with 32 vowels and diphthong forms. The alphabet was adapted to the typewriter by U.S. missionaries in 1891. The native tongue of the Chinese minority is Teochiu, that of the Thai Malay is Malay.

English is the universal second language. In many private schools it is taught from the elementary grades on, while in public schools it is taught as a compulsory foreign language. English is used extensively, particularly by the Thai elite and businessmen. Many official documents are published in both Thai and English. Bangkok has four English newspapers.

Each of the smaller ethnic minorities forms a linguistic group. The most prominent among these are the Karen dialects of Skaw and Pwo, Meo, Lawa, Mon, Khmer, Yao, Lisu, Lahu and Akha.

Official linguistic policy is directed toward the propagation of Central Thai as the standard official language, discouragement of the use of minority languages and promotion of the knowledge of English.

RELIGIONS

The state religion is Buddhism in its Theravada or Hinayana form, which is professed by 95.5% of the population. Religion is perhaps the most pervasive and visible force in national life and temples—known as wats—dot the landscape as Buddhist festivals do the calendar. The number of monks in the population has led to the description of the country as "the land of the yellow robes."

Thai Buddhism is an amalgam of pre-Buddhist Hindu beliefs and practices and animist spirit worship interwoven with Buddhist theology and rituals. Popular religious beliefs and institutions have changed little over the centuries. Cosmological and astrological concepts pervade not only religious but also social and economic life.

Buddhism in Thailand has an elaborate ecclesiastical structure. That structure is headed by the supreme patriarch of the Sangha whose title is Sakala Sanghaparinayaka Somdech Phra Sangharaja. The Sangha, or the order of Buddhist monks, with a membership of over 250,000, is the nearest thing to a clergy that Buddhism has. The patriarch, who is appointed by the king, presides over the supreme council, Mahathera Samagom, which has both judicial and legislative functions.

The king is required by the constitution to be a practicing Buddhist. The affairs of the Sangha are regulated by the Department of Religious Affairs in the Ministry of Culture. The state is closely involved in the promotion of Buddhism, and the relations between the two are defined in the Buddhist Order Act of 1962. The government is the legal owner of all wat lands, administers religious education and operates a large Buddhist publishing house. The monarch himself maintains 115 royal wats and two ecclesiastical colleges.

Minority religious groups constitute an estimated 7% of the population, but they have contributed little to Thai cultural traditions. The Chinese practice a traditional mixture of Mahayana Buddhism, Taoism, Confucianism and ancestor worship. The vast majority of Muslims are the ethnic Malay of the southern region; the remainder are Pakistanis in urban centers and the ethnic Thais, known as Thai Islam, in rural areas of the central region. The government provides financial assistance to Thai Muslims for their annual pilgrimage to Mecca. The head of the Muslim establishment, the chularajamontri, has a semi-official status. Most of the Indians are Hindus.

Although Christianity was introduced into Thailand as early as 1511, it has had only modest success in winning converts. The size of the Christian community is estimated at around 200,000, including Catholic Chinese, Vietnamese and Laos. The Catholic Church, accounting for nearly half the Christian population, has two archdioceses, at Bangkok and Sakonnakohn. The Church of Christ in Thailand, the major Protestant denomination, has over 140 congregations; independent Protestant denominations have another 180. Christian missions have played an influential role in the Westernization of Thailand. Catholic missions run 125 schools and six hospitals, and the Protestants operate 50 schools and ten hospitals.

COLONIAL EXPERIENCE

Thailand has never been under foreign rule in modern times.

CONSTITUTION & GOVERNMENT

The modern constitutional history of Thailand begins with the constitution of 1932, which was amended by 11 other constitutions: 1932, 1946, 1947, 1949, 1952, 1959, 1968, 1971, 1974, 1976, 1977 and 1978. The only principle common to all these constitutions is the inviolability of the monarch. Successive changes of government have not diminished the role of the monarchy as the most visible symbol of national unity. The monarch also provides the imprimatur of legitimacy to both civilian and military administrations. But, at the same time, his effectiveness in influencing the composition and policies of the government is limited.

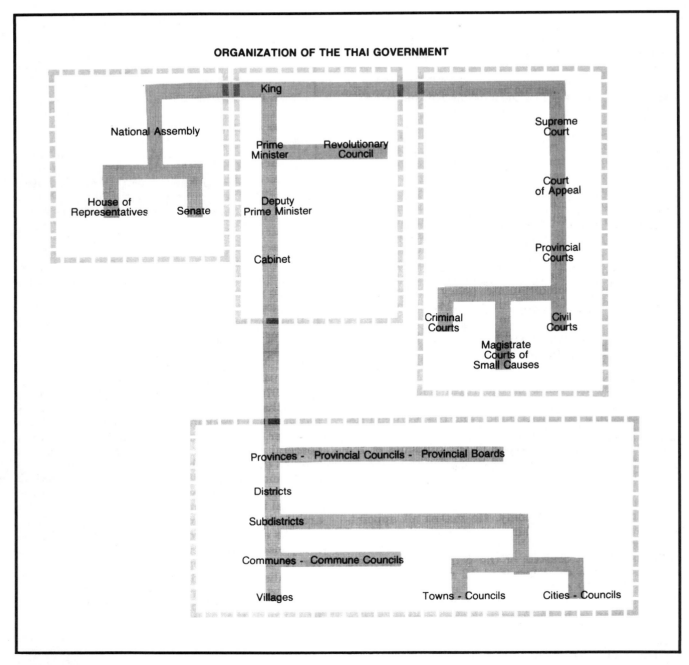

ORGANIZATION OF THE THAI GOVERNMENT

King

National Assembly

Prime Minister   Revolutionary Council

House of Representatives   Senate

Deputy Prime Minister

Cabinet

Supreme Court

Court of Appeal

Provincial Courts

Criminal Courts   Civil Courts

Magistrate Courts of Small Causes

Provinces - Provincial Councils - Provincial Boards

Districts

Subdistricts

Communes - Commune Councils

Villages   Towns - Councils   Cities - Councils

The 1978 constitution made no drastic changes in the form of government and the concessions it made to democracy actually made parliament a "fig-leaf" in the words of veteran Thai statesman, Thanat Khoman, than an effective arm of government.

Despite a constitutional facade, Thailand has since 1932 been ruled, except for brief, intermittent periods, by military strongmen supported by an elite and conservative oligarchy. The main organs of government are the cabinet, which formulates policy jointly with 14-member Privy Council which advises the king.

Under the 1978 constitution, as under its predecessors, the most important government office is that of the prime minister, who is usually the leader of the ruling group and the chief executive. He also supervises the office of the royal household and heads the National Economic Development Board, the National Security Council and the National Research Council. Under military governments he is also the commander of one of the branches of the armed forces. All laws and royal decrees must be countersigned by him. He presides over cabinet meetings and controls their agenda. In a national emergency he has unlimited powers over national security and the economy. He makes all appointments and conducts all investigations in the name of the king.

The cabinet consists of the prime minister, two deputy prime ministers and 12 ministers. Under each ministry are a number of quasi-autonomous statutory agencies, each headed by a director general appointed by the king with the approval of the prime minister. Within these departments are divisions and sections as well as provincial and district offices. Under the 1978 and previous constitutions, cabinet members were barred from membership in the national assembly, although ministers were permitted to participate without vote in senate and assembly debates. The concept of executive answerability to the legislature has not been acknowledged in Thai constitutions.

Thailand's security apparatus operates within a constitutionally mandated framework, but numerous police, civilian and military agencies share responsibility, often with overlapping jurisdictions and ill-defined mandates. Reflecting the strong executive orientation of the government, the security services have formidable powers. Although these powers are sometimes utilized in a heavy-handed or uneven way, human rights abuses attributable to the security services are not believed to be systematic and have been infrequent in recent years.

RULERS OF THAILAND
(from 1945)

PRIME MINISTERS:
1945 (August to September)
      Thawi Bunyakhet
1945 (September) to 1946 (January)
      Mom Rachawongse Seni Pramoj
1946 (January to March)
      Nai Khuang Aphaiwong
1946 (March to August)
      Nai Pridi Phanomyong
1946 (August) to 1947 (September)
      Luang Thamrong Nawasawat
1947 (September) to 1948 (April)
      Nai Khuang Aphaiwong
1948 (April) to 1957 (September)
      Luang Phibun Songgram
1957 (September) Sarit Thanarat
1957 (September to December)
      Nai Pote Sarasin
1957 (December) to 1958 (October)
      Thanom Kittikatchorn
1958 (October) to 1963 (December)
      Sarit Thanarat
1963 (December) to 1973 (October)
      Thanom Kittikatchorn
1973 (October) to 1975 (January)
      Sanya Dharmasakti Thammasak
1975 (January to March)
      Seni Pramoj
1975 (March) to 1976 (April)
      Kukrit Pramoj
1976 (April to September)
      Seni Pramoj
1976 (October) to 1977 (October)
      Thanin Kraivichien
1977 (October) to 1980 (February
      Kriangsak Chamanand
1980 (Feb) — Prem Tinsulanonda

CABINET LIST (1985)

King	Bhumibol Adulyadej
Prime Minister	Gen. (Ret.) Prem Tinsulanonda
Deputy Prime Minister	Gen. (Ret.) Prachuap Suntharangkun
Deputy Prime Minister	Boontheng Thongswasdi
Deputy Prime Minister	Bhichai Rattakul
Deputy Prime Minister	Adm. (Ret.) Sontee Boonyachai
Minister Attached to Office of Prime Minister	Kramol Thongthammachart
Minister Attached to Office of Prime Minister	Meechai Ruchpan
Minister Attached to Office of Prime Minister	Pol. Lt. (Ret.) Charn Manootham
Minister Attached to Office of Prime Minister	Flying Officer Suli Mahasanthana
Minister Attached to Office of Prime Minister	Sawas Khamprakob
Minister Attached to Office of Prime Minister	Chaisiri Ruangkanchanases
Minister Attached to Office of Prime Minister	Banyat Bantadtan
Minister of Agriculture & Cooperatives	Narong Wongwan
Minister of Commerce	Kosol Krairerk
Minister of Communications	Samak Sundaravej
Minister of Defense	Gen. (Ret.) Prem Tinsulanonda
Minister of Education	Chuan Leekpai
Minister of Finance	Sommai Huntrakun
Minister of Foreign Affairs	Air Ch. Mar. (Ret.) Siddhi Savetsila
Minister of Industry	Ob Vasuratna
Minister of Interior	Gen. (Ret.) Sitthi Chirarot
Minister of Justice	Phiphob Atisrirat
Minister of Public Health	Marut Bunnak

Between 1932 and 1985 there were 13 elections, most of them managed by the group in power. Suffrage is universal over age 20. The voter turnout in the last elections in 1976 was 40%. A 1974 electoral law forbade candidates from running as independents, which led to a proliferation of political parties.

There have been five coups d'etat in Thailand since 1946, four of them by the military (in 1948, 1958, 1976 and 1977). Of these, only the 1973 student revolt that toppled Thanom Khittikachorn involved any violence, break in continuity or shift in the locus of power. In this sense Thailand is a stable, largely peaceful nation that has been spared much of the turmoil experienced by other Southeast Asian countries since World War II. This relative stability stems from a number of factors: a strong sense of national identity, respect for the institution of monarchy, the absence of large disaffected minorities, relative economic prosperity and a long history of independence. Particularly because of this last factor, revolutionary appeals of Communism and anti-colonialism have had little impact on the Thais.

Communist insurgents, Muslim separatists, and Mafia-type criminal gangs operate in rural areas and use terrorism to advance their respective aims. Communist strength has declined markedly in recent years due to several factors, including an amnesty program for defectors and financial assistance to help them reintegrate into society. The government is also continuing efforts to integrate Thailand's Muslim community into the mainstream of national life. Sporadic low-level violence in southern Thailand in 1985 continued to call attention both to Communist and Muslim separatist activities in provinces along the Malaysian border.

Nevertheless, internal security is a major consideration in national policy, and all governments since World War II have been obsessed with the fear of Thailand's becoming the next domino to fall in Southeast Asia. Communist infiltration and subversion came into the open in 1965 with armed insurgent attacks and systematic assassinations of village leaders in northeast Thailand, the country's poorest region. In 1967 insurgency broke out in the far north where Communist agents had recruited Meo hill tribesmen, exploiting their grievances against government efforts to stamp out their profitable opium trade and promising to establish a separate Meo kingdom. The insurgency was directed by the pro-Beijing Communist Party, the Beijing-based Thailand Independence Movement and the Thailand Patriotic Front. China also supplied strategic guidance and material support. Communist propaganda was beamed to Thailand, until 1979 when it was suspended, by a clandestine radio station called Voice of the People of Thailand. Currently, guerrillas are being trained in Vietnam and Laos. Insurgents are active in the southern region in concert with remnants of clandestine Malayan Communist terrorist organizations. Since the fall of Laos and Cambodia to Communist forces in 1975, insurgents have escalated their activities in those border areas, forcing the Thai government to conduct full-scale military operations against them.

FREEDOM & HUMAN RIGHTS

In terms of civil and political rights, Thailand is considered as a partly-free nation with a negative rating of 3 in political rights and 4 in political rights (on a descending scale in which 1 is the highest and 7 the lowest in rights).

Thailand has a mixed track record in human rights just as it has a mixed form of government. It is a military dictatorship that is also a constitutional monarchy and a modified democracy. That the administration is sensitive to civilian interests or pressures was demonstrated in 1980 when Prime Minister Kriangsak Chamanand resigned in the face of public dissatisfaction with his government's economic performance. The current government of Prem Tinsulanonda has made an effort to curb the reported excesses and abuses of authority by paramilitary forces, especially in rural areas. Although restrictive and undemocratic laws remain on the statute books they are only lightly enforced. The main problems seem to come not so much from official policies as from venal and insensitive officials. The Coordinating Group for Religion in Society, the principal Thai human rights organization, has alleged scattered instances of brutality by police and military personnel but, at the same time, has reported that such cases have declined in recent years because of unfavorable publicity. Under the Anti-Communist Act, persons accused of Communist activities may be detained for up to 480 days with the approval of a military or criminal court. During the pre-trial or investigative period accused persons may be denied the right to legal counsel. In 1980 the Thai National Legislative Assembly shifted certain categories of offenses from the military back to the civilian courts. Military courts, however, retain jurisdiction over cases involving internal and internal national security and offenses against the royal family and public peace.

CIVIL SERVICE

The civil service comprises the personnel of all ministries, provincial and district government officials, school teachers and university professors and policemen, but excludes military personnel, judges and public prosecutors, and municipal employees. Civil servants are governed by the Civil Service Act of 1928 and administered by the Civil Service Commission, a statutory body under the immediate control of the prime minister. They are divided into five main grades, four numerical and one special, of which the last and fourth grade is clerical and manual. The third grade includes senior officers in districts and sections. The second grade comprises executive district officers, governors of small provinces. The first grade includes governors of large provinces. The highest grade, called the special grade, includes directors general and undersecretaries of government departments. In each ministry the civil service is headed by the undersecretary, who often wields more effective power than the minister. Each department and ministry has its own civil service subcommittee responsible for personnel administration and promotion. Recruitment is based upon public examinations conducted by the Civil Service Commission. Civil servants are barred from participation in politics and are not subject to excessive political interference.

LOCAL GOVERNMENT

For purposes of local government, Thailand is divided into seven levels of administrative units as follows:

The largest territorial units are the changwads, of which there are 72.

Local government bodies have very little autonomy and are only units of the national government. However, there are no central government officials below the district level. Kamnans, heads of the communes, are chosen from among the headmen of the constituent villages; the phu yai bans are chosen by the villagers for fixed terms of five years, although they tend to remain in office until death or retirement.

Self-governing institutions at the local level are the provincial councils, the commune councils, the municipal councils and the sanitation councils. These last-

Unit	Number	Title of Administrator	Council
Changwad (Provinces)	72	Phuwarachakan	Khana Kromakhan Changwad
Amphoe (Districts) King Amphoe	565	Nai Amphoe	N.A.
(Sub Districts) Tambon	34	N.A.	N.A.
(Communes)	5,036	Kamnan	Sapa Tambon
Muban (Villages)	44,606	Phu Yai Ban	N.A.
Muang (Towns)	82	N.A.	Tesaban Sukapiban
Nakhon (Cities)	3	N.A.	N.A. . . . 6

CHANGWADS

Ang Thong	Buri Ram	Chacheoeng Sao	Chainat
Chaiyaphum	Chanthaburi	Chiang Mai	Chiang Rai
Chon Buri	Chumphon	Kalasin	Kamphaeng
Kanchanaburi	Kohn Kaen	Krabi	Lampang
Lamphun	Loei	Lop Buri	Maehong Son
Maha Sara Khan	Nakhon Nayok	Nakhon Pathom	Nakhon Ratchasima
Nakhon Sawan	Nakhon Si Thammarat	Nakhorn Phanom	Nan
Narathiwat	Nong Khai	Nonthaburi	Pathum Thani
Pattani	Phangnga	Phattthalung	Phetchabun
Phetchaburi	Phichit	Phit Sanulok Prae	Phra Nakhon Si Aytthaya
Phra Nakhon	Phuket	Phrachin Burin	Prachuap Khiri Khan
Ranong	Ratchaburi	Rayong	Roi Et
Sakon Nakhon	Samut Prakan	Samut Sakhon	Samut Songkhram
Saraburi	Satun	Si Sa Ket	Singh Buri
Songkhla	Sukhothai	Suphan Buri	Surat Thani
Surin	Tak	Thon Buri	Trang
Trat	Ubon Ratchathani	Udon Thai	Uthai Thani
Uttaradit	Yala	Yasothon	

named function in areas smaller than regular municipalities.

FOREIGN POLICY

Currently, in the late 1970s, Thailand is reassessing its foreign policy, aiming to regain flexibility in dealing with the new power alignments in Southeast Asia. Until the end of the Vietnam War, the main determinants of Thai foreign policy were its militant anti-Communism and its support for the political and military leadership of the United States. Thailand was one of the few Asian nations to reject a non-aligned posture in the Cold War and to send troops to both Korea and Vietnam. The keystone of the Thai-U.S. alliance is the pledge made by then U.S. Secretary of State Dean Rusk in 1962 to defend Thailand against external attack. On the basis of this pledge Thailand permitted the building of U.S. bases on Thai soil. At the peak of the Vietnam War, these bases had a strength of 45,000 U.S. troops. The alliance, however, was diluted with President Richard Nixon's Guam Doctrine, (1969), under which the United States lowered its military profile in Asia and required Asian wars to be fought by Asians themselves. Thai troops in Korea and Vietnam were withdrawn in 1972, and U.S. troops and bases in Thailand were phased out by 1976. Another major issue between Thailand and the United States concerns the Thai connection in narcotics and dangerous drugs. The Golden Triangle, the area where Burma, Thailand and Laos converge, is one of the major opium-growing areas in the world. The two countries are cooperating on a broad range of programs to stem this traffic.

Since the end of the Vietnam War, Thailand has pursued two opposing lines of foreign policy toward its neighbors: a traditional anti-Communism reinforced by Communist victories in Vietnam, Laos and Cambodia on the one hand and a desire to come to terms with the new power realities following U.S. withdrawal on the other. The two democratically elected governments of Kukrit Pramoj (March 1975 to April 1976) and his elder brother Seni (April to October 1976) had set out to improve relations with Hanoi and Beijing. The pace of detente with Hanoi was uncertain, but solid progress was achieved in negotiations with Beijing, with which diplomatic relations were resumed in 1975. Thai foreign relations entered a new phase in 1976 when the right-wing government that took office after the military coup reversed most of the policies of the democratic period. The army had always been critical of Kukrit's policies of detente and was convinced that he was capitulating to Hanoi by forcing U.S. withdrawal from Thailand without a parallel withdrawal of the 40,000 Vietnamese troops stationed in Laos. But Thanin Kravichien's dogmatic anti-Communism caused a precipitous deterioration in relations with Cambodia and Laos, both of which denounced the new Thai regime. Phnom Penh re-opened the border questions on which the Kukrit government had achieved a measure of accord. Two months after the October 1976 coup the first of a series of border clashes with Cambodia began; it lasted well into the middle of the following year. The danger of a confrontation with Cambodia and Laos alarmed the Thai generals, and they deposed Kravichien in 1977 and resumed a rapprochement with Beijing and Phnom Penh. Gen. Kriangsak, the strongman in the new regime, favored a general relaxation of tensions in the Southeast Asia region.

With the invasion and conquest of Cambodia by Vietnam, Thailand became a frontline state deeply concerned about its own security. Hanoi's grand plan to create an Indo-China federation had robbed Thailand of its last buffer against Communist aggression. It also led Thailand to re-examine its relations with Peking which now appeared in much friendlier light.) The problem was compounded by the seemingly endless influx of refugees posing severe economic strains on an already overheated economy. One development which served to ease Thai anxieties was the first ever visit of a Thai premier to Vientiane where the Laotians greeted him with a pledge not to allow its territory to be used as a base for infiltration or aggression.

Thailand's relations with Burma and Malaysia have been generally friendly. Although the grant of political asylum to President Gen. Nu Win's Burmese opponents in Thailand is a source of minor irritation, both countries have cooperated in putting down the Shan insurgency in the border areas. Relations with Malaysia are closer, reinforced by joint military operations against Malayan guerrillas in southern Thailand. Relations with Japan are ambivalent; growing trade relations between the two countries are offset by Thai resentment against the deteriorating trade balance with Japan.

Thailand has been very active in regional alliances. It was one of the signers of the South East Asia Collective Defense Treaty that established SEATO in 1954, with headquarters at Bangkok. It is a charter member of both ASPAC (The Asian and Pacific Council) and ASEAN (The Association of South East Asian Nations) and played a seminal role in the Colombo Plan.

Thailand and the United States are parties to 30 treaties and agreements covering agricultural commodities, atomic energy, aviation, defense, economic and technical cooperation, education, extradition, health, investment guaranties, mapping, mutual security, narcotic drugs, Peace Corps, postal matters, publications seismic observations, telecommunications, trade and commerce and visas.

Thailand joined the U.N. in 1946; its share of the U.N. budget is 0.11%. It is a member of 14 U.N. organizations and 23 other international organizations.
U.S. Ambassador in Bangkok: William A. Brown
U.K. Ambassador in Bangkok: H.A.J. Staples
Thai Ambassador in Washington, D.C.: Kasem S. Kasemsri
Thai Ambassador in London: Phan Wannamethee

PARLIAMENT

The bicameral national assembly established under the constitution of 1978 consists of a lower house (Saphaphutan), or the House of Representatives, and an upper house (Wuthisapha), or the Senate. The Senate consisted of 244 members appointed by the king for six-year terms. The House had a maximum of 324 members elected for four-year terms.

The Thai legislature is the least powerful organ of the nation's government and is subordinate to the executive both in form and practice. In Thai political traditions, power is centered in the monarchy, the army and the bureaucracy; an elected body is seen as a threat to stability and continuity. The legislature, when it functions, is viewed as an instrument of cabinet rule rather than as a partner in the political decision-making process.

Because the Senate is an appointed body and because joint meetings of the two houses are required

for the passage of money bills, important legislation and no-confidence motions, the government is always assured of a majority and the passage of bills sponsored by the government. Furthermore, money bills initiated by either house need the approval of the prime minister. Unfavorable action by house committees may be overruled by the executive. Draft bills submitted by private members require the permission of the Extraordinary Commission to Study Bills, half of whose membership is appointed by the cabinet.

HOUSE OF REPRESENTATIVES (1983 elections)	
Party	Seats
Social Action	92
Chart Thai	73
Democratic	56
Prachakorn Thai	36
Siam Democratic Party	18
National Democratic Party	15
Thai People	4
Progressive Party	3
Social Democratic Party	2
People's Freedom	1
Independents	24

POLITICAL PARTIES

Thai political parties operate intermittently and are, in fact, irrelevant. Nevertheless, power groups have found it expedient to organize front parties to confer legitimacy on their activities. More than 42 parties contested the 1976 and 1983 elections. The fractionalization of the party system is cited as one of the reasons for the suspension of all political parties by the military-backed government of Thanin Kravichien in 1976. At that time there were nine major parties, of which four were right-wing, two were centrist and three were left-wing.

•The right-wing parties were Thai Nation Party, Thai Citizens Party, Siam Democratic Party, People's Freedom, Thai People's Party and United Nation.

•The centrist parties were the Democratic Party, the Social Action Party, National Democracy Party, Thai People, People's Party and the New Force.

•The one left-wing party was the Social Democratic Party.

The strength of the proscribed Communist Party is about 1,200; Thai Communist insurgents throughout Thailand total about 9,400.

ECONOMY

Thailand is one of the 39 lower middle-income countries of the world with a free-market economy, in which the dominant sector is private.

The National Economic Development Board (NEDB) was established in 1959 to coordinate and stimulate development, and the first Economic Development Plan was implemented from 1961 to 1966.

PRINCIPAL ECONOMIC INDICATORS

Gross National Product: $40.380 billion (1983)
  GNP Annual Growth Rate: 6.5% (1973-82)
  Per Capita GNP: $810 (1983)
  Per Capita GNP Annual Growth Rate: 4.0% (1973-82)

Gross Domestic Product: B991.75 billion (1984)
  GDP at 1980 Prices B850.31 billion (1984)
  GDP Deflator (1980=100) 116.6
  GDP Annual Growth Rate: 6.9% (1973-83)
  Per Capita GDP: B19,835 (1984)
  Per Capita GDP Annual Growth Rate: 4.6% (1970-81)

Income Distribution: 15% of national income is received by
  the lowest 40%; 50% of the national income is received by
  the highest 20%.

Percentage of Population in Absolute Poverty: 15% urban;
  34% rural

Consumer Price Index (1970=100):
  All Items: 320.4 (June 1985)
  Food: 314.9 (June 1985)

Wholesale Price Index (1980=100): Agricultural products
  94.0; Industrial products 13
  Domestic goods: 107.0 (March 1985)

Average Annual Rate of Inflation (1973-83): 8.7%

Money Supply: B90.0 billion (April 1985)
  Reserve Money: B78.0 billion (April 1985)

Currency in Circulation: B63.54 billion (1984)

International Reserves: $1.921 billion, of which foreign ex-
  change reserves were $1.890 billion (1984).

BALANCE OF PAYMENTS (1984)
(million $)

Current Account Balance	−2,100
Merchandise Exports	7,340
Merchandise Imports	−9,270
Trade Balance	−1,930
Other Goods, Services & Income	+2,228
Other Goods, Services & Income	−3,454
Other Goods, Services & Income Net	−1,226
Private Unrequited Transfers	946
Official Unrequited Transfers	109
Capital Other Than Reserves	2,531
Net Errors & Omissions	114
Total (Lines 1,10 and 11)	544
Counterpart Items	−111
Total (Lines 12 and 13)	433
Liabilities Constituting Foreign Authorities' Reserves	—
Total Change in Reserves	−433

This was the only plan to achieve either overall or sec-toral targets, and subsequent plans, although based on sounder statistics and more sophisticated tech-niques, have fallen short of expectations.

In the second and third plans, regional elements became more important, with particular emphasis placed on the North-East with its extreme poverty and increasing Communist insurgency. Under the third plan (1972-76), separate regional plans were drawn up but, because of the shortage of funds, the failure to complete the infrastructure projects of the second plan and widespread unrest, greater emphasis was placed on low-cost self-help schemes in rural areas. A shift of expenditure to social projects was matched by a change of name for the NEDB to the National Economic and Social Development Board.

These trends were continued in the fourth plan (1977-81), drafted under the more liberal civilian regime. This plan was implemented under the very different political conditions which prevailed after the 1977 coup d'état and amid a rapidly worsening eco-nomic situation. The social measures were largely abandoned. By 1981, not only were many of the tar-gets of the fourth plan not realized, but a number from the third plan remained uncompleted.

The Fifth Plan (1982-86) shifted the emphasis from national and regional planning to broad structional changes which will reduce regulations and state in-volvement. It had a target annual growth rate of 6.6% and aimed to promote small industries, placing em-phasis on agriculturally based and light manufactur-ing concerns. In the mid-term review of the Fifth Plan in 1984, the annual growth rate was revised down to 5.5% and a slower export growth was predicted. A scheme that was introduced in 1980, inviting foreign multinationals to invest in activities previously lim-ited to the Thai public sector, has led to improvements in social and economic conditions.

GROSS DOMESTIC PRODUCT BY ECONOMIC ACTIVITY
(1982)

	%	Rate of Change % 1970-81
Agriculture	20.6	4.6
Mining	1.8	6.0
Manufacturing	20.6	10.4
Construction	5.2	8.3
Electricity, Gas & Water	1.4	12.6
Transport & Communications	8.0	7.6
Trade	19.5	7.5
Finance	7.1	7.5
Public Administration & Defense	4.3	6.6
Services	10.1	7.3
Other	1.4	7.3

During 1979-81, Thailand received $624.4 million in foreign aid, or $13.40 per capita.

FOREIGN ECONOMIC ASSISTANCE

Source	Period	Amount ($ million)
United States Loans	1946-83	163.3
United States Grants	1946-83	674.7
International Organizations	1946-83	5,007.2
(Of which World Bank)	1946-83	(3,316.9)

BUDGET

The Thai fiscal year runs from October 1 through September 30. The national budget is prepared by the Bureau of the Budget, an office under the direct con-trol of the prime minister. Development expenditures are based on the recommendations of the National Economic and Social Development Plan.

BUDGET ESTIMATES
(million baht, year ending 30 September)

Revenue	1982/83	1983/84	1984/85
Taxation	127,865.8	136,616.7	159,462.8
Sale of property and services	3,940.6	4,218.4	5,103.4
State enterprises	7,145.7	6,993.4	7,106.1
Others	6,047.9	6,171.5	6,327.7
New taxes and tax revisions	6,000.0	6,000.0	—
TOTAL REVENUE	151,000.0	160,000.0	178,000.0
Total borrowing	24,000.0	30,000.0	35,000.0
Treasury reserves	2,000.0	2,000.0	—
TOTAL RECEIPTS	177,000.0	192,000.0	213,000.0

Expenditure	1982/83	1983/84	1984/85
Education	37,142.9	38,794.6	40,290.8
Defense	35,235.4	37,988.5	41,421.6
Economic services	33,869.4	34,194.8	35,029.4
Internal security	9,611.5	10,400.0	11,006.2
Public health	7,673.8	9,078.9	9,912.3
Public utilities	11,153.2	12,065.5	13,538.9
General administration	5,214.4	5,394.8	5,978.5
Debt services	27,150.3	33,444.7	44,400.0
Others	9,949.1	10,638.2	11,422.3
TOTAL	177,000.0	192,000.0	213,000.0

Of current revenues, 21.4% comes from taxes on income, profit and capital gain, 47.7% on domestic taxes on goods and services, 18.9% from taxes on international trade and transactions, 1.9% from other taxes and 10.1% from non-tax revenues. Current revenues represented 13.9% of GNP. Of current expenditures, 20.6% goes to defense, 20.7% to education, 5.0% to health, 4.9% to housing, social security and welfare, 22.2% to economic services and 26.5% to other functions. Current expenditures represented 19.9% of GNP and overall deficit 5.9% of GNP.

In 1984 government consumption totaled B133.05 billion and private consumption B657.69 billion. During 1973-83 public consumption grew by 9.4% and private consumption by 5.9%.

During 1983, total outstanding disbursed external debt was $9.731 billion of which $7.060 billion was publicly guaranteed debt. Of the publicly guaranteed debt, $4.312 billion was owed to official creditors and $2.748 billion was owed to private creditors. Total debt service was $949.2 million of which $418.6 million was repayment of principal and $530.7 million was interest. Total external debt represented 84.2% of export revenues and 18% of GNP. Total debt service represented 11.3% of export revenues and 2.4% of GNP.

FINANCE

The Thai unit of currency is the baht divided into 100 satangs. Coins are issued in denominations of ½, 1, 5, 10, 20, 25 and 50 satangs and 1 baht; notes are issued in denominations of 1, 5, 10, 20, 100 and 500 baht. The baht's dollar exchange value has remained fairly stable at $1=B26.750.

The central bank is the Bank of Thailand which acts as the bank of issue, banker to the government, banker to and regulator of the commercial banking system and fiscal agent to the treasury.

There are five development finance institutions under state auspices: the Bank for Agriculture and Agricultural Cooperatives, the Government Housing Bank, the Industrial Finance Corporation of Thailand, the Small Industries Finance Office and the Thai Development Bank. The commercial banking system includes 16 domestic banks and 13 branches of foreign banks. The commercial banks have 690 branches in Thailand and 11 abroad. About one-third of the branches are located in Bangkok, but every province except Maehong Son has at least one banking facility. In June 1984 the commercial banks had reserves of B14.61 billion, demand deposits of B29.09 billion and time and savings deposits of B450.54 billion. The discount rate was 12%.

GROWTH PROFILE
Annual Growth Rates (%)

Population 1980-2000	1.7
Birthrate 1965-83	-37.2
Deathrate 1965-83	-35.5
Urban Population 1973-83	3.6
Labor Force 1980-2000	2.1
GNP 1973-82	6.5
GNP per capita 1973-82	4.0
GDP 1973-83	6.9
GDP per capita 1970-81	4.6
Consumer Prices 1970-81	10.1
Wholesale Prices 1970-81	11.2
Inflation 1973-83	8.7
Agriculture 1973-83	3.8
Manufacturing 1973-83	8.9
Industry 1973-83	9.0
Services 1973-83	7.6
Mining 1970-81	6.0
Construction 1970-81	8.3
Electricity 1970-81	12.6
Transportation 1970-81	7.6
Trade 1970-81	7.5
Public Administration & Defense 1970-81	6.6
Export Price Index 1975-81	8.0
Import Price Index 1975-81	16.3
Terms of Trade 1975-81	-7.0
Exports 1973-83	9.0
Imports 1973-83	3.3
Public Consumption 1970-78	9.4
Private Consumption 1970-78	5.9
Gross Domestic Investment 1970-78	6.2
Energy Consumption 1970-78	5.4
Energy Production 1974-78	13.7

AGRICULTURE

Of the total land area of 51,400,000 hectares (127,009,400 acres), 24% is classified as farmland, or 0.27 hectare (0.66 acre) per capita. Based on 1974-76=100, the index of agricultural production in 1982 was 135, the index of food production 135 and the index of per capita food production 112. Agriculture employs 76% of the labor force. The agricultural sector contributes 23% to the GDP and 52% to export earnings; its rate of growth during 1973-83 was 3.8%.

The value added in the agricultural sector in 1983 was $9.444 billion.

Land use patterns vary from region to region. The breadbasket of the country is the central lowlands, where over 26% of the land area is under cultivation, most of it in rice paddies. In the peninsular region, 27.3% of the land area is under cultivation, most of it planted with rubber, coconut and fruit trees. Land utilization is lowest in the northern and western mountain region where only 8% is cultivated, most of it in irrigated land, and the northeastern Khorat Plateau, where poor soils, water scarcity and infertility limit farmholdings to 19% of the land.

Most farms are owned and cultivated by small-scale peasant farmers. But many of these farms are modest plots, and their owners work as tenants or employees on other farms. The average size of landholdings vary from 2.59 hectares (6.4 acres) in the north to 4.33 hectares (10.7 acres) in the central lowlands, with a nationwide average of 3.48 hectares (8.6 acres). In some localities, about one half the farmers are tenants, and 95% are deeply in debt. Another problem is the continued fragmentation of land as a result of inheritance laws under which all children, both sons and daughters, inherit land equally from the father. The usual term of tenancy is one year with payment in kind or cash equal to 50% of the crop, with the tenant furnishing work animals and implements. Rents increase toward the north, where most farms are double-cropped.

Agricultural techniques are primitive and labor-intensive. Mechanized equipment is used only in the central lowlands, where 72,000 tractors were in operation in 1982. In the same year 323,800 tons of fertilizers were consumed or 18.3 kg (40.3 lb) per hectare of farmland. Slash and burn cultivation is practiced by the hill tribes.

Although crop cultivation is dependent on rainfall rather than on irrigation, over 1,878,763 hectares (4,642,360 acres) are irrigated, particularly in the central lowlands which is crisscrossed by canals. Major irrigation projects are the Pasom Dam, the Greater Mae Klong project, the Pran project, the Kud Dam project and the Uttaradit and Phitsanulok diversion dams.

The chief crop is rice, of which Thailand is one of the world's largest exporters. Rice farming accounts for 60% of the cultivated acreage. During the 1960s and 1970s there was some diversification with greater emphasis on non-rice crops such as rubber, coconuts, sugarcane, tobacco, cotton, corn and tapioca.

Livestock of some kind is raised on all farms. The most common animals are buffaloes, cattle, pigs and poultry. The livestock population in 1983 consisted of 6,150,000 buffaloes, 4,600,000 cattle, 3,800,000 pigs, 19,000 horses, 30,000 goats and 65,000,000 chickens. The buffaloes are used in the rice paddies as draft animals.

Forests cover nearly 56% of the land area, especially in the peninsula and the mountains of the north and northeast. Virtually all forest land is state-

PRINCIPAL CROP PRODUCTION (1983)		
	Area (000 hectares)	Production (000 metric tons)
Rice	8,288	18,535
Corn	1,400	3,552
Sorghum	100	327
Sweet potatoes	37	355
Cassava	709	17,000
Dry beans	244	283
Soybeans	175	126
Groundnuts	125	157
Cottonseed	65	87
Cotton (lint)	n.a.	44
Coconuts	n.a.	800
Copra	n.a.	56
Water melons	50	525
Sugar cane	567	24,407
Bananas	n.a.	2,035
Kenaf	n.a.	234
Natural rubber	n.a.	570
Pineapples	n.a.	1,439
Onions	26	133
Tobacco	153	93
Castor beans	42	33

owned. Thai forests are noted for their teak, considered the finest in the world and the best for shipbuilding. A major export, teak accounts for about one-fourth of total lumber production. Output, however, has been declining because of excessive clearcutting and inadequate replanting. In 1982 Thailand produced 39.472 million cubic meters (1.394 million cubic ft) of roundwood and 879,000 cubic meters (31 million cubic ft) of sawn wood.

In 1983 the total fish catch was 2,259 million tons, consisting of both freshwater fish in rivers and canals and marine fish. Most of the fish is sold fresh; the remainder is smoked, dried and pickled or made into the popular fish paste called nampla. Pla tu, or little mackerel, is the most common fish in Thai waters. Some fish and prawns are exported.

Agricultural credit is provided mainly by private moneylenders. There are also 9,784 credit cooperatives. The Bank for Agriculture and Agricultural Cooperatives is the state agency concerned with extending credit to farmers.

INDUSTRY

There is virtually no heavy industry in Thailand. The most important industries are textiles and the processing of agricultural products. Manufacturing employs 8% of the work force and contributes 19% of the GDP, and its rate of growth during 1973-83 was 8.9%. In 1982 the value added in manufacturing was $4.837 billion, of which agro-based products accounted for 45%, textiles 17%, machinery and transport equipment 8%, and chemicals 15%.

The Thai economy is relatively free of controls on private enterprise that are common in other developing countries. The Industrial Finance Corporation was set up in 1959 as part of the government's efforts to stimulate private entrepreneurial activity. Government funds have been directed to private enterprise projects. But despite the government's commitment to private enterprise, there is a relatively large public sector known as the Ratwisahakit, consisting of 108 enterprises with a total capital of B9 billion. They are in the four sectors of agriculture, manufacturing, transportation and energy and include major public utilities, such as the State Railways, the Port Authority of Bangkok and the Telephone Organization. About 10% of the manufacturing output is government-owned. The government also has a monopoly in tobacco, arms, opium and alcohol.

The concentration of economic and political power within a small elite group and relative freedom from economic control are two factors that have helped to create a favorable climate for foreign investment in Thailand. A new investment law was introduced in 1977, and the prime minister placed himself at the head of the Board of Investment. A one-stop investment center for prospective investors was set up. Under the Industries Promotion Act of 1962 industries are guaranteed against nationalization and are granted exemption from import and export duties, taxes on corporate income for a specified period and business taxes on plant, machinery, spare parts, and raw materials and are permitted to repatriate capital and remit profits abroad. Net direct private investment in 1983 was $348 million.

Few major multinational developments have taken place in Thailand, because there have hitherto been more attractive and secure areas for investment in South-East Asia. Between 1959 and 1982, 1,420 firms were issued with the "promotional certificates" which exempt them from restrictions on repatriating profits and capital and on foreign ownership of land, import duties and taxes on equipment, as well as giving guarantees against nationalization or competition from state enterprises and other tax or tariff advantages. Only 1,037 companies have actually started operations. Total investment under this scheme amounts to $5,729.8 million, of which 73.4% is Thai. The largest foreign investors are Japan (with 27.4%), Taiwan (11.2%) and the USA (10.9%). Thai industry remains generally small in scale, with family control still a dominant feature. However, some large groups appeared during the 1970s, notably Siam City Cement. Since 1973 it has acquired controlling interests in a wide range of firms.

ENERGY

In 1982 Thailand produced 3.084 million metric tons of coal equivalent and consumed 16.454 million metric tons of coal equivalent, or 339 kg (747 lb) per capita. The national energy deficit is 13.37 million metric tons of coal equivalent. The annual growth rates during 1973-83 were 13.7% for energy production and 5.4% energy consumption. Energy imports account for 39% of all merchandise imports. Apparent per capita consumption of gasoline is 17 gallons per year.

In 1983 Thailand produced 4 million barrels of petroleum. Proved reserves are estimated at 45 million barrels, sufficient to last 11 years. Annual refinery capacity is 176,000 barrels per day. In 1984 production of electric power totaled 19.1 billion kwh, or 370 kwh per capita. Proved reserves of natural gas are estimated at 241 billion cubic meters (8.510 trillion cubic feet), and production in 1984 was 1.5 billion cubic meters (53 billion cubic ft). A 560-km (348-mi) submarine and overland pipeline was built from the well-head to Bangkok at an estimated cost of $180 million. The concessions are being exploited by two U.S. firms, Texas Pacific and Union Oil.

LABOR

The economically active population is estimated at 24.8 million, of which women made up 47.3%.

ECONOMICALLY ACTIVE POPULATION ('000 persons aged 11 and over)	
	July-Sept. 1982
Agriculture, forestry, hunting and fishing	16,984.9
Mining and quarrying	64.6
Manufacturing	2,006.7
Construction, repair and demolition	520.3
Electricity, gas, water and sanitary services .	76.3
Commerce	2,298.2
Transport, storage and communications	500.9
Services	2,378.2
Activities not adequately described	0.5
Total in employment	24,831.3

While agricultural labor is almost entirely ethnic Thai, more than half the nonagricultural and skilled labor force is Chinese. Most of the Indians, Malays and Vietnamese are self-employed in business or fishing.

Working conditions and wages are governed by legislation, especially the Labor Code of 1956. The workweek varies from 30 to 49 hours, with one day of rest. Workers are entitled to at least six days of paid vacation, a minimum of 12 paid public holidays and 30 days of sick leave each year. Wages vary considerably according to geographical region, sex and occupation. Foreign companies generally pay higher wages than Thai firms and Chinese workers receive more than Thais. In the larger enterprises workers receive low-cost housing, medical care and subsidized food. The Labor Code prohibits dismissal without cause or severance pay of workers with more than 180 days of service.

Although organized labor was suppressed during the period 1977-79, the right of labor to organize has been unrestricted since then. A minimum of only 10 persons can form a labor union. Labor unions exist in both the private and state enterprise sectors. Only about 10% of the labor force in non-agrarian occupations is unionized, but this low percentage stems from the newness and fragmentation of the labor movement in Thailand, and from the economic slowdown of the past few years. Labor unions in Thailand maintain unrestricted relations with recognized international labor bodies and with the Association of Southeast Asian Nations (ASEAN) Trade Union Congress. The same is true for relations with other national labor bodies, notably those from the United States, West Germany, Japan and Israel.

The right to strike is recognized and unrestricted in private sector enterprises. State enterprise workers, however, do not have the right to strike. Many of them have struck on occasion anyway, often without penalty to the strikers. On the other hand, the government has attempted to discourage labor demonstrations which have political connotations. A system of labor courts, to which unions elect one-third of the judges, serves as a frequently used medium for dispute settlement. Thailand's largest labor congress attempted to play an active role in Thai politics and its leaders helped found a political party designed to promote labor interests through electoral politics. It met with little success at the ballot box and the union leaders subsequently decided to concentrate more on economic issues while distancing the union movement from day-to-day political infighting. Unions in the private sector as well as some state enterprises have the right to strike if negotiations conducted in accordance with Thai labor laws fail to resolve the dispute. In practice, the government has rarely acted against strikers, even when they ignored the cumbersome negotiating procedures required under labor law. Workers are represented on the government wage committee, the national labor advisory board, and on the labor courts which arbitrate labor disputes and grievances. Unions freely exercise the right to maintain relations with international organizations that promote the interests of labor.

Thai law prohibits the employment of children under age 12. Employment of children aged 12 to 15 is permitted for "light work." A recent study sponsored by the government concludes that the laws governing child labor are inadequate by International Labor Organization (ILO) standards, poorly enforced, and that both children and adults work in substandard conditions. A major part of the problem is that the Thai labor protection law is vague, difficult to enforce, lacks severe punishment for offenders, and does not differentiate between adult and child workers. Although each year the press carries reports of employers tried and punished for violating the law, child labor abuse remains a chronic problem.

The labor movement is represented on a tripartite committee which makes an annual recommendation on minimum wage levels. In Bangkok and surrounding provinces, where most industry is located, the minimum wage is B70 ($2.66) per day. This standard has been difficult to enforce, however, and many workers receive less than the minimum, especially in construction and the domestic non-export oriented sectors of the economy. Work conditions vary widely in Thailand. Medium and large factories, which produce most of Thailand's exported goods, work standard eight-hour shifts and have working conditions which are reasonable by international standards.

Where there are deficiencies, including child labor abuse and inadequate provision for health and safety, they are confined to the more difficult-to-enforce sectors of small manufacturing enterprises which produce lower quality goods for the local market.

A report issued in 1980 by the Anti-Slavery Society for the Protection of Human rights charged that child labor abuse is widespread in Thailand and that the government is not effectively addressing the problem. The report estimates that there are 3.2 million working children in Thailand between the ages of 11 and 15 years, the vast majority working illegally and, consequently, under very poor conditions. The children come mainly from the poverty-stricken northeast and are hired out on long term contracts (commonly 1-3 years) for a fee paid to their parents of only $25 to $100 per year. Room and board, often inadequate, are provided by the employer but not much else.

The government has responded that the report greatly exaggerates the problem and that in fact only about 60,000 children between the ages of 12-18 years are employed legally in the industrial sector and about 5,000 children are employed illegally under the age of 12. The vast majority of child laborers work with their families in the traditional agriculture.

The Thanin Kravichien government banned all labor unions in 1976 but they were legalized again in 1977.

In July 1984, an estimated 70,000 workers were members of the 185 officially registered unions, 98 of which are in Bangkok. Union membershipis concentrated in a few large unions located predominantly in the Bangkok area. More than half of all union members work in the public sector. Unions are strong in public utilities, particularly electricity, water, and telephones, but they are also found in transportation, petroleum refining, in private industry, textiles, and garments.

In February 1978 the Labor Congress of Thailand (LCT) became the country's first broadly based officially registered labor federation. With 44 member unions, the LCT draws its strength from 18 larger labor unions in key sectors of the Bangkok economy; electricity, water, tobacco, buses, and trucking.

A second labor federation is the National Free Labor Union Congress (NFLUC), which was registered in March 1978. It consists of 16 smaller private sector unions. Strikes are illegal, although other rights of workers are acknowledged. The Settlement of Labor Disputes Act of 1965 prescribes collective bargaining procedures that must be followed by both employers and employees.

FOREIGN COMMERCE

The foreign commerce of Thailand consisted in 1984 of exports of $7.401 billion and imports of $10.347 billion, leaving an unfavorable trade balance of $2.946 billion. Of the imports, fuels constituted 29.5%, machinery 9.9%, iron and steel 7.7%, electrical machinery 7.0%, organic chemicals 3.2%, fertilizers

1.7% and paper and paper products 1.3%. Of the exports, rice constituted 14.1%, tapioca products 12.4%, sugar 8.1%, rubber 5.9%, corn 5.2%, tin 4.9% and shrimp 2.0%.

The major import sources are: Japan 23.4%, Saudi Arabia 15.2%, West Germany 13.9%, the United States 13.3%, Singapore 6.3% and Malaysia 5.2%. The major export destinations are: Japan 13.7%, the Netherlands 13.2%, the United States 12.7%, Singapore 7.3%, Malaysia 5.2% and Hong Kong 5.0%.

Based on 1975=100, the import price index in 1981 was 227, the export price index was 140 and the terms of trade (export prices divided by import prices × 100) 62.

FOREIGN TRADE INDICATORS (1984)

Annual Growth Rate, Imports:	3.3% (1973-83)
Annual Growth Rate, Exports:	9.0 (1973-83)
Ratio of Exports to Imports:	42:58
Exports per capita:	$140
Imports per capita:	$196
Balance of Trade:	$2.946 billion
Ratio of International Reserves to Imports (in months)	2.5
Exports as % of GDP:	22.1
Imports as % of GDP:	26.5
Value of Manufactured Exports:	$2.014 billion
Commodity Concentration:	31.0%

Direction of Trade (%)

	Imports	Exports
EEC	12.8	25.8
U.S.	16.6	12.7
Industrialized Market Economies	58.8	56.6
East European Economies	0.6	1.3
High Income Oil Exporters	9.7	7.6
Developing Economies	37.4	41.3

Composition of Trade (%)

	Imports	Exports
Food	4.4	55.5
Agricultural Raw Materials	4.0	9.0
Fuels	29.8	—
Ores & Minerals	9.6	8.6
Manufactured Goods	48.2	25.1
of which Chemicals	12.2	0.8
of which Machinery	25.9	5.2

TRANSPORTATION & COMMUNICATIONS

The state-owned railway system, consisting of 3,800 km (2,360 mi) of track, radiates from Bangkok in four main lines: the northern line to Chiang Mai, the northeastern line to Ubon Ratchathani and Nong Khai on the Laotian border, the eastern line to Aranyaprathet on the Cambodian border and the southern line to Sungai Kolok and Sadao on the Malaysian border. In 1982 rail traffic consisted of 9.455 billion passenger-km and 2.374 billion net-ton-km.

The inland waterways, 3,999 km (2,483 mi) long, make up the country's oldest transportation system and, together with the Chao Phraya River, form an interconnected network of canals that are navigable for shallow-draft craft throughout the year. The canals of Bangkok, called klongs, also function as marketplaces where much trading activity takes place on shop-boats. There are floating markets in other towns such as Ayutthaya.

Bangkok is the country's only major port, accounting for 98% of the imports and 65% of the exports. Songkhla and Phuket also serve as international ports for southern Thailand. There are 15 minor ports serving coastal traffic. In 1982 these ports together handled 31,400,000 tons of cargo. There are three Thai steamship companies with 219 vessels amounting to a total gross registered tonnage of 868,000.

In 1982 the length of the road system was 34,950 km (21,704 mi), of which 16,244 km (10,087 mi) were paved national highways. One of the important new roads is the Friendship Highway, built with U.S. aid, linking Bangkok with Nong Khai. Thailand has already completed its portion of the Asian Highway. In 1982 these roads were used by 451,001 passenger cars and 535,735 commercial vehicles. Per capita passenger car ownership is 8.5 per 1,000 inhabitants.

The national airlines are Thai Airways International, with 10 aircraft flying to 11 foreign cities, and Thai Airways Company, with 20 aircraft, operating domestic services and also flying to Vientiane and Penang. In 1982 these airlines flew 50.8 million km (31.5 million mi) and carried 3,155,000 passengers. Don Muang, outside Bangkok, is the principal international airport. In addition there are 131 other airfields, of which 106 are usable, 56 have permanent-surface runways and 12 have runways over 2,500 meters (8,000 ft).

In 1984 there were 496,558 telephones in use in the country, or 1.1 per 100 inhabitants.

Thailand's 555 post offices, 341 district post offices and 545 railway station post offices handled 252,436,000 pieces of mail and 6,871,000 telegrams in 1982. Per capita volume of mail traffic was 4.8 pieces. There are 3,040 telex subscriber lines.

Tourism is the country's third largest earner of foreign exchange. In 1982, 2,179,000 tourists visited Thailand. Of these, 119,900 were from the United States, 160,100 from the United Kingdom, 446,700 from Malaysia, 214,600 from Japan, 68,000 from Australia, 89,100 from West Germany, 70,600 from France, 86,400 from Singapore, 45,600 from Italy, 23,000 from Switzerland, 83,100 from India, 33,900 from Indonesia, 23,300 from the Netherlands, 21,900 from Sweden and 20,200 from Canada. Tourist revenues totaled $983 million and expenditures by nationals abroad $257 million. There are 148,000 hotel beds and the average length of stay was 5 days.

MINING

Thailand ranks third among world tin producers, accounting for 14% of the world output. The richest tin mines are located in the southern region and are operated by British, Australian and Chinese concessionaires. The country's only smelter, owned 70% by Union Carbide, has an annual capacity of 20,000 tons. Production in 1983 was 27,208 tons of tin concentrate, 5,900 tons of manganese, and 1,866,083 tons of brown coal and lignite.

Thailand's other mineral resources include iron ore, zinc and tungsten.

DEFENSE

The defense structure is headed by the king who is also the commander in chief of the armed forces. Real control, however, is exercised by the prime minister and the defense minister. The line of command runs through the supreme commander of the armed forces to the commanders in chief of the three armed services. Defense policy is determined by the National Security Council, presided over by the prime minister, while budget allocations, mobilization, training and deployment are supervised by the Defense Council.

Thailand is divided into four military regions. First, Second and Third Armies and the Fifth Military Circle. The First Army which provides the King's Guard also oversees the central and northern areas. The second with headquarters at Korat oversees the northeast. The Third Army with headquarters at Phitsanulok oversees the southeast. The Fifth Military Circle with headquarters at Nakhon Si Thmmarat oversees the isthmus and Malay border.

Military manpower is obtained through conscription. Under the law all male Thais must register for military service when they reach the age of 18 and become liable for compulsory service when they reach 21. The conscript service period is two years.

The total strength of the armed forces is 253,300. This number represents 4.9 armed persons per 1,000 civilians.

ARMY:

Personnel: 160,000

Organization: 4 regions; 4 army HQ; 1 cavalry division; 1 armored division; 7 infantry divisions; 2 special forces divisions; 1 royal guard; 1 artillery division; 1 AA division; 11 engineer battalions; 8 independent infantry battalions; 4 reconnaissance companies; 3 airmobile companies.

Equipment: 390 heavy tanks; 144 light tanks; 88 armored combat vehicles; 750 armored personnel carriers; 472 howitzers; mortars; recoilless launchers; rocket launchers; antitank guided weapons; air defense guns; SAM

Army Aviation: 88 light aircraft; 23 trainers; 94 helicopters.

NAVY:

Personnel: 32,200 (including 13,000 marines)

Units: 6 frigates; 7 fast attack craft with guns; 3 fast attack craft; 94 patrol craft; 4 mine countermeasures vessels; 60 landing craft; 3 training ships; 2 transports; 1 tanker

Naval Air: 28 combat aircraft; 1 maritime reconnaissance/antisubmarine warfare squadron; 1 maritime reconnaissance/search and rescue squadron; 1 maritime reconnaissance/counterinsurgency squadron; 1 helicopter training squadron; 1 observation squadron

Marines: 1 brigade; 1 infantry regiments; 1 artillery regiment; 1 amphibious assault battalion; 40 armored personnel carriers; 24 guns/howitzers.

Naval Bases: Paknam and Sattahip

AIR FORCE:

Personnel: 43,100

Organization: 183 combat aircraft; 1 fighter ground attack squadron; 2 air defense squadrons; 7 counterinsurgency squadrons; 1 reconnaissance squadron; 3 transport squadrons; 3 liaison squadrons; 2 helicopter squadrons; 68 trainers; air-to-air missiles

Para Military: Thahan Phran, 14,000-strong volunteer irregular force, 32 regiments, 196 independent companies serving as 6th Army Region Border Guard.

Air Bases: Bangkok, Udon Thani, Don Muang, Khorat Takhli, Ubon, Nongkai, Prachuab, Kokethion, Utapao and Nakhon Phanom

In 1985/86 military expenditures totaled $1.411 billion, representing 19.9% of the national budget, 3.9% of the GNP, $19.9 per capita, $6,575 per soldier and $2,980 per sq km of national territory.

The Thais have no military tradition despite the fact that throughout history the Thais have waged a constant struggle to maintain their freedom and national identity. The military establishment had no professional capability until 1950 when the United States undertook a military assistance program to modernize the armed forces. Since then the combatworthiness, morale and logistical reach of the Thai forces have become at least equal to those of its hostile neighbors, Cambodia and Laos. Most of the forces are deployed on the eastern border where they are engaged in a drawn-out struggle with guerrillas supported by the Communist regimes across the border.

During the period 1947-83, Thailand received $374 million in loans and $1.522 billion in grants under the U.S. military assistance programs. Arms purchases abroad during 1973-83 totaled $1.890 billion including $850 million from the United States.

Thailand has no internal defense production. A small arms and munitions factory is being set up at Takhili.

EDUCATION

The national literacy rate is 81.8% (88.9% for males and 74.9% for females). Of the population over 15, 18.7% have had no schooling, 67.7% have reached up to the fourth grade, 9.9% have completed at least the seventh grade, 2.7% have completed secondary school, and 1.0% have completed some kind of post-secondary training.

Schooling is free, universal and compulsory for seven years from the ages of seven to 15. In 1982 the gross school enrollment ratios were 96% in the first level (7 to 12) and 29% in the second level (13 to 18), for a combined enrollment ratio of 64%. The third level enrollment ratio is 22.3%. Girls constitute 48% of the primary school school enrollment, 46% of secondary school enrollment and 40% of postsecondary enrollment.

Schooling lasts for 12 years, divided into six years of elementary and primary education (prathom) and six years of secondary education (matthayom). Prathom itself is divided into two cycles, a lower cycle of three years and an upper cycle of three years; matthayom is divided similarly into a lower cycle of three years and an upper cycle of three years. In the mid-1980s, there were 32,194 primary schools and 1,547 secondary schools. Of the secondary schools, 80% are run by private organizations, including Christian missions. Nearly 11% of the primary students and 32% of the secondary students are enrolled in private schools. Coeducation is the exception rather than the rule and is discouraged by the state.

The school year runs from the middle of April to the end of March. The language of instruction is Thai, but English is taught as a compulsory second language in the secondary grades.

There has long been a shortage of teachers in rural elementary schools caused by poor salary scales and urban migration. Nearly a third of rural teachers are without diplomas. The national teacher-pupil ratio is 1:23 at the primary level, 1:19 at the secondary level and 1:9 at the tertiary level.

Vocational education is offered in 172 vocational institutes. There has been a recent trend toward comprehensive schools that offer both academic and vocational training. Nearly 15.5% of secondary school students are enrolled in the vocational stream.

Control over education is centralized in the Ministry of Education. In 1982, the ministry's budget was B32,364,600,000, of which 75.9% was current expenditure. This amount represented 3.9% of GNP, 20.3% of the national budget and $31 per capita.

EDUCATIONAL ENROLLMENT (1980)

	Schools	Teachers	Students
First Level	32,194	319,015	7,392,563
Second Level	1,547	83,379	1,617,465
Vocational	417	22,385	427,302
Third Level(1977)	12	12,483	113,351

Higher education is provided in 12 universities: the Asian Institute of Technology, Chiang Mai University, Chulalongkorn University, Kasetsart University, Khonkaen University, King Mongkut's Institute of Technology, Mahidol University, Prince of Songkla University, Rankhamhaeng University, Silpakorn University, Sri Nakharinwirot University and Thammasat University, with a total enrollment of 113,351 in 1980. Per capita university enrollment was 675 per 100,000 inhabitants.

In 1982, 8,868 Thai students were enrolled in institutions of higher learning abroad. Of these, 5,388 were in the United States, 767 in India, 238 in Australia, 266 in West Germany, 319 in Japan, 200 in the United Kingdom, 1,096 in the Philippines and 89 in Canada.

Thailand ranks 49th in the world in contribution to world scientific authorship with a share of 0.0330% (U.S., 42%).

LEGAL SYSTEM

The criminal justice system provides for three levels of courts: the courts of first instance, the court of appeals and the supreme court. There are 108 courts of first instance belonging to five types: Sarn Kwaeng, or magistrate courts of small causes; Sarn Kadee Dek Lae Yaochon, or juvenile courts; Sarn Paeng, or civil courts with two judges; Sarn Aya, or criminal courts; and Sarn Changwad, or provincial courts.

The Sarn Uthorn, or the court of appeal, is composed of a chief judge and 51 other judges, divided into 17 divisions. The supreme court is the highest court in the land and consists of a president and 21 judges. The court sits in plenary session only occasionally to determine cases of exceptional importance. Appeals are taken to the king for clemency in criminal cases. The courts are supervised, and their integrity is ensured by the Judicial Service Commission, composed of 11 members.

Thailand's criminal and civil codes follow Western European models, and the rights of suspects are similar to those in Western Europe. Except in cases of crimes in progress, arrest warrants are generally required, and specific charges must be brought against those detained within a limited time period. A small number of Communist insurgents and Muslim separatists have been detained without trial under martial law provisions. Otherwise, the only legal basis for arrest and detention without specific charges for long periods (up to 480 days) is the Anti-Communist Activities Act. These powers are infrequently used, and fewer than 100 persons are being detained under this act.

The constitution guarantees Thai citizens the presumption of innocence and access to courts or administrative bodies to seek redress. Suspects can be denied the right to legal counsel during the pretrial or investigative period of their case, but before trial can have access to a lawyer of their own choosing. In recent cases with political overtones, such as the arrests of persons suspected of violating the Anti-Communist Activities Act, the government moved quickly to allow rapid access by legal counsel and visitors during the pretrial period of the case. There is a functioning bail system. The leaders of the September 1985 coup attempt thus far have been treated according to prescribed statutes and due process. There have been no summary punishments.

A number of amendments to the criminal code to improve rights of defendants are under active consideration. One amendment, adopted in October 1984 contains specific provisions that mandate confidential legal counsel for suspects. Proposals that remain under consideration would guarantee counsel during the investigative phase, access by visitors during this period, and the right to contest extensions of the pretrial period of detention.

The Thai legal system reaches decisions on the basis of evidence presented by the parties to a judge rather than a jury. Criminal cases are heard on the basis of specific charges by a panel of judges. During the martial law period (October 1976 — August 1984) military courts had jurisdiction over cases involving internal and external national security, Thai relations with other nations, and offenses against the royal family and public peace. Military courts are now used solely in cases involving military personnel. All other cases, including those having mixed military and civilian participants, come under the jurisdiction of civilian courts. A pilot government program to provide free legal advice to the poor continues in operation. Most free legal aid, however, comes from private organizations including the Lawyers' Association and the Women's Lawyers' Association.

The court and investigatory apparatus in the Bangkok area have been overtaxed in recent years. As a consequence, the time required for criminal trials has at times exceeded three years in the court of first instance. Defendants acquitted after such lengthy proceedings receive no compensation. Persons tried in both the military and civilian courts enjoy a broad range of legal rights, including the right to counsel both in the trial and appellate stages. Although a civilian court decision can be appealed to a higher court, no such appeal process exists in the case of a military court verdict. Both court systems, however, allow for a royal pardon. Moreover, prisoners sometimes benefit from periodic royal amnesties, which take the form of commutation or abrogation of sentences. The courts are relatively independent of external pressures. There have been allegations, however, of both government and private influence being brought to bear on the courts and prosecutors in certain cases, often those involving narcotics.

The corrections or penal system consists of 46 institutions, including seven central and five regional prisons, 23 prison camps, seven correctional institutions, one detention home and three reformatories. In addition, each of the 84 provincial and district and 45 metropolitan police stations are used as temporary prisons. The oldest and the largest prison is the Khlong Prem Central Prison at Bangkok with 6,000 inmates. There is a maximum security institution for habitual criminals at Nakhon Pathom and a penal island in the Strait of Malacca. Illiterate prisoners are enrolled in compulsory adult education programs. Vocational training is also provided in workshops in most prisons.

LAW ENFORCEMENT

The national police force has a strength of 60,000 men, divided into four bureaus: the Provincial Police, including the Border Police; the Metropolitan Police of the City of Bangkok; the Police Education Bureau; and the Criminal Investigation Bureau. The per capita strength of the force is one policeman for every 683 inhabitants.

Police organization is quasi military in character, and all ranks except that of the constable correspond to military ranks. The director general of the force holds the rank of general, and his two deputies and one assistant hold the rank of lieutenant generals.

The Provincial Police are headed by a commissioner, under whom there are nine police regions, each region consisting of six to 11 provinces. Each police region is headed by a commander, and each of the provinces within each region is in the charge of a police superintendent. The Border Patrol Police, although a unit of the Provincial Police, operate with a great deal of autonomy. Their prime responsibility is the protection of the borders against smuggling and the infiltration of subversives. Each Border Patrol unit consists of a platoon of 30 men. The Criminal Investigation Bureau includes the Special Branch Police, which is in charge of surveillance of political opposition, intelligence gathering and related activities.

Published crime statistics are non-existent because the police department does not release crime figures. However, it is known that the opium trade is the most important area of criminal activity. Juvenile delinquency has emerged in recent years as a serious law enforcement problem.

HEALTH

In 1980, there were 615 hospitals in the country with 71,858 beds, or one bed per 661 inhabitants. In the same year there were 6,803 physicians, or one physician per 6,980 inhabitants, 1,084 dentists and 10,118 nursing personnel. Availability of health care is heavily tilted in favor of Bangkok. While the capital had 3,425 doctors, 344 of Thailand's 659 administrative districts had no full-time doctors. Of the hospitals 77.3% are state-run, 2.8% are run by private nonprofit agencies and 19.9% are run by private for-profit agencies. The admissions/discharge rate is 590 per 10,000 inhabitants, the bed occupancy rate is 66.1% and the average length of stay is five days.

Thailand has made rapid strides to expand the quality of the national health care system. In 1982 health expenditures constituted 4.2% of the national budget, and $5.70 per capita. The principal health problems are tuberculosis, pneumonia and typhoid. Only 22% of the population have access to safe water.

PRINCIPAL HEALTH INDICATORS (1984)

Crude Death Rate: 7.7 per 1,000

Decline in Death Rate: –35.5%

Infant Mortality Rate: 50.0 per 1,000 live births

Child Death Rate (Ages 1-4) per 1,000: 4

Life Expectancy at Birth: 60.8 (Males): 64.8 (Females)

FOOD

The staple food is rice (khao) and dishes such as curry eaten with rice (kab khao). Fish is the major source of protein. The per capita daily intake of food is 2,301 calories and 47.5 grams of protein, 28 grams of fats and 466 grams of carbohydrates.

MEDIA & CULTURE

In 1982, 69 daily newspapers and 275 non-dailies were published in the country with aggregate circulations of 2,580,000 and 2,000,000, respectively. Per capita newspaper circulation was 53 for dailies and 37 for nondailies per 1,000 inhabitants. With the exception of one daily in Chiang Mai, all dailies are published in Bangkok, and many are linked by common ownership. Of the dailies six are published in Chinese and three in English. The most influential English daily, and most widely read outside Thailand, is the *Bangkok Post* owned by The Thomson Group. Newspapers in Thai suffer from the high cost of typesetting machinery. The periodical press consists of 990 titles. In 1982 annual newsprint consumption was 110,200 tons, or 2,290 kg (3.0 lb) per 1,000 inhabitants.

While the press is privately owned and there is no pre-publication censorship, the media are always under pressure to conform to government-established guidelines. However, there is lively criticism of government policies within the framework of the regulations, and wide latitude is permitted in reporting non-political news. The principal restraints on the press are contained in the Printing Act of 1941, the Anti-Communist Act of 1952, Announcement Number 17 of the Revolutionary Party of 1958, Section 33 of the 1968 constitution Martial Law Order 42. These prohibit the publication of materials that offend the king, discredit the government or contribute to the growth of Communism. In 1980 Thailand's largest-circulation daily newspaper the *Thai Rath*, was closed by the police and the editor was arrested for publishing an article on alleged corruption in the police department. Three other episodes served to heighten the distrust abetween the media and the government: a police search of the editorial offices of *Matichon*, the closure of *Ban Muong*, and the indefinite closure of *Siam Nikorn*. In October 1980, the government banned 15 books allegedly advocating violent overthrow of the government. In terms of press freedom, Thailand is ranked 51st in the world with a rating of +0.70 (on a scale in which +4 is the highest and –4 is the lowest).

The press continues to operate under the restrictions imposed by the Press Law of 1941 and remnants of past martial law orders. These laws permit the government to close newspapers and revoke the licenses of editors of newspapers which publish stories deemed to be libelous or contrary to national security interests. In 1985 a new press law remained under discussion in the Parliament. If finally approved, certain restrictions it allows would have uncertain repercussions for press freedom. The government's relations with the domestic media remain generally good. The government infrequently uses its statutory power over the press, although awareness of this power contributes to self-censorship, which is a restraint on local press activities. In 1985, one national publication was closed but was allowed to publish under a different masthead for a few months and then reappear in its original form. As in similar cases which occurred in 1983 and 1984, the authorities judged a number of its articles to be inaccurate and detrimental to the public order, and hence contrary to national security interests. The journalistic community advocates full press freedom but has not regarded these closures as a threat to existing levels of press freedom.

In past years, the local press has noted the large number of journalists killed in rural areas for a variety of reasons other than political. The killings diminished sharply in 1983 and 1984. Local human rights activists regard the situation as distinctly improved, but would like the government to examine further the circumstances surrounding some 1982 deaths. The human rights aspect of this problem is difficult to assess. Some of the murdered journalists had published exposes of corruption or illegal activity. At the same time, however, some Thai journalists have in fact only a nominal attachment to the journalistic profession, and often become involved in extortion, blackmail, and similar activities which can lead their victims to use murder as a means of retaliation.

There is no national news agency. Twenty two foreign news agencies, three radio and eight television services and three photographic agencies are represented in Bangkok, including AP, UPI, AFP, Reuters and Tass.

There are 42 commercial publishers in Thailand belonging to the Publishers' and Booksellers' Association. Their total output in 1982 was 5,645 titles. Thailand adheres to the Berne and Florence Conventions.

Radio broadcasting is a state monopoly. Most of the 39 radio stations are owned by the government either directly or indirectly through the Royal Thai Army, the Office of the Prime Minister, the Public Relations Department, the Ministry of Education, the National Police Department and the Royal Household. The national broadcasting station, Radio Thailand, operates 23 medium-wave transmitters and short-wave transmitters. Its home service is on the air for 166 hours a week in Thai and in seven regional vernaculars. The overseas service of Radio Thailand is on the air for 38 hours a week in English and five other languages. A 1,000-kw medium-wave transmitter, the Voice of Free Asia, at Ban Pachi broadcasts in English and Thai. In 1982 there were 7,197,000 radio receivers in the country, or 149 per 1,000 inhabitants.

Television, introduced in 1955, is operated by Television of Thailand, which operates one color station in Bangkok and five black-and-white stations at Lampang, Khonkhaen, Surat Thani, Phuket and Haadyai/Songkla. These stations are on the air for 2,596 program-hours a year. In addition, the Thai Television Company, a commercial concern with state participation, the Royal Thai Army and two smaller companies also operate networks, some in color. In 1982 there were 830,000 television sets in the country, or 17 per 1,000 inhabitants.

Thailand has an active film industry with an annual production of 55 full length feature films in 1975. Most of the 260 films imported annually are Chinese but 23.1% are of U.S. origin. There are 376 fixed cinemas with 267,200 seats, or 6.1 per 1,000 inhabitants. Annual movie attendance was 71 million, or 1.7 per capita.

The library system consists of 526 public libraries, with an aggregate holding of 586,000 books, 38 special libraries, with an aggregate holding of 551,000 books, 85 college and university libraries, with an aggregate holding of 1,297,000 books, and one national library, with a holding of 882,000 volumes. Per capita there are 14 volumes and 4 registered borrowers per 1,000 inhabitants.

There are 119 museums, including 5 private museums, reporting an annual attendance of 15.5 million. There are 60 nature preservation sites.

SOCIAL WELFARE

Public welfare activities are coordinated by the Department of Public Welfare. There are also a number of voluntary organizations providing social assistance such as the Red Cross and the Catholic Association. The share of social welfare in the national budget is 1.3%. Family assistance is provided to families with many children. A nationwide social security scheme is under study.

GLOSSARY

amphoe: a district, subdivision of a province.
changwad: a province, largest territorial division
kamnan: the elected head of a commune.
khana kromakhan changwad: provincial advisory board.
khanarathamontri: the council of ministers or cabinet.
king amphoe: subdistrict, administrative unit into which some amphoe are divided.
klong: any one of the latticework of canals of central Thailand.
krasung: a ministry of the national government.

krom: a government department or agency.
krut: the state emblem, featuring a mythological bird.
muang: any one of a class of municipalities with a population of over 10,000.
muban: a village with at least five households.
nai amphoe: the chief administrative officer of a district.
nakhon: a city.
phu yai ban: the elected headman of a village.
phuywarachakan: the governor of a province.
rathabanklang: the central government including the executive, legislature and judiciary.
ratwisahakit: the state-owned enterprises comprising the public sector.
sakala sangha parinayaka somdech phra sangharaja: the patriarch of the Buddhist faith in Thailand.
sapha: council, as in sapha changwad, provincial council.
saphaphutan: the house of representatives, lower house of the national legislature.
sarn: court, as in sarn uthorn, court of appeal, or sarn dika, supreme court.
sukapiban: local sanitation or health district smaller than a municipality.
tambon: the commune, a unit of local government consisting of a group of villages.
tesaban: a town council.
uparaja: a heir apparent.
wat: Buddhist monastery consisting of a complex of buildings within the temple compound.
wuthisapha: the senate, upper house of the national legislature.

CHRONOLOGY (from 1945)

1946— Pridi Phanomyong's party wins national elections; Khuang Aphaiwong is elected prime minister.
1946— Khuang resigns; Pridi is elected prime minister. . . . King Ananda Mahidol (Rama VIII) dies under mysterious circumstances; his brother Bhumidol Adulyadej is proclaimed king. . . . Pridi resigns and is succeeded as prime minister by Thamrong Nawasawat.
1947— Military strongman Phibun Songkhram returns to power in a bloodless coup; Pridi is exiled; Khuang is reelected prime minister.
1948— Phibun replaces Khuang as prime minister.
1949— Pridi leads unsuccessful coup and later flees to Peking. . . . Siam is discarded as the official name of the country and the name of Thailand is restored.
1951— Phibun is kidnapped by naval malcontents, but the uprising is quelled by loyal army and air force units. . . . Phibun is ousted by Sarit Thanarat and Phao Siyanon but is reinstated after 10 days.
1952— Anti-Communist Act is passed by legislature.
1954— Thailand signs the South East Asia Collective Defense Treaty establishing SEATO with headquarters at Bangkok.

1955— Seri Manang Khasila Party is victorious in elections.

1957— Sarit replaces Phibun as virtual dictator; new government is formed by Pote Sarasin, former secretary general of SEATO; Sarit organizes a new party, Chat Sangkhom (National Socialist) Party, under General Thanom Khittikachorn.

1958— Sarit, now a field marshal, assumes dictatorial powers, suspends the constitution, proclaims martial law, bans all political parties, dissolves the national assembly, and arrests all leftist leaders.... Thanom is prime minister briefly but later yields office to Sarit.

1959— Sarit proclaims new constitution.

1962— World Court rules in favor of Cambodia in Thai-Cambodian dispute over border temple.

1963— Sarit dies; Thanom succeeds him as prime minister.

1968— New constitution is proclaimed, the eighth since 1932.

1969— Elections are held under the new constitution.

1971— Thanom proclaims martial law, citing Communist insurgency in the northeast region.

1973— Mass student demonstrations against government lead to two days of street fighting in which at least 100 persons are killed; Thanom falls; the king appoints Sanya Dharmasakdi as prime minister; a 299-member interim national assembly is elected.... United States begins closing air bases in Thailand.

1975— Kukrit Pramoj is elected prime minister; Kukrit moves toward rapprochement with Peking and Hanoi; diplomatic relations are established with China.

1976— U.S. bases in Thailand are phased out.... Seni Pramoj replaces his brother Kukrit Pramoj as prime minister following national elections.... Military junta under Admiral Sangad Chaloryoo deposes Seni and suspends the legislature; new constitution is promulgated.... Thanin Kravichien is named prime minister; Kravichien reverses the left-wing domestic and foreign policies of the former democratic administrations.

1977— Clashes occur on the Thai-Cambodian border as relations between Thailand and its Communist neighbors deteriorate.... Kravichien is deposed by a moderate military group led by Kriangsak Chamanand who is named prime minister; the new Revolutionary Council proclaims interim constitution and pledges return to civilian government by 1979.

1979— In first parliamentary elections since 1976, no party wins clear majority in the lower house but Kukrit Pramoj's Social Action Party wins largest largest block of votes.... Prime Minister Kriangsak visits Laos.... Thailand condemns Vietnamese invasion of Cambodia.

1980— Prime Minister Kriangsak Chamanand steps down in face of public criticisms of his handling of the economy... Defense Minister Prem Tinsulanonda is named prime minister

1981— An abortive coup by disgruntled army colonels is foiled when the king publicly supports Gen. Prem.... Social Action Party is brought into the government.

1983— The National Assembly is dissolved.... In new elections no party gains absolute majority.... Prem heads a coalition government.... Amnesty is offered to outlawed Communists.

BIBLIOGRAPHY (from 1970)

Akrasanee, Narongchai, *Thailand and Asian Economic Cooperation* (London: 1981).

Bailey, Nigel, *Thailand and the Fall of Singapore: A Frustrated Asian Revolution* (Boulder, Co., 1985).

Bangkok. Color film, 18 min. Films International.

Basche, James, *Thailand, Land of the Free* (New York, 1971).

Batson, Benjamin A., *Siam's Political Future* (Ithaca, N.Y., 1974).

————, *The End of the Absolute Monarchy in Siam* (New York, 1985).

Bhuangkasem, Corine, *Thailand's Foreign Relations, 1964-1980* (London, 1984).

Bradley, Williams, *Thailand: Domino by Default?* (Athens, Oh., 1977)

Bruce, London, *Metropolis & Nation in Thailand: The Political Economy of Uneven Development* (Boulder, Col., 1979).

Children of the World: Thailand. Color film, 29 min. National Educational Television.

Davies, David, *Thailand: The Rice Bowl of Asia* (New York, 1974).

Elliott, David, *Origins of Military Rule* (Belfast, Me., 1979).

Emery, R. F., *Financial Institutions of South East Asia* (New York, 1974).

Floating Market: Bangkok. Color film, 10 min. Producer: not available.

Focus on Thailand. B&W film, 14 min. Producer: not available.

Girling, John L., *Thailand: Society and Politics* (Ithaca, N.Y., 1981).

Haas, David F., *Interaction in the Thai Bureaucracy* (Boulder, Col., 1979).

Ho, Robert and E. C. Chapman, *Studies of Contemporary Thailand* (Melbourne, Australia, 1973).

Ingram, James C., *Economic Change in Thailand, 1850-1970* (Stanford, Calif., 1971).

Jain, R.K., *China and Thailand, 1945-1981* (Atlantic Highlands, N.J., 1984).

Jha, Ganganath, *Foreign Policy of Thailand* (New York, 1979).

Jumsai, M. L., *Popular History of Thailand* (New York, 1972).

Kaufman, Howard K., *Bangkhuad: A Community Study in Thailand* (Rutland, Vt., 1976).

Krannich, Ronald, L., *Mayors & Managers in Thailand: The Struggle for Political Life in Administrative Settings* (Athens, Oh., 1978).

Kunstadter, Peter, *Farmers in the Forest: Economic Development & Marginal Agriculture in Northern Thailand* (Honolulu, Hi., 1978).

Lissak, Moshe, *Military Roles in Modernization: Civil-Military Relations in Thailand and Burma* (Beverly Hills, Calif., 1976).

Mabry, Bevars D., *Development of Labor Institutions in Thailand* (Ithaca, N.Y., 1979).

Maxwell, W. David and W. Lee Baldwin, *The Role of Foreign Financial Assistance to Thailand in the 1980s* (Lexington, Mass., 1975).

Moore, Frank J. and Clark D. Neher, *Thailand: Its People, Its Society, Its Culture* (New Haven, Conn., 1974).

Murray, Charles A., *A Behavioral Study of Rural Modernization: Social & Economic Change in Thai Viallages* (New York, 1977).

Neher, Clark D., *Modern Thai Politics: From Village to Nation* (Cambridge, Mass., 1981).

Nicol, Gladys, *Thailand* (New York, 1980).

Northern Capital (Chiang Mai). Color film, 13 min. Sterling.

Prizzia, Ross, *Thailand in Transition: The Rise of Oppositional Forces* (Honolulu, 1985).

Ray, J. K., *Portraits of Thai Politics* (New York, 1972).

Rice Farmer in Thailand. Color film, 18 min. Films International.

Samudavanija, Chai-Anan, *The Young Turks* (London, 1982).

Siam. Color film, 32 min. Walt Disney.

Siffin, William J. and Woodworth G. Thronmbley, *Thailand: Politics, Economy, and Sociocultural Setting: A Selective Guide to the Literature* (Bloomington, Ind., 1971).

Smith, Harold E., *Historical and Cultural Dictionary of Thailand* (Metuchen, N.J., 1976).

Suksamran, Somboon, *Buddhism and Politics in Thailand* (London, 1982).

Terwiel, B.J., *A History of Modern Thailand* (Brisbane, Australia, 1984).

Thailand. Color film, 19 min. Canadian Broadcasting Corp.

Thailand Farmer's Life. Color film, 13 min. Tribune Films.

Thailand: Land of Rice. Color film, 14 min. Encyclopaedia Britannica.

Thailand: Land of Smiles. Color film, 27 min. Seabourne Enterprises.

Thailand: Past and Present. Color film, 16 min. Coronet Films.

Thailand: Winds of Change. Color film, 17 min. Contemporary Films.

Thompson, W.S., *Unequal Partners: Philippine and Thai Relations with the United States* (Lexington, Mass., 1975).

Town on the Water: Bangkok. Color film, 12 min. Fleetwood Films.

van der Mehden, Fred R. and David A. Wilson, *Local Authority and Administration in Thailand,* (Los Angeles, Calif., 1970).

Van Roy, Edward, *Economic Systems of Northern Thailand* (Ithaca, N.Y., 1971).

Wilson, David A., *The United States and the Future of Thailand* (New York, 1970).

Wilson, Constance M., *Thailand: A Handbook of Historical Statistics* (Boston, 1983).

Wyatt, David K., *Thailand: A Short History* (New Haven, Conn., 1984).

OFFICIAL PUBLICATIONS

Comptroller General's Department, *Allotments and Expenditures Report, Central Offices.*
———, *Expenditures Classified by Project.*
———, *Nonbudgetary Funds.*
———, *Records on External Public Debt.*
———, *Revenue Report, Provincial Offices.*
———, *Statement of Receipts and Expenditures, Provincial Offices.*
———, *Summary Report of Central Revenue.*
———, *Trial Balances of Treasury Accounts.*
Technical & Economic Cooperation Department, *Disbursement of Counterpart Fund Account Report.*
Thailand Bank, *Detailed Report on Government Securities.*
———, *Detailed Report on Internal Public Debt.*
———, *Report on Treasury Cash Balance Account.*

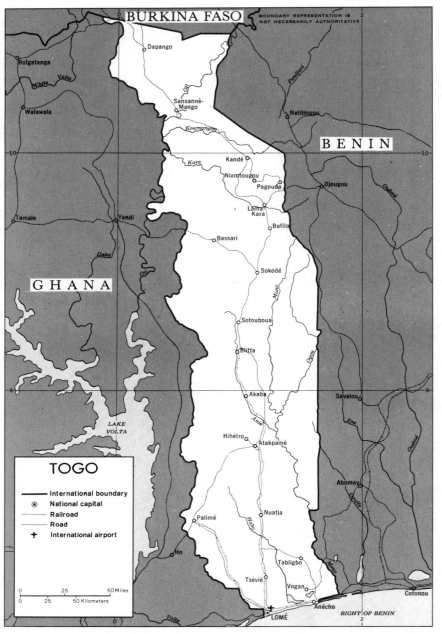

BURKINA FASO

BOUNDARY REPRESENTATION IS
NOT NECESSARILY AUTHORITATIVE

Dapango

Bolgatanga

White Volta

Walewale

Sansanné-
Mango

Natitingou

Pendjari

Koumongou

BENIN

Kandé

Kara

Niamtougou

Pagouda

Djougou

Ouémé

Lama-
Kara

Bafilo

Tamale

Yendi

Bassari

Dako

Oti

GHANA

Sokodé

Mono

Sotouboua

Blitta

Ogou

LAKE
VOLTA

Akaba

Savalou

Anié

Zou

Hihétro

Atakpamé

Abomey

Couffo

TOGO

International boundary
⊛ National capital
⋯⋯ Railroad
⎯⎯ Road
✛ International airport

Palimé

Nuatja

Hoho

Ho

Tabligbo

Tsévié

Vogan

Mono

Cotonou

0   25   50 Miles

0   25   50 Kilometers

LOMÉ

Anécho

BIGHT OF BENIN

Volta

TOGO

LOCATION & AREA

Togo is located in West Africa with an area of 56,000 sq km (21,622 sq mi), extending 510 km (317 mi) N to S and 110 km (68 mi) E to W. Its coastline on the Gulf of Guinea stretches 50 km (31 mi).

Togo shares its international border of 1,623 km (1,008 mi) with three neighbors: Benin (620 km, 385 mi); Ghana (877 km, 545 mi); and Upper Volta 126 km, 78 mi). The borders are based on the Anglo-German and Franco-German treaties of 1897 and 1899. There are no current border disputes.

The capital is Lome with a 1983 population of 366,476. The other major urban centers are Sokode (33,500), Palime (25,500), Atakpame (17,800), Bassari (16,000), Tsevie (13,600), Anecho (11,400), Mango (9,600), Bafilo (9,100) and Taligbo (4,400).

The country consists primarily of two savanna plains separated by a southwest to northeast range of hills known as the Chaine du Togo. From south to north, the country is composed of six topographical regions: (1) the sandy beaches, estuaries and inland lagoons of the coastal plain; (2) the Ouatchi Plains in the immediate hinterland; (3) the higher Mono tableland; (4) the Chaine du Togo that begins in Benin's Atakora Mountains and ends in Ghana's Akwapim Hills (Togo's highest elevation is found here at Pic Baumann (986 meters, 3,235 ft); (5) the northern sandstone Oti Plateau; and (6) the northwestern granite regions in the vicinity of Dapango.

The Mono Basin and its affluents occupy the southern half of the country. Northern Togo is drained by the Oti, a tributary of the Volta, and the Kara and the Mo Rivers, which drain into the Oti. The only rivers whose mouths are in Togo are the Sio (Chio) and the Haho. Of the many inland lagoons, the largest is Lac Togo.

WEATHER

Togo is a tropical country. In the south there are two rainy seasons; from March to early July and from the end of September to early November. The north has only one rainy season, between April and July. The heaviest rainfall occurs in the mountains of the west, southwest and center, while the coastal regions are essentially dry. Annual rainfall averages 102 cm (40 in.) in the north and 178 cm (70 in.) in the west, southwest and center. Average temperatures range from 22°C to 35°C (72°F to 95°F). Temperatures increase inland from the coast. Northern Togo has a savanna climate with longer dry seasons.

POPULATION

The population of Togo was estimated in 1985 at 3,018,000 on the basis of the last official census held in 1981 when it was 2,700,982. The population is expected to reach 4.7 million by 2000 and 8.3 million by 2020. The annual growth rate is 2.86% on the basis of the estimated annual birth rate of 45.4 per 1,000.

The population is concentrated in the south, where the average density approaches 200 per sq km (518 per sq mi). The highest densities are recorded in the Maritime Region, where Lome has a density of 669 per sq km (1,732 per sq mi), Anecho 170 per sq km (440 per sq mi) and Vogan 176 per sq km (456 per sq mi). The central region records the lowest densities, with 9 per sq km (23 per sq mi) in Sotouboua and 15 per sq km (39 per sq mi) in Bassari. The overall density is 52 per sq km (130 per sq mi).

The urban component of the population is 20% and is growing annually by 5.8%. Lome, the capital, is the only city with a population of over 100,000 inhabitants. Nearly 75% of the population of Lome live in slums and squatter settlements. The size of urban settlements progressively decreases toward the north.

The age profile shows 44.5% in the under-14 age group, 52.3% between 15 and 64 and 3.2% over 65. In the 1981 census, the male/female ratio was 48.2:51.8. The reasons for this imbalance, not unusual in tribal societies, are not known.

The 19th century border arrangements between the Germans and the British, on the one hand, and the French and the Germans, on the other, resulted in splitting the Ewe, Adja-Watyi, Fon and other peoples. As a result, there is today a steady migration across the borders, mostly Togolese going to Ghana and Benin in search of work. There are some politically motivated exiles in Togo, mostly secessionist Ewes from Ghana, who enjoy equal civil rights as nationals. These population movements are unrecorded and have proved difficult to control.

The economic and social rights of Togolese women are spelled out in the Family and Individual Code which was adopted in early 1980. Under this code, women's rights include the ownership of property, control of all money earned and maternity leave benefits. Article 88 of the labor code stipulates equal pay for equal work, qualifications and production for both sexes. Women dominate local market activities and commerce with Togo's neighbors. They often amass considerable wealth. Formal equality under the law and success in the local marketplace do not mean total equality for all women throughout Togo, however. Traditional law places barriers in the path of women seeking to break with custom. Civil law, for example, recognizes a woman's property rights, but customary law gives all property to the male in the event of separation or divorce. Economic conditions in rural areas

DEMOGRAPHIC INDICATORS (1984)

Population, total (in 1,000)	3,018.0
Population ages (% of total)	
0-14	44.5
15-64	52.3
65+	3.2
Youth 15-24	553
Women ages 15-49 (000)	669
Dependency ratios	91.1
Child-woman ratios	776
Sex ratios (per 100 females)	97.3
Median ages (years)	17.7
Decline in birthrate (%, 1965-83)	–1.2
Proportion of urban (%)	20.12
Population density (per sq. km.)	52
per hectare of arable land	1.33
Rates of growth (%)	2.86
urban %	5.8
rural %	2.2
Natural increase rates (per 1,000)	28.5
Crude birth rates (per 1,000)	45.4
Crude death rates (per 1,000)	16.9
Gross reproduction rates	3.0
Net reproduction rates	2.17
Total fertility rates	6.09
General fertility rates (per 1,000)	198
Life expectancy, males (years)	47.0
Life expectancy, females (years)	50.5
Life expectancy, total (years)	48.7
Population doubling time in years at current rate	25
Average household size	5.0

also often leave women little time for anything other than carrying water, finding firewood, cooking, caring for the family, and helping to raise food crops. The government has undertaken a campaign to make women throughout Togo aware of their expanded opportunities under the new family code. The government's priority emphasis on developing water resources in rural Togo should also help to mitigate one of the most onerous burdens on rural women, that of carrying water over long distances.

Togo has no official birth control programs or policies.

ETHNIC COMPOSITION

Over 37 tribal groups make up Togo's heterogeneous ethnic configuration, and most of these have more in common with racial groups living outside the national borders than with other groups within the country.

A major distinction is sometimes made between tribes of Sudanic origin inhabiting the northern regions and those of the Negroid type found in the south. The Ewe, concentrated in the Tsevie and Kluoto regions, are not only numerically dominant in the south but have also, until the advent of Gen. Eyadema, dominated Togolese politics, administration, commerce and education. They have never developed a centralized social organization but have remained dispersed in 120 clans. The related Adja are of Yoruba origin and are found mostly in the Anecho and Atakpame areas. The Ana, also of Yoruba origin, are found between Atakpame and Sokode along the

ETHNIC GROUPS IN TOGO		
Cluster & Group	Population	Percentage
Ewe Cluster	763,000	44
Ewe	(362,000)	(21)
Ouatchi, Mina, Fon, Adja, etc.	(391,000)	(23)
Kabre Cluster	399,000	23
Kabre	(241,000)	(14)
Losso, Lamba, Tamberma, Mossi,Logba, etc.	(158,000)	(9)
Moba Cluster (Moba and Konkomba)	122,000	7
Kotokoli Cluster (Kotokoli, Bassari and Tchamba)	122,000	7
Central Togo Cluster	77,000	5
Gurma	76,000	5
Yoruba Cluster (Nago, Ana)	46,000	3
Hausa and Fulani	29,000	2

Benin border. The Chokossi are of Mandingo origin and are famed for their martial skills. The Ane are usually lumped together with Ga as Mina; the two groups, although relatively small in number, from an important part of the Togolese elite. The Hausa and the Yoruba are Muslim groups of Nigerian origin. The Gurma, also called Binumba, live in the Sansanne-Mango and Dapango areas. The Kabre, called in French the Cabrais, are concentrated in the northern Centrale Region. With the rise of Gen. Eyadema (a Kabre), they have become predominant in the army and administration. The Kotokoli, also known as the Temba, are Muslims of Gurma descent, living in the Sokode area. The Ouatchi live in the vicinity of Anecho and Tabligbo. The Moba live in the northern Dapango area, the Losso in the Lama Kara and Sansanne-Mango areas and the Akposso in the Aposso district in the Plateaux region. Known for their rebellious and anarchic spirit, the Akposso are among the few African tribes without chiefs or kings. The Konkomba (also known as Kpunkpamba) are concentrated along the Oti River.

Non-Africans in the population include some 2,000 Europeans and a few Lebanese.

In terms of ethnic and linguistic homogeneity, Togo ranks 27th in the world with 29% homogeneity (on an ascending scale in which North and South Korea are ranked 135th with 100% homogeneity and Tanzania is ranked first with 7% homogeneity).

LANGUAGES

The official language is French, also the language of commerce and the media.

More than 44 different dialects are spoken in Togo, of which the principal one in the south is Evegbe, the language of the Ewes. Evegbe has many subdialects, such as Anlo, Mina or Ge, and Ouatchi. There is a considerable body of vernacular literature, especially in Anlo. Of the numerous languages spoken in the north, Hausa, Twi, Dagomba, Tim, Cabrais and Fongbi are the most widely used. Most of the traders in the major market towns use a form of pidgin English.

RELIGIONS

The majority of the Togolese, estimated at over 75%, adhere to some form of traditional religion, while Christians make up 20% and Muslims 5%, although these percentages vary with the source. Of the 521,185 Christians reported in the last census, 402,476 were Catholics and 118,709 Protestants. Under the Roman Catholic archdiocese of Lome, there are over 5,407 mission centers. There are 170 Protestant mission centers under the administrative control of a Conseil Synodal.

COLONIAL EXPERIENCE

Togo was Germany's first African acquisition. In 1884 a treaty was signed between Gustav Nachtigal, a German explorer, and the chief of the tiny coastal village of Togo, on which basis the German flag was raised over the area and the German penetration of the hinterland began. At the Berlin Convention of 1884/85, the German occupation of Togo was acknowledged by France; the western borders were settled with the United Kingdom by the Treaty of Zanzibar of 1890 and the Treaty of Paris of 1897.

The German era falls into two periods: pacification, until 1900, and development, until 1914, when Germany tried to transform Togo into a Musterkolonie (model colony). The Germans also went further than other Western powers in protecting the natives from non-African, especially Christian, influences. Despite its brevity and certain harsh aspects, such as forced labor, the Togolese remember German rule fondly and, in the inter-war period, petitioned the League of Nations to return Togo to Germany. German rule ended in 1914 when French troops moved into Togo from what was then called Dahomey and occupied Lome. At the same time, British troops invaded the colony from the Gold Coast (today Ghana). Togo was subsequently divided into French and British spheres of occupation. After World War I, the allies redrew the borders, with France occupying two-thirds of the country, and were granted mandates by the League of Nations over what came to be called British and French Togoland.

Except for a brief period, French Togo was not a part of French West Africa; from 1922 to 1934 it was under the direct control of the Minister of Overseas France and, between 1934 and 1936, it was merged with Dahomey as an economy measure. With the end of World War II and the establishment of the U.N., Togo became a U.N. Trusteeship Territory administered by the United Kingdom and France. In 1945 the French Union was created, and Togo was given representation in the French National Assembly. Within the Union, Togo was classified as an associated territory rather than as a colony. In 1955 the passage toward autonomy was accelerated by the creation of the Autonomous Republic of the Togo. In 1956 a plebiscite in British Togo resulted in a 3:2 vote in favor of merger with Gold Coast, shattering Togolese hopes of an eventual union of the two territories under the control of Lome.

French Togo became independent in 1960 following a U.N.-supervised election. Current relations between France and her former colony are good despite Togo's gradual drift to the left since the rise to power of Gen. Eyadema.

CONSTITUTION & GOVERNMENT

In 1979 President Eyadema proclaimed the Third Republic with a new constitution that was originally drafted 10 years ago. The latest constitution, approved by a reported 98% of the registered electorate, provides for a highly centralized government with a strong executive who is empowered to dissolve the legislature after consulting with the Political Bureau of the Rally of the Togolese People, the country's sole political party. Eyadema was elected for another seven-year term under the new constitution. A constitutional committee was set up in 1967, which drew up a draft constitution for the country, later rejected by the Central Committee (now known as Politburo) of Togo's new party, the Rassemblement du Peuple Togolais. Since independence, the country has had four constitutions: the provisional constitution of 1960, providing for a parliamentary form of government; the constitution of 1961 and the constitution of 1963, both providing for a strong presidential form of government and the constitution of 1979. A presidential referendum was held in 1972 when Gen. Eyadema was elected for an indefinite term in office.

Assisting the president is an Economic and Social Council whose 25 members include five labor leaders, five representatives of commerce and industry, five representatives of agriculture, five economists and sociologists and five technologists.

Suffrage under the suspended constitution was universal for all adults. Togo's first elections were held in 1979.

Since independence, Togo has suffered from prolonged instability. There were two attempted coups, in 1966 and 1970, and two successful coups, in 1963, when the first president, Sylvanus Olympio, was assassinated, and in 1967, when the present president Gen. Eyadema, seized power. Eyadema's position currently seems secure; he is believed to have a strong following and continues to receive massive demonstrations of public support; each announcement that the army's mission has been accomplished has been followed by public pleas for its continued rule. Eyadema has also genuinely tried to follow a policy of unity and reconciliation, as a result of which many former members of Olympio's government have joined the Rassemblement du Peuple Togolaise. He has also significantly reduced the inequalities between the north and south by giving more representation in the cabinet to

---

CABINET LIST (1985)

President	*Gen.* Gnassingbé Eyadéma
Minister of Civil Service & Labor	Nyandi Seibou Napo
Minister of Commerce & Transport	Pali Yao Tchalla
Minister of Equipment & Telecommunications	Barry Moussa Barqué
Minister of Finance & Economy	Komlan Alipui
Minister of Foreign Affairs & Cooperation	Koffi Amega
Minister of Interior	Kpotivi Têvi Djidjogbé Laclé
Minister of Justice, Keeper of the Seal	Ayite Mawuko Ajavon
Minister of Natl. Defense	*Gen.* Gnassingbé Eyadéma
Minister of National Education & Scientific Research	Komlan Agbetiafa
Minister of Plan & Industry	Yaovi Adodo
Minister of Public Health, Social Affairs & Women's Affairs	Ayssah Agbetra
Minister of Rural Development	Koffi Kadanga Walla
Minister of Rural Management	Samon Korto
Minister of State Corporations	Koffi Djondo
Minister of Technical Education & Professional Training	Koffi Edoh
Minister of Youth, Sports & Culture	Yao Agbo
Minister Delegate at the Presidency in Charge of Information	Gbenyon Amegboh

---

RULERS OF TOGO

1961 (April) to 1963 (January) Sylvanus Olympio
1963 (January) to 1967 (January) Nicolas Grunitzky
1967 (Jan) —   Etienne (later Gnassingbe) Eyadema

---

the formerly underrepresented northerners. The Kabre and the Kotokoli tribes, respectively accounting for 23% and 7% of the population, have 42% and 17% representation in the cabinet, whereas the Ewe, accounting for 44% of the population, occupy only 25% of cabinet posts.

FREEDOM & HUMAN RIGHTS

In terms of civil and political rights, Togo is classified as a not-free country with a rating of 7 in political rights and 6 in civil rights (on a descending scale in which 1 is the highest and 7 the lowest in rights).

Togo is a one-party authoritarian state. The adoption of a new constitution in 1979 and the proclamation of a so-called Third Republic has made no difference in the nature and philosophy of government. The laws themselves do not grant the basic rights, such as freedom from torture, habeas corpus, and freedom of assembly and speech. Although there are some undocumented reports of torture, it does not seem to be part of official policy. However, prison conditions are harsh and primitive. In the main detention facilities at Lome, Lama-Kara and Temedja, forced marches and hard labor are standard. Unconfirmed estimates of approximately 200 political detainees are discounted by the government which admit of only six (37 were released in early 1980). Legal procedures are still

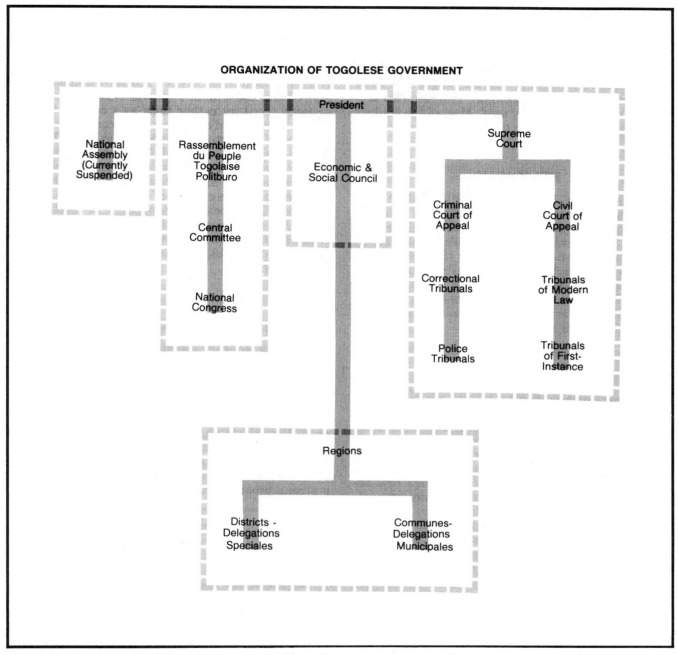

ORGANIZATION OF TOGOLESE GOVERNMENT

President

National Assembly (Currently Suspended)

Rassemblement du Peuple Togolaise Politburo

Central Committee

National Congress

Economic & Social Council

Supreme Court

Criminal Court of Appeal

Correctional Tribunals

Police Tribunals

Civil Court of Appeal

Tribunals of Modern Law

Tribunals of First-Instance

Regions

Districts - Delegations Speciales

Communes- Delegations Municipales

based on the French system and thus afford some semblance of due process. There are no media to speak of outside of government owned publications. Amnesty International and the government have made several charges and countercharges against each other. However, even President Eyadema's opponents concede that there has been a relaxation of many of the rigorous restraints which characterized his rule in the beginning.

President Eyadema publicly stated in 1980 that Togo had six political prisoners. This referred to persons convicted of crimes against the state. In January 1982, President Eyadema announced the release of two of these persons, Kouassivi Alphonse de Souza and Abdo de Souza. Unconfirmed reports, which do not include names or any other case specifics, estimate that perhaps up to 200 political detainees are currently held in Togolese prisons. It is unknown what portion may have committed acts of violent protest. The number of political exiles is unknown, but is believed to number about a dozen.

CIVIL SERVICE

No current information is available on the Togolese civil service.

LOCAL GOVERNMENT

For purpose of local government, Togo is divided into five administrative regions, Maritime, Plateaux, Centrale, Savanes, and La Kara, each administered by an inspector appointed by the president. Each region is subdivided into districts headed by presidentially appointed district chiefs. There are local advisory councils at the district level, known as delegations speciales (formerly conseils de circonscriptions from 1946 to 1973 and conseils de notables from 1922 to 1946). There are currently 21 delegations speciales, one for each district. These councils are composed of five or six members appointed by presidential decree.

Each of the six fully established communes —Anecho, Atakpame, Lome, Palime, Sokode and Tsevie—has a popularly elected municipal council (delegation municipale) and a mayor elected by the council; the urban center of Bassari has a delegation municipale and a presidentially appointed mayor.

FOREIGN POLICY

On achieving independence, Togo was subjected to constant harassment from Ghana, whose president, Kwame Nkrumah, had assisted Togo in her struggle to gain independence with the object of bringing about the political merger of Ghana and Togo. Failing this objective, Nkrumah used trade embargoes and border closures against Togo. But relations improved after the assassination of President Olympio in 1963 and have remained cordial since then.

Relations have been close with two countries for differing reasons. From Zaire, Eyadema has adopted the national authenticity campaign, under which vestiges of colonialism, such as foreign place and personal names have been replaced by African ones. Eyadema himself dropped Etienne, his European former name, and adopted Gnassingbe. In a major policy shift, Togo worked closely with Nigeria in 1975 to organize the Economic Community of West African States (ECOWAS), a new grouping that would embrace both French- and English-speaking states. Eyadema rejects the French view that French-speaking African states are threatened by their stronger English-speaking neighbors. Relations have been mixed with neighboring Benin, whose president, Mathieu Kerekou, has accused Eyadema of involvement in a plot to overthrow his regime. For a while, in 1976, Benin closed its border with Togo.

Togo and the United States are parties to six agreements and treaties covering economic and technical cooperation, investment guaranties, judicial assistance, Peace Corps, social security, and trade and commerce.

Togo joined the U.N. in 1960; its share of the U.N. budget is 0.02%. It is a member of 14 U.N. organizations and 17 other international organizations.
U.S. Ambassador in Lome: Owew W. Roberts

Togolese Ambassador in Washington, D.C.: Ellom Kodjo Schuppius

PARLIAMENT

One of the first acts of the Eyadema regime was to suspend the National Assembly (Assemblee Nationale du Togo, ANT), a 51-member body that replaced the Chambre des Deputes in 1961. The Chambre des Deputes was itself the successor to the Assemblee Legislativ du Togo (1955-58), the Assemblee Territoriale du Togo (1952-55) and the Assemblee Representative du Togo (1946-52). All these bodies were plagued by factional strife.

Under the new constitution the single-chambered General Assembly is composed of 77 members, all of whom are nominated by the party and are popularly elected for five-year terms.

POLITICAL PARTIES

The country's sole political party since 1969 has been the Assembly of the Togolese People (Rassemblement du Peuple Togolaise, RPT), founded in 1969 by President Eyadema. The party's administrative organs are the National Congress that meets every three years; a 23-member Central Committee that meets every three months; and the Politburo, a 10-member body that functions as the country's effective decision-maker. A women's section, the Union Nationale des Femmes du Togo, and a youth wing, the Union Nationale de la Jeunesse Togolaise, are staffed by loyal Eyadema supporters. Membership is voluntary, but membership drives have been successful, especially in urban areas.

ECONOMY

Togo is one of the 49 low-income countries of the world, with a free-market economy dominated by the private sector.

Development planning began with the 1971-75 Plan, which provided for a total investment of CFAF175.9 billion. This was followed by the 1976-80 Development Plan, with a projected investment of CFAF250 billion. Preparation is now underway for Togo's Fourth Five Year Plan (1981-1985). Preliminary reports indicate that the Plan will emphasize transforming industries, agricultural development, storage facilities and possibly solar energy development. The Plan forecast a role for the government in general service industries and large industrial operations.

The 1981-85 Plan projects investment, under a priority program, at the same level as in 1976-80, which means a reduction of about one-third in real terms (i.e. if inflation is taken into account), with infrastructure receiving CFAF74,100 million, industry 73,400 million and rural development 66,600 million. A supplementary "optional" program provides for an additional

PRINCIPAL ECONOMIC INDICATORS

Gross National Product: $790 million (1983)
  GNP Annual Growth Rate: 3.0% (1973-82)
  Per Capita GNP: $280 (1983)
  Per Capita GNP Annual Growth Rate: 0.4% (1973-82)
Gross Domestic Product: CFAF 248.72 billion (1983)
  GDP Annual Growth Rate: 2.3% (1973-83)
  Per Capita GDP: CFAF103,159 (1984)
  Per Capita GDP Annual Growth Rate: 0.7% (1970-81)
Income Distribution: Information not available
Percentage of Population in Absolute Poverty: 42
Consumer Price Index (1970=100):
  All Items: 353.5 (December 1984)
  Food: 359.8 (December 1984)
Average Annual Rate of Inflation: (1973-83) 8.3%
Money Supply: CFAF86.0 billion (March 1985)
  Reserve Money: CFAF115.0 billion (March 1985)
Currency in Circulation: CFAF36.99 billion (1984)
International Reserves: $203.3 million, of which foreign exchange reserves were $201.1 million (1984)

FOURTH DEVELOPMENT PLAN (1981-85)
(Estimates — million francs CFA)

Source of Finance

Internal resources	
State	44,000
Parastatal companies	10,000
Collectives	12,600
Private sector	23,000
External sources	
Bilateral grants and loans	93,000
Multilateral grants and loans	63,300
Total	250,900

Investment Expenditure

Industry	73,400
Rural development	66,500
Infrastructure	74,100
Employment	1,200
Social and cultural development	23,600
Administration	12,000
Total	250,800

BALANCE OF PAYMENTS (1984)
(million $)

Current Account Balance	16.0
Merchandise Exports	253.3
Merchandise Imports	−237.4
Trade Balance	16.0
Other Goods, Services & Income	—
Other Goods, Services & Income	—
Other Goods, Services & Income Net	—
Private Unrequited Transfers	—
Official Unrequited Transfers	—
Direct Investment	—
Portfolio Investment	—
Other Long-term Capital	—
Other Short-term Capital	—
Net Errors & Omissions	25.3
Counterpart Items	−21.6
Exceptional Financing	—
Liabilities Constituting Foreign Authorities' Reserves	—
Total Change in Reserves	−19.7

FOREIGN ECONOMIC ASSISTANCE

Source	Period	Amount ($ million)
United States Grants	1946-83	75.2
International Organizations	1946-83	404.8
(Of which World Bank)	1946-83	(3.5)
All Sources	1979-81	107.0

NATIONAL BUDGET

1980: budget balanced at CFAF67,300 million.

1981: budget balanced at CFAF70,658 million.

1982: budget balanced at CFAF72,300 million (investment expenditure CFAF5,580 million).

1983: budget balanced at CFAF75,800 million (investment expenditure CFAF3,820 million).

1984: budget balanced at CFAF76,970 million (investment expenditure CFAF3,500 million).

1985: draft budget balanced at CFAF81,890 million.

CFAF117,500 million in development spending. Foreign aid is expected to cover two-thirds of the program.

GROSS DOMESTIC PRODUCT BY ECONOMIC ACTIVITY
(1982)

	%	Rate of Change % 1970-81
Agriculture	27.2	1.5
Mining	8.9	—
Manufacturing	6.4	6.1
Construction	6.3	—
Electricity, Gas & Water	1.6	—
Transport & Communications	6.7	—
Trade & Finance	20.7	—
Public Administration & Defense	10.1	—
Other Branches	14.1	3.1

During 1979-81 Togo received $40.70 per capita in foreign aid.

BUDGET

The Togolese fiscal year is the calendar year. The national budget is generally balanced, reflecting conservative fiscal policies.

Of the current revenues, 33.7% comes from taxes on income, profit, and capital gain, 6.4% from social security contributions, 15.3% from domestic taxes on goods and services, 33.0% from taxes on international trade and transactions, −1.0% from other and 12.7% from non-tax revenues. Current revenues represented 29.1% of GNP. Of current expenditures, 7.1% goes to defense, 22.9% to education, 6.1% to health, 11.0% to housing, social security and welfare, 22.2% to economic services and 30.8% to other functions. Current expenditures represented 32.8% of GNP and overall deficit 1.8% of GNP.

In 1983 public consumption was CFAF41.80 billion and private consumption CFAF231.96 billion. During

1973-83 public consumption grew by 8.4% and private consumption by 3.3%.

In 1983 total disbursed outstanding external debt was $805.3 million of which $646.3 million was owed to official creditors and $159.0 million to private creditors. Total debt service was $44.6 million of which $16.6 million was repayment of principal and $28.0 million interest. Total debt service was 16.8% of export revenues and 6.3% of GNP. Total debt was 302.3% of export revenues and 113.9% of GNP.

FINANCE

The Togolese unit of currency is the CFA (Communaute Financiere Africaine) franc, divided into 100 centimes. Coins are issued in denominations of 1, 2, 5, 10, 25, 50, 100 and 500 francs CFA; notes are issued in denominations of 50, 100, 500, 1,000 and 5,000 francs CFA.

In August 1985 the dollar and sterling exchange rates were $1=CFAF424.98.

The central bank and the bank of issue of CFAF is the Banque Centrale des Etats de l'Afrique de l'Ouest (BCEAO) whose headquarters are in Dakar, Senegal. Togo has a 10% share in the central bank along with other members of the monetary union, Benin, the Ivory Coast, Niger, Senegal and Burkina.

The commercial banking system consists of six domestic banks, one foreign bank and two development banks, including the Togolese Development Bank and the National Investment Society. In 1980 commercial banks had reserves of of CFAF63.11 billion, demand deposits of CFAF52.70 billion and time deposits of CFAF45.39 billion.

AGRICULTURE

Of the total land area of 5,600,000 hectares (13,837,600 acres), 42% is classified as agricultural land, or 1.2 hectares (3 acres) per capita. Based on 1974-76=100, the index of agricultural production in 1982 was 126, the index of food production was 125 and the index of per capita food production was 99. Agriculture employs 67% of the labor force and contributes 22% of the GDP and about 50% of export earnings. The annual rate of agricultural growth during 1973-83 was 1.1%. The value added in agriculture in 1983 was $238 million.

About 15% of the land area is under actual cultivation. Traditional farming is small scale and is unaffected by mechanization or chemicalization. In 1982 there were 220 tractors in use in the country, and annual consumption of fertilizers was 3,500 tons or 1.9 kg. The Office des Produits Agricoles du Togo (OPAT) is the state organization responsible for the pricing of agricultural products, marketing and research. There are five regional development authorities concerned with crop production, credit, agricultural techniques and land use. The principal cash crops include cocoa, coffee, palm kernerls, cotton, peanuts and shea nuts.

GROWTH PROFILE Annual Growth Rates (%)	
Population 1980-2000	3.2
Birthrate 1965-83	−1.2
Deathrate 1965-83	−20.4
Urban Population 1973-83	6.6
Labor Force 1980-2000	2.9
GNP 1973-82	3.0
GNP per capita 1973-82	0.4
GDP 1973-83	2.3
GDP per capita 1970-81	0.7
Consumer Prices 1970-81	11.2
Wholesale Prices	—
Inflation 1973-83	8.3
Agriculture 1973-83	1.1
Manufacturing 1970-81	6.1
Industry 1973-83	2.6
Services 1973-83	3.0
Mining	—
Construction	—
Electricity	—
Transportation	—
Trade	—
Public Administration & Defense	—
Export Price Index 1975-81	3.6
Import Price Index 1975-81	11.4
Terms of Trade 1975-81	−7.0
Exports 1973-83	3.5
Imports 1973-83	7.4
Public Consumption 1973-83	8.4
Private Consumption 1973-83	3.3
Gross Domestic Investment 1973-83	−0.2
Energy Consumption 1973-83	13.9
Energy Production 1973-83	27.4

Several product oriented, para-public corporations are charged with the execution of agovernment agricultural policies. The SRCC (Societe National pour la Renovation et le Developpement de la Cacaoyere et de la Cafeiere Togolaises) handles cocoa and Coffee. SONAPH (Societe National pour le Developpement des Palmeraies et des Huileries) has jurisdiction over palm oil. TOGOFRUIT controls fruits and SOTOCO (Societe Togolaise du Coton) deals with cotton. Since their creation, these organizations have furnished planting materials, provided extension services and marketing mechanisms and established processing facilities. Through the CNCA, Caisse Nationale de Credit Agricole, these agencies also extend credit to small farmers. In addition to these para-public agencies, the Ministry of Commerce supervises the marketing entities of OPAT (Office des Produits Agricoles du Togo) and TOGOGRAIN. OPAT, which markets coffee, cocoa, cotton, palm oil and palm kernels, produces surplus revenues which are used for development. A small but growing portion of these surpluses is being reinvested in agriculture. TOGOGRAIN plays a stabilizing role in food crop marketing through market intervention and construction of grain storage facilities.

The chief livestock raising areas are in the north and the far south. Most of the national herd is of the humpless, West African shorthorn variety. The breeds are affected by the prevalence of tsetse fly south of the Togo Hills. Grazing is on communal lands. The livestock population in 1982 consisted of

PRINCIPAL CROP PRODUCTION (1982)
(000 tons)

Corn	150
Millet & sorghum	170
Rice	22
Sweet potatoes	7
Cassava	480
Other roots & tubers	542
Dry beans	13
Other Pulses	9
Bananas	15
Oranges	11
Other fruit	18
Tomatoes	5
Other vegetables	65
Palm kernels	22
Groundnuts	36
Sesame seed	2
Cottonseed	13
Cotton (lint)	7
Coconuts	14
Copra	2
Coffee	13
Cocoa beans	16
Tobacco	2

250,000 cattle, 835,000 sheep, 360,000 pigs, 750,000 goats, 3,000 horses, 1,000 asses and 3,150,000 chickens.

The country's forests, half of which are located in the central region, have been depleted by indiscriminate cutting and inadequate reafforestation programs. Roundwood removals in 1982 totaled 724,000 cubic meters (25.5 million cubic ft).

Fishing is relatively negligible; the annual production in 1982 was 14,530 tons, most of it consumed locally either smoked or dried.

INDUSTRY

The manufacturing sector is small and underdeveloped, employing 14% of the work force, contribution 6.4% to the GDP, with about 52 establishments generating a total value added of $13 million in 1982. The annual rate of industrial growth during 1973-83 was 6.1%. The leading industries are textiles, beverages, cement and footwear in that order. Togo has a moderately developed import substitution sector of about 40 medium-sized manufacturing plants, which receive a number of tax and customs benefits under the investment code. However, most of the recent growth in the industrial sector has occurred in heavy industry, particularly phosphates, oil steel, power generation and cement. Under the 1975-80 Development Plan, the most important single industrial project is the phosphate fertilizer factory that entered production in 1978. A new cement plant with an initial capacity of 1.2 million tons was built at Sikakondji by Ciments de l'Afrique de l'Ouest.

The Investment Code of 1965, as modified in 1973, favors companies that export finished products and grants exemption from taxes and export and import duties on a scale based on the size of the investments. The government has an open door investment policy and 100% owned foreign businesses can be established in Togo. The investment code provides for tax holidays, customs exonerations and the right of profit repatriation. The code applies to businesses of all sizes and types, such as agro-businesses, extractive industries, energy producing industries as well as repackaging and assembling operations. The government has established an Industrial Zone surrounding the port of Lome covering some 640 heactares of land. Fifty hectares have been reserved for small and medium sized businesses with Togolese partners. Additionally, some 70 hectares have been alloted to the Free Port Zone, and the government is seeking financing for the development of another 36 hectares.

ENERGY

In 1982 Togo produced 2,000 tons of energy and consumed 542,000 million metric tons of coal equivalent, or 202 kg (445 lb) per capita. The annual growth rate during 1973-82 was 27.4% energy production and 13.9% for energy consumption. Energy imports account for 18% of all merchandise imports. Apparent per capita consumption of gasoline is 13 gallons per year.

The STH (Society Togalaise des Hydrocarbures) manages the government owned million ton capacity oil refinery. The refinery operates on crude oil imports from Nigeria. It opened in January 1978, closed in August 1978 because of financial difficulties and reopened in April of 1979. The refinery has apparently resolved its financial problems and in 1982 had a throughput of 20,000 barrels per day.

Total electric power production in 1984 was 452 million kwh, or 154 kwh per capita.

LABOR

The labor force of 1,104,000 includes 30,000 wage-earners, evenly divided between the public and private sectors. Women make up nearly 34.9% of the force.

Labor practices in Togo are set by the Togolese Labor Code adopted in 1974, which is generally respected in practice. The code specifically stipulates that there should be equal pay for equal work, qualifications, and production for both sexes; working hours of all employees in any enterprise, except for agricultural enterprises, should not normally exceed 40 hours per week; the employment of children under 14 in any enterprise is prohibited; at least one period of 24 hours of rest per week is compulsory; and workers earn 30 days of paid leave each year. Enterprises must run a regular medical service for its employees. Health and safety standards in the workplace are determined by a technical consulting committee at the Ministry of Labor and instituted by decrees. There are penalties for employers who do not meet the conditions of the decree.

The labor union movement has been incorporated within the RPT one-party system. All labor unions in Togo were dissolved in 1972 and replaced by the Confederation Nationale des Travailleurs du Togo (CNTT, National Confederation of Workers of Togo). CNTT is governed by a bureau of 19 members.

FOREIGN COMMERCE

The foreign commerce of Togo consisted in 1984 of exports of $254.12 million and imports of $402.02 million, leaving an unfavorable trade balance of $148.08 million. Of the imports, cotton textiles constituted 17.5%, food 12.7%, petroleum 11.8%, beverages and tobacco 10.6%, machinery and mechanical equipment 6.9% and transport equipment and parts 6.2%. Of the exports, phosphates constituted 45.7%, clinker 14.3%, coffee 10.6%, cacao beans 9.6%, raw cotton 8.6% and cement 2.5%.

The major import sources are: France 27.1%, the Netherlands 11.0%, the United Kingdom 10.1%, West Germany 7.1%, Japan 6.4% and the United States 4.4%. The major export destinations are: France 22.1%, the Netherlands 18.4%, Yugoslavia 9.6%, Ivory Coast 7.9%, Ghana 6.8% and West Germany 5.1%.

Based on 1975=100, the import price index in 1981 was 173, the export price index 109 and the terms of trade (export prices divided by import prices × 100) 63.

FOREIGN TRADE INDICATORS (1984)		
Annual Growth Rate, Imports:		7.4% (1973-83)
Annual Growth Rate, Exports:		3.5% (1973-83)
Ratio of Exports to Imports:		39:61
Exports per capita:		$85
Imports per capita:		$134
Balance of Trade:		–$148 million
Ratio of International Reserves to Imports (in months)		7.1
Exports as % of GDP:		29.5
Imports as % of GDP:		43.6
Value of Manufactured Exports:		$32 million
Commodity Concentration:		51.5%
Direction of Trade (%)		
	Imports	Exports
EEC	59.0	63.6
U.S.	3.7	1.8
Industrialized Market Economies	73.0	63.3
East European Economies	0.9	4.5
High Income Oil Exporters	1.0	—
Developing Economies	22.6	32.1
Composition of Trade (%)		
	Imports	Exports
Food	25.7	26.1
Agricultural Raw Materials	1.8	6.4
Fuels	8.4	1.3
Ores & Minerals	3.1	51.5
Manufactured Goods	61.1	14.6
of which Chemicals	6.2	0.2
of which Machinery	21.3	1.4

Togo is a signatory of the Lome Convention and a member of the Economic Community of West African States.

TRANSPORTATION & COMMUNICATIONS

The state-owned Chemin de Fer Togolais operates 570 km (354 mi) of meter gauge track. The major lines run from Lome to Palime, from Lome to Anecho and from Lome to Atakpame and Blitta. In 1982 rail traffic consisted of 78 million passenger-km and 5.368 billion net-ton-km. of freight.

There are 50 km (31 mi) of navigable waterways, including coastal lagoons and tidal creeks. A section of the Mono River is also navigable.

The major port is Lome. Kpeme, built by the Companie Togolaise des Mines du Benin (CTMB), is used mainly for the export of phosphates. In 1982 these ports handled 1,699,000 tons of cargo.

In relation to its size Togo has a fairly extensive road transport system of 7,562 km (4,696 mi), of which 1,505 km (935 mi) are paved. The principal roads radiate from Lome to the borders of Ghana, Burkina and Benin. In 1982 these roads were used by 29,447 passenger cars and 5,132 commercial vehicles. Per capita passenger car ownership is 9.8 per 1,000 inhabitants.

The national airline is Air Togo, which operates scheduled internal services and external services to Lagos with two aircraft (Cessna 402). Togo has also a 7% share in Air Afrique, West Africa's multinational airline. In 1982 these lines flew 188 million passenger-km and carried 18 million ton-km of freight. There are 11 usable airfields and airports in the country of which one, at Lome, has a permanent-surface runway over 2,500 meters (8,000 ft).

In 1984 there were 9,800 telephones in use, or 0.4 per 100 inhabitants.

In 1980 the postal system handled 32,055,000 pieces of mail and 26,000 telegrams. Per capita volume of mail was 10.6 pieces. In 1982, 131,000 tourists visited Togo, of these 4,100 were from the United States, 3,900 from the United Kingdom, 19,800 from France, 10,000 from West Germany and 8,200 from Switzerland. In the same year, tourist revenues were $17 million and expenditures by nationals abroad $19 million. There are 4,000 hotel beds and the average length of stay was 3.3 days.

MINING

Togo's principal mineral resource is phosphates; since the quadrupling of phosphate prices in 1974 their importance in the economy has increased. In an average year, phosphates provide about 80% of the export earnings. Production from the main deposits at Akoupame was controlled until 1974 by the French-owned Compagnie Togolaise des Mines du Benin; in that year the company was taken over by the state and is now run by the Togolese Office of Phosphates. Production in 1982 totaled 2,100,000 tons.

DEFENSE

The defense structure is headed by the president, who holds the positions of commander in chief, minister of defense, chief of staff and commander of the first battalion of Togolese Infantry. As a result, the president has direct operational control of the armed forces, and there is no extended chain of command. There is no conscription and enlistment is voluntary.

The total strength of the armed forces (including gendarmerie) is 5,110, or 2.1 armed persons per 1,000 civilians.

ARMY:

Personnel: 4,000
Organization: 2 infantry regiments, one with 1 mechanized battalion and 1 motorized battalion, and one with 2 armored squadrons, 3 infantry companies, and special units. 1 presidential guard; 1 parachute commando regiment; 1 support regiment, with 1 field artillery battery, 2 AA artillery batteries, and 1 logistics/transport and engineer battalion
Equipment: 9 tanks; 55 armored combat vehicles; 34 armored personnel carriers; 24 guns and mortars; 27 rocket launchers; 38 air defense guns

NAVY:

Personnel: 100
Units: 2 patrol vessels
Naval Base: Lome

AIR FORCE:

Personnel: 260
Organization: 11 combat aircraft: 6 counterinsurgency; 8 trainers; 1 transport; 3 helicopters
In 1985 the defense budget totaled $17.316 million, representing 6.8% of the national budget, 2.4% of the GNP, $6 per capita, $5,500 per soldier and $386 per sq km of national territory.

The Togolese armed forces have no offensive capability and have only limited defensive capability.

The bulk of the military aid has been obtained from France. Arms purchases abroad during 1973-83 totaled $110 million.

EDUCATION

The national literacy rate is 15.9% (26.9% for males and 7.1% for females). Of the population over 25, 89.8% have had no schooling, 5.8% have attended first level, 3.3% have completed first level, 0.7% have attended second level, 0.2% have completed second level and 0.1% have completed post-secondary education.

Education is compulsory, free and universal for six years between the ages of 6 and 12. The gross school enrollment ratios are 106% at the first level (6 to 11) and 27% at the second level (12 to 18), for a combined

enrollment ratio of 68%. The third-level enrollment ratio is 1.7%. Girls constitute 40% of primary school enrollment, 25% of secondary school enrollment and 14% of post-secondary enrollment.

Schooling lasts for 13 years, divided into six years of primary school, four years of lower secondary cycle and three years of upper secondary cycle. Christian mission schools account for nearly half of the total enrollment. In 1982 there were 2,251 primary schools, 248 secondary schools and 22 technical schools in the system.

The school year runs from October to June. The language of instruction is French, but the prevailing vernaculars are used in pre-primary and primary grades in rural schools.

Enrollment in teacher-training institutions in 1982 was 308. The national teacher-pupil ratios in the same year were 1:48 in primary classes, 1:31 in secondary classes, and 1:14 in tertiary classes. Nearly 5% of secondary students are enrolled in the vocational stream.

Educational expenditures in 1982 totaled CFAF14,859,236,000, of which current expenditures accounted for 98.2%. This amount represented 19.6% of the national budget, 5.8% of the GNP and $19 per capita.

EDUCATIONAL ENROLLMENT (1982)			
Level	Schools	Teachers	Students
First Level	2,291	10,214	492,329
Second Level	248	3,982	122,925
Vocational	22	348	7,306
Third Level	1	285	4,131

Higher education is provided by the University of Benin at Lome, which also serves the Republic of Benin and Upper Volta. University enrollment in 1982 was 4,131, of which about 70% was from Togo. Per capita university enrollment is 138 per 100,000 inhabitants.

In 1982, 1,827 Togolese students were enrolled in institutions of higher learning abroad. Of these, 52 were in the United States, 1,261 in France, 43 in Canada, 85 in West Germany, 183 in Senegal, 93 in the Ivory Coast and 1 in the United Kingdom. In 1980 1,114 foreign students were enrolled in Togo.

LEGAL SYSTEM

Togolese jurisprudence is based on French civil law and African customary law.

The judiciary is headed by the Supreme Court at Lome with four chambers: constitutional, judicial, administrative and audit. Below the Supreme Court, criminal justice is administered by a Cour d'Appel, four Tribunaux Correctionnels, and eight Tribunaux de Simple Police, while civil and commercial law is enforced by a Cour d'Appel, four Tribunaux de Droit Moderne and eight Tribunaux Coutumiers de Premier Instance. A State Security Court was established in

1970 to deal with crimes against internal and external state security.

The Togolese legal system does not include the right of habeas corpus, nor does this right exist in practice. Detention without trial or administrative detention is used in Togo against those whom the government considers guilty of "crimes against the public trust" (i.e., corruption or political opposition thought to pose a security threat). Those held in administrative detention are usually not formally charged and cannot obtain redress through the courts. Preventive detention has no fixed term. Pretrial proceedings are sometimes protracted. A crowded court docket and shortage of judges inhibit speedy trials. Defendants accused of nonpolitical crimes are generally accorded the right to a public trial and the right to be represented by counsel. When the defendant cannot afford the cost of an attorney, counsel is appointed by the government. An attorney is accorded permission to talk with the defendant.

No information is available on the nature of the penal system or the number and location of penal institutions.

LAW ENFORCEMENT

The Gendarmerie Nationale, Togo's police force, is an integral part of the armed forces, though with a separate command. The force is led by one of President Eyadema's most trusted lieutenants, Col. Menveyinoyu Alidou Djafalo. The total strength of the force (including that of a related para-military organization) is 1,250; fully 60% of the rank and file are Kotokoli and Kabre.

Reports indicate that the national gendarmerie has almost unlimited power to arrest and detain persons in Togo for whatever reason. Present practice allows any permanent officer of the gendarmerie to arrest and detain persons without seeking prior permission or submitting a subsequent report. There are reported instances of gendarmerie officers being bribed to make arrests as a solution to personal disputes not having any relation to matters of state, security or local laws. These arrest cases are not subject to the usual judicial review.

Prisoners accused of crimes unrelated to political security are usually held for no longer than 48 hours prior to indictment or provisional release pending investigation. No legal basis exists to prevent authorities from holding a person beyond that time without charge. Administrative sanctions against officials have also included suspension from their jobs and assignment to residences in their home villages, where they are required to report weekly to the regional gendarmerie office. There was one reported case of this type in 1984. The number of detainees held by the gendarmerie in its Lome prison, outside the strictures of local judicial process, varies but has been reported to be as high as 50. Detentions made by the military are processed through the military judicial system. There is no functioning system of bail in Togo.

No information is available on the nature and incidence of crime in the country.

HEALTH

In 1980 there were 65 hospitals in the country with 3,600 beds, or one bed per 729 inhabitants. In the same year there were 132 physicians in the country, or one physician per 19,900 inhabitants, 4 dentists and 773 nursing personnel. Health expenditures represent 5.6% of the national budget and $7.30 per capita.

PRINCIPAL HEALTH INDICATORS (1984)
Crude Death Rate: 16.9 per 1,000
Decline in Death Rate: –20.4% (1965-83)
Life Expectancy at Birth: 47.0 (Males); 50.5 (Females)
Infant Mortality Rate: 114.7 per 1,000 Live Births
Child Death Rate (Ages 1-4) per 1,000: 17

The major health problems are yaws, malaria and leprosy, while the leading causes of death are measles and tetanus. Only 16% of the population have access to safe water.

FOOD

The staple food is manioc (cassava), generally supplemented by yams. Corn is also popular. Meat consumption is high among the nomads, but fish ranks low in food preference. The national drink is coffee.

Per capita daily consumption of food is 2,106 calories and 46.5 grams of protein, both below the recommended minimums of 2,600 calories and 65 grams of protein, 31 grams of fats and 420 grams of carbohydrates.

MEDIA & CULTURE

Two daily newspapers are published in the country, with an aggregate circulation of 13,000, or 6 per 1,000 inhabitants. Both are owned by the government, and are published in French. Most of the periodicals are also published by the government, except for the distinguished Catholic periodical, *Presence Chretienne*.

The national news agency is the Agence Togolaise de Presse. Both AFP and DPA have bureaus in Lome.

The principal book publisher is the state-owned Les Establissements des Editions du Togo (EDITOGO). Togo adheres to the Berne Convention.

The state-owned Radiodiffusion Television de la Nouvelle Marche and Radiodiffusion Kara broadcast on two medium-wave transmitters and three short-wave transmitters for 89 hours a week in French and six vernaculars: Evegbe, Hausa, Bassari, Moba, Cotocolis and Cabrais. In 1982 there were 575,000 radio receivers in the country, or 209 per 1,000 inhabitants. Of the total 11,024 annual radio broadcasting hours, 3,136 hours are devoted to information, 868 hours to education, 894 hours to culture, 26 hours to religion and 5,741 hours to entertainment.

Television, introduced in 1973, is operated by Television Togolaise, which is on the air for 3½ hours each evening with programs in French and the vernaculars. Of the 1,564 annual television broadcasting hours 586 hours are devoted to information, 91 hours to education, 205 hours to culture and 234 hours to entertainment. The number of television sets is estimated at 12,000 or 4.4 per 1,000 inhabitants.

There is no domestic film production. There are four fixed cinemas with 2,000 seats, or one seat per 1,000 inhabitants. Annual movie attendance was 600,000, or 0.3 per capita.

The largest libraries are the National Library of the Togolese Institute of Humane Sciences, with 5,600 volumes, and the library of the University of Benin in Lome, with 5,000 volumes.

There is only one museum in the country with a reported annual attendance of 8,000.

SOCIAL WELFARE

A modest social welfare program provides family allowances for workers, but generally it is the extended family or tribe, rather than the state, that is concerned with providing social assistance.

GLOSSARY

asafohene: nominal chief of a dou or Ewe clan.
authenticity: term applied to de-Westernization programs, especially those that Africanize personal and place names.
Brazilian: name for Togolese of mixed Euro-African parentage, because many of them are descended from those repatriated from Brazil.
circonscription: former name for a district.
commune: a municipality.
delegation special: a district council.
dou: a clan of Ewe origin.
revendeuses: retail merchants who constitute one-third of Togo's working population and the core of Rassemblement du Peuple Togolaise membership.
uro: title of the paramount chief of the Kotokoli.

CHRONOLOGY (from 1960)

1960— Republic of Togo becomes a sovereign nation with Sylvanus Olympio as president.
1963— Olympio is assassinated by military insurgents; Nicolas Gruntizky, exiled leader of the Togolese Party for Progress, returns to Togo at the request of the insurgents and forms government as president.
1966— Popular uprising by Olympio's supporters in Lome is put down by the military.

1967— A plot led by Noe Kutuklui is foiled; the military decide that Grunitzky is a political liability and force him to step down in favor of a military junta led by Kleber Dadjo and Etienne Eyadema; Eyadema assumes supreme power as president; the constitution and legislature are suspended.
1969— Rassemblement du Peuple Togolaise is founded.
1970— Anti-Eyadema coup is uncovered and plotters are arrested.
1972— National referendum approves indefinite continuation of the Eyadema regime.
1974— Eyadema launches cultural authenticity campaign by renaming people and places.... French-owned phosphate mines are nationalized.
1978— At West African summit meeting, Togo supports the Economic Community of West African States (ECOWAS).
1980— Eyadema proclaims Third Republic under a new constitution and has himself elected again for another seven-year term.
1985— Multi-candidate elections are held for the National Assembly.

BIBLIOGRAPHY (from 1968)

Aithnard, K.M., *Some Aspects of Cultural Policy in Togo* (Paris, 1976).
Crowder, Michael, *West Africa Under Colonial Rule* (London, 1968).
Decalo, Samuel, *Historical Dictionary of Togo* (Metuchen, N.J., 1976).
Hargreaves, John D., *West Africa: The Former French States* (Englewood Cliffs, N.J., 1967).

OFFICIAL PUBLICATIONS

Benin University, *Rapport Annuel de l'Universite de Benin* (unpublished).
Finance Ministry, *Balance Generale des Comptes du Tresor, Definitive* (Treasury Accounts) (December 31 issue of monthly publication).
———*Compte Definitif du Budget General* (Statement of General Budget Execution). Direction des Finances (Direcorate of Finances) (annual).
———*Releves Recapulatifs des Paiements et des Recouvrements Effectues au Budget General et au Budget d'Investissement, au 31 Decembre* (Receipts and Expenditure Statements of the General Budget and the Capital Budget). Tresor (December 31 issue of monthly publication).
———*Situation des Comptes de l'Etat au 31 Decembre* (Statement of treasury Accounts), Tresor (December 31 issue of monthly publication).
———*Situation Detaille des Operations au Tresors au 31 Decembre* (Detailed Statement of Trea-

sury Operations), Tresor (December 31 issue of monthly publication).

Regional Development Agencies, *Rayport Annuel des Organismes de Developpement Regional* (Annual Report of the Regional Development Agencies).

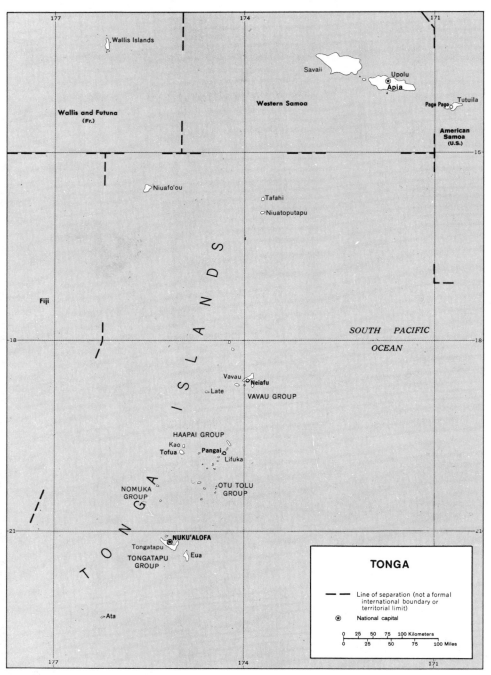

177 | 174 | 171

Wallis Islands

Savaii | Upolu | Tutuila
Apia | Page Pago

Western Samoa

Wallis and Futuna
(Fr.)

American Samoa (U.S.)

15

Niuafo'ou

Tafahi
Niuatoputapu

I S L A N D S

Fiji

SOUTH PACIFIC

18 | *OCEAN* | 18

Vavau | Neiafu
Late | VAVAU GROUP

HAAPAI GROUP
Kao
Tofua | **Pangai**
Lifuka

T O N G A

NOMUKA | OTU TOLU
GROUP | GROUP

21 | **NUKU'ALOFA** | 21
Tongatapu
TONGATAPU | Eua
GROUP

Ata

TONGA

— — — Line of separation (not a formal
international boundary or
territorial limit)
⊛ National capital

0 25 50 75 100 Kilometers
0 25 50 75 100 Miles

177 | 174 | 171

TONGA

LOCATION & AREA

Tonga is an archipelago, also known as the Friendly Islands, located in the SW Pacific, about 643 km (400 mi) E of Fiji, and about 1,770 km (1,100 mi) from Auckland, New Zealand. It comprises 169 islands, of which only 36 are permanently inhabited. Including the Minerva reefs, which it has recently claimed, the total land area is 749 sq km (289 sq mi), extending 631 km (392 mi) NNE to SSW and 209 km (130 mi) ESE to WNW. The areas of the main islands and island groups are: Tongatapu and Eua (350 sq km, 135 sq mi), Haapai (119 sq km, 46 sq mi), Vavau (143 sq km, 55 sq mi), Niuatoputapu and Tafahi (18 sq km, 7 sq mi) and Niuafoou (52 sq km, 20 sq mi). Tonga's total coastline stretches 560 km (348 mi).

The capital is Nukualofa with a 1983 population of 20,564.

The Tonga Islands are dispersed in two parallel chains, volcanic in the west with limestone formations superimposed on them and upifted coral formations in the east. The islands fall into three latitudinal groups: a northern or Vavau group including Hunga, Kapa and Vavau; a central or Haapai group; and a southern or Tongatapu group. The Tongatapu group contains seven major islands; the largest is Tongatapu on which the capital, Nukualofa, is located. Other major islands in this group include Eua, Ata, Atata, Euaki, Kalaau and Kenatea. Of the 36 islands in the Haapi group, only 20 are inhabited and one is an active volcano containing a steaming lake. Of the 34 islands in the Vavau group, 14 are uninhabited. Toward the east the islands are bordered by the Tonga Trench over 11.2 km (7 mi) deep. Most of the uninhabited islands are active or extinct volcanic cones; at least one, Falcon, rises above sea level only during eruptions and disappears at other times.

Except for creeks on Eua and a stream on Niuatoputapu, there is no running water on any of the other islands. Their inhabitants rely on wells and stored rainwater.

WEATHER

The climate is subtropical with a warm period from December to April and a cool period from May to November. The mean annual temperature varies from about 10°C (50°F) in winter to 32°C (90°F) in summer. Both temperature and rainfall increase from the south to the north. Most of the rainfall is concentrated in the period from December to March. Average rainfall is 168 cm (66 in.) with the least rainfall in Tongatapu and the most on Vavau.

The prevailing winds are the southwest trades.

POPULATION

The population of Tonga was estimated in 1985 at 107,000 on the basis of the last official census held in 1976 when the population was 90,128. The population is expected to reach 140,000 by 2000. The annual growth rate is estimated at 2.72% on the basis of an annual birth rate of 36.8 per 1,000.

Almost two-thirds of the population live on the main island of Tongatapu. The overall density of population is 152.5 per sq km (245.4 per sq mi). The only urban and commercial center is the capital, Nukualofa, into which thousands of Tongans have moved in recent decades. However, a strong rural tradition persists on most of the other islands.

DEMOGRAPHIC INDICATORS (1985)	
Population (000)	107
Annual rate of growth (1980-85) (%)	2.72
Crude birthrate 1/1000	36.8
Crude death rate 1/1000	4.9
Total fertility rate	5.60
Gross reproduction rate	2.70
Net reproduction rate	2.59
Life expectancy at birth: years	
Males	68.3
Females	73.1
Average household size	6.1
Density per sq km	152.5
% Urban	20
Sex distribution:	
Males	51
Females	49
Age Breakdown (%)	
0-14	44.2
15-29	26.0
30-44	14.7
45-59	9.5
60-74	4.0
75 and over	1.6
Population doubling time in years at current rate	30
Natural increase rate	23.8
Marriage rate 1/1000	6.9
Divorce rate 1/1000	0.9

Because of land shortage, immigration is restricted. For the same reason there is considerable emigration to New Zealand and Fiji. In 1976 New Zealand imposed ceilings on the number of visas for Tongan workers, provoking a mild diplomatic crisis.

There is a limited birth control program with 8,892 acceptors.

ETHNIC COMPOSITION

The population is extremely homogeneous, with native Tongans constituting 98% of the population. Europeans and part-Europeans make up the remainder.

The Tongans are of pure Polynesian origin with only a trace of Melanesian traits. They are generally tall, large-boned, light-skinned with wavy or straight hair.

LANGUAGE

The official language is Tongan, properly called Tongatabu, a member of the Polynesian subfamily of the Malayo-Polynesian family of languages. It was not until the 19th Century that it acquired a script as a result of the efforts of Christian missionaries.

English is extensively used. It is taught as a second language in the schools, and all official publications are issued in both Tongan and English. In addition to being bilingual in both these languages, Tongans find no difficulty in learning other Polynesian subdialects, such as Hawaiian.

RELIGIONS

Almost all Tongans are professed Christians; there are no vestiges of the ancient indigenous religions. Most of the people belong to the Free Wesleyan Church of Tonga, which had nearly 39,000 adherents in the early 1970s. The strength of the other denominations are: Roman Catholics (12,363), Free Church of Tonga (10,622), Church of Tonga (6,891) and Latter-Day Saints (5,455).

COLONIAL EXPERIENCE

The Tongan archipelago was first visited by the Dutch explorer Abel Tasman in 1643. However, continuous contacts with Europeans began only in 1773 with the visit of Captain James Cook to these islands, which he named the Friendly Islands. With the conversion of Prince Taufaahau and his ascension to the throne as King George Tupou I, Christianity began to spread throughout the islands. Tonga came under British protection in 1900 with the signing of the Treaty of Friendship and Protection. Tonga retained its independence and autonomy, while the United Kingdom agreed to handle its foreign affairs and guarantee its security from external attack. Two more treaties were signed in 1958 and 1968, both of which reaffirmed Tonga's internal autonomy. Full independence, which came in 1970, made few changes other than adding foreign affairs to the government's responsibilities. Strong links are maintained by independent Tonga with Britain, Australia and New Zealand.

CONSTITUTION & GOVERNMENT

Tonga is a hereditary constitutional monarchy governed by a constitution first promulgated in 1875 and little modified since then. Under this constitution, the sovereign is assisted by a Privy Council consisting of

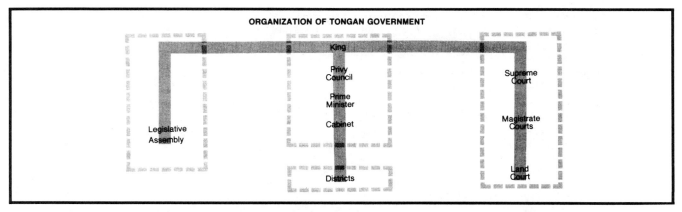

ORGANIZATION OF TONGAN GOVERNMENT

seven other members, including the prime minister. It advises the monarch on affairs of state and, between legislative sessions, makes ordinances that become law when confirmed by the legislature. Lesser executive decisions are made by the cabinet, which consists of Privy Council members presided over by the prime minister. The governors of Vavau and Haapai are members of the Privy Council and are responsible to it for the administration of the islands under their jurisdiction.

CABINET LIST (1985)

King	Taufa'ahau Tupou IV
Premier	*Prince* Fatafehi Tu'ipelehake
Deputy Premier	S. L. Tuita
Minister of Agriculture	*Prince* Fatafehi Tu'ipelehake
Minister of Defense	*Prince* Tupouto'a
Minister of Education	S. Langi Kavaliku
Minister of Finance	Cecil Cocker
Minister of Foreign Affairs	*Prince* Tupouto'a
Minister of Health	*Dr.* Sione Tapa
Minister of Industry, Trade & Commerce	Baron Vaea
Minister of Lands, Survey & Natural Resources	S. L. Tuita
Minister of Police	George Akau'ola
Minister of Works	S. Langi Kavaliku

Suffrage is limited to literate citizens who pay taxes. Elections are held every three years. Women voted for the first time in 1960.

Its geographical isolation has helped Tonga to preserve many of its old traditions, including respect for the monarchy and the nobility. With the greater penetration of Western political and social ideas, there are signs of incipient dissent. However, none of this dissent is as yet serious enough to pose a threat to the monarchy.

FREEDOM & HUMAN RIGHTS

In terms of civil and political rights, Tonga is classified as a partly free country with a rating of 5 in political rights and 3 in civil rights (on a descending scale in which 1 is the highest and 7 the lowest in rights).

CIVIL SERVICE

No current information is available on the Tongan civil service.

LOCAL GOVERNMENT

For purposes of local government Tonga is divided into three districts: Vavau, Haapai and Tongatapu, corresponding to the three island groups. The first two are administered by governors who are members of the Privy Council. Town and district officials have been popularly elected since 1965.

FOREIGN POLICY

Tonga maintains cordial relations with all its Pacific neighbors. By special agreement, New Zealand assists in the maintenance of the Tongan Defense Force.

Tonga currently has only one diplomatic mission abroad, in the United Kingdom, and only one resident mission, that of the United Kingdom. Recently it has obtained help from the Soviet Union to build an air strip near the capital. The U.S. Embassy in Fiji is also accredited to Tonga. There is a small U.S. Peace Corps contingent in the country engaged primarily in teaching and public health. Tonga is not a member of the U.N.

In 1972 Tonga laid claim to the tide-washed Minerva Reefs, some 482 km (300 mi) SW of Nukualofa, to forestall efforts by a private Anglo-American group called the Ocean Life Research Foundation to establish an independent Republic of Minerva.

U.K. High Commissioner in Nukualofa: Gerald F.J. Rance

Tongan High Commissioner in London: Sonatane Tu'a Taumoepeau-Tupou

PARLIAMENT

The unicameral Legislative Assembly is made up of nine nobles, who are elected by the 33 hereditary nobles of Tonga, nine People's Representatives, elected by universal adult suffrage for three-year terms, and the premier and the cabinet ministers. In addition, the governors of Haapai and Vavau serve as ex officio members. The Assembly is presided over by a speaker appointed by the king from among the members. Of the seven elected members, three represent Tongatapu and two each Haapai and Vavau. Sessions are required to be held at least once every calendar year, and they generally last two or three months. Legislation is usually introduced by the government, and all Privy Council decrees are required to be confirmed by parliament.

POLITICAL PARTIES

There are no political parties in Tonga. The people's representatives are elected as independents.

ECONOMY

Tonga is one of the 49 low-income countries of the world with a free-market economy in which the dominant sector is private.

PRINCIPAL ECONOMIC INDICATORS

Gross National Product: $80 million (1983)
  GNP Annual Growth Rate: 5.5% (1973-82)
  Per Capita GNP: $780 (1983)
  Per Capita GNP Annual Growth Rate: 3.9% (1973-82)
Gross Domestic Product: P59.9 million (1982)
  GDP Annual Growth Rate: Information not available
  Per Capita GDP: P551 (1983)
  Per Capita GDP Annual Growth Rate: Information not available
Income Distribution: Information not available
Consumer Price Index (1970=100)
  All Items: 407.2 (June 1984)
  Food: 446.7 (June 1984)
Money Supply: Information not available
Currency in Circulation: Information not available
International Reserves: Information not available
  *No information available on balance of payments.

In 1975 Tonga launched its third five-year plan (1975-80). The earlier two Five-Year Development Plans (1965-70, 1970-75) aimed at stimulating the coconut industry and tourism and improving internal and external communications.

GROSS DOMESTIC PRODUCT BY ECONOMIC ACTIVITY (1982)

	(%)
Agriculture	31.0
Mining	0.8
Manufacturing	4.3
Electricity	0.5
Construction	4.7
Trade	14.9
Transport	7.7
Other	36.1

During the period 1979-81 Tonga received $19.5 million in foreign aid from all sources, or $195.00 per capita. During 1970-75 Tonga received £1.5 million from the United Kingdom under various development assistance programs.

BUDGET

The Tongan fiscal year runs from July 1 through June 30.

The 1984/85 national budget consisted of revenues of P19,156,904 and expenditures of P19,144,145.

Of the revenues, 31.4% came from import duties, 13.6% from income and wealth tax and 1.3% from license, stamp duties and registration fees. Of the expenditures, 37.2% went to investments, 22.2% to social services, 13.9% to economic services and 2.7% to defense.

Outstanding external debt in 1982 totaled $16 million.

FINANCE

The Tongan unit of currency is the Paanga, divided into 100 senitis. Coins are issued in denominations of 1, 2, 5, 10, 20 and 50 senitis and 1 and 2 paangas; notes are issued in denominations of 1, 2, 5 and 10 paangas.

The Tongan paanga is linked to the Australian dollar with which it is at par. In 1985 the dollar exchange rate was $1 = P1.0778.

The banking system consists of only two institutions, the Bank of Tonga, owned by the government of Tonga, and the Tongan Development Bank.

AGRICULTURE

Of the total land area of 74,900 hectares (185,077 acres), 77% is considered arable, 3% pasture, 13% forest, and 3% inland water. Per capita agricultural land is 0.6 hectare (1.4 acre). Based on 1974-76 = 100, the index of agricultural and food production was 113 in 1982. More than 90% of the population is involved in farming, usually as smallholders. Agriculture contributes 31.0% of the GDP.

Cultivation is generally carried on by the bush-fallow method, under which land is allowed to lie fallow for four or five years after intensive cultivation for an equal period. Mechanization is making slow progress. In 1982 there were 55 tractors in use.

Traditionally, all land belongs to the crown, which makes grants to the nobles who, in turn, lease it to commoners. Land tenure is based on the Land Act of 1927. Under this act every male Tongan is entitled, on attaining the age of 16, to one api (3.33 hectares, 8.25 acres) of bushland and land for a house in town. These allotments are hereditary, pass from generation to generation and may not be sold. Every tenant is legally required to plant 200 coconut trees and keep them free of weeds. A tenant may be evicted for failing to observe this condition as well as for nonpayment of rent. Because of the growth of population, it has not been possible to grant all applications from Tongan males reaching adulthood.

PRINCIPAL CROP PRODUCTION (1982)		
	Area (000 hectares)	Production (000 metric tons)
Sweet Potatoes	6	81
Cassava	2	14
Bananas	2	2
Coconuts	—	122
Copra	n.a.	16
Oranges	n.a.	3

Beef cattle are raised chiefly on European-owned plantations, but some are raised by native Tongans. Pigs are raised by smallholders throughout the kingdom but are used only for ceremonial purposes and are not sold. The livestock population in 1983 consisted of 90,000 hogs, 15,000 horses, 8,000 cattle and 18,000 goats.

Forests cover 10,926 hectares (27,000 acres) mainly on Vavau and Eua but, because of poor exploitation, the kingdom lacks sufficient usable timber to meet construction needs; thus lumber must be imported.

The fish catch is also inadequate to meet domestic demand, although the potential is large. In 1982 government-owned fishing vessel reported an annual catch of 1,993 tons, principally tuna and shark. Shellfish and turtles are also plentiful in coastal waters. In 1984, 60 new boats were added to the fishing fleet and a new dockyard was built in the Ha'apai group.

INDUSTRY

In the mid-1980s manufacturing contributed only 4.3% to the GDP. Some 35 companies are officially registered in the kingdom. Principal industries include coconut processing, sawmills and brush and mat manufacture.

Foreign investment is welcome, but not much of it has been forthcoming in recent years.

ENERGY

In 1984 Tonga produced 8 million kwh of electric power, or 75 kwh per capita. No other forms of energy are produced in the islands. Total consumption of energy was 21,000 tons or 208 kg (459 lb) per capita.

LABOR

The economically active population of the kingdom is estimated at 25,400, predominantly employed in the non-monetary subsistence agriculture sector. However, the size of the paid labor force is expanding as reduced opportunities in agriculture drive workers to either full-time or part-time employment in the towns.

Compensation and working conditions are prescribed by law. However, there is no workmen's compensation legislation, and there are no labor unions. Unemployment is estimated at 13.1%.

FOREIGN COMMERCE

In 1982 foreign trade consisted of imports of P41.198 million and exports of P4.185 million. Of the imports, fish and live animals constituted 24.0%, machinery and transport equipment 14.7%, consumer goods 14.2%, fuels 13.9% and chemicals 6.4%. Of the exports, coconut oil constituted 31.2%, vanilla beans 15.0%, metal products 9.3%, desiccated coconuts 7.0%, watermelons 7.0% and textiles 2.5%.

The major import sources are: New Zealand 37.1%, Australia 23.6%, the United States 9.5%, Fiji 7.5%, Japan 6.1%, Singapore 6.1%, China 3.0% and Hong Kong 1.3%. The major export destinations are: Australia 45.4%, New Zealand 36.8%, the United States 9.7%, Fiji 2.5% and Western Samoa 1.3%.

TRANSPORTATION & COMMUNICATIONS

There are no railways on Tonga. The chief ports are Nukualofa and Neiafu on Vavau. In 1982 these ports handled 97,000 tons. Services to Australia, New Zealand and Fiji are provided by the Pacific Navigation Company.

There are 198 km (123 mi) of all-weather roads on Tongatapu and 74 km (46 mi) on Vavau. There are no bridges in the kingdom, but three islands of the Vavau group are connected by causeways. In 1984 there were 1,082 passenger cars and 1,294 commercial vehicles in use. Per capita passenger car ownership is 10 per 1,000 inhabitants.

Inter-island air services are provided by TAS (Tonga Air Services). Air Pacific and Polynesian Airlines also serve Tonga. The principal airport is Fua'amotu, near Nukualofa, which has a grass runway less than 2,500 meters (8,000 ft). There are three other usable airports.

In 1984 there were 1,285 telephones in the kingdom, or 1.4 per 100 inhabitants.

In 1981 the postal service handled 1,063,000 pieces of foreign mail (all inter-island mail is considered foreign mail). Per capita volume of mail was 10 pieces.

Nukualofa is a major port of call for cruise ships. Tourist revenues in 1982 totaled $3.9 million from 92,494 tourists.

MINING

Tonga has no known mineral reserves.

DEFENSE

The defense structure is headed by the king. The armed forces consist of the Royal Guard and the Tongan Defense Force, commanded by a New Zealander. A defense services patrol boat was commissioned in 1973 to patrol coastal waters.

EDUCATION

The national literacy rate is estimated at 99.6% (99.7% for males and 99.5% for females).

Education is universal and compulsory for all Tongans for eight years from the ages of 6 to 14. Education is free in government schools; mission schools charge small fees. Most primary schools are coeducational. Girls make up 47% of primary enrollment, 48% of secondary enrollment and 43% of tertiary enrollment.

Schooling lasts for 13 years, divided into six years of primary school, four years of middle school and three years of secondary school. Selected students prepare for the New Zealand Secondary School Certificate examination. In 1982 there were 110 government denominational primary schools and two government and 48 mission and private schools providing post-primary education.

The academic year runs from February to December. The language of instruction is Tongan, but English is also taught from middle grades on.

A teacher-training college, with an enrollment of 125 in 1982, offers a two-year course. The teacher pupil ratio is 1:21 at the primary stage and 1:24 at the secondary stage. In the same year there were 612 students in the country's five technical and vocational schools.

In 1981 the annual educational budget was P1,909,000 of which 99.1% was current expenditure. This amount represented 3.4% of the GNP and P17.80 per capita.

EDUCATIONAL ENROLLMENT (1982)			
	Schools	Teachers	Students
First Level	110	793	16,701
Second Level	50	668	17,085
Vocational	11	N.A.	693
Third level	1	64	125

In 1982, 308 Tongans were enrolled in institutions of higher learning abroad. Of these, 150 were in the United States, 89 in New Zealand, 5 in United Kingdom and 48 in Australia.

LEGAL SYSTEM

The legal system is based on English common law.

The judiciary consists of a Supreme Court, a Court of Appeal, a land court and magistrates' courts. There are eight magistrate courts; appeals from them are heard by the Supreme Court. In cases which come before the Supreme Court the accused or either party in a civil suit may elect for a jury trial. Appeals from the Supreme Court are heard by the Privy Council sitting as a court of appeal.

Tonga's penal system consists of a prison at Huatolitoli near Nukualofa and three smaller jails at Haapai, Vavau and Niuatoputapu. Prisoners sentenced to six months or more are incarcerated in Huatolitoli. Most prisoners are required to perform labor on public works.

LAW ENFORCEMENT

The national police force, commanded by a commissioner of police, has a strength of over 200 officers and men deployed in three territorial districts, corresponding to the local government divisions: Tongatapu, Haapai and Vavau. The bulk of the force is stationed on Tongatapu, where the capital is located, and where two-thirds of the population resides. There are many small and remote islands without resident policemen. The force is unarmed, but batons are held in reserve and are issued in cases of emergency.

The incidence of crime is low, and most of the 2,500 cases handled by the police every year are misdemeanors. The three most common offenses are adultery, offenses against property and cruelty to animals.

HEALTH

Tongans are generally healthy, aided by a national health service that provides free medical and dental treatment for all citizens. The major health problems are tuberculosis, typhoid fever, dysentery, filariasis and skin and eye conditions. A WHO-UNICEF yaws-elimination project has resulted in the near-elimination of that disease.

PRINCIPAL HEALTH INDICATORS (1984)
Crude Death Rate: 4.9 per 1,000
Infant Mortality Rate: 6.4 per 1,000 Live Births
Life Expectancy at Birth: (males) 68.3
(females) 73.1

In 1981 there were nine hospitals in the country with 325 beds, or one bed per 294 inhabitants. In the same year there were 38 physicians, or one physician per 2,605 inhabitants, 9 dentists and 147 nurses. The admissions/discharge rate was 612 per 10,000 inhabitants in 1982, the bed occupancy rate was 43.8% and the average length of stay was 8 days.

FOOD

The staple foods are sweet potatoes and cassava supplemented by bananas and coconuts. A traditional and popular food is poi, made of boiled taro roots softened and pounded in a stone mortar and later mixed with water and fermented. The national drink is kava, a mild narcotic made from the roots of a species of pepper plant.

The daily per capita intake of energy, protein, fats and carbohydrates are 3,221 calories, 66.7 grams, 59 grams, and 467 grams respectively.

MEDIA & CULTURE

Three non-daily newspapers are published, of which the *Tonga Chronicle* is an illustrated weekly issued by the government with 6,000 copies in Tongan and 1,200 in English. Various missions issue church newspapers periodically. There is no national news agency. In 1982, 33 books were published locally.

The government-sponsored Tonga Broadcasting Commission operates two medium-wave transmitters, on the air for 60 hours weekly, broadcasting in Tongan, English, Fijian and Samoan. In 1983 there were 20,000 radio receivers, or 187 per 1,000 inhabitants There is no television service.

All feature films are imported. In 1982 there were three fixed cinemas with 2,000 seats, or 18 seats per 1,000 inhabitants. Annual movie attendance was 0.1 million, or 1 per capita.

The kingdom has 20 small public libraries with a total of 250,000 volumes.

SOCIAL WELFARE

There is no social welfare department; welfare services are provided primarily by the Christian missions. The Ministry of Health provides free medical and dental care for all citizens.

GLOSSARY

api: one parcel of land (3.33 hectares, 8.25 acres) to which every adult Togan is entitled under the Land Act.

CHRONOLOGY (from 1970)

1970— Tonga becomes a fully independent nation within the Commonwealth.
1972— Tonga claims the Minerva Reefs, some 482 km (300 mi) SW of Nakualofa.
1975— Tonga signs the Lome Convention.

BIBLIOGRAPHY (from 1970)

Gerstle, Donna, *Gentle People: Into the Heart of Vavua, Kingdom of Tonga, 1781-1973* (San Diego, Calif., 1973).
———, and Helen Raitt, *Tonga Pictorial* (San Diego, Calif., 1974).
Latukefu, Sione, *Church and State in Tonga* (Honolulu, 1974).
Marcus, George E., *The Nobility and the Chiefly Tradition in the Modern Kingdom of Tonga* (Honolulu, 1978).
Rutherford, Noel, *Shirley Baker and the King of Tonga* (New York, 1972).
———, *Friendly Islands: A History of Tonga* (New York, 1978).

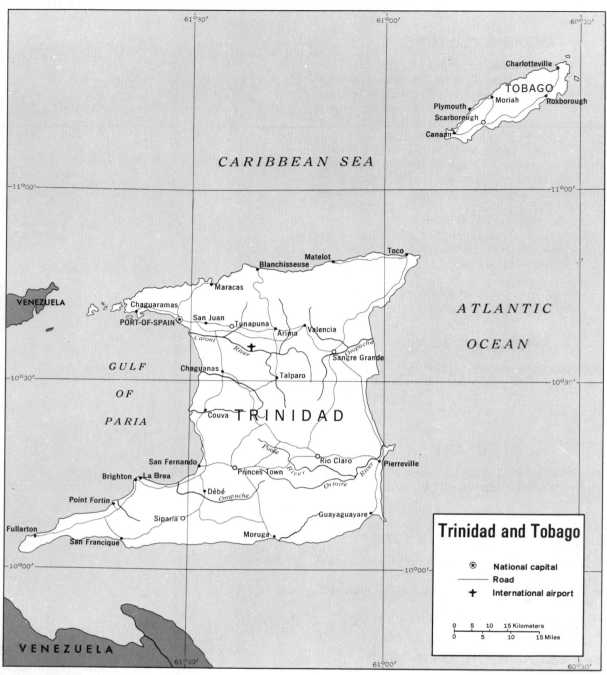

Trinidad and Tobago

⊛   National capital

⋯⋯   Road

✛   International airport

```
0    5    10   15 Kilometers
0    5    10   15 Miles
```

CARIBBEAN SEA

TOBAGO

Charlotteville
Plymouth   Moriah
Scarborough   Roxborough
Canaan

VENEZUELA

ATLANTIC

OCEAN

Matelot   Toco
Blanchisseuse
Maracas
Chaguaramas
San Juan
PORT-OF-SPAIN   Tunapuna   Arima   Valencia
Caroni   River
GULF   Chaguanas   Sangre Grande
Oropuche
OF   Talparo
Couva   TRINIDAD
PARIA
Poole   River
San Fernando   Rio Claro   Pierreville
Brighton   La Brea   Princes Town
Point Fortin   Débé   Ortoire   River
Oropuche
Fullarton   Siparia   Guayaguayare
San Francique   Moruga

TOGETHER WE ASPIRE   TOGETHER WE ACHIEVE

TRINIDAD & TOBAGO

BASIC FACT SHEET

OFFICIAL NAME: Republic of Trinidad & Tobago

ABBREVIATION: TR

CAPITAL: Port of Spain

HEAD OF STATE: President Ellis Emmanuel Innocent Clarke (Governor General from 1972; President from 1976)

HEAD OF GOVERNMENT: Prime Minister George Michael Chambers (from 1981)

NATURE OF GOVERNMENT: Parliamentary democracy

POPULATION: 1,185,000 (1985)

AREA: 5,128 sq km (1,980 sq mi)

ETHNIC MAJORITY: Negro and East Indian

LANGUAGE: English

RELIGION: Christianity

UNIT OF CURRENCY: Trinidad & Tobago dollar ($1=TT$2.4, August 1985)

NATIONAL FLAG: Black band edged with white, extending from top left to bottom right on a red field

NATIONAL EMBLEM: A shield divided by a triangular white border with two gold hummingbirds in the black upper portion and three gold, white-sailed ships on a red background (representing the vessels of Christopher Columbus when he discovered the islands) in the lower and larger part. The shield is flanked by a long-billed scarlet ibis standing on an island with three peaks (the trinity from which Trinidad derives its name), while a brown, white and yellow strutting cocrico bird perches on an island representing Tobago. The device is crested by a golden queen's helmet with a red and white mantle, on which is placed a helmsman's wheel and a green palm tree. A scroll at the bottom proclaims the national motto: "Together We Aspire—Together We Achieve."

NATIONAL ANTHEM: "Forged from the Love of Liberty, In the Fires of Hope and Prayer"

NATIONAL HOLIDAYS: August 31 (Independence Day, National Day); January 1 (New Year's Day); May 1 (May Day); First Monday in August (Discovery Day); September 24 (Republic Day); also Christian festivals including Good Friday, Easter Monday, Boxing Day, Whit Monday and Corpus Christi; one Hindu and one Islamic festival are also celebrated.

NATIONAL CALENDAR: Gregorian

PHYSICAL QUALITY OF LIFE INDEX: 91 (up from 88 in 1976) (On an ascending scale in which 100 is the maximum. U.S. 95)

DATE OF INDEPENDENCE: August 31, 1962

DATE OF CONSTITUTION: August 1, 1976

WEIGHTS & MEASURES: Imperial units are in use.

LOCATION & AREA

Trinidad & Tobago are the southernmost islands of the Lesser Antilles chain in the Caribbean, separated from Venezuela by 11 km (7 mi) of the Gulf of Paria. The islands cover an area of 5,128 sq km (1,980 sq mi), with a length of 210 km (130 mi) NE to SW and a width of 93 km (58 mi) NW to SE. Trinidad, the larger of the islands, has an area of 4,828 sq km (1,864 sq mi), extending 143 km (89 mi) N to S and 61 km (38 mi) E to W, while Tobago, 31 km (19 mi) NE of Trinidad, has an area of 300 sq km (116 sq mi), extending 42 km (26 mi) NE to SW and 12 km (7 mi) NW to SE. The country also includes 16 smaller islands. The length of the coastline on the Atlantic Ocean, the Caribbean Sea and the Gulf of Paria is 470 km (292 mi).

The capital is Port of Spain with a 1981 population of 65,906. The other major urban centers are San Fernando (33,490) and Arima (11,390).

The most prominent natural features of Trinidad are the three east-to-west mountain ranges called the Northern, Central and Southern Ranges. The Northern Range, a rugged chain that is a continuation of the mountains of the Paria Peninsula of Venezuela, includes the highest point in the country, Cerro del Aripo, with an elevation of 940 meters (3,048 ft). The elevations of the Central and Southern Ranges are somewhat lower. Between the Northern and the Central Ranges is the broad Caroni Plain and between the Central and Southern Ranges are the Naparima and Nariva Plains. There are extensive swamps along the eastern, southern and western coasts, such as the Caronia Swamp, the Nariva Swamp and the Oropuche Lagoon. Satellite islands near the coast of Trinidad include the Chacachacare and Monos islands. Tobago is geologically part of the Lesser Antilles and has an uneven terrain dominated by the Main Ridge, a series of volcanic mountains rising to 550 meters (1,800 ft). The southwestern part of the island consists of an extensive coral platform. Tobago has a number of satellite islands, such as Little Tobago and St. Giles.

Rivers are numerous on both islands. The longest on Trinidad are the the Ortoire, flowing into the Atlantic in the south, and the Caroni, flowing into the Gulf of Paria in the north. On Tobago, the Courland runs westward into the Caribbean Sea. There are no natural lakes, but Trinidad has the world's largest natural asphalt bog, the 46-hectares (114-acre) Pitch Lake at La Brea on the southwestern coast, containing 45 million tons of pure asphalt. In the 16th Century, Sir Walter Raleigh used pitch from this lake to caulk his ships. Geologically the islands are unstable, and earthquakes are common.

WEATHER

Although located within the tropics, the climate of Trinidad is moderated by the cooling effects of the trade winds and its marine environment. Climatically, the year is divided into two seasons: a dry season from January to May and a wet season from June to December. The mean temperatures are 27.8°C (82°F) in the daytime and 23.3°C (74°F) at night; the mean annual average is 21°C (70°F). In Port of Spain, where the annual average is 25°C (77°F), the variation between the warmest month of July and the coldest month of January is only 19.4 degrees centigrade (35 degrees Fahrenheit). The climate of Tobago is similar to that of Trinidad, although temperature levels are generally lower because of the island's small size and greater exposure to the trade winds.

The wettest months are June through November; rainfall, although occasionally heavy, is of short duration and is interspersed with periods of bright sunshine. On the Northern and Central Ranges in Trinidad and on the Main Ridge in Tobago, rainfall ranges from 254 cm to 381 cm (100 to 150 in.) annually, but it decreases to between 150 cm and 195 cm (59 in. to 77 in.) on the western belt of Trinidad and 114 cm (45 in.) on the coastal platform of Tobago. There are occasional droughts in the drier areas of both islands.

The islands lie outside the track of maximum velocity hurricanes; nevertheless Hurricane Flora struck Tobago in 1962, bringing heavy devastation. Tropical storm Alma also slashed across it in 1974.

POPULATION

The population of Trinidad & Tobago was estimated in 1985 at 1,185,000, on the basis of the last official census held in 1980, when it was 1,059,825. The population is expected to reach 1.5 million by 2000 and 1.7 million by 2020.

The annual growth rate is 0.92% on the basis of an estimated annual birth rate of 24.6 per 1,000.

The population is concentrated in an almost continuous urban area extending eastward from Port of Spain to Tunapuna, westward to Chaguaramas and northward into the Northern Range. About one-third of the population lives within 16 km (10 mi) of Port of Spain. The overall density of population is 218 per sq km (565 per sq mi).

DEMOGRAPHIC INDICATORS (1984)	
Population, total (in 1,000)	1,185.0
Population ages (% of total)	
0-14	31.6
15-64	62.6
65+	5.8
Youth 15-24 (000)	243
Women ages 15-49 (000)	293
Dependency ratios	59.8
Child-woman ratios	440
Sex ratios (per 100 females)	99.6
Median ages (years)	23.4
Marriage Rate (per 1,000)	7.4
Divorce Rate (per 1,000)	0.6
Average size of Household	4.2
Decline in birthrate (%, 1960-78)	−10.8
Proportion of urban (%)	22.63
Population density (per sq. km.)	218
per hectare of arable land	2.62
Rates of growth (%)	0.92
urban %	1.9
rural %	0.6
Natural increase rates (per 1,000)	18.3
Crude birth rates (per 1,000)	24.6
Crude death rates (per 1,000)	6.2
Gross reproduction rates	1.40
% Illegitimate births	43.7
Net reproduction rates	1.36
Total fertility rates	2.90
General fertility rates (per 1,000)	95
Life expectancy, males (years)	67.8
Life expectancy, females (years)	72.6
Life expectancy, total (years)	70.1
Population doubling time in years at current rate	37

Because of the small size of the islands, the distinction between an urban and a rural area is often clouded. The urban component of the population is reported as 22% (according to the World Bank). According to a Trinidadian source, 56.7% of the urban population lives in the two cities of Port of Spain and San Fernando. Some suburban areas or counties surrounding cities have acquired urban characteristics without the official designation of a town or urban locality. In fact, both Port of Spain and San Fernando reported a negative growth rate of –27.8% and –6.3%, respectively, during the intercensal period of 1960 to 1970; the national urban growth rate during 1973-83 was only 1.9%. Moreover, the prevailing pattern of settlement is still rural, and there are no big urban centers other than Port of Spain and San Fernand. On Tobago, Scarborough, its only real town, has a population of only 4,000; the remaining settlements are villages.

The age profile shows 31.6% under 14, 62.6% between 15 and 64 and 5.8% over 65. Over half the population is under the age of 20.

The 1980 census revealed a rise in the proportion of males in the population, from 97.8 in 1970 to 99.6 in 1980 per 100 females.

The flow of migrants out of the country, particularly unskilled domestics, to the United Kingdom and North America, officially encouraged by the government at one time, declined after 1970 as a result of stringent controls imposed by Canada, the United

States and the United Kingdom. Among the emigrants 15.1% were professional and skilled workers; of these, doctors, engineers and nurses were the most numerous. Furthermore, an estimated 30 to 40% of Trinidadians engaged in studies abroad did not return to the country. Emigration has therefore been costly for the country in terms of the loss of skilled manpower. Immigration is controlled by stringent restrictions on the employment of aliens, who are attracted by the high Trinidadian wages. With the rise in unemployment in the mid-1970s, the flow of immigrants has declined to a trickle.

Women enjoy equality under the law. Many have positions in the government, civil service, political party leadership, business, and other professions, although their presence in these positions is not in proportion to their numbers in the population. Women currently serve in Parliament and women's groups are quick to speak out on women's rights.

Organized family planning efforts date from 1967 when the Population Council was established by the government. The Council includes representatives of the private Family Planning Association (an affiliate of the International Planned Parenthood Federation) and the Catholic Marriage Advisory Council. By the mid-1970s, 46 clinics had been established, including 36 operated by the government. The official goal is 90 clinics by 1980. Nearly one-fourth of married women of childbearing age are believed to use family planning services. Trinidad and Tobago is one of about six countries in Latin America and the Caribbean in which the birthrate has registered a decline since 1960. A long-range objective is to achieve a crude birthrate of 15.5 per 1,000 by 1990.

ETHNIC COMPOSITION

Trinidadian society is based on the complex interaction of as many as 13 ethnic groups, of which two predominate: the Negroes—descendants of African slaves—and East Indians—descendants of indentured laborers imported from India between 1845 and 1917. In between, there are five groups of whites (foreign whites or bekes, local whites or French Creoles, Portuguese, Middle Easterners and Spanish-speaking Venezuelans), three groups of coloreds (including one simply described as douglas or bastards) and one group of Chinese. On a different level are the 2,000 Caribs and Arawaks (both called Caribs), who represent the original Amerindian population, although it is doubtful if they are unmixed. According to the official census of 1970, Negroes constituted 42.83%, East Indians 40.12%, whites about 2%, Chinese 0.86% and mixed 14.17%. Based on color and ethnic background, these groups are broadly divided into Creole and non-Creole, with the East Indians, Chinese, Portuguese, Middle Easterners, Jews and Spanish-speaking Latin Americans falling into the non-Creole category. The presence of these diverse races within a small country makes Trinidad & Tobago a microcosm of the world.

Despite government efforts to develop a black culture rooted in the African past and to introduce black pride as a viable cultural concept, Creole society is essentially white-oriented and is deeply imbued with European, specifically British, values. On the other hand, the East Indians have been, as elsewhere in all the countries to which they have migrated, most resistant to assimilation and have succeeded in maintaining their separate identity and social norms. Four institutions have helped the East Indians to preserve their cultural autonomy: the caste system, religion, kinship ties and material culture, including language, clothing and food, which have become hallmarks of their separatism. The East Indians' impact on Trinidadian society has been profound. Their percentage of the total population has also increased rapidly, growing by nearly 5% between 1959 and 1970, while the percentage of the Negro population has actually decreased. By 1980 East Indians outnumbered the Negroes because of their higher birth rate and their strict practice of endogamy. Of the other non-Creole groups, only the Chinese enjoy a social status comparable — or even superior—to the Creoles. The Chinese are mainly urban; many of them are wealthy and, unlike the East Indians, have readily adopted Western values.

Ethnic differences are reinforced by occupational and even geographic segregation. Most residential areas are divided into Negro, white or East Indian districts. Negroes are concentrated in industrial urban areas in and around Port of Spain, San Fernando, Arima and Pitch Lake and in the oil fields in the southwest. East Indians provide the bulk of rural agricultural labor, especially in the sugar belt in the west. Other non-Creole groups are generally urban. Those of French descent live in the north. On Tobago the bulk of the population is Negro.

In terms of ethnic and linguistic homogeneity, Trinidad & Tobago is ranked 48th in the world with 44% homogeneity (on an ascending scale in which North and South Korea are ranked 135th with 100% homogeneity and Tanzania is ranked first with 7% homogeneity).

LANGUAGES

The official language is English, but varieties of English are spoken in Trinidad & Tobago, ranging from the Creole of the lower classes to the standard English of the upper classes. The most common form of English spoken on the islands is called Trinidad English, a Creole form which differs from standard English in both the flexibility of its pronunciation and the incorporation of African and other words. In fact, it is so different that some linguists classify it as a separate language. Because its distance from standard English is related to the social class of the speaker, Trinidad English is very innovative and has no fixed forms or rules. It is the sole form of communication among the lower classes, and others use varying degrees of Trinidad English depending on their audience. However, more recently, there has been a drive to popularize and destigmatize the language by writers, scholars and writers of calypso music.

One of the most interesting characteristics of Trinidad's language scene is the persistence of French and Spanish patois. French patois, not readily intelligible to a Frenchman, is widely spoken particularly in the rural areas in the north. French and Spanish have also influenced Trinidad English in its vocabulary, intonation and tempo of speech.

The older East Indians still speak any one of numerous Indian languages, particularly Hindustani, also called Desi Bhasa, but their use is decreasing and may eventually die out.

RELIGIONS

The 1970 census listed about 63% of the population as belonging to various Christian denominations, 25% as Hindu, 6% as Muslim and 6% as other. The majority of the Christians are Roman Catholic (33.6%) or Anglican (18.1%), and the remainder belong to smaller groups, none of which makes up more than 5% of the population. There is a Roman Catholic archbishopric and an Anglican bishopric at Port of Spain.

There are two kinds of sects of African origin: Shouter and Shango, the latter including a variant called Rada. The Shouters, who call themselves Spiritual Baptists, are a fundamentalist cult who place great emphasis on participatory and demonstrative worship with hand-clapping, singing, dancing, shouting and trances. The Shango are only marginally Christian, and most of their beliefs and practices, as well as their pantheon of gods, are derived from African animism.

The constitution guarantees freedom of religion and also authorizes grants to religious organizations for ecclesiastical expenses. Under this provision aid is extended to 16 religious groups.

COLONIAL EXPERIENCE

Trinidad was discovered by Christopher Columbus in 1984, but the Spanish ignored the islands and did not appoint a governor until 1552. The three centuries of Spanish rule were uneventful except for skirmishes with the native Arawak Indians and raids by English buccaneers. In time, the colonists established plantations and imported slaves from West Africa to work them. In 1797 a British expedition from Martinique captured Trinidad, which was ceded formally to the United Kingdom in 1820 by the Treaty of Amiens. Tobago, also discovered by Columbus in 1498, changed hands many times before coming under the British crown in 1814. Tobago was at first ruled as a separate colony; during the 19th Century it was under the administrative jurisdiction of Grenada. It became a crown colony in 1877 and was amalgamated with Trinidad in 1888. In 1958 the Federation of the West Indies was formed together with Jamaica, Barbados, and the Windward and Leeward Islands; Port of Spain was the capital. The Federation collapsed in 1961. The ethnic configuration of the two islands had changed in the meanwhile as a result of the importation of indentured workers from India. Full independence, which came in 1962, has not loosened the strong economic and cultural ties with the United Kingdom.

CONSTITUTION & GOVERNMENT

Trinidad & Tobago is a parliamentary democracy under the republican constitution of 1976. The constitution provides for a largely ceremonial president, a prime minister as the effective head of government, and a bicameral legislature. The principal provisions of the constitution are described as "entrenched" and the more important of these are described as "specially entrenched." The entrenched provisions relate to human rights, prorogation of parliament, appointment and dismissal of judicial and police officers and protection of pension rights. The specially entrenched provisions relate to parliament, elections and amendments to the constitution.

The prime minister is formally appointed by the president and is always the leader of the party that commands the support of the majority of the members of the House of Representatives. The prime minister chooses the ministers of the cabinet and also allocates their portfolios. The cabinet also includes an attorney general appointed by the president on the advice of the prime minister.

Suffrage is universal over the age of 18. Elections are held every five years (the last one in 1976) and are supervised by an Elections Commission comprising a chairman and two to four other members. The members of this commission are also members of the Boundaries Commission.

The president is elected by an electoral college of members of both the Senate and the House of Representatives. His term of office is five years.

The first significant threat to the Eric Williams government since independence occurred in 1970 when a black power movement organized by students of the University of the West Indies and supported by various dissident groups launched a series of disturbances, which they called "revolution." Some 10,000 persons joined in a black power march through Port of Spain, and over 65,000 attended the funeral of a young student shot dead by a policeman. Shortly thereafter, a small army group mutinied and tried to organize a march on the capital but was foiled by the intervention of the coast guard. Williams survived the crisis, but he was often accused by the opposition of being intolerant. An unsuccessful attempt was made in 1970 to pass the National Security Act, to curtail civil rights during emergencies. However, criticism of the government is expressed openly, the press is ungagged and there is no discernible trend toward absolutism or one-party rule.

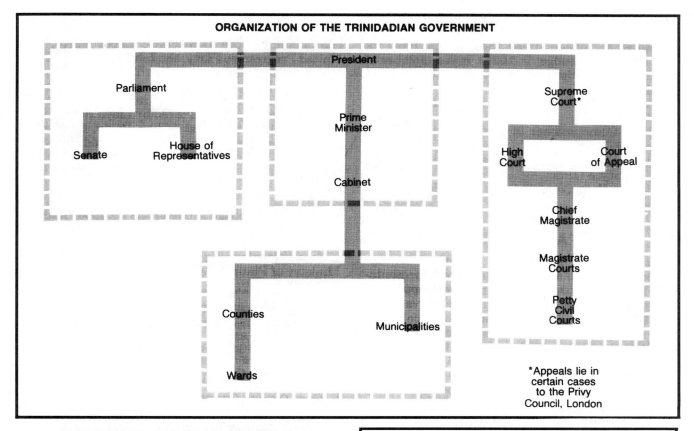

ORGANIZATION OF THE TRINIDADIAN GOVERNMENT

*Appeals lie in certain cases to the Privy Council, London

FREEDOM & HUMAN RIGHTS

In terms of civil and political rights Trinidad & Tobago is classified as a free country with a rating of 2 in civil rights and 2 in political rights (on a descending scale in which 1 is the highest and 7 the lowest in rights).

As in many other former British Colonies, democracy has taken firm roots in Trinidad & Tobago. Multiracial, multireligious, and multilingual, the country is a stable, multiparty parliamentary democracy with a good track record in human rights. The judiciary is independent, the economy is based on free enterprise with mixed ownership of major sectors, the tax system is progressive, the elections are based on universal adult suffrage and fair elections are held regularly. the constitutional guarantees of fundamental rights and freedoms are generally observed in practice, as well as the constitutional prohibitions of cruel and inhuman punishment, torture and invasion of the home. Political participation is open to all citizens and is reinforced by the freedoms of speech, press, and assembly.

CIVIL SERVICE

The civil service, modeled on that of the United Kingdom, is administered by three service commissions: the Public Service Commission, the Judicial and Legal Service Commission and the Police Service Commission. The commsssions are responsible for recruitment, promotion, transfer and discipline.

PRIME MINISTERS OF TRINIDAD AND TOBAGO
1962 to 1981 (March) Eric Eustace Williams
1981 (March) — George Chambers

LOCAL GOVERNMENT

There are 10 local government bodies: three municipal councils and seven county councils. The three municipalities are: Port of Spain, San Fernando and Arima. The seven county councils are: St. George, St. David-St. Andrew, Narive-Mayaro, Caroni, Victoria, St. Patrick and Tobago. Municipalities have elected mayors and deputy mayors; councillors and aldermen serve for three-year terms. In each county council there is one councillor for each electoral district and two aldermen. One alderman is elected from all the qualified persons in the electoral area and another from qualified persons who are members of village councils in the electoral area. The chairmen and vice chairmen of the county councils are elected annually, but councillors and aldermen serve three-year terms.

The counties of Trinidad are in turn subdivided into 29 wards; Tobago is subdivided into nine parishes.

FOREIGN POLICY

The broad goals of Trinidadian foreign policy are diversifying and expanding sources of trade, continuing the quest for Caribbean unity and integration,

```
CABINET LIST (1985)
President . . . . . . . . . . . . Ellis Emmanuel Innocent Clarke
Prime Minister . . . . . . . . . . . . . . . . . . George Chambers
Minister of Agriculture, Lands
   & Food Production . . . . . . . . . Kamaluddin Mohammed
Minister of Community Development
   & Local Government . . . . . . . . . . . . . . Neville Connell
Minister of Education . . . . . . . . . . . . . . Marilyn Gordon
Minister of Energy
   & Natural Resources . . . . . . . . . . . . . Patrick Manning
Minister of External Affairs . . . . . . . . . . . . Errol Mahabir
Minister of Finance & Planning . . . . . . . George Chambers
Minister of Health & Environment . . . . . . . John Eckstein
Minister of Housing & Resettlement . . . . Desmond Cartey
Minister of Industry, Commerce
   & Consumer Affairs . . . . . . . . . . . . . . Wendell Mottley
Minister of Information . . . . . . . . . . . . . . . Muriel Green
Minister of Labor, Social Security
   & Cooperatives . . . . . . . . . . . . . . . . John S. Donaldson
Minister of Legal Affairs . . . . . . . . . . . Russell Martineau
Minister of Natl. Security . . . . . . . . . . . Overand Padmore
Minister of Public Utilities & National
   Transportation . . . . . . . . . . . . . . . . . . Cuthbert Joseph
Minister of Sport, Culture & Youth Affairs . . . . . . Basil Ince
Minister of State Enterprises . . . . . . . . . Ronald J. Williams
Minister of Works, Maintenance
   & Drainage . . . . . . . . . . . . . . . . . . . . . . Hugh Francis
Minister in the Ministry of
   Community Development
   & Local Government . . . . . . Muriel Donawa-McDavidson
Minister in the Ministry of Finance
   & Planning . . . . . . . . . . . . . . Charles Anthony Jacelon
Minister in the Ministry of Health
   & Environment . . . . . . . . . . . . . . . Norma Lewis-Phillips
Minister in the Ministry of Housing
   & Resettlement . . . . . . . . . . . . . . . Elmina Clarke-Allen
Minister in the Ministry of Legal Affairs . . . . . Carlton Alert
Attorney General . . . . . . . . . . . . . . . . Russell Martineau
```

maintaining special relations with the United Kingdom and developing closer rapport with black African and Third World nations.

Relations with other Caribbean nations are the prime concern of foreign policy. Trinidad & Tobago is a founding member of CARICOM (Caribbean Common Market) and participates in the periodic summit conferences of the Commonwealth Caribbean Heads of Government. Trinidad & Tobago was the first Commonwealth country to seek membership in the OAS, where its admission was initially opposed by Venezuela, Guatemala and Argentina (because of long-standing disputes between these countries and the U.K. colonies in the Western Hemisphere). A number of disputes with Venezuela—such as those involving delimitation of territorial waters, illegal immigration, smuggling and fishing—were resolved shortly after independence. But a continuing dispute over Venezuela's territorial claims to offshore islands in the Caribbean is still active. Since the transfer of the Chaguaramas U.S. Naval Base to Trinidad & Tobago in 1967 (assigned to the United States by the United Kingdom under World War II arrangements),

there are no outstanding issues in U.S. relations with Trinidad & Tobago. The country's generally pro-Western posture has, however, not precluded it from seeking advantageous, although limited, relations with Cuba, China and the Soviet Union.

Trinidad & Tobago and the United States are parties to 25 agreements and treaties covering aviation, claims, consuls, defense, economic and technical cooperation, extradition, investment guaranties, mutual security, postal matters, property, taxation, telecommunications, trade and commerce, trade marks, visas and weather stations.

Trinidad & Tobago joined the U.N. in 1962; its share of the U.N. budget is 0.02%. It is a member of 13 U.N. organizations and 18 other international organizations.

U.S. Ambassador in Port of Spain: Sheldon J. Krys
U.K. High Commissioner in Port of Spain: Martin Berthoud
Trinidadian Ambassador in Washington, D.C.: James O'Neil-Lewis
Trinidadian High Commissioner in London: F.O. Abdullah

PARLIAMENT

The bicameral Parliament comprises an appointed Senate and an elected House of Representatives. The Senate consists of 31 members appointed by the president for a maximum term of five years: 16 of the senators are named on the advice of the prime ministers, six on the advice of the leader of the opposition, and nine at the president's discretion. The House of Representatives has 36 members directly elected for five-year terms. The House initiates money bills, but other bills may be initiated by either house.

Following the 1981 elections, party strength in the House of Representatives was as follows: People's National Movement, 26; Trinidad & Tobago National Alliance (comprising United Labor Front, Democratic Action Congress and Tapia House Movement) 10.

In 1980 Tobago was granted its own parliament instead of the two seats it had in the national parliament. In the first elections to this local parliament, the separatist Democratic Action Congress won 54% of the vote and eight of the 12 seats.

POLITICAL PARTIES

Trinidad & Tobago has an effective multiparty system dominated by two parties, the ruling People's National Movement (PNM) and the opposition United Labor Front (ULF). PNM, founded in 1956 by the country's first prime minister, Eric Williams, is predominantly African in ideology and membership, but it lays great stress on national unity and social reform. In 1981 the party gained 53.3% of the votes cast. The opposition United Labor Front is a coalition in which the senior partner is the East Indian-dominated Sugar Workers' Union and the minor partners are the black-dominated Oil Workers' Union, the United National Independence Party and the Liberation Action Party. The Democratic Action Congress is led by a former associate of Prime Minister Williams, A. N. Raymond Robinson. It is relatively conservative in outlook.

PNM has in the past obtained electoral support from Commonwealth Caribbean citizens who have immigrated and become legal residents of Trinidad and Tobago. The PNM has historically obtained support from lower-middle and working-class blacks and Christian and Muslim East Indians. The opposition has drawn support from rural Hindus, Tobagonians, and middle- and upper-class people of various ethnic groups.

Several opposition parties joined to form a single National Alliance for Reconstruction (NAR) in 1985. These parties individually won control of 6 of the 7 country councils in the 1983 local elections. The United Labor Front, the Tapia House Movement and the Democratic Action Congress formed the Trinidad and Tobago National Alliance which won 10 seats in the 1981 elections.

There are three parties without legislative representation but with substantial national followings, The Democratic Labor Party, the principal opposition before 1976, is essentially an East Indian group. In 1972 it split into two: an official group led by Allen Lequoy and an unofficial, and exclusively Hindu, group led by Vernon Jamadar that renamed itself the Social Democratic Party. The United Democratic Labor Party is a coalition embracing the official faction of the Democratic Labor Party, the United Progressive Party, the Liberal Party and the African National Congress. The Tapia (literally, the mud wall) Party is an offshoot of the black power movement calling for nationalization of all foreign-controlled enterprises. It is led by Lloyd Best. Minor parties include the West Indian Party, the Democratic Liberation Party, the United Freedom Party, the National Joint Action Committee and the Fargo House Movement.

ECONOMY

Trinidad & Tobago is one of the 35 upper middle-income countries of the world with a free-market economy dominated by the private sector.

Economic planning is the responsibility of the Ministry of Planning and Development. Four development plans have been drafted, three of which have been implemented: The First Five-Year Plan, 1958-62, the Second Five-Year Plan, 1964-68, the Third Five-Year Plan, 1969-73, and the Fourth Five-Year Plan, 1974-78. The Fourth Plan has not been implemented because the rapid increase in oil revenues from 1973 made an upward revision of the targets and the number and size of the projects necessary. In addition to the national plans, a number of regional plans have been prepared and implemented. These include the Tobago Regional Development Plan, the Port of Spain Capital Regional Plan, the Northwest Penin-

---

PRINCIPAL ECONOMIC INDICATORS

Gross National Product: $7.870 billion (1983)
   GNP Annual Growth Rate: 5.6% (1973-82)
   Per Capita GNP: $6,900 (1983)
   Per Capita GNP Annual Growth Rate: 5.2% (1973-82)

Gross Domestic Product: TT$17.558 billion (1982)
   GDP at 1980 prices: TT$15.403 billion (1982)
   GDP Deflator (1980=100): 114.0
   GDP Annual Growth Rate: 5.2% (1973-83)
   Per Capita GDP: TT$15,538 (1982)
   Per Capita GDP Annual Growth Rate: 3.6% (1970-81)

Income Distribution: 4.2% of national income is received by the lowest 20%; 31.8% of the national income is received by the top 10%.

Percentage of Population in Absolute Poverty: 7; 39% Rural

Consumer Price Index (1970=100):
   All Items: 615.1 (June 1985)
   Food: 695.1 (June 1985)

Money Supply: TT$2.061 billion (March 1985)
   Reserve Money: TT$2.305 billion (April 1985)

Currency in Circulation: TT$709.7 million (1984)

Average Annual Rate of Inflation: 15.6% (1973-83)

International Reserves: $1.356 billion, of which foreign exchange reserves were $1.131 billion (1984)

BALANCE OF PAYMENTS (1982)
(million $)

Current Account Balance	−909.1
Merchandise Exports	2,211.2
Merchandise Imports	−2,441.5
Trade Balance	−230.3
Other Goods, Services & Income	+880.8
Other Goods, Services & Income	−1,419.9
Other Goods, Services & Income Net	−539.1
Private Unrequited Transfers	−81.3
Official Unrequited Transfers	−58.5
Capital Other Than Reserves	551.9
Net Errors & Omissions	265.3
Total (Lines 1, 10 and 11)	−91.9
Counterpart Items	−175.1
Total (Lines 12 and 13)	−267.0
Liabilities Constituting Foreign Authorities' Reserves	—
Total Change in Reserves	267.0

---

sula Plan, the West Coast Region Plan and the South-Western Region Plan.

GROSS DOMESTIC PRODUCT BY ECONOMIC ACTIVITY
(1970-81)

	%	Rate of Change %
Agriculture	3.0	−1.8
Mining	28.7	2.4
Manufacturing	13.9	1.3
Construction	7.9	10.9
Electricity, Gas & Water	1.4	7.4
Transport & Communications	11.1	8.4
Trade & Finance	19.5	7.6
Public Administration & Defense	8.3	4.7
Other Branches	8.2	3.2

As a result of increasing oil revenues, in the 1970s Trinidad & Tobago became for a while a donor as well as a beneficiary country. Its Caribbean Aid Council gave contributions to neighboring countries equal to 2.2% of GDP.

FOREIGN ECONOMIC ASSISTANCE

Sources	Period	Amount (in Million $)
United States Grants	1946-83	40.9
International Organizations	1946-83	176.9
(Of which World Bank)	1946-83	119.9
ODA & OOF (£ million)	1970-82	118.0
All Sources	1979-81	4.8

During 1979-81 Trinidad & Tobago received $4.10 in per capita foreign aid.

BUDGET

The Trinidadian fiscal year is the calendar year. Budgets are generally modified by supplemental appropriations so that they do not always reflect actual expenditures. The current account is in surplus in most years and the capital account in deficit. Both municipalities and counties receive annual transfers for their operations.

BUDGET ESTIMATES
(TT $ million)

Revenue	1981	1982
Capital receipts	123.8	710.6
Customs and excise	505.0	547.6
Direct taxes	4,899.2	4,862.8
Other current revenue	1,224.6	1,756.8
Total	6,752.6	7,877.8
Expenditure	**1981**	**1982**
Recurrent expenditure	3,812.4	4,421.8
Development program	155.0	230.0
Funds for long-term projects	2,933.1	3,505.5
Public debt charges	59.8	59.5
Other capital expenditure	613.9	1,094.9
Total	7,574.2	9,311.7

Of current revenues, 70.0% came from taxes on income profit and capital gain, 2.0% from social security contributions, 4.1% from domestic taxes on goods and services, 6.5% from taxes on international trade and transactions, 0.6% from other taxes and 16.8% from non-tax revenues. Total current revenues represent 44.1% of GNP. Of current expenditures, 2.0% goes to defense, 11.2% to education, 5.9% to health, 17.3% to housing, social security and welfare, 31.1% to economic services and 32.4% to other functions. Current expenditures represented 31% of GNP and overall deficit 3.3% of GNP.

In 1982 public consumption was TT$2.371 billion and private consumption TT$10.286 billion. During 1973-83 public and private consumption grew by 7.7%.

In 1983, total outstanding disbursed external debt amounted to $892.1 million of which $242.2 million was owed to official creditors and $649.8 million to private creditors. The total debt service was $217.4 million of which $117.5 million was repayment of principal and $99.9 million interest. Total external debt represented 10.7% of GNP and total debt service 2.6% of GNP.

FINANCE

The Trinidadian unit of currency is the Trinidad & Tobago dollar, divided into 100 cents. Coins are issued in denominations of 1, 5, 10, 25, 50 cents and 1 dollar; notes are issued in denominations of 1, 5, 10 and 20 dollars.

The Trinidad & Tobago dollar was introduced in 1965, replacing at par the West Indian dollar. Until 1976 it was linked to sterling, but in that year the link was broken and the currency was pegged to the U.S. dollar at the rate of $1=TT$2.40.

The banking sector is headed by the Central Bank with a capital of TT$3 million. There are a number of specialized financial institutions owned by the government: the Industrial Development Corporation, the Agricultural Development Bank, the National Commercial Bank, the Post Office Savings Bank and the Credit Union Bank. There are over eight commercial banks with 85 branches. Five of these banks are branches of British, Canadian and U.S. banks. In 1984 the commercial banks had reserves of TT$1.497 billion, demand deposits of TT$1.390 billion and time and savings deposits of TT$5.883 billion. The prevailing bank rate in 1984 was 7.50%.

GROWTH PROFILE
Annual Growth Rates (%)

Population 1980-2000	1.7
Birthrate 1965-83	−10.8
Deathrate 1965-83	−1.4
Urban Population 1973-83	1.0
Labor Force 1980-2000	2.3
GNP 1973-82	5.6
GNP per capita 1973-82	5.2
GDP 1973-83	5.2
GDP per capita 1970-81	3.6
Consumer Prices 1970-81	13.7
Wholesale Prices	—
Inflation 1973-83	15.6
Agriculture 1970-81	−1.8
Manufacturing 1970-81	1.3
Industry 1973-82	4.0
Services 1973-82	6.9
Mining 1970-81	2.4
Construction 1970-81	10.9
Electricity 1970-81	7.4
Transportation 1970-81	8.4
Trade 1970-81	7.6
Public Administration & Defense 1970-81	4.7
Export Price Index 1975-81	23.4
Import Price Index 1975-81	19.8
Terms of Trade 1975-81	3.1
Exports 1973-83	−7.7
Imports 1973-83	−5.1
Public Consumption	7.7
Private Consumption 1973-83	7.7
Gross Domestic Investment 1973-83	13.0
Energy Consumption 1973-83	3.9
Energy Production 1973-83	0.8

AGRICULTURE

Of the total land area of 512,800 hectares (1,267,128 acres), 28% is classified as agricultural land, or 0.2 hectare (0.4 acre) per capita. Based on 1974-76=100, the index of agricultural production in 1982 was 61, the index of food production was 60 and the index of per capita food production was 70. Agriculture employs 10% of the labor force. Agriculture contributes 3% of the GDP, and its rate of growth during 1970-81 was −1.8%. Agricultural products contribute less than 5% to export earnings, and even this share is declining.

An agricultural census in 1972 reported 35,800 farms in the country with 128,937 hectares (318,600 acres) under crops. The average farm size is about 6 hectares (14.8 acres); 25,800 farms are between 0.4 and 3.6 hectares (1 and 9 acres); 7,500 farms are between 4 and 9.7 hectares (10 and 24 acres); the rest are over 10 hectares (25 acres). Forty-two of the largest farms have more than 400 hectares (1,000 acres), each with a total average area of 53,016 hectares (131,000 acres), while 25,800 small farms at the other end of the scale have a total area of only 38,325 hectares (94,700 acres). Disparities in ownership are greater on Tobago where 800 of the largest farms account for 13,476 hectares (33,300 acres), while the remaining 3,200 farms account for only 5,058 hectares (12,500 acres). More than 18,000 farms, or 50% of the total, are operated by the owner, 10,600 or 30% of the total by renters and the balance operate under mixed tenure arrangements. Farms operated by owners occupy 67% of the total farmland, while rented farms occupy 9%. Nevertheless, land reform has not been a major issue because large areas of state lands are available for distribution.

Agricultural techniques are primitive and utilize hand labor. Most of the 2,420 tractors in use in 1982 were owned by the large estates or plantations. In 1982 the annual consumption of fertilizers was 6,500 tons or 30.4 kg (67 lb) per arable hectare. The main commercial crops are sugar, cocoa and coffee. Levels of production have fallen steeply. Whereas the country was a net exporter of food in the 1960s, it imported 295,000 tons in 1982, or 75% of requirements.

```
PRINCIPAL CROP PRODUCTION (1982)
(000 tons)
Sugar Cane ......................... 1,000
Cocoa .............................. 3
Coconuts & Copra ................... 68
Orange ............................. 7
Grapefruit ......................... 7
```

There is not much livestock in the country. Most East Indian farmers keep water buffalo, while some 10,000 farmers keep either dairy or beef cattle. The percentage of pasture in the farmland is the smallest in Latin America. The livestock population in 1982 consisted of 79,000 cattle, 8,000 buffaloes, 61,000 pigs, 12,000 sheep, 48,000 goats and 7.6 million chickens.

Forests cover about 43% of the land area, most of them government-owned. More than 60 different species are exploited including teak, mora, carapa, mahoe, cedar and other hardwoods. There are more than 60 sawmills in the country. Production has been declining from the high of 4.9 million cubic meters (173 million cubic ft) in the early 1970s.

Fishing, like livestock, is underdeveloped as a result of past neglect. There are an estimated 3,300 full-time and 2,200 part-time fishermen and about 1,000 registered craft operating from 63 fishing beaches. There are also about 100 tuna and shrimp trawlers, mostly foreign-owned, operating out of Trinidad ports. There are few cold-storage or other handling facilities. A wide variety of fish is caught including carite, kingfish, snapper, grouper, salmon and herring. The catch in 1982 was 4,500 tons.

Agricultural credit is provided by the Agricultural Development Bank and credit unions.

INDUSTRY

The manufacturing sector consists of more than 600 establishments producing or assembling over 400 categories of goods and generating 13.9% of the GDP. The annual growth rate of the manufacturing sector during 1970-81 was 1.3%. Employment in this sector has been relatively stable at around 20%. In 1983, the value added in manufacturing was $434 million, of which agro-based products accounted for 54%. The principal industries are textiles and food processing.

Many new industrial plants have been established under the "Pioneer" category. These are granted remission of taxes on profits during the early years, remission of import duties on production equipment and raw materials and accelerated depreciation allowances. The Aid to Pioneer Industries Ordinance also reserves certain areas of crown lands for industrial purposes at modest rentals.

Industry is concentrated in the Port of Spain and San Fernando area, but the dispersion of manufacturing facilities is a major development priority. A second industrial area at Point Fortin, in St. Patrick's County, where light manufacturing industries established.

There is a greater degree of state participation in the industrial sector in Trinidad & Tobago than in any other Caribbean country. The government is the largest investor in the sugar industry, petroleum production and distribution, meat packing, hotels and related industries. The government owns a few of the banks and most of the utilities and telecommunications. However, all acquisitions, both foreign and domestic, have been by purchase at mutually agreed prices, and there have been no cases of expropriation.

The government's concern to widen the country's economic base and to reduce the overwhelming dependence on petroleum has led to heavy investment in a number of planned industries. The first of these, the TRINGEN ammonia plant, came into production in 1977. The success of this operation has prompted the government to consider the construction of more ammonia plants, to make the country a major world producer. Urea and methanol plants commenced operations in mid-1984, and large contracts have been placed for the export of urea to India and the People's Republic of China. Other projects include petrochemicals, fertilizers, furfural, plastics and electronics.

The Industrial Development Corporation serves as the principal agency in promoting industrial investment and development. It has created the Point Lisas Port industrial park and also provides financing to small businesses.

Foreign investment is actively solicited. Major incentives include an adequate labor pool, duty-free imports of equipment and raw materials, an income tax holiday, accelerated depreciation allowances, unlimited carryover of losses, repatriation of capital and profit and preferential tariff rates in Commonwealth markets. However, government thinking has been moving in the direction of restricting certain manufacturing activities to domestic ownership and of preferring joint ventures rather than outright foreign ownership. Foreign firms are not permitted to dominate any sector, and no public contracts are awarded to firms without local participation. Net direct foreign private investment in 1983 was $341 million.

The number of foreign firms operating in the country is variously reported from 100 to 180 companies. Foreign firms employ about 25,000 Trinidadians and have a book value of about $1 billion, of which $500 million is held by U.S. firms, mainly in petroleum and petrochemicals. Other major investors are the United Kingom, Japan, Canada, and the Netherlands. The largest share of foreign investment, about 71%, is in petroleum, 6% in food processing, 4% in assembly operations, 3% each in chemicals, marketing and services and the balance in other sectors.

ENERGY

In 1982 Trinidad & Tobago's total production of energy was 17.35 million metric tons of coal equivalent; consumption was 6.726 million metric tons of coal equivalent, or 6,222 kg (13,719 lb) per capita. The national energy surplus is 10.62 million metric tons of coal equivalent. The annual growth rates during 1973-83 were 0.8% for energy production and 3.9% energy consumption. Energy imports account for 4% of all merchandise imports. Apparent per capita consumption of gasoline is 192 gallons per year.

Trinidad is one of the major oil-producing countries in the world, with reserves of 630 million barrels (enough to last for 11 years at current extraction rates) of petroleum and 371 billion cubic meters (13.102 trillion cubic ft) of natural gas. Production in 1982 totaled 58 million barrels of petroleum and 3 billion cubic meters (106 billion cubic ft) of natural gas. By the 1980s petroleum accounted for 50% of GDP and 90% of export income. The main producing areas are the Amoco offshore field, the Soldado field in the Gulf of Paria and smaller wells in the southern part of the island. Nearly 72% of the production is from 579 offshore wells and 28% from the 7,058 land wells. Production is handled by seven companies, of which the Amoco Trinidad Oil Company is the largest, accounting for over half of the total production. The government owns one company, the Trinidad & Tobago Oil Company, formerly Shell Trinidad, purchased in 1974.

The strategic geographic location of the islands has favored the establishment of a large refining complex. The rated capacity of the two existing refineries exceeds 375,000 barrels per day. The larger of these refineries is located at Point-a-Pierre and is owned by Texaco Trinidad, slated to be acquired by the government. The other is the state-owned Trinidad and Tobago Oil Company refinery at Point Fortin. Because of the excess capacity of the refineries, it is necessary to import over 75% of the crude oil input.

Electric power production in 1984 totaled 2.6 billion kwh, or 2,226 kwh per capita.

LABOR

The economically active population is estimated at 473,000, yielding a participation rate (percentage of total population in the labor force) of 40%. Women constitute 31.6% of the total number of economically active persons. By occupational sectors, 13.5% are engaged in agriculture, 20% in manufacturing and mining, 15.7% in construction, 17.4% in commerce, 7.5% in transport and communications and 23.0% in services. Some 76.7% are wage earners, 13.8% are self-employed, 6.9% are employers and 2.6% are unpaid family workers. An interesting characteristic of the Trinidadian labor force is its ethnic correlation. Most of the agricultural labor is performed by East Indians; the civil service, industry and commerce are dominated by Negroes; professional, technical and managerial occupations are monopolized by whites; while the Chinese and Middle Easterners are small businessmen.

There is little protective labor legislation. Work rules are subject to labor-management negotiations.

Trinidad & Tobago had one of the highest unemployment rates in Latin America, estimated at 20%, although official sources in 1982 reported it at 10.4%. As a result of the rapid expansion of the economy in recent years, particularly in the construction sector, the country has recorded a significant reduction in the rate of unemployment and labor shortages are reported in some skilled and semi-skilled jobs. In order to protect the domestic labor market, the employment of aliens is effectively banned. Strikes are frequent and often prolonged and bitter.

There is no minimum wage rate in Trinidad and Tobago. However, minimum wages have been set in three occupational categories (gas station attendants, shop clerks and domestic servants) by order of the minister of labor. The minister's rationale was that these industries were difficult to organize and that, therefore, the workers wouldn't be protected by collective bargaining.

Occupational health and safety is covered by the 1948 Factories Ordinance Bill. Because of shortcomings of the 1948 bill, a new Occupational Safety and Health Bill reflecting changes in Trinidad and Tobago's industry has been circulated for public comment, but has not yet come before Parliament. The new bill is expected to prompt extensive debate when brought before Parliament some time during 1986.

The laws of Trinidad and Tobago prohibit the employment of children under the age of 12. Children between the ages of 12 and 18 may be employed only in family businesses with the exception that children between the ages of 16 and 18 may be employed in certain industries specifically exempted from the law by order of the president.

The most powerful representative of organized labor is the Trinidad & Tobago Labor Congress with 24 affiliated unions and 50,000 members. In addition, there are some 14 nonaffiliated unions with a combined membership of 5,000.

FOREIGN COMMERCE

The foreign commerce of Trinidad & Tobago in 1984 consisted of exports of $2.106 billion and imports of $1.878 billion, leaving a trade surplus of $228 million. Of the imports, fuels constitute 25.2%, industrial supplies 23.6%, capital equipment 20.5% and transport equipment 10.7%. Of the exports, petroleum products constitute 87.9%, chemicals 5.2%, transport equipment 2.6% and food 1.7%.

The major import sources are: the United States 35.4%, Saudi Arabia 11.6%, Indonesia 9.5%, the United Kingdom 8.2%, Japan 7.2% and Canada 3.7%. The major export destinations are: the United States 50.2%, the Netherlands 7.3%, Italy 4.4%, Guyana 3.6%, Suriname 3.6% and Honduras 3.1%.

Based on 1975=100, the import price index in 1981 was 270, the export price index was 349 and the terms of trade (export prices divided by import prices × 100) 129.

Trinidad & Tobago is a member of the Caribbean Common Market (CARICOM), successor to the CARIFTA (Caribbean Free Trade Association).

TRANSPORTATION & COMMUNICATIONS

Trinidad's former rail system was phased out and is not currently in operation. The island's major industrial product, petroleum, is moved by a 1,032 km (641 mi) pipeline. There is also a 19 km (11.7 mi) pipeline for refined products and a 904 km (561 mi) pipeline for natural gas.

The country has nine seaports: Port of Spain for general cargo, Point-a-Pierre and Point Fortin for petroleum, Brighton for asphalt, Chaguaramas and Tembladora for transshipment of bauxite, Goodrich Bay and Point Lisas for sugar and Scarborough, the

FOREIGN TRADE INDICATORS (1984)	
Annual Growth Rate, Imports:	–5.1% (1973-83)
Annual Growth Rate, Exports:	–7.7% (1973-83)
Ratio of Exports to Imports:	53:47
Exports per capita:	$1,777
Imports per capita:	$1,585
Balance of Trade:	$228 million
Ratio of International Reserves to Imports (in months)	9.6
Exports as % of GDP:	46.6
Imports as % of GDP:	36.5
Value of Manufactured Exports:	$322 million
Commodity Concentration:	46.4%

Direction of Trade (%)

	Imports	Exports
EEC	14.3	14.4
U.S.	26.1	58.9
Industrialized Market Economies	80.7	74.9
East European Economies	—	—
High Income Oil Exporters	—	—
Developing Economies	16.9	22.0

Composition of Trade (%)

	Imports	Exports
Food	12.9	2.0
Agricultural Raw Materials	1.7	—
Fuels	36.6	89.6
Ores & Minerals	4.2	0.3
Manufactured Goods	44.4	8.0
of which Chemicals	5.2	3.8
of which Machinery	22.4	3.2

only port on Tobago, for inter-island cargo. In 1982 these ports handled 23,892,000 tons of cargo.

The road system is 8,000 km (4,968 mi) long, of which 4,300 km (2,670 mi) are paved. In 1983 these roads were used by 180,948 passenger cars and 49,800 commercial vehicles. Per capita passenger car ownership is 152 per 1,000 inhabitants. There is an extensive bus transportation system operated by the Public Transport Service Corporation.

The national airline is British West Indian Airways, which operates a fleet of 14 aircraft (including seven Boeing 707s) to Barbados, St. Lucia, Puerto Rico, Jamaica, Guyana, Toronto, Miami, London and Havana. The Trinidad & Tobago Air Services, with two aircraft, operates services between Trinidad and Tobago. In 1982 these airlines flew 13.9 million km (8.6 million mi) and carried 1,381,000 passengers. There are seven airports in the country, of which five are usable, three have permanent-surface runways and one—Piarco International Airport on Trinidad— has a runway over 2,500 meters (8,000 ft). There are also two seaplane stations.

In 1984 there were 86,900 telephones in use, or 7.0 per 100 inhabitants.

In 1984 Trinidad & Tobago's 63 post offices and 170 postal agencies handled 50,137,000 pieces and 491,000 telegrams. Per capita volume of mail was 42 pieces. There are 265 telex subscriber lines.

In 1982, 200,000 tourists visited Trinidad & Tobago, generating $163 million in revenues. Expenditures by nationals abroad totaled $167 million. There are 3,000 hotel beds and the average length of stay was 6.1 days.

MINING

Trinidad's principal mineral resource is asphalt from the Pitch Lake. Iron ore deposits have been reported in the Northern Range.

DEFENSE

The defense structure is headed by the president, but the prime minister is in direct command through the Ministry of National Security. The defense force is commanded by a brigadier.

Enlistment is voluntary. The usual term of enlistment is six years.

The total strength of the armed forces is 2,130, or 1.8 armed persons for every 1,000 civilians.

ARMY:
Personnel: 1,500
Organization: 1 infantry battalion; 1 reserve battalion of 3 companies; 1 support battalion
Equipment: mortars; rocket launchers

NAVY:
Personnel: 580
Units: 6 patrol craft
Naval Bases: Port of Spain and Chaguaramas

AIR FORCE:
Personnel: 50
Equipment: 1 light aircraft; 1 helicopter

In 1984 the defense budget totaled $75.0 million, representing 5.3% of the national budget, 3.2% of the GNP, $203.0 per capita, $23,000 per soldier and $9,200 per sq km of national territory.

The Trinidadian armed forces have no offensive capability. In fact, the lack of a purposeful mission is cited as one of the causes for low morale and restiveness in the army.

Military aid has been received almost exclusively from the United Kingdom.

EDUCATION

The national literacy rate is estimated at 92.3% (94.8% for males and 89.9% for females). Of the population over 25, 11.6% have had no schooling, 74.6% have completed the first level, 12.6% have completed the second level, and 1.2% have completed post-secondary training.

Education is free, universal and compulsory for seven years between the ages of six and 12. The gross school enrollment ratios are 99% at the first level (5 to 11) and 62% at the second level (12 to 16) for a combined enrollment ratio of 78%. The third level ratio is 4.6%. Girls constitute 50% of primary school enroll-

ment, 49% of secondary enrollment and 36% of tertiary enrollment.

Schooling lasts for 12 years, divided into seven primary grades (known as standards), three years of secondary school (known as forms) and a two-year pre-university course known as sixth form. Those completing the five primary grades are required to take a Common Entrance Examination. Those who are not admitted to the secondary school take a two-year senior primary cycle or a five-year intermediate cycle. On completion of form five of secondary school, students take the General Certificate of Eduction 'O' Level Examination; on completion of the two-year sixth form they take the General Certificate of Education 'A' Level Examination. The dropout rates are low by Caribbean standards. However, only 13% of students taking the crucial 'O' level examination receive passing grades. Educational reforms now under consideration include abolition of the Common Entrance Examination and the replacement of 'O' and 'A' level examinations (both administered from the United Kingdom) with tests more responsive to the needs of the Caribbean. In 1982 the school system consisted of 465 primary and secondary schools.

The school year runs from September to July. The language of instruction is English throughout.

Primary school teachers are trained at three government and two private colleges. There is no institution for the training of secondary school teachers. The national teacher-pupil ratio is 1:26 in primary and intermediate schools, 1:21 in secondary schools and 1:6 in the post-secondary classes.

About 41% of secondary school enrollment is private. Vocational and technical programs offered in state as well as private institutions are two or three years in duration and account for 8.3% of secondary enrollment. Part-time students make up one-half of the enrollment in the vocational stream.

Because Trinidad & Tobago claims the highest rate of literacy in the Caribbean and South America, adult education programs are directed to the teaching of useful skills such as nutrition, culture and handicrafts.

Both government and assisted schools (the latter owned and operated by voluntary agencies) are financed by the government. Educational expenditures 1982 totaled TT$1,034,355,000, of which 83.4% was current expenditure. This amount represented 5.9% of the GNP, 9.5% of the national budget, and $416 per capita.

EDUCATIONAL ENROLLMENT (1980)		
Level	Teachers	Students
First Level	6,443	166,763
Second Level	1,631	84,482
Vocational	114	4,092
Third Level	500	1,878

Higher education is provided by the University of the West Indies at its St. Augustine campus with an enrollment, in 1980, of 1,878 students. Per capita enrollment in higher education is 515 per 100,000 inhabitants.

In 1982, 2,282 Trinidadian students were enrolled in institutions of higher learning abroad. Of these, 1,194 were in the United States, 838 in Canada, 196 in the United Kingdom and 17 in Ireland.

LEGAL SYSTEM

The legal system is based on English common law.

The Supreme Court consists of a High Court and Court of Appeal. The High Court comprises a chief justice and 10 junior judges; the Court of Appeal comprises a chief justice and four other judges.

The lower judicature is headed by a chief magistrate. Under him are seven magisterial districts: St. George West, St. George East, Eastern Counties, Caroni, Victoria, St. Patrick and Tobago, each presided over by a senior magistrate. There are also 18 stipendiary magistrates presiding over petty civil courts.

An unusual constitutional feature is the right of appeal to the Privy Council in the United Kingdom in grave civil or criminal cases.

There are three prisons in the country: the Royal Gaol in Port of Spain, the island prison on Carrera Island and Golden Grove Prison near Arouca. The annual average prison population is around 1,100, of which women make up only 5%.

LAW ENFORCEMENT

The national police service is headed by a commissioner assisted by three deputy commissioners respectively in charge of administration, operation and Special Branch. The Special Branch is concerned with intelligence, subversion and related matters. The force is divided into two units: a north unit and a south unit, and the country is divided into nine police divisions with a total of 60 police stations. The total strength of the force in the mid-1970s was 3,800, including 2,446 constables, 72 inspectors and 63 officers. Per capita there was one policeman for every 281 inhabitants.

In addition to the regular police, there are special units, called the special reserve police, commanded by a senior superintendent, and a municipal police in Port of Spain. Recruitment to and discipline of the force are the constitutional responsibilities of the Police Service Commission. The force is predominantly (about 95%) Negro in its ethnic composition, leading to frequent complaints by East Indians.

Criminal statistics are published annually. Since the early 1960s, serious crimes have risen by over 200%, while prosecutions and convictions have risen by only 77% and 30%, respectively. Convictions for narcotics trafficking have risen by 600% since 1968.

HEALTH

In 1980 there were 25 hospitals in the country with 4,465 beds, or one bed per 246 inhabitants. In the same year there were 710 physicians, or one physician per 1,490 inhabitants, 69 dentists and 2,836 nursing personnel. Of the hospitals 60% are state-run and 40% run by private nonprofit agencies. The admissions/discharge rate per 10,000 is 865, the bed occupancy rate is 86.6% and the average length of stay is five days.

```
PRINCIPAL HEALTH INDICATORS (1984)
Crude Death Rate: 6.2 per 1,000
Decline in Death Rate: –1.4% (1965-83)
Life Expectancy at Birth: 67.8 (Males); 72.6 (Females)
Infant Mortality Rate: 26.4 per 1,000 Live Births
Child Death Rate (Ages 1-4) per 1,000: 1
```

Health conditions are generally good, reflecting a declining incidence of disease. The major health problems are cancer, respiratory diseases, and circulatory diseases. Other significant causes of mortality are gastritis, enteritis, tuberculosis and tetanus. Health expenditures in 1982 represented 6.4% of the annual national budget, and $83.90 per capita. Fifty percent of the population has access to safe water.

FOOD

Food consumption patterns and preferences vary according to race and religion. The staple Negro food is bread, while East Indians consume either rice or wheat flour in the form of pancakes called rotis or chappathis. Hindus eat little flesh other than fish, Muslims eat no pork, but Negroes have few food taboos. Trinidadians are reported to be the second heaviest chicken eaters in the world, and their consumption of fish is also above average.

Trinidadian cookery is one of the most varied in the world and features dishes from all parts of the world: British, East Indian, Spanish, North American, African, European, Chinese and Creole. The national beverage is rum, of which the country produces some of the best in the world.

The daily per capita intake of food is 2,702 calories and 75.1 grams of protein (both below the recommended minimums of 2,600 calories and 65 grams of protein), 64 grams of fats and 424 grams of carbohydrates.

MEDIA & CULTURE

Four daily newspapers are published in the country, with an aggregate circulation of 177,100, or 149 per 1,000 inhabitants. Two non-dailies and 24 other periodicals are also published (including one in Chinese). Annual consumption of newsprint in 1981 was 5,100 tons, or 4,304 kg (9,490 lb) per 1,000 inhabitants.

The Trinidadian press has a long tradition of freedom. Its boldness and irreverence have occasionally alarmed the authorities, but few government efforts have been made to muzzle it or make it subservient to the ruling party's interests. Press censorship laws have been enforced only sporadically. Until 1974 Prime Minister Williams conducted a campaign against the two leading newspapers, the *Guardian* and the *Evening News*, both owned by Lord Roy Thomson, which resulted in his relinquishing ownership.

There is no national news agency. Reuters, UPI, AP and ADN have bureaus in Port of Spain.

There are about seven book publishers, all located in Port of Spain. Annual output in 1982 was 101 titles.

There are two radio networks: the National Broadcasting Service or Radio 610, with one FM and one medium-wave transmitter, broadcasts a home service in English for 119 hours a week; Radio Trinidad, a subsidiary of Radiodiffusion International of London, with one FM and one medium-wave transmitter, broadcasts for 130 hours a week. Of the total 13,505 annual broadcasting hours, 1,726 are devoted to information, 38 to education, 584 to culture, 751 to religion, 2,035 to commercials and 5,615 to entertainment. In 1982 there were 350,000 radio receivers in the country, or 291 per 1,000 inhabitants.

Television, introduced in 1961, is operated by the Trinidad & Tobago Television Company, in which the government holds 90% and the U.S. Columbia Broadcasting System, 10%. It is on the air for 73 hours a week. Of the total 4,525 annual television broadcasting hours, 356 are devoted to information, 702 to education, 95 to religion, 185 to commercials and 3,187 to entertainment. In 1982 there were 300,000 television sets in the country, or 250 per 1,000 inhabitants.

No feature films are produced locally and of the imported ones 50.4% come from the United States. There are 72 fixed cinemas with 57,000 seats, or 52.4 seats per 1,000 inhabitants.

The largest library is the Central Library in Port of Spain with 447,000 volumes. There is one university library and two other public libraries. Per capita, there are 385 volumes and 112 registered borrowers per 1,000 inhabitants.

There are three museums reporting an annual attendance of over 36,000.

SOCIAL WELFARE

The country's first broad-based social security program went into effect in 1972. Its benefits include an old-age pension at 65, or a reduced pension at 60 after completing 750 weeks of contributions; widows' pensions and stipends for children, sickness and maternity benefits up to 60% of the earnings; and blindness and funeral allowances. Employers pay two-thirds of the insurance costs, workers one-third. The welfare of the sugar industry workers is promoted by the Sugar Industry Welfare Committee. Unemployed workers receive some limited relief.

GLOSSARY

beke: a white Trinidadian born abroad.
Creole: person of African or European descent who belongs to the cultural mainstream, as opposed to East Indians, Chinese and others outside it.

CHRONOLOGY (from 1962)

1962— Following the breakup of the West Indies Federation, Trinidad & Tobago is granted independence with Eric Eustace Williams as prime minister.

1967— The United States returns the Chaguamaras Naval Base to Trinidad.

1970— Black-power inspired riots lead to declaration of a state of emergency; radical armed force units mutiny and try to march on the capital but are foiled by the coast guard.

1971— Opposition boycotts elections; as a result, the ruling People's National Movement wins all seats in the House of Representatives.

1976— Trinidad & Tobago adopts a republican constitution; Governor General Ellis Clarke becomes first president of the republic; in national elections People's National Movement gains 24 seats, thus retaining its solid majority.

1980— Tobago is granted internal autonomy and a parliament; in first elections to the Tobago Parliament separatist Democratic Action Congress wins 54% of the vote and eight of the 12 seats.

1981— Prime Minister Eric Williams dies... George Chambers is named premier.... In new legislative elections, PNM retains its majority in Parliament.

BIBLIOGRAPHY (from 1970)

Boyki, Roy, *Patterns of Progress: Trinidad & Tobago, Ten Years of Independence* (Port of Spain, 1972).

Brereton, Bridget, *A History of Modern Trinidad* (London, 1982).

La Guerre, John, *Calcutta to Caroni: The East Indians of Trinidad* (New York, 1974).

Lieber, Michael, *Street Scenes: Afro-American Culture in Urban Trinidad* (Cambridge, Mass., 1981).

Malik, Yogendra, *East Indians in Trinidad: A Study in Minority Politics* (London, 1971).

Naipaul, V.S., *Loss of El Dorado* (New York, 1970).

Niddrie, David L., *Tobago* (London, 1981).

Otley, C.R., *The Story of Tobago* (London, 1973)

Oxaal, Ivar, *Race & Revolutionary Consciousness: A Report on the 1970 Black Power Revolt in Trinidad* (Cambridge, Mass., 1971).

———, *Black Intellectuals and the Dilemmas of Race and Class in Trinidad* (Cambridge, Mass., 1982).

Ryan, Selwyn D., *Race & Nationalism in Trinidad & Tobago* (Toronto, 1972).

Szulc, Tad, *The United States and the Caribbean* (Englewood Cliffs, N.J., 1971).

Williams, Eric, *Inward Hunger* (London, 1972).

———, *History of the People of Trinidad & Tobago* (New York, 1970).

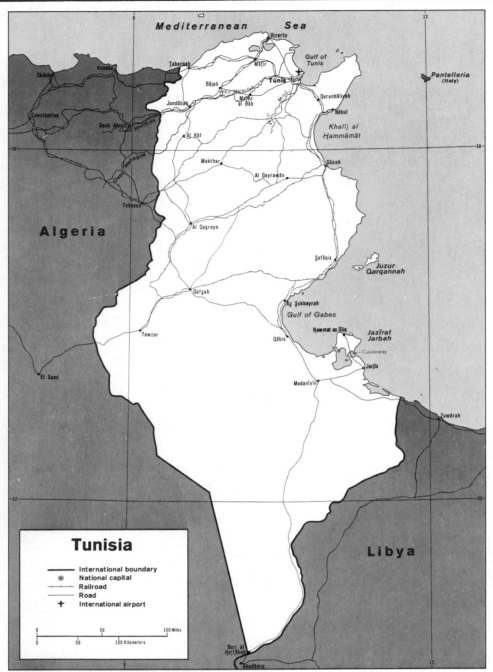

Mediterranean Sea

Skikda
Annaba
Constantine
Souk Ahras

ALGERIA

El Oued

Ţabarqah
Bizerte
Maţir
Gulf of Tunis
Bājah
Wādi Majardah
Tūnis
Jundūbah
Maʿtiz al Bāb
Milyān
Qurunbāliyah
Nābul
Al Kāf
Khalīj al Ḥammāmāt
Oued Mellegue
Makthar
Al Qayrawān
Sūsah
Tebessa
Al Qaşrayn
Şafāqis
Juzur Qarqannah
Qafşah
Aş Şukhayrah
Gulf of Gabes
Tawzar
Ḥawmat as Sūq
Jazīrat Jarbah
Qābis
Causeway
Jarjīs
Madanīyīn
Zuwārah

Pantelleria
(Italy)

LIBYA

Burj al Ḥaṭṭābah
Ghudāmis

Tunisia

—— International boundary
⊛ National capital
┼┼┼ Railroad
—— Road
✛ International airport

0   50   100 Miles
0   50   100 Kilometers

TUNISIA

LOCATION & AREA

Tunisia is the smallest and the easternmost of the three countries that together form the Maghreb of North Africa. It is bordered by Algeria to the west and Libya to the southeast. Because the country has not been completely surveyed, there is disagreement on the total area but official estimates place it at 164,150 sq km (63,378 sq mi). It has a total coastline of 1,028 km (639 mi) including offshore islands. The greatest distance north-south is 792 km (492 mi) and east-west is 350 km (217 mi).

The boundaries with Algeria and Libya, largely undemarcated, run 958 km (595 mi) and 459 km (285 mi) respectively.

Tunis is the capital and the commercial and intellectual center. It had a population of 596,654 in 1984. The other major urban centers are Sfax (231,911), Sousse (85,509), Ariana (98,665), Djerba(92,369), Bizerta (94,509), Kairouan (72,254), Bardo (65,669), La Goulette (61,609), Gabes (92,258), and Monastir (40,000).

Tunisia has three distinct physical regions. In the north are the mountains of the Tell Atlas and the Dorsale separated by the fertile valley of the Medjerda River. The Tell is generally divided into the coastal, central and high Tells. South of the Dorsale ridge is a wide expanse of barren plateau, which the Tunisians call the center. Its western half is known as the high steppe and its eastern half as the low steppe. Eastward the low steppes give way to the flat coastal plain of the Sahel between the Gulf of Hammamet and the Gulf of Gabes. Southward, beyond the extensive salt lakes dominated by the Chott el-Djerid, lies the country's vast Saharan desert sector.

Tunisia's only major river is the Medjerda, which rises in Algeria and flows into the Gulf of Tunis. It flows within the country for 367 km (228 mi). The Medjerda's seasonal variations in flow reduce its usefulness. At the peak of summer it almost dries up.

Only 1% of the land surface is more than 900 meters (3,000 ft) above sea level, while two-thirds of the country has an average elevation of only 183 meters (600 ft). The basins of the great shatts of the south are all below sea level.

WEATHER

Tunisia has two distinct Mediterranean-type seasons: a cool, rainy season from October to May and a warm, dry season from May to September. There are no proper autumn or spring transitional periods. The temperature in the Tell regions varies between 5°C and 26°C (41°F and 79°F) with a mean of 17.8°C (64°F), while southern Tunisia experiences desert conditions with temperatures rising to 40°C (104°F). Rainfall, concentrated during the winter months, is greatest to the north of the Dorsale where it exceeds 46 cm (16 in.) a year, reaching over 152 cm (60 in.) in the Kroumirie Mountains, which is the wettest area in North Africa. South of the Dorsale the rainfall is reduced to 20 to 40 cm (8 to 16 in.) annually. In the southern desert rainfall is less than 35 cm (10 in.) and occurs only at rare intervals.

POPULATION

The population of Tunisia was estimated at 7,352,000 in 1985 on the basis of the last official census in 1984 when the population was 6,966,173. The population is expected to reach 9.7 million by 2000 and 12.9 million by 2020. The annual rate of population growth in 2.4% for the population as a whole and 4.0% for the urban population.

The annual birthrate is 34.1 per 1,000 inhabitants.

The average density is 44 per sq km (93 per sq mi) for the country as a whole and 88 per sq km (155 per sq mi) of arable land.

At the 1984 census the national male/female ratio was 101 males to 100 females. The ratio may be skewed by the usual underreporting of females in Islamic countries. The population is young with 39.6% under 14 years of age; 56.1% were in the 15 to 64 age bracket and 4.3% were over 65. In 1980 the relative percentages were 45%, 51% and 4%.

The urban component of the population is estimated at 57%, with 25.6% of Tunisians living in cities over 100,000. Nearly 20% of the population lives in the capital city, Tunis. Nearly 43% of the population of Tunis live in slums and squatter settlements. There are three cities of over 100,000 inhabitants and eight cities of over 25,000 inhabitants.

Since the 1950s the net flow of migration has been outward. An estimated 225,000 Tunisians work abroad, most of them in France.

A drive to lower the birthrate began in 1960, and a national campaign was launched in 1966. The ban on contraceptives was lifted in 1961. The minimum age of marriage was raised to 20 for men and 17 for women, and from 1965 free and legal abortions were made available to all women having five or more children. Family planning centers are set up in each governorate and mobile birth control clinics tour rural

DEMOGRAPHIC INDICATORS (1984)	
Population, total (in 1,000)	7,352.0
Population ages (% of total)	
0-14	39.6
15-64	56.1
65+	4.3
Youth 15-24 (000)	1,558
Women ages 15-49 (000)	1,731
Dependency ratios	78.3
Child-woman ratios	667
Sex ratios (per 100 females)	101.2
Median ages (years)	19.5
Marriage Rate (per 1,000)	14.9
Divorce Rate (per 1,000)	0.9
Average size of Household	4.0
Decline in birthrate (%, 1965-83)	−29.3
Proportion of urban (%)	56.76
Population density (per sq. km.)	44
per hectare of arable land	0.75
Rates of growth (%)	2.41
Urban %	4.0
Rural %	0.5
Natural increase rates (per 1,000)	24.0
Crude birth rates (per 1,000)	34.1
Crude death rates (per 1,000)	10.1
Gross reproduction rates	2.40
Net reproduction rates	2.01
Total fertility rates	4.92
General fertility rates (per 1,000)	144
Life expectancy, males (years)	60.1
Life expectancy, females (years)	61.1
Life expectancy, total (years)	60.6
Population doubling time in years at current rate	30

areas. Nearly 12% of married women of child-bearing age are believed to practice contraception.

Legal equality between men and women is vigorously supported by the government. Equal rights in the areas of divorce and child custody are, for example, guaranteed by legislation. A small number of women serve in the government at all levels; for example there are two women cabinet ministers out of 26, there are at least five women jurists who have direct impact on cases they hear or review, and there are seven women in the 132-member Chamber of Deputies. Nevertheless, the centralized nature of decision making generally limits the influence of women at the national level. Despite the government's efforts, traditional practices in many cases keep women, especially in the rural areas, from full attainment of their legal rights.

ETHNIC COMPOSITION

Though Tunisians are the most completely Arabized people of the Maghreb, persons of pure Arab blood have never constituted more than 10% of the population. Most Tunisians belong to a mixed Berber-Arab stock. Because elements of the traditional Berber culture were adopted by the Arabs, the term Berber now properly refers to the few small, scattered communities that have completely rejected Arabization. The largest of these Berber communities are found in enclaves on the island of Djerba, in the Ksour Mountains, around Qafsah near the Libyan border, and in the mountains bordering Algeria. The ethnic composition of the Arab-Berber population has been only slightly affected as a result of Turkish, and later French, domination.

The country's Jewish population, numbering 60,000 in 1956, has declined to a few thousand. The French presence has been similarly eroded after the nationalization of the French estates. Europeans are estimated to number no more than 50,000. The main non-French foreign communities are Greek and Italian.

In terms of ethnic and linguistic homogeneity, Tunisia ranks 92nd among the nations of the world with 84% homogeneity (on an ascending scale on which North and South Korea are ranked 135th with 100% homogeneity and Tanzania 1st with 7% homogeneity).

LANGUAGE

Arabic is the official language, but French remains entrenched as the language most widely used by businessmen, by the media and even by the government itself. About 2 million persons are estimated to have some knowledge of French, of whom about 15% use it fluently. The native Berber language is no longer a written language and survives only in remote speech islands.

RELIGION

Islam in its Sunni form is the state religion, and Muslims form about 98% of the population. Both Christianity and Judaism are represented by small numbers. Carthage is a Roman Catholic archbishopric.

Despite the official status of Islam and the generally traditionalist character of Tunisian society, Bourguiba has initiated a number of reforms in areas where Muslim religious injunctions and observances seemed to conflict with the secular needs of modern Tunisia. He was successful in his efforts to abolish polygamy, the use of the veil, and Muslim inheritance laws, but he had to beat a retreat when he tried to abolish the fast of the Ramadan.

Although Islam is the state religion, the constitution guarantees religious freedom. Proselytizing for religions other than Islam is prohibited. There is no religious discrimination in private commerce and employment, although government employment is generally reserved for Muslims. The Jewish community worships freely and maintains indigenous organizations with official protection. Synagogues and Jewish-owned shops have been subject, however, to attack during periods of tension. In one incident two Jews and one Muslim policeman were killed when a second policeman guarding a synagogue on the island of Djerba opened fire on passersby. Throughout the tense aftermath of the Israeli raid October 1, 1985, on PLO headquarters outside Tunis, the government took extraordinary measures to protect the Jewish community. Expatriate Christians freely attend church services. Under an agreement between the Vatican and the Tunisian government, several Roman Catholic orders remain active. The Bahai's have been given government protection in the past but in November 1984 the government ordered them to cease all religious gatherings. Since that time the community has not been the object of any further restrictions, although the ban on its religious gatherings is still in effect.

COLONIAL EXPERIENCE

Tunisia was under French rule from 1881 to 1956. The French were the last of a series of invaders and masters who had ruled Tunisia since Roman times and their rule was the briefest and most intensive. Beside the French language, French legacies include the civil and criminal justice system and educational system. The French civil administrative structure, however, has been dismantled under Bourguiba. The manner in which the French left Tunisia and the subsequent expropriation of French estates and expulsion of French citizens have left a residue of bitterness on both sides. It was not until the late 1960s that relations between France and Tunisia were renormalized.

CONSTITUTION & GOVERNMENT

The constitution was proclaimed on June 1, 1959 by the National Constituent Assembly. It established a strong presidential form of government with a single political party, the Destourian (constitutional) Socialist Party. The president enjoys exceptionally wide powers while the National Assembly has only limited authority in theory and much less in practice. Destourian socialism is proclaimed as the philosophy of the nation. The ruling party, with its highly developed, all-pervasive organization, serves as the principal instrument of its propagation and implementation.

Tunisia has had only one president in its history as a republic: Habib Bourguiba, who was elected president for life in 1974. Under the constitution the president must be a Muslim of Tunisian descent, and he is elected by direct, universal and secret suffrage for five-year terms, and may be reelected for three consecutive terms. He holds supreme command of the armed forces and makes all civil and military appointments. He has the right to legislate by decree, to veto legislation passed by the National Assembly, and to dissolve the Assembly if his veto is overridden. In his role as chief executive he is assisted by a prime minister and cabinet directly responsible to him and not to the legislature. Cabinet members are advisers rather than directors of general policy. Most cabinet members are also deputies in the Assembly, and the more important ones also sit on the Political Bureau, the

ORGANIZATION OF TUNISIAN GOVERNMENT

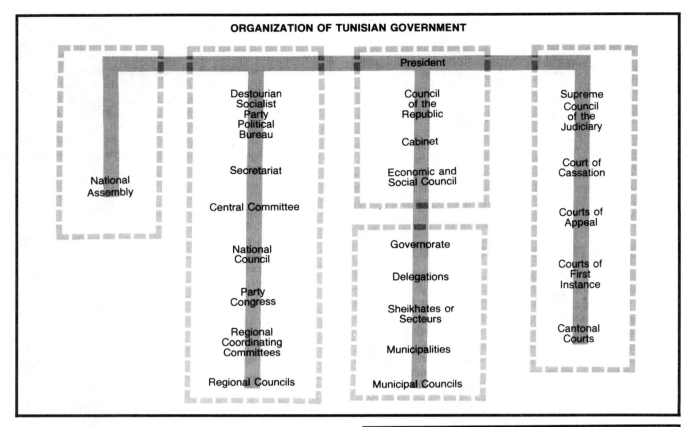

policy-making organ of the Destourian Socialist Party.

In 1966 a Council of the Republic was created that includes the president, cabinet and the Political Bureau of Destourian Socialist Party. Sessions of the Council are sometimes expanded to include regional governors and heads of state enterprises. The Council meets at the call of the president to review policy, coordinate executive and political programs, and formalize major decisions on national and foreign affairs.

Tunisians have voted in seven national elections since independence: 1956, 1959, 1964, 1969, 1974, 1979 and 1981. The electoral law of 1957 formalized election procedures. The franchise was extended to women in 1957. Candidates are restricted to a single official list drawn up by the Destourian Socialist Party. Voting is not fully secret as the ballot is filled out in a public room. Suffrage is universal over age 21.

Tunisia enjoyed prolonged political stability until January 1978 when strikes—partly inspired by political motives—led to violent rioting resulting in over 100 deaths. Apart from minor riots in 1967, 1968, 1970 and 1984, the country had been relatively free of internal strife and dissidence.

FREEDOM & HUMAN RIGHTS

In terms of civil and political rights, Tunisia is classified as a partly-free country with a negative rating of 6 in political rights and 5 in civil rights (on a descending scale where 1 denotes the highest and 7 the lowest in civil and political rights).

CABINET LIST (1985)	
President	Habib Bourguiba
Prime Minister	Mohamed Mzali
Special Adviser to the President	Habib Bourguiba, Jr.
Minister of Agriculture	Lassad Ben Osman
Minister of Culture	Bechir Ben Slama
Minister of Family & Women's Advancement	Fathia Mzali
Minister of Finance	Salah Ben Mbarka
Minister of Foreign Affairs	Beji Caid Essebsi
Minister of Higher Education & Scientific Research	Abdelaziz Ben Dhia
Minister of Information	Abderrazak Kefi
Minister of Interior (Acting)	Mohamed Mzali
Minister of Justice	Ridha Ben Ali
Minister of Natl. Defense	Slaheddine Baly
Minister of Natl. Economy	Rachid Sfar
Minister of Natl. Education	Mohamed Fredj Chedli
Minister of Plan	Ismail Khelil
Minister of Public Health	Souad Yacoubi
Minister of Public Works & Housing	Mohamed Sayah
Minister of Social Affairs	Mohamed Ennaceur
Minister of Tourism & Handicrafts	Ezzedine Chelbi
Minister of Transport & Communications	Brahim Khouaja
Minister of Youth & Sports	Mohammed Kraiem
Minister Attached to the President	Mongi Kooli
Minister Attached to the Prime Minister for Civil Service & Admin. Reform	Mezri Chekir

Tunisia has made impressive strides toward achieving a more open and responsive society. All political prisoners have been released and some exiles have been permitted to return. Efforts are being made by the prime minister, Mohamed Mzali, who is designated as Bourguiba's successor, to ensure probity in government. Trade union freedoms have been restored and students have national representation. Although cases of police abuse still occur authorities do not condone or acquiesce in such practices. Following the terrorist attack on Gafsa, 13 were executed by hanging but generally such executions are rare. Further, fair trials are the rule rather than the exception. The new government has also taken steps to enhance the independence of the judiciary. To this end, the office of the general prosecutor of the republic was abrogated in August 1980.

There has been a loosening of the controls over the media and over the rights of public assembly. The opposition and independent press has continued to voice constant, if guarded, criticism. There are no clear guidelines for editors and publishers, but those who go too far risk being closed down temporarily as happened to *Moujtamaa*, or permanently, as in the case of two Islamic magazines. Some radical groups have been denied the right to start publications. Many Western newspapers and periodicals are freely available, but from time to time an individual issue is not permitted on the newsstands. Foreign correspondents are occasionally denied entry, as in the case of *Le Monde*/UPI correspondent in 1980. Non-Muslims are generally tolerated, but are never employed in the government. Although the Destourian Socialist Party is the sole political organization, opposition groups are permitted de facto. As part of a liberalization program, several ministerial positions were reportedly offered to Social Democratic leaders.

The key political event of 1984 was the bread riots in January, an outgrowth of the economic downturn of the early eighties. The government rescinded its subsidies for bread and cereal products with the result that the price of those staples doubled. Riots quickly spread from the southern cities and eventually touched all major cities. On January 6, President Bourguiba restored the subsidies and the rioting ceased, but not before the army had been called out to impose order. There were substantial losses of property through looting, and it is officially estimated that 92 persons died. Widespread arrests and trials ensued in which judicial procedure was not always scrupulously observed. Later in the year the government pardoned many of those arrested during the riots.

The key political events of 1985 which had a bearing on human rights were the municipal elections, boycotted by the opposition, in May; the dramatic deterioration of relations between Tunisia and Libya following Libya's decision to expel the Tunisian workers, leading to the severing of diplomatic ties at the end of September, as well as increased measures by security forces as the government sought to counter possible Libyan subversion; and pressures on the main trade union movement. The Israeli raid on the headquarters of the PLO on October 1 led to tension throughout the country, especially in the Tunisian Jewish community. Tension between labor and government has posed problems, and continuing poor relations with Libya may bring further security measures.

CIVIL SERVICE

Employment in the civil service is regulated by the General Civil Servants' Law of 1968. Although political appointments are common at the highest levels, 70% of civil service vacancies are filled by competitive examinations, 20% by specialized examinations, and 10% by internal promotions. Lateral entry is encouraged for technicians and teachers. A National School of Administration was established in 1962. The Destourian Socialist Party holds a monopoly over recruitment to sensitive political posts. Choice posts in the national ministries and the governorates are filled only by dependable party members.

LOCAL GOVERNMENT

In 1956 the civil and military zones of the French Protectorate period were abolished and the country was divided into 13 wilayats, or governorates, each named after the major city in the area: Tunis, Beja, Bizerta, Nabeul, Gabes, Kairouan, Le Kef, Gafsa, Medenine, Kasserine, Jendouba, Sfax and Sousse. In a later reorganization the number of governorates was raised to 18 by adding Tunis-Sud, Siliana, Sidibou-Zid, Mahdia and Monastir. Each wilayat is headed by a wali. The wilayats are divided into delegations, or mutamadiyats, administered by a civil servant called a delegate. The smallest unit of local administration is the secteur, formerly known as sheikhat. There are now 136 delegations and 1,113 secteurs.

The civil administration has its parallel in the Destourian Socialist Party regional organization. Regional Committees of Coordination have been created at the governorate level composed of party members and presided over by the governors. The secretary general of the committee is also the governor's first assistant. The Committee's wide responsibilities include supervision of the cooperation between party and state apparatus. There is also a Regional Council composed of national organizations and Committees of Coordination. The regional councils examine the regional budgets and establish development priorities.

Municipal government, though less important in the political system, is more democratic. There are 94 municipalities, or balads, each with an elected council, or majlis al balad, and an elected major, or rais. Council members are elected by universal direct suffrage for three-year terms. The councils meet four times annually for a maximum of 40 days.

FOREIGN POLICY

The foreign policy of Tunisia has been consistently moderate and ideologically uncommitted, but this has not prevented a number of diplomatic crises. Relations with France were periodically strained in the first years of independence and came to a breaking point over the Tunisian demand for French evacuation of Bizerta in 1961 and the expropriation of French lands in 1964. The ties of history and culture, however, proved strong enough to prevent irreparable damage.

Though Maghrebian and Arab solidarity is a central consideration in Tunisian foreign policy, relations with Arab countries have had ups and downs. Relations with Morocco were suspended for four years following Tunisia's recognition of Mauritania. In 1963 Tunisia severed relations with Algeria, accusing the latter of conspiring against the Bourguiba regime. Algerian dissidents found asylum in Tunisia, and Bourguiba's enemies found asylum in Algeria. A border dispute with Algeria was settled in 1968. Relations with Libya were tense and acrimonious after an ill-conceived merger between the two countries, proposed by the Libyan leader Colonel Muammar el-QadHafi, was abandoned in 1974. On the Arab-Israeli conflict Bourguiba adopted a position radically different from other Arab leaders and his initiative resulted in bitter controversies. In 1965 he criticized Arab League policy on Palestine and advocated direct negotiations with Israel. This provoked severe attacks from the U.A.R. and other Arab states, most of which recalled their ambassadors. Syria and Iraq broke off diplomatic relations in 1965 and the U.A.R. in 1966. The rift widened when Tunisia refused to follow other Arab states in breaking off relations with West Germany, which had exchanged ambassadors with Israel. At this point Tunisia suspended her participation in the Arab League. The 1967 Arab-Israeli War brought Tunisia back to the Arab fold, but the reconciliation was short-lived. Relations were again suspended with Syria in 1968 and with Jordan in 1973, though they were resumed by 1974. From 1974 Tunisia's relations with its neighbors and other Arab states improved, and it once again began playing an active role in the Arab League. In 1979, after the expulsion of Egypt forced it to choose a new site, the Arab League established its headquarters at Tunis and subsequently, a Tunisian., Chedli Klibi, was named the secretary general. Many of the estimated 6,000 PLO fighters who had agreed in August 1982 to leave Lebanon were evacuated to Tunisia, while the PLO temporarily transferred its headquarters to Tunis. However, relations with Libya continued to worsen following allegations of Libyan complicity in the attack on Gafsa and the Libyan takeover of Chad.

In 1983, Tunisia signed a Maghreb Fraternity and Cooperation Treaty with Algeria to which Mauritania acceded later. Relations with Libya, although reestablished in 1982, remained troubled. Tunisia suspected Libyan involvement in the 1983 sabotage of a pipeline and the bread riots of 1984. Following charges that Tunisia had sanctioned transit for an anti-Qaddhafi group involved in a May 1984 gun battle in Tripoli, Mzali recalled his country's ambassador to Libya. In 1985 all Tunisian workers were expelled from Libya thus bringing the two country's relations to its lowest point in years.

Although fundamentally nonaligned, Tunisia is Western-oriented and has placed particular emphasis on good relations with the United States, which has provided substantial economic and technical assistance from 1957 through the Agency for International Development, from 1961 through the Peace Corps, and from 1966 through a military mission. Tunisia has developed cautious, but practical, relations with the Soviet Union and Eastern European governments. Tunisia recognized the People's Republic of China in 1964, but before relations became active Chinese diplomats in Tunis were asked to depart in 1967.

Tunisia and the United States are parties to 23 treaties and agreements covering agricultural commodities, cultural relations, defense, economic and technical cooperation, education, investment guaranties, Oceanographic research, Peace Corps, postal matters, scientific cooperation, telecommunications, and visas.

Tunisia is a founding member of the Organization of African Unity. It joined the Arab League in 1958 but boycotted its meetings from 1958 to 1961 and again in 1966. It became a member of the U.N. in 1956 and holds membership in 16 U.N. organizations and 26 other international organizations. Its share of the U.N. budget is 0.02%.

U.S. Ambassador in Tunis: Peter Sebastian
U.K. Ambassador in Tunis: James Adams
Tunisian Ambassador in Washington, D.C.: Habib Ben Yahya
Tunisian Ambassador in London: Sadek Bouzayen

PARLIAMENT

The National Assembly (Majlis al-Umma) is a unicameral body of 136 members elected by direct popular vote for five-year terms, coinciding with the presidential terms. Members of the governing Destourian Socialist Party have occupied all seats since 1959 under the one-party system. The Assembly holds two annual sessions of three months' duration each. The real legislative work is done by four permanent committees (Political, General Legislation, Economic and Financial, and Social and Cultural), which remain in constant session. The president of the republic has the right to propose legislation. He may also decree laws when the Assembly is not in session, but they must be ratified by the National Assembly.

Ultimate control of legislation rests with a body known as the Assembly Bureau, whose members are chosen by the Political Bureau of the Destourian Socialist Party. No item can be placed on the Assembly agenda until it has been discussed in committee. The

Assembly Bureau coordinates the work of the committees and decides which proposal shall pass out of committee to be considered in plenary sessions.

POLITICAL PARTIES

Tunisia is a one-party state in which all members of the legislature and executive belong to the Destourian Socialist Party (PSD). The party is descended from the Neo-Destour Party founded by Bourguiba in 1934. It was renamed the Destourian Socialist Party at its 1964 congress, the "Congress of Destiny," which endorsed a socialist program. It is moderately left-wing in tendency, but it has no rigid ideology and conceives its role more as a catalyst and mobilizer for social and economic development. Its lack of a clearly defined ideological base is more than made up for by its organizational strength derived in part from its affiliated syndicates: The General Union of Tunisian Workers, the General Union of Tunisian Students, the National Union of Tunisian Farmers, the Tunisian Union of Commerce, Industry and Handicrafts, and the National Union of Tunisian Women.

At the bottom of the party pyramid is the cellule, or local branch, of which there are two types: territorial and professional. The cellules are grouped into 14 regions, each with a coordinating committee elected by the membership but presided over by the governor and centrally appointed officials. At the national level, the supreme representative body is the party congress which meets every three years. In between congresses the National Council acts as a surrogate. Above the Congress is the Central Committee of 29 members of whom 15 are elected and the others nominated. At the apex of the pyramid is the Political Bureau of 15 to 20 members appointed by the president and responsible only to him. The Bureau determines state and party policy and draws up statutes for ratification by the National Assembly and the party congress. The president of the party is Habib Bourguiba, who holds the title of "Supreme Combatant." The prime minister is the secretary general. Although opposition parties are not legal, at least three groups are permitted to function unofficially as a de facto opposition: Mouvement des Democrates Socialistes (MDS), Mouvement de l'Unité Populaire (MUP) and Parti Communiste Tunisien (PCT).

The one-party system was ended in July 1981, when the PCT was officially recognized. President Bourguiba announced that any political group which gained 5% of votes cast in the legislative elections in November would also be recognized as a party. The PCT, the MUP and the MDS all protested against these conditions, and subsequently suffered an overwhelming defeat by the Front National, a joint front presented by the PSD and UGTT (Union Générale des Travailleurs Tunisiens), which gained 94.6% of votes cast in elections to the National Assembly. The three other groups complained of "electoral irregularities." The government also faced illegal opposition from the fundamentalist Islamic Tendency Movement (MIT).

ECONOMY

Tunisia is a lower-middle-income country, according to the U.N., with a modest resource base and a heavy dependence on foreign aid. The private sector predominates in Tunisia's free market economy.

Tunisia's overall economic performance during the 1970's and early 1980s was excellent. Tunisia's ability to maintain this growth has been largely due to favorable social and political conditions. Tunisia's well-educated, homogeneous population has an aptitude for industry and short-term sacrifice, as evidenced by recent private savings ratios of over 20% of GDP. Since independence in 1956, Tunisia under Bourguiba has enjoyed political stability. An experiment with the socialist planned-economy model of development during the 1960's proved unsuccessful, and the 1970's were characterized by the dismantling of many of the programs of this period.

Development planning began with the 10-Year Perspective Plan of 1961 and was continued with the three-year plan of 1962-64, and three successive four-year plans (1965-68, 1969-72 and 1973-76). The five-year plan of 1977-81 involved a total investment of $10 billion aimed at creating 60,000 new jobs and achieving an annual growth rate of 9.4%. The Sixth Development Plan (1982-86) envisaged total investment of D8,200 million, of which one-third was to be provided by foreign sources: Arab investment is being particularly encouraged, and several joint investment banks have been established. The plan aimed at self-sufficiency in food production and emphasized job creation. It envisaged an average annual increase of 6.3% in real GDP. Planning is administered by the Ministry of State for Planning and National Development.

Over 40% of development expenditure over the last decade has been financed by foreign aid. The United States has been the major donor, and assistance through 1983 has been over $967.5 million. Since 1967 other countries have also become donors, notably West Germany and the Persian Gulf States. World Bank loans to Tunisia through 1983 amounted to $1.2036 billion. EEC aid totaled $41 million through 1983. Soviet and East European aid has been on a more limited scale. During 1979-81 Tunisia received $257.3 million in bilateral and multilateral aid. Per capita aid received was $40.30.

BUDGET

The Tunisian fiscal year is the calendar year. The national budget is drawn up in two parts: an ordinary or administrative budget and a capital or investment budget. The capital budget is the equivalent of a yearly development plan.

Of current revenues, 14.7% comes from taxes on income, profit and capital gain, 8.9% from social security contributions, 21.0% from domestic taxes on goods and services, 27.3% from taxes on international trade and transactions, 4.4% from other taxes and

PRINCIPAL ECONOMIC INDICATORS

Gross National Product: $8.860 billion (1983)
  GNP Annual Growth Rate: 6.6% (1973-82)
  Per Capita GNP: $1,290 (1983)
  Per Capita GNP Annual Growth Rate: 4.1% (1973-82)

Gross Domestic Product: D6.235 billion (1984)
  GDP at 1980 prices D3.888 billion
  DGP Deflator (1980=100) 142.0
  GDP Annual Growth Rate: 6.0% (1973-82)
  Per Capita GDP: D848 (1984)
  Per Capita GDP Annual Growth Rate: 5.0% (1970-81)

Income Distribution: 6% of the national income is received by
  the lowest 20%; 17% of the national income is received by
  the top 5%.

Percentage of Population in Absolute Poverty: 20% urban;
  15% rural

Wholesale Price Index (1980=100): Domestic Supply 156
  (December 1984)

Imported Goods: 149 (December 1984)
  Average Annual Rate of Inflation 1973-83: 9.4%

Consumer Price Index (1970=100)
  All Items: 190.3 (December 1984)
  Food: 202.1 (December 1984)

Money Supply: D1.717 billion (March 1985)
  Reserve Money: D649 million (April 1985)

Currency in Circulation: D573.0 million (1984)

International Reserves: $406.3 million of which foreign ex-
  change reserves were $375.6 million (1984)

BALANCE OF PAYMENTS (1983)
(million $)

Current Account Balance	−693
Merchandise Exports	1,492
Merchandise Imports	−2,669
Trade Balance	−1,178
Other Goods, Services & Income	+1,095
Other Goods, Services & Income	−998
Other Goods, Services & Income Net	97
Private Unrequited Transfers	346
Official Unrequited Transfers	41
Capital Other Than Reserves	448
Net Errors & Omissions	301
Total (Lines 1,10 and 11)	56
Counterpart Items	−95
Total (Lines 12 and 13)	−39
Liabilities Constituting Foreign Authorities Reserves	—
Total Change in Reserves	39

GROSS DOMESTIC PRODUCT BY ECONOMIC ACTIVITY
(1970-81)

	%	Rate of Change %
Agriculture	18.3	4.1
Mining	10.5	3.9
Manufacturing	12.3	11.7
Construction	7.5	10.0
Electricity, Gas & Water	1.8	8.5
Transport & Communications	6.0	7.9
Trade & Finance	—	—
Public Administration & Defense	12.8	8.6
Other Branches	30.8	6.9

23.6% from current non-tax revenues. Current revenues represented 33.9% of GNP.

Of current expenditures, 9.63% goes to general
public services, 8.35% to defense, 15.29% to education,
7.65% to health, 8.26% to social security and welfare,
5.38% to housing, 2.50% to other community and social services, 33.95% to economic services, 17.03% to
agriculture, 1.51% to roads, 5.04% to other transportation and communications and 14.76% to other functions. Current expenditures represented 36.9% of
GNP and overall deficit 5.1% of GNP.

In 1984 government consumption was D1.030 billion and private consumption D3.940 billion. During
1973-83 public consumption grew by 8.1% and private
consumption by 7.2%.

In 1983 total outstanding disbursed external debt
was $3.427 billion of which $2.518 billion was owed to
official creditors and $908.2 million to private credi-
tors. Total debt service was $598.1 million of which
$403.5 million was repayment of principal and $194.6
million interest. Total external debt represented
127.7% of export revenues and 42.4% of GNP. Total
debt service represented 22.3% of export revenues
and 7.4% of GNP.

CURRENT BUDGET
(estimates in '000 dinars)

Ministry	1981	1982
Prime Minister's office	7,050	9,254
Plan and finance	19,390	22,721
Education	142,220	162,400
Defense	60,928	70,000
Public health	69,300	83,200
Interior	56,846	64,000
Agriculture	50,052	56,565
Social affairs	15,459	17,334
Youth & sports	12,900	15,000
Communications & transport	7,531	9,220
Information and cultural affairs	13,961	15,356
Justice	7,801	9,030
TOTAL (incl. others)	677,800	797,000

Capital Budget ('000 dinars): 554,000 in 1981; 645,000 in
1982.

FINANCE

The Tunisian unit of currency is the dinar divided
into 1,000 millemes. Coins are issued in denominations of 1, 2, 5, 10, 20, 50, 100 and 500 millemes and
notes in denominations of 500 millemes, and 1, 5 and
10 dinars. The dinar is linked to the French franc, and
thus its exchange rate with the dollar varies widely
and is fixed from month to month. In August 1985 the
exchange rate was $1 = D0.824. The sterling ex-
change rate on this basis was £1=D1.0015.

The Tunisian banking system consists of a central
bank (Banque Centrale de Tunisie) with assets of 355
million dinars, seven major domestic commercial
banks and four major foreign banks. In the absence
of a well developed money market, the Banque de

Developpement de l'Economie de la Tunisie is the main source of long-term and equity finance. The post office checking and savings service provides an important source of funds for the state. In 1984 the commercial banks had reserves of D68.0 million and demand deposits of D1.107 billion. The discount rate was 7.0% in 1982.

GROWTH PROFILE Annual Growth Rates (%)	
Population 1980-2000	2.2
Birthrate 1965-83	–29.3
Deathrate 1965-83	–48.6
Urban Population 1973-83	3.7
Labor Force 1980-2000	2.9
GNP 1973-82	6.6
GNP per capita 1973-82	4.1
GDP 1973-83	6.0
GDP per capita 1973-83	5.0
Consumer Prices 1970-81	6.3
Wholesale Prices 1970-81	7.3
Inflation 1973-83	9.4
Agriculture 1973-83	1.6
Manufacturing 1973-83	11.1
Industry 1973-83	8.1
Services 1973-83	6.3
Mining 1970-81	3.9
Construction 1970-81	10.0
Electricity 1970-81	8.5
Transportation 1970-81	7.9
Trade	—
Public Administration & Defense 1970-81	8.6
Export Price Index 1975-81	14.3
Import Price Index 1975-81	12.9
Terms of Trade 1975-81	1.1
Exports 1973-83	0.2
Imports 1973-83	5.3
Public Consumption 1973-83	8.1
Private Consumption 1973-83	7.2
Gross Domestic Investment 1973-83	9.5
Energy Consumption 1973-83	8.2
Energy Production 1973-83	4.3

AGRICULTURE

Of the total land area of 16,415,000 hectares (40,561,465 acres), about 47% is prime agricultural land, or 1.21 hectares (3 acres) per capita. The agricultural production index in 1982 was 109 (based on 1974-76=100), the index of food production was 109 and per capita food production 87. The agricultural sector employs 35% of the labor force. The value added in agriculture in 1983 was $1,191 billion.

Agriculture normally contributes 14% of the gross domestic product, but this may vary by as much as 10% depending on the rainfall. In a cycle of five years the yield is excellent in one year, fair in two years, and poor in the remaining two. In good years the country is self-sufficient in food production, in poor years it imports up to 40% of its food needs. In 1983 it imported 1,131,000 tons of cereals. Exports of agricultural commodities account for 50 to 60% of the country's export earnings in normal years. The annual rate of

growth of the agricultural sector during 1973-83 was 1.6%.

The country's prime grain land is the Medjerda Valley. Vineyards cover the northeast and olives the eastern plateau region. The oases of the southern desert produce dates while the central hinterland produces esparto grass. Although intensive and modern farming is practiced in the Tell, Cape Bon, Medjerda and northern Sahel, traditional agriculture predominates. Over 113,000 hectares (279,229 acres) are irrigated, and a number of dams are planned, including the Sidi Salem dam. Some 35,500 tractors and 3,600 harvester-threshers were in use in 1982. Annual consumption of fertilizers in 1982 was 83,900 tons, or 16.8 kg (37 lb) per arable hectare.

During the period 1958 to 1964, the government acquired or expropriated 637,380 hectares (1,575,000 acres) of French-owned land. By a comprehensive land reform act in 1963, large collective agricultural units of 500 to 1,000 hectares (1,235 to 2,471 acres) were formed through consolidation of expropriated estates and small peasant holdings. State control over these cooperatives was exercised through the Regional Unions of Cooperatives, the Regional Commission for Agricultural Cooperation, and the Regional Development Union. By the Code of Real Property Rights, fragmentation of property by traditional Muslim laws of inheritance was prohibited. By 1969 the system of cooperatives was extended to the entire cultivated area. But following the downfall of the minister for planning, Ahmed Ben Salah, in 1969, the system was modified and farmers were given a chance to opt out of the state system. The former French estates, however, remained under state control, some as cooperatives, others as agrocombinats (collective farms on state land). By 1975 half the cultivated area was back in private hands, while about 849,606 hectares (2.1 million acres) were worked by production cooperatives and the remainder was farmed by state or religious institutions. Mixed cooperatives and service cooperatives have been organized outside the northern regions. The average size of smallholdings was 10.1 hectares (25 acres).

PRINCIPAL CROP PRODUCTION (1982) (000 metric tons)	
Wheat	1,000
Barley	300
Potatoes	140
Olives	410
Tomatoes	380
Chillies & peppers	125
Onions	23
Water melons & melons	283
Grapes	100
Dates	52
Sugar beet	104
Apricots	30
Citrus fruit	146
Almonds	38
Tobacco	5

Tunisia's livestock population in 1982 consisted of 600,000 cattle, 52,000 horses, 206,000 asses, 179,000 camels, 4,500,000 sheep, 800,000 goats and 14,000,000 chickens. Some 70,000 hectares (173,000 acres) of land are set apart for grazing.

Of the 889,769 hectares (2.2 million acres) classified as domain forests, only 299,842 hectares (741,000 acres) are wooded. The total roundwood production in 1982 was 2.634 million cubic meters (93 million cubic ft).

Fishing is an important industry and employs 14,000 people and over 4,000 boats, with Sfax as the main center. The total fish catch in 1982 was 62,800 metric tons.

Agricultural credit is provided by the National Agricultural Bank and the Mutual Credit Program.

INDUSTRY

Of all the sectors of the economy, manufacturing is the fastest-growing with a growth rate of 11.1% during 1973-83. It contributes 14% to the GDP and employs 21.7% of the labor force. The index of industrial production in 1982 was 107 (1975=100). The value added in manufacturing was $841 million, of which agro-based products accounted for 22%, textiles for 12%, chemicals for 16% and machinery and transport equipment for 13%.

Over half the industry is located in Tunis. Manufacturing is concentrated on the processing of raw materials, particularly foodstuffs, but has recently diversified with substantial production of textiles, cellulose, paper and pulp, cement, chemicals, automobiles, steel, ceramics, glass and electrical goods. In 1980 there were 1,408 manufacturing establishments, each employing over five workers.

The government takes an active role in fostering industry through direct investment and through incentive programs. The public sector is relatively small and is restricted to heavy industry, automobile assembly and public utilities. As part of the government's drive to encourage foreign investment in export-oriented industries, a law was enacted in 1972 offering extremely generous concessions to foreign companies setting up factories in Tunisia producing export goods. The law provides a 10-year exemption from corporation tax with a 10% reduction in tax for the second 10-year period. The law also waives tax on the rental value of the premises, customs duties, and turnover tax for a period of 20 years. It permits complete freedom to recruit foreign personnel and to repatriate earnings. The Agence de Promotion des Investissement oversees foreign investment. Current investment policy represents a shift in emphasis from larger, capital-intensive projects to the smaller, medium-sized projects which create more jobs per dinar invested.

Industry is highly concentrated in Tunis. About one-half the total number of manufacturing establishments and the same proportion of total industrial employment are located in the city. It accounts for an even larger percentage of total industrial production. In some branches of industry, as many as 80% of the factories are located in Tunis. In other cities, there is a concentration of factories manufacturing particular products, such as carpets in Kairouan, ceramics in Nabul and textiles in Monastir. The government is making an effort to obtain more even distribution of manufacturing by locating many of the new industrial sites in the smaller cities of the interior, and by providing tax incentives for projects that are away from Tunis and the coast.

Handicrafts hold an important place in the economy because of the large number of people working their traditional trades. Exposure to different cultures and customs over the centuries has developed a distinctive and widespread handicrafts industry. Handicrafts can be divided into two sectors: the utilitarian and the artistic. The former is rapidly being made obsolete by imports and by the cheaper products of the modern domestic manufacturing sector. The latter is an important part of the economy, which government planners seek to preserve and promote for tourist and export purposes. More than 100,000 people depend on handicrafts to provide for all or part of their livelihood. The major handicraft products include textiles, rugs and carpets, pottery and ceramics, leather goods, brasswork, copperware, jewelry, embroidery and wrought iron. A National Handicraft Office supervises the quality of products for export, promotes marketing at home and abroad, and helps form cooperatives of craftsmen. Dozens of cooperatives comprising several thousand members have been formed to buy raw materials and sell the finished products. They help alleviate shortages of credit and supplies, which traditionally threaten the artisans.

Industrial credit is provided by Banque de Developpement de l'Economie de la Tunisie.

ENERGY

Tunisia's total energy production in 1982 was the equivalent of 8.144 million tons of coal and consumption was equivalent to 4.309 million tons of coal, or 642 kg (1,416 lb) per capita. Total electric power production in 1984 was 3.271 billion kwh, and per capita consumption was 454 kwh. The annual growth rates during 1973-83 were 4.3% for energy production and 8.2% energy consumption. Energy imports accounts for 31% of all merchandise imports. Apparent per capita consumption of gasoline is 23 gallons per year.

In 1964 oil was found at El Borma in the south near the Algerian border. Recoverable reserves nationwide are estimated at 1.820 billion barrels sufficient to last 43 years at current rates of production. The field went into production in 1965, and output reached 42 million barrels in 1983. Crude oil accounts for 42.2% of export revenues.

Small amounts of natural gas are produced, mainly in the Cape Bon area. In 1975 discoveries of gas were made near the Kerkenna Islands. Tunisia's total reserves of natural gas are estimated at 118 billion cubic meters (4.167 trillion cubic ft). Annual natural gas output in 1983 was 476 million cubic meters (16.809 billion cubic ft).

The state-owned Bizerta refinery and Gabes refinery have a throughput of 34,000 barrels per day.

Oil exploration and production is a state monopoly controlled by Societe Recherches et d'Exploitations des Petroles en Tunisie.

Crude petroleum is produced mainly from two fields. The El Borma field in southwestern Tunisia near the Algerian border has been exploited since 1966 and is operated by the Société Italo-Tunisian d'Exploitation Pétrolière (SIETP). The Ashtart field, offshore in the Gulf of Gabes has been exploited since 1974 and operated by the Franco-Tunisian firm, Entreprise Tunisienne d'Activities Pétrolières (ETAP). The Tunisian government took 50% participation in both firms under an agreement concluded with the companies in January 1978. Tunisia's mainland oil fields are dwarfed by the deposits believed to exist offshore adjacent to Libyan waters in the Gulf of Gabes. However, further exploration of this area has been halted due to a border dispute with Libya. Most of Tunisia's petroleum production, which is light-density crude oil, is exported. To meet domestic requirements, lower-quality heavy crude oil is imported, mainly from Saudi Arabia and Iraq.

LABOR

Of the total population about 25.3%, or 1.9 million, are economically active. Women constitute about 22.3% of the labor force.

By economic sector, the 1982 labor force was engaged as follows: Agriculture, forestry, hunting and fishing, 32.4%; mining and quarrying, 0.9%; manufacturing, 21.7%; construction, 10.8%; public utilities, 0.6%; commerce, 8.9%; transport and communications, 3.8%; finance and services, 16.8%; and other 4.0%.

Shortly after independence, Tunisia adopted an enlightened labor code which provided for standards of work, hours of work, and a minimum wage. These conditions apply directly to some 60% of the labor force who work in government jobs, parastatal companies, and in professions such as teaching. Another 20% of the labor force who work in agriculture and the private sector are indirectly affected by these provisions. About 20% of the work force, principally domestics and migrant agricultural labor, are not covered by the labor code. Tunisian labor legislation consists of the April 1966 Labor Code, which defines basic employment conditions, and a number of collective bargaining agreements which have been signed to date. These include the five-year Social Contract concluded between the government and labor in January 1977. This covers productivity norms, the indexing of wages to the cost of living, and improvements in working conditions. Legislation provides for a 40-to 48-hour week, depending upon the occupation. The working day must not exceed 10 hours. Overtime pay for those who work a 48-hour week is 70%. For those on a 40-hour week, the premium is 25% up to 48 hours total and 50% over 48 hours. Heads of families are allowed one day of leave for a birth in the family. Mothers are granted maternity leave of four to six weeks. A worker is allowed a 24-hour rest period each week, generally taken on a Friday, Saturday, or Sunday. There are a minimum of four paid holidays: May 1, June 1, July 25, and October 15. Leave is given for other holidays. Social security benefits are administered by the National Social Security Fund. The system provides medical insurance and family allowances for workers' children. The basic labor costs to the employer over and above pay for time worked and supplementary bonuses and allowances amount to 35.5% of payroll. These costs include such things as contributions to the social security fund, paid annual leave and national holidays, and vocational training tax. Tunisia's minimum wage system is based on the French pattern for industry (Salarie Minimum Interprofessional Garanti, SMIG) and agriculture (Salarie Minimum Agricole Granti, SMAG). The base minimum wage in the industrial sector is D96 (approximately $125) for a 40-hour week. In agriculture the base minimum wage is D76 (approximately $100) per week, although this only directly applies to some 3% of the agricultural work force. Employees who are covered under the minimum wage also by law receive other benefits including social security, disability and health insurance, transportation and family allowances, and paid leave. The labor code also requires employers to pay overtime, a night work differential, and holiday pay. In the major urban areas a minimum wage employee with a family of four will net between D120-150 (approximately $160-$200) per month when allowances (nontaxable) are included. Child labor is prohibited prior to 16 years of age. Moreover, these provisions are widely enforced through an oversight program directed by the Labor Ministry. Private sector wages are reviewed annually and revised when prices rise by more than 5%.

Employment creation in recent years has fallen 25% short of planned levels. In a country where the official unemployment rate is 16%, and where many observers place the true rate even higher at 25%, this is a source of major concern to the government. While much of the pressure on the labor market during the 1977-79 period has been relieved by a sharp increase in emigration, mainly to Libya, the 1985 expulsion of Tunisian workers from Libya has placed this safety valve in severe jeopardy.

An estimated 225,000 Tunisian workers work abroad. It is estimated that a minimum of 316,000 Tunisians are overseas, of whom around 200,000 are working males. The estimates by country are: France, 183,000; Libya, 64,000; Algeria, 27,000; West Germany, 18,000; Belgium, 12,000; all others, 12,000. The government promotes emigration through its Central Emigration Service. The hiring of foreign workers by Tunisian employers is permitted though under stringent conditions. Such workers have to obtain residence permits which are valid only for a maximum of two years.

The major representative of organized labor in Tunisia is Union Generale Tunisienne du Travail (UGTT), which is affiliated to the Destourian Socialist Party. The UGTT claims a total membership of 350,000, or about 20% of the labor force, divided ino 11 federations. A second federation, the National Federation of Tunisian Workers, was formed in 1984 by UGTT dissidents. Agricultural workers, though constituting 46% of the labor force, have been highly resistant to unionization. The power of the UGTT in the economy is limited because of its function as an organ of the government party and because wages are fixed not by collective bargaining but by government decree. Strikes, almost nonexistent until 1970, have increased over recent years. In January 1978, the UGTT called a general strike to press demands for higher wages. The strike was perfectly legal but in the subsequent riots and clashes between the police and the workers, described as the worst in Tunisian history, more than 46 persons were killed and hundreds injured. Tunisian officials feared that the strike was inspired by pro-Libya forces within the country. All but one member of the UGTT's Executive Board, virtually the entire national leadership of the labor movement, were jailed.

The government imposed a public sector wage freeze in 1984 and 1985. The UGTT strongly opposed this policy and salary negotiations remained at an impasse, adding to internal social tensions. To combat these tensions the government has followed a carrot and stick approach, alternately negotiating and settling with some unions and then, where strikes were still threatened, imposing temporary restrictions on specific union activity. Current restrictions include a ban on workplace meetings and a suspension of dues checkoff privileges for public sector employees. The period of rising tensions over Libya's expulsion of Tunisian workers further exacerbated government-UGTT relations when the labor union refused to halt strikes for 90 days in support of the government. In reaction, the government launched a media campaign to discredit the UGTT Secretary General and called on ruling party members within the union to take over the leadership of all UGTT locals.

Tunisian security forces on October 31, 1985 occupied major trade union offices in Tunis and elsewhere throughout the country and arrested trade union members. Subsequent strikes in Gafsa, Gabes, and Sfax led to confrontations with the police. On November 10 Habib Achour, the UGTT Secretary General, was placed under de facto house arrest. No court order accompanied the action. While many of the union officials and members who had been detained were released, police rounded up 30-40 Islamic leaders on the university campus and sent them to perform their required one year military service with the Saharan Development Brigade.

In a communique issued on December 5, Labor Minister Noureddine Hached and the UGTT Executive Board agreed that the position of the trade union would be normalized under the supervision of the UGTT Executive Board, that those union members who had continued under detention would be released, that those expelled from work for union activities would be reinstated, and that government-UGTT negotiations would resume. On the same day, the press reported that Achour had been fired as UGTT Secretary General and that Sadok Allouche had been elected to succeed him. After 7 weeks of house arrest Achour was convicted on January 1 of usurping union authority at a cooperative in Sfax and sentenced to one year in prison. At the end of 1985, it was estimated that between 20 and 25 trade unionists were still in jail.

On January 19, 1977, a Social Pact was concluded by the government, the Political Bureau of the Party, the Executive Bureau of the UGTT, the UTICA and the UNA. The 5-year agreement covered productivity, improvements in living and working conditions, indexing of wages to the cost of living, production norms, subsidies of basic food items, remuneration of public employees, annual reviews of salaries in the private sector, and included a provision that collective agreements which expired and which the social partners agreed to revise will not entail new costs for the enterprise during 1977-81.

The Social Pact became a thorny issue between the then union leaders and the government in a period of growing confrontation over political issues in late 1977. The Pact was subsequently repudiated by the UGTT but after a change of leadership in early 1978, the union reaffirmed its support for the Pact.

FOREIGN COMMERCE

The foreign commerce of Tunisia consisted in 1984 of exports of $1.798 billion and imports of $3.182 billion, giving an unfavorable trade balance of $1.384 billion. Of the imports, machinery and transportation vehicles constituted 4.9%, chemicals and pharmaceuticals 3.4%, textiles 3.2%, crude oil 2.5% and wheat 2.3%. Of the exports, crude oil constituted 42.2%, clothing 12.6%, phosphoric acid 5.9%, olive oil 4.9%, crude phosphates 1.9% and dates 0.7%.

The major import sources are: France 25.9%, Italy 14.8%, West Germany 11.5%, the United States 7.8%, the Netherlands 5.1% and Spain 4.1%. The major export destinations are: the United States 23.0%, France 19.3%, Italy 16.2%, West Germany 10.4%, Greece 2.7% and the Netherlands 2.4%. The import price index in 1981 was 189 baseu on 1975=100. In the same year and on the same basis, the export price index was 198 and the terms of trade (export price divided by import price × 100) was 104.

An international fair is held annually at Tunis.

FOREIGN TRADE INDICATORS (1984)

Annual Growth Rate, Imports:	5.3% (1973-83)
Annual Growth Rate, Exports:	0.2% (1973-83)
Ratio of Exports to Imports:	36:64
Exports per capita:	$244
Imports per capita:	$433
Balance of Trade:	−$1.384 billion
Ratio of International Reserves to Imports (in months)	2.1
Exports as % of GDP:	34.2
Imports as % of GDP:	40.3
Value of Manufactured Exports:	$835 million
Commodity Concentration:	81.0%

Direction of Trade (%)

	Imports	Exports
EEC	63.8	71.7
U.S.	5.9	14.5
Industrialized Market Economies	79.9	74.8
East European Economies	3.9	0.9
High Income Oil Exporters	2.8	5.6
Developing Economies	13.9	17.9

Composition of Trade (%)

	Imports	Exports
Food	14.3	9.2
Agricultural Raw Materials	3.1	0.7
Fuels	20.5	54.0
Ores & Minerals	9.4	2.8
Manufactured Goods	52.5	33.2
of which Chemicals	6.7	12.8
of which Machinery	27.2	2.3

TRANSPORTATION & COMMUNICATIONS

Rail transport is controlled by the state-owned Societe Nationale des Chemins de Fer Tunisiens. The total length of track is 2,089 km (1,298 mi). In addition, there is an electrified line from Tunis to La Marsa. In 1983 rail traffic consisted of 802 million passenger-kilometers and 1.896 billion net-ton kilometers of freight.

There is a 797-km (495-mi) crude oil pipeline, an 86 km (53 mi) refined products pipeline and a 742-km (461 mi) natural gas pipeline from El Borma oilfield to the port of La Skhirra.

The only indigenous shipping company is the Compagnie Tunisienne de Navigation in which the state holds controlling shares. Tunisia has four major ports: Tunis-La Goulette, Bizerta, Sousse and Sfax. There is a special petroleum port at La Skhirra and a new port complex at Gabes. Total seaborne traffic at these ports in 1982 was 13,764,000 metric tons.

In 1984 there were 17,762 km (11,030 mi) of roads in the country, of which 9,970 km (6,191 mi) were paved. The state-owned Societe Nationale des Transports has a monopoly of bus transport and runs 85 local and 169 long-distance domestic and international bus routes. The total number of passenger cars in the country in 1982 was 141,185, and commercial vehicles totalled 147,571. Vehicle ownership was 19 per 1,000 inhabitants.

The national airline is Tunis Air, which has a fleet of 16 aircraft and flies to 12 countries. It carried 1,729,000 passengers and flew 23.753 million km (14.75 million mi) in 1982. There are four international airports, of which Tunis-Carthage is the most important. The others are Monastir-Skanes, Djerba-Mellita and Tozeur-Nefta. The country had a total of 28 airfields, of which 25 are usable, 12 with permanent-surface runways, and five with runways over 2,500 m (8,000 ft).

In 1984 Tunisia had 188,500 telephones, or 3.0 per 100 inhabitants.

In 1982 over 403 post offices handled 144,355,000 pieces of mail, and 628,000 telegrams. The volume of mail per capita was 19.6 pieces. There are 1,828 telex subscriber lines.

In 1983 1,355,000 tourists visited Tunisia, of whom 10,300 were from the United States, 150,800 from the United Kingdom, 378,100 from France, 327,900 from West Germany, 36,400 from Belgium, 71,600 from Italy and 36,400 from the Netherlands. Total tourist receipts were $577 million and expenditures by nationals abroad $102 million. There are 63,000 hotel beds and the average length of stay is 8.3 days.

MINING

Tunisia is poorly endowed with natural resources except for substantial deposits of phosphates. The share of mining in the GDP is 10.5%. Phosphate is produced and marketed — largely for export — by a public enterprise, the Compagnie des Phosphates de Gafsa (CPG). Seven out of the eight major phosphate mines in Tunisia are located in the south central area of the country in the vicinity of the city of Gafsa. All but one are underground mines. Exploitation of a new mine with large phosphate deposits at Sehib, in the south region, has recently begun. The mines are operated by the CPG. Tunisia is the world's fourth largest exporter of phosphate rock and a major world supplier of derivative fertilizers.

The six main phosphate centers are owned by the government but are worked by concessionaires. Mineral production in 1983 consisted of 5,924,000 metric tons of phosphate and 314,000 metric tons of iron ore.

DEFENSE

The defense structure is headed by the president of the republic who is also the commander in chief of the armed forces.

Manpower is provided by conscription at age 20 followed by one year of active service.

The strength of the armed forces is 35,100, excluding para-military forces, or 4.0 military personnel per 1,000 civilians.

ARMY:

Personnel: 30,000 (Reserves: 25,000)
Organization: 2 combined armored brigades; 1 Sahara brigade; 1 parachute commando brigade; 2 ar-

mored reconnaissance regiments; 3 field and 2 AA artillery regiments; 1 engineer regiment

Equipment: 68 heavy tanks; 50 light tanks; 60 armored combat vehicles; 68 armored personnel carriers; 6 guns/howitzers; 77 howitzers; mortars; antitank guns; rocket launchers; antitank guided weapons; 45 air defense guns; SAM

NAVY:

Personnel: 2,600 (Reserves: 3,000)
Naval Bases: Tunis and Bizerte
Units: 1 frigate; 2 fast attack craft; 17 patrol craft

AIR FORCE:

Personnel: 2,500 (Reserves: 2,500)
Organization & Equipment: 20 combat aircraft; 12 fighter ground attack; 1 counterinsurgency squadron; 2 transport; 4 liaison; 48 trainers; 1 helicopter wing
Air Bases: Tunis (El Aouina), Monastir, Bizerte, Gabes, Sfax and Djerba

The annual military budget in 1985 was $402.036 million, or 2.9% of the GNP and 9.0% of the national budget, $35 per capita, $12,448 per soldier and $2,201 per sq km of national territory.

From 1960 the United States has been the major supplier of arms. Between 1966 and 1983 military aid from the United States consisted of $319.5 million in loans and $70.7 million in grants. A formal U.S. Military Assistance and Advisory Group was established in Tunis in 1968. Arms purcases abroad during 1973-83 totaled $490 million, of which $110 million came from the United States and $130 million from France.

Tunisia has no defense-related industries.

EDUCATION

Tunisia has a literacy rate of 47.4% (61.2% for males and 33.7% for females). Of the population over 25, 96.1% have had no schooling, 7.1% have completed the first level, 3.0% have completed the second level and 0.7% have completed post-secondary training.

Schooling is free but neither universal nor compulsory in primary and secondary schools. In 1982 the gross student enrollment was 89% in the 6-11 age group and 29% in the 12-18 age group. The percentage of girls was 43% in primary schools, 38% in the secondary schools and 33% at the university level. The teacher-pupil ratio was 1:36 in primary classes, 1:20 in secondary classes and 1:8 in post-secondary classes.

The academic year runs from October 1 through June 30. The language of instruction is Arabic for the first two years in primary school. Thereafter French and Arabic are both used.

The school system is organized in three levels: elementary, intermediate or secondary, and higher. Since 1958 the traditional Koranic, or Zitouna, schools have been incorporated within the secular school system. The elementary level consists of six years. The secondary level is divided into an academically oriented seven-year program of a three-year lower cycle and a four-year upper cycle, and an intermediate trade-oriented three-year program, which is terminal. The secondary level consists of six tracks of which four are general, one is commercial and one is technical. Nearly 17% of secondary students are enrolled in the last track. Private schools account for 1% of primary enrollment and 6% of secondary enrollment.

Adult education is emphasized as a development process. The Institute of Adult Education is charged with two programs: short-term literacy training and a continuing course of social education. Of a total of 316 literacy training centers, 172 are run by the army which uses mandatory conscription to combat illiteracy.

Control of education is centralized in the state; all educational facilities are nationalized and integrated within a single system. A large corps of inspectors is charged with monitoring the school system to ensure conformity with officially established standards. Curricula are drawn up by technical committees appointed by the secretary of state for national education; textbooks are authorized and approved in a similar manner. The education budget in 1982 was D253,963,000, of which 90.7% was current expenditure. This expenditure was 5.4% of the GNP and 14.2% of the national budget. Per capita expenditure on education was $70.00.

EDUCATIONAL ENROLLMENT (1984)			
	Institutions	Teachers	Students
First Level	3,066	33,026	1,191,408
Second Level	335	17,943	364,492
Third Level	15	4,397	35,426

The country's sole institution of higher learning, the University of Tunis, has 20 faculties and institutes and 35,426 students. French is almost exclusively used at the university level. University enrollment was 817 per 100,000 inhabitants.

In 1982, 4,938 students graduated from the University of Tunis. By fields of study 886 were awarded degrees in medicine, 445 in engineering, 398 in natural sciences, 184 in social sciences, 116 in law, 414 in education and 252 in agriculture. In 1982, 9,737 Tunisian students were enrolled in institutions of higher learning abroad, including 258 in the United States, 8,071 in France, 279 in Belgium, and 258 in West Germany. In the same year 1,042 foreign students were enrolled in Tunisia.

Fifteen scientific journals are published in the country. Tunisia's contribution to world scientific authorship is 0.0060% (U.S.=42%).

LEGAL SYSTEM

The Tunisian legal system is an amalgam of French, Sharia and executive laws. The whole body of Tunisian law has been codified and includes seven codes promulgated since independence. The most important of these codes is the Code of Personal Status, which secularized the legal system, raised the status of women, abolished polygamy, made divorce subject to court decisions and raised the age of marriage.

At the apex of the court system is the Court of Cassation, consisting of four chambers, each with a president, the first president being the chief justice. Immediately below are the three Courts of Appeal located in Tunis, Sousse and Sfax. Courts of first instance are located in all principal administrative centers and comprise the third tier of the judicial system. At the base of the system are the cantonal (nahiyah) courts, which have taken the place of the old Sharia courts. Special courts include boards of arbitration, realty courts, the High Court of Justice to try cases of treason, the Security Court and administrative courts.

The judiciary is not independent but is subject to the executive. Judges are appointed by the president on the recommendation of the Supreme Council of the Magistracy.

LAW ENFORCEMENT

Internal security is maintained by the National Police in urban areas and the National Guard in other areas. The two forces are integrated under a director general of national security forces, but the National Guard is headed by a commandant and the National Police by a director. The total strength of the two forces is around 10,000, or 4 per 1,000 working inhabitants. In contrast to the National Police, the National Guard also functions as a paramilitary organization in times of emergency.

Crime is not a serious social problem. The crime rate is increasing but is still low compared to most countries. The latest available statistics (1968) showed a per capita crime rate of 11.7 per 1,000 inhabitants and an annual growth rate of 6.6%. Urban areas had 2½ times as much crime in proportion to the population as rural areas. Juvenile delinquents form one of the largest groups of criminals.

Secret service functions are performed by the special services branch of the National Police.

HEALTH

In 1981 there were 98 hospitals in the country with 14,071 beds, or 1 bed per 478 persons. In the same year there were 1,732 doctors, or 1 doctor per 3,883 persons, 330 dentists and 4,919 nursing personnel. The admissions/discharge rate is 621 per 10,000 inhabitants, the bed occupancy rate is 66.8% and the average length of stay is 8 days.

Nearly 70% of the population have access to safe water. In 1982, health expenditures accounted for 7.1% of gross government expenditures and $31.20 per capita.

> **PRINCIPAL HEALTH INDICATORS (1984)**
> Crude Death Rate: 10.1 per 1,000
> Decline in Death Rate: −48.6% (1965-83)
> Life Expectancy at Birth: 60.1 (Males); 61.1 (Females)
> Infant Mortality Rate: 106.5 per 1,000 Live Births
> Child Death Rate (Ages 1-4) per 1,000: 8

FOOD

The staple food is couscous, consisting of semolina cooked over steam of vegetable soup and served on a dish with pieces of meat around it. Per capita food intake is 72.8 grams of protein and 2,751 calories a day, which falls below the minimum of 2,600 calories recommended by WHO, 50 grams of fats and 394 grams of carbohydrates.

MEDIA & CULTURE

Five daily newspapers are published in Tunisia with a total circulation of 250,000, or 34 per 1,000 inhabitants. The daily press consists of two organs of the Destourian Socialist Party, including *L'Action*, two government newspapers in French, and one private newspaper in Arabic, all published in Tunis. Thirteen non-daily newspapers are published with a total circulation 732,000 (121 per 1,000 inhabitants). The periodical press consists of 230 magazines with a combined circulation of 870,000 (144 per 1,000 inhabitants). Of these the best known is *Jeune Afrique* which circulates widely in Francophone Africa and is the best-selling magazine in 10 African countries. "Visas" are required for books, periodicals and newspapers imported from abroad. Annual consumption of newsprint in 1982 was 5,500 tons, or 843 kg (1,859 lb) per 1,000 inhabitants.

The National Press Code of 1957 gives the government considerable restrictive powers, but these are rarely enforced and the press enjoys some freedom in practice. Newspapers and journals that stray too far from the official line are subject to suspension. The government also influences editorial policy through subsidized newsprint and state advertising. Tunisian law requires government permission prior to publication. During 1984, the government suspended publication or seized issues of at least 10 publications. One independent publication failed due to financial losses during its suspension. The normal period of suspension is three to six months. Seizure depends upon the offending topic and varies with individual publications. Tunisia ranks 66th among the nations of the world in press freedom, in which it is scaled at −0.66 (on an index with +4 as the maximum and −4 as the minimum).

The national news agency is Tunis-Afrique Presse (TAP), a public corporation, founded in 1961. Major foreign news bureaus in Tunis include AFP, UPI, Reuters and Tass.

Societe Tunisienne de Diffusion (STD), a semiofficial publishing and distributing company, controls and assists the small book industry. In 1981, 172 books were published in the country. Tunisia adheres to the Universal Copyright and Berne Conventions.

Broadcasting is a state monopoly controlled by Radiodiffusion Television Tunisienne (RTT), which operates two medium-wave stations at Djedeida, near Tunis, and Sidi Mansour, near Sfax, of 600 kw and 100 kw, respectively. In addition, three short-wave services (50 and 100 kw) are beamed to North Africa and the Middle East. Total program time is 248½ hours a week. The total number of radio receivers is 1,100,000, or 164 per 1,000 inhabitants.

Television was introduced in 1966 with a transmitter at Jabal Zaghwan. Practically the whole country is covered by RTT's seven main TV transmitters, which broadcast a national program for 26½ hours a week with a further 18 hours a week in French. A second channel was introduced in 1983. The total number of TV sets is 350,000, or 52 per 1,000 inhabitants.

In 1957 the government established a semiofficial company for the production and distribution of films called Societe Nationale Anonyme Tunisienne de Production et Exploitation Cinematographique (SAT-PEC). Imported films numbered 261, of which 77 came from the United States. There were 82 cinemas in the country, half of them in Tunis and Bizerta, with a combined seating capacity of 41,000, or 6.8 per 1,000 persons. Annual attendance was 9.1 million, or 1.5 per inhabitant. Annual box office receipts in 1980 totaled D2.1 million.

The largest library is the National Library at Tunis with 520,000 volumes in 1967. There are 168 other libraries. Per capita there are 71 volumes and nine registered borrowers per 1,000 inhabitants.

There are 25 museums in the country, reporting an average annual attendance of 981,000. There are 12 nature preservation sites.

There are 12 theaters (seven in the capital) serving 10 professional companies and 54 amateur troupes.

SOCIAL WELFARE

A social security program was established between 1960 and 1964 under the direction of the National Social Security Fund. Benefits are provided in the form of maternity and family allowances, disability and life insurance, and old-age insurance. Programs in the field of child welfare include day nurseries and a children's village for orphaned and homeless children. Relief work is coordinated by the Tunisian Red Crescent.

GLOSSARY

afaqi: Muslim social class consisting of sedentary villagers.
Arabi: tribesmen of central and southern Tunisia.

arch: land held collectively without right of alienation.
balad: municipality.
baldi: traditional urban aristocracy.
chefaa: right of a partner to sell his share of an undivided property.
couscous: staple dish of semolina cooked twice over steam of vegetable soup and garnished with meat and vegetables.
delegate: administrator of a delegation, or subdivision of a governorate.
enzel: perpetual lease of land for a fixed rent (compare **kirdar**).
farra: a four-year primary school in the Muslim school system.
gourbiville: a slum or squatter settlement in towns.
habous: agricultural land held in mortmain by a charitable trust or religious organization.
khammes: traditional sharecropping practice under which the tenant receives one-fifth of the harvest (compare **rebaa**).
kirdar: land held on the basis of varying annual rents (compare **enzel**).
kuttab: Koranic school, often attached to a mosque.
majlis: assembly, as in Majlis al-Umma, the National Assembly.
melk: private land with full right of alienation.
mutamadiyat: a delegation or subdivision of a governorate.
nahiyah: cantonal court.
rais: mayor of a municipality.
rebaa: traditional sharecropping practice under which the tenant received one-fourth of the harvest (compare **khammes**).
shatt: a large salt lake in central and southern Tunisia.
sheikhate: formerly, the smallest unit of local administration.
tunsi: the urban proletariat.
wadi: streambed or valley in desert regions.
wilayat: governorate, administered by a **wali.**

CHRONOLOGY (from 1956)

1955— France ends protectorate and grants independence to Tunisia. . . . Neo-Destour Party wins absolute majority in elections to the Constituent Assembly. . . . Habib Bourguiba is elected premier. . . . New constitution is enacted. . . . Tunisia joins U.N.
1957— Bey of Tunis is deposed. . . . Republic of Tunisia is proclaimed with Bourguiba as its first president.
1958— Tunisia joins Arab League. . . . Dinar is introduced as unit of currency. . . . Central Bank is established.
1959— Constitution of the republic is promulgated. . . . National elections are held. . . . Under the Code of Personal Status polygamy is outlawed, legal system is secularized, Muslim marriage and divorce laws reformed, and status of women is raised.

1960— Bourguiba makes unsuccessful attempt to abolish Muslim fast of Ramadan.

1961— University of Tunis is reorganized... Crisis occurs over Tunisian call for withdrawal of French forces from naval base at Bizerta.... The 10-Year Perspective of Development Plan is launched.

1962— Relations with Algeria are suspended.

1963— Tunisia joins the Organization of African Unity.

1964— French evacuate Bizerta; all French-owned estates are nationalized.... Dinar is devalued.... Name of Neo-Destour Party is changed to Destourian Socialist Party at Congress of Destiny; new socialist program is adopted.... National elections are held.

1965— Bourguiba calls for Arab negotiations with Israel; this counsel of moderation is rejected by Arab nations; war of words with U.A.R. breaks out; Tunisia breaks relations with Syria and Iraq.

1966— Tunisia breaks relations with U.A.R.... Television is introduced.... Oil is found at El Borma field.

1967— Ties are restored with Arab countries following Arab-Israeli War.

1968— Students riot against U.S. and U.K. embassies.

1969— National elections are held.... Ben Salah, the powerful minister of planning and finance, is dismissed.

1970— Hedi Nouira replaces Bahi Ladgham as prime minister.... Treaty is concluded with Algeria.

1971— Ahmed Mestiri, minister of the interior, falls into disgrace and is dismissed.

1974— National elections are held; Bourguiba is elected president for life and given enlarged powers.... Union with Libya is first proposed, then repudiated.

1978— UGTT-led general strike erupts into violent riots, the worst in nation's history, in which 46 are killed.... Habib Achour, secretary general of the UGTT, is sentenced to 10 years in prison for part in fomenting the strike

1979— Arab League establishes new headquarters in Tunis, following expulsion of Egypt.

1980— Prime Minister Hedi Nouira leaves office on account of illness; moderate Mohamed Mzali is named to succeed him as prime minister and secretary general of the ruling party.

1981— One-party political system ends with three opposition parties being accorded legitimacy.

1982— Diplomatic relations are reestablished with Libya.

1983— Tunisia signs Maghreb Fraternity and Cooperation Treaty with Algeria.

1984— Bread riots break out following steep hike in food prices... Bourguiba rescinds price increases.

1985— Libya expels Tunisian workers.

BIBLIOGRAPHY (from 1965)

Amin, Samir, *The Maghreb in the Modern World: Algeria, Tunisia, Morocco* (Baltimore, Md., 1970).

Bennet, Norman R., *A Study Guide for Tunisia* (Boston, 1968).

Duvignaud, Jean, *Change at Shebika* (New York, 1970).

Duwagi, Ghazi, *Economic Development in Tunisia* (New York, 1967).

Hawrylshyn, Oli. *Planning for Economic Development: The Construction and Use of a Multisectoral Model for Tunisia* (New York, 1976).

Knapp, Wilfred, *Tunisia* (New York, 1970).

Ling, Dwight D., *Tunisia, from Protectorate to Republic* (Bloomington, Ind., 1967).

Moore, Clement H., *Tunisia Since Independence* (Berkeley, Calif., 1965).

Rossi, Pierre, *Bourguiba's Tunisia* (Tunis, 1967).

Rudebeck, Lars, *Party and People: A Study of Political Change in Tunisia* (New York, 1969).

Said, Rafik, *Cultural Policy in Tunisia* (New York, 1971).

Salem, Norma, *Habib Bourguiba: Islam and the Creation of Tunisia* (London, 1984).

Schliephake, Konrad, *Oil and Regional Development: Examples form Algeria and Tunisia* (New York, 1977). 049

Simmon, John and Russell A. Stone, *Change in Tunisia* (Albany, N.Y., 1976).

Sylvester, Anthony, *Tunisia* (London, 1969).

OFFICIAL PUBLICATIONS

Central Bank, *Financial Statistics.*

———, National Institute of Statistics, *Monthly Bulletin of Statistics.*

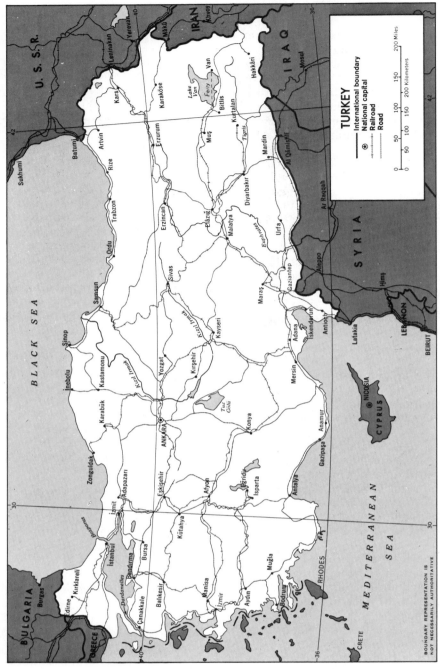

TURKEY

- International boundary
- ⊛ National capital
- ┼┼┼ Railroad
- Road

Miles: 0 50 100 150 200 Miles
Kilometers: 0 50 100 150 200 Kilometers

U.S.S.R.

IRAN

IRAQ

SYRIA

LEBANON

BULGARIA

GREECE

BLACK SEA

MEDITERRANEAN SEA

CYPRUS

⊛ NICOSIA

CRETE

RHODES

Sukhumi
Batumi
Leninakan
Yerevan
MAKÜ
Khvoy
Kars
Karaköse
Van
Ferry
Lake Van
Bitlis
Hakkâri
Mosul
Kurtalan
Artvin
Rize
Erzurum
Muş
Tigris
Mardin
Al Qāmishlī
Trabzon
Erzincan
Elâzığ
Diyarbakır
Ordu
Malatya
Urfa
Euphrates
Ar Raqqah
Sivas
Maraş
Gaziantep
Aleppo
Ḥimş
Samsun
Kayseri
Adana
İskenderun
Antioch
Latakia
BEIRUT
Sinop
Kızıl Irmak
Yozgat
Kırşehir
Mersin
İnebolu
Kastamonu
Konya
Tuz Gölü
Kızıl Irmak
ANKARA ⊛
Anamur
Gazipaşa
Karabük
Eskişehir
Afyon
Eğridir
Isparta
Antalya
Zonguldak
Adapazarı
İzmit
Kütahya
Bodrum
Muğla
İstanbul
Bandırma
Bursa
Manisa
Aydın
İzmir
Bosporus
Dardanelles
Balıkesir
Çanakkale
Kırklareli
Edirne
Burgas

BOUNDARY REPRESENTATION IS
NOT NECESSARILY AUTHORITATIVE

TÜRKİYE CUMHURİYETİ

TURKEY

BASIC FACT SHEET

OFFICIAL NAME: Republic of Turkey (Turkiye Cumhuriyeti)

ABBREVIATION: TU

CAPITAL: Ankara

HEAD OF STATE: President Gen. Kenan Evren (from 1980)

HEAD OF GOVERNMENT: Prime Minister Turgut Ozal (from 1983)

NATURE OF GOVERNMENT: Partial Democracy

POPULATION: 51,259,000 (1985)

AREA: 780,576 sq km (301,302 sq mi)

ETHNIC MAJORITY: Turks

RELIGION: Sunni Islam

LANGUAGE: Turkish

UNIT OF CURRENCY: Turkish Lira ($1=L532.125, August 1985)

NATIONAL FLAG: White crescent and star on red field

NATIONAL EMBLEM: An elliptical red shield bearing the republic's name in gold at the top with a white crescent beneath it and a white star in the center. The Turkish national colors are red and white.

NATIONAL ANTHEM: Istiklal Marsi ("The March of Independence")

NATIONAL HOLIDAYS: October 29 (National Day, Anniversary of the Declaration of the Republic); January 1; April 23 (National Sovereignty and Children's Day); May 1 (Spring Day); May 19 (Youth and Sports Day); May 27 (Freedom and Constitution Day); August 30 (Victory Day); October 29 (Republic Day); also variable Islamic festivals, Seker Bayram and Kurban Bayram.

NATIONAL CALENDAR: Gregorian

PHYSICAL QUALITY OF LIFE INDEX: 67 (up from 54 in 1976) (On an ascending scale with 100 as the maximum. U.S. 95)

DATE OF INDEPENDENCE: October 29, 1923

DATE OF CONSTITUTION: November 7, 1982

WEIGHTS & MEASURES: The metric system prevails.

LOCATION & AREA

Turkey occupies the land mass of the Anatolian Peninsula in West Asia together with the city of Istanbul and its Thracian hinterland. The Asian and European portions of Turkey are divided from each other by the Bosporus Strait, the Sea of Marmara and the Dardanelles Strait. Of its total area of 780,576 sq km (301,302 sq mi), the area in Europe consists of 23,721 sq km (9,158 sq mi) and the area in Asia 756,855 sq km (292,221 sq mi). It is the sixth largest nation in Asia. The greatest distance north-south is 650 km (403 mi) and east-west, 1,600 km (993 mi). The total length of the coastline is 8,210 km (5,098 mi). Turkey shares its total international border of 2,753 km (1,710 mi) with six nations: Bulgaria (269 km, 167 mi), Greece (212 km, 132 mi), the Soviet Union (610 km, 379 mi), Iran (454 km, 282 mi), Iraq (331 km, 205 mi) and Syria (877 km, 545 mi). The only active boundary dispute is with Syria over Hatay Province, including the towns of Antakya (Antioch) and Iskanderun (Alexandretta), obtained from France in 1939.

Turkey is one of the most earthquake-prone regions of the world with a major structural fault line running from the Sea of Marmara in the general direction of Ankara. Over 85% of the land is over 450 meters, (1,476 ft), and the median altitude is 1,125 meters (3,691 ft).

The capital is Ankara with an estimated population in 1980 of 1,877,755. But the commercial and intellectual center of Turkey is Istanbul (2,772,708). The other major urban centers are: Izmir (757,854), Adana (574,515), Bursa (445,113), Gaziantep (374,290), Eskisehir (309,431), Konya (329,139), Diyarbakir (235,617), Kayseri (281,320), Kahraman Maras (178,557), Erzurum (190,241), Samsun (198,749), Sivas (172,864), Malatya (179,074), Kocaeli or Izmit (190,423), Mersin or Icel (216,308) and Antalya (173,501).

Turkey is divided into five physical regions. The heartland of the country is the Anatolian Plateau, an arid steppe-like region with limited rainfall and cold winters. The eastern highlands, consisting of the entire eastern third of Turkey, is a vast stretch of wild, barren wasteland with higher elevations and a more severe climate. The productive regions of the country are the Aegean coastlands, which contain half the agricultural wealth in the broad, cultivated valleys of the Bursa Plains, the Plains of Troy, the Ismit Valley, the Mediterranean coastland and the narrow coastal ribbon of the Black Sea Region.

The longest river completely within Turkey is the Kizil Irmak, which runs 96 km (60 mi) east of Sivas and reaches the Black Sea at Bafra. The other major rivers are the Firat (Euphrates) and Dicle (Tigris) in the east, the Coruh, Yesil Irmak and Sakarya, all feeding the Black Sea; the Simav Cayi discharging into the Sea of Marmara; the Maritsa, flowing into the Aegean Sea; the Gediz draining into the Gulf of Izmir; and the Buyuk Menderes with its estuary on the Aegean. Most rivers are unsuitable for navigation, but they are harnessed for hydroelectric power.

WEATHER

Because of the closeness of mountain ranges to the coast and the great elevation of the interior plateaus, the Turkish climate is characterized by great extremes and wide temperature variations between regions and seasons—sometimes over 50°C (122°F). The coastal regions have a continental temperate climate with mild winters and moderately hot summers and a median of 19°C to 20°C (66.2°F to 68°F). August is the hottest month, with a mean temperature of 28°C, (82.4°F) and January the coldest, with a mean temperature of 8°C to 11°C (46.4°F to 51.8°F). In the interior plateaus winters are cold and frost occurs for more than 100 days a year. The summers are hot, with temperatures rising to 43°C (109.4°F). The climate of Eastern Turkey is inhospitable with bitter, cold winters and hot summers. Around the Aegean the summers are tempered by the northerly Meltemi, or Etesian, wind. Rainfall too is variable. Winters are generally the wettest months on the coast. Rainfall averages from 50.8 cm to 72.2 cm (20 to 30 in.) per annum along the Aegean and Mediterranean seas to over 254 cm (100 in.) along the Black Sea. May is generally the wettest month in the interior, where the annual amount of rainfall measures only between 25.4 cm to 43.1 cm (10 and 17 in.).

POPULATION

The population of Turkey in 1985 was estimated at 51,259,000 on the basis of the last official census, held in 1980, when the population was 44,736,957. The population is expected to reach 71.3 million by 2000 and 97 million by 2020.

The annual rate of population growth is 2.33% nationwide and 3.8% in urban areas. The annual birth rate is 32.5 per 1,000.

The population is concentrated in European Turkey and the lowlands of the Marmara, Aegean and Black Sea coasts, which together account for 25% of the territory but 42% of the inhabitants. The central regions, with 62% of the area, have only 46% of the population. The average density of population is 64 per sq km (166 per sq mi) and 116 per sq km (300 per sq mi) in agricultural land.

The urban component of the population is 48%. Between 1965 and 1972 the number of urban settle-

DEMOGRAPHIC INDICATORS (1985)	
Population, total (in 1,000)	51,259
Population ages (% of total)	
0-14	37.1
15-64	58.6
65+	4.2
Youth 15-24 (000)	10,215
Women ages 15-49 (000)	11,828
Dependency ratios	70.5
Child-woman ratios	569
Sex ratios (per 100 females)	105.6
Median ages (years)	21.1
Marriage Rate (per 1,000)	3.6
Divorce Rate (per 1,000)	0.4
Average size of Household	5.2
Decline in birthrate (%, 1965-83)	−25.7
Proportion of urban (%)	48.11
Population density (per sq. km.)	64
per hectare of arable land	0.99
Rates of growth (%)	2.33
urban %	3.8
rural %	1.1
Natural increase rates (per 1,000)	23.5
Crude birth rates (per 1,000)	32.5
Crude death rates (per 1,000)	9.0
Gross reproduction rates	2.17
Net reproduction rates	1.91
Total fertility rates	4.45
General fertility rates (per 1,000)	139
Life expectancy, males (years)	60.8
Life expectancy, females (years)	65.3
Life expectancy, total (years)	63.0
Population doubling time in years at current rate	28

ments over 50,000 increased from 30 to 40. Over 5 million Turks live in cities over 100,000 and over 6% live in the three largest cities of Istanbul, Ankara and Izmir. The urban birthrate is lower than the rural, and the increase in urban population (currently 3.8% per year) is attributable almost entirely to migration.

Nationwide 25% of the Turks live in slums and squatter settlements; the proportion is highest in Izmir (65%) Ankara (60%) and Istanbul (40%).

Historically, Turkey had a preponderance of females over males in numbers, but this trend was reversed by 1945. In the 1980 census the male-female ratio was 51.60 to 48.40. The population is young, with 37.1% under 14 years of age; 58.6% between 15 and 64; and 4.2% over 65.

Since the beginning of the 20th Century the nation has witnessed large population transfers with a substantial out-migration of foreign minority groups, such as the Armenians and the Greeks, and an influx of Muslim refugees and immigrants from the Balkans and the Soviet Union. During the 1960s a steady out-migration of Turkish workers seeking employment abroad assumed massive proportions. By 1974 there were 810,498 Turks working abroad, of whom 29% were women. Of these, 649,257 were employed in West Germany and the balance in Austria, Belgium, the Netherlands and Switzerland. In the early 1970s an increasing number were emigrating to Australia. Workers' emigration has been officially encouraged because of its beneficial effects on domestic unemployment and the balance of payments. In 1978 there were 730,000 Turks working abroad, of these 16,000 were employed in Australia, 27,000 in Australia; 16,000 in Belgium; 42,000 in France; 506,000 F.R.G.; 18,000 in Libya; 44,000 in the Netherlands and 16,000 in Switzerland.

Turkey has long been in the forefront of Muslim nations in the promotion and protection of women's rights. Although some conservative elements in Parliament and in society at large have resisted advances in women's rights, President Evren has been a consistent champion of equality for women. Women have full suffrage, occasionally attain high public office, and are represented—albeit not always in significant numbers—in all Turkish professions and institutions. Women have served or are currently employed at the rank of university rector and dean, ambassador, political party vice president and army colonel. Turkish businesswomen play significant roles in many industries, and a few sit on the boards of some of Turkey's largest private firms. Female lawyers and judges are no rarity, and female doctors are dominant in some specialties.

Despite government policies to promote and protect women's rights, the role of women in smaller communities and rural areas, especially in the southeast, is still defined by centuries of traditional practice. Many women and girls in the southeast are still partially or fully veiled. Prevailing cultural values make it difficult for some women to receive primary or secondary education or to pursue careers outside of the home.

Equal political rights for men and women are guaranteed by the constitution. A dozen women hold leadership roles in two opposition parties, though the 22-member Cabinet is all male. Women are strongly encouraged to exercise their franchise; the fine imposed upon adults who do not vote applies equally to men and women. In December 1984, female educators and parliamentarians joined forces to conduct a government-approved conference on the role of women in Turkish society, in commemoration of the 50th anniversary of passage of women's rights legislation.

From 1920 to 1960 population growth was officially encouraged, and financial incentives were provided for large families. The annual growth rate reached 3% in the 1950s and led to a reconsideration and reversal of this policy. A family planning law was passed in 1965 advocating voluntary birth control. A family planning division was established within the Ministry of Health and Social Assistance. A liberalized abortion law was passed in 1967. The official goal was to reduce the birth rate from 39.6 to 26 per 1,000. Birth control services are provided under government auspices through 500 state clinics and 200 private clinics, with emphasis on intrauterine devices and oral contraceptives. The government program is complemented by private organizations, such as the Turkish Family Planning Association, the Institute of Population Studies at Haceteppe University and the U.S. Population Council. Approximately 8.2% of married women of reproductive age are believed to practice contraception.

ETHNIC COMPOSITION

Officially, there are no ethnic minorities in Turkey, and the only distinctions are those of language and religion. However, ethnic homogeneity has been the historic goal of the Turkish state, and national identity is limited to ethnic Turks. Succeeding governments have worked hard to create a feeling of Turkishness by laying down rigid requirements for the definition of a true Turk. Thus, only a person who speaks Turkish as his primary language, follows Islam as his religion and owes allegiance to the Republic of Turkey is considered a Turk. Members of ethnic minorities are treated as second-class citizens and are excluded from full participation and acceptance in Turkish life. Some assimilation has taken place among the Muslim Kurds and even Arabs, but Jews, Armenians and Greeks seem destined to remain distinct and unassimilable.

Unofficial estimates placed the percentage of Turks at 92 in 1973. In the 1965 census their number totalled 28,317,579. Of these, only 5% can claim Turki or Western Mongoloid ancestry on the basis of physical characteristics such as color and build. The remaining 95% are the descendants of conquered peoples particularly Greeks who were Turkicized through forcible conversion, coercion and intermarriage. A number of regional variants may also be distinguished among the Turks. The most important of these are the Anatolian Turks, who form the core of the peasantry of Asiatic Turkey; the Rumelian Turks, including immigrants from the former Balkan territories of the empire; and Central Asian Turks, including Crimean Tatars and Turkomans. There are also numbers of Caucasians, particularly Circassians and Georgians, who have contributed to the racial structure of Turkey.

The Kurds form the most important Muslim minority, estimated at between 2 and 2.5 million. Two-thirds of them belong to the Sunni and one-third to the Shia or Alevi sect. They are traditionally a mountain people, largely pastoral, but some have settled in permanent villages and cities, notably Diyarbakir. Intermittent demands for an independent Kurdish state have been suppressed, and the government has gradually disarmed the tribes and dismantled the tribal organization. Recent efforts to integrate them into national life through education have been only partly successful. In the early 1970s there were approximately 300,000 Arabs concentrated along the Syrian border in the province of Hattay. Both the Arabs and Kurds engage in systematic smuggling across the Syrian and Iraqi borders.

There is also an interesting community, known as the Donme, who are descendants of the Jewish followers of the false messiah, Sabbatai Zebi in the 17th Century. They consider themselves Muslim, but are not accepted as such by the Turks in general.

Except for the Kurds and the Arabs no ethnic minority numbers over 100,000. Deportations and periodic exchanges of population have eroded the number of Greeks to around 70,000. There are about the same number of Armenians, survivors of the Armenian holocausts of the 19th and 20th Centuries. About 30,000 Jews are left in the country, less than their number in 1948. The Greeks, Armenians and the Jews are concentrated in Istanbul.

Almost all major Western communities are represented in Istanbul.

Turkey ranks 77th in the world in ethnic and linguistic homogeneity with 75% homogeneity (on an ascending scale in which Tanzania is ranked 1st as the least homogeneous and South and North Korea are rank 135th as the most homogeneous).

LANGUAGES

The official language of Turkey is Turkish, spoken by an estimated 92% of the population as their mother tongue. The most basic of Kemal Ataturk's reforms was the Dil Devrimi, or the language revolution, which produced a new language that was more practical and precise, made it a central symbol of Turkish national identity, and used it as a powerful mechanism for a radical reorientation of the nation toward the West away from the Islamic past. Dil Devrimi consisted of two elements: introduction of a new alphabet and purification of the vocabulary by purging it of Arabic and Persian words. The new Turkish alphabet is composed of Latin letters or variants with one symbol for each sound in standard Turkish. The Turkish Linguistic Society was founded in 1932 and charged with the task of collecting and approving Turkish words and phrases to replace foreign words. But by the late 1940s opposition to the purification movement began to surface, and official policy was in retreat by the 1950s. Some Arabic words began to reappear in official use, and the Turkish Linguistic Society lost its official status as the arbiter of Turkish language.

Minority languages include two Kurdish dialects (Kermanji and Zaza), Arabic, Greek, Armenian and Ladino, the last spoken by Jews. The right of indigenous minority groups to use their own languages is limited. The constitution states that the official language of the country is Turkish. Although one article bans discrimination on the basis of language, others prohibit the public use of "languages prohibited by law." However, legislation has never been enacted prohibiting specific languages. The government has stated that the intent of these articles is to foster Turkish as the language of all citizens for all uses, as part of its effort to inculcate in all Turkish citizens a sense of identity with the Turkish state and nation as opposed to identification with any particular groups within the nation. The Treaty of Lausanne guarantees the use of Greek and Armenian in schools and religious education. The government honors that guarantee. In practice, the severity of restrictions on the use of a minority language appears to depend on the perceived threat the group in question presents to the integrity of the Turkish State. For example, the use of Kurdish, which the government believes fosters separatist tendencies, is severely restricted. Use of Arabic, about which there are no such concerns, is not similarly restricted. The use of Syriac, however, is not protected by the Treaty of Lausanne, and in 1984 five court cases were brought against a Syrian Christian publisher of religious materials. One case was dismissed in martial law court based on the testimony of an outside expert called in by the court, who determined that the publication (a calendar with biblical quotes) did not violate Turkish law. Four cases in civil court are still outstanding.

Traditionally, both French and German have been the principal foreign languages, but since World War II English has replaced them in higher education.

RELIGION

Turkey is officially a secular state, but over 98% of Turks are Sunni Muslims. The reforms of Ataturk disestablished religion and destroyed the institutional structures of Islam. These reforms included abolition of the office of seyhulislam, or the head of Islamic establishment, the change from the Muslim to the Gregorian calendar and from the use of Arabic to Roman script; the displacement of the seriat or Muslim law; the outlawing of the veil for women, the fez for men and clerical garbs for clerics; the closing of the medrese or religious schools and the abolition of the tarikatlars, or Sufi religious orders. The mosque of Santa Sophia was converted to a museum. The administration of Muslim organizations was vested in the Presidency of Religious Affairs and the Directorate of Pious Foundations, independent regulatory agencies under lay civil servants.

Since the 1940s there has been a retreat from Kemalist secularism, accelerated under the Democrat Party's rule from 1950 to 1960. Provision was made for public education in Islam based on the Koran, and a Higher Islamic Institute was established at Ankara. Over 1,500 mosques were built every year from 1950 to 1964. The annual Haj pilgrimage to Mecca was once again permitted, and muezzin calls for prayer were permitted in Arabic. The Tarikatlar (dervish groups) re-emerged and gained substantial followings. The revolution of 1960 brought about a return to the earlier secularism, but Bulent Ecevit's coalition government of 1974 and Suleyman Demirel's coalition government, which succeeded it, re-established the links between church and state, primarily through the influence of the National Salvation Party, a junior member of the coalition, which is committed to break with secularism and return to traditional Islamic values.

The Political Parties Law prohibits the establishment of any political party advocating theocracy or the foundation of law and government, even partially, on religious principles. Several former administrators of the now-dissolved National Salvation Party, convicted in 1983 of "turning a legally established party into a front working for the establishment of a regime based on theocratic principles,'' were acquitted by an appellate court in September 1985.

Under the constitution, Islamic religious instruction, following a state-prepared curriculum, is compulsory for all students except those who declare themselves non-Muslim. The courses of about two hours per week are taught by lay teachers. Extracurricular Koran courses using government-approved texts are permitted.

Armenian Orthodox, Greek Orthodox, Greek Catholic, Jewish, Syrian Christian, Roman Catholic, and Protestant religious minorities are found throughout Turkey but are primarily concentrated in Istanbul. These groups operate churches, monasteries, synagogues, schools and charitable religious foundations, such as hospitals and orphanages. Guarantees of minority rights, beyond those contained in the constitution, are included in the Treaty of Lausanne (1923), which provides that non-Muslim minority communities may maintain separate schools for their children. Non-Muslim minority groups have repeatedly complained about government policies and procedures concerning the operation of community schools, the formation of parish councils, and the registration and repair of church property. Government claims on property endowed by religious charitable organizations have also been cited as a major concern. There were complaints in 1985 about a government ruling that a 1984 law, which permits religious foundations to increase property rents, applies only to Muslims. Of continuing concern to some non-Muslim religious communities is the dearth of new clergy. The lack of clerics for these communities stems partly from the closure of some seminaries and partly from the inability of the communities to generate enough candidates for the religious life from their indigenous populations.

The Greek Orthodox community is concerned about its inability to obtain permission to rebuild a part of the Patriarchate administration building, although some progress was made on this issue in 1985. Relations between the church and the government were improved when Archbishop Iakovos, the Primate of the Greek Orthodox Archdiocese of North and South America, was permitted to visit Turkey in 1985. Iakovos had not been allowed to enter Turkey since 1961.

A dispute between the Greek community and the government arose in May 1985 over alterations to a Greek Orthodox church in an Istanbul suburb which the Greek community claimed was protected by the Treaty of Lausanne. The government asserted that the alterations were necessitated by a compelling public need for road-widening and did not prevent continued use of the church for religious services. Further, the government pointed out that several mosques were razed in a similar project. The alterations have now been completed.

The daily use of languages other than Turkish by non-Muslim religious minorities, such as Greek, Armenian, Hebrew, and Arabic, in religious services is allowed but is declining.

Istanbul is the seat of the Ecumenical Patriarch of the Orthodox Church. The Armenians have two patriarchates, one at Istanbul and the other at Beirut, Lebanon. The Chaldeans, the Syrian Jacobites, and the Roman Catholics are also represented. The Jews, who are nearly all Sephardim, have a grand rabbi (hahambasi) in Istanbul. In the 1965 census Christians of all denominations numbered 254,000 and Jews 38,000.

COLONIAL EXPERIENCE

Turkey has never been under colonial rule in modern times.

CONSTITUTION & GOVERNMENT

For the third time in three decades, Turkey returned to military authoritarian rule in 1980. When the generals acted, they did so reluctantly, fed up with a wrangling parliament that was unable to elect a president for five months, political street violence claiming 16 lives a day, and a stagnant economy and only after half a dozen warnings to the politicians. From the first hours of the coup the generals made it clear that they regarded the 1961 constitution as chiefly responsible for the dissipation of state authority under civilian rule and that they do not intend to return power to the civilians again under the same political framework. The generals immediately set up a junta known as the National Security Council.

The 1961 constitution, which the generals suspended, was one of the most liberal in the world with so many checks and balances that there was no chance of returning to authoritarian rule—barring, of course, a military coup. The document was a direct reaction to the strongman rule of Adnan Menderes, prime minister from 1950 to 1960. The constitution succeeded but too well. Its principal failings were a weak executive, malfunctioning legislature, an overly powerful judiciary, university autonomy, and a lack of curbs on the proliferation of political groups.

The key to understanding the 1980 coup is the role of the military as the guardians of the legacy of Ataturk. Since the republic was formed in 1923 only one of its six presidents has been a civilian. Ever since the introduction of full democracy and a multi-party system in 1945, the country has been under martial law, off and on, for 15 years. The military is also a political party in its own right, perhaps the most cohesive and progressive force in Turkish society. The army has always regarded itself as the guardian of both the state and the Kemalist revolution, and it has intervened in political life four times since 1961, twice through memoranda threatening a coup and twice through actual coups.

The 1961 constitution contained 157 articles and 11 provisional articles. The constitution declared Turkey to be a national, democratic, secular and social state

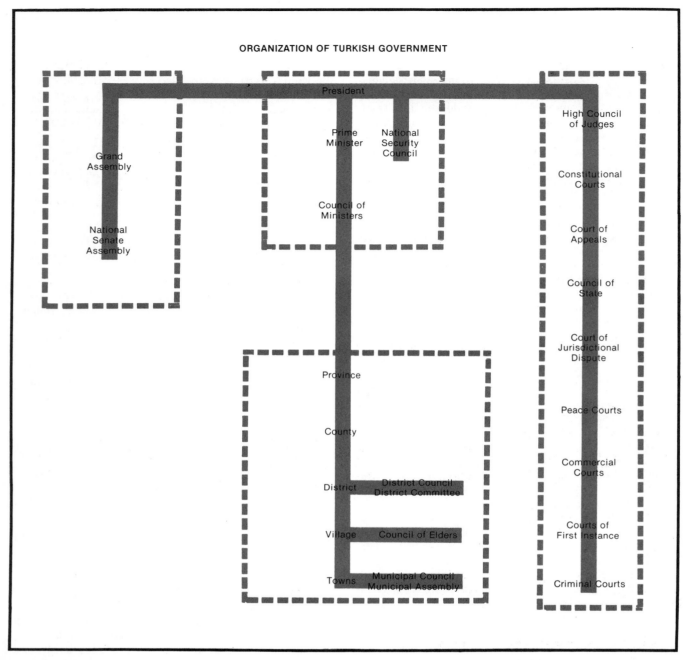

ORGANIZATION OF TURKISH GOVERNMENT

President

Grand Assembly
National Senate Assembly

Prime Minister
National Security Council
Council of Ministers

High Council of Judges
Constitutional Courts
Court of Appeals
Council of State
Court of Jurisdictional Dispute
Peace Courts
Commercial Courts
Courts of First Instance
Criminal Courts

Province
County
District — District Council District Committee
Village — Council of Elders
Towns — Municipal Council Municipal Assembly

governed by the rule of law based on human rights. It also contained a detailed bill of rights and a set of social welfare provisions. It embodied a number of curbs on executive authority and a system of checks and balances among the executive, legislative and judicial branches.

In 1971, 35 articles of the constitution were amended and nine new articles added. The amendments were aimed at ensuring that the freedom enjoyed by universities, trade unions, the media and other institutions could not be exercised to jeopardize the integrity, security, morality or public order of the state.

In June 1981 the National Security Council appointed a 160-member National Consultative Council, whose constitutional committee was charged with drafting a new basic law. The document in question, published in draft on July 17, 1982, and approved by the electorate in a referendum on November 7, provided, inter alia, for the following: (1) a unicameral, 400-member Grand National Assembly elected for a five-year term; (2) a president who, at the conclusion of General Evren's seven-year incumbency, would be elected by the Assembly for a nonrenewable term of like duration, and who would be advised by a State Consultative Council of 30 members (20 presidentially appointed); (3) a four-member Presidential Council of senior military figures, continuing the role of the other members of the existing NSC as of the second year of the initial presidential term; and (4) an advisory Economic and Social Council. In addition, the president is empowered to appoint and dismiss the prime minister and other cabinet members; to dissolve the Assembly and call for a new election, if faced with a government crisis of more than 30 days' duration; to declare a state of emergency, during which the government may rule by decree; and to appoint a variety of leading government officials, including senior judges and the governor of the Central Bank. Political parties may be formed if they are not class based, linked to trade unions, or committed to Communism, Fascism, or religious fundamentalism. However, leading members of the former parties are barred from political activity for periods of up to 10 years, while an electoral law enacted in June 1983 empowers the president to deny registration to groups suspected of being linked to the earlier formations. Strikes that exceed 60 days duration are subject to compulsory arbitration, while strict controls are exercised over the media.

RULERS OF TURKEY
(from 1945)

PRESIDENTS:
1938 (November) to 1950 (May) Ismet Inonu
1950 (May) to 1960 (May) Celal Bayar
1960 (May) to 1966 (March) Cemal Gursel
1966 (March) to 1973 (March) Cevdet Sunay
1973 (April) to 1980 (September) Fahri Koruturk
1980 (Sep) —   Kenan Evren
PRIME MINISTERS:
1943 (March) to 1946 (August) Sukru Saracoglu
1946 (August) to 1947 (September) Recep Peker
1947 (September) to 1948 (June) Hasan Saka
1948 (June) to 1949 (January) Hasan Saka
1949 (January) to 1950 (May) Semsettin Gunaltay
1950 (May) to 1960 (May) Adnan Menderes
1960 (May) to 1961 (October) Cemal Gursel (See also presidents)
1961 (November) to 1965 (February) Ismet Inonu
1965 (February to October) Suat Hayri Urguplu
1965 (October) to 1971 (March) Suleyman Demirel
1971 (March) to 1972 (April) Nihat Erim
1972 (April) to 1974 (January) Naim Talu
1974 (January to September) Bulent Ecevit
1974 (November) to 1975 (March) Sadilrmak
1975 (March) to 1977 (July) Suleyman Demirel
Note: Bulent Ecevit was prime minister for 10 days during this period)
1977 (August to December) Suleyman Demirel
1977 (December) to 1979 (October)
            Bulent Ecevit
1979 (November) to 1980 (September)
            Suleyman Demirel
1980 (Sep) to 1983 (Dec)
            Bulend Ulusu
1983 (December) —
            Turgut Ozal

The ideological basis of the constitution was Ataturk's manifesto of 1931 containing six fundamental and unchanging principles, sometimes called "the six arrows of Kemalism." They are republicanism, nationalism, populism, statism, secularism and reformism. Commonly referred to as Ataturkism, the meaning and continued validity and applicability of

---

CABINET LIST (1985)

President	*Gen.* Kenan Evren
Prime Minister	Turgut Özal
Deputy Prime Minister	Kaya Erdem
Minister of Agriculture, Forests & Village Affairs	Hüsnü Dogan
Minister of Communications	Veysel Atasoy
Minister of Culture & Tourism	Mükerrem Taşçioglu
Minister of Energy & Natural Resources	Sudi Turel
Minister of Finance & Customs	Ahmet Alptemocin
Minister of Foreign Affairs	Vahit Halefoglu
Minister of Health & Social Assistance	Mehmet Aydin
Minister of Industry & Technology	Cahit Aral
Minister of Interior	Akbulut Yildirim
Minister of Justice	Necat Eldem
Minister of Labor	Mustafa Kalemi
Minister of Natl. Defense	Zeki Yavuztürk
Minister of Natl. Education, Youth & Sports	Vehbi Dinçerler
Minister of Public Works & Resettlement	Safa Giray
Minister of State	Kazim Oksay
Minister of State	Mustafa Tinaz Titiz
Minister of State	Abdullah Tenekeci
Minister of State	Mesut Yilmaz
Minister of State	Ahmet Karaevli
Minister of State	Cemal Büyükbas

the "six arrows" are the subjects of frequent discussion and debate in Turkish political life.

Since 1961 Turkey has been plagued by unstable cabinets and governments based on patchwork alliances between disparate political parties, though only one government since 1923 has been violently overthrown—in 1961—and that at the cost of just four lives. In 1977 Bulent Ecevit's cabinet lasted only 10 days. Turkey has thus alternated between stable governments without legitimacy and legitimate governments without stability.

FREEDOM & HUMAN RIGHTS

In terms of civil and political rights, Turkey is classified as a partly-free country with a favorable ranking of 5 in political rights and 5 in civil rights (on a descending scale where 1 denotes the highest and 7 the lowest in rights).

The overall status of human rights in Turkey in 1985 showed continuing improvement, but there are important shortcomings. Chief among the latter is the persistence of credible reports of torture, usually at the hands of poorly educated police officials during initial periods of incommunicado detention. Politicians and the press have publicized allegations of torture. A parliamentary report released in November 1985 recommended that the government introduce legislation to put more teeth into its laws against torture, although several hundred security officials, according to official sources, have been prosecuted and punished for acts of torture. The press has publicized domestic and foreign criticism of human rights practices and has publicized the views of banned politicians with increasing frequency. With a few notable exceptions, most of the mass trials of recent years have concluded with substantial numbers of convictions.

The constitution requires a warrant for any arrest, except in certain limited circumstances, e.g., when a person is caught redhanded. The Police Powers Act of June 1985 reduced from 48 hours to 24 hours the time within which a person taken into custody must be charged or released. This provision was applied to two police officers in Giresun Province who were under indictment as of October 1985 for detaining two suspects for 37 hours without a warrant and for beating them. The law did not change the period of detention without charge (15 days) in cases of "offenses committed collectively." In the nine provinces under martial law or the 16 under state-of-emergency rule, an individual may be detained without charge for 15 to 30 days. Martial law authorities do not need warrants to detain suspects. Martial law commanders, subject to prescribed judicial procedures, may impose "internal exile" for up to five years on individuals believed to be acting against the "general security and public order." No such cases were reported in 1985. In its May 1985 Report, Amnesty International charged that torture was "widespread and systematic" in Turkey. The government responded that the organization had raised old, not current, incidents, and that, while occasional cases of mistreatment unfortunately still occurred, the perpetrators were punished. In September, the Ministry of Justice published statistics on the number of security officials who have been prosecuted for mistreatment of prisoners since the 1980 military takeover. According to ministry figures, investigations have been opened into accusations of torture involving 4,623 civilian security officers. Of these, 2,052 defendants have been acquitted, 439 have been found guilty, and charges against 410 have been dropped. The remainder are still under investigation. From among the 624 cases that involved martial law authorities, some 105 persons have been found guilty.

Some 125 armed clashes occurred between government security forces and separatist terrorists. In an October 16, 1985 statement to the Parliament, the interior minister noted that a total of 59 soldiers and 108 insurgents had been killed to date. There have also been about 74 civilian deaths related to the conflict since August 1984. As of August 1985, the government reported that 272 persons were under detention, 133 were being questioned, and 186 were on trial in connection with this conflict.

The Turkish General Staff (TGS) describes the insurgents as "terrorists/separatists" whose aim is to establish a separate Kurdish state incorporating parts of Turkey, Iran and Iraq. Drug smugglers, Armenian terrorists, and Kurdish guerrillas operating from bases in Iraq, Iran and elsewhere are also involved in the incidents, according to the TGS.

The Turkish National Police are responsible for maintaining public order in most of the country. In martial law areas (nine out of 67 provinces compared to 34 out of 67 at the end of 1984) military authorities oversee security throught the gendarmerie, which functions as the police in rural areas. These nine provinces are in eastern Turkey where government forces are under attack by Kurdish separatist insurgents.

CIVIL SERVICE

Each ministry does its own recruiting and develops its own training programs. The Institute of Public Administration at Ankara provides additional training for civil servants above the level of district administrators. Civil servants are prohibited from participating in politics. The civil service has recently suffered a decline in social status because of relatively low salaries and competition from managers of private industry.

LOCAL GOVERNMENT

Turkey is divided for purpose of regional administration into 67 vilayetlar (sing: vilayet) or iller (sing: il), or provinces each under a provincial governor or vali

PROVINCES OF TURKEY (1977)

Adana	Cankiri	Izmir	Ordu
Adiyaman	Corum	Kars	Rize
Afyonkarahisar	Denizli	Kastamonu	Sakarya
Agri	Diyarbekir	Kayseri	Samsun
Amasya	Edirne	Kirklareli	Siirt
Ankara	Elazig	Kirsehir	Sinop
Antalya	Erzincan	Kocaeli	Sivas
Artvin	Erzurum	Konya	Tekirdag
Aydin	Eskisehir	Kutahya	Tokat
Balikesir	Gaziantep	Malatya	Trabazon
Bilecik	Giresun	Manisa	Tunseli
Bingol	Gumusane	Maras	Urfa
Bitlis	Hakkari	Mardin	Usak
Bolu	Hatay	Mugla	Van
Burdur	Icel	Mus	Yozgat
Bursa	Isparta	Nevesehir	Zonguldak
Canakkale	Istanbul	Nigde	

The provinces are divided into counties (kazalar; sing: kaza; also ilceler; sing: ilce) each headed by an administrator known as a kaymakam. In 1977 there were over 600 counties, each divided into bucaklar, or districts, and each under a bucak mudur, or director. The smallest administrative units are koys, or villages, in the charge of muhtars, or headmen. Each provincial and district capital, regardless of size, and each town of more than 2,000 people is organized as a belediye, or municipality, under a belediye reise, or mayor. At each level there are elected representative assemblies with limited administrative powers: the vilayet genel meclisi in the provinces, the kaza idare heyeti in the counties, the bucak heyti, or district council, and the bucak encumeni, or district committee, in the districts, the ihtiar heyti, or council of elders, in the villages, and the municipal assembly and municipal council in towns.

FOREIGN POLICY

The North Atlantic Treaty Organization, which Turkey joined as a full member in 1952, was the cornerstone of Turkish foreign policy until 1962. Relations with the Soviet Union were locked in cold war patterns until the mid-1960s when Turkey adopted a more flexible stance in world affairs.

The central problem in Turkish foreign relations is the Cyprus dispute, which revolves around the fate of the Turkish Cypriot community and has been critical since Cyprus achieved independence in 1960. It nearly led to war with Greece (in 1967) and strained relations with the United States and the West to the limit of estrangement. In 1974 Turkish forces invaded Cyprus and occupied one-third of the island. Following the invasion, the United States banned all military aid to Turkey, while Turkey retaliated by placing U.S. bases under Turkish control. Relations were improved following an agreement reached at Brussels in December 1975; U.S. aid was resumed, and U.S. bases were reopened in 1976. The other sensitive issue in U.S.-Turkish relations concerns the illicit trade in opium originating in Turkey. Recent years have witnessed a number of anti-American and anti-NATO riots as these issues were exploited by the left and the right. In 1978 Prime Minister Bulent Ecevit indicated his willingness to sign a treaty of friendship with the Soviet Union.

Turkey recognized Israel in 1949 and, despite contrary pressures from Arab countries, has succeeded in maintaining a neutral posture on the Arab-Israeli conflict. A departure from the strict secular foreign policy was Turkey's participation in the Islamic Summit conference at Rabat, Morocco in 1969. Relations are generally cordial with Arab and Muslim states, but Syria's lingering resentment over the loss of Hattay Province in 1939 continues to be an irritant in Syrian-Turkish relations. Relations with West Germany have been close for a number of years based on the economic link provided by migrant Turkish workers.

Turkey's internal political and economic problems have been exacerbated by its continuing isolation in foreign affairs. Although the U.S. embargo was finally lifted in 1978 (with the stipulation that Turkey continue to seek a negotiated settlement on the Cyprus issue), the very next year witnessed the crumbling of CENTO, one of the cornerstones of Turkish foreign policy and military strategy. The hesitant attempts that were made during the 1970s to identify more closely with the Islamic bloc were halted by the 1980 coup which left Turkey, as it always was, without a niche of its own — neither West nor East, neither Europe nor Asia.

In the EEC councils, Turkey continues to be treated as a poor relation, and has been chastised on a number of occasions. In 1981 the EEC imposed restrictions on the import of Turkish goods. In 1984 the credentials of the Turkish delegates to the Parliamentary Assembly of the Council of Europe were suspended in protest against continuing violations of human rights.

Turkey and the United States are parties to 45 treaties and agreements covering agricultural commodities, atomic, energy, aviation, defense, economic and technical cooperation, education, extradition, finance, investment guaranties, judicial assistance, lend-lease, mutual security, narcotic deugs, patents, Peace Corps, postal matters, surplus property, taxation, trade and commerce, and visas.

Turkey is a founding member of the United Nations; its share of the U.N. budget is 0.029%. It is also a member of 16 U.N. organizations and 39 other international organizations.

U.S. Ambassador in Ankara: Robert Strausz-Hupe
U.K. Ambassador in Ankara: Sir Mark Russell
Turkish Ambassador in Washington, D.C.: Sukru Elekdag
Turkish Ambassador in London: Rahmi Gumrukcuoglu

PARLIAMENT

Following the coup of 1980, the junta suspended the Grand National Assembly. The Grand National Assembly was composed of two houses, the National Assembly and the Senate of the Republic. The National Assembly (Millet Meclisi) consisted of 450 members elected on a proportional basis for four-year terms. The Senate (Cumhuriyet Senatosu) consisted of 184 members popularly elected to six-year terms, with one-third elected every two years. In addition there were 15 members chosen by the president, along with an unlimited number of lifetime senators, including former members of the Committee of National Unity and former presidents of the republic. The 1982 constitution abolished the bicameral legislature and established in its place a unicameral 400-member Grand National Assembly elected for four-year terms. In the 1983 elections, the Motherland Party obtained 212 seats, the Populist Party 117 seats and the National Democracy Party 71 seats. The Grand National Assembly convenes on the first day of November every year and could adjourn for no more than five months a year. The president could return a law to the Grand National Assembly within 10 days but, if it passed a second time it was published without his approval.

POLITICAL PARTIES

All political parties were suspended in 1980. The 1982 constitution virtually eliminated all pre-coup political parties and ensured that they will not return to the political scene. In order to qualify for the 1983 parliamentary elections, new parties were required to obtain the signatures of at least 30 founding members, subject to veto by the National Security Council. Most were rejected by the NSC without explanation and only three groups were registered for the balloting. Further, any political party that failed to obtain at least 5% of the national vote was disqualified from the Assembly. This provision sounded the death knell for the small parties that proliferated in pre-coup Turkey.

Parties Registered for the 1983 Election were:

• Motherland Party: A nationalist and pro-Islamic party that favors private enterprise. At the 1984 local elections, it obtained control of the municipal councils in the capitals of 55 out of 67 provinces.

• Populist Party: A left-of-center group.

• Nationalist Democracy Party: A center-right group backed by the military.

The former major parties have their counterparts in the parties that were not granted recognition by the NSC. These include the Social Democratic Party and the Democratic Left Party (the old Republican People's Party); True Path Party (the old Justice Party); and the Welfare Party (the old National Salvation Party). A few Kemalist parties sponsored by former army officers have sprouted since 1983, including the Banner Party, the New Order Party and Virtue Party.

Permanent restrictions on political activity include barring of certain political and social groups from operating independently in political arenas and the banning of leading figures of the old political system from political activities. In the first category, no political party may be formed which advocates, or is organized according to principles which would result in, a theocratic basis for the state and the law; no party may advocate the superiority or dictatorship of a particular social class or group, or "exclusivist" or "elitist" political philosophies; and no party may be formed around a particular ethnic or cultural group. Prohibited political groupings would include a Communist or other Marxist party based on class, a Fascist "elitist" party, a party based on an ethnic or minority group such as the Kurds, or an Islamic fundamentalist party. There is no prohibition on the participation of members of ethnic or religious minorities in political parties so long as the parties do not adopt prohibited principles. Persons regarded as Communists and Fascists are banned from party membership. Other groups permanently banned from joining, or actively participating in, political parties include members of the armed forces and certain categories of civil servants.

The second category of "permanent" restrictions bans leaders of the pre-September 1980 political parties from participating in politics or in organization and control of political parties for up to 10 years. These restrictions range from five-year bans on some former politicians from holding leadership positions in the new political parties (but without restrictions on the right to join a party and to run for office), up to complete bans on all political activities for 10 years for former party leaders, including ex-prime ministers Ecevit and Demirel. These restrictions represent an attempt by the military to remove from the political process for a time those elements which it blames

for the anarchy and political stalemate that existed before the 1980 military takeover. Finally, the new elections law establishes a minimum percentage requirement for a party to win seats in Parliament, setting the threshold at 10%. The intent of this provision is to prevent recurrence of the situation that existed in the late 1970s when several small parties, notably extremist parties of the right, held the balance of power in Parliament and extracted concessions from the major parties as their price for support in coalition governments.

The illegal opposition consists of the Labor Party and the Communist Party. The former is a Marxist group founded in 1961 with a heterogeneous constituency consisting of intellectuals and peasants. It received less than 3% of the vote in 1969 and was banned in 1971 by the Constitutional Court. The Communist Party has been proscribed since 1925 but claims a membership of over 1,000 and the support of thousands of fellow-travelers. It is pro-Soviet.

Under the constitution, political parties are considered indispensable entities of democratic life. The government provides financial assistance to political parties that receive at least 5% of the total popular vote in national elections. But they are required at the same time to submit accounts of their sources of income and expenditure to the Constitutional Court, which has the power to dissolve parties. Public associations are not permitted to make financial contributions to political parties. Under the 1971 constitutional amendment, party programs must conform to the principles of democracy, nationalism, secularism, the 1960 revolution and Ataturkism. Parties not complying with this provision may be permanently dissolved.

ECONOMY

Turkey is one of the 35 higher middle-income countries of the world with a free-market economy dominated by the private sector.

In 1960 the State Planning Organization was established to implement a series of five-year economic and social development plans. It consisted of a Supreme Planning Council responsible for initiation, policy formulation, and audit control, and a Central Planning Organization charged with implementation and investment. The first Five-Year Plan was inaugurated in 1963 and achieved an annual GNP growth rate of 6.3%; the second plan, launched in 1968, followed in the same direction as the first, emphasizing manufacturing, housing, transportation, agriculture and energy, in that order, at a projected cost of L110 billion. The third plan (1973-78) was projected to achieve an 8% annual increase in GDP and a 7% annual increase in the GNP. The overall cost of the plan was projected at about L280 billion in constant 1971 prices, of which 56% would take place in the public sector and 44% in the private sector. In sectoral allocations, manufacturing led the field, with 31%, followed by housing, transportation, agriculture, power and mining, in that

PRINCIPAL ECONOMIC INDICATORS

Gross National Product: $58.260 billion (1983)
  GNP Annual Growth Rate: 3.6% (1973-82)
  Per Capita GNP: $1,230 (1983)
  Per Capita GNP Annual Growth Rate: 1.4% (1973-82)

Gross Domestic Product: L11.467 trillion (1983)
  GDP at 1980 Prices: L4.989 trillion
  GDP Deflator (1980=100): 230.6
  GDP Annual Growth Rate: 4.1% (1973-83)
  Per Capita GDP: L242,550 (1983)
  Per Capita GDP Annual Growth Rate: 2.8% (1970-81)

Income Distribution: 12% of the national income is received by the bottom 40%; 57% of the national income is received by the top 20%.

Percentage of Population in Absolute Poverty: 11

Consumer Price Index (1970=100);
  All Items: 268.8 (June 1985)
  Food: 257.6 (June 1985)

Wholesale Price Index: (1980=100)
  General: 445 (March 1985)

Average Annual Rate of Inflation: 42.0% (1973-83)

Money Supply: L2.292 trillion (December 1984)
  Reserve Money: L2.101 trillion (December 1984)

Currency in Circulation: L547.6 billion (1983)

International Reserves: $1.271 billion, of which foreign exchange reserves were $1.239 billion (1984)

BALANCE OF PAYMENTS (1984)
(million $)

Current Account Balance	−1,407
Merchandise Exports	7,389
Merchandise Imports	−10,331
Trade Balance	−2,942
Other Goods, Services & Income	+2,366
Other Goods, Services & Income	−2,945
Other Goods, Services & Income Net	−579
Private Unrequited Transfers	1,885
Official Unrequited Transfers	229
Capital Other Than Reserves	1,194
Net Errors & Omissions	318
Total (Lines 1, 10 and 11)	105
Counterpart Items	−830
Total (Lines 12 and 13)	−724
Liabilities Constituting Foreign Authorities' Reserves	—
Total Change in Reserves	724

order. Among the long-term objectives of the plan were a reduction in unemployment, improved income distribution and a higher standard of living.

Etatism has also been historically a salient feature of the Turkish economy. In recent years more than half of fixed capital investment has been undertaken by the public sector, and the country's Fourth Five Year Plan (1979-1983) called for more than half of public sector ianvestment to be made in directly productive enterprises, rather than infrastructure. Typically, more than 40% of national industrial production has been in the public sector.

A five-year plan, announced in June 1984, envisaged an average real annual growth in GDP of 6.3% from 1985, while inflation was to be reduced to 10% by 1990. Private investment was expected to grow by 11% annually, and public investment by 6.8%,

while industrial production was to rise by 7.5% per year. Per capita GNP was to rise by about 2.5% annually to $1,353 (at 1983 prices) by 1990.

GROSS DOMESTIC PRODUCT BY ECONOMIC ACTIVITY
(1970-81)

	%	Rate of Change %
Agriculture	23.8	3.2
Mining	1.9	9.7
Manufacturing	20.5	5.5
Construction	5.1	5.2
Electricity, Gas & Water	1.9	10.8
Transport & Communications	10.1	5.7
Trade & Finance	17.5	7.5
Public Administration & Defense	9.6	5.9
Other Branches	9.7	5.0

Turkey continues to be dependent in part on external assistance for economic development. The Organization for Economic Cooperation and Development (OECD) provided about $3.4 billion from 1963 through 1973, while the IMF and the European Monetary Agreement have also assisted Turkey with short-term credits. In 1979 the OECD members pledged more than $900 million to Turkey in grants and credits as balance of payments assistance. In April 1980 these same countries pledged an additional $1.2 billion. From 1946 through 1983 the United States provided $3.780 billion in economic aid and $6.435 billion in military support programs. Aid received from international organizations during the same period totaled $5.561 billion of which the World Bank share was $4.435 billion.

Turkey signed an agreement of association with the EEC in 1963. In mid-1971 Turkey entered the second or transitional stage of its association with the Common Market, which provides free entry of Turkish industrial exports to EEC countries, improved access to agricultural goods and up to $195 million in credit for investment in industrial products. In turn, Turkish tariffs will be progressively reduced or curtailed for EEC products over a 30-year period. Full association with the EEC is envisaged in 1992, or soon thereafter.

BUDGET

The fiscal year runs from March 1 through February 28. The consolidated national budget includes, in addition to the budget of the central government, 16 annexed budgets relating to partially autonomous agencies, state monopolies, airports, forests and universities.

Of current revenues, 51.7% comes from taxes on income, profit and capital gain, 19.9% from domestic taxes on goods and services, 5.3% from taxes on international trade and transactions, 6.7% from other taxes and 16.4% from non-tax revenues. Current revenues represented 22.0% of GNP. Of current expenditures, 15.2% goes to defense, 16.8% to education, 2.1%

GENERAL BUDGET ESTIMATES
(L million)

Revenue	1982*	1983
Tax revenues	1,303,038	1,933,338
Direct taxes	825,725	1,148,771
Taxes on income	804,131	1,109,071
Taxes on capital	21,594	39,700
Indirect taxes	477,313	784,567
Taxes on commodities	201,458	278,015
Taxes on services	131,102	252,390
Taxes on foreign trade	144,753	254,162
Non-tax ordinary revenues	109,933	307,668
Special revenues and funds	50,919	63,502
Domestic borrowing	54,266	198,463
Annexed budget revenues	34,428	65,562
TOTAL REVENUE	1,552,584	2,568,533

Expenditure	1982*	1983
Current expenditure	700,095	1,050,490
Investment expenditure	351,616	548,998
Transfer and capital formation expenditure	606,354	1,196,160
TOTAL EXPENDITURE	1,658,065	2,795,648

* The 1982 budget covered only 10 months (1 March–31 December), to bring the financial year into line with the calendar year.

1984 (L million): Total expenditure 3,250,000 (current 1,495,000; investment 740,700; transfer and capital formation 1,014,300).

1985 (L million): Total expenditure 5,508,000 (current 2,153,000; investment 1,010,000; transfer and capital formation 2,345,000).

to health, 8.9% to health, social security and welfare, 25.7% to economic services and 31.3% to other functions. Current expenditures represented 23.3% of GNP and overall deficit 1.8% of GNP.

In 1981 public consumption was L700.1 billion and private consumption L4.494 trillion. During 1973 to 1983, public consumption grew by 5.8% and private consumption by 2.2%.

In 1983 total outstanding disbursed external debt was $15.886 billion of which $10.721 billion was owed to official creditors and $4.675 billion to private creditors. The total debt service was $2.344 billion of which $1.174 billion was rempayment of principal and $1.169 billion interest. Total external debt represented 191% of export revenues and 30.7% of GNP. Debt service represented 29.1% of export revenues and 4.7% of GNP.

FINANCE

The Turkish unit of currency is the Turkish pound or lira divided into 100 kurus or 4,000 paralar (sing: para). Coins are issued in denominations of l, 5, 10, 25, and 50 kurus and 1, 2, 5, and 10 liras; notes are issued in denominations of 5, 10, 20, 50, 100, 500, and 1,000 liras.

Until 1960 the exchange rate was U.S. $1=L2.80 In 1970 the lira was devalued to L15 per U.S. $1. When the dollar was devalued in 1971, the rate was changed to L14 per U.S. $1. The lira maintained its relationship to the dollar when the latter was again devalued in 1973. Since 1974, the rates have been adjusted frequently with an export or buying rate and an import or selling rate. The lira was again devalued in 1978 for a whopping 49%. The rate in 1984 was U.S. $1=L532.125.

The banking system consists of the central bank, Turkiye Cumhuriyet Merkez Bankasi, 13 state-controlled banks, 29 private banks and five foreign-owned banks with over 3,400 branches. The central bank, reorganized in 1970, is the bank of issue and is responsible for the supervison of the credit system, implementation of monetary and credit policies and regulation of the exchange value of the lira. It also supplies many of the credit requirements of the public sector and finances the central government's budgetary deficits. Short-term advances to the treasury are limited by law to 15% of the national budget.

Of the 13 state-owned banks the largest is the Agricultural Bank, with over 30% of deposits in the country. There are other specialized state banks dealing with tourism, municipalities, real estate credit, mining and electrical power, the merchant marine and manufacturing. The largest of the private banks, Turkiye Is Bankasi, has over 700 branches and 25% of deposits. In 1984 the commercial banks had reserves of L827.1 billion, demand deposits of L1.371 trillion and time and savings deposits of L1.353 trillion.

The three most important development and investment banks are the Industrial Development Bank, the Industrial Investment and Credit Bank and the State Investment Bank. The principal source of savings is the Social Insurance Fund, which covers over a million workers.

The average rate of interest in 1981 was 31.5%.

AGRICULTURE

Agriculture is the largest sector of the Turkish economy. Of the total land area of 78,057,600 hectares (192,880,320 acres), 65 million hectares (160.6 million acres) are classified as arable, divided among field crops (24 million hectares, 59.3 million acres with some one-third fallow), orchards, vineyards and vegetables (2.4 million hectares, 5.9 million acres), meadows and pastures, (26 million hectares, 64.2 million acres) and forests (12.6 million hectares, 31.1 million acres). Per capita agricultural land is 1.4 hectares (3.4 acres). The index of agricultural production in 1982 was 122; the index of food production was 126 and the per capita index of food production 104 (both indices based on 1974-76=100). Some 54% of the labor force was employed in agriculture in 1981; women constitute almost 50% of that number. Agriculture's contribution to GDP was 19% in 1983 and its growth rate 3.4% (1973-83). Agricultural products made up one-third of the value of exports. The value added in agriculture in 1983 was $12.890 billion.

Turkish agriculture is beset by a large number of problems, not the least of which is the physical environment which restricts the range of crops. Turkish planners have tended to neglect agriculture in favor

GROWTH PROFILE Annual Growth Rates (%)	
Population 1980-2000	1.9
Birthrate 1965-83	−25.7
Deathrate 1965-83	−40.3
Urban Population 1973-83	3.7
Labor Force 1973-83	2.1
GNP 1973-82	3.6%
GNP per capita 1973-82	1.4%
GDP 1973-83	4.1%
GDP per capita 1970-81	2.8%
Consumer Prices 1970-81	32.9
Wholesale Prices 1970-81	31.8
Inflation 1973-83	42.0
Agriculture 1973-83	3.4
Manufacturing 1973-83	3.7
Industry 1973-83	4.2
Services 1973-83	4.3
Mining 1970-81	9.7
Construction 1970-81	5.2
Electricity 1970-81	10.8
Transportation 1970-81	5.7
Trade 1970-81	7.5
Public Administration & Defense 1970-81	5.9
Export Price Index 1975-81	8.9
Import Price Index 1975-81	16.7
Terms of Trade 1975-81	−6.8
Exports 1973-83	6.3
Imports 1973-83	−0.2
Public Consumption 1973-83	5.8
Private Consumption 1973-83	2.2
Gross Domestic Investment 1973-83	2.3
Energy Consumption 1973-83	4.6
Energy Production 1973-83	3.8

of industry; agriculture received only 18% of investment in the first Five-Year Plan, 15% in the second plan and 12% in the third plan. Although Turkey is traditionally self-sufficient in foodstuffs except wheat, the growth of agricultural output has fallen below target and has barely kept up with population growth.

Before the 1973 land reforms, the patterns of land ownership showed a predominance of small holdings.

PATTERN OF LAND OWNERSHIP		
Percentage of Holdings	Acres per Holding	Percentage of Cultivated Area
69	less than 12.4 acres	25
18	12.4 to 24.7 acres	25
13	over 24.7 acres	50

There were fewer than 500 holdings over 607 hectares (1,500 acres). Most of the farms were still owner-managed, though there was sharecropping and absentee ownership especially in the east.

The Land and Agrarian Reform Bill passed in 1973 is designed to redistribute 3.2 million hectares (8 million acres) to 500,000 peasants over 15 years. Of the total area, 0.8 million hectares (2 million acres) will be nationalized private land. The maximum holding of each family was set at 32 hectares (80 acres) of irrigated land and 101 hectares (250 acres) of unirrigated land. The excess will be expropriated and distributed to landless peasants in units of from 34 to 101 hectares (85 to 250 acres). The new owners are prohibited

from subdividing them for inheritance purposes but are encouraged to join production cooperatives.

Although the proportion of cultivable land is greater in Turkey than in most Middle Eastern countries, much of the area is subject to limited and variable rainfall, less that 50 cm (20 in.) per year. Irrigation has thus assumed a crucial role in agricultural development plans. In the early 1970s less than 2 million hectares (5 million acres), or 12% of the planted crop area, were under irrigation. This was only one-fourth to one-third of land considered irrigable. During the first and second plans, the land under irrigation increased at an average rate of 100,000 hectares (247,100 acres) a year. Much of this activity was carried out by the Soil and Water General Directorate, known as Topraksu, which was also responsible for soil conservation and extension activities.

Over 70% of the area under crops is cultivated by draft animals and only 30% by tractors. The number of tractors in use in 1982 was 457,425 and the number of harvester-threshers 13,100. Annual consumption of fertilizers in 1982 was 1,293,700 tons or 53.5 kg (118 lb) per arable hectare.

The government maintains a comprehensive system of price supports for most agricultural commodities and subsidizes the sales of seed, fertilizers, pesticides, and agricultural equipment.

Of the total area sown, food grains account for 85% with 60% under wheat, 17% under barley, 8% under rye and corn and 3% under pulses. The principal wheat-growing area is the Anatolian plateau. The most important industrial crop is cotton, which accounts for 22% of exports by value and contributes 7% to agriculture's share of the GDP. Turkey is ranked among the world's largest producers of sultana grapes and hazelnuts. The country is also noted for its fine tobacco, produced in the southwestern provinces.

Turkey is one of the seven countries permitted by the U.N. Commission on Narcotic Drugs to export opium and is the second largest exporter, after India, with about 20% of the market. A significant proportion of the opium is smuggled out of the country to France where it is processed into heroin for eventual sale in the United States. U.S. efforts to suppress the production of opium at the source led to an official ban on opium-poppy cultivation in Turkey after the 1972 harvest. In 1974 the government rescinded the ban but retained the ban on lancing poppy pods and authorized harvesting only through the collection of the entire pod, a practice known as straw process, which is less conducive to illegal trafficking. Under this procedure no opium is produced but morphine is extracted directly.

Livestock production accounts for about 30% of agricultural output and one-fifth of agriculture's contribution to GDP. Most livestock is raised in the eastern highlands. The Angora goat produces the fine, soft wool known as mohair, of which Turkey is the largest producer in the world with an annual production of 9,000 tons. Livestock population in 1982 consisted of 49.636 million sheep, 18.213 million goats,

PRINCIPAL CROP PRODUCTION (1984)		
	Area (000 hectares)	Production (000 metric tons)
Wheat	9,300	17,200
Spelt	46	40
Rye	470	360
Barley	2,600	6,200
Oats	225	324
Corn	580	1,500
Millet	20	14
Rice	70	270
Mixed grain	170	90
Dry beans	100	190
Chick peas	168	350
Lentils	177	650
Vetch	156	142
Broad beans	31	82
Potatoes	180	3,135
Onions	70	1,090
Garlic	13	81
Tomatoes	87	3,500
Cabbages	30	610
Melons & water-melons	131	4,600
Eggplants	36	700
Cotton (lint)		601
Cottonseed	653	790
Tobacco	304	210
Sugar beet	277	12,000
Sesame seed	35	33
Sunflower seed	415	715
Olives		1,200
Olive oil	81.1	120
Tea	53	500

14.484 million cattle, 1.252 million asses, 744,000 horses, 56.616 million chickens, 808,000 buffaloes, 9,000 camels, 3.072 million turkeys, 285,000 mules and 14,000 pigs.

The 1961 constitution has a special provision placing all forest areas under state management and control. Total forest land in 1973 was estimated at 19.14 million hectares (47.2 million acres) or about 23% of the land area. More than half of this area was either unproductive or low grade. Roundwood production in 1982 was 21.883 million cubic meters (772 million cubic ft).

Fishing is comparatively undeveloped and contributes only 1% of the agricultural share of the GDP. The total fish catch in 1982 was 514,900 metric tons.

Agricultural credit is provided by the Agricultural Bank, with 859 branches, either through direct loans to farmers or indirectly through 2,000 credit cooperatives.

INDUSTRY

The growth rate of the manufacturing sector declined during 1973-83 to 3.7% compared to 9.5% during 1965-73. Its contribution to the GDP was 24% and it overtook agriculture as the primary contributor to the GDP by 1980. Though manufacturing employed only 10.7% of labor, as against 54% employed in agriculture, labor productivity in industry was 4.8 times as great as in agriculture. The growing importance of industry is also attested by the relative proportions of investment that went to industry and agriculture in the three five-year plans: 31% to industry and 18% to agriculture in the first, 34% to industry and 15% to agriculture in the second and 31% to industry and 12% to agriculture in the third. The gross manufacturing output in 1981 was L3.471 trillion. The value added in manufacturing in 1982 was $6.898 billion of which agro-based products accounted for 24%, textiles for 11%, machinery and transport equipment for 14% and chemicals for 12%. Based on 1975=100 the index of industrial production in 1980 was 108.

Industrialization, however, is characterized by a number of sharp imbalances. The first is the concentration of industries in a small geographical area: in Ankara and the industrial zone around the Sea of Marmara and the Gulfs of Izmir and Iskenderun. Istanbul alone accounts for 40% of the industrial output. The second contrast is between large and small-scale units and between traditional and modern subsectors. In 1982 the dozen largest state enterprises and the 100 largest private enterprises produced 50% of the net output of the manufacturing sector while employing only 20% of industrial labor.

The total number of industrial plants was estimated in 1981 at 9,488, each employing 10 or more persons. Of these consumer goods industries accounted for 55%, secondary goods industries 30% and capital goods industries 14.1%. Industrial development is geared principally to the home market, and manufactured goods account for only about 4% of total exports.

The Turkish economy is best described as mixed, in which contributions to the GDP are more or less evenly divided between the public and private sectors. Most heavy industry and almost all utilities are concentrated in the public sector, but the private sector dominates the production of consumer goods. The state provides industrial leadership through some 20 to 25 major public sector undertakings and about 100 lesser ones collectively called Iktisadi Devlet Tesekkulleri (IDT). Together they control all sensitive areas of public ownership: minerals, power, transportation, communications and heavy industry, employ over 400,000 persons and account for 10% of the GNP, 20% of gross fixed investment and 40% of the manufacturing output. The public sector suffers from a lack of efficient planning and the intervention of political and social considerations. The government planned to sell 40 State Economic Enterprises to private investors in 1985, in an attempt to revive the moribund securities market, raise revenue and increase efficiency. Since 1950 private enterprise has been actively encouraged and now provides nearly half the investment capital and about two-thirds of total industrial output. Private sector firms are either individually owned or partnerships. Joint-stock operations are comparatively rare.

The largest industrial subsector is food processing (33%), followed by textiles (15%) and machinery (12%). The other major industries are iron and steel, paper and board, cement, automobiles and petrochemicals.

With the exception of petroleum there has been little foreign participation in industry, and the government has traditionally discouraged large-scale foreign investment. Private foreign investment capital coming into Turkey has increased in each of the past four years, but was still only $72 million in 1983. Industrial credit is provided by the Industrial Development Bank of Turkey and the State Investment Bank.

ENERGY

Total energy production in Turkey in 1982 was 16.950 million metric tons of coal equivalent and consumption 36.642 million metric tons of coal equivalent, or 787 kg (1,735 lbs) per capita. The annual growth rates during 1973-83 were 3.8% for energy production and 4.6% energy consumption. Energy imports accounts for 66% of all merchandise imports. Apparent per capita consumption of gasoline is 37 gallons per year.

The weak spot in Turkey's energy picture is the relatively small amount of petroleum and natural gas discovered within the country. Despite intensive prospecting, only one significant field has been discovered, at Ramandag in south-east Turkey. Reserves are estimated at 370 million barrels of petroleum and about 16 billion cubic meters (565 billion cubic ft) of natural gas. Production of petroleum crude was 16 million barrels in 1982, which met one-seventh of the country's requirements. The production of natural gas was 787 million cubic meters (27.792 billion cubic ft). The largest of the four companies producing oil was Shell with 58%, followed by the Turkish Petroleum Corporation, in which the government has 51% controlling interest, and Mobil. Four existing oil refineries at Mersin, Izmit, Batman and Izmir have a combined capacity of 472,000 barrels per day.

Coal, which supplies about 14% of energy needs, is produced entirely by state enterprises. Production of coal was 20,168,000 tons in 1982. Turkey also has substantial reserves of lignite, estimated at 5.9 billion tons.

Production of electricity in 1984 was 32 billion kwh and per capita output was 640 kwh. Some 70 to 75% of the installed capacity was thermal and the remainder hydroelectric. Turkey's most ambitious power project, the Keban Dam on the Euphrates, has an initial capacity of 620,000 kw rising to 1,240,000 kw. Turkey's first nuclear power station, with a capacity of 400 MW, went on stream in 1977.

LABOR

Turkey's economically active population was estimated at 19,027,000, or 41% of the total population, in 1982 with 54% employed in agriculture, 13% in industry and 33% in government and services. Of the total, 32.9% were women and 12% children. Over 59% were self-employed, mostly in agriculture.

ECONOMICALLY ACTIVE POPULATION ('000 persons employed in 1983)	
Agriculture, hunting, forestry and fishing	9,451
Mining and quarrying	113
Manufacturing	1,676
Energy, gas and water	119
Construction	596
Wholesale and retail trade	684
Transport, storage and communications	515
Finance, insurance and real estate	224
Public and personal services (including restaurants and hotels)	1,933
Other activities (not adequately described)	1,933
Total	15,682

WORKERS ABROAD ('000)	1982	1983
Australia	15	13
Austria	30	30
Belgium	25	25
France	64	64
Germany, Federal Republic	653	653
Libya	80	80
Netherlands	70	69
Saudi Arabia	80	80
Switzerland	24	24
Total (incl. others)	1,082	1,086

A significant feature of the labor market is the large number of Turkish workers abroad, estimated at 1.086 million in 1983. Workers' remittances from abroad, amounting to $1.554 billion in 1983, constitute a major item of foreign exchange. As demand for foreign labor has eased in Europe, increasing numbers of Turkish workers are being employed elsewhere abroad, notably in Saudi Arabia and Libya. In terms of the number of Turkish guest workers employed, Saudi Arabia has climbed to third place, following West Germany and France. A General Directorate for the Problems of Workers Abroad coordinates the export of Turkish manpower.

Conditions of labor are regulated by the Labor Act of 1967, which covers all places of work employing more than three persons outside agriculture. The constitution guarantees the right to reasonable conditions of labor suited to the worker's age, sex, and capacity, and grants the right to rest and leisure and a fair wage. The labor law forbids the employment of children under 13, and restricts children under 15 to "light work which will not harm their health and physical development, prevent their attendance at occupational training and orientation programs, or their ability to benefit from education." Children between 15 and 18 years of age may not be employed in underground or underwater work, nor may they be employed at night. Girls and women may not be employed in underground or underwater work, but, if over the age of 18, may work night shifts under conditions specified jointly by the Ministry of Health and Social Welfare and the Ministry of Industry and Commerce. A board composed of government, private sector, and labor representatives establishes national minimum wages for the agricultural and nonagricultural sectors. The labor law provides for a 7.5-hour day and a 45-hour workweek. Acceptable conditions of work are both guaranteed by the constitution and sought after by the workers, though there remains a considerable gap, especially in the area of occupational safety and health, between society's goals and laws, on the one hand, and actual practice on the other. The trade unions have repeatedly complained that existing regulations governing health, safety and working conditions are not adequately enforced.

Turkey has suffered chronic and severe unemployment, averaging 9 to 20% annually since 1971. Urban unemployment is reported to grow by about two percentage points a year. Depressed wage scales and spiraling prices have combined to accentuate the distance between the poor and the rich. Average wages in nonagricultural jobs in 1980 were L426.96 per day.

Organized labor is a comparatively new phenomenon in Turkey. Strikes, lockouts and collective pargaining were legalized in 1963 but were restricted under the constitutional amendments of 1971. The laws on associations and trade unions prohibit all associations and trade unions from having any ties to political parties. The trade union law and the constitution also prohibit any political activity by trade unions, including the endorsement of parties or candidates and contributions to their campaigns. However, trade union activity in the defense of workers' social and economic interests is not considered political activity. The unions have taken advantage of this exception to mount strenuous public campaigns against various government policies and to lobby government and opposition parliamentarians in support of labor positions. Those unions and confederations which are organized in accordance with the 1983 Labor Law have been allowed to organize workplaces freely.

There are four national labor federations of which the most important and largest is Turk-Is, the Confederation of Turkish Trade Unions, with 35 member unions and over 1,500,000 members. There are 625 other unions.

The September 20 1980 amendments to the Martial Law Act empower the government to prohibit strikes and to impose a permit requirement for unions to strike. Disk, the leftist labor federation, and Misk, the rightist labor federation, have had their assets blocked and activities suspended from September 1980. However, Turk-Is, the largest labor federation, has been allowed to continue functioning. Many labor leaders were taken into custody following the coup but were released later. The government appointed trustees to handle the financial affairs of suspended federations.

FOREIGN COMMERCE

The foreign commerce of Turkey in 1984 consisted of exports of $6.924 billion and imports of $10.499 billion, leaving an unfavorable trade balance of $3.575 billion. Of the imports, petroleum constituted 35.9%,

nonelectrical machinery 20.5% (of which transport equipment 4.9%), chemicals 12.4% and iron and steel products 8.9%. Of the exports, cereals, livestock and foodstuffs constituted 42.7%, textiles 22.7%, petroleum products 4.1% and machinery and transport equipment 4.0%.

The major import sources were Iran 13.7%, West Germany 10.6%, Iraq 9.8%, Libya 8.6% and the United States 7.5%. The major export destinations were Iran 19.0%, West Germany 14.6%, Italy 7.4%, Saudi Arabia 6.4% and Iraq 5.6%. Based on 1975=100, the import price index in 1981 was 222, the export price index 149 and the terms of trade 73. Persistent trade deficits were partly offset by a net surplus in invisible items such as tourism and migrant workers' remittances from Western Europe.

FOREIGN TRADE INDICATORS (1984)

Annual Growth Rate, Imports:	−0.2 (1973-83)
Annual Growth Rate, Exports:	6.3 (1973-83)
Ratio of Exports to Imports:	40:60
Exports per capita:	$135.00
Imports per capita:	$205.00
Balance of Trade:	−$3.575 billion
Ratio of International Reserves to Imports (in months)	2.8
Exports as % of GDP:	8.1
Imports as % of GDP:	14.3
Value of Manufactured Exports:	$2.475 billion
Commodity Concentration:	20.4%

Direction of Trade (%)

	Imports	Exports
EEC	27.9	32.0
U.S.	6.5	5.7
Industrialized Market Economies	52.0	50.5
East European Economies	6.0	2.5
High Income Oil Exporters	33.3	39.5
Developing Economies	41.6	46.5

Composition of Trade (%)

	Imports	Exports
Food	2.8	46.0
Agricultural Raw Materials	1.8	10.0
Fuels	44.2	2.3
Ores & Minerals	9.2	6.1
Manufactured Goods	42.0	35.6
of which Chemicals	14.9	2.1
of which Machinery	22.0	4.4

As part of the economic stabilization program of 1970, a Ministry of Foreign Economic Relations was established whose main task was to reduce imports. This ministry was renamed the Ministry of Commerce in 1972. A vast array of restrictions have been imposed on importers on addition to five different taxes on imported articles.

The principal Turkish international trade fair is held at Izmir annually during August-September.

TRANSPORTATION & COMMUNICATIONS

The Turkish Republic State Railways operates 8,156 km (5,064 mi) of railroad track, mostly standard gauge, including 204 km (127 mi) of electrified line. Modernization of the railways is a major target of the five-year plans. The rail system is linked to Iran (under a CENTO plan) and to Bulgaria. Traffic in 1983 consisted of 5.7 billion passenger-km and 6.301 billion net-ton-km of freight.

Maritime transport is controlled by two state-owned organizations: the Turkish Maritime Bank, which operates 17 ships and 80 ferries on coastal and Mediterranean routes, five shipyards and dry docks, and six hotels; and the Turkish Cargo Lines, which operates 62 cargo ships, bulk ore carriers and tankers. A number of private companies are engaged in ocean shipping. The gross registered tonnage of the 688-vessel Turkish merchant marine was 4,088,800 in 1983. Of this, tankers accounted for 709,000 and ore and bulk carriers 758,000. In 1982 the six ports of Mersin, Iskenderun, Istanbul, Izmir, Izmit and Samsun handled 68,796,000 metric tons of freight.

With the closure of Persian Gulf ports due to disturbances in the Middle East, Turkish overland routes have become a major connecting point to the Middle East. While transportation fees are a major foreign exchange earner, the greatly increased traffic has caused strains on highway infrastructure. Turkey has no significant navigable rivers. The railroad ferry over Lake Van forms part of the railroad link between Istanbul and Teheran. Istanbul is linked to the Asian continent by a rail ferry service and by a bridge over the Bosporus. This bridge, completed in 1975, is the fourth largest bridge in the world. Construction of a second bridge and a tube-tunnel under the Bosporus is planned.

The pipeline system is 3,433 km (2,132 mi) long, of which 1,288 km (800 mi) carry crude oil and 2,145 km (1,332 mi) carry refined products.

The road network consists of 67 km (41 mi) of expressways, 31,895 km (19,807 mi) of national highways, 19,644 km (12,199 mi) of provincial roads, and 87,473 km (54,320 mi) of village roads. Of these, 21,031 km (13,060 mi) of national highways and expressways are hardsurfaced. The total number of passenger cars in 1983 was 812,122 and that of commercial vehicles 392,927, excluding 85,200 buses. Per capita passenger car ownership was 16.0 per 1,000 inhabitants.

The Turkish national airlines is Turk Hava Yollari (THY), which is 97.35% state-owned. Its fleet of 30 aircraft services an extensive internal network, and it also has international flights to over 17 foreign cities. In 1982 it flew 12.2 million km (7.5 million mi) and carried 646,000 passengers. The major international airports are Yesilkoy (Istanbul), Esenboga (Ankara), Cigli (Izmir), and Adana. There are 113 other airfields, 93 usable, 57 with permanent-surface runways and 22 with runways over 2,500 meters (8,000 ft).

In 1984 Turkey had 2.39 million telephones, or 5.3 per 100 inhabitants.

In 1980 the postal service's 10,335 post offices handled 770,714,000 pieces of mail and 12,788,000 telegrams. The volume of mail per capita was 15 pieces. There are 7,265 telex subscriber lines.

In 1982, 1,026,000 tourists visited Turkey, of whom 36,300 were from the United States, 33,000 from the United Kingdom, 109,100 from France, 45,400 from Italy, 11,000 from Switzerland, and 100,200 from West Germany. Total tourist receipts were $370 million and expenditure by nationals abroad $108.917 million. There are 44,100 hotel beds and the average length of stay was 2.5 days.

MINING

Turkey is rich in mineral resources, including bauxite, borax, chrome, copper, iron ore, manganese and sulphur. The mining sector employed 113,000 workers and contributed 1.9% to the GDP in 1983. Mining was allocated 5.8% investment outlay in the Third Five-Year Plan.

The mining sector is dominated by two state corporations, Etibank and State Iron Mines, which together account for 70% of mineral production and export. The remaining 30% is accounted for by some 200 small and medium private sectors firms. In 1983 mineral production was (in '000 metric tons): iron ore, 3,151; chrome, 482; copper, 19; sulphur, 29; and manganese, 3.

DEFENSE

The defense structure is headed by the president of the republic who is also the commander in chief of the armed forces. The line of command runs from him through the prime minister and the minister of defense to the chief of the general staff. There are three institutions linking the government and the armed forces: The Ministry of National Defense, the National Security Council which advises and is presided over by the president, and the Supreme Military Council which advises and is presided over by the prime minister.

The armed forces, once heavily deployed on the Soviet and Bulgarian borders, are now poised also on the Aegean front in view of the ever-present possibility of a war with Greece. Turkey's commitment to the NATO has diminished since 1974, but Turkish leaders have reaffirmed their intention to stay in the alliance because of the undeniable benefits it reaps in military aid and hardware.

Manpower is provided by conscription. The length of service is fixed at 20 months for all services. The principle of universal service was abandoned as the supply of manpower began to exceed requirements. Instead the general staff determines the necessary yearly number of recruits, who are then chosen by lot.

The total strength of the armed forces is 630,000, which makes it one of the largest standing armies in the world and second only to the United States within the NATO alliance. The size of the armed forces is enhanced by a proud national military tradition and the toughness and fighting quality of the Turkish soldier. Military personnel constitute 16.7 armed persons per 1,000 civilians.

In addition to its role as defender of the country, the Turkish Army has also played an active role in politics and views itself as guardian of the Kemalist legacy. Under this concept the Army stays out of politics but retains the right to intervene if the civilian government departs substantially from Ataturk's policies, as in 1961 and 1980. Both the National Military Council and the Supreme Military Council wield potent influence on national policy.

ARMY:

Personnel: 520,000; Reserves: 800,000

Organization: Four armies: The First Army, with headquarters at Istanbul, the Second Army, with headquarters at Konya in the South, and the Third Army, with headquarters at Erzincan near the Soviet border. The newly created Fourth Army at headquarters at Izmir is responsible for the security of Aegean coastal region. 4 army HQ; 10 corps HQ; 1 armored division; 2 mechanized divisions; 14 infantry divisions; 6 armored brigades; 4 mechanized brigades; 11 infantry brigades; 1 parachute brigade; 1 commando brigade; 4 SSM battalions with Honest John; 1 SAM battery

Equipment: 2,922 tanks; 2,000 armored personnel carriers; 2,225 artillery including 186 guns, 2,039 howitzers; 18 Honest John SSM; 1,750 mortars; 2,590 antitank rocket launchers; 85 antitank guided weapons; 1,200 air defense guns; SAM

Army Aviation: 175 aircraft; 160 helicopters

NAVY:

Personnel: 55,000; Reserves: 70,000

Organization: Northern Sea Area Command at Istanbul; the Fleet Command at Golcuk; Southern Sea Area Command at Izmir; Marine Corps (three battalions)

Units: 16 submarines; 12 destroyers; 6 frigates; 9 fast attack craft; 29 patrol craft; 7 minelayers; 26 minesweepers; 68 amphibious landing craft; 56 auxiliary ships

Naval Aviation: 20 combat aircraft; 7 combat helicopters; 1 antisubmarine squadron

Marines: 1 brigade; 3 battalions; 1 artillery battalion

Naval Bases: Ankara, Golcuk, Istanbul, Izmir, Eregli, Bosphorus, Dardanelles, Heybeli and Iskenderun

AIR FORCE:

Personnel: 55,000; Reserves: 66,000

Organization: The First Tactical Air Force, with headquarters at Eskesehir; the Third Tactical Air Force, with headquarters at Diyarbekir; an air defense and warning command, with a 24-hour radar warning network as the Second Tactical Air Force Command

Units: 2 tactical air commands; 1 transport command; 1 training command; 368 combat aircraft; 17 fighter ground attack squadrons; 2 fighter squadrons; 2 reconnaissance squadrons; 5 transport squadrons; 1 VIP fleet; 3 liaison fleets; 3 Operational Conversion Unit squadrons; 3 training squadrons; 8 SAM squadrons

Forces Abroad: Cyprus, 1 corps of 2 infantry divisions

Air Bases: Izmir, Adana, Bandirma, Diyarbakir, Esluboga, Sivas, Etimesgut, Eskisehir, Yesilkoy, Mersifon and Balikesir

Light military equipment and ammunition are produced under the auspices of Mkek, a state-owned enterprise. Leopard II tanks, armored cars and troop carriers are manufactured by the Ground Forces Support Foundation and fighter-bombers by TUSAS.

The annual military budget in 1985 was $1.645 billion, which constituted 21.4% of the national budget, or 4.9% of the GNP, $55 per capita, $4,216 per soldier and $4,151 per sq km of national territory.

The Turkish armed forces rank with those of Israel as the best-organized, best-equipped and best-led in the Middle East. Turkish military strength is based not only on the fierce and ruthless fighting qualities of the average soldier but also on $6.435 billion worth of equipment received from the United States from 1946 through 1983. However, the arms embargo imposed by the United States following the Turkish invasion of Cyprus and lifted only in mid-1978 has seriously affected Turkey's ability to obtain spare parts for its sophisticated weaponry. The armed forces are heavily concentrated on the Greek border in Thrace and on the Soviet border in the east.

Turkey has received over $6.4 billion in U.S. aid since 1946. Of this, more than half has been in the form of direct military assistance. Other NATO countries have also assisted Turkey. From 1964 onward military aid from West Germany was estimated at $20 million annually. Izmir is a major NATO base and also a base for the U.S. Sixth Fleet. There are still about 6,000 U.S. military personnel stationed in Turkey and at least 200 military aircraft, beside extensive radar installations. Arms purchases abroad for 1973 through 1983 totaled $3.480 billion, of which $750 million was supplied by the United States and $850 million by West Germany.

EDUCATION

The national literacy rate is 60.2% (77.2% for males and 43.1% for females). Illiteracy is highest among females (66%) and among the rural population (60%). Of the population over 15, 39.5% have had no schooling, 52.4% have completed primary school, 6.7% have completed secondary school, and 1.4% have completed post-secondary education.

Education is free, universal and compulsory from the ages of 6 to 14. In 1982 the school enrollment ratio in the primary 6-10 age group was 102% and 39% in the secondary age group of 11 to 16 for a combined enrollment ratio of 69%. The third-level enrollment ratio is 5.9%.

The academic year runs from September to June. The language of instruction is Turkish, except at the university level, where English is adopted in some colleges and courses.

Schooling consists of 11 years divided into primary and secondary sections. Primary education is again divided into a three-year lower and a two-year upper stage. Secondary education lasts for six years, divided into two stages: middle schools and lycees. The middle school is designed to give a complete education to students who, at the end of the course, may elect to go to work. The lycee, also known as lise, is a university preparatory course. The study of modern languages, English, French or German, is compulsory in the middle schools and lycees. The teaching methods in the primary schools are based on the Austrian and German model, those in the middle school on the French model and those in the technical schools on the Belgian model.

All state schools are coeducational. Girls represent 46% of primary education, 35% of secondary education and 30% of higher education enrollment.

Non-Muslim communities in Istanbul maintain their own private schools which, like other private schools, are subject to state supervision. Islamic religious instruction, following a state-prepared curriculum, is compulsory for all students except those who declare themselves non-Muslim. The courses of about two hours per week are taught by lay teachers. Extracurricular Koran courses using government-approved texts are permitted. Private schools account for 2% of secondary enrollment. The government has long resisted recurrent demands for nationalization of private schools, but the American-run Robert College, one of the most prestigious institutions in the Middle East, was taken over in 1971 and renamed Bosporus University.

Teacher training institutions are divided into two-year institutes for the primary schools, three-year institutes for the middle schools, and four-year colleges for the lycees. In 1982 there were 16,819 students enrolled in 42 teacher training colleges. The supply of primary school teachers is considered satisfactory, but there is a severe shortage of technical teachers. The average student-teacher ratio is 1:28 at the primary level and 1:18 at the secondary level and 1:17 at the post-secondary level.

In 1982, 22% of the students at the secondary level were in the technical stream. Technical education is offered in lower secondary and upper secondary schools. During the 1960s a number of trade institutes and technical schools was established, and in 1982 their total enrollment was 524,128.

The education system is highly centralized in the Ministry of National Education. Curricula, textbooks and the recruitment and posting of teachers are controlled by Ankara. The National Council on Education serves as a high-level advisory body on educational reforms. Adult education programs are supervised by the General Directorate for Adult Education. Ninety-two percent of public education funds are provided by the central government, while local authorities provide the balance mainly for school construction and maintenance. The national education budget in 1982 was L253,575,968,000, of which 82.9% were current expenditures and 87.3% teachers' salaries. Educational expenditures were 2.9% of the GNP and 16.8% of the national budget. Per capita expenditure on education was $38.

EDUCATIONAL ENROLLMENT (1982)			
	Schools	Teachers	Students
First Level	45,842	212,795	5,859,711
Second Level	5,062	129,268	2,393,477
Vocational	1,718	39,682	524,128
Third Level	331	21,814	281,929

There are 18 universities and 102 institutions of higher education in Turkey, with a total enrollment of 281,929 in 1982. Enrollment in higher education has grown at a rate of 14% annually since 1965. University enrollment was 1,788 per 100,000 inhabitants. With the exception of Ataturk University and Black Sea Technical University, both of which are administered by the Ministry of National Education, all universities are autonomous bodies.

The universities are: Anatolia University (Eskesehir), Ankara University (Ankara), Ataturk University (Erzurum), Bosporus University (formerly Robert College, Istanbul), Bursa University (Bursa), Cukurova University (Adana), Republic University (Sivas), Diyarbakir University (Diyarbakir), Aegean University (Izmir), Euphrates University (Elazig), Hacettepe University (Ankara), Inonu University (Malatya), Istanbul University (Istanbul), Istanbul Technical University (Istanbul), 19 May University (Sarnsua), Middle East Technical University (Ankara) and Seljuk University (Konya). Turkish university students are heavily politicized and a number of laws have been passed during the military regime against student organizations. Conflicts between students and the military are frequent.

The government has moved since 1980 to bring universities under tight, centralized control through a Higher Education Council. The constitution and the Political Parties Law prohibit faculty members and students from becoming members of political parties or involved in political activities. Thus, faculty or student political associations or any type are banned, and political parties are also forbidden to form youth branches. Some faculty members who were fired when martial law was in effect throughout the country have unsuccessfully petitioned the Higher Education Council for reinstatement. There is a court case pending to determine the constitutionality of the earlier dismissals.

In 1981, 44,542 Turkish students graduated from Turkish universities, including 12,379 women. Of these, 4,071 were awarded degrees in medicine, 9,698 in engineering, 1,266 in natural sciences, 5,387 in social sciences, 1,510 in law, 1,095 in agriculture and 5,543 in education.

In 1982, 15,262 Turkish students attended institutions of higher learning abroad, of whom 2,356 were in the United States, 8,838 in West Germany, 484 in the United Kingdom, 284 in the Netherlands, 278 in Switzerland, 1,234 in France and 152 in Canada. In the same year, 6,030 foreign students were enrolled in Turkey.

Scientific research is coordinated by the Scientific and Technical Research Council. In 1982 there were 7,747 scientists and engineers engaged in research and development. Expenditures on scientific research in the same year total L27.22 billion. Ninety scientific journals are published in the country. Turkish contribution to world scientific authorship was 0.0450% (U.S.=42%), and Turkey was ranked 42nd in the world in this respect.

LEGAL SYSTEM

Until the proclamation of the Turkish Republic in 1923, Turkish civil law was based on the Sharia and was administered by special religious courts. The reforms of 1926 secularized the legal system. The Swiss Civil Code and the Code of Obligation, the Italian Penal Code, the Neuchatel Code of Civil Procedure and the German Code of Maritime Commerce were adopted with certain modifications. The new codes revolutionized the legal basis of property, inheritance, contracts, marriage, divorce and other personal matters.

The court system consists of five higher courts and four types of ordinary courts. At the apex is the Constitutional Court consisting of 15 regular and five ordinary members. It is empowered to review the constitutionality of laws passed by the Grand National Assembly and to try, for offenses related to their functions, the president of the republic, the prime minister, and other senior ministers of state. The Council of State, with nine judicial chambers of five members each, is the highest administrative court. The Council also expresses opinions of draft legislation and government regulations and contracts. Most of the Council's cases are initiated by aggrieved citizens. The Court of Appeals, or the Court of Cassation, is the court of last resort with original and appellate jurisdiction. The Court of Jurisdictional Dispute settles disputes arising among civil, administrative and military courts as to jurisdictional limits. The State Security Court was set up in 1973 to prosecute offenses against the integrity of the state.

Ordinary courts include three types of civil courts: peace courts, courts of first instance and commercial courts. Criminal courts are organized on two levels: peace courts with a single judge and criminal courts with three judges. The military court structure is headed by the Military Court of Cassation and the High Military Administrative Court.

The constitution guarantees the independence of the judiciary. Judges may not be dismissed, retired or deprived of salaries except when they have been convicted of offenses or are mentally or physically incapacitated. Disciplinary action against judges can be initiated only by the High Council of Judges, consisting of 11 regular and three reserve members.

The system of justice includes a bail system under which the arraigning judge may release the accused on presentation of an appropriate guarantee, or order him held in preventive detention if the court determines that there is a risk that he may flee or destroy evidence. While Turkish law has no specific provision for habeas corpus, the constitution includes the right of detainees to request speedy conclusion of arraignment and trial, or release "if the restriction placed upon them is not lawful." Especially in mass trials, the speed with which court proceedings are concluded or provisional release is granted is not so rapid as constitutional provisions would suggest. Indeed, due process provisions of Turkish jurisprudence often tend to prolong both civil and criminal cases. Trials themselves are usually conducted under rules of procedure based on the constitution and the Martial Law Regulations. Civilian and military courts generally conduct trials under the same rules of precedure. Convictions in either system may be appealed to civilian and military appeals courts, respectively. In some types of cases, particularly capital cases, appeals are automatic to the Supreme Court or the High Court of Military Appeals, after which they must be approved by the Parliament and, finally, the president. It is not unusual for mass trials to last two or three years, often with many defendants in custody for part or all of the duration of the trial.

The corrections system is headed by the General Directorate of Prisons and Houses of Detention. There is a prison in every town and at least one in every district. The older penal institutions are being replaced by new penitentiary labor establishments emphasizing a rehabilitative regime and compulsory labor.

LAW ENFORCEMENT

The two principal agencies of law enforcement and internal security are the General Directorate of Security, which administers the National Police, and the Gendarmerie General Command, which administers the rural constabulary. The total personnel strength of the National Police in 1973 was estimated at 30,000, while the gendarmerie had a strength of 75,000, meaning that 6.5 persons were employed in law enforcement per 1,000 working population. Turkey ranks 11th in the world in terms of per capita strength of internal security forces.

The National Police is headed by a director general, assisted by six operational staff offices of which the first is concerned with political and media surveillance. Highly specialized squads focus on particular crime areas, such as smuggling and narcotics. A director of security is stationed in each of the 67 provinces. Below them are local police chiefs at the county and district levels. At the end of the scale are the bekciler (sing:bekci), or night watchmen in rural towns and villages. About 70% of the police are deployed in the Istanbul area.

The gendarmerie (jendarma) is a paramilitary force under a General Command at Ankara, headed by a four-star officer as commanding general. Armed with light weapons, it is a rural police force of constabulary with the usual functions of guarding land borders and of enforcing the law outside urban areas. In the provinces the operational units are three mobile infantry brigades under 13 district commands. The provincial gendarmerie functions under a commander, usually a colonel. At the county and district levels there are commanders who control gendarmerie posts, located at intervals of 10 to 12 miles along the roads. These posts are manned by six to twelve gendarmerie soldiers under a sergeant. In wartime the gendarmerie is fully under army control.

Surveillance and counter-subversion activities are carried out by the Political Branch of the National Police.

The rate of ordinary, nonpolitical crime has been consistently low in Turkey in relation to other countries. Crimes against persons dominate in frequency of occurrence in both rural and urban areas, while smuggling and black marketing are chronic problems. Juvenile offenses have increased to about 15% of the total reported crime. The death penalty is limited to offenses against the state, premeditated murder and espionage in wartime.

HEALTH

The most prevalent communicable diseases in the country are trachoma and tuberculosis. Diarrhea and enteritis are the major causes of death among infants and young children. Over 75% of the population have access to safe water.

PRINCIPAL HEALTH INDICATORS (1984)
Crude Death Rate: 9.0 per 1,000
Decline in Death Rate: −40.3% (1965-83)
Infant Mortality Rate: 131 per 1,000 Live Births
Child Death Rate (Ages 1-4) per 1,000: 8
Life Expectancy at Birth: Males: 60.8 females: 65.3

In 1981 there were 831 hospitals in the country with 97,765 beds, or one bed per 464 inhabitants. The total number of physicians was 28,411, or one physician per 1,597 inhabitants, 6,790 dentists and 22,998 nursing personnel. Some 30% of Turkish medical graduates are believed to be practicing in foreign countries. Of the hospitals 85.1% are state-run, 3.5% are run by private nonprofit agencies and 11.4% are run by private for-profit agencies. The admissions/discharge rate is 406 per 10,000 inhabitants. The bed occupancy rate is 44.1% and the average length of hospital stay is 9 days. Expenditures on health services account for 3.6% of the national budget and $11.70 per capita.

FOOD

Staple items of the Turkish diet are wheat and rye bread, vegetables and fruits. Meat is scarce and expensive, but fish are plentiful. The national drink is raki, distilled from fermented raisins and flavored with anise.

The per capita food intake is 83.3 grams of protein and 2,965 calories per day, 57 grams of fats and 504 grams of carbohydrates.

MEDIA & CULTURE

The total number of dailies in Turkey is placed at 1,115, and, while no exact figures are published, total daily circulation is now estimated to exceed 3.8 million copies. Istanbul has about 40 dailies, Ankara has around 25 (in addition to same-day issues of Istanbul titles), and Izmir six. Most of the dailies are privately owned and the majority are politically independent, though a small number are associated with political parties. Apart from a few titles in Armenian, Greek, English and French, all are published in Turkish. Fifteen dailies have circulations of over 100,000, of which *Hurriyet*, with a circulation of 767,000 in 1980, is the largest newspaper in the Middle East. The others are *Adalet* (174,000), *Ankara Tikaret* (100,000), *Baris* (180,000), *Hur Vatan* (165,000), *Tasvir* (141,000), *Yenigun* (153,000), *Yeni Tanin* (300,000), *Bulvar* (130,000), *Gunes* (290,000), *Yeni Nesil* (450,000), *Gunaydin* (300,000), *Tercuman* (225,000), *Milliyet* (210,000) and *Cumhuriyet* (90,000). Both *Hurriyet* and *Milliyet* are part of chain groups. Per capita newspaper circulation is estimated at 88 per 1,000.

The non-daily press consists of 618 titles, and the periodical press of between 1,300 and 2,000 titles, including 56 in English. The newsprint consumption was 148,400 tons, or 3,200 kg (7,056 lb) per 1,000 inhabitants in 1981.

Under the Constitution of 1961 "the press is free within the limits of law." This freedom was abridged by the constitutional amendment of 1971, which prohibits the publication of materials that might jeopardize public order, security or morality. Following student violence and terrorist activities during 1968-71, full censorship was imposed, and over 220 journalists were convicted. Communist propaganda and the defamation of national institutions are punishable offenses. A further measure of press control is provided by the Press Council, which imposes a code of self-discipline. The government also influences editorial policy through a system of indirect subsidies in the form of state advertisements. Turkey is ranked +1.66 in terms of press freedom (on scale with +4 as the maximum and −4 as the minimum: Switzerland +3.06; U.S. +2.72).

The official news agency is Anadolu Ajansi, which is state-owned with 517 domestic correspondents but no foreign bureaus. There are five private agencies: Turk Haberler Ajansi, IKA Haber Ajansi, Anatolian

News Agency, Hurriyet Haber Ajansi and ANKA Ajansi. Foreign agencies with bureaus in Ankara are AP, ANSA, AFP, UPI, Reuters and DPA.

Turkey has an extensive book publishing industry. Over 4,793 books were published in 1981. Turkey adheres to the Berne Copyright Convention and Florence Agreement.

Radio and television broadcasting is controlled by the Turkish Radio and Television Corporation (TRT), a state-owned autonomous enterprise until 1971, when it lost its autonomous status. A national program is on the air for 18 hours a day and is broadcast from Ankara (1,200 kw), Erzurum (100 kw), Antalya (600 kw), Cukurova (300 kw), Istanbul (150 kw), Izmir (100 kw) and Diyarbekir (300 kw). A second program is broadcast for seven hours daily from Ankara, Istanbul and Izmir. The Turkish police, the Turkish State Meteorological Service, American Forces Radio and Television Service, Istanbul University, and Istanbul Technical University operate transmitters of lower wattage. Regular school broadcasts are carried out by TRT in conjunction with the Ministry of Education. External broadcasting emanates from Ankara with two short-wave transmitters (250 and 100 kw). The foreign service, known as the Voice of Turkey, broadcasts for 47 hours a week in 11 languages. A licence fee is payable for non-portable receivers at different rates for cities and villages. The total number of receivers in 1983 was estimated at 4,300,000, or 83 per 1,000 inhabitants. Of the 52,104 annual radio broadcasting hours, 7,421 are devoted to information, 2,563 hours to education, 308 hours to culture, 146 hours to religion, 2,130 hours to commercials and 42,556 hours to entertainment.

Television was introduced in 1968 and now covers about 50% of the population with seven stations at Istanbul, Ankara, Eskesehir, Balikesir, Edirne, Izmir and Kirikkale. These stations are on the air for five days a week totaling 17 hours of program time, of which 13 are devoted to domestic programs and two to educational programs. A licence fee is payable for nonportable sets. The number of receivers in the country was estimated in 1983 at 3,610,000 or 70 per 1,000 inhabitants. Of the 2,053 annual television broadcasting hours, 419 hours are devoted to information, 250 hours to education, 195 hours to culture, 46 hours to religion, 142 hours to commercials and 915 hours to entertainment.

In 1981 some 65 feature films were produced by private film producers, almost entirely for the domestic market compared to 160 in 1975, 208 in 1976 and 111 in 1977. Some 208 feature films were imported in 1981 from the United States, Italy and France, down from 198 in 1976. In 1980 there were 938 cinemas in the country with 506,300 seats, or 11.3 per 1,000 inhabitants. Annual attendance was 62.5 million, or 1.4 per inhabitant.

There were 406 libraries in the country with 2.3 million volumes. The largest is the National Library at Ankara with over half a million volumes. Per capita there are 44 volumes per 1,000 inhabitants.

There are 89 museums, including the famous Topkapi, reporting an annual attendance of 5.1 million.

There are 15 theaters (four in the capital), and 14 nature preservation sites.

SOCIAL WELFARE

Turkey's social security system is based on two organizations: the Pension Fund and the Social Insurance Organization. The Pension Fund covers all public servants, and benefits include retirement pensions, disability insurance, pensions for widows and orphans, marriage grants, children's allowances, supplementary pensions and death grants. The Social Insurance Organization covers all other workers outside agriculture and provides the same benefits. Other organizations active in the field of welfare include the Red Crescent Society and the Army Mutual Aid Organization.

GLOSSARY

bekciler (sing: **bekci):** night watchmen charged with peacekeeping duties in rural areas

belediye: municipality as a unit of local administration.

bucak mudur: director of a district.

bucaklar (sing: **bucak):** districts, subdivisions of counties.

Buyuk Millet Meclisi: Turkish Grand National Assembly.

dil devrimi: literally, language revolution; introduction of the Roman alphabet and purification of the vocabulary under Ataturk in 1928.

dolmus: private cab operated like a bus on fixed routes.

gacekondu: literally, built by night; squattertowns near large cities inhabited by poor rural migrants.

iller (sing: **il):** provinces, as units of local administration.

jandarma: gendarmerie.

kaymakam: administrator of a county.

kazaler (sing: **kaza):** counties, as units of local administration.

koy: a village, as unit of local administration.

lise: lycee.

Millet Meclisi: National Assembly.

muhtar: headman of a village.

raki: national drink of Turkey distilled from fermented raisins and flavored with anise.

reise: mayor of a municipality.

seriat: the Sharia or Muslim religious legal system.

taksim: partition, especially partition of Cyprus as opposed to enosis, or union with Greece.

tarikatlar: a dervish order among the Sufi sects.

vali: governor of a province.

vilayet: a province, as unit of local administration.

yagligures: greased wrestling, the national sport of Turkey.

CHRONOLOGY (from 1945)

1945— Turkey joins the United Nations.

1946— Group of Republican People's Party dissidents led by Adnan Menderes and Celal Bayar form Democrat Party and wins 46 seats in the National Assembly.

1950— Democratic Party wins absolute majority in country's first free elections; Adnan Menderes is elected prime minister and Celal Bayar president.... Turkey sends troops to Korea under U.N. command.

1951— Turkey joins NATO.

1954— Democratic Party retains majority in national elections.

1955— Anti-Greek riots erupt in Istanbul over Cyprus issue.... Turkey joins CENTO.

1957— Democratic Party majority is reduced in national elections.... Student unrest erupts.

1960— Military coup under Cemal Gursel topples Menderes government; Menderes and Bayar are placed under arrest; provisional military government is formed headed by Committee of National Unity.... Turkish lira is devalued.

1961— Menderes and two other cabinet members are tried, found guilty of misuse of power, and hanged; Bayar is jailed.... New constitution is promulgated.... Gursel is elected president; in new national elections Republican People's Party gains plurality; new government is formed by Ismet Inonu in coalition with the Justice Party.

1962— Army attempts coup.

1963— Second army coup is unsuccessful.

1964— Turkey joins the Regional Cooperation for Development.

1965— Inonu resigns; Suat Hayri Urguplu forms interim government.... Justice Party wins clear majority in general elections; Suleyman Demirel heads new government.

1966— Cevdet Sunay succeeds Gursel as president.

1967— Pope Paul visits Istanbul.

1968— Television is introduced.

1969— Justice Party retains majority in national elections.

1970— Turkish lira is devalued.

1971— Armed forces threaten to intervene again; Demirel steps down; Nihat Erim forms a national union, non-party government with military support; martial law is proclaimed in 11 provinces, including Istanbul; constitution of 1961 is amended to abridge freedom of association.... Israeli consul-general, Ephraim Elrom is kidnaped and murdered by terrorists.

1972— Erim resigns; Suat Urguplu and Ferit Melen head brief governments.

1973— Fahri Koruturk is elected president on the 14th ballot to succeed Sunay; Melen resigns and is succeeded by Naim Talu; National Assembly passes Agrarian Reform Bill setting ceilings on land holdings.... New bridge is opened over the Bosporus.... Opium cultivation is banned under agreement with United States.... Gen. Illhami Sancar, chief of staff, limits military intervention in politics; martial law is lifted.... In new general elections Republican People's Party replaces Justice Party as majority in National Assembly.

1974— Bulent Ecevit, leader of RPP, forms coalition government; amnesty is granted to 50,000 political prisoners on the 50th anniversary of the Republic.... Ban on opium cultivation is removed.... Turkey invades Cyprus and occupies one-third of the island; United States halts arms aid.... Ecevit resigns as coalition breaks up; Sadi Irmak forms caretaker government.

1975— Suleyman Demirel returns to power leading a right-wing coalition.... United States partially lifts embargo on arms to Turkey.

1977— RPP emerges as leading party in national elections; Bulent Ecevit forms cabinet, which lasts for 10 days.... Turkish lira is devalued for the fourth time.... Demirel forms a new cabinet but resigns toward end of the year.

1978— Ecevit is sworn in as prime minister for the third time.... U.S. arms embargo is lifted.

1979— In national elections Rightists win clear lead; Ecevit resigns and Demirel returns to the prime minister's office.... Turkish lira is devalued in a desperate move to shore up the economy.

1980— Turkish military ousts the civilian government, suspends parliament, and imposes martial law; chief of staff, Kenan Evren takes over as head of state and chairman of the newly set up National Security Council; retired Admiral Bulend Ulusu is named prime minister; Ecevit and Demirel are arrested but later released while rightwing extremist leaders are held; Strikes are banned.... New accord is asigned with the United States regarding U.S. bases in the country giving Turkey controlling rights.

1982— New constitution is approved in popular referendum.

1983— Ban on political parties is lifted; of the 15 new political parties that are established, three are permitted to contest parliamentary elections... The Motherland Party wins 211 out of 400 seats in the new Grand National Assembly, and its leader, Turgut Ozal, is named prime minister.

1984— In local elections, the Motherland Party wins decisively.... Northern Cyprus and Turkey exchange ambassadors.

BIBLIOGRAPHY (from 1970)

Ahmad, Feriz, *The Turkish Experiment in Democracy* (Boulder, Col., 1977).

Alford, Jonathan, *Greece & Turkey: Adversity in Alliance* (New York, 1984).

Ankara & Central Turkey. Color film, 11 min. International Film Bureau.

Asfour, Edmound, *Turkey: Prospects and Problems of an Expanding Economy* (Baltimore, 1975).

Barchard, David, *Turkey and the West* (London, 1985).

Berberoglu, B., *Turkey in Crisis: From State Capitalism to Neo-Colonialism* (London, 1982).

Bianchi, Robert, *Interest Groups and Political Development in Turkey* (Princeton, N.J., 1984).

Cohn, Edwin J. *Turkish Economic, Social and Political Change.* (New York, 1970).

Couloumbis, Theodore A., *The United States, Greece and Turkey: The Troubled Triangle* (New York, 1983).

Dewdney, J. C., *Turkey.* (London, 1971).

Dodd, C. *Crisis of Turkish Democracy* (London, 1983).

Durdag, M., *Some Problems of Development Financing: A Case Study of the Turkish First Five-Year Plan, 1963-1967* (Hingham, Mass., 1973).

Geyikdaqi, Mehmet, *Political Parties in Turkey: The Role of Islam* (New York, 1984).

Guclu, Meral, *Turkey* [World Bibliographical Series] (Santa Barbara, Calif., 1981).

Hale, William, *The Political and Economic Development of Modern Turkey* (New York, 1981).

Harris, George S., *Troubled Alliance: Turkish-American Problems in Historical Perspective, 1945-1971* (Washington, D.C., 1972).

Hotham, David, *The Turks.* (London, 1972).

Introducing Turkey. B&W film, 22 min. NATO.

Issawai, Charles, *The Economic History of Turkey, 1800-1914* (Chicago, Ill., 1981).

Kemal, Karpat, et al., *Social Change and Politics in Turkey* (Leiden, Netherlands, 1973).

Kim, Chong Lim, *The Legislative Connection: The Politics of Representation in Kenya, Korea and Turkey* (Durham, N.C., 1984).

Kuniholm, Bruce, R., *The Origins of the Cold War in the Middle East. Great Power Conflict and Diplomacy in Iran, Turkey & Greece* (Princeton, N.J., 1979.

Landau, Jacob M., *Pan-Turkism in Turkey: A Study of Irredentism* (Hamden, Conn., 1981).

Lewis, Bernard, *The Emergence of Modern Turkey* (New York, 1970).

Lewis, Geoffrey, *Modern Turkey* (New York, 1974).

Mango, A., *Discovering Turkey* (London, 1971).

———, *Turkey: A Delicately Poised Ally* (Beverly Hills, Calif., 1975).

Ozbodun, Ergun, *Social Change and Political Participation in Turkey* (Princeton, N.J., 1976).

——— and Ayden Ulusan, *The Political Economy of Income Distribution in Turkey* (New York, 1980).

Paine, Suzanne, *Exporting Workers: The Turkish Case.* (Cambridge, Mass., 1974).

Ramazanoglu, Huseyin, *Industrialization, Power and Class: Turkey in the World Capitalist System* (London, 1985).

Renda, Gunsel and C. M. Kortepeter, *The Transformation of Turkish Culture: The Ataturk Legacy* (Princeton, N.J., 1985).

Roos, Leslie L. and P. Noralou, *Managers of Modernization and Elites in Turkey* (Cambridge, Mass., 1971).

Shabon, Anwar and Isik U. Zeytinoglu, *The Political, Economic and Labor Climate in Turkey* (Philadelphia, Pa., 1985).

Stone, Frank A., *The Rub of Cultures in Modern Turkey: Literary Views of Education* (Bloomington, Ind., 1973).

Tamkoc, Metin, *The Warrior Diplomats: Guardians of the National Security and Modernization of Turkey* (Salt Lake City, Ut., 1976).

Toprak, Binnaz, *Islam and Political Development in Turkey* (Atlantic Highlands, N.J., 1981).

Trask, Roger R., *United States Response to Turkish Nationalism and Reform, 1914-1939* (Minneapolis, 1971).

Turkey. Color film, 20 min. Canadian Broadcasting Corp.

Turkey. Color film, 15 min. Claude Lelough.

Turkey: A Middle East Bridgeland. Color film, 18 min. Universal.

Turkey: A Strategic Land and Its People. Color film, 11 min. Coronet.

Turkey: Crossroads of the Ancient World. Color film, 27 min. Centron Educational Films.

Turkey: Emergence of a Modern Nation. Color/B&W film, 17 min. Encyclopaedia Britannica.

Turkey: Key to the Middle East. B&W film, 20 min. British Information Services.

Turkey: Modern Reforms. Color film, 17 min. Producer: not available.

Turkey: Nation in Transition. Color film, 26 min. Julien Bryan.

Turkey: Rebirth of a Nation. Color film, 18 min. Universal.

Vali, Ferenc, *Bridge Across the Bosporus: The Foreign Policy of Turkey* (Baltimore, 1970).

———, *The Turkish Straits and NATO* (Stanford, Calif., 1972).

Weisband, Edward, *Turkish Foreign Policy, 1943-1945* (Princeton, N.J., 1973).

OFFICIAL PUBLICATIONS

Finance Ministry, *Budget Revenues Yearbook* (annual, English).

——— *Economic Report* (annual).

———, *Final Accounts* (annual).

———, *Government Accounts Bulletin* (monthly, unpublished).

———, *Monthly Economic Indicators* (English).

State Statistical Institute, *Budget and Final Accounts* (irregular).

———, *Monthly Bulletin of Statistics.*

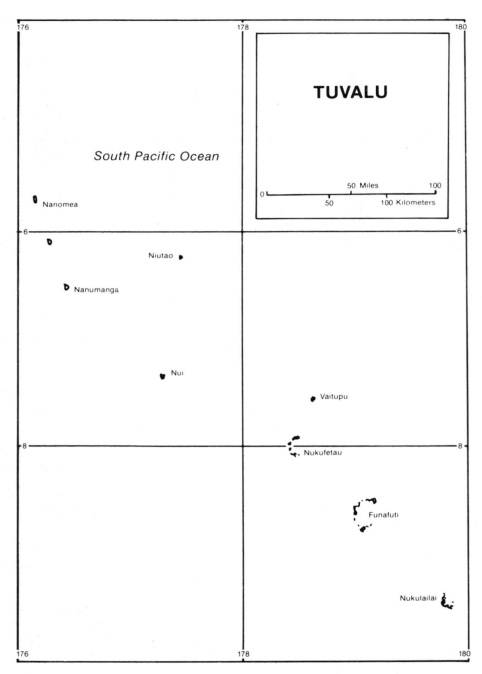

TUVALU

South Pacific Ocean

Nanomea

Niutao

Nanumanga

Nui

Vaitupu

Nukufetau

Funafuti

Nukulailai

50 Miles
0   50   100
50   100 Kilometers

Source: American Geographical Society

Emblem not available

TUVALU

BASIC FACT SHEET

OFFICIAL NAME: Tuvalu (formerly, Ellice, or Lagoon, Islands)

ABBREVIATION: TV

CAPITAL: Funafuti Island; strictly, Fongafale

HEAD OF STATE: Governor General Sir Fiatau Pentala Teo (from 1978)

HEAD OF GOVERNMENT: Prime Minister Tomasi Puapua (from 1981)

NATURE OF GOVERNMENT: Parliamentary Democracy

POPULATION: 8,000 (1985)

AREA: 26 sq km (10sq mi)

ETHNIC MAJORITY: Polynesian

LANGUAGES: English and Tuvaluan

RELIGION: Christianity

UNIT OF CURRENCY: Australian Dollar ($1=A$1.375, 1985). A Tuvaluan coinage, as yet unnamed, was introduced in 1977 at par with the Australian dollar largely for numismatic purposes.

NATIONAL FLAG: Light blue field with the United Kingdom flag as a canton in the upper hoist and nine white five-pointed stars

NATIONAL EMBLEM:

NATIONAL ANTHEM:

NATIONAL HOLIDAYS: October 1 (Tuvalu day); also, Queen's Birthday; Prince of Wales' Birthday; Christmas; New Year's Day; Easter Monday

NATIONAL CALENDAR: Gregorian

PHYSICAL QUALITY OF LIFE INDEX: Not Available

DATE OF INDEPENDENCE: October 1, 1978

DATE OF CONSTITUTION: October 1, 1978

WEIGHTS & MEASURES: The metric system is in force

LOCATION & AREA

Tuvalu is a widely scattered group of nine islands in the western Pacific bounded by Fiji to the south, Kiribati to the north, and Solomon Islands to the west. The islands are Funafuti, Nanomea, Nanumanga, Niulakita, Niutao, Nui, Nukufetau, Nukulailai, and Vaitupu. The islands extend 560 km (350 mi) north to south and cover an area of 26 sq km (10 sq mi). The length of the coastline is about 24 km (15 mi).

The capital is on Funafuti atoll (2,620) and is called Fongafale by the natives. There are no other urban settlements.

WEATHER

The climate is uniformly hot, seldom varying more than a degree or two from the mean annual temperature of 26.7°C (80°F). Most of the annual rainfall of 3,00 mm (120 in.) is derived from the cyclonic storms; the terrain is too low to provoke much precipitation from the clouds borne by the southeast trades.

POPULATION

The population of Tuvalu is estimated at 8,000 in 1985 based on the last census held in 1979 when the population was 7,349. The population is expected to reach 15,800 by 2000.

The annual growth rate is estimated at 2.67% on the basis of a crude birth rate of 34.9 per 1,000.

DEMOGRAPHIC INDICATORS 1984

Population (000)	8.0
Annual rate of growth (1980-85)	2.67%
Crude birthrate 1/1000	34.9
Crude death rate 1/1000	8.5
Total fertility rate	4.98
Gross reproduction rate	2.43
Net reproduction rate	2.15
Density per sq km	362
% Urban	31.3
Sex Distribution (%):	
Male	46.77
Female	53.23
Age profile: (%)	
0-14	33.8
15-29	31.0
30-44	14.3
45-59	13.2
60-74	6.1
Over 75	1.6
Population in 2000	15,800
Population doubling time in years at current rate	19
Life expectancy at birth: years	
Males	60.9
Females	64.5

ETHNIC COMPOSITION

The population is 91.2% Polynesian, mixed 1-Kiribati 6.0%, pure I-Kiribati 1.3% and European and other Pacific peoples 1.4%.

LANGUAGE

English is the official language of the islands. Tuvaluan is widely spoken.

RELIGION

The population is almost entirely Christian, about 97% belonging to the Church of Tuvalu, derived from the Congregationalist foundation of the London Missionary Society.

COLONIAL EXPERIENCE

The islands came under the hegemony of the United Kingdom between 1850 and 1875 as a result of the activities of slave-traders. They were placed under the jurisdiction of the Western Pacific High Commission in 1875 and 17 years later they were linked administratively with the Gilbert Islands to the north. In 1916 the two groups were renamed the Gilbert and Ellice Islands Colony under the responsibility of the High Commissioner for the Western Pacific represented locally by a resident commissioner. In 1974 the colony began to move toward self-government with the replacement of the Legislative Council by a House of Assembly and the election of a chief minister. In 1972 the British government appointed a commission to study the separatist claims of the Polynesian Ellice Islands who chafed under the domination of the Gilbert Islanders, who are Micronesians. On the basis of the commission's recommendations a referendum was held in the Ellice Islands in 1974 when over 90% of the voters favored separate status. The islands became a separate British dependency in 1975 under the name of Tuvalu (an old native term, meaning "eight standing together") with a separate House of Assembly and chief minister. An independence constitution was approved in London in 1978 and after a few months of guided internal self-government Tuvalu achieved independence in October 1978.

CONSTITUTION & GOVERNMENT

Tuvalu is a constitutional monarchy with the Queen of England, represented in the nation by the governor general, as the head of state and the leader of the majority in the parliament as the prime minister and head of government. The governor general is required by the constitution to be a citizen of Tuvalu appointed on the recommendation of the prime minister. The cabinet consists of the prime minister and up to four other ministers appointed by the governor general in consultation with the prime minister.

CABINET LIST (1985)

Governor General	*Sir* Fiatau Penitala Teo
Prime Minister	*Dr.* Tomasi Puapua
Deputy Prime Minister	Henry Naisali
Minister of Commerce	Lale Seluka
Minister of Finance	Henry Naisali
Minister of Foreign Affairs	*Dr.* Tomasi Puapua
Minister of Local Government	*Dr.* Tomasi Puapua
Minister of Natural Resources	Lale Seluka
Minister of Social Services	Falaile Pilitati
Minister of Works & Communications	Metia Tealof

FREEDOM & HUMAN RIGHTS

In terms of civil and political rights Tuvalu is classified as a free country with a rating of 2 in civil rights and 2 in political rights (on a scale in which 1 is the highest and 7 the lowest).

CIVIL SERVICE

No information is available on the Tuvaluan civil service.

LOCAL GOVERNMENT

Each of the eight inhabited islands has its own island council which is responsible for local government. The councils are held in the maneabas or council halls that are so large that they can sleep as many as 1,000 persons, which is necessary when an entire island population comes together for the periodic communal feasts lasting for several weeks.

FOREIGN RELATIONS

Tuvalu is a special member of the Commonwealth without the right to participate in heads of states meetings. It is also a full member of the South Pacific Forum and the South Pacific Commission, but has not yet applied for U.N. membership.

Tuvalu and the United States are parties to eight treaties and agreements covering aviation, consuls, extradition, Peace Corps, telecommunications, trademarks, and visas. Under a special treaty of friendship signed in 1979 the United States acknowledged Tuvaluan sovereignty over four island (Funafuti, Nukufetau, Nukulailai, and Niulakita) claimed by the United States for over a hundred years.

PARLIAMENT

The national legislature is the Parliament (formerly, the House of Assembly) consisting of 12 elected members, two each from the more populous Funafuti, Nanumea, Niutao, and Vaitupu and 1 each from the remaining inhabited islands. The 12 seats

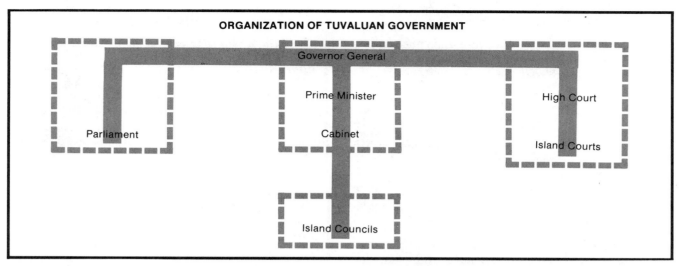

ORGANIZATION OF TUVALUAN GOVERNMENT

Governor General

Prime Minister

Cabinet

Parliament

High Court

Island Courts

Island Councils

were contested by 31 candidates in the last elections held in 1981.

POLITICAL PARTIES

There are no political parties in Tuvalu.

ECONOMY

Tuvalu is one of the upper middle income countries of the world with a free-market economy in which the private sector is dominant.

> **PRINCIPAL ECONOMIC INDICATORS (1981)**
> Gross National Product: $5 million
> GNP per capita: $680

There is very little economic activity on the islands. Most of the foreign exchange is earned through the sale of postage stamps and coins and from remittances sent home by Tuvaluans working abroad, particularly in Nauru and Kiribati and on foreign ships.

In 1983, Tuvalu received A$7.1 million in grant and loan funds from the United Kingdom, New Zealand, Australia, Canada, Japan, the Federal Republic of Germany, the EDF and UNDP.

In 1982 the government planned to spend A$156,140 on social services and education, A$948,166 on commerce and natural resources and A$180,022 on communications and works.

By economic sectors, agriculture contributes 16% to the GDP, manufacturing 1.0%, construction 13.0%, trade 34%, transportation and communication 4% and finance, public administration and services 32.0%.

BUDGET

The fiscal year is the calendar year.

The 1981 national budget consisted of revenues of A$5,433,141 and expenditures of A$5,048,250. Of the revenues, 59.8% came from external aid, 14.5% from philatelic sales, 8.5% from customs and excise, 4.1% from income tax and 13.3% from other. Of the expenditures, 28.3% went to transportation and communications, 19.7% to administration, 15.5% to public works and local administration, 12.5% to education, 6.8% to health and 17.2% to other.

No information is available on the national debt.

FINANCE

The Tuvaluan unit of currency is the Australian Dollar divided into 100 cents. Coins are issued in denominations of 1, 2, 5, 10, 20 and 50 cents and notes in denominations of 1, 2, 5, 10, and 50 dollars.

In 1977 Tuvaluan coinage of denominations 1, 2, 5, 10, 20 and 50 cents and 1 dollar was introduced and they continue to be current along with the Australian dollar.

The exchange rate in 1985 was $1 = A$1.375.

The only commercial bank on the islands is the National Bank of Tuvalu, founded in 1980.

AGRICULTURE

Because of the poor quality of the soil there is very little cultivation. Much of the land is covered with coconut palms which provided 1,000 tons of copra, the only export, in 1982. Cattle raising has been prevented by the lack of suitable grass. Fishing is done mostly on a small scale although the national territorial sea extends over 1.3 million sq km (500,000 sq mi).

INDUSTRY

There is virtually no manufacturing activity on the islands.

ENERGY

No energy is produced in Tuvalu and consumption is insignficant. Production of electric power in 1984 was 3 million kwh or 375 kwh per capita.

LABOR

The economically active population numbered 4,010 in 1980, of which females constituted 51.4%. Nearly 73% is employed in agriculture, 1.5% in manufacturing, 5.7% in construction, 2.5% in trade, 0.4% in public utilities, 2.8% in transportation and communications, 9.4% in finance, services and public administration and 4.0% in other.

About a quarter of the labor force is overseas, some 300 on foreign ships, 255 on Nauru and a smaller number on Kiribati. The unemployment rate is 4.0%.

FOREIGN COMMERCE

In 1982 foreign commerce consisted of exports of A\$36,766 and imports of A\$2,890,377. Of the imports, food and live animals constituted 22.4%, basic manufactures 19.1%, petroleum 16.7% and machinery and transport equipment 16.1%. Of the exports, copra constituted 72.5%. The major import sources are: Fiji 47.5%, Australia 39.7% and New Zealand 5.3%.

TRANSPORTATION & COMMUNICATIONS

There are no paved roads on the islands and the length of the graveled roads is only 8 km (5 mi).

The main port of entry is Funafuti, which is served by irregular shipping services. Inter-island transportation is handled by a government-owned ship.

There is one airfield at Funafuti, which is served by Air Pacific

There are 300 telephones (mostly on the capital atoll), or 0.5 per 100 inhabitants.

In 1980 the mail traffic consisted of 2,313,000 pieces of mail.

Because of the remoteness of the islands tourism is ill developed. The country's only hotel is on Funafuti. In 1979 there were 474 tourists.

MINING

Tuvalu has no mineral resources.

DEFENSE

Tuvalu has no defense force but is covered by British military guarantees in case of external attack.

EDUCATION

The national literacy rate is 95.5% (for both males and females).

Education is free and almost all children receive primary education. There are nine primary schools (one in each inhabited atoll) attended in 1983 by 965 students. The country's only secondary school located on Vaitupu had an enrollment of 250 in the same year. Students requiring higher or vocational training have to go to Fiji or Kiribati. The total number of teachers is 72.

EDUCATIONAL ENROLLMENT 1983			
Level	Schools	Teachers	Students
First	9	41	966
Second	1	15	250
Vocational	8	16	354

The teacher enrollment ratios are 1:23 in primary schools, 1:17 in secondary school and 1:22 in vocational schools.

LEGAL SYSTEM

The judicial system comprises eight island courts with limited jurisdiction and magistrate courts. Appeals from these courts lie with the High Court presided over by the chief justice. In some cases, the Judicial Committee of the Privy Council in the United Kingdom serves as the ultimate court of appeal.

No information is available on prisons or the incidence of crime.

LAW ENFORCEMENT

The Tuvalu Constabulary is a centrally controlled and administered law enforcement agency under a chief police officer assisted by superintendents, inspectors, NCO's and constables. In addition, an Island Police is employed to support the work of the regular constabulary. The latter is a decentralized force of part-time policemen operating under the administration officer of the island. It has no set strength, but is organized to meet the needs of the individual islands.

HEALTH

In 1981 there were eight hospitals with 64 beds (1 per 102 persons) and five doctors (or one per 1,470 persons) and 2 dentists. The admissions/discharge rate is 770 per 10,000 inhabitants. The bed occupancy rate is 52.1% and the average length of hospital stay is 11 days. Each inhabited atoll has a dispensary.

FOOD

No information is available on the food habits and intake in Tuvalu.

```
┌─────────────────────────────────────────────┐
│      PRINCIPAL HEALTH INDICATORS (1984)        │
│ Crude Death Rate (per 1,000): 8.5             │
│ Life Expectancy at Birth (Males): 60.9        │
│ (Females): 64.5                               │
│ Infant Mortality Rate: 42 per 1,000 live births│
└─────────────────────────────────────────────┘
```

MEDIA & CULTURE

The country's only newspaper is *Tuvalu Echoes (Sikuleo o Tuvalu)* published by the Broadcasting and Information Division at Funafuti. The paper which is published every two weeks has a circulation of around 200 in Tuvalu and 250 in English.

Radio Tuvalu broadcasts for about six hours daily from the Funafuti atoll in both English and Tuvaluan. The number of radio receivers is estimated at 2,000 or 330 per 1,000 inhabitants. There is no television service.

The country's only library is located in the Funafuti atoll.

SOCIAL WELFARE

No information is available on social welfare programs in the islands.

GLOSSARY

Maneaba: local town council hall

CHRONOLOGY

1979— Tuvalu becomes an independent nation but retains status as a special member of the Commonwealth. . . . Tuvalu and the United States sign treaty of friendship by which the latter renounces claims to the four southernmost atolls.

1981— Prime minister Toalipi Lauti is replaced by Tomasi Puapua.

BIBLIOGRAPHY

Sabatier, Ernest, *Astride the Equator* (New York, 1978).

UGANDA

International boundary
⊛ National capital
┼ Railroad
 Road

0   25   50 Miles
0   25   50 Kilometers

SUDAN

KENYA

ZAIRE

TANZANIA

RWANDA

Moyo
Kaabong
Kitgum
Pager
Arua
Albert Nile
Gulu
Achwa
Moroto
Pakwach
Victoria Nile
Lira
Bunia
LAKE ALBERT
Masindi
LAKE KWANIA
Lake Salisbury
Soroti
Ituri
Hoima
Kafu
LAKE KYOGA
Kapchorwa
Nkusi
Mpongo
Victoria Nile
Mbale
Kitale
Semliki
Fort Portal
Mubende
Bombo
Iganga
Tororo
Beni
Mityana
Jinja
Eldoret
Kasese
Katonga
KAMPALA
Entebbe
Butere
Lake George
Rusangue
Nzoia
KENYA
LAKE EDWARD
Lyantonde
Masaka
SESE ISLANDS
Kisumu
Mbarara
LAKE VICTORIA
Kabale
Kagera
Kyaka
Bukoba
Musoma

Bahr al Jabal

Turkwel

Suam

FOR GOD AND MY COUNTRY

UGANDA

LOCATION & AREA

Landlocked Uganda is located in east-central Africa, straddling the equator, with a total area of 243,411 sq km (93,981 sq mi), including 35,454 sq km (13,689 sq mi) of water and swamps. The country extends 787 km (489 mi) NNE to SSW and 486 km (302 mi) ESE to WNW.

Uganda shares its total international border of 2,558 km (1,590 mi) with five neighbors: Sudan (435 km, 270 mi); Kenya (772 km, 480 mi); Tanzania (418 km, 260 mi); Rwanda (169 km, 105 mi); and Zaire (764 km, 475 mi). The borders were demarcated in the late 19th Century among the United Kingdom, Germany and Belgium, but some territory has been ceded since then to Kenya. There are no current border disputes.

The capital is Kampala with a 1980 population of 458,000. The other major urban centers are Jinja (45,100), Mbale (28,039), Mbarara (23,160), Masaka (29,120), Entebbe (21,096) and Gulu (14,958).

The country is one vast plateau; there are no natural geographic regions. The main mountain masses are the Mufumbiro and the Ruwenzori in the west and Mount Elgon in the east. The Mufumbiro are volcanic highlands over 1,524 meters (5,000 ft) above sea level, extending northeastward. The range includes Mount Sabinio (3,645 meters, 11,960 ft), at the tripoint of Uganda, Rwanda and Zaire, and Mount Mahavura (4,127 meters, 13,540 ft). These highlands are separated from the Ruwenzori Mountains ("The Mountains of the Moon") by a low valley containing Lake George and the Kazinga Channel. The Ruwenzori Range, about 80 km (50 mi) long, has a number of peaks, of which the highest is Margherita (5,109 meters, 16,763 ft). The plateau's eastern boundary is marked by a number of peaks: Mount Elgon (4,321 meters, 14,178 ft), Mount Debasien (3,068 meters, 10,067 ft), Mount Moroto (3,083 meters, 10,116 ft), Mount Morungole (2,750 meters, 9,022 ft) and Mount Zulia (2,148 meters, 7,048 ft). The Labwor Hills west of these ranges and the Imatong Mountains on the northern border are between 1,829 meters (6,000 ft) and 2,530 meters (8,300 ft). By contrast, the Western Rift Valley, which runs from north to south through the western half, is as low as 900 meters (3,000 ft) below sea level on the floor of Lake Edward.

Uganda is within the upper basin of the White Nile. The Victoria Nile runs from Lake Victoria at Jinja over Owen Falls north into Lake Kyoga. After Karuma Falls, the river follows a westward course over Murchison Falls into Lake Albert. From Lake Albert it runs as the Albert Nile, leaving Uganda at Nimule on the Sudan border. There are numerous smaller rivers that are for the most part not navigable. These include the Katonga, the Kafu, the Aswa, the Pager, the Dopeth-Okok and the Mpongo.

There are almost as many lakes as rivers in the country. Uganda shares Lakes Albert, Edward and Victoria with its neighbors, while Lakes Salisbury, Wamala, Kyoga, George and Kwania are entirely within Uganda. West of Lake Victoria is a group of some six lakes connected by swamps.

WEATHER

Uganda has an equatorial climate with with temperatures moderated by altitude. In most of the country the main dry season occurs between November and March. Mean annual temperatures range between 20°C to 22°C (68°F to 72°F). Kampala has a January average of 22°C (72°F) and a July average of 20°C (68°F). At Entebbe, south of the Equator at an altitude of 1,000 meters (3,280 ft), the January average is 22°C (72°F) and the July average is 21°C (70°F). Throughout the country July is the coolest month.

On the basis of climatic features, particularly rainfall, the country is divided into six zones as follows:
• The Lake Victoria Region has two dry seasons, from December to March and from June to July, and two wet seasons, from March to May and during October and November. On the shores rain falls for 160 to 170 days a year; the average rainfall is 152 cm to 178 cm (60 in. to 70 in.).
• The Karamoja Region is a semi-arid plain with an intense dry season lasting from November to March and a wet season from April to October. Annual average rainfall ranges from 38 cm to 89 cm (15 in. to 35 in.).
• The Western Region of the three Rift Valley lakes is one of the hottest parts of the country with an intense dry season from December to February, a secondary dry season from June to August and two wet seasons from September to October and from April to May. Nearer the lakes, rain falls for 80 to 100 days a year, the average annual rainfall is 76 to 101 cm (34 to 40 in.) and on the slopes of Ruwenzori it rains for 100 to 150 days a year; the average annual rainfall is 152 to 203 cm (60 to 80 in.).
• The Acholi-Kyoga Region is a flat plain with many swamps. Rain falls for 140 to 170 days a year from April to October and varies between 89 to 127 cm (35 to 50 in.).

• The Ankole-Buganda Region, including most of the former kingdom of Buganda, has two rainy seasons, from September to November and during April and May, for a total of 90 to 130 days of rain. Average annual rainfall is about 101 cm (40 in.). Because of its elevation, this region has moderate temperatures.
• The Mount Elgon Region has high rainfall on the southern slopes.

POPULATION

The population of Uganda was estimated in 1985 at 14,733,000, on the basis of the last official census held in 1980, when it was 12,630,076. The population is expected to reach 24.5 million by 2000 and 43.7 million by 2020. The annual growth rate is 3.5% based on an estimated annual birth rate of 49.9 per 1,000.

The most densely populated areas are the central plateau north and west of Lake Victoria and the slopes of Mount Elgon. Elsewhere, settlement is sparse. The overall density is 67 per sq km (173 per sq mi). However, the highest rate of increase has occurred in the western region (bordering Rwanda and Zaire) and the northern region (bordering Sudan) with increases of 54.3% and 52.3%, respectively, since 1962.

The population is overwhelmingly rural with only 14% living in urban areas but the urban growth rate of 7.3% is double the national growth rate. Nearly one-third of the urban population is concentrated in Kampala. There are only five other cities with over 20,000 inhabitants.

The age profile shows 48.5% in the under-14 age group, 49% between 15 and 64 and 2.5% over 65. There is no significant imbalance in the sex ratio; in 1980 there were 49.5 males to every 50.5 females.

Uganda's geographical location has drawn migrants and refugees from all its neighbors. Rwanda, Burundi, Kenya, Zaire and the Sudan are all sources of migrant laborers, and there have also been political refugees from Burundi, Zaire and the Sudan. Migrants from Kenya, especially the Luohave, have settled in Jinja and Kampala. The largest population movement out of Uganda followed the expulsion of an estimated 40,000 Asians in 1972. Some 25,000 of these Asians were resettled in the United Kingdom (as holders of U.K. passports) and the rest found new homes in Canada or India.

Women are not legally discriminated against or officially restricted from education or employment. However, their access to education has been declining, according to United Nations International Children's Emergency Fund, as the educational system deteriorates and the economy declines. Families withdraw daughters rather than sons from school in times of economic hardship. At the same time, women have been active in politics at the grass roots level and have held several senior positions in national parties as well as in government. There were no women of cabinet-level rank in the IMG government.

DEMOGRAPHIC INDICATORS (1985)

Population, total (in 1,000)	14,733.0
Population ages (% of total)	
0-14	48.5
15-64	49.0
65+	2.5
Youth 15-24 (000)	2,961
Women ages 15-49 (000)	3,398
Dependency ratios	104.2
Child-woman ratios	914
Sex ratios (per 100 females)	98.3
Median ages (years)	15.7
Proportion of urban (%)	14.39
Population density (per sq. km.)	67
per hectare of arable land	2.56
Rates of growth (%)	3.50
Urban %	7.3
Rural %	2.9
Natural increase rates (per 1,000)	35.2
Crude birth rates (per 1,000)	49.9
Crude death rates (per 1,000)	14.7
Gross reproduction rates	3.40
Net reproduction rates	2.59
Total fertility rates	6.90
General fertility rates (per 1,000)	230
Life expectancy, males (years)	50.3
Life expectancy, females (years)	53.8
Life expectancy, total (years)	52.0
Population doubling time in years at current rate	20
Change in birthrate % 1965-83	2.2
Average size of household	5.2

A private Family Planning Association is active in the country, but there are few official programs directed toward control of population growth.

ETHNIC COMPOSITION

Uganda ranks as the second most heterogeneous nation in the world with only 10% ethnic and linguistic homogeneity (on an ascending scale in which North and South Korea are ranked 135th with 100% homogeneity and Tanzania is ranked first with 7% homogeneity). The approximately 40 African tribes are grouped according to language into four large categories: Bantu, Eastern Nilotic, Western Nilotic and Central Sudanic. The numerically dominant Bantus live in the densely populated southern half of the country, while the Eastern and Western Nilotics live north of Lake Kyoga, and the Central Sudanics inhabits the West Nile district.

MAJOR TRIBES OF UGANDA

Tribe	%	Tribe	%
Baganda	16.2	Bagisu	5.1
Iteso	8.1	Acholi	4.4
Basoga	7.7	Lugbara	3.6
Banyankore	8.0	Banyoro	2.9
Banyaruanda	5.8	Batoro	3.2
Bakiga	7.1	Karamojong	2.0
Lango	5.6		

The Bantu-speakers make up two-thirds of the population. The group is broadly classified into Eastern Lacustrine Bantu (Baganda Soga, Gwe, Gisu, Nyuli, Samia and Kenyi) and the Western Lacustrine Bantu (Nkole, Toro, Nyoro, Kiga, Amba and Konjo). Western Nilotic speakers make up about 15% of the population and are often referred to collectively as the Luo. They include the Acholi, Alur, Padhola, Kuman, Jonam and Paluo. The Eastern Nilotics make up 12% of the population and comprise four major tribes: the Karamaojong, Dodoth, Jie and Teso, and a number of minor tribes such as the Kakwa, Sebei, Labwor, Nyakwai, Tepeth, Napore-Nyangea and Teuso. The Central Sudanics are represented by the Lugbara and the Madi, who together make up less than 5% of the population. Intertribal relations are conditioned by historic animosities and rivalries and, paradoxically, the process of modernization has tended to reinforce these attitudes rather than soften them.

Until 1972 there was a flourishing Asian community in Uganda engaged in the middle-level professions. Most of them lived in urban areas and held British passports. In 1972 President Amin ordered the expulsion within 90 days of all Asians with British passports in a move designed, in his words, "to teach Britain a lesson." Despite British efforts to extend the time limit and to ensure compensation, over 40,000 penniless Asians were airlifted from Uganda within six weeks. Of these, the United Kingdom took in an estimated 25,000. Amin's action was strongly supported by many African countries (in all of which Asians were intensely disliked), but Uganda's expectations of benefits from the Asian departure proved unfounded. All Asian property was appropriated by Ugandan soldiers and officials. The resulting shortage of trained personnel, including doctors, teachers and mechanics, reduced the Ugandan economy to chaos. Ironically, Amin sent a delegation to Pakistan in 1974 to recruit skilled personnel.

Ethnic minorities include about 73,000 Rwandans, 30,000 Sudanese, 34,000 Zaireans and an undetermined number of Kenyans, in addition to about 3,000 Arabs, descendants of slavers who ravaged East Africa in the 19th Century. No reliable information is available on Western communities in Uganda.

Perhaps as many as 500,000 persons have been displaced by conflict within Uganda since 1980. Many have sought sanctuary in neighboring states. The great majority of these displaced persons and refugees fled to eastern Zaire and southern Sudan in the aftermath of the 1979 liberation war and UNLA excesses in repulsing a 1980 guerrilla attack in the west Nile region. At its peak, the numbers of Ugandans in Zaire and Sudan totaled approximately 150,000. During the first half of 1985 over 20,000 of these people returned to Uganda with the help of the United Nations High Commissioner for Refugees. Since the coup, a large number of persons living in southern Sudan have returned spontaneously to Uganda, several thousand of whom were young men of military age who have come back to serve in government fighting forces.

Approximately 40,000 Banyarwanda fled Uganda to Rwanda in 1982-83 as a result of quasi-official harassment of this minority group. The majority were Ugandan citizens, but some were Rwandese nationals. Although the Obote government publicly invited these persons to return to Uganda as part of its stated policy of reconciliation and no revenge, it was reluctant to support a full-scale repatriation of the Banyarwanda, including those with valid legal claims to Ugandan nationality. Possibly 25,000 Banyarwanda have spontaneously repatriated themselves since the coup, mainly settling in southwestern Uganda, an area under NRA control. There were credible reports that some Banyarwanda returnees had been recruited into NRA forces. At the end of 1985, an estimated 200,000 persons out of Uganda's population of 15 million still lived abroad.

LANGUAGES

The official language of Uganda is English, spoken by only a small fraction of the population. Ki-Swahili (also known as Swahili) has been selected as the national language and is designated to supersede English eventually as the official language.

There are as many languages in the country as there are tribes, and the system of classification is the same for race as for language. Each language is generally unintelligible to speakers of other languages, and dialect differences exist within the larger tribes. The two languages that have emerged as lingua francas are Luganda in the south and Ki-Swahili in the Lango, Acholi and Teso areas. A considerable body of literature exists in Luganda. The Uganda Broadcasting Corporation broadcasts in 21 vernaculars in addition to English, French, Arabic and Ki-Swahili. These are Luganda, Luo, Runyoro, Rutoro, Ateso, Runyankore, Rukiga, Lusoga, Lumasaba, Lunyole, Lusamia, Lugwe, Ngakarimojong, Madi, Alur, Kupsabiny, Lugbara, Rukonjo, Dhopadhola, Kumam and Kakwa.

RELIGIONS

Uganda is one of the most Christianized countries in Africa, with 60% professing the Christian faith. Some 35% retain African traditional beliefs, while 5% are Muslim. Uganda has been the scene of intense Catholic and Protestant missionary activity since the 19th Century. Except among the animist tribes of the northwest — Dodoth, Jie and Karamojong — Christianity claims about one-half of the rural population. The Christians are almost evenly divided between Roman Catholic and Protestant denominations. The Roman Catholic is organized into one archdiocese at Kampala (headed by a cardinal), 10 dioceses and 227 parishes. In addition, the Catholics maintain three major seminaries, 10 minor seminaries and over 1,425 schools. The Anglican Church of Uganda is composed of five dioceses under an archbishop.

Islam, introduced in the 19th Century, was not a major factor in national life until the rise of Idi Amin and has ceased to be one after his fall.

The Amin regime had banned over 15 Christian religious sects and 18 foreign missionaries were expelled in 1975. Christian bishops and priests are among the 25,000 to 250,000 persons murdered by Amin, according to the International Commission of Jurists.

COLONIAL EXPERIENCE

Uganda was under British colonial rule from around 1888 to 1962. In 1888 the Imperial British East African Company was granted a charter to administer the British sphere of East Africa, assigned to the United Kingdom by the Anglo-German Agreement of 1890. As the company was unable to mediate religious conflicts in the country or to establish a sound administration, the British Parliament announced a protectorate over Buganda in 1894. The area of the protectorate was consolidated between 1894 and 1919. The only major challenge to its hegemony came in 1897 when Mwanga, the kabaka of Buganda, rose in revolt; but he was quickly defeated, deposed and replaced by his son, Dawdi Chwa. The British administrative system in the colony was based on the Uganda Agreement of 1900, signed between British Special Commissioner Sir Harry Johnston and the chiefs of Buganda. Under this Agreement Buganda was ruled indirectly by the British, who in turn used the Baganda leadership to extend British control. The agreement confirmed the privileged position of the Baganda tribe in the country and the semi-independence of the Buganda kingdom. The agreement also established a system of land tenure under which half the land area was granted to the chiefs and subchiefs as private holdings and the other half became crown land, whose rights were vested in the commissioner. In 1907 the commissioner became the governor. The first step toward self-government came in 1921 with the creation of a Legislative Council without African representation. Later constitutional evolution was marked by Bagandan attempts to ensure their supremacy in the emerging Ugandan state. A British commission of inquiry accepted that Buganda should have federal status within an independent Uganda and that the other three kingdoms, Ankole, Bunyoro and Toro, should enjoy a quasi-federal status. This arrangement did not survive the post-independence conflicts.

Uganda is still a member of the Commonwealth, but as a result of Amin's policies, relations between the United Kingdom and her former colony were strained. Uganda is the only Commonwealth country with which the United Kingdom had to suspend diplomatic relations, which occurred in 1976.

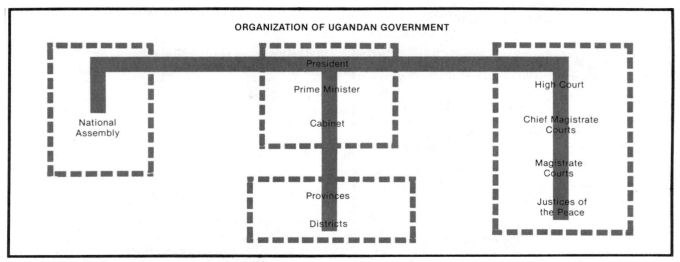

ORGANIZATION OF UGANDAN GOVERNMENT

CONSTITUTION & GOVERNMENT

Although Dictator Idi Amin was overthrown in 1979, Uganda is still struggling with his legacies. The post-Amin period has been marked by economic decline, political instability, a breakdown in the institutions of law and order, and generally inefficient administration. The rate of inflation soared to well over 100%; there was no foreign exchange even to buy food; parts of Uganda were severly affected by drought producing near-famine conditions; acts of political violence and murder were commonplace, and the police and the military created as much crime as they prevented. Much of this could be rightly placed at the door of the eight-year misrule of Idi Amin who virtually shattered the economy and the political cohesion of the country. The first and second post-Amin governments headed by Yusuf Lule and Godfrey Binaisa respectively, had only short lives; and the 1980 elections which returned Milton Obote to power ironically brought the country full circle to the leadership that was at the helm when Amin had interrupted Ugandan history.

Elements of the Ugandan National Liberation Army (UNLA), led by senior military officers primarily from the Acholi ethnic group, overthrew the government of President A. Milton Obote on July 27, 1985. An Interim Military Government (IMG) headed by a Military Council was installed with General Tito Okello Lutwa, formerly chief of the defense forces, as head of state and Military Council chairman. Immediately after assuming power, the Military Council began appointing a broad-based civilian cabinet, comprising all major ethnic groups as well as representatives of the four political parties which had contested the disputed 1980 election. The council subsequently included members of four insurgent groups, but not Yoweri Museveni's National Resistance Army/Movement (NRA/NRM), which is dominated by Bantus, in particular the Banyankole. Museveni's NRM/NRA forces continued hostilities against the interim government but also agreed to enter into peace talks with the IMG in Nairobi under the

chairmanship of Kenyan President Daniel Arap Moi. The talks culminated in a peace accord signed on December 17, in Nairobi between Okello and Museveni, who agreed to join the government, as vice chairman of the Military Council when the terms of the accord implemented, and further fighting took place.

By early 1986 Museveni's army (mostly teenagers, but fanatically devoted to their leader) had taken over Kampala, driven out Okello and installed Museveni as president. The new president appointed Samson Kisekka as prime minister.

RULERS OF UGANDA

1963 (October) to 1966 (February) Sir Edward Frederick Mutesa II
1966 (February) to 1971 (January) Milton Obote
1971 (January) to 1979 (April) Idi Amin
1979 (April-June) Yusuf K. Lule
1979 (June) to 1980 (December) Godfrey Lukongwa Binaisa
1980 (December) to 1985 (July) Milton Obote
1985 (July) to 1986 (January) Tito Okello Lutwa
1986 (January) — Yoweri Museveni

FREEDOM & HUMAN RIGHTS

In terms of political and civil rights, Uganda is classified as a partly-free country with a maximum negative of 5 on both counts (on a descending scale in which 1 is the highest and 7 the lowest in rights).

Human rights issues have played a major role in Uganda's turbulent 23-year postindependence history. The depredations of the Amin years are well-known and well documented. Chaos and widespread human rights violations continued during the 1979-80 interim governments. After initial promise, the 1980-85 Obote government was widely discredited by the time it fell because of its unwillingness or inability to halt or prevent large-scale violations of human rights, particularly perpetrated by ill-disciplined soldiers during military operations against the NRA, as

CABINET LIST (1986)

President . . . . Yoweri Museveni
Prime Minister . . . . Samson Kisekka
Minister of Agriculture & Forestry . . . . Robert Kitariko
Minister of Animal Industry . . . . .Henry Masaba
Minister of Commerce . . . . Evaristo Nyanzi
Minister of Cooperatives & Marketing . . Chrispus Kiyonga
Minister of Defense . . . . .Yoweri Museveni
Minister of Education . . . . .Joshua Mayanja Nkangi
Minister of Energy . . . . Andrew Kayiira
Minister of Environmental
  Protection . . . . David Livingston Lwanga
Minister of Finance . . . . Ponsiano Mulema
Minister of Foreign Affairs . . . . .Ibrahim Mukibi
Minister of Health . . . . Dr. Ruhakana Rugunda
Minister of Industry
  & Technology . . . . Stanley Elly Tuhinruie Tumwine
Minister of Information
  & Broadcasting . . . . .Abubakar Mayanja
Minister of Internal Affairs . . . Paul Kawanga Ssemogerere
Minister of Justice . . . . Joseph Mulenga
Minister of Labor . . . . .Jaberi Bidandi Ssali
Minister of Lands & Surveys . . . . .James Obol Ochola
Minister of Local Government . . . . E. Kakongwe
Minister of Planning & Economic
  Development . . . . .Joseph Okune
Minister of Public Service
  & Cabinet Affairs . . . . .David Kibirango
Minister of Regional Cooperation . . John Ssebaana Kizito
Minister of Rehabilitation . . . . Ali Kivejinja Kivenjinja
Minister of Tourism & Wildlife . . . . Antony Butele
Minister of Transportation
  & Communications . . . . Stanislaus A. Okurut
Minister of Water & Mineral
  Development . . . . Dr. B. Chanyo Macho
Minister of Works . . . . Daniel Serwango Kigozi
Minister of Youth, Culture & Sports . . . . Alex Ofumbi
Minister Without Portfolio . . . . Tom Rubale
Minister of State
  Attached to the Presidency . . . . .Balaki Kirya
Minister of State, Office of the
  Prime Minister . . . . Eriya Kategaya
Minister of State
  for Constitutional Affairs . . . . Dr. Sam Njuba
Minister of State for Defense . . . . Dr. Ronald Bata
Minister of State for Education . . . . .John Ntimba
Minister of State for Internal Affairs . . . . Kiiza Besigye
Assistant Minister of Defense
  & Commissar of the NRA . . . . . . Col. Amanya Mushanga
Attorney General . . . . Joseph Mulenga

well as unrestrained activities of civilian intelligence, security and ruling-party agents. Various guerrilla groups bent on the violent overthrow of the Obote government also contributed to human rights violations through the use of both indiscriminate and selective terrorism. A special Amnesty International Report released in June 1985, indicated that the government security forces had been involved in mass detentions, routine torture, widespread abductions and frequent killings of prisoners.

CIVIL SERVICE

The civil service has been completely Africanized and is under the control of the Public Service Commission. Public Service commissioners are appointed and may be dismissed by the president. There are three grades of civil servants: clerical or technical, executive and aministrative. In the third class are permanent secretaries who head the ministerial staffs, under-secretaries, commissioners and other departmental heads.

LOCAL GOVERNMENT

For purposes of local government, Uganda is divided into 10 provinces and 34 districts. The 10 provinces are Nile, Northern, Karamoja, Eastern, North Buganda, Busoga, South Buganda, Western, Southern and Kampala. Provincial governors are appointed by the president, and district commissioners are appointed by the governors. There are no institutions of local self-government.

FOREIGN POLICY

Despite its domestic problems since 1971, Uganda enjoys substantial goodwill among African and Asian as well as Western countries. The ideological gears of the Musaweni government's foreign affairs ministry have not yet started functioning so it is difficult to determine the new direction that it will take.

Uganda and the United States are parties to four treaties and agreements covering agricultural commodities, economic and technical cooperation, investment guaranties, and Peace Corps.

Uganda joined the U.N. in 1962; its share of the U.N. budget is 0.02%. It is a member of 14 U.N. organizations and 22 other international organizations.
U.S. Ambassador in Kampala: Allen C. Davis
U.K. High Commissioner in Kampala: Colin McLean
Ugandan Ambassador in Washington D.C.: John Wycliffe Lwamafa
Ugandan High Commissioner in London: Shafiq Arain

PARLIAMENT

The former unicameral National Assembly was dissolved in 1971. It consisted, at the time of dissolution, of 82 members elected for five-year terms. The new parliment that met after the 1980 election was a 120-member body. It was dissolved in 1985.

POLITICAL PARTIES

All political parties were suspended in 1986. The two main political parties that contested the 1980 elections were the ruling Uganda People's Congress (led by Milton Obote) and the Democratic Party.

ECONOMY

Uganda is one of the 49 low-income countries of the world, one of the 29 least-developed countries, and one of the 45 countries considered by the U.N. as most seriously affected by recent adverse economic conditions. It has a free-market economy in which the private sector is dominant.

PRINCIPAL ECONOMIC INDICATORS

Gross National Product: $3.090 billion (1983)
  GNP Annual Growth Rate: –3.0% (1973-82)
  Per Capita GNP: $220 (1983)
  Per Capita GNP Annual Growth Rate: –5.6% (1973-82)
Gross Domestic Product at 1975 prices: Sh22.557 billion (1983)
  GDP Annual Growth Rate: –2.1% (1973-83)
  Per Capita GDP: Sh1,541 (1983)
  Per Capita GDP Annual Growth Rate: –4.2% (1970-81)
Income Distribution: 6.2% of the national income is received by the bottom 20%; 20% is received by the top 5%
Percentage of Population in Absolute Poverty: 64
Consumer Price Index (1970=100):
  All Items: 1632.8 (May 1980)
  Food: 1655.7 (May 1980): No information available after 1980.
Average Annual Rate of Inflation: 62.7% (1973-83)
Money Supply: Sh88.041 billion (December 1984)
Reserve Money: Sh60.106 billion (December 1984)
Currency in Circulation: Sh18.92 billion (1984)
International Reserves: Information not available

BALANCE OF PAYMENTS (1981)
(million $)

Current Account Balance	31.9
Merchandise Exports	229.3
Merchandise Imports	–278.3
Trade Balance	–49.0
Other Goods, Services & Income	+45.1
Other Goods, Services & Income	–113.6
Other Goods, Services & Income Net	–68.5
Private Unrequited Transfers	–2
Official Unrequited Transfers	149.6
Capital Other Than Reserves	–88.5
Net Errors & Omissions	–38.1
Total (Lines 1, 10 and 11)	–94.7
Counterpart Items	–3.4
Total (Lines 12 and 13)	–98.1
Liabilities Constituting Foreign Authorities' Reserves	—
Total Change in Reserves	98.1

Development planning began with the First Five-Year Development Plan, 1961-66, which invested Sh1.88 billion over the plan period, followed by the Second Five-Year Plan, 1966-71, which invested Sh4.6 billion, and the Third Five-Year Plan, 1971-76, which invested Sh7.7 Billion. The plans were formulated by the Central Planning Bureau from 1964 to 1966, after which it became the Ministry of Planning and Community Development.

The Three-Year Plan (1976-79), which provided for total spending of Sh. 11,300 million, had little chance of being fulfilled, since the economy was by that time operating at the most basic level.

In March 1981 Obote announced an economic recovery plan which aimed at, among other things, providing greater encouragement and protection for foreign investors. This was followed in March 1982 by a two-year recovery program, to run from July 1982 to June 1984. This $557.5 million program concentrated on the strengthening of the main export commodity sectors, on projects which would bring a quick return, either in export earnings or foreign exchange savings, and on schemes of an urgent humanitarian or social nature, particularly the rehabilitation of hospitals. During 1983 the government decided to "roll over" the recovery program, and in November a revised program was announced, covering the two years from 1983 to 1985. The program included 105 projects. It allocated to the industrial sector 35% of the envisaged resources, while agriculture, which was granted the largest share under the earlier program, received 27%, social infrastructure 20% of resources, transport and telecommunications 14% and mining 4%.

GROSS DOMESTIC PRODUCT BY ECONOMIC ACTIVITY (1970-81)

	%	Rate of Change %
Agriculture	65.0	–0.8
Mining	0.7	–26.7
Manufacturing	7.1	–9.3
Construction	1.4	–10.3
Electricity, Gas & Water	0.6	–4.9
Transport & Communications	2.6	–7.1
Trade & Finance	11.4	–6.3
Public Administration & Defense	4.6	5.4
Other Branches	6.6	1.9

With the establishment of the Second Republic, patterns of aid have changed drastically. Since the overthrow of Idi Amin, Uganda has received three reconstruction aid packages from a group that includes the World Bank, totaling $265 million. The U.N. Development Program provided $60 million during 1982-86. The EEC pledged $78.9 million under Lome I and $104.0 million under Lome II. Uganda has also received bilateral aid from other countries, and some, such as the United Kingdom and West Germany, have waived all debt repayments on pre-1979 loans. The IMF has provided three generous stand-by facilities and the Club of Paris has rescheduled arrears in repayments.

During 1979-81, Uganda received $7.60 in per capita foreign aid.

BUDGET

The Ugandan fiscal year runs from July 1 through June 30. Two budgets are drawn up annually: the recurrent budget covers ordinary government expenditures and is financed by taxation. The capital

FOREIGN ECONOMIC ASSISTANCE		
Sources	Period	Amount (in million $)
United States Loans	1946-83	11.6
United States Grants	1946-83	66.2
International Organizations	1946-83	487.8
(Of which World Bank)	1946-83	(8.4)
Soviet Union	1954-76	16.0
China	1954-76	15.0
United Kingdom	1970-75	(£ million) 13.6
All Sources	1979-81	99.7

budget is the instrument of the development plan and is financed by foreign economic assistance. The recurrent budget generally shows a surplus.

RECURRENT BUDGET (million shillings, year ending 30 June)			
Revenue	1979/80	1980/81*	1981/82*
Income tax	425.3	387.5	951.4
Selective income levy	23.5	15.4	18.7
Export taxes	1,319.8	300.0	6,860.8
Customs duties	372.6	625.0	6,363.8
Excise duties	76.0	130.0	2,280.0
Public sector investment contribution	354.5	300.0	—
Sales tax	1,129.1	950.0	8,660.0
Service and production taxes and commercial transactions levy	16.1	27.0	50.0
Fees and licences	92.5	100.2	106.8
TOTAL	3,809.5	2,835.1	25,291.5
Expenditure	1979/80	1980/81*	1981/82*
Office of the president	129.6	278.4	861.7
Foreign affairs	100.9	102.2	671.7
Finance	211.5	395.0	1,467.8
Agriculture and forestry	191.9	306.8	742.1
Animal industry and fisheries	115.7	159.7	362.7
Lands, mineral and water resources	83.6	156.5	583.7
Education	947.6	1,284.5	4,053.9
Health	346.2	493.1	1,242.3
Works	159.0	241.0	644.8
Defense	639.1	1,902.7	4,774.3
Police force	209.5	439.6	962.1
Prison service	208.5	439.7	1,126.7
Local administrations	225.6	380.7	1,017.0
TOTAL (incl. others)	4,223.8	7,568.3	21,421.9†

* Estimates.

† Before deducting appropriations-in-aid (480.0 million shillings).

Of current revenues, 9.7% comes from taxes on income, profit and capital gain, 31.5% from domestic taxes on goods and services, 56.0% from taxes on international trade and transactions, 0.1% from other taxes and 2.7% from non-tax revenues. Current revenues represent 3.1% of GNP. Of current expenditures, 19.8% goes to defense, 14.9% to education, 5.2% to health, 6.5% to housing, social security and welfare, 11.7% to economic services and 42.0% to other functions. Total expenditures represented 5.0% of GNP and overall deficit 1.5% of GNP. During 1973-83 public and private consumption declined by 6.4%.

In 1983 total outstanding disbursed external debt was $623.2 million of which $543 million was owed to official creditors and $80.2 million was owed to private creditors. Total debt service was $81.8 million of which $64.8 million was repayment of principal and $17.0 million was interest. Total external debt represented 10.3% of GNP and total debt service 1.4% of GNP.

FINANCE

The Ugandan unit of currency is the shilling, divided into 100 cents. Coins are issued in denominations of 5, 10 and 50 cents and 1 shilling; notes are issued in denominations of 5, 10, 20, 50 and 100 shillings.

The Uganda shilling was introduced in 1966, replacing at par the East African shilling. Until 1975 the shilling was tied to the U.S. dollar, but in that year the link was broken, and the shilling's value was tied to the IMF Special Drawing Right (SDR) based on a weighted basket of 16 national currencies. The exchange rate against the U.S. dollar is adjusted from month to month. In 1985 the dollar exchange rate was $1=Sh600.

The Bank of Uganda was established in 1966 as the bank of issue, replacing the East African Currency Board at Nairobi. Three state banks provide the bulk of the commerical and development financial services: the Uganda Commercial Bank, the Uganda Cooperative Bank and the Uganda Development Bank. All commercial banks are required to be locally incorporated. Of the five foreign banks, there are British, one is Indian and one is Libyan.

In 1983 commercial banks had reserves of Sh5.964 billion, demand deposits of Sh23.528 billion and time and savings deposits of Sh10.886 billion.

AGRICULTURE

Of the total land area of 24,341,100 hectares (60,146,858 acres), 42% is classified as agricultural area, or 0.8 hectare (2 acres) per capita. Based on 1974-76=100, the index of agricultural production in 1982 was 108, the index of per capita agricultural production was 82, the index of food production was 112 and the index of per capita food production was 91. Agriculture employs 83% of the labor force and contributes 65% of the GDP; its rate of growth during 1970-81 was –0.8%. Agricultural products earn 85% of the export revenues. The value added in agriculture in 1983 was $2.614 billion.

The country is endowed with the potential for rich and varied agriculture. Over three-quarters of the land area receives at least the minimum amount of rainfall required for intensive cultivation. However, only 21% of the land area is under actual cultivation. Most of the cultivated land is located in the three southern regions. The major obstacle to the extension of cultivation and herding is the prevalence of the tsetse fly over some 30% of the land surface, but from the 1940s large areas have been reclaimed in northern

GROWTH PROFILE
Annual Growth Rates (%)

Population 1980-2000	3.3
Birthrate 1965-83	2.2
Deathrate 1965-83	-12.4
Urban Population 1973-83	7.3%
Labor Force 1980-2000	3.4
GNP 1973-82	-3.0
GNP per capita 1973-82	-5.6
GDP 1973-83	-2.1
GDP per capita 1970-81	-4.2
Consumer Prices 1970-81	36.0
Wholesale Prices	—
Inflation 1973-83	62.7
Agriculture 1973-83	-1.6
Manufacturing 1970-81	-9.3
Industry 1973-83	-10.1
Services 1973-83	-1.0
Mining 1970-81	-26.7
Construction 1970-81	-10.3
Electricity 1970-81	-4.9
Transportation 1970-81	-7.1
Trade 1970-81	-6.3
Public Administration & Defense 1970-81	5.4
Export Price Index 1975-81	8.5
Import Price Index 1975-81	10.0
Terms of Trade 1975-81	-1.3
Exports 1973-83	-8.6
Imports 1973-83	1.9
Public Consumption	
Private Consumption 1973-83	-6.4
Gross Domestic Investment 1973-83	-5.2
Energy Consumption 1973-83	-5.8
Energy Production 1973-83	-2.6

and central Uganda. Land shortage is therefore not a problem for the country as a whole, although the fallow period under the shifting form of cultivation has been abridged as the supply of virgin land became more restricted.

The basic unit of production is the small-scale family holding with an average size of 1.6 hectares (4 acres) around Lake Victoria, 1.6 hectares to 2.8 hectares (4 to 7 acres) in other areas of the south and 3.2 hectares (8 acres) in the north. The hoe is still the most common agricultural implement; ox-drawn plows are used only in the Teso and Lango districts. In 1982 there were 2,200 tractors and 10 harvester-threshers in use. Annual consumption of fertilizers in the same year was only 600 tons. Irrigation is confined to large sugar estates or experimental projects in the Toro district. Intensive cultivation has consisted mainly of increased intercropping and cultivation of higher-yielding food crops, such as cassava.

Customary forms of land tenure vary from tribe to tribe. The majority of the tribes recognize the right of continuous use of a specific area of tribal land by a family, which amounts to virtual ownership. This right is secure so long as the land is occupied and cultivated, but when it ceases to be so, it reverts to common ownership. The rights of sale or lease are not part of the traditional rules of tenure but have come to be accepted in practice. In most areas, the assignment of land is the function of the clan or lineage head and in others the function of the local councils. Of privately held lands, 12.5% was in the form of mailo es-

tates, originally granted by the Buganda Agreement of 1900 to the chiefs of Buganda, Toro and Ankole. All Asian-owned estates were nationalized in 1972.

Cotton and coffee are the principal cash crops; between them they generate 32% of the monetary income from agriculture.

Uganda remains one of the few African nations self-sufficient in food, despite the complete collapse of its economic infrastructure due to the civil war.

PRINCIPAL CROP PRODUCTION (1982)
(000 tons)

Wheat	9
Rice	18
Corn	293
Millet	528
Sorghum	400
Potatoes	196
Sweet potatoes	690
Cassava	1,425
Beans	361
Field peas (dry)	1
Chick-peas	3
Soybeans	6
Groundnuts	90
Sesame seed	35
Sugar cane	700
Plantains	3,380
Coffee	155
Tea	14
Tobacco	4
Cotton (lint)	18

Crop and animal husbandry are practiced side by side in a system known as parallel husbandry. However, three tribes in the northeast—the Karamojong, Jie and Dodoth—and the Hima in the southwest practice subsistence pastoralism. About 70% of the national herd are the short-horned zebu, and the remainder are the long-horned Ankole and Ngandu. Expansion of livestock is limited by poor ranch management, disease and poor offtake rates for slaughter because of the cultural value of cattle. The government has established some large ranches, such as the Ankole-Masaka Ranch on about 161,880 hectares (400,000 acres) and the Teso Ranch on 18,211 hectares (45,000 acres). The livestock population in 1982 included 5 million cattle, 1.078 million sheep, 2.165 million goats, 260,000 pigs, 16,000 asses and 13,400,000 chickens.

Forests cover about 8% of the land area, mostly in the western rift valley area. About 30 to 40 species of wood are exploited, including mahogany, muzizi, nongo, satinwood, muhimbi, Elgon olive and mvule. The most productive forests are the Budongo at the northern end of Lake Albert, Kibale in Toro district, Kalinzu in the Ankole district, Mabira in the Lake Victoria region, and those of Mount Elgon and the Ruwenzori Mountains. Roundwood removals in 1982 totaled 25.441 million cubic meters (898 million cubic ft).

Lakes Victoria and Kyoga are the main commercial fishing areas, but some fishing is carried on in all the lakes and rivers. Processing and marketing are handled by the Uganda Fish Marketing Corporation. The annual catch in 1981 was 166,600 tons.

Agricultural credit is provided by the Agriculture and Livestock Development Fund.

INDUSTRY

Manufacturing employs 14% of the workforce, contributes 7.1% of the GDP, and its rate of growth during 1973-83 was –9.3%. The value added in manufacturing in 1982 was $81 million, of which agro-based products accounted for 54% and textiles 25%. Most of the manufacturing plants are small; the few large ones account for a disproportionate share of employees and total capacity. Manufacturing is concentrated in the Lake Victoria Region. About 90% of all firms with over 10 employees are located in the southeast and south-central region, and 49% of all industrial employees work in Kampala and Jinja. There has been very little growth in manufacturing outside of food processing (including beverages), cement, textiles and footwear. The state-owned Uganda Development Corporation has dominated industrial investment since the 1960s.

Nationalization of foreign-owned enterprises was one of the five stages of Amin's so-called "Economic War." In 1972 Amin nationalized the British-owned tea estates, the Madhvani Group of Companies and the Mehta Industrial Group, the two latter controlled by Asians. In the same year Amin announced the takeover of numerous British concerns, such as Brooke Bond, British American Tobacco, Chillington Tool and the British Metal Corporation. In 1973 Amin took over German, Dutch, Danish, French and Italian firms. Expropriated British interests in Uganda are estimated to be worth between £40 million and £50 million, while Asian claims total over £100 million. Most of the expropriated companies are operated by government agencies. Amin stated in 1973 that between 3,500 and 4,000 businesses had been handed over to Ugandans from their former owners. In 1983 property expropriated by Amin was restored to the former owners. The current stock of foreign investment is estimated at $19 million.

ENERGY

In 1982 Uganda's production of energy was 81,000 metric tons of coal equivalent and consumption was 342,000 metric tons of coal equivalent, or 24 kg (53 lb) per capita. The annual growth rates during 1973-83 were –2.6% for energy production and –5.8% energy consumption. Apparent per capita consumption of gasoline is 11 gallons per year.

In 1984 Uganda produced 525 million kwh of electric power, or 35 kwh per capita.

LABOR

The economically active population is estimated at 5.706 million of which women make up one-third. By sectors, 83% is employed in agriculture, 6% in industry and 11% in services. The annual growth rate of the labor force during 1973-83 was 1.7%. The Ugandan labor force is one of the most completely Africanized in African as a result of the government's drastic indigenization (also called localization) programs. However, a considerable percentage of the labor force comes from African countries outside Uganda, such as Rwanda, Burundi, Zaire, Sudan and Kenya. Wage-earners account for 6% of the economically active population, and government servants account for 37% of all wage-earners.

Wages are determined by the Minimum Wages Order of 1965, revised periodically. Fringe benefits include subsidized housing, pension rights, free medical services and liberal leave pensions. The law guarantees an annual paid vacation of at least 30 days. Retirement is at age 50. Working conditions are governed by the Employment Ordinance Act of 1955. The work-week is generally 48 hours in industry and 44 hours in government. Severance pay in lieu of notice is mandatory in all cases of retrenchment.

Industrial relations are governed by the Industrial Relations Charter of 1964, which set up conciliation and arbitration machinery and an industrial court. Strikes and lockouts are prohibited before conciliation mechanisms have been exhausted.

In 1973 all labor unions were consolidated within a state-sponsored National Organization of Trade Unions, whose membership is reported at 125,000.

FOREIGN COMMERCE

The foreign commerce of Uganda in 1984 consisted of exports of $394.52 million and imports of $323.52 million, leaving a trade surplus of $71 million. Of the imports, machinery and transport equipment make up 48.4%, metal and metal products 4.6% and paper and paper products 2.2%. Of the exports, coffee constituted 96.8% and raw cotton 1.0%. The major import sources are: Kenya and Tanzania 33.8%, the United Kingdom 23.3% and India 13.4%. The major export destinations are: the United Kingdom 17.1%, the United States 14.8%, the Netherlands 13.5%, Japan 9.5% and West Germany 3.4%.

Based on 1975=100, the import price index in 1981 was 159, the export price index was 168 and the terms of trade (export prices divided by import prices × 100) 106.

TRANSPORTATION & COMMUNICATIONS

As a landlocked country, Uganda depends on Kenya and Tanzania for access to the sea. A direct rail line links Kampala with Kilindini Harbor in Mom-

FOREIGN TRADE INDICATORS (1984)	
Annual Growth Rate, Imports:	−1.9% (1973-83)
Annual Growth Rate, Exports:	−8.0% (1973-83)
Ratio of Exports to Imports:	55:45
Exports per capita:	$27
Imports per capita:	$22
Balance of Trade:	$71 million
Ratio of International Reserves to Imports (in months)	—
Exports as % of GDP:	4.6
Imports as % of GDP:	4.9
Value of Manufactured Exports:	—
Commodity Concentration:	44.1%

Direction of Trade (%)	Imports	Exports
EEC	29.1	31.6
U.S.	—	48.4
Industrialized Market Economies	42.5	88.9
East European Economies	—	—
High Income Oil Exporters	2.9	1.7
Developing Economies	51.3	11.0

Composition of Trade (%)	Imports	Exports
Food	7.9	89.8
Agricultural Raw Materials	0.6	6.8
Fuels	29.6	0.8
Ores & Minerals	3.1	2.2
Manufactured Goods	58.7	0.4
of which Chemicals	11.1	—
of which Machinery	26.8	—

basa, Kenya, through Jinja and Tororo. The other main lines are those linking Kampala with the West Nile district and one running west to Kasese. Including the northern extension completed in 1972, the total trackage is 1,216 km (755 mi).

Lake services are important only on Lake Victoria, and the Albert Nile and river services on the Kagera River, with a combined length of 610 km (379 mi) of navigable waterways.

The length of the road system is 27,540 km (4,200 mi), of which 2,504 km (1,201 mi) are paved. In 1982 these roads were used by 10,633 passenger cars and 11,245 commercial vehicles including 1,566 buses. Per capita passenger car ownership is 0.7 per 1,000 inhabitants.

The national airline is Uganda Airlines Corporation (UAC), which operates four aircraft on domestic and foreign routes. The airline flew 5.1 million km (3.1 million mi) in 1982 and carried 56,000 passengers. There are 38 airports and airfields in the country, of which 34 are usable, five have permanent-surface runways, and three have runways over 2,500 meters (8,000 ft). The principal international airport is Entebbe, near Kampala; a second international airport is being built at Arua.

In 1984 there were 61,600 telephones in use, or 0.5 per 100 inhabitants.

In 1981 the postal system handled 28,275,000 pieces of mail and 64,000 telegrams. Per capita volume of mail was 1.9 pieces. There are 419 telex subscriber lines.

In 1982, 9,000 tourists visited Uganda. Tourist revenues in 1982 totaled $5 million, down from $10 million in 1972. Expenditures by nationals abroad totaled $20 million. There are 4,000 hotel beds and the average length of stay is 3.6 days.

MINING

The principal mineral resource is copper, but the only known deposit at Kilembe is being rapidly exhausted and may not be commercially exploitable after the 1980s. Production in 1982 totaled 2,000 tons, down from a high of 18,000 in 1964. There are two known phosphate deposits in the vicinity of Tororo with proven reserves of more than 180 million tons.

DEFENSE

The defense structure is headed by the president, who is the commander in chief of the armed forces, and the chief of staff. The chain of command runs through the army chief of staff and the commanders of the air force. Enlistment is entirely voluntary.

The total strength of the armed forces is estimated at 18,000, or 0.9 armed persons for every 1,000 civilians.

Very little information is available on the construction and size of the Ugandan armed forces after the fall of Obote. The new NRA regime has its own men and materiel. They captured much of the hardware left behind by the Acholi forces.

ARMY:
Personnel: 18,000
Organization: 3 brigade HQ; 18 infantry battalions
Equipment: 13 tanks; 150 armored personnel carriers; 80 guns; 40 antitank guided weapons; 40 air defense guns; SAM
The Air Force is part of the army. It has six training planes.

NAVY:
There is a Pioneers of Uganda Naval force but no navy.
The defense budget in 1982/83 was $94.153 million, representing 18.5% of the national budget, 1.0% of the GNP, $4 per capita, $7,800 per soldier and $165 per sq km of national territory.

EDUCATION

The national literacy rate is 52.5% (64.6% for males and 40.5% for females). Of the population over 25, 71.8% have had no schooling, 26.5% have attended and/or completed the first level, 1.8% have attended and/or completed the second level, and 0.1% have completed post-secondary education.

Uganda has not yet introduced free, universal and compulsory education. The gross school enrollment ratios are 60% at the first level (6 to 12) and 8% at the second level (13 to 18) for a combined enrollment ratio of 39%. The third-level enrollment ratio is 0.6%. Girls make up 43% of primary school enrollment, 33% of secondary enrollment and 27% of tertiary enrollment.

Schooling lasts for 13 years, divided into seven years of primary schooling, four years of general secondary school (forms I through IV) and two years of higher secondary school (forms IV through VI). The primary school-leaving examination is administered by the Ministry of Education. The general cycle of secondary education leads to the Cambridge Overseas School Certificate or the General Certificate of Education; the higher cycle leads to the to the Higher School Certificate, which permits university entrance. There is a high dropout rate before the seventh year of primary school. In 1982 the school system comprised 4,945 primary schools, 118 secondary schools, 48 vocational and technical secondary schools and 29 teacher-training schools. Mission schools continue a prominent role in education and receive direct grants-in-aid.

The school year runs from January through December. The language of instruction is English, but seven African languages are permitted to be used in primary schools: Akaramojong, Ateso, Luganda, Lugbara, Luo, Runyankole-Rukiga and Runyoro-Rutoro.

Total enrollment in teacher-training institutions in 1982 was 9,157. The National Institute of Education at Makrere is concerned with the professional improvement of teachers, and it also undertakes educational research. The national teacher-pupil ratios are 1:34 in primary schools, 1:21 in secondary schools and 1:10 in post-secondary classes.

Vocational training is provided in four types of institutions: technical schools, farm schools, rural trade schools and industrial training schools, with a total enrollment in 1982 of 4,181, or 2.8% of total secondary school enrollment. The senior four–year course leads to the First Craft Certificate of the City and Guilds of London Institute.

The educational system is under the jurisdiction of the Ministry of Education with four divisions: schools and colleges under the chief education officer; higher education; finance and establishment; and the Inspectorate. Primary school education (including finance) is under the operational control of local authorities, but secondary education is controlled and financed by the national government. In 1981 the Ministry of Education's budget totaled Sh6,733,700,000, of which 84.6% was current expenditure. This amount represented 1.3% of the GDP (as compared to a UNESCO recommendation of 4%), 12.3% of the national budget and $4 per capita.

Higher education is provided by the Makrere University with about 7,312 students. Per capita university enrollment is 50 per 100,000 inhabitants.

In 1982, 1,529 students (including 386 women) graduated from Makrere University. Of these, 92 received degrees in medicine, 92 in engineering, 60 in natural sciences, 284 in social sciences, 57 in law, 181 in education and 66 in agriculture.

In 1982, 1,011 Ugandan students were enrolled in institutions of higher learning abroad. Of these, 401 were in the United States, 172 in the United Kingdom, 52 in Canada, 83 in West Germany and 35 at the Vatican. In the same year, 42 foreign students were enrolled in Uganda.

LEGAL SYSTEM

The legal system is based on English common law and African customary law. However, customary law is effective only when not in conflict with statutory law.

The judiciary is a four-level structure headed by the High Court, comprising a chief justice and 14 junior judges. The High Court has also supervisory and review responsibilities over the lower courts, of which the chief magistrate courts are the most important. Each chief magistrate has under him three types of magistrate courts, Grades I, II and III. At the bottom level are justices of the peace with very limited jurisdiction.

The Prison Service operates 30 prisons, including special prisons for long-term prisoners and habitual criminals. Prisoners under the death sentence are confined at Upper Prison at Murchison Bay, Kampala. Political prisoners are incarcerated and tortured at Makindye Prison.

LAW ENFORCEMENT

The Uganda Police Force is commanded by an Inspector General of Police, assisted by four regional commanders who direct police operations within their regions. Law enforcement policy is decided upon by the Police Council of six members headed by the Inspector General. There is a special Police Tracker Force in charge of suppressing cattle-raiding. The total strength of the police has varied in recent times because of the large-scale murders of non-Muslim members of the force, but reliable sources place it at around 14,000, or one policeman for every 880 inhabitants.

Violent crime has increased since the establishment of the Second Republic, and it is doubtful if all crimes are reported. No criminal statistics have been published since 1971.

HEALTH

In 1981 there were 485 hospitals in the country with 19,782 beds, or one bed per 690 inhabitants. In the

EDUCATIONAL ENROLLMENT (1982)			
Level	Schools	Teachers	Students
First Level	4,945	44,426	1,616,791
Second Level	118	7,022	145,389
Vocational	48	n.a.	4,181
Third Level	4	540	7,312

same year there were 611 physicians, or one physician per 22,324 inhabitants, 17 dentists and 6,778 nursing personnel. Of the hospitals 84.5% are state-run and 15.5% are run by private nonprofit agencies.

PRINCIPAL HEALTH INDICATORS (1984)

Crude Death Rate: 14.7 per 1,000
Decline in Death Rate: −12.4 (1965-83)
Life Expectancy at Birth: 50.3 (Males); 53.8 (Females)
Infant Mortality Rate: 100.5 per 1,000 Live Births
Child Death Rate (Ages 1-4) per 1,000: 21

Free medical treatment is provided in government dispensaries and hospitals. In 1982 health expenditures constituted 6.1% of the national budget, and $4.30 per capita. The principal health problems are malaria, sleeping sickness, leprosy, kwashiorkor, hookworm, schistosomiasis, tuberculosis, syphilis, gonorrhea, yaws, smallpox, typhoid and poliomyelitis. Only 35% of the population have access to safe water.

FOOD

The staple food around Lake Victoria is a starchy mixture of baked bananas known as matoke. In the west and northwest, the staple foods are millet and sorghum supplemented by peanuts and cassava. The pastoral tribes have a high intake of animal products, including animal blood and meat. Fish is popular where available.

The daily per capita intake of food is 1,862 calories and 49.4 grams of protein (compared to recommended minimums of 2,600 calories and 65 grams of protein), 32 grams of fats and 409 grams of carbohydrates.

MEDIA & CULTURE

Five daily newspapers are published in Kampala of which the *Uganda Times* and the *Star* are in English. Aggregate circulation is 35,000 per issue, or 2.3 per 1,000 inhabitants. The non-daily and periodical press includes a number of government and mission publications. Annual consumption of newsprint in 1982 was 200 tons, or 15 kg (0.04 lb) per 1,000 inhabitants.

The national news agency is the Uganda News Agency run by the Ministry of Information. Novosti and Tass have bureaus in Kampala, and Reuters and AP are represented.

Book publishing is carried on in a limited way. The major publishing houses are Longman and the Uganda Publishing House (formerly owned partly by Macmillan of London).

The state-owned Radio Uganda operates short-wave and medium-wave transmitters and is on the air for 230 hours a week in English and 21 vernaculars. In 1982 there were 310,000 radio receivers in the country, or 22 per 1,000 inhabitants.

The Uganda Television Service, founded in 1963, operates a main station in Kampala and five relay sta-

tions at Masaka, Mbale, Mbarara, Lira and Soroti, and is on the air for nine hours a day. In 1982 there were an estimated 78,000 television receivers, or 6.0 per 1,000 inhabitants.

There is no domestic film production. There are 17 fixed cinemas with 10,000 seats, or 1.1 seats per 1,000 inhabitants. Annual movie attendance is 1.6 million or 0.2 per capita. In 1977, 936 films were imported, 328 from the United States.

The Public Libraries Board administers the Uganda Library Service, with approximately 20 branches. The largest library is the library of the Makrere University, whose central library with 300,000 volumes also functions as the National Reference Library. Per capita, there are eight volumes and three registered borrowers per 1,000 inhabitants.

There are nine museums reporting an annual attendance of 170,000. There are 17 nature preservation sites.

SOCIAL WELFARE

A national provident fund scheme initiated in 1965 provides pension benefits at age 60 or retirement. Contributions are at the rate of 10% of wages, shared equally by worker and employer, with no input by government. There are numerous voluntary, religious and tribal associations offering a wide array of social welfare services.

GLOSSARY

bataka: the traditional chief of the Baganda clans.
gombolola: a territorial unit under British administration.
kabaka: title of the traditional ruler of the Buganda Kingdom.
katikiri: title of the prime minister of the Buganda Kingdom.
lukiko: government council of the Buganda Kingdom.
mailo: lands assigned to the chiefs of Buganda under the Buganda Agreement of 1900.
mugabe: title of the traditional ruler of the Kingdom of Ankole.
mukama: title of the traditional ruler of the Kingdoms of Bunyoro and Toro.
rukurato: government council of the Kingdom of Bunyoro.
saza: county, as a unit of local administration.

CHRONOLOGY (from 1962)

1962— Uganda becomes an independent member of the Commonwealth with Milton Obote as prime minister at the head of a Kabaka Yekka-Uganda People's Congress coalition.
1963— Uganda proclaims itself a republic with Sir Edward Mutesa, the kabaka of Buganda, as first president.

1966— Struggle for power between the kabaka and the prime minister culminates in Obote's suspending the constitution and assuming full executive powers; under new constitution Obote names himself president; the federal character of the republic is abrogated; and Uganda becomes a unitary state.... Obote declares state of emergency following clashes between the Baganda and the police; the army storms the kabaka's palace, and the kabaka flees to England.

1967— The four kingdoms—Buganda, Ankole, Bunyoro and Toro—are abolished under the new republican constitution.

1969— Obote introduces a Common Man's Charter, signaling a turn to the left.

1971— Obote is overthrown by an army coup led by Maj. Gen. Idi Amin; the Suspension of Political Activities Decree abolishes all constitutional rights; the Armed Forces (Power of Arrest) Decree places the armed forces above the law; the Detention (Presumption of Time Limit) Decree grants the armed forces wide powers of detention without trial and the power to shoot on sight.... "Disappearances" of prominent Ugandans begin; among the first to "disappear" are two Americans, the journalist Nicholas Stroh and the sociologist Robert Siedle, and the chief justice of the Ugandan High Court, Benedicto Kiwanuka.

1972— Obote's supporters launch unsuccessful invasion from Tanzania that is easily repulsed by the Ugandan army, now manned by mercenaries and Muslims.... Last major elements of the Langi and Acholi tribes in the police and armed forces are massacred.... Over 40,000 Asians are expelled within 90 days.

1973— British and other foreign businesses are expropriated without compensation and distributed among the military and the police.

1974— International Commission of Jurists, in a report to the U.N., accuses Amin of murdering up to 250,000 people.

1975— British lecturer Denis Hills is sentenced to death for writing a defamatory article about Amin but is reprieved after appeals from 50 countries.

1976— Amin claims territories in Sudan and Kenya; Kenya, in retaliation, closes the border to Ugandan goods bound for Mombasa; Amin backs down.... Israeli commandoes raid Entebbe Airport to release Jewish hostages in plane hijacked by Palestinian guerrillas.... United Kingdom suspends diplomatic relations with Uganda.

1979— Uganda forces claiming Tanzanian territory advance and occupy the Kagera salient and cross the Kagera River; Tanzanians counterattack with Ugandan dissidents, push back the Ugandan forces, and continue advancing, despite stiff resistance into Uganda; Tanzanians seize Kampala and force Amin to flee; a provisional government, the National Executive Council, is established from the ranks of the Uganda National Liberation Front, a broad coalition of exiled groups, under the leadership of Yusuf Lule; Lule is replaced as president by Godfrey Binaisa.

1980— As ethnic divisions within the government grow to crisis proportions, the military seize the president and place him under house arrest; the promised elections are held with Commonwealth monitors; Milton Obote, former president, and leader of the Uganda People's Congress, is elected president by popular vote; Obote appeals for national unity.

1985— Elements of the Ugandan National Liberation Army, led by Gen. Tito Okello, overthrow Milton Obote and establish an Interim Military Government... Okello Lutwa is installed as president and head of Military Council; Council includes members of four insurgent groups excepting the National Resistance Army (NRA).

1986— The National Resistance Army takes over Kampala and drives out the Northerners... NRA leader Yoweri Museveni is installed as president.

BIBLIOGRAPHY (from 1970)

Avirgan, Tony and Martha Honey, *War in Uganda: The Legacy of Idi Amin* (Westport, Conn., 1982).

Baird, Mark, *Uganda: Country Economic Memorandum* (Washington, D.C., 1982).

Collison, Robert L., *Uganda* [World Bibliographical Series] (Santa Barbara, Calif., 1981).

East Africa: Kenya, Tanganyika, Uganda. Color film, 21 min. Encyclopaedia Britannica.

Gukiina, Peter, *Uganda: A Case Sudy of African Political Development* (Notre Dame, Ind., 1972).

Gupta, Vijay, *Obote: Second Liberation* (New York, 1983).

Gwyn, David, *Idi Amin: Death Light of Africa* (Boston, 1977).

Heymann, Micheal, *The Uganda Controversy* (New Brunswick, N.J., 1978).

Ibingira, G.S., *The Forging of an African Nation: The Political and Constitutional Evolution of Uganda from Colonial Rule to Independence, 1894-1962* (New York, 1973).

International Commission of Jurists, *Violations of Human Rights and the Rule of Law in Uganda* (Geneva, 1974).

Jameson, J.P., *Agriculture in Uganda* (London, 1971).

Jorgensen, Jan, *Uganda: A Modern History* (New York, 1981).

Kasfir, Nelson, *The Shrinking Political Arena: Participation and Ethnicity in African Politics with a case of Uganda* (Chicago, 1976).

Kyemba, Henry, *A State of Blood: the Inside Story of Idi Amin* (New York, 1977).

Ladefoged, Peter, *Language in Uganda* (New York, 1972).

Listowel, Judith, *Amin* (Dublin, 1973).

Mamdani, Mahmood, *Politics and Class Formation in Uganda* (New York, 1976).
——, *Imperialism and Fascism in Uganda* (Trenton, N.J., 1984).
Martin, David, *General Amin* (London, 1974).
Mazrui Ali, *Soldiers & Kinsmen in Uganda: The Making of a Military Ethnocracy* (Beverly Hills, Calif., 1975).
Melady, Thomas and Margaret Melady, *Uganda: The Asian Exiles* (Maryknoll, N.Y., 1976).
——, *Idi Amin: Hitler in Africa* (New York, 1977).
Mittelman, James H., *Ideology and Politics in Uganda: From Obote to Amin* (Ithaca, N.Y., 1975).
Nadudere, D. Wadada, *Imperialism & Revolution in Uganda* (New York, 1980).
Rowe, John, *Revolution in Buganda, 1856-1900* (Ann Arbor, Mich., 1974).
Shorter, Aylward, *East African Societies* (London, 1974).
Stevenson, William and Dan Stevenson, *Ninety Minutes at Entebbe* (New York, 1976).
Toko Gad W., *Intervention in Uganda:* (Pittsburgh, Pa., 1979).
Twaddle, Michael, *Expulsion of a Minority: Essays on Ugandan Asians* (London, 1974).
Uchendu, *The Last Days of Idi Amin* (Buffalo, N.Y., 1981).
Uzoigwe, Godfrey N., *Uganda: The Politics of Decolonization* (New York, 1981).
——, *Uganda: The Dilemma of Nationhood* (New York, 1982).
Wooding, Dan and Ray Barnett, *Uganda Holocaust.* (Grand Rapids, Mich., 1980).
Zwanenberg, R.M. van and Anne King, *An Economic History of Kenya and Uganda 1800-1970* (New York, 1975).

OFFICIAL PUBLICATIONS

Education Ministry, *Accounts of Government-Aided Schools.*
——, *Accounts of Makerere University.*
Finance Ministry, *Background to the Budget.*
——, *Detailed Estimates of Recurrent Expenditure.*
——, *Estimates of Development Expenditure.*
——, *Financial Statement and Revenue Estimates.*
——, *Public Accounts of the Republic of Uganda.*
Planning and Economic Development Ministry, *Quarterly Economic and Statistical Bulletin.*
——, *Statistical Abstract.*
Uganda Bank, *Annual Report.*
——, *Quarterly Bulletin.*

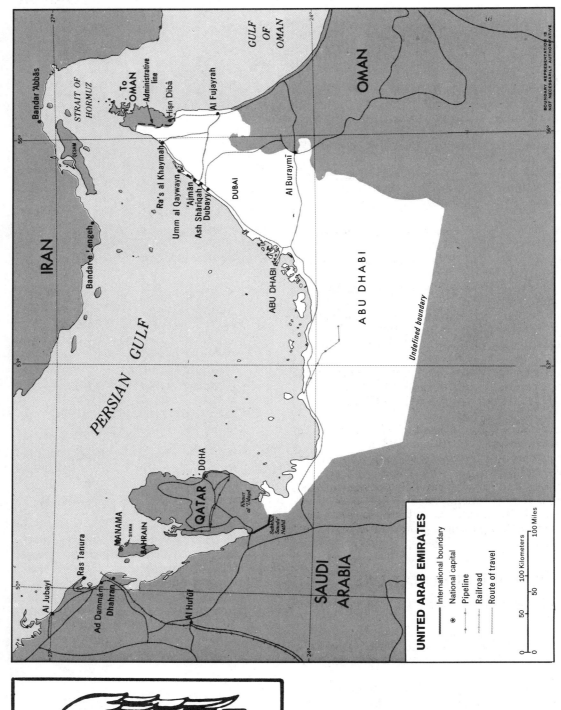

IRAN

Bandar 'Abbās

STRAIT OF
HORMUZ

QESHM

GULF
OF
OMAN

OMAN

To
OMAN

Administrative
line

Hisn Dibā

Al Fujayrah

Bandar-e 'Lengeh

Ra's al Khaymah

Umm al Qaywayn

'Ajmān

Ash Shāriqah

Dubayy

DUBAI

Al Buraymi

PERSIAN

GULF

ABU DHABI

ABU DHABI

ABU DHABI

Undefined boundary

DOHA

QATAR

Khawr
al 'Udayd

MANAMA

SITRAH

BAHRAIN

Sabkhat
Sawdā'
Nathil

Ras Tanura

Al Jubayl

Ad Dammām

Dhahrān

Al Hufūf

SAUDI
ARABIA

UNITED ARAB EMIRATES

—⊛— International boundary

⊛ National capital

╫╫ Pipeline

+++ Railroad

—— Route of travel

50   0   50   100 Kilometers

0   50   100 Miles

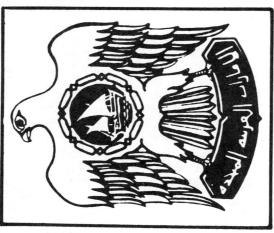

UNITED ARAB EMIRATES

BASIC FACT SHEET

OFFICIAL NAME: The State of the United Arab Emirates (Dawlat al-Imaaraat al-Arabiyya al-Muutahidah. (Formerly the Trucial States)

ABBREVIATION: UE

CAPITAL: Abu Dhabi (provisional)

HEAD OF STATE: President Sheikh Zaid ibn Al Nuhayan, Ruler of Abu Dhabi (from 1971)

HEAD OF GOVERNMENT: Prime Minister Sheikh Rashid ibn Said al-Maktum, Ruler of Dubai (from 1979)

NATURE OF GOVERNMENT: Confederation of absolute monarchies

POPULATION: 1,320,000 (1985)

AREA: 77,700 sq km (30,000 sq mi)

ETHNIC MAJORITY: Arab

LANGUAGE: Arabic

RELIGION: Sunni Islam

UNIT OF CURRENCY: Dirham ($1=UD3.671, August 1985)

NATIONAL FLAG: A vertical red stripe on the hoist and three equal horizontal stripes of green, white and black on the right

NATIONAL EMBLEM: An outstretched Arab eagle with an Arab dhow displayed in a circle on its chest. Beneath appears the name of the country in Arabic.

NATIONAL ANTHEM: Instrumental piece without words

NATIONAL HOLIDAYS: December 2 (National Day); January 1 (New Year's Day); December 25 and 26 (Christmas and Boxing Day). Also, variable Islamic festivals.

NATIONAL CALENDAR: Islamic and Gregorian

PHYSICAL QUALITY OF LIFE INDEX: 69 (up from 34 in 1976) (On an ascending scale in which 100 is the maximum; U.S. 95)

DATE OF INDEPENDENCE: December 2, 1971

DATE OF CONSTITUTION: December 2, 1971

WEIGHTS & MEASURES: Metric and Imperial systems are used. Full conversion to the metric system is planned by stages.

LOCATION & AREA

The United Arab Emirates is located on the southeastern end of the Arabian Peninsula and extends from Sha'am to Khor al Odeid. Formerly known as the Trucial Sheikhdoms, Trucial Coast, Trucial Oman and the Trucial States, the Emirates consist of seven states: Abu Dhabi (67,340 sq km, 26,000 sq mi), Dubai (3,885 sq km, 1,500 sq mi); Ras al-Khaimah (1,683 sq km, 650 sq mi); Fujairah (1,166 sq km, 450 sq mi), Umm al-Qaywayn (777 sq km, 300 sq mi); Sharjah (2,590 sq km, 1,000 sq mi); and Ajman (259 sq km, 100 sq mi). Disputed and undefined boundaries make the geographical extent of this region difficult to define precisely, but the most commonly cited figure is 77,700 sq km (30,000 sq mi). This figure does not include a number of sandbars and islands of which the largest are Dalma, Al Ghubbah, Abu Musa, Az Zarqa, Das and Mubarak. The greatest distance NE to SW is 544 km (338 mi) and that SE to NW 361 km (224 mi).

The total length of international borders is 1,173 km (723 mi). The border with Oman runs 513 km (319 mi), that with Saudi Arabia 586 km (364 mi), and that with Qatar 64 km (40 mi). The Persian Gulf coastline stretches for 777 km (483 mi). Although there are no serious boundary disputes between the emirates, the internal divisions of the smaller states are complicated by noncontinuous enclaves. Sharjah, for example, consists of three parts. In addition, there are unresolved and potentially divisive border disputes with Saudi Arabia and Qatar.

The provisional capital is Abu Dhabi with a 1980 population of 243,000. The other major urban centers are Dubai (266,000), Sharjah (125,000), Ras al Khaimah (42,000), Fujairah, Ajman and Umm al-Qaywayn. Dubai is the undisputed leader in finance and maritime activity.

The UAE is an arid and inhospitable desert. The Trucial coast is characterized by shallow seas, coral reefs, sand bars and islets. Inland the coastal plain gives way to rolling sand dunes with occasional tiny oases fed by shallow ground water. This region is bounded on the west by an immense sabkha, or salt flat, extending southward for nearly 112 km (70 miles) and merging with the vast wastes of the Rub al-Khali. Toward the east, as the desert reaches the Musandam Peninsula, the foothills of the Western Hajar range of mountains begin to rise, in places to 2,500 meters (8,000 ft), and their spurs run down in steep cliffs to the shore except for small embayments, as at Fujairah. A cluster of oases, known as the Liwa, form an arc along the southern edge of the sandy desert. On the east coast a fertile coastal strip, known as the Batinah Coast, runs between the mountains and the sea and continues into Oman.

WEATHER

The UAE has an arid, sub-tropical climate. Average maximum temperatures in July and August, the summer months, run over 48°C (118.4°F), while average minimum temperatures in the winter months of January and February are between 10°C (50°F) and 14°C (57°F). Humidity exceeds 85% on the coast during summer. Rainfall is slight and erratic. It usually falls in January and February. Average annual rainfall varies between 25mm (1 in.) and 125 mm (5 in.), with the higher limits being received by the eastern mountains. Rain tends to fall in short, torrential outbursts flooding the wadis. Droughts are frequent. The scarcity of the rainwater is compounded by the limited supply of groundwater, generally confined to oases.

The main wind is the Sharqi, a humid southeastern wind, that blows along the Trucial Coast making the summer heat oppressive.

POPULATION

The population of the UAE in 1985 was 1,320,000, on the basis of the last census held in 1981 when the population was 1,043,225. The population is expected to reach 1.9 million by 2000 and 2.5 million by 2020. By state the population is as follows: Abu Dhabi (521,000), Dubai (307,000), Sharjah (185,000), Ras al-Khaimah (86,000), Fujairah (38,000), Ajman (44,000) and Umm al-Qaywayn (14,000). There are also 20,000 nomads.

The annual growth rate in population during 1973-83 was 12.0%. The population of Abu Dhabi state has quadrupled and that of the city of Abu Dhabi decupled between 1968 and 1975. The population of Dubai city rose by 300% in the same period. The annual birthrate is estimated at 27 per 1,000.

The density of population is estimated at 16 per sq km (35 per sq mi). The population is almost entirely concentrated in the coastal towns and in the Liwa and Buraimi Oases.

The median age is heavily weighted in favor of the middle aged and early adult, reflecting the heavy influx of immigrants. Only 30.7% are below 14 years of age, 66.8% are between 15 and 64, and 2.4% are over 65.

The urban population, replenished by a constant stream of immigrants, constitutes over 78% of the total, up from 26% in 1970.

The most important demographic fact about the UAE is the large numbers of external migrants who have been attracted since 1968 by the booming economy of the country. The UAE is perhaps the only country, other than Kuwait, where immigrants form the majority of the population. Of its total economically active population, UAE citizens form only 2%;

DEMOGRAPHIC INDICATORS (1984)	
Population total (000)	1,320.0
Population ages (% of Total)	
0-14	30.7
15-64	66.8
Age 65+	2.4
Youth 15-24 (000)	201
Women 15-49 (000)	179
Dependency ratio	49.6
Child-woman ratio	875
Sex ratio (per 100 females)	219.2
Median age (Years)	26.6
% Urban	77.76
Population density (per sq km)	16
per hectare of arable land	N.A.
Rate of growth (%)	5.83
urban (%)	5.0
rural (%)	9.2
Natural increase rate (per 1,000)	23.0
Crude birthrate 1/1000	27.0
Crude death rate 1/1000	4.0
Gross reproduction rate	2.90
Net reproduction rate	2.72
Total fertility rate	5.94
General fertility rate (per 1,000)	194
Life expectancy years: Male	68.2
Female	73.2
Total	70.6
Decline in birthrate 1965-83 (%)	−34.1
Population doubling time in years at current rate	30.0
Average household size	3.8

non-UAE Arabs constitute 7%, and Indians, Pakistanis and Iranians constitute 91%. Overall, migrants form 56% of the population. The number of annual work permits reached a peak in 1977 and then began to drop, particularly in Dubai and Sharjah, although it continued to rise in Abu Dhabi. Changes in the distribution of immigrant workers by country of origin showed a sizeable decrease in the number of Arab nationals and Iranians and a lesser drop in the number of Pakistanis and Indians, while showing an increase in the number of other Asians.

UAE has no birth control policies or programs and may not need them so long as its economic resources far outrun the growth rate of its population.

ETHNIC COMPOSITION

Ethnically the population of UAE presents a mosaic, reflecting the country's need for foreign labor to man the rapidly growing economic and social services sectors. The dominant strain is Adnani, or Northern, Arab who constitute 10% of the population in Abu Dhabi and 25% nationwide. There are significant numbers of Negroes, recalling the region's prominence in the slave trade of the 18th and 19th centuries.

Three major ethnic groups—Iranians, Indians and Pakistanis—constitute 75% of the population. Almost all of them are foreign-born and recent arrivals. There are also groups of non-UAE Arabs, such as Palestinians, Egyptians, Iraqis and Lebanese, found throughout the country. The immigrant population is concentrated in the towns along the coast, particularly Abu Dhabi and Dubai.

Historically, the UAE's native population has tolerated, and even welcomed, outsiders and displayed a freedom from the xenophobia common in many Arab countries. Nevertheless, there has been increasing concern at the numerical strength of immigrants and some resentment at their growing economic power.

Traditional conservatism and strong family pressures, plus the still honored tradition of girls marrying in their early teens, have prevented many women citizens from continuing their education beyond the primary level. This in turn has limited their role in the economic and cultural life of the country. The number of Emirate women in the workforce is minimal. However, the government is encouraging women to pursue their education, and they are beginning to find employment in the news media and government offices, as well as in the traditionally accepted fields of health and education. Women are permitted to drive automobiles and may appear in public unveiled.

LANGUAGE

The official language of the UAE is Arabic. Gulf Arabic is akin to the Arabic of Saudi Arabia and Iraq but different from the Arabic spoken in Egypt and Lebanon.

English is universally understood among the commercial and administrative elite and is taught as the second language in secondary schools.

RELIGION

Islam is the state religion and the majority of the natives and immigrants are Sunni Muslims. Shiite Muslims are found in Dubai but not in numbers to challenge Sunni dominance.

Toleration, remarkable by Arab standards, is extended to Christians of all denominations and some churches, missions and schools are permitted to function openly. Religious hostility is exercised only against the Jews whose small communities have virtually disappeared.

CONSTITUTION & GOVERNMENT

A provisional constitution for the UAE was set up in 1971. This constitution established a Supreme Federal Council as the highest organ of government, the presidency and council of ministers as the executive, a Federal Council as the legislature, and a federal supreme court. Under the constitution considerable reserved powers remain to each emirate, including control over mineral rights, taxation and police powers. There has been, however, a slow but persistent growth in federal powers. A significant portion of the oil revenues of the three oil-producing emirates goes to the UAE's central budget. There has also been growing integration of defense forces, communications facilities and courts. In 1975 a committee was appointed to draft a permanent federal constitution which, it is expected, will introduce radical changes in the interrelationships of the emirates within the union without affecting the monarchist and absolutist character of each unit.

The principal federal institution is the Supreme Federal Council, which is composed of the rulers of the seven emirates and is charged with the formulation and supervision of all state policies, ratification of federal laws, and preparation of the union budget. All important decisions require the votes of at least five members, including the rulers of Abu Dhabi and Dubai. The president and the vice president are elected for a period of five years and may be reelected.

SUPREME COUNCIL OF RULERS
(with each ruler's date of accession)

Ruler of Abu Dhabi: Sheikh Zayed Bin Sultan Al-Nahayan (1966).

Ruler of Dubai: Sheikh Rashid Bin Said Al-Maktoum (1958).

Ruler of Sharjah: Sheikh Sultan Bin Muhammad Al-Qasimi (1972).

Ruler of Ras al-Khaimah: Sheikh Saqr Bin Muhammad Al-Qasimi (1948).

Ruler of Umm al-Qaiwain: Sheikh Rashid Bin Ahmad Al-Mu'alla (1981).

Ruler of Ajman: Sheikh Humaid Bin Rashid Al-Nuami (1981).

Ruler of Fujairah: Sheikh Hamad Bin Muhammad Al-Sharqi (1974).

The president is assisted by a Council of Ministers presided over by the prime minister. The member states are represented in the cabinet in proportion to their size and importance.

The UAE has never held an election in its history, and there is no constitutional provision for elections. Consequenly, there is no suffrage. The chief political effect of Iranian events has been to heighten awareness of the UAE's own political divisions and to hasten efforts of its leaders to solve internal problems. Because the country is a federation of seven independent-minded emirates, the UAE federal government has always been weak. Disagreements among the individual emirates over such important economic issues as the creation of a central bank, immigration and labor laws, as well as over other political and defense matters, have sapped the effectiveness of the national government. National economic planning and coordination have also been hampered.

Emirate rulers are accessible to any subject who has a problem or a request. The choice of a new ruler falls to the ruling family, which is supposed to choose its most capable and respected eligible member. In practice, to avoid violent succession disputes which were common in the past, primogeniture has become increasingly common. The political dominance of the ruling families is intertwined with their substantial involvement and influence in economic life. The ruling families and their close allies control and profit from

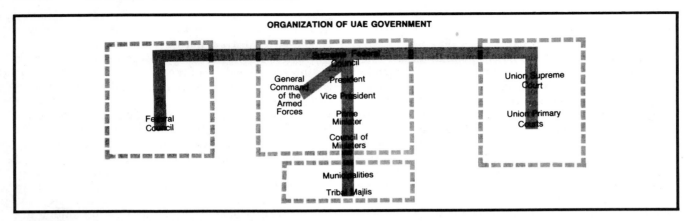

ORGANIZATION OF UAE GOVERNMENT

Supreme Federal Council
President
Vice President
Prime Minister
Council of Ministers
General Command of the Armed Forces
Federal Council
Union Supreme Court
Union Primary Courts
Municipalities
Tribal Majlis

CABINET LIST (1985)

President . . . . .Zayid bin Sultan Al Nuhayyan
Vice President . . . . Rashid bin Sa'id Al Maktum
Prime Minister . . . . Rashid bin Sa'id Al Maktum
Deputy Prime Minister . . . .Maktum bin Rashid Al Maktum
Deputy Prime
 Minister . . . . Hamdan bin Muhammad Al Nuhayyan
Minister of Agriculture & Fisheries . . . . . .Sa'id al- Raqbani
Minister of Communications . . .Muhammad Sa'id al- Mulla
Minister of
 Defense . . . Muhammad bin Rashid bin Sa'id Al Maktum
Minister of Economy & Commerce . . . Sayf' Ali al- Jarwan
Minister of Education & Youth . . . . . Faraj Fahdil al- Mazrui
Minister of Electricity & Water . . .Humayd Nasir al- 'Uways
Minister of Finance
 & Industry . . . . Hamdan bin Rashid bin Sa'id Al Maktum
Minister of Health . . . . . Hamad 'Abd al-Rahman al- Madfa
Minister of Information
 & Culture . . . . Ahmad bin Hamid Al Nuhayyan
Minister of Islamic Affairs
 and Awqaf . . . . Muhammad bin Hasan al- Khazraji
Minister of Justice . . . . Abdallah Hamid al- Mazrui
Minister of Labor
 & Social Affairs . . . . Khalfan Muhammad al- Rumi
Minister of Petroleum & Mineral
 Resources . . . . Mani Sa'id al- 'Utayba
Minister of Public Works
 & Housing . . . . .Muhammad Khalifa al- Kindi
Minister of State . . . . Ahmad bin Sultan al- Qasimi
Minister of State for Cabinet Affairs . . . . . Sa'id al- Ghayth
Minister of State for Financial and
 Industrial Affairs . . . . Ahmad Humayd al- Tayir
Minister of State for Foreign
 Affairs . . . . Rashid 'Abdallah 'Ali al- Nu'aymi
Minister of State for Interior
 Affairs . . . . *Maj. Gen.*Hammuda bin 'Ali al- Dhuhiri
Minister of State for Supreme Council
 Affairs . . . .'Abd al- 'Aziz bin Hamid al- Qasimi

---

petroleum production, and, with important merchant families, have a major stake in the UAE's commercial life. Women play virtually no public role in the UAE's conservative male-dominated society. However, pressure for change may come from the generally superior educational performance of girls (who are restricted from educational opportunities abroad) and their increasing secondary and university enrollment.

The UAE has had a stable government reinforced by economic prosperity. In the absence of representative institutions and political parties, there is no forum for political expression. Pockets of dissidence, however, exist. In 1972-73 a number of army officers and civil servants were arrested as subversives. Supporters of the Palestinian Front for the Liberation of the Arabian Gulf and other leftist organizations are known to be active, particularly in Abu Dhabi.

FREEDOM & HUMAN RIGHTS

In terms of political and civil rights the UAE is classified as a partly free country with a rating of 5 in civil rights and 5 in political rights (on a descending scale in which 7 is the lowest and 1 the highest in civil and political rights).

The Emirates' egalitarian Islamic and Bedouin traditions shape their outlook on human rights and political organization. In some emirates, particularly, Abu Dhabi, criminal cases are tried in the Islamic (Sharia) courts which apply traditional and harsh procedures and penalties. Muslims may be flogged for drunkeness and for violating the Ramadan fast. But all capital sentences must be personally approved by the ruler. Prolonged detention without trial is rare. Although no public defender system exists, defendants may be represented by counsel of their choice. Mild criticism of the government is generally tolerated but "irresponsible" opposition is discouraged. Newspapers that deviate from official guidelines are suspended. All books, films, and periodicals are subject to censorship if they contain materials considered pornographic, politically subversive, or derogatory of Islam and the Arabs. Visits by foreign journalists require official permission. Several journalists were arrested in 1980 for photographing military installations. A new press law is being codified that will incorporate stringent terms, but there are as yet no indications that this law will give the government any more powers than it enjoys now. There are no political parties or popularly elected legislatures. Expatriates who constitute the numerical majority are expected to refrain from political activity and are, further, not permitted to organize.

CIVIL SERVICE

No current information is available on the UAE civil service.

LOCAL GOVERNMENT

All the principal towns of the emirates have their own appointed municipal governments. These include Abu Dhabi, al-Ain, Dubai, Ras al-Khaimah, Fujairah, Ajman and Umm al-Qaywayn. In addition, the tribes have their own traditional councils known as majlis and amiri diwans.

FOREIGN POLICY

Since independence the UAE has settled two outstanding border disputes: one with Iran over the Gulf Median Line and the other with Saudi Arabia over the Buraimi Oasis. Under the 1974 agreement with Saudi Arabia the six disputed villages of the oasis were awarded to Abu Dhabi in return for the grant of a land corridor to Saudi Arabia. This corridor runs through Abu Dhabi to the Persian Gulf port of Khor al-Adad. The dispute with Iran over the Gulf Median Line has become dormant since 1972.

Although one of the most conservative Arab states, the UAE gave considerable support to the front-line Arab states in the October War of 1973 and participated in the petroleum production cutbacks and boycotts following it. It was the first state to impose a total ban on oil exports to the United States. It has also used its economic clout to promote Arab and Muslim interests in Asia and Africa.

In 1981 UAE joined its five neighbors, Saudi Arabia, Oman, Bahrain, Qatar and Kuwait, in founding the Gulf Cooperation Council; it also participated in 1983 in the Peninsula Shield military exercises in Oman. Nevertheless, it has been the most conciliatory Arab state in the Iraq-Iran Gulf conflict and maintains an active trade with Iran despite the war.

United Arab Emirates and the United States are parties to three agreements and treaties covering defense and economic and technical cooperation.

Abu Dhabi became a member of the U.N. in 1971, and its share of the U.N. budget is 0.02%. It is also a member of 12 U.N. agencies and regional associations, such as the Arab League, OPEC, and OAPEC. U.S. Ambassador in Abu Dhabi: G. Quincey Lumsden, Jr.
U.K. Ambassador in Abu Dhabi: Harold B. Walker
UAE Ambassador in Washington, D.C.: Ahmed S. Al-Mokarrab
UAE Ambassador in London: Sayed Mohamed Mahdi Al-Tajir

PARLIAMENT

The legislature is the 40-member Federal Council, a purely consultative assembly of delegates appointed by the rulers of the constituent states for two-year terms. There are eight delegates each from Abu Dhabi and Dubai, six each from Sharjah and Ras al-Khaimah, and four each from Fujairah, Ajman and Umm al-Qaywayn.

POLITICAL PARTIES

No political parties are permitted to function in the UAE. The major illegal opposition is the National Front for the Liberation of the Occupied Arabian Gulf, which until 1975 was actively supported by the People's Democratic Republic of Yemen. This support was withdrawn in 1975 following the normalization of relations between, the UAE and Yemen. Since then the National Front has ceased to be a threat to the UAE.

ECONOMY

The UAE is one of the 39 high-income countries. In fact, in relation to its size and population, it is one of the richest countries of the world. In 1983 its per capita income of $21,340 —considered the highest in the world—was derived entirely from its oil wealth. The UAE has a free market economy with a dominant private sector.

PRINCIPAL ECONOMIC INDICATORS

Gross National Product: $25.770 billion (1983)
  GNP Annual Growth Rate: 11.5% (1973-82)
  Per Capita GNP: $21,340 (1983)
  Per Capita GNP Annual Growth Rate: –0.4% (1973-82)
Gross Domestic Product: D101.2 billion (1983)
  GDP Annual Rate: 10.8% (1973-83)
  GDP at 1980 Prices D94.3 billion
  GDP Deflator (1980=100) 106.3 (1982)
  Per Capita GDP: D84,333 (1983)
  Per Capita GDP Annual Growth Rate: –1.2% (1970-81)
Income Distribution: Information not available
Average Annual Rate of Inflation: 12.7% (1973-83)
Price Indices: Information not available
Money Supply: D8.565 billion (October 1984)
  Reserve Money: D5.974 billion (October 1984)
Currency in Circulation: D2.879 billion (1984)
International Reserves: $2.072 billion, of which foreign exchange reserves were $1.783 billion (1984)

No information is available on balance of payments. In 1983 a current surplus of D16.7 billion was reported.

There is no central economic planning body, but development projects are centralized under the authority of the federal government. The three primary objectives of development policy are the strengthening of the physical and social infrastructure, the diversification of the economy and expansion of entrepot trade.

UAE, specifically Abu Dhabi, is one of the most generous donors of foreign aid in relation to its GNP and population. Most of this aid is channeled through

ORIGIN OF GDP BY ECONOMIC SECTORS 1982 (%)	
Agriculture	1.0
Mining	49.5
Manufacturing	9.0
Construction	9.7
Trade	9.2
Public Utilities	1.6
Transportation & Communications	4.8
Other	15.2

the Abu Dhabi Fund for Arab Economic Development with a paid-up capital of $500 million. The principal beneficiaries of this fund are the Arab and Muslim countries of Asia and Africa, particularly Egypt, Syria, Sudan, Tunisia, Jordan, Yemen, Morocco, Mauritania and Bangladesh. Between 1974 and 1979 the ADFAED had extended 60 loans totaling D2.925 billion to 31 developing countries. Of this amount, Arab countries received 83.8%, non-Arab Asian countries 11.1%, non-Arab African countries 4.1% and European countries 1%. In addition, the Abu Dhabi Investment Board handles a portfolio of $2 billion, mostly in property, equities and bonds.

BUDGET

The UAE fiscal year is the calendar year. The federal budget is also the main instrument of development policy. Individual emirates draw up separate budgets for municipal expenditures and local industrial projects. Abu Dhabi itself contributes more than 90% of the federal budget revenue, and oil-derived renenue constitutes 85% of the total revenue. There are no federal taxes and no taxes of any kind in Ras al-Khaimah, Fujairah, Umm al-Qaywayn, Ajman and Sharjah. In Abu Dhabi and Dubai an income tax is levied on oil producers and banks, but not on individuals or firms.

The revenues are almost entirely derived from oil. Of the expenditures, 36.4% goes to defense, 7.5% to education, 7.1% to health, 3.7% to housing, social security and welfare, 7.0% to economic services and 38.4% to other functions. Total expenditures represented 18.4% of GNP.

The UAE has no external debt.

FINANCE

The UAE unit of currency is the dirham divided into 100 fils. Coins are issued in denominations of 1, 5, 10, 25 and 50 fils and 1 dirham; notes are issued in denominations of 1, 5, 10, 50 and 100 dirhams.

The official exchange rate in 1985 was $1=D3.671. The sterling exchange rate was £1=D4.255.

Before 1966 the common currency of the Trucial states was the Persian Gulf Indian rupee. In 1966 it was replaced by the Bahrain dinar in Abu Dhabi and the Saudi Arabian rial in other states. In the same year the Qatar/Dubai rial was introduced to replace

FEDERAL BUDGET EXPENDITURE* (million UAE dirhams)			
	1981	1982	1983
Current budget			
State†	105.2	177.7	102.8
Finance and industry	49.4	62.3	55.5
Economy and trade	9.6	14.9	12.8
Interior, justice and defense	9,298.3	7,555.1	8,508.4
Housing and public works	50.6	63.4	54.6
Communications	67.1	98.0	77.6
Health	955.1	1,343.4	1,121.7
Agriculture and fisheries	79.3	107.1	86.7
Education and youth	1,127.4	1,495.4	1,419.8
Petroleum	27.8	23.3	18.1
Electricity and water	254.0	402.2	238.4
TOTAL (including others)	17,547.3	18,719.6	14,269.4
Development budget			
Interior, justice and defense	176.7	263.7	149.6
Electricity and water	295.9	500.0	242.8
Housing	188.4	185.0	196.4
Communications	203.4	300.0	151.5
Health	51.5	143.5	64.2
Agriculture	72.8	195.0	106.6
Education and youth	256.4	214.1	126.1
TOTAL (including others)	1,280.9	1,950.3	1,107.2
Equity participation	1,537.7	1,589.6	286.9
TOTAL EXPENDITURE	20,365.9	22,259.5	15,663.5

*Provisional figures.

†Includes the Council of Ministers and the National Federal Council.

Revenue (million dirhams): 22,592.3 in 1981; 19,959.5 in 1982; 12,944.7 (estimate) in 1983.

1984 (estimates, million dirhams): Revenue 12,854; Expenditure 17,239.

the Saudi Arabian rial. The UAE adopted the dirham as its common currency in 1973.

The most important step in the financial integration of the UAE was the establishment of the Currency Board in 1973 to take on the functions of a central bank. Until the formation of the Currency Board, there was no banking legislation in effect and no liquidity ratios were required to be maintained. The board introduced a measure of fiscal control and also served as licensing authority for new banks. There are 53 banks in the UAE with 370 branches.

In 1980 the UAE Central Bank replaced the Currency Board.

Virtually every major international bank is represented in the country. In 1975 the Currency Board imposed a moratorium on the establishment of further banks, although this was temporarily lifted in 1976. It was later reimposed. No new commercial bank has been licensed since 1978. In March 1978 the Currency Board established a Banking Supervision Department, with the broad objectives of promoting sound banking practices and ensuring compliance of banks with the Board's directives. New requirements include 80% local ownership of banks. In 1984 commercial banks had reserves of D3.590 billion, demand deposits of D5.963 billion and time and savings deposits of D37.978 billion.

AGRICULTURE

The agricultural potential of the UAE is negligible. Only 10% of the land area is considered cultivable, and the actual cultivated area is estimated at only 4,000 hectares (9,884 acres). Agriculture employs 5% of the population, but its contribution to the GDP is less than 1%. Agricultural land per capita is about 1 hectare (2.3 acres).

Principal agricultural areas are Al Ain in Abu Dhabi, Ras al-Khaimah and Meleiha in Sharjah. The Buraimi and Liwa Oases and the Batinah coastal plain are also cultivated. Ras al-Khaimah supplies 50% of the food produced in the UAE. The Arid Lands Research Center on Sadiyat Island, Abu Dhabi, produces vegetables in an artificial environment based on hydroponics. Another hydroponics unit is planned for Mazaid in Abu Dhabi. There are experimental farm complexes at Rawaya and Al Ain and a trial station and training school at Digdigga in Ras al-Khaimah. The principal crops are tomatoes, cucumbers and aubergines.

PRINCIPAL CROPS ('000 metric tons)	
	1982*
Cereals	2
Tomatoes	36
Cucumbers and gherkins	4
Aubergines	7
Chillies and peppers (green)	2
Watermelons	26
Melons	17
Dates	52
Tobacco	2
*FAO estimates.	

Animal husbandry has declined as the Bedouins have abandoned herding and moved to the cities. There is a 100-hectare (247-acre) dairy farm at Al Ain with 600 head of imported Australian cattle. In 1982, the livestock population consisted of 27,000 cattle, 70,000 camels, 140,000 sheep and 400,000 goats.

Forests are virtually nonexistent. A 1,618-hectare (3,998-acre) afforestation program is under way in Abu Dhabi.

Exploitation of the rich Persian Gulf and Gulf of Oman fisheries is a major development program. A nucleus of a modern fishing fleet has been created with 1,150 power boats and refrigeration plants. Fishmeal factories also are planned. The total fish catch in 1982 was 70,100 metric tons.

INDUSTRY

Industrial development is concentrated on hydrocarbon-based projects. The major industrial plant is the $600-million gas liquefaction unit on Das Island in Abu Dhabi. Other industrial enterprises include a $333-million dry dock in Dubai, a $300-million aluminium smelter in Dubai, an industrial complex at Mafraq in Abu Dhabi including a petrochemicals plant and a steel plant, a steel complex at Jebel Ali, and an oil equipment factory at Rams in Ras al-Khaimah. Light industry is relatively small and its growth slow. Apart from a few food processing plants and four cement works serving the construction industry there has been no significant trend toward diversification.

ENERGY

In 1982 the UAE's total production of energy was equivalent to 107.755 million metric tons of coal and consumption to 21.560 million metric tons of coal. Per capita production was 19,046 kg (41,996 lbs) per inhabitant, the second highest in the world, after Qatar.

Total electric power production in 1984 was 13.58 billion kwh and per capita output 10,760 kwh per year.

The UAE is the 12th largest oil producer in the world and 5th largest in the Middle East, accounting for 1.1% of total world production. Its proven reserves are estimated at 32.4 billion barrels (9.3% of total OAPEC reserves) of which Abu Dhabi alone accounts for 75%. This figure, however, does not include the reserves of the Upper Zakum field estimated at 48 billion barrels. The proved reserves are expected to last 72 years at current rate of extraction.

OIL PRODUCTION & REVENUES			
	1980	1981	1982
Crude Petroleum (million barrels)	626.2	648.1	462.4
Export Revenues (million dirhams)	...	67,000	53,100
Liquified Gas (000 metric tons)	2,032.4	2,325.2	2,331.9

The major concessions in Abu Dhabi are held by Abu Dhari Marine Areas Ltd. and Abu Dhabi Petroleum Company Ltd., in both of which the government of Abu Dhabi holds a 60% interest, through the Abu Dhabi National Oil Company, a state corporation. The remaining 40% of the Abu Dhabi Petroleum Company is divided among U.K., U.S. and Dutch interests, while 40% of Abu Dhabi Marine Areas is held by British, Japanese and French interests. Other producing companies include Abu Dhabi Oil Company (a Japanese consortium), Bunduq Oil Company (a consortium of Japanese, British and French interests), and Total Abu al Bukhoosh (owned by French and American interests). The major Oil fields are Zakum, Umm Shaif, Bu Hasa, Bab, Asab and Abu al-Bukhoosh. The principal onshore oil terminal and port, Jebel Dhanna, is supplied by pipeline from oil fields at Al Dhafra. The offshore oil tanker loading facility at Das Island is supplied by submarine pipelines from the Al Zukum and Umm Shaif oilfields. Abu Dhabi also has large reserves of natural gas, estimated at 2.520 trillion cubic meters (89 trillion cubic ft). The gasfield at Shamis is connected by a 100-km (247-mi) pipeline to Abu Dhabi. The Abu Dhabi Gas Liquefaction Company, in which the government holds 51% interest, is building a liquefaction plant at Jebel Dhanna in addition to the $600-million gas liquefaction plant completed in 1976 on Das Island.

The producing company in Dubai is the Dubai Petroleum Company, in which the government acquired 100% interest in 1975. All of the output comes from the offshore Fateh field. Reserves are estimated at 185 million tons.

Production from an offshore field near the island of Abu Musa, jointly owned by Sharjah and Iran, is operated by the Buttes Group in which U.S. interests own 75%. Revenues from the field are shared by Iran, Sharjah and Umm al-Qaywayn in the ratio of 50:35:15. There is extensive onshore and offshore exploration in all the emirates.

Abu Dhabi's first refinery at Umm al-Nar, with a capacity of 15,000 barrels per day, was opened in 1976 and another refinery at Ruwais with a capacity of 230,000 barrels per day was completed in 1981. The refinery at Umm al-Nar Island is owned by the Abu Dhabi National Oil Company.

LABOR

The UAE has a small labor force of 557,521 of which foreigners make up 80%. Skilled manpower is imported from abroad to fill the needs of the booming economy. Non-UAE Arabs are employed at all levels, while manual labor is performed mostly by Pakistanis and Iranians and clerical work by Indians. Most managerial positions are held by Europeans. Of the economically active population, native UAE subjects account for only 7%; non-UAE Arabs for 12%, and Indians, Pakistanis and Iranians for 79%. Construction employs the majority of the emirate population (27%) and its share of the labor market is increasing. Next comes government services (16%), although its abnormal growth has slowed somewhat. Unemployment, nonexistent in 1968, first appeared in 1975 (2.1%) but has remained limited. Few women hold any kinds of jobs. The 1975 census showed 9,961 active women as opposed to 286,555 employed men; 76.8% of active women are employed in social and personal services.

DISTRIBUTION OF LABOR FORCE BY INDUSTRY (1980)		
		%
Agriculture, fruits & fisheries	14,580	4.6
Petroleum & mining	10,200	2.1
Manufacturing industries	36,200	6.3
Electricity, gas, water	11,500	2.0
Construction	157,150	27.8
Commerce, hotels	74,690	13.3
Transport, communications	52,350	7.5
Finance, insurance, real est.	13,300	2.7
Government services	72,130	16.3
Personal & social services	34,500	17.4

There are marked variations between emirates in patterns of employment; 40% of the labor force is employed in construction in Abu Dhabi, while over 80% is engaged in agriculture in Fujairah. Labor is not permitted to organize and there is no legal provision for the right to strike or to engage in collective bargaining. Foreign workers dare not strike; they would be summarily deported. Individual workers, or even small groups, may bring grievances to a conciliation committee at the Ministry of Labor, which will arbitrate the dispute. The rulings are widely regarded as fair. However, because of language barriers and the ignorance of many foreign laborers about the avenue for redress of grievances, the facility is not utilized as much as it might be. The government is concerned about the labor conditions of foreign employees, particularly the semiskilled and unskilled. Aware that many have been misled and exploited by unscrupulous labor agents, it has tightened up considerably on visa procedures and work permits. The declining need for unskilled labor has engendered even more firmness in this regard, and people without proper documentation are promptly deported. The government continues to improve the labor law covering conditions of employment, compensation, inspection of the workplace and enforcement procedures. Some abuse of foreign labor persists, contrary to government policy, as enforcement is difficult and intermittent.

Labor regulations prohibit employment of youths below 18 and restrict hours of work to 8 hours per day, 6 days per week. There is no minimum wage. The government has adopted some occupational safety standards which are generally enforced.

FOREIGN COMMERCE

The foreign commerce of the UAE consisted in 1984 of exports of $17.636 billion and imports of $7.030 billion, producing a favorable trade balance of $10.606 billion. Petroleum constituted 88.6% of the exports and natural gas 2.7%. Of the imports, nonelectrical machinery constituted 16.7%, electrical machinery 9.5%, transport equipment 9.5%, food and live animals 9.1%, iron and steel 6.9%, textiles 5.8% and chemicals 5.1%. The major import sources are: Japan 21.5%, the United States 11.1%, the United Kingdom 9.5%, West Germany 6.6%, Italy 4.6%, Bahrain 4.1% and France 3.5%. The major export destinations are: Japan 34.5%, the United States 13.5%, France 8.0%, the Netherlands Antilles 6.7% and West Germany 6.3%.

Dubai, the major entrepot of the Persian Gulf, is a free-trade zone and free port with no restrictions on imports or exports. The other emirates exert no control over imports and exports except for licensing.

TRANSPORTATION & COMMUNICATIONS

The UAE has no railways or inland waterways.

FOREIGN TRADE INDICATORS 1984

Annual growth rate: exports %	–2.1 (1973-83)
Annual growth rate: imports %	14.3 (1973-83)
Ratio of exports to imports	71:29
Exports per capita	$13,360
Imports per capita	$5,325
Balance of trade	+$10.606 billion
Ratio of international reserves to imports in months	3.2
Exports as % of GDP	73.4
Imports as % of GDP	33.6
Value of manufactured exports	$777 million
Commodity concentration	93.7%

Dubai's Port Rashid, currently being expanded to 47 berths, is the largest harbor in the Middle East. Abu Dhabi has also become an important port since the opening of its artificial harbor, Port Zayed, with 17 deep-water berths. Minor ports include Sharjah's six-berth port, Ras al-Khaimah's port complex at Khor Kwayr and Fujairah's deep-water port. Work on a dry dock was begun in Dubai in 1973. It will have two docks capable of handling 500,000-ton tankers, a third dock capable of accommodating 1,000,000-ton tankers, and seven repair berths. In 1982 UAE ports handled 73,288,000 tons of cargo. The UAE also had a merchant marine of 202 vessels with a gross registered tonnage of 450,300 in 1983.

Paved coastal roads link all the emirate capitals, Abu Dhabi and Al Ain, and Abu Dhabi and Sila via Tarif. An underwater tunnel linking Dubai and Deira was completed in 1975. Eventually the UAE road network will link up with the trans-Arabian highway. The total length of the road network is 2,000 km (1,200 mi). In 1982 there were 108,589 passenger cars and 3,505 commercial vehicles. Per capita passenger car ownership is 82 per 1,000 inhabitants.

The national airline is Gulf Air Dubai with 18 aircraft. There are international airports at Abu Dhabi, Dubai, Sharjah and Ras al-Khaimah. The new Nadia International airport opened at Abu Dhabi in 1982. The emirates have a total of 43 airfields, of which 30 are usable, 20 have permanent-surface runways, eight with runways over 2,500 meters (8,000 ft).

There are 830 km (515 mi) of crude oil pipeline and 870 km (540 mi) of natural gas pipeline from Al Dhafra to the port of Jebel Dhanna and from Al Zukum and Umm Shaif to Das Island.

In 1984 there were 241,000 telephones in the country, or 20 per 100 inhabitants. Some 36% of the phones are in Abu Dhabi.

In 1984 the postal service handled 238,896,000 pieces of mail, or 180 pieces per capita.

In 1976 the government set up the UAE Communications Corporation to take over all telecommunications operations in six emirates (excluding Ras al-Khaimah). There is an earth satellite station at Jebel Ali.

No statistics are available on the number of tourists or on receipts from tourism.

MINING

The UAE has no known mineral wealth other than oil.

DEFENSE

The defense structure of the federation is headed by the president, who is the chairman of the Defense Council. In 1976 the armed forces of the UAE were unified under a single central command known as the General Command of the Armed Forces with three military regions—Western, Central and Northern—with a General Staff Command. The unified nature of the military high command is largely a fiction for sheikhly rivalries continue unabated. For all practical purposes, each of the three major military regions - Abu Dhabi, Dubai and Ras al-Khaimah- retain full operational independence. The Al-Yarmuk Brigade consists of federal forces and the National Guard in Sharjah and Umm al-Qaywayn. The line of command runs from the president as the supreme commander through the deputy supreme commander and the defense minister to the chief of staff. British officers and non-commissioned officers continue to be employed in the higher echelons. About 40% of the manpower is provided by local recruitment, another 30% comes from Muscat and Oman, and the rest from India, Pakistan and Iran.

The total strength of the armed forces is 43,000, or 40.8 armed persons per 1,000 civilians.

ARMY:
Personnel: 40,000
Organization; 3 regional commands: Western (Abu Dhabi), Central (Dubai) and Northern (Ras al Khaimah); 1 Royal Guard Brigade; 1 armored brigade; 1 mechanized infantry brigade; 2 infantry brigades; 1 artillery; 1 air defense brigade
Equipment: 136 heavy tanks; 60 light tanks; 90 armored combat vehicles; 360 armored personnel carriers; 50 guns; howitzers; mortars; rocket launchers; air defense guns; SAM

NAVY:
Personnel: 1,500
Units: 6 fast attack craft with guns; 9 patrol craft; 2 support vessels.

AIR FORCE:
Personnel: 1,500
Organization & Equipment: 42 combat aircraft; 2 interceptor squadrons; 1 fighter ground attack squadron; 1 counterinsurgency squadron; 21 transports; 47 helicopters; 11 trainers; AAM; ASM

Annual military expenditures were $579.255 million in 1984, representing 36.4% of the national budget, 7.9% of GNP, $1,492 per capita, $40,729 per soldier and $23,274 per sq km of national territory.

The equipment is mostly British but some hardware is obtained from France, the United States and

Italy. Initially, the personnel were mostly British but assistance is now being received from Pakistan and other Arab countries.

The deterrent capability and combatworthiness of the UAE's armed forces have not been tested in the field except briefly in 1972 when Union forces joined local security forces in putting down an attempted coup in Sharjah. Both the navy and the air force are being built up at an accelerated pace, but they are heavily dependent on overseas personnel and equipment. Arms purchases abroad during 1973-83 totaled $990 million, of which $350 million came from France.

EDUCATION

The national literacy rate is 68.6% (71% for males and 61.0% for females). Education is free, universal and compulsory, in principle, for six years between the ages of 6 and 12. School uniforms, books, equipment and transport are also free. Schooling consists of six years of primary school, three years of middle school, and three years of secondary school for a total of 12 years.

In 1982 the school enrollment ratio was 132% in the primary grades (6-11), and 87% in the secondary grades (12-17) for a combined enrollment ratio of 103%. The third level enrollment ratio is 6.8%. The percentage of girls enrolled is 48% at the primary level, 47% at the secondary level, and 50% at the tertiary level.

The academic year runs from September to June. The medium of instruction is Arabic, but English is taught in secondary grades.

As in the rest of the Gulf countries, the majority of the school teachers are either Egyptian, Lebanese or Palestinian. The teacher-pupil ratio is 1:17 in primary grades, 1:11 in secondary grades and 1:15 in post-secondary classes.

Special adult education is provided for 7,000 adults at 26 centers. In 1983, 722 students were enrolled in technical and vocational schools, constituting 1.5% of total secondary school enrollment.

The annual education budget in 1982 was D1,495,443,000, which was 6.6% of the national budget, 1.5% of GNP and $348 per capita.

EDUCATIONAL ENROLLMENT (1983)			
	Schools	Teachers	Students
First Level	244	6,599	115,411
Second Level	68	4,081	45,442
Vocational	4	154	722
Third Level	318	8,343	125,209

The UAE's first university opened in Abu Dhabi in 1976. In 1982, 595 students graduated from the University of Abu Dhabi, including 291 women. Of these, 124 were awarded degrees in education, 47 in law, 75 in social and behavioral sciences, 21 in mass communications and 68 in natural science. In 1982, 1,006 UAE students were enrolled in colleges and universities abroad, including 707 in the United States, 92 in the United Kingdom, 98 in Egypt, 23 in Pakistan and 38 in Kuwait.

LEGAL SYSTEM

The constitution of 1971 set up a Union Supreme Court and Union primary tribunals as the first step toward the unification of the separate legal and judicial systems. The Supreme Court consists of a chief justice and a maximum of five judges, all of whom are appointed by presidential decree. The constitution guarantees the independence of the judiciary.

The traditional emirate courts, which dispensed justice according to the Sharia, are being brought under the administrative control of the Union Ministry of Justice. A modern code of law is being drafted for Abu Dhabi, which has also a Ruler's Court presided over by a professional judge. In other emirates the courts are presided over either by a qadi, or Islamic jurist, or by the ruler himself.

LAW ENFORCEMENT

Each emirate has its own police force with the ruler's personal bodyguards as the nucleus. Information on the composition and functions of these forces has not been published.

The Emirate courts provide trials before experienced civil or religious judges. The judges are mainly Egyptians, Sudanese, and Palestinians since there are as yet few Emirate-citizen jurists. As foreign judges serve on limited employment contracts, they may not be independent enough to restrain the government in a politically sensitive case. Interference in the judicial process by rulers of various emirates does occur. Dubai is a notable exception. The provisional constitution provides for broad judicial review powers. Except for the rare cases involving national security, ruling families and the executive agencies usually respect the independence of the courts. A ruler will occasionally pardon a convicted person or commute a sentence, but only subsequent to judicial proceedings.

There are no jury trials. In civil courts, the accused may be represented by counsel of his choice. No public defender system exists. Criminal courts based on European models function alongside the Islamic courts. Crimes and penalties are defined by law — civil or Shari'a — and the accused is presumed innocent until found guilty. In Shari'a court, counsel is not permitted. Definition of the crime and the penalty are drawn from religious sources.

Public access to trials may be limited to those with a concern in the case. If political or security matters are involved, access is severely restricted. No such trials took place in 1984. Special labor courts have been established to handle disputes between workers and employers and are widely believed to be fair in their judgments.

Legal counsel is readily available and permitted to represent a defendant in both court systems. The court may appoint legal counsel if counsel agrees to provide services free; no system of state payment of public defenders exists.

HEALTH

The UAE provides comprehensive and free health services for all its subjects. Medical care is also free for patients referred to foreign hospitals. In 1982 Abu Dhabi had four hospitals with 672 beds and two tuberculosis sanatoria with 100 beds. Dubai had four hospitals with 1,142 beds in addition to a hospital and sanatorium built by Kuwait. There are other general hospitals at Sharjah, Ras al-Khaimah, Umm al-Qaywayn and Dibba. Further hospital complexes are planned in Abu Dhabi, Al Ain, Fujairah and Ras al-Khaimah. Small towns and rural areas are served by clinics. Existing medical services provide 3,260 beds or one bed for every 319 inhabitants. In 1981 there were 1,491 doctors or one doctor per 698 inhabitants, 76 dentists and 907 nursing personnel. Of the hospitals 95.5% are state-run and 4.5% are run by private nonprofit agencies. The admissions/discharge rate per 10,000 inhabitants is 1,385 the bed, occupancy rate is 62.1% and the average length of hospital stay is 7 days.

PRINCIPAL HEALTH INDICATORS (1984)
Crude Death Rate: 4 per 1,000
Infant Mortality Rate: 80.9 per 1,000 Live Births
Life Expectancy at Birth: (males) 62.8 (females) 73.2
Decline in death rate (1965-83) −73.3%
Child death rate (Age 1-4) 2

Traditionally the most prevalent diseases in UAE have included tuberculosis, malaria, trachoma, dysentery, rickets, typhus and smallpox. Although health statistics are unavailable in complete form, there is evidence that, with the improvement of sanitation and medical services, great strides have been made in eradicating or reducing the incidence of many of these diseases. Public health expenditures constitute 7.9% of the national budget and $319.30 per capita.

FOOD

No statistics are available on the patterns of food consumption or per capita food intake in the UAE.

MEDIA & CULTURE

Nine daily newspapers are published in the UAE, four in Arabic and five in English; six are published from Abu Dhabi and three from Dubai. They have an aggregate circulation of 220,000, or 160 per 1,000 inhabitants. The best-selling dailies are *Al Ittihad* (60,000) in Arabic and *Khaleej Times* (46,000) in English. There are also three non-dailies, of which the most widely read is the *Gulf Weekly Mirror*, which is published in English in Bahrain and eight periodicals. Official gazettes are published by the governments of Abu Dhabi and Dubai. Sharjah and Ras al-Khaimah have monthly publications in Arabic.

The official news agency is the Emirates News Agency, founded in 1977. There is a small book publishing industry with an annual output in 1982 of six titles. It does not adhere to any copyright convention.

The Abu Dhabi Radio broadcasts a home service for Abu Dhabi for 17 ½ hours a day in Arabic and two hours a day in English with one medium-wave transmitter, four short-wave transmitters, and one FM transmitter. Abu Dhabi Radio and UAE Radio and Television broadcast with two medium-wave transmitters and one short-wave transmitter and are on the air in Arabic for 20 hours a day and English for 13 hours a day. Radio Ras al-Khaimah has one medium-wave transmitter. Radio Sharjah has two stations, one in English and the other in Arabic. Capital Radio is an English language FM music and news radio in Abu Dhabi. The number of radio receivers is estimated at 270,000, or 342 per 1,000 inhabitants. Of the 17,355 annual radio broadcasting hours, 1,594 hours are devoted to information, 851 hours to education, 953 hours to culture, 2,300 hours to religion, 1,460 hours to commercials, and 10,207 hours to entertainment.

The UAE Television Service operates a color television network with transmitters at Dubai and Abu Dhabi. The service broadcasts for six hours daily. The number of television receivers is estimated at 105,000, or 133 per 100 inhabitants. Of the 4,588 annual television broadcasting hours, 460 hours are devoted to information, 134 hours to education, 310 hours to culture, 660 hours to religion, 180 hours to commercials, and 2,550 hours to entertainment.

In 1977 there were 21 cinemas with 29,000 seats (43.5 per 1,000 inhabitants). Movie attendance was 6.9 million, or 103 per capita. Annual import of feature films in 1980 was 142 including 90 from the United States, and 28 from India.

There are public libraries in Abu Dhabi, Dubai, Sharjah and other towns. The British Council runs two libraries in the UAE.

SOCIAL WELFARE

There is no social security legislation in the UAE, but subjects receive most benefits of a welfare state including free medical aid, subsidized education and subsidized food. Under the National Assistance Law, state aid is also provided for victims of catastrophic illnesses and disasters. Social security payments of between D225 and D675 can be claimed by any resident who is unable to support himself of herself. All UAE subjects are entitled to free housing with subsidized furnishings. The UAE Development Bank and the Dubai Development Council also extend loans to residents at an interest rate of 1%.

GLOSSARY

diwan (pl. dawawin): an advisory council assisting the ruler, consisting of representatives of various interest groups, as well as tribal sheikhs.

majlis (pl. majalis): an audience or assembly; properly, an informal meeting between the ruler and any group of his subjects.

sabkah (pl. sibakh): salt marsh, usually located near the sea coast consisting of a treacherous layer of hard sand covering a slushy mixture of salt water and sand.

sharqi: a humid southeastern wind that blows along the Gulf coast of the UAE.

Trucial States: former name of the UAE; so named because the states were bound by truces with the paramount British power.

CHRONOLOGY (from 1971)

1971— United Kingdom withdraws its forces from the Persian Gulf region and ends treaty obligations with the Trucial States.... Six of the Trucial States—Abu Dhabi, Dubai, Sharjah, Ajman, Umm al-Qaywayn, and Fujairah—federate themselves as a sovereign and independent nation.... Provisional constitution of UAE is promulgated.

1972— Ras al-Khaimah joins the Federation.... Sheikh Khalid of Sharjah is killed in coup led by his cousin Sheikh Saqr; UAE forces capture the rebels and restore Khalid's brother, Sheikh Sultan, to the emirate.

1973— The dirham is adopted as the national currency of the UAE; Currency Board is established as UAE's central bank... Hundreds of alleged subversives belonging to the National Front for the Liberation of the Arab Gulf are arrested.

1974— Accord is reached with Saudi Arabia over border disputes relating to the Liwa and Buraimi Oases; diplomatic relations are established with Saudi Arabia.

1975— Committee is appointed to draft permanent constitution for UAE.

1976— University of Abu Dhabi is established.... As a further step toward integration the separate emirate defense forces are unified into a single general command with three military regions.

1977— Abu Dhabi is chosen as the headquarters of the newly established Arab Monetary Fund.

1979— Prime Minister Sheikh Maktum ibn Rashid al-Maktum is replaced by Sheikh Rashid ibn Said al-Maktum.... Egypt severs diplomatic relations with the Emirates.

1980— In the Iraq-Iran war the Emirates cautiously sides with Iraq.

1981— UAE joins the Gulf Cooperation Council.

BIBLIOGRAPHY (from 1970)

Anthony, John Duke, *Arab States of the Lower Gulf: People, Politics, Petroleum* (Washington, D.C., 1975).

—, *Historical and Cultural Dictionary of the Sultanate of Oman and the Emirates of Eastern Arabia* (Metuchen, N.J., 1976).

Belgrave, Sir Charles, *The Pirate Coast* (Beirut, 1972).

Daniels, John, *Abu Dhabi: A Portrait* (London, 1974).

Fenelon, Kelvin G., *The United Arab Emirates: An Economic and Social Survey* (London, 1973).

Hawley, Donald Frederick, *The Trucial States* (London, 1971).

Hopwood, D., *The Arabian Peninsula* (London, 1972).

Khalifa, Ali M., *The United Arab Emirates: Unity in Fragmentation* (Boulder, Co., 1979).

Koury, Enver M., *The United Arab Emirates: Its Political System and Politics* (Hyattsville, Md., 1980).

Lorimer, J.G., *Gazetteer of the Persian Gulf* (London, 1970).

Lundy, Frederic K., *The Economic Prospects of the Persian Gulf Emirates* (Washington, D.C., 1974).

Sadik, Muhammad T. and William P. Snavely, *Bahrain, Qatar, and the United Arab Emirates: Colonial Past, Present Problems, and Future Prospects* (Concord, Mass. 1972).

OFFICIAL PUBLICATIONS

Planning Department, Abu Dhabi, *Statistical Abstract and Statistical Yearbook*.

United Arab Emirates Currency Board, *Annual Report*.

———, *Bulletin*.

Uruguay

- —— International boundary
- ⊛ National capital
- +++ Railroad
- —— Road
- ✛ International airport

0   25   50 Miles
0   25   50 Kilometers

Argentina

Brazil

Paso de los Libres
Uruguaiana
Alegrete
Monte Caseros
Bella Union
Artigas
Rosário do Sul
Santana do Livramento
Rivera
Rio Ibicui
Rio Santa Maria
Rio Cuareim
Rio Arapey Grande
Concordia
Salto
Bagé
Rio Daymán
Tacuarembó
Aceguá
Rio Queguay Grande
Colón
Melo
Paysandú
Embalse de Rio Negro
Rio Tacuarembó
Rio Negro
Concepción del Uruguay
Paso de los Toros
Rio Branco
Jaguarão
Gualeguaychú
Rio Negro
Laguna Merín
Fray Bentos
Mercedes
Rio Yí
Durazno
Trienta y Tres
Trinidad
Rio Cebollatí
Carmelo
Chuy
Isla Martín Garcia (under jurisdiction of Argentina)
Florida
Buenos Aires
San Jose
Minas
Rocha
Colonia
Canelones
La Paloma
La Plata
Rio de la Plata
Montevideo
Maldonado
Punta del Este
Atlantic Ocean

URUGUAY

BASIC FACT SHEET

OFFICIAL NAME: Oriental Republic of Uruguay (Republica Oriental del Uruguay) (*Note:* The designation Oriental in the official name refers to the location of the country on the east bank of the Uruguay River. [Uruguayans sometimes call themselves Orientals.])

ABBREVIATION: UY

CAPITAL: Montevideo

HEAD OF STATE & HEAD OF GOVERNMENT: President Julio Maria Sanguinetti Cairolo (from 1985)

NATURE OF GOVERNMENT: Constitutional Democracy

POPULATION: 2,936,000 (1985)

AREA: 177,508 sq km (68,536 sq mi)

ETHNIC MAJORITY: Europeans of Spanish and Italian descent

LANGUAGE: Spanish

RELIGION: Roman Catholicism

UNIT OF CURRENCY: New Peso ($1=P102.5, August 1985)

NATIONAL FLAG: Four azure blue horizontal stripes on a white background. On a white canton on the hoist side is the "Sun of May," a golden sun with 16 rays of which eight are wavy and the others are straight.

NATIONAL EMBLEM: A quartered blue and white elliptical badge on which are displayed gold scales of justice, the green cerro, or mountain island of Montevideo, a dark brown stallion, and a gold longhorn bull. The badge is enclosed within olive and laurel branches tied at the base with a silver ribbon. A golden "Sun of May" rises over the top.

NATIONAL ANTHEM: "Orientals, [Uruguayans] Our Country or Death"

NATIONAL HOLIDAYS: August 25 (National Day, Independence Day); January 1 (New Year's Day); April 19 (Landing of the 33 Patriots); May 1 (Labor Day); May 18 (Battle of Las Piedras); June119 (Birthday of Gen. Artigas); July 18 (Constitution Day); October 12 (Discovery of America Day); December 8 (Blessing of the Waters); Also Christmas, All Souls' Day and Epiphany. Many business firms close during Carnival Week (February/March) and Tourist Week (Easter Week).

NATIONAL CALENDAR: Gregorian

PHYSICAL QUALITY OF LIFE INDEX: 90 (down from 88 in 1976) (On an ascending scale in which 100 is the maximum. U.S. 95)

DATE OF INDEPENDENCE: August 25, 1828

DATE OF CONSTITUTION: February 1967 (Partially suspended)

WEIGHTS & MEASURES: The metric system is in force.

LOCATION & AREA

Uruguay is located in the southeastern part of the South American continent, east of the Uruguay River. With a total land area of 177,508 sq km (68,536 sq mi), it extends 555 km (345 mi) NNW to SSE and 504 km (313 mi) ENE to WSW. Its Atlantic coastline stretches 565 km (351 mi).

Uruguay shares its international land boundary of 1,498 km (930 mi) with two neighbors: Argentina (495 km, 308 mi) and Brazil (1,004 km, 623 mi). The Uruguay River and the Rio de la Plata separate Argentina and Uruguay, and the Cuareim and Yaguaron Rivers and the Laguna Merin separate Brazil and Uruguay. Most of the boundaries are fully demarcated, but the sovereignty of some river islands remain in dispute. The dispute with Argentina was settled by an agreement in 1973, by which Argentina was to retain control over navigation on the largest part of the channel, but the geographical middle point was to be the official frontier for purpose of mineral exploitation. The agreement also ceded the island of Timoteo Dominguez to Uruguay.

The capital is Montevideo with a 1980 population of 1,261,000. The other major urban centers are Salto (72,000), Paysandu (62,000), Mercedes (53,000), Las Piedras (54,000), Rivera (42,000), Minas (40,000) and Melo (38,000).

Southern Uruguay is an extension of the Argentine Pampas and northern Uruguay an extension of the basaltic plateau of Brazil. In between, the country consists of a rolling plateau whose most prominent features are ranges of low hills known as cuchillas, none of which are over 500 meters (1,600 ft). The two major cuchillas are Cuchilla Grande and the Cuchilla de Haedo.

Uruguay can claim only partial title to the river that bears its name, and the Rio de la Plata is actually an estuary of the Atlantic Ocean (and is considered by many nations as an international waterway). The longest of the internal rivers is the Rio Negro, which rises in Brazil and bisects the country as it flows southward to join the Uruguay River. Its main tributary is the Rio Yi which rises in the Cuchilla Grande. Among the rivers flowing east is the Rio Cebollati, which flows into the country's largest lake, Laguna Merin.

WEATHER

Uruguay is the only country in the Western Hemisphere other than Canada that lies entirely outside the tropics. Weather conditions are uniformly temperate, but the absence of high relief causes some variations. The average temperature in June, the coolest month, is about 10°C (50°F), while the average for January, the warmest month, is 23°C (74°F). Rainfall, evenly distributed throughout the year, averages about 109 cm (36 in.) varying from an average of 91 cm (36 in.) in Punta del Este to 127 cm (50 in.) in Artigas, the northernmost province.

The prevailing wind systems are the zonda, a hot wind blowing from the north in summer, and the pampero, a chilly wind blowing from the south in the winter.

POPULATION

The population of Uruguay was estimated in 1985 at 2,936,000 on the basis of the last official census held in 1975, when the population was 2,763,964. The population is expected to reach 3.4 million by 2000 and 3.8 million by 2020.

The annual growth rate is estimated at 0.7% based on an annual birth rate of 19.5 per 1,000.

Uruguay is the only South American country with no large uninhabited areas; even so the population is concentrated in the department of Montevideo, which accounts for 47% of national population. Population density per sq km in Montevideo is 2,072.6 (5,368 per sq mi). There are only four other departments with over 10 persons per sq km (26 persons per sq mi): Canelones (54.3 per sq km, 141 per sq mi); Colonia (18.5 per sq km, 48 per sq mi); Maldonado (14.9 per sq km, 38 per sq mi); and San Jose (11.4 per sq km, 29 per sq mi). The lowest densities are recorded in Durazno and Tacuarembo, both with 3.7 per sq km (9.5 per sq mi). The nationwide density is 17 per sq km (44 per sq mi).

Nearly 85% of Uruguayans live in urban areas. Montevideo itself accounts for 54% of the urban population. However, the urban population has remained more or less stable and the annual rate of urban growth is only 1.0%.

The population is extraordinarily mature as a result of the low birthrate and greater longevity. Only 30% are under 14 while 63% are between 15 and 64 and 9%—thrice the normal proportion—is over 65. The male/female ratio at the time of the 1975 census was

DEMOGRAPHIC INDICATORS (1984)	
Population, total (in 1,000)	2,936.0
Population ages (% of total)	
0-14	26.9
15-64	62.4
65+	10.7
Youth 15-24 (000)	486
Women ages 15-49 (000)	701
Dependency ratios	60.3
Child-woman ratios	400
Sex ratios (per 100 females)	96.9
Median ages (years)	29.8
Marriage Rate (per 1,000)	7.8
Divorce Rate (per 1,000)	1.8
Average size of Household	3.5
Decline in birthrate (%, 1965-83)	−14.6
Proportion of urban (%)	85.06
Population density (per sq. km.)	17
per hectare of arable land	0.20
Rates of growth (%)	0.70
Urban %	1
Rural %	−0.7
Natural increase rates (per 1,000)	9.3
Crude birth rates (per 1,000)	19.5
Crude death rates (per 1,000)	10.2
Gross reproduction rates	1.35
Net reproduction rates	1.29
Total fertility rates	2.76
General fertility rates (per 1,000)	83
Life expectancy, males (years)	67.1
Life expectancy, females (years)	73.7
Life expectancy, total (years)	70.3
% Illegitimate	24.6
Population doubling time in years at current rate	72

49:51, with females showing an even greater numerical predominance in urban areas.

The government's efforts to promote immigration are undermined by an alarming rate of emigration. The favorite destinations of emigrants are, in order of preference, the United States, Argentina, West Germany, Spain, Brazil, Venezuela, Canada, Italy and France. While no statistics are available, the total Uruguayan diaspora is estimated at over 2 million, of which some 500,000 are believed to be resident in Buenos Aires and an equal number in Brazil. Although professionals constitute only a minority of the emigrants, the continued pace of emigration is causing official concern.

Women in Uruguay are accorded equality before the law. They attend the National University and pursue professional careers in large numbers. Women serve on the cabinet, in the Supreme Court, and in the diplomatic corps, including at the ambassadorial level. Although there are currently no women in Congress, several serve as alternates. Some barriers to equality still exist as a result of traditional social patterns and restricted employment opportunities. Pay is not always equal for men and women, especially for the less skilled workers in the private sector. Uruguay is a signatory of the 1948 Interamerican Convention on Political Rights for Women, but has not yet acceded to the 1953 U.N. Convention on Political Rights of Women.

Uruguay's low growth rate is partly attributable to the sustained efforts of the Association for Family

Planning and Research on Reproduction, founded in 1962. The Association, which is supported by government funds, facilities and personnel, operates six clinics in addition to family planning services in the lower income residential areas.

ETHNIC COMPOSITION

The population is predominantly white, and its European character was reinforced by successive waves of immigrants from almost all countries of Europe in the 19th Century. The core ethnic group is the criollos, descendants of Spanish settlers who are generally found in the northern interior. There is very little to distinguish them from later immigrants, particularly the Italians who form the next most important element in the population. Approximately 54% of the European majority is of Spanish origin and 22% is of Italian origin.

Other Europeans represented in the population are French, German, British, Sephardic and Ashkenazic Jews. There are also small colonies of Slavs, Armenians, Lebanese and Syrians contributing to the ethnic variety. Although assimilation is not officially encouraged, most immigrants are Hispanicized quickly and easily, and very few tend to retain separate ethnic identities.

Through intermarriage and deliberate extermination, the pureblooded Indian community has become extinct. Some of their ethnic characteristics survive in the mestizo population, which represents some 5% of the total population and is concentrated in the northern interior. The mestizos are the descendants of the nomadic Charrua and Chana Indian tribes.

During the late 18th and 19th Centuries, Negroes constituted as much as 20% of the population, but their numbers have dwindled and by the mid-1970s there were less than 60,000 people of African descent in the country, of whom less than 1% may be strictly classified as Negro rather than mulatto. There is very little race discrimination in the country, and blacks enjoy equal social and political rights.

In terms of ethnic and linguistic homogeneity, Uruguay ranks 84th in the world with 80% homogeneity (on an ascending scale in which North and South Korea rank 135th with 100% homogeneity and Tanzania ranks first with 7% homogeneity).

LANGUAGES

Spanish is the official language, spoken by virtually all Uruguayans. The spoken Spanish of Uruguay is almost identical to that of Buenos Aires, called the porteno or Rio Platense. The accent is characterized by the linguistic trait known as yeismo in which vowels are thickened, a marked deviation from classical Spanish. The language also includes words and idioms borrowed from each of the many immigrant communities as well as some derived from Quechua and Guarani. Near the northern Brazilian border over 70%

of the inhabitants are bilingual in Spanish and Portuguese, and in some border towns Portuguese is spoken exclusively. This bilingualism has also helped to create a border dialect called dialecto fronterizo in which Portuguese and Spanish elements are combined.

English is the most popular second language, displacing French, which was the traditional language of the elite before World War II.

RELIGIONS

Uruguay is perhaps the most secularized nation in Latin America as a result of the unremitting anticlerical efforts of the Colorado Party, which has dominated Uruguayan politics for nearly a century. Church and state were separated by the constitution of 1919 culminating the campaign for secularization waged by Uruguayan social reformer and president (1903-07, 1911-15) Jose Batlle y Ordonnez. The Church was however allowed to retain its ecclesiastical properties. Religious instruction is not permitted in public schools; divorce is legal; civil marriages are compulsory; and cemeteries are under public ownership. Some religious holidays have been given secular names. The state has also taken over some of the social welfare and educational functions of the Church.

Nevertheless, Roman Catholicism remains the national religion and the imprint of religious beliefs is still strong, especially in the interior. The ratio of priests to the laity, about 1 to 4,000, is high compared to other Latin American countries. But over half of all the priests live in Montevideo, and many of the interior rural settlements may be visited by a priest only once or twice in a year. Ecclesiastically, the church is organized under one metropolitan see, the Archdiocese of Montevideo, and nine suffragan dioceses: Florida, Salto, Melo, San Jose de Mayo, Minas, Tacuarembo, Mercedes, Canelones and Maldonado. The dioceses are further subdivided into 205 parishes, over a third of which are in Montevideo.

The Church's political and social roles have become more sharply defined in the 1960s and 1970s as a result of its involvement in the liberalization movements under the guidance of the Archbishop of Montevideo, Carlos Parteli, and his successor, Antonio Maria Berbieri. Conservative forces among the clergy are in the minority, and a few members of the clergy even belong to radical urban guerrilla groups. The church's main political wing is the Christian Democratic Party, which advocates social transformation through democratic means. It has only a small following and gained only a fraction of the electoral vote in the last free elections in 1971. In addition, there are numerous lay organizations engaged in enhancing the social relevance of the church: Catholic Workers' Circle, Catholic Action, the Christian Democratic Youth Movement and the Catholic Family Movement.

About 2% of the population is Protestant, divided among nearly 25 different sects and denominations. However, the Protestants have a high minister-to-laity ratio of 1:200, and nearly one-half of the membership attends church on Sundays. Protestant missionary efforts suffer from their association with foreign countries, but, nonetheless, Protestantism has developed a significant appeal among the middle classes and the lower segments of society. Since the Second Vatican Council, relations between Catholics and Protestants are harmonious. Jews, estimated to number around 50,000, constitute the largest religious minority.

COLONIAL EXPERIENCE

The earliest European settlers were Jesuit and Franciscan missionaries. From 1680, when the Portuguese founded Colonia de Sacramento as a rival to Buenos Aires on the eastern bank of the Rio de la Plata, to 1828, when Uruguay achieved independence, the country was a battleground between Argentina and Brazil. Uruguay became part of the new viceroyalty of Buenos Aires established in 1776. In 1815 Jose Gervasio Artigas declared Uruguay's independence, but the next year the country was invaded by Brazil. After a four-year struggle Uruguay was annexed to Brazil as the Cisplatine Province. In 1825 Juan Antonio Lavalleja returned secretly to Uruguay from Argentina at the head of the "33 Orientales" (Trienta y Tres) and resumed the struggle for independence that ended in 1828 with a peace treaty in which Uruguay's independence was acknowledged by both Argentina and Brazil.

CONSTITUTION & GOVERNMENT

Since independence Uruguay has had five constitutions (1830, 1917, 1934, 1952 and 1967). The last constitution was ratified by plebiscite when the country voted to return to the presidential form of government after 15 years of collegiate government.

In 1973 the military intervened once again and compelled President Juan Maria Bordaberry Arocena to accede to a 19-point reorganization program that suspended the democratic process. A National Security Council was created to oversee the administration. Congress was dissolved and replaced by a Council of State, and municipal and local councils were supplanted by appointed bodies. The National Confederation of Workers was proscribed and opposition political leaders were placed in detention. The National University of Montevideo was closed and all leftist groups, including the Frente Amplio, were banned. In 1976, President Bordaberry was deposed after he opposed the military's limited democracy. The newly constituted Council of the Nation (incorporating the Council of State, the three heads of the armed services, and other high-ranking officers) designated Aparicio Mendez Manfredini as president for a five-year term. In 1980 the military unveiled a basic law which would give them an effective veto power within a restricted democracy. The law was rejected by more

than 57% of the voters in a national referendum. In 1981 the Council of the Nation designated retired army commander Lt. Gen. Gregario Conrado Alvarez Armellino as transitional president for a term which was scheduled to end upon a promised reversion to civilian rule in 1985. Fourteen months later, on November 28, 1982, nationwide balloting was held to select delegates to a convention of three legally recognized groups — the Colorado and Blanco parties and the Civic Union — in order to draft a constitution to be presented to the voters. In the elections, the antimilitary candidates outpolled the promilitary candidates within each party by almost five to one. Thereupon, the military initiated a series of talks that resulted in an accord between the regime and the Multipartidaria (multiparty group); it confirmed the end of military rule in 1985 following national elections and the inauguration of a civilian president. In the 1985 elections, the Colorado candidate, Julio Maria Sanguinetti Cairolo, won handily while his party won a slim plurality in both houses.

On March 1, 1985, the Uruguayan military ended its 12-year rule and handed over power to the elected civilian government of President Julio Maria Sanguinetti. Thus Uruguay returned to its traditional form of government — an elected constitutional democracy with an executive branch, and independent bicameral legislature, and an autonomous judicial system. The return to democracy was marked by a high level of political participation by all sectors of the population, unrestricted political debate, and broad access to the media by the major political parties.

The year 1985 saw the culmination of the gradual loosening of political restrictions, a process initiated in 1983 and continued in 1984. Soon after taking office, the Sanguinetti government released all remaining political prisoners, lifted remaining censorship, and lifted proscriptions from those few political groups still outlawed, including the Uruguayan Communist Party and the National Liberation Movement-Tupamaros. The legislature and judiciary began to function normally without outside interference. University autonomy was reinstated, and proscribed student organizations re-emerged, holding in September their first free elections since 1973. An independent labor movement also reappeared and by the end of 1985 most labor unions had held elections for new officers. Opposition leaders were included in the Cabinet.

In accordance with Institutional Act No. 19, the August 1984 agreement between the Alvarez regime and the Multipartidaria, the army, navy, and air force commanders participate in an advisory National Defense Council, which also includes the president, the vice president, and the defense, foreign and interior ministers. The council's actions are subject to the approval of Congress. Other provisions of the act require the president to appoint military commanders from a list presented by the armed forces, limit the scope of military justice to crimes committed by members of the armed forces, and preclude the declaration of a state of siege without congressional approval.

ORGANIZATION OF URUGUAYAN GOVERNMENT

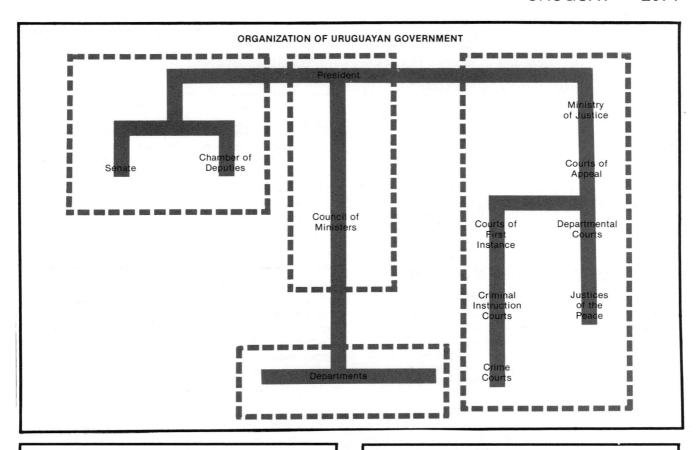

RULERS OF URUGUAY
(from 1945)

1943 (March) to 1947 (March) Juan Jose de Amezaga
1947 (March) 1947 (August) Tomas Berreta
1947 (August) to 1951 (March) Luis Batlle y Barres
1951 (March) to 1953 (March) Andres Martinez Trueba
1953 (March) to 1955 (March) Luis Batlle y Barres
1955 (March) to 1957 (March) Alberto F. Zubiria
1957 (March) to 1958 (March) Arturo Lezama
1958 (March) to 1959 (March) Carlos A. Fischer
1959 (March) to 1960 (March) Martin R. Etchegoyen
1960 (March) to 1961 (March) Benito Nardone
1961 (March) to 1962 (March) Eduardo Victor Haedo
1962 (March) to 1963 (March) Faustino Harrison
1963 (March) to 1964 (March) Daniel Fernandez Crespo
1964 (March) to 1965 (February) Luis Giannattasio
1965 (February) to 1966 (March) Washington Beltran
1966 (March) to 1967 (March) Alberto Heber Usher
1967 (March to December) Oscar Gestido
1967 (December) to 1972 (February) Jorge Pacheco Areco
1972 (March) to 1976 (June) Juan Maria Bordaberry Arocena
1976 (June to July) Alberto Demichelli
1976 (July) to 1981 (September) Aparicio Mendez Manfredini
1981 (September) to 1985 (February) Gregario Conrado Alvarez
1985 (March) —Julio Maria Sanguinetti Cairolo

Note: (1) Since the 1973 coup the country had been governed de facto by the military through the National Security Council.
(2) The presidency was suspended from 1952 through 1966 and the country was ruled by a colegiado with a rotating presidency.

The presidential cabinet comprises 11 ministries.

CABINET LIST (1985)

President .Julio María Sanguinetti
Vice President . . . . Enrique Tarigo
Minister of Agriculture
   & Fishing . . . . Roberto Vázquez Platero
Minister of Economy & Finance . . . . Ricardo Zerbino
Minister of Education & Culture . . . . Dr. Adela Reta
Minister of Foreign Affairs . . . . .Enrique Iglesias
Minister of Industry & Energy . . . . .Dr. Carlos Piran
Minister of Interior . . . . .Dr. Carlos Manini Rios
Minister of Justice . . . . Dr. Adela Reta
Minister of Labor &
   Social Welfare . . . . Hugo Fernández Faingold
Minister of Natl. Defense . . . . Juan Vicente Chiarino
Minister of Public Health . . . . .Dr. Raúl Ugarte
Minister of Transportation
   & Public Works . . . . Jorge Sanguinetti
Secretary of Planning, Coordination
   & Information . . . . José María Puppo Riveiro

Elections are conducted under the supervision of the Electoral Court, made up of nine members of whom five were designated by the General Assembly by a two-thirds majority and four were designated by the General Assembly as party representatives. Suffrage is universal over age 18, and the government maintains a National Civic Register of all eligible voters.

Until the 1970s Uruguay had enjoyed relative political stability and a reasonable measure of civil liberties. Elements contributing to the stability were racial and ethnic homogeneity, a high level of literacy and the lack of marked disparities in income. This tradition has been severely battered in recent years. An urban guerrilla group called Tupamaros (so called after Tupac Amaru, the legendary Inca ruler who led a revolt against the Spaniards in the 16th century) began the cycle of violence with a brutal campaign of urban terrorism. The Tupamaros aimed to create conditions that would help to discredit the democratic system but instead provoked harsh repression and the eventual military takeover. The Tupamaros had been eliminated as a significant force by 1975.

FREEDOM & HUMAN RIGHTS

In terms of civil and political rights, Uruguay is classified as a free country with a positive rating of 3 in civil and political rights (on a descending scale in which 1 is the highest and 7 the lowest in rights).

Uruguay's political transition brought with it dramatic improvements in the area of human rights. Accusations of political killings, torture and disappearances ceased. Restrictive laws and acts passed under military rule were repealed, and the 1967 constitution, which guarantees habeas corpus and freedom from arbitrary arrest, was reinstated. Congress set up commissions to handle the issues of restitution for those who had lost their jobs for political activities and to investigate violations of human rights which occurred during the military regime. President Sanguinetti indicated before his inauguration that the policy of his government would be "justice, not revenge," and that obstacles would not be placed in the way of legal proceedings against those accused of human rights violations. In general, Uruguayans enjoyed a freedom and openness in political life that they had not experienced since the late 1960s, and they responded to it with a high level of civic consciousness and political involvement.

There are currently no political prisoners in Uruguay. Those who, like Blanco Party President Wilson Ferreira Aldunate, were free on bail pending trial had the charges against them dropped. Others, who had already been tried, were pardoned by President Sanguinetti.

CIVIL SERVICE

It is estimated that nearly one-fifth of the labor force is employed by the government and the 22 autonomous corporations. Under the constitution, civil service regulations have been established governing recruitment, promotions and working conditions. In addition, each department has its own regulations.

LOCAL GOVERNMENT

For purpose of local government Uruguay is divided into 19 departments or provinces.

PROVINCES OF URUGUAY			
Departments	Capitals	Departments	Capitals
Artigas	Artigas	Paysandu	Paysandu
Canelones	Canelones	Rio Negro	Fray Bentos
Cerro-Largo	Melo	Rivera	Rivera
Colonia	Colonia	Rocha	Rocha
Durazno	Durazno	Salto	Salto
Flores	Trinidad	San Jose	San Jose
Florida	Florida	Soriano	Mercedes
Lavalleja	Minas	Tacuarembo	Tacuarembo
Maldonado	Maldonado	Treinta y Tres	Treinta y Tres
Montevideo	Montevideo City		

Under the 1967 constitution each department was administered by an intendente, who served as the mayor of the capital city of the department and governor of the rest of the territory. These intendentes were elected by direct popular vote for five-year terms and could be re-elected only once. Each department had a unicameral legislature, the junta departmental, with 31 members who were elected for four-year terms. Towns outside the departmental capitals had local five-member juntas.

Since 1973 all intendentes have been appointed by the national government.

FOREIGN POLICY

As a small buffer state located between the two giants of South America, Uruguay has pursued a cautious policy emphasizing regional cooperation, national self-determination and pacific settlement of disputes. Traditionally, the Colorado Party has oriented the country toward Brazil and the Blanco Party toward Argentina, but the military regime maintained a scrupulous balance between the two. Despite occasional disagreements, relations with the United States have always been amicable and the nation has no tradition of anti-American sentiments. Among Western European nations, the United Kingdom enjoys a special place because of historical political and economic ties beginning in 1828, when the United Kingdom guaranteed the creation of Uruguay. Relations with the Soviet Union have been marred by frequent expulsions of Soviet diplomats for engaging in subversive activities.

Uruguay and the United States are parties to 21 treaties and agreements covering agricultural commodities, aviation, customs, defense, economic and technical cooperation, education, extradition, air force missions, nationality, Peace Corps, pacific settlement of disputes, telecommunications, trade and commerce and visas.

Uruguay joined the U.N. in 1945; its share of the U.N. budget is 0.06%. It is a member of 13 U.N. organizations and 31 other international organizations.

U.S. Ambassador in Montevideo: Thomas Aranda, Jr.
U.K. Ambassador in Montevideo: Charles W. Wallace
Uruguayan Ambassador in Washington, D.C.: Hector Luisi
Uruguayan Ambassador in London: Luis M. de Posadas

PARLIAMENT

Under the 1967 constitution the Congress, properly called the General Assembly, consists of a 30-member Senate and a 99-member Chamber of Deputies. Both senators and representatives are directly elected for five-year terms. The senators are elected by a system of proportional representation. Each of the 19 departments has at least two representatives in the chamber, but the actual number is determined by the Electoral Court on the basis of the number of voters in each district. The General Assembly convenes on March 15 every year and remains in session until December 15. The functions of the Assembly include the election of the members of the Supreme Court and the Electoral Court. When the Assembly is not in session, a permanent commission consisting of four senators and seven representatives assume its functions.

CONGRESO

Senate Election, 25 November 1984

Party	Seats
Partido Colorado	13
Partido Nacional	11
Frente Amplio	6
Total	**30**

Federal Chamber of Deputies Election, 25 November 1984

Party	Seats
Partido Colorado	41
Partido Nacional	35
Frente Amplio	21
Unión Cívica	2
Total	**99**

POLITICAL PARTIES

Uruguay has a vigorous two-party political system dominated by two traditional parties, the radical, anticlerical and liberal Colorado Party and the relatively more conservative Blanco or National Party. (Both parties derive their names from the colors of their flags in the 1836 civil war). Neither Colorado nor Blanco are disciplined political groups in the conventional sense but only broad alliances, called lemas, of factions called sub-lemas. Each sub-lema has its own leaders and organizational structure, but present a united front with other sub-lemas at election times. The Colorado Party was in power from 1865 to 1958 and is identified with the social welfare system, secularism and urban cosmopolitanism that distinguish modern Uruguay. The policies and organizational structure of the Colorado Party reflect the influence of its most important leader in the 20th Century, Jose Batlle y Ordonnez, and each of the numerous factions of the party claims his legacy as its own. The largest of such groups is the Batllista (Lista 15 or Unidad y Reforma) led by Jorge Batlle Ibanez. Other factions include the Gestidistas Union (Colorado y Batllista or Lista 123, itself a coalition of Lista 14 and Lista 515), the left-wing Lista 99 (or Evolucion y Gobierno del Pueblo), Lista 315 (or the Antorcha de Batlle), and the Lista 10, which supported a collegiate form of government. Since 1973 new factions have emerged in the Colorado Party, particularly the promilitary *pachequistas* and the antimilitary Libertad y Cambio and Batllismo Radical.

The Blanco Party (Partido Nacional) represents conservative, rural and clerical elements and also favors a more isolationist foreign policy. For the greater part of the last century, Blanco functioned as a loyal opposition. It was in power only briefly from 1958 through 1962. The Blancos are also divided into five factions: Union Blanca Democratica, Herreristas, Ortodoxos Movimiento Popular Nacionalista, Azul y Blanco and Movimiento de Rocha. The Blancos are also divided into promilitary and antimilitary factions; the latter represented by Por la Patria, Movimiento de Rocha and Consejo Nacional Herrerista.

Fringe parties included the now outlawed Leftist Liberty Front (Frente Izquierda de Libertad, FIdeL), a coalition of the Partido Socialista, the pro-Cuban Movimiento Revolucionario Oriental and the Partido Comunista. In 1971 FIdeL was largely superseded by the Frente Amplio, a coalition of more or less the same partners. There are also two Catholic-oriented parties, the Christian Democratic Party and the Civic Union, both with small followings.

The only major insurgent opposition to the government in recent times was the National Liberation Front, commonly known as the Tupamaros. Originally regarded as latter-day Robin Hoods, their tactics became more violent after the mid-1960s. The last recorded Tupamaro clash with the police was in 1974, and the movement is now believed to have been crushed.

ECONOMY

Uruguay is one of the 35 upper-middle-income countries of the world with a free-market economy dominated by the private sector.

The Committee on Investment and Economic Development was in charge of economic development planning until 1974, when its functions were taken over by the Economic and Social Council. The 1965-75 10-year plan was superseded in 1973 by the National Development Plan, 1973-77. The plan projected an annual growth rate of 3.8% in real GDP and an export growth rate of 10.1%. The increase in domestic investment was projected at an annual rate of 15.1%.

Foreign aid flow has been modest, but it has been received uninterruptedly from a variety of sources.

PRINCIPAL ECONOMIC INDICATORS

Gross National Product: $7.390 billion (1983)
  GNP Annual Growth Rate: 3.4% (1973-82)
  Per Capita GNP: $2,490 (1983)
  Per Capita GNP Annual Growth Rate: 2.9% (1973-82)

Gross Domestic Product: NP295.546 billion (1984)
  GDP at 1980 Prices: NP79.420 billion
  GDP Deflator 1980=100: 372.1
  GDP Annual Growth Rate: 2.5% (1973-83)
  Per Capita GDP: NP98,845 (1984)
  Per Capita GDP Annual Growth Rate: 2.7% (1970-81)

Income Distribution: 4.4% of the national income is received by the bottom 20%; 19% of the national income is received by the top 5%.

Percentage of Population in Absolute Poverty: 6

Consumer Price Index (1970=100):
  All Items: 74,381.2 (April 1985)
  Food: 74,745.3 (April 1985)

Wholesale Price Index (1980=100):
  Domestic supply: 636 (March 1985)
  Farm Products: 607 (March 1985)

Average Annual Rate of Inflation: 51% (1973-83)

Money Supply: NP12.201 billion (March 1984)
  Reserve Money: NP33.902 billion (March 1984)

Currency in Circulation: NP8.401 billion (1984)

International Reserves: $134 million, of which foreign exchange reserves were $129 million (1984)

BALANCE OF PAYMENTS (1984)
(million $)

Current Account Balance	−124.4
Merchandise Exports	924.6
Merchandise Imports	−733.2
Trade Balance	191.4
Other Goods, Services & Income	+452.0
Other Goods, Services & Income	−777.8
Other Goods, Services & Income Net	−325.8
Private Unrequited Transfers	10.0
Official Unrequited Transfers	—
Capital Other Than Reserves	189.2
Net Errors & Omissions	−148.6
Total (Lines 1, 10 and 11)	−83.8
Counterpart Items	22.0
Total (Lines 12 and 13)	−61.8
Liabilities Constituting Foreign Authorities' Reserves	−1.2
Total Change in Reserves	63.0

GROSS DOMESTIC PRODUCT BY ECONOMIC ACTIVITY
(1970-81)

	%	Rate of Change %
Agriculture	10.2	1.2
Mining	—	—
Manufacturing	26.9	3.4
Construction	5.1	9.4
Electricity, Gas & Water	1.3	4.0
Transport & Communications	6.7	3.3
Trade & Finance	21.5	4.3
Public Administration & Defense	11.0	—
Other Branches	17.3	2.1

Per capita aid received during 1979-81 was $5.90.

FOREIGN ECONOMIC ASSISTANCE

Sources	Period	Amount (million $)
United States Grants	1946-83	32.5
United States Loans	1946-83	128.8
International Organizations	1946-83	768.9
(Of which World Bank)	1946-83	442.2
Other Western Nations, ODA & OOF	1970-82	124.0
Soviet Union and East European Countries	1970-83	65.0
All Sources	1979-81	17.1

BUDGET

The Uruguayan fiscal year is the calendar year. The national budget is prepared by the National Office of Planning and Budget. The budget also covers the finances of the decentralized autonomous agencies, and the recurrent deficits of these agencies have been a particularly burdensome charge on the national government.

NATIONAL BUDGET (1983)
(in million new pesos)

Revenue	29,486.4
Expenditure	36,897.3

Of current revenues, 5.8% comes from taxes on income, profit and capital gain, 26.2% from social security contributions, 43.2% from domestic taxes on goods and services, 10.3% from taxes on international trade and transactions, 5.8% from other taxes and 8.7% from non-tax revenues. Current revenues represented 21.6% of GNP. Of current expenditures 13.6% goes to defense, 7.7% to education, 3.3% to health, 54.3% to housing, social security and welfare, 9.4% to economic services and 11.8% to other functions. Current expenditures represented 30.1% of GNP and overall deficit 9.2% of GNP.

In 1983 public consumption was NP34.003 billion and private consumption NP222.138 billion. During 1973-83 public consumption grew by 3.7% and private consumption by 1.1%.

In 1983, total outstanding disbursed external debt was $2.681 billion of which $2.522 billion was publicly guaranteed. Of the publicly guaranteed debt, $382 million was owed to official creditors and $2.140 billion to private creditors. Total debt service was $292.4 million of which $94 million was repayment of principal and $198.3 million interest. Total debt represented 171.2% of export revenues and 48.4% of GNP. Debt service represented 19.8% of export revenues and 5.6% of GNP.

FINANCE

The Uruguayan unit of currency is the new peso divided into 100 centisimos. Coins are issued in denominations of 1, 2, 5 and 10 centisimos; notes are issued in denominations of 5, 10 and 50 centisimos and 1, 5 and 10 new pesos.

The new peso was introduced in 1975 replacing the old peso at the rate of 1 new peso=1,000 old pesos. At that point the value of the old peso had depreciated to $1=OP2,330 compared to $1=OP250 in 1969. Since 1975 the exchange rate, linked to the U.S. dollar, has been frequently adjusted. In February 1985 it was $1=P102.5. The sterling exchange rate on that basis was £1=P19.73/P1= £0.0506.

The banking sector is headed by the central bank, Banco Central, which is a decentralized autonomous agency under the constitution. There are three government-owned financial institutions: Banco de la Republica Oriental del Uruguay, which operates both as a commercial bank and as the fiscal agent of the government; Banco Hipotecario del Uruguay; and the Banco de Prevision Social. There are 13 principal domestic commercial banks and eight foreign banks including the Citibank and Bank of America. In 1984 the commercial banks had reserves of NP16.939 billion, demand deposits of NP3.716 billion and time and savings deposits of NP74.310 billion.

GROWTH PROFILE
Annual Growth Rates (%)

Population 1980-2000	0.7
Birthrate 1965-83	−14.6
Deathrate 1965-83	−4.2
Urban Population 1973-83	0.8
Labor Force 1980-2000	0.9
GNP 1973-82	3.4
GNP per capita 1973-82	2.9
GDP 1973-83	2.5
GDP per capita 1970-81	2.7
Consumer Prices 1970-81	63.8
Wholesale Prices 1970-81	63.2
Inflation 1973-83	51.0
Agriculture 1973-83	1.5
Manufacturing 1970-81	3.4
Industry 1973-82	2.4
Services 1973-83	2.7
Mining	—
Construction 1970-81	9.4
Electricity 1970-81	4.0
Transportation 1970-81	3.3
Trade 1970-81	4.3
Public Administration & Defense	—
Export Price Index 1975-81	16.4
Import Price Index 1975-81	17.6
Terms of Trade 1975-81	−0.9
Exports 1973-83	9.2
Imports 1973-83	−1.5
Public Consumption 1973-83	3.7
Private Consumption 1973-83	1.1
Gross Domestic Investment 1973-83	7.0
Energy Consumption 1973-83	0.7
Energy Production 1973-83	18.2

AGRICULTURE

Of the total land area of 17,750,800 hectares (43,862,225 acres), 87% is classified as agricultural area, or 4.8 hectares (12 acres) per capita. Based on

1974-76=100, the index of agricultural production in 1982 was 104, the index of food production was 103 and the index of per capita food production was 106. Agriculture employs 11% of the labor force. Agriculture contributes 12% to the GDP, and its annual growth rate during 1973-83 was only 1.5%. The value added in agriculture in 1983 was $893 million.

Of the land classified as agricultural, only 1.2 million hectares (3 million acres) are under cultivation. The principal production areas are in the south and west for wheat and corn, along the Rio Uruguay for sugar and oil crops and in the Laguna Merin Basin for rice. Land ownership is marked by high concentration and disparities. Some 4.9% of farms are 1,011 hectares (2,500 acres) or more in extent and comprise 62.4% of all farm lands. At the other end of the scale, 30% of farms are less than 10 hectares (25 acres) in size and account for less than 0.7% of the farmland. Increasing numbers of landowners are incorporating their properties as agricultural societies to benefit from tax exemptions and to avoid division of holdings through inheritance. In the mid-1980s almost two-thirds of the holdings were controlled by some 3,000 such enterprises.

About 50% of farmland is under some form of tenancy, including cash-rentals and sharecropping. Tenancy is regulated by the law of 1954. The minimum period of a tenancy contract is five years with an additional three-year extension at the request of the tenant. The landlord is required to provide certain basic improvements to the land. Rentals are subject to renegotiation every two years. Resettlement programs are administered by the National Land Settlement Institute. Although investments in improved agricultural techniques have not reached optimum levels, cultivation is highly mechanized. In 1982 there were 28,400 tractors and 5,600 harvester-threshers in use. Annual consumption of fertilizers was 63,600 tons, or 37.6 kg (83 lb) per cultivated hectare.

In 1981 work began on the India Muerta Dam in the Department of Rocha, which, when completed, will provide irrigation for an area of 7,000 hectares (17,297 acres). In June 1984 an agricultural trade agreement was signed by Uruguay, Brazil and Argentina which eliminated custom tariffs and established a free-trade system.

PRINCIPAL CROP PRODUCTION (1983)
(000 metric tons)

Wheat	450
Corn	103
Barley	90
Oats	40
Sorghum	100
Rice	332
Potatoes	100
Sugar cane	495
Sugar beet	377
Sunflower seed	26
Linseed	6

About 70% of the land area is devoted to raising livestock, accounting for more than two-thirds of the total agricultural production. Uruguay has more cattle and sheep in relation to its area than any other Latin American country. Animals and animal products constitute over 65% of the exports by value. Cattle are evenly distributed throughout the country, but the dairy breeds are heavily concentrated in the south. In 1983 the livestock population consisted of 9.7 million cattle, 20.4 million sheep, 440,000 pigs and 530,000 horses. A reduction in the number of livestock resulted in a substantial decline in meat exports in 1984. In 1983 Uruguay produced an estimated 418,000 metric tons of beef and veal. Low world prices caused a 10% drop in wool production in 1981, after reaching a peak of 80,000 metric tons in 1980. In 1983 Uruguay's exports of raw wool and wool products amounted to $13.2 million, which represented a decline of 34.3% on the figures for 1982.

Forests cover about 3% of the land area, and timber resources are limited. State-owned forests cover about 16,997 hectares (42,000 acres). Roundwood removals totaled 1.144 million cubic meters (40.4 million cubic ft) in 1982.

Uruguay's fishing grounds extending from Colonia to the Brazilian border are rich in corvina negra (a kind of bass), mullet, sole, anchovy, mackerel, whiting and shark. The annual catch in 1983 was 123,200 tons.

INDUSTRY

Manufacturing contributes 26.9% to the GDP and employs about 20.3% of the labor force. Its rate of growth during 1973-83 was 3.4%. The principal industries are food processing, hides and leather, textiles, construction, metallurgy and rubber. An industrial development law has boosted non-traditional manufactures, which now account for 50% of the exports. Most industries are concentrated in the Montevideo area, and smaller centers are found in Paysandu, Rio Negro, Lavalleja, Artigas and Colonia. The value added in manufacturing in 1982 was $787 million, of which food products accounted for 37%, textiles for 18%, machinery and transport equipment for 9% and chemicals for 9%. The index of industrial production in 1982 (1975=100) was 102.

The food, beverages and tobacco group employs 21% of the industrial labor force, followed by clothing and footwear (19%), metal products (also 19%), textiles (10%) and wood products and chemicals (8% each).

U.S. private investments account for the bulk of foreign investments. British investments, once dominant, now amount to only $20 million. Net direct private investment in 1983 was $6 million. Under investment laws passed in 1973 new industries are exempt from income taxes for 10 years.

ENERGY

In 1982 Uruguay's total production of energy was equivalent to 616,000 metric tons of coal and consumption to 2.738 million metric tons of coal, or 929 kg (2,048 lb) per capita. The national energy deficit is 2.122 million metric tons of coal equivalent. The petroleum refinery capacity is 45,000 barrels per day. The annual growth rates during 1973-83 were 18.2% for energy production and 0.7% energy consumption. Energy imports account for 28% of all merchandise imports. Apparent per capita consumption of gasoline is 67 gallons per year.

In 1984 production of electric power totaled 5.0 billion kwh, or 1,709 kwh per capita.

LABOR

The economically active population is estimated at 1,148,000, yielding a participation rate (ratio of economically active persons to the total population) of 38.7%. Women constitute about 27% of this force. By occupational sectors, 18.6% are employed in the government and army, 11.6% in agriculture, 0.2% in mining, 20.3% in manufacturing, 5.8% in construction, 15% in trade, 1.4% in public utilities, 5.1% in transportation and 22% in other.

Uruguay has long been one of the most advanced countries in Latin America in terms of worker rights. Child labor is not permitted until after a child has obtained primary education. Children are generally not employed below the age of 15, but children of 12 or above can work with special permits from the government. Dangerous, fatiguing or night work, apart from domestic service, cannot be performed by children under 18, and hours and pay are more strictly regulated than for adults. Children 16 or over can sue in court for payment of wages, and the right of child laborers to dispose of their own wages is mandated by law. Children working in the informal sector (street vendors, itinerant laborers and others without a permanent seat of operations) or in agrarian work are less strictly regulated and generally lower paid.

The basic workweek is 48 hours, or six working days of eight hours each, for manual workers and 44 hours for office and professional workers. However, the civil service and banks work on a 30-hour workweek schedule, shortened still further during summer. In addition to Sundays and national holidays, work comes to stop during the carnival days that precede Lent and during Holy Week (designated Tourist Week). Workers generally receive 20 days of paid vacation every year but vacation credits do not accumulate.

Wages are determined by comprehensive wage laws setting minimum wages and maximum wage limits. Before 1968 wage rates were set for different industries by management-labor negotiations leading to contracts or awards by salary councils, but since then this function has been taken over by the tripartite Commission on Productivity, Prices and Incomes.

In addition to regular wages, all employees are entitled to receive a Christmas bonus equal to one month's earnings, family allowance contributions and other fringe benefits. Most workers are eligible for unemployment compensation and a comprehensive pension program.

Until 1973 Uruguay was plagued by considerable labor unrest resulting in frequent strikes, work stoppages and industrial violence. In response, the government introduced security laws, prohibited union meetings, arrested union leaders, placed public services under military control and suppressed public information concerning strikes. In 1973 the Confederacion Nacional de Trabajadores (CNT, National Workers' Confederation), which claimed 400,000 members, was declared illegal. In 1974 new legislation was passed restricting labor union membership to free and nonpolitical labor unions.

No reliable figures are available on unemployment, but there has been a sharp rise in unemployment and unofficial sources have cited an unemployment rate as high as 25%. However, the unemployment figures are believed to be much lower in the countryside.

FOREIGN COMMERCE

The foreign commerce of Uruguay in 1984 consisted of exports of $1.508 and imports of $810.9 million, leaving a favorable balance of $697 million. Of the imports, mineral products account for 41.6%, machinery and appliances for 13.4%, chemicals for 10.6%, transport equipment for 10.4%, plastics and rubber for 4.3% and base metals and products for 4.3%. Of the exports, textiles account for 28.6%, animals and animal products for 28.4%, vegetable products for 14.9%, skin and hides for 13.6%, chemicals for 4.2% and plastics and rubber for 1.9%.

The major import sources are: the United States 12.4%, Nigeria 12.1%, Brazil 11.8%, Venezuela 8.6% and Mexico 7.9%. The major export destinations are: Brazil 14.3%, Argentina 10.7%, Germany 9.0%, the Soviet Union 7.7% and the United States 7.4%.

Based on 1975=100, the import price index in 1981 was 242, the export price index was 209 and the terms of trade (export prices divided by import prices × 100) 87.

Uruguay is one of the founding members of the Latin American Free Trade Association (LAFTA), commonly known as the Montevideo Treaty, under which it enjoys special treatment granted to less developed countries. It is also a member of ALADI and SELA.

TRANSPORTATION & COMMUNICATIONS

The State Railways Administration administers 3,000 km (1,863 mi) of track. Montevideo is the hub of the rail system with four main lines radiating north, south and west linking with the Brazilian and Argen-

FOREIGN TRADE INDICATORS (1984)		
Annual Growth Rate, Imports:		−1.5% (1973-83)
Annual Growth Rate, Exports:		9.2% (1973-83)
Ratio of Exports to Imports:		65:35
Exports per capita:		$514
Imports per capita:		$276
Balance of Trade:		$697 million
Ratio of International Reserves to Imports (in months)		9.3
Exports as % of GDP:		15.6
Imports as % of GDP:		19.7
Value of Manufactured Exports:		$332 million
Commodity Concentration:		39.5%
Direction of Trade (%)		
	Imports	Exports
EEC	17.9	30.0
U.S.	9.8	7.8
Industrialized Market Economies	38.1	53.7
East European Economies	1.5	5.1
High Income Oil Exporters	3.4	16.7
Developing Economies	60.0	38.8
Composition of Trade (%)		
	Imports	Exports
Food	6.8	47.4
Agricultural Raw Materials	3.1	21.2
Fuels	31.6	1.0
Ores & Minerals	4.8	0.9
Manufactured Goods	53.6	29.3
of which Chemicals	10.8	3.3
of which Machinery	32.1	2.1

tine systems. Railways carry 15% of all freight. Rail traffic in 1982 consisted of 274 million passenger-km and 180 million net-ton-km.

There are about 1,600 km (994 mi) of inland waterways handling about 5% of all freight. On the Rio Uruguay, oceangoing vessels up to 4.2 meters (14 ft) in draft can reach Paysandu and vessels of up to 2.7 meters (9 ft) can reach Salto. The Rio Negro is navigable by coastal vessels for about 72 km (45 mi) upstream. Other navigable rivers include the Yi, Quequay Grande, Santa Lucia and the Cebollati. There is a daily hydrofoil service between Colonia and Buenos Aires.

The country has four major ports: Montevideo, Colonia, Fray Bentos and Paysandu. In 1982 these ports handled 1,034,000 tons of cargo. In 1983 the national merchant marine consisted of 88 ships with a total GRT of 331,000, of which oil tankers accounted for 95,000 tons.

Uruguay has one of the most extensive, modern road networks in South America with a total length of 49,900 km (30,988 mi), of which 6,700 km (4,160 mi) are paved. Road transport handles 80% of all freight. The national highways link Montevideo with Colonia and Mercedes on the Rio Negro and with the interior of the country as far as Paso Toros and eastward through Minas and Treinta y Tres to the Brazilian frontier. Another road links Montevideo with Punta del Este. In 1982 these roads were used by 281,275 passenger cars and 49,813 commercial vehicles. Per capita passenger car ownership was 96 per 1,000 inhabitants.

The national airline is PLUNA (Primeras Lineas Uruguayas de Navegacion Aerea), which operates 14 major aircraft on internal and external routes to Brazil, Paraguay and Argentina. In 1982 the airline flew 5.5 million km (3.4 million mi) and carried 356,000 passengers. The primary international airport is Carrasco, outside of Montevideo. There are 95 airfields in the country, of which 91 are usable, 14 have permanent-surface runways and one has a runway over 2,500 meters (8,000 ft). There are also two seaplane stations.

In 1984 there were 294,300 telephones in use, or 9.9 per 100 inhabitants.

In 1982, mail traffic consisted of 35,356,000 pieces of mail and 1,673,000 telegrams. The volume of mail per capita was 12 pieces. There are 1,043 telex subscriber lines.

In 1982, 622,000 tourists visited Uruguay. In the same year tourist revenues totaled $149 million and expenditures by nationals abroad $304 million.

MINING

Known mineral resources are limited and production is insignificant. The country's inventory of proved mineral deposits include manganese, iron, lead and copper as well as heavy minerals, such as ilmenite, rutile, zircon and monazite.

DEFENSE

The defense structure is headed by the president as commander in chief.

There is no conscription. Military manpower is obtained through voluntary enlistment of males between the ages of 18 and 45, who serve for one or two years.

The total strength of the armed forces is 31,900, or 10.3 armed persons for every 1,000 civilians.

ARMY:
Personnel: 22,300
Organization: 4 military regions; 1 presidential escort (1 cavalry regiment); 1 infantry brigade (1 airborne, 1 motorized battalion); 1 engineer brigade; 1 signals brigade; 4 infantry divisions (3 cavalry brigades with 4 mechanized, 1 horsed regiments); 5 infantry brigades; 15 battalions; 5 field artillery groups; 1 AA group; 6 engineer battalions
Equipment: 57 tanks; 53 armored combat vehicles; 70 armored personnel carriers; 46 howitzers; mortars; antitank rocket launchers; 6 air defense guns

NAVY:
Personnel: 6,600
Units: 3 frigates; 1 corvette; 7 patrol craft; 8 landing craft
Naval Air Force: 7 combat aircraft; 1 fleet antisubmarine warfare; 1 fleet maritime reconnaissance; 3 transports; 7 trainers; 1 helicopter fleet

Naval Base: Montevideo

AIR FORCE:
Personnel: 3,000
Organization: 41 combat aircraft; 2 counterinsurgency squadrons; 1 reconnaissance/training squadron; 1 search and rescue squadron; 3 transport squadrons; 36 trainers
Air Bases: Carrasco, Isla de la Libertad, Laguna del Sauce, Punta del Este, Melilla and Laguna Negra

In 1982 military expenditures totaled $395.43 million, or 12.4% of the national budget, 3.3% of the GNP, $93 per capita, $13,600 per soldier and $2,318 per sq km of national territory.

Since the 1870s the Uruguayan armed forces have not participated in any military action. Their present strength is designed only for domestic peacekeeping because the nation does not face any conceivable external threat.

From 1946 through 1983 Uruguay received $89.2 million in military assistance from the United States, including $41.0 million in MAP grants, $18.3 million in credit sales and $20.4 million in excess stock sales. Arms purchases abroad during 1973-83 totaled $185 million of which $70 million was received from France.

Uruguay's defense production is limited to naval supplies.

EDUCATION

The national literacy rate is 90.5% (90.7% for males and 90.4% for females).

Education is free, universal and compulsory for nine years from the ages of six to 15. The gross school enrollment ratios are 114% at the first level (6 to 11) and 63% at the second level (12 to 17), for a combined enrollment ratio of 89%. The third-level enrollment ratio is 20.4%. Girls constitute 48% of primary school enrollment, 58% of secondary school enrollment and 56% of post-secondary enrollment.

Schooling lasts for 12 years divided into a primary cycle of six years, a general secondary cycle of three years and a university preparatory cycle of three years. Full six-year primary schooling is offered only in a few rural schools, which are, in most cases, simple one-room affairs where all age groups are taught simultaneously. Dropping out and grade-repetition are frequent in the lower grades. Secondary education is administered by the National Council of Secondary Education and is offered in three types of schools: liceos or general secondary schools, offering academic courses leading to the bachillerato certificate; pilot secondary schools with a five-year curriculum, generally patterned on that of the United States in which the fifth year involves specialization in a technical or vocational field; and technical and vocational secondary schools. In 1982 the school system comprised 2,292 state and private primary schools, 135 state secondary schools, 125 private secondary schools and 87 technical and vocational schools. Private schools account for 17% of primary and secondary enrollment.

The school year runs from March to late November or early December. The medium of instruction is Spanish throughout.

Teachers are generally professionally trained and competent, and the national teacher-pupil ratios are slightly higher than the Latin American average at 1:22 in primary classes, 1:10 in secondary classes and 1:18 in post-secondary classes. Secondary school teachers are trained at the Artigas Institute.

Adult education is administered by the National Board of Adult Education and is offered by cultural and welfare institutions, hospitals and binational centers such as the Uruguay-United States Cultural Alliance. Because of the country's high rate of literacy, adult education programs have lost much of their earlier urgency and importance.

Technical and vocation education is centralized under an autonomous agency called the Labor University. Labor University programs are generally of two or three years' duration, but completion of these programs does not lead to university enrollment. There is also a small church-run private secondary vocational system. In 1982, 14.2% of secondary students were enrolled in the vocational track.

Public education is financed by the national budget, but in each department educational administration is vested in the governor or intendente. Each level of education is under the immediate control of one of four autonomous agencies: the National Council of Primary and Normal Instruction, the National Council on Secondary Education, the National Council of Vocational and Technical Training and the University of the Republic. In 1981 educational expenditures totaled P2,958,337,000, representing 2.4% of the GNP, 12.8% of the national budget and $86 per capita.

EDUCATIONAL ENROLLMENT (1982)			
Levels	Schools	Teachers	Pupils
State Primary	2,292	16,821	363,179
Private Primary			
State Secondary	135	N.A.	187,190
Private Secondary	125		
Technical	87	N.A.	26,654
University	1	4,149	48,234

Higher education is provided by the Universidad de la Republica with an enrollment in 1982 of 48,234. Per capita university enrollment is 1,663 per 100,000 inhabitants.

In 1982, 1,894 students graduated from the national university, including 945 women. Of these, 479 were awarded degrees in medicine, 121 in engineering, 67 in natural sciences, 110 in social sciences, 463 in law and 232 in agriculture.

In 1982, 1,403 Uruguayan students were enrolled in institutions of higher learning abroad. Of these, 193 were in the United States, 880 in Argentina, 44 in Switzerland, 4 in Canada, 48 in West Germany, 11 in the United Kingdom and 122 in Spain.

LEGAL SYSTEM

The Uruguayan legal system is based on Spanish civil law. The judiciary is headed by the Supreme Court, which has general administrative control over the entire judicial system and the power to declare laws unconstitutional. Under the constitution the Supreme Court has five judges appointed for 10-year terms by a two-thirds vote of the full membership of the General Assembly. They are eligible for reelection only after a five-year interval.

Under the Supreme Court are four appellate courts, three for civil cases and one for criminal cases, all located in Montevideo and each with three judges. These courts hear appeals from a series of "lawyer-courts," or juzgados letrados, presided over by "lawyer-judges," or jueces letrados. These include 35 courts sitting in Montevideo and departmental courts in the capitals of each of the 19 departments. The Montevideo courts include 18 courts of first instance, three financial courts, five criminal instruction courts, six crime courts, two juvenile courts and one customs court. Each of the 224 judicial divisions of the country has a justice of the peace court.

Full autonomy of the judiciary returned with the Sanguinetti government, and military officers who had been appointed to the Supreme Court or the higher Appeals Courts retired from their posts. According to the 1967 constitution, all trials shall be public, and trials by commission or in absentia are prohibited. Each trial must be opened by a public statement of the charge by a public prosecutor or complaining witness. Uruguayan legal tradition calls for judges, without the use of juries, to hand down decisions on the basis of written summaries, which are not available to the public. Several lawyers and human rights groups have advocated re-examination of the current judicial process in an effort to make it more efficient. Ideas include the institution of jury trials, tighter juridical supervision over pre-trial investigations by police, and the institution of a judicial police force. At present judges have to call on local police forces to carry out judicial decrees, which often slows the process considerably due to the volume of other work for which the police are responsible.

All prisons are administered by the Ministry of Culture. There are temporary jails in each of the 19 departments, but prisoners who have been sentenced are confined in one of three federal prisons and one work colony. Two of these prisons are for men and the third one is for women. Prisoners are obliged by law to work on road-building, quarrying, clearing, and similar projects. Prison conditions are generally unsatisfactory, and abuses of prisoners during interrogation and confinement are routine.

LAW ENFORCEMENT

The national police force has four operating agencies: the Montevideo Police, the Interior Police, the Highway Police and the National Corps of Firemen. The chief of police of Montevideo also controls two paramilitary organizations: the Republican Guard, a mounted unit of some 450 officers and men, and a Metropolitan Guard of 600 officers and men in infantry-type units armed with machine guns. The chiefs of police of Montevideo and eight of the departments are either active or retired army colonels. There are also three specialized units: the Technical Police concerned with laboratory work, criminal identification and fingerprinting; the Quick Action Unit; and the Maritime Police. In the early 1970s the police numbered about 17,000 officers and men, or one policeman for every 166 inhabitants.

Thefts and burglaries lead reported crimes followed by crimes against persons. Arrest rates are high because of the number of people arrested on mere suspicion, but the conviction rate is low. The highest crime rates prevail in Montevideo.

HEALTH

Uruguay has one of the healthiest populations in Latin America as reflected in the highest average life expectancy. Free medical services are available under a wide variety of public and mutual aid programs. Most of the hospitals and health facilities are government-operated. The major causes of death are heart diseases, cancer, diarrhea and enteritis.

```
PRINCIPAL HEALTH INDICATORS (1984)
Crude Death Rate: 10.2 per 1,000
Decline in Death Rate: –4.2 (1973-83)
Life Expectancy at Birth: 67.1 (Males); 73.7 (Females)
Infant Mortality Rate: 33.7 per 1,000 Live Births
Child Death Rate (Ages 1-4) per 1,000: 2
```

In 1980 there were 66 hospitals in the country with 23,000 beds or one bed per 127 inhabitants. In 1981 there were 5,600 physicians, or one physician per 523 inhabitants, 2,300 dentists and 15,200 nurses. Nearly 84% of the population have access to safe water. Health expenditures account for 4.8% of the national budget and $37.10 per capita. The admissions/discharge rate is 378 per 10,000 inhabitants, the bed occupancy rate is 61.1% and the average length of stay is 10 days.

FOOD

The Uruguayans are among the best-fed people in the Western Hemisphere with a daily per capita intake of 2,868 calories and 86.8 grams of protein (compared to recommended minimums of 2,600 calories and 65 grams of protein), 102 grams of fats and 421 grams of carbohydrates.

Meat is the staple and key article of diet and the annual per capita meat consumption of 103 kg (227 lb) is believed to be among the world's highest. Almost all of the country's noted dishes are based on meat: asado (a form of barbecue), churrasco (grilled beafsteak), parillada (mixed grill), puchero (meat and vegetables), carbonada (meat stew with rice) and milanesa (beef cutlet). The national beverage is Paraguayan tea, but ordinary tea and coffee are also popular.

MEDIA & CULTURE

In 1982, 24 daily newspapers and 58 non-dailies were published in the country. Daily newspapers had an aggregate circulation of 558,000, or 190 per 1,000 inhabitants. Fifteen of these dailies are published in the capital, accounting for 90% of the total circulation. The non-daily press includes one English-language weekly. The periodical press consists of 396 titles. Annual consumption of newsprint was 21,800 tons, or 7,400 kg (16,317 lb) per 1,000 inhabitants in 1982.

Following the signing of the August 3, 1985 transition document, the government revoked its August 1983 decree which prohibited reporting on political activity. This action along with the discontinuance in February 1985 of "prior censorship" of political party weeklies, has freed Uruguay's information media to report political developments as they occur. Recently, the growth of publications has been constrained primarily by economic factors.

Uruguay has no national news agency. Foreign news agencies represented in Montevideo include Reuters, ANSA, DPA, Efe, UPI and AP.

Uruguay has an active book publishing industry with 11 publishers accounting for most of the 837 titles published in 1981. Uruguay adheres to the Berne and Buenos Aires Copyright Conventions.

Broadcasting is partly private and partly public. In 1982 there were 35 medium- and short-wave stations and four FM stations in the Montevideo area and 65 radio stations outside the capital. The government service, Servicio Oficial de Difusion Radio Electrica (SODRE), has three medium-wave transmitters and four short-wave transmitters and is on the air for 15 hours a day. Over 75% of program hours are locally produced. Of the total 678,165 annual radio broadcasting hours, 154,630 hours are devoted to information, 11,425 to education, 5,460 to culture, 2,980 to religion, 121,000 to commercials and 380,400 hours to entertainment. In 1982 there were 1,700,000 radio receivers in the country, or 577 per 1,000 inhabitants.

Television, introduced in 1956, now covers nearly 90% of the population. There are three networks, SAETA, Teledoce and the government-owned SODRE, with four commercial stations in the capital each broadcasting for 15 hours each day and 16 stations in the provincial capitals. Of the 810 program-hours a week, between 40% and 60% are imported programs. Of the 42,165 annual television broadcasting hours,

2,585 hours are devoted to information, 840 to education, 55 to culture, 90 to religion, 8,400 to commercials and 30,195 hours to entertainment. In 1982 there were 370,000 television sets, or 126 per 1,000 inhabitants.

Feature films are produced only occasionally. In 1981 there were 120 fixed cinemas with 80,000 seats, or 27.3 seats per 1,000 inhabitants. Annual movie attendance was 6.2 million or 2.1 per capita. Box office receipts totaled P86.5 million.

The largest library is the National Library with over 500,000 volumes. There are 56 museums.

SOCIAL WELFARE

Uruguay is a welfare state with one of the most comprehensive social security systems in the world. At the core of this system is a series of seven retirement and pension funds, covering industry and commerce, civil servants and teachers, rural workers and domestic servants, banking, university graduates, notaries and the military. Membership in an appropriate fund is mandatory for wage earners as well as the self-employed. The amount of benefits varies from fund to fund, but generally it is 80% of the average wage earned during the last 60 months of active service. Eligibility usually begins after 30 years of service. In addition, the Central Family Allowances Fund administers a system of dependency allowances for wage earners in the lower economic brackets. Workers also receive unemployment and sickness benefits and accident and occupational disease compensation. Under the Children's Code of 1933, care of children is vested with the Children's Council, which operates kindergartens, school milk services and holiday camps and homes. The poor receive free medical attention and low-cost living quarters. In the early 1970s social security costs averaged about 7% of the GDP, among the highest in the world.

GLOSSARY

cantegrile: a shantytown on the outskirts of a city.
colegiado: a collegial executive as an alternative to a strong presidency, first suggested by President Batlle y Ordonez. It functioned as an organ of government between 1919 and 1934 and between 1952 and 1967.
estancia: a large ranch.
intendente: governor of a department.
junta departmental: departmental board set up under the 1966 constitution as a local legislature.
juzgado letrado: a single-judge lawyer court with original and appellate jurisdiction.
lema: a union of political factions, equivalent to a conventional political party.
pampero: a chilly wind blowing from the south in winter.
sub-lema: a political faction, usually revolving around a national leader.

zonda: a hot wind blowing from the north in the summer.

CHRONOLOGY (from 1945)

1945— Uruguay declares war on Germany.
1946— Tomas Berreta is elected president on the Colorado ticket.
1947— Berreta dies and is succeeded in office by Vice President Luis Batlle Barres.
1951— Andres Martinez Trueba is elected president on the Colorado ticket.
1952— The presidency is abolished and is replaced by a nine-man council known as the colegiado with an annually rotating presidency.
1955— Luis Batlle Barres is named chairman of the colegiado.
1956— Albert F. Zubaira is named chairman of the colegiado.
1958— In a historic upset the Blancos win power for the first time in the 20th Century; Luis Alberto de Herrera, 80-year old Conservative leader, is named chairman of the colegiado but dies within five weeks of taking office; Benito Nardone assumes leadership of the Blanco party and the state.
1959— Martin R. Etchegoyen is named chairman of the colegiado.
1961— Eduardo Victor Haedo is named chairman of the colegiado.
1962— Faustino Harrison is named chairman of the colegiado.
1963— Daniel Fernandez Crespo is named chairman of the colegiado.
1964— Luis Giannattasio is named chairman of the colegiado.
1965— Washington Beltran is named chairman of the colegiado.
1966— Alberto Heber Usher is named chairman of the colegiado. . . . In a national referendum the people vote to abandon the colegiado and to restore the presidency. . . . The Colorados win a decisive victory and return to office under the leadership of Oscar Gestido.
1967— Gestido dies and is succeeded in office by Vice President Jorge Pacheco Areco. . . . Tupamaros launch their insurgency.
1971— Juan Maria Bordaberry, the Colorado candidate, is elected president.
1973— Bordaberry suspends the constitution and all political activity; the General Assembly is replaced by a Council of State.
1976— The military ousts Bordaberry and promises a return to civilian government within 15 years; Vice President Alberto Demicheli is named provisional president. . . . Newly established Council of the Nation, functioning as an electoral college, elects Aparicio Mendez Manfredini as president for a five-year term.
1977— Supreme Court is abolished and is replaced by the Ministry of Justice.

1978— Gen. Gregario Alvarez is named commander in chief, head of the ruling junta and, in effect, the ruler of the country.

1980— Military-inspired new constitutional proposals are defeated in national referendum; Lt. Gen. Louis V. Queirolo is named head of the ruling junta.

1981— Gregorio Conrado Alvarez is named "transitional" president by the Council of the Nation.

1982— In nationwide balloting to select delegates to a constitutional convention, antimilitary delegates win a five-to-one majority.

1983— On return to civilian rule, the military initiates talks with the Multipartidaria; they break down over the extent of military oversight.

1984— Blanco leader Wilson Ferreira Aldunate is arrested on his return from exile.... Agreement is reached between the Multipartidaria and the military on the basic law governing restoration of civilian rule.

1985— President Alvarez resigns in February naming Supreme Court President Rafael Addiego Bruno as interim president.... In national elections Colorado candidate Julio Maria Sanguinetti Cairolo is elected president and his party wins slim plurality in both houses; Sanguinetti is inaugurated as president... All political prisoners are released; censorship is lifted; all restrictions imposed by the military on labor unions, the judiciary, and the university are removed.

BIBLIOGRAPHY (from 1960)

Alisky, Marvin, *Uruguay: A Contemporary Survey* (New York, 1969).

Argentina, Paraguay, Uruguay. Color film, 11 min. Coronet.

Finch, M. H., *A Political Economy of Uruguay Since 1870* (New York, 1981).

Gilo, Maria Esther, *The Tupamaro Guerrillas* (New York, 1972).

Pendle, George, *Uruguay* (London, 1965).

Uruguay. B&W film, 18 min. Producer: not available.

Weinstein, Martin, *Uruguay: The Politics of Failure* (Westport, Conn., 1975).

Willis, Jean, *Historical Dictionary of Uruguay* (Metuchen, N.J., 1974).

Young Uruguay. B&W film, 17 min. Universal.

OFFICIAL PUBLICATIONS

Accountant General, *Balance de Ejecucion Presupuestal* (Statement of Budget Performance) (annual).

———, *Movimientos de Fondos y sus Anexos* (Operations of Funds and their Annexes) (monthly).

Central Bank, *Boletin Estadistico* (Statistical Bulletin) (monthly).

———, *Estados de Cuentas Bancaries*, (Statement of Bank Accounts) (daily).

Municipal Accounting Offices, *Balances de Ejecucion Presupuestal* (Statements of Budgetary Performance) (monthly).

——— *Statistical Bulletin.*

——— *Indicators of Economic and Financial Activity.*

Social Security Movement Funds, *Movimientos de Fondos del Sector Seguro Social.*

Transport Ministry and Public Works, *Estados de Cuentas del Ministerio de Transporte y Obras Publicas* (Statement of Accounts of the Transport Ministry and Public Works) (monthly).

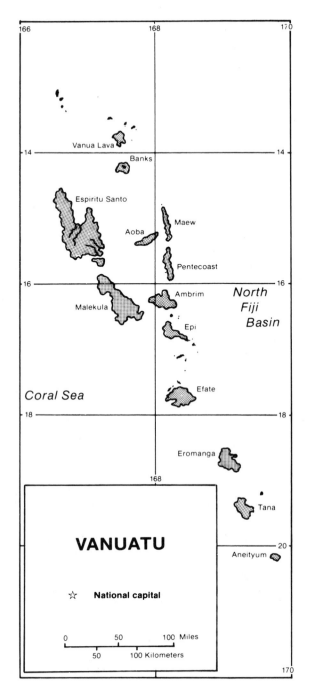

166   168   170

Vanua Lava

14

Banks

Espiritu Santo

Maew

Aoba

Pentecoast

16

Ambrim

*North
Fiji
Basin*

Malekula

Epi

Coral Sea

Efate

18

Eromanga

168

Tana

VANUATU

Aneityum

20

☆   **National capital**

0   50   100 Miles

50   100 Kilometers

170

Source: American Geographical Society

VANUATU

BASIC FACT SHEET

OFFICIAL NAME: Vanuatu (formerly The New Hebrides)

ABBREVIATION: VA

CAPITAL: Vila (on Efate Island)

HEAD OF STATE: President George Ati Sokomanu (from 1980)

HEAD OF GOVERNMENT: Prime Minister Father Walter Lini (from 1980)

NATURE OF GOVERNMENT: Parliamentary Democracy

POPULATION: 134,000 (1985)

AREA: 14,763 sq km (5,700 sq mi)

ETHNIC MAJORITY: Melanesian

LANGUAGES: English & French

RELIGION: Christiantiy

UNIT OF CURRENCY: Vatu ($1 = V106.210, 1985)

NATIONAL FLAG: A yellow Y with black borders dividing a field of dark red at the top and mint green at the bottom; the black triangle between the arms of the Y based on the hoist containing the national emblem in the middle.

NATIONAL EMBLEM: A figure in the form of a 9 with the inner end tapering; inside the 9 are two crossed branches.

NATIONAL ANTHEM: Not available

NATIONAL HOLIDAYS: July 29 (Independence Day); also, New Year's Day; Christmas and most other Christian festival days

NATIONAL CALENDAR: Gregorian

PHYSICAL QUALITY OF LIFE INDEX: Not available

DATE OF INDEPENDENCE: July 29, 1980

DATE OF CONSTITUTION: July 29, 1980

WEIGHTS & MEASURES: The metric system is in force

LOCATION & AREA

Vanuatu is a chain of 13 large and about 70 small islands stretching from south of the Solomon Islands to the east of New Caledonia with a combined land area of 14,763 sq km (5,700 sq mi). The Y-shaped archipelago whose open end is in the north has a total coastline of 2,528 km (1,570 mi). The 13 large islands are Vanua Lava, Banks, Espiritu Santo, Maew, Pentecost, Aoba, Malekula, Ambrim, Epi, Efate, Eromanga, Tana, and Aneityum. These are all high islands, quite mountainous and containing extensive rain forests. The other islands are of the coral atoll or almost atoll types. There are at least three active volcanoes: Tanna, Ambrym, and Lopevi.

The capital is Vila on Efate Island with a 1979 population of 9,971. The only other major town is Santo on Luganville with a population of 5,183.

WEATHER

The climate is quite hot and humid. Vila has an average year-round humidity of 83% and an average rainfall of about 2,300 mm (90 in). The winter months are fairly cool. The archipelago lies within the hurricane zone and suffers hurricane damage at least once or twice a year.

POPULATION

The population of Vanuatu is estimated at 134,000 on the basis of the last census taken in 1979 when the population was 111,251. The population is expected to reach 200,000 by 2000 and 300,000 by 2020.

The annual growth rate is estimated at 3.56% on the basis of a crude birth rate of 39.9 per 1,000. The population density is 11 per sq km (28 per sq mi).

At the time of the first census males constituted 53% of the population, an unusually high male coefficient. The two major cities, Vila, the capital, and Santo account for 23% of the population.

The government runs a family planning service as part of a U.N.-sponsored family health project.

Women have equal legal rights, but traditional culture has hampered their moving into leadership roles. The only female candidate for the National Parliament in 1983 was defeated by a small margin. Several women hold senior positions in the government bureaucracy.

ETHNIC COMPOSITION

Vanuatuans are basically Melanesian by race. Melanesians are an amalgam of Negritoid, Ainoid and Veddoid stock, but Negritoid physical characteristics remain predominant.

DEMOGRAPHIC INDICATORS (1985)

Population (000)	134.0
Annual growth rate (%) 1980-85	3.56
Density per sq km	11.0
% Urban	17.8%
Sex distribution (%)	
Male	53.10
Female	46.90
Age profile (%)	
0-14	45.4
15-29	27.5
30-44	15.0
45-59	7.7
60-74	3.4
Over 75	1.1
Population doubling time in years at current rate	25.0
Crude birthrate 1/000	39.9
Crude death rate 1/100	6.6
Total fertility rate	5.98
Gross reproduction rate	2.90
Net reproduction rate	2.70
Life expectancy at birth (Years)	
Males	64.7
Females	69.1

Non-Melanesians form about 8% of the population, about 3% are European or mixed European and the rest are Vietnamese. Chinese or other Pacific Islanders.

LANGUAGE

As a former British and French Condominium, both English and French are spoken in the country with English having a slight edge. A language calledBislama is spoken by those without formal English or French training. A variety of other Melanesian languages and dialects are also spoken on some islands but many of them are dying out.

RELIGION

Nearly 84% of Vanuatuans are Christians. Eight churches and denominations are represented, the strongest being Presbyterian, Anglican and Roman Catholic. The Roman Catholic diocese is based at Vila.

COLONIAL EXPERIENCE

The islands were governed since 1906 as an Anglo-French condominium under which each power was responsible for its own citizens and conducted its administration in its own language. The first representative assembly was not established until 1974, but thereafter the country made quick strides toward full independence following a timetable drawn up by the British and the French. In 1979 a government of internal autonomy was formed under Father Walter Lini. As the date of independence drew closer separatist movements became more militant; one, led by Jimmy Stevens in the island of Espiritu Santo, established a provisional government for a time until suppressed by British, French and Papua New Guinea troops.

The unrest did not delay the end of the British and French joint rule which took place at midnight on July 29, 1980 as the new nation of Vanuatu was born and the name New Hebrides was discarded.

CONSTITUTION & GOVERNMENT

Under the new constitution which took effect in 1980, Vanuatu is a republic with the president as head of state and the prime minister as head of government. The prime minister is also the leader of the majority party in the Representative Assembly and heads a cabinet consisting of a deputy prime minister and other ministers.

The constitution provides for periodical elections on the basis of universal adult suffrage.

CABINET LIST (1985)

President	George Ati Sokomanu
Prime Minister	*Father* Walter Lini
Deputy Prime Minister	Sethy J. Regenvanu
Minister of Agriculture, Fisheries & Forestry . . .	Jack Hopa
Minister of Education, Youth & Sports	Onneyn Tahi
Minister of Finance, Industry, Commerce & Tourism	Kalpokor Kalsakau
Minister of Foreign Affairs & Trade	Sela Molisa
Minister of Health	Willie Korisa
Minister of Home Affairs	Sethy J. Regenvanu
Minister of Justice	*Father* Walter Lini
Minister of Lands	Donald Kalpokas
Minister of Public Services	*Father* Walter Lini
Minister of Transport, Communications & Public Works	Albert Sande

FREEDOM & HUMAN RIGHTS

In terms of civil and political rights Vanuatu is classified as a partly-free country, with a rating of 4 in civil and political rights on a scale in which 1 is the highest and 7 the lowest.

CIVIL SERVICE

No information is available on the civil service on Vanuatu.

LOCAL GOVERNMENT

For purposes of local government the country is divided into four administrative districts with headquarters at Lenakel (Tanna), Vila, Lamap (Malekula) and Espiritu Santo. More than half the island have local councils and Vila and Santo have municipal councils.

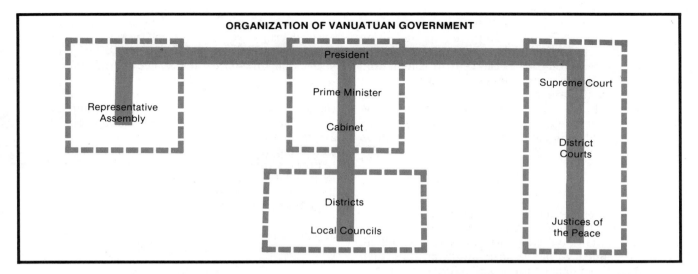

ORGANIZATION OF VANUATUAN GOVERNMENT

President

Prime Minister

Cabinet

Representative Assembly

Supreme Court

District Courts

Districts

Local Councils

Justices of the Peace

FOREIGN POLICY

As of the end of 1985 Vanuatu has not applied for membership in the United Nations or established diplomatic relations. At the time of the attempted secession of Espiritu Santo, Vanuatu accused U.S. and French interests of backing the revolt, but the transfer of power was smooth and helped to reconcile the differences between the new government and the former colonial powers.

As a nonaligned nation, Vanuatu has no diplomatic relations with either the United States or the Soviet Union, although ambassadors were exchanged with Cuba in 1983. Increasing Cuban influence has caused much concern both within the island's conservative groups and in other Pacific governments. In February 1981 the French ambassador to Vanuatu was expelled, following the deportation from New Caledonia of the VP secretary-general, who was due to attend an assembly of the New Caledonian Independence Front. France immediately withdrew aid to Vanuatu but, after relations between the countries improved in March, a V855.6 million aid agreement was signed and a new ambassador appointed. In June 1982 Vanuatu laid claim to the small, uninhabited islands of Matthew and Hunter, lying about 200 km (120 mi) south-east of Vanuatu's southern island of Aneityum, thus greatly increasing the size of the country's exclusive economic zone, although France disputed the claim.

PARLIAMENT

The national legislature is the Representative Assembly consisting of 39 members elected by universal adult suffrage for three-year terms. After the 1983 elections the Vanuaaku Pati gained 24 of the 39 seats, while the Union of Moderate Parties won 12 seats and Na-Griamel, Namake Aute and Fren Melanesia won 1 each.

POLITICAL PARTIES

The ruling party is the Vanuaaku Pati headed by Father Walter Lini, which was the most militant of the New Hebridean groups seeking independence. It also advocates the transfer of lands held by non-natives to the indigenes.

The principal opposition party is the Union of Moderate Parties, the successor to the former New Hebrides Federal Party, an alliance of predominantly francophone groups, including the Na-Griamel. Following the Na-Griamel inspired Santo rebellion, the moderate elements of the party regrouped under the present name winning 12 seats in Parliament. Other parties with parliamentary representation include the Na-Griamel, Namake Auti and Fren Melanesia; the first two represent Santo interests and the last represents Malakula Island interests. The Vanuatu Independent Alliance Party, another Santo-based group, failed to win any seats in 1983.

ECONOMY

Vanuatu is one of the lower middle income countries of the world with a free-market economy in which the private sector is dominant.

PRINCIPAL ECONOMIC INDICATORS

Gross National Product: $70 million (1980)
  GNP Per Capita: $585 (1980)
Consumer Price Index (1970=100): All items: 187.9 (December 1984) Food: 173.8 (December 1984)
Money Supply: V2.664 billion (June 1985)
Reserve Money:V998 million (June 1985)
Currency Outside Banks: V922 million (1984)
International Reserves: $8.09 million, of which foreign exchange $6.45 million (1984)

The Transitional Development Plan prepared by the Planning Office in 1978 provides for a balanced program of development. Vanuatu's first Five-Year Development Plan (1982-86), with a budget of

V11,000 million, aims at self-sufficiency for the economy within 10-15 years. Regional specialization is planned, with priority to be given to cocoa in the north, forestry and cattle in the central islands and coffee in the south. Industrial centers are to be expanded in Port Vila and on the islands of Tanna and Espiritu Santo. During 1979-81 Vanuatu received $37.6 million in foreign aid or $313.30 per capita. Between 1980 and 1983 Australia supplied $14.4 million in aid.

BUDGET

The fiscal year is the calendar year.

The national budget in 1983 consisted of revenues of V2.372 billion and expenditures of V2.876 billion. Of the revenues, 37.9% came from grant aid, 34.8% from import and export duties and 8.6% from non-tax revenues. Of the expenditures, more than 25% went to education. The total outstanding external debt in 1982 was $4.1 million.

FINANCE

The Vanuatuan unit of currency is the vatu, which is divided into 100 centimes. Coins are issued in denominations of 1, 2, 5, 10, 20 and 50 vatu and notes in denominations of 100, 500 and 1,000 vatu.

The exchange rate in 1985 was $1 = V106.210 and £1 = V118.95.

Vanuatu is developing rapidly as a tax haven and off-shore banking center because of the lack of direct taxation. There are 10 major international banks in Vila and two in Santo. In 1979 the estimated "invisible" export earnings from the use, by about 500 overseas companies, of the tax haven facility reached V450 million, thus making it the fourth largest source of foreign exchange. In Port Vila a financial center has developed within the framework of British company law, and a shipping register was established in 1981, offering a flag of convenience.

AGRICULTURE

Of the total land area of 1,476,300 hectares (3,647,937 acres) 95,000 hectares (234,745 acres) are cultivated, mostly on the coastal plains. Official policy favors the protection of Vanuatuan land ownership and to this end land has been reserved for specific native groups and cannot be alienated without official permission. Western concepts of buying and selling land are only slowly making headway, hampered by the lack of clear titles. Following the abolition of foreign-owned freehold title, upon the country's independence in 1980, a Land Leasing Act of April 1983 provided for secure leases of land from traditional owners and was expected to encourage many new projects.

Many of the larger plantations, however, are owned by Europeans although locally owned planta-tions account for some 60% of the production. The major cash crops are coconuts, cocoa, and coffee. In 1982 production consisted of 250,000 tons of coconuts and 48,102 tons of copra, 1,000 tons of corn, 1,000 tons of bananas, and 1,000 tons of cocoa.

Cattle are raised for grazing on coconut plantations, particularly on the islands of Efate and Espiritu Santo. The livestock population in 1982 consisted of 100,000 cattle, 69,000 pigs, and 8,000 goats. Pigs are raised mostly for ceremonial purposes.

Forests cover 16,000 hectares (39,536 acres). Those on the islands of Eromanga, Aneityum, and Efate have timber of commercial value but exploitation is impeded by lack of transportation facilities.

Deep sea fishing is carried on in adjacent waters by Japanese fishing boats. The catch, mostly tuna, is exported to the United States. The total catch was 2,819 tons in 1982.

INDUSTRY

There is very little manufacturing activity other than small factories canning meat, producing soda, and making bricks. A plant for freezing tuna is located on Santo.

ENERGY

Vanuatu does not produce any form of energy, but consumes 19,000 tons of coal equivalent or 150 kg (331 lb) per capita.

In 1984 electric power production was 20 million kwh or 154 kwh per capita.

LABOR

The economically active population is estimated at around 62,000, of which 76.8% is employed in agriculture, 10.8% in services, 1.9% in manufacturing, 2.2% in construction, 4.3% in trade and 2.6% in transportation and communications.

Vanuatuans are consistently averse to paid employment on a full time basis except on islands where the supply of agricultural land is insufficient. This has led to a shortage of workers which has been usually met by the importation of labor from Asia and other island groups from time to time. Some of these workers were permitted to remain as free citizens on the expiration of their contracts. Many Europeans are employed in teaching, planting, and trading. Females constitute 43.3% of the economically active population.

Industrial disputes are governed by the Joint Regulation 8 of 1957, and wages and hours and other conditions of employment by comprehensive legislation enacted in 1966. A minimum wage law was enacted in 1985. Vanuatu has a small but active trade union movement with the right to organize, strike, and bargain collectively. As of 1984, there were 21 registered trade unions and 6 employer associations. In February 1984, a labor council, called the Vanuatu Trade Union Congress, was formed and became a member of the International Confederation of Free Trade Unions.

FOREIGN COMMERCE

Vanuatu's foreign commerce consisted in 1984 of imports of $29.20 and exports of $43.30 million leaving a trade deficit of $14.10 million. Of the imports, food and beverages constitute 25%, machinery and transport equipment 15.9%, fuels 13.7%, textiles 8.5% and fish 1.5%. Of the exports, copra constitute 32.2%, frozen fish 31.2% and cocoa 2.6%. The major import sources are: Australia 33.8%, Japan 12.9%, New Zealand 10.6%, France 9.4% and Fiji 9.2%. The major export destinations are: Belgium 34.0%, the Netherlands 32.8%, New Caledonia 13.5%, France 12.0% and the United States 25.0%.

TRANSPORTATION & COMMUNICATIONS

The islands have no railways. There are 240 km (150 mi) of all-weather or sealed roads maintained by the public works department on seven of the larger islands. Most of the other islands have tracks usable by motor vehicles. These roads were used in 1984 by 3,087 passenger cars (28 per 1,000 inhabitants) and 242 commercial vehicles. Per capita passenger car ownership is 23 per 1,000 inhabitants.

The chief ports of Vila and Santo are linked by international shipping services with Australia, New Zealand, Hong Kong, Japan, North America and Europe. In 1982 these ports handled 172,000 tons of cargo. Smaller ships provide inter-island services. In 1982 12 ships were registered in Vanuatu with a GRT of 38,600.

The principal airports are Bauer Field at Vila and Pekoa at Santo. There are 28 other airfields of which 22 are usable. The national airline is Air Vanuatu, founded in 1981. Inter-island flights are provided by Air Melanesiae.

There are automatic telephone exchanges at Vila and Santo; outlying islands are served by a network of teleradio stations. In 1984 there were 2,400 telephones, or 2.4 per 100 inhabitants. There are 51 telex subscriber lines.

Vanuatu is a favorite destination of Australian tourists. In 1982, 32,180 tourists and 65,300 cruise-ship passengers called on the islands.

MINING

The principal mineral resource is manganese. The deposit, which occurs at Forare on the east coast of Efate, is reported to contain about 1 million metric tons of commercially valuable ore. The lease, held by a French company until 1970, was taken over by an Australian firm. Production in 1977 was 11,300 tons.

DEFENSE

Vanuatu has no standing army or defense force. During the short-lived revolt on Espiritu Santo, the government had to call in British and French troops in the beginning and later Papua New Guinean troops for military assistance.

EDUCATION

The national literacy rate is between 10 and 20%.

Until 1980, the school system was divided into two sectors; the British sector with 136 primary schools and five secondary schools and the French sector with 111 primary schools and two secondary schools. Education is neither universal nor compulsory. Schooling lasts for 13 years divided into six years of primary school, four years of middle school and three years of secondary school. Girls constitute 46% of primary enrollment and 38% of secondary enrollment. The national teacher-pupil rate is 1:22 at the primary level and 1:16 at the secondary level. Twenty-two primary schools receive grant-in-aid. The school year lasts from February through December. The language of instruction is English.

In 1982 educational expenditures totaled V627 million. This amount constituted 25% of the national budget.

EDUCATIONAL ENROLLMENT (1982)			
	Schools	Teachers	Pupils
First Level	244	934	22,244
Second Level	9	126	2,067
Vocational	2	40	351

Vanuatuans seeking higher education have to go abroad.

LEGAL SYSTEM

The judiciary comprises the Supreme Court at Vila, district courts and justices of the peace. Justices of the peace have only limited jurisdiction and often act as conciliators in civil and commercial matters. District courts consist of a single judge sitting in each of the four administrative districts.

There are four prisons and one rehabilitation center. The prisons are located at Vila and at each police headquarters. Sentences are automatically remitted by as much as one-third for good behavior; the average prison population is therefore not large and rarely exceeds seventy. The rehabilitation center is located at Pialulub.

LAW ENFORCEMENT

Headed by an officer who bears the title of commandant (after the French style) the Vanuatuan police force is an amalgam of the former British and French police corps. Below the headquarters level, the country is divided into four operating police districts with headquarters at Vila, Santo, Lakatoro (on Malekula) and Tana Island. The Vila district is commanded by an inspector, the Santo district by an assistant superintendant of police, the Lakatoro district by an NCO and the Tana district also by an NCO.

HEALTH

Medical care is provided through a network of 112 hospitals, health centers, clinics and dispensaries, of which the 21 full-fledged hospitals have 711 beds, or 1 bed per 153 inhabitants. These hospitals are staffed by 20 physicians, or 1 physician per 5,600 inhabitants. There are also two dentists and 255 nursing personnel. Of the hospitals 47.6% are state-run and 52.4% are run by private nonprofit agencies. The admissions/discharge rate is 970 per 10,000 inhabitants, the bed occupancy rate is 33.6% and the average length of hospital stay is 8 days.

PRINCIPAL HEALTH INDICATORS (1984)
Crude Death Rate (per 1,000): 6.6
Life Expectancy at Birth (Males): 64.7 (Female): 69.1
Infant Mortality Rate: 41 per 1,000 live births

The islands' most serious health problems include malaria, tuberculosis, leprosy filiariasis, and venereal diseases.

FOOD

The diet relies heavily on vegetarian foods, especially foods high in starch content. The staples are chosen from among roots and tubers, such as yams, sweet potatoes, taro, maniota (also called cassava, manioc or tapioca) and starch taken from the pith of sago palm tres. Protein is gained mostly from seafood and occasionally from fowl or small game.

The daily per capita availability of energy, protein, fats and carbohydrates is 2,477 calories, 65.1 grams, 94 grams and 311 grams respectively.

MEDIA & CULTURE

There are no privately owned daily or weekly newspapers. There are two fortnightlies and a quarterly journal published by Vanuaaku Pati.

There is no book publishing activity.

The government owned broadcasting station is Radio Vanuatu which broadcasts in English, French and Bislama to 15,500 radio receivers (155 per 1,000 inhabitants)

There are three cinemas with 1,300 seats or 13.4 seats per 1,000. Annual movie attendance was 100,000 or 1 per 1,000 inhabitants.

The nation's only public library at Vila has 12,000 volumes, or 36 volumes per 1,000 inhabitants.

SOCIAL WELFARE

No information is available on social welfare programs in Vanuatu.

CHRONOLOGY

1980— Vanuatu becomes an independent republic as the Anglo-French Condominium is terminated... Jimmy Stevens, backed by an American right-wing organization known as the Phoenix Foundation, leads a secessionist uprising on Espiritu Santo and proclaims an independent republic; the revolt is suppressed with the help of British, French, and Papua New Guinean troops.

1982— Vatu is introduced as national currency replacing the Australian dollar.

1983— The Land Leasing Act provides security for agricultural tenants.... Vanuatu establishes diplomatic relations with Cuba.... In national parliamentary election VP gains 24 seats and the Union of Moderate Parties 12.

BIBLIOGRAPHY

Deacon, Bernard, Malekula, *A Vanishing People in the New Hebrides* (New York, 1970).

Gourguechon, Charlene *Journey to the End of the World: A Three-Year Adventure in the New Hebrides* (New York, 1977).

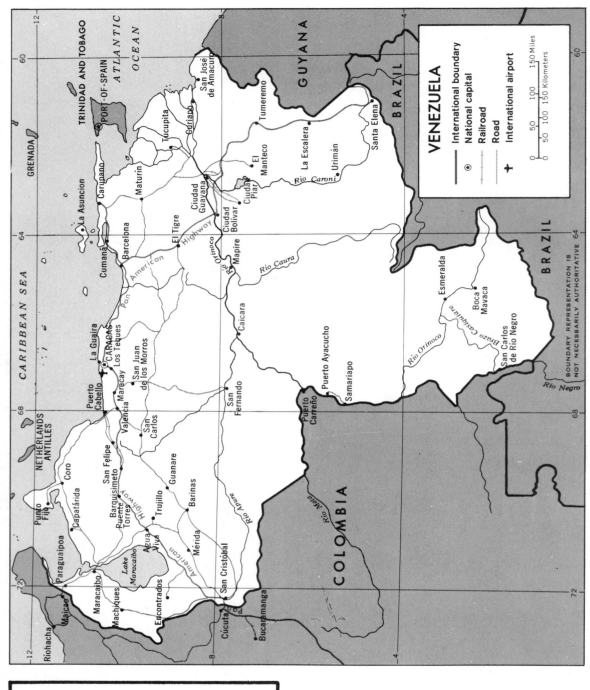

VENEZUELA

- International boundary
- ⊛ National capital
- Railroad
- Road
- ✈ International airport

0 50 100 150 Miles
0 50 100 150 Kilometers

BOUNDARY REPRESENTATION IS
NOT NECESSARILY AUTHORITATIVE

ATLANTIC OCEAN

CARIBBEAN SEA

GRENADA

NETHERLANDS ANTILLES

TRINIDAD AND TOBAGO

PORT-OF-SPAIN

GUYANA

BRAZIL

COLOMBIA

San José de Amacuro

Tumeremo

Santa Elena

La Escalera

Uriman

El Manteco

Río Caroní

Tucupita

Pedernales

Carúpano

La Asunción

Cumaná

Barcelona

Maturín

El Tigre

Ciudad Guayana

Ciudad Bolívar

Ciudad Piar

Orinoco

Mapire

Río Caura

Esmeralda

Boca Mavaca

San Carlos de Río Negro

Brazo Casiquiare

Río Orinoco

Río Negro

Pan American Highway

Caicara

Puerto Ayacucho

Samariapo

Puerto Carreño

San Fernando

CARACAS

La Guaira

Los Teques

San Juan de los Morros

Maracay

Valencia

Puerto Cabello

San Carlos

San Felipe

Coro

Capatárida

Punto Fijo

Paraguaipoa

Maracaibo

Machiques

Encontrados

Barquisimeto

Puente Torres

Agua Viva

Trujillo

Guanare

Barinas

Mérida

San Cristóbal

Cúcuta

Bucaramanga

Pan American Highway

Río Apure

Río Meta

Lake Maracaibo

Majagua

Riohacha

Río Negro

VENEZUELA

BASIC FACT SHEET

OFFICIAL NAME: Republic of Venezuela (Republica de Venezuela)

ABBREVIATION: VE

CAPITAL: Caracas

HEAD OF STATE & HEAD OF GOVERNMENT: President Jaime Lusinchi (from 1983)

NATURE OF GOVERNMENT: Parliamentary democracy

POPULATION: 17,810,000 (1985)

AREA: 912,050 sq km (352,143 sq mi)

ETHNIC MAJORITY: Mestizos

LANGUAGE: Spanish

RELIGION: Roman Catholicism

UNIT OF CURRENCY: Bolivar ($1=B7.5, August 1985)

NATIONAL FLAG: Tricolor of yellow, blue and red horizontal stripes. An arc of seven white stars appears on the central blue stripe.

NATIONAL EMBLEM: A shield divided into three parts, two upper and one lower. The upper left segment features a sheaf of 20 stalks of grain arranged in a fan against a red background. At the upper right a trophy of arms and national flags appears. The bottom half shows a white stallion prancing on a green ground under a light blue sky. On the top of the shield are two cornucopias, their stems crossed in saltire. A yellow, red and blue ribbon elaborately tied at the base proclaims: "19 de Abril 1810 Independencia" (the date of independence); "20 de Febrero de 1859 Federacion" (the date of the Federation of Venezuela; until 1953 the nation was known as the United States of Venezuela) and Republica de Venezuela.

NATIONAL ANTHEM: "Glory to the Brave People"

NATIONAL HOLIDAYS: July 5 (National Day, Independence Day); January 1 (New Year's Day); April 19 (Declaration of Independence and the Day of the Indian); May 1 (Labor Day); June 24 (Army Day and the Battle of Carabobo Day); July 24 (Bolivar's Birthday); October 12 (Columbus Day); December 17 (Death of Bolivar Day); all major Catholic festivals are observed including Epiphany, St. Joseph's Day, Assumption, All Saints' Day, Immaculate Conception, Ascension, Corpus Christi and the Holy Week.

NATIONAL CALENDAR: Gregorian

PHYSICAL QUALITY OF LIFE INDEX: 83 (up from 80 in 1976) (On an ascending scale in which 100 is the maximum. U.S. 95)

DATE OF INDEPENDENCE: July 5, 1811

DATE OF CONSTITUTION: January 23, 1961

WEIGHTS & MEASURES: The metric system is in force.

LOCATION & AREA

Venezuela is located on the northern coast of South America with an area of 912,050 sq km (352,143 sq mi) extending 1,487 km (924 mi) WNW to ESE and 1,175 km (730 mi) NNE to SSW. The national territory also includes 72 islands in the Antilles, the largest of which is Margarita in the Nueva Esparta group. The length of the coastline is 3,500 km (2,175 mi).

Venezuela shares its international land border of 4,793 km (2,976 mi) with three neighbors: Guyana (743 km, 462 mi); Brazil (2,000 km, 1,243 mi); and Colombia (2,050 km, 1,274 mi). The border with Colombia was the subject of an arbitration by the Spanish monarch (whose decision was rejected by Venezuela), and the two countries reached an agreement on the border line only by the Treaty of 1941. Two small problems remained unresolved in the mid-1970s: the change in the course of the Arauca River and offshore border beyond the Gujaira Peninsula. The border with Brazil is based on the Treaty of 1859 confirmed by the protocol of 1905, but in 1974 Venezuela claimed an additional 4,400 sq km (1,700 sq mi) of land based on a survey of the source of the Orinoco River. The most serious boundary problem is with Guyana, more than half of which west of the Essequibo River is claimed by Venezuela. In 1966 the dispute was submitted to a mixed Guyana-Venezuela Commission established by the Geneva Agreement. In 1970 by a protocol signed in Port of Spain, Trinidad, the two countries agreed on a 12-year moratorium on the issue, but all Venezuelan maps continue to show the disputed territory within the national borders.

The capital is Caracas with a 1981 population of 2,299,700. The other major urban centers are Maracaibo (929,000), Valencia (523,000), Barquisimeto (504,000), Maracay (255,134), San Cristobal (152,239), Cumana (119,751) and Ciudad Bolivar (103,728).

Venezuela is divided topographically into four regions: the Maracaibo Lowlands, the Northern Mountains, the Llanos or the Orinoco Lowlands and the Guyana Highlands.

The Maracaibo Lowlands comprise some 51,800 sq km (20,000 sq mi) of coastal plains starting in the narrow western strip between the Perija Mountains and the sea and broadening out eastward to embrace Lake Maracaibo. The region, which also includes the Paraguana Peninsula, is delimited on the west by the Sierra de Perija (also known as the Serrania de las Motilones) and on the south and east by the Cordillera de Merida and the Segovia Highlands. The Northern Mountains, which is sometimes called the Venezuelan Andes, extend from the Colombian border on the west to the Paria Peninsula on the east. The mountains are an extension of the Eastern Cordillera of the Andes, which divides near the border into the Sierra de Perija and the Cordillera de Merida. The latter broadens northward to form the Segovia Highlands. Between the Cordillera de Merida and the Colombian Andes is the Tachira Gap, which serves as the communication route between Colombia and Venezuela. At Pico Bolivar the Cordillera de Merida reaches the highest elevation in the country (5,000 meters, 16,400 ft). This region, known as the Roof of Venezuela, terminates at the Yaracuy Gap, while a coastal range continues to the tip of the Paria Peninsula. The coastal range comprises two parallel series of mountains. The fertile valleys between these two ranges contain some of the country's largest cities including Caracas, Maracay and Valencia. One part of the coastal range terminates at Cape Codera; the continuation of the other beyond Barcelona is called the Eastern, or Cumana, Highlands.

The Orinoco Lowlands are the great plains that extend from the Colombian border south of the Andes to the Atlantic, bounded by the Northern Mountains and the Orinoco River. This region, covering nearly 259,000 sq km (100,000 sq mi), is also called the llanos or plains and consists of pastureland, forests, sandy tablelands and swamps.

The Guyana Highlands, comprising 57% of the national territory, consists principally of plateaus between the Brazilian border and the Orinoco River. It includes the Gran Sabana in the southeast, a 36,000 sq km (14,000 sq mi) plateau covered with grass and scrub from which emerge massive flat-topped bluffs, some of them 2,750 meters (9,000 ft) above sea level. The Rio Churun tumbles over an opening in these cliffs to create the Angel Falls, at 979 meters (3,212 ft) the highest in the world. The Guyana Highlands is one of the least explored regions left in the world.

There are over 1,000 rivers in the country. About four-fifths of the country is drained by the Orinoco River, the world's eighth largest river and South America's second largest, after the Amazon. Rising in the Parima Mountains near the Brazilian frontier it is 2,815 km (1,750 mi) long and 21 km (13 ½ mi) across at its widest point. The river with its 436 tributaries is connected to the Amazon by a channel, the Casi-quiare, which joins up with the Rio Negro. The major tributaries of the Orinoco are the Apure and the Caroni. Among the rivers flowing from the Northern Mountains into Lake Maracaibo and the Caribbean Sea are the Tuy and the Unare.

Lake Maracaibo is the largest lake in South America and it is also accessible to ocean shipping. There are hundreds of other lakes in the country, of which only Lake Valencia is geographically significant.

WEATHER

Venezuela lies entirely within the tropic zone; climatic variations are determined primarily by elevations. The rainy months are customarily referred to as winter and the remainder of the year as summer.

Based on altitude Venezuela is divided into four climatic regions:

The tierra caliente comprising the coastal plains, the central prairies, the valleys and deltas of the Orinoco and the jungles with elevations of less than 800 meters (2,600 ft). Average temperatures in this zone range from 24.4°C to 34.4°C (76°F to 96°F).

The tierra templada comprising the lower mountain slopes and plateaus between 800 meters and 2,000 meters (2,600 ft and 6,500 ft) where the average temperatures range between 10°C and 25°C (50°F and 77°F). Caracas is located in this zone.

The tierra fria, the sub-alpine zone of the mountains with elevations from 2,000 meters to 3,000 meters (6,500 ft and 9,800 ft) with temperatures below 23.9°C (75°F) throughout the year.

The paramos above the timber line where the temperatures seldom rise above 14.4°C (58°F).

The rainy season lasts from May through November. The average annual rainfall varies from 140 cm (55 in.) in the Andes to 76 cm (30 in.) in Caracas and 28 cm (11 in.) at La Guaira on the coast. The heaviest rainfall occurs in the south and southeast and the least in the Paraguana Peninsula.

Venezuela lies to the south of the customary path of the hurricanes, and cyclones are therefore infrequent. Prevailing trade winds exert a significant influence on climatic conditions. These winds include the barines from the northwest, the calderetes from the south and a Caribbean wind called the Red Wind of Coro.

POPULATION

The population of Venezuela was estimated in 1985 at 17,810,000 on the basis of the last official census held in 1981, when the population was 14,516,735. The population is expected to reach 24.7 million by 2000 and 35.4 million by 2020.

The annual growth rate is 3.26% on the basis of an estimated annual birth rate of 35.2 per 1,000.

Although one-half of the country lies south and east of the Orinoco, it is inhabited by only 4% of the population, while 50% of the population is concentrated around Caracas and Valencia (the former capital of the country). The percentage distribution by regions on the basis of the 1971 census showed that 25.2% lived in Caracas, 15.4% in the North-Central Region, 13.8% in the West-Central (Llanos) Region, 12% in Zulia-Lake Maracaibo Region, 14.8% in Los Andes, 13.6% in the North-East Region, 3.9% in the Guyana Region and 1.8% in the south. The overall density of population is 20 per sq km (51.8 per sq mi).

Venezuela is the second most urbanized nation in South America (after Uruguay). In the mid-1980s nearly 86% of the population lived in urban areas, defined as localities with more than 2,500 inhabitants. Until the 1950s Venezuela was predominantly rural with two-thirds of the population classified as rural in the 1941 census. The shift to an overwhelmingly urban population took less than three decades beginning in 1950, when the urban population became for the first time in a majority. The rural population has remained unchanged in absolute numbers between 1941 and 1971, and the entire population growth during this period has been absorbed by the cities. In 1941 there were only two cities with over 20,000 inhabitants, while in 1971 there were 61 cities in this category and 11 had populations of over 100,000. Nearly one out of every five Venezuelans lives in the city of Caracas, and the city's annual growth rate is 5%. Nearly 42% of the population of Caracas live in slums and squatter settlements. The slum population has an annual growth rate of 5.4%.

The age profile shows 41% in the under-14 age group, 56% between 15 and 64 and 2.9% over 65. The sex ratio is perfectly balanced at 50:50.

Venezuela was among the first Latin American countries to open its doors to refugees and displaced persons after World War II. As a result nearly 1 million people are estimated to have entered the country between 1948 and 1958, although not all of them settled permanently. The policy of actively encouraging immigration was supended in 1959, and the flow of immigrants has slowed since then. About 30% of the foreign born in 1971 were Colombians, 25% Spaniards, 15% Italians and 14% Portuguese. The remainder includes an estimated 50,000 political refugees from Chile, Argentina and Uruguay. In addition to legal migrants, a large pool of illegal migrants from Colombia, estimated at over 500,000, are believed to be permanently residing in the country. Many are farm workers entering the country to work as harvest-hands and deciding to remain indefinitely. Because of the length of the border and the similarity in ethnic and physical characteristics, the illegal migration has proved impossible to control, but it remains a matter of concern for both countries.

The constitution prohibits discrimination on the basis of sex and accords women and children "special protection" in the workplace. Women workers receive extensive maternity leave benefits, and laws limit their amount of involuntary overtime. Women are heavily represented in many of the professions but

DEMOGRAPHIC INDICATORS (1985)	
Population, total (in 1,000)	17,810.0
Population ages (% of total)	
0-14	41.0
15-64	56.0
65+	2.9
Youth 15-24 (000)	3,753
Women ages 15-49 (000)	4,525
Dependency ratios	78.5
Child-woman ratios	673
Sex ratios (per 100 females)	100.0
Median ages (years)	19.2
Marriage Rate (per 1,000)	7.0
Divorce Rate (per 1,000)	0.4
Average size of Household	5.3
Decline in birthrate (%, 1965-83)	−14.6
Proportion of urban (%)	85.70
Population density (per sq. km.)	20
per hectare of arable land	0.89
Rates of growth (%)	3.26
urban %	3.8
rural %	0.2
Natural increase rates (per 1,000)	29.6
Crude birth rates (per 1,000)	35.2
Crude death rates (per 1,000)	5.6
Gross reproduction rates	2.11
Net reproduction rates	2.0
Total fertility rates	4.33
General fertility rates (per 1,000)	144
Life expectancy, males (years)	65.1
Life expectancy, females (years)	70.6
Life expectancy, total (years)	67.8
Population doubling time in years at current rate	25
% Illegitimate births	53.4

continue to be underrepresented in the political and economic sectors and differences still exist in wage and employment opportunities. Overall there is a firm trend toward greater equality for women. Recent reforms in Venezuelan laws have been designed to promote greater economic rights for women.

Women are increasingly active in all political parties, professions, public administration and the judiciary. About a dozen are members of the Chamber of Deputies, including one who is the assistant leader of the AD parliamentary faction and another who is a vice president of a permanent committee. Both major political parties have women members on the national executive committees.

Family planning became a national priority after the election of President Carlos Andres Perez in 1973. The private Association of Family Planning was integrated with the Ministry of Health in 1974. About 140 hospitals and clinics offer free family-planning services and the number of acceptors is estimated at 86,000. Expenditures on family-planning programs in 1975 totaled $4 million, or $0.34 per capita. Official policy in this area has not been opposed by the Roman Catholic hierarchy, although it remains opposed to abortion and sterilization. Abortion is permitted only in medically approved cases and after the authorization of a committee of doctors.

ETHNIC COMPOSITION

Since 1926 ethnic background has been excluded from the census questionnaire; so the ethnic composition of the country can be determined only in approximate terms. In the mid-1970s mestizos are believed to constitute the majority, with 67% of the population, while the whites, Negroes and Indians make up the remainder, accounting for 21%, 10% and 2%, respectively. Through a process known as mestizaje, which involves the cultural as well as the genetic fusion of the white, black and Indian races, ethnic distinctions are bound to decrease in course of time and the percentage of mestizos in the population to increase.

The Indians occupy a special niche in the national ethnic structure, although their numbers are reported to be decreasing with every census. A 1970 source estimated their number at 36,000, but their decline is so rapid that many of the tribes are reported to have become extinct since then and few of them are expected to survive the end of the century. The Indian population is divided into at least 40 groups speaking as many as 170 languages and dialects. They are primarily concentrated in the Amazonas territory, although smaller numbers are to be found in the states of Zulia, Bolivar, Apure and Sucre. A few of them have adopted Roman Catholicism, but otherwise they have retained their traditional culture. The 1961 constitution defines the government's responsibilities toward the Indians and extends to them special protection. The largest of Venezuelan Indian tribes are the Guajiro, Achagua, Arawak, Caberre, Caracas, Chaima, Chake, Warrau, Karinya, Makiritare, Piaroa, Motilones, Cumanagoto, Gandule, Guahibo, Guayupe, Jirajira, Marakapan, Mariche, Omegua, Otomac, Palenque, Paria, Quiriquire, Saliva, Teques, Timote, Tumuzu and Zorca.

The number of aliens legally residing in the country is estimated at over 1 million, including 134,786 Colombians, 236,830 Spaniards, 220,219 Italians and 98,276 Portuguese.

In terms of ethnic and linguistic homogeneity, Venezuela is ranked 107th in the world with 89% homogeneity (on an ascending scale in which North and South Korea are ranked 135th with 100% homogeneity and Tanzania is ranked first with 7% homogeneity).

LANGUAGE

The official language is Spanish, which is spoken by virtually the entire population outside of isolated Indian groups.

RELIGION

Nearly 94% of the population are baptized Catholics, and Roman Catholicism functions as the national religion, although there is no constitutional provision for a state religion. Relations between state and church are harmonious and are reinforced by a number of common activities. Through a special division of the Ministry of Justice, the government contributes to the operating expenses of the Church, such as the salaries of the hierarchy and construction and repair of religious buildings. The Church also has a dominant position in education and the media. There are four Catholic radio and television stations, and the Church's daily newspaper, La Religion, is one of the leading newspapers in Caracas. The government also supports and finances the Church's mission work among the Indians. As in other parts of Latin America, the Church's growing social consciousness and concern for the problems of injustice and economic disparities has led it to adopt a progressive stand on many political issues.

The primate of Venezuela is the archbishop of Caracas, who is also a cardinal. There are five other metropolitan sees at Barquisimeto, Ciudad Bolivar, Maracaibo, Merida and Valencia.

Religious minorities include Protestants who make up some 2% of the population and several thousand Jews.

COLONIAL EXPERIENCE

Venezuela was under Spanish rule from 1498, when it was discovered by Christopher Columbus on his third voyage. The country received its name, meaning "Little Venice," because the native huts built on stilts over the water reminded Alonso de Ojeda, who sailed into the Gulf of Venezuela in 1499, of Venice. From 1528 until 1546 the territory was under the control of the Weslers, a German banking firm, in settlement of a debt owed by Charles I of Spain. Indian resistance to the Spanish rule continued until 1580, when the natives were decimated by smallpox. After two unsuccessful revolts against Spain, Francisco de Miranda, "El Precursor," the leader of the Congress of Cabildos, declared the independence of the country in 1811 only to be overthrown by royalist factions, captured and sent to die in a dungeon in Cadiz. The cause of independence was taken up by Simon Bolivar, who issued his famous declaration calling for a war to the death against all Spaniards. In 1813 Bolivar entered Caracas as the Liberator and established the Second Republic. The Second Republic was also short-lived, and in 1814 Bolivar was driven out of the country by the royalists. After regrouping his forces in Haiti, Bolivar launched a new attack on eastern Venezuela and, with the help of Jose Antonio Paez, freed part of the country and proclaimed the Third Republic at Angostura in 1819. The end of the war of independence came with Bolivar's decisive victory at Carabobo in 1821; the death toll in the 10-year war was over 300,000, representing one-third of the population. The Cucuta Congress proclaimed the union of Venezuela and Colombia in the Republic of Gran Colombia, but the new republic disintegrated in a power struggle between Paez, the military commander of the Venezuela region, and Francisco de Paula Santander, the Colombian leader. In 1829 Paez declared Venezuela an independent state.

CONSTITUTION & GOVERNMENT

The legal basis of the government is the constitution of 1961, the nation's 26th, which established a federal republic with a strong presidential form of government. Six articles and 74 clauses deal with basic human rights and freedoms. Private enterprise and private ownership are protected, but the state is charged with the ultimate responsibility for the national economy and social welfare.

RULERS OF VENEZUELA
(from 1945)

1941 (May) to 1945 (October)
    Isias Medina Angarita
1945 (October) to 1948 (February)
    Romulo Betancourt
1948 (February to November)
    Romulo Gallegos
1948 (November) to 1950 (November)
    Carlos Delgado Chaulbaud
1950 (November) to 1952 (December)
    German Suarez Flammerich
1952 (December) to 1958 (January)
    Marcos Perez Jimenez / Dictator
1958 (January to November)
    Wolfgang Larrazabal
1958 (November)
    Edgar Sanabria
1959 (February) to 1964 (February)
    Romulo Betancourt
1964 (February) to 1969 (March)
    Raul Leoni
1969 (March) to 1974 (March)
    Rafael Caldera Rodriguez
1974 (March) to 1979 (March)
    Carlos Andres Perez Rodriguez
1979 (March) to 1984 (February)
    Luis Herrera Campins
1984 (February) —
    Jaime Lusinchi

The executive branch is headed by the president, who is elected by universal suffrage for five-year terms. He is not eligible for reelection until 10 years have elapsed from the last day of his previous term. The president wields considerable powers in practice: he appoints and removes members of the Council of Ministers as well as the governors of the states, territories and the Federal District; conducts foreign relations; convenes extraordinary sessions of the Congress; and administers national finance. He has the right to introduce bills and defend them before Congress. As the commander in chief of the armed forces, he is charged with the defense of the national territory. His most important power is that of declaring a state of emergency (or state of siege) and suspending constitutional guarantees in the event of a national crisis. The declaration of a state of emergency must be authorized subsequently by the Congress or by its steering committee, when the Congress is not in session, within 90 days. The only constitutional checks on

---

CABINET LIST (1985)

President . . . . Jaime Lusinchi
Minister of Agriculture
    & Livestock . . . . Felipe Gómez Alvarez
Minister of Coordination
    and Planning . . . . Leopoldo Carnevali
Minister of Culture . . . . .Ignacio Iribarren Borges
Minister of Development . . . . .Héctor Hurtado Navarro
Minister of Education . . . . .Luis Manuel Carbonell
Minister of Energy & Mines . . . . *Acting* Hernán Anzola
Minister of Environment
    & Natural Resources . . . . .Juan Francisco Otaola
Minister of Finance . . . . Manuel Azpúrua Arreaza
Minister of Foreign Affairs . . . . Simón Alberto Consalvi
Minister of Health
    & Social Welfare . . . . Otto Hernández Pieretti
Minister of Interior . . . . Octavio Lepage Barretto
Minister of Justice . . . . .José Manzo González
Minister of Labor . . . . Simón Antoni Paván
Minister of Natl. Defense . .Andrés Eduardo Brito Martínez
Minister of Transport
    & Communications . . . . Juan Pedro Del Moral
Minister of Urban Development . . . . Rafael Martín Guédez
Minister of Youth . . . . Milena Sardi de Selle
Minister of State for Guyana
    Development . . . . .Leopoldo Sucre Figarella
Minister of State for Science
    & Technology . . . . .Tulio Arends
Minister of State, President of the
    Investment Fund . . . . Carlos Rafael Silva
Minister & Adviser to the Presidency
    for International Economic
    Affairs . . . . Manuel Pérez Guerrero
Minister, Secretariat
    of the Presidency . . . . .Carmelo Lauría Lesseur
Governor,
    Federal District . . . . . . Miguel Angel Contreras Laguado

---

his power are congressional control over the budget and the congressional approval required for certain appointments, contracts with foreign states and declarations of states of emergency. The constitution does not provide for a vice president; in case of a vacancy the president of the Congress acts as chief executive until Congress, meeting in a joint session within 30 days, elects a new president by secret vote.

As head of government the president presides over the Council of Ministers. Ministers are appointed by and removed by the president but are accountable to Congress, before which they may be called upon to explain their policies.

Suffrage is universal and compulsory over age 18. The penalty for not voting is the loss of certain civil rights, but these penalties have not been strictly enforced. Elections are held every five years, and there are no by-elections or mid-term elections. The president is elected by a simple majority; congressional representatives are elected by a simple majority; congressional representatives are elected on the basis of a system of proportional representation. Voters cast their ballots for lists rather than candidates. Voting is by colored ballot slips to enable illiterates to exercise

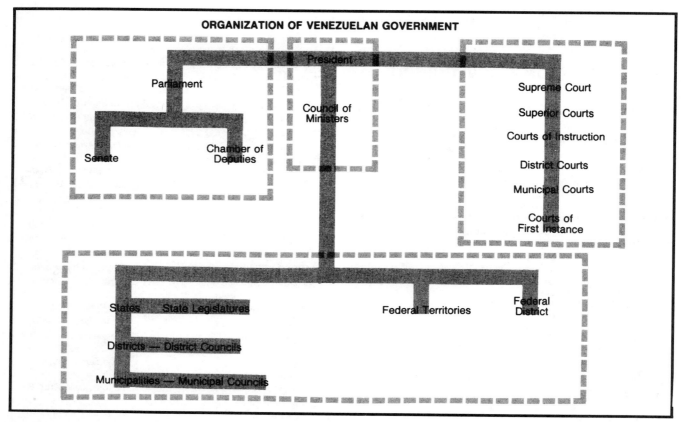

ORGANIZATION OF VENEZUELAN GOVERNMENT

their franchise. Each party is preassigned a specific color so that voters in practice choose colors in the act of voting.

Elections are supervised by the Consejo Supremo Electoral (CSE, Supreme Electoral Council), a 13-member body chosen every two years by the Congress in which no political party may have a majority. The four elections since 1958 have been characterized by a high voter turnout, averaging about 90% of eligible voters.

In a continent dominated by right-wing military governments, Venezuela has managed to achieve both stability and freedom within a left-of-center democratic framework. Threats to the nation's internal security are fewer than at any previous time in its history. The activities of dissidents and guerrilla organizations have very little political impact, and even student groups and activists seem to have lost their revolutionary fervor. The country's new economic affluence has accelerated a maturing of political attitudes and traditions.

FREEDOM & HUMAN RIGHTS

In terms of civil and political rights, Venezuela is classified as a free country with a rating of 1 in political rights and 2 in civil rights (on a descending scale in which 1 is the highest and 7 the lowest in rights).

In 27 years of uninterrupted democratic experience Venezuela has developed into a free and pluralistic society with the resiliency to adapt to massive social changes. It has also repeatedly demonstrated its ability to effect peaceful transfer of power between opposing political parties while maintaining a clear commitment to human rights, not only at home but also in other Latin American countries. Individual liberties are reinforced and protected by an independent judiciary, a free press, and an open and competitive political system. It has successfully co-opted former advocates of violence into the mainstream of politics. The president of the country's third largest party is a former guerrilla who has renounced violence for the pursuit of legitimate politics. There are no prisoners of conscience since the implementation of President Herrera's amnesty program. There are occasional confrontations between the government and the media, but restrictions on media freedoms are rare and generally do not seem to bother the media very much. In many areas, Venezuela is a model nation for the defenders of human rights.

Human rights violations, when they occur, tend to be well-publicized and investigated. Venezuela is one of the most active participants in international human rights forums and is noted within the hemisphere as a proponent of civil liberties and democratic rule. The principal focus of human rights debate within Venezuela is on deficiencies in the country's judicial system; delays in the trials of detainees are frequent, and there have been allegations of improper influence in the courts. Inadequate prison conditions have been the subject of recent official reports.

Restrictions on property rights based on sex, religion or social status do not exist, but there are some restrictions on ownership of business property based on nationality.

CIVIL SERVICE

The constitution provides for a career civil service and sets standards for recruitment, promotion and discipline. Despite many attempts at reform, recruitment is still based on political patronage. In 1969 President Rafael Caldera set up a Commission on Public Administration to prepare an overall administrative reform plan. The commission's plan, submitted in 1972, is being implemented in a piecemeal fashion. The total strength of the civil service is 300,000, including those employed in autonomous agencies.

LOCAL GOVERNMENT

For administrative purposes Venezuela is divided into 20 states, two federal territories, the Federal District and 69 island dependencies. The states are subdivided into 156 districts and these, in turn, into 613 municipalities.

The constitution describes the states as "autonomous and equal political entites," but despite its federal form (until 1953 the Republic of Venezuela was called the United States of Venezuela), the government is unitary in structure and authority. Furthermore, the 20 state governors are appointed by the president and thus function as agents of the central government. The states have only restricted financial powers and are dependent on the central government for most of their revenues.

STATES OF VENEZUELA

State	Capital	Governor
Anzoategui	Barcelona	Guillermo Alvares Bajares
Apure	San Fernando	Rafael Felice Bolivar
Aragua	Maracay	Jose Ignacio Arnal
Barinas	Barinas	Jose Napoleon Paredes
Bolivar	Ciudad Bolivar	Alberto Palazzi
Carabobo	Valencia	Raul Gomez
Cojedes	San Carlos	Jose Herrera La Riva
Falcon	Coro	Raul Valeri Salvatierra
Guarico	San Juan	Facundo Camero
Lara	Barquisimeto	Carlos Zapata Escalona
Merida	Merida	Reinaldo Chalbaud Zerpa
Miranda	Los Teques	Jose Rafael Unda Briceno
Monagas	Maturin	Pablo Morillo Robles
Nueva Esparta	La Asuncion	Pedro Luis Briceno
Portuguesa	Guanare	Manuel Ricardo Martinez Azcu
Sucre	Cumana	Carmelo Rios
Tachira	San Cristobal	Pedro Contreras Pulido
Trujillo	Trujillo	Dore Maldonado De Falcon
Yaracuy	San Felipe	Juan Jose Caldera
Zulia	Maracaibo	Gilberto Urdaneta Besson
Distrito Federal	Caracas	Dr.Enrique Perez Olivares
Federal Territories:		
Amazonas	Puerto Ayacucho	Luis Jose Gonzalez Herrera
Delta Amacuro	Tucupita	Simplicio Hernandez

Popular representative institutions at the local level include the unicameral state legislatures and district councils. The district councils, whose membership varies according to the size of the district, are headed by elected chairmen holding office for one-year terms. Council members are elected at the same time as national officials for five-year terms. Similarly, the municipalities have elected municipal councils. These councils have no decision-making powers but function as instruments for the implementation of the decisions of the central government.

FOREIGN POLICY

As one of the few functioning democracies in Latin America, Venezuela has emerged as the spokesman of progressive countries in the Western Hemisphere. It has also become the leading advocate of the so-called New Economic Order, whereby developing countries are seeking economic independence by acquiring full control over their natural resources and by obtaining a stronger bargaining position vis-a-vis the industrialized countries in the formulation of international economic policies. The pursuit of these goals has been facilitated by Venezuela's growing economic clout as a powerful OPEC member.

Much of Venezuela's wealth is being used to enlarge its sphere of influence in the Central American and Caribbean region. It has extended substantial credit and development loans and has also channeled some of its resources through the Central American Common Market and the Caribbean Common Market. It was estimated in 1974 that Venezuela recycled abroad more than one-third of its trade surplus, or about one-tenth of its total GNP. On average, between $2 and $3 billion are being committed annually to the Central American and Caribbean region. The extent of these investments led Prime Minister Eric Williams of Trinidad & Tobago to state that the "Caribbean is being recolonized, this time by Venezuela." A related aspect of this policy is Venezuela's active participation in regional organizations, such as the Andean Common Market (ANCOM), the Latin American Economic System (SELA),the Latin American Free Trade Association (LAFTA) and the Contadora group. Regional integration through these organizations has become one of the primary goals of Venezuelan foreign policy. Significantly, the United States was not invited to join SELA, among whose objectives are the formulation of a specifically Latin American position on international economic issues, creation of Latin American multinational enterprises, protection of Latin American commodity prices, financing of Latin American development projects and the pooling of technological and scientific information and capability.

Venezuela's relations have been traditionally weakest with its neighbors in South America. In the 1960s it broke off relations with a number of Latin American countries because of the so-called Betancourt Doctrine, under which diplomatic relations were suspended with any country whose government came to power through extraconstitutional means. This policy was abandoned under President Rafael Caldera but continues to affect Venezuela's relations with the right-wing dictatorships on the continent, most recently in 1976 when relations with Uruguay were suspended. Venezuela also has made little progress in resolving border disputes with two of its neighbors: Guyana and Colombia. On the other hand, President Perez was one of the most ardent supporters President Omar Torrijos' efforts to secure sovereignty over the Panama Canal.

Venezuela was one of the harshest critics of Castro's Cuba and led the successful campaign in the OAS to impose an economic and diplomatic embargo against it in 1964. Ten years later Venezuela led another campaign in the OAS to lift the sanctions it had helped impose, citing changed conditions in Cuba. This reversal of policy also reflected Venezuela's increasing self-confidence and sense of security as well as renewed interest in regional politics. Diplomatic relations with Cuba also were resumed in 1974. However, by 1976 new strains appeared in these relations over Cuba's intervention in Angola and the alleged involvement of two Venezuelans in the sabotage of a Cuban airliner in the Caribbean.

The most important bilateral relationship is that with the United States. The core of this relationship is economic for the United States as the largest customer of Venezuelan oil. Nevertheless, there is a strong anti-Yankee undercurrent in national politics, as was demonstrated when Vice President Richard M. Nixon's motorcade was stoned at Caracas in 1958 (one of Nixon's "six crises"). Current relations between the U.S. and Venezuela are good.

Venezuela and the United States are parties to 31 agreements and treaties covering agricultural commodities, amity, atomic energy, aviation, customs, defense, economic and technical cooperation, extradition, investment guaranties, judicial assistance, mapping, maritime matters, air force, army, and naval missions, narcotic drugs, pacific settlement of disputes, Peace Corps, telecommunications, trade and commerce and visas.

Venezuela joined the U.N. in 1945; its share of the U.N. budget is 0.32%. It is a member of 13 U.N. organizations and 36 other international organizations.
U.S. Ambassador in Caracas: (Vacant)
U.K. Ambassador in Caracas: M. I. Newington
Venezuelan Ambassador in Washington, D.C.: Valentin Hernandez
Venezuelan Ambassador in London: Jose Luis Salcedo-Bastardo

PARLIAMENT

The bicameral National Congress (Congreso Nacional) comprises a Senate and a Chamber of Deputies, both elected for five-year terms by direct popular vote.

The Senate consists of two members elected from each of the 20 states and the Federal District by direct vote. Additional members (three in 1983) are selected by a system of proportional representation to ensure seats for minority parties that receive a certain per-

centage of the total vote. Former presidents, if they were popularly elected and served more than one-half of their terms, are ex officio members of the Senate. Senate membership was 47 in 1985.

The Chamber of Deputies consists of 196 deputies, apportioned among the states, territories and the Federal District at the rate of one per 63,000 voters and one more if the remainder is over 32,000. Each state is entitled to a minimum of two deputies. Because there are no by-elections, each congressman has an alternate, named by his party, to serve in his stead in case he dies, resigns, is incapacitated or is removed.

The Congress is in session from March 2 to July 6 and from October 1 to November 30, except in election years when there is a single session from March 2 to August 15. Special sessions may be called by the president and joint sessions may be held to break deadlocks or to authorize the declaration of a state of emergency.

Bills may be introduced in either house but must be passed by both. Bills may also be introduced by the executive branch, the Supreme Court and by the petition of a minimum of 20,000 voters. The president has the authority to override legislation and the Congress to override his veto. The Senate is responsible for the initiation of bills relating to international agreements and treaties and for the approval of major presidential appointments. Much of the legislative work is done through committees, of which the lower house has 11 and the upper house 10. The most important of these is the delegated or steering committee created by the constitution. Made up of the president and the vice president of the Congress and 21 other members on the basis of party representation, the committee serves as the legislative watchdog between sessions of Congress. It also has the power to convene extraordinary sessions of Congress.

PARTY POSITION IN CONGRESS (1984)
Senate
President: Reinaldo Leandro Mora

Party	Seats
Acción Democrática (AD)	27
Partido Social-Cristiano (COPEI)	16
Movimiento al Socialismo (MAS)	2
Unión Republicana Democrática (URD)	2
Total	**47**

Chamber of Deputies
President: Leonardo Ferrer (Copei)

Party	Seats
Acción Democrática (AD)	109
Partido Social-Cristiano (COPEI)	60
Movimiento al Socialismo (MAS)	10
Unión Republicana Democrática (URD)	8
Opinión Nacional (OPINA)	3
Movimiento de Izquierda Revolucionaria (MIR)	2
Partido Comunista de Venezuela (PCV)	2
Movimiento de Integración Nacional (MIN)	1
Nueva Alternativa (NA)	1
Total	**196**

POLITICAL PARTIES

In recent years Venezuela has been moving in the direction of a two-party system and away from fragmented political groupings. The senior and the larger of these two parties is the Accion Democratica (AD). AD was founded in 1937; it went underground during Perez Jimenez's dictatorship but emerged in 1958 to win the presidency. In its early years, AD was a militant revolutionary party but the years in exile until 1958 mellowed its ideology until it espoused a form of democratic socialism similar to that of the British Labor Party. It is fully committed to representative democracy, a mixed economy, agrarian reform, rapid economic development and social welfare. It is also strongly anti-Communist and pro-Western. The party's organizational structure is headed by an executive committee below which are three national bodies, each with a progressively larger membership: the steering committee, a disciplinary tribunal and a national convention.

The other leading party is the Comite Organizado Pro Elecciones Independientes (COPEI), also known as the Christian Socialist Party, a moderately conservative and Catholic-oriented party founded in 1946. Its original ideological base in Catholic doctrine and its geographic base in the Andean southwest have expanded until it currently attracts professionals, farmers, labor and urban intellectuals. COPEI has also been more pragmatic than most other Latin American Christian Democratic parties and has espoused a broad array of popular causes such as agrarian reform, economic nationalism and a more equitable distribution of income. The very catholicity of its programs has led to tensions between its right and left wings.

Fringe parties in the political system include:
- National Opinion, founded in 1961.
- New Generation, a right-wing group, founded in 1979.
- National Redemption, founded in 1983.
- National Integration Movement, formed in 1977.
- Movement to Socialism. Originally a radical left-wing group that split from the Communist Party, it subsequently became Eurocommunist and in 1983 became democratic socialist rather than Marxist.
- Movement of the Revolutionary Left. A radical urban terrorist guerrilla group in the 1960s, it entered legitimate politics in 1973 by capturing a chamber seat. In 1980 it split into pro-Moscow and anti-Moscow factions.
- Alliance for the Unity of the People. An electoral alliance of leftist parties, including the pro-Moscow Union for the New Alternative, Communist Party of Venezuela, Democratic Republican Union, People's Electoral Movement, the People's Advance, Revolutionary Action Group, Socialist League, Radical Cause and the Socialist Fatherland Movement.
- The clandestine guerrilla groups of the 1960s have now died out except for the Maoist America Silva Guerrilla Front of the Red Flag and the Agrimiro Ga-

baldon Revolutionary Command. One of the best known guerrila groups, the Armed Forces of National Revolution, turned into the Party of the Venezuelan Revolution.

ECONOMY

Venezuela is one of the 35 upper-middle-income countries of the world with a free-market economy in which the dominant sector is private.

President Jaime Lusinchi came to power in 1983 on a platform of returning the country to a more disciplined style of economic management, emphasizing social projects rather than expansion of the state industrial sector. He has succeeded in a number of areas. Less has been achieved however, in instilling confidence in the private sector and getting social projects off the drawing board, and inflation has become a political constraint on carrying some policies much further.

PRINCIPAL ECONOMIC INDICATORS

Gross National Products: $70.820 billion (1983)
GNP Annual Growth Rate: 3.5% (1973-82)
Per Capita GNP: $4,100 (1983)
Per Capita GNP Annual Growth Rate: 0.0% (1973-82)

Gross Domestic Product: B290.49 billion (1984)
GDP at 1980 Prices: B240.83 billion
GDP Deflator (1980=100): 120.6
GDP Annual Growth Rate: 2.5% (1973-83)
Per Capita GDP: B17,723 (1984)
Per Capita GDP Annual Growth Rate: 1.1% (1970-81)

Income Distribution: 15% of the national income is received by the bottom 40%; 48% of the national income is received by the top 20%.

Percentage of Population in Absolute Poverty: 5

Consumer Price Index (1970=100):
All Items: 373.1 (March 1985)
Food: 602.8 (March 1985)

Wholesale Price Index (1970=100):
General: 175.0 (February 1985)
Farm Products: 192.0 (February 1985)

Average Annual Rate of Inflation: 11.7% (1973-83)

Money Supply: B81.449 billion (March 1985)
Reserve Money: B54.803 billion (March 1985)

Currency in Circulation: B15.132 billion (1984)

International Reserves: $8.901 billion, of which foreign exchange reserves were $7.716 billion (1984)

Development planning is the responsibility of the Central Office of Coordination and Planning (Oficina Central de Coordinacion y Planificacion, CORDIPLAN). CORDIPLAN's Five-Year National Plan, 1976-80, provided for an investment of B119 billion, 35% of which was supplied by the government. Petroleum and iron are designated as the development bases and agriculture, energy and heavy industry as the priority sectors. The plan also aimed at a more equitable distribution of wealth and a massive program of public works. The projected annual economic growth was 8.3%. Major development projects include the establishment of an aircraft industry, a zinc refinery, four petrochemical complexes, a new railway sys-

BALANCE OF PAYMENTS (1983) (million $)	
Current Account Balance	4,427
Merchandise Exports	14,571
Merchandise Imports	−6,409
Trade Balance	8,162
Other Goods, Services & Income	+2,770
Other Goods, Services & Income	−6,294
Other Goods, Services & Income Net	−3,524
Private Unrequited Transfers	−187
Official Unrequited Transfers	−24
Capital Other Than Reserves	−4,099
Net Errors & Omissions	11
Total (Lines 1, 10 and 11)	339
Counterpart Items	−244
Total (Lines 12 and 13)	95
Liabilities Constituting Foreign Authorities' Reserves	—
Total Change in Reserves	−95

GROSS DOMESTIC PRODUCT BY ECONOMIC ACTIVITY (1970-81)		
	%	Rate of Change %
Agriculture	5.9	3.4
Mining	22.6	−4.8
Manufacturing	16.2	5.3
Construction	6.0	9.3
Electricity, Gas & Water	1.3	9.8
Transport & Communications	10.5	6.8
Trade & Finance	20.9	3.4
Public Administration & Defense	11.3	7.3
Other Branches	5.3	10.2

FOREIGN ECONOMIC ASSISTANCE		
Source	Period	Amount (million $)
United States Loans	1946-83	127.9
United States Grants	1946-83	72.2
International Organizations	1946-83	6,423
(Of which World Bank)	1946-83	(348.0)
All Sources	1979-81	−17.2

tem and a shipbuilding and repair industry. Agricultural output was to be increased to meet 92% of the country's requirements. The plan also solved two major constraints on rapid development: the lack of a large home market by expanding vigorously into Andean Pact countries and the lack of skilled labor by encouraging immigration and an accelerated program of scholarships for study abroad.

The Sixth National Development Plan covered the period 1981-85. Plans for key projects called for over $16 billion in spending to include housing, coal and steel, water and sewer, hydroelectricity, and the Caracas metro. The rate of government investment in new industrial projects was moderate and tilted in favor of socially oriented projects including health, education, housing, urban and municipal services, and recreation and culture. Government planners targeted a 6% annual increase in real GDP during the five-year period.

The Sixth Plan envisaged a broadened industrial base, a gradual and selective import substitution policy starting with the metal-mechanical and petrochemical industries, and more autonomy and control over technology and engineering. In addition, the following industries are targeted for government stimulation: steel, aluminum, plastics, fertilizers, and electrical and electronics. Nontraditional exports were also to be promoted. Agriculture was once again accorded high priority with $4.3 billion slated over 1981-85.

Although Venezuela is currently a donor country, it received substantial economic assistance until 1973 when increased oil made such assistance unnecessary.

During 1979-81 Venezuela received −$1.2 per capita in foreign aid. The Venezuelan Investment Fund with resources of over B23 billion aids investment projects throughout Latin America and the Caribbean. Venezuela also lends special funds to the World Bank for Latin American development.

BUDGET

The Venezuelan fiscal year is the calendar year. The national budget is financed principally from oil revenues and the bulk of the non-petroleum revenues is derived from tariffs and income taxes. The states and territories are supported primarily by central government grants, while the municipalities raise the bulk of their own revenues.

Of current revenues, 62.2% comes from taxes on income, profit and capital gain, 4.4% from social security contributions, 4.8% from domestic taxes on goods and services, 8.4% from taxes on international trade and transactions, 1.0% from other taxes and 19.2% from non-tax revenues. Current revenues represented 29.3% of GNP. Of current expenditures, 5.8% goes to defense, 15.7% to education, 7.6% to health, 9.4% to housing, social security and welfare, 24.0% to economic services and 37.4% to other functions. Current expenditures represented 29.6% of GNP and overall deficit 5.4% of GNP.

In 1983 public consumption was B41.34 billion and private consumption B183.44 billion. During 1973-83 public consumption grew by 5.2% and private consumption by 7.1%.

In 1983 total outstanding disbursed external debt was $12.911 billion, of which 47% was short-term. During 1976 and 1981 external debt grew by an average of 52% per year. By 1984 Venezuela had secured its fifth moratorium on debt repayments and had accumulated interest arrears of $400 million. Of the disbursed debt only $237 million was owed to official creditors and $12.674 billion was owed to private creditors. The debt service was $2.595 billion of which $936.7 million was repayment of principal and $1.658 billion was interest. Total external debt represented 74.4% of export revenues and 18.2% of GNP. Debt ser-

BUDGET (million bolívares)			
Revenue*	1981	1982	1983
Tax revenue	85,715	67,385	64,599
Withholding taxes on individuals	4,073	4,079	2,124
Taxes on corporate income	68,955	47,811	40,441
Petroleum enterprises	63,215	42,560	34,028
Social security contributions	3,546	3,663	3,170
Taxes on property	508	561	562
Registration fees	338	376	373
Excises	2,698	3,868	4,266
Liquor	897	1,157	1,160
Cigarettes	1,170	1,563	1,624
Motor gasoline (petrol)	591	1,103	1,441
Import duties	5,542	7,003	3,529
Customs duties, etc.	4,016	5,214	2,517
Other current revenue	11,544	15,993	12,211
Property income	10,380	14,088	9,815
Central Bank	1,897	6,332	2,245
Petroleum exploitation	7,237	6,258	6,150
Gas exploitation	344	343	311
Dividends	703	937	921
Administrative fees, charges, etc.	283	463	629
Capital revenue	89	1	53
TOTAL	97,348	83,379	76,863
Expenditure†	1981	1982	1983
General public services	6,072	5,004	4,917
Defense	3,264	4,924	4,025
Education	13,648	13,280	14,627
Health	6,398	6,398	6,114
Social security and welfare	5,944	5,871	5,470
Housing and community amenities	1,799	2,056	2,256
Other community and social services	1,191	1,684	1,487
Economic services	27,614	20,259	15,884
General administration, regulation and research	203	286	246
Agriculture, forestry and fishing	6,259	4,000	2,986
Mining, manufacturing and construction	1,427	1,544	2,710
Electricity, gas and water	2,283	5,540	3,355
Roads	1,930	2,020	2,057
Inland and coastal waterways	1,085	2,917	318
Other transport and communications	3,271	2,704	3,268
Other economic services	11,156	1,248	944
Other purposes	18,715	25,259	21,265
Transfers to regional and local governments	12,286	12,565	12,631
Interest on public debt	5,615	6,149	6,844
SUB-TOTAL	84,645	84,735	76,045
Adjustment	−223	−379	−784
TOTAL	84,422	84,356	75,261

*Excluding grants received (million bolívares): 479 in 1981; 638 in 1982; 50 in 1983.

†Excluding lending minus repayments (million bolívares): 19,746 in 1981; 15,164 in 1982; 5,838 in 1983.

1983, the government announced import controls on over 400 items.

In February 1984 the new government, under President Lusinchi, announced a series of economic measures, including more flexible price controls, a realignment of the currency exchange system, an increase in domestic fuel prices of 20%, a relaxation of restrictive foreign investment regulations and the creation of 200,000 jobs in 1984. The government also announced a de facto devaluation of the bolivar by 78%. Government spending was to be reduced by 10%. In March President Lusinchi was granted special powers by Congress to enable him to introduce austerity measures and reforms to reactivate the private sector. Public spending was cut by 30% and domestic fuel prices rose by 100%, as the government attempted to tackle the worsening economic situation. After lifting food subsidies, the government introduced a system of food distribution to poor families.

FINANCE

The Venezuelan unit of currency is the bolivar (plural: bolivares) divided into 100 centisimos. Coins are issued in denominations of 5, 10, 25 and 50 centisimos and 1, 2 and 5 bolivares; notes are issued in denominations of 5, 10, 20, 50 and 100 bolivares.

In 1985 the dollar and sterling exchange rates of the bolivar were $1=B7.500 and £1=B8.69.

The monetary system is controlled by the Superintendency of Banks. The Central Bank is the fiscal agency of the government and also the bank of issue. The banking sector consists of both official and private banks. The official banks include the Industrial Bank of Venezuela, the Labor Bank, seven regional development banks, controlled by the Venezuelan Development Corporation, and the Agriculture and Livestock Bank. The private sector consists of over 44 banks, of which eight are foreign banks. Under the Bank Law of 1970, all banks are required to be at least 70% Venezuelan-owned. In addition, there are financing companies known as financieras and a savings and loan system consisting of the publicly owned National Savings and Loan Bank and numerous private savings and loan societies. In 1984 the commercial banks had reserves of B19.867 billion, demand deposits of B47.652 billion and time and foreign currency deposits of B78.266 billion. The prevailing discount rate in 1984 was 13%.

AGRICULTURE

Of the total land area of 91,205,000 hectares (225,367,550 acres), 21% is classified as agricultural land, or 1.4 hectares (3.6 acres) per capita. Based on 1974-76=100, the index of agricultural production in 1982 was 122, the index of food production was 124 and the index of per capita food production was 91. Agriculture employs 18% of the labor force. Agriculture contributes 7% of the GDP, and its rate of

vice represented 15.0% of export revenues and 3.7% of GNP.

In March 1983 the government introduced a three-tier exchange rate system incorporating a de facto 28.7% devaluation of the bolivar. In an attempt to check capital flight and reduce imports by 25% in

```
                    GROWTH PROFILE
                 Annual Growth Rates (%)

Population 1980-2000                              2.6
Birthrate 1965-83                               -19.7
Deathrate 1965-83                               -40.2
Urban Population 1973-83                          4.3
Labor Force 1973-83                              3.4
GNP 1973-82                                       3.5
GNP per capita 1973-82                            0.0
GDP 1973-83                                       2.5
GDP per capita 1970-81                            1.1
Consumer Prices 1970-81                          8.8
Wholesale Prices 1970-81                         10.3
Inflation 1973-83                               11.7
Agriculture 1973-83                              2.6
Manufacturing 1973-83                            3.7
Industry 1973-83                                 1.5
Services 1973-83                                 3.1
Mining 1970-81                                   -4.8
Construction 1970-81                             9.3
Electricity 1970-81                              9.8
Transportation 1970-81                           6.8
Trade 1970-81                                     3.4
Public Administration & Defense 1970-81          7.3
Export Price Index 1975-81                       22.4
Import Price Index 1975-81                        9.4
Terms of Trade 1975-81                          11.8
Exports 1973-83                                  -6.8
Imports 1973-83                                  4.7
Public Consumption 1973-83                       5.2
Private Consumption 1973-83                      7.1
Gross Domestic Investment 1973-83                2.5
Energy Consumption 1973-83                       4.5
Energy Production 1973-83                        -3.5
```

growth during 1973-83 was 2.6%. Agriculture's share of export earnings is negligible. The value added in agriculture in 1983 was $1.616 billion.

Only 4% of the land area is under actual cultivation, most of it in the Northen Mountains. The most highly developed agricultural region is the basin of Lake Valencia. Venezuela does not have the rich soil of other Latin American countries; the alluvial deposits of the mountain slopes are quickly leached out as they are cleared of their covering. Food production meets only about half of the country's requirements. In 1983, 2.555 million tons of cereals were imported.

Venezuela's land reform program is considered one of the most successful in Latin America. Under this program, 122,796 farm families have been resettled at a cost of B1.35 billion and 50,000 farmers have received titles to the land they work. The Instituto Agrario Nacional has established agricultural colonies where farmers are settled on smallholdings. Three kinds of land are subject to expropriation by the government: uncultivated lands, lands worked indirectly through renters, sharecropper and other intermediaries, and lands suitable for cultivation but devoted to livestock raising. Venezuelan demand growth consistently outstrips agricultural production (an estimated 40% of all food is imported), and substantial imports, including sophisticated frozen products, will continue.

Nearly 82,234 hectares (203,200 acres) are under some form of irrigation, of which half is in the El Guarico irrigation system. The target is to expand the irrigated area to 800,000 hectares (1,976,000 acres). In 1982, 39,000 tractors and 3,500 harvester-threshers were in use and the annual consumption of fertilizers was 145,700 tons (40.8 kg: 57.71 lb) per hectare of cultivated land.

```
            PRINCIPAL CROP PRODUCTION (1983)
                      (000 tons)

Corn  . . . . . . . . . . . . . . . . . . . . . . . . . . . . . . .      429
Rice  . . . . . . . . . . . . . . . . . . . . . . . . . . . . . . .      509
Potatoes  . . . . . . . . . . . . . . . . . . . . . . . . . . . .      238
Sesame  . . . . . . . . . . . . . . . . . . . . . . . . . . . . .       51
Raw cotton  . . . . . . . . . . . . . . . . . . . . . . . . . .       15
Coffee  . . . . . . . . . . . . . . . . . . . . . . . . . . . . . .       61
Cocoa  . . . . . . . . . . . . . . . . . . . . . . . . . . . . . .       14
Tobacco  . . . . . . . . . . . . . . . . . . . . . . . . . . . . .       16
Cassava  . . . . . . . . . . . . . . . . . . . . . . . . . . . . .      365
Oranges  . . . . . . . . . . . . . . . . . . . . . . . . . . . . .      384
Tomatoes  . . . . . . . . . . . . . . . . . . . . . . . . . . . .      130
Coconuts  . . . . . . . . . . . . . . . . . . . . . . . . . . . .      161
Bananas  . . . . . . . . . . . . . . . . . . . . . . . . . . . . .      944
Sugar cane  . . . . . . . . . . . . . . . . . . . . . . . . . . .    5,132
```

Cattle raising is a major economic activity in the Orinoco lowlands and the Maracaibo lowlands; the herds tend to be large in the former region and smaller in the latter. The principal breeds are Brahmin and Criollo crossed with Zebu, Brown Swiss and Santa Gertrudis. In 1983 the livestock population consisted of 12.092 million cattle, 3,200,000 pigs and 1.734 million goats and sheep.

Forest covers 40% of the land area, but they are largely unexplored and commercially unexploited. The Administration for the Protection of Natural Resources manages forest reserves (including 36 government-owned forest plantations), authorizes lumber cutting and undertakes reafforestation. In 1982 roundwood removals totaled 1.678 million cubic meters (59.2 million cubic ft).

Although Venezuela has the highest per capita fish consumption in Lation America (three times that of the United States), fishing is underdeveloped in relation to available resources. The bulk of the fishing takes place around the fishing ports of Maracaibo, Punto Fijo, Cumana and on Margarita Island. In addition, the major rivers (the Orinoco, Apure, Arauca and Portuguesa) and their numerous tributaries now provide about 6% of the annual catch. Some 3% of the population obtain a livelihood from fishing, and some 2,000 boats are operating in the lakes and rivers and some 7,500 deep-sea boats from the east coast. Commercial catches consist mainly of red snapper, anchovy, herring, bonito, sardines and shrimps; the last two accounted for the bulk of the export earnings from fish products of $38.231 million in 1982. In the same year the fish catch totaled 213.4 million tons.

Agricultural credit is provided by the Agriculture and Livestock Bank.

INDUSTRY

Venezuelan industry is in a process of transition from small, labor intensive units engaged in the production of intermediate and consumer goods to large enterprises producing heavy and capital goods. This process is fueled by a strategy known as "Sembandro el Petroleo" (sowing back petroleum), which means, essentially, plowing back oil revenues into industrial development and diversification in order to replace oil as a source of revenue when the reserves are exhausted.

Manufacturing accounts for 16% of the GDP, employs 15.2% of the labor force, and its rate of growth during 1970-81 was 5.3%. Based on 1975=100, the index of industrial production in 1982 was 240. In 1979 there were 10,348 manufacturing establishments, employing 448,700 workers and generating B107.35 billion in gross value of output. Of the value added in manufacturing, ($5.709 billion in 1982) agro-based products account for 27%, textiles for 6%, machinery and transport equipment for 8% and chemicals for 8%.

About 31% of industry is located in the Federal District and another 30% in Miranda state. In a massive decentralization program, new industries are being located away from these areas. The first of these new complexes was Ciudad Guyana, which is being developed as the hub of a vast Latin American Ruhr. Ciudad Guyana is being developed by Corporacion Venezolana de Guayana, but private enterprises are encouraged to establish industries and businesses in the region. Other large-scale industries established in the last decade include: the National Steel Mills at Matanzas, better known as SIDOR (Siderurgica del Orinoco) with a total capacity of 2.2 million tons; an integrated steel complex at Zulia, with an output of 10 million tons by 1980; Alumino del Caroni, a joint venture with Reynolds International with an annual capacity of nearly 25,000 tons; and the petrochemical complex at Moron established by Instituto Venezolano de Petroquimica (IVP). A second petrochemical complex at El Tablazo is the harbinger of 12 industrial enterprises undertaken by IVP to produce synthetic rubber, ammonia, plastics and related chemicals. Automobile vehicle production has increased to 94,000 in 1982. Observers predict a doubling of industrial output during the coming decade.

Aluminium has replaced iron ore as the second export industry. However, in 1982 low world prices and falling export demand caused the industry to decline. Output fell by 12.8% to 274,000 metric tons, and exports fell by 14.5% in volume to 205,000 tons. The one million metric ton Interalumina plant began operations in March 1983. Interalumina planned to export 200,000 tons of alumina in 1984. Recent discoveries of 500 million tons of bauxite mean that Venezuelan aluminium plants can be supplied entirely with local bauxite. In 1984 the government announced plans to mine up to 4.4 million metric tons annually of high-grade bauxite at the Los Pijiguas zone in Bolivar state. Open-cast mining operations were due to commence in mid-1986 and full production was planned in 1990.

Total foreign investment is estimated at $5.5 billion, of which 85% is in oil. Of this amount, U.S. private investment is $4.2 billion, representing one-fourth of all U.S. investment in Latin America. Of the remainder, 9% is of Dutch and 7% of British origin. Until 1973 Venezuela imposed few restrictions on foreign investment. Since 1974 new foreign investors are required to obtain prior authorization from the Superintendency of Foreign Investment. Special permission is required for repatriation of capital over 14% and for reinvestment of more than 5% of total capital each year. To receive Andean Pact tariff benefits, foreign companies must sell at least 51% of the stock to local investors within 15 years. Net direct private investment in 1983 was –$62 million.

ENERGY

In 1982 Venezuela produced 174.532 million metric tons of coal equivalent of energy and consumed 51.818 million metric tons of coal equivalent, or 3,102 kg (6,641 lb) per capita. The national energy suplus is 122.714 million metric tons of coal equivalent. The annual growth rates during 1973-83 were –3.5% for energy production and 4.5% energy consumption. Apparent per capita consumption of gasoline is 377 gallons per year.

Venezuela is the fifth largest producer and second largest exporter of oil in the world. Venezuelan production accounts for 9.9% of world petroleum trade and 6.5% of total production. Before the mid-1980s slump in oil prices, oil revenues provided 90% of foreign exchange, 15% of the GNP and 66% of annual budget.

Venezuela's current proven reserves are estimated at 24.85 billion barrels of petroleum and 1.545 trillion cubic meters (55 trillion cubic ft) of natural gas. About three-fourths of the output comes from the Maracaibo petroleum basin, and most of the remainder comes from the Orinoco basin south of Puerto La Cruz and the Apure-Barinas basin. Though proved Venezuelan reserves are small compared to Middle Eastern reserves, Venezuela has an additional and potentially richer field in the Orinoco Tar Belt (also known as the Orinoco Heavy Oil Belt), a 33,700 sq km (13,000 sq mi) belt containing 700 billion barrels of highly viscous oil impregnated with metals and sulfur. Its extraction is not yet technologically feasible.

The oil industry consisted until 1975 of 21 private companies, all but two of which were foreign. In 1975 President Perez signed into law the Oil Industry Nationalization Act, by which all concessions were rescinded and a state holding company, Petroleos de Venezuela (PETROVEN), was created. Total compensation to the nationalized companies exceeds B5 billion, of which B3.9 billion is to be paid in tax-free, five-year bonds at 6% interest redeemable only in Venezuelan oil. Operations have been consolidated in PETROVEN's four fully integrated operating subsidiaries, LAGOVEN, MARAVEN, MENEVEN, and CORPOVEN, with research conducted by the Venezuelan Petroleum Technology Institute (INTEVEP) and basic petrochemicals produced by a sixth subsidiary, PEQUIVEN. A number of the major foreign oil companies which previously had operated in Venezuela continue to provide the industry with technical services under contract and other outside firms are being contracted to provide specialized assistance and services.

Petroleum output in 1983 was 654 million barrels and natural gas output was 15.835 billion cubic meters (559 billion cubic ft). In January 1985 the government announced plans to reduce production from 1.56 million b/d to 1.44 million b/d, in accordance with the new OPEC limit established in October 1984. Income generated in 1985 was expected to amount to $13.9 billion. Venezuela is a charter member of OPEC and hosted the organization's 55th Conference in December 1979. The U.S. is the major market for Venezuela's petroleum, taking about 50% of total crude and product export, including indirect exports through Caribbean refineries.

The percentage of crude refined in the country has grown to 38%. The annual capacity of the two refineries at Moron is 80.2 million tons. The Amuay refinery on the Paraguana peninsula, with a planned capacity of 630,000 b/d, was inaugurated in February 1983. Initial production was to be 450,000 b/d.

In 1985 electric power production totaled 36.5 billion kwh, or 2,110 kwh per capita. The first stage of the 9,000 MW Guri project, on the Caroni River, was completed in 1982. It provides 40% of domestic energy requirements.

LABOR

The economically active population is estimated at 5.5 million, of whom 17% are women. By occupational sectors, 16% are employed in agriculture, 9% in construction, 16% in manufacturing, 7% in transport, 22% in commerce, 27% in services and 3% in petroleum and utilities.

EMPLOYMENT (survey, January—June 1981)	
Agriculture, forestry and fishing	633,762
Mining and quarrying	54,613
Manufacturing	672,542
Electricity, gas and water	48,501
Construction	380,931
Trade, restaurants and hotels	800,751
Transport, storage and communications	314,931
Financing, insurance, real estate and business services	201,270
Community, social and personal services	1,161,234
Activities not adequately defined	3,448
Total	4,271,991
Unemployment:	289,052.

The basic Labor Law of 1936, as amended in 1945, 1947, and 1966 is still in force, implemented by labor regulations. The present Labor Law (Ley de Trabajo) covers all enterprises, public and private, except when special legislation applies to particular categories. White collar government employees, for example, are covered by separate legislation, and do not have the right to bargain collectively or to strike. Agricultural labor has some special provisions under law. Domestic workers also are covered separately.

The statutory workweek is 44 hours (40 for night-shift workers) for salaried employees, and 48 hours (42 at night) for wage earners, or "obreros." For both wage earners and salaried employees the basic workday is 8 daytime hours, and 7 at night. Overtime must be paid at 125% of the basic rate. Union contracts frequently provide for time and one-half for overtime during the day, and double time at night. Contracts increasingly provide for a reduced workweek of 42 to 45 hours for wage earners. More and more salaried employees work a 40-hour week. A regular night shift commands an 20% premium over daytime wages. A wage earner who works his regular days is paid for the compulsory weekly day of rest at a rate equal to 1 day's wages.

A national minimum wage of 15 bolivares per day, for all workers except domestics, was introduced in 1974. At that time, the president decreed a general salary increase of between 5% and 25% for all salaried workers in both public and private sectors who earned less than 5,000 bolivars (US $1,170) per month. Wages are very high by Latin American standards and compare favorably with those in the poorer countries of Europe. Although the minimum wage for industrial workers is $7 plus a day, most workers receive higher compensation. In 1978, blue collar workers averaged $592 a month while white collar employees received $960. Skilled workers are compensated at rates similar to their U.S. counterparts.

Inflation and falling living standards led to enactment of the Law for a General Salary Increase, which provided wage raises for all workers as of January 1, 1980. The legislated increase varied from 30% for the lowest paid workers to 5% for those making between $1,100 and $1,400 per month.

Organized labor has a strong voice in Venezuela and resultant labor laws protect its interest. Legally required benefits include severance pay amounting to 30 days wages for each year of service, a profit-sharing bonus equal to at least 15 days pay, 15 days vacation, plus 15 days as a vacation bonus yearly. Social security taxes are 4% of the worker's salary and 7-9% paid by the employer. Collective bargaining contracts often provide significantly larger fringe benefits. In addition, the law against unjustified dismissals provides for double the normal amount of severance pay to workers deemed unjustly dismissed. Labor laws restrict the percentage of foreigners in firms of more than five employees to 25% of total salaries.

Strikes are legal but may not be called before a conciliation attempt has been made. Voluntary arbitration is encouraged, but in some cases arbitration may be imposed by the Ministry of Labor. In 1975, 100 strikes were reported in the country involving 25,752 workers and leading to the loss of 100,662 man-days. Illegal strikes may also be settled by conciliation and arbitration, or may be terminated by government decree. Participants in illegal strikes can be jailed, but that provision is seldom invoked. In 1977 and 1978 there were no legal strikes, and in 1976 only one. The number of illegal strikes has risen in recent years, but strikes are usually short.

More than 45% of the labor force is unionized. The largest union is the Confederacion de Trabajadores de Venezuela (CTV) with 1.3 million members in 23 regional and 16 industrial federations. There are 8,427 other unions, including the COPEI-affiliated Confederacion de Sindicatas Autonomos de Venezuela (CODESA), the left-wing Central Unitaria de Trabajadores de Venezuela and the right-wing Movimiento Nacional de Trabajadores para la Liberacion.

FOREIGN COMMERCE

The foreign commerce of Venezuela consisted in 1984 of exports of $15.424 billion and imports of $6.843 billion, leaving a trade surplus of $8.581 billion. Of the imports, nonelectrical machinery constituted 22.1% (of which motor vehicles 11.6%), chemicals 10.5%, electrical machinery 9.3%, iron and steel 7.0% and cereals 3.5%. Of the exports, petroleum and petroleum products constituted 92.6%.

The major import sources are: the United States 46.1%, Japan 8.2%, West Germany 7.0% and Canada 4.2%. The major export destinations are: the United States 37.3%, the Netherlands Antilles 21.7%, Canada 10.1% and the United Kingdom 2.4%.

Based on 1975=100, the import price index in 1981 was 155, the export price index 328, and the terms of trade (export prices divided by imports prices × 100) 212.

Venezuela is a member of three trade groupings: ANCOM, SELA ALADI and LAFTA.

TRANSPORTATION & COMMUNICATIONS

The state-owned Instituto Autonomo de Administracion de Ferrocarriles del Estado operates 419 km (232 mi) of track. The main line connects Baraquisimeto with Puerto Cabello. The government plans to construct a 3,900-km (2,418 mi) rail network by 1990 at a cost of 9,397 million bolivares. The basic network will comprise two north-south routes and a third running from west to east. The first north-south line, crossing the western part of the country, was completed in 1984.

Plans are under way for building a 50-km (31 mi) underground railway in Caracas. The first stage, a 20-km (12 mi) east-west rapid transit line, was begun in 1976 and it was completed in 1983 at a total cost of over 7,000 million bolivares.

FOREIGN TRADE INDICATORS (1984)		
Annual Growth Rate, Imports:		4.7% (1973-83)
Annual Growth Rate, Exports:		-6.8% (1973-83)
Ratio of Exports to Imports:		69:31
Exports per capita:		$866
Imports per capita:		$384
Balance of Trade:		$8.581 billion
Ratio of International Reserves to Imports (in months)		10.7
Exports as % of GDP:		30.5
Imports as % of GDP:		26.9
Value of Manufactured Exports:		$417 million
Commodity Concentration:		67.4%
Direction of Trade (%)		
	Imports	Exports
EEC	19.8	12.9
U.S.	48.1	27.3
Industrialized Market Economies	83.4	65.7
East European Economies	—	—
High Income Oil Exporters	—	—
Developing Economies	15.7	32.8
Composition of Trade (%)		
	Imports	Exports
Food	16.9	0.4
Agricultural Raw Materials	2.4	—
Fuels	0.8	94.0
Ores & Minerals	7.8	4.5
Manufactured Goods	72.1	1.1
of which Chemicals	10.4	0.5
of which Machinery	43.4	0.4

Venezuela has an extensive pipeline system serving its oil industry. Of this system, 6,370 km (3,956 mi) carry crude oil, 450 km (279 mi) refined oil and 2,480 km (1,540 mi) natural gas.

The total length of inland waterways is 7,100 km (4,409 mi). Shallow-draft boats are able to reach the Colombian ports in the wet season. The principal navigable rivers are the Orinoco and its tributaries, the Apure and Arauca, from San Fernando to Tucupita through Ciudad Bolivar, Puerto Ordaz and San Felix; the San Juan from Caripito to the Gulf of Paria; and the Esculante to Lake Maracaibo.

There are 33 ports located on the Caribbean coast, on Lake Maracaiba and on the Orinoco. Traffic is heaviest at Puerto Cabello, followed by Puerto La Cruz, Amuay and La Guaira. In 1982 these ports handled 72,914,000 tons of cargo. Oil is handled by Maracaibo, general cargo by Puerto Cabello and iron ore by Puerto Ordaz. In 1983 the country's merchant marine consisted of 244 vessels with a total GRT of 1,357,000, of which oil tankers accounted for 458,000 GRT. In 1974 a state shipbuilding corporation was established at Puerto Cabello.

There are 77,785 km (48,304 mi) of roads, of which 22,780 km (14,146 mi) are paved. Caracas is the hub of the highway system. Divided superhighways, called autopistas, link the airport at Maiquetia with Caracas and the capital with the industrial center of Valencia before veering north to Puerto Cabello. The 968-km (602-mi) Venezuelan section of the Pan-American Highway connects Caracas with the Colombian border, while another road links with the Brazilian system through the jungles of the southeast. The General Rafael Urdaneta Bridge crosses the narrow neck of water connecting Lake Maracibo with the Gulf of Venezuela. A new marginal highway is under construction along the western fringe of the Amazon basin in Venezuela. In 1982 these roads were used by 1,501,382 passenger cars and 795,856 commercial vehicles. Per capita vehicle ownership was 84 passenger cars per 1,000 inhabitants.

The national airline is Venezolana-Internacional de Aviacion S.A. (VIASA), in which the Pan American World Airways has a minority interest. There are two other national airlines providing domestic services: Aerovias Venezolanas (AVENSA) and Linea Aeropostal Venezolana (LAV). With 72 aircraft, these airlines flew 58.1 million km (36 million mi) and carried 5,434,000 passengers in 1982. There are 259 aiports and airfields in the country, of which 238 are usable, 104 have permanent-surface runways, and seven have runways over 2,500 meters (8,000 ft). There are also two seaplane stations. The largest international airport is the Simon Bolivar International Airport at Maiquetia.

In 1984 there were 1.38 million telephones in use, or 8.5 per 100 inhabitants.

The country's 809 postal districts and branch post offices handled 347,500,000 pieces of mail and 5,148,000 telegrams in 1982. Per capita volume of mail was 19 pieces. There are 15,915 telex subscriber lines.

In 1982, 260,000 tourists visited Venezuela, generating revenues of $251 million. Expenditures by nationals abroad totaled $2.349 billion. There are 96,000 hotel beds and the average length of stay is 8.4 days.

MINING

Of Venezuela's varied mineral resources, only iron is currently being exploited. The country's iron reserves are estimated at 2 billion tons of high grade ore and 7.5 million tons of low-grade ore. Ore produced in the mid-1970s had an average iron content of 64%. Iron mining is concentrated in two areas, El Pao and Cerro Bolivar, both near Ciudad Bolivar. Production in 1981 totaled 15,530,000 tons. The iron industry was developed by two U.S. firms, subsidiaries of U.S. Steel and Bethlehem Steel, respectively. In 1975 both were nationalized with a total compensation of $175 million. Production is now controlled by Orinoco Ferrominerals Company, a state corporation.

Production of other known minerals such as coal, gold and diamonds has been declining. On the other hand, aluminum production has been increasing. Other minerals known to exist but not yet exploited include manganese, mercury, nickel, magnesite, cobalt and mica.

DEFENSE

The defense structure is headed by the president. The chain of command runs through the minister of defense, who is generally the chief of the joint staff. Military policy is formulated by the Supreme Council of National Defense, which, however, functions outside the chain of command.

Conscription is mandatory by law but is rarely enforced. Only 10% of those eligible are drafted each year. The selective service period is two years.

The total strength of the armed forces is 49,000, or 3.3 armed persons for every 1,000 civilians.

ARMY:
Personnel: 34,000

Organization: HQ 5 divisions; 1 armored brigade; 6 infantry brigades; 1 cavalry regiment; 5 artillery groups; 2 AA artillery groups; 5 engineer battalions; 1 airborne group

Equipment: 80 heavy tanks; 422 light tanks; 100 armored combat vehicles; 126 armored personnel carriers; 115 howitzers; 25 rocket launchers; 185 mortars; 35 antitank guns; antitank guided weapons; 48 air defense guns

Army Aviation: 1 transport squadron; 1 helicopter squadron; 2 submarines; 8 frigates; 19 amphibious vehicles; 2 transports

NAVY:
Personnel: 10,000

Units: 4 Naval Aviation: 4 combat aircraft; 6 combat helicopters; 1 maritime reconnaissance squadron; 1 antisubmarine warfare helicopter squadron; 1 search and rescue squadron; 1 transport squadron

Marines: 4 battalions, with 47 armored personnel carriers and 18 howitzers

AIR FORCE:
Personnel: 5,000

Organization: 91 combat aircraft; 2 bomber/reconnaissance squadrons; 1 fighter ground attack squadron; 3 interceptor squadrons; 1 counterinsurgency squadron; 1 presidential transport squadron; 2 transport squadrons; 2 utility/liaison squadrons; 1 helicopter squadron; 12 trainers; 1 parachute battalion

Air Bases: Caracas, Maracay, Maiquetia, La Carlota, Maturin, Maracaibo, Palo Negro, Barquisimeto and Barcelona

The defense budget in 1984 was $1.069 billion, representing 1.3% of the GNP, 5.0% of the national budget, $52 per capita, $28,342 per soldier and $1,274 per sq km of national territory.

The Venezuelan armed forces are among the most modern and professional in Latin America. With its vast petroleum revenues, the government has embarked on a program of rapidly modernizing the military establishment, providing it with a deterrent capability far in excess of the nation's needs. The large annual defense budgets have drawn criticism from the opposition, who fear that Venezuela is not only fueling an arms race in Latin America but creating a military Frankenstein that might engulf their freedoms.

Almost all military aid has been obtained from the United States, which has supplied $152.4 million worth of military assistance since 1946. Arms purchases abroad during 1973-83 totaled $1.260 billion including $110 million from the United States, $30 million from France, and $550 million from Italy.

EDUCATION

The national literacy rate is 76.5% (79.7% for males and 73.4% for females). Of the population over 25, 49.1% have had no schooling, 44.1% have attended and/or completed first level, 5.3% have attended and/or completed second level and 1.5% have completed post-secondary education.

Education is free, universal and compulsory for six years between the ages of seven and 14. The gross school enrollment ratios are 105% in the first level (7 to 12) and 40% in the second level (13-17), for a combined enrollment ratio of 74%. Girls constitute 49% of primary school enrollment, 48% of secondary school enrollment and 41% of post-secondary enrollment.

Schooling lasts for 12 years divided into six years of primary school, three years of intermediate school and three years of secondary school. The last two years of the secondary cycle offer specialization in sciences and humanities. Upon graduation the students receive the bachillerato degree in secondary and technical schools and the maestro degree in normal schools. In rural areas most of the schools are unitarias, or one-room schools with one teacher for all classes. In 1982 the school system consisted of 12,788 primary schools and 1,754 secondary schools.

The school year runs from October to July. The language of instruction is Spanish throughout.

Primary school teachers are trained in normal schools and secondary school teachers are trained in four pedagogical institutes at Caracas, Maracay, Matorin and Barquisimeto. The national teacher-pupil ratios are 1:27 in primary schools, 1:21 in secondary schools and 1:11 in post-secondary classes.

In 1980 nearly 43,000 students were enrolled in vocational courses in 400 technical and vocational schools, representing 4.8% of total secondary school enrollment. Private schools account for 11% of primary enrollment and 18% of secondary enrollment.

Educational administration is centralized in the Ministry of Education. Within the ministry are various directorates dealing with primary, normal, secondary, higher, special and technical and commercial education. The ministry's budget in 1981 totaled B17,018,635,000 of which 95.6% was current expenditure. This amount represented 5.8% of the GNP, 15.0% of the national budget and $276 per capita.

Higher education is provided by 11 universities with a total enrollment 307,133. Per capita university enrollment is 1,725 per 100,000 inhabitants.

In 1982, 20,121 students graduated from Venezuelan universities. Of these, 2,391 received degrees in medicine, 4,016 in engineering, 258 in natural

EDUCATIONAL ENROLLMENT (1981)			
Level	Schools	Teachers	Students
First Level	12,788	97,045	2,591,051
Second Level	1,754	45,888	958,233
Third Level	68	28,052	307,133

UNIVERSITIES OF VENEZUELA	
Institution	Location
Universidad de Carabobo	Valencia
Universidad Catolica Andre Bello	Caracas
Universidad Central de Venezuela	Caracas
Universidad Centro-Occidental	Baraquisimeto
Universidad de los Andes	Merida
Universidad Metropolitana	Caracas
Universidad de Oriente	Sucre
Universidad Rafael Urdaneta	Maracaibo
Universidad de Santa Maria	Caracas
Universidad Simon Bolivar	Caracas
Universidad del Zulia	Maracaibo

sciences, 1,135 in social sciences, 985 in law, 5,110 in education and 1,409 in agriculture.

In 1982, 14,818 Venezuelan students were enrolled in institutions of higher learning abroad. Of these, 11,174 were in the United States, 342 in Canada, 748 in France, 192 in West Germany, 334 in the United Kingdom, 643 in Italy, 948 in Spain, 146 in Portugal and 33 in Switzerland

Venezuela ranks 42nd in the world in contributions to world scientific authorship with a share of 0.061% (U.S., 42%). Ninety scientific journals are published in the country. In 1980, 3,673 Venezuelan scientists were engaged in basic research. In 1981 scientific expenditures totaled B1.012 billion.

LEGAL SYSTEM

Venezuelan law is derived from Napoleonic and Italian sources.

The judiciary is headed by the Supreme Court comprising nine members and nine alternates, divided among three chambers known as salas. Judges are elected by the Congress in joint session for nine-year terms, with one-third of the judges retiring every three years. Each of the three salas—Politico-Administrative, Civil Cassation and Criminal Cassation—is composed of no fewer than five justices. The Supreme Court has broad powers of judicial review.

Below the Supreme Court, the country is divided into 20 judicial areas that correspond to a state, except in three instances: the state of Miranda falls within the jurisdiction of the Federal District, the federal territory of Amazonas lies within the jurisdiction of Apure State and the federal territory of Delta Amacuro falls within the jurisdiction of Monagas State. Each judicial district has a superior court composed of either one or three judges. Other judicial bodies within each judicial district include courts of instruction, district courts, municipal courts and courts of first instance. In the mid-1980s there were 144 courts of first instance, 174 district courts, 457 municipal courts and 53 courts of instruction. The conduct, efficiency and independence of the judiciary are supervised by the Council of the Judiciary.

There are 25 prisons including 17 judicial detainment centers, seven national jails and the national institute of female orientation. The annual average prison population in the mid-1980s was around 15,000, which is more than what the prisons are designed to house. The resulting overcrowding and poor living conditions have led to many strikes by inmates.

LAW ENFORCEMENT

Venezuela does not have a single unified national police force. Law enforcement responsibilities are divided among four national police agencies and among 450 metropolitan, state and municipal police agencies with a total strength of 37,000, or one policeman for every 324 inhabitants. In 1974 a bill was introduced in Congress providing for the integration of all law enforcement agencies into a single agency, but nothing came out of it.

The largest, best trained and equipped and most efficient law enforcement agency is the 12,000-man National Guard (also known as the Armed Forces of Cooperation), a volunteer force organized along military lines and commanded by an officer with the rank of a general directly responsible to the minister of national defense. The general command headquarters is in Caracas and there are three regional commands. The basic unit is the detachment, composed of a variable number of companies subdivided into platoons and squads. The second most significant law enforcement agency is the Directorate of Intelligence and Prevention Services (Direccion de Seguridad e Intelligencia Policial, DISIP), a non-uniformed political police force and counterintelligence service responsible for investigation of crimes involving subversion, narcotics and arms smuggling. DISIP is headed by a director. Another national force is the Technical and Judicial Police, a corps of about 1,500 plainclothesmen, who handle investigative police work, apprehension of criminals and criminal identification, under a director appointed by the president. A fourth national force is the Traffic Police, a corps of 1,500 uniformed men stationed in all the major cities. The 450 state, municipal and metropolitan police forces operate as independent entities and have a combined strength of about 12,000 men. The largest of these is the 8,600-man Metropolitan Force of Caracas.

The rapid changes in the country's economic and social life caused by the influx of petroleum revenues are reflected in the upsurge of crime in urban areas. Caracas, the capital, with one-fifth of the national population, accounts for about one-half of all crimes committed in the country. Significantly, criminal activity is becoming a male phenomenon; less than 3% of the crimes are committed by women. By category, the greatest increase is reported in crimes against property.

HEALTH

Venezuela is virtually free of endemic diseases that afflict other tropical countries. Major causes of death are heart disease and cancer.

PRINCIPAL HEALTH INDICATORS (1984)
Crude Death Rate: 5.6 per 1,000
Decline in Death Rate −40.2% (1965-83)
Life Expectancy at Birth: 65.1 (Males); 70.6 (Females)
Infant Mortality Rate: 44.8 per 1,000 Live Births
Child Death Rate (Ages 1-4) per 1,000: 2

In 1979 there were 446 hospitals with 41,386 beds, or one bed per 317 inhabitants. In the same year there were 15,359 physicians, or one physician per 888 inhabitants, 4,645 dentists and 9,077 nurses. Of the hospitals 42.1% are state-run, 4.3% are run by private nonprofit agencies and 53.6% are run by private for-profit agencies. In 1982 health expenditures accounted for 8.7% of the national budget and $89.70 per capita. Nearly 80% of the population has access to safe water.

FOOD

The staple foods are corn and rice. The daily per capita intake of food is 2,649 calories and 70.8 grams of protein (both below the recommended minimums of 2,600 calories and 65 grams of protein per day), 57 grams of fats and 409 grams of carbohydrates.

MEDIA & CULTURE

In 1982, 36 daily newspapers were published in the country with an aggregate circulation of 2,383,000, or 176 per 1,000 inhabitants. Ten of these dailies are published in Caracas (including one in English). The periodical press consists of over 300 titles. Annual consumption of newsprint is 140,000 tons, or 8,666 kg (19,108 lb) per 1,000 inhabitants

The Venezuelan press is one of the freest in Latin America and compares favorably with that of the United States. It is ranked 13th in the world in press freedom with a rating of +2.54 (on a scale in which +4 is the highest and −4 is the lowest).

The national news agency is Prensa Venezolana (PEVE). Foreign news agencies represented in Caracas include AFP, ANSA, AP, DPA, Efe, Europa Press, Novosti, Prensa Latina, Reuter-Latin, Tass and UPI.

Venezuela is one of the centers of the Latin American book industry with an annual title output of 3,596 in 1982. It adheres to the Universal Copyright Convention.

The official broadcasting network, Radio Nacional, operates eight medium-wave transmitters, 10 short-wave transmitters and two FM transmitters. There are 148 other commercial stations, of which only four are on the air for 24 hours a day, while 60 are on the air for 18 hours a day and the remainder for 12 hours a day. In 1982 there were 6,000,000 radio receivers in the country, or 408 per 1,000 inhabitants.

Television, introduced in 1952, is operated by one official station, Televisora Nacional (TVN-5) and seven other stations, of which five are commercial. TVN-5 is on the air for 49 hours a week; broadcasting hours vary for other stations. In 1980 the government introduced regulations for the television services to prevent the lowering of standards and curtail large profits from advertising. Programs broadcast on government stations must be submitted to the ministry 48 hours before being transmitted, will be classified according to suitability of content and must be "educational, cultural, informative, sporting or recreational" and "contribute to the spiritual enrichment" of the viewers. Private stations are expected to conform to these standards and may be subject to sanctions if the regulations are contravened. In 1982 there were 1,850,000 television sets in use, or 126 per 1,000 inhabitants.

Domestic feature film production was two in 1981. In 1981 there were 535 cinemas in the country with 256,000 seats, or 20.1 seats per 1,000 inhabitants. Annual movie attendance was 67.6 million, or 4.7 per capita. In 1982, 606 films were imported, of which 330 were from the United States. Annual box office receipts were B376 million.

Venezuela has over 100 public libraries, of which the largest is the National Library at Caracas with 400,000 volumes. Per capita there are six volumes per 1,000 inhabitants.

There are 133 museums reporting an annual attendance of 1.385 million, and 35 nature preservation sites.

There are nine theaters (seven in the capital) and six other performance areas serving 29 professional companies and seven amateur troupes. In 1977 these groups performed in 80 dramas, 239 operas and ballets, and seven traditional dances.

SOCIAL WELFARE

The social security system is administered by the Bureau of Social Security. Coverage includes sickness and maternity benefits and benefits for occupational accidents, deaths and disabilities. Maternity and sickness benefits are restricted to low-income workers, and their costs are met by contributions by both employee and employer. All other benefits are financed solely from employers' contributions. In the mid-1970s nearly 1.2 million workers were covered by social security.

GLOSSARY

adeco: a member of the AD (Accion Democratica) Party.
barrio: an urban slum.

mestizaje: cultural and genetic mixing of Indian, white and Negro races producing a mestizo.
sembrando el petroleo: literally, sowing the petroleum. Plowing back oil revenues into industrial development.

CHRONOLOGY (from 1945)

1945— President Angarita Isaias Medina is overthrown in an army-inspired coup, which sets up a seven-man junta led by Romulo Betancourt, AD leader.
1946— Newly elected constituent assembly draws up nation's 25th constitution, which goes into effect in 1947.
1948— In free, universal and secret elections, Romulo Gallegos is elected president.
1948— Disgruntled army group deposes Gallegos; military triumvirate consisting of Carlos Delgado Chalbaud, Perez Jimenez and Luis F. Llovera Paez takes over the government.
1950— Delgado is assassinated in mysterious circumstances; Jimenez becomes virtual dictator.
1952— Jimenez holds sham plebiscitè on his reelection and declares himself the winner.
1957— Jimenez holds sham plebiscite on his relection and declares himself elected for another term even before the votes are counted.
1958— Jimenez is overthrown by military junta led by Admiral Wolfgang Larrazabal.
1959— Romulo Betancourt is elected president and forms a coalition government.
1960— Led by Venezuela, oil exporting nations form OPEC.
1961— New constitution, the nation's 26th, is promulgated.
1963— OAS charges Cuba with aggression against Venezuela. . . . Raul Leoni is elected president in nation's first peaceful transfer of power.
1968— Rafael Caldera, founder of COPEI, is elected president.
1973— Carlos Andres Perez of AD is elected president. . . . Venezuela joins the Andean Common Market.
1976— All foreign mining companies are nationalized.
1978— Luis Herrera Campins of COPEI is elected president in national elections.
1979— Herrera is inaugurated president; vows austerity program and reduction in state role in commerce and industry.
1980— Former president Perez is censured by Congress for role in scandal involving purchase of a Norwegian ship at an inflated price.
1983— Jaime Lusinchi, the AD candidate, is elected president.
1984— AD consolidates its electoral control of local governments.

BIBLIOGRAPHY (from 1970)

Allen, Robert Loring, *Venezuelan Economic Development* (Greenwich, Conn., 1976).

Assignment Venezuela. B&W film, 24 min. Creole Petroleum Corp.

Betancourt, Romulo, *Venezuela's Oil* (London, 1978).

Blank, David Eugene, *Politics in Venezuela* (Boston, 1973).

Bond, Robert D., *Contemporary Venezuela and its Role in International Affairs* (New York, 1977).

Bonilla, Frank and Jose A. Michelana, *The Politics of Change in Venezuela* (Cambridge, Mass., 1971).

Braveboy-Wagner, Jacqueline, *The Venezuela-Guyana Border Dispute: Britain's Colonial Legacy in Latin America* (Boulder, Colo., 1984).

Burggraff, Winfield J., *The Venezuelan Armed Forces in Politics 1939-1959* (Columbia, Mo., 1972).

Carlisle, Douglas H., *Venezuelan Foreign Policy* (Washington, D.C., 1978).

Childers, Victor E., *Human Resources Development in Venezuela* (Bloomington, Ind., 1974).

Colombia and Venezuela. B&W film, 17 min. Encyclopaedia Britannica.

Colombia and Venezuela. Color film, 17 min. S. Sterling.

Coronel, Gustavo, *The Nationalization of the Venezuelan Oil Industry: From Technocratic Success to Political Failure* (Lexington, Mass., 1983).

Ewell, Judith, *Venezuela: A Century of Change* (Stanford, Calif., 1984).

Five Northern Countries. Color film, 11 min. Coronet.

Gall, Norman, *Oil and Democracy in Venezuela* (Hanover, N.H., 1974).

Gilbert, Alan and Patsy Healey, *The Political Economy of Land: The State and Urban Development in Venezuela* (London, 1985).

Gilyepes, Jose A., *The Challenge of Venezuelan Democracy* (New Brunswick, N.J., 1981).

Herman, Donald L., *Christian Democracy in Venezuela* (Durham, N.C., 1980).

Kolb, Glen L., *Democracy and Dictatorship in Venezuela, 1945-1958* (Hamden, Conn., 1974).

Levine, Daniel H., *Conflict and Political Change in Venezuela* (Princeton, N.J., 1973).

Liss, Sheldon B., *Diplomacy & Dependency: Venezuela, The United States and The Americas* (Salisbury, N.C., 1978).

Lombardi, John V., *Venezuela: The Search for Order, The Dream of Progress* (New York, 1982).

Martz, John D. and David J. Myers, *Venezuela: The Democratic Experience* (New York, 1977).

Martz, John D. and Enrique Baloyra, *Electoral Mobilization and Public Opinion: The Venezuelan Campaign of 1973* (Chapel Hill, N.C., 1973).

Myers, David J., *Venezuela's Pursuit of Caribbean Basin Interests: Implications for U.S. National Security* (Santa Monica, Calif., 1983).

Oropeza, Luis, *Venezuela's Tutelary Pluralism: A Critical Approach to Venezuelan Democracy* (Lanham, Md., 1981).

Petras, James F., *The Nationalization of Venezuelan Oil* (New York, 1977).

Powell, John D., *Political Mobilization of the Venezuelan Peasant* (Cambridge, Mass., 1971).

Rabe, Stephen G., *The Road to OPEC: United States Relations with Venezuela, 1919-1976* (Austin, Texas, 1982).

Roseberry, William, *Coffee and Capitalism in the Venezuelan Andes* (Austin, Texas, 1984).

Rudolph, Donna K. and G. A. Rudolph, *Historical Dictionary of Venezuela* (Metuchen, N.J., 1971).

Salazar-Carrillo, Jorge, *Oil in the Economic Development of Venezuela* (New York, 1976).

Steiner, Stan, *In Search of the Jaguar: Growth & Paradox in Venezuela* (New York, 1979).

Stewart, Bill, *Change & Bureaucracy: Public Administration in Venezuela* (Durham, N.C., 1978).

Tugwell, Franklin, *The Politics of Oil in Venezuela* (Stanford, Calif., 1975).

Valente, Cecilia, M., *The Political, Economic & Labor Climate in Venezuela* (Philadelphia, Pa., 1979).

Venezuela. Color film, 16 min. Contemporary Films.

Venezuela: Oil Builds A Nation. Color film, 17 min. Sleeping Giant Films.

Venezuela: The Last Chance for Democracy. B&W film, 60 min. National Education Television.

Venezuela: The Making of a Government. B&W film, 59 min. National Education Television.

OFFICIAL PUBLICATIONS

Treasury, *Cuenta del Gobierno General* (Central Government Account).

Finance Ministry, *Resumen Ley de Presupuesto* (Budget Law Summary), Ministerio de Haciendo.

Central Bank, *Informe Economico* (Economic Report).

VIETNAM

NORTH

CENTER

SOUTH

Lai Chau
Hoang Lien Son
Ha Tuyen
Bac Thai
Cao Lang
Son La
Vinh Phu
Ha Bac
Quang Ninh
HANOI
Hai Hung
Ha Son Binh
Thai Binh
Ho Nam Ninh
Thanh Hoa
Nghe Tinh
Binh Tri Thien
Quang Nam-Da Nang
Gia Lai-Cong Tum
Nghia Binh
Dac Lac
Phu Khanh
Song Be
Tay Ninh
Lam Dong
Dong Nai
Thuan Hai
An Giang
Long An
Tien Giang
Ho Chi Minh City (Saigon)
Ho Chi Minh
Kien Giang
Cuu Long
Ben Tre
Hau Giang
Minh Hai

0 — 150 Miles
0 — 150 Kilometers

Names and boundary representation
are not necessarily authoritative

VIỆT NAM
DANG CHU CONG HOA

VIETNAM

BASIC FACT SHEET

OFFICIAL NAME: Socialist Republic of Vietnam (Cong Hoa Xa Hoi Chu Nghia VietNam); Also, Viet-Nam, Viet Nam

ABBREVIATION: VN

CAPITAL: Hanoi

HEAD OF STATE: President Nguyen Huu Tho (Acting from 1980)

HEAD OF GOVERNMENT: Prime Minister Pham Van Dong (from 1955)

NATURE OF GOVERNMENT: One-party Communist dictatorship

POPULATION: 60,492,000 (1985)

AREA: 332,559 sq km (128,401 sq mi)

ETHNIC MAJORITY: Vietnamese

LANGUAGE: Vietnamese (Quoc-Ngu)

RELIGIONS: Mahayana Buddhism, Taoism, Confucianism, Hoa Hao, Cao Dai and Roman Catholicism

UNIT OF CURRENCY: Dong ($1=D10.588, 1984)

NATIONAL FLAG: A red field with a five-pointed gold star in the middle

NATIONAL EMBLEM: A gold five-pointed star on a circular red badge surrounded by golden ears of rice. At the base is an industrial cog-wheel. A red ribbon draped around the device carries the name of the republic.

NATIONAL ANTHEM: "Forward, Soldiers"

NATIONAL HOLIDAYS: September 2 (National Day); January 1 (New Year's Day); April 30 (Liberation Day); May 1 (May Day); May 19 (Ho Chi Minh's Birthday); December 19 (Resistance Day); December 22 (People's Army Day)

NATIONAL CALENDAR: Gregorian and Am Lich, the Chinese lunar calendar

PHYSICAL QUALITY OF LIFE INDEX: 75 (up from 60 in 1976) (On an ascending scale in which 100 is the maximum. U.S. 95)

DATE OF INDEPENDENCE: July 21, 1954

DATE OF CONSTITUTION: December 18, 1980

WEIGHTS & MEASURES: The metric system is in force, but traditional measures are also used. These include the mau (0.36 hectare, 0.89 acre in North Vietnam and 0.5 hectare, 1.24 acres in South Vietnam); the gia (0.38 hectoliter, 1.1 bushels); and the thung (0.19 hectoliter, 0.55 bushel).

LOCATION & AREA

Vietnam is located in Southeast Asia with an area of 332,559 sq km (128,401 sq mi) extending 1,650 km (1,025 mi) N to S and 600 km (373 mi) E to W. Its total coastline on the South China Sea and the Gulfs of Siam and Tonkin stretches 2,309 km (1,435 mi).

Vietnam shares its total international border of 3,818 km (2,371 mi) with three neighbors, all Communist countries: China (1,281 km, 796 mi); Cambodia (982 km, 610 mi); and Laos (1,555 km, 966 mi).

The capital is Hanoi with a 1979 population of 2,767,000. The other major urban centers are Ho Chi Minh City, formerly Saigon (3,419,978), Haiphong (1,279,067), Da Nang (492,194), Nha Trang (216,227), Qui Nhon (213,757), Hue (209,043), Can Tho (182,424), Mytho (119,892), Cam-Ranh (118,111), Vungtau (108,436) and Dalat (105,072).

Most of North Vietnam is mountainous, particularly the northern and northwestern sections. The lowlands consist of the Red River Delta and the coastal plains which extend northeast and south from the delta. South Vietnam is divided into four topographical regions. The lower third of the country is dominated by the estuary of the Mekong River system, a low and marshy flatland. Immediately north and east of Ho Chi Minh City the topography becomes more varied with upland forests and rugged terrain. Central Vietnam is divided into a narrow coastal strip and a broad plateau separated from the coastal lowlands by the Annamite chain. The country also includes six islands or island groups: Cat-Ba Island in the Gulf of Tonkin, Con-Son Island in the southeast, Cu-Lao Island in the South China Sea, the Paracel Islands in the South China Sea, Phu-Quoc Island in the Gulf of Siam, and the Spratley Islands in the South China Sea.

There are 14 mountain ranges: An-Khe, Bacson, Chiem-Hoa, Dong-Trieu, Hoang-Lien-Son, Hoanh-Son, Lao-Cai, Nam-Kim, Ngan-Son, Sa-Phin, Song Gam, Truong-Son, Yen-Binh and Yen-Lac.

The principal river systems are the Red River in the north and the Mekong in the south. The Red River, also known as Song Nhi-Ha, Song Coi or Song Cai, is about 1,167 km (725 mi) long. It originates in China's Yunan Province and has two main tributaries, the Lo and the Da-Giang. It enters Vietnam at Lao Cai and passing through the city of Hanoi empties into the South China Sea at five locations. The river is navigable beyond Hanoi and up to Yen-Bay. The Thai-Binh River parallels the Red River, and the two are linked by a system of canals. The Red River delta is considered to be the cradle of Vietnamese civilization. The Mekong, also known as Song Cuu Long, or the River of the Nine Dragons, is about 4,500 km (2,800 mi) long and originates in Tibet. At Phnom-Penh in Cambodia it splits into two main branches: the Hau-Giang, the Lower River, also called the Bassac River, and the Tien-Giang, or the Upper River, which splits into several branches and empties into the South China Sea at six locations. Often included in the Mekong Delta are the delta areas of the Vam-Co, Sai-Gon and Dong-Ni Rivers. Other minor rivers provide supplementary drainage: the Cau, Ca, Cai, Con, Da-Giang, Da Bach, Bac-Giang, Bach-Dang, Ben-Hai, Chu, Da-Rang, Dai-Giang, Dai-Thuong, Gam, Hieu-Giang, Khinh-Tay, Ky-Cung, Lach-Tray, Lai-Giang, Lo, Luoc, Luy, Ma, Perfume, Rang, Tra-Bong, Tra-Khuc, Van-Uc, Ve and Vam-Co.

There are three large lakes in the country, Ba-Be, Ho-Tay and Hoan-Kiem, of which the largest is Ba-Be situated at an elevation of 145 meters (400 ft).

WEATHER

The climate of Vietnam ranges from tropical in the south to subtropical in the north. North Vietnam has a monsoon climate with a hot and humid wet season from mid-May to mid-September, a relatively warm and humid dry season from mid-October to mid-March and two short transitional seasons. From late December through April the climate of the coastal lowlands is characterized by a phenomenon called crachin, which is a prolonged period of fog, cloudiness and drizzle. In the southern panhandle the monsoon is shorter and comes later in the year.

Daily temperatures fluctuate widely in the Red River region. The average temperature for Hanoi is 28°C (82°F) in June and 17°C (63°F) in January, but the temperature often drops as low as 6°C (43°F). The temperatures of Ho Chi Minh City are representative of the south and range between 18°C and 33.4°C (64°F and 92°F). Temperatures in the highland areas are somewhat cooler ranging from a mean of about 15.6°C (60°F) in winter to 20°C (68°F) in summer.

The rainy season in the north extends from mid-April to mid-October with maximum rainfall in July and August. In central Vietnam the heaviest rains occur from September through January and in the south from April through December with peak periods in June and in September. The average rainfall is 183 cm (72 in.) in Hanoi, 297 cm (117 in.) in Hue and 206 cm (81 in.) in Ho Chi Minh City. In certain areas of the Annamite Cordillera the rainfall exceeds 406 cm (160 in.).

The typhoon season lasts from July through November. The plateaus in the central highlands are subject to hot, dry and sometimes violent summer winds known as Gio-Lao, the winds of Laos.

POPULATION

The population of Vietnam was estimated in 1985 at 60,492,000. The last official census in North Vietnam was taken in 1979, when the population was 52,741,766. The population is expected to reach 79.5 million by 2000 and 102.2 million by 2020.

The annual growth rate is estimated at 2.02% on the basis of an annual birth rate of 31.2 per 1,000.

The population is concentrated in the Red River delta in the North and the Mekong River delta in the South, where densities approach 800 per sq km (2,072 per sq mi). Disparities in density are being corrected through enforced relocation of over 10 million Vietnamese to areas designated as New Economic Zones. The overall density is 179 per sq km (464 per sq mi).

The urban component of the population is 20%, but because of the 3.4 million inhabitants of Ho Chi Minh City the south is more urbanized than the north. There are 12 cities with over 100,000 inhabitants

DEMOGRAPHIC INDICATORS (1984)	
Population, total (in 1,000)	60,492.0
Population ages (% of total)	
0-14	40.2
15-64	55.9
65+	3.9
Youth 15-24 (000)	11,518
Women ages 15-49 (000)	14,575
Dependency ratios	78.9
Child-woman ratios	698
Sex ratios (per 100 females)	94.7
Median ages (years)	19.7
Decline in birthrate (1960-78)	−22.2
Proportion of urban (%)	20.29
Population density (per sq. km.)	179
per hectare of arable land	6.7
Rates of growth (%)	2.02
urban %	3.1
rural %	1.8
Natural increase rates (per 1,000)	21.1
Crude birth rates (per 1,000)	31.2
Crude death rates (per 1,000)	10.1
Gross reproduction rates	2.10
Net reproduction rates	1.78
Total fertility rates	4.30
General fertility rates (per 1,000)	129
Life expectancy, males (years)	56.7
Life expectancy, females (years)	61.1
Life expectancy, total (years)	58.8
Population doubling time in years at current rate	28

Migration has taken place in the past only in response to the severe disruptions caused by war. Engulfed by war and destruction, many non-Communist Vietnamese fled first from the North to the South, then from the rural areas to Saigon (as Ho Chi Minh City was then called) and finally, in the weeks prior to the collapse of the Republic of Vietnam Government, out of the country in a massive air and sea lift supported by the U.S. government. The number of those evacuated to the United States in 1975 was estimated at 137,000. Many others have fled since, often in small fishing boats, to other Southeast Asian countries.

Many factors, in addition to the generally repressive political situation, have caused a mass exodus from Vietnam since 1975. Among them are ethnic and religious persecution, discrimination with regard to economic and educational opportunities, fear of imprisonment or of forced resettlement in remote areas, and fear of conscription to fight in Cambodia.

Vietnam's program to "facilitate" the departure of ethnic Chinese and others as refugees, which led in the spring of 1979 to an exodus of over 40,000 a month by boat, was apparently suspended in July 1979. Information from refugees who have left Vietnam since then indicates that the authorities are no longer officially assisting such departures. In May 1979 the UNHCR reached agreement with the government on the legal departure of people from Vietnam under the Orderly Departure Program. This program started slowly but in fiscal year 1984, 28,340 people left Vietnam and in fiscal year 1985 the number was 28,478. A significant number of these people are ethnic Chinese who consistently find it easier than ethnic Vietnamese to obtain official approval for departure. Another significant portion is composed of children fathered by Americans in Vietnam, known as "Amerasians." The government wants them to leave, and they are often subject to discrimination in Vietnam. In order to be placed on Orderly Departure Program lists, people must often bribe officials. Refugees from the Mekong Delta have reported that some people have paid officials from $4,800 to $6,000 in gold per person to be placed on tentative lists with no guarantee as to when or if they would be permitted to leave. People who have applied for exit permits reportedly are subject to recurring security checks and harassment.

Refugees continued to leave Vietnam clandestinely, although at a reduced rate compared to past years. They leave because of a combination of political, economic, and personal factors. Hanoi radio has broadcast reports of executions or of lengthy jail sentences for organizers of failed escape attempts, as well as of punishments dealt to others implicated. Currently, men can expect sentences ranging from three to 15 years at hard labor — depending on their role in the departure attempt — while women receive one to three months, with childless women often receiving longer sentences. Those released from reeducation camps who attempt flight can expect to be returned to the camps for an indefinite term. Property, often including the means of livelihood, is confiscated from those caught trying to escape. During the past few years there have been credible reports of Vietnamese patrol boats firing upon and sinking helpless refugee boats attempting to flee clandestinely. Hundreds of refugees reportedly have been killed and others captured and imprisoned as a result of these attacks.

Despite the promises of the Communist Party to emancipate women and the important administrative and productive roles filled by women in the war to take over the South, women in Vietnam today do not have positions in the leadership of the country which their numbers would warrant. There are no women in the Politburo and only four women in the 116-member Central Committee. There is only one woman member, the education minister, in the Council of Ministers. Vietnamese women have retreated from management positions they held during the war.

Family planning was launched in 1962 and contraception and abortion services are readily available to the population. The government plans the reduction of population growth rate to 2.1% by 1981 and 1.8% by 1986.

ETHNIC COMPOSITION

The Vietnamese are among the most vigorous people in Asia. Their remarkable cohesion and strong sense of national identity have enabled them to survive as a nation centuries of Chinese and French occupation and one of the most destructive wars in the 20th Century. The basic racial stock is Vietnamese, who constitute 85% to 90% of the population. Also called Annamese or Annamites, they are a mixture of Chinese and Thai ethnic stock. They are pale yellow with straight black hair with prominent cheek bones and oblique eyes; most of them are short.

The ethnic Chinese are the largest minority group, constituting 6.6% of the population, mostly in the south. Vietnamese hostility toward the Chinese resurfaced in 1978 when government restrictions on shopkeepers were generally perceived by the Chinese and the government of Communist China as racially motivated. As a result, many Chinese crossed the border into China after being stripped of their possessions.

The second largest minority is the Khmer group making up about 4% of the total population.

There are also over 60 minority groups thinly spread in the extensive mountainous regions. Collectively, they were known formerly as Montagnards.

Gradual assimilation appears to be the government's long-run strategy for most minorities. The government has created special schools in the Hanoi area to train minority cadres destined to be the "eyes and ears" of the party among their own people. Highland minorities in central Vietnam are subject to repression if suspected of ties with resistance groups. Officially sponsored settlement of ethnic Vietnamese into the highlands is designed to enhance lowlander control and to restrict minorities, some of whom are being forced away from their traditional farming practices and into settled agriculture. Southern minorities such as the Chinese, Indian, and Khmer have been encouraged to leave the country. One effect of Vietnam's history has been on the Vietnamese attitude toward the ethnic Chinese minority, whom the government perceives as a potential fifth column, to be expelled if possible, and if not, to be watched and closely controlled. Ethnic Chinese are severely discriminated against through denial of officially sanctioned employment and educational opportunities.

MINOR ETHNIC GROUPS OF VIETNAM

Group	Region	Population (in last census)
Bahnar	Pleiku, Phu bon	100,000
Black Thai	North	350,000
Bru	Quang Tri	22,000
Caolan	Tuyen-Quang, Ha-Bac, Bac-Thai	22,543
Cham	Central	56,820
Chroo	Central Highlands	15,000
Chru	Dran Valley	5,000
Cil	Central Highlands	18,000
Cua	Quang-Ngai	11,500
Die (Jeh)	Quang-Nam, Quang-Tin, Kontum	15,000
Duan	Upper Song Thanh River	3,500
Halang	Kontum	10,000
Han	Quang-Ninh, Ha-Bac, Lang-Son, Ha-Giang	174,644
Hre	Quang-Ngai	43,051
Hroy	Phu-Yen, Phu-Bon	8,000
Jarai	Central	150,000
Katu	Quang-Nam, Quang-Tin	30,000
Koho	Sai-Gon, Khanh-Hoa	65,000
Lat	Central Highlands	10,000
Lolo	Ha-Giang, Lao-Cai	6,398
Maa	Quang-Duc	15,000
Meo	Ha-Giang, Lao-Cai	219,514
M'Nong	Central Highlands	36,000
Monom	Kontum	2,100
Muong	Thanh-Hoa, Son-La, Ha-Tay, Nghia-Lo, Hoa-Binh	515,658
Nhang	Lao-Cai, Ha-Giang	16,429
Nung	Lang-Son, Bac-Thai, Cao-Bang, Ha-Giang, Ha-Bac	313,998
Pacoh	Thua-Thien	6,500
Red Thai	Thanh-Hoa	15,000
Rengao	Kontum	15,000
Rhade (Ete)	Darlac Plateau	100,000
Roglai	Central Highlands	40,000
Sanchi	Bac-Thai, Quang-Ninh, Ha-Bac	14,382
Sanziu	Bac-Thai, Ha-Bac, Quang-Ninh	33,913
Sedang	Kontum	30,000
Sre	Di-Linh	21,000
Stieng	Phuoc-Long, Binh-Long	50,000
Tau-Oi	Quang-Tri	11,000
Tay	Viet-Bac Autonomous Region	503,988
Thai	Lai-Chau, Nghia-Lo, Son-La	385,000
Van-Kieu	Quang-Tri, Quang-Binh, Thua-Thien	30,000
Xa	Tay-Bac Autonomous Region	22,500

LANGUAGES

The official language is Vietnamese, or Quoc-Ngu. The latter name is properly used to designate the Romanized writing script developed in the early 17th Century by Catholic missionaries as a means of translating catechisms and prayer books. It was initially used only by the Catholic Church and displaced the earlier Chinese characters, known as Chu Nho, only in this century. Vietnamese is a tonal monosyllabic language that belongs to the Mon-Khmer family, which, in turn, belongs to the Austro-Asiatic superfamily. At least one-third of the vocabulary is derived from Chinese. The modern history of the language begins with the famous dictionary published by Father Alexandre de Rhodes.

The other languages spoken in Vietnam are divided into five families: (1) Kadai or Thai spoken by the Thai, Tho and Nung groups; (2) Sino-Tibetan, or Tibeto-Burman, spoken in North Vietnam; (3) Miao-Yao spoken by the Meo and Man of North Vietnam; (4) Austronesian or Malayo-Polynesian spoken by the Cham, Rhade and Jarai groups; (5) Austroasiatic, including the Mon-Khmer languages such as Koho.

French, the colonial language, has fallen into disuse and is spoken only by older persons. English is looked upon with disfavor as the language of the Americans. Russian is gaining in importance and is taught along with Chinese in schools.

RELIGIONS

Vietnam has no national or official religion. The three traditional religions of the country, collectively known as tam-giao, are Buddhism, Taoism and Confucianism. Buddhism is the predominant religion in the number of followers. Introduced from China around 194-95 A.D. it became the official religion by the 10th Century. The Mahayana, or the Greater Wheel (Bac-Tong or Dai-Thua), is practiced in North and central Vietnam, whereas the Theravada Buddhism, or the Lesser Wheel (Nam-Thong or Tieu-Thua), is practiced in South Vietnam. Confucianism (Nho-Giao or Khong-Giao) while not a formal organized religion has been an important force in shaping social thought and structure by prescribing rules for social interaction, setting up the patriarchal family as the ideal human institution and introducing the cult of ancestor worship. Taoism, derived from the teachings of Lao Tse, has contributed much to the mysticism, magic and sorcery that is popular in Vietnam.

Catholicism, introduced in the 16th Century and proscribed and severely repressed in the 17th and 18th Centuries, flourished under the French and currently claims over 2 million followers. There are three archbishoprics at Hanoi, Hue and Ho Chi Minh City; the primate of the country, the archbishop of Hanoi, is a cardinal.

In addition to organized religions, there are at least two powerful sects which have played an important role in the social and political history of the country. The first is the Cao Dai, also known as Dai-Dao Tam Ky Pho-Do, founded by a visionary and spiritualist called Ngo Van-Chieu around 1920. Cao-Daism is actually a composite of several religions and among its saints are Winston Churchill, Victor Hugo and Sun Yat-sen. Centered in Tay-Ninh, Cao-Daism is strongest in the Mekong Delta. It has been a formidable political force under the French and the Japanese and maintained for a time an independent army. One sect of Cao-Daism, the Tien-Thien, has been represented in the National Liberation Front. Hoa Hao (Phat Giao Hoa Hao) is a Buddhist-oriented sect founded in 1939 by Huynh Phu-So. The sect is named after the Hoa Hao village in Chau-Doc Province. At one time it claimed nearly 1.5 million adherents, but its postwar fate is uncertain because of its strong anti-Communism.

Traditional religions are being modified under the current Marxist and atheist regime. Ironically, the religion that has adjusted itself best to the regime is the Catholic Church, whose cardinal, Archbishop Joseph Marie Trin Nhu Khue, was permitted to lead a delegation to Rome in 1975. The regime has sought the Church's help in persuading people to move to the New Economic Zones. Unlike the Catholic hierarchy, the most important group among the Buddhists, the An Quong Pagoda, has remained uncooperative. They have resented the official takeover of their schools and orphanages and discouragement of the reclusive and "unproductive" life of the monks and have staged several immolations in protest.

The government tolerates the existence of religious groups and allows religious services but has consistently attempted to divide and control the Catholic, Buddhist, and Cao Dai religions, the Islamic community, and other religious groups. The government perceives them as potential seedbeds of subversion and political opposition. It has attempted to prevent their growth and to inhibit proselytizing activities by, among other things, prohibiting publication of religious materials and severely limiting the training and mobility of clergy. The government has attempted to coopt religious groups by promoting parallel organizations and leaders who are subservient to it.

Refugees have reported constant harassment of the Catholic church by government authorities. Sermons require government approval. Uncooperative priests are subject to confinement in remote villages or incarceration in "reeducation camps." Many priests have been arrested, or are under house arrest. There are reportedly more than 100 priests detained in reeducation camps, and most former South Vietnamese military chaplains of all religions have remained in prison since 1975. Catholic priests and nuns are subject to police surveillance, and most of them are required by the authorities to work full time in secular occupations, thus limiting their participation in religious activities. The teaching role of the church has been severely restricted, and many churches and all but one Catholic seminary in the South have been closed; reportedly, no priest has been ordained since 1980. The government has restricted communication between rural parishes and their bishops. It also prohibits the printing of Bibles or their importation. Authorities routinely cut lists of parishioners applying to attend services by at least half, and an individual can attend only the church at which he is registered. Catholics are required to register as such with the authorities and are discriminated against in employment, although Buddhists are not. "Voluntary" work and other required activities are scheduled by the authorities during times of regular church services. As a result of this harassment, the size of Catholic congregations has shrunk steadily since 1975. In central Vietnam, thousands of Catholics have been forcibly relocated and made to work on government construction projects.

Protestant churches have been similarly restricted. Church buildings have been taken over by the authorities under various pretexts. Churches in the highlands (where most Protestants are located) have all been closed, as was the sole Protestant college and theological seminary. There have been continued reports of harassment among those evangelical churches which have been allowed — albeit within narrow limits — to continue to hold services in urban areas.

Most of the 30,000 Vietnamese Muslims are members of the Cham minority, which the regime distrusts and harasses. Links between the Cham, Khmer Krom (ethnic Khmer living in Vietnam) and hill tribes (Montagnards) have created the only sizable resistance movement in Vietnam: the United Liberation Front of Oppressed Races, or FULRO. In its repression of the Cham the government has eliminated the position of Mufti, or Islamic religious leader, within the Muslim communities; disbanded the organized Islamic association; and forced them to sever their links with overseas Islamic organizations. The regime forbids pilgrimage to Mecca and has not given permission for the Islamic community to participate in the Koran reading contest held annually in Malaysia. Many Islamic schools have been closed. Importation of the Koran is forbidden and the Koran printing house has been closed.

About 30 million people of Vietnam's population of 59 million are Buddhists, the great majority of them Mahayana. Vietnamese authorities have tried repeatedly since 1975 to suppress and intimidate the Mahayana Buddhist leadership. The authorities have closed temples and transformed them into public buildings. They have arrested monks intermittently since 1975 and hundreds remain in reeducation camps. Several monks were reportedly arrested in 1984. Many monks ramain under house arrest, and the travel of those not under detention is severely restricted. Government permission is required for monks to travel and stay overnight away from their home temples. Some reports allege that local authorities seek to control and restrict the community of Buddhist monks by forbidding the donation of food. The majority of pre-1975 monks in the South have been forced to leave the monkhood and few young men are allowed to join the community. Teaching of seminarians must often be conducted in secret and pagoda schools have been closed. Monks of the formerly politically active An Quang, Xa Loi, and Vinh Nghiem pagodas are kept under close government surveillance and are rarely allowed visitors.

The regime organized a conference in November 1981 to establish the Unified Vietnam Buddhist Church. Its charter provides that it is "the only Buddhist organization representing Vietnamese Buddhism in all other relations in the country and with other countries." Reports suggest that the new church has no appeal to most Buddhists who view it simply as a creature of the regime.

Most of Vietnam's Therevada Buddhists are Khmer Krom. This group numbers about 800,000 people living in southern and southwestern Vietnam, and has provided the Vietnamese army of occupation in Cambodia with interpreters and staff for its government in Cambodia. Nevertheless, the Khmer Krom continue to be distrusted by the Vietnamese, partly for historical reasons. A number of former Therevada leaders have been imprisoned.

Other religious groups have also been persecuted by the regime. The Hoa Hao strongly resisted the Communist takeover in 1975. As a result, the government violently repressed the sect and arrested virtually all of its leaders. The regime maintains tight control over Hoa Hao areas. Similarly, the regime has arrested many of the leaders of the Cao Dai. Refugees have reported police occupation of the Cao Dai Holy See in Tay Ninh City. The official press has claimed that the Cao Dai leaders have used the Holy See to establish an anti-government subversive organization, broadcasting and printing anti-government messages and storing arms for an uprising. Some leaders have been tried and executed for these alleged activities, according to the official news media. A trial of two leaders and 31 accomplices was publicized in August 1983.

Since the regime views religion as a possible source of political opposition, adherence to a religious sect is incompatible with membership in the Communist Party. Party membership is a prerequisite for advancement in society.

COLONIAL EXPERIENCE

The division of Vietnam into two states in the 18th Century, Tonkin in the north and Cochinchina in the south, permitted French political intervention and expansion in the region. Cochinchina became a French colony in 1867, and Annam and Tonkin became French protectorates in 1883. Later all three were merged with Laos and Cambodia to form French Indochina. Throughout French colonial rule, Vietnam was beset by strong nationalist and revolutionary movements, some of them with religious overtones. With the collapse of France in 1940, the Vichy regime yielded Indochina to the Japanese who set up a puppet administration under Bao Dai, emperor of Annam. Following Japan's surrender, the league for the Independence of Vietnam (Viet-Nam Doc Lap Dong Minh Hoi), commonly known as the Viet-Minh, a nationalist coalition led by a Communist known as Nguyen Ai Quoc (who had adopted the pseudonym of Ho Chi Minh in 1943) proclaimed the Democratic Republic of Vietnam in Hanoi in 1945. French resistance to the Viet-Minh led to a war that lasted eight years culminating in the siege of Dien Bien Phu. A ceasefire agreement was signed at Geneva in 1954, which provisionally partitioned Vietnam along the 17th parallel pending general elections to bring about the unification of the country. These elections were never held, but in a referendum the South proclaimed itself the Republic of Vietnam with Ngo Dinh Diem as president and its capital at Saigon. The anti-Communist regime in the South was opposed by a growing resistance movement composed of former members of the Viet-Minh who became known as the Viet-Cong. Diem was overthrown in 1963 and a series of short-lived military regimes followed. Earlier, in 1961, the United States had joined the war between the North and the South, committing large ground forces on the side of the Saigon government and carrying out bombing attacks against the North from 1965 to 1968. These bombings did not deter the Viet-Cong from stepping up their insurgent activity and gaining control of large areas in the South. Meanwhile, peace negotiations begun in 1969 between the Hanoi government and the United States (spurred by the failure of U.S. military policy and growing internal opposition to an unpopular war) led to the Paris Peace Agreement on January 27, 1973. The last of the U.S. forces in South Vietnam left on March 29, 1973; the U.S. combat death roll in Vietnam was 46,079.

The conflict dragged on for another two years until the Hanoi-led National Liberation Front forces, in a massive offensive, swept through to the gates of Saigon. President Nguyen Van Thieu resigned and fled and was replaced by Gen. Duong Van Minh, who announced the Republic of Vietnam's unconditional surrender. The war, which had raged for three decades, ended after killing 2 million Vietnamese, maiming and injuring another 4 million, rendering 57% of the population homeless, and desolating most of its cultivated areas.

The nation that emerged united from the war had no reason to remember its colonial experience with gratitude. However, the bitterest feelings of the Vietnamese are directed not against the French but against the Americans who, paradoxically, have never ruled the country.

CONSTITUTION & GOVERNMENT

The constitution of the Democratic Republic of Vietnam was adopted by the National Assembly on December 18, 1980. It contains a preamble and 12 chapters with 147 articles. The constitution established two executive organs of government, the Council of State and the Council of Ministers. Executive power is vested in these two organs, plus the president, who is elected by the National Assembly for a four-year term. In practice all power lies with the Vietnam Communist Party.

Suffrage is universal over age 18. Pro forma elections are held for national and local assemblies, the last being the elections for the National Assembly held in 1981.

Either because opposition is stifled at its source or because there are no channels through which dissent could gain national attention or support, Vietnam presents the picture of a monolithic state solidly united behind its new masters. There are no ways of assessing the success of the regime's efforts to elimi-

ORGANIZATION OF VIETNAMESE GOVERNMENT

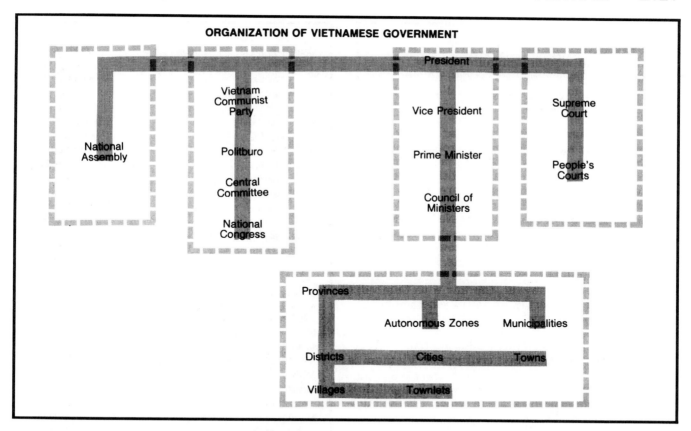

nate all survivals of the old order. Nevertheless, the government has made phenomenal strides in rebuilding the country. It has also shown considerable moderation and pragmatism in its efforts to integrate unassimilated groups, such as the Roman Catholic Church. However, the war with Cambodia may set back its efforts to complete the reconstruction of the country by several years. There are also occasional reports of anti-Communist guerrillas operating in remote areas.

FREEDOM & HUMAN RIGHTS

In terms of political and civil rights, Vietnam is classified as a not-free country with a maximum negative rating of 7 in civil rights and 7 in political rights (on a descending scale in which 1 is the highest and 7 the lowest in rights).

During six years of existence, Vietnam has still not achieved complete normalcy either at home or abroad. In its efforts to consolidate its power it treats its internal opponents like war criminals. The government encouraged and at times coerced the departure of nearly one million Vietnamese, half of them ethnic Chinese, until universal outcry forced Hanoi to stop the outflow. The government maintains close surveillance over religious groups many of whose members are denied employment until they receive re-education. Government approval is required for all internal and external travel. No one is allowed to change his residence or work location without permis-

sion from authorities. Although Southerners have been appointed to some ministerial positions, distrust of Southerners is a significant factor in the delegation of political responsibilities. The ethnic Chinese are the most severely discriminated against. Corruption has become widespread in the country with petty officials requiring bribes for providing any service as well as ignoring minor infractions of the law.

There is a pervasive system of population surveillance by party-appointed local wardens, who use informants to keep track of each person's political and economic activities. The system works imperfectly in the South, however, partly because of a shortage of trusted party workers. There have been reports of officials and even unofficial security wardens conducting without warrants midnight searches of homes for draft-age males in order to fill draft quotas. There continue to be reliable reports that the Interior Ministry inspects and sometimes confiscates international mail and packages sent to Vietnam, particularly to politically suspect people or those of Chinese origin. Outgoing mail is also subject to inspection and censorship.

The regime has widely publicized its program to relocate millions of people to "new economic zones" in virgin or unproductive rural areas in order to expand agricultural production. Hundreds of thousands were resettled in these remote zones in the South in the years immediately following the fall of South Vietnam. The resettlement process has involved forms of coercion in most cases. It targeted for resettlement those whose views and background made them politi-

COUNCIL OF STATE

President: Truong Chinh.
Vice-Presidents: Le Thanh Nghi, Chu Huy Man, Huynh Tan Phat.
General Secretary: Le Thanh Nghi.
Members of the Council: Nguyen Duc Thuan, Nguyen Thi Dinh, Ngo Duy Dong, Le Thanh Dao, Y Ngong Niek Dam, Dam Quang Trung, Vu Quang.

cally suspect and often unable to find employment. Conditions in these zones are widely reported to range from poor to life-theatening with inadequate provision of basic services. Many of those so relocated have left the zones, returning to the cities where they are forced to live on an already marginal economy, without the ration or neighborhood registration cards essential to procuring employment, food and other essential services. Without these documents they can be arrested arbitrarily and returned to the new economic zone. The government continues its relocation program, despite its cost in human suffering. The 1981-85 plan calls for the relocation of one million people. A Ministry of Labor official claimed in August 1985 that the 1985 goal of relocating 200,000 workers would be met. The official rationale for this massive dislocation of people is increased economic production, particularly of cash crops such as coffee and rubber. Although the government speaks of "volunteers" when discussing people resettled in these zones, it is clear that arbitrary resettlement interferes with a person's right to live in a place of his own choosing.

Those suspected of political crimes may be sent to reeducation camps without trial or charge. The government continues to hold large numbers of people in the camps, including both those whom the government distrusts because of their association with the former Republic of Vietnam, and those whose current political views are suspect. These camps remove dissident elements from society, particularly competent and/or charismatic leaders. The camps attempt to produce conformity through confinement, hard labor, self-criticism and a minimum amount of indoctrination. While several thousand prisoners have been released, including officers up to the rank of colonel (and a handful of generals, mostly from the medical services), some have been rearrested. Decisions on most releases appear arbitrary and often the result of bribery. The Vietnamese government officially maintains that the number of people associated with the former regime detained in the camps since 1975 is on the order of 10,000. Others incarcerated in the system include post-1975 dissidents, those caught trying to emigrate illegally and common criminals.

Forced labor has been used by Vietnamese and local authorities in Cambodia for projects to improve the logistical infrastructure for Vietnamese occupation troops. This labor cannot be justified as a normal civic obligation or an emergency response to catastrophe.

COUNCIL OF MINISTERS (1985)	
Chairman, National Assembly	Nguyen Huu Tho
Chairman, State Council	Truong Chinh
Vice Chairman	Nguyen Huu Tho
Vice Chairman	Le Thanh Nghi
Vice Chairman	Chu Huy Man
Vice Chairman	Huynh Tan Phat
Chairman, Council of Ministers	Pham Van Dong
Vice Chairman	Vo Van Kiet
Vice Chairman	*Gen.* Vo Nguyen Giap
Vice Chairman	Pham Hung
Vice Chairman	To Huu
Vice Chairman	Vu Dinh Lieu
Vice Chairman	Do Muoi
Vice Chairman	Dong Sy Nguyen
Vice Chairman	Tran Phuong
Vice Chairman	Tran Quynh
Minister of Agriculture	Nguyen Ngoc Triu
Minister of Building	Phan Ngoc Tuong
Minister of Communications & Transportation	Dong Sy Nguyen
Minister of Culture	Nguyen Van Hieu
Minister of Education	Nguyen Thi Binh
Minister of Engineering & Metals	Nguyen Van Kha
Minister of Finance	Chu Tam Thuc
Minister of Food	Nguyen Van Chinh
Minister of Food Industry	Vu Tuan
Minister of Foreign Affairs	Nguyen Co Thach
Minister of Foreign Trade	Le Khac
Minister of Forestry	Phan Xuan Dot
Minister of Higher & Vocational Education	Nguyen Dinh Tu
Minister of Home Trade	Le Duc Thinh
Minister of Interior	Pham Hung
Minister of Justice	Phan Hien
Minister of Labor	Dao Thien Thi
Minister of Light Industry	Nguyen Chi Vu
Minister of Marine Products	Nguyen Tien Trinh
Minister of Mines & Coal	Nguyen Chan
Minister of Natl. Defense	*Gen.* Van Tien Dung
Minister of Power	Pham Khai
Minister of Public Health	Dang Hoi Xuan
Minister of Supply	Hoang Duc Nghi
Minister of War Invalids & Social Welfare	Song Hao
Minister of Water Conservancy	Nguyen Canh Dinh
Chairman, State Capital Construction Comn.	Do Quoc Sam
Chairman, State Inspection Comn.	Bui Quang Tao
Chairman, State Law Comn.	Tran Quang Huy
Chairman, State Nationalities Comn.	Hoang Van Kieu
Chairman, State Planning Comn.	Vo Van Kiet
Chairman, State Science & Technology Comn.	Dang Huu
Director General, State Bank	Nguyen Duy Gia

CIVIL SERVICE

No current information is available on the Vietnamese civil service.

LOCAL GOVERNMENT

For administrative purposes the country is divided into 35 provinces, autonomous zones and municipalities. Provinces are further subdivided into districts, cities and towns; districts, in turn, are subdivided into villages and townlets.

PROVINCES OF VIETNAM	
Province	Area (sq km)
Lai Chau	17,408
Son La	14,656
Hoang Lien Son	14,125
Ha Tuyen	13,519
Cao Lang	13,731
Bac Thai	8,615
Quang Ninh	7,076
Vinh Phu	5,187
Ha Bac	4,708
Ha Son Binh	6,860
Hai Hung	2,526
Thai Binh	1,344
Ha Nam Ninh	3,522
Thanh Hoa	11,138
Nghe Tinh	22,380
Binh Tri Thien	19,048
Quang Nam-Do Nang	11,376
Nghia Binh	14,700
Gia Lai-Kontum	18,480
Dac Lac	18,300
Phu Kanh	9,620
Lam Dong	10,000
Thuan Hai	11,000
Dong Nai	12,130
Song Be	9,500
Tay Ninh	4,100
Long An	5,100
Dong Thap	3,120
Tien Giang	2,350
Ben Tre	2,400
Cuu Long	4,200
An Giang	4,140
Hau Giang	5,100
Kien Giang	6,000
Minh Hai	8,000

The three cities are Ho Chi Minh City, Hanoi and Haiphong.

At each of the three levels, people's councils have been set up; the councils, in turn, elect people's committees to run the day-to-day administration.

FOREIGN POLICY

Vietnam's long march toward nationhood culminated in its being admitted in 1977 as a member of the U.N., following the United States' withdrawal of its opposition. In his first speech at the U.N., Foreign Minister Nguyen Duy Trinh listed the foreign policy priorities, in order of importance, as follows: friendship and cooperation with the Soviet Union and other socialist countries, preservation of a special relationship with Laos and Cambodia, solidarity with nonaligned countries and support for all national independence movements.

The special relationship with Laos and Cambodia turned out to be a quest for hegemony over all of Indochina, which Vietnam has achieved within five years of its establishment as a unified republic. through a number of Hanoi-dictated "mutual cooperation agreements," Laos has become little more than a province of Vietnam. Over 40,000 Vietnamese troops are believed to be permanently stationed in Laos. When Cambodia resisted Vietnamese demands, relations between the two countries deteriorated sharply, leading to military encounters and border clashes, later escalating into full-scale warfare. In a 14-day blitzkreig, ending on January 7, 1919, Vietnam overran its neighbor and captured Phnom Penh, installing a puppet government headed by a former member of the Cambodian general staff, Heng Samrin. A month later the Chinese, long unhappy over the Hanoi-Moscow axis, launched a punitive attack across the border that served very little purpose except to demonstrate Chinese weaknesses.

In the end, the conquest of Cambodia has proved a pyrrhic victory for Vietnam. Not only has it drawn condemnation from virtually every country outside of the Soviet bloc but also made it necessary for Vietnam to deploy its troops on two fronts: on the Chinese border in the north and on the Thai border to the west in addition to maintaining an army of occupation in both Cambodia and Laos. While the military advantages are obvious, the political and economic liabilities may prove disastrous in the future.

In 1977 the Communist Party supremo Le Duan, visited Moscow to attend the 60th anniversary of the Russian Revolution and the occasion was marked with exhibitions, lectures and cultural programs throughout Vietnam praising the Soviet Union as the model Communist country. Hanoi also confirmed that the Soviet Union had written off Vietnam's wartime debts and committed $2.6 billion to Vietnam's Second Five-Year Plan (1976-80). In 1978 Vietnam became a member of CMEA (Council for Mutual Economic Assistance) and signed a treaty of friendship and cooperation with the Soviet Union. Soviet and Cuban help enabled Vietnam to unseat Pol Pot's representatives at the Havana Summit of Non-Aligned Nations but not at the United Nations.

Vietnam has also come a long way from its earlier hostility to its ASEAN (Association of South-East Asian Nations) neighbors. Governmental ties and commercial relations have been established with all ASEAN members. Vietnam also enjoys a rather close relationship with India, which has offered funds for agricultural and cattle-breeding projects.

More significant has been the restoration of relations with France to prewar levels. Premier Pham Van Dong visited France in 1977 and signed an agreement settling all outstanding issues including payment for French property in Vietnam. French aid has been promised for a steel mill and offshore oil exploration.

Vietnam's share of the U.N. budget is 0.02%. Vietnam and the United States have no diplomatic relations.

U.K. Ambassador in Hanoi: R. G. Tallboys
Vietnamese Ambassador in London: Dang Nghiem
Bai

PARLIAMENT

The National Assembly (Quoc Hai) is a unicameral body of 496 members, of whom 251 are from the North and 245 from the South. These 496 members were elected from 605 candidates nominated by political parties and revolutionary mass organizations. Of the total number, 67 are members of ethnic minorities and 13 are members of religious communities. The Assembly is elected for the same term as the president, i.e. five years. It meets twice a year or for extraordinary sessions.

Between sessions the Assembly's functions are performed by a Standing Committee comprising a chairman, seven vice chairmen, 13 permanent members and two alternate members.

POLITICAL PARTIES

The ruling political party is the Communist Party of Vietnam (Dang Cong san Viet-Nam), founded in 1976 as the successor to the Vietnam Workers' Party. The party is governed by a politburo of 13 full and two alternate members and its secretariat is headed by the general secretary, Truong Chinh, who succeeded Le Duan in 1986. The party's chairmanship has been left vacant in deference to its former chairman, Ho Chi Minh. The Central Committee of the party is the second-ranking organ with 116 full and 36 alternate members. The party's fifth congress, which met at Hanoi in 1982, was attended by 1,033 delegates. Its total membership is estimated at over two million.

In addition to the Vietnam Communist Party, there are a number of satellite political organizations operating under its umbrella. Together they constitute the National United Front. These parties include the Vietnam Socialist Party, the Vietnam Democratic Party, the Vietnam Alliance of National, Democratic and Peace Forces and the Vietnam Fatherland Front. The purpose of permitting these parties to function is to create the impression of a multiparty system.

ECONOMY

Vietnam is one of the 49 low-income countries of the world with a centrally planned economy in which the dominant sector is public. Since the Communist takeover of the South very little economic information has been published or permitted to reach the West. No financial statistics are reported to the IMF. What statistics are available relate to the pre-1975 divided Vietnam or are estimates based on fragmentary information.

The evolution of the Vietnamese economy has gone through three phases: the first phase was that of a so-

cialist transformation in order to destroy the feudal and capitalist elements; the second that of socialist construction, based on state control and planning; and the third phase one of pragmatism based on the realities of Vietnam's political and economic isolation, financial debt and depleted resources.

For historical reasons, these three phases have had differing chronological time frames in the North and the South. In the North the first phase involved a Maoist mass mobilization effort and its concrete result was the redistribution of land and the elimination of both landlords and rich peasants as a class. This was a prelude to the cooperativization movement by bureaucratic methods. When the deficiencies of the cooperative movement became obvious, there emerged a system of contracting out cooperative land to individual families or small production teams. Although this un-Marxist practice was periodically condemned by the party faithful, it has subsequently spread to all sectors of the economy. The contracts are given on the basis that a certain quota of the output be given to the state. Any excess may be sold by the peasants on the open market, in much the same way as produce from the private plots is sold. Private plots still constitute 5% of the land area. By 1982 the contractual quota system was said to be operating in fully 98% of the cooperatives in the northern delta and in northern and central Vietnam and in 90% of the cooperatives in the South. In the South, private ownership of land was permitted until 1977, when it was decided to accelerate the process of socialist transformation. However, it was reported in the mid-1980s that individual ownership was still widespread, with production collectives limited to 21.3% of the farm households and 15% of the arable land area. Transformation of southern industry has proceeded even more slowly than has been the case with agriculture, with most small-scale enterprises still in private hands and even some of the larger nationalized industries retaining their former executives as managers. Only in the sphere of private trading has all private initiative and ownership been effectively removed, but even here private enterprise does continue to play a significant role.

PRINCIPAL ECONOMIC INDICATORS

Gross National Product: $14.8 billion (1983)
  GNP Annual Growth Rate: Information not available
  Per Capita GNP: $245 (1983)
  Per Capita GNP Annual Growth Rate: Information not available

Gross Domestic Product: Information not available

Income Distribution: Information not available

Consumer Price Index: Information not available

Money Supply: Information not available

International Reserves: Information not available
  *no information available on balance of payments.

The Second Five-Year Plan was designated for the years 1976-80 (corresponding to the Soviet and Eastern European planning cycle), but its content was still being debated throughout 1976 and it was not formally approved until the fourth party congress in December that year. By then the formal incorporation of the South into a united Vietnam meant that the plan was broadened into what is now considered as the First National Plan. The new plan continued to pay lip service to the concept of heavy industry, but in practice it retreated from the ambitious objectives of 1960-63. Much greater emphasis was to be placed on agriculture and light industry, which would contribute both to the improvement of material living standards within Vietnam and to the development of exports to earn foreign exchange. In this context, the South was to revert to its former role as the main supplier of the nation's food needs, as well as the source of agricultural exports and light industrial goods. The plan ran into difficulties in 1977-78, however, and targets were drastically revised. While one of the reasons for this may have been the disastrous weather of these two years, it now seems that the plan depended heavily on foreign investments. It was anticipated that the bulk of the investment would come from the U.S. With the U.S. refusing to normalize relations, none of this aid has been forthcoming and foreign aid in general has been further reduced in reaction to Vietnam's action in invading Cambodia. This and the subsequent war and general state of hostility with the People's Republic of China has drawn further resources away from the economic development effort and it is now estimated that over 40% of the country's budget is being spent on defense. In such circumstances, it is hardly surprising that most of the plan targets were subsequently revised and abandoned.

In 1980 discussions began on the Second National Plan (1981-85), also to be set within the framework of the CMEA, but this was finally revealed only at the fifth party congress in March-April 1982. The delay of over a year probably relates to the failure of Vietnam's CMEA partners to confirm their aid commitments. Even now, the plan remains more a statement of intentions than a detailed outline for action, but it is nevertheless clear that the new plan will be much less ambitious than its ill-starred predecessor. Many grandiose construction projects have been suspended, while the emphasis is on small, practical projects within Vietnam's capabilities and, in sectoral terms, on agriculture, consumer goods industries, energy, exports and communications. The plan also marks a return to a more decentralized management structure, with the delegation of powers to regional and grassroots echelons in line with the stress upon a balance of the "three interests" of society, the collective and the worker. In the past, the latter has been rather neglected and the new emphasis is in line with the more liberal attitudes toward individual responsibilities and incentives.

No information is available on the current breakdown of the GDP by economic activity.

In 1976 Vietnam joined the IMF, the World Bank and the Asian Development Bank on the strength of South Vietnam's previous membership of these bodies. In 1977 and 1978 the IMF and World Bank extended some loans, but since that time has turned down further requests for loans. The ADB, under Japan's leadership, has been unwilling to extend aid because of opposition to the occupation of Cambodia. Thus most multilateral development aid has come from the relatively limited resources of the United Nations Development Program which has provided $118 million, mostly for irrigation and agricultural projects. Development aid from capitalist countries has been mainly from France, Japan and Scandinavian countries, expecially Sweden. Aid from France, in mixed credits, is estimated at $363 million; aid from Japan $65 million; aid from Sweden $100 million; aid from Denmark $75 million; aid from Finland $37 million and aid from Norway $52 million. Aid from multilateral agencies has been more recently oriented toward humanitarian efforts.

Since joining CMEA in 1977, the bulk of foreign aid comes from Communist countries. During the 1976-80 plan, the economic aid disbursed by the USSR and its allies has been estimated at between $1.450 and $3.500 billion. Much of the Soviet aid was for specific large projects, such as the Black River Hydroelectric project, the Pha Lai power plant, the Bim Son Cement Works, the Cao Son coal mine, and the rehabilitation of the Haiphong Harbor. East Germany is the second most generous donor with $200 million, followed by Hungary with $188 million, Czechoslovakia with $150 million and Bulgaria with $143 million. During 1979-81 aid from all sources totaled $266 million or $4.90 per capita.

BUDGET

The Vietnamese fiscal year is the calendar year. In 1982 the national budget consisted of revenues of $4.120 billion and expenditures of $5.560 billion. In March 1983 a series of changes in the tax system were introduced in an effort to reduce the budget deficit, which stood at 4,000 million dong (U.S. $440 million) at the end of 1982. The deficit was reduced from 19% of GDP in 1982 to 11% in 1983. It was hoped that the amendments would also curb the expansion of private trading. In 1983 tax revenues from private enterprise rose by 55%. More than one-half of the national budget is thought to be spent on defense. Although small by world standards, Vietnam's external debt now totals $3.5 billion of which $1.600 billion is in convertible currencies. Annual repayments in convertible currencies are 200% of annual hard currency exports.

FINANCE

The Vietnamese unit of currency is the dong divided into 100 xu and 10 hao. Coins are issued in denominations of 1, 2 and 5 xu; notes are issued in denominations of 2 and 5 xu, 1, 2 and 5 hao, and 1, 2, 5, 10 and 20 dong.

The new dong was introduced in 1959 with a par value of 1 new dong for 1,000 old dong. In 1975 the piastre, the monetary unit of South Vietnam, was abolished and the dong was made the national currency in the South as well as the North. In 1984 the exchange rates were $1 = D10.588 and £ = D12.272.

The country's sole bank is the State Bank of Vietnam, which also functions as the central bank and the bank of issue of the dong. It has 612 branches and sub-branches. The Bank of Foreign Trade is authorized to deal with foreign currencies and international payments, while the Commercial Credit Bank is entrusted with certain foreign transactions.

AGRICULTURE

Of the total land area of 33,255,900 hectares (82,175,328 acres), some 16.5% is classified as cultivated land, or 0.1 hectare (0.2 acre) per capita. The agricultural sector employs 60% of the labor force. Agriculture is concentrated in the lowland areas: the Red River delta in the North and the Mekong River delta in the South, the latter one of the great rice-producing regions of the world. In the North almost the entire arable area is under intensive cultivation, while in the South only 71% of the arable area is under cultivation. In the North two (and in some cases three crops a year, as in Thai-Binh and Nam-Dinh provinces) are made possible through an extensive system of irrigation utilizing over 4,000 km (2,484 mi) of dikes. On the other hand, in the South only single cropping is possible because heavy rains during six months alternate with dry conditions in the other six.

Agriculture is being systematically collectivized. In the North the socialist sector covers 95% of the farmlands, including some 63 state farms covering more than 200,000 hectares (494,200 acres). In the South all large holdings have been expropriated and redistributed to landless peasants and families of National Liberation Front soldiers killed during the war. Over 800 agricultural cooperatives have been organized by 1979. However, small- and medium-scale farmers have been permitted to continue to operate their farms for the time being. More than 1 million persons are being resettled in the so-called New Economic Zones in the central plateau regions.

By far the greatest part of the arable land — 5.74 million hectares out of 7.6 million hectares (14.18 million acres) — is used for rice cultivation and in many areas it is possible to harvest two crops per year from the same land, especially where there is a double monsoon or the land is irrigated. Since the 1970s the high-yielding varieties of rice have been a prominent feature of Vietnamese agriculture, although some parts of the Mekong delta are unsuited for such varieties. A large area of arable land is devoted to dry crops, such as corn, sweet potatoes, cassava and pulses. Such secondary crops are generally regarded as an insurance against bad rice harvests.

Although expansion of agriculture has been a recurring theme in Vietnamese planning since the 1960s — especially since 1963 when it was accepted that industry must serve agriculture — periodic natural disasters have plagued this sector. Until 1983, when for the first time the country was self-sufficient in foodstuffs, there were chronic food shortages. The basic food ration dropped to a mere 13 kg (28.66 lb) of grain per person per month, of which only 6.7kg (14.77 lb) were of the favored rice staple. By mid-1981 there was widespread and serious malnutrition. But agriculture was depressed not merely by unfavorable weather but also by the collectivist policies of the Hanoi regime, particularly the work-point system used in the cooperatives. Part of the grain deficit was due to the government's inability to obtain its full quota of rice production from the peasants in the South, where there were reports of grain being fed to the livestock rather than being offered to the government at unattractive prices.

Since the early 1980s the picture has changed as a result of the use of production contracts and increased procurement prices. In 1983 food production reached 16.71 million tons (despite the loss of 400,000 tons as a result of typhoons). During 1983 and 1984 Vietnam did not have to import foodstuffs, and although farming is still at the mercy of the elements, the downward trend of the 1970s has been reversed.

The mechanization of agriculture is inhibited by the shortage of petroleum. The country's 38,000 tractors, not all of them serviceable, serve less than one-half of agricultural requirements. This explains the recent shift in policy to encourage the production of draft animals. Since 1979 some 15% of communal land has been set aside for collective stockbreeding in an effort to reverse the alarming downward trend in the total cattle herd since 1961. The Chinese invasion of 1979 is believed to have resulted in the deaths of 250,000 heads of cattle, and flooding and the outbreak of epidemics decimated an equal number.

Annual consumption of fertilizers in 1982 was 250,000 tons, or 50 kg (110 lb) per arable hectare. The country is badly short of the hydrocarbon base for nitrogenous fertilizers, and increasing use is made of green fertilizers, such as the plant *Azolla pinata* grown as a natural fertilizer on flooded paddy fields, and cattle manure.

The raising of draft animals, especially water buffalo, is the most significant aspect of animal husbandry. Hogs which provide about 80% of the meat are raised mainly in the north. The livestock population in 1982 consisted of 1.970 million cattle and 11.393 million pigs, 140,000 horses, 2.5 million buffaloes, 16,000 sheep, 197,000 goats and 46.068 million chickens.

Forests cover about 40.3% of the land area, but their commercial potential has been hurt by the defoliation programs conducted by the U.S. Air Force during the war. Roundwood removals in 1982 totaled 23.191 million cubic meters (819 million cubic ft), including rosewood, mahogany, ebony, sandalwood, pine, lat-hoa and gu.

PRINCIPAL CROP PRODUCTION (1982)		
	Area (000 hectares)	Production (000 tons)
Rice	4,889	13,786
Corn	450	487
Sorghum	30	40
Sweet potatoes	350	1,665
Cassava	400	2,665
Dry beans	90	60
Other pulses	120	133
Soybeans	45	100
Groundnuts	110	85
Cottonseed	10	3
Cotton (lint)	10	2
Coconuts	n.a.	355
Vegetables	n.a.	2,719
Fruit)	n.a.	2,856
Sugar cane	70	4,400
Coffee	13	8
Tea	45	25
Tobacco	26	30
Jute & substitutes	33	36
Natural rubber	n.a.	50

In addition to its rich offshore fishing grounds, Vietnam has over 122,275 hectares (303,019 acres) of lakes, ponds, rivers and marshes where over 50 commercial species of fish are found. Ha-Long Bay, the major fishing area in the North, is rich in prawns, crayfish, shrimp and lobster. Most of the fish catch is consumed domestically (the fish sauce known as nuoc mam is a major ingredient of the Vietnamese diet). The annual fish catch in 1982 totaled 1,000,000 tons. Collectivization of the fishing industry and nationalization of most oceangoing vessels have lowered fishermen's income severely. The fishing industry has been further curtailed by strict government limits on the amount of fuel and water permitted aboard. These measures have been adopted to prevent refugee ecapes. Depletion of the fishing fleet through loss of boats to transport refugees has also hurt the industry.

INDUSTRY

Industry is mainly concentrated in the North. Heavy U.S. bombing from 1965 to 1973 destroyed an estimated 70% of the productive capacity, but by 1976 output in many sectors had regained prewar levels. Heavy industries in the North include the Hanoi Engineering Plant, producing lathes, machine tools and tractors, an iron and steel plant at Thai Nguyen, and a Chinese-aided nitrogenous fertilizer plant at Ha-Bac. Industrial production in the South consists of light manufactures and processed agricultural and forest products. Although all large industries have been brought under state control, there exists a very small private industrial sector. In 1983 industry employed only 10% of the work force.

Industrial production, which by 1980 had fallen overall to only 87% of the 1976 level, is reported to have increased at an annual rate of 11.8% in 1980-83, but progress has been uneven. Whereas there has been a 15.2% increase in locally run (small-scale and privately or co-operatively-owned) industries and a 19.7% increase in handicrafts, production in the larger-scale, centrally run state industries has been less sucessful, with a mere 3.2% increase in output. Many existing consumer industries inherited from the former regime in the South required the import of raw materials and parts from the West, for which foreign exchange is not available at present. Shortfalls in the agricultural sector have also affected supplies of raw materials, while the refugee outflow of 1979-81 has left the country short of a good many skilled workers and managerial staff. Equally, if not more serious, is the power shortage in the country which condemns many plants to work at only 30% – 40% of total capacity.

ENERGY

In 1982 Vietnam's total production of energy was 6.297 million metric tons of coal equivalent and consumption 7.138 million metric tons of coal equivalent, or 127 kg (280 lb) per capita. In 1984 production of electric power totaled 4.5 billion kwh, or 75 kwh per capita. There are plans for intensive offshore exploration to tap large suspected oil basins. The annual growth rates during 1973-83 were 5.6% for energy production and –2.1% energy consumption. Apparent per capita consumption of gasoline is 11 gallons per year.

The first stage of the Pha Lai thermal power station, which will have an eventual total capacity of 110,000 kw, came into operation in October 1983, thus easing energy problems. Vietnam's first nuclear research reactor, at Da Lat, was inaugurated in March 1984, with a capacity of 500 kw.

LABOR

The economically active population is estimated at 25.362 million, of whom 45.5% are women. Nearly 70% are employed in agriculture, 3% in manufacturing, 1.8% in construction, 0.7% in transportation and communications and 24.5% in other. The dismantling of the South Vietnamese army at the end of the war, along with the economic reorganization launched by the new regime, contributed to heavy unemployment, estimated to affect 2.5 million workers. Many of those unemployed are being sent to work in the rice paddies.

Wages and hours of work are regulated by the government, and wages are at near subsistence levels for most workers. Wage increases for civil servants have not kept pace with inflation, forcing many city dwellers, especially government cadre and workers, to hold two jobs. It is not known whether child labor or occupational safety and health laws exist in Vietnam.

At least 55,000 Vietnamese workers have been sent under contract to work in various occupations in the Soviet Union and other East European countries. A significant portion of their wages is deducted to help pay for Vietnam's debt to these countries. It appears that even with these deductions, however, workers are eager to participate in this program so as to escape the extreme poverty and unemployment of present-day Vietnam.

The sole labor union in the country is the Viet-Nam General Federation of Trade Unions formed in 1976 through the merger of the Southern Viet-Nam Trade Union Federation and the Tong Cong Doan Viet-Nam, based in Hanoi with a membership of 1.2 million.

FOREIGN COMMERCE

In 1984 the foreign commerce of Vietnam consisted of exports of $253.8 million and imports of $596 million, leaving a trade deficit of $342.2 million. Of the imports, fuels and raw materials constituted 44.7%, machinery 23.2% and food products 17.2%. Of the exports, manufactured goods constituted 72.8%, handicrafts 18.6% and agricultural products 8.6%. The major import sources are: the Soviet Union 18.3%, Japan 15.8%, India 12.9%, Singapore 6.9% and Hong Kong 6.2%. The major export destinations are: Japan 31.0%, Hong Kong 14.1%, the Soviet Union 11.6% and Singapore 11.4%.

TRANSPORTATION & COMMUNICATIONS

The government-owned Duong Sat Vietnam operates 2,816 km (1,749 mi) of track. Hanoi is the center of the rail network in the North and is linked to the Chinese rail system. A major achievement in 1976 was the opening of the trans-Vietnam railway between Hanoi and Ho Chi Minh City after 30 years of interruption. However, the rail system still suffers from the ravages of the war and contains many provisional bridges and makeshift stations. Rail traffic in 1982 consisted of 4.554 billion passenger-km and 779 million ton-km of freight.

The total length of inland waterways is 17,702 km (10,992 mi), of which 5,149 km (3,179 mi) are navigable all year round. The principal waterways are the Red River and its tributaries in the North and the Mekong in the South.

There are six major ports: Haiphong, Ho Chi Minh City, Nha Trang, Da Nang, Qui Nhon and Hong-Gai. A new harbor has been built at Vinh with Cuban aid. In 1982 these ports handled 5,680,000 tons of cargo. Vietnam has only a small merchant marine of 114 ships with a GRT of 389,600. Most of the coastal trade is carried on in sampans

There are 41,190 km (22,579 mi) of roads, of which 5,471 km (3,397 mi) are paved. Long-distance and municipal bus services are handled by the National Automobile Transport Undertaking. In 1982 there were 100,000 passenger cars and 200,000 commercial vehicles in the country. Per capita vehicle ownership is 1.6 per 1,000 inhabitants. The basic means of transportation, however, are not motorized vehicles but three-wheeled pedicabs known as cyclos. In rural areas loads are carried by a bamboo carrying pole (with baskets hanging at either end) known as don ganh.

The national airline is Hang Khong Vietnam, which has an old fleet of DC-4s and two Boeings inherited from the South as well as Soviet AN-26s, Ilyushins and Antonous. It operates primarily on domestic routes. There are a total of 217 airports and airfields in the country, of which 128 are usable, 40 have permanent-surface runways, and 12 have runways over 2,500 meters (8,000 ft). The largest of these airports is Gia Lam near Hanoi, but it cannot handle big jets. There are also two seaplane stations.

In 1982 there were 118,000 telephones in use, or 0.2 per 100 inhabitants.

MINING

Principal mineral resources include coal, tin, chrome, apatite and phosphate. Most of these mineral deposits are found in the North. The coal mines of Hong-Quong are among the largest in Southeast Asia; apatite is found in Lao Kay province and phosphate on the Paracel Islands (also claimed by China). The mineral production in 1982 consisted of 800,000 tons of coal, and at the present pace of production coal reserves will last for 235 years.

DEFENSE

Vietnam is divided into seven military zones: Four are in the north (the North, Northwestern, South and the fourth with headquarters at Vinh). The South is divided into three military regions: Coastal Plains, the Highlands and Extreme South or Cochinchina.

The defense structure is controlled by the Communist Party of Vietnam, but direct control is exercised through the minister of defense, Gen. Vo Nguyen Giap. The chain of command runs through the General Staff, the Political Directorate, the Training Directorate and the Logistics Directorate. Military policy is formulated by the National Defense Council, one of the most powerful institutions of government, with the president of the republic as chairman, the prime minister as vice chairman and eight members.

Military service is compulsory, and the minimum conscript service period is two years.

The total strength of the armed forces is 1,027,000, or 20.8 military men for every 1,000 civilians.

ARMY:
Personnel: 1,000,000
Organization: 16 corps HQ 1 armored division; 65 infantry divisions; 10 marine brigades; 8 engineer and 16 construction divisions; 5 field artillery divisions; 4 independent engineer brigades; 10 independent armored regiments
Equipment: Tanks 1,000; light tanks 450; 2,700 armored personnel carriers; armored combat vehicles;

500 guns; 190 howitzers; mortars; rocket launchers. 3,000 air defense guns; SAMs

NAVY:
Personnel: 12,000
Units: 8 frigates; 22 fast attack craft; 54 patrol craft; 7 amphibious craft
Naval Bases: Haiphong, Vinh and Quang Khe

AIR FORCE:
Personnel: 15,000
Organization: 270 combat aircraft; 65 combat helicopters; 4 air divisions; 1 fighter ground attack regiment; 4 fighter regiments; 3 transport regiments; 1 helicopter division; 3 training regiments; AAM
Air Defense Force: 60,000; 4 AA divisions
Forces Abroad: Laos 40,000; Cambodia 160,000
Air Bases: Gia Lam, Dien Bien Phu, Dong Hoi, Vinh and Hoa Lae

The defense budget is treated as classified information and therefore not published.

The Vietnamese armed forces are perhaps the best trained and best equipped as well as the largest in East Asia outside of China. In discipline, morale, tenacity, skill and endurance the average Vietnamese soldier has no equal in Southeast Asia. In Gen. Giap, the defense minister, the forces had one of the best tactical and guerrilla experts of modern times. They have also on tap sophisticated weaponry and spare parts and replacements from the Soviet Union. The Vietnamese armed forces have never suffered a military defeat since 1945, having been successful against France, the United States and, most recently, Cambodia.

A major effect of the armed Sino-Vietnamese conflict was a sharp rise in Soviet presence in Vietnam. At the height of the Sino-Vietnamese war, a Soviet naval task force of 14 vessels entered Vietnamese waters for the first time. Several ships later dropped anchor at Cam Ranh Bay and Danang, and there were visits by Soviet long-range reconnaissance aircraft and submarines. According to intelligence reports, Moscow was building an electronics listening post at Cam Ranh Bay. Soviet personnel also increased, with "maritime workers and volunteers" arriving in Haiphong and Saigon port. As deliveries of Soviet military hardware were stepped up, the number of Soviet advisers also went up to an estimated 5,000-8,000. Arms purchases from 1973-83 totaled $5.980 billion.

Military aid has been received from both the Soviet Union and China.

EDUCATION

The government claims a literacy rate of 85% for the whole country, but the actual rate may be closer to 65%. Even the latter rate represents a remarkable improvement over the 25% literacy during World War II years.

Education is universal and compulsory for five years from 6 to 11 but nominal fees are charged. School enrollment ratios are 113% for the first level (6-10) and 48% for the second level (11-17), for a combined ratio of 78%. The third level ratio is 2.5%. Girls constitute 47% of primary school enrollment, 47% of secondary school (general programs) enrollment and 24% of post-secondary enrollment.

Schooling lasts for 12 years divided into five years of primary school, four years of middle school and three years of secondary school. The educational system in the South has been restructured to conform to that of the North. Over 20,000 teachers in the South have been subjected to hoctap, or reeducation (political indoctrination) programs. All textbooks formerly used in the South have been burned and replaced with books shipped from the North. Over 1,000 former private schools, many of them run by Roman Catholics, have been brought under state control.

The school year runs from September to May. The language of instruction is Vietnamese throughout, but Russian is taught as a second language.

The number of students in teacher-training institutions was 20,397. The national teacher-pupil ratios are 1:39 in primary grades, 1:26 in secondary grades and 1:10 in post-secondary classes.

No information is available on educational expenditures.

EDUCATIONAL ENROLLMENT (1982/83)			
Level	Schools	Teachers	Students
First Level	12,200	383,700	11,700,000
Second Level (1980)	N.A.	148,973	3,846,737
Vocational	319	16,614	138,000
Third Level	87	16,400	160,000

Higher education is provided by 87 institutions of higher learning and universities, with a total enrollment of 160,000 in 1982/83. Per capita university enrollment is 265 per 100,000 inhabitants. The largest of these universities are the University of Cantho, the University of Hanoi, the University of Hue and Ho Chi Minh University.

In 1982, 7,424 Vietnamese students were attending institutions of higher learning abroad.

LEGAL SYSTEM

The Vietnamese legal system is based on Communist legal theory and French civil law.

The highest court is the Supreme Court in Hanoi, whose members are appointed for five-year terms by the National Assembly. People's Courts function in all district towns headed by judges appointed for three-year terms by the local administrative committees. The chief prosecutor is the director of the People's Office of Public Prosecution.

Arbitrary detention without charge, trial or any form of legal proceedings under the guise of "reeducation" has subverted the rudimentary legal system which exists. Even for those who are given a trial, for the most part those charged with nonpolitical crimes or specific prohibited political acts, the judicial process cannot be considered fair to the accused. A case brought to trial almost invariably leads to conviction.

Initially, a people's committee, an administrative body, holds a preliminary hearing. Upon its recommendation, the case is brought before a local or high people's court, depending upon the severity of the sentence to which the accused is liable. The high court tries those accused of serious criminal or political crimes for which the sentence is greater than two, or in some locales five, years imprisonment or death. The court consists of a presiding judge, two or three people's judges, a prosecutor and a court-appointed defense counsel. The defense counsel ensures that the proper legal procedures are followed in accordance with the defendant's rights under the constitution and explains the proceedings to the defendant. However, the defense counsel is not an advocate for the defendant in the Western sense. The trial is normally a formality at which the judges present their ruling on evidence which they have studied prior to the trial. Following the verdict of the judges, the defendant has 15 days to appeal the verdict to the National Assembly if the case has been tried by the high people's court. There is no appeal from local courts. In general, the entire legal system operates as an agency for the enforcement of regime directives; it has no independence from political intervention.

No information is available on the nature of the penal system or the number and location of prisons in the country.

LAW ENFORCEMENT

Law enforcement is the concern of the People's Organs of Control under a Supreme People's Organ of Control. No other information is available on the operation of the law enforcement forces or on the nature and incidence of crime in the country.

HEALTH

In 1976 the government claimed to have eliminated most of the tropical diseases that afflicted the country: tuberculosis, smallpox, malaria, venereal diseases, leprosy and bubonic plague. In addition, opiate addition, formerly a major health problem, has been reduced through severe penalties. However, many medical establishments were totally destroyed during the war including 28 provincial hospitals, 94 district hospitals and 533 community health centers. Expenditures on health services account for $1 per capita. Only 15% of the population has access to safe water.

In 1981 there were 11,550 hospitals in the country with 208,000 beds, or one bed per 258 inhabitants. In the same year there were 14,000 physicians, or one physician per 4,007 inhabitants, 409 dentists and 33,108 nurses. The admissions/discharge rate was

---

PRINCIPAL HEALTH INDICATORS (1984)

Crude Death Rate: 10.1 per 1,000
Decline in Death Rate: –53.5% (1965-83)
Life Expectancy at Birth: 56.7 (Males); 61.1 (Females)
Infant Mortality Rate: 75 per 1,000 live births
Child Death Rate (Ages 1-4) per 1,000: 9

1,587 per 10,000 inhabitants, the bed occupancy rate was 80.7% and the length of hospital stay was 7 days.

FOOD

The staple food is rice supplemented by corn, sweet potatoes and cassava. Fish sauce, called nuoc mam, is used with almost every meal. Vietnamese cooking has been heavily influenced by Chinese, French and Malay cooking. The per capita availability of energy, proteins, fats and carbohydrates is 2,029 calories, 49.3 grams, 27 grams and 455 grams respectively.

MEDIA & CULTURE

Four daily newspapers are published in the country, of which three are published in Hanoi and one in Ho Chi Minh City with an aggregate circulation of 500,000 or 5 per 1,000 inhabitants. All are published by the Communist Party or by official agencies. The official organ of the Communist party is *Nhan Dan* (The People) with a circulation of 300,000. Fifteen non-periodicals are published with an aggregate circulation of 257,000, or 5 per capita. Over 173 periodicals are also published, all of them by state or party agencies except for two published by the Catholic Church. The annual consumption of newsprint in 1981 was 2,000 tons, or 36 kg per 1,000 inhabitants.

The national news agency is Vietnam Thong Tin Xa (Vietnam News Agency, VNA) founded in 1946. The Liberation News Agency also supplies news to the domestic and foreign press. Tass, Novosti and CTK have bureaus in Hanoi.

Of the over 16 publishing houses reported as active, the largest is the Foreign Languages Publishing House in Hanoi. Annual output in 1981 was 1,495 titles. Vietnam does not adhere to any international copyright agreement.

The official broadcasting organization is the Voice of Vietnam, controlled by the Council of Ministers. There are 11 regional stations including one at Ho Chi Minh City. The home service program is on the air for 24 hours a day in Vietnamese in addition to broadcasting in minority languages for five hours daily. The foreign service is broadcast daily in English, Khmer, French, Loatian, Indonesian, Japanese, Korean, Thai and Chinese for a combined total of 19½ hours daily. In 1984 there were 6 million radio receivers in the country, or 99 per 1,000 inhabitants.

Television was introduced into South Vietnam in 1966 and in North Vietnam in 1970. There are seven television stations at Hanoi, Hue, Qui Nhon, Danang,

Nha Trang, Ho Chi Minh City and Can Tho. In 1984 there were approximately 2.25 million television receivers, or 37 per 1,000 inhabitants.

No information is available on the film industry in North Vietnam or on the number of cinemas, but at the end of the war the South had a flourishing film industry with an annual production of some 18 feature films and 92 short films. In 1975 film production declined to 7 films. In 1979, 229 films were imported. There are 210 fixed cinemas with 178,000 seats, or 3.5 seats per 1,000 inhabitants. Annual movie attendance was 264 million, or 5.2 per capita, and box office receipts were D41 billion.

The largest library is the National Library with 1 million volumes. The former National Library in Ho Chi Minh City has about 160,000 volumes. In addition, there are 76 municipal and provincial libraries. Per capita there are six volumes and five registered borrowers per 1,000 inhabitants.

There are nine museums in the country with a reported annual attendance of 1.918 million.

There are 148 professional companies and 7,762 amateur troupes.

SOCIAL WELFARE

Vietnam has no social security system, but there is an extensive social welfare program financed by the national government.

GLOSSARY

hoc tap: reeducation or indoctrination programs for members of the former South Vietnamese army and government.

New Economic Zone: one of several regions in the Central Plateau where people from the overpopulated districts are forcibly resettled.

Quoc Hai: the National Assembly.

Quoc-Ngu: the Romanized writing script of the Vietnamese language devised by Roman Catholic missionaries.

tem-giao: collective name for the three traditional religions of Vietnam: Buddhism, Confucianism and Taoism.

CHRONOLOGY (from 1945)

1945— The League for the Independence of Vietnam, known as the Viet-Minh, led by Ho Chi Minh, proclaims the Democratic Republic of Vietnam in Hanoi.

1946— The French, returning to the colony, recognize the Democratic Republic of Vietnam (DRV) as a free state within the French Union; clashes between the Viet-Minh and French forces escalate into full-scale war.

1954— French forces capitulate following 56-day siege of the French stronghold Dien Bien Phu by Viet-Minh forces; Geneva Ceasefire Agreement provisionally partitions the country along the 17th parallel pending general elections to unify the country; International Control Commission is set up.

1955— Last French forces leave the country, now divided effectively into North and South; in the South Ngo Dinh Diem is chosen chief of state in popular referendum replacing Emperor Bao Dai; Republic of Vietnam (RVN) is proclaimed with capital at Saigon.

1960— National Liberation Front (NLF), composed of South Vietnamese guerrillas supported by Hanoi, launches open insurrection against RVN through its military arm, the National Liberation Army (popularly known as Viet-Cong)... The Democratic Republic of Vietnam (DRV) promulgates new constitution.

1961— United States and the RVN sign treaty of amity; U.S. military presence in the country increases tenfold from the 1960 level of 685.

1963— Military junta led by Gen. Duong Van Minh overthrows and assassinates Diem in a coup with the alleged connivance of the U.S. government.

1964— U.S. destroyer *Maddox* patrolling the Tonkin Gulf is allegedly attacked by three of Hanoi's torpedo boats; United States orders retaliatory assaults.

1965— President Johnson orders continuous bombing raids on North Vietnam below the 20th parallel.... After a series of internal upheavals, air force commander Nguyen Cao Ky emerges as chief of state.

1967— In national elections army chief of staff Nguyen Van Thieu is elected president with Ky as vice president.

1968— NLF and DRV launch a Tet (last month of the Vietnamese New Year) offensive attacking Saigon and 30 provincial capitals.... President Johnson orders halt to bombing.

1969— President Richard M. Nixon announces Vietnamization policy under which the United States begins phased withdrawal of its troops.... Ho Chi Minh dies; after an intense struggle for power Le Duan is named to the powerful post of party general secretary.

1972— United States resumes intensive bombing of the North.

1973— Paris Peace Agreement ending U.S. involvement in the Vietnam War is signed by Secretary of State Henry Kissinger and NLF representative Le Duc Tho; last U.S. forces leave Vietnam.

1975— In a stunning offensive the NLF sweep across the South to Saigon; Thieu resigns and flees; his successor, Gen. Duong Van Minh, announces unconditional surrender of the Republic of Vietnam; the banner of the Provisional Revolutionary Government is raised over the presidential palace at Saigon ending the 11-year war.

1976— The Military Management Committee of the Provisional Revolutionary Government, which had ruled the South since the end of the war, is replaced by a civilian administration.... Following nation-wide elections, the first National Assembly of united Vietnam meets in Hanoi and proclaims the establishment of the Socialist Republic of Vietnam.... Saigon is renamed Ho Chi Minh City; the Vietnam Workers' Party is renamed Vietnam Communist Party (VCP).... Fourth congress of the VCP is held in Hanoi.... Vietnam launches its Second Five-Year Development Plan, 1976-80.

1977— Vietnam is admitted to the U.N.... Relations with Cambodia worsen.

1978— Border clashes with Cambodia lead to full-scale hostilities.... Relations with China worsen as China takes Cambodia's side in the conflict.... Thousands of Chinese leave under severe economic pressures.... Small businesses are nationalized; widespread persecution forces ethnic Chinese to flee the country; North and South currencies are unified; Vietnam signs Treaty of Peace and Friendship with the Soviet Union and joins the COMECON.

1979— In swift invasion lasting less than three weeks Vietnam overruns Cambodia, seizes Phnom Penh, ousts the Pol Pot government and installs its own puppet government headed by Heng Samrin; Invasion is condemned by all nations outside of the Moscow orbit; China, in retaliation, launches a punitive attack and advances 25 miles into Vietnamese territory despite stiff resistance; China withdraws from captured territory; Veteran party member Hoang Van Hoan defects to China; The presidium and the National Assembly approve a new constitution to replace the 1959 constitution.

1980— President Ton Duc Thang dies and is succeeded in office by Acting President Nguyen Huu Tho.

1985— Vietnam launches large-scale offensive against Cambodia and gains control of all guerrilla bases.

BIBLIOGRAPHY (from 1970)

Boettcher, Thomas D., *Vietnam: The Valor and the Sorrow* (Boston, 1985).

Burchett, Wilfred, *The China-Cambodia-Vietnam Triangle* (New York, 1982).

————, *Catapult to Freedom: The Survival of the Vietnamese People* (London, 1982).

Cao Ky, Nguyen, *Twenty Years and Twenty Days* (Briarcliff Manor, N.Y., 1976)

David Schoenbraun on Vietnam. B&W film, 33 min. American Documentary Films.

Duiker, William, *The Communist Road to Power in Vietnam* (Boulder, Col., 1980).

————, *Vietnam since the Fall of Saigon* (Athens, Ohio, 1985).

————, *Vietnam: Nation in Revolution,* (Boulder, Colo., 1983).

End of an Empire. B&W film, 25 min. CBS.

Fall, Bernard B., *The Two Vietnams: A Political and Military Analysis* (Boulder, Colo., 1985).

Gettleman, Marvin E., *Vietnam: History, Documents & Opinions on a Major World Crisis* (Gloucester, Mass., 1970)

Hodgkin, Thomas, *Vietnam: The Revolutionary Path* (New York, 1980).

Hung, G. Nguyen, *Economic Development of Socialist Vietnam* (New York, 1977).

Indochina. B&W film, 22 min. Producer: not available.

Karnow, Stanley, *Vietnam: A History* (New York, 1981).

Lam, Truong B., *Resistance, Rebellion, Revolution: Popular Movements in Vietnamese History* (London, 1984).

Lawson, Eugene K., *The Sino-Vietnamese Conflict* (New York, 1984).

Long, Nguyen and Harry H. Kendall, *After Saigon Fell: Daily Life under the Vietnamese Communists* (Berkeley, Calif., 1981).

Marr, David G., *Vietnamese Tradition on Trial* (Berkeley, Calif., 1983).

McAlister, Jr., John T. and Paul Mus, *The Vietnamese and their Revolution* (New York, 1970).

Pike, Douglas, *History of Vietnamese Communism, 1925-76* (Stanford, Calif., 1978)

Popkin, Samuel, *The Rational Peasant: The Political Economy of Rural Society in Vietnam* (Berkeley, Calif., 1979).

Porter, Gareth, *Vietnam: A History in Documents* (New York, 1981).

Ray, Hemen, *China's Vietnam War* (Atlantic Highlands, N.J., 1983).

Rosenberger, Leif. *The Soviet Union and Vietnam: An Uneasy Alliance* (Boulder, Colo., 1986).

Scholl-Latour, Peter, *Death in the Ricefields: An Eyewitness Account of Vietnam's Three Wars* (New York, 1985).

Smith, Ralph, *Vietnam and the West* (Ithaca, N.Y., 1971).

South Vietnam: People of Saigon. Color film, 17 min. Lem Bailey Production.

Taylor, Keith W., *The Birth of Vietnam* (Berkeley, Calif., 1983).

Thayer, Carl, *Vietnam: Politics, Economics and Society* (Boulder, Colo., 1986).

Van Canh, Nguyen, *Vietnam Under Communism, 1975-82* (Stanford, Calif., 1983).

Van Dyke, J.M., *North Vietnam's Strategy for Survival* (Palo Alto, Calif., 1972).

Vietnam Today. Color film, 18 min. Oxford Films.

Vo Nguyen Giap, *Banner of People's War: The Party's Military Line* (New York, 1970).

Whitfield, Danny J., *Historical and Cultural Dictionary of Vietnam* (Metuchen, N.J., 1976).

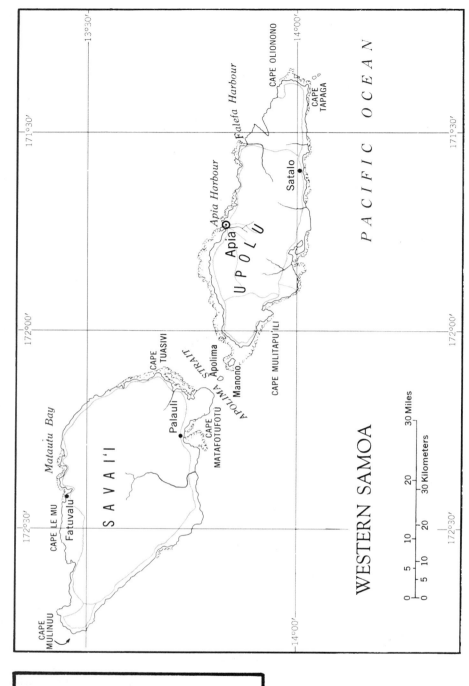

WESTERN SAMOA

PACIFIC OCEAN

S A V A I ' I

U P O L U

CAPE MULINUU

Mataautu Bay

CAPE LE MU

Fatuvalu

CAPE TUASIVI

Palauli

CAPE MATAFOTUFOTU

APOLIMA STRAIT

Apolima

Manono

CAPE MULITAPU'ILI

Apia Harbour

Apia

Falefa Harbour

CAPE OLIONONO

CAPE TAPAGA

Satalo

171°30'

172°00'

172°30'

13°30'

14°00'

171°30'

172°00'

172°30'

14°00'

| 0 | 5 | 10 | 20 | 30 Miles |
| 0 | 5 | 10 | 20 | 30 Kilometers |

FA'AVAE I LE ATUA SAMOA

WESTERN SAMOA

BASIC FACT SHEET

OFFICIAL NAME: The independent State of Western Samoa (Samoa i Sisifo)

ABBREVIATION; WS

CAPITAL: Apia

HEAD OF STATE: Ao O Le Malo Malietoa Tnaumafili II (joint Ao O Le Malo from 1962; sole Ao O Le Malo from 1963)

HEAD OF GOVERNMENT: Prime Minister Vaai Kolone (from 1985)

NATURE OF GOVERNMENT: Constitutional monarchy

POPULATION: 163,000 (1985)

AREA: 2,841 sq km (1,097 sq mi)

ETHNIC MAJORITY: Samoan

LANGUAGE: Samoan

RELIGION: Christianity

UNIT OF CURRENCY: Tala ($1=T2.79, December 1984)

NATIONAL FLAG: Red field with a blue quarter on the hoist bearing five white stars of the Southern Cross

NATIONAL EMBLEM: A shield displaying the constellation of the Southern Cross on a blue field from which sprouts a brown palm tree with green fronds against a white background broken by wavy green lines. The device is encircled by a stylized wreath and is crested by a cross.

NATIONAL ANTHEM: "The Flag of Freedom"

NATIONAL HOLIDAYS: January 1 (National Day); April 25 (ANZAC Day), June 3, 4, 5, (Independence Days); also variable Christian and Western festivals, including Good Friday, Easter Monday and Whit Monday, Christmas and Boxing Day.

NATIONAL CALENDAR: Gregorian

PHYSICAL QUALITY OF LIFE INDEX: 84 (down from 86 in 1976) (On an ascending scale in which 100 is the maximum. U.S. 95)

DATE OF INDEPENDENCE: January 1, 1962

DATE OF CONSTITUTION: October 28, 1960

WEIGHTS & MEASURES: Imperial units are used.

LOCATION & AREA

Western Samoa is located in the Pacific Ocean, 2,574 km (1,600 mi) NE of Auckland, New Zealand. It consists of two large islands, Upolu and Savaii, and the smaller islands of Apolima, Fanuatapu, Manono, Namua, Nuusafee and Nuutele. Of these, only Upolu and Savaii, separated by 18 km (11 mi), are inhabited. The total land area is 2,841 sq km (1,097 sq mi), extending 150 km (93 mi) ESE to WNW and 39 km (24 mi) NNE to SSW. Savaii and Upolu have a combined coastline of 371 km (231 mi).

The capital is Apia with a population of 35,000. There are no other large urban centers.

The islands are of volcanic origin, and the coasts are surrounded by coral reefs. There are many dormant volcanoes; the most recent period of volcanic activity was between 1905 and 1911. Rugged mountain ranges form the core of both Savaii (1,709 sq km, 660 sq mi) and Upolu (1,113 sq km, 430 sq mi). The highest elevations are 1,857 meters on Savaii (6,094 ft) and 1,099 meters (3,608 ft) on Upolu. Because of large areas laid waste by lava flows on Savaii, the island supports less population than the smaller Upolu.

WEATHER

Western Samoa has a tropical climate with two seasons: dry from May to October and wet from November to April. The hottest month is December, the coldest is July. The mean daily temperature is 27°C (80°F). The average rainfall is 287 cm (113 in.) per year, of which two-thirds falls during the wet season. Although Samoa lies outside the normal track of hurricanes, there are occasional severe storms.

POPULATION

The population of Western Samoa was estimated in 1985 at 163,000 on the basis of the last official census held in 1981, when it numbered 156,349. The population is expected to reach 178,000 by 2000. The annual growth rate is 0.87% on the basis of an annual birth rate of 36.8 per 1,000.

Of the total population, 106,053 live on Upolu, where the capital is located. The overall density is 56.4 per sq km (146 per sq mi). Apart from Apia there are no major towns. Most people live in some 400 coastal villages ranging in population from 100 to over 2,000. The urban component of the population is 21.2%. The age profile shows 44.3% in the under-14 age group, 50.3% in the 15-60 age group and 5.4% in the over-60 age group. The sex ratio favors males by 51.8:48.2.

DEMOGRAPHIC INDICATORS (1984)	
Population (000)	163
Annual rates of growth (1975-80)	0.87
Crude birthrates (per 1,000)	36.8
Crude death rates (per 1,000)	4.9
Gross reproduction rates (per woman, 1975-80)	2.70
Life expectancy at birth (males, 1975-80)	68.3
Life expectancy at birth (females, 1975-80)	73.1
Density per sq km	56.4
% urban	21.2%
Sex Distribution (%)	
Male	51.82
Female	48.18
Age profile (%)	
0-14	44.3
15-29	29.1
30-44	12.2
45-59	9.0
60-74	3.8
over 75	1.6
Population projection in 2000	178,000
Population doubling time in years at current rate	43
Marriage rate 1/1000	5.5
Divorce rate 1/1000	0.29
Average household size	7.8
% Illegitimate births	66.5
Natural increase rate 1/1000	16.4
Total fertility rate	5.60
Net reproduction rate	2.59

The heavy annual growth rate is partially offset by an annual loss of population through migration. New Zealand is the destination of most emigrants who are either students or workers. There is a nominal family planning program, but it appears to have little effect on population growth.

ETHNIC COMPOSITION

Samoans constitute nearly 90% of the population; the remaining 10% is made up by 12,000 Euronesians (mixed Europeans and Polynesians) and 700 Europeans.

The Samoans belong to the Polynesian race, which came to the islands in migratory waves over 2,000 years ago. Samoans are the second largest branch of the Polynesian race, after the Maoris of New Zealand. They are generally tall, large-boned and light-skinned with wavy or straight hair.

LANGUAGES

The official languages are Samoan and English. Samoan, a Polynesian dialect, is spoken universally. It is a vowel language containing 10 distinct vowel sounds but only a few consonants. In some words the vowel sounds are doubled or even tripled resulting in three aaa's or eee's in the same word. English is taught in schools and is used in the administration and commerce. Though statistics are not available, most Samoans are familiar with English.

RELIGIONS

As in race and language, there is considerable homogeneity in the religious background of Samoans. Nearly 99.7% are Christians and 50% belong to the London Missionary Society, now known as the Congregational Christian Church of Western Samoa. The Roman Catholic and Methodist Churches each have about 20% membership. The Roman Catholic Church in Samoa is headed by a cardinal, Pio Taofinu'u. Religious observance is strong among all groups.

COLONIAL EXPERIENCE

The earliest contacts between Samoa and the West were through the London Missionary Society, a branch of which was established in Apia in 1832. Between 1847 and 1861 representatives of Germany, the United Kingdom and the United States were stationed in Apia where they became actively involved in the intrigues and civil wars among the various paramount tribal chiefs. By a series of conventions signed in 1900, Western Samoa became a German protectorate. On the outbreak of World War I in 1914, New Zealand occupied the islands and administered them from 1919 to 1946 as a mandate of the League of Nations. From 1927 to 1936 the New Zealand administration faced a serious challenge from a nationalistic organization known as Mau, which embarked on a program of civil disobedience.

In 1946 the League of Nations mandate was converted into a trusteeship agreement, under which New Zealand was committed to the promotion of Samoan self-government. A native cabinet was introduced in 1959, and in 1960 the constitution of the independent state of Western Samoa was adopted. In a plebiscite under U.N. supervision in 1961, an overwhelming majority approved full independence, which was granted in 1962. Even after independence, Western Samoa is dependent on New Zealand for economic and military assistance, and the links between the two countries are therefore as close as ever before.

CONSTITUTION & GOVERNMENT

The constitution of 1960 established a British or Westminster-style parliamentary democracy. It provides for a head of state, known as ao o le malo. The present head of state is the scion of an old royal line and holds the position for life, but future heads of state will be elected by the legislative assembly for five-year terms. Although the constitution does not make it mandatory, the future heads of state will be selected from the holders of the four paramount titles. The cabinet, introduced in 1959, is headed by a prime minister appointed by the head of state, and in-

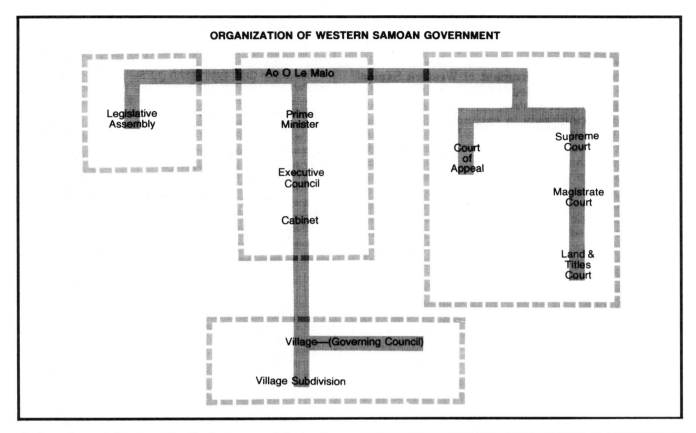

ORGANIZATION OF WESTERN SAMOAN GOVERNMENT

Ao O Le Malo

Legislative Assembly

Prime Minister

Executive Council

Cabinet

Court of Appeal

Supreme Court

Magistrate Court

Land & Titles Court

Village—(Governing Council)

Village Subdivision

cludes nine ministers collectively responsible to the legislative assembly. The prime minister requires the confidence of the assembly, although he and the cabinet are not necessarily dismissed when he loses that confidence. This is because there is no conventional party structure and also because such a dismissal is contrary to traditional Samoan concepts of government. Decisions of the cabinet are subject to review by the executive council, a joint body composed of the head of state, the prime minister and the cabinet. The council does not formulate policy but issues regulations and makes important appointments.

Suffrage is universal for Western Samoan citizens of non-matai status (either Westernized Samoans or part-Samoans), but in the territorial constituencies only the matai are eligible to vote or stand for election to office. Elections are held triennially; the last elections were held in 1976.

The main element of Samoan stability is the conservative character of the political system, which is moderately representative while preserving older traditions. Decision making at the political level is dominated by the concept of consensus, described as essential to the fa'a Samoa, or the Samoan Way. The Samoan political and social systems interact at every level. Samoan society is composed of a number of extended families(or aiga) whose heads bear the official title of matai. The number of such patriarchs is not fixed because as new extended families are formed new titleholders are created. This exclusive group of matais functions as the reservoir from which Samoan political leadership is always drawn. Traditionally

CABINET LIST (1985)	
Head of State	Malietoa Tanumafili II
Prime Minister	Va'ai Kolone
Deputy Prime Minister	Tupuola Efi
Minister of Agriculture & Forests	Fuimaono Mimio
Minister of Broadcasting	Le Tagaloa Pita
Minister of Economic Development	Le Tagaloa Pita
Minister of Education	Lemamea Ropati
Minister of Foreign Affairs	Va'ai Kolone
Minister of Finance	Semu Faasootauloa
Minister of Fisheries	Fuimaono Mimio
Minister of Health	Toelesulusulu Siueva
Minister of Immigration	Va'ai Kolone
Minister of Justice	George Michael Lober
Minister of Labor	George Michael Lober
Minister of Lands & Surveys	Faumuina Anapapa
Minister of Police & Prisons	Va'ai Kolone
Minister of Post Office	Le Tagaloa Pita
Minister of Public Works	Tupuola Efi
Minister of Transportation & Civil Aviation	Toelesulusulu Siueva
Attorney General	Va'ai Kolone
Minister of Youth, Sports & Culture	Lemamea Ropati

matais have the authority to impose their views on other members of the extended family. However, they have also well-defined responsibilities and they may be removed if they do not meet these responsibilities. Apart from fa'a Samoa, there are no other political ideologies strong enough to influence voters.

Recently, however, there have been moves toward universal suffrage and a reduction of matai powers.

FREEDOM & HUMAN RIGHTS

In terms of civil and political rights, Western Samoa is classified as a partly free country with a rating of 4 in political rights and 3 in civil rights (on a descending scale in which 1 is the highest and 7 is the lowest in rights).

Although described only as a partly free country, human rights are well secured both by constitution and by custom. The political system is traditionally elitist, but this has not polarized society and there are no deep divisions between the power-holders and the powerless. The judiciary is independent and the legislature is not entirely a rubber stamp of the executive.

CIVIL SERVICE

The civil service is being Samoanized, but a number of New Zealanders (on assignment from the New Zealand public service) are found at the higher echelons. A Public Service Commission, headed by a chairman and including two other commissioners, is a statutory body.

LOCAL GOVERNMENT

There is no formal system of local government; apart from an administrative officer on Savaii, there is no administrative corps at the district level. Administrative districts drawn up in 1956 are used mainly as units for the operation of health, agriculture, police and educational service.

The basic territorial units are the nu'u (village) and pitonu'u (subvillage). The governing body of the nu'u is the fono, whose members are the matai, or titled elders each of whom heads an extended family. The chief of the fono is known as the ali'i, while the executive agent is the tulafale (orator). The frequency of the fono's meetings may vary from weekly to a few times a year.

FOREIGN POLICY

In accordance with the Treaty of Friendship of 1962, New Zealand acts as the channel of communication between the government of Western Samoa and other governments outside the Pacific islands. In contrast to other developing nations, Western Samoa moved cautiously in expanding its international contacts. It was not until 1976, when the nation's first non-royal prime minister, Taisi Tupuola Efi, took office that it chose to submit an application for membership to the U.N. This move was condemned by the more conservative leaders because of the costs of membership. In the same year it established diplomatic relations with the Soviet Union, which has offered to set up a fish cannery.

Relations with the country's principal trading partner, New Zealand, which had been cordial since independence, cooled in 1978-1979 as a result of Wellington's attempt to expel some 200 Samoan "overstayers" who had been assured New Zealand citizenship. Subsequently, the Privy Council at London ruled that all Western Samoans born between 1928 and 1949 (when New Zealand passed legislation separating its own citizenship from that of Britain), as well as their children, were entitled to such rights. However, the decision was effectively invalidated by an agreement concluded in mid-1982 by Prime Ministers Kolone and Muldoon whereby only the estimated 50,000 Samoans currently resident in New Zealand could claim citizenship. Western Samoa and the United States are parties to two treaties and agreements covering Peace Corps and Investment Guaranties. Both the U.S. Ambassador, and the U.K. High Commissioner, reside in Wellington, New Zealand. Western Samoa is represented in the United States by Malavai Iulai Toma (1985)

Western Samoa joined the U.N. in 1976; its share of the U.N. budget is 0.02%. It is a member of seven U.N. organizations, the Commonwealth and the South Pacific Commission.

PARLIAMENT

The unicameral Legislative Assembly (*Fono*) is elected for three-year terms and consists of 47 members, of whom 45 are elected from territorial constituencies by the matai and two members are elected by universal suffrage by persons outside the matai system, such as Euronesians and Europeans with West Samoan citizenship.

POLITICAL PARTIES

Until 1979 there were no political parties in Western Samoa. In that year, Vaai Kolone organized the kingdom's first political party, the Human Rights Protection Party, which won 22 out of 47 seats in the 1982 election. Following legal wrangles, Kolone turned over party leadership to Tofilau Eti, who led the HRPP to a landslide 31-16 victory in the 1985 election. Meanwhile, a pro-private enterprise Labor Party was formed in 1981, while former prime minister Tupuola Efi organized the Christian Democratic Party. HRPP dissidents and the Christian Democratic Party toppled the government of Tofilau Eti in December 1985 and reinstated Vaai Kolone as prime minister.

ECONOMY

Western Samoa is one of the 39 lower middle-income countries; it is also one of the 29 countries considered by the U.N. as one of the least developed countries (LLDC) and one of the 45 countries considered to be most seriously affected by recent adverse economic conditions. Western Samoa has a free-market economy in which the private sector is dominant.

PRINCIPAL ECONOMIC INDICATORS

Gross National Product: $130 million (1983)
  GNP Annual Growth Rate: Not available
  Per Capita GNP: $770
  Per Capita GNP Annual Growth Rate: Not available

Gross Domestic Product: Not available
  GDP Annual Growth Rate: 0.5% (1983)
  Per Capita GDP: Not available
  Per Capita GDP Annual Growth Rate: Not available
  Average Annual Rate of Inflation: 11.9% (1984)

Income Distribution: Not available

Consumer Price Index (1980-100):
  All Items: 185.7 (1984)

Money Supply: T18.85 million (1984)
  Currency in Circulation: T6,200,000 (1983)

International Reserves: $10.56 million, of which foreign exchange reserves were $10.41 million (1984)

BALANCE OF PAYMENTS (1984)
(million $)

Current Account Balance	0.51
Merchandise Exports	20.0
Merchandise Imports	−45.59
Trade Balance	−25.59
Other Goods, Services & Income	+6.78
Other Goods, Services & Income	−11.58
Other Goods, Services & Income Net	−4.80
Private Unrequited Transfers	20.27
Official Unrequited Transfers	10.63
Capital Other Than Reserves	1.52
Net Errors & Omissions	1.20
Total (Lines 1, 10 and 11)	3.23
Counterpart Items	−2.16
Total (Lines 12 and 13)	1.07
Liabilities Constituting Foreign Authorities' Reserves	—
Total Change in Reserves	−1.07

In 1964, two years after independence, an economic development board was established. In 1965 the board launched the first five-year development plan (1966-70) covering agriculture, tourism, secondary industry, public works, health and education, trade development and telecommunications. Projects under later development plans have included a hydroelectric plant on Upolu.

The largest foreign aid donor is New Zealand. During 1970-82 non-U.S. Western nations supplied $144 million in aid through ODA and OOF, while the United States supplied $10 million from 1970-83. During the period 1979-81 Western Samoa received $27.0 million in aid from all sources, or $168.80 per capita.

BUDGET

The Western Samoan fiscal year is the calendar year.

The 1982 national budget consisted of revenues of T38.506 million and expenditures of T26.246 million. Of current revenues, 46.4% came from customs duties, 17.5% from taxes, 10.6% from treasury department, 8.5% from public works, 8.1% from postal service and 3.2% from transport fees and licenses. Of current expenditures, 19.3% went to public works, 17.0% to health, 16.5% to education, 11.8% to treasury department and 7.3% to justice, police and prisons.

The external public debt in 1983 totaled $60.5 million, of which $57.5 million was owed to official creditors and $3.1 million to private creditors. Total debt service was $3.7 million of which $2.7 million was repayment of principal and $1.0 million was interest.

FINANCE

The Western Samoan unit of currency is the tala, divided into 100 sene. Coins are issued in denominations of 1, 2, 5, 10, 20 and 50 sene; notes are issued in denominations of 1, 2 and 10 tala.

The tala was introduced in 1967, replacing the West Samoan pound at the rate of 1 West Samoan pound=2 tala. The West Samoan pound had been introduced at independence replacing the New Zealand pound at par. The initial value of the tala in relation to the dollar was pegged at $1=T0.719. In 1975 the tala's direct link with the the U.S. dollar was broken, and it was pegged to a basket of currencies as used by New Zealand. In 1984 the exchange value of the tala was $1=T2.179. The sterling exchange rate was £1=T2.525.

The banking system consists of the bank of issue, the Central Bank of Western Samoa founded in 1984, and two commercial banks, the Bank of Western Samoa and the Pacific Commercial Bank. The post office also offers savings facilities.

AGRICULTURE

Of the total land area of 284,100 hectares (701,011 acres), only 42,000 hectares (103,782 acres) are considered arable, or 0.276 hectare (0.68 acre) per capita. Agricultural products contribute 100% of the export earnings.

The chief method of production, known as village agriculture, is confined to the villages. About 80.5% of the total arable land is held in customary tenure, that is its ownership is vested in the extended family group. The chief or the head of the family controls the actual use of the land and permits members of the family to cultivate land in return for various services. Public land accounts for 11.3% of the total arable land and mission land for 3.7%. In addition, 4.5% is owned by the Western Samoa Trust Estates Corporation, which consists of 11 estates on Upolu confiscated as reparations from the Germans after World War I. Land under customary tenure may be leased only to chiefs or foreigners and then only for an initial period of 20 years with one renewal period.

In the absence of proper fertilization, most land is cultivated until the soil fertility is exhausted and then abandoned and allowed to lie fallow for up to 10 years. In 1982 there were only 30 tractors in use, and the consumption of fertilizers was 300 tons.

The three major commercial crops are coconuts, cocoa and bananas. Other cash crops include coffee, papayas, mangoes, nutmeg, and mace.

PRINCIPAL CROP PRODUCTION (1982) (000 tons)	
Taro (Coco yam)	38
Coconuts	202
Copra	19
Bananas	22
Cocoa beans	2.0

About one-half of the cattle population of 27,000 in 1982 was owned by the Western Samoa Trust Estates Corporation. Pigs are raised by almost all small farmers and numbered 62,000 in 1982.

Forests cover 167,000 hectares (412,657 acres); commercial exploitation is in the hands of foreign firms. The production of roundwood in 1982 was 131,000 cubic meters (4.626 million cubic ft). Timber and plywood exports in 1974 totaled $400,000.

Subsistence fishing is carried on along the reefs and coasts, but there are no organized commercial fisheries. In 1977 the annual fish catch totaled 4,020 metric tons.

INDUSTRY

There is little industry apart from timber dressing, manufacture of beverages and coffee processing. In an effort to attract foreign capital, the Enterprises Incentives Act was passed in 1965. This act provides income-tax holidays, duty-free imports and other incentives to new or expanding industries. The act is administered by the Enterprises Incentives Board and has resulted in the number of companies registered in Samoa rising to 120.

ENERGY

Western Samoa does not produce any form of mineral energy. Its total consumption in 1982 was 55,000 million metric tons of coal equivalent, or 344 kg (758 lb) per capita. Total electric power production in 1983 was 51 million kwh, or 315 kwh per capita.

LABOR

The economically active population in 1983 was 41,506, of whom 45.4% were employed in agriculture, 6.8% in manufacturing, 7.0% in construction, 7.5% in commerce, 6% in transport and communications and 27.3% in services and finance.

Because of the structure of the social system, under which every member shares in the products of his family lands, there is little incentive to work for wages. Of the 12,000 wage earners, about half are employed in the government or on the Trust Estates.

The Labor and Employment Act of 1972 and 1973 regulations establish a 40-hour workweek for the private sector and a minimum wage, currently about $.25 an hour. It is illegal to employ children under 15 years of age except in "safe and light work." The law also establishes certain rudimentary safety and health provisions, such as a requirement for fencing around dangerous machine parts. Independent observers say, however, that the safety laws are not enforced except when accidents highlight noncompliance and that many agricultural workers, among others, are inadequately protected from pesticides and other health hazards. Part of the problem is low safety consciousness, which government education programs are addressing. The law does not apply to service rendered to the matai, some of whom require children to work at what might be considered "child labor." Government employees are covered under different and more stringent regulations, which are adequately enforced.

There is a relatively large Western Samoan labor force in New Zealand, but in the mid-1970s New Zealand drastically reduced the number of annual visas for Western Samoan workers.

Although labor unions are permitted under the law, none has been established.

FOREIGN COMMERCE

The foreign commerce of Western Samoa consisted in 1984 of exports of $20.59 million and imports of $66.41 million, leaving an unfavorable trade balance of $45.82 million. Of the imports, food constituted 22.0%, machinery and transport equipment 18.2%, petroleum and petroleum products 14.4%, manufactured metal products 9.5%, miscellaneous manufactures 7.1%, chemicals 5.8% and animal oils and fats 3.6%. Of the exports, coconut oil constituted 24.4%, taros, fruits and vegetables 14.0%, timber 7.2%, re-exports 6.6%, cocoa and shell 6.2%, coconut cream 5.6%, beer 4.2% and bananas 3.2%.

The major import sources are: New Zealand 31.0%, Australia 21.4%, Japan 11.9%, the United States 9.7%, China 7.0% and Singapore 5.7%. The major export destinations are: the United States 28.6%, New Zealand 27.1%, Australia 9.8%, American Samoa 9.5%, Japan 7.9% and West Germany 5.8%.

TRANSPORTATION & COMMUNICATIONS

Western Samoa has no railroads. The main port is Apia, which handled 123,000 tons of cargo in 1982. Inter-island transportation is provided by diesel-powered launches. Fortnightly cargo and passenger services are maintained with New Zealand, and there are other scheduled services with Australia and North America.

The road system consists of 784 km (486 mi) of roads, of which 375 km (233 mi) are paved. Most of these roads are on the northern coast of Upolu. In 1982 these roads were used by 3,254 passenger cars and 410 commercial vehicles. Per capita passenger car ownership is 20 per 1,000 inhabitants.

Air service is provided by the Polynesian Airlines, which operates two aircraft for flights to American Samoa, Fiji, Niue and Tonga. There are four usable airfields in the country, of which Faleolo, near Apia, is the major international terminal.

In 1984 there were 3,800 telephones in the country, or 2.5 per 100 inhabitants. In 1982 the postal service handled 14,589,000 pieces of mail. Volume of mail per capita is 89 pieces.

In 1982, 32,752 tourists visited Western Samoa. Tourism is a recent phenomenon because until 1965 official policy was opposed to the presence of overseas visitors in the kingdom. Tourist revenues in 1982 totaled $6 million.

MINING

Western Samoa has no known mineral reserves.

DEFENSE

Western Samoa has no defense forces. New Zealand is responsible for the country's defense.

EDUCATION

The national literacy rate is 97%. Western Samoa has not introduced universal, free, compulsory education. The enrollment ratio is 91% in primary schools. Girls constitute 48% of primary school enrollment, 50% of secondary school enrollment and 47% of post-secondary enrollment.

Schooling lasts for 14 years, divided into seven years of primary school, four years of lower secondary or middle school and three years of upper secondary school. However, village schools provide only four years of primary schooling. The curriculum and textbooks are similar to those used in New Zealand. The school system, including both public and mission schools, consists of 162 primary schools, and 38 intermediate and secondary schools. The teacher-pupil ratio is 1:22 at the first level, 1:24 at the secondary level and 1:5 at the post-secondary level.

The Western Samoan school year is the calendar year. The language of instruction is Samoan in primary schools and English in secondary schools. Most Samoan children therefore are bilingual. Almost all Samoan teachers in the public school system hold teachers' certificates. Mission schools account for 15% of primary school enrollment, 19% of intermediate school enrollment and 46% of secondary school en-

rollment. Nearly 2.7% of secondary school students are enrolled in the vocational stream.

In 1982 the education budget was T4.330 million, representing 16.5% of the national budget.

EDUCATIONAL ENROLLMENT (1981-82)			
	Schools	Teachers	Students
First Level	162	1,460	40,475
Second Level	38	495	11,839
Vocational	4	55	454
Third Level	6	53	263

Western Samoan students go abroad for higher education. In 1982, 214 Western Samoan students were enrolled in foreign universities. Of these, 64 were in the United States, 29 in Australia and 101 in New Zealand. In the same year 21 foreign students were enrolled in Western Samoa.

LEGAL SYSTEM

The legal system is based on English common law but with elements of Samoan customary law.

The judiciary is headed by the Supreme Court, consisting of a chief justice and a junior judge, appointed by the head of state acting on the advice of the prime minister. Appeals from the Supreme Court lie with the Court of Appeal, consisting of the chief justice and three other judges. The subordinate courts are the magistrates' courts. The highest magistrate's court consists of a magistrate and two senior judges assisted by seven junior judges. The Land and Titles Court has jurisdiction in disputes over Samoan land and succession to Samoan titles.

The Judicial Service Commission is composed of the chief justice, the attorney general and some other person nominated by the minister of justice. It advises the head of state on the appointment, promotion and transfers of judges except the chief justice.

The corrections system consists of two penal institutions—a conventional prison at Tafa'igata near Apia and a prison farm at Vaia'ata on Savaii Island—with an average prison population of 200.

LAW ENFORCEMENT

The national police force is commanded by a commissioner of police. There are no territorial divisions, but units are assigned to three stations on Upolu and three on Savaii, each of which is responsible for policing outlying islands in their immediate vicinity. The total strength of the force is about 170, or one policeman for every 882 inhabitants.

Because the matai system has an effective self-policing influence, major crimes are rare. Major law enforcement problems are petty theft, disorderly conduct, and the unlicensed production, sale and consumption of beer.

HEALTH

Because of Western Samoa's geographic isolation, most tropical diseases are unknown in the country with the exception of filariasis. Only 16% of the population has access to safe water.

```
PRINCIPAL HEALTH INDICATORS (1984)
Crude Death Rate: 4.9 per 1,000
Infant Mortality Rate: 42.0 per 1,000 Live Births
Life Expectancy at Birth: 68.3 (Males); 73.1 (Females)
```

In 1981 there were 16 hospitals in the country with 735 beds, or one bed per 214 inhabitants. In the same year there were 63 physicians, or one physician per 2,482 inhabitants. The admissions/discharge rate was 746 per 10,000 inhabitants, the bed occupancy rate was 39.3% and the average length of hospital stay was 8 days.

FOOD

The daily diet consists of cakes made of breadfruit and boiled bananas, pumpkins, yams and taro sprinkled with coconut milk. A traditional food is poi, a starchy paste made from boiled taro roots softened by pounding in a stone mortar. A seasonal delicacy is palolo, the spawn of a sea creature that resembles a miniature lobster. Food is usually cooked by baking in a shallow pit lined with a single layer of volcanic or basaltic stones.

The daily per capita availability of energy, proteins, fats and carbohydrates is 2,289 calories, 50.5 grams, 87 grams, and 321 grams respectively.

MEDIA & CULTURE

In 1984 four non-daily newspapers were published in the country with an aggregate circulation of 11,500, or 70 per 1,000 inhabitants. All papers are published in English and Samoan.

There is no domestic news agency. Overseas news is obtained through the New Zealand Press Association, which has a part-time correspondent at Apia. In 1982, 79 books were published locally.

The government-controlled Western Samoa Broadcasting Service operates a medium-wave transmitter at Apia, which is on the air for 105 hours a week, with programs in Samoan and English. In 1983 there were 70,000 radio receivers in the country, or 430 per 1,000 inhabitants. Although there is no local television service, 60% of the population is within range of transmitters in American Samoa. In 1982 there were 2,500 television sets, or 16 per 1,000 inhabitants.

In 1982 there were six fixed cinemas with 6,000 seats, or 37.5 per 1,000 inhabitants. Annual movie attendance in the same year was 500,000, or 3.2 per capita.

The largest public library is the Nelson Memorial Library at Apia with over 28,000 volumes. Per capita, there are 203 volumes and 54 registered borrowers per 1,000 inhabitants.

SOCIAL WELFARE

There are no organized social welfare programs.

GLOSSARY

aiga: an extended family headed by a matai.

ali'i: chief of a village governing council.

ao o le malo: title of the West Samoan head of state.

fa'a Samoa: literally, the Samoan Way. The customs and traditions of Samoa, especially as contrasted with those of Westerners.

fautua: the title of adviser held by certain heads of families in the traditional Samoan society.

fono (shortened form of fono a faipule): The village governing body.

ifoga: local custom, as distinguished from court-administered law.

matai: title of the head of a traditional extended family who represents all members of the family in political and social transactions.

nu'u: village considered as the basic territorial unit.

pitonu'u: subdivision of a village.

tulafale: title, meaning orator, of the executive agent of a village council.

CHRONOLOGY (from 1962)

1962— Following a U.N.-supervised plebiscite in which Samoans vote in favor of full independence, Western Samoa becomes the first Pacific Islands Trust Territory to achieve nationhood.

1963— Joint ao o le malo Tupua Tamasese Meaoli dies, and Malietoa Tanumafili becomes sole head of state.

1970— Western Samoa joins the Commonwealth of Nations.... Following legislative assembly elections, Tupua Tamasese Lealofi is elected prime minister replacing Fiame Mataafa.

1973— Fiame Mataafa returns as prime minister.

1975— Fiame Mataafa dies and Lealofi is chosen to serve as prime minister for the remaining months of Mataafa's term.... Western Samoa signs the Lome Convention.

1976— Taisi Tupuola Efi becomes the nation's first commoner to be elected prime minister.... Western Samoa joins the U.N.... Diplomatic ties are set with the Soviet Union.

1977— Western Samoa receives development loan from the World Bank.

1982— The islands' first political party, the Human Rights Protection Party is formed and wins a plurality of 22 seats in Legislative Assembly... HRPP leader Tofilau Eti forms government.

1985— HRPP captures 31 out of 47 Assembly seats in general elections.... In December Vaai Kolone, with the backing of HRPP dissidents and the Christian Democratic Party, recaptures leadership of HRPP, ousts Tofilau Eti and is installed as prime minister.

BIBLIOGRAPHY (from 1963)

Davidson, J.W., *Samoa Mo Samoa: The Emergence of the Independent State of Western Samoa* (New York, 1967).

Fairbairn, Ian, *The National Income of Western Samoa* (New York, 1974).

Fox, J. W., *Western Samoa* (Auckland, New Zealand, 1963).

Gilson, R. P., *Samoa 1830 to 1900: The Politics of a Multicultural Community* (New York, 1970).

Lockwood, Brian, *Samoan Village Economy* (New York, 1971).

Pitt, David, *Tradition and Economic Progress in Samoa* (New York, 1970).

Shankman, Paul, *Migration and Underdevelopment: The Case of Western Samoa* (Boulder, Colo., 1976).

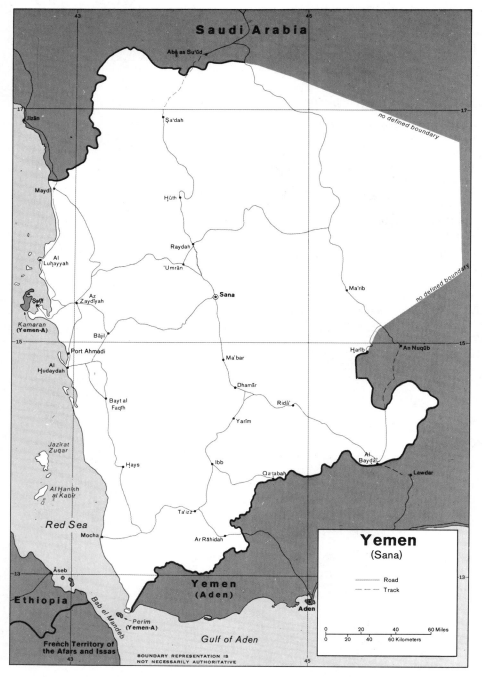

Saudi Arabia

Abā as Suʿūd

17 Jizān

Saʿdah

no defined boundary

Maydī

Ḥūth

Raydah

Al Luḥayyah

ʿUmrān

no defined boundary

Salīf

Az Zaydīyah

Sana

Maʿrib

Kamaran (Yemen-A)

Bājil

15

Port Ahmadi

Ma'bar

Ḥarīb

An Nuqūb

15

Al Ḥudaydah

Dhamār

Bayt al Faqīh

Ridāʿ

Jazīrat Zuqar

Yarīm

Ḥays

Ibb

Al Bayḍāʿ

Al Hanīsh al Kabīr

Qaʿtabah

Lawdar

Red Sea

Taʿizz

Mocha

Ar Rāhidah

13 Āseb

Yemen (Aden)

Aden

Ethiopia

Bab el Mandeb

Perim (Yemen-A)

Gulf of Aden

French Territory of the Afars and Issas

BOUNDARY REPRESENTATION IS
NOT NECESSARILY AUTHORITATIVE

Yemen
(Sana)

——— Road
– – – Track

0   20   40   60 Miles
0 20 40 60 Kilometers

YEMEN

BASIC FACT SHEET

OFFICIAL NAME: Yemen Arab Republic (Al-Jumhouriyya al-Arabiyya al Yamaniyya)

ABBREVIATION: YE

CAPITAL: Sana'a

HEAD OF STATE: Chairman of the Military Command Council Ali Abdullah Saleh (from 1978)

HEAD OF GOVERNMENT: Prime Minister Abd al-Aziz Abd al-Ghani (from 1983)

NATURE OF GOVERNMENT: Military dictatorship

POPULATION: 6,058,000 (1985)

AREA: 195,000 sq km (75,290 sq mi)

ETHNIC MAJORITY: Arab

LANGUAGE: Arabic

RELIGION: Islam (Sunni and Shia)

UNIT OF CURRENCY: Rial ($1=R 6.485, August 1985)

NATIONAL FLAG: Tricolor with red, white and black horizontal stripes and a green star on the white stripe

NATIONAL EMBLEM: A left-facing eagle bears a triangular shield with wavy blue and white lines below and black and gold stripes above and a green tree over them. Crossed national flags appear in an arc around the device. A green scroll at the base carries the nation's name in Arabic script.

NATIONAL ANTHEM: "Peace to the Land"

NATIONAL HOLIDAYS: September 26 (National Day, Revolution Day); June 13 (Corrective Movement Anniversary); variable Islamic festivals

NATIONAL CALENDAR: Islamic calendar based on the Hegira

PHYSICAL QUALITY OF LIFE INDEX: 28 (up from 27 in 1976) (On an ascending scale with 100 as the maximum. U.S. 95)

DATE OF INDEPENDENCE: 1918

DATE OF CONSTITUTION: 1965 (amended in 1967, 1971 and 1974)

WEIGHTS & MEASURES: The main units of weight are the waqiyah (34 grams, 1.2 ounces) and the rotl, of which there are three kinds: the small rotl (17 waqiyah), the medium rotl (20 waqiyah) and the large rotl (24 waqiyah). The unit of length is the dhra (66.04 cm, 24 in.). The unit of capacity is the qadah (33.1 liters, 35 quarts), divided into 64 nafar.

LOCATION & AREA

Yemen (YAR) is situated in the southwestern corner of the Arabian Peninsula just north of the passage between the Red Sea and the Gulf of Aden. Its total area is estimated at 195,000 sq km (75,290 sq mi). It extends 540 km (336 mi) north-south and 418 km (260 mi) east-west. Its total land boundary length is 1,209 km (751 mi) of which its border with Saudi Arabia is 628 km (390 mi) and that with the People's Democratic Republic of Yemen 581 km (361 mi). The total length of the Red Sea coastline is 452 km (281 mi).

The capital is Sana'a with an estimated 1981 population of 277,820. The major urban centers are Taiz (119,580), the capital from 1948 to 1962, and Hodeida (126,390), the main Red Sea port. The only other towns with populations of over 10,000 are Dhamar and Yarim.

The country includes two distinct topographical regions. The Tilhama, a sandy strip of about 65 km (40 mi) in width separates the Red Sea coast from the mountainous interior. The average elevation of the interior highlands ranges from about 2100 meters (7,000 ft) to 3,000 meters (10,000 ft) with the highest peak, the summit of Jabal Hadhur, rising to 3,760 meters (12,336 ft). Toward the eastern border with Saudi Arabia the mountains fade into the Rub al-Khali, the largest sand desert in the world.

The abundant rain in the highlands produces flash flood rivers, or wadis. To the northeast rise the tributaries of Wadi Najran and Dawasir; Wadi Bana and Wadi Tiban drain the southern slopes into the Gulf of Aden; while Wadi Siham, Wadi Zabid and Wadi Surdud flow into the Red Sea.

WEATHER

The Tihama Plain is characterized by heat, aridity and high humidity. The temperature often rises in the summer to 54.4°C (130°F), and there is little rainfall, less than 127 mm (5 in.) a year. The highlands of the interior, on the other hand, enjoy the best climate in Arabia, with a temperate, rainy summer and a cool, moderately dry winter. Average temperatures ranges from 14.°C (57°F) in January to 21.6°C (71°F) in June. Snow and frost are common in winter, particularly at high altitudes. Rainfall varies from 91.44 cm (36 in.) in the SW monsoon area to 50 cm (20 in.) in other parts, including Sana'a. Rainfall, however, is unpredictable, and both drought and severe floods are common.

POPULATION

The population of Yemen was estimated at 6,058,000 in 1985 according to the census conducted in 1981. The population is expected to reach 9.1 million by 2000 and 14.0 million by 2020.

The population growth rate during 1973-85 was 2.37% nationwide and 7.38% in urban areas. The annual birth rate was 48.5 per 1,000 during 1965-70.

The Yemenis are almost all settled and live in scattered towns and villages. Unlike other Arab countries, Yemen has no nomadic population. Most of the population is concentrated in the Tihama foothills and in the central highlands. Only 20% of the population lives in towns of any size. The average density is 34 persons per sq km (88 per sq mi), which makes Yemen one of the most densely populated countries in the Middle East. The density in agricultural areas is 72 per sq km (186 per sq mi).

DEMOGRAPHIC INDICATORS (1985)	
Population, total (in 1,000)	6,058.0
Population ages (% of total)	
0-14	45.3
15-64	51.4
65+	3.3
Youth 15-24 (000)	1,327
Women ages 15-49 (000)	1,578
Dependency ratios	94.6
Child-woman ratios	735
Sex ratios (per 100 females)	89.9
Median ages (years)	17.1
Decline in birthrate (1965-83)	−1.6
Proportion of urban (%)	20.04
Population density (per sq. km.)	34
per hectare of arable land	1.60
Rates of growth (%)	2.37
Urban %	7.8
Rural %	1.2
Natural increase rates (per 1,000)	26.9
Crude birth rates (per 1,000)	48.5
Crude death rates (per 1,000)	21.6
Gross reproduction rates	3.30
Net reproduction rates	2.13
Total fertility rates	6.76
General fertility rates (per 1,000)	201
Life expectancy, males (years)	43.0
Life expectancy, females (years)	45.0
Life expectancy, total (years)	44.0
Population doubling time in years at current rate	26
Net migration %	−3.2

Although Yemeni rulers have discouraged both immigration and emigration, there has been demographically significant migration over the years, mainly to Aden and Saudi Arabia. In 1975 1,234,000 Yemenis were working in Arabia, Indonesia and Singapore. Several refugee groups have sought asylum in Yemen. Approximately 2,700 armed members of the

Palestinian Liberation Organization sought refuge in North Yemen in the fall of 1982 and December 1983 following their evacuation from Lebanon; many have since departed. Perhaps 250,000 South Yemenis have settled in North Yemen to escape political persecution or economic hardship in the south. Refugee groups from countries in the Horn of Africa have frequently sought residence in Yemen, often for economic rather than political reasons. The authorities have taken measures to restrict the flow of these national groups. For example, many Somalis and Ethiopians, who have no claim to Yemeni citizenship or clear demonstration of being political refugees, find it difficult to obtain work permits and visa extensions.

Living in a conservative Islamic society which remained largely isolated from the modern world prior to 1962, few Yemeni women are employed outside the home or play an active role in other aspects of public life. Additionally, education for women in significant numbers began only at the end of the civil war in 1970. The government does not restrict women's access to employment and is trying to expand their educational opportunities. However, lack of manpower continues to inhibit the opening of new schools and the staffing of existing institutions. Traditional Islamic norms, more stringently followed in rural areas, as well as the considerable time expended by women in water and fuel collection, constrain the number of women attending classes.

Women are now present in the middle levels of several ministries such as the Central Planning Organization, and one woman is in the Constituent Assembly. A few were elected to Local Development Councils. Prevailing social norms frequently dictate, however, that women defer to the guidance of their male colleagues and accept close supervision of their activities by male relatives. Women seeking exit permits for travel outside the country are frequently asked to provide evidence that male relatives have no objection to their travel.

Yemen has no official birth control policy or programs.

ETHNIC COMPOSITION

The Yemenis are almost entirely Semitic and, with the departure in 1948 of Yemenite Jews for Israel, almost entirely Arab, though inhabitants of the Tihama belt show Negroid strains. Within the Arab community the historic division is between the Qahtani or Southern Arabs and the Adnani or Northern Arabs and between the Zeidi and Shafi tribes. The latter distinction is based on religious rather than ethnic factors. Nevertheless, the division and rivalry between the two tribes permit only limited social cohesion. The Zeidis, who are Shiites, claim as their imam descendants of the Prophet Muhammad through his son-in-law Ali and Ali's grandson, Zeid. Zeidi tribes are concentrated in northern and eastern Yemen and in the central plateau. More warlike than the Shafis, the Zeidis have dominated the country. The Shafis, who are

Sunnis, live along the Tihama coast and in the southern region where they form the local majority. The Shafis, unlike the Zeidis, are mainly town-dwellers and are also much more active in the commercial professions.

In terms of linguistic and ethnic homgeneity Yemen, ranks 121st among nations of the world with 99.06% homogeneity (on an ascending scale in which North and South Korea are ranked 135th with 100% homogeneity and Tanzania is ranked 1st with 7% homogeneity).

Yemen is virtually a closed society; there are only a few thousand aliens or foreigners permanently resident in the country.

LANGUAGE

The official and national language of Yemen is Arabic, which is spoken by all Yemenis. The study of Western languages is not encouraged.

RELIGION

Islam is the state religion and that of the vast majority of Yemenis. Members of the Zaydi (Shi'a) sect have historically enjoyed greater political influence than those of the Shafei (Sunni) sect, although this distinction has often been as much based on geographical and tribal considerations as on sectarian grounds. For the most part, the two major Islamic communities coexist without friction and seek to minimize the significance of doctrinal differences. Muslim associations with ties to Pan-Islamic or foreign organizations enjoy some degree of freedom, including the right to operate schools which are largely independent of the national education system.

Although almost all of the once substantial Yemeni Jewish population has emigrated to Israel, the small number of Jews remaining live in peace with the Muslim majority. These Jews practice their religion freely, and suffer no unusual economic hardships. They maintain only very limited contact with Jews abroad. Communications between Yemeni Jews and their coreligionists and relatives in Israel are strictly proscribed.

There is no indigenous Christian population. Foreign Christians are allowed to conduct private services, although the establishment of churches is not permitted. Foreign clergy are not permitted into the country.

There is also a small Ismaili community, numbering over 50,000. The Ismailis follow the religious practices of the Shias but differ from them in their devotion to Ismail, the seventh imam.

COLONIAL EXPERIENCE

Yemen was never under a Western colonial power.

CABINET LIST (1985)

President	Col. 'Ali 'Abdallah Salih
Vice President	'Abd al-Karim al- 'Arashi
Prime Minister	'Abd al-'Aziz 'Abd al-Ghani
Deputy Prime Minister	'Abd al-Karim al- Iryani
Deputy Prime Minister	Muhammad Sa'id al- 'Attar
Deputy Prime Minister for Domestic Affairs	Lt. Col. Mujahid Yahya Abu Shawarib
Minister of Agriculture & Fisheries	Ahmad Muhammad al- Hamdani
Minister of Awqaf & Guidance	Qadi 'Ali ibn 'Ali Samman
Minister of Civil Service & Administrative Reform	Isma'il Ahmad al- Wazir
Minister of Communications & Transport	Ahmad Muhammad al- Ansi
Minister of Development	Muhammad Sa'id al- 'Attar
Minister of Economy & Industry	Ahmad Qa'id Barakat
Minister of Education	Husayn Abdallah al- Amri
Minister of Electricity, Water & Sewage Works	Muhammad Hasan Sabra
Minister of Finance	Muhammad al-Khadam al- Wajih
Minister of Foreign Affairs	'Abd al-Karim al- Iryani
Minister of Health	Dr. Muhammad Ahmad al- Kabab
Minister of Information & Culture	Hasan Ahmad al- Lawzi
Minister of Interior	Lt. Col. Muhsin Muhammad al- 'Ulufi
Minister of Justice	Ahmad Muhammad al- Jubi
Minister of Labor, Social Affairs & Youth	Muhammad Ahmad al- Asbahi
Minister of Local Government	Muhammad 'Abdallah al- Jayfi
Minister of Municipalities & Housing	Ahmad Muhammad Luqman
Minister of Petroleum & Mineral Resources	Muhammad al-Khadam al- Wajih
Minister of Public Works	'Abdallah Husayn al- Kurshumi
Minister of Supply & Trade	Fuad Qayd Muhammad
Minister of State	Husayn 'Ali al- Hubayshi
Minister of State for the Affairs of Yemeni Unity	Yahya Husayn al- 'Arashi
Minister of State for Cabinet Affairs	Ahmad Salih al- Ru'ayni
Minister of State for Youth & Sports	Abdallah Nasir al- Darafi

CONSTITUTION & GOVERNMENT

Yemen's constitutional development began only in 1962, and successive governments have functioned under interim constitutions. Under the constitution of 1971, the first nationwide elections took place, and an assembly of 159 members was elected as the new legislative body. The assembly subsequently elected a Republican Council whose chairman served as the head of state. In 1974 the constitution was temporarily suspended, and the country was ruled by a five-member Command Council and an appointed prime minister and cabinet. Later the constitution was restored in a somewhat modified form that strengthened the role of the Command Council. In 1975 Lt. Col. Ibrahim Muhammad al-Hamadi dis-

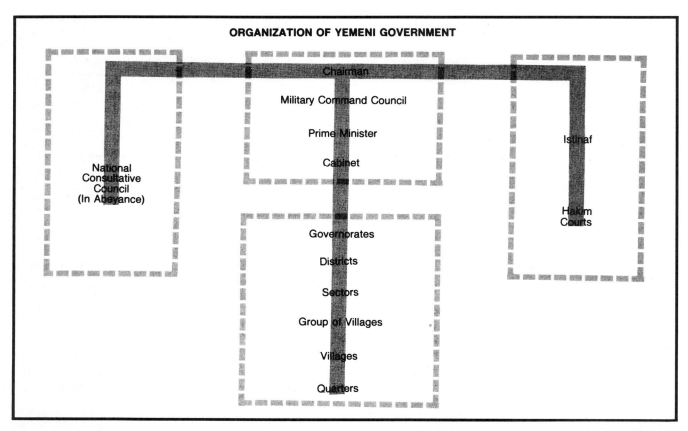

ORGANIZATION OF YEMENI GOVERNMENT

Chairman

Military Command Council

Prime Minister

Cabinet

National Consultative Council (In Abeyance)

Istinaf

Hakim Courts

Governorates

Districts

Sectors

Group of Villages

Villages

Quarters

solved the consultative body that had served as a nominal legislature. In 1982 the government convoked a People's General Congress to discuss the National Charter.

The government is currently headed by a seven-member Command Council, which serves as the policy-making body. The Council appoints the prime minister, who is essentially an administrative official. The cabinet, chosen by the prime minister, includes two deputy ministers and 16 ministers.

RULERS OF YEMEN ARAB REPUBLIC

IMAMS:
1904 to 1948 (February)
    Yahya Muhammad ibn Muhammad
1948 (March) to 1962 (September)
    Ahmad an-Nasir li-din Allah
1962 (September) to 1970 (May)
    Muhammad Mansur bi-illah

(In September 1962 civil war broke out; the imam served as head of the royalist forces until the conclusion of the civil war and establishment of a republic)

PRESIDENTS
1962 (October) to 1967 (November)
    Abdullah as-Sallal
1967 (November) to 1974 (June)
    Abdur Rahman al-Iriani
1974 (June) to 1977 (October)
    Ibrahim Muhammad al-Hamadi
1977 (October) to 1978 (June)
    Ahmad Husayn al-Ghashmi
1978 (June) — Ali Abdullah Saleh

Seven hundred of the 1,000 delegates to the People's General Congress were elected in 1982. Women, as a rule absent from public life, hold a few seats in the Congress, and have the right to vote in general elections. Reportedly debate at times has been vigorous within the Congress, but the president and his key advisers control the agenda closely. Elections were held in July 1984 to fill 17,507 positions on newly created Local Development Councils which are responsible for local government as well as local development projects. For the first time in North Yemen's history, the balloting was secret, and it included all citizens over 18 years of age except for the mentally handicapped and certain criminals. Well received by the population, the elections were a step toward extending government control in the countryside.

Yemen remains an essentially tribalized society alien to modern political organization. In the mountain regions power rests with the largely autonomous tribes. Political stability depends on the ability of the Sana'a government to contain tribal rivalries that periodically erupt into open hostilities. Three coup attempts were reported in 1975 and 1976, all by tribal sheikhs trying to resist the central government. From 1948 to 1967 the country witnessed nine coups, making Yemen one of the most unstable countries in the Middle East. In 1977 the chairman of the Military Command Council Col. Ibrahim Muhammad al-Hamadi and his brother were assassinated on the eve of a trip to Southern Yemen. The same fate befell his successor, Ahmed Hussein al-Ghashmi who was killed in 1978 when a bomb concealed in the briefcase of a visiting Southern Yemeni emissary exploded in his office. It is widely believed that the assassination was masterminded by President Rubayi Ali of Southern Yemen who himself was deposed and shot within weeks.

FREEDOM & HUMAN RIGHTS

In terms of civil and political and rights, Yemen is classified as a not-free country with a negative rating of 6 in political rights and 5 in civil rights (on a descending scale in which 7 is the lowest and 1 the highest in civil and political rights).

The Yemen Arab Republic has had a checkered and violent history. After the fall of the imam, it emerged from centuries-old isolation only to experience a bloody civil war, followed by political instability and the assassination of two presidents within four years. There is a border war with South Yemen and continuing guerrilla activity in the south-central part. Because of these conditions, the government has not been overly zealous in its efforts to prevent torture of prisoners, especially in areas where it has only a nominal control over local officials.

Overall there was little change in the state of human rights in 1985. In the early 1980s human rights practices were strongly affected by the activities of the National Democratic Front (NDF), a foreign-supported, Marxist-oriented rural guerrilla movement operating in the central and southern regions of the country. Fighting between government forces and the guerrillas was at times heavy and basic human rights of the population living in the affected areas were often violated in the wake of the Front's terrorism and the frequently repressive antiterrorist campaigns.

The state of human rights is greatly influenced by tribal and Islamic traditions. Most males bear arms and will use them to defend the integrity of their person and family. The state has a limited capability to govern and does not have a monopoly on the use of force.

Association of citizens with foreigners is closely monitored. The names of those visiting embassies or attending social functions hosted by foreigners are routinely monitored, and access is sometimes denied. Security officials have on occasion detained citizens for investigations of their possible links with foreigners.

Although government officials are not exempt from politically motivated arrest, prominent public figures whose opposition to government policies falls short of subversion are rarely detained by the security police. Instead, they are generally forced to withdraw from public life and their activities are closely monitored by government authorities. Usually, such persons are not subject to formal house arrest, but are simply told not to work for a time.

Those formally charged with espionage or other antigovernment activities are tried in special security courts. These courts are convened at the direction of the president to handle specific cases. Rights normally afforded the accused may be suspended in security cases. All decisions made by the security court are subject to review and confirmation by the president. The number of political prisoners held in Yemeni prisons may, by rough estimate, number 100 or more.

The Yemeni press is government controlled and all foreign newspapers and magazines are routinely censored. Books are also closely monitored but not as closely controlled.

CIVIL SERVICE

No current information is available on the Yemeni civil service.

LOCAL GOVERNMENT

Yemen is divided into seven governorates (muhafaza), each headed by a governor, or emir, who may also be the commander of the armed forces in the area. The governorates are Taiz, Ibb and Al Bayda in the south, Hodeida along the Red Sea coast, Sana'a in the center, and the Hajja and Sa'dah in the northwest and northeast, respectively. The governorates are divided into districts (qada) and these again into sectors or nahiya. At the lower level traditional structures prevail. A group of mahallahs, or quarters, form a qarya, or village, under the authority of a sheikh, and a number of villages constitute an ozlah. In 1974 Yemen had 41 qada, 165 nahiya, 1,680 ozlah, 15,418 qarya and 14,384 mahallah. There are no popular representative institutions at any of these levels.

FOREIGN POLICY

Since the end of the civil war Yemen has pursued a moderate course in its foreign policy. However, relations with Western nations are still less cordial than those with Eastern-bloc countries. The Soviet Union, in particular, has provided substantial economic and military aid to Yemen. The Chinese aid mission, established in 1958 under the imam, was expanded under the Republicans. In a dramatic policy reversal, relations with Saudi Arabia have improved to the point where it has become the principal aid donor in recent years.

Relations with the United States, suspended in 1967 in line with other Arab nations, were resumed in 1972, in which year the U.S. AID program was renewed.

A critical element in Yemeni foreign policy is its relations with the People's Democratic Republic of Yemen, its southern neighbor. Although both governments subscribe to the goal of eventual reunification, relations have been badly strained since 1967. A series of unification committees established in 1972 have achieved little progress in view of ideological differences between Sana'a and Pro-Soviet and Communist-dominated Aden.

Another round of hostilities between Sana and Aden began on February 15, 1979 when South Yemeni forces crossed into North Yemen along with rebels of the National Democratic Front, advancing within 10 days to Qataba and Harib, towns deep inside the border. A ceasefire was arranged by the Arab League and South Yemen withdrew its forces. The border was reopened five days later and President Saleh and President Ismail of South Yemen met in Kuwait for three days of talks which concluded with a mutual pledge to unite their two countries. However, this agreement displeased Saudi Arabia which thereupon withheld delivery of weapons forcing Saleh to turn to Moscow to military aid. Although the restoration of Saudi aid in 1980 was predicated on the pledge that Soviet aid would be phased out, relations with Moscow have grown stronger since then. In 1981 President Saleh visited Moscow and in 1984 signed a 20-year Friendship Treaty with the Soviet Union.

Yemen Arab Republic and the United States are parties to four treaties and agreements covering economic and technical cooperation, investment guaranties, Peace Corps, and trade and commerce.

Yemen joined the U.N. in 1947; its share of the U.N. budget is 0.02%. It is a member of eight U.N. organizations and three other organizations, including the Arab League.

U.S. Ambassador in Sana'a: William A. Rugh
U.K. Ambassador in Sana'a: David Tatham
Yemeni Ambassador in Washington, D.C.: Mohsin A. Alaini
Yemeni Ambassador in London: Ahmed Daifellah Alazeib

PARLIAMENT

The 1970 constitution provided for a Consultative Assembly of 179 members, of whom 159 were to be elected. An election was held in 1971. The Council was dissolved in 1974, reconvened later that year and dissolved again in 1975.

The Constituent Assembly was reconstituted in 1978 and expanded to its full membership. It is responsible for the ratification of laws and treaties, budget review, codification of Islamic laws, and provisions for new elections. It has ratified the selection of the last two presidents.

The People's Constituent Assembly reviews and ratifies legislation proposed by the president and the cabinet ministers he appoints. The Assembly has never disapproved the president's policies, but on occasion in 1985 called ministers and other ranking government officials to explain proposed legislation. The members of this legislative body were appointed by presidential decree in 1978. Once scheduled for 1983, parliamentary elections have not taken place and their timing remains uncertain.

The People's General Congress is the only national political organization whose members have been selected in competitive elections. Convoked in 1982 to discuss the National Charter, it held its second national convention in August 1984 to endorse government policies. The 1,000 delegates (700 elected) represent most segments of Yemeni society.

There are organizations which provide alternative channels for political expression for Yemenis living outside the few urban centers. Large segments of the population in local communities play a role in selecting the leadership of so called Local Development Associations and influence their policies. These organizations use a mixture of local and national funding for economic and social infrastructure development. In any areas where the effective presence of the central government is minimal, tribal leaders make key decisions in consultation with other prominent members of their community. Gradually, however, the authority of the National Security Organization has slowly penetrated previously autonomous local communities.

POLITICAL PARTIES

Political parties in the accepted sense have not developed in Yemen where loyalties and alignments are determined by religious and tribal ties. For a brief period there were groups, such as the Popular Revolutionary Union and the Yemeni Union. None of these groups survived the coup of 1974.

ECONOMY

Yemen is one of the 49 low-income countries of the world. It is considered by the United Nations as one of the 29 least developed countries (LLDC) and also one of the countries most seriously affected (MSA) by recent adverse economic conditions. The private sector prodominates in Yemen's basically free-market economic system.

PRINCIPAL ECONOMIC INDICATORS

Gross National Product: $3.930 billion (1983)
  GNP Annual Growth Rate: 6.6% (1973-82)
  Per Capita GNP: $510 (1983)
  Per Capita GNP Growth Rate: 3.5% (1973-82)
Gross Domestic Product: YR14.637 billion (1982)
  GDP Average Annual Growth Rate: 8.2% (1973-83)
  GDP at 1980 Prices: YR13.285 billion (1982)
  GDP Deflator (1980=100): 110.2
  Per Capita GDP: YR2403 (1982)
  Per Capita GDP Average Annual Growth Rate: 5.7% (1970-81)
  Average Annual Rate of Inflation: 13.9% (1973-83)
Consumer Price Index (108=100): Food: 108 (1982)
Money Supply: YR18.049 billion (May 1985)
  Reserve Money: YR19.246 billion (May 1985)
Currency in Circulation: YR13.314 billion (1984)
International Reserves: $318.5 million of which foreign exchange reserves were $304 million (1984)

In 1973 Yemen's newly established Central Planning Office issued the first Three-Year Development Plan (1973-76). The plan called for an expenditure of

BALANCE OF PAYMENTS (1983) (million $)	
Current Account Balance	−559.0
Merchandise Exports	9.6
Merchandise Imports	−1,765.5
Trade Balance	−1,755.9
Other Goods, Services & Income	+294.2
Other Goods, Services & Income	−341.6
Other Goods, Services & Income Net	—
Private Unrequited Transfers	1,084.4
Official Unrequited Transfers	159.9
Direct Investment	7.6
Portfolio Investment	−2.4
Other Long-term Capital	152.1
Other Short-term Capital	13.2
Net Errors & Omissions	181.7
Counterpart Items	−9.2
Exceptional Financing	—
Liabilities Constituting Foreign Authorities' Reserves	17.3
Total Change in Reserves	198.6

YR935.6 million ($205.8 million), of which 75.1% was to be financed by foreign grants and loans.

The Second Five-Year Development Plan (1977-81) and the Third Five-Year Plan (1982-86) had allotments of YR16.5 billion and YR27.4 billion respectively. Foreign financing constituted 42% of the second plan and 45% of the third plan. The 1982 earthquake in Dhamar severely set back the second plan.

DEVELOPMENT PLAN, 1982-86 (proposed fixed capital investment in million riyals)	
Agriculture	4,430
Mining	905
Manufacturing	3,510
Electricity and water	2,040
Construction	640
Trade, restaurants and hotels	2,870
Transport and communications	4,640
Finance	100
Dwellings and real estate services	3,745
Government services	4,250
Other services	270
Total	27,400

GROSS DOMESTIC PRODUCT BY ECONOMIC ACTIVITY (1970-81)		
	%	Rate of Change %
Agriculture	33.8	3.7
Mining	1.1	12.2
Manufacturing	5.2	12.3
Construction	7.9	15.0
Electricity, Gas & Water	0.4	19.1
Transport & Communications	3.5	9.5
Trade & Finance	22.6	15.3
Public Administration & Defense	11.7	10.6
Other Branches	13.7	11.2

Yemen began to accept foreign aid shortly after it emerged from its centuries-old isolation in the late fifties. The United States was one of the early donors and its program ran until it was terminated by Yemen in 1967. The United States constructed a road from Mocha to Sana'a through Taiz, installed a public water system at Taiz and undertook a series of small self-help rural development projects. Total U.S. aid from 1946 through 1967 amounted to $42.8 million and, after resumption in 1972, its level reached $3 million a year. Among Western donors West Germany ranks first with a number of loans tied to specific development projects, but the Soviet Union and China have outdistanced Western donors. The Soviet aid program began in 1956 with a $20 million loan for construction of Sana'a's airport and the modernization of the Hodeida harbor. Other Soviet-financed projects include a power house, a radio station, the Hodeida-Taiz highway, a cement factory, a hospital in Sana'a and a number of technical schools. Chinese aid was used to build Yemen's first asphalted road from Hodeida to Sana'a and the first textile factory.

In recent years Saudi Arabia has become the largest aid donor with both direct financial assistance and project aid. Direct annual Saudi assistance is estimated to exceed $120 million. Generous aid, directed to health, education and social welfare projects, has also flowed into Yemen from other oil-rich Arab countries, mainly Kuwait, Iraq, Qatar, the United Arab Emirates and Algeria.

From 1946 through 1983, U.S. aid provided approximately $196.9 million and Saudi Arabia provided an estimated $250 million in budget support alone to Yemen. The U.N. Development Assistance Program in Yemen is one of the world's largest. Total aid received from international organizations from 1946 through 1983 was $392.9 million.

During 1979-81 Yemen received $137.5 million in bilateral and multilateral aid or $23.70 per capita.

BUDGET

The Yemeni fiscal year runs from April 1 through March 31. The national budget and tax system are recent developments dating back to the mid-1960s. Government revenues continue to be derived primarily from customs, agricultural and capital taxes, and the Islamic zakat (or charity) tax. Collection varies from area to area, from harvest to harvest; often the government is left without any source of income in periods of drought. The Central Budget Bureau supervises budgetary and accounting procedures.

Of current revenues, 11.7% comes from taxes on income, profit and capital gain, 7.3% from domestic taxes on goods and services, 49.8% from taxes on international trade and transactions, 13.5% from other taxes and 17.6% from non-tax revenues. Current revenues represented 20.4% of GNP. Of current expenditures, 35.5% goes to defense, 16.4% to education, 4.5% to health, 8.8% to economic services, 34.7% to other functions. Current expenditures represent 45.7% of GNP and overall deficit 29.1% of GNP.

In 1982, public consumption was YR3.899 billion and private consumption YR13.927 billion. During

1973-83 public consumption grew by 20.6% and private consumption by 5.8%.

In 1983, total external disbursed and outstanding debt was $1.594 billion of which $1.555 billion was owed to official creditors and $18 billion was owed to private creditors. Total debt service was $42.1 million of which $28.9 million was repayment of principal and $13.2 million interest. Total external debt represented 517.7% of export revenues and 39.2% of GNP. Total debt service represented 13.9% of export revenues and 1.0% of GNP.

BUDGET ('000 riyals, year ending 30 June)		
	Revenue	Expenditure
1981/82	5,280,000	8,470,000
1982/83	5,460,000	8,720,000
1984/85	5,455,700	8,123,800
1985/86: Budget estimates: Revenue 6,228,200,000 riyals: Expenditure 8,895,372,000 riyals.		

FINANCE

The Yemeni unit of currency is the rial divided into 100 fils. Coins are issued in denominations of 1, 5, 10, 25 and 50 fils; notes are issued in denominations of 1, 5, 10, 20 and 50 rials. Before 1975 the rial was divided into 40 buqsha, and coins of ½, 1 and 2 buqsha are still in use.

In 1985 the official exchange value of the rial was YR 1=$6.485. The sterling exchange rate was £1=YR 6.79.

The banking system consists of the Central Bank of Yemen, the Yemeni Bank for Reconstruction and Development and five foreign commercial banks. The Yemeni Bank for Reconstruction and Development dominates the banking business and controls over 70% of the outstanding loans. In 1985 the commercial banks had reserves of YR 3.704 billion, demand deposits of YR 2.501 billion and time and savings deposits of YR 3.814 billion.

AGRICULTURE

Yemen has the largest farming sector on the Arabian peninsula. It employs 75% of the economically active population and contributes 21% of the GDP and 90% of the value of exports. The rate of growth during 1973-83 was 2.1%. Of the total land area of 19,500,000 hectares (48,184,500 acres), 42% or 8,158,000 hectares (17,988,390 acres) is agricultural land. Per capita agricultural land is 1.5 hectares (3.7 acres). On the basis of 1974-76=100, the index of agricultural production in 1982 was 99, the index of food production was 99 and the index of per capita food production 80. Nearly 80% of the farm families work as sharecroppers. Through the centuries a dry farming system has been used that conserves soil and moisture through an intricate terracing system. Differences in elevation and climate permit the cultiva-

GROWTH PROFILE Annual Growth Rates (%)	
Population 1980-2000	2.4
Birthrate 1965-83	−4.0
Deathrate 1965-83	−29.3
Urban Population 1973-83	3.5
Labor Force 1980-2000	3.3
GNP 1973-83	6.6
GNP per capita 1973-83	3.5
GDP 1973-83	8.2
GDP per capita 1973-83	5.7
Consumer Prices 1970-81	23.4
Wholesale Prices	—
Inflation 1973-83	13.9
Agriculture 1973-83	2.1
Manufacturing 1970-81	12.3
Industry 1973-83	13.2
Services 1973-83	11.3
Mining 1970-81	12.2
Construction 1970-81	15.0
Electricity 1970-81	19.1
Transportation 1970-81	9.5
Trade 1970-81	13.3
Public Administration & Defense 1970-81	10.6
Export Price Index	—
Import Price Index	—
Terms of Trade	—
Exports	—
Imports	—
Public Consumption 1973-83	20.6
Private Consumption 1973-83	5.8
Gross Domestic Investment 1973-83	18.2
Energy Consumption 1973-83	22.4
Energy Production	—

tion of a broad variety of cereals, vegetables and fruits. Approximately 90% of the total agricultural production consists of cereals. The major crops in the north are sorghum, wheat and barley, while in the south sorghum and corn constitute the main crops. The value added in agriculture in 1983 was $761 million.

Until the civil war Yemen was self sufficient in foodstuffs. But the hostilities, combined with long periods of drought, caused a decline in production. As a result Yemen has become a net importer of food and has also received food relief under the United Nations World Food Program. In 1983 it imported 556,000 tons of cereals.

Because droughts are so frequent, one of the major concerns of the development plans is the creation of irrigation and water storage systems. The largest project as yet undertaken is the agricultural scheme for the Tihama region, assisted by the United Nations, the International Development Association and the Kuwait Fund for Arab Economic Development. The scheme involves irrigation works in the Wadi Zebid area and the development of 60,000 hectares (148,260 acres) at Wadi Mawr. The rebuilding of the ancient Marib Dam is also under consideration. In 1982, 2,050 tractors were in use and consumption of fertilizer totaled 12,100 tons, or 5.1 kg (11.2 lb) per hectare of arable land.

Yemeni farmers are shifting to crops with high cash returns. Qat is a particular case in point. It is a swiftly growing tree requiring very little care. If chewed while still fresh, qat leaves produce a mild narcotic effect. Chewing qat is a very common Yemeni social activity even though, according to some experts, a Yemeni may spend more than 20% of his disposable annual income on qat. It is not uncommon for people to spend $22 to $45 per day for qat, making it Yemen's most lucrative crop. Because of its profitability, some areas which once produced other products, such as coffee, now product qat.

The major export crops are cotton, qat and coffee. Coffee was the principal export earner until the mid-1960s when it was overtaken by qat, which has now been replaced by cotton.

```
┌─────────────────────────────────────────────────┐
│        PRINCIPAL CROP PRODUCTION (1978)           │
│              (000 metric tons)                    │
│  Wheat . . . . . . . . . . . . . . . . . . .   27 │
│  Barley . . . . . . . . . . . . . . . . . . .  10 │
│  Corn . . . . . . . . . . . . . . . . . . . .  59 │
│  Sorghum . . . . . . . . . . . . . . . . . .  248 │
│  Potatoes . . . . . . . . . . . . . . . . .   140 │
│  Pulses . . . . . . . . . . . . . . . . . . .  15 │
│  Vegetables . . . . . . . . . . . . . . . .   285 │
│  Grapes . . . . . . . . . . . . . . . . . . .  59 │
│  Coffee . . . . . . . . . . . . . . . . . . .   4 │
│  Tobacco . . . . . . . . . . . . . . . . . . .  6 │
│  Cotton (lint) . . . . . . . . . . . . . . . .  5 │
│  Dates . . . . . . . . . . . . . . . . . . . . 84 │
│  Sesame . . . . . . . . . . . . . . . . . . . . 6 │
└─────────────────────────────────────────────────┘
```

Breeding of humped cattle occurs throughout the country, camels are bred in the highlands and lowlands, and the export of hides and skins is an important source of foreign exchange. The livestock population in 1982 consisted of 3,000 horses, 740,000 asses, 950,000 cattle, 108,000 camels, 3.150 million sheep, 7.5 million goats and 4.0 million chickens.

Most of the forests which once covered the Yemeni highlands have been cleared, and today there are few forest areas.

Fishing is a minor activity employing only a few thousand. The annual catch is estimated at around 17,000 tons in 1982. A fish processing plant has been built at Hodeida with Chinese help. An agricultural credit bank was established in 1975.

INDUSTRY

Manufacturing employs 11% of the population and contributes only 8.6% to the GDP. Its rate of growth during 1973-83 was 12.3%. The value added in manufacturing in 1983 was $118 million. With the exception of a few manufacturing plants, industry is characterized by handicrafts and family ventures. Only 270 enterprises employ more than five workers and they are concentrated in Sana'a, Taiz and Hodeida.

Weaving, tanning, dyeing and traditional local handicrafts are the main forms of industrial activity. Public sector industry is a recent development, established solely through foreign aid programs. Industrial projects initiated during the 1960s and 1970s include a textile mill, a cement factory, a pharmaceutical plant and an aluminum factory. The textile industry is the most promising line of industrial development. A rock salt factory at Salif utilizes local rock deposits. The Yemeni Company for Industrial Development is engaged in the development of light industry.

In July 1975, the government promulgated a new law on investments which guaranteed freedom of investments, equal treatment with national capital in the case of foreign investors, transferability of net profits abroad, protection against nationalization, and exemption from all customs and duties on imports of machinery and imported raw materials.

ENERGY

Yemen does not produce any form of energy other than electric power. In 1982 its total consumption of power was equivalent to 740,000 metric tons of coal, or 122 kg (269 lb) per capita. Annual growth rate in energy consumption during 1973-83 was 22.4%. The total production of electric power was 500 million kwh in 1984; the per capita output was 80 kwh per year.

The Yemen Petroleum Company, a joint venture of Yemen and Southern Yemen, has a monopoly of imports, storage and distribution of oil products.

In July 1984 the Yemen Hunt Oil Company (a subsidiary of the U.S. Hunt Oil Company) made the first discovery of oil in commercial quantities in the YAR, in the Marib al-Jawf basin in the northeast of the country. The find, known as the Alef field, was producing about 10,000 b/d at the end of 1984 from a total of three wells, which were to be increased to six by April 1985. The field's reserves have been estimated at 200 million barrels and production levels should be a minimum of 75,000 b/d and a maximum of 300,000 b/d. Yemen's annual oil consumption is only 17,000 b/d and the potential for the country to become an oil exporter, and thereby to transform its economy, is clear. The government set up a Supreme Council for Oil and Mineral Resources in February 1985, and appointed Deputy Prime Minister Abdul Karim al-Iryani as its chairman. The council is designed to encourage investment in the oil and minerals sector, and to examine means of exploiting the country's energy resources. There are plans to establish a refinery and a 400-km (248 mi) export pipeline, expected to run from Alef to the Red Sea. In December 1984 President Ali Abdullah Saleh said that the Yemen could begin to export oil within two years. Revenues from oil could make the Yemen independent of foreign aid.

LABOR

The Yemeni labor force is estimated at 1.668 million of whom 11% are women. By sectors 75% are employed in agriculture, 11% in industry and 14% in services. Nearly 50% of the labor force consists of emigrant workers. The government encourages the emigration of workers to Saudi Arabia and other countries because of the beneficial effects of workers' remittances on the national budget. An estimated 1,395,123 Yemenis work abroad, about one million in Saudi Arabia. Workers' remittances brought in $1.3 billion in 1983, but have declined since then as a result of the decline in the petroleum industry. Although domestic wages are as high as those in Saudi Arabia and Gulf states, the flow of Yemenis in search of work abroad has continued unabated. This has resulted in a labor shortage at home. Even though immigration and conscription laws enacted in September 1979 have modestly limited the numbers of Yemenis who legally go abroad, the only real solution to the shortage has been increased use of expatriate labor. There are approximately 5,000 Indians and the same number of Pakistanis working in Yemen. In addition to these, there are Sudanis, Somalis, Egyptians, Koreans, westerners, and numerous other foreigners. They now provide everything from manual labor to the expertise vital for a modern economy. These people in turn send money back to their homes, which increases the outflow of currency and thus impacts on the balance of payments. Yemen's first labor union, the Yemen General Trade Union, has a small membership limited to construction workers.

FOREIGN COMMERCE

Yemen's foreign trade in 1984 consisted of exports of $67.2 million and imports of $1.6 billion, leaving a trade deficit of $1.533 billion. Of the imports, machinery and transport equipment constituted 27.8% (of which vehicles 11.7%, electrical machinery 4.3%), food and live animals 26.1%, petroleum products 7.1%, iron and steel 6.2%, chemicals 5.1% and cement 3.2%. Of the exports, food and live animals constituted 43.8%, civil engineering equipment 16%, textiles and yarn 5.9% and road vehicles 4.0%. The major import sources are: Saudi Arabia 19.3%, Japan 12.7%, France 7.9%, West Germany 5.9%, the United Kingdom 5.2% and Italy 5.0%. The major export destinations are: Southern Yemen 42.4%, France 11.5%, China 9.3%, the United States 8.8%, Italy 6.5% and Saudi Arabia 5.4%.

TRANSPORTATION & COMMUNICATIONS

Yemen has no rail system or inland waterways. There are three ports, Hodeida, Mocha and Salif, of which the largest at present is Hodeida. The Hodeida harbor, completed in 1962 by Soviet engineers and expanded later with Egyptian and Iraqi aid, can accommodate ocean-going vessels. It is no longer as congested as it once was. This is due to the new berths constructed at Hodeidah and Ras al-Katib, a sandpit extending 15 km. north of the main port, as well as to more efficient off-loading procedures. In 1982 40,000 tons of cargo were loaded and 2,000,000 tons unloaded at this port. Both Salif and Mocha have been

FOREIGN TRADE INDICATORS (1984)	
Annual Growth Rate, Imports:	—
Annual Growth Rate, Exports:	—
Ratio of Exports to Imports:	4:96
Exports per capita:	$11
Imports per capita:	$264
Balance of Trade:	$1.533 billion
Ratio of International Reserves to Imports (in months)	2.1
Exports as % of GDP:	5.3
Imports as % of GDP:	56.9
Value of Manufactured Exports:	—
Commodity Concentration:	—

Direction of Trade (%)

	Imports	Exports
EEC	32.7	24.6
U.S.	—	8.8
Industrialized Market Economies	55.0	33.6
East European Economies	1.0	—
High Income Oil Exporters	14.7	44.4
Developing Economies	36.9	62.5

Composition of Trade (%)

	Imports	Exports
Food	28.4	45.0
Agricultural Raw Materials	0.2	3.9
Fuels	7.2	0.1
Ores & Minerals	6.7	4.4
Manufactured Goods	57.1	42.6
of which Chemicals	5.1	2.8
of which Machinery	27.7	25.1

expanded, and Salif may eventually replace Hodeida as the principal port. Cargo and passenger services are run by the Yemen Navigation Company.

There are about 4,000 km (2,484 mi) of main roads, of which 1,775 km (1,102 mi) are asphalted and the rest graveled. Highways run from Hodeida to Sana'a and from Mocha to Taiz. The number of passenger cars in the country in 1982 was 80,375 and commercial vehicles totalled 115,018. Per capita vehicle ownership is 13 per 1,000 inhabitants.

Yemen Airways, with a fleet of nine aircraft, operates internal and overseas flights. During 1982 it carried 352,000 passengers and flew 6.3 million km (3.9 million miles). There are three airports of international standard: Al Ganad at Taiz, Hodeida and Al Rahaba at Sana'a, the last built with West German assistance. There are 18 other airfields, 12 of them usable, three with permanent-surface runways, and one with runway over 2,500 meters (8,000 ft).

In 1984 Yemen had 35,000 telephones, or 0.6 per 100 inhabitants.

In 1980 the postal service handled 7,802,000 pieces of mail or 1.2 per capita.

Under the imamate foreigners were prohibited from entering Yemen. Though the republican governments have reversed this policy, lack of facilities has discouraged travelers. In 1982 23,000 tourists visited Yemen generating $34 million in revenues. Of the visitors, 2,300 were from the United States, 3,800 from the United Kingdom, 1,900 from Syria, 4,100 from France, 4,100 from West Germany and 3,900 from Egypt. Expenditures by nationals abroad totaled $44 million. There are 4,000 hotel beds and the average length of stay was 5.2 days.

MINING

Salt is the only mineral at present exploited in Yemen on any scale. Salt deposits exist at Maarib in the east and at Qumah, near Salif. Other known minerals include coal, copper, lead, zinc, silver, gold, iron, sulphur and uranium.

DEFENSE

The defense structure is headed by the military command council whose chairman is the head of state and commander in chief. There is no minister of defense and the armed forces stand directly under the president's authority. The head of the Central National Security Organization (also referred to as the Director of Military Intelligence) reports directly to the president. Because of tribal rivalries, the institutional structure is weak and can be overthrown by any determined group. The conflict between the ruling Zaidi officers and the Sunni Shafai tribes is carried over into military politics. The fact that the Shafai are politically leftist and more enthusiastic about reunion with Southern Yemen adds to the confusion and divisiveness of the military's role. Military manpower is provided by conscription of all able-bodied males between the ages of 18 and 30 for three years of obligatory service.

The total strength of the armed forces is 36,550, excluding tribal paramilitary levies of 20,000. This strength constitutes 3.9 armed persons per 1,000 civilians. The present regime has the cooperation of the major tribes and their military potential is an important consideration. The major tribes are capable of fielding 200,000 men at short notice and represent a formidable force in themselves.

ARMY:
Personnel: 35,000
Organization: 1 armored brigade; 1 mechanized and 5 infantry brigades; 1 special forces brigade; 1 parachute/commando brigade; 1 marine brigade; 1 central guard force; 3 artillery brigades; 3 AA artillery and 2 air defense battalions
Equipment: 664 tanks; 50 combat armored vehicles; 390 armored personnel carriers; 230 guns; 65 rocket launchers; howitzers; 200 mortars; 72 air defense guns; antitank guided weapons; SAMs

NAVY:
Personnel: 550
Fleet: 2 fast attack craft with guns; 6 patrol craft; 2 mine counter measures vessels; 4 amphibious craft
Naval Base: Hodeida

AIR FORCE:
Personnel: 1,000
Organization: 76 combat aircraft; 5 fighter squadrons; 11 transports; 8 trainers; 33 helicopters; 1 air defense regiment with 12 SAMs; antiaircraft missiles

The annual military budget in 1984 was $579.255 million, or 15.4% of the GNP, 32% of the national budget, $100 per capita, $16,812 per soldier and $2,759 per sq km of national territory.

Yemen has a strong military tradition reinforced during the civil war period. But relative to its two neighbors, the armed forces are weak in both manpower and firepower. Arms purchases from 1973 to 1983 totaled $2.515 billion.

Yemen has received substantial military aid from Egypt and the Soviet Union. Most of the officers were trained in Egypt, and the equipment is almost entirely Soviet.

EDUCATION

Until recently Yemen was one of the most illiterate countries of the world with some 90% of its men and almost 100% of its women illiterate. The current national literacy rate is 8.3% (15.9% for males and 0.5% for females).

The government provides free, compulsory and universal education for six years at the elementary level from age 6 to 12. School enrollment ratios are 59% at the elementary level (6 to 12) and 7% at the secondary level (13 to 18) for a combined enrollment ratio of 35%. The third level enrollment ratio is 1.2%. Girls constitute 15% of the elementary enrollment, 12% of secondary enrollment, and 11% of post-secondary enrollment.

Most primary education is provided by the kuttab, the traditional religious school. The secular school system, introduced during the imamate of Ahmad, provides a six-year primary course, a three-year intermediate course and three-year secondary course. The academic year runs from September through June. The medium of instruction is Arabic at all levels.

Until 1967 the schools were staffed mainly by Egyptian teachers, most of whom left when Egyptian troops withdrew from the country. The government invited a number of teachers from other Arab countries to take the place of the Egyptians. The teacher-pupil ratio is 1:46 in primary schools and 1:14 in secondary schools.

About 1.6% of the students in the secondary schools are enrolled in the vocational stream. There are three commercial schools, five teacher training schools and one technical school.

Control of the educational system rests with the Ministry of Education. The annual education budget in 1980 was YR682,978,000, of which 65.1% was current expenditure. This amount constituted 15.1% of the national budget and 4.8% of the GNP (as against a UNESCO recommendation of 4%). Per capita educational expenditures equalled $54.

Higher education began with the establishment of the Sana'a University in 1970. In addition there is a college of telecommunications and a college of avia-

EDUCATIONAL ENROLLMENT (1980/81)			
	Institutions	Teachers	Students
First Level	4,169	13,165	602,212
Second Level	314	2,023	28,852
Vocational	29	196	4,023
Third Level (1977)	—	58	4,220

tion. Total enrollment in higher education is 4,220, or 70 per 100,000 inhabitants. In 1980 374 students graduated from institutions of higher education. Of these 94 were awarded degrees in law, 95 in education, 17 in natural science, 120 in commerce and 25 in social and behavioral sciences. In 1982 2,445 Yemeni students were enrolled in institutions of higher learning abroad. Of these 307 were in the United States, 214 in Egypt, 1,302 in Saudi Arabia, 177 in Indian, 103 in Hungary, 93 in Czechoslovakia and 34 in the United Kingdom. In the same year, 192 foreign students were enrolled in Yemen.

Yemen's contribution to world scientific authorship was 0.0060% (U.S. = 42%), and its rank among the nations of the world in this respect, 106th.

LEGAL SYSTEM

As a strict Muslim nation, Yemen is governed primarily through the Sharia, Islamic religious law, which covers worship, family law, commercial transactions and taxes. In each district the Sharia system is headed by a hakim with appeals going to the Istinaf, the highest court in Sana'a. Under the Sharia's strict code, corporal punishment is applied for certain crimes. A man can lose his right hand if convicted of stealing.

Two other legal systems also operate along with the Sharia. Civil law is administered through civil judges appointed by the Ministry of Justice. Tribal law, or urf, governs violations of tribal customs and is applied through tribal courts.

There are several types of courts in the Yemen, including traditional Shari'a (Islamic) courts, commercial courts and special security courts. The Shari'a courts have jurisdiction in all cases that do not fall into the latter two categories, although there is overlapping jurisdiction in some commercial law cases. The Shari'a courts appear to be fair and impartial, within the context of the Islamic tradition. The judge plays an active role in questioning the witnesses, seeking to establish the guilt or innocence of the accused. Attorneys may counsel their clients, but do not address the court or examine witnesses. If the defendant is to be brought to trial, he is informed of the charges against him at the conclusion of the police investigation.

There is a possibility of appeal to political authorities outside the Shari'a system. Persons often seek to bring the influence of prominent people or government officials to bear in a case. The ability to do so varies according to the status of the defendant. In the commercial court, litigants can also expect a fair and open trial with legal counsel. The Shari'a and commercial courts remain largely independent of the executive, though all decisions are subject to review and confirmation by the president.

No criminal statistics are available for Yemen.

LAW ENFORCEMENT

In the absence of reliable statistics, the strength of the national police is estimated at 3,000. The force is recruited mostly from the Zeidi population in the highlands.

There is a relatively high crime rate, which is often attributed to the consumption of qat, a mild narcotic.

HEALTH

In 1981 there were 28 hospitals with 4,000 beds, or 1 bed per 1,900 inhabitants. In the same year there were 896 doctors (of whom 116 were foreigners), or 1 physician per 6,629 inhabitants, 26 dentists and 896 nursing personnel. Of the hospitals 89.3% are state-run and 10.7% are run by private nonprofit agencies. The admissions/discharge rate is 1,186 per 10,000 inhabitants, the bed occupancy rate is 87.3% and the average length of stay is 16 days. In 1976, health expenditures represented 3.6% of national budget and $5.70 per capita.

PRINCIPAL HEALTH INDICATORS (1984)
Crude Death Rate: 21.6 per 1,000
Decline in Death Rate: –19.6% (1965-83)
Infant Mortality: 169.16 per 1,000 Live Births
Child Death Rate (ages 1-4) per 1,000: 33
Life Expectancy at Birth: 43.00 (Males); 45.00 (Females)

Malaria, typhus, tuberculosis, dysentery, whooping cough, measles, hepatitis, schistosomiasis and typhoid fever are among Yemen's major health problems. Poor hygiene and sewage disposal practices, a generally inadequate diet and a scarcity of trained personnel all contribute to the low level of health. Only 4% of the population have access to safe water.

FOOD

The Yemeni diet is qualitatively inadequate. The staple foods are grains, mainly corn, millet, wheat and barley. Little meat or poultry is consumed. Per capita food intake is 2,272 calories and 70.5 grams of protein, 30 grams of fats and 372 grams of carbohydrates.

MEDIA & CULTURE

Two daily newspapers, *Al Gumhuryyah* and *Al Thawra*, are published in the capital, Sana'a, and one in Taiz, all in Arabic. An officially sponsored printing and publishing company, the Yemen Printing and

Publishing Company, produces six periodicals. The official news agency is the SABA News Agency, with headquarters at Sana'a. Foreign news agencies respresented in Sana'a include Tass and MENA.

Yemen has no book publishers of any size, nor does it adhere to any copyright convention.

The government station, Radio Sana'a, with three medium-wave transmitters and two short-wave transmitters, broadcasts a home service in Arabic for about 15 hours daily. Radio Hodeida and Radio Taiz broadcast in Arabic for four hours daily. There are an estimated 110,000 radio receivers in Yemen, or 18 per 1,000 inhabitants. A limited television service was introduced in 1975 with one station. There are 27,000 television sets (or 4.5 per 1,000 inhabitants) in use.

In 1981 there were 35 cinemas in the country with 28,000 seats (4.6 per 1,000 inhabitants). Annual attendance was 13 million or 2.2 per capita.

Yemen's largest library, which is not open to the public, is at the great mosque in Sana'a.

There are two museums reporting an annual attendance of 10,000.

SOCIAL WELFARE

The state operates a few orphanages, but otherwise there are no public social welfare programs. The auqaf, or religious foundations, provide some limited charity.

GLOSSARY

hakim: judge of a Sharia court.
imam: (in the Shiite sect) a divinely appointed religious leader of the family of Ali.
kuttab: Muslim religious school.
mahallah: a quarter of a town.
muhafaza: governorate
nahiya: a sector of a district.
ozlah: a group of villages.
qada: a district
qarya: a village
urf: traditional tribal law.
wadi: a river or riverbed, usually dry in the summer.

CHRONOLOGY (from 1946)

1945— Yemen joins the Arab League.
1947— Yemen joins the U.N.
1948— Imam Yahya is killed in coup; his son Saif al Islam Ahmad succeeds as imam.
1955— A coup against the imam is suppressed.... Yemen concludes aid agreement with the Soviet Union.... Imam appoints first royal cabinet.
1956— Yemen recognizes the People's Republic of China and obtains Chinese economic and technical assistance.
1958— Yemen joins Egypt and Syria in a confederation known as the United Arab States.

1959— The United States opens first mission in Sana'a.
1961— The United Arab States is dissolved.... Egypt launches propaganda campaign against the imam.
1962— Imam Ahmad dies and is succeeded by son Muhammad al-Badr as imam.... Within weeks Brigadier Abdallah al-Salal leads successful coup and seizes power; Imam Badr escapes to the highlands where he organizes a royalist army, and a civil war begins.
1963— The civil war becomes an international conflict as Egyptian troops land in Yemen to aid the republican forces and the Saudis lend arms and equipment to the royalists.
1964— A new republican government is announced under a new constitution with Hamud al-Jaifi as premier.
1965— Hassan al-Amri replaces Jaifi as premier but later yields office to Muhammad Ahmad Noman.... Noman falls out of favor with the Egyptians, and Amri becomes premier again.
1966— Amri is dismissed; Salal assumes the office of premier in addition to that of the president.
1967— President Nasser and King Faisal, meeting in Khartoum, agree to a ceasefire in Yemen and a pullout of both Egyptian and Saudi Arabian forces.... Withdrawal of Egyptian troops is followed by a coup in which Salal is overthrown and Abd al-Rahman Iryani becomes president with Mohsin al-Aini as premier.... Yemen breaks off diplomatic relations with the United States.... Hassan al-Amri replaces Aini as premier.
1968— In fierce fighting the royalist forces lay siege to Sana'a but are repelled.
1969— Abdullah Kurshoumi is named premier.
1970— New constitution is promulgated.... Muhsin al-Aini is recalled to succeed Kurshoumi as premier.
1971— Yemen holds the first elections in its history under the new constitution.
1972— Diplomatic relations are resumed with the United States.... Fighting breaks out with the People's Democratic Republic of Yemen.... A peace agreement and an agreement on eventual unification of the two countries are signed at Cairo but border incidents continue.... Aini resigns and is succeeded in office by Abdullah al-Hajari.
1974— A new government under Premier Hassan Makki takes office.... In a successful coup Ibrahim Muhammad al-Hamadi ousts Iryani and seizes power.... The Revolutionary Command Council is established as the supreme state body under an amended constitution.... Aini is recalled as premier.
1975— Abdul Aziz Abdul Ghani is named premier.
1977— President Ibrahim al-Hamadi and his brother are assassinated on the eve of their trip to Southern Yemen; new President Lt. Col. Ahmed Hussein al-Ghashmi escapes assassination attempt.

1978— President Ghashmi is killed when a bomb concealed in the briefcase of a visiting Southern Yemeni emissary explodes in his office; The People's Council elects Ali Abdullah Saleh as president.

1979— Southern Yemen forces, joined by guerrilla forces of National Democratic Front, cross into Yemen and advance 30 miles; Under a ceasefire arranged by the Arab League, Southern Yemen's troops withdraw; President Saleh and President Ismail of Southern Yemen meet in Kuwait and agree to a peaceful resolution of the conflict and eventual reunification of the two countries; Saudi Arabia, angered by this conclusion, withholds military aid; Yemen turns to the Soviet Union which begins delivery of planes and military equipment.

1982— Earthquake devastates large areas in Yemen.... The General People's Congress is convened.

1983— President Saleh is reelected for another term in office.... Abd al Aziz Abd al Ghani is reinstated as prime minister and Iriyani is placed in charge of reconstruction of earthquake-struck areas.

1984— 20-year Treaty is signed with the Soviet Union.

BIBLIOGRAPHY (from 1970)

Al-Rashid, Ibrahim, *Yemen Under the Rule of Imam Ahmad* (Chapel Hill, N.C., 1985).

Bidwell, Robin, *The Two Yemens* (Boulder, Colo., 1983).

Doe, Brian, *Southern Arabia* (London, 1972).

Ingrams, Harold, *The Yemen* (London, 1963).

O'Ballance, Edgar, *The War in Yemen* (Hamden, Conn., 1971).

Peterson, John E., *Yemen: The Search for a Modern State* (Baltimore, Md., 1982).

Pridham, Brian, *Economy, Society and Culture in Contemporary Yemen* (London, 1985).

———, *Contemporary Yemen: Politics and Historical Development* (New York, 1985).

Rahmy Ali, A., *The Egyptian Policy in the Arab World: Intervention in Yemen, 1962-67* (Lanham, Md., 1983).

Schmidt, Dana Adams, *Yemen: The Unknown War* (New York, 1968).

Smith, Rex, *The Yemens* [World Bibliographical Series] (Santa Barbara, Calif., 1984).

Stokey, R., *Yemen* (Boulder, Col., 1978).

Wenner, Manfred W., *Modern Yemen, 1919-1966* (Baltimore, Md., 1967).

———, *North Yemen* (Boulder, Colo., 1986).

World Bank, *Yemen Arab Republic: Development of a Traditional Economy* (Washington, D.C. 1979).

Zabarah, Mohammed, Yemen: *Traditionalism versus Modernity* (New York, 1982).

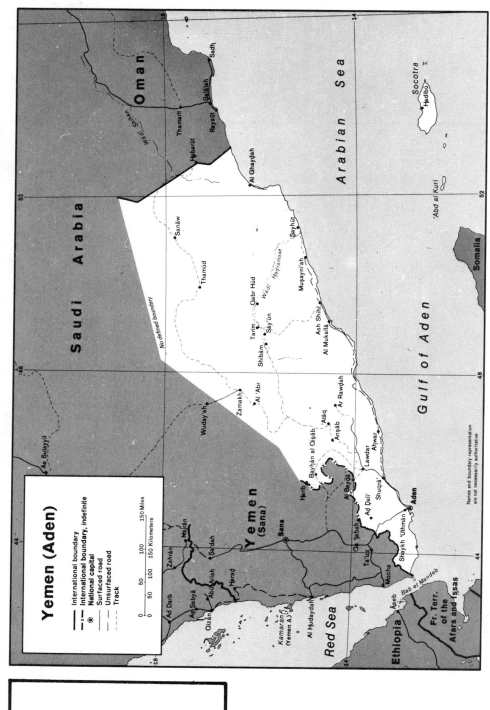

Yemen (Aden)

International boundary
International boundary, indefinite
⊛ National capital
Surfaced road
Unsurfaced road
Track

0	50	100	150 Miles
0	50	100	150 Kilometers

Saudi Arabia

Oman

Wādī Shiḥan

Sadḥ
Salālah
Ṭhamarīt
Rayṣūt
Ḥabarūt

Al Ghaydah

Arabian Sea

Socotra
Ḩadibū

'Abd al Kuri

Sanāw

Thamūd

Wādī Ḥaḑramawt

Shaḩṭ

Musayni'ah

Qabr Hūd
Tarīm
Sayūn
Shibām
Ash Shiḩr
Al Mukallā

No defined boundary

Al 'Abr

Zamakh

Ar Rawḑah

Gulf of Aden

Wuday'ah

'Ataq
Anṣāb
Bayḩān al Qiṣāb

Lawdar
Ahwar

Shuqrā'
Al Bayḑā'
Aḑ Ḑāli'

Ḩarīb

Aden

Somalia

As Sulayyil

Yemen (Sana)

⊛ **Sana**

Najrān
Zāhān
Sa'dah

Shaykh 'Uthmān

Al Qabah
Ta'izz

As Sabyā
Abū 'Arīsh
Ḩarad

Mocha

Ad Darb
Qīzān

Kamarān (Yemen A.)
Al Ḩudaydah

Bab el Mandeb

Aseb

Red Sea

Ethiopia

Fr. Terr. of the Afars and Issas

Names and boundary representation are not necessarily authoritative

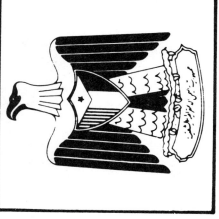

YEMEN (SOUTHERN)

BASIC FACT SHEET

OFFICIAL NAME: People's Democratic Republic of Yemen (Jumhouriyyat al-Yemen ad-Dimuqraatiyya esh-Sha'biyya) Commonly called Southern Yemen

ABBREVIATION: YS

CAPITAL: Aden; **Administrative Capital:** Madinat al-Sha'ab (al-Ittihad)

HEAD OF STATE & HEAD OF GOVERNMENT: Chairman of Presidential Council Haydar Bakr Al-Attas (from 1986)

NATURE OF GOVERNMENT: One-party dictatorship

POPULATION: 2,211,000 (1985)

AREA: 287,683 sq km (111,075 sq mi)

ETHNIC MAJORITY: Arab

LANGUAGE: Arabic

RELIGION: Sunni Islam

UNIT OF CURRENCY: South Yemen Dinar (SYD) ($1=SYD 0.3454, August 1985)

NATIONAL FLAG: A tricolor of red, white, and black horizontal stripes with a red star on a blue triangular field at the hoist

NATIONAL EMBLEM: The black and gold Saladin's eagle. On its breast appears a shield with three vertical stripes in red, white and black, with a light blue triangle above them displaying a red star. A gold scroll at the bottom carries the state's name in Arabic.

NATIONAL ANTHEM: "The Presidential Salute"

NATIONAL HOLIDAYS: October 14 (National Day Revolution Day); November 30 (Independence Day); variable Islamic festivals

NATIONAL CALENDAR: Gregorian and Islamic

PHYSICAL QUALITY OF LIFE INDEX: 38 (up from 27 in 1976) (On an ascending scale in which 100 is the maximum. U.S. 95)

DATE OF INDEPENDENCE: November 30, 1967

DATE OF CONSTITUTION: 1970

WEIGHTS & MEASURES: The imperial system is used in Aden while the rest of the country uses local weights and measures. [See Yemen Arab Republic]

LOCATION & AREA

Southern Yemen is located at the southern end of the Arabian Peninsula facing the Gulf of Aden. It has a total area of 287,683 sq km (111,075 sq mi) and extends 1,127 km (700 mi) NE to SW and 412 km (256 mi) SE to NW. It also includes the 3,626 sq km (1,400 sq mi) island of Socotra and the smaller islands of Perim and Kamaran. Its total international land frontiers of 1,699 km (1,056 mi) are mostly undemarcated. The border length with Yemen Arab Republic is 581 km (361 mi), Saudi Arabia 830 km (516 mi) and Oman 288 km (179 mi). The mainland's coastline stretches some 1,210 km (752 mi) along the Gulf of Aden and the Arabian Sea. The border with Yemen Arab Republic is the subject of dispute and has never been settled.

The capital is Aden with a metropolitan population in 1981 of 365,100. The administrative capital is Madinat Al-Sha'ab al-Ittihad, situated between Little Aden and Shaikh Othman. Aden itself is composed of a number of townships: Steamer Point, Ma'alla, Khormaksar, Crater and Little Aden. The only other towns of any size are Mukalla (65,000), Say'un, Lawdar, Lahij and Bahyan.

Topographically the country is divided into a littoral region varying between 6½ km (4 mi) and 64 km (40 mi) in width, a maritime range between 300 meters (1,000 feet) and 600 meters (2,000 feet) above sea level, and a highland plateau, ranging from 1,500 meters (5,000 feet) to 2,400 meters (8,000 feet), which falls steeply into the Rub al-Khali desert. An important feature is the Wadi Hadhramaut, a wide and imposing valley running parallel to the coast about 200 km (125 mi) inland. The broad upper and middle parts of the Hadhramaut are relatively fertile, but at its lower end it turns sharply to the south and becomes a narrow, barren gorge as it descends to the sea. The land is totally devoid of natural vegetation except for a light cover of thorn scrub.

WEATHER

Temperatures are high throughout the country except in the mountainous region of the west where winter temperatures hover near 0°C (32°F). The coastal region has a hot season lasting from April until October with temperatures between 30°C (86°F) to 40°C (104°F) followed by a cooler season between October and April when temperatures range from 20°C (68°F) to 30°C (86°F). Temperatures up to 54.4°C (130°F) have been recorded in Aden. Humidity is very high, particularly at the beginning and end of the hot season. Rainfall, limited to the monsoon months of July and September, is sparse. The average rainfall is 76 mm (3 in.) but there are marked regional variations. The Hadhramaut and the western highlands receive as much as 50 cm (20 in.) to 76 cm (30 in.) a year while the northern and eastern sections may receive rain only once in five or ten years.

POPULATION

The population of Southern Yemen was estimated in 1985 at 2,211,000 on the basis of the country's first official census, taken in 1973, which showed a population of 1,590,275. The population is expected to reach 3.3 million by 2000 and 5.2 million by 2020. The annual growth rate in population is estimated at 1.9%, based on a crudely estimated birthrate of 50 per 1,000.

The population is relatively concentrated in Aden, in the cluster of settlements along the coast and in the Hadhramaut. The average nationwide density is 6 per sq km (15 per sq mi) rising to 14 per sq km (35 per sq mi) in arable areas. At the 1973 census, the total population of 1,590,275 consisted of 787,017 males and 803,258 females, giving females a slight numerical majority and a male/female ratio of 49.49/50.51. Compared to other undeveloped countries, the median age is high. 45.2% of the population is under 14, while 52.1% is between 15 and 64 and 2.7% is over 65.

DEMOGRAPHIC INDICATORS (1985)	
Population, total (in 1,000)	2,211.0
Population ages (% of total)	
0-14	45.2
15-64	52.1
65+	2.7
Youth 15-24 (000)	438
Women ages 15-49 (000)	491
Dependency ratios	92.0
Child-woman ratios	773
Sex ratios (per 100 females)	97.9
Median ages (years)	17.2
Decline in birthrate (1960-78)	−4.0
Proportion of urban (%)	39.92
Population density (per sq. km.)	6
per hectare of arable land	5.89
Rates of growth (%)	2.68
Urban %	4.2
Rural %	1.7
Natural increase rates (per 1,000)	28.8
Crude birth rates (per 1,000)	47.6
Crude death rates (per 1,000)	18.8
Gross reproduction rates	3.35
Net reproduction rates	2.26
Total fertility rates	6.87
General fertility rates (per 1,000)	207
Life expectancy, males (years)	45.5
Life expectancy, females (years)	47.5
Life expectancy, total (years)	46.5
Population doubling time in years at current rate	24
Average household size	5.5

Despite a steep fall in the population of Aden due to emigration, the urban component of the population has remained stable at 37%. Urban growth rate during 1973-83 was 4.2%. Some 50% of the population is rural and 10% is nomadic. About 15% of the total population lives in the greater Aden region. The rest of the urban population is scattered among a number of small towns of which the largest is Mukalla, the only port in the east and the trading center for the Hadhramaut.

Before independence in 1967, Southern Yemen attracted a substantial number of immigrants, the largest flow of which came from the Yemen Arab Republic; at one time the Yemenis numbered over 80,000. The 1955 census enumerated other major migrants: Indians, Pakistanis, Baluchis, Ethiopians, Danakils and Somalis. The decline in the fortune of the Aden port because of the eight-year closure of the Suez Canal (1967-75) has resulted in the exodus of most of these migrants. Other changes in population took place when the Jews departed for Israel after the Palestine War of 1948 and the British left after independence. A reverse migratory trend is the return to their homeland of a large group of Hadhramis who had emigrated to Indonesia and Malaysia before independence. Some 85,000 Hadhramis are believed to be still living in Indonesia.

Settlement of the nomadic Bedouin has been a major government effort. The government has also sought to destroy the influence of the mercantile community in Aden. As a result of these efforts to restructure traditional society, large numbers of South Yemenis, perhaps 300,000 to 500,000 (or 15 to 25% of the population), have left the country, many for residence in neighboring North Yemen. Many thousands of others have emigrated to Saudi Arabia and the Persian Gulf states in search of employment.

Equality of the sexes is guaranteed by law, and women frequently hold government and service jobs. Polygamy, child marriages, and arranged marriages are forbidden.

Southern Yemen has no official birth control policy or programs.

ETHNIC COMPOSITION

Like most Arab nations, Southern Yemen has a relatively homogeneous population. The native population is almost entirely of Arab stock, though purists have established a distinction between Adnani, or Northern, and Qahtani, or Southern Arabs. The tribal configuration is extremely varied, and there are an estimated 1,300 to 1,400 separate tribes organized in large confederations called zei. The most important of these zei are Subaihi, Abdali, Aqrabi, Haushabi, Amiri, Alawi, Fadhli, Yafa, Aulaqi, Audhali, Dathina, Beihan, Wahidi, Shenafir, Seibani, Quaiti and Hamuni.

The inhabitants of the island of Socotra differ from mainland Arabs and are believed to be a mixture of Greek, Portuguese, African and Arab stock. The

Mahra tribes of the eastern region are believed to be of Himyarite descent.

Southern Yemen ranks 134th in the world in ethnic linguistic homogeneity with 99.9% homogeneity (on an ascending scale in which North and South Korea are ranked 135th with 100% homogeneity and Tanzania is ranked first with 7% homogeneity).

The population of Aden, unlike that of the hinterland, is diverse and contains many small ethnic communities. Though no post-independence statistics are available, there are unquestionably large numbers of Indians, Pakistanis, Somalis and Yemenis still living in the republic, but their numbers are decreasing every year. The once flourishing British community has virtually disappeared. Adenis are generally tolerant of foreigners and do not display the deep-rooted xenophobia of inland Arabs.

LANGUAGES

Since 1967 Arabic has been the official language of Southern Yemen. English is widely understood, particularly in Aden. However, Yemen's growing political isolation from the West makes its future uncertain.

The only two groups in the country who do not speak modern Arabic are the Socotrans and the Mahra tribes of the east. Both of them speak a variety of the ancient Himyarite language, spoken in pre-Islamic Arabia for many centuries.

RELIGIONS

Islam was established as the state religion in 1970 and is followed, in its Shafai form, by all native Arabs.

The only sizable non-Muslim community until recent times was the Jews, who all emigrated to Israel in 1948. There are scattered groups of Christians and Hindus among the alien communities.

COLONIAL EXPERIENCE

Aden and other parts of Southern Yemen were under British hegemony as East and West Aden Protectorates for 128 years until 1967. They were among the last outposts of the empire to be relinquished by the British. British political penetration was visible only in Aden, but in the rest of the country British influence was nominal. The British impact on the social and cultural life on the country was even more negligible. Further, power was transferred in 1967 to a government deeply hostile to Britain and the West. Few legacies of British rule remain except some elements of the legal and educational systems.

CONSTITUTION & GOVERNMENT

The basis of the Southern Yemeni government is the draft constitution of 1970 that was ratified by the general command of the National Front Political Organization. The constitution created the main organs of government: the People's Supreme Council as the legislative body and the Presidential Council and Council of Ministers as the executive organs. The Presidential Council consists of the president, the secretary general of the National Front Political Organization and the prime minister. It proposes draft laws, formulates state policies, promulgates the laws approved by the People's Supreme Council and nominates the prime minister and the Council of Ministers.

The constitution grants suffrage to all citizens over 18 years of age. However, no elections have been held and no electoral mechanisms or agencies have been set up.

The power of the head of state is absolute, though theoretically subject to the decisions of the party and the presidential council. The prime minister and the cabinet are in practice named by him and in turn are responsible to him. The Yemen Socialist Party hierarchy comprises the ruling group. Policy questions are decided by a small group of party and government officials, who have often demonstrated bitter factionalism. Officials losing power struggles have been placed under house arrest, forced into political exile or executed.

RULERS OF SOUTHERN YEMEN

1967 (November) to 1969 (June)
    Qahtan Muhammad ash-Shaabi
1969 (June) to 1978 (June)
    Salim Rubai Ali
1978 (June) to 1980 (April)
    Abd al-Fattah Ismail
1980 (April) to 1986 (March)
    Ali Nasir Muhammad al-Hasani
1986 (March) —Haydar Bakr Al- Attas

In the 10 years of its existence as a free nation, Southern Yemen has experienced most of vicissitudes that can plague a young state including tribal uprisings, armed dissidence, border clashes, two successful and several abortive coups and virtual financial bankruptcy. The state has been held together only by external support, notably from the Soviet Union and the People's Republic of China. The political dynamics are further complicated by tribal divisions and by ideological divisions within the National Front Political Organization, which led the nation to independence. These internal contradictions were best illustrated by Southern Yemen's acceptance in 1976 of aid from Saudi Arabia and the United Arab Emirates, whose conservative governments it long opposed bitterly.

In the power struggle (that followed the 1978 slaying of North Yemeni President Ahmed Hussein al-Ghashmi) between President Rubayi Ali and the pro-Soviet faction led by NLF Secretary Abdel Fattah Ismail, the latter emerged successful. Rubayi Ali's supporters were crushed and Ali himself was arrested, convicted of treason, and shot. It is believed

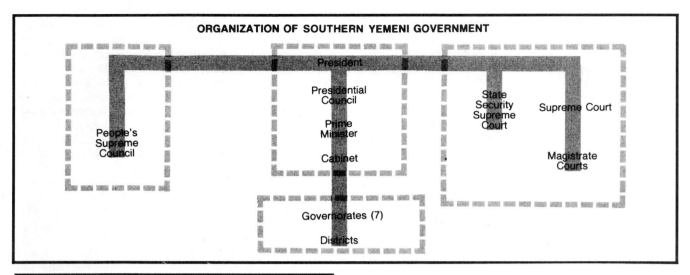

ORGANIZATION OF SOUTHERN YEMENI GOVERNMENT

President
Presidential Council
Prime Minister
Cabinet
People's Supreme Council
State Security Supreme Court
Supreme Court
Magistrate Courts
Governorates (7)
Districts

CABINET LIST (1986)

Chairman, Supreme People's
Council Presidium . . . . Haydar Abu Bakr al-'Attas

Chairman, Council of Ministers . . . Dr. Yasin Sa'id Nu'man

Deputy Prime Minister . . . . . Salih Abu Bakr bin Husaynun

Deputy Prime Minister . . . . Salih Munassir al- Sayayli

Minister of Agriculture &
Agrarian Reform . . . . Ahmad 'Ali Muqbil

Minister of Culture
& Information . . . . Muhammad Ahmad Jirghum

Minister of Defense . . . . Maj. Salih 'Ubayd Ahmad

Minister of Education . . . . Salim Ba Salim

Minister of Energy
& Minerals . . . . Salih Abu Bakr bin Husaynun

Minister of Finance . . . . Mahmud Sa'id al- Madhi

Minister of Fisheries . . . . 'Abd al-Jabir Rashid'Uthman

Minister of Foreign Affairs . . . . Dr. 'Abd al-'Aziz al- Dali

Minister of Health . . . . Sa'id Sharaf

Minister of Housing
& Building . . . . Muhammad Ahmad Salman

Minister of Industry, Trade
& Supply . . . .'Abdallah Muhammad 'Uthman

Minister of Installations . . . . . . Muhammad Ahmad Salman

Minister of Interior . . . . Salih Munassir al- Sayayli

Minister of Justice & Religious
Endowments . . . . 'Abd al-Wasi Salim

Minister of Labor & Civil Service . . Dr. Yasin Sa'id Nu'man

Minister of Planning . . . . Dr. Faraj ibn Ghanim

Minister of State Security . . . . Sa'id Salih Salim

Minister of Transport . . . . Salih 'Abdallah Muthana

Minister of State for
Union Affairs . . . . Rashid Muhammad Thabit

---

that Rubayi Ali had favored improved relations with the United States and Saudi Arabia and had also opposed Soviet use of Aden as a link in its airlift of arms and troops to Ethiopia. The new triumvirate that seized power included beside Ismail, the new head of state, Ali Nassar Mohammed Hasani and the Defense Minister Ali Antar, all of whom were vehemently pro-Soviet.

In 1986 the drama was reenacted when President al-Hasani was ousted in a bloody struggle that is believed to have taken up to 13,000 lives, and an even more pro-Soviet regime was installed under Haydar Bakr Al-Attas.

FREEDOM & HUMAN RIGHTS

In terms of civil and political rights Southern Yemen is ranked as a not-free nation with a maximum negative rating of 7 in political rights and 7 in civil rights (on a descending scale in which 7 is the lowest and 1 the highest in civil and political rights).

South Yemen is one of the Arab countries with the worst human rights records. According to one account there might be as many as 10,000 political prisoners in the country. The Yemen Socialist Party is the only legal political party and even within the party infighting is so violent that there is high turnover in leadership. Because of the unsettled conditions between 300,- and 500,000 persons are believed to have fled the country. South Yemen also serves as a staging point for Soviet troops and material en route to African countries.

CIVIL SERVICE

No current information is available on the civil service of Southern Yemen.

LOCAL GOVERNMENT

Southern Yemen is divided into seven governorates as follows:

First Governorate: Aden and the nearby villages of Dar Saad and Imran and the islands of Perim, Kamaran and Socotra.

Second Governorate: Lahij, Subbeyha, Haushabi, Alawi, Radfan, Shaib, Halmain and Muflahi.

Third Governorate: Upper and Lower Yafa, Fadhli, Audhali, Dathina and Lower Awlaqi.

Fourth Governorate: Beihan, Upper Awlaqi, Wahidi and northwestern Hadhramaut.

Fifth Governorate: Hadhramaut except Thamoud.

Sixth Governorate: Mahra
Seventh Governorate: Thamoud.

Each governorate has an appointed governor, and the districts into which the governorates are divided are also administered by appointed officials.

FOREIGN POLICY

The principal determinant of South Yemeni foreign policy is its leftwing ideology. Pursuit of this ideology has facilitated cordial relations with the Soviet Union and Eastern European countries. These relations have been reinforced by an unbroken record of Soviet military and financial assistance, which has been a major factor in Southern Yemen's economic survival.

Until recently, Southern Yemen has remained politically isolated from the Arab world because of its opposition to the conservative regimes on the Arabian peninsula. In line with that policy, it voted against the admission of the Persian Gulf Sheikhdoms to the Arab League. Serious tensions also existed with Saudi Arabia and Yemen Arab Republic resulting in armed clashes. Southern Yemen also extended military support to the radical Dhofar guerrillas in southwestern Oman.

In an effort to end this isolation, Southern Yemen launched a diplomatic offensive in 1975 which gained notable successes. Contacts were reestablished with the United Arab Emirates. Relations between the two Yemeni republics also improved to the point where a positive union between the two countries was regarded as a desirable goal. Perhaps the most important development was the growing rapprochement between Saudi Arabia and Southern Yemen, culminating in the resumption of diplomatic links in 1976. Unlike other Arab states Southern Yemen was actively involved in providing direct military assistance to Ethiopia during the 1977-78 war in the Ogaden region with Somalia. Southern Yemen's role in this conflict served to widen the rift between it and Western nations, particularly the United States.

Since a meeting between the heads of state of North and South Yemen in May 1982, a relatively stable truce has been in effect, under which the government has withdrawn military support from the National Democratic Front. Meetings between the two Yemeni leaders take place periodically and have resulted in reduced tensions between the two countries.

Relations continue to improve between South Yemen and Oman since they announced their agreement to establish diplomatic relations in October 1983. The delineation of the South Yemen-Oman border is under negotiation and has still to be resolved; however, the Dhofar region near the border area has been relatively calm in the past several years. There is currently an agreement in effect with Oman which facilitates the return to Oman of Omani insurgents who were residing in South Yemen.

In 1981 PDRY, Libya and Ethiopia signed a trilateral treaty, and in 1982 PDRY signed a political and economic cooperation treaty with Iran.

Following the dramatic events that led to the assassination of the president of Yemen Arab Republic and the execution of the president of South Yemen in 1978, South Yemen launched an attack on its neighbor with the assistance of the exiled guerrillas of the National Democratic Front. Within weeks, South Yemen was in control of three of the main North Yemeni towns along the border: Qataba, Bayda and Harib. The situation was defused by the mediation of the Arab League and the South Yemen forces withdrew. Subsequently the presidents of the two countries met in Kuwait to reaffirm their desire to seek a peaceful solution to the crisis and an eventual reunification.

Southern Yemen's relations with the West remain unfriendly. Relations with the United States, suspended in 1969 because of American support for Israel, have never been resumed, and United States interests in Aden are represented by the United Kingdom.

Southern Yemen joined the U.N. in 1967, and its share of the U.N. budget is 0.02%. It is also a member of 12 specialized U.N. agencies and of the Arab League.

PARLIAMENT

The legislature of Southern Yemen is the People's Supreme Assembly, a 111-member body whose membership is appointed by the Supreme General Command of the National Liberation Front to represent the party, professional groups and labor unions. Though the constitution specifies election of members there is no electoral apparatus. The term of the Council is three years. In theory, the council elects the president and the presidential council and also enacts laws and controls the executive. Some Communists and Baathists are also represented in the council.

POLITICAL PARTIES

The Yemen Socialist Party is the only legal party in the country. Founded in 1978, it is the successor to the United Political Organization-National Front which represented a merger of the National Liberation Front, the Baathist Popular Vanguard Party and the Communist Popular Democratic Union. Its organizational structure is modeled after the Soviet Communist Party and includes a nine-man Political Bureau and a 51-member Central Committee. Its left-wing ideology is closer to Moscow than to Peking, though the country has received economic aid from both the Soviet Union and China.

Exiled political parties, notably the South Arabian League and the Front for the Liberation of Occupied South Yemen, continue to operate illegally from the neighboring Yemen Arab Republic and Saudi Arabia.

ECONOMY

Southern Yemen is one of the 49 low-income countries. It is considered by the United Nations as one of the 29 least developed (LLDC) countries in the world and one of the 45 most seriously affected (MSA) by recent adverse economic conditions. The public sector is dominant in Southern Yemen's centrally planned socialist economy.

PRINCIPAL ECONOMIC INDICATORS

Gross National Product: $1.020 million (1983)
  GNP Annual Growth Rate: 9.0% (1973-82)
  Per Capita GNP: $510 (1983)
  Per Capita GNP Annual Growth Rate: 6.4% (1973-82)

Gross Domestic Product: $850 million (1983)
  GDP per Capita: $393 (1983)
  Percentage of Population below Poverty Level: 20

Price Index: Information not available

Money Supply: SYD 398 million (May 1985)
  Reserve Money: SYD 476 million (May 1985)

Currency in Circulation: SYD 244.31 million (1983)

International Reserves: $248.72 million of which foreign exchange reserves were $229.36 million (1984)

BALANCE OF PAYMENTS (1983)
(million $)

Current Account Balance	−308.9
Merchandise Exports	40.2
Merchandise Imports	−768.1
Trade Balance	−727.9
Other Goods, Services & Income	+141.6
Other Goods, Services & Income	−210.5
Other Goods, Services & Income Net	—
Private Unrequited Transfers	436.3
Official Unrequited Transfers	51.5
Direct Investment	—
Portfolio Investment	—
Other Long-term Capital	253.0
Other Short-term Capital	2.9
Net Errors & Omissions	59.5
Counterpart Items	−17.1
Exceptional Financing	0.1
Liabilities Constituting Foreign Authorities' Reserves	7.8
Total Change in Reserves	2.7

The Five-Year Plan 1974-79, formulated on the basis of the experiences gained from the Three-Year Plan 1971-74, called for a total investment of SYD 75,358,000.

The deteriorating finances of the Southern Yemen Republic has made foreign aid crucial to its ability to survive. The Soviet Union, the earliest donor, began its aid program in 1969. Beside aid tied to specific projects, the Soviets lent 7 million rubles in 1970 and 18 million rubles in 1976, both at low interest. The German Democratic Republic agreed to a loan of $22 million in 1969, and China granted a loan of $18 million in 1970, both part of large aid-and-trade package deals. The Chinese aid was directed to roadbuilding and the GDR aid to light industries and communications. The richer Arab countries, including Libya, Iraq, Algeria,

---

THREE-YEAR PLAN (1971-74)

Agriculture	36.8%
Transport & Communications	25.4%
Industry	17.9%
Education	8.0%
Health	4.5%
Housing	4.7%
Geological Research	1.2%
Information & Social Welfare	1.5%

The Five Year Plan 1980 called for expenditures of D425 million.

No information has been available on the sectoral origin of GDP since 1970.

Kuwait and the United Arab Emirates, have more recently joined the ranks of donor countries. At the same time, Southern Yemen is one of the few developing countries that has not received aid from the United States.

Total foreign aid during 1979-81 was $51 million or $25.90 per capita.

BUDGET

The Southern Yemeni fiscal year runs from April 1 through March 31.

The 1980-81 budget provided for revenues of D86.020 million and expenditures of D96.020 million.

The total external debt in 1982 was $817 million.

FINANCE

The unit of currency of Southern Yemen is the Southern Yemen dinar (SYD) divided into 1,000 fils. Coins are issued in denominations of 1, 2½, 5, 25 and 50 fils; notes are issued in denominations of 250 and 500 fils and 1, 5 and 10 dinars.

The dinar was at par with the pound sterling until the latter was allowed to float in 1972. The exchange rate in 1984 was /$1=SYD 0.3454. The sterling exchange rate was £1=D0.400. The dinar is not freely convertible.

The central bank is the Bank of Yemen, which replaced the Yemeni Currency Authority in 1972. All commercial banks were nationalized in 1969 to form the National Bank of Yemen, Southern Yemen's only bank. The National Bank had reserves of SYD 123.98 million in 1983, demand deposits of SYD 87.28 million and time and savings deposits of SYD 115.59 million.

AGRICULTURE

Of the total land area of 28,768,000 hectares (71,085,728 acres), 6,300,000 hectares (15,567,300 acres) are cultivable land, but only 1,260,000 hectares (3,113,460 acres) are cultivated. Agricultural land per capita is 5.38 hectares (13.3 acres). Based on 1974-76=100, the index of agricultural production in 1982 was 98, the index of food production was 98, and the per capita index of food production was 84. Agriculture employs about 45% of the economically active population; its contribution to the GDP was 29%.

The most intensively cultivated areas are Abyan, where the Abyan Dam was completed in 1977, and Lahij. The river valleys of the Hadhramaut are also fertile and well developed. Over 80% of the cultivated area is under irrigation. Farming methods are traditional and primitive except in state-run farms. The number of tractors in the country in 1982 was 1,265. Fertilizer consumption was 1,800 tons or 10.9 kg (24 lb) per arable hectare.

Sorghum, sesame, millet and dates are the principal crops grown along the coast. Wheat and barley are raised in the highlands, and coffee and tobacco in the Hadhramaut. The country is self-sufficient in vegetables and fruits, but imported 205,000 tons of cereals in 1983. Bananas in particular are produced in quantity and exported to China. The most important cash crop is long-staple cotton, grown in the Abyan Delta.

By the Agrarian Reform Law of 1970 ownership of agricultural land is limited to a maximum of 20 hectares (50 acres) per person. Lands confiscated under this law were distributed to landless peasants. Some of this land was formed into cooperative farms, some into state farms.

Agriculture and fisheries received the largest proportion of capital expenditure under the Five-Year Plans, and 80% of this investment was earmarked for irrigation projects. The plan envisaged a 54% increase in agricultural production and a 30% increase in cultivated area.

PRINCIPAL CROP PRODUCTION (1983)

	Area (000 hectares)	Production (000 tons)
Millet	40	80
Wheat	15	15
Barley	2	2
Sesame seed	4	4
Cotton Lint	12	10
Cotton seed	12	5

Livestock breeding is limited by poor and inadequate grazing land. In 1983 the livestock population consisted of 120,000 cattle, 1 million sheep, 1.35 million goats, 170,000 asses and 100,000 camels. Most hides and skins are exported.

Southern Yemen has no forests.

The Arabian Sea fishing grounds are among the richest in the world. However, until recently Southern Yemen's 10,000 fishermen were unable to exploit this wealth because of poor equipment and marketing. The fishing industry, centered on Mukalla, primarily served internal markets.

Under the Five-Year Plan, fishing has been allocated SYD 9,447,000, and plan projects include expansion of the fishing fleet with aid from Abu Dhabi, the Soviet Union and Cuba; the development of Nakhtun fishing port with Danish aid; and the construction of a fish-meal plant and canning factory at Muakalla with Kuwaiti aid. In 1975 a $30-million joint deep-sea fishing enterprise with Iraq was announced. The total fish catch was 69,700 metric tons in 1982.

There is no specialized agricultural credit institution in Southern Yemen.

INDUSTRY

Industry contributes 27% to the GDP, but 80% of the output comes from the petroleum refinery at Little Aden, which was nationalized in 1977, and is the only major industrial concern in the country, accounting for 80% of the total industrial output. Existing light industry, concentrated in Aden, consists of small factories producing cement, tiles, and bricks, cloth goods, soft drinks and other consumer goods for local demand. There are 525 establishments employing over five workers. Of the total industrial output, the public sector accounts for 43%, the mixed sector 3%, the private sector 36% and the cooperative sector 18%. The industrial sector was allocated SYD 13,456,800 under the Five-Year Plan, out of which public sector enterprises received 95.8%. Most of the new enterprises are agro-industries based on conversion of locally available raw materials including cotton, hides and tobacco.

The government is committed to complete nationalization of all industry. In 1971 the government adopted the tactic of fomenting "spontaneous workers' uprisings" as a form of revolution from below by which all businesses were taken over by workers' committees.

ENERGY

Southern Yemen does not produce any form of energy other than electric power. The total consumption of energy in 1982 was equivalent to 1.588 million metric tons of coal or 811 kg (1,788 lbs) per capita. The total production of electric power in 1984 was 427 million kwh, and the per capita production 200 kwh per year.

The petroleum refinery at Little Aden can process 8.9 million tons of crude oil a year but is operating at less than half capacity. The refinery produces at present bunker oil, gasoline, kerosene and industrial gases.

In 1975 the government invited foreign oil companies to bid for exploration and exploitation concessions. Siebens Oil and Gas of Canada and Technoexport of the Soviet Union are now involved in oil exploration. A Ministry of Energy and Minerals was set up in 1985.

LABOR

The total economically active population in 1982 census was 500,000. Men constituted 97% and women 3%. About 45% were engaged in agriculture, about 15% in industry and 40% in services. Some 9% were unemployed.

Since independence the only government-approved labor union has been the General Confederation of Workers of the People's Democratic Republic of Yemen. Though its influence is limited, it supervises social insurance and concludes wage agreements.

FOREIGN COMMERCE

The foreign commerce of Southern Yemen consisted in 1984 of exports of $378.67 million (excluding petroleum) and imports of $906.79 million, giving an unfavorable trade balance of $538.12 million. Of the imports, machinery and transport equipment constituted 34.8%, food and live animals 23.4%, petroleum products 18.2% and chemicals 2.9%. Of the exports, petroleum products constituted 95%. The major import sources are: Kuwait 11%, Qatar 11%, the United Arab Emirates 8%, Japan 6%, the Soviet Union 6% and Saudi Arabia 6%. The major export destinations are: the United Arab Emirates 22%, Italy 11% and India 5%.

FOREIGN TRADE INDICATORS (1984)	
Annual Growth Rate, Imports:	—
Annual Growth Rate, Exports:	—
Ratio of Exports to Imports:	29:71
Exports per capita:	$172
Imports per capita:	$412
Balance of Trade:	−$538.12 million
Ratio of International Reserves to Imports (in months)	3.6
Exports as % of GDP:	—
Imports as % of GDP:	—
Value of Manufactured Exports:	—
Commodity Concentration:	2.2%

TRANSPORTATION & COMMUNICATIONS

Southern Yemen has no railroads, the old line from Aden to Lahij having been dismantled.

Aden is one of the great ports of the world and was expanded to its present capacity by a $9.8 million project completed before independence. The inner harbor has 20 first-class berths and seven second-class berths. The 600-foot cargo wharf can accommodate vessels of 300 feet length and 18 feet draught, while the oil harbor can handle four tankers of 42,000 tons. The closure of the Suez Canal 1967-75 dealt the harbor a blow from which it may never recover, although traffic has doubled since the canal reopened. Traffic through the port averaged 150 ships a month in 1975 compared with an average of 500 before the Suez closure. In 1982 the port handled 8,409,000 tons of cargo. Other minor ports along the Gulf of Aden include Mukalla and Khalif.

Aden has 5,600 km (3,478 mi) of roads, of which about 1,700 km (1,056 mi) are paved. The hinterland has 10,260 km (6,382 mi) of tracks, of which 1,150 km (716 mi) are hard surfaced. The Five-Year Plan increased the asphalted road network by 776 km (480 mi). A new state transport monopoly, the Yemen Land Transport Company, operates bus transport in Aden and between Aden and other towns. In 1980 the number of registered motor vehicles was 11,900 cars and 10,500 commercial vehicles. Per capita vehicle ownership is 5.3 per 1,000.

The national airline is the Alyemda Airways, which provides domestic and international services. The major international airport is at Khormaksar, 11 km (7 mi) from the port of Aden. In addition there are 44 airfields of which 29 are usable, eight with runways over 2,500 meters and one with a permanent-surface runway.

In 1984 the country had 10,000 telephones, or 0.6 per 100 inhabitants.

In 1981 the postal service handled 15,058,000 pieces of mail or 6.8 pieces per capita. There are 149 telex subscriber lines.

In 1982, income from tourism was estimated at $4 million. Expenditures by nationals abroad totaled $10 million.

MINING

A large-scale mineral exploration program was launched in 1975. Minerals known to exist in commercial quantities include copper, silver, gold, titanium and zircon. However, no production figures are available.

DEFENSE

The defense structure is headed by the president who is also the supreme commander of the armed forces. The line of command runs through the defense minister who is also the prime minister and the head of the armed forces to the chief of the general staff. Military manpower is provided by conscription of able-bodied males for a two-year obligatory service.

The total strength of the armed forces is 27,500, or 11.9 armed persons per 1,000 civilians.

ARMY:
Personnel: 24,000
Organization: 1 armored brigade; 1 mechanized brigade; 10 infantry brigades; 1 artillery brigade; 10 artillery battalions; 1 SSM brigade; 2 SAM batteries
Equipment: 450 tanks; 100 mechanized infantry combat vehicles; 300 armored personnel carriers; 350 guns; howitzers; rocket launchers; 18 SSM; mortars; 200 air defense guns; 9 SAMs

NAVY:
Personnel: 1,000
Fleet: 8 fast attack craft with guns; 4 patrol craft; 5 landing craft
Naval Bases: Aden and Mukalla

AIR FORCE:

Personnel: 2,500

Organization: 103 combat aircraft; 15 armored helicopters; 4 fighter ground attack squadrons; 3 interceptor squadrons; 1 transport squadron; 1 helicopter squadron; 1 SAM regiment; 3 trainers; AAM; ASM

Air Bases: Khormaksar (Aden), Ad Dali, Mukayris, Lawdar, Bayshan al Qisab, Ansab, Ataq, Mukalla, Zamaka and Ir Fadhi

In 1982 the defense budget was $159.409 million, which was 21.0% of the national budget, 17.4% of the GNP, $82 per capita, $6,000 per soldier and $468 per sq km of national territory.

The South Yemeni armed forces are almost entirely equipped by the Soviet Union under an arms agreement concluded in 1968. Cuban and Soviet military technicians and instructor-advisers are present in the country. Arms purchases abroad during 1973-83 totaled $1.940 billion, of which $1.5 billion was supplied by the Soviet Union. There is a Soviet naval base in the island of Socotra and an air base in Aden. There are reports that Socotra is only an anchorage, and its usefulness to the Soviet navy is limited.

In relation to its size and population, Southern Yemen has an effective armed force trained by Soviet advisers and supported by Soviet equipment. Its combatworthiness has been tried in the field in recent years in border clashes with Yemen Arab Republic and Saudi Arabia.

EDUCATION

The national adult literacy rate is 38.9% (66.6% for males and 10.9% for females). Of the population over 10, 72.9% have had no schooling, 21.1% have completed first level, 5.1% have completed second level or the post secondary level.

Education is free and compulsory for seven years up to the age of 14. Schooling consists of eight years of primary school, and four years of secondary school for a total of 12 years.

In 1982 the school enrollment ratio was 64% in the primary school age group (7-14) and 18% in the secondary school age group (15-18), for a combined enrollment ratio of 51%. The third-level enrollment ratio is 2.3%. The percentage of female enrollment is 26% at the primary level, 31% at the secondary level and 52% at the tertiary level.

The academic year runs from September to June. The medium of instruction is Arabic, but English is taught as a second language from the middle grades in Aden.

In much of the interior the prevalent form of education remains the kuttab, or the traditional Muslim school for boys where little is taught beside the Koran. There are five private primary schools and four private intermediate schools.

Adult education is provided by evening classes. The number of teachers is 10,832 at the primary level, 2,016 at the secondary level and 403 at the tertiary level. The teacher-pupil ratio is 1:21 at the primary level, 1:16 at the secondary level and 1:9 at the post-secondary level. Only 10% of students at the secondary level are enrolled in the vocational stream.

Education at all levels is controlled and directed by the Ministry of Education. In 1982 the public education budget was SYD 24,136,000, of which 80% was current expenditure. This expenditure was 7.2% of GNP (as against a UNESCO recommendation of 4%) and 16.9% of the national budget for that year. Per capita expenditure on education was $34.

EDUCATIONAL ENROLLMENT (1982)			
	Schools	Teachers	Students
First Level	861	10,832	270,167
Second Level	46	2,016	31,705
Vocational	13	173	1,556
Third Level	N.A.	403	3,645

Higher education is provided by the University of Aden, established in 1975. University enrollment is 165 per 100,000 inhabitants. In 1982, 1,650 Southern Yemeni students were enrolled in institutions of higher learning abroad. Of these six were in the United States, 15 in the United Kingdom, 731 in Egypt, 67 in Kuwait, 723 in Saudi Arabia and 8 in West Germany.

Southern Yemen's contribution to world scientific authorship is 0.0330% (U.S.=42%). It ranks 106th in the world in this respect.

LEGAL SYSTEM

Southern Yemen inherited a modern system of legal administration from the British. Aden has secular codes for ciminal and civil cases, while the rest of the country has a mix of Sharia, tribal and civil jurisprudence. The court system consists of a number of magistrates' courts and a Supreme Court in Aden. A Security division of the Supreme Court was established in 1969 to try political prisoners and enemies of state.

No criminal statistics are published. The nature of the penal system is not known.

LAW ENFORCEMENT

The composition, structure and divisions of the law enforcement agency in Southern Yemen have not been revealed. Similarly, the extent and type of crime cannot be determined in the absence of statistics.

HEALTH

In 1981 there were 48 hospitals in the country with 2,900 beds, or 1 bed per 641 inhabitants. The number of doctors in the country in the same year was 264, or 1 per 7,390 persons, 9 dentists and 150 nursing personnel.

A reasonably good health care program exists only in Aden. In the hinterland malaria, tuberculosis, dys-

```
PRINCIPAL HEALTH INDICATORS (1984)
Crude Death Rate: 18.8 per 1,000
Decline in Death Rate: –29.3% (1965-83)
Infant Mortaliy Rate: 153.3 per 1,000 Live Births
Child Death Rate (Ages 1-4) per 1,000: 27
Life Expectancy at Birth: 45.5 (Males); 47.5 (Females)
```

entery and trachoma are fairly widespread. Only 24% of the population have access to safe water. Health expenditures represent 5.1% of the national budget and $2.10 per capita.

FOOD

The per capita daily intake of food is 2,103 calories, 53.2 grams of protein, 42 grams of fats and 365 grams of carbohydrates.

MEDIA & CULTURE

Two daily newspapers are published in the capital, Aden, with a total circulation of 25,000, or 11.3 per 1,000 inhabitants. All are published in Arabic. Two of these newspapers are sponsored by the government Ministry of Information. Nine non-daily newspapers are published, including one in English. All except one are based in Aden. All news media are subject to strict censorship by the Ministry of Information. The national news agency is the Aden News Agency with headquarters in Aden. Annual consumption of newsprint in 1982 was 800 tons or 420 kg (926 lb) per 1,000 inhabitants.

Southern Yemen has no active book publishing industry. The 14th October Corporation has the sole right to import and distribute books. Southern Yemen does not adhere to any copyright convention.

Radio and television broadcasting is operated by Democratic Yemen Broadcasting Service. Radio Aden broadcasts 100 hours a week in Arabic on one medium-wave and one short-wave transmitter. In 1982 there were 115,000 radio receivers in the country, or 55 per 1,000 inhabitants. Television was introduced in 1964. DYBS broadcasts 4 ½ hours daily in the evenings with stations at Al-Airahr, Al-Bargh and Ga'ar. In 1982 there were 37,000 television receivers in the country, or 18 per 1,000.

In 1980 Southern Yemen had 21 cinemas with 20,900 seats, or 11.6 per 1,000 inhabitants. Annual attendance was 5.6 million, or 3.1 per inhabitant.

The largest library is the Miswat Library, the former Lake Library with some 35,000 volumes. A central national library is planned. Per capita, there are 22 volumes and 1 registered borrower per 1,000 inhabitants.

There are three museums with a reported annual attendance of 7,000.

SOCIAL WELFARE

The state role in public welfare assistance has not been clearly defined. Social security programs have not been established. The mosque remains the principal channel of assistance for the sick, widows, orphans and the handicapped.

GLOSSARY

Adnani: northern Arab.
Hadhrami; native of Hadhramaut region of Southern Yemen.
kuttab: traditional Muslim school, often adjacent to a mosque.
Qahtani: southern Arab.
zei: tribal confederation.

CHRONOLOGY (from 1967)

1967— Southern Yemen gains independence from Britain with Qahtan al-Shaab, leader of the National Liberation Front, as president of the republic.

1968— Following the Zingibar conference, conflict between the moderate and radical elements within the National Liberation Front intensifies. . . . Short-lived revolts and uprisings occur in the First, Third, Fifth and Sixth governorates.

1969— Qahtan al-Shaab is ousted in a power struggle and replaced by Salim Rubayi Ali, leader of the pro-Moscow extremist faction.

1970— New constitution is promulgated; name of the republic is changed to People's Democratic Republic of Yemen. . . . 36 foreign firms are nationalized.

1971— Muhammed Ali Haithem reigns as prime minister and is replaced by Ali Nasir Muhammad Hasani.

1972— Border clashes with Yemen Arab Republic lead to intervention by the Arab League, which mediates a ceasefire. . . . The two Yemens agree in principle on the concept of a united Greater Yemen.

1973— Southern Yemen conducts its first official census. . . . A seventh governorate is established at Thamoud.

1975— The National Liberation Front, the Popular Vanguard Party and the Democratic People's Union merge to form the National Front Political Organization.

1976— Southern Yemen, in dramatic reversal of policy, resumes diplomatic relations with Saudi Arabia and agrees to accept Saudi aid.

1977— Southern Yemen supports Ethiopia in the latter's war with Somalia over Ogaden; Soviet arms are airlifted to Ethiopia via Aden.

1978— President Rubayi Ali is accused of complicity in the assassination of North Yemeni President Ahmed Hussein al-Ghashmi and is deposed, arrested, and shot by a firing squad; pro-Soviet triumvirate consisting of NLF Secretary Abdel Fatteh

Ismail, Defense Minister Ali Antar, and Ali Nassar Mohammed Hasani seizes power; Hasani is named head of state; Ismail announces formation of a new Communist party called the Vanguard Party.

1979— South Yemeni forces cross into North Yemen and seize three important towns; South Yemen withdraws forces from captured territory under truce arranged by Arab League; President Ismail meets with President Abdullah Saleh of North Yemen in Kuwait and agrees to peaceful negotiations leading to eventual reunification of the two Yemens.

1980— President Ismail steps down and Prime Minister Ali Nasir Muhammad assumes the presidency.... Guerrilla forces supported by South Yemen step up activity in North Yemen.

1981— PDRY, Libya and Ethiopia conclude Treaty of Friendship and Cooperation.

1982— PDRY and Yemen Arab Republic agree to terms of truce between the two countries.

1983— Diplomatic relations with Oman are reestablished.

1986— President al-Hasani is ousted in a bloody power struggle and Moscow-backed Haydar Bakr Al-Attas is installed as president.

BIBLIOGRAPHY (from 1970)

Bernard, Bernard, *Aden and the Yemen* (London, 1960)

Bidwell, Robin, *The Two Yemens* (Boulder, Colo., 1983).

Brinton, J. Y., *Aden and the Federation of South Arabia* (Washington, D.C., 1964).

Gavin, R. J., *Aden 1839-1967* (London, 1973).

Little, Tom, *South Arabia* (New York, 1968).

O'Ballance, Edgar, *The War in Yemen* (Hamden, Conn., 1971).

Smith, Rex, *The Yemens* [World Bibliographic Series] (Santa Barbara, Calif., 1984).

Stookey, Robert W., *South Yemen: A Marxist Regime* (Boulder, Colo., 1982).

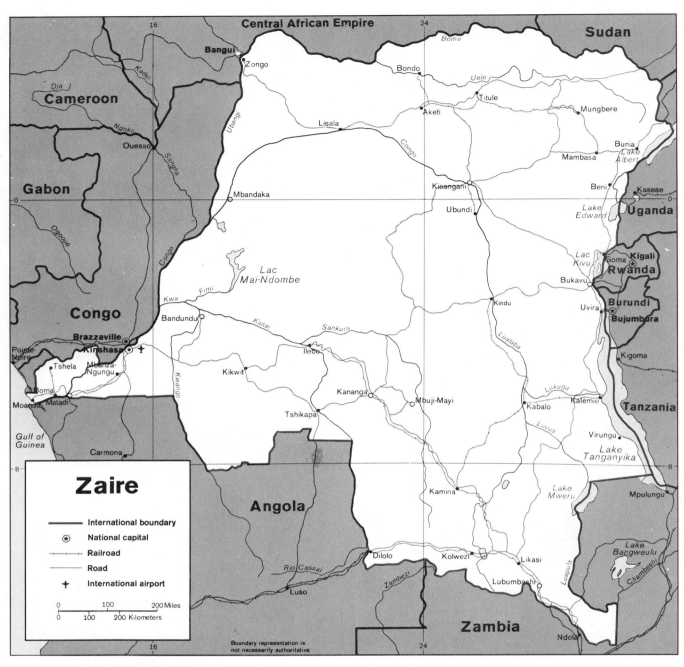

Zaire

- —— International boundary
- ⊛ National capital
- +++ Railroad
- —— Road
- + International airport

0 ——— 100 ——— 200 Miles
0 ——— 100 ——— 200 Kilometers

Boundary representation is
not necessarily authoritative

Central African Empire

Sudan

Cameroon

Gabon

Congo

Brazzaville
Kinshasa

Pointe-Noire
Boma
Moanda Matadi
Tshela
Mbanza-Ngungu

Gulf of Guinea

Carmona

Angola

Zambia

Ndola

Bangui
Zongo
Bondo
Titule
Mungbere
Aketi
Mambasa
Bunia
Lake Albert
Beni
Kasese
Uganda

Lisala
Congo
Kisangani
Ubundi
Lake Edward

Mbandaka

Lac Mai-Ndombe

Goma Kigali
Lac Kivu Rwanda
Bukavu
Uvira Burundi
Bujumbura

Kindu

Kigoma

Bandundu
Kwa Fimi
Kasai
Sankuru
Lualaba
Lukuga

Kikwit
Ilebo
Kananga
Mbuji-Mayi
Kabalo
Kalemie
Tanzania

Tshikapa

Luvua
Virungu
Lake Tanganyika

Kamina
Lake Mweru
Mpulungu

Dilolo
Kolwezi
Likasi
Lake Bangweulu
Chambeshi

Rio Cassai
Luso
Zambezi
Lubumbashi
Luapula

Kwango
Kwilu

Dja
Ngoko
Kadei
Ubangi
Sangha
Ogooue
Bomu
Uele

JUSTICE PAIX TRAVAIL

ZAIRE

BASIC FACT SHEET

OFFICIAL NAME: Republic of Zaire (Republique du Zaire); Former Name: Congo

ABBREVIATION: ZR

CAPITAL: Kinshasa

HEAD OF STATE & HEAD OF GOVERNMENT: President Lt. Gen. Mobutu Sese Seko Kuku Ngbendu Wa Za Banga (from 1965)

NATURE OF GOVERNMENT: One-party dictatorship

POPULATION: 32,985,000 (1985)

AREA: 2,344,932 sq km (905,381 sq. miles)

ETHNIC MAJORITY: Bantu tribes

LANGUAGES: French (official), Lingala, Kingwana, Kikongo, Tshiluba, Swahili

RELIGIONS: Roman Catholicism and Animism

UNIT OF CURRENCY: Zaire ($1=Z50.650, June 1985)

NATIONAL FLAG: Green with gold ball in center displaying an arm bearing a torch of brown and red

NATIONAL EMBLEM: A leopard head in the center framed by a crossed arrow and a spear, and a palm branch to the left, an elephant tusk to the right and a scroll underneath them with the national motto in French "Peace, Justice, Work"

NATIONAL ANTHEM: "Song of Independence"

NATIONAL CALENDAR: Gregorian

NATIONAL HOLIDAYS: National Day (Anniversary of the regime; November 24); January 1; January 4 (Martyrs of Independence Day); Easter Monday; May 1 (Labor Day); Ascension Day; Whit Monday; May 20 (Mouvement Populaire de la Revolution Day); June 24 (Zaire Day); June 30 (Independence Day); August 1 (Parents' Day); Assumption Day; All Saints' Day; October 27 (Three Z Day); December 25.

PHYSICAL QUALITY OF LIFE INDEX: 51 (up from 28 in 1976) (On an ascending scale with 100 as the maximum: U.S. 95)

DATE OF INDEPENDENCE: June 30, 1960

DATE OF CONSTITUTION: June 24, 1967

WEIGHTS & MEASURES: The metric system, introduced in 1910, prevails.

LOCATION & AREA

Zaire is a rectangle-shaped inland nation located in the south-central part of the African continent, with a narrow strip of land on the north bank of the Zaire estuary as the only outlet to the Atlantic. It includes the greater part of the Zaire River basin and lies on the equator with one-third of the country to the north and two-thirds to the south. It is the third largest nation in Africa with a land area of 2,344,932 sq km (905,381 sq mi). The length of the coastline is 40 km (25 mi). The greatest distance both north-south and east-west is about 2,250 km (1,400 mi). Zaire shares its total international border of 10,120 km (6,284 mi) with nine neighbors as follows: Central African Republic (1,577 km, 980 mi); Sudan (628 km, 390 mi); Uganda (764 km, 475 mi); Rwanda (217 km, 135 mi); Burundi (233 km, 145 mi); Tanzania (459 km, 285 mi); Zambia (2,017 km, 1,309 mi); Angola (2,285 km, 1,420 mi); Cabinda (225 km, 140 mi); Congo (1,625 km, 1,010 mi). There are no current border disputes but Zaire has intermittently claimed the Angolan exclave of Cabinda.

The capital is Kinshasa (formerly Leopoldville) with a 1976 population of 2,443,876. The other major urban centers (former names within parentheses are: Kisangani (Stanleyville), 339,210; Lubumbashi (Elisabethville), 451,332; Kananga (Luluabourg), 704,211; Likasi (Jadotville), 146,394; Mbandaka (Coquilhatville), 149,118; Mbuji Mayi, 382,632; Kikwit, 172,450; Matadi, 162,396; Bukavu, 209,051.

Zaire is divided into four physical regions. The vast low-lying central area is a basin-shaped plateau sloping toward the west with an average elevation of 400 meters (1,300 ft). This area is surrounded by mountainous terraces in the west, plateaus merging into savannas in the south and southeast, and dense grasslands in the northwest, with an elevation in the south between 1,000 and 2,000 meters (3,300 and 6,500 ft) and in the north between 600 and 800 meters (2,000 and 2,600 ft). High mountains enclose the country in the north including the Ngoma, the Virunga, the Ruwenzori, the Blue Mountains, the Kundelunga, and the Marungu with the altitude rising to 5,000 meters (16,400 ft). The coastline of Zaire is bordered by a small plain 100 km (62 m) wide.

The country is almost entirely drained by the 4,505-km (2800-mi) long Zaire River and its many tributaries. The lower Zaire is not navigable but the Upper and Middle Zaire is navigable for 2,575 km (1600 mi). The Zaire is the world's second largest river, next to the Amazon, in terms of volume of water 339,600 cubic meters per sec (12 million cubic feet per sec) and area drained 3,263,250 sq km (1,425,000 sq mi).

WEATHER

The seasons are reversed north and south of the equator. Both regions have two short wet and two short dry seasons. North of the equator the rainy season lasts from early April to late October and the dry season from early November to March. The hours of daylight remain practically unchanged throughout the year. On the southern plateau—farthest from the equator—there is one long rainy season and one dry season with a characteristic tropical climate influenced by the trade winds. Eastern Zaire and Upper Shaba have a mountainous climate with lower temperatures sometimes falling to 0°C (32°F) at night. The average rainfall for the entire country is about 107 cm (42 in.), and it falls more or less regularly every year. The central region receives over 152 cm to 203 cm (60 to 80 in.) a year and the rainy season extends to 130 days a year. Storms are violent but seldom last for more than a few hours. At the equator temperature varies from 15.6°C to 37.8°C (60°F to 100°F) with the mean maximum around 32.2°C (90°F). The hottest month is February. Humidity is always high ranging upward from 65%. Temperatures drop on the edges of the Zaire Basin to around 25°C (77°F) with cooler nights.

POPULATION

The population of Zaire was estimated at 32,985,000 in 1985 on the basis of the last official census held in 1976 when the population was 25,697,575. The population is expected to reach 52.4 million by 2000 and 93.3 million by 2020.

The annual rate of population growth is 2.9% nationwide and 5.2% in urban areas. The crude birth rate is estimated at 45.2% per 1,000 but there are striking regional differences in fertility between regions and between urban areas and rural areas attributable perhaps to variations in marriage and sex customs and to the quality of health care.

There is no part of the country where settlement is impossible, but more than half the country is thinly populated and about 10% is almost totally uninhabited. Half the country has fewer than 1.1 per sq km (3 per sq mi), while two-thirds of the people live on one-fourth of the land area. The densest settlements are found in Kinshasa Province with an average density of 649 per sq km (1,681 per sq mi) and Lower Zaire with an average density of 23.7 per sq km (61 per sq mi). The average density is 6 per sq km (15 per sq mi) in Equator and Shaba Provinces. The average density nationwide is 14 per sq km (36 per sq mi), and the average density per sq km in agricultural areas is 186 (481 per sq mi).

DEMOGRAPHIC INDICATORS (1985)	
Population, total (in 1,000)	32,985.0
Population ages (% of total)	
0-14	45.1
15-64	52.0
65+	2.9
Youth 15-24 (000)	6,184
Women ages 15-49 (000)	7,489
Dependency ratios (per 1,000)	92.5
Child-woman ratios (per 1)	794
Sex ratios (per 100 females)	97.2
Median ages (years)	17.4
Decline in birthrate (1965-83)	−4.0
Proportion of urban (%)	44.17
Population density (per sq. km.)	14
per hectare of arable land	3.61
Rates of growth (%)	2.94
Urban %	5.2
Rural %	1.3
Natural increase rates (per 1,000)	29.4
Crude birth rates (per 1,000)	45.2
Crude death rates (per 1,000)	15.8
Gross reproduction rates	3.00
Net reproduction rates	2.22
Total fertility rates	6.09
General fertility rates (per 1,000)	198
Life expectancy, males (years)	48.3
Life expectancy, females (years)	51.7
Life expectancy, total (years)	50.0
Population doubling in years at current rate	24
Average household size	5.6
Marriage rate 1/1000	7.5
Divorce rate 1/1000	0.03

Towns and urban centers are relatively recent developments but since the 1940s the population movement has been from rural to urban areas. This shift was intensified by the civil strife following independence and reached an annual growth rate of 7.2%. Most of this increase in urban population growth was in the form of squatters' villages on the outskirts of larger cities. In 1984 there were two cities with over 500,000 inhabitants. The urban component of the population is 44%. Nearly 60% of the population of Kinshasa live in slums and squatter settlements.

There is an estimated female surplus in the countryside with about 109 women to 100 men. The ratio is distorted by outmigration to cities, where there is a higher proportion of men to women.

Uncontrolled and continuing migration in and out of Zaire has a significant impact on population patterns. During the period beginning in the mid-1950s large numbers of refugees entered from neighboring countries as a result of political and social disruptions. By the 1960s Zaire had the largest number of refugees of any African country. These included Christians from southern Sudan, the Kongo from Angola, and the Tutsi from Rwanda. There was also some offsetting out-migration, but Zaire may have gained nearly half a million people through migration in the 1960s.

In May 1985, Zaire was providing a safehaven to approximately 330,000 displaced persons from neighboring countries. Generally such people pass freely into Zaire and are allowed to settle on the land or seek employment. They tend to become self-sufficient and are often integrated into the Zairian economic system within a few years of arrival. The government considers them to be resettled until such time as they decide to return to their country of origin. Although the Zairian government generally accepts displaced persons, it does not have the resources to provide assistance beyond free land, and international agencies play an active role in providing humanitarian assistance. At times, displaced persons from neighboring countries (particularly Angola) have been detained or harassed by security forces on suspicion of illegal political activity.

The role of women in Zairian society is given great emphasis in party doctrine. Women's rights to own property and participate in the political and economic sectors are protected by law, and a growing number of women work in the professions, government service and the universities. Nevertheless, custom, tradition, and existing law continue to constrain women from attaining a position of complete equality in society. Women generally earn less than their male counterparts in the same jobs. In addition, married women must obtain their husband's authorization before opening a bank account, accepting a job or renting or selling real estate.

In 1972 President Mobutu expressed interest in limiting births to "desirable" ones. In 1974 official policy became formally in favor of family planning for reasons of health and as a human right, although not as primary objective of national development. A governmental agency, Fonds Medical de Coordination, has initiated family planning clinics in Kinshasa and other cities but the response to these programs is not known.

ETHNIC COMPOSITION

More than 99% of the Zaireans are of African descent divided into over 200 tribes. In physical features these tribes are almost exclusively Negroid. No single ethnic group can claim a majority on the national level but each has its own territory where it is predominant.

Based on cultural and historical criteria three ethnic zones exist in the Congo: Northern and Southern Savanna, Central Rain Forest and Eastern Highlands. Each has its own tribes or tribal clusters as follows:

Southern Savanna: Kongo, Kuba, Teke, Boma-Sakata, Yans-Mbun, Lunda, Songye, Luba, Yaka, Mbala, Pende, Lunda, Aushi, Kaone, Lala, Lamba, Lembe, Lembwe, Ngoma, Nweshi, Sanga, Seba, Yeke, Luba, Hembe, Bemba.

Northern Savanna: Zande, Nazkara, Mamvu, Mangbetu, Mangutu.

Central Rain Forest: Apagibeti-Boa, Ubangi, Mba, Binza, Water Peoples, Eso, Ngombe-Doko, Ndunga, Mongo, Bira, Nyari, Bali, Budu, Nyintu, Lega, Binja, Lengolo, Bembe, Pygmies.

Eastern Highlands: Furiiru, Shi, Havu, Hunde, Tembo, Yira, Nyanga, Hutu, Rundi, Lugbara, Alur.

The most important of these ethnic groups are the Kongo, Luba, Lunda, Mongo and Zande. None of these groups number over 3 million. The primary feelings of identity among these groups are ethnic rather than national, but the pressure of the events of the independence period has created a rudimentary consciousness of common interests.

The resident alien population numbers roughly 900,000, including Angolans, Sudanese, Zambians, and West Africans. Since 1970 the non-African alien population has declined, and their number is estimated at around 50,000, half the pre-independence figure. The Belgians still constitute the majority, followed by Portuguese, Italians, Greeks, Arabs, Lebanese, Pakistanis and Indians. Most of them are employed as civil servants, missionaries, traders, teachers and planters. In terms of ethnic and linguistic homogeneity, Zaire is ranked second in the world with 10% homogeneity (on an ascending scale in which North and South Korea are ranked 135th with 100% homogeneity and Tanzania is ranked first with 7% homogeneity).

LANGUAGES

French is the official language and the medium of instruction in secondary and higher education, but only a small percentage of the population have a working knowledge of it and efforts to introduce it into the primary schools have failed. Nearly all Zaireans speak languages of the Bantu subgroup of the Central Branch of the Niger-Congo Family. The Eastern branch of the Niger-Congo Family and the Central Sudanic Family are also represented. The principal language is Bantu with its 14 clusters of languages spoken by over 11 million people. The Kongo, Luba, Mongo and Lunda belong to this family. Zande is the most important of the Eastern Branch and Moru-Mangbetu of the Central Sudanic. The total number of languages and dialects is estimated at 700.

A number of hybrid languages have been developed as means of communication between different groups. The most widespread of these lingua francas are:

(1) Lingala, developed along the Zaire River as a trade language in the 1880s. In time it was given written form and a standardized vocabulary by Catholic missionaries and it is now used along the Zaire River and in the north and northwest. It is the language of the Zairean Army.

(2) Kingwana, an upcountry dialect of Kiswahili introduced by the Arabs in the course of 19th century slaving operations, is spoken in Kisangani, Orientale, Kivu, Katanga and parts of Kasai Provinces. For some it has been written in Roman alphabet with a large number of loan words from European languages. A substandard variant, spoken in Katanga, is known as Katanga Swahili.

(3) Kikongo, spoken in the region immediately east of Kinshasa.

(4) Tshiluba, spoken by the Luba of south-central Luba, has acquired considerable prestige as a literary medium.

Other languages that serve as lingua francas within limited areas are Lomongo, Lokele, Pazande, Lingombe, Kicokwe and Kinyarwande.

RELIGIONS

It is estimated that about half of the Zaireans are, at least nominally, Christians. Of these, three-quarters are Roman Catholic and one-quarter Protestant. Most of the non-Christian population is comprised of adherents of traditional religions or syncretic sects. The traditional religions are not formalized but they embody some common concepts such as animism, belief in spirits and ancestor worship. The syncretic sects are a mixture of Christianity and traditional beliefs centered around new prophets. One of these Kimbanguism, has about 3 million members and in 1969 became the first independent African Church to be admitted to the World Council of Churches.

Zaire has been the scene of one of the most intense Christian missionary efforts and both Catholic and Protestant organizations have had a profound impact on the development of the nation particularly in the fields of education and health. At one time there were over 7,000 missionaries, and two universities were run by church bodies. Many missionaries, however, lost their lives in the civil war of the 1960s, many were mistreated, and others left. The churches have been largely Africanized since independence. Of the 40 Roman Catholic bishops, 22 are Zairean, including five archbishops and a cardinal. The number of present missions is around 700. All Catholic activities are coordinated by the Interdiocesan Center in Kinshasa. Protestant churches function as a united group under the title United Churches of Christ. Freedom of religion is guaranteed under the constitution of 1960 and the Loi Fondamentale of 1967. Relations between the church and state have been considerably strained since Mobutu launched his authenticity program under which religious instruction was prohibited in schools, Christian names were replaced by Zairean ones, church schools were nationalized, and religious holidays secularized. However, by the end of the 1970s many of Mobutu's anti-Christian excesses had been curbed and, in some instances, Church schools and property had been handed back to their owners. Pope John Paul II's visit to Zaire in 1980 marked a reconciliation between church and state and an end to the authenticity campaign. Religious minorities include nearly 200,000 Muslims.

COLONIAL EXPERIENCE

Two men were responsible for the Belgian colonization of the Congo region: Henry M. Stanley and King Leopold of the Belgians. Stanley's historic trip down the Congo in 1877 (following David Livingstone's explorations in eastern Africa) aroused European interest in the Congo basin. King Leopold was the first to realize the potentials of Stanley's discoveries and commissioned him to create a chain of stations along the Congo River and bind the tribal chiefs by treaties. Leopold undertook this work independently of Belgium and in 1878 formed the International Association of the Congo with himself as its chief stockholder. By masterful diplomacy Leopold induced the Berlin Conference of 1884-85 to recognize the association as the master of the Congo, a territory 80 times the size of Belgium. By capitalizing on the booming world demand for rubber, the colony's chief product, Leopold made a handsome profit on his investments but his very success was his undoing. The methods used in the collection of rubber involved ghastly atrocities, news of which led to the formation of the Congo Reform Campaign and diplomatic pressures on Belgium to take over the administration of the territory. In 1908 with the passage of the Colonial Charter Congo became a Belgian colony.

Belgium was thus a reluctant and unprepared colonial power, a role which it assumed only out of a sense of obligation to the royal family, and it had no reserves of imperial expertise to draw upon, as the British and the French had. Belgium's modest colonial goals included extension of a rudimentary administrative structure to prevent the recurrence of the kind of abuses under Leopold, the development of the economy solely with a view to profit and the Christianization of the tribes. The administration, the big companies and the missions thus formed a kind of triumvirate and the main instruments of change. Administratively the Belgians had no interest in introducing Belgian structures but rather in regulating traditional units of government. It was only in the field of religion that any fundamental change took place. Initially there was tension between Christian emphasis on individuality and the essentially communal nature of African life and the Western distinctions between the natural and the supernatural and the secular and the religious and the African tendency to disregard such boundaries. But the impact of Christianity has been profound and in many cases permanent even where Africanized in such messianic movements as Kimbanguism.

The earlier ad hoc response of Belgian rulers to their new colonial responsibilities became institutionalized only after World War I, when the Belgians made a serious effort to devise permanent channels of authority. They also created a new African urban class called evolues who by a process called immatriculation (including learning French language, adopting Western customs and accepting the orderly transition to a mercantile from a tribal culture) were given the same legal status as Europeans—although not given entry into European society. It was these evolues who spearheaded the nationalist movement that ultimately forced the Belgians to grant independence at the Brussels Round Table Conference in

1960. But the nationalist movement in the Congo had not had time to mature, and therefore the Congo was ill-prepared for independence when it came. By its failure to prepare the Africans to take over authority and exercise it responsibly, the Belgians were partly responsible for the upheavals that followed soon after independence. Many of the valuable legacies of Belgian rule were obliterated in the bloody events of the 1960s.

CONSTITUTION & GOVERNMENT

Under the constitution of 1967 as amended in 1974 the supreme state organ is the Political Bureau of the Mouvement Populaire de la Revolution (MPR), which was established in 1967 as the country's only political party. The relationship of the Bureau to the government has been defined in the phrase, "the Bureau decides, the government executes." The decisions of the Bureau are binding on both the executive and legislative branches. The president of the MPR serves concurrently as the president of the republic. The synthesis of government and party is further reinforced by the National Executive Council, which represents a fusion of the former cabinet and executive council of the MPR. Members of the Council are styled state commissioners. The main locus of power is the president of the republic, elected for a five-year term, renewable for a second term. He presides over the MPR Political Bureau, the MPR congress, and executive, judicial and legislative councils. He is empowered to legislate with the consent of the legislative council and renders account directly to the people by means of an annual policy statement. He appoints all political commissioners, regional commissioners and judges. He is also commander in chief of armed forces. He is empowered to declare a state of emergency for as long a period as he may deem necessary. The Political Bureau was enlarged to 31 members in 1974 to include representatives of the judiciary, university communities and the military. After Mobutu's tenure a president will be permitted to change only one-third of the membership of the Political Bureau during his term of office. The Bureau may remove a president, other than Mobutu, for deviation from party doctrine. Permanent presidential succession is by way of popular election, the single MPR candidate being chosen by the Political Bureau. The executive departments of the government are administered by state commissioners who are selected by the president and together with him comprise the National Executive Council. In 1980 the president held the posts of defense and planning in the national executive council.

In addition to the National Executive Council a permanent committee of MPR Political Bureau has been established consisting of 10 members who will always be at the president's disposal for policy formulation and implementation.

Elections are by universal, direct and secret suffrage. The age of eligibility is 18. An electoral district,

called a circumscription, consists of 50,000 citizens. There is only one slate of candidates for every circumscription chosen by the Political Bureau of the MPR. The number of candidates on every slate is one-

NATIONAL EXECUTIVE COUNCIL (1985)

President . . . . *Marshal* Mobutu Sese Seko
First State Commissioner . . . . Kengo wa Dondo
State Commissioner for Agriculture & Rural Development . . . . Bokana W'Ondangela
State Commissioner for Civil Service . . . . Kembukuswa ne Nlaza
State Commissioner for Culture & Arts . . . . Pendje Demodetdo Yako
State Commissioner for Economy & Industry . . . . Tshibambe Kabamba
State Commissioner for Environment, Preservation of Nature & Tourism . . . . Ndjoli Balanga
State Commissioner for External Trade . . . Lengema Dulia
State Commissioner for Finance & Budget . . . . Djamboleka Loma Okitongono
State Commissioner for Foreign Affairs & International Cooperation . . . . . . Mokolo wa Mpombo
State Commissioner for Higher & University Education . . . . Mokondo Bonza
State Commissioner for Idealogy & Formation of Cadres . . . Kangafu Vingi Gudumbangana
State Commissioner for Information & Press . . . . Ramazani Baya
State Commissioner for Justice . . . . *Marshal* Mobutu Sese Seko
State Commissioner for Labor & Social Security . . . . Mbaya Ngang
State Commissioner for Land Affairs . . . . Ileka Nkumu
State Commissioner for Mines & Energy . . . . Umba Kyamitala
State Commissioner for Mobilization, Propaganda & Political Action . . . . Takizala Luyan Muis Mbingin
State Commissioner for National Defense . . . . *Marshal* Mobutu Sese Seko
State Commissioner for Planning . . . Sambwa Pida Nbagui
State Commissioner for Posts, Telephone & Telegraph . . . . Mukuku W'Etonda
State Commissioner for Primary & Secondary Education . . . . Mokondo Bonza
State Commissioner for Public Health . . . . . Mushobekwa Kalimba wa Katana
State Commissioner for Public Works & Territorial Development . . . . Thambwe Mwamba
State Commissioner for Scientific Research . . . . Kande Buloba Kasumpata
State Commissioner for Sports & Leisure . . . . Tshimpumpu wa Tshimpumpu
State Commissioner for Social Affairs . . . . Kilolo Musampa Lubemba
State Commissioner for State Enterprises . . . . . Unen Can
State Commissioner for Territorial Administration . . . . Mozagba Ngbuka
State Commissioner for Transport & Communications . . . . Muyulu Mombanga
State Commissioner for Women's & Family Affairs . . . . Soki Fuanti Eyenga
State Commissioner for Youth . . . . Sampassa Kaweta Milombe

ORGANIZATION OF ZAIRE GOVERNMENT

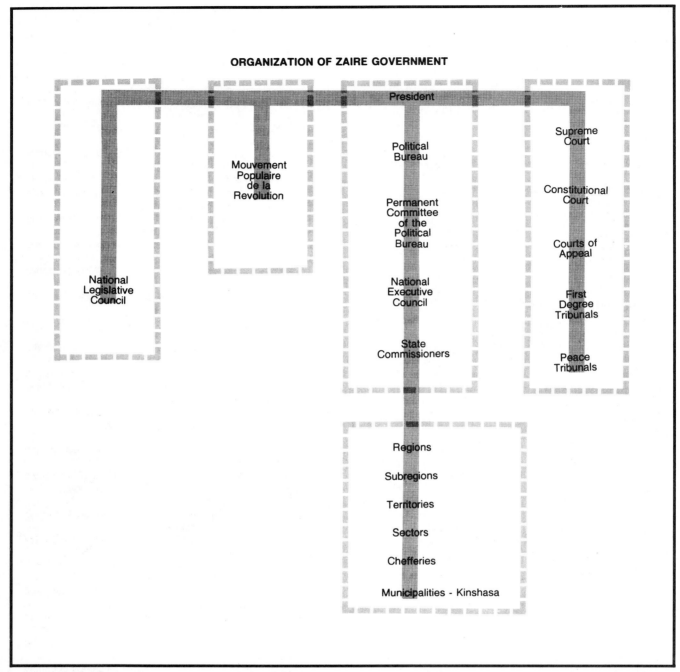

President

Mouvement Populaire de la Revolution

National Legislative Council

Political Bureau

Permanent Committee of the Political Bureau

National Executive Council

State Commissioners

Supreme Court

Constitutional Court

Courts of Appeal

First Degree Tribunals

Peace Tribunals

Regions

Subregions

Territories

Sectors

Chefferies

Municipalities - Kinshasa

third more than the actual number of seats. The slate is adopted if it receives over 50% of the votes cast. The candidates who receive the largest number of votes are elected deputies while the remaining third are substitutes to fill vacancies as they occur.

Suffrage is universal over age 18 and voting is mandatory, enforced by penalties including fines or arrest. The national Parliament, municipal councils, rural and urban zone councils are chosen by direct popular elections which take place every 5 years, with the most recent having been in 1982. All candidates are members of the party (as are all citizens of Zaire) and are screened by party committees at the appropriate level, but voters generally have a choice of candi-

dates (in the 1982 parliamentary election there were an average of five candidates per district). The president is popularly elected for a 7-year term, after nomination by the party central committee. President Mobutu was reelected in 1984 to a third term in office.

The official philosophy of Zaire is Mobutism, which is more of a personal cult than a strict ideology. Mobutu is publicly referred to as "The Guide" and as the "Father of the Nation." Mobutism includes a campaign for authenticity and national identity under which colonial place names and Christian names have been replaced by mandate. References to ancestors are now part of public ceremonies. Much of the thrust of the militant Africanization programs generated by

---

RULERS OF ZAIRE

PRESIDENTS:
1960 (June) to 1965 (November) Joseph Kasavubu
1965 (Nov) to— Mobutu Sese Seko (formerly Joseph
        Mobutu)
PRIME MINISTERS:
1960 (June) to 1960 (September) Patrice Lumumba
1960 (September) Joseph Ileo
1960 (September) to 1961 (February)
        College of Commissioners
1961 (February) to 1961 (July) Joseph Ileo
1961 (August) to 1964 (June) Cyrille Adoula
1964 (July) to 1965 (October) Moise Tshombe
1965 (October) to 1965 (November) Evariste Kimba
1965 (November) to 1966 (October) Mulamba Nyunyu wa
Kadima
From 1966 (October) the president also prime minister

---

the ideology of Mobutism was blunted by the economic and military failures of the Mobutu regime in the late 1970s. This forced Mobutu to depend more and more on Western powers and to generally retrace his steps toward a more pragmatic stance in political and social matters. By the time Pope John Paul II visited Zaire in 1980, it ws clear that Mobutu had abandoned the more audacious of his indigenization policies and had adopted a different set of priorities.

After almost a decade of prosperity, Zaire relapsed into near civil war in 1977 following the invasion of Shaba province in 1977 and 1978 by the National Front for the Liberation of the Congo. The Mobutu regime was rescued solely by the intervention of French forces, although some assistance was received from a number of other states, such as Uganda, Morocco, Central African Republic and Saudi Arabia, as well as Belgium. The proximity of a Soviet- and Cuban-backed regime in Angola has altered radically the balance of power in Africa and may pose further problems for Mobutu.

In May 1983, following the publication of a highly critical report on Zaire by the human rights organization, Amnesty International, Mobutu offered an amnesty to all political exiles who returned to Zaire by 30 June. A number of exiles accepted the offer, including Mungul Diaka, leader of the Council for the Liberation of the Congo, but a substantial opposition movement remained in Belgium. The 13 imprisoned members of the National Legislative Council were released in May; their fate was not known for certain, but Mobutu claimed at a press conference in Belgium, in July 1984, that five of them had accompanied him on his trip. Opposition to Mobutu's regime continued to manifest itself in Zaire during 1984: in January and March a number of bombs exploded in Kinshasa, causing loss of life, and a rebel force occupied the town of Moba, in Shaba province, for two days in November, before it was recaptured by Zairian troops. Zaire accused Belgium of harboring the groups responsible for such violent opposition, and claimed that the rebels had crossed into Zaire from neighboring Tanzania. However, the main opposition groups in Belgium did not acknowledge involvement in the occupation of Moba, suggesting instead that

rebellious Zairian troops had been responsible. It was widely believed that the violent opposition in Zaire had been orchestrated in order to disrupt the proceedings for the election and inauguration of the country's president, which were due to take place in 1984. However, Mobutu was reelected to the post without hindrance in July, and was inaugurated in December. A reduction by one-third of the number of members of the Central Committee of the MPR, from 120 to 80, in January 1985, and a major ministerial reshuffle in February, followed an announcement by the president that, with the exception of himself and the first state commissioner, nobody might concurrently be involved in government and be a member of the Central Committee.

FREEDOM & HUMAN RIGHTS

In terms of civil and political rights Zaire is ranked as a not-free nation with a maximum negative rating of 6 in political rights and 6 in civil rights (on a descending scale where 1 is the highest and 7 the lowest).

Although the military and economic reverses of the late 1970s had forced Mobutu to adopt a more responsive and flexible political strategy, the government remained authoritarian, personalized and highly centralized. The president heads both the party (Popular Movement of the Revolution) and the state, appointing the first state commissioner or prime minister and his cabinet. He retains the right to promulgate laws by decree although in theory he shares legislative powers with the Legislative Council.

Nevertheless, there have been significant improvements in the human rights situation in Zaire. The government continued a policy of amnesty towards political exiles. By 1980 judicial reforms were implemented that abolished the oppressive judicial council and reinforced the independence of the bar. The ministry of justice also launched a campaign to improve prison conditions by reducing overcrowding, prohibiting the use of torture and other inhuman treatment, and improving food, water and sanitation facilities. Despite these reforms, overcrowding is so bad that prisoners must take turns sleeping on the floor for lack of space. some are held for months without charges being filed. Occasional disappearances of prisoners are attributed to administrative incompetence rather than official policy. Under Article 49 of the 1978 constitution the president can declare a state of national siege or emergency under which security or military police may arrest suspects without filing formal charges and hold them for interrogation for an unlimited period. Often ill-paid soldiers and policemen detain citizens without provocation or on flimsy grounds in order to extract bribes or accept money to arrest citizens. Trials are almost always public but are not always fair. Although civil judges are now more independent, they are still supervised by the department of justice and are subject to political pressures. Because judges are poorly paid, corruption is rampant in the judiciary.

The government controls the press and the broadcast media. Articles and opinion pieces must be approved by a government review commission before publication. Journalists and writers are required to exercise self-censorship and must take care not to criticize directly the president—a criminal offense—or his close associates. From time-to-time, certain issues of foreign magazines are censored or banned by the government.

Right of assembly is qualified by the requirement that groups be legally recognized. Groups of more than a few persons may not assemble without a permit and all social, political, sport or youth associations must be affiliated to the MPR. Although the right to strike is restricted by both legal and political considerations, there were a number of job actions in 1980 which won higher benefits for workers.

The changes in the human rights situation in 1985 were mixed. The continuing instability in eastern Zaire led to a sharply deteriorating human rights situation there, with many civilian casualties caused by the fighting between government military forces and the rebels. A number of members of a group advocating a second political party were rearrested and banned to the interior of the country in October and November. Harassment of citizens by law enforcement personnel and inordinate delays in processing of detainees remained serious problems. There were, however, concerted efforts by the government to reconcile differences with political dissidents, notably former prime minister Nguza Karl-I-Bond who returned to Zaire, as well as signs of greater government awareness of shortcomings in the judicial and penal systems. President Mobutu took over the minister of justice portfolio early in the year and named a commission to investigate prison and judicial performance which did effect at least short-term reforms in some parts of the country. Less successful but still positive efforts were undertaken to end the corruption in prison administration which permits poor conditions, beatings, and in some cases prisoners to starve to death. Zaire continues to provide sanctuary to over 300,000 refugees and displaced persons from neighboring countries, primarily Angola.

A complex of security organizations, notably the civilian National Documentation Agency, the paramilitary gendarmerie and Civil Guard, and the armed forces (particularly the military intelligence action service and the Special Presidential Brigade) share responsibility for identifying and controlling potential internal and external threats to Zaire and the Mobutu government. These organizations wield broad powers and influence, which allows arbitrary harassment and detention of ordinary citizens as well as suspected political opponents of the government. Throughout 1985, continued instability affected the region along Lake Tanganyika in Eastern Zaire, from Uvira in Kivu region down to Moba, with rebel attacks against Kalemie and, once again in May, Moba itself, which had been a rebel target in 1984.

The government claims not to condone torture and denies allegations that torture is administered by its officials during interrogation. However, Amnesty International maintains that torture and physical mistreatment of detainees is routine in most Zairian places of detention. There is little question that mistreatment of detainees, particularly beatings at time of arrest and during preliminary interrogation, is the rule rather than the exception. Criminal penalties do not include physical punishment or mutilation. In fact, however, abuses of all kinds are endemic in Zaire's jails and prisons, with reports of unsanitary and crowded facilities, malnutrition and starvation among prisoners. The reasons for this situation include lack of concern at senior levels, incompetence, corruption, and budget reductions imposed as a result of the economic reform program. The government has begun to take steps to correct some of these abuses. President Mobutu took personal charge of the Ministry of Justice early in 1985, primarily in response to evidence of malfeasance in the administration of justice and prisons.

Arbitrary arrest and prolonged detention without charges remain common occurrences, affecting most people who come into contact with the criminal justice system. Although habeas corpus or its equivalent and bail do not exist, by law those arrested must be brought before a magistrate to hear charges within 48 hours of arrest. In practice, however, suspects are often arrested and held for months without a hearing. Detainees with financial resources are known to buy their way out of detention without ever having charges formally filed.

The party and state security organizations extend down to neighborhood level, and both maintain liaison offices in all government agencies (including military units, universities, legislative council, ministries, etc.). All Zairians 18 years or older are automatically members of the party. Party officials, civil servants, armed forces personnel, parliamentarians and employees of state enterprises pay an obligatory tax to support the activities of the party's major organs (cadre training, mobilization, propaganda and youth). These party cadres are also required to attend the party's training institute. Non-attendance can result in reprimands and suspensions. Government employees, market women, and blue-collar workers are often required to participate in public events— parades, official arrival and departure ceremonies, etc.—or risk being suspended from work.

Mail is opened sporadically by security services, some telephone conversations are tapped, and government informers monitor places of residence as well as work. In line with the party-state's ideology of "Zairian authenticity," Zairian men are forbidden to wear ties and women to wear pants or wigs. Zairians are also forbidden to use non-African names.

CIVIL SERVICE

The corps of Zairean civil servants functions under the Ministry of Public Function. To help offset the critical shortage of civil servants the government initiated a program of obligatory civil service in 1966, requiring all university graduates to perform a two-year term of public service.

LOCAL GOVERNMENT

There are two types of local government units: administrative circumscriptions, which depend entirely on the central authority, and decentralized territorial collectivities, which enjoy a certain administrative autonomy. The circumscriptions consist of eight provinces (Lower Zaire, Bandundu, Upper Zaire, Equator, West Kasai, East Kasai, Shaba and Kivu), 23 districts and 135 territories. The provinces are administered by governors, districts by district commissioners, and territories by territorial administrators. The territorial collectivities include 446 sectors and 360 chefferies administered by chiefs and local councils. Provincial cities constitute communes administered by a first burgomaster and a city council. The capital city of Kinshasa constitutes a separate unit under a governor and urban commissioners appointed by the president of the republic. Under the reorganized local government structure in 1975 the provinces were renamed regions, the governors regional commissioners, and the districts subregions.

FOREIGN POLICY

Since coming to power Mobutu has generally pursued a moderate line in foreign policy and avoided involvement in non-African issues. Zaire's relationship with Belgium remains important to both countries but has been periodically impaired by economic nationalism. In 1974 Zaire and the Belgian Societe Generale reached a final agreement on compensation for nationalization of its former mining properties. Mobutu has called for an economic alliance of the oppressed against the developed countries and has called for cartel action by producers of primary raw materials. Zaire is one of the four members of the Intergovernmental Council of Copper Exporting Countries.

In the fall of 1973 Zaire's role was crucial in the swing of black African support from Israel to the Arabs. In 1982, Mobutu reversed himself and reestablished relations with Israel. In retaliation, many Arab governments suspended relations with Zaire. Israeli Defense Minister Ariel Sharon visited Kinshasa and promised arms aid and training for Zairian troops.

Relations with former French territories in central Africa, especially Congo (Brazzaville) are less smooth; its memberships in the Union of Central African States (UEAC) and the Afro-Malgasy Common Organization (OCAM) were terminated by 1972.

During the Angolan independence movement, Zaire supported the Front for the National Liberation of Angola against the Popular Movement for the Liberation of Angola, which eventually seized power with Soviet and Cuban aid. With the establishment of the Republic of Angola relations between the two countries deteriorated. Zaire's Shaba Province (formerly Katanga) was invaded in 1977 and 1978 by guerrillas of the Congolese National Liberation Front based in Angola and supported by Cuban and Angolan troops and equipment. The rebel forces made rapid gains due in part to support from the local Lunda tribe among whom secessionist feelings were strong. The conflict soon assumed international proportions and a number of Western and African nations sent men and materiel to the aid of Zaire. Relations with the Soviet Union and East European nations received a setback and relations with Cuba and East Germany were suspended. As a result of the events of 1977 and 1978 Mobutu's Zaire is now firmly in the Western camp. It is reported that the French and the Belgians have imposed a number of conditions as quid pro quo for their intervention in 1978. To this extent Zaire's ability to provide a leadership to black Africa has been seriously impaired.

The hostile confrontation of Angola and Zaire was apparently defused by the state visit of late president Neto to Zaire in 1979 and the signing of a cooperation agreement establishing a four nation control commission under the OAU to guard against rebel violations, on either side, of their common border.

The conference between France and African states held in Kinshasa in 1982 enhanced Zaire's role in Africa as the bellwether of generally conservative or moderate francophone nations. This role was reinforced when Zaire sent 2,000 troops to Chad to defend President Habre. In 1984 Mobutu called for the creation of an Organization of Sub-Saharan African States as a counterthrust to North African and Islamic interests.

Zaire and the United States are parties to 25 treaties and agreements covering agricultural commodities, aviation, defense, economic and technical cooperation, finance, investment guaranties, Peace Corps, remote sensing, and taxation.

Zaire is an active member of the Organization of African Unity. It joined the U.N. in 1960 and is a member of 14 U.N. organizations and 16 other international organizations. Its share of the U.N. budget is 0.02%.

U.S. Ambassador in Kinshasa: Brandon H. Grove
U.K. Ambassador in Kinshasa: Nicholas Peter Bayne
Zairean Ambassador in Washington, D.C.: Kasongo Mutuale
Zairean Ambassador in London: (Vacant)

PARLIAMENT

The National Legislative Council is a unicameral body of 310 members elected for five-year terms from a single slate of the ruling Popular Movement of the

Revolution. It meets twice annually from April to July and from October to January. Its powers, including those over the purse, are unsubstantial and in practice the National Legislative Council only serves as the fifth wheel in the administration.

POLITICAL PARTIES

The sole channel of political activity in Zaire is the Mouvement Populaire de la Revolution (MPR) founded by Mobutu in 1967. By a constitutional amendment in 1970 the MPR was established not only as the sole political party but as a public institution of the republic and thus, in effect, an organ of government. MPR's territorial organization follows the administrative structure of regional government. The central organs are the president, the Congress, the Political Bureau, and the National Executive Committee. The local organs of the party are committees of three members each who head the different territorial subdivisions. The president of the MPR is also automatically the president of the republic and the Political Bureau of the MPR acts as a super cabinet setting the goals and policies of national government. Government administrators fill dual roles in the state and in the party. MPR also had two wings—a youth wing and a labor wing, Jeunesse du Mouvement Populaire de la Revolution (JMPR) and Union Nationale des Travailleurs du Zaire (UNTZ)—which enjoy monopoly positions in their respective fields.

The official ideology of the MPR is embodied in the Manifesto of Nsele (so called because it was issued from the presidential palace at Nsele). The manifesto set a middle course between capitalism and socialism and emphasized Zairean solutions to Zairean problems. National goals and priorities were described as economic independence, national unity and social development.

ECONOMY

As a result of the enormous capital flow into the country during the colonial period Zaire was one of the most economically advanced countries in Sub-Saharan Africa. Yet Zaire has become virtually "growthproof"; it is an undeveloped country plagued by the triple ills of corruption, mismanagement and decline in producer prices. In the eyes of many Western bankers, and particularly the IMF, however, Zaire is a test case for applying theories of fiscal and monetary austerity to a moribund economy. Zaire plunged into an economic quagmire in 1975 as a result of prodigal spending and corruption of legendary proportions. Nearly 25 years after independence agriculture has remained at little more than subsistence level. Education is declining in real terms even at the primary level. There are few passable roads, except in the towns. Healthcare is almost impossible to obtain. Whereas Zaire was self-sufficient in food at independence, today it imports 60% of its food.

Zaire hewed to the IMF plan for recovery unflinchingly for more than three years. Mobutu's dictatorial powers and the lack of public opposition were among the reasons why the IMF regimen went through. The steps taken included an immediate rise in farm prices, a drastic devaluation of the zaire, a reorganization of the mining company, and large cuts in government spending. One result of the program has been a dramatic increase in the price of staples, such as millet, sorghum and cooking oil. Bus and train fares have doubled and urban jobs are difficult to find. Sticking to the IMF plan has meant the diversion of more than half the state revenues to servicing the nation's $4.5 billion debt. There is little money to spend on schools, hospitals, roads, electrification and clean drinking water. Zaire is faced with the classic dilemma of a developing country: to gain respectability in international banking circles, it has to forgo every claim to economic development or growth.

PRINCIPAL ECONOMIC INDICATORS

Gross National Product: $5.050 billion (1983)
  GNP Annual Growth Rate: −1.2% (1973-82)
  Per Capita GNP: $160
  Per Capita GNP Annual Growth Rate: −4.2% (1973-82)

Gross Domestic Product: Z59.134 billion (1983)
  GDP in 1980 Prices: Z17.35 billion
  GDP Deflator (1980=100): 340.8
  GDP Annual Growth Rate: −1.0% (1973-83)
  Per Capita GDP: Z179 (1983)
  Per Capita GDP Annual Growth Rate: −3.1% (1970-81)

Income Distribution: Information not available

Percentage of Population in Absolute Poverty: 60; 80 (rural)

Consumer Price Index (1970=100):
  All Items: 1,813.1 (1981)
  Food: 1,828.1 (1981)

Average Annual Rate of Inflation: 48.2% (1973-83)

Money Supply: Z14.775 billion (March 1984)
  Reserve Money: Z13.161 billion (March 1984)

Currency in Circulation: Z6.141 billion (1984)

International Reserves: $137.37 million, of which foreign exchange were $137.37 million (1984)

BALANCE OF PAYMENTS (1980)
(in million $)

Current Account Balance	332.4
Merchandise Exports	1,953.6
Merchandise Imports	−1,201.3
Trade Balance	752.3
Other Goods, Services & Income	+133.5
Other Goods, Services & Income	−762.4
Other Goods, Services & Income Net	−628.9
Private Unrequited Transfers	—
Official Unrequited Transfers	209.0
Capital Other Than Reserves	69.9
Net Errors & Omissions	−415.3
Total (Lines 1, 10 and 11)	12.9
Counterpart Items	28.5
Total (Lines 12 and 13)	15.5
Liabilities Constituting Foreign Authorities' Reserves	—
Total Change in Reserves	−15.5

Zaire has no formal economic planning.

Foreign aid plays an important role in the Zairean economy but its volume, source, and nature have changed over the years. Total U.S. bilateral economic aid to Zaire through 1983 was $733.4 million in addition to another $500 million in direct loans and guarantees through the Export-Import Bank. Belgian and U.N. aid have also fallen off after 1972. Zaire received $1.084 billion from international organizations, of which $227.1 million came from the World Bank and $192.4 million from the EEC. Total bilateral and multilateral aid during 1979-81 was $410.9 million or $15.60 per capita.

Beginning in 1973 Zairean economy began to falter under the impact of new stresses. Large budget deficits weakened the currency. The cost of living rose precipitately—40% in 1974 alone—while the government kept a firm lid on wages. A decline in the price of copper, which brings in 70% of Zaire's currency earnings, and a fall off in agricultural production following the takeover of foreign farms accelerated the economic downturn. Zaire became the first nation to default on its Eurocurrency loans in 1975.

GROSS DOMESTIC PRODUCT BY ECONOMIC ACTIVITY (1970-81)

	%	Rate of Change %
Agriculture	28.7	1.5
Mining	17.1	–0.1
Manufacturing	4.4	–2.3
Construction	4.2	–3.0
Electricity, Gas & Water	0.2	2.4
Transport & Communications	2.5	–2.7
Trade & Finance	18.0	–1.7
Public Administration & Defense	10.7	–8.2
Other Branches	14.3	–9.5

BUDGET

The Zairean fiscal year is the calendar year. Since 1967 the budget has consisted of two parts: an ordinary budget and an extraordinary or investment budget. The provincial budgets are included in the central government's budgets and disbursements are centralized in Kinshasa.

Of current revenues, 32.5% comes from taxes on income, profit and capital gain, 1.4% from social security contributions, 22.3% from domestic taxes on goods and services, 25.0% from taxes on international trade and transactions, 6.5% from other taxes and 12.3% from non-tax revenues. Current revenues represented 21.6% of GNP. Of current expenditures, 21.3% goes to civil service salaries and 7.9% to servicing of domestic debt. No other breakdowns are available.

In 1983 public consumption totaled Z9.629 billion and private consumption Z36.201 billion. During 1973-83 public consumption grew by 2.2% and private consumption declined by 7.7%.

ORDINARY BUDGET ('000 zaires)

Revenue	1980	1981	1982
Direct taxes	655,354	1,734,823	2,748,274
Income tax	513,041	1,474,823	2,049,752
Turnover tax	142,313	260,000	698,522
Indirect taxes	1,684,471	2,596,002	2,144,061
Export duties	860,819	1,299,468	93,122
Import duties	324,820	569,400	1,121,800
Consumption tax	70,920	180,701	400,879
Non-tax revenue	839,776	965,195	1,538,229
TOTAL REVENUE	3,335,921	5,616,428	7,839,814

Expenditure	1980	1981	1982
Current expenditure	3,312,642	3,733,103	7,649,871
Presidency	30,000	60,000	105,514
National defense	271,614	366,336	583,326
Foreign affairs	83,144	130,711	109,654
Education	589,944	995,018	1,672,711
Agriculture	27,899	101,133	180,480
Public health	97,040	118,034	286,361
Public works	127,452	205,967	282,738
Public debt	932,491	957,846	1,357,208
Towns and regions	66,353	259,124	150,000
Capital expenditure	373,281	383,973	1,189,973
TOTAL EXPENDITURE (incl. others)	3,685,923	6,117,076	8,839,844

1985 (draft budget, '000 zaires): Revenue 30,700,000; Expenditure 34,700,000 (incl. Capital expenditure 2,600,000).

In 1983 total outstanding disbursed external debt was $4.022 billion of which $3.152 billion was owed to public creditors and $870 million to private creditors. Total debt service was $126.8 million of which $39.3 million was repayment of principal and $87.5 million interest. Total external debt was 91.5% of GNP and total debt service 2.9% of GNP.

FINANCE

The unit of currency is the zaire divided into 100 makuta (singular: likuta), each likuta being divided into 100 sengi. Notes are issued in denominations of 10, 5, 1 zaire and 50, 20, 10 makuta; coins are issued in denominations of 5 makuta, 1 likuta and 10 sengi. The zaire was introduced in 1967 and was accompanied by a devaluation of the currency by 70%. Zaire remained aligned with the American dollar in the devaluations of 1971 and 1973, in effect being devalued by 25%. In 1976 the link between the zaire and the U.S. dollar was ended and its value was pegged to the SDR based on a weighted basket of 16 national currencies. The exchange rate in August 1985 was U.S.$1= Z50.65. The sterling exchange rate in 1984 was £1= Z46.88.

The Zairean banking system consists of a central bank, Banque du Zaire, and over 24 commercial banking institutions and development banks. The only publicly owned commercial bank is the Banque du Peuple. There are a number of specialized credit institutions of which the most important are the Caisse Nationale d'Epargne et de Credit Immobilier, established by presidential decree in 1971 and the Societe Financiere de Developpement. In 1983 commercial banks reported reserves of Z3.110 billion, demand deposits of

Z7.406 billion, and time and foreign currency deposits of Z887.0 million. The general absence of commercial banking facilities in rural areas is partially offset by the existence of a postal checking system whose prime objective is the collection and management of voluntary savings.

GROWTH PROFILE Annual Growth Rates (%)	
Population 1980-2000	3.1
Birthrate 1965-83	-4.0
Deathrate 1965-83	-32.6
Urban Population 1973-83	6.9
Labor Force 1980-2000	3.6
GNP 1973-82	-1.2
GNP per capita 1973-82	-4.2
GDP 1973-83	-1.0
GDP per capita 1970-81	-3.1
Consumer Prices 1970-81	43.7
Wholesale Prices	—
Inflation 1973-83	48.2
Agriculture 1973-83	1.4
Manufacturing 1970-81	-2.3
Industry 1973-83	-2.0
Services 1973-83	-1.1
Mining 1970-81	-0.1
Construction 1970-81	4.2
Electricity 1970-81	0.2
Transportation 1970-81	2.5
Trade 1970-81	18.0
Public Administration & Defense 1970-81	10.7
Export Price Index 1975-81	7.1
Import Price Index 1975-81	12.7
Terms of Trade 1975-81	-49
Exports 1973-83	-8.7
Imports 1973-83	-13.7
Public Consumption 1973-83	2.2
Private Consumption 1973-83	-7.7
Gross Domestic Investment 1973-83	4.9
Energy Consumption 1973-83	1.5
Energy Production 1973-83	9.1

AGRICULTURE

Of the total land area of 234,493,200 hectares (579,432,690 acres), only one-half is potentially arable, and only an estimated 1.2% is planted in field or tree crops, while an additional 15 to 20% lies fallow. About 90% of the cultivated area is planted in food crops and 10% in export crops. Per capita agricultural land area is 3.2 hectares (8 acres). The index of agricultural production in 1982 was 108, the food production index was 108 and the per capita food production index was 93 (based on 1974-76=100). Agriculture employs 75% of the labor force. The value added in agriculture in 1983 was $1.866 billion.

Agriculture contributed 36% of GDP in 1982, and its growth rate during 1973-83 was 1.4%. Agricultural products account for 11% of export earnings.

The agricultural sector consists of three categories of farms: large plantations and ranches formerly owned by Europeans and expropriated in 1973, small-scale traditional family holdings, and intermediate paysannats, units of 4 to 9 hectares (10 to 22 acres) in-

troduced by the colonial government in order to supervise an intensive form of cultivation. The paysannats are characterized by soil conservation, use of fertilizers, mechanization, scientific layout, time-sequenced planting, and better harvesting. The concept of outright individual ownership of land was introduced into Zaire by the Belgians and has no basis in traditional law, which regards all land as communally owned. During the colonial period concessions of vacant state-owned land were sold to European companies and individuals, particularly the Special Committee for Katanga which received 46.5 million hectares (115 million acres) and the National Committee for Kivu which received 303,000 hectares (750,000 acres). Leased land that was not developed in the designated way reverted to the public domain. Less than 1% of the land area was occupied under customary rules of tenure. In 1966 the state cancelled all land, forest and mining concessions granted before 1960 and required all titleholders to apply for reissuance of their titles. In 1973 all foreign-owned plantations and farms were nationalized in a sweeping law. At the time of expropriation these foreign planters had freehold rights to approximately 1.49 million hectares (3.7 million acres) and concessionary rights to 1.1 million hectares (2.8 million acres).

Zairean agriculture continued to stagnate during the late 1970s as a result of the disastrous Zaireanization policies, unrealistic price controls and deterioration in transportation and marketing channels. Zaire imported 273,000 tons of cereals in 1983.

Over 80% of export crops are grown on plantations formerly owned by Europeans. Oil palm products, which account for about 42% of agricultural export earnings, and coffee, which accounts for 31%, are the two major cash crops. Rubber is the third, followed by tea and cocoa. Sugar and cotton are produced for domestic use beside small amounts of tobacco and urena, a fiber crop.

Until independence Zaire was self-sufficient in foodstuffs, but agriculture suffered more than any other sector as a result of the disorders of the 60s and now the country spends more than 60% of its foreign exchange to pay for imported foodstuffs. The predominant food crop is cassava, which is grown in all parts of the country and accounts for 22% of the total cultivated area and 40% of the area devoted to food crops. In volume of production, plantains are second and sweet potatoes third. Corn is the most important cereal crop and rice the second. Peanuts, an important protein source in Zairean diet, are grown in the savanna areas. In 1982 2,000 tractors were in use. Annual consumption of fertilizers in 1983 was 7,600 tons, or 0.8 kg (1.76 lb) per arable hectare.

The prevalence of the tsetse fly is a limiting factor in animal husbandry. Other restricting factors are the low rates of growth of domestic breeds and poor range management practices. In 1982 the livestock population consisted of 1.266 million cattle, 764,000 sheep, 2.9 million goats, 749,000 pigs and 16.268 million chickens. The best livestock breeding areas are

PRINCIPAL CROP PRODUCTION (1982)
(000 Metric tons)

Wheat	5
Rice	255
Corn	527
Oats	25
Millet	25
Potatoes	31
Sweet potatoes & yams	309
Cassava	13,173
Pulses	141
Groundnuts	323
Sesame seed	1
Cottonseed	19
Palm kernels	65
Palm oil	155
Cabbages	19
Tomatoes	30
Onions	26
Sugar cane	620
Oranges	141
Grapefruit	9
Avocados	24
Mangoes	137
Pineapples	153
Bananas	313
Plantains	1,469
Coffee	85
Cocoa beans	4
Tea	7
Tobacco	5
Kenaf	1
Cotton (lint)	10
Natural rubber	23

Shaba, Kasai plateau, Oubangui plateau and the eastern mountains. The country is not self sufficient in animal products and imports sizable quantities of meat and dairy products.

Forests cover half the total land area, but only 1.5% of the forest are worked. More than 90% of the forests are state-owned. The forests produce over 2,000 types of economically valuable wood including the limba, fuma, lobeche, wenge, lifaki, boleke, kamba, kamelala, bwana, lossasa, bonkoto and khaya. The total roundwood production in 1982 was 30.391 million cubic meters (1.073 billion cubic feet).

Fish are abundant in all lakes and rivers with the exception of Lake Kivu; over 1,000 fresh-water species have been identified. Lake fishing is done by private fishermen while ocean fishing is controlled by the state-owned Societe de Pecherie Maritime du Zaire (PEMARZA), which owns 12 trawlers and a 180-ton refrigerator ship. The total fish catch in 1982 was 100,700 metric tons, but Zaire had to import nearly 19,000 metric tons to meet home demand.

Agricultural credit is provided by Le Credit Agricole Controle (CAC).

INDUSTRY

Zaire has a large and diversified manufacturing base centered on Kinshasa and Lubumbashi. It employed 13% of the worce force, contributed 4.4% to the GDP, and its annual rate of growth during 1973-83 was -2.3%. The value added in manufacturing in 1982 was $253 million, of which agro-based products accounted for 59%, textiles for 10%, machinery and transport equipment for 5% and chemicals for 4%. The largest production gains have occurred in consumer goods, particularly processed food and clothing. It also produces supplies for the construction and mining industries. Government policy places increased emphasis on heavy industry, such as chemicals, steel, fertilizers, paper and rubber. Industrial credit is provided by the Societe Financiere de Developpement (SOFIDE) and Societe de Credit aux Classes Moyennes et a l'Industrie (SCCMI)

Zaire has one of the most industrialized economies in black Africa. Beverages (brewing, soft drinks), textiles and food (flour, sugar, vegetable oil, margarine, fish) are the major industries, followed by leather goods, tobacco, chemicals (paint), metal engineering, cement, timber and river transport equipment. Manufacturing output is almost wholly for the domestic market and is composed mainly of consumer products (66%), plus some capital goods and inputs. The industrial sector has slightly expanded since 1960 but without doing anything to cure the structural weaknesses of manufacturing. In the early 1980s factories were operating well below capacity because of extreme reluctance on the part of investors, inadequate inputs and the absence of spare parts, caused by a shortage of foreign currency and restrictions on imports. Manufacturing has become ever more tightly concentrated in certain locations. One-half of the total industrial activity is in Kinshasa, which is also the political and administrative capital, a key point of transhipment for cargo and well supplied with cheap electricity. Shaba (the main mining center), also well supplied with electric power, accounts for another 25% of the total.

Concentration on a number of branches which enjoy geographical protection (cement, glassware), are highly labor-intensive (textiles, vehicle assembly) or operate "downstream" of agriculture (tobacco, soap, sugar, timber) has not been lessened either. It reflects a failure to integrate industrial processing activities, both among themselves and with other branches of the economy, and also industry's dependence on external sources for inputs, plant and machinery, and capital, management skills and technology.

Shortly after 1965 Mobutu began injecting the government more forcefully into the working of the economy and expanding its investment portfolio. Public control is total in the fields of transportation and mining and the state also controls electric power production. In 1965 a new institute was established, called L'Institute de Gastion du Portefeuille (IGP) to manage various state enterprises. Its other functions include promotion of private investments according to general government policy, creation of or participation in new enterprises, and the management of state shares in over 500 companies. In 1969 the government enacted a new investment code establishing two systems of benefits for investors: the general system and the convention system. The transfer of profits after taxes was guaranteed as was also the repatriation of capital in the event of liquidation. The government also offered reduced taxes on reinvested profits and foreign exchange for debt service. The new code along with the government's monetary reform revived investor confidence and by 1971 foreign investment in Zaire had reached $3.5 billion. Foreign investment covered by the code was exempted from the Zaireanization measures of 1973 and 1974. The government, however, declared its intention to take 50% of the equity in all new mining ventures and to progressively Zaireanize the management of foreign-owned companies. U.S. investment in Zaire in 1980 was on the order of $250 million, primarily in oil exploration, copper mining, auto assembly, textiles, tire and battery production and hotels. Some U.S. firms were nationalized in 1974. Net direct private investment in 1983 was $331 million.

Zaire's investment policy is characterized by the predominance of major projects. There are two reasons for this, one being the political significance, internal and external, of such schemes, which express the regime's desire to present a thrusting, go-ahead image, and demonstrate its commitment to industrialization as a rapid route to development. The second reason is of an economic nature. Decisions on investment are taken at the top, without reference to a comprehensive master-plan or to any concept of financial responsibility, since the capital—Zairian public money or foreign aid—is not subject to the requirement to show a return. The small group which takes the decisions is composed of people whose income derives from their high positions in the state and profits earned as middlemen between the government and multinational corporations. These large-scale projects are mainly in energy, telecommunications, services and manufacturing. They include the Inga dam, the 1,820-km (1,130 mi) Inga–Shaba power line, the port of Banana, the Banana–Matadi rail project, the Matadi bridge, the electrification of the Matadi–Kinshasa railway, the Kinshasa–Ilebo (Shaba) rail link, a clutch of airports, the Voix du Zaire radio complex and the World Trade Center in Kinshasa, the Maluku steel works, the national cement works in Bas-Zaïre, the Géména agro-industrial complex and the Kaniama-Kasese maize project.

Despite government efforts to diversify ownership a small number of firms account for a disproportionate share of labor force, capital and output. Concentration is particularly pronounced in consumer industries. The private manufacturing sector is limited to small-scale enterprises such as agricultural processing, brickmaking and woodworking. Limited financing and technical know-how have acted as constraints on the emergence of a strong private entrepreneurial class.

ENERGY

Total energy production in Zaire in 1982 was equivalent to 2.32 million metric tons of coal and con-

sumption equivalent to 2.116 million metric tons of coal, or 70 kg (154 lb) per capita. The annual growth rates during 1973-83 were 9.1% for energy production and 1.5% energy consumption. Energy imports account for 24.6% of all merchandise imports. Apparent per capita consumption of gasoline is 7 gallons per year.

Oil was discovered offshore by the Gulf Oil Company in 1970 and first pumped into a tanker at Moanda in 1975. Production is handled by a consortium in which the Zaire government has 15% stake. Output reached 9 million barrels in 1982 —enough to meet Zaire's internal consumption needs. Total crude petroleum reserves are estimated at 110 million barrels, enough to last 12 years. The crude is refined at the 850,000 ton-refinery at Moanda run by SOZIR (Societe Zairo-Italienne de Raffinage), in which the Zaire government holds a 50% interest. Zaire has two coalfields in operation. The Lukiga Basin produces coal with a high clinker content which is not considered suitable for making coke. The Luena Basin also produces poor quality non-coking coal. Total proved reserves of the two coalfields are estimated at 720 million tons. Annual output in 1982 was 120,000 tons. The uranium deposits at Shinkolobwe, in Shaba, are estimated at between 1 and 5 million tons but production was stopped in 1961.

Zaire's main energy resource is hydroelectricity with a potential of about 103 million kilowatts. At Inga alone, on the Zaire River, near Kinshasa, there is a potential of 30,000 Mw. In 1984 total electric power production was 4.96 billion kwh. Some 74% of this power is used by the copper refining industry in Shaba. Per capita electric power output is 154 kwh.

LABOR

Of the total economically active population of 12.445 million in 1982, 73.7% were employed in agriculture and 13% in mining and manufacturing. Women made up 42.3% of the labor force. Of the total labor force, 87% worked in the subsistence sector and only 13% worked for wages. Skills are in short supply at all levels. The public sector employed over 12,000 foreign personnel at independence in 1960. All but a few have left, and it has not been possible to replace them by nationals with the same qualifications. Zaireanization of managerial and supervisory positions is official policy, but its implementation is slow and uneven.

An estimated two-thirds, at least, of Zaire's population stands outside the modern trading economy and lives mainly or wholly within a subsistence economy, based on traditional primitive farming activities.

In 1959 the total number of persons employed (wage-earners plus "free" workers, non-wage earning workers renumerated for their labor in kind) in all sectors of the modern economy (production and services) was estimated at 1,473,000, but by 1977 the figure had fallen to approximately 928,000. The largest branch of activity is modern plantation agriculture, which accounted for more than one-quarter of those employed in 1977. It was followed by education (23%), other services in the public sector (15%) and industry (12%). The complement of free plantation workers shrank by a startling 80%, which has naturally had serious effects on rural cash incomes, and goes some way toward explaining the lack of development in the interior, the drift of population to the towns and the return to a subsistence economy. The number of wage-earners employed in industry has stagnated or may even have contracted. Employment in the public sector, on the other hand, rose by about 150% between 1959 and 1977. The structure of employment, therefore, has changed. The public sector, which in 1959 engaged 25% of those in employment, accounted for 39% in 1977 (including 24% as teachers). In broader terms, more than one-half of the registered jobs in 1977 were in non-productive sectors (administration and services), compared with less than one-fifth before independence.

Labor conditions are regulated by the comprehensive Code de Travail of 1967, which covers all workers except public servants and the military. The workweek is eight hours a day, six days a week with strict limits on overtime. Health and safety conditions are regulated by Labor Inspectorates. The Code also established a National Employment Service and a National Labor Council to study wages, manpower and welfare needs and set up a National Vocational Preparation Institute.

Worker rights are protected by law, but the fact that such a large percentage of the work force is in the unofficial sector limits the effectiveness of those laws. The minimum age for employment in Zaire is 14 years. However, many children younger than 14 engage in various income-earning activities and are often a major source of family income. The same is true with regard to conditions of work. Workers employed in the public and organized private sector have generally acceptable conditions of work: working hours are set by law and collective bargaining and do not exceed 48 hours a week; workers enjoy a full 24-hour rest day per week, and many have a 48 hour weekend; paid holidays and vacations are required by law and are included in all labor contracts; and workplaces are required to meet minimum health standards set by law. While wages are generally above the minimum wage, that minimum, by itself, is insufficient to provide a decent living for a worker. In the official private sector, benefits often make up more than half of the total wage package, but in the public sector total remuneration does not provide a decent living. The results are corruption and workers taking on second jobs, often in the unregulated informal sector.

The minimum legal wage in 1983 ranged from Z20 per day for an unskilled worker to Z30 per day for a highly skilled worker. Wages have not kept pace with the high inflation rates and, by 1983, a wage-earner's purchasing power was less than 5% of its 1960 value. Thus, wages do not suffice to maintain an average-sized family of six people; such a family would need at least Z1,900 per month to maintain an above-poverty level of existence. The situation is no better outside Kinshasa, where prices are not necessarily lower but wages are. To maintain minimum living standards, workers supplement their pay packet with other alternative sources of income: bribery and theft in the case of those in public employment, prostitution in the case of women, and petty crafts and casual jobs in the case of others. The calorie and protein requirements of the majority of town dwellers are no longer being met, leading to a dramatic increase in morbidity and mortality. Agricultural prices, which provide the bulk of peasants' incomes, are also low.

Urban unemployment, a result of the quadrupling of urban population since independence, is a more socially catastrophic and politically dangerous phenomenon than rural underemployment. Although precise statistics are lacking, it is estimated that more than 50% of urban males are unemployed (women constitute only an insignificant proportion of wage-earners). In Kinshasa unemployment is upwards of 40%, and in the larger nonmining towns, the situation is worse with some reporting an unemployment rate of 70 to 80%.

The sole labor union organization is the official Union Nationale des Travailleurs Zairois (UNTZ) which is affiliated to the Mouvement Populaire de la Revolution. Communists are excluded from the Union. UNTZ is organized regionally by occupations represented by affiliated unions. The politicization of the UNTZ has made it, in effect, an agency for carrying out the political decisions of the government. The over 800,000 workers employed in the public and private sectors are members of the organization and pay dues to it. However, about 55% of Zairian workers are employed in unregulated small commerce and agriculture and are not covered by the union. The leaders of the union, who are also party members, ensure that relations with international labor organizations are kept consistent with general Zairian foreign policy. The union participates actively in the International Labor Organization and the Organization of African Trade Union Unity, and maintains relations with various foreign trade union confederations. Basic collective bargaining procedures are outlined in the 1967 Labor Code. Strikes are permitted but all conciliation and arbitration procedures have to be exhausted before a strike can be called.

FOREIGN TRADE

The foreign commerce of Zaire consisted in 1984 of exports of $1.583 billion and imports of $1.098 billion giving a favorable trade balance of $485 million. Based on 1975=100, the import price index in 1981 was 186, the export price index 138, and the terms of trade (export prices divided by import prices × 100) 74.

Of the imports, consumer goods constituted 33.3% (of which food 16.4%), petroleum 24.6% and primary manufactures 19.5%. Of the exports, copper con-

FOREIGN TRADE INDICATORS (1984)

Annual Growth Rate, Imports:	–13.7% (1973-83)
Annual Growth Rate, Exports:	–8.7% (1973-83)
Ratio of Exports to Imports:	59:41
Exports per capita:	$48
Imports per capita:	$33
Balance of Trade:	$485 million
Ratio of International Reserves to Imports (in months)	—
Exports as % of GDP:	31.0
Imports as % of GDP:	38.7
Value of Manufactured Exports:	—
Commodity Concentration:	92.7%

Direction of Trade (%)

	Imports	Exports
EEC	54.0	72.0
U.S.	—	3.6
Industrialized Market Economies	74.7	91.9
East European Economies	—	0.3
High Income Oil Exporters	0.2	0.5
Developing Economies	24.4	7.5

Composition of Trade (%)

	Imports	Exports
Food	20.3	18.8
Agricultural Raw Materials	2.7	2.8
Fuels	3.3	0.1
Ores & Minerals	6.5	73.1
Manufactured Goods	66.2	3.2
of which Chemicals	13.5	0.1
of which Machinery	33.6	1.1

stituted 54.7%, cobalt 25.4%, coffee 10.1% and diamonds 5.3%. The major import sources are: Belgium-Luxembourg 22.0%, France 13.2%, the United States 10.3%, West Germany 10.1%, Japan 6.3% and Italy 5.2%. The major export destinations are: the United States 36.2%, Belgium-Luxembourg 31.2%, France 6.3% and West Germany 5.4%.

The Kinshasa International Trade Fair is held annually at the capital and is a major African trade event.

TRANSPORTATION & COMMUNICATIONS

Railways and waterways are the most important sectors of the transportation system and are controlled and coordinated by the government. The total length of railways is 5,254 km (3,263 mi) including 679 km (421 mi) of electrified line. The main line runs from Lubumbashi to Matadi via Kinshasa. International connections running to Dar-es-Salaam and Lobito link Zaire's railroads with the Zambian, Zimbabwean, Mozambican and South African systems. The railway network within Zaire is divided into four different zones: north, south, east, and west, disposing of 1,023 km (635 mi), 2,642 km (1,529 mi), 1,087 km (675 mi) and 502 km (312 mi), respectively of track.

The most important zones in terms of tonnage transported and tonnage per kilometer are the south and west zones. The north, south, and east zones are run by the state railway company, Societe Nationale des Chemins de Fer Zairois (SNCZ), while the Office

National des Transports du Zaire (ONATRA) runs the west zone. SNCZ and ONATRA together own approximately 184 locomotives, 117 shunters, and 8,994 units of rolling stock. A substantial number of the locomotives are over 20 years old and are liable to frequent breakdowns. Rail traffic in 1982 consisted of 389 million passenger-km and 1.772 billion net-ton-km. There is also a small pipeline 390 km (242 mi) long for refined petroleum products.

The total length of inland waterways is 16,400 km (10,184 mi). The River Zaire is navigable for 1,600 km (993 mi) from Bukama to Kongolo, from Kindu to Ubudnu, from Kisangani to Kinshasa and from Matadi to the sea. River transportation is controlled for the most part by ONATRA. However, private competition, in the form both of small shipping companies and of industrial and agricultural producers' own shipping transport, accounts for over 20% of the market share and is increasing. ONATRA's operational fleet in 1982 consisted of 280 barges, 255 light barges, 85 tugboats, and 62 passenger vessels. The country has only two deep-water harbors, Boma, the old capital of the country, and Matadi. Seaborne traffic at these ports in 1982 consisted of 2,358,000 metric tons. There are four important inland river ports: Kinshasa, Mbandaka, Kisangani and Ilebo. The national merchant shipping company is Compagnie Maritime Zairoise, which was nationalized in 1973. In 1982 the merchant fleet had 34 vessels with a gross registered tonnage of 133,300. The port of Matadi is administered by the Office d'Exploitation des Transports au Zaire (OTRAZ)

Road transport plays a secondary role in Zaire. There are 145,050 km (90,076 mi) of roads, of which 2,350 km (1,459 mi) are paved. In 1982 the number of passenger vehicles was 89,471 and that of commercial vehicles 16,807. Per capita vehicle ownership was 2.7 cars per 1,000 population.

The national airline is Air Zaire, which operates 57 aircraft which flew 8.3 million km (5.1 million mi) and carried 378,000 passengers in 1982. The country has three international airports at Kinshasa (Ndjili), Lubumbashi (Luano) and Kisangani, 316 other airfields, of which 280 are usable, 23 had permanent-surface runways, and three have runways over 2,500 meters (8,000 ft).

In 1984 the total number of telephones in the country was 30,300, or 0.1 per 100 inhabitants.

In 1983 351 post offices handled 60,860,000 pieces of mail, and 234,000 telegrams. Per capita volume of mail was 1.8 pieces. There is a ground satellite communications station at Mboma-Mbomu, near Kinshasa. There are 804 telex subscriber lines.

In 1982, 24,000 tourists visited Zaire generating receipts of $23 million. There are 5,000 hotel beds and the average length of stay is 3.8 days.

MINING

The copper deposits of Shaba are among the richest in the world; the province also produces between one-half and two-thirds of the world's supply of cobalt. Industrial diamond mines in Kasai account for almost 75% of the total produced in the non-Communist world. Zaire is the sixth largest producer of copper, the largest producer of cobalt and industrial diamonds, and the 10th largest producer of zinc. Mineral exports account for 87% of Zaire's export revenues. Zaire's greatly increased dependence on mineral exports, and the greater relative predominance of copper and cobalt, make the country more vulnerable than ever to international market conditions. Mining contributed 17% of the GDP during 1970-81, although it employed only 10% of the labor force. Copper is mined exclusively by the state-owned Generale des Carrieres et des Mines (GECAMINES), which took over the assets of the Belgian Union Miniere du Haut Katanga in 1966. The two other major copper mining firms are Societe Developpement Industriel et Mines du Zaire and Societe Miniere de Tenke-Fungarume.

MINERAL PRODUCTION (1983) (metric tons)		
Copper Ore	metric tons	465,792
Tin Concentrates	metric tons	2,468 (1981)
Manganese Ore	metric tons	4,000 (1982)
Coal	metric tons	139,506 (1980)
Zinc Concentrates	metric tons	69,500 (1981)
Cobalt Ore	metric tons	5,370
Cadmium	metric tons	308
Tungsten	metric tons	134 (1980)
Industrial Diamonds	'000 carats	8,001 (1980)
Gem Diamonds	'000 carats	2,234 (1980)
Silver	kilogrammes	78,825 (1980)
Gold	kilogrammes	1,117 (1980)

DEFENSE

The defense structure is headed by the president of the republic, who is also the defense minister. Control is exercised through the Military High Command.

The main source of military manpower is voluntary enlistment, but the government attempts to achieve an ethnic balance through controlled recruitment.

The total strength of the armed forces is 48,000 including Gendarmerie of 22,000 (1.3 armed persons per 1,000 civilians).

ARMY:

Personnel: 22,000

Organization: 3 military regions; 1 infantry division consisting of 1 armored brigade and 2 infantry brigades; 1 special forces division consisting of 1 parachute brigade; 1 special force (commando/counterinsurgency) brigade; 1 presidential guard brigade

Equipment: 50 tanks; 150 armored combat vehicles; 129 armored personnel carriers; 88 guns/howitzers; mortars; antitank rocket launchers; air defense guns

NAVY:

Personnel: 1,500 (including 600 marines)

Units: 4 fast attack craft; 46 patrol craft

AIR FORCE:

Personnel: 2,500

Organization & Equipment: 40 combat aircraft; 1 fighter squadron; 3 counterinsurgency squadrons; 1 transport wing; 1 helicopter squadron; 29 trainers

Air Bases: Kinshasa, Kisangani, Lubumbashi, Luluabourg, Mbandaka, Kamina, Likasi and Kolwezi.

Annual military expenditures in 1983 were $139.654 million, which constituted 1.5% of the GNP and 4.3% of the national budget, $2 per capita, $3,231 per soldier and $36 per sq km of national territory. Despite heavy military aid and arms transfers from the West, the Zairean army has a poor track record. It has fared badly against Angola-backed Shaba dissidents in both 1977 and 1978 and was saved from total disaster by French and Belgian paratroopers and allied African forces. Ethnicity is one of the influences contributing to the poor combat performance. The armed forces are heavily concentrated on the southern border and in the Shaba province.

U.S. military aid from 1946 through 1983 was $183.8 million. Belgian aid has been slightly over $1 million a year. An organization known as WIGMO (Western International Ground Maintenance Organization, believed to be a U.S. covert operation) has kept the air force in operation and provided the pilots. Arms purchases abroad during 1973-83 totaled $480 million, of which $50 million was supplied by France, $30 million by the United States, $50 million by Italy and $40 million by China.

EDUCATION

The national literacy rate is 55% (73.6% for males and 36.7% for females).

The 1964 constitution states that all Zaireans have "the right to education." The state provides theoretically free, universal and compulsory education for six years from the ages 6 to 12. The 1978 school enrollment ratio in the primary age group of 6 to 11 was 90% and in the secondary age group of 12 to 17 23%, for a combined enrollment ratio of 60%. Girls represent 42% of primary school enrollment, and 27% of secondary school enrollment. University enrollment of women is less than 5%. Adult education programs are particularly directed toward women, over 64% of whom are illiterate.

The academic year runs from September to July. The medium of instruction is Kikongo, Tshiluba, Lingala or Swahili in the primary grades and French in the secondary and university levels. Schooling consists of 12 years with six years of primary education divided into three two-year sections: elementary, middle, and terminal. Students are not divided into formal grades at the first level. The secondary program consists of a lower and an upper cycle. The lower, or orientation program, lasts for two years and is followed by a four-year upper cycle, which provides two options: a long humanities cycle or a short vocational cycle which accounts for 14% of secondary enrollment. The orientation cycle terminates in a diploma called a brevet and the upper humanities cycle in a diploma or certificate. The school system includes two types of schools: state schools and schools administered by religious congregations but subsidized by the government. There are also a few unsubsidized private schools. Over 92% of the primary and secondary school population attend subsidized schools, over 70% of which are run by the Roman Catholic Church. In 1982 the school system consisted of 7,909 primary schools and 2,511 secondary schools.

There is a critical shortage of trained teachers. Only 24.4% of primary school teachers have diplomas. The national teacher-pupil ratio is 1:41 at the primary level and 1:23 at the secondary level. The Compulsory Civic Service was instituted in 1966 to create a pool of trained personnel by making a two-year teaching stint mandatory for all students who received a license after 1966.

The education budget in 1980 was Z947,891,000 which was 32.3% of the national budget and 5.8% of the GNP (as against the 4% recommended by UNESCO). The per capita educational expenditure was $11 in 1982.

EDUCATIONAL ENROLLMENT (1980)			
	Schools	Teachers	Students
First Level	7,909	132,759	3,919,395
Second Level	2,511	42,212	611,349
Vocational	20	N.A.	192,329
Third Level (1974)	9	2,782	28,430

All universities in Zaire were reorganized and nationalized in 1971 as the National University with three campuses at Kisangani, Kinshasa and Lubumbashi, with a total enrollment of 28,430 students. University enrollment was 86 per 100,000 inhabitants.

In 1982 Zairean students in universities abroad numbered 4,011 of whom 177 were in the United States, 1,468 in France, 1,545 in Belgium and 136 in West Germany.

Zaire's contribution to world scientific authorship was .0070% (U.S.=42%) and its world rank in this respect was 106th.

LEGAL SYSTEM

The basis of Zairean law is the Belgian Penal Code with certain modifications to provide for African traditions.

The court system consists of the Supreme Court of Justice, three courts of appeal at Kinshasa, Kisangani and Lubumbashi, first degree tribunals in each region and the city of Kinshasa, district tribunals in each district and city, and peace tribunals in each city and territory. The constitution also provides for a Constitutional Court to rule on the constitutionality of laws. Judges and public prosecutors are appointed by the president of the republic on the advice of the superior council of the magistrature. They are irremovable but may be transferred.

Defendants are guaranteed by the constitution the right to a public trial and defense counsel. In practice, however, most citizens are not aware of those rights, and there are insufficient lawyers in Zaire to provide adequate counsel to most defendants. When available, defense counsel generally function freely and without coercion from the government. Most defendants who are aware of their rights avail themselves of the right to appeal. Decisions of the court of state security involving national security, armed robbery, and smuggling are not subject to appeal (appeal to the Court of Cassation is permitted only on questions of law, not of fact), although all other procedural protections of the criminal code do apply. Military court procedures also do not provide for appeal. While military courts generally try only cases involving military personnel, in time of emergency or during military operations (as was done in the Moba-Kalemie area in late 1984), the president can suspend civilian courts and transfer jurisdiction over all cases to military courts.

The fairness of trials is uneven. Poorly paid magistrates are known to accept bribes, and it is essentially those unable to pay such bribes who are subject to the full rigor of the judicial system. All judges are members of the sole political party and are subject to party discipline. The result is that, while judges are nominally independent and in fact perform their function without political interference in the great majority of cases, in sensitive or highly politicized cases the judges operate under instructions from the executive or security forces.

The corrections system consists of three tiers: central prisons, district prisons and territorial prisons under the Department of Prisons.

LAW ENFORCEMENT

The national police force functions under an inspector general with five divisions: an Intelligence Exploitation Service and four directorates. There are nine detachments of varying strength, one assigned to each of the eight regions and one to the national capital. The strength of the internal security forces was 22,000 (in 1969), or 2.4 per 1,000 working inhabitants.

The National Records Center is in charge of sensitive national security work under the immediate control of President Mobutu. It has broad and undefined powers and maintains its own network of communications.

No statistics on crime have been published since 1959. Although there has been a progressive restoration of law and order since 1965, crimes of all types have increased appreciably. Crimes with the highest incidence are armed banditry and diamond smuggling.

HEALTH

In 1980 Zaire had 942 hospitals with 78,938 hospital beds, or 1 bed per 352 inhabitants. The total number of physicians was 1,900, or 1 physician per 15,065 inhabitants, 54 dentists and 4,097 nursing personnel. Of the hospitals 40.9% were state-run, 44.6% were run by private nonprofit agencies, and 14.5% were run by private for-profit agencies. The admissions/discharge rate was 474 per 10,000 inhabitants, the bed occupancy rate was 71.6% and the average length of hospital stay was 12 days. Only 16% of the population have access to safe water.

```
PRINCIPAL HEALTH INDICATORS (1984)
Crude Death Rate: 15.8 per 1,000
Decline in Death Rate: –32.6% (1965-83)
Life Expectancy at Birth: 48.3 (Males): 51.7 (Females)
Infant Mortality Rate: 116.6 per 1,000 Live Births
Child Death Rate (Ages 1-4) per 1,000: 20
```

In 1982, health expenditures constituted 3.0% of the national budget and $1.20 per capita.

FOOD

The Zairean diet is limited to a few staple foods such as manioc, bananas, sweet potatoes, peanuts and papaya among forest peoples and rice, corn and millet among urban peoples. Meat is in short supply, milk is seldom consumed, and fish are eaten mainly in towns. The per capita food intake is 33.4 grams of protein per day and 2,133 calories per day, which falls below the WHO recommendation of 2,600 calories, 29 grams of fats and 364 grams of carbohydrates.

MEDIA & CULTURE

Four daily newspapers are published in Zaire, of which two are published in the capital, one in Lubumbashi and one in Kisangani. All are published in French. The total circulation is 45,000, or 1.3 per 1,000 inhabitants. Six weekly or fortnightly journals are also published, all in French. The periodical press consists of 43 titles. Annual newsprint consumption was 1,400 tons or 48 kg (105.8 lb) per 1,000 inhabitants in 1982.

Freedom of the press is implicitly guaranteed in the constitution, but newspapers that stray from the official line are frequently suspended. In terms of press freedom Zaire is scaled at −.45 (on an index with +4 as the maximum and −4 as the minimum).

The official news agency is Agence Zaire Presse (AZAP) based in Kinshasa with 15 regional correspondents and a foreign bureau at Brussels. A second agency, DIA (Documentation and Information for and about Africa), founded by the Catholic Church in 1956, functions as an independent private company.

In 1982 there were eight major book publishers of whom the largest were the Centre Protestant d'Edi-tions et de Diffusion (CEDI) and Presses Universitaire du Zaire. Annual title output in 1982 was 194, or 6 per 1 million inhabitants. Zaire adheres to the Berne Convention and the Florence Agreement.

The state-owned La Voix du Zaire operates 16 transmitters of which three are medium-wave (total 1,200 kw), 12 are short-wave and one is FM. Three of the stations are located in Kinshasa; they are on the air for 23 hours a day. The provincial stations broadcast for 13 hours a day. An international service, known as the Voice of African Brotherhood, is broadcast from Lubumbashi for 42 hours a week. In 1982 there were about 2,500,000 radio receivers, or 76 per 1,000 inhabitants.

Television was introduced in 1966. Two stations, one in Kinshasa and the other in Lubumbashi, broadcast for a total of 46 hours a week. The total number of television receivers was 11,000, or 0.4 per 1,000 inhabitants.

In 1980 there were 18 cinemas in the country with a total of 23,400 seats or 1 per 1,000 inhabitants. The annual attendance was 1.6 million, or 0.1 per inhabitant.

In 1980 there were 436 public and institutional libraries in the country, of which the largest was the National Library at Kinshasa. Public libraries are also located in each of the regional capitals. Per capita there are 10 volumes per 1,000 inhabitants.

There are 12 museums with a reported annual attendance of 100,000, and 12 nature preservation sites.

There are three theaters, all in the capital, serving four professional companies and 28 amateur troupes.

SOCIAL WELFARE

A social security system was established in 1961 with the formation of Institut National de Securite Sociale (INSS). The social security fund is derived from progressive deductions from the wages of employees and contributions from employers. Benefits include compensations for occupational injuries, unemployment insurance, family allowances, and pensions. The number of covered workers is estimated at 800,000.

GLOSSARY

bula matari: literally, he who can break the rocks. Nickname of Belgian governors and administrators.

cheffery: chiefdom ruled by a traditional chief.

circumscription: a traditional subdistrict; also an electoral district.

etuka: a property-controlling group within a tribe.

evolue: formerly, a Congolese who had evolved through education or assimilation and accepted European values and patterns of behavior.

immatriculation: process by which evolues were given the same legal status as Europeans.

limba: principal hardwood of Zaire, used for plywood and veneers.

ngunzism: indigenous prophetic movements, as Kimbanguism, which combined Christian and tribal religious forms centered around a black prophet. From ngunza, prophet.

paysannat: a planned native agricultural settlement.

CHRONOLOGY (from 1960)

1960— Belgium grants independence to the Congo; replaces colonial charter with the Loi Fondamentale establishing a republican and parliamentary form of government.... In national elections contested by over 100 parties, the Mouvement National Congolaise wins a plurality; Patrice Lumumba, leader of the MNC, forms a government with Joseph Kasavubu, president of the Alliance des Bakongo, as president of the republic.... Fighting erupts between ethnic groups; the province of Katanga declares independence under Moise Tshombe, head of the Confederation des Associations du Katanga.... Congolese soldiers mutiny; Belgian commanders are dismissed; Victor Lundula, Lumumba's uncle, is appointed new commanding officer of the Congolese National Army (ANC) with Joseph Mobutu as chief of staff.... Belgian paratroopers land in Katanga to aid secessionists.... U.N. Security Council, responding to a Congo government request, authorizes dispatch of U.N. troops to the country; Belgians withdraw; Albert Kalondji proclaims independence of South Kasai.... Lumumba declares martial law, arrests opponents, and requests Soviet aid; Lumumba is dismissed by Kasavubu and in turn dismisses Kasavubu; parliament refuses to confirm dismissals; Mobutu seizes power, establishes a college of commissioners made up of recent university graduates, orders expulsion of Soviet diplomats.... Lumumbists organize counter government at Stanleyville; Lumumba attempts to flee to Stanleyville, but is arrested, transferred to Katanga, where he is mysteriously assassinated;

1961— College of commissioners is dissolved; provisional government is formed by Joseph Ileo.... U.N. Security Council resolution calls for end to anarchy and removal of foreign personnel.... Tananarive agreement between the Leopoldville government and the secessionist governments of Katanga and Kasai establishes a confederal government.... A second conference at Coquilhatville establishes a federal form of government.... Parliament reopens under U.N. protection; coalition government, headed by Cyrille Adoula as prime minister, is approved by parliament.... Diplomatic relations with Belgium are reestablished.... U.N. troops move against Katanga; Dag Hammarskjold dies in air crash en route to Ndola in Northern Rhodesia for talks with Tshombe.

1962— Katanga secession is ended by Kitona agreement.... Stanleyville government is dissolved; Antoine Gizenga and Kalondji are arrested.

1963— President Kasavubu declares state of emergency.... Tshombe is appointed Congo's fourth prime minister.

1964— Constitution is drawn up by a commission headed by Joseph Ileo with U.N. assistance.... The country's name changed from Republic of Congo to Democratic Republic of Congo.... Government moves against two rebel movements: the Kwilu Rebellion under Pierre Mulele and the Eastern Rebellion; rebels capture Stanleyville; Katangan gendarmerie and white mercenaries spearhead attacks against rebel strongholds; rebels under Christophe Gbenye use white hostages as a means of halting government forces.... Stanleyville is retaken in a bloody offensive operation.... U.N. forces leave.

1965— Tshombe wins majority in new parliamentary elections.... Tshombe is dismissed by Kasavubu; Evariste Kimba is appointed premier; parliament refuses to confirm Kimba.... As the parliament remains deadlocked, Gen. Mobutu seizes power for a second time and names a government of national unity with Leonard Mulamba as premier.

1966— Mobutu abolishes parliament and assumes legislative powers.... Premier Mulamba is dismissed.... Number of provinces is reduced from 21 to 12.... Names of Congolese cities with foreign names are changed.... Former prime minister Kimba is executed.... New mutiny by Katangan and white mercenary troops breaks out in Katanga.... New copper mining company is formed to replace the Union Miniere du Haut-Katanga.... Corps des Volontaires de la Republique is launched.

1967— New constitution is promulgated.... All political parties are outlawed; Mouvement Populaire de la Revolution is founded as the country's sole political party.... Union Miniere is nationalized.... Plane carrying Tshombe is hijacked over Algeria.... Mercenaries launch rebellion in the east and gain initial successes, but rebellion collapses and rebels flee to Rwanda.... Manifesto of Nsele is issued embodying the goals of the MPR.... Zaire is introduced as the new unit of currency.... The country's sole labor union, Union Nationale des Travailleurs Zairois, is launched.

1968— Relations with Rwanda and Congo (Brazzaville) are suspended.

1969— Patrice Lumumba is declared a national hero.

1970— Mobutu is elected president in first presidential election.

1971— Name of Congo is changed to Zaire and the name of River Congo is changed to River Zaire.... National University is founded through amalgamation of three existing universities.

1972— National Executive Council is formed to replace former cabinet.... Provinces are renamed as regions and districts as subregions.

1973— All foreign-owned firms, plantations and mining companies are nationalized.

1974— The constitution is revised to make the MPR synonymous with the state.

1975— The economy falters and government promulgates austerity measures.

1976— Zaire defaults on foreign loans. . . . Currency is devalued.

1977— Guerrillas of the Congolese National Liberation Front based in Angola invade Shaba province with Cuban aid, straining relations with Soviet Union; Zaire receives aid from Morocco, Sudan, Uganda and Western nations in drive against rebels.

1978— Guerrillas of the Congolese National Liberation Front invade Shaba again through Zambia and occupy Kolwezi and Mutshalaha; rebels are reportedly backed by Angola, Cuba and Soviet Union; Nearly 400 whites are reported killed or missing; French and Belgian troops launch successful rescue operations.

1979— President Neto of Angola visits Kinshasa and reaches agreement with Mobutu regarding creation of a supervisory body to prevent guerrilla operations across the common border.

1980— Pope John Paul II visits Zaire signaling Zaire's return to traditional relations with the Vatican.

1982— Zaire restablishes diplomatic relations with Israel.... Zaire hosts francophone African summit in Kinshasa.

BIBLIOGRAPHY (from 1970)

Bustin, Edouard, *Lunda under Belgian Rule: The Politics of Ethnicity* (Cambridge, Mass., 1975).

Callaghy, Thomas M., *The State-Society Struggle: Zaire in Comparative Perspective* (New York, 1984).

Gran, Guy, *Zaire, The Political Economy of Underdevelopment* (New York, 1979).

Kanza, Thomas, *Conflict in the Congo: The Rise and Fall of Lumumba* (Harmondsworth, England, 1972).

Lefever, Ernest W., *Spear and Scepter: Army, Police, and Politics in Tropical Africa* (Washington, D.C., 1970).

Lemarchand, Rene, *Political Awakening in the Belgian Congo* (Westport, Conn., 1982).

Markowitz, Marvin D., *Cross & Sword: The Political Role of Christian Missions in Belgian Congo, 1908-1960* (Stanford, Calif., 1973).

Schatzberg, Micheal C., *Politics & Class in Zaire: Bureacracy, Business & Beer in Lisala* (New York, 1980).

Vengroff, Richard, *Development Administration at the Local Level: The Case of Zaire* (Syracuse, N.Y., 1983).

Weissman, Stephen R., *American Foreign Policy in the Congo, 1960-1964.* (Ithaca, N.Y., 1974).

Williame, Jean-Claude, *Patrimonialism and Political Change in the Congo* (Stanford, Calif., 1972).

Young, Crawford and Thomas Turner, *The Rise and Decline of the Zairian State* (Madison, Wis., 1985).

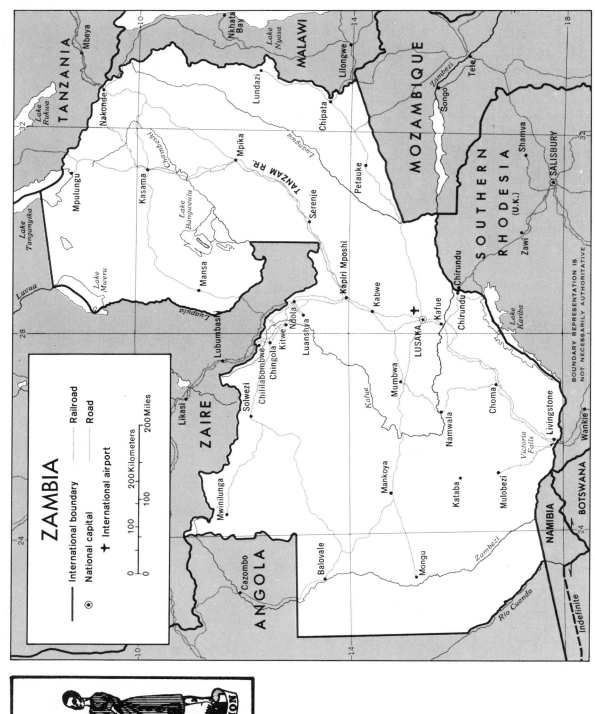

ZAMBIA

— International boundary
— Railroad
⊛ National capital
— Road
✈ International airport

200 Kilometers
200 Miles

TANZANIA
Mbeya
Lake Rukwa
Nakonde
Mpulungu
Lake Tanganyika
Luvua
Lake Mweru
Lungu
Likasi
Lubumbashi
ZAIRE
Solwezi
Chililabombwe
Chingola
Kitwe
Luanshya
Ndola
Mwinilunga
Cazombo
ANGOLA
Balovale
Mongu
Kataba
Mankoya
Mulobezi
NAMIBIA
Rio Cuando
Indefinite
BOTSWANA
Wankie
Livingstone
Victoria Falls
Lake Kariba
Choma
Namwala
Zambezi
Mumbwa
Kafue
Chirundu
Kafue
LUSAKA
Kabwe
Kapiri Mposhi
SOUTHERN RHODESIA (U.K.)
SALISBURY
Zawi
Shamva
Songo
Tete
Zambezi
MOZAMBIQUE
Petauke
Serenje
TANZAM R.R.
Mpika
Luangwa
Chipata
Lundazi
Lilongwe
MALAWI
Lake Nyasa
Nkhata Bay
Kasama
Lake Bangweulu
Mansa
Chambeshi
Luapula

BOUNDARY REPRESENTATION IS NOT NECESSARILY AUTHORITATIVE

ONE ZAMBIA ONE NATION

ZAMBIA

BASIC FACT SHEET

OFFICIAL NAME: Republic of Zambia

ABBREVIATION: ZA

CAPITAL: Lusaka

HEAD OF STATE: President Kenneth David Kaunda (from 1964)

HEAD OF GOVERNMENT: Prime Minister Kebby Musokotwane (from 1985)

NATURE OF GOVERNMENT: One-party modified democracy

POPULATION: 6,770,000 (1985)

AREA: 752,618 sq km (290,586 sq mi)

ETHNIC MAJORITY: Bantu

LANGUAGE: English (official); Bemba (lingua franca)

RELIGION: Animism and Christianity

UNIT OF CURRENCY: Kwacha ($1=K2.237, July 1985)

NATIONAL FLAG: Green field with a tricolor at the lower corner of the fly, under an orange flying eagle. The tricolor consists of red, black, and orange vertical stripes.

NATIONAL EMBLEM: A shield made up of wavy narrow black and white vertical lines, called pallets, symbolizing the Victoria Falls. The shield is flanked by an African man in a green bush shirt and shorts and an African woman in a red traditional dress. They stand on a green mound on which appear a zebra (for game), a shafthead (for mining), and an ear of corn (for agriculture). Above the emblem an orange eagle is perched on a crossed pickaxe and mattocklike hoe. The national motto appears on a scroll on the base, "One Zambia, One Nation"

NATIONAL ANTHEM: "Stand and Sing for Zambia"

NATIONAL HOLIDAYS: October 24 (National Day, Independence Day); January 1 (New Year's Day); First Monday in May (Labor Day); May 24 (Commonwealth Day); May 25 (African Freedom Day); First Monday in July (Heroes' Day); First Tuesday in July (Unity Day); August 9 (Youth Day); Christian festivals include Christmas, Boxing Day, Good Friday, Easter Monday and Whit Monday

NATIONAL CALENDAR: Gregorian

PHYSICAL QUALITY OF LIFE INDEX: 48 (up from 28 in 1976) (On an ascending scale with 100 is the maximum. U.S. 95).

DATE OF INDEPENDENCE: October 24, 1964

DATE OF CONSTITUTION: August 1973

WEIGHTS & MEASURES: The metric system is in force.

LOCATION & AREA

Zambia is a landlocked country located in southern Africa between the Zambezi River and the southern rim of the Congo Basin, extending 1,206 km (749 mi) E to W and 815 km (506 mi) N to S with a total land area of 752,618 sq km (290,586 sq mi).

Zambia shares its total international boundary of 5,627 km (3,496 mi) with eight countries: Mozambique (424 km, 263 mi); Zimbabwe (739 km, 459 mi); Botswana (100 meters, 109.4 yards); South-West Africa (203 km, 126 mi); Angola (1,086 km, 675 mi); Zaire (2,107 km, 1,309 mi); Tanzania (322 km, 200 mi) and Malawi (746 km, 464 mi). The border with Tanzania is based on an agreement between the United Kingdom and Germany in 1901. Except for the border with Rhodesia, which follows the Zambezi River and Lake Kariba, most of the other borders are arbitrary lines reflecting territorial adjustments in colonial times. There are no current border disputes.

The capital is Lusaka, with a 1980 population of 538,469. The other major urban centers are Kitwe (in-cluding Kalulushi, 314,794), Ndola (282,439), Chingola (including Chililabombwe, formerly Bancroft, 145,869), Mufulira (149,778), Luanshya (184,000), Kabwe (143,635) and Livingstone (71,987).

The Zambian plateau is a mosaic of savanna, swamps and deserts, with five distinct topographic regions: the central highlands, including the Copperbelt sloping toward the Kafue Basin toward the west and the Zambezi Valley toward the east with an average elevation of 1,230 meters (4,000 ft); the western plains consisting of the swamps of Barotseland, the flat Liuwa and Mulonga Plains and semiarid deserts; the Rift Valley, represented by the Luangwa-Luano Trench together with the Zambezi lowlands; the Muchinga uplands northwest of the Luangwa Valley; and Northeastern Zambia, including the Bangweulu Swamps, part of the Luapula Basin, and the Mweru-Wantipa fault zone lying between Lakes Mweru and Tanganyika.

The country's main drainage system is the River Zambezi with its three major tributaries, the Kabompo, the Kafue and the Luangwa Rivers. Near

Livingstone, the Zambezi drops down the Victoria Falls, 107 meters high and 1.6 km broad (350 ft high and 1 mile wide). At flood season, the flow rate is 3,785,410 liters (1 million gallons) per second. Downstream, the river enters Lake Kariba, the world's largest man-made lake. The northern regions are drained by three rivers, the Chambesi, the Luapula and the Luvua, all of which eventually flow into the Atlantic through the Zaire River. Zambian rivers are noted for their great seasonal variations in flow and frequent rapids and falls.

There are three large natural lakes: the Bangweulu, the Mweru and the Tanganyika, all in the north. Of these, only Lake Bangweulu is entirely within the national territory.

WEATHER

Zambia is part of a broad belt of temperate highlands with a mild tropical climate. There are three sharply defined seasons: cool and dry from May to August, hot and dry from September to November and warm and wet from December to April. A second period of high temperatures occurs in April and May.

Temperatures are closely related to altitude. Nationwide, the temperatures range from 16°C to 27°C (60°F to 80°F) in the cool season and from 27°C to 38°C (80°F to 100°F) in the hot season. There are occasional frosts in winter.

The pattern of rainfall is fairly uniform. The northern parts of the plateau have an annual precipitation of between 100 and 140 cm (40 and 50 in.). It decreases southward to about 51 cm (20 in.). Lusaka in the middle receives an average rainfall of about 76 cm (30 in.). For half the year, during the cool season, there is no rain anywhere in the country.

Heavy tropical storms occur at the start of the rainy season, and there are thunderstorms during October.

POPULATION

The population of Zambia was estimated in 1985 at 6,770,000 on the basis of the last official census, held in 1980, when the population was 5,679,808. The population is expected to reach 10.9 million by 2000 and 20.7 million by 2020. The annual growth rate is 3.31%, on the basis of an annual birthrate of 48.1 per 1,000.

One-third of the population lives along what is known as the line-of-rail belt in the central highlands, in the adjacent high plains area, and in the Copperbelt. Population is also dense in the Mozambique and Malawi border areas in the southeast, in the Lake Bangweulu-Luapula complex of swamps and islands in the northern region and in the flats of the Zambezi River in the western part of the country. In contrast, parts of Barotse and Northwestern Provinces, in the west, and the Luangwa Valley in the southeast, comprising 10% of the national territory, hold less than 0.2% of the population. The Luangwa

Valley is virtually unpopulated. Overall, the density is 9 per sq km (23.3 per sq mi), while the density in agricultural areas is 14.1 per sq km (36.5 per sq mi).

DEMOGRAPHIC INDICATORS (1985)	
Population, total (in 1,000)	6,770.0
Population ages (% of total)	
0-14	47.3
15-64	50.0
65+	2.7
Youth 15-24 (000)	1,256
Women ages 15-49 (000)	1,458
Dependency ratios	100
Child-woman ratios	872
Sex ratios (per 100 females)	98.8
Median ages (years)	16.3
Average size of household	4.6
Decline in birthrate (1965-83)	−4.0
Proportion of urban (%)	49.46
Population density (per sq. km.)	9
per hectare of arable land	0.73
Rates of growth (%)	3.31
Urban %	6.2
Rural %	0.8
Natural increase rates (per 1,000)	33.1
Crude birth rates (per 1,000)	48.1
Crude death rates (per 1,000)	15.1
Gross reproduction rates	3.33
Net reproduction rates	2.51
Total fertility rates	6.76
General fertility rates (per 1,000)	219
Life expectancy, males (years)	49.6
Life expectancy, females (years)	53.1
Life expectancy, total (years)	51.3
Population doubling time in years at current rate	21

The urban component of the population is 50%, and its annual growth rate is an 6.2%. There are ten major urban centers, of which six, including Lusaka, have populations of over 100,000. Nearly 50% of the population of Lusaka live in slums and squatter settlements. Seven of the ten towns are located in the Copperbelt, and eight of the towns are located near mines. Furthermore, the vast bulk of the European and Asian residents are concentrated in these towns.

The age profile shows 47% in the under-14 age group, 50% in the 15-to-64 age group and 3% over 65. Based on the 1980 census, the male/female ratio was 49:51.

Before independence there was a sporadic immigration of Europeans and Asians who came to work as miners, farmers, traders and administrators. After independence many Europeans left, and the new immigrants were South African black nationalists. Current population gain through immigration is slight. There is a floating refugee population of around 17,000.

Zambia has long played host to a considerable refugee and asylum-seeking population that originates in several strife-torn southern African countries. The United Nations High Commissioner for Refugees (UNHCR) estimates that there are about 97,000 refugees in Zambia. The largest group of refugees is from Angola, with significant numbers from Zaire, Namibia and South Africa. Smaller numbers are from

Malawi, Mozambique and Zimbabwe. Many of the Angolans and Zaireans have spontaneously resettled in western and northwestern provinces since the ethnic compositions on both sides of the border are similar. The Zambian government operates two large refugee resettlement centers, and the Southwest African People's Organization operates one camp. Urban refugees number approximately 700.

Under statutory law, women generally enjoy full equality with men, and women participate increasingly in Zambia's social, economic and political life. They hold some senior positions in the party, the government, and the judiciary, and are gaining increasing representation in the professions and higher education. In 1983, the number of women on the party's 25-member central committee was increased from two to four. Nevertheless, the majority of Zambian women still occupy traditional roles. Customary law and practice still compete on a de facto basis in most rural areas with Zambia's constitution and codified laws. Some customary statutes place women in subordinate or unequal status with respect to property inheritances and marriage. The Law Development Commission is seeking ways to remove such anomalies. In Zambia's traditional society, women's primary role is bearing and raising children.

Official policy toward family planning is positive. A private group, the Family Planning and Welfare Association, trains workers to teach family planning and nutrition through home visits.

ETHNIC COMPOSITION

Nearly 98.7% of Zambians are Africans belonging to more than 70 Bantu-speaking tribes. Although the term tribe is used in official sources to designate an ethnic group with a common name, territory, custom, language, history and socio-political organization, tribal affiliations are often fluid and modified through assimilation, migration and circumstances of history. There are 18 tribes in the Bemba-speaking group, accounting for 34.9% of the population; eight tribes in the Tonga-speaking group, accounting for 17.4%; five tribes in the Nyanja-speaking group, accounting for 15.9%; six tribes in the Lunda-Luvale group, accounting for 12.1%; 14 tribes in the Barotse language group, accounting for 9.7%; five tribes in the Mambwe language group, accounting for 5.3%; and three tribes in the Tumbuka language group, accounting for 3%.

The others include nine tribes of the Luyana subgroup, accounting for 4.7%; two tribes of the Totela sub-group, accounting for 1.2%; and four tribes of the Nkoya sub-group, accounting for 1.1%. All these tribes speak Barotse languages.

Although tribal divisions no longer have political significance, tribalism, defined as social values rooted in tribal affiliations and cultural differences, is an important source of identification and fellowship in a changing society. Zambia has been described by President Kenneth Kaunda as a federation of tribes rather than a nation. Despite new divisions based on

MAJOR TRIBES OF ZAMBIA				
Geographical Region	Tribe	Racial Stock	Language	%
Southwest Lunda	Lozi	Congolese	Barotse	2.7
Northwest	Lunda	Congolese	Lunda-Luvale	2.1
	Luvale	Congolese	Lunda-Luvale	2.4
	Mbunda	Congolese	Lunda-Luvale	1.5
	Luchazi	Congolese	Lunda-Luvale	1.1
	Ndembu	Congolese	Lunda-Luvale	1.1
	Chokwe	Congolese	Lunda-Luvale	0.6
	Kaonde	Congolese	Kaonde	3.3
South Central	Tonga	Bantu-Botatwe	Tonga	11.4
	Lenje	Bantu-Botatwe	Tonga	2.8
	Soli	Bantu-Botatwe	Tonga	0.9
	Ila	Bantu-Botatwe	Tonga	0.8
	Toka	Bantu-Botatwe	Tonga	0.5
	Leya	Bantu-Botatwe	Tonga	0.4
	Sala	Bantu-Botatwe	Tonga	0.3
	Gowa	Bantu-Botatwe	Tonga	0.3
North Luapula Valley	Bemba	Congolese Luba	Bemba	8.8
	Lunda	Congolese Lunda	Bemba	5.2
	Lala	Congolese Lunda	Bemba	3.1
	Bisa	Congolese Lunda	Bemba	3.0
	Ushi	Congolese Lunda	Bemba	2.5
	Chishinga	Congolese Lunda	Bemba	1.9
	Ngumbo	Congolese Lunda	Bemba	1.7
	Lamba	Congolese Lunda	Bemba	1.6
	Kabende	Congolese Lunda	Bemba	1.0
	Tabwa	Congolese Lunda	Bemba	1.0
	Swaka	Congolese Lunda	Bemba	1.0
	Mukulu	Congolese Lunda	Bemba	0.9
	Ambo	Congolese Lunda	Bemba	0.9
	Lima	Congolese Lunda	Bemba	0.8
	Shila	Congolese Lunda	Bemba	0.6
	Unga	Congolese Lunda	Bemba	0.5
	Bwile	Congolese Lunda	Bemba	0.2
	Luano	Congolese Lunda	Bemba	0.2
Northeast	Tambo	Tanzanian	Mambwe	0.3
	Lungu	Tanzanian	Mambwe	2.2
	Mambwe	Tanzanian	Mambwe	1.4
	Namwanga	Tanzanian	Mambwe	0.7
	Iwa	Tanzanian	Mambwe	0.7
Eastern	Tumbuka	Congolese Luba	Tumbuka	1.8
	Senga	Congolese Luba	Tumbuka	1.0
	Yombe	Congolese Luba	Tumbuka	0.2
Southeast	Chewa	Congolese Luba	Nyanja	6.1
	Nsenga	Congolese Luba	Nyanja	4.2
	Kunda	Congolese Luba	Nyanja	1.4
	Chikunda	Congolese Luba	Nyanja	0.2
	Ngoni	Zulu	Nyanja	4.0

economic class, geography and occupations, tribal loyalties and prejudices remain powerful determinants of social and political attitudes.

There are three major ethnic minorities: Asians, Coloreds and Europeans. The Asian population numbers nearly 10,000 persons of Indian origin, most of whom are Gujarati Hindus. Asians are found in all large towns as traders and free businessmen. Coloreds are persons of mixed racial origin, most of whom are Euro-Africans in a variety of combinations, while a small percentage is Indo-African. The European community, numbering 76,000 at independence, but only half that number in the mid-1970s, is mainly of British stock. The remainder is of diverse origin — Greeks, Italians, Lithuanians, Jews, Lebanese and Americans. Unlike European communities in other parts of Africa, there is a substantial European working class in the country. Although President Kaunda has repeatedly characterized Zambia as a multi-racial society, the Europeans and Asians feel that they have no real future there because of the growing emphasis on Zambianization of the economy. Accordingly, the non-African component of the population has been declining since independence.

In terms of ethnic and linguistic homogeneity, Zambia is ranked 12th in the world with 18% homogeneity (on an ascending scale in which North and South Korea are ranked 135th with 100% homogeneity and Tanzania is ranked first with 7% homogeneity).

LANGUAGES

The official language of Zambia is English. Although spoken by a very small minority of Europeans, Asians and educated Africans, it is often the only language in which Africans speaking different vernaculars can communicate.

Communication between English-speaking Europeans and Asians on the one hand and non-English-speaking Africans on the other is carried on through the medium of a pidgin language called Kitchen Kaffir (or Chilapalapa, Chilolo, Chikabanga, Chiboi and Fanagolo) a hybrid of Zulu, Afrikaans and English, heavily interlarded with Bemba words and phrases. Because Kitchen Kaffir is basically a master-servant language, its use is often resented by Africans.

There are more than 30 vernaculars spoken in Zambia, of which Bemba, Tonga, Nyanja, Lunda, Luvale, Lozi and Kaounde have official status. Although Bemba is the dominant language of the Copperbelt, no one language can claim to be the lingua franca. Two-thirds of the Africans speak Bemba, Tonga or Nyanja. Each ethnic group has its own language or at least a dialect, but their linguistic relationships have not yet been determined.

RELIGIONS

Although there are no reliable statistics, 82% of Zambians follow traditional African beliefs, 17% are Christian and the remaining 1% belong to the Asian religions of Hinduism and Islam. Other sources place the percentage of Christians as high as 45.

Christianity was introduced into what is now Zambia in the late 19th Century by the successors of David Livingstone. But it was not until the early part of the 20th Century that Christianity began to displace tribal religions and become a spiritual force in the country. However, even today, elements of pre-Christian faiths, such as beliefs in ancestral spirits, witchcraft and magic, persist in disguised forms. Christianity has its strongest hold among educated and urban residents.

Somewhat more than three-fifths of the Christians are Roman Catholics, one fifth Protestant and the remainder members of independent African churches. The Roman Catholic Church is organized in two archdioceses, at Lusaka and Kasama, and six dioceses at Livingstone, Chipata, Monze, Ndola, Mbala and Mansa. Protestants are fragmented into a number of churches, of which the largest are the Anglican Church, the United Church of Zambia and the Church of Scotland. Except for denominations that cater exclusively to Europeans, all denominations are formally interracial, but there is continuing de facto segregation, not only between Europeans and Africans but also among African tribes.

Under President Kaunda's leadership, Zambianization of the churches has made significant progress. The Roman Catholic archbishop of Lusaka and the Anglican bishop are both native Zambians, and an increasing number of clergy and seminarians are also Zambians. New Roman Catholic masses incorporate African drums, rhythms and hymns. Church and state cooperate in many areas of national concern. The Christian Council of Zambia, comprising Roman Catholic, Anglican and United Church leaders, meet regularly with President Kaunda to explore the church's role in national development.

As in other parts of Africa, there are a number of independent African Christian movements founded and headed by self-styled prophets of uncertain orthodoxy. At one time in the early 1970s, nearly 40 such churches were reported, but many had only a short life. The best known of these churches is the Lumpa Church, founded in 1953 by one Alice Lenshina, who claimed to possess the "real" Bible and to have a divine mandate to extirpate witchcraft and sorcery. By the 1960s, her church claimed a membership of between 50,000 and 100,000 members. In 1964 it came into conflict with the government, as a result of which Alice Lenshina was arrested, the church was banned and between 13,000 and 65,000 of its adherents were forced to seek refuge in Zaire. Another sect in trouble with the government is the Jehovah's Witnesses, which, although not under a ban, is viewed with suspicion. The sect claims some 100,000 active members.

African traditional beliefs and practices vary from tribe to tribe, but belief in sorcery and witchcraft is one aspect common to all tribal systems. Almost all tribes have a notion of a high god, but spirits play a more important role in determining the details of religious belief and ritual.

COLONIAL EXPERIENCE

Zambia's first European contacts were through Christian missionaries, such as David Livingstone and Francois Coillard. In the 1890s Cecil Rhodes's British South Africa Company extended its charter to the north of the Zambezi. From 1891 to 1923, the territory known as Northern Rhodesia was ruled by this private company. After the transfer of power from the company to the crown in 1923, Northern Rhodesia became a protectorate under the British Colonial Office, and Southern Rhodesia became a self-governing colony. While the British Parliament remained the ultimate source of law, an executive council and a legislative council were set up, both composed of British officials and presided over by the governor. Africans were not considered British subjects and were excluded from all political institutions. In 1953 Northern

Rhodesia became a member of the Federation of Rhodesia and Nyasaland, despite the opposition of an overwhelming majority of Africans. Following the federation the government underwent constitutional changes with growing African participation in the political process. In 1963 the federation was formally dissolved, and in 1964 Northern Rhodesia became an independent republic under the name of Zambia with Kenneth David Kaunda as its first president. Zambia has since then played a key role in the movement toward black majority rule in southern African countries, but this has not affected its relations with the United Kingdom or its membership in the Commonwealth of Nations. While stressing Zambianization as a national ideology, President Kaunda has displayed considerable moderation and shown no desire to break completely with the colonial past.

CONSTITUTION & GOVERNMENT

Under the Constitutional Amendment Bill of 1972, Zambia is a "One-Party Participatory Democracy" with a strong presidential form of government. The sole party of the republic, the United National Independence Party, is integrated with the government on all levels. The president of the republic is concurrently the president of the party. The party nominates the sole candidate for presidential elections. If the presidency becomes vacant through death, disability or resignation, the secretary general of the party acts

---

CABINET LIST (1985)

President . . . . Kenneth David Kaunda
Prime Minister . . . . Kebby Musokotwane
Secretary General, United Natl.
  Independence Party . . . . Alexander Grey Zulu
Secretary of State for Defense & Security . . . . Alex Shapi
Minister of Agriculture & Water
  Development . . . . *Gen.*Kingsley Chinkuli
Minister of Commerce, Industry
  & Foreign Trade . . . . Leonard S. Subulwu
Minister of Cooperatives . . . . .Justin Mukando
Minister of Decentralization . . . . *Dr.* Henry Meebelo
Minister of Defense . . . . *Gen.* Malimba Masheke
Minister of Finance & Technical
  Cooperation . . . . Luke J. Mwananshiku
Minister of Foreign Affairs . . . . Lameck K. H. Goma
Minister of General Education
  & Culture . . . . Basil Kabwe
Minister of Health . . . . Mark M. Tambatamba
Minister of Higher Education . . . . .Rajah Kunda
Minister of Home Affairs . . . . Frederick M. Chomba
Minister of Information & Broadcasting
  Services .Cosmas Chibanda
Minister of Labor & Social
  Services . . . . .Frederick Shumba Hapunda
Minister of Lands & Natural Resources . . .Fabiano Chelah
Minister of Legal Affairs . . . . Gibson Chigaga
Minister of Mines . . . . Jameson K. M. Kalaluka
Minister of Natl. Guidance . . . . Arnold K. Simuchimba

---

CABINET LIST (1985) (CONTINUED)

Minister of Power, Transport &
  Communications . . . . Fitzpatrick Chuula
Minister of Tourism . . . . Rodger C. Sakuhuka
Minister of Works & Supply . . . . Haswell Y. Mwale
Minister of Youth & Sports . . . . .Ben Kakoma
Minister of State for Agriculture &
  Water Development . . . . .Daniel Munkombwe
Minister of State for Civil Service . . . . .J. Mwondela
Minister of State for Commerce
  & Industry . . . . Richard S. Zimba
Minister of State for
  Decentralization . . . . *Mrs.* Mavis Muyanda
Minister of State for Finance . . . . Mbambo M. Sianga
Minister of State for Foreign Affairs . . . . . . Otema Musuka
Minister of State for General Education
  & Culture . . . . .Kennedy Shepande
Minister of State for General Education
  & Culture . . . . Raphael Chota
Minister of State for Health . . . . .Peter Chansi
Minister of State for Higher Education . . . .
Minister of State for Home Affairs . . . . .E. Nkomeshya
Minister of State for Information
  & Broadcasting . . . . Samson Mukando
Minister of State for Labor & Social
  Services . . . . Richard K. Banda
Minister of State for Lands & Natural
  Resources . . . . C. Masongo
Minister of State for Mines . . . . Nathan Siafwa
Minister of State for Natl. Planning
  & Development . . . . Lavu Mulimba
Minister of State for Power, Transport
  & Communications . . . . Simon C. Kalaba
Minister of State for Power, Transport
  & Communications . . . . Kenneth Musango Kakoma
Minister of State for Tourism . . . . Enos Haimbe
Minister of State for Works & Supply . . . . .Noah Dilamonu
Minister of State for Youth & Sports . .Joseph C. Kasongo
Attorney General . . . . Gibson Chigaga

---

as president for up to three months pending a new presidential election. The president is formally elected for a five-year term, but there is no constitutional limitation on the number of terms he may seek. The president is empowered to veto any legislation; should the National Assembly over-ride any vetoed legislation, the president may order its dissolution. The president appoints the prime minister, the secretary general of the party, the attorney general, the chief justice and the judges of the supreme court.

National policy is formulated by the 25-member Central Committee of the UNIP and is implemented by the cabinet headed by the prime minister. The prime minister is required to be an ex officio member of the UNIP Central Committee.

Suffrage is universal over age 18. Under the 1973 constitution all candidates are required to be members of UNIP. The elections proceed through primary and final stages, with the party leadership specifying up to four candidates in each district, among whom

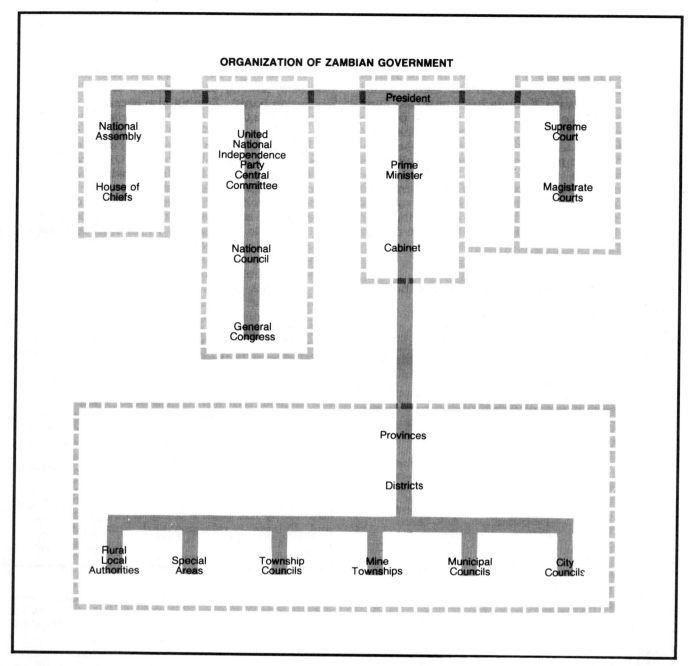

ORGANIZATION OF ZAMBIAN GOVERNMENT

President

National Assembly

House of Chiefs

United National Independence Party Central Committee

National Council

General Congress

Prime Minister

Cabinet

Supreme Court

Magistrate Courts

Provinces

Districts

Rural Local Authorities

Special Areas

Township Councils

Mine Townships

Municipal Councils

City Councils

the voters can choose one. Balloting for the presidency is separate from the balloting for the National Assembly, but both are held at the same time.

A staunch opponent of racism, President Kaunda has based his policies on an ideology that he terms Zambian Humanism. This concept draws its inspiration from specifically Christian and African socialist ideas. It rejects capitalism, Marxism and African tribalism. It demands a return to the traditional egalitarian value-systems of African society based on mutual assistance. Kaunda has dominated Zambian politics since independence, and his position has never been seriously challenged. At the same time, there are deep-rooted, persisting tribal divisions that lead to periodical outbreaks of politically inspired violence.

Zambia political system is open to individuals of divergent opinions provided they are willing to work within the one-party structure and not challenge the president's preeminent position. In the latest parliamentary elections in 1983, 760 candidates contested 125 seats; 40 incumbents were defeated, including seven ministers of state.

The National Assembly is reflective of constituent interests and sometimes thwarts or modifies executive branch policies and programs. It can also be very critical of such policies, as was demonstrated a number of times in 1985 when members of Parliament railed against government expenditures, poor services and land allocations. Presidential and general elections are by universal suffrage but the numbering of ballots, which could be cross-checked against voter registration numbers, could undermine the secrecy of the ballot. In the 1983 presidential election, voters had the option of voting for or against the single candidate or abstaining. A total of 63.4% of registered voters went to the polls, of whom 93% voted in favor of the president.

FREEDOM & HUMAN RIGHTS

In terms of civil and political rights, Zambia is classified as a partially free country with a rating of 5 in civil and 6 in political rights (on a descending scale in which 1 is the highest and 7 the lowest in rights).

One of the most stable nations in Africa, Zambia has shown considerable ability to combine a powerful presidency and a one-party system of government with extensive constitutional guarantees of human rights, an independent judicary, and substantial political activity.

Under the state of emergency which has been in effect since independence in 1964, the president has broad discretion to detain or restrict the movements of individuals, a power not exercised since 1982. Detention procedures have been revised to conform with provisions of the constitution and have increased the president's authority. Under the state of emergency, law officers and defense personnel have extraordinary powers. Police officers of assistant inspector rank and above may arrest without a warrant and detain an individual for up to 28 days if the officer has reason to believe grounds exist to justify a presidential detention order. However, police must within 14 days provide the detainee with reasons for his detention, or his incarceration is void. This requirement is followed rigorously.

The president can incarcerate a detainee indefinitely and is not legally bound to accept a court's acquittal if he still believes that the detainee is guilty. In practice, detainees are almost always released if the court finds in their favor. By law, presidential detainees are entitled to: formal notice of the reasons for their detention; publication of their detention in the government *Gazette*; access to counsel; frequent visitation by family and colleagues; immediate representation to the detaining authority; and the right to seek judicial review of the detention order by an independent and impartial tribunal after one year. Presidential detainees must have their cases heard by the High Court and have the right to appeal to the Supreme Court. Habeas corpus is available to persons detained under presidential order, but the government is not obliged to accept the recommendation of the review tribunal. Six detainees were among the 243 prisoners amnestied in October 1984 in conjunction with Zambia's 20th anniversary celebrations. It is estimated that there are fewer than 15 presidential detainees currently held in Zambia.

The media enjoy some freedom within limits. Both national dailies are owned by the government and the party, but some muted critism is permitted as long as it avoids direct critism of the head of state and his philosophy of humanism. Censorship exists but is not stringent. Observers have noted that only two or three persons have been convicted since independence for attacking the president in print. Although the Zambia Congress of Trade Unions operates under government supervision, it maintains its freedom of action and frequently challenges government policy. Within the one-party structure, there is considerable latitude for differing opinions.

There was no major change in the status of human rights in Zambia in 1985. Zambian institutions such as the press, trade unions, and churches have come under some pressure from central authorities to be more responsive to the wishes of the government but have maintained to the best of their ability their objectivity, status and influence. There is strong competition for parliamentary seats within the single-party structure. The National Assembly provides a platform for the spirited consideration of issues. The judiciary is independent and takes full account of the rights of the accused. The trade union movement continues to be one of the best organized and most democratic in Africa, and the churches remain a strong independent force which can unite to defend common interests. Zambia continues to serve as a place of first asylum for refugees in the region.

CIVIL SERVICE

No current information is available on the Zambian civil service.

LOCAL GOVERNMENT

For purposes of local government, Zambia is divided into nine provinces, each under a minister of state of sub-cabinet rank.

ZAMBIAN PROVINCES

Province	Capital
Eastern	Chipata
Central	Kabwe
Copperbelt	Ndola
Western	Mongu
Luapula	Mansa
Southern	Livingstone
North-Western	Solwezi
Northern	Kasama
Lusaka	Lusaka

Within the provinces are 35 districts and 113 local government units above the ward level, including 34 rural local authorities, 39 special areas, 24 township councils, eight mine township management boards, six municipal councils and two city councils.

The minister of state for each province serves as the link between the national and local governments. The administrative head in each province is the resident secretary, who is the senior civil servant in that province. District administrations are conducted by district governors.

The municipal and town councils are modeled on the English county boroughs. They have the power to levy taxes, manage housing projects and control roads, water, power, town planning and health facilities. Both urban and rural councils have appointed members, but the majority are elected on the basis of universal adult suffrage.

FOREIGN POLICY

Zambia has been in the front line of African states committed to ending white minority rule in South Africa. The Kaunda regime has consistently supported African liberation movements; by 1973 these groups posed a substantial threat to Rhodesia, leading to the closure of the Zambian-Rhodesian border. Zambia also became a haven for more than 33,000 black refugees from South Africa and Rhodesia. In 1969 President Kaunda sponsored the Lusaka Manifesto, subsequently approved by the U.N. General Assembly and the OAU, which justified intervention in the affairs of white-ruled countries of southern Africa on the ground that they lacked commitment to the principles of human equality and self-determination. At the same time, the Manifesto expressed a willingness to consider the possibility of peaceful change rather than confrontation. In 1975 Kaunda attended the unsuccessful Victoria Falls talks between African nationalists and Rhodesia. Following the failure of the Geneva Conference on Rhodesia in 1976, Kaunda authorized black guerrillas to operate across the border and declared his support for the Patriotic Front led by Robert Mugabe and Joshua Nkomo.

Relations with the Communist government in Angola continues to be strained because of Zambian support for the pro-Western faction, UNITA, during the Angolan civil war. On the other hand, relations with Mozambique, in whose independence negotiations Zambia played a major role, are very close; a permanent commission has been established to promote mutual cooperation. Zambia and South Africa have come close to open confrontation a number of times over the use of Zambian territory by Namibian guerrillas. Relations with Malawi have been strained by the latter's policy of maintaining trade and diplomatic relations with South Africa. But Zambia has opposed moves by other East and Central African states to expel Malawi from the OAU for this reason.

Zambia's strongest fraternal ties are with Tanzania and Zimbabwe with whom it is bound by a common colonial tradition and a common outlook on African and world problems. The friendship between Kaunda and Julius Nyerere of Tanzania also led Zambia to oppose the Idi Amin regime in Uganda. Relations with Zaire are based on mutual economic and cultural interests and parallel policies with respect to African nationalism.

Of the many countries outside Africa with which Zambia has diplomatic relations, only those with the United Kingdom, China and the United States have important political or economic significance. Zambia continues to look to the United Kingdom for economic and political support, and basic ties remain strong. Zambia shares U.S. concern over Soviet and Cuban intervention in African affairs. Relations with China are primarily economic. Chinese aid programs have incluced the construction of the TanZam Railway from Kapiri Mposhi in Zambia to Dar es Salaam and the building of three radio stations.

Zambia and the United States are parties to 18 treaties and agreements covering agricultural commodities, aviation, consuls, economic and techinal cooperation, extradition, investment guaranties, mutual security, property, taxation and trademarks.

Zambia joined the U.N. in 1964; its share of the U.N. budget is 0.02%. It is a member of 13 U.N. organizations and 10 other international organizations.

U.S. Ambassador in Lusaka: Paul J. Hare
U.K. High Commissioner in Lusaka: W. K. K. White
Zambian Ambassador in Washington, D.C.: Nalumino Mundia
Zambian High Commissioner in London: Peter D. Zuze

PARLIAMENT

The Zambian National Assembly is a unicameral body consisting of 135 members, of whom 125 are elected by universal adult suffrage for five-year terms and 10 are appointed by the president. All candidates must be members of the nation's sole party, United National Independence Party (UNIP) and must be confirmed in a primary, in which only party members may cast ballots. A speaker is elected by the members from outside their own ranks.

Although the supremacy of the parliament is built into the constitution, its role is limited in practice. Among its extensive powers are the rights to impeach the president, amend the constitution, challenge the constitutionality of any ordinance and extend or revoke a presidentially imposed emergency. All bills receive three readings in the house; those which pass and receive the assent of the president become acts of parliament with the force of law.

The constitution also provides for a House of Chiefs of 27 members, four each from the Northern, Western, Southern and Eastern provinces, three each from the North-western, Luapula and Central provinces and two from the Copperbelt. It submits resolutions to be discussed in the Assembly and considers matters referred to it by the president. Its constitutional role is purely advisory.

POLITICAL PARTIES

Under the constitution, the United National Independence Party is the country's sole political party.

UNIP was formed in 1958 as a result of the withdrawal of Kenneth David Kaunda, Simon M. Kapwepwe and others from the older African National Congress led by Harry Nkumbula. UNIP led Zambia to independence in 1964 and has ruled the country ever since.

The three principal organs of the party are the party central committee, the National Council and the General Conference of more than 5,000 members. The composition and powers of the Central Committee are defined in the constitution. It consists of the president and secretary general and not more than 23 members: 20 of whom are elected at the party's General Conference held every five years and three who are nominated by the president. The Central Committee ranks above the cabinet; its general secretary is the second ranking person in the official hierarchy. Within the committee are eight subcommittees dealing with defense and security; elections, publicity and strategy; economics and finance; political, constitutional, legal and foreign affairs; new appointments and discipline; social and cultural affairs; rural development; and youth and sports. No member of the Central Committee may serve in the cabinet, with the exception of the prime minister.

The political ideology of UNIP is the philosophy of Zambian Humanism formulated by President Kaunda. Until the 1970s, the party was held together by the momentum generated by its successful drive for national independence, but internal divisions, based not only on ethnic and regional rivalries but also the political ambitions of the middle leadership, began to pose serious threats to its dominance. The establishment of a one-party state was in part an effort to prevent the further disintegration of the party in the face of a more dynamic leftist opposition.

ECONOMY

Zambia is one of the 39 lower middle income countries of the world with a free market economy in which the dominant sector is public.

The Third National Development Plan, originally sheduled for 1977-81, was launched in October 1979. Total planned investment up to 1983 was K3,354 million.

Independent Zambia has had two four-year development plans (1966-70 and 1972-76). Development expenditures totaled Z £430 million in the first plan period and K1.956 billion in the second plan period. Allotments in the second plan were K716.5 million for economic facilities and transport, K655 million for industrial and mining development, K314.9 for social facilities, K117.5 for education and K152.5 for agriculture.

Per capita aid received during 1979-81 was $49.86. The Chinese aid, the largest from any country, was in the form of a loan for the construction of the TanZam Railway. The loan was an indirect one consisting of Chinese goods whose sale proceeds were retained by the Zambian government.

PRINCIPAL ECONOMIC INDICATORS

Gross National Product: $3.630 billion (1983)
  GNP Annual Growth Rate: 0.6% (1973-82)
  Per Capita GNP: $580 (1983)
  Per Capita GNP Annual Growth Rate: −2.5% (1973-82)
Gross Domestic Product: K4.733 billion (1984)
  GDP at 1980 Prices: K3.058 billion
  GDP Deflator (1980=100): 154.8
  GDP Annual Growth Rate: 0.2% (1973-83)
  Per Capita GDP: K758 (1984)
  Per Capita GDP Annual Growth Rate: −2.6% (1970-81)
Income Distribution: 11% of national income is received by the bottom 40%; 57% of national income is received by the top 20%.
Percentage of Population in Absolute Poverty: 25
Consumer Price Index (1970=100):
  All Items: 639.8 (March 1985)
  Food: 696.4 (March 1985)
Wholesale Price Index (1980=100):
  Agricultural Products 209 (December 1984)
  Consumer Goods: 191 (December 1984)
Average Annual Rate of Inflation: 10.3% (1973-83)
Money Supply: K860.00 million (March 1985)
  Reserve Money: K478.00 million (March 1985)
Currency in Circulation: K285.6 million (1984)
International Reserves: $54.2 million (September 1980), of which foreign exchange reserves were $54.2 million

---

BALANCE OF PAYMENTS (1984)
(million $)

Current Account Balance	−115
Merchandise Exports	916
Merchandise Imports	−612
Trade Balance	304
Other Goods, Services & Income	+85
Other Goods, Services & Income	−500
Other Goods, Services & Income Net	−414
Private Unrequited Transfers	−26
Official Unrequited Transfers	21
Capital Other Than Reserves	233
Net Errors & Omissions	−77
Total (Lines 1,10 and 11)	41
Counterpart Items	−105
Total (Lines 12 and 13)	−64
Liabilities Constituting Foreign Authorities' Reserves	—
Total Change in Reserves	64

GROSS DOMESTIC PRODUCT BY ECONOMIC ACTIVITY
(1982)

		Rate of Change % 1970-81
Agriculture	15.1	1.8
Mining	6.0	−1.5
Manufacturing	18.3	0.3
Construction	4.3	−2.4
Electricity, Gas & Water	2.0	13.0
Transport & Communications	6.5	2.1
Trade & Finance	13.4	−0.4
Public Administration & Defense	—	1.7
Other Branches	34.3	2.7

FOREIGN ECONOMIC ASSISTANCE TO ZAMBIA		
Sources	Period	Amount (million $)
United States Loans	1946-83	227.5
United States Grants	1946-83	403
International Organizations	1946-79	922.8
(Of which World Bank)	1946-79	580.6
China	1954-79	330.0
EEC	1946-83	42.0
Soviet Union	1954-84	30.0
East European Countries	1954-84	165.0
All Sources	1979-81	290.1

BUDGET

The Zambian fiscal year is the calendar year. Zambia has a narrow tax base, but it has a rich source of public revenue in its mining industry. Expenditures are divided into recurrent and capital, but balanced budgets are not considered essential in view of investment needs.

BUDGET (K million)			
Revenue	1981*	1982	1983
Income Tax	307.8	296.4	366.6
Customs and excise	424.1	451.0	488.2
Fines, licenses and other taxes	4.9	5.1	4.6
Mineral revenue	10.5	—	41.7
Interest	0.6	1.0	0.8
Court fees and earnings of ministries	46.7	51.0	44.9
OSAS reimbursements	1.4	1.2	1.0
Miscellaneous	2.5	13.3	0.8
Loans	21.9	21.4	7.7
TOTAL	820.4	840.4	956.5
Expenditure	1981*	1982	1983
Planning and finance	166.2	68.7	46.8
Police	33.7	54.8	52.2
Local government and housing	11.0	42.0	31.8
Home affairs	11.5	17.6	16.8
Commerce, industry and mines	3.7	4.8	6.0
Health	72.6	106.0	95.8
Power, transport and works	44.1	65.2	66.6
Education	83.0	108.0	120.0
Lands, natural resources and development	140.9	202.6	146.7
Constitutional and statutory	522.4	407.0	317.3
TOTAL (incl. others)	1,230.5	1,323.0	1,150.3

*Provisional.
1984 (K million, estimates): Revenue 1,240; Expenditure 1,508.

Of current revenues 32.9% comes from taxes on income, profit and capital gain, 48.3% comes from domestic taxes on goods and services, 8.8% from taxes on international trade and transactions, 3.2% from other taxes and 6.6% from non-tax revenues. Current revenues represented 24.9% of GNP. Of current expenditures, 15.2% goes to education, 8.4% goes to health, 1.8% goes to housing, social security and welfare, 23.9% to economic services and 50.7% to other functions, including defense. Current expenditures represented 41.9% of GNP and overall deficit 20.0% of GNP.

In 1983 public consumption was K1.070 billion and private consumption K2.935 billion. During 1973-83 public consumption declined by 0.8% and private consumption grew by 3.9%.

In 1983 total outstanding disbursed external debt was $2.638 billion of which $2.034 billion was owed to official creditors and $604 million to private creditors. Total debt service was $126.2 million of which $48.1 million was repayment of principal and $78.1 million was interest. Total external debt represented 263.6% of export revenues and 83.9% of GNP. Total debt service represented 12.6% of export revenues and 4.0% of GNP.

FINANCE

The Zambian unit of currency is the kwacha divided into 100 ngwee. Coins are issued in denominations of 1, 2, 5, 10, 20 and 50 ngwee; and notes are issued in denominations of 50 ngwee and 1, 2, 5, 10 and 20 kwacha.

The Zambian kwacha was introduced in 1968, replacing the Zambian pound at the rate of Z £1=K2. Initially, the kwacha was linked to the dollar at the rate of $1=K0.7143. In 1976 the kwacha's link with the U.S. dollar was ended, and the currency was pegged to the SDR (Special Drawing Rights) at the rate of SDR1=K0.92184. The market rate against the U.S. dollar is adjusted from month to month. In August 1980 the dollar exchange rate was $1=K2.237. The sterling exchange rate in 1984 was £1=K2.551.

The central bank is the Bank of Zambia, which is also the bank of issue and regulator of the fiscal system. The two largest commercial banks, the Commercial Bank of Zambia and the National Commercial Bank, are state-owned. All foreign banks are required to be incorporated in Zambia, to be capitalized at not less than K2 million, and to have native Zambian citizens as half of its board of directors. Development finance is provided by the State Finance and Development Corporation and the Development Bank of Zambia. In July 1984 commercial banks had reserves of K275.8 million, demand deposits of K581.5 million and time and savings deposits of K833.9 million.

AGRICULTURE

Of the total land area of 75,261,800 hectares (185,971,900 acres), 5% is cultivated, an additional 5% is considered arable, and another 40% is considered potentially cultivable. Per capita agricultural land is 7.6 hectares (19 acres). Based on 1974-76=100, the index of agricultural production in 1982 was 89, the index of food production was 89 and the index of per capita food production was 74. Agriculture employs

```
┌────────────────────────────────────────────────┐
│                GROWTH PROFILE                   │
│            Annual Growth Rates (%)              │
│ Population 1980-2000                      3.3    │
│ Birthrate 1965-83                        1.7    │
│ Deathrate 1965-83                      −21.4    │
│ Urban Population 1973-83                 6.5    │
│ Labor Force 1980-2000                    3.3    │
│ GNP 1973-82                              0.6    │
│ GNP per capita 1973-82                  −2.5    │
│ GDP 1973-83                              0.2    │
│ GDP per capita 1970-81                  −2.0    │
│ Consumer Prices 1970-81                 11.9    │
│ Wholesale Prices 1970-81                 9.4    │
│ Inflation 1973-83                       10.3    │
│ Agriculture 1973-83                      1.4    │
│ Manufacturing 1970-81                    0.3    │
│ Industry 1973-83                        −0.3    │
│ Services 1973-83                         0.6    │
│ Mining 1970-81                          −1.5    │
│ Construction 1970-81                    −2.4    │
│ Electricity 1970-81                     13.0    │
│ Transportation 1970-81                   2.1    │
│ Trade 1970-81                           −0.4    │
│ Public Administration & Defense 1970-81  1.7    │
│ Export Price Index 1975-81               7.9    │
│ Import Price Index 1975-81              14.5    │
│ Terms of Trade 1975-81                  −5.8    │
│ Exports 1973-83                         −0.8    │
│ Imports 1973-83                         −7.3    │
│ Public Consumption 1973-83              −0.8    │
│ Private Consumption 1973-83              3.9    │
│ Gross Domestic Investment 1973-83      −12.5    │
│ Energy Consumption 1973-83               1.9    │
│ Energy Production 1973-83                6.4    │
└────────────────────────────────────────────────┘
```

67% of the economically active population. The agricultural sector contributes 14% to the GDP, and its rate of growth during 1973-83 was 1.4%. Agriculture's share of export earnings is not significant. The value added in agriculture in 1983 was $562 million.

Zambian agriculture is characterized by a sharp contrast between commercial farming for cash developed by European settlers and subsistence farming carried on by the vast majority of Africans. The large-scale commercial farms are concentrated in the so-called line-of-rail between Livingstone and Kabwe. Subsistence or shifting cultivation is the rule elsewhere. The country is not self-sufficient in food; 247,000 tons of cereals were imported in 1983.

The prevailing land-use practices in African farms are both primitive and wasteful. The most common methods of farming are mound cultivation, chitemene or slash and burn, grassland cultivation, flood-plain or dambo and cattle grazing. These methods are sometimes used in combination. In mound cultivation the mounds from the first crop or season are used for sowing the second crop and the weeds used as green manure. In the chitemene system the wood of felled trees is gathered and built into stacks, usually in the form of a circle. The stacks are burned at the end of the dry season resulting in a fine ash garden temporarily enriched in potash, phosphate and nitrate. The ash gardens from larger stacks may be used for a succession of crops for up to five years. Chitemene is usually practiced only by shifting cultivators because woodlands may take 20 to 40 years to recover for

renewed cutting. Other causes of low productivity are a shortage of male labor, lack of fencing for livestock and the small size and fragmentation of landholdings. The average farm size varies between 0.40 and 1.6 hectares (1 and 4 acres). Most Africans employ the hoe as the principal agricultural implement, and mechanization and application of fertilizers are limited to the large-scale sector. In 1982 there were 4,650 tractors and 285 harvester-threshers in the country. Consumption of fertilizers in the same year was 85,400 tons, or 18.5 kg (41 lb) per arable hectare.

The transition from tribal to modern cultivation has been hindered by the traditional forms of tenure. Under customary law, ownership of land is theoretically vested in the tribe, with the paramount chief as custodian. But land rights could be conveyed to individuals, and there was some security of tenure. Sale of land is not permitted, but land may be transferred by a farmer to members of his family, usually through matrilineal inheritance. At independence, the government took over all land in an effort to detribalize tenure. It also encouraged sale and acquisition of land and its disposition by individual testament. Although lands under cultivation by Europeans have not been taken over, those abandoned by European farmers leaving Zambia have been redistributed to Africans.

```
┌────────────────────────────────────────────────┐
│         PRINCIPAL CROP PRODUCTION (1982)        │
│               (000 metric tons)                 │
│ Corn ....................................   810 │
│ Millet ...................................    60 │
│ Sorghum .................................    40 │
│ Sugar cane .............................. 1,050 │
│ Potatoes ................................     3 │
│ Sweet potatoes ..........................    21 │
│ Cassava .................................   180 │
│ Onions ..................................    22 │
│ Tomatoes ................................    25 │
│ Sunflower seed ..........................    16 │
│ Pulses ..................................    13 │
│ Bananas .................................     1 │
│ Groundnuts ..............................     9 │
│ Cottonseed ..............................    12 │
│ Cotton (lint) ...........................     4 │
│ Tobacco .................................     3 │
└────────────────────────────────────────────────┘
```

Cattle production is limited by the prevalence of the tsetse fly, poor grazing and breeding practices and low rate of reproduction. Furthermore, as in other African countries, cattle are regarded primarily as a store of wealth and as status symbols; the annual rate of takeoff for slaughter is only 6%—including ceremonial and ritual slaughter—compared to 30% in advanced countries. In order to improve the quality and management of livestock, the Rural Development Corporation has established a number of cattle ranches. Despite these efforts, only half of domestic beef requirements are supplied locally. The livestock population in 1980 consisted of 2.250 million cattle, 38,000 sheep, 343,000 goats, 240,000 pigs and 13 million chickens.

Nearly 13% of the land area is covered by forests, mostly in the Copperbelt and southern Barotseland.

The principal timber is Rhodesian teak, also known as Zambezi Redwood, a hardwood used in mine props and railroad ties. Roundwood removals in 1982 totaled 5.707 million cubic meters (201 million cubic ft).

Fishing is carried on in the major lakes, the Kariba, the Tanganyika and the Mweru and in the upper Zambezi and Bangweulu-Luapula basins, mostly as a subsistence occupation by part-time and full-time fishermen. The principal fishing concern is a state-owned firm set up with Norwegian assistance that provides storage, transportation and marketing facilities and equipment. The total fish catch in 1982 was 55,809 tons.

Agricultural finance is provided by the Agricultural Finance Corporation.

INDUSTRY

In 1982 manufacturing constituted the largest economic sector, contributing 18.3% to the GDP, with an annual rate of growth during 1973-83 of 0.3% and employing 2.2% of the wage-earning labor force. In 1982 the index of industrial production (1975=100) was 97. The value-added in manufacturing in 1982 was $427 million, of which agro-based products accounted for 16%, textiles for 24%, machinery and transport equipment for 10% and chemicals for 12%.

Foodstuffs, beverages and tobacco together form the largest subsector in terms of employment, investment and output, followed by textiles, sawmilling, manufacture of cement products, chemicals and pharmaceuticals, in approximate order. However, the greatest growth in manufacturing output has been in newer industries such as basic metals (71.1%), paper and paper products (20.2%) and chemicals, rubber and plastic products (15.3%).

Since independence the government has acquired a commanding position in manufacturing through the Industrial Development Corporation (INDECO), successor to the Nothern Rhodesia Industrial Development Corporation, which controls about 90 subsidiaries and associated companies in brewing, chemicals, real estate and manufacturing. INDECO expanded its role in the economy after the Mulungushi Declaration, under which it was given authority to take over 51% or more of the shares of 25 companies. INDECO has recently move into fertilizers, motor assembly and batteries. Over 60 foreign corporations have been nationalized since independence under a Zambianization program. These firms include Tate and Lyle, the giant British sugar concern.

Zambia always had had what can be described as a mixed economy despite substantial government participation in the industrial and marketing sectors through the parastatal system. Basic inefficiencies, caused by a number of factors, have been financed or subsidized by copper revenues. Zambia's philosophy of humanism which militates against exploitation by any one economic class, is the basic reason behind government's participation in, or control of, the mining sector, agricultural marketing, the food processing sector and other basic industries. The economic decline of recent years, however, has made the functioning of the parastatal system a drag on the economy rather than a net contributor to basic human needs and development. While recent policy decisions do not represent a policy change with respect to the private sector, they clearly suggest a change in emphasis. The first clear indication of this came with the introduction of the Industrial Development Act of 1977. It provides a basis for both domestic and foreign investor participation in the economy and certain guaranties and incentives.

Foreign investments in Zambia have been progressively reduced through nationalization. At the same time foreign investments are encouraged through a liberal policy permitting unlimited remittances of profits abroad.

ENERGY

In 1982 Zambia produced 1.807 million metric tons of coal equivalent of energy and consumed 2.335 million metric tons of coal equivalent, or 387 kg (853 lb) per capita. The annual energy deficit is 1.572 million metric tons of coal equivalent.

The annual growth rates during 1973-83 were 6.4% for energy production and 1.9% for energy consumption. Energy imports account for 22% of all merchandise imports. Apparent per capita consumption of gasoline is 33 gallons per year.

The domestic refinery capacity is 24,000 barrels of petroleum per day.

In 1984 total electric power production was 10.091 billion kwh, or 1,539 kwh per capita.

LABOR

The economically active population is estimated at close to 2.204 million, of which 17% is female. The wage-earning labor force is estimated at 402,000, consisting of 375,000 Africans and 27,000 Europeans and Asians. By occupation, nearly 66% of the labor force is employed in agriculture, 15% of wage-earners are in mining, 9% in agriculture, 9% in domestic service, 19% in construction, 9% in commerce, 10% in manufacturing, 23% in government service and 6% in transport.

In many cases wages are determined through collective bargaining. Where there are no established trade unions, minimum wage rates are determined by Wage Councils, in the case of specific industries, and Wages and Conditions of Employment Boards, in the case of geographical areas. Average monthly wages in 1980 ranged from K202 for Zambians to K1,000 for non-Zambians. This dual wage structure continues to be a source of considerable dissatisfaction for African workers. In April 1983 the government said that there would be a 10% ceiling on wage increases for low-paid workers. This followed threats by the Zambian Congress to Trade Unions (ZCTU) to organize a general strike unless the government reconsidered the 5% freeze which had been introduced in January. The ZCTU rejected the 10% ceiling in May. By September, however, President Kaunda announced that the 10% limit had been accepted by the unions. Working conditions are governed by legislation consistent with International Labor Organization (ILO) standards. These regulations cover provision of public holidays with pay, dismissal, housing and medical care. The Factories Act provides for stringent, comprehensive standards relating to working environments. The workweek varies from 40 to 48 hours. A majority of the wage-earning native labor force is covered by the National Provident Fund that provides retirement and permanent disability benefits. There is a similar fund for workmen's compensation.

Zambian law regulates minimum health and safety standards and worker rights in any industrial undertaking. Boards appointed by the government and including worker and employer representatives fix minimum wages, overtime pay and conditions of employment. Women are excluded from night work and a variety of hazardous occupations. Although age restrictions apply to the industrial sector, with few cases of employees under age 16, in the commercial and agricultural sectors persons under age 14 are often employed.

Since independence, the government has adopted Zambianization as an official policy. A committee was appointed to speed up this process in both the public and private sectors. In the mid-1980s, 94.7% of the jobs in the public sector and 88.4% of the jobs in the private sector were filled by Africans.

The country is faced with both unemployment among unskilled workers and a shortage of skilled workers. Extensive training programs are being undertaken under the four-year development plans to train craftsmen, technicians and scientists.

Zambia has a vigorous labor movement. The largest labor confederation is the Zambia Congress of Trade Unions (ZCTU), with 18 affiliated unions and 140,000 members. The largest single union is the Zambian African Mining Union, with 40,000 members.

Labor relations have been difficult throughout the 1970s. Virtually all strikes are illegal, since they almost always commence before the mandatory process of mediation has run its course. However, the government has normally relied on persuasion and continued mediation to end strikes once they have begun. A series of wildcat strikes during 1985, involving workers in such important sectors as finance and mining, resulted in a government decree declaring workers in most sectors of the economy "essential" and therefore liable to prosecution for illegal strike action. However, the government has yet to invoke this decree. The ZCTU is not controlled by the party or government, and union leaders frequently criticize government policy on such subjects as wages, economic policy, conditions of service and labor representation in party and government organs.

FOREIGN COMMERCE

The foreign commerce of Zambia consisted in 1984 of exports of $843.7 million and imports of $548.9 million, resulting in a trade surplus of $294.8 million. Of the imports, machinery and transport equipment constituted 34.8%, energy 22.0%, basic manufactures 20.6%, chemicals 12.4% and food 4.4%. Of the exports, copper constituted 86.8%, cobalt 8.2%, zinc 2.0% and lead 0.7%.

The major import sources are: the United Kingdom 22.4%, South Africa 15.7%, the United States 7.0%, West Germany 6.9%, Japan 5.0% and China 0.6%. The major export destinations are: Japan 16.4%, the United Kingdom 13.8%, the United States 11.2%, West Germany 8.3%, China 2.9% and South Africa 0.6%.

Based on 1975=100, the import price index in 1981 was 204, the export price index 137 and the terms of trade (export prices divided by import prices × 100) 67.

FOREIGN TRADE INDICATORS (1984)

Annual Growth Rate, Imports:	-7.3% (1973-83)
Annual Growth Rate, Exports:	-0.8% (1973-83)
Ratio of Exports to Imports:	60:40
Exports per capita:	$125
Imports per capita:	$81
Balance of Trade:	$294.8 million
Ratio of International Reserves to Imports (in months)	1.3
Exports as % of GDP:	41.9
Imports as % of GDP:	41.4
Value of Manufactured Exports:	—
Commodity Concentration:	98.6%

Direction of Trade (%)

	Imports	Exports
EEC	46.0	47.9
U.S.	7.8	10.2
Industrialized Market Economies	62.3	68.3
East European Economies	1.1	1.2
High Income Oil Exporters	20.2	0.7
Developing Economies	36.4	30.2

Composition of Trade (%)

	Imports	Exports
Food	8.6	0.4
Agricultural Raw Materials	1.2	—
Fuels	17.9	1.2
Ores & Minerals	5.8	97.6
Manufactured Goods	66.4	0.7
of which Chemicals	13.4	0.2
of which Machinery	33.9	0.1

TRANSPORTATION & COMMUNICATIONS

Zambia's rail system, 1,204 km (748 mi) long, is almost entirely single track. In 1975 the Tanzara line, a new 1,860-km (1,155-mi) rail link between Kapiri Mposhi and Dar es Salaam was opened to traffic. The line was built with technical and financial aid from China.

The length of the domestic pipeline is 1,724 km (1,071 mi).

Inland waterways are 2,250 km (1,397 mi) long and include both the Zambezi and other rivers and the three lakes: the Kariba, the Tanganyika and the Bangweulu. Mpulungu on Lake Tanganyika is Zambia's only port.

Zambia's road system is 36,370 km (22,586 mi) long including 6,500 km (4,036 mi) of paved roads. The main arterial roads run from Beit Bridge to Tunduma (the Great North Road, formerly nicknamed Hell's Run), from Beit Bridge to Chingola and Chililabombwe on the Zairean border, from Livingstone to the junction of the Kafue River and from Lusaka to the Malawi border. These roads were used in 1983 by 103,000 passenger cars and 90,000 commercial vehicles. Per capita passenger car ownership is 15.3 per 1,000 inhabitants. Freight and transport services are provided by the National Transport Corporation of Zambia and the Zambia-Tanzania Road Services.

The national airline is Zambia Airways Corporation, which operates nine aircraft on domestic and foreign routes, flying to 12 countries in Africa and Europe. In 1982 this airline carried 253,000 passengers and flew 8.4 million km (5.2 million mi). The main international airport is at Lusaka. In addition there are 127 airfields, of which 113 are usable, 10 have permanent-surface runways and three have runways over 2,500 meters (8,000 ft).

In 1984 there were 67,300 telephones in the country, or 1.0 per 100 inhabitants.

In 1982 Zambia's postal service handled 69,175,000 pieces of mail and 14,446,000 telegrams. Per capita volume was 10.2 pieces. There are 1,292 telex subscriber lines.

Zambia's impressive tourist attractions—including the Victoria Falls, known in the native language as Musi-O-Tunya, the Smoke that Thunders, and 17 national parks—were visited by 117,000 visitors in 1982. Of these, 3,800 were from the United States, 10,900 from the United Kingdom, 4,300 from South Africa, 1,700 from Italy, 2,300 from India and 2,100 from West Germany. Annual tourist revenues in the same year totaled $59 million and expenditures by nationals abroad $43 million. There are 4,000 hotel beds and the average length of stay was 4.8 days.

MINING

Zambia's copper-ore reserves are among the richest in the world. It has about one-fifth of the world's known reserves, some 880.3 million tons of high grade ore ranging from 2.41% to 4.6% copper content. The mines are administered by the Mining and Development Corporation, a statutory body controlled by the Zambia Industrial and Mining Corporation.

Metal mining is the country's most important economic activity, usually providing about 95% of foreign exchange earnings and 16%–18% of GDP, although its share of the latter fell considerably in 1981 and 1982, recovering to 16% in 1983. The contribution of mining to government revenue has declined since 1975, owing to rising costs, falling copper prices and constraints on copper output. By 1982 it was almost nil. New tax measures restored government revenue from mining in 1983.

The mining industry in Zambia was developed by two major groups, Zambian Anglo American (later Nchanga Consolidated Copper Mines) and Roan Selection Trust (later RCM), which first became involved in Zambia in the 1920s. Production of unrefined copper rose from virtually nil before 1930 to a peak of 747,500 metric tons in 1969, accounting for about 12% of world production and making Zambia the world's third largest copper producer. However, production fell to 564,000 tons in 1981, the lowest level since independence. Production is affected by falling ore grades and by increased processing losses; the industry suffers from shortages of foreign exchange (although the share of foreign exchange earnings that ZCCM may retain was increased from 25% to 35% in August 1983), from exacerbating problems of aging capital stock, from lack of maintenance and from shortages of skilled labor. As a result, Zambia's share of world copper output fell to just over 6% by 1982 from 12% in 1969.

The mining sector is now faced with a real prospect of exhaustion. Estimated reserves will last less than 20 years at current production rates. The 1983 annual report of ZCCM showed that fully developed reserves were equivalent to less than one year's output. Loans to finance a rehabilitation program have now been secured from the EEC (SYSMIN), the African Development Bank and, despite considerable opposition from U.S. producer interests, from the World Bank ($75 million approved in March 1984). It is estimated that the full rehabilitation project will cost $300 million and will take about five years to complete.

The copper price has given no comfort, and the long-term outlook for copper consumption is also gloomy. In 1983 the U.S. producer price averaged 78 cents per lb, while the price on the London Metal Exchange averaged £953 per metric ton: such prices are not sufficient to maintain ZCCM's short-term profitability, and clearly do not leave a sufficient margin for investment. ZCCM made operating losses in 1981/82 (K106 million) and in 1982/83 (K63 million). The first half of 1983/84 showed a considerable improvement, with operating profit at K120 million, reduced to K10 million after financing charges and tax.

ZCCM is still among the world's largest copper companies (only Chile's CODELCO produces more copper and employs more workers). In 1983 the company employed 57,700 Zambians and just over 2,000 expatriates; employment has been reduced by cost-cutting measures that were begun in May 1982. Zambia's copper is mostly exported in refined but unwrought form, through MEMACO, the state-owned marketing organization.

Mineral production in 1983 also included 452,870 tons of coal, 2,444 tons of cobalt, 14,800 tons of lead and 37,800 tons of zinc.

DEFENSE

The defense structure is headed by the president who is also the commander in chief of the armed forces and Minister of Defense. A Defense Council consisting of civilian and military members formulates military policy. The armed forces do not have a general staff, but each branch has its commander who reports to the permanent secretary of defense. Military manpower is obtained through voluntary enlistment.

Total strength of the armed forces is 16,200. Per capita strength is 2.5 armed persons per 1,000 civilians.

ARMY:

Personnel: 15,000

Organization: 1 armored regiment; 9 infantry battalions; 3 artillery batteries; 2 AA artillery batteries; 1 engineer battalion; 2 signals squadrons

Equipment: 30 heavy tanks and 50 light tanks; 60 armored combat vehicles; 13 armored personnel carriers; 65 guns; 43 howitzers; 50 rocket launchers; 12 antitank recoilless launchers; 161 air defense guns; antitank guided weapons; SAMs

AIR FORCE:

Personnel: 1,200

Organization: 44 combat aircraft; 2 fighter squadrons; 1 counter-insurgency squadron; 2 transport squadrons; 40 trainers; 1 helicopter squadron; 1 SAM regiment

Air Bases: Lusaka, Livingstone, Kalabo, Broken Hill, Ndola, Abercorn, Kasama, Mpika, Luwingu, N'changa and Chingola.

There is no navy.

No information is available on annual military expenditures since 1980.

The defense establishment is composed principally of ground troops, particularly infantry. The air force is essentially a supporting element without tactical combat capability. The army units are deployed along the line-of-rail stretching from the northern to the southern borders. It is doubtful whether the armed forces would be able to hold their own in the event of a conflict with white-ruled South Africa.

The United Kingdom and China have been the principal sources of military assistance, contributing $14 million and $18 million respectively. Arms purchases abroad during 1973-83 totaled $420 million, of which $180 million was supplied by the Soviet Union.

EDUCATION

The national literacy rate is 68.6% (79.3% for males and 58.3% for females). Of the population over 25, 63.9% have had no schooling, 31.9% have attended and/or completed first level, 3.7% have attended and/or completed second level, and 0.6% have completed secondary education.

Zambia has not yet introduced universal and compulsory education, but primary education is free for seven years. In 1980 the gross enrollment ratios were 96% in the first level (7-13) and 17% in the second level (14-18) for a combined enrollment ratio of 67%. The third-level enrollment ratio is 1.8%. Girls constitute 47% of primary school enrollment, 35% of secondary school enrollment and 22% of postsecondary enrollment.

Schooling lasts for 12 years divided into seven years of primary school, three years of junior secondary school and two years of senior secondary school. The primary cycle consists of two segments: a lower primary of four years and an upper primary of three years. At the end of the seventh year all students take the Upper-Primary School Leaving Examination and the Secondary Selection Examination; at the end of the 10th year they take the Junior Secondary School Leaving Examination. On completion of their secondary school studies, students receive the Cambridge Overseas School Certificate. The curriculum has been Zambianized to emphasize Zambian content and include material from Zambian sources. Textbooks are produced locally by the National Education Company. In 1982 the school system comprised 2,854 primary school and 135 secondary schools.

The school year runs from January through December. The language of instruction is English, but regional vernaculars are also emphasized.

There are adequate facilities for training primary school teachers in the nation's nine teacher training colleges. But there is an acute scarcity of qualified Zambian secondary school teachers, and enrollment in the country's two secondary school teacher training institutions is inadequate. Secondary schools rely on British and Asian teachers, who constitute nearly 90% of the staff. The national teacher-pupil ratio is 1:46 at the primary level, 1:21 at the secondary level and 1:11 at the postsecondary level.

There are two types of private schools: aided schools administered by churches or missions or other similar bodies, which charge no fees, and unaided schools, administered by private agencies, which sometimes charge tuition fees. Private schools account for 24% of primary and 2% of secondary enrollment.

Technical training institutions and vocational training schools are administered by the Commission for Vocational and Technical Training. Nearly 2.4% of the secondary school enrollment is in the vocational stream. However, teachers of technical subjects are in short supply. Literacy programs for adults are conducted by a number of organizations but primarily by the Adult Literacy Program through centers scattered throughout the country. Large numbers are also reached through radio programs in different vernaculars.

The educational system is administered by the Ministry of Education. A chief inspector of schools supervises the school system; each province has its own chief education officer. In 1981 educational expenditures totaled K139,810,000, of which 97.1% was current expenditure. This amount represented 10.0% of the national budget, 5.1% of the GNP and $35 per capita.

EDUCATIONAL ENROLLMENT (1981)			
	Schools	Teachers	Students
First Level	2,854	23,100	1,068,314
Second Level	135	4,650	98,862
Vocational	28	406	9,972
Third Level	1	334	3,603

Higher education is provided by the University of Zambia with 3,603 students. Per capita university enrollment is 54 per 100,000 inhabitants.

In 1982, 1,141 Zambian students were enrolled in institutions of higher learning abroad. Of these, 299 were in the United States, 484 in the United Kingdom, 163 in India, 70 in Canada and 17 in Australia.

Zambia ranks 106th in the world in contribution to world scientific authorship, with a share of 0.0060% (U.S., 42%).

LEGAL SYSTEM

The basis of Zambian jurisprudence is English common law. Under the 1972 constitution, the highest court in the land is the Supreme Court, consisting of a chief justice and six lower judges appointed by the president. Resident magistrate courts in various centers administer customary law. The independence and integrity of the judiciary are ensured by the Judicial Service Commission.

There are 60 penal institutions under the control of the Prison Service. Long-term prisoners are housed in 12 central prisons distributed among the provincial capitals and major cities. Of these, the maximum security institution is at Kabwe. In addition, there are 33 local prisons, nine remand prisons for those awaiting trial, a pre-release camp, a reformatory for juvenile offenders and institutions for first offenders. All prisoners are required to work and participate in literacy programs. A number of prison farms are also maintained.

LAW ENFORCEMENT

The Zambian Police Force, commanded by an inspector general, is the primary agency concerned with internal peacekeeping. It consists of a central headquarters at Lusaka, with nine divisions in each of the provinces and in the capital. Its total strength in the mid-1970s was 6,250, or one policeman for every 800 inhabitants.

Division police units differ in size and capability but generally comprise a number of police stations. The grade structure conforms closely to the British pattern. Police are permitted to carry firearms, but are subject to strict limitations on their use.

The police are assisted by a number of specialized support units, including a mobile battalion, a light aircraft and helicopter unit and a paramilitary battalion. The mobile force and the paramilitary battalion are organized and trained along military lines.

Crime has increased by over 300% over the last 30 years; all types of criminal activity have contributed to this staggering increase. Nearly 60% of the crimes relate to offenses against property, and a large number of offenses are committed under the influence of drink. The juvenile share of both total crimes and serious crimes has risen sharply, but women represent a decreasing minority among law-breakers.

HEALTH

Health services have been expanded since independence to provide free medical treatment to Zambian nationals at both rural and urban health centers. One successful innovation has been the Flying Doctor Service, with five light aircraft and seven physicians delivering health care to remote areas. Health expenditures in 1982 constituted 6.1% of the national budget and $15.30 per capita.

PRINCIPAL HEALTH INDICATORS (1984)
Crude Death Rate: 15.1 per 1,000
Decline in Death Rate: −21.4% (1965-83)
Life Expectancy at Birth: 49.6 (Males); 53.1 (Females)
Infant Mortality Rate: 110.5 per 1,000 Live Births
Child Death Rate (Ages 1-4) per 1,000: 19

In 1981 there were 636 hospitals with 20,638 beds, or one bed per 282 inhabitants. The number of physicians was 821, or one physician per 7,101 inhabitants, 52 dentists and 871 nursing personnel. Of the hospitals 63.8% are state-run, 14.5% are run by private nonprofit agencies and 1.7% by private for-profit agencies. The admissions/discharge rate is 391 per 10,000 inhabitants, the bed occupancy rate is 76.0% and the average length of hospital stay is 7 days. Only 42% of the population have access to safe water.

FOOD

The staple foods are corn, millet and cassava, supplemented by sweet potatoes and peanuts. The main source of protein is fish.

The daily per capita intake of food is 1,992 calories, 54.5 grams of protein, 35 grams of fats and 367 grams of carbohydrates.

MEDIA & CULTURE

Two daily newspapers, The Times of Zambia and the Zambia Daily Mail, both owned by the government, are published in the country, with a combined circulation of 115,000, or 17 per 1,000 inhabitants. Both are published in English. Of non-daily general interest newspapers, three appear weekly and 10 bi-weekly, either in English alone or in both English and regional vernaculars. A number of biweeklies are published by the Zambian Information Services. Annual consumption of newsprint in 1982 was 1,200 tons, or 0.17 kg (0.3 lb) per capita.

The influential daily press is almost entirely controlled by the government, and there are numerous restrictions on other types of media. Criticism of government policies is usually frowned upon; the press, therefore, always presents official policies in a favorable light. There is no opposition press.

The national news agency is Zambia News Agency. Reuters, AFP and DPA are represented in Lusaka.

Zambia's book publishing industry, once one of the most active in English-speaking Africa, has declined in recent years. There are at least seven commercial publishers, including the Oxford University Press. The National Educational Company is a subsidiary of the Kenneth Kaunda Foundation. Annual output in 1981 was 7 titles.

Zambia Broadcasting Services operate eight medium-wave radio stations and 10 short-wave stations, broadcasting for about 240 hours a week, principally in English, but also in the seven main vernaculars: Bemba, Nyanja, Lozi, Tonga, Kaounde, Lunda and Luvale. In 1982 there were 160,000 radio receivers in the country, or 26 per 1,000 inhabitants. Of the 10,589 annual radio broadcasting hours, 2,172 hours are devoted to information, 2,212 hours to education, 648 hours to culture, 328 hours to religion, 432 hours to commercials and 3,162 hours to entertainment.

Television, introduced in 1961, is operated by Television Zambia, with two stations at Lusaka and Kabwe. Programs are broadcast for six hours daily on three channels, with an additional educational program for 1 ½ hours on school days. In 1982 there were 75,000 television sets, or 12 per 1,000 inhabitants.

Domestic film production is limited to documentaries. There are 12 fixed cinemas with 4,100 seats, or 0.8 seats per 1,000 inhabitants. Annual attendance is 1.6 million, or 0.3 per capita.

The largest libraries in the country are the University of Lusaka Library with 70,000 volumes and the Central Library of the Zambia Library Service, with 300,000 volumes. The Zambia Library Service maintains 750 library centers, six regional libraries and three branch libraries.

There are three museums reporting an annual attendance of 300,000, and 18 nature preservation sites.

SOCIAL WELFARE

The Department of Welfare provides a wide range of welfare services, including emergency relief, care for the aged and protection of children. A contributory social security system in the form of the National Provident Fund was established in 1966 and covers urban workers.

GLOSSARY

chitemene: slash-and-burn cultivation practiced by African farmers.
kitchen kaffir: pidgin language used by Asians and Europeans in communicating with Africans.

CHRONOLOGY (from 1964)

1964— Northern Rhodesia becomes an independent republic under the name of Zambia with Kenneth David Kaunda as first president.... Government efforts to suppress the Lumpa sect lead to clashes in which 650 are killed.

1968— Kwacha is introduced as the national currency replacing the Zambian pound.... Kaunda issues Mulungushi Declaration announcing state takeover of 51% ownership in 25 major companies through the Industrial Development Corporation.... United Party is banned following election violence.... Ruling United National Independence Party (UNIP) wins decisive electoral victory; Kaunda names new cabinet.... Amnesty granted to Lumpa cultists is rejected by its leader, Alice Lenshina.

1969— Kaunda sponsors the Lusaka Manifesto condemning South Africa and Rhodesia but calling for peaceful change rather than confrontation as the means of eliminating racism in southern Africa.... Licenses of Indian merchants are not renewed.... Anti-judiciary riots follow High Court ruling exonerating white Portuguese soldiers who violated Zambian territory.... Official campaign against Jehovah's Witnesses begins.

1970— Kaunda announces steps for eventual takeover of all foreign-owned mining interests.

1971— Prime Minister John Vorster of South Africa embarrasses Kaunda by revealing confidential state correspondence between the two in which Kaunda had sought economic aid.... New constitution is announced for UNIP.

1972— Simon Kapwepwe's United Progressive Party is banned

1973— Kaunda signs into law new constitution establishing Zambia as a "one party participatory democracy."... Rhodesia closes border with Zambia.

1974— Kaunda nationalizes the country's two major copper mining companies.... Lusaka Agreement opens the way for constitutional talks in Rhodesia.

1975— TanZam rail link between Dar es Salaam and Kapiri Mposhi is opened.... Kaunda attends the unsuccessful Victoria Falls Talks between the Ian Smith regime and Zimbabwe nationalists.

1976— Kaunda declares emergency as depressed copper prices cause severe economic difficulties; kiwacha is devalued.

1977— Mainza Chona replaces Elijah Mudenda as prime minister.

1978— Copper output is cut and austerity measures are introduced.... President Kaunda is re-

elected.... Prime Minister Chona is replaced by
Daniel Lisulo.
1983— President Kaunda is reelected to another
term in office.... President Kaunda visits London
for the first time since the UDI of Rhodesia.
1986— South African planes raid Lusaka and other
targets in pursuit of ANC rebels.

BIBLIOGRAPHY (from 1970)

Anglin, Douglas G., and Timothy M. Shaw, *Zambia's Foreign Policy: Studies in Diplomacy & Dependence* (Boulder, Col., 1979).

Beveridge, Andrew A., and Oberschall, Anthony R., *African Businessmen and Development in Zambia* (Princeton, N.J., 1979).

Bond, George C., *The Politics of Change in a Zambian Community* (Chicago, 1976).

Bratton, Michael, *The Local Politics of Rural Development: Peasant & Party-State in Zambia* (Hanover, N.H., 1980).

Burdette, Marcia, *Zambia* [profiles Nations of Contemporary Africa] (Boulder, Colo., 1986).

Central Statistical Office, *Statistical Yearbook* (Lusaka, Zambia, Annual).

Chanock, Martin, *Law, Custom and Social Order: The Colonial Experience in Malawi and Zambia* (New York, 1985).

Daniel P., *Africanization, Nationalization & Inequality* (New York, 1979).

De Gaay Fortman, Bastiaaen, *After Mulungushi: The Economics of Zambian Humanism* (New York, 1969).

Dodge, Doris J., *Agricultural Policy & Performance in Zambia* (Berkeley, Calif., 1977).

Elliott, Charles, *Constraints on the Economic Development of Zambia* (New York, 1972).

Epstein, A.L., *Urbanization and Kinship: The Domestic Domain on the Copperbelt of Zambia* (Orlando, Fla., 1982).

Gertzel, Cheryl, *The Dynamics of the One-Party State in Zambia* (Manchester, England, 1984).

Grotpeter, John J., *Historical Dictionary of Zambia* (Metuchen, N.J., 1979).

Hall, Richard, *The High Price of Principles: Kaunda & the White South* (New York, 1970).

——, *Zambia, 1890-1964: The Colonial Period* (New York, 1976).

Harries-Jones, Peter, *Freedom and Labour: Mobilization and Political Control on the Zambian Copperbelt* (New York, 1975).

Johnson, Walter R., *Worship & Freedom: A Black American Church in Zambia* (New York, 1978).

Kaunda, Kenneth, *Letter to My Children* (New York, 1973).

Macpherson, F., *The Anatomy of a Conquest: The British Occupation of Zambia, 1884-1924* (London, 1982).

Madu, Oliver, V., *Models of Class Domination in Plural Societies of Central Africa* (Washington, D.C., 1978).

Meebelo, Henry, *Reaction to Colonialism: A Prelude to the Politics of Independence in Northern Zambia, 1893-1939* (New York, 1971)

Obidwegwu, Chukwuma F. and Mudziwiri Nziramasanga, *Copper and Zambia: An Econometric Analysis* (Lexington, Mass., 1981).

Osei-Hwedie, Kwaku and Muna Ndulo, *Issues in Zambian Development* (Roxbury, Mass., 1985).

Pettman, Jan, *Zambia: Security and Conflict, 1964-1973* (New York, 1974).

Roberts, Andrew, *A History of Zambia* (New York, 1976).

Rotberg, Robert I., *Black Heart: Gore-Brown and the Politics of Multiracial Zambia* (Berkeley, Calif., 1979).

Schultz, Jurgen, *The Basically Traditional Land Use Systems of Zambia and their Regions* (New York, 1976).

Shaw, Timothy M., *Dependence and Underdevelopment: The Development and Foreign Policies of Zambia* (Athens, Ohio, 1976).

——, and Douglas G. Anglin, *Alternative Sources of Event Data on Zambian Foreign Policy* (Syracuse, N.Y., 1981).

Simonis, Heide and Uldo Ernst, *Socioeconomic Development in Dual Economies: The Example of Zambia* (New York, 1971).

Sklar, Richard L., *Corporate Power in an African State: The Political Impact of Multinational Mining Companies in Zambia* (Berkeley, Calif., 1975).

Tordoff, William, *Politics in Zambia* (Berkeley, Calif., 1975).

——, *Administration in Zambia* (Madison, Wis., 1981).

Turok, Ben, *Development in Zambia: A Reader* (London, 1981).

Williams, Geoffrey J., *Independent Zambia: A Bibliography of the Social Sciences* (Boston, Mass., 1984).

Young, Alistair, *Industrial Diversification in Zambia* (New York, 1973).

OFFICIAL PUBLICATIONS

Central Statistical Office, *Monthly Digest of Statistics.*

Zambia Bank, *Report and Statement of Accounts.*

——, *Quarterly Statistical Review.*

Boundary representation is
not necessarily authoritative.

28   32

Lusaka
Namwala   Kafue
Mazabuka   Kanyemba   Feira   *Cabora Bassa Dam*
Chirundu   Songo

16   MOZAMBIQUE   16

ZAMBIA

Kariba Dam   Kariba
Mulobezi   Choma   *Zambezi*   *Mazoe*   Changara
Lake Kariba   Mangula   Mount Darwin
Zawi   Kildonan   Bindura   Shamva
Sinoia   Mtoko
Kazungula   Binga   *Hunyani*   *Sanyati*
Livingstone   **Salisbury**   Catandica
Victoria Falls   Marandellas   Inyanga
Victoria Falls   *Umniati*   Gatooma   Rusape   Chimoio
Wankie   *Gwai*   Que Que   *Sabi*   Umtali   Chimoio
Shangani   Umvuma   *Chicamba*   *Rio Revué*
Lupane   Gwelo   Selukwe   Melsetter
Eastnor   *Gwai*   Dombe   20
20   Fort Victoria   *Rio Buzi*
Nata   Bulawayo   Shabani   Espungabera

BOTSWANA   Plumtree   *Lundi*   Nandi
Gwanda   *Rio Save*
Francistown   West Nicholson   *Nuanetsi*   Rutenga

Zimbabwe

——— International boundary
★   National capital
⊹⊹⊹ Railroad
——— Road
✛   International airport

0 25 50 75 Kilometers
0 25 50 75 Miles

Umzingwane   MOZAMBIQUE
Beitbridge   Chicualacuala   *Rio Chefu*
Limpopo   Messina   *Limpopo*
SOUTH AFRICA   32

ZIMBABWE

BASIC FACT SHEET

OFFICIAL NAME: The Republic of Zimbabwe (formerly Southern Rhodesia)

ABBREVIATION: ZI

CAPITAL: Harare

HEAD OF STATE: President Canaan Banana (from 1980)

HEAD OF GOVERNMENT: Prime Minister Robert Mugabe (from 1980)

NATURE OF GOVERNMENT: Parliamentary Democracy

POPULATION: 8,667,000 (1985)

AREA: 390,580 sq km (150,803 sq mi)

ETHNIC MAJORITY: Shona and Ndebele Tribes

LANGUAGE: English; Shona and Ndebele spoken by Africans

RELIGIONS: Christianity, Animism

UNIT OF CURRENCY: Zimbabwe Dollar ($1=Z$1.548, 1985)

NATIONAL FLAG: Seven horizontal stripes of green, yellow, red, black, red, yellow and green; on a white triangle in the hoist a red star surmounted by a Zimbabwe bird in yellow

NATIONAL EMBLEM: Red star surmounted by a Zimbabwe bird in yellow.

NATIONAL ANTHEM: "Ishe Komborera Africa'

NATIONAL HOLIDAYS: April 18 (Independence Day); New Year's Day; March 8 (International Women's Day); March 18 (Thiupepo Day); April 28 (Chimurenjo Day); May 1 (Day of the International Working Day); May 6 (Heroes Day); May 25 (African Liberation Day); June 1 (International Children's Day); June 15 (Pakawira Day); August 8 (ZANU Day); August 9 (Nyadzonya Day); November 23 (Rededication Day); Christmas; December 26 (Boxing Day)

NATIONAL CALENDAR: Gregorian

PHYSICAL QUALITY OF LIFE INDEX: 64, up from 46 in 1980. (On an ascending scale in which 100 is the maximum; U.S. 95).

DATE OF INDEPENDENCE: April 18, 1980

DATE OF CONSTITUTION: April 18, 1980

WEIGHTS & MEASURES: The metric system is in force

LOCATION & AREA

Located in south central Africa, between the Zambezi River on the north and Limpopo River on the South, Zimbabwe has an area of 390,580 sq km (150,803 sq mi) extending 852 km (529 mi) WNW to ESE and 710 km (441 mi) NNE to SSW.

Zimbabwe's total international border of 2,988 km (1,857 mi) is shared with four neighbors; Mozambique (1,223 km, 760 mi); South Africa (225 km, 140 mi); Botswana (813 km, 505 mi) and Zambia (727 km, 452 mi). Except for the border with Zambia, the boundaries were established during colonial rule. The Limpopo River was accepted as the boundary with South Africa by the convention of 1881. The border with Mozambique dates from 1891 with only minor changes until 1912 and again during the 1930s. The Zambezi formed the administrative dividing line between northern and southern Rhodesia and was tacitly accepted when Zambia became independent. There are no current boundary disputes.

The capital is Harare, formerly Salisbury, with a 1982 population of 656,000. The other principal towns are: Bulawayo (413,800), Chitungwiza (172,600), Gweru, formerly Gwelo (78,900), Mutare, formerly Umtali (69,600), Kwekwe, formerly Que Que (47,600), Kadoma, formerly Gatooma (44,600), Hwanga, formerly Wankie (39,200), Masuingo, formerly Fort Victoria (30,600), Zvishavani, formerly Shabani (26,800), Chinhoyi, formerly Sinoia (24,300), Radeliff (22,000) and Marondera, formerly Marandellas (20,300).

A rolling plateau known as the veld covers most of Zimbabwe. The veld slopes gently downward forming three distinct topographical regions: the High Veld, the Middle Veld and the Low Veld. The High Veld is some 640 km (400 mi) long and 80 km (50 mi) wide stretching northeast and southwest with a mean elevation of between 1,219 meters (4,000 ft) and 1,675 meters (5,500 ft). Its relatively smooth terrain is frequently interrupted by rocky hills known locally as kopjes. The eastern mountain complex around Umtali is the highest in the country with peaks between 1,829 meters (6,000 ft) and 2,438 meters (8,000 ft). The highest peak, Mount Inyangi, reaches 2,595 meters (8,514 ft). The central High Veld is marked by the Great Dyke, a series of eroded ridges, such as the Doro Range, the Selondi Range, the Mashona Hills, and the Umvukwe Range. The Middle Veld is no more than

120 km (75 mi) wide in its southeastern flank, but is twice as broad in western and northwestern Zimbabwe. The Low Veld, generally land below 914 meters (3,000 ft) extends from the of the Middle Veld to the southern and southeastern borders covering nearly one-fifth of the national territory.

Only one major river originates in Zimbabwe: the Sabi which has its watershed west of Umtali in the High Veld. Thence the Sabi flows southwest into the Low Veld where it is joined by the Lundi and turns eastward, reaching eventually the Indian Ocean in Mozambique. But the principal drainage system is provided by two rivers originating outside Zimbabwe: the Zambezi and the Limpopo. The longest of all African rivers flowing into the Indian Ocean, the Zambezi drains water from all of Zimbabwe northwest of the central ridgeline of the High Veld. In western Zimbabwe the river drops over the Victoria Falls, one of the most spectacular and largest falls in the world, 109 meters (360 ft) high and 1.6 km (1 mi) wide. Some 480 km (300 mi) below the falls is Lake Kariba, one of the largest man-made lakes in the world, flooding 5,180 sq km (2,000 sq mi) in Zimbabwe and Zambia. Runoff from the eastern and southeastern slopes is carried off by the Limpopo, which rises in South Africa.

WEATHER

Zimbabwe lies within the southern intertropical zone with four distinct climatic seasons: a warm rainy season from November to March, a transitional season during April and May, a cool and dry winter season from May to August and a warm and dry season from August through October. Throughout most of the High Veld, the climate is generally pleasant, with daily maximum temperatures hovering between 26.7°C and 32.2°C (80°F and 90°F) in summer and 12°C and 13°C (53.6°F and 55.4°F) in winter. On the Low Veld, temperatures are generally 5.5 degrees centigrade (10° Fahrenheit) higher and up to 38°C (100°F) in the Zambezi and Limpopo valleys.

Rainfall is highest in the High Veld which receives as much as 102 cm (40 in.) annually. The eastern highlands and southeastern Veld also receive small amounts of precipitation during winter when most of the country is dry. Annual rainfall averages 41 to 61 cm (16 to 24 in.) in the Middle Veld but declines to less than 40 cm (12 in.) in Low Veld regions. Beitbridge, in the country's most arid zone, receives less than 50 mm (2 in.) in some years.

POPULATION

The population of Zimbabwe was estimated in 1985 at 8,667,000 on the basis of the last census held in 1982 when the population was 7,532,000. The population is expected to reach 14.5 million by 2000 and 28.1 million by 2020.

The annual growth rate is estimated at 3.5% on the basis of a birthrate of 47.2 per 1,000 and a natural increase of 34.9 per 1,000. These rates are more than twice those for the small Asian minority and thrice those of the whites.

The population estimates reveal an average density of 22 per sq km (44 per sq mi) up from 13 per sq km (34 per sq mi) in 1969. The patterns of density remain uneven with much of the former white areas in the High Veld reporting much lower densities as compared to the African populated Middle and Low Veld.

In 1982, 82 localities were classified as urban including 12 described as cities. Nearly 23% of the population live in these urban areas as compared to 20% in 1969. But the pace of urban growth has accelerated since the late 1970's and is now estimated at close to 5.8%. More than 18% of the total population was concentrated in the 12 largest towns and Harare itself accounts for 50% of the urban population. Eighty percent of the white, Asian and Colored minorities live in the major towns. More than two-fifths of the white population live in Harare and one-fifth in Bulawayo.

Nearly 47.6% of the population is less than 14 years of age, 49.6% between 15 and 64 years of age constituting the economically active population, and 2.7% over 65 years.

Males are in a slight majority forming 50.3% of the population and there is no evidence that the white exodus after independence has significantly changed this percentage.

Zimbabwe attracted a steady stream of white immigrants until the late 1970's. The rate of arrivals and departures varied according to the changing political situation in the country. Except for the years 1961 through 1964 and 1966, there has been a net gain in white immigration since 1954. The largest gain was in 1956 when the net immigration was 11,000 people and the largest loss was in 1963 when the net loss was also 11,000. About 55% of the British, South African, Indian and other minorities were born outside of the then colony. Most of the white immigrants, called Europeans locally, arriving in the 1970's have settled either in Harare or in Bulawayo. African immigration has also been substantial, although extending over several decades. The 1969 census reported that 6.9% of the African population was born outside of the country, about one half from Malawi and one third from Mozambique. There was a net loss in African immigration only from 1968 through 1972.

Precise figures are difficult to obtain on the number of black Zimbabweans in self-imposed exile in Zambia and Botswana. As a result of political violence in Matabeleland, a significant number of Ndebele-speakers are living in a United Nations High Commissioner for Refugees-sponsored camp in Botswana and in several Botswanan towns close to the border with Zimbabwe. The government views the camp as a staging base for dissidents and "bandits" operating in Matebeleland and has urged the Botswana government to be more active in policing the sector and to turn over suspected dissidents to Zimbabwean

DEMOGRAPHIC INDICATORS (1985)	
Population, total (000)	8,667
Population ages (% of total)	
0-14	47.6
15-64	49.6
65 +	2.7
Youth 15-24 (000)	1,660
Women 15-49 (000)	1,918
Dependency, total	101.4
Child-Woman ratio	215
Sex ratio (per 1,000 Females)	98.2
Median age	16.1
Average size of household	4.5
% Illegitimate births	4.2
Decline in birthrate 1965-83 (%)	4.4
Proportion of urban	25.46
Population density per sq km	22
per hectare of arable land	1.72
Annual rate of growth (%)	3.50
Urban	5.8
Rural	2.8
Natural increase 1/1000	34.9
Crude birthrate 1/1000	47.2
Crude death rate 1/1000	12.3
Gross reproduction rate	3.25
Net reproduction rate	2.62
Total fertility rate	6.60
General fertility rate 1/1000	215
Life expectancy: males years	53.5
Life expectancy: females years	57.9
Life expectancy total years	55.7
Population doubling time in years at current rate	20

authorities. An improvement in the political climate in Matabeleland could result in the return to Zimbabwe of many of these exiles.

Migration of persons from Mozambique into Zimbabwe continued in 1985. An estimated 6,000 Mozambicans are now located in camps along the border. The flow is due partly to political instability in areas of Mozambique and partly to expectations of better economic opportunities in Zimbabwe. With few exceptions, the Zimbabwean government does not consider these temporary residents to be "refugees" as defined by the U.N. Protocol Relating to the Status of Refugees.

Despite efforts to clarify and modernize the situation, the legal status of women in Zimbabwean society remains ambiguous. In 1980, the government passed the Legal Age of Majority Act which gave all women over the age of 18 equal legal rights, including the right to arrange their own marriages and to own property apart from their husbands. On the other hand, the system of "Lobola," or bride price, is still the social norm, and the reality of equal rights remains elusive. A recent ruling by the Supreme Court found that fathers may no longer sue for "seduction damages" from a male suitor who has impregnated a daughter over the age of 18; the woman herself may sue, however. The widespread public reaction against this ruling is indicative of the power of traditional norms.

Until independence, African leaders opposed birth control programs as efforts by the then dominant white majority to restrict African growth while encouraging white immigration. This attitude has changed and the Mugabe regime has called for the creation of a ministry to deal with population explosion.

ETHNIC COMPOSITION

Ethnically, Zimbabwe is composed of four distinct groups: black Africans, whites (called Europeans, irrespective of national origins), Asians (mainly East Indians) and Coloreds (people of mixed European-African or Indian African origin). Blacks constite 96% of the population, whites, 3.55% and Indians and Coloreds 0.5%. Despite fears of a white exodus following independence, the European percentage has not been substantially reduced. In the first year of independence only 20,000 whites left Zimbawe out of a total of over 200,000.

Most Africans belong to one of two major ethnic groups: Shona or Ndebele. Because of historical assimilation, ethnicity is determined by the language spoken by each tribe. On this basis, nearly 71% of the population is Shona, 16% Ndebele, and 13% members of smaller ethnic groups. The Shona, often called Mashona, are actually a group of different ethnic tribes speaking variants of the same Bantu language and displaying considerable similarities in social organization. The Ndebele, called the Matabele by British historians, are a pastoral and later warrior people who invaded present-day Zimbabwe in the 19th century and subjugated the Shona. Under their king Mzilikazi they were in the process of carving out a nation when the British arrived and put an end to their ambitions.

ETHNIC GROUPS OF ZIMBABWE	
	(%)
Shona	70.8
Shona	26.0
Karanga	15.5
Zezeru	13.4
Manyika	7.2
Ndau	3.7
Korekore	3.0
Kalanga	1.8
Other	0.2
Ndebele and Nguni	15.8
Minor Indigenous Tribes	4.9
SenaChikunda	1.9
Tonga	1.2
Venda	0.8
Sotho-Tswana	0.6
Thonga-Hlengwe	0.1
Other	0.3
Minor Non Indigenous Tribes	7.8
Nyanja (Malawi)	5.2
Yao (Malawi)	0.4
Senga (Zambia)	0.3
Lozi (Zambia)	0.2
Ngoni (Mozambique)	0.1
Xosa (South Africa)	0.1
Bemba (Zambia)	0.1
Other	1.4
Other	0.7

Coloreds and Asians occupy a somewhat ambiguous position in Zimbabwean society. The proportion of

Asians has remained more or less stable over the years while that of Coloreds has risen.

LANGUAGES

English is the official language and is spoken by an increasing number of Africans.

Africans speak the language or dialect of their tribe and although of Bantu origin they are not mutually intelligible. The predominant African languages are Shona and Ngoni (or Ndebele). A form of pidgin called Kitchen kaffir based on Bantu with an admixture of Portuguese, English and Afrikaans, is dying out.

RELIGIONS

The religious affiliations of Zimbabweans generally conform to those of the rest of Black Africa. Available statistics indicate that around 20% is nominally Christian while the majority follow either traditional beliefs or a syncretist faith blending Christian and traditional tenets and practices. Of the Europeans and Coloreds some 33% are Anglican, 11% Presbyterian, 15% Roman Catholic, 9% Methodist and 9% Dutch Reformed. The Asian population is divided roughly into Hindu and Muslim. There are Jewish congregations in Harare and Bulawayo.

The trend among African Christians is toward independent and separatist churches presenting typically Africanized responses to the Biblical message. There are two kinds of independent churches: one called Ethiopian (which had split from the mother churches in protest against white control and racial discrimination) ministered only to black congregations; the second called Zionist churches attracted people from a non-Christian background, people who had very little formal education, and those who wished to retain their own traditional culture. Similar to the Messianic cults of central Africa, these churches coalesced around a charismatic leader and claimed to follow the Bible literally and stressed healing and speaking in tongues.

COLONIAL EXPERIENCE

The home of the Shona people, Zimbabwe was ruled by the Ndebele when Cecil Rhodes and his British South Africa Company obtained a royal charter for the exploitation of mineral rights in what was then called Mashonaland. Rhodes sent a group of settlers with a force of police and founded the town of Salisbury. Later, he gained the right to dispose of the land to settlers. With the defeat of the Ndebele rulers between 1893 and 1897, Mashonaland became British territory under the name of Rhodesia. In 1923 Southern Rhodesia was annexed to the crown and the colony received its first constitution. Ten years later, the government acquired the mineral rights to the territory from the British South Africa Company.

From the beginning the white settlers made every effort to institutionalize their supremacy. The British government, however, retained certain powers to safeguard the rights of Africans. In 1930, under pressure from the settlers, the British government adopted a land apportionment act under which about half the total land area, including all the mining and industrial regions, was reserved for Europeans. Most of the remaining territory was designated as Tribal Trust Land. The Land Tenure Act of 1969 gave Europeans and Africans 18.19 million hectares (44.95 million acres) each, although the former constituted only 4% of the population.

In 1953 Southern Rhodesia joined with Northern Rhodesia and Nyasaland in the short-lived Central African Federation. After its demise in 1963, Southern Rhodesia began to seek independence, but the whites and the blacks set their own conditions; the latter insisting on African majority rule and the former on the continuance of the status quo. After the breakdown of negotiations, the government of Southern Rhodesia, led by Prime Minister Ian Smith, issued a Unilateral Declaration of Independence in 1965. Five years later, Rhodesia declared itself a republic. Both acts were condemned by the United Kingdom, United Nations, and most African countries as illegal and unconstitutional. Following a call by the U.N. Security Council, many countries imposed severe economic sanctions against the so-called Republic of Rhodesia. Mounting international political pressure and guerrilla activities forced the Smith government to alternate between increased repression and efforts to seek an accord with the nationalists, represented by three organizations, the Zimbabwe African National Union, the African National Union, and the Zimbabwe National People's Union. In 1977 Ian Smith accepted the principle of universal adult suffrage and a settlement was signed in 1978 with bishop Muzorewa's United African National Council, the Ndabaningi Sithole faction of the Zimbabwe African National Union and Jeremiah Chirau's Zimbabwe United People's Organization. In 1978, the newly created Executive Council consisting of Smith, Muzorewa, Chirau and Sithole released all political detainees in an effort to bring about a ceasefire. In 1979 a majority rule constitution, with entrenched safeguards for the white minority, was approved by the House of Assembly. In the first elections held under this constitution, Muzorewa's UANC emerged as the majority party winning 51 of 72 African seats. Muzorewa was named as the first black prime minister of the nation (now renamed Zimbabwe) and his government of national unity included European members. The new government did not win either domestic or international acceptance and further efforts to resolve the crisis led to the constitutional conference at Lancaster House in London in September 1979, attended by both the Muzorewa group and the Patriotic Front representing the guerrilla forces. Complete agreement was reached on a new constitution (including special representation for the whites) and on transitional arrangements following a ceasefire. "Rebel" rule, which had lasted for 14 years, ended when the Zimbabwe-Rhodesian parliament renounced "independence" and reverted to the status of a British colony. The new British governor, Lord Soames, supervised new elections to the House of Assembly in which Robert Mugabe's ZANU emerged as the largest single party winning 57 out of 80 African seats. On April 18, 1980 the new state of Zimbabwe was born with Rev. Canaan Banana as president and Robert Mugabe as prime minister. Current relations with Great Britain are good.

CONSTITUTION & GOVERNMENT

Under the terms of the independence constitution of 1980, Zimbabwe is a sovereign republic with a president as head of state and a prime minister, elected by the House of Assembly, as the head of government. Legislative power is vested in the bicameral parliament consisting of the House of Assembly and the Senate. The constitution provides for separate voting rolls for blacks and whites, the latter having 20% of the seats in the House of Assembly and 25% of the Senate.

The president is elected by an electoral college consisting of the House of Assembly and the Senate and holds office for renewable terms of six years.

The constitution contains what are known as entrenched clauses dividing voter list into two categories: African and European. Voters on the European list elect 20 members of the House of Assembly and 10 members of the Senate. Amendments to this clause require the approval of all members of the House of Assembly. Other amendments require the approval of not less than two thirds of the Senate and of not fewer than 70 members of the House of Assembly.

Zimbabwe is a multiparty, parliamentary-style democracy fashioned after the Westminster model. Members of Parliament represent electoral districts and are chosen by direct, universal suffrage. The prime minister is elected by a parliamentary majority and is responsible to Parliament. Prime Minister Mugabe has pledged to transform Zimbabwe into a one-party state — an action that, if carried out, would fundamentally alter the political landscape and possibly deprive Zimbabweans of many of the political rights they now enjoy.

Zimbabwe's first general election since independence was held in July 1985. The Zimbabwe African National Union (ZANU), led by Prime Minister Mugabe, enlarged its existing parliamentary majority by winning 64 of the 80 seats reserved under the 1980 Lancaster House agreement for representatives of the black electorate. ZANU support came from the Shona-speaking majority, which is concentrated in northern and central Zimbabwe. The Zimbabwe African Peoples' Union (ZAPU), led by Joshua Nkomo, captured 15 parliamentary seats in largely Ndebele-speaking areas in the south and west. A splinter party, ZANU-S, won one seat in the predominantly Ndau tribal region in the southeast. On the white elec-

CABINET LIST (1985)	
President	Canaan Banana
Prime Minister	Robert Mugabe
Deputy Prime Minister	Simon Vengai Muzenda
Minister of Defense	Robert Mugabe
Minister of Education	Dzingai Mutumbuka
Minister of Energy, Water Resources & Development	Kumbirai Kangai
Minister of Finance, Economic Planning & Development	Dr. Bernard Chidzero
Minister of Foreign Affairs	Dr. Witness Mangwende
Minister of Health	Dr. Sydney Sekeramayi
Minister of Home Affairs	Enos Nkala
Minister of Industry & Technology	Dr. Callistus Ndlovu
Minister of Information, Posts & Telecommunications	Dr. Nathan Shamuyarira
Minister of Justice, Legal & Parliamentary Affairs	Eddison Zvobgo
Minister of Labor, Manpower Planning & Social Welfare	Frederick Shava
Minister of Lands, Agriculture & Rural Settlement	Moven Mahachi
Minister of Local Government, Rural & Urban Development	Enos Chikowore
Minister of Mines	Richard Hove
Minister of Natl. Supplies	Simbi Mubako
Minister of Natural Resources & Tourism	Victoria Chitepo
Minister of Public Construction & Natl. Housing	Simbarashe Mumbengegwi
Minister of Trade & Commerce	Dr. Oliver Munyaradzi
Minister of Transport	Herbert Ushewokunze
Minister of Youth, Sport & Culture	David Karimanzira
Minister of State in the Prime Minister's Office (Community Development & Women's Affairs)	Teurai Ropa Nhongo
Minister of State in the Prime Minister's Office (Defense)	Ernest Kadungure
Minister of State in the Prime Minister's Office (Political Affairs)	Maurice Nyagumbo
Minister of State in the Prime Minister's Office (Public Service)	Chris Andersen
Minister of State in the Prime Minister's Office (Security)	Emmerson Munangagwa

toral roll, former prime minister Ian Smith's Conservative Alliance for Zimbabwe (CAZ) won 15 of the 20 available seats. The Independent Zimbabwe Group (IZG), representing whites seeking accommodation and cooperation with the current government, won the other five seats. Voter turnout was heavy nationwide.

In postelection statements, Prime Minister Mugabe interpreted his party's victory as a mandate to proceed toward establishment of a one-party state. It is not clear, however, whether all those who voted for ZANU share Mugabe's interpretation. Mugabe also castigated whites who voted for Ian Smith's CAZ, vowing to eliminate the separate electoral roll for whites as soon as possible. Under the constitution, however, the white roll cannot be abolished before 1987. Thereafter, abolition of the special white roll would require a 7/10 majority vote in Parliament. ZANU, with 64 parliamentary seats, is six votes short

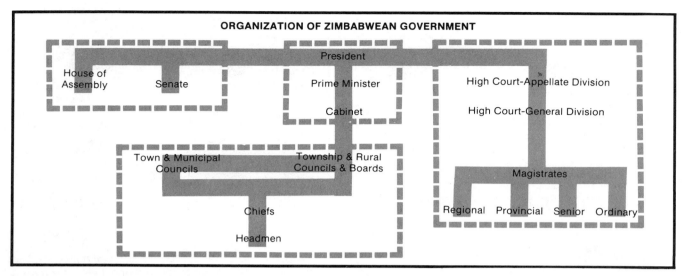

ORGANIZATION OF ZIMBABWEAN GOVERNMENT

President

House of Assembly   Senate   Prime Minister   High Court-Appellate Division

Cabinet   High Court-General Division

Town & Municipal Councils   Township & Rural Councils & Boards   Magistrates

Chiefs   Regional   Provincial   Senior   Ordinary

Headmen

of the necessary majority. Institution of a one-party state cannot occur legally before 1990 unless Parliament votes unanimously to amend the constitution. Despite obvious impatience on both these issues, Prime Minister Mugabe has not set a specific timetable for attaining ZANU goals. He has indicated that he will follow constitutional guidelines on revising Zimbabwe's political system.

The first year of Mugabe's administration dispelled many pre-independence fears of an early end to the privileges of whites and predictions of economic and political disaster. Although Mugabe claimed to be a dedicated Marxist during the guerrilla struggle days, he modified his pre-revolutionary ideology and goals after assuming power to avoid alienating the skilled white population. Mugabe also gained the confidence of the whites by including them in his coalition government. As a result, according to one Western diplomat, Zimbabwe "is in better shape than any other country in Africa except South Africa."

FREEDOM & HUMAN RIGHTS

In terms of civil and political rights Zimbabwe is classified as a partly free country with a rating of 3 in political rights and 4 in civil rights (on a scale in which 1 is the highest and 7 is the lowest in rights).

The human rights climate in Zimbabwe in 1985 continued to be clouded by internal security problems. The present government respects the 1980 constitution's provisions that preserve multiracial democracy and the rights of property but maintains the legal state of emergency, proclaimed in 1960, in force. The government has made full use of its emergency powers to override constitutional guarantees of several basic human rights, such as freedom from arbitrary arrest and the right to a prompt and fair trial. The emergency powers have also been used to detain without trial opponents of the government, possibly as many as 3,000 in 1985, including five ZAPU members of Parliament and several ZAPU Bulawayo city councilors. Government efforts to control dissident

activity and banditry, concentrated primarily in Ndebele-speaking areas in the southwestern part of the country, and ZANU zealots' harassment of minority party members have strained relations between the two major black parties — ZANU and ZAPU — and elicited international attention due to the substantial violations of human rights that resulted on both sides. The judicial system functions independently, frequently ruling against the state on sensitive issues and defending human rights through the rule of law.

Political killings increased in 1985. Two main factors are responsible for this trend: government efforts to stamp out dissident activity and the tensions that emerged among various political party supporters during the preelection period. Dissident-related killings by security forces are extremely difficult to quantify. However, evidence suggests that some summary executions have occurred in reprisals against rural populations (primarily in Ndebele-speaking areas) believed to have harbored dissident bands. While it is commonly alleged that this practice is widespread, supporting evidence is difficult to obtain, and cases where security forces have been brought to trial are extremely rare. No adequate mechanism exists to ensure that the police investigate crimes that the security forces are alleged to have committed.

Dissident attacks on civilians continued during the year and on a somewhat larger scale than in 1984. The government has estimated that dissidents killed over 100 civilians, including many local ZANU party officials. There was a clear pattern of targeting of these officials for elimination or harassment by dissidents of uncertain origin. Credible theories as to the indentity of the criminals have ranged from ZAPU militants to South African-backed elements to government troops masquerading as dissidents. The government has made no formal comment on allegations that members of its security forces have posed as dissidents. ZANU members of Parliament have repeatedly denied such charges.

Youth members of ZANU, the ruling party, have been responsible for between 150-200 deaths over the past year, according to the estimates of knowledgeable sources. Victims were, with the exception of two individuals, members of minority parties. Informed sources report that government security forces, including the police, the military and the CIO, have been responsible for a broad range of mistreatment of suspected dissidents, suspected dissident sympathizers, and minority party members at various government installations. Types of cruel, inhuman, or degrading treatment which have been alleged include repeated beatings, rape, and torture involving electric shock equipment and water suffocation. Cases involving confinement in crowded cells with little or no ventilation and detention for several days in open-air cages have also been well documented.

Informed sources report that the use of torture is routine in a few government facilities, particularly during interrogation or suspected dissidents and dissident sympathizers. The bulk of these abuses reportedly take place in Stops Camp, a police holding center in Bulawayo. Information on the number of persons tortured and on the number of deaths that have resulted from torture is difficult to obtain. However, reliable sources indicate that some deaths have occurred.

At least 5,000 people are believed to have been detained during the curfew in Matabeleland. At any one time the number of people under detention has probably averaged between 800 and 1,200 through 1984. Most of the detainees were never formally charged and their detention was never widely known. Others, such as UANC leader Bishop Muzorewa, who was held for ten months until his release in September, and four leaders of ZAPU's former military wing, have drawn considerable international attention. The latter remain in detention on the advice of the detention review tribunal.

Police permits are required for public meetings and political rallies. All opposition parties complained repeatedly in 1985 of government abuse of this rule. Numerous opposition political meetings were banned during the year, with public safety most often cited as the reason. There were far fewer instances during the same period where the government prohibited meetings or demonstrations of the ruling ZANU Party. Moreover, in the first half of 1985, several legal opposition rallies were attacked and broken up by gangs of thugs. Evidence strongly suggests that most of these attacks were carried out by the ZANU youth wing. The government has disclaimed responsibility for this political violence.

CIVIL SERVICE

There are over 24,000 civil servants, of whom over 13,000 hold tenured positions, including 3,300 teachers and 1,900 medical personnel. Of the tenured civil servants, nearly 8,000 were white at the time of independence. In the first year of independence 1,600 whites had left the civil service, including 400 who were over 55 and thus eligible for retirement. In the same period 2,000 black officials were hired. The administration and discipline of the civil service are controlled by the Public Service Board.

LOCAL GOVERNMENT

For administrative purposes Zimbabwe is divided into seven provinces but no governmental structures exist at the provincial level. Government statistics, however, are collected province by province.

The principal agency of local government, thus, are the cities and town municipalities of which there are seven including two cities. Each municipality is governed by a mayor and council. The councils are composed of six to 24 members elected for terms of three to four years. They have wide property taxing powers making the municipalities entirely self-supporting. Smaller urban centers are governed by town management boards with less authority.

Townships and rural areas have councils and boards, of which there are over 253. All chiefs and headmen are included in the councils but the majority of the members are popularly elected.

The lowest level of local government is that of chiefs and headmen. Unlike traditional hereditary chiefs, present-day chiefs are appointed government officials responsible for tax collection and maintenance of law and order. They also combine the powers of the local constable and judge. Below the chiefs are the headmen who are charged with the supervision of a segment of a tribal area called ward and supervising the work of heads of kraals or hamlets consisting of a few households. There are advisory councils of chiefs at the provincial and national levels.

FOREIGN POLICY

Until Joshua Nkomo's ouster in 1982 the Mugabe government's foreign policy was characterized by caution, moderation and pragmatism. Within months of independence Mugabe visited the United States where he assured Americans that the Marxist rhetoric of his election campaigns was largely propaganda "not to be taken seriously." In 1983, on being elected to the U.N. Security Council Zimbabwe adopted a distinctly anti-American posture: it abstained from a U.S.-sponsored resolution condemning the Soviet shooting of a South Korean jetliner while cosponsoring a resolution against the U.S. invasion of Grenada. In regional affairs, Harare has taken a leading position among the Front-line States bordering South Africa, concluding a mutual security pact with Mozambique in late 1980 and hosting several meetings of the Southern African Development Coordination Conference (SADCC). While declining for the sake of "the process of [domestic] reconciliation," to provide bases for black nationalist attacks on South Africa, Mugabe's anti-Pretoria rhetoric has escalated particularly in light of allegations of South African support for unrest in Matabeleland.

Zimbabwe is a member of the Commonwealth, OAU and the United Nations.

U.S. Ambassador in Harare: David C. Miller, *Jr.*

U.K. High Commissioner in Harare: Ramsay Melhuish

Zimbabwean Ambassador in Washington, D.C.: Edmund Richard Mashoko Garwe

Zimbabwean High Commissioner in London: M. Murerwa

PARLIAMENT

The national legislature is the bicameral parliament consisting of a Senate and a House of Assembly. The Senate consists of 40 members of whom 14 are elected by an electoral college consisting of those members of the House of Assembly elected by voters registered on the common roll. Ten are elected by those members elected by voters on the separate white roll. Five chiefs of Mashonaland are elected to the Senate by the Council of Chiefs. Five chiefs of Metabeleland are similarly elected and six members are appointed by the president. The House of Assembly consists of 100 members elected by universal adult suffrage from 80 common roll constituencies and 20 white roll constituencies. The life of the parliament is five years.

In the 1985 elections some three million blacks, out of a total population of eight million, cast ballots. Approximately 77% voted for Mugabe's ruling ZANU party (up from 62% in the 1980 elections), while 20% voted for Nkomo's ZAPU (down from 24% in 1980). The remaining vote went to two tiny opposition parties: ZANU (Sithole), led by exiled Rev. Ndabaningi Sithole, and the United African National Congress, led by Bishop Abel Muzorewa. Out of 79 contested seats, ZANU won 63 and ZAPU took 15, with ZANU (Sithole) winning a single seat. Muzorewa's party lost the three seats it had previously held. ZAPU's 15 victories came in Matabeleland province, home to Nkomo and his minority Ndebele tribe. The party lost the five seats it had held in other areas of the country. ZAPU's electoral sweep in Matabeleland underlined the tribal division — between the Ndebele and Mugabe's majority Shona tribe — that continued to plague Zimbabwe.

POLITICAL PARTIES

The independence struggle brought to the forefront a number of political parties that not only epoused different political ideologies, but also promoted different ethnic interests. The two largest are the ruling Zimbabwe African National Union (ZANU) and the Patriotic Front, formerly the Zimbabwe African People's Union. ZANU, which considers itself one of the partners of the Patriotic Front, has its largest following among the majority Shona tribe. Led by Prime Minister Robert Mugabe, it describes itself as Marxist in orientation but follows a moderate political course. A splinter group of ZANU that follows a more centrist line is led by Rev. Ndabaningi Sithole. The Patriotic Front headed by Joshua Nkomo is a largely Ndebele organization that waged the guerrilla warfare against white minority rule in alliance with ZANU but broke with it before the 1980 elections. The third major African national party is the United African National Council led by former Prime Minister Abel Muzorewa, a bishop of the Methodist Church. It supported the internal settlement with the Smith regime and thereby lost much of its following among the less moderate Africans.

There are a number of minor political parties, none of which are represented in the House of Assembly. These include the National Democratic Union, a conservative grouping with minority Zezeru support, the United National Federal Party, a conservative group that supports the federation of Mashonaland and Mtabeleland, the traditionalist Zimbabwe Democratic Party, the Zimbabwe National Front, and the Zimbabwe United People's Organization. The last-named party was a member of Abel Muzorewa's interim government.

The whites are represented by the Conservative Alliance (formerly the Rhodesian Front until 1981 and the Republican Front from 1981 to 1984), led by former Prime Minister Ian Smith. Fanatically devoted to the preservation of white privileges, its influence has been seriously whittled down by Mugabe's moderate racial and political policies. Its claim to be the exclusive spokesman of the white community was challenged in 1981 with the establishment of a moderate white party called the Democratic Party led by Andre Holland, a former minister in the Smith government.

ECONOMY

Zimbabwe is one of the 39 lower middle income countries of the world with a free-market economy in which the private sector is dominant.

Ostracized by the international community Zimbabwe received very little foreign aid during the years of rebel rule. The spigots of foreign aid were again turned on in 1981; at the Zimcord Conference attended by delegates from 31 nations and 26 international agencies $1.8 billion was pledged, including $225 million from the United States, $307 million from the United Kingdom and $459 million from the World Bank. Per capita the pledges amounted to $250. From 1980-1983 the United States disbursed $190.1 million in economic aid. International aid totaled $522.8 million, of which the World Bank share was $381 million. Total aid from all sources during 1979-81 was $136.1 million or $18.50 per capita.

Because it was preoccupied with the civil war and in counteracting the debilitating economic effects of the international boycott, the Smith regime did not devote any attention to development planning. the new post-independence government created a department of

PRINCIPAL ECONOMIC INDICATORS

Gross National Product: $5.820 billion (1983)
GNP Annual Growth Rate: 1.7% (1973-82)
Per Capita GNP: $740 (1983)
Per Capita GNP Annual Growth Rate: 0.4% (1973-82)

Gross Domestic Product: Z$5.005 billion (1982)
GDP at 1980 Prices: Z$3.735 billion
GDP Deflator 1980=100: 134.0
GDP Annual Growth Rate: 1.8% (1973-83)
GDP Per Capita: Z$577 (1982)
GDP Per Capital Annual Growth Rate: −1.4% (1970-81)

Income Distribution: The lower 50% of the population receive 12% of the national income; the upper 5% receive 48% of the national income

Consumer Price Index (1970=100)
All Items: 192.1 (October 1984)
Food: 207.3 (October 1984)

Average Annual Growth Rate of Inflation: 9.7% (1973-83)

Money Supply: Z$769 million (March 1985)

Reserve money: Z$416 million (April 1985)

Currency in Circulation: Z$258.8 million (1984)

International Reserves: $45.4 million of which foreign reserves $43.1 million (1984)

GDP BY ECONOMIC ACTIVITY 1982 (%)

		Annual Growth Rate 1970-81
Agriculture	15.0	−0.5
Mining	5.4	3.4
Manufacturing	24.5	2.8
Construction	3.4	−4.5
Public Utilities	1.7	0.4
Transportation & Communications	8.0	1.5
Trade	14.7	0.6
Finance	6.2	0.6
Public Administration & Defense	8.0	9.5
Health and Education	9.4	0.1
Other	3.7	0.1

BALANCE OF PAYMENTS (1984)
(million $)

Current Account	−100.0
Merchandise Exports	1,173.6
Merchandise Imports	−989.3
Trade Balance	184.3
Other Goods, Services	+205.0
Other Goods, services	−538.9
Private Unrequited Transfers	−38.5
Official Unrequited Transfers	88.2
Direct Investment	−2.5
Portfolio Investment	2.8
Other Long-term Capital	168.4
Total	68.8
Other Short-term Capital	−160.1
Net Errors & Omissions Counterpart to Monetization/Demonetization of Gold	22.7
Counterpart to Valuation Changes	−39.7
Total Change in Reserves	63.3

economic planning to initiate and coordinate planning efforts.

The first major policy statement by the government after independence was "Growth with Equity: an Economic Policy Statement," issued in February 1981, seen by the government as providing a framework for overall sectoral policies as well as constituting "the policy basis for the first National Development Plan." It was directed "toward the attainment of a socialist and egalitarian society to which the government is committed."

Volume one of the Three Year Transitional National Development Plan was published after long delays at the end of November 1982. The major objectives of the plan are stated as being the reconstruction of the war-damaged and sanctions-distorted economy, achievement of a high real rate of economic growth; generation of maximum employment opportunities; greater equitable sharing of income and wealth (particularly land); provision, extension and improvement of social services; and the undertaking of measures for economic restructuring. More specific global targets were the achievement of an 8% real annual growth rate; an annual increase of 3% in formal employment; a total investment over the plan period of Z$6,096 million, constituting about 26% of GDP; a large increase in foreign trade and foreign capital inflows; a rise in gross domestic savings from 16% to 20% of GDP; and an annual rate of inflation not exceeding 15%.

Much of the plan has been overtaken by events, and it is generally agreed that few, if any, of the targets will be achieved or even approached.

BUDGET

The fiscal year runs from July 1 through June 30.

The current expenditure budget is known as revenue account and usually yields a small surplus. This surplus is used to finance a small part of the deficit on the capital budget which is known as the loan account. Zimbabwe does not published a consolidated budget.

Of current revenues, 46.7% comes from taxes on income, profit and capital gain, 31.4% from domestic taxes on goods and services, 11.1% from taxes on international trade and transactions, 1.0% from other taxes and 9.8% from non-tax revenues. Current revenues represented 31.3% of GNP. Of current expenditures, 17.3% goes to defense, 21.9% to education, 6.4% to health, 6.7% to housing, social security and welfare, 23.3% to economic services and 24.4% to other functions. Current expenditures represented 39.0% of GNP and overall deficit 11.3% of GNP.

In 1982 public consumption was Z$994 million and private consumption Z$2.975 billion. During 1973-83 public consumption grew by 10.8% and private consumption by 2.9%.

In 1983 total disbursed and outstanding publicly guaranteed external debt was $1.497 billion of which $347 billion was owed to official creditors and $1.149 billion to private creditors. Total debt service was $434.8 million of which $329.5 million was repayment of principal and $105 million interest. Total external debt represented 108.8% of export revenues and 27.9% of GNP. Total debt service represented 31.6% of export revenues and 8.1% of GNP.

BUDGET ESTIMATES – REVENUE
(Z $'000, year ending 30 June)

Revenue	1980/81	1981/82*	1982/83†
Taxes on income and profits:			
Income tax	418,866	631,488	815,000
Nonresident shareholders' tax	16,706	25,500	30,000
Nonresident's tax on interest	—	1,805	2,000
Resident shareholders' tax	—	2,501	5,000
Branch profits tax	1,880	2,885	3,500
Capital gains tax	—	42	4,000
Total	437,452	664,221	859,500
Taxes on goods and services:			
Sales tax	180,427	230,748	440,000
Customs duties	59,627	140,125	244,000
Excise duties	83,040	130,109	161,000
Betting tax	3,992	4,327	5,200
Other	902	774	850
Total	327,988	556,083	851,050
Miscellaneous taxes:			
Stamp duties and fees	9,888	10,541	12,600
Estate duty	2,395	2,246	4,500
Other	7	6	5
Total	12,290	12,793	17,105
Revenue from investments and property:			
Interest, dividends and profits	58,694	46,243	57,690
Rents	2,825	3,045	3,000
Total	62,437	49,727	61,700
Fees: Departmental facilities and services:			
Agriculture	533	785	700
Civil aviation	1,476	1,406	1,700
Companies, trade marks and patents	1,150	1,121	1,300
Education	4,605	4,982	6,595
Health	1,666	1,249	1,500
National parks	1,099	1,621	1,900
Roads and road traffic	1,300	1,469	1,650
Water development	311	350	550
Other	1,788	2,178	2,350
Total	13,938	15,161	18,245
Recoveries of development expenditure	941	675	1,100
International aid grants	—	5,419	63,300
Other:			
Pension contributions	21,383	32,286	36,000
Judicial fines	2,817	4,408	4,500
Sale of state property	3,515	3,408	3,700
Refunds of miscellaneous payments from votes	6,836	8,953	6,000
Miscellaneous	61,279	8,733	26,000
Total	95,830	57,788	76,200
Grand Total	950,876	1,361,867	1,948,200

*Provisional.
†Estimates.

BUDGET ESTIMATES – EXPENDITURE
(Z $'000, year ending 30 June)

Expenditure	1980/81	1981/82*	1982/83†
Recurrent expenditure:			
Goods and services:			
Salaries, wages and allowances	374,500	475,497	552,036
Subsistence and transport	33,311	41,423	50,022
Incidental expenses	21,354	26,268	42,524
Other recurrent expenditure	175,986	226,353	253,598
Total	605,151	769,361	898,180
Transfers:			
Interest	99,815	139,188	193,239
Subsidies	106,418	138,152	146,556
Parastatal bodies	13,498	15,169	19,171
Pensions	72,248	73,773	84,130
Grants and transfers	239,311	321,749	506,605
Total	531,290	688,031	949,701
Capital expenditure:			
Land purchase	3,844	21,597	28,262
Buildings	24,244	37,988	124,148
Land development	1,864	2,095	25,106
Civil engineering	27,923	39,950	80,376
Plant, machinery and equipment	6,484	6,957	15,188
Office equipment and furniture	1,414	4,362	7,638
Other capital expenditure	28	31	685
Total	65,801	112,980	281,403
Grand Total	1,202,242	1,570,372	2,129,284

*Provisional.
†Estimates.
1983/84: Total expenditure estimated at Z.$2,400,000.

The Zimbabwe dollar was introduced in 1980 replacing at par the Zimbabwe Rhodesia dollar, which in itself was the successor to the Rhodesian dollar and the Rhodesian pound. The unofficial exchange rates are: $2 = Z$1.548 and £ = Z$1.741.

Zimbabwe's financial system, originally established to serve the Federation of Rhodesia and Nyasaland, is larger than that required for the country's present state of economic development. Banking activities are regulated by the Banking Act of 1964 as amended in 1979. The Reserve Bank of Zimbabwe, in addition to being the bank of issue and the government's banker, may also grant loans and advances to both the government and the private sector.

There are five commercial banks, four merchant banks and one development bank.

AGRICULTURE

Of the total land area of 39,058,000 hectares (96,512,318 acres) 40% is considered arable (although only 6% is cultivated), 60% available for cattle grazing; 39% is owned by Europeans and 48% worked communally by Africans; 7% is national land and 6% is not alienated.

Agriculture employs 60% of the work force, provides 40% of the raw materials for industry and accounts for 11% of the GDP and its growth rate during

FINANCE

The Zimbabwean unit of currency is the Zimbabwe Dollar divided into 100 cents. Coins are issued in denominations of 1/2, 1, 2½, 5, 10, 20 and 25 cents and notes in denominations of 1, 2, 5, and 10 dollars.

GROWTH PROFILE
Annual Growth Rates (%)

Population 1980-2000	3.6
Birthrate 1965-83	-4.4
Death rate 1965-83	-9.3
Urban Population 1973-83	6.0
Labor Force 1980-2000	4.4
GNP 1973-82	1.7
GNP per Capita 1973-82	0.4
GDP 1973-83	1.8
GDP per Capita 1970-81	-1.4
Consumer Prices 1970-81	8.0
Wholesale Prices 1970-81	10.9
Inflation 1973-83	9.7
Agriculture 1973-83	1.2
Industry 1973-83	(.)
Manufacturing 1970-81	2.8
Services 1973-83	3.3
Mining 1970-81	3.4
Construction 1970-81	-4.5
Electricity 1970-81	0.4
Transportation 1970-81	1.5
Trade 1970-81	0.6
Public Administration & Defense 1970-81	0.5
Export Price Index 1975-81	12.3
Import Price Index 1975-81	14.7
Terms of Trade 1975-81	-7.1
Exports 1973-83	—
Imports 1973-83	—
Public Consumption 1973-83	10.8
Private Consumption 1973-83	2.9
Gross Domestic Investment 1973-83	1.9
Energy Production 1973-83	-2.6
Energy Consumption 1973-83	0.5

1973-83 was 1.2%. Based on 1970=100, the index of food production per capita was 102 in 1976-78. Based on 1974-76=100, the index of agricultural production was 97, the index of food production was 95 and the index of per capita food production was 79, all in 1982. The value added in agriculture in 1982 was $673 million.

The principal characteristic of Zimbabwean agriculture is the dichotomy between European and African agriculture. The nearly 7,000 white farmers, well organized and supported by extensive research and marketing services, are reported to be among the best in the world in terms of productivity. On the other hand, the 700,000 Africans officially described as farmers, fail to produce a surplus even in a good crop year. The excessive rate of population growth and race-based restrictions introduced by white governments have actually diminished the productive capacity of the average African farmer over the last century. The average African family of five or six members have the use of only 2.7 hectares (six acres) of arable land and five or six head of inferior cattle.

Statistical information about African agriculture is fragmentary. No data are collected on total output in the African areas. Official policy during white rule favored the creation of two categories of African farmland: African Purchase Areas with 8,500 farmers and 1.49 million hectares (3.68 million acres) and Tribal Trust Lands with 600,000 farmers and 16.1 million hectares (40 million acres). Purchase Areas are designed to permit Africans to acquire registered title to land under freehold tenure. The average farm in Purchase Areas produces three times the average farm in a Tribal Trust Land and further 68% of Purchase Area production is for sale as compared to 13% in Tribal Trust Lands. Because they own title to their land, Purchase Area farmers have better access to credit and marketing facilities. On the other hand, of the 600,000 farmers in Tribal Trust Lands, only 29,439 use fertilizers, 42,940 own farm carts and 300,000 own plows. The average farm income is only between $50 to $70 per year.

One root cause of low productivity in African lands is the small size of the holding. A closely related one is the unfavorable climate and the low inherent fertility of African areas. Further, excessive use and poor cultivation and grazing practices have long depleted the soil. But the most serious one is the practice of most adult male farmers emigrating to the towns or to the white farms. This means that at any one time between 40 and 50% of ablebodied males will be absent from their farms leaving routine agricultural operations to be performed by the women. The arable plots of absent migrants are only partially used, thus adding a further cause of low average productivity.

A sample survey estimated that 50% of African land under crops is planted with maize and 40% with millet and sorghum. Much smaller areas ore planted with peanuts, rice and other crops. In addition, most villagers have kitchen plots planted with beans, root crops, vegetables and condiments. Most farms are strip fields demarcated by a regular succession of graded conservation ridges.

The country has little inherently fertile land. Because intensive farming is possible only on 27.5% of white areas and 10.6% of African areas, agriculture depends heavily on water conservation, intensive use of pesticides and fertilizers and extension services. Severe drought cuts output periodically, as in 1968, 1970 and 1973. In 1982, 20,500 tractors and 570 combined harvester-threshers were in use. In 1982, 182,500 tons of fertilizers were consumed, nearly half of them nitrogenous, or 53.2 kg (117 lb) per arable hectare.

The principal crops are maize, tobacco (30% of total crop sales), cotton (18% of total crop sales), soybean, coffee, sugarcane, peanuts and potatoes. In recent years new crops, such as wheat, have been successfully introduced. A significant proportion of agricultural output is exported, with tobacco exports being predominant. In 1982 these were valued at Z$195 million, constituting 24% of total exports.

Most of Zimbabwe is covered by large tracts of natural grassland where beef cattle are produced in large numbers, making the country self-sufficient in meat and dairy products. In the drier regions of the Low Veld and the Middle Veld ranching is the only viable activity.

About 755,022 hectares (1,865,635 acres) are designated as forest lands in European areas and 172,005 hectares (425,019 acres) in African areas. In addition, 1,774,053 hectares (4,383,625 acres) are reserved as

PRINCIPAL CROP PRODUCTION (1982)
(000 tons)

Wheat	182
Corn	1,800
Millet	190
Sorghum	131
Sugarcane	3,612
Potatoes	23
Cassava	60
Seed Cotton	143
Tobacco	90
Tea	10
Cotton (Lint)	51
Coffee	6
Dry Beans	24
Soybeans	91
Oranges	31
Bananas	58
Peanuts	115
Cottonseed	93

LIVESTOCK POPULATION (1982)
(000)

Cattle	5,600
Sheep	360
Pigs	170
Goats	1,000

PRODUCTION OF DAIRY PRODUCTS (1982)
(000 tons)

Beef & Veal	67
Pork	10
Mutton & Lamb	1
Milk	200

parks and wildlife refuges in European areas and 255,007 hectares (630,115 acres) in African areas. Most of the hardwood stands are in the eastern mountains. In the rest of the country, the main stands are baobab, mopani, and acacia. Roundwood production in 1982 totaled 8.679 million cubic meters (306 million cubic ft) and sawnwood production 198,000 cubic meters (6.99 million cubic ft).

Commercial fishing is limited to the Kariba Lake and annual fish catch does not exceed 18,100 tons.

INDUSTRY

Since World War II Zimbabwe has experienced substantial, if unsteady, industrial growth. Manufacturing employs 17.3% of the labor force and accounts for 24.5% of GDP and its rate of growth during 1970-81 was 2.8%.

Geographically, manufacturing was fairly concentrated around a few areas: 48.1% in Harare, 27.4% in Bulawayo, 8.4% in Kwekwe -Redcliff, 4.3% in Gweru, and 3.1% in Mutare.

Despite growing diversification, food processing remains the largest single branch of manufacturing and the largest employer of labor accounting for 21% of the labor force. Value added in manufacturing of $925 million in 1982. Textiles follow with 19%, chemicals with 11%, and machinery and transport equipment with 10%. The greatest gains in gross output in recent years have been in textiles, metals and metal products, wood and furniture and transport equipment.

Despite international sanctions, Zimbabwean industry actually grew during the rebel years and reached an intermediate stage of development. Before independence there was no great need to force the pace of industrialization and manufacturing was limited to processing of domestic goods and low-quality consumer goods. An additional drawback was the country's landlocked location entailing high transportation costs both for imports and exports. As a consequence of the imposition of sanctions, exchange controls were placed on the repatriation of dividends by foreign firms and they were forced to reinvest more of their earnings within the colony. The imposition of import controls stimulated the expansion and diversification of domestic manufactures. Not only the level but the range of output increased significantly. There was a strengthening of basic industries and a more active involvement of the government in the formulation of industrial policy and its execution. There was also an increasing trend toward monopoly production and larger average size of plants. Nearly 65% of all products were produced by only one firm each without any competition.

The government's investment plans were spelled out in the Transitional Development Plan (1982/83–84/85). In the Public Sector Investment Program (PSIP), government and parastatal gross investment (including stock increases) was expected to total Z$3,618 million over the three year period. It was expected that the private sector would invest Z$2,478 million over the same period, giving a breakdown of 51% from the public sector and 49% from the private. The largest component of the PSIP is the provision of Z$878 million for energy, transport and communication. Major projects are the Wankie thermal power station (total cost of Z$218 million), railway electrification (Z$160 million), roads (Z$87 million), and posts and telecommunications (Z$140 million). Of the Z$610 million earmarked for social services, the major expenditures are for education (Z$163 million), and housing (Z$390 million). The education budget includes Z$24 million for vocational training, which is intended to double the output of skilled workers from the technical colleges.

The dramatic downturn in the economy in 1982 and 1983 has meant that most of these plans have not materialized and the government has been forced to revise its program of investments. It is generally agreed that the growth which Zimbabwe experienced in the post-independence period was the result of a consumer-led boom, caused in part by increased minimum wages, the removal of restrictions on exports and increased business optimism. The subsequent deterioration of the sector is due to a number of factors. The opening up of the economy after years of enforced protection has placed a large number of producers in the economy as a whole, but particularly in this sector, under increased competitive pressures. This problem has been compounded by the severe foreign exchange shortages which have resulted from problems with traditional exports, particularly from the mining sector which has suffered from the world recession. The cuts in foreign exchange allocations have hit manufacturing industries particularly hard, as they tend to have a high import content in their production processes.

In 1963 the government established the Industrial Development Corporation funded largely by the government. The National Export Promotion Council was established in 1964 to assist manufacturers to find foreign markets.

ENERGY

In 1982, Zimbabwe produced 2.846 million metric tons of coal equivalent and consumed 3.898 million metric tons of coal equivalent, or 494 kg (1,089 lb) per capita. The national energy deficit is 1.052 million tons of coal equivalent. The average annual growth rate during 1973-83 was -2.6% for energy production and 0.5% for energy consumption. The oil refinery at Umtali has a capacity of 1 million tons.

Electric power production in 1984 was 5.606 billion kwh, or 670 kwh per capita. Most of the power is produced by the Kariba North generating plant and the new thermal power station at Wankie.

LABOR

The total labor force is estimated at 2.485 million (estimated to rise to 4.551 million by 2000) of which 29.6% is female. The number of wage-earners is estimated at 990,000. Agriculture accounts for 26.2%, mining for 8.1%, manufacturing for 17.3%, construction for 4.9%, trade for 7.6%, public utilities for 0.6%, transportation and communication for 4.8%, finance for 1.4%, health and education for 8.7%, public administration and defense for 7.8% and other for 14.6%. The annual growth rate of the labor force was 1.4% from 1973 to 1983 but is expected to jump to 4.4% for the rest of this century.

A major characteristic of Zimbabwean labor is the significant proportion of Africans from neighboring countries, such as Malawi and Zambia, estimated at about 20% of the total work force. There are two categories of foreign labor: contract labor and free flow labor. The latter is restricted to the eastern districts. All other migrants are required to register with the Labor Supply Commission.

The government introduced a Minimum Wage Act in 1980 providing a minimum wage of Z$85 a month for those covered by the Industrial Conciliation Act in industrial, commercial and services sectors and Z$70 per month for others. There is a dual wage gap: between the wages paid to whites and those paid to blacks and between the wages paid to blacks in farming and domestic service and those paid to blacks in other occupations. The gap between the blacks and the whites has narrowed substantially since 1958 when it was 12.9 to one, but in absolute terms it has widened. The African wage bill constitutes 8% of gross output in manufacturing, 15% in mining and 31% in white farming.

There are occasional shortages of skilled labor, especially with the emigration of whites since independence.

Until 1960, African workers were excluded from the definition of employee. The 1959 Industrial Conciliation Act gave workers trade union rights but did not apply to farm workers and a large number of government employees. It permitted the establishment of trade unions on a racial basis, but prohibited them from accepting assistance from the international trade union movement. The Act's 1971 amendment provided for the registration and regulation of trade unions and set up industrial boards.

The 1985 labor relations legislation guarantees a 24-hour rest period sometime during the workweek. The workweek can range up to 60 hours. The new law also calls for strict enforcement of acceptable standards of health and safety. By Zimbabwe law, the working age for the formalized economy is 18, but it is possible to begin an apprenticeship at age 16. The law also codifies the government's right to set minimum wage standards. However, the government's constant adjustments of minimum wage levels have become a bone of contention with both the unions and the business/farming community. Since a large share of unionized workers are paid the minimum wage, the unions complained that the government usurped their main bargaining power by its continual adjustments of the minimum wage. Business and farming interests, on the other hand, feared that the government's recent decision — now partly overturned — to double the minimum wage for agro-industrial and plantation workers (e.g., in the sugar, citrus, tea, coffee, timber and poultry industries) threatened 40,000 jobs, and could have resulted in lost export revenues and some liquidations of businesses. The new labor act permits the formation of worker committees which could serve the purpose of shop floor stewards to industry and in mines. Realizing that these committees could usurp their power, the unions are monitoring their development very closely and intend to incorporate them into the union structure.

There are 64 unions in Zimbabwe including eight federations: The African Trades Union Congress, National African Federation of Unions, National African Trades Union Congress, National Association of Local Government Officers and Employees, Trade Union Congress of Zimbabwe, Zimbabwe African Congress of Unions, Zimbabwe Federation of Labor, and Zimbabwe Trades Union Congress.

Conditions of service for all workers outside of agriculture are negotiated through 27 industrial councils and 54 industrial boards. Training is provided by apprenticeship committees established under the Apprenticeship Act. Workmen's compensation is through compulsory insurance administered by a government fund. Health and safety in industry is the responsibility of supervisors appointed under the Factories and Works Act.

FOREIGN COMMERCE

The foreign commerce of Zimbabwe consisted in 1984 of exports of $791.7 million and imports of $760.6 million leaving a trade surplus of $31.1 million. Of the imports, machinery and transport equipment constituted 40.7%, basic manufactures 14.5% (of which textiles 4.2% and iron and steel 4.1%), petroleum products 14.3% and chemicals 11.6%. Of the exports, tobacco constituted 20.1%, gold 14.5%, ferroalloys 8.0%, asbestos 6.3%, cotton 5.4%, sugar 5.4%, nickel 4.7% and corn 4.1%. The major import sources are: South Africa 22.1%, the United Kingdom 15.0%, the United States 9.6%, West Germany 8.2% and Japan 5.2%. The major export destinations are: South Africa 17.1%, the United Kingdom 9.5%, West Germany 8.0%, the United States 7.9% and the Netherlands 4.5%.

TRANSPORTATION & COMMUNICATIONS

The 3,394 km (2,108 mi) rail system is managed by the National Railways of Zimbabwe. The trackage is entirely narrow guage. Trunk lines run from Bulawayo south through Botswana to the border with South Africa, northwest to the Victoria Falls, connecting with the Zambia Railways, northeast to Harare and Mutare connecting with the Mozambique rail line from Beira. From a point near Gwery a line runs to the southeast making connection with the Mozambique Railway's Limpopo line and with the port of Maputo. Another connection runs from Rutenga to the South African rail system at Beitbridge. In an effort to discourage competition from truckers, the railways also operate their own fleet of trucks. Rail traffic carried 6.259 billion net ton-km of freight and 2,050,000 passengers in 1983.

Some use is made of navigable rivers. There is a barge route for chrome ore linking Salisbury with Mozambique by the Mazoe and Zambezi Rivers.

There is an oil pipeline from the port of Beira in Mozambique to the refinery at Umtali, but it was effectively closed down by the British blockade during the white minority rule.

The road system is best developed in the white areas of the High Veld. There are 85,237 km (52,932 mi) of roads, of which 12,243 km (7,603 mi) are paved. About 8,367 km (5,200 mi) are maintained by the central government and another 22,526 km (14,000 mi) are maintained by local roads councils. The government also controlled the road sector through the Road Services Board. The number of passengers cars and

commercial vehicles on the roads in 1982 was 224,453 and 24,246, respectively. Per capita there were 26 passenger cars and 2.8 commercial vehicles per 1,000 inhabitants.

The national airline is the Air Zimbabwe Corporation, which operates 12 aircraft on regular scheduled services to South Africa, Malawi, Mauritius and Mozambique. The principal airports are at Harare and Bulawayo, both of which have regular scheduled international flights. There are 482 other airfields, 446 usable and 19 with permanent-surface runways. In 1982, Air Zimbabwe carried 449,000 passengers and flew 8.8 million km (5.46 million mi).

Zimbabwe's telecommunications system is one of the best in Africa and consists of radio-relay links, open wire lines, and radiocommunications stations. The number of telephones in use in 1984 was 236,500, or 3.1 per 100 inhabitants.

In 1982 there were 155 post offices and 42 postal agencies. Mail traffic in the same year consisted of 137,085,000 pieces of mail and 433,000 telegrams, or 16 letters per capita. There are 1,190 telex subscriber lines.

The principal tourist attractions are the Victoria Falls, the Kariba Dam, the Wankie Game reserve and the ruins of the ancient city of Zimbabwe. In 1982 256,000 tourists visited Zimbabwe generating $46 million in revenues. Of these 144,600 were from South Africa, 24,500 from the United Kingdom, 11,600 from Canada and 6,100 from West Germany. There are 9,000 hotel beds.

MINING

Mining provides 6% of GDP and over a third of its exports. Zimbabwe now produces more than 40 different minerals. The most important of these (with their 1982 share of total mineral production) are: gold (32.5%); asbestos (20.0%); nickel (13.0%); coal (9.4%); copper (7.0%); chrome (5.2%); and iron (3.6%). Other minerals which are mined in significant amounts are silver, cobalt, tin, phosphate, barytes, mica, tungsten, tantalite, magnesite, lithium, limestone and precious stones (including beryl, kyanite, quartz, topaz, tourmaline and emerald). Despite the international sanctions, both the volume and value of mining production had doubled since 1965, partly because minerals proved the easiest product to sell abroad and partly because of the opening of new nickel deposits. Zimbabwe is believed to contain the world's largest reserves of high grade chrome ore and its sales were boosted by the Byrd Amendment passed by the U.S. Senate in 1971 ending the ban on American imports from Rhodesia of certain strategic minerals. Gold overtook chrome as the most valuable export in 1979, a position it held until 1940. Many dormant gold mines have been reopened for renewed prospecting.

Mining is almost entirely dominated by subsidiaries of British, South African and U.S. firms: Asbestos by the British firm of Turner & Newall, Chrome by the U.S. firms of Foote Minerals, Union Carbide, and

Vanadium Corporation, nickel by the British firm of Rio Tinto, Copper by the South African Messina Group, lithium by the U.S. firms of American Metal Climax and Bikita Mineral and coal by Anglo-American of South Africa. In addition, the U.S.-owned Roan Selection trust and the British-owned Lonrho had large investments spread throughout the mining sector.

MINERAL PRODUCTION (1983) (000 tons)	
Coal	3,326
Iron Ore	924
Chromium	431.4
Copper	21.6
Gold (troy oz)	453,000
Nickel Ore (tons)	10.147
Tin Ore (tons)	1,235
Asbestos	153
Cobalt (tons)	73
Silver (troy oz)	935

DEFENSE

The defense structure is headed by the president who is also the titular commander in chief. The prime minister, Robert Mugabe, also holds the defense portfolio and he is assisted in the direction of the armed forces by the army and air force commanders.

Military manpower is provided by compulsory military service consisting of 12 to 18 months of training followed by three years of part-time training in territorial battalions, in active duty or on reserve duty.

Formerly entirely white in its officer corps, the Zimbabwe armed forces are being gradually Africanized through the integration of the members of the former Zimbabwe National Liberation Army and the Zimbabwe People's Revolutionary Army. About half of the officers resigned immediately upon independence, and the number of white personnel was down to about 1,500 in mid-1981. Total strength of the armed forces is 42,000 or 5.7 per 1,000 civilians.

ARMY:

Personnel: 41,000

Organization: 6 brigade HQ (including 1 presidential guard); 1 armored regiment; 23 infantry battalions; 1 artillery regiment; 1 air defense regiment; 7 engineer and 7 signals squadrons

Equipment: 31 tanks; 122 combat vehicles; 25 armored personnel carriers; 58 guns/howitzers; 100 mortars; 12 antitank rocket launchers; air defense guns; SAMs

AIR FORCE:

Personnel: 1,000

Organization: 53 combat aircraft; 1 bomber squadron; 2 fighter ground attack squadrons; 1 fighter squadron; 1 counterinsurgency squadron; 2 training squadrons; 1 transport squadron; 2 helicopter squadrons; 2 security squadrons

Air Bases: Harare, Gweru, Bulawayo, Chireczi, Mutare

The annual military budget in 1984/85 was $238.953 million, representing 11.9% of the national budget, 6.4% of GNP, $47.0 per capita, $6,825 per soldier and $1,100 per sq km of national territory.

The emerging Zimbabwe regular army, manned by former guerrilla fighters, is a seasoned force, but it is unlikely that it will be called upon in the near future to repulse any external attack.

EDUCATION

The national literacy rate is 70.8% (78% for males and 63.8% for females), excluding the white population, which has a near 100% literacy.

The school enrollment ratios are 98% for the primary level (7-13) and 23% for the secondary level (14-19), yielding a combined enrollment ratio of 85%. Until independence there were two school systems, one for the whites, Asians and Coloreds and the other for the blacks. For both systems, education is free and compulsory from the ages 7 to 15. For the first system, primary education consisted of a seven-year program (including two years called Infants One and Infants Two) and secondary education consisted of one of four streams: academic, slow academic, general and technical-commercial, leading to one of several types of degrees letterd O, M or A. The African system consisted of a seven-year primary program, including two initiatory years called Sub-Standard-A and Sub-Standard-B, three years called Lower Primary and two years called Upper Primary, followed by six-year secondary program or a shorter two-year junior secondary program. Of the combined enrollment, girls constitute 48% at the primary level, 41% at the secondary level and 22% at the post-secondary level.

Vocational training is provided by five institutions at Harare, Bulawayo, Mutare, Kwekwe and Gweru.

One of the major problems of Zimbabwean education is obtaining qualified teachers. About 95% of all primary school teachers are qualified as compared to only 33% of secondary school teachers. The exodus of white teachers following independence has reduced the stock of qualified teachers, particularly in science, mathematics and technical subjects. The teacher-pupil ratio is 1:38 at the primary level, 1:26 at the secondary level and 1:9 at the post-secondary level.

The school year is the calendar year. The medium of instruction is English throughout.

Educational expenditures for 1980, the latest reported year, was Z$223,845,000 representing 6.4% of GNP (as against a UNESCO recommendation of 4%), 13.7% of the national budget and $72 per capita.

Higher education is provided at the University College of Zimbabwe with a 1982 enrollment of 3,091, or 36 per 100,000 inhabitants. In 1982, 1,580 Zimbabwean students were enrolled in institutions of higher

EDUCATIONAL ENROLLMENT (1982)			
	Schools	Teachers	Pupils
Primary	3,880	49,588	2,044,029
Secondary	186	8,549	227,613
Vocational/Commercial	N.A.	20	319
University	1	325	3,091

learning abroad. Of these 520 were in the United States, 820 in the United Kingdom, 50 in Australia and 48 in Canada.

LEGAL SYSTEM

The legal system is Roman-Dutch based on the prevailing system in South Africa in the 19th century.

At the apex of the legal system is the high court with two divisions: appellate and general. The Appellate Court is the court of final review, hearing appeals from the General Division of the High Court as well as lower courts and comprises the chief justice, the judge president of the division and at least one judge of appeal. The General Division, also presided over by the chief justice, consists of a number of puisne judges. Below the High Court are four levels of magistrate courts presided over by the chief magistrate: regional, provincial, senior, and ordinary. In criminal cases, the four levels have different limits of jurisdiction, but appeals from all levels lie directly with the High Court and all levels have equal jurisdiction in civil cases. All civil matters involving over Z$400 are automatically referred to the General division of the High Court and all criminal cases tried before a magistrate court, except petty cases, are automatically reviewed by a judge of the General Division and sentences cannot become effective until he confirms them.

The judiciary continues to function independently of the government and frequently rules against the state on sensitive issues. In addition, the government has made an effort to appoint well-qualified and experienced judges, even if this has meant recruiting expatriate judges or those with links to minority parties. Several judges have emphasized their freedom from government interference in those cases over which they have presided.

Approximately 500 people were tried for "political" crimes in 1985. The bulk of them were convicted. Most had been charged under the Emergency Powers Law and Order Maintenance Act for their alleged involvement with dissident groups. No more than 10% of them were represented by counsel.

No information is available on Zimbabwean prisons.

LAW ENFORCEMENT

The Zimbabwe Police, formerly known as the British South African Police (BSAP) is a well trained paramilitary force of some 7,500 active members. The force is currently being reorganized following the resignation of nearly half of its white officer corps.

The police units are divided into rural and urban. Urban police are controlled from the headquarters in Salisbury and in each of the provincial administrative centers. Rural units report directly to the headquarters. Overt use of force by the police is a matter of frequent public criticism.

In 1972, the latest year for which criminal statistics are available, 223,000 criminal offenses were reported including 158 murders, 10,935 other crimes against the person, 28,100 thefts, and 16,740 housebreaking.

HEALTH

Africans in Zimbabwe generally suffer from poor health as a result of ignorance of basic hygiene, poor housing, contaminated water, and inadequate medical care. The main causes of death among them are tuberculosis, pneumonia, avitaminosis, gastroenteritis, colitis, malaria, and parasitic infections, such as schistosomiasis. Medical care is adequate only in urban areas. In 1980 there were 254 hospitals with 21,418 beds, or 1 bed per 344 inhabitants. In 1981 there were 1,148 physicians, or one physician per 6,411 inhabitants, 158 dentists and 5,094 nursing personnel. The admissions/discharge rate per 10,000 inhabitants was 1,043, the bed occupancy rate was 67.5% and the average length of hospital stay was 7 days.

PRINCIPAL HEALTH INDICATORS (1984)
Crude Death Rate (per 1,000): 12.3
Decline in Death rate (%, 1965-83): –9.3%
Life Expectancy at Birth (Males) 53.5 (Females) 57.9
Infant Mortality Rate (per 1,000) Live Births: 78.8
Child Death Rate (Ages 1-4) (per 1,000): 7

In 1982 national health expenditures represented 6.4% of national budget and $10 per capita.

FOOD

The average African diet is ill-balanced and deficient in essential nutrients. The staple food is a stiff porridge made from maize meal and eatan with a spicy sauce. Milk, meat and eggs do not form part of the regular diet. Meat is eaten only during ceremonial functions. The most popular drink is beer made from maize or millet or both.

The daily per capita availability of energy, protein, fats and carbohydrates is 1,911 calories, 51.0 grams, 51 grams and 432 grams, respectively.

MEDIA & CULTURE

The national press consists of two dailies (*Herald* published at Harare with a circulation of 107,000 and *The Chronicle* published at Bulawayo with a circulation of 45,547), the thrice weekly *Umtali Post*, two Sunday papers and 10 weeklies including *The National Observer, The Zimbabwe Times, Zimbabwe Government Gazette, Umtali Post* and *Look & Listen*, four fortnightlies, 16 monthlies, and five periodicals published at intervals longer than a month. Aggregate newspaper circulation is 155,000 or 21 per 1,000 inhabitants. Annual consumption of newsprint is 25,503 tons, or 3,334 kg (7,351 lb) per 1,000 inhabitants.

Although there is no censorship of the media, the press is remarkably subdued. Opposition speeches and activities receive no coverage in the nation's press. In 1981 the government took over the two dailies. Zimbabwe's constitution guarantees freedom of expression, and the right to free speech is widely exercised. However, control of the mass media rests with the government. Major daily newspapers are controlled by the Mass Media Trust in which the government has a controlling interest. The Zimbabwe Broadcasting Corporation, which operates the nation's three radio stations and the sole television station, is wholly government-owned. While there is no evidence of systematic government meddling in the editorial policies of these media, senior media officials tend either to be strong exponents of the ruling party/government line or to practice a high degree of self-censorship. Two prominent exceptions are a Catholic Church-sponsored monthly magazine *(Moto)*, which often includes articles critical of government policies, and a private weekly financial newspaper *(The Financial Gazette)*.

Criticism of the government is tolerated, but personal attacks on the president are prohibited by law. Senior officials of the Mass Media Trust have sometimes interfered in editorial policy at the newspapers. Two pseudonymous columnists for the major Sunday newspaper, who frequently wrote articles critical of the government, no longer appear in print. This has served to reinforce the willingness of other reporters and columnists to practice "self-censorship" on contentious issues and to stress ZANU positions. Nevertheless, it appears that most senior editorial personnel generally share and support the government's policies and programs and do not hesitate to criticize incompetent or corrupt officials.

Zimbabwe has no national news agency, but the privately owned Inter-African News Agency fills that role. Foreign news bureaus in Harare include AFP, UPI, AP, Reuters and South African News Agency (SANA).

Book publishing is a well developed activity as a result of the stimuli from South Africa, Great Britain and missionary groups. There are over 20 major publishing houses in operation including University of Zimbabwe Publications. Zimbabwe does not subscribe to any copyright conventions. Annual title output was 32 in 1982.

The Zimbabwe Broadcasting Corporation, successor to the Rhodesian Broadcasting Corporation, is a statutory body under the direct control of the Ministry of Information. It operates two main services and three regional ones. The General Home Service is broadcast by six medium-wave transmitters and four short-wave transmitters for 17 hours daily. All programs in this service are in English. The African Service is broadcast over three medium-wave transmitters and four using short-wave frequencies for 15 hours daily. Programs are in English, Ndebele, Nyanja and Shona. The three regional services include Radio Jacaranda in Harare, Radio Matopos in Bulawayo, and Radio Manica in Mutare. Each of these services broadcasts for about 17 hours daily. A Foreign Service broadcasts to Mozambique in Portuguese and three vernaculars. In 1982 there were 300,000 radio receivers in the country, or 40 per 1,000 inhabitants. Of the 18,200 annual radio broadcasting hours, 6,000 hours are devoted to information, 1,000 hours to education, 4,000 hours to culture, 150 hours to religion, 1,000 hours to commercials and 4,900 hours to entertainment.

Television was introduced in 1960 as a commercial venture and is now operated by Zimbabwe Television Corporation with a main station at Harare and a second studio in Bulawayo. In 1982 there were 80,000 television sets, or 11 per 1,000 inhabitants. Of the 1,800 annual television broadcasting hours, 550 hours are devoted to information, 50 hours to education, 80 hours to culture, 30 hours to religion, 250 hours to commercials and 640 hours to entertainment. No information is available on cinemas and the film media.

The oldest library is the Bulawayo Public Library, founded in 1896, with a collection of over 50,000 volumes. The largest is the University of Zimbabwe Library with 190,000 books. Other major libraries include the Library of Parliament with 70,000 volumes, the National Free Library and the Queen Victoria Memorial Library in Harare, both with 50,000 volumes.

There are seven museums, reporting an annual attendance of over 500,000. The largest are the National Museum at Bulawayo, the Queen Victoria Museum at Harare and the Mutare Museum. There are 25 nature preservation sites.

SOCIAL WELFARE

A Department of Social Welfare was established in 1971 under the Ministry of Labor. The department offers a range of social services including child welfare, public assistance, care of the aged, and old age pensions. A voluntary program known as Medical Aid provide health care to some. Disabled people receive monthly allowances under the Workmen's Compensation Act. In addition, 723 voluntary welfare organizations provide a wide spectrum of social services.

GLOSSARY

Abezansi: the upper or noble caste of the Ndebele
Ishe: Hereditary chiefdoms of the Shona

Izinduna (sing: unduna): Hereditary chiefdoms of the Ndebele

Kraal: a village or hamlet composed of several households

Samusha: head of a kraal who allocates the land to eligible members

CHRONOLOGY (from 1980)

1980— Zimbabwe-Rhodesia gains legal independence as the Republic of Zimbabwe with a coalition government headed by Prime Minister Robert Mugabe; Joshua Nkomo is named home minister; Air, road and rail links with Mozambique and Zambia are restored. . . Zimbabwe severs diplomatic relations with South Africa. . . Robert Mugabe, on his first visit to the United States as prime minister, assures Americans that much of his Marxist rhetoric was mere propaganda. . . Lt. Gen. Peter Walls , the white commander of the Zimbabwean army is dismissed for interference in politics

1981— New press curbs are set requiring foreign correspondents to seek monthly registration. . . at the Zimcord Conference 31 nations and 26 international agencies pledge $1.8 million in economic aid. . . . Joshua Nkomo is demoted as rift between Mugabe and Nkomo surfaces but the two men reach accord. . . Edgar Z. Tekere, manpower and planning minister and ZANU secretary general is dismissed after his trial and acquittal on murder charges.

1983— Nkomo and two Patriotic Front Cabinet ministers are ousted from Cabinet following discovery of arms caches in Matabeleland.

1984— ZANU Party holds congress demanding one-party rule and end to white electoral districts. . . . Nkomo flees the country.

1985— In national elections Mugabe gains striking victory with 64 seats out of 80 for Africans.

BIBLIOGRAPHY (from 1970)

Akers, M., *Encyclopaedia Rhodesia* (Salisbury, 1977).

Astrow, Andre, *Zimbabwe: A Revolution that Lost its Way?* (London, 1983).

Blake, R., *A History of Rhodesia* (London, 1977).

Botsio, Utete C., *The Road to Zimbabwe* (Washington, D.C., 1978).

Bowman, Larry W., *Politics in Rhodesia* (Cambridge, Mass., 1973).

Channock, Martin, *Britain, Rhodesia and South Africa, 1900-1945* (Totowa, N.J., 1977).

Davies, D.K., *Race Relations in Rhodesia* (London, 1973).

Dorman, James E., *Rhodesia Alone* (Washington, D.C., 1977).

Frederiske, Julie, *None But Ourselves: Masses vs. Media in the Making of Zimbabwe* (New York, 1984).

Gibson, Richard, *African Liberation Movements* (London, 1972).

Good, Robert C., *The International Politics of the Rhodesian Rebellion* (Princeton, N.J., 1973).

Hills, Denis, *Rebel People: Rhodesia in Crisis* (New York, 1978).

Hudson, Miles, *Triumph or Tragedy: Rhodesia to Zimbabwe* (London, 1981).

Kapungu, Leonard, *The United Nations and Economic Sanctions Against Rhodesia* (Lexington, Mass., 1973).

Kay, George, *Rhodesia: A Human Geography* (New York, 1970).

Kinloch, Graham, C., *Racial Conflict in Rhodesia: A Socio-Historical Study* (Washington, D.C., 1978).

Kumbula, Tendayi J., *Education & Social Control in Southern Rhodesia* (San Francisco, 1979).

Martin, David and Phyllis Johnson, *The Struggle for Zimbabwe* (New York, 1982).

Meredith M., *The Past is Another Century: Rhodesia, 1890-1979* (London, 1979).

Mlambo, Eshmael, *Rhodesia: The Struggle for a Birthright* (New York, 1972).

Morris-Jones, W.H., *From Rhodesia to Zimbabwe* (Totowa, N.J. 1980).

Mosley, Paul, *The Settler Economies: Studies in the Economic History of Kenya and Southern Rhodesia* (New York, 1983).

Nyangoni, Christopher & Gideon Nyandoro, *Zimbabwe Independence Movements: Select Documents* (New York, 1979).

O'Meara, P., *Rhodesia: Racial Conflict or Coexistence* (Ithaca, N.Y., 1975).

Palmer, Robin, *Land & Racial Domination in Rhodesia* (London, 1977).

Peterson, Robert W., *Rhodesian Independence* (New York, 1971).

Ranger, T.O., *African Voice in Southern Rhodesia* (Evanston, Ill., 1970).

———, *Peasant Consciousness and Guerrilla War in Zimbabwe* (Berkely, Calif., 1985).

Rasmussen R. Kent., *Historical Dictionary of Rhodesia-Zimbabwe* (Metuchen, N.J., 1979).

Schatzberg, Michael G., *The Political Economy of Zimbabwe* (New York, 1984).

Sithole, N., *Roots of a Revolution* (London, 1977).

Skimin, Robert, *The Rhodesian Sellout* (Roslyn Heights, N.Y., 1978).

Strack, Harry R., *Sanctions: The Case of Rhodesia* (Syracuse, N.Y., 1978).

Vambe L., *From Rhodesia to Zimbabwe* (London, 1976).

Weinrich, A.K., *African Farmers in Rhodesia* (New York, 1975).

———, *Black & White Elites in Rural Rhodesia* (Totowa, N.J., 1973).

Weinrich, Elaine, *Britain and the Politics of Rhodesian Independence* (London, 1978).

Wiseman, Henry and Alastair M. Taylor, *From Rhodesia to Zimbabwe: The Politics of Transition* (London, 1981).

APPENDICES

APPENDIX I: COMPARATIVE TABLE

	Year of Independence	Former Colonial Power(s)	Income Group	Area (Sq. Km.)
Afghanistan	1775	—	Low	652,090
Algeria	1962	France	Upper Middle	2,381,741
Angola	1975	Portugal	Lower Middle	1,246,700
Antigua & Barbuda	1981	U.K.	Upper Middle	280
Argentina	1816	Spain	Upper Middle	2,791,810
Bahamas	1973	U.K.	High	13,935
Bahrain	1971	U.K.	High	622
Bangladesh	1971	U.K.	Low	142,776
Barbados	1966	U.K.	Upper Middle	430
Benin	1960	France	Low	112,622
Belize	1981	U.K.	Upper Middle	22,963
Bhutan	—	—	Low	46,620
Bolivia	1825	Spain	Lower Middle	1,098,579
Botswana	1966	U.K.	Lower Middle	600,372
Brazil	1822	Portugal	Upper Middle	8,511,965
Brunei	1984	U.K.	High	5,765
Burma	1948	U.K.	Low	678,033
Burundi	1962	Belgium	Low	27,834
Cambodia	1953	France	Low	181,035
Cameroon	1960	France	Lower Middle	475,442
Cape Verde Islands	1975	Portugal	Low	4,033
Central African Republic	1960	France	Low	622,984
Chad	1960	France	Low	1,284,000
Chile	1818	Spain	Upper Middle	756,945
Colombia	1819	Spain	Upper Middle	1,138,914
Comoros	1975	France	Low	1,795
Congo	1960	France	Upper Middle	342,000
Costa Rica	1821	Spain	Upper Middle	50,900
Cuba	1902	Spain	Lower Middle	114,520
Djibouti	1977	France	Lower Middle	23,000
Domenica	1978	France & U.K.	Lower Middle	752
Dominican Republic	1844	Spain	Upper Middle	48,734
Ecuador	1822	Spain	Upper Middle	270,670
Egypt	1922	U.K.	Lower Middle	1,001,449
El Salvador	1841	Spain	Lower Middle	20,935
Equatorial Guinea	1968	Spain	Low	27,972
Ethiopia	—	—²	Low	1,221,900
Fiji	1970	U.K.	Upper Middle	18,272
Gabon	1960	France	High	267,667
Gambia	1965	U.K.	Low	11,570
Ghana	1957	U.K.	Low	238,539
Grenada	1974	U.K.	Lower Middle	344
Guatemala	1821	Spain	Upper Middle	108,889
Guinea	1958	France	Low	245,857
Guinea-Bissau	1974	Portugal	Low	36,125
Guyana	1966	U.K.	Lower Middle	214,970
Haiti	1804	France	Low	27,750
Honduras	1821	Spain	Lower Middle	112,088
India	1947	U.K.	Low	3,287,588
Indonesia	1945	The Netherlands	Lower Middle	1,904,345
Iran	—	—	Upper Middle	1,648,195
Iraq	1932	U.K.	Upper Middle	438,446
Ivory Coast	1960	France	Lower Middle	322,463
Jamaica	1962	U.K.	Upper Middle	11,424
Jordan	1946	U.K.	Upper Middle	97,740
Kenya	1963	U.K.	Low	582,646
Kiribati	1979	U.K.	Upper Middle	684
Korea (North)	1948	Japan	Upper Middle	120,538
Korea (South)	1948	Japan	Upper Middle	98,485
Kuwait	1961	U.K.	High	17,818
Laos	1953	France	Low	236,800
Lebanon	1946	France	Upper Middle	10,400
Lesotho	1966	U.K.	Lower Middle	30,355
Liberia	—	—	Lower Middle	111,370
Libya	1951	Italy	High	1,759,540
Madagascar	1958	France	Low	587,041
Malawi	1964	U.K.	Low	118,485
Malaysia	1957	U.K.	Upper Middle	329,745
Maldives	1965	U.K.	Low	298
Mali	1960	France	Lower Middle	1,204,021
Mauritania	1960	France	Low	1,118,700
Mauritius	1968	France & U.K.	Upper Middle	1,974
Mexico		Spain	Upper Middle	1,972,547
Morocco	1956	France	Lower Middle	624,550
Mozambique	1975	Portugal	Low	783,030
Nauru	1968	U.K. & Australia	High	21
Nepal	—	—	Low	141,499
Nicaragua	1821	Spain	Lower Middle	140,621
Niger	1960	France	Low	1,267,000
Nigeria	1960	U.K.	Lower Middle	923,768
Oman	—	—	High	212,457
Pakistan	1947	U.K.	Low	803,943
Panama	1819	Spain	Upper Middle	75,650
Papua New Guinea	1975	Australia	Lower Middle	475,368
Paraguay	1811	Spain	Upper Middle	406,752
Peru	1821	Spain	Upper Middle	1,285,215
Phillippines	1946	Spain & U.S.	Lower Middle	299,404
Qatar	1971	U.K.	High	11,000
Rwanda	1962	Belgium	Low	26,388
Saint Lucas	1979	France	Lower Middle	616
Saint Vincent	1979	U.K.	Lower Middle	389
Sao Tome & Principe	1975	Portugal	Low	963
Saudi Arabia	—	—	High	2,149,690
Senegal	1960	France	Lower Middle	197,161
Seychelles	1976	France & U.K.	Upper Middle	285
Sierra Leone	1961	U.K.	Low	71,740
Singapore	1965	U.K.	High	581
Solomon Islands	1978	U.K.	Lower Middle	28,530
Somalia	1960	U.K. & Italy	Low	637,140
Sri Lanka	1948	U.K.	Low	65,610
St Kitts	1983	U.K.	Lower Middle	261
Sudan	1956	U.K.	Lower Middle	2,505,813
Suriname	1975	The Netherlands	Upper Middle	163,265
Swaziland	1968	U.K.	Lower Middle	17,364
Syria	1946	France	Upper Middle	185,180
Tanzania	1964	U.K.	Low	939-361
Thailand	—	—	Lower Middle	514,000
Togo	1960	France	Low	56,000
Tonga	1970	U.K.	Lower Middle	749
Trinidad & Tobago	1962	U.K.	High	5,128
Tunisia	1956	France	Upper Middle	164,150
Turkey	—	—	Upper Middle	779,452
Tuvalu	1978	U.K.	Upper Middle	26
Uganda	1962	U.K.	Low	243,411
United Arab Emirates	—	—	High	77,700
Upper Volta	1960	France	Low	274,200
Uruguay	1825	Spain	Upper Middle	177,508
Vanuata	1980	U.K. & France	Lower Middle	14,763
Venezuela	1811	Spain	High	912,050
Vietnam	1945	France	Low	332,559
Western Samoa	1962	U.K.	Lower Middle	2,841
Yemen (P.D.R.)	1967	—	Lower Middle	287,683
Yemen Arab Republic	—	—	Lower Middle	195,000
Zaire	1960	Belgium	Low	2,344,932
Zambia	1964	U.K.	Lower Middle	752,618
Zimbabwe	1980	U.K.	Lower Middle	380,580

¹estimate
²Briefly under Italian occupation, 1935-41
³in 1974

APPENDIX II: CLASSIFICATION OF COUNTRIES BY PER CAPITA INCOME (1984)

1. Gross National Product Per Capita, 1984 (in 1984 U.S. $)

More than $10,000: Bahrain, Bermuda, Brunei, Canada, Denmark, Greenland, Japan, Kuwait, Liechtenstein, Nauru, Norway, Qatar, Saudi Arabia, Sweden, Switzerland, United Arab Emirates, United States, West Germany.

$5,001 to $10,000: American Samoa, Australia, Austria, Belgium, Bulgaria, Czechoslovakia, East Germany, Faroe Islands, Finland, France, French Polynesia, Gabon, Guam, Hong Kong, Hungary, Iceland, Ireland, Israel, Italy, Libya, Luxembourg, Martinique, Monaco, Netherlands, New Caledonia, New Zealand, Oman, Poland, Romania, Singapore, Trinidad and Tobago, United Kingdom, USSR, Virgin Islands (US), Yugoslavia.

$1,001 to $5,000: Algeria, Andorra, Antigua and Barbuda, Argentina, Bahamas, Barbados, Belize, Brazil, Chile, China-Taiwan, Colombia, Cook Islands, Costa Rica, Cuba, Cyprus, Dominica, Dominican Republic, Ecuador, Falkland Islands, Fiji, French Guiana, Gibraltar, Greece, Guadeloupe, Guatemala, Iran, Iraq, Ivory Coast, Jamaica, Jordan, Macau, Malaysia, Malta, Mauritius, Mexico, Mongolia, Montserrat, Morocco, Netherlands Antilles, Panama, Paraguay, Peru, Portugal, Puerto Rico, Reunion, St. Lucia, San Marino, Seychelles, South Africa, South Korea, Spain, Suriname, Syria, Thailand, Tunisia, Turkey, Uruguay, Venezuela.

$401 to $1,000: Albania, Angola, Anguilla, Bolivia, Botswana, Cameroon, Congo, Djibouti, Egypt, El Salvador, Equatorial Guinea, Gambia, Ghana, Grenada, Guyana, Honduras, Indonesia, Kenya, Kiribati, Lebanon, Liberia, Madagascar, Maldives, Mauritania, Namibia, Nicaragua, Nigeria, North Korea, Pakistan, Papua New Guinea, Philippines, St. Kitts and Nevis, St. Vincent and the Grenadines, Senegal, Solomon Islands, Sri Lanka, Sudan, Swaziland, Tonga, Turks and Caicos Islands, Tuvalu, Vanuatu, Wallis and Futuna Islands, Western Samoa, Yemen Arab Republic, Yemen, People's Democratic Republic of, Zambia, Zimbabwe.

Less than $401: Afghanistan, Bangladesh, Benin, Bhutan, Burkina, Burma, Burundi, Cambodia, Cape Verde, Central African Republic, Chad, China-Mainland, Comoros, Ethiopia, Guinea, Guinea-Bissau, Haiti, India, Laos, Lesotho, Malawi, Mali, Mozambique, Nepal, Niger, Rwanda, Sao Tome and Principe, Sierre Leone, Somalia, Tanzania, Togo, Uganda, Vietnam, Western Sahara, Zaire.

Source: *Handbook of Economic Statistics*, 1985, Central Intelligence Agency

APPENDIX III: GLOBAL INDICATORS

1. Annual Changes in Selected Economic and Financial Indicators, 1973-84 (%)

	1973	1974	1975	1976	1977	1978	1979	1980	1981	1982	1983	1984
OUTPUT												
Industrial countries	6.1	0.5	-0.6	5.0	3.9	4.1	3.5	1.3	1.6	-0.2	2.6	4.9
Oil-exporting countries	10.7	8.0	-0.3	12.3	6.3	2.3	3.7	-2.1	-4.1	-4.2	-0.8	3.8
Non-oil developing countries	...	...	...	...	5.8	6.4	5.0	5.0	3.1	1.7	1.8	3.7
CONSUMER PRICES												
Industrial countries	7.7	13.1	11.1	8.3	8.4	7.2	9.0	11.8	9.9	7.4	4.9	4.9
Oil-exporting countries	11.3	17.1	18.8	16.8	15.2	12.0	10.9	13.2	13.2	8.1	10.0	10.8
Non-oil developing countries	...	...	...	...	23.6	20.8	24.8	31.4	30.1	30.3	41.4	44.5
EXPORT VOLUMES												
Industrial countries	13.2	7.0	-4.2	10.6	5.3	6.2	7.6	3.9	3.3	-2.3	2.6	8.6
Oil-exporting countries	14.2	-1.6	-11.7	14.3	0.4	-3.2	1.6	-12.2	-15.2	-18.5	-7.5	6.0
Non-oil developing countries	9.3	-0.1	-0.3	11.3	4.2	9.7	8.1	9.0	7.7	1.7	5.8	9.1
IMPORT VOLUMES												
Industrial countries	11.5	1.4	-8.1	13.3	4.4	5.2	8.6	-1.5	-2.2	-0.6	4.4	11.9
Oil-exporting countries	20.6	38.5	41.4	20.6	16.7	3.4	-8.5	12.4	21.3	5.9	-10.9	-2.7
Non-oil developing countries	11.5	7.6	-4.1	4.5	7.4	8.6	10.6	7.3	3.1	-8.2	-1.8	6.4
TERMS OF TRADE												
Industrial countries	-1.8	-10.6	2.5	-1.0	-1.2	2.8	-3.5	-6.9	-1.6	2.0	2.2	0.3
Oil-exporting countries	13.3	140.0	-5.1	5.8	1.1	-10.2	28.3	43.4	11.3	-0.3	-9.3	-2.3
Non-oil developing countries	5.3	-5.9	-8.5	5.9	6.7	-4.1	0.7	-3.8	-5.1	-3.3	0.8	1.7
U.S. REAL INTEREST RATES												
Money Market rates	8.7	10.5	5.8	5.1	5.5	7.9	11.2	13.4	16.4	12.3	9.1	10.5*
Inflation rates	6.2	11.0	9.1	5.8	6.5	7.6	11.3	13.5	10.4	6.2	3.2	4.3*
Real interest rates	2.5	-0.5	-3.3	-0.7	-1.0	0.3	-0.1	-0.1	6.0	6.1	5.9	6.2*
EXTERNAL DEBT RATIO												
(as % of exports—goods & services)												
Non-oil developing countries	...	...	...	...	129.5	131.0	119.5	113.1	125.0	148.3	154.4	147.4

* Based on three-quarters of 1984.

Sources: *World Economic Outlook*, 1984 (IMF) and *Financial Statistics* (IMF) various issues.

2. Selected World Statistics

	1960	1965	1970	1975	1980	1981	1982	1983	1984
Gross national product (billion 1984 U.S. $)	5,300	6,780	8,770	10,900	12,900	13,100	13,200	13,500	14,000
Population (million persons, midyear)	3,063	3,357	3,722	4,107	4,478	4,559	4,641	4,721	4,800
Agricultural production index (1975=100)	65	73	88	100	110	114	117	117	122
Exports (billion U.S. $)	129.8	189.9	313.1	873.8	1,995.4	1,974.3	1,849.7	1,808.8	1,897.0
Crude oil, excluding natural gas liquids (million b/d)	21.0	30.3	45.7	53.0	59.5	55.8	53.0	52.6	53.8
Natural gas (trillion cubic feet)	NA	24.5	38.1	46.5	54.4	55.7	55.1	55.4	58.9
Hard coal (million metric tons)	1.985[a]	2,034[a]	2,141	2,361	2,728	2,728	2,829	2,829	2,997
Brown coal and lignite (million metric tons)	640	742	794	869	1,005	1,034	1,069	1,091	1,127
Electricity (billion kilowatt hours)	2,348	3,412	4,953	6,519	8,247	8,397	8,477	8,797	8,953
Iron ore (million metric tons)	522	621	769	892	896	861	796	800	839
Bauxite (million metric tons)	27.6	37.4	57.8	75.1	88.8	86.0	73.2	77.4	85.2
Pig iron (million metric tons)	259	335	431	468	510	501	454	466	480
Crude steel (million metric tons)	346	459	594	651	714	704	641	644	690
Refined copper (thousand metric tons)	NA	6,157	7,543	8,344	8,916	9,171	9,119	9,340	9,680
Primary aluminium (million metric tons)	4.5	6.3	9.7	12.0	15.4	15.1	13.3	14.8	16.5
Smelter lead (thousand metric tons)	2,313	2,641	3,292	3,369	3,205	3,159	3,237	3,910	3,590
Refined zinc (thousand metric tons)	3,025	3,949	4,827	5,460	6,057	6,140	5,881	6,175	6,310
Primary tin (thousand metric tons)	192	200	227	226	248	242	241	210	223
Mineral fertilizer[b] (million metric tons, nutrient content)	NA	42.8	66.3	93.3	119.0	124.9	119.0	119.6	130.2
Nitrogen fertilizer[b] (million metric tons of N)	NA	16.8	30.2	42.5	59.7	62.8	62.0	63.5	68.6
Phosphate fertilizer[b] (million metric tons of P_2O_5)	NA	13.8	19.2	27.1	33.4	34.6	31.1	31.7	33.8
Potassium fertilizer[b] (million metric tons of K_2O)	NA	12.1	16.9	23.7	25.9	27.5	25.9	24.4	27.8
Synthetic fibers (thousand metric tons)	700	2,050	4,870	7,450	10,475	10,830	10,142	9,538	9,513
Automobiles (thousands units)	12,800	19,100	22,500	25,220	28,997	27,567	26,130	29,686	30,413
Cement (million metric tons)	NA	439	585	720	867	875	888	890	911
Grain (million metric tons)	929	1,010	1,220	1,330	1,530	1,610	1,660	1,600	1,750
Wheat (million metric tons)	240	262	319	360	446	454	485	496	521
Coarse grain (million metric tons)	414	441	540	613	682	747	753	655	764
Rice (million metric tons)	162	166	312	359	399	412	423	450	468
Potatoes (million metric tons)	285	285	312	285	264	288	284	286	306
Sugar (million metric tons)	61.4	67.2	76.7	81.7	87.7	96.1	107	101	102
Coffee (thousand metric tons)	NA	4,929	3,566	4,393	4,793	6,026	4,963	5,518	NA
Fish catch (million metric tons)	40.2	53.2	65.6	66.0	72.3	75.1	76.8	NA	NA
Cattle (million head)	901	1,072	1,096	1,202	1,205	1,214	1,257	1,260	1,266
Hogs (million head)	519	575	594	655	793	778	767	777	778
Meat (million metric tons)	65.4	73.3	102	117	138	132	133	137	139
Milk (million metric tons)	315	342	362	392	428	430	432	448	449
Wool (thousand metric tons)	2,450	2,540	2,840	2,722	2,773	2,820	2,854	2,866	2,905
Ginned cotton (million metric tons)	10.4	12.2	11.8	11.7	14.0	15.4	14.7	14.7	18.4
Tobacco (thousand metric tons)	NA	4,581	4,675	5,445	5,289	5,974	6,882	5,923	NA
Railroad freight (billion ton-kilometers)	3,338	4,195	5,020	5,958	6,766	6,797	6,775	NA	NA
Fishing fleet inventory (number)	NA	NA	12,889	18,940	21,523	21,800	21,926	22,231	21,913
(thousand GRT)	NA	NA	7,804	11,339	12,669	12,923	12,819	13,031	12,806
Merchant fleet inventory (number)	17,229	17,825	19,503	22,353	23,855	24,247	24,467	24,503	24,699
(million DWT)	171.6	214.1	325.1	556.4	638.1	653.0	660.2	647.1	646.9
Tanker fleet inventory (number)	3,371	3,533	4,119	5,177	5,439	5,606	5,647	5,600	5,574
(million DWT)	63.7	89.6	152.4	301.7	379.9	378.8	374.0	352.6	337.9

[a] Including brown coal at its hard coal equivalent.

[b] Fertilizer year ending 30 June of the stated year.

Source: Handbook, Economic Statistics, 1985 Central Intelligence Agency.

3. Selected Economic Indicators, Regional Summary
Average annual real growth and shares in Gross National Product (GNP)
1960-70, 1970-80, 1981, 1982, 1983, and 1984

(percentages)

Region and indicator	1960-70	1970-80	1981	1982	1983	1984(P)
All developing regions						
REAL RATE OF GROWTH						
Total GNP	6.0	5.8	2.8	0.9	0.3	3.9
Agricultural production	3.0	2.8	4.6	2.4	5.4	3.7
Manufacturing production	8.6	7.7	0.5	1.7	3.4	n.a
Population	2.4	2.3	2.1	2.2	2.0	2.0
GNP per capita	3.5	3.5	0.7	-1.2	-1.7	1.8
Gross investment	7.6	8.8	2.6	-2.8	-0.1	n.a.
SHARE IN GNP						
Gross investment	20.5	25.5	25.6	24.7	24.0	n.a.
Gross national savings	18.4	25.4	25.1	23.3	21.8	n.a.
Africa, south of the Sahara						
REAL RATE OF GROWTH						
Total GNP	4.9	3.8	1.0	-2.0	-2.7	-0.7
Agricultural production	2.2	1.3	4.1	2.1	-0.1	4.0
Manufacturing production	8.2	4.1	6.3	-4.2	-7.5	n.a.
Population	2.5	2.8	3.1	3.1	3.2	3.2
GNP per capita	2.4	1.0	-2.1	-5.0	-5.7	-3.8
Gross investment	8.2	6.0	9.4	-0.4	-13.0	n.a.
SHARE IN GNP						
Gross investment	18.8	24.3	23.8	20.9	18.9	n.a.
Gross national savings	16.2	22.3	15.8	13.3	14.5	n.a.
East Asia and Pacific						
REAL RATE OF GROWTH						
Total GNP	7.3	6.9	5.2	5.6	7.1	8.8
Agricultural production	4.6	3.5	6.2	5.7	5.2	4.0
Manufacturing production	11.9	10.8	5.3	4.8	10.4	13.7
Population	2.3	2.0	1.5	1.8	1.3	1.3
GNP per capita	4.9	4.8	3.6	3.8	5.7	7.4
Gross investment	13.9	8.9	1.4	6.2	9.8	7.2
SHARE IN GNP						
Gross investment	19.0	28.6	28.6	28.0	28.8	28.3
Gross national savings	14.6	27.0	26.0	25.9	26.7	n.a.
Latin America and the Caribbean						
REAL RATE OF GROWTH						
Total GNP	5.7	5.8	0.0	-2.0	-3.4	2.7
Agricultural production	3.2	3.2	5.4	-0.4	0.3	3.0
Manufacturing production	6.6	6.1	-9.1	-2.1	-4.0	n.a.
Population	2.8	2.5	2.4	2.3	2.3	2.3
GNP per capita	2.9	3.2	-2.3	-4.2	-5.6	0.3
Gross investment	6.6	7.1	-2.5	-14.8	-16.4	0.9
SHARE IN GNP						
Gross investment	21.4	24.7	23.7	22.0	17.1	17.5
Gross national savings	20.3	22.1	19.3	17.6	15.6	n.a.
North Africa and the Middle East						
REAL RATE OF GROWTH						
Total GNP	7.9	8.3	4.2	-0.2	-6.6	1.2
Agricultural production	1.5	3.0	-8.3	3.4	28.9	9.9
Manufacturing production	8.4	7.5	5.7	2.8	1.3	n.a.
Population	2.7	3.0	2.9	2.9	2.9	2.9
GNP per capita	5.2	5.3	1.3	-3.1	-9.2	-1.6
Gross investment	4.4	18.7	15.6	-2.8	9.5	4.1
SHARE IN GNP						
Gross investment	23.2	25.6	26.1	25.7	31.0	32.5
Gross national savings	26.7	44.4	47.1	39.5	30.7	n.a.
South Asia						
REAL RATE OF GROWTH						
Total GNP	4.3	3.5	5.9	2.8	7.1	4.6
Agricultural production	2.5	2.2	6.0	-1.6	10.8	1.9
Manufacturing production	6.5	3.8	8.2	4.8	5.2	7.4
Population	2.4	2.4	2.2	2.3	2.3	2.3
GNP per capita	1.9	1.1	3.7	0.5	4.7	2.2
Gross investment	5.4	5.1	0.0	0.4	6.7	5.5
SHARE IN GNP						
Gross investment	17.2	19.8	22.7	22.9	22.7	22.7
Gross national savings	12.4	16.2	17.9	18.4	19.2	19.1

3. Selected Economic Indicators, Regional Summary (continued)
Average annual real growth and shares in Gross National Product (GNP)
1960-70, 1970-80, 1981, 1982, 1983, and 1984

(percentages)

Region and indicator	1960-70	1970-80	1981	1982	1983	1984(P)
Southern Europe and other Mediterranean countries						
REAL RATE OF GROWTH						
Total GNP	6.6	5.2	1.7	1.6	0.7	0.9
Agricultural production	3.4	3.1	-0.1	5.9	-3.3	4.1
Manufacturing production	9.6	6.8	4.3	0.6	2.1	3.1
Population	1.6	1.6	1.4	1.4	1.4	1.4
GNP per capita	5.0	3.5	0.3	0.2	-0.7	-0.5
Gross investment	8.0	4.9	-2.2	1.0	-4.2	-3.4
SHARE IN GNP						
Gross investment	24.5	27.5	28.2	27.2	24.8	22.8
Gross national savings	19.4	19.9	19.6	19.5	19.6	n.a.
Industrialized countries						
REAL RATE OF GROWTH						
Total GNP	4.9	3.2	1.3	-0.4	2.4	4.9
Agricultural production	1.9	1.8	3.7	1.2	-6.0	7.9
Manufacturing production	6.1	3.1	0.5	-3.7	3.5	8.1
Population	1.1	0.8	0.6	0.6	0.6	0.6
GNP per capita	3.8	2.4	0.7	-1.0	1.7	4.2
Gross investment	6.6	2.5	-0.5	-1.6	1.2	1.7
SHARE IN GNP						
Gross investment	22.8	22.7	21.6	19.8	19.5	19.5
Gross national savings	23.5	23.1	21.8	20.2	20.0	19.5

Note: All the countries listed below (excluding Lebanon) have been included for the estimates of the real rates of growth of GNP and population. For other indicators, some countries or other areas have been omitted because of lack of data.

Industrialized countries—Australia, Austria, Belgium, Canada, Denmark, Finland, France, Federal Republic of Germany, Iceland, Ireland, Italy, Japan, Luxembourg, Netherlands, New Zealand, Norway, Spain, Sweden, Switzerland, United Kingdom, United States.

Developing countries or other areas—All other countries except China, high income oil exporters, South Africa and planned central economies.

(P) Preliminary.

Source: *World Bank Annual Report*, 1985.

APPENDIX IV: SELECTED ECONOMIC AND SOCIAL INDICATORS

1. Sectoral distribution of Labor Force in Developing Countries (%)

Region	Agriculture		Industry		Services	
	1960	1980	1960	1980	1960	1980
Developing countries	70.7	59.0	11.2	16.0	18.0	25.0
by region:						
America	47.9	34.5	20.0	22.5	32.1	43.0
Africa	78.8	67.8	7.6	14.0	13.5	18.1
West Asia	67.7	47.2	14.5	21.8	17.7	31.0
South and South-East Asia	73.3	62.8	10.2	14.5	16.5	22.6
Memo item:						
Developed market-economy countries	28.4	12.3	34.6	39.5	37.0	48.2

Note: Components may not add to 100 due to rounding.

Source: *UNCTAD Statistical Pocketbook*, 1984

2. Selected Economic and Social Indicators of Developing Countries: Population, Labor Force, Health, Education, Food Production per capita and Nutrition (1982 or latest year available)

Indicator / Country	Population % of urban (1)	Labor force Total (2)	Labor force % in agric. (3)	Health % infant mortal. (4)	Health % pub. expend (5)	Health pop. per doctor (6)	Health access to safe water (7)	Education illit. rate (8)	Education % pub. expend (9)	Index per capita food pro. duction (10)	Phones per 100 inhab. (11)
Afghanistan	17	7 738	77	205	2.5	18 633	10.0	80.0	9	96	0.2
Algeria	64	4 427	48	111	7.4	2 610	..	73.6	24	75	2.5
American Samoa	..	..	..	..	..	1 240	100.0	2.2	..	..	..
Angola	23	1 944	57	165	5.3	15 580	21.4	97.0	..	77	0.7
Antigua & Barbuda	..	..	..	..	14.8	2 313	..	11.3	11	136	..
Argentina	83	10 568	12	44	1.7	521	56.6	7.4	15	122	9.3
Bahamas	..	..	..	..	13.9	1 162	..	10.3	23	85	34.3
Bahrain	78	..	..	..	7.7	832	..	20.9	10	..	19.8
Bangladesh	13	31 872	83	133	5.3	9 081	38.4	74.2	8	94	0.1
Barbados	40	111	16	..	11.2	1 249	..	0.7	23	85	26.6
Belize	..	..	..	..	..	3 239	..	8.8	..	108	4.4
Benin	35	1 706	45	117	..	17 304	20.1	72.1	..	100	0.5
Bermuda	..	..	..	..	10.2	931	..	1.6	16	..	84.6
Bhutan	4	..	..	163	8.6	..	7.5	..	..	107	..
Bolivia	35	1 912	49	126	5.4	1 845	36.5	36.8	25	100	..
Botswana	36	400	79	80	7.4	7 396	..	59.0	12	70	1.5
Brazil	67	42 101	37	73	..	1 700	70.7	23.9	11	133	6.3
British Virgin Is.	..	..	..	..	..	1 200	..	1.7	15	..	24.0
Brunei Darussalam	..	..	..	..	4.9	2 031	97.8	36.1	11	133	8.0
Burkina	9	3 838	80	157	6.4	55 858	30.5	91.2	20	95	0.1
Burma	29	14 634	50	96	4.7	4 940	21.0	34.1	12	113	0.1
Burundi	2	2 249	82	123	5.1	47 167	23.6	73.2	18	96	0.1
Cameroon	38	4 042	80	92	6.5	13 678	..	59.5	21	102	..
Cape Verde	6	107	55	..	8.5	6 352	50.0	63.1	11	88	0.6
Cayman Islands	..	..	..	..	9.1	750	100.0	2.5	16	..	39.2
Central Afr. Rep.	43	1 245	86	119	..	22 434	..	67.0	20	104	..
Chad	20	1 813	82	161	4.2	47 933	..	94.4	..	95	0.1
Chile	82	3 854	18	27	6.9	1 925	84.2	11.0	12	98	5.0
Colombia	72	8 468	26	54	10.5	1 966	92.4	19.2	14	124	6.4
Comoros	13	125	63	..	16.5	16 000	..	41.6	..	93	0.4
Congo	39	549	33	68	6.1	5 325	..	84.4	19	81	1.1
Cook Islands	..	..	..	..	..	1 474	10.5	8.2	..	100	..
Costa Rica	45	787	34	18	5.1	1 436	83.9	11.6	22	100	10.7
Cuba	67	..	..	17	..	728	..	4.6	30	113	3.7
Cyprus	48	290	33	..	6.1	1 088	..	11.0	13	103	17.9
Dem. Kampuchea	15	..	..	190	..	16 598	..	63.9	..	55	..
Democratic Yemen	39	..	..	140	..	7 326	44.4	72.9	17	92	..
Djibouti	..	..	..	..	5.9	2 179	44.8	..	12	..	1.2
Dominica	..	..	..	..	8.8	7 800	..	5.9	..	93	1.0
Dominican Rep.	54	1 640	55	65	9.3	4 467	59.4	32.8	16	104	2.9
East Timor	11	..	..	..	13.3	25 667	..	..	..	..	..
Ecuador	46	2 734	43	78	7.4	1 570	45.2	25.8	33	101	3.3
Egypt	47	12 451	50	104	3.0	807	74.9	61.8	9	85	1.2
El Salvador	42	1 590	49	72	8.7	3 220	51.3	38.0	17	97	1.9
Equatorial Guinea	57	111	74	..	..	64 600	..	80.0	..	..	..
Ethiopia	16	14 001	78	122	4.5	76 271	..	95.8	11	82	2.8
Falkland Is. (Malvinas)	..	..	..	..	11.1	667	..	..	14	..	..
Fiji	44	214	39	..	8.1	2 180	76.6	21.0	20	104	6.8
French Guiana	..	..	..	..	..	1 169	..	26.1	..	..	24.0
French Polynesia	..	..	..	..	10.5	1 084	..	5.5	..	85	15.5
Gabon	38	266	75	..	5.6	2 570	..	87.6	16	94	..
Gambia	20	306	77	..	6.3	11 653	15.6	79.9	10	75	0.5
Ghana	38	4 580	49	86	7.0	7 239	47.1	69.8	22	72	0.7
Greenland	..	..	..	..	..	912	..	..	..	..	..
Grenada	..	..	..	..	15.6	388	..	2.2	13	100	5.0
Guadeloupe	45	..	..	..	..	1 051	..	16.8	..	83	14.0
Guam	..	..	..	..	..	1 714	..	3.0	..	..	..
Guatemala	40	2 338	54	66	10.9	8 606	44.5	54.0	11	114	..
Guinea	21	2 324	79	190	..	51 440	17.1	91.4	..	89	..
Guinea-Bissau	26	180	81	150	9.8	5 036	9.8	81.1	13	87	..
Guyana	22	308	21	43	5.7	10 177	72.0	8.4	14	89	2.7
Haiti	27	3 032	65	110	13.3	9 462	..	78.7	11	85	..
Honduras	38	1 165	62	83	8.0	3 124	43.8	43.1	10	79	0.8
Hong Kong	91	2 380	2	10	10.5	1 193	99.6	22.7	15	71	32.6
India	23	276 647	62	94	1.7	2 641	41.2	65.9	10	101	0.4
Indonesia	21	54 116	57	102	2.5	11 973	24.2	43.4	9	117	0.3
Iran (Islamic Rep.)	52	11 187	37	102	4.4	2 586	..	63.8	16	111	3.2
Iraq	74	3 421	38	73	5.4	1 774	..	75.8	7	87	1.7
Ivory Coast	40	4 188	78	119	3.9	20 903	..	65.0	30	107	1.3
Jamaica	43	801	19	10	7.8	2 848	..	3.9	13	90	6.0
Jordan	58	809	24	65	4.1	1 678	98.3	32.4	12	70	5..
Kenya	16	6 608	77	77	7.8	10 355	25.8	52.9	18	88	2.1
Kiribati	..	..	..	..	..	4 188	43.6	9.9	13	..	..
Korea, Republic of	58	15 242	36	32	1.2	1 438	77.7	12.4	14	125	7.7

2. Selected Economic and Social Indicators of Developing Countries: Population, Labor Force, Health, Education, Food Production per capita and Nutrition (continued)
(1982 or latest year available)

Indicator / Country	Population % of urban (1)	Labor force Total (2)	% in agric. (3)	% infant mortal. (4)	% pub. expend (5)	pop. per doctor (6)	access to safe water (7)	illit. rate (8)	% pub. expend (9)	Index per capita food pro- duction (10)	Phones per 100 inhab. (11)
Kuwait	90	393	2	32	4.9	680	..	40.4	8	..	15.9
Lao People's Dem. Rep.	15	..	..	159	2.3	21 667	..	56.4	..	122	0.2
Lebanon	78	..	..	39	3.5	614	..	14.0	22	134	..
Lesotho	5	727	82	94	7.8	18 642	13.9	41.4	..	84	..
Liberia	35	718	69	91	7.6	9 259	..	79.0	24	88	..
Libyan Arab Jamah.	56	801	13	95	10.4	660	98.0	49.9	13	127	..
Macau	..	..	..	..	6.9	949	100.0	20.6	..	53	..
Madagascar	20	4 445	82	116	8.1	9 970	21.5	66.5	19	94	0.4
Malawi	41	2 905	82	137	5.5	48 198	40.6	77.9	13	99	0.5
Malaysia	31	4 897	46	29	6.5	..	63.3	..	16	150	4.5
Maldives	..	..	..	..	..	19 000	5.0	18.0	..	90	..
Mali	22	3 739	86	132	3.1	25 174	6.4	90.6	31	83	..
Malta	84	120	5	..	10.0	859	100.0	33.5	8	113	25.3
Martinique	69	..	..	..	..	896	..	12.2	..	83	16.0
Mauritania	42	525	82	132	2.8	15 161	83.7	82.6	22	73	..
Mauritius	55	379	27	34	7.0	1 978	98.9	21.0	12	91	3.9
Mexico	68	21 602	34	53	2.4	1 233	56.2	17.3	14	104	7.2
Montserrat	..	..	..	..	9.5	1 857	..	3.4	..	..	18.3
Morocco	42	5 738	50	125	3.4	18 187	41.8	78.6	19	84	1.2
Mozambique	10	4 096	62	105	4.2	33 893	..	66.8	..	68	0.4
Namibia	48	338	47	..	..	..	..	61.6	..	87	5.0
Nepal	5	7 019	92	145	5.2	29 273	12.1	80.8	8	83	..
Neth. Antilles	..	..	..	..	7.9	1 783	..	7.5	22	5	22.1
New Caledonia	..	..	..	..	16.9	946	52.2	8.7	..	86	19.1
Nicaragua	55	869	41	86	14.6	2 258	53.2	42.5	10	77	2.2
Niger	14	1 741	87	132	4.1	37 321	33.1	90.2	23	88	0.2
Nigeria	22	30 613	51	109	2.2	9 591	..	66.0	16	92	..
Niue	..	..	..	..	8.3	3 000	..	6.0	..	92	..
Oman	8	..	..	123	3.2	1 519	..	44.0	5	95	2.0
Pacific Islands	..	..	..	..	15.2	2 673	37.6	..	24	..	..
Pakistan	30	23 586	52	121	1.5	3 192	34.6	79.3	5	105	0.4
Panama	56	669	33	33	13.2	1 167	82.3	12.9	18	103	9.5
Papua New Guinea	..	1 561	82	99	6.9	16 052	15.6	67.9	14	99	1.0
Paraguay	41	1 050	48	45	3.5	1 752	20.9	19.9	12	111	1.8
Peru	70	5 564	36	83	4.5	1 480	51.3	27.5	17	87	2.0
Philippines	38	18 583	45	51	4.1	7 118	50.8	17.4	10	124	1.5
Puerto Rico	73	1 173	3	..	13.9	847	..	12.2	..	77	20.0
Qatar	87	..	..	..	..	1 237	..	90.0	4	..	..
Reunion	57	168	26	..	..	1 360	..	37.1	..	108	10.0
Rwanda	5	2 644	89	126	4.7	27 203	54.2	50.3	22	105	0.1
Saint Christ. & Nevis	..	..	..	..	12.6	4 643	..	2.4	..	..	5.3
Saint Helena	..	..	..	..	..	1 667	..	2.9	10	..	..
Saint Lucia	..	..	..	..	8.8	2 775	..	18.3	17	92	6.9
St. Pierre and Miquelon	..	..	..	..	..	1 000	..	1.1	..	..	..
St. Vincent & Grenadines	..	..	..	..	11.8	4 182	..	4.4	..	107	4.0
Samoa	..	..	..	..	9.9	2 587	94.8	2.2	20	98	3.7
Sao Tome & Principe	..	..	..	..	10.7	2 263	..	..	..	78	..
Saudi Arabia	70	2 276	59	108	..	2 414	91.0	75.4	9	9	5.3
Senegal	26	2 439	73	155	6.0	12 942	41.6	94.4	9	9	5.3
Seychelles	..	..	..	..	13.1	2 370	..	42.3	14	..	9.9
Sierra Leone	27	1 353	64	190	4.1	18 284	16.0	93.3	18	81	0.4
Singapore	74	1 008	2	11	6.9	1 110	100.0	17.1	8	91	29.1
Somalia	32	1 464	79	184	3.1	12 191	..	93.9	9	60	..
Sri Lanka	28	5 434	3	32	6.0	7 706	30.6	14.0	9	154	0.6
Sudan	27	5 990	76	119	1.4	8 711	..	85.3	9	87	0.3
Suriname	45	105	17	..	8.7	1 748	..	35.0	25	182	4.0
Swaziland	10	265	71	..	7.2	7 000	..	44.8	14	111	2.2
Syrian Arab Rep.	52	2 346	47	58	3.6	2 515	70.7	60.0	8	168	3.2
Thailand	15	22 448	74	51	4.3	6 942	63.2	21.4	21	138	1.1
Togo	19	1 164	67	122	5.6	19 417	42.2	84.1	19	89	0.4
Tokelau	..	..	..	..	..	..	..	2.8	..	..	..
Tonga	..	..	..	..	14.1	2 553	74.5	0.4	16	118	..
Trinidad & Tobago	22	454	15	26	6.4	1 449	97.6	7.8	8	62	6.8
Tunisia	54	1 610	39	65	7.1	3 625	63.0	62.0	17	128	3.0
Turkey	50	19 560	52	83	3.6	1 636	76.2	31.2	11	115	4.2
Turks & Caicos Is.	..	..	..	..	..	2 000	..	1.9	14	..	..
U.S. Virgin Is.	..	..	..	..	..	927	..	5.0	..	..	39.0
Uganda	13	5 705	80	120	6.1	22 296	..	47.7	11	86	0.4
U. Arab Emirates	75	..	..	50	7.9	563	93.2	46.5	28	..	20.1
U. Rep. of Tanzania	13	7 699	80	98	5.4	16 282	..	26.5	11	88	0.5
Uruguay	85	1 148	11	34	4.8	538	80.5	6.1	10	109	9.9
Vanuatu	..	..	..	..	..	5 045	55.1	..	..	98	..
Venezuela	85	4 921	17	39	8.7	946	81.1	23.5	15	95	5.8

2. Selected Economic and Social Indicators of Developing Countries: Population, Labor Force, Health, Education, Food Production per capita and Nutrition (continued)
(1982 or latest year available)

Indicator / Country	Popu-lation % of urban (1)	Labor force Total (2)	% in agric. (3)	% infant mortal. (4)	% pub. expend (5)	pop. per doctor (6)	access to safe water (7)	illit. rate (8)	% pub. expend (9)	Index per capita food pro-duction (10)	Phones per 100 inhab. (11)
						Labor force	Health		Education		
Wallis & Futuna Is.	..	..	..	..	..	2 250		..	..	..	..
Yemen	11	..	..	163	4.0	6 776	27.3	91.4	15	93	..
Zaire	42	12 425	73	106	3.8	14 484	..	45.5	..	87	0.1
Zambia	40	2 153	65	105	6.1	7 101	..	52.7	10	87	1.1
Zimbabwe	25	2 561	58	83	6.7	6 443	..	31.2	..	87	2.8

Sources: (Column 1) Urban population as percent of total population in 1982:
Population Division of the United Nations.

(Columns 2,3) Labor force: total in thousands and percent in agriculture in 1982:
Department of International Economic and Social Affairs, United Nations.

(Column 4) Infant mortality rate per 1,000 live births. Deaths of under one year old in 1982:
World Development Report, 1984; The World Bank, 1984.

(Column 5) Public expenditure on health as percent of total public expenditure in 1980:
World Health Organization, *World Health Statistics Reports*, various issues.
International Monetary Fund, *Government Finance Statistics Yearbook*, various issues.

(Column 6) Population per physician:
United Nations, *Statistical Yearbook*, various issues.

(Column 7) Percentage of population with access to drinking water in 1980:
World Health Organization, *Review of National Baseline data*, WHO/HQ, September 1984.

(Column 8) Illiteracy rate:
UNESCO, *Statistical Yearbook*, 1983.

(Column 9) Public expenditure on education as percent of total public expenditure in 1980:
UNESCO, *Statistical Yearbook*, 1983.

(Column 10) Average of food production per capita. 1969-1971=100:
World Development Report, 1984: The World Bank, 1984. FAO, *Production Yearbook*, 1982.

(Column 11) Telephones per 100:
United Nations, *Statistical Yearbook*, various issues.

APPENDIX V: POPULATION

1. Population Growth, 1965-84 and Projected to 2000

Country group	1984 population (millions)	Average annual growth (%) 1965-73	1973-80	1980-84	1984-90	1990-2000
Developing countries	3,386	2.4	2.0	2.0	1.8	1.8
Low-income countries	2,263	2.4	1.8	1.8	1.8	1.7
Asia	2,040	2.4	1.7	1.7	1.6	1.4
India	749	2.3	2.3	2.2	2.0	1.7
China	1,032	2.4	1.2	1.3	1.0	0.9
Africa	223	2.6	2.8	3.1	3.3	3.4
Middle-income countries	1,123	2.4	2.4	2.4	2.2	2.1
Oil exporters	491	2.5	2.6	2.6	2.5	2.4
Oil importers	632	2.4	2.2	2.2	2.1	1.9
Major exporters of manufactures	413	2.3	2.1	2.0	1.9	1.7
High-income oil exporters	19	4.5	5.3	4.4	3.9	3.4
Industrial market economies	729	0.9	0.7	0.5	0.5	0.4
World, excluding nonmarket industrial economies	4,134	2.1	1.8	1.8	1.6	1.6
Nonmarket industrial economies	390	0.8	0.8	0.8	0.7	0.6

2. Population and GNP per capita, 1980, and Growth Rates, 1965-84

Country group	1980 GNP (bilions of dollars)	1980 population (millions)	1980 GNP per capita (dollars)	Average annual growth of GNP per capita					
				1965-73	1973-80	1981	1982	1983[a]	1984[b]
Developing countries	2,059	3,119	660	4.1	3.3	0.8	-0.7	-0.1	2.1
Low-income countries	547	2,098	260	3.0	3.1	2.0	2.8	5.2	4.7
Asia	495	1,901	260	3.2	3.5	2.5	3.4	6.0	5.3
China	284	980	290	4.9	4.5	1.6	5.8	7.6	7.7
India	162	687	240	1.7	1.9	3.5	0.4	4.2	2.0
Africa	52	197	270	1.3	0.0	-1.7	-2.6	-2.6	-1.5
Middle-income oil importers	962	579	1,660	4.6	3.1	-0.8	-2.0	-1.6	1.1
East Asia and Pacific	212	162	1,310	5.6	5.7	3.7	1.9	4.5	3.4
Middle East and North Africa	25	31	830	3.5	4.3	-2.5	2.6	0.5	-1.3
Sub-Saharan Africa	26	33	780	2.0	0.5	4.1	-4.8	-5.4	-5.4
Southern Europe	214	91	2,350	5.4	2.9	0.2	0.3	-0.5	0.2
Latin America and Caribbean	409	234	1,750	4.5	2.9	-4.1	-4.8	-4.5	1.1
Middle-income oil exporters	550	442	1,240	4.6	3.1	1.5	-2.3	-3.6	0.1
High-income oil exporters	229	16	14,050	4.1	6.2	-1.1	-7.8	-14.1	-6.4
Industrial market economies	7,477	714	10,480	3.7	2.1	0.7	-1.0	1.5	4.3

a. Estimated.
b. Projected.

Source: *World Development Report*, 1985

---

3. Population Trends and Vital Statistics for the World, by Development Status and Geographic Region, 1960-2020

Category	World	DEVELOPMENT STATUS[a]		GEOGRAPHIC REGION								
		Less developed	More developed	Africa	East Asia[b]	Balance of Asia	Oceania	Latin America	Northern America	Europe	USSR
Population (in millions)											
1960	3,014	2,069	945	278	801	864	15.8	217	199	425	214
1980	4,453	3,317	1,136	476	1,183	1,408	23.0	362	252	484	265
1984 (estimate)	4,763	3,597	1,166	537	1,239	1,539	24.5	397	261	490	276
2000 (medium proj.)[c]	6,127	4,851	1,276	877	1,470	2,074	30.4	550	298	513	315
2020 (medium proj.)[c]	7,806	6,429	1,377	1,489	1,662	2,654	37.8	742	339	525	357
% Population increase											
1960-1980	48	60	20	71	48	63	46	67	27	14	24
1980-2000	38	46	12	84	24	47	32	52	18	6	19
2000-2020	27	33	8	70	13	28	24	35	14	2	13
Population distribution by region (%)											
1960	100.0	68.6	31.4	9.2	26.6	28.7	0.5	7.2	6.6	14.1	7.1
1984 (estimate)	100.0	75.5	24.5	11.3	26.0	32.3	0.5	8.3	5.5	10.3	5.8
2000 (medium proj.)	100.0	79.2	20.8	14.3	24.0	33.8	0.5	9.0	4.9	8.4	5.1
2020 (medium proj.)	100.0	82.4	17.6	19.1	21.3	34.0	0.5	9.5	4.3	6.7	4.6
% Population increase by age, 2000 (medium proj.) over 1980											
All ages	38	46	12	84	24	47	32	52	18	6	19
Under 5 years	21	25	4	77	9	11	18	22	15	-3	7
5-14 years	15	18	0.3	89	-27	25	17	33	12	-10	19
15-64 years	48	62	13	85	44	64	37	66	19	8	17
65 years and over	58	88	30	83	83	94	51	83	25	18	40
Women aged 15-29	32	44	-7	88	15	50	20	47	-14	-9	-2
Women aged 15-44	46	61	6	87	42	62	34	63	9	3	12
Population distribution by age (%), 1980 (all ages = 100)											
0-14 years	35.7	40.0	23.0	45.2	35.5	40.8	29.5	39.4	22.6	22.3	24.4
15-64 years	58.6	56.2	65.6	51.7	59.5	55.9	62.6	56.3	66.3	64.7	65.6
65 years and over	5.7	3.8	11.4	3.1	5.1	3.3	7.9	4.3	11.1	13.0	10.0
Dependency ratio, 1980[d]	71	78	53	93	68	79	60	78	51	55	52

3. Population Trends and Vital Statistics for the World, by Development Status and Geographic Region, 1960-2020 (Continued)

Category	World	DEVELOPMENT STATUS[a] Less developed	More developed	Africa	East Asia[b]	GEOGRAPHIC REGION Balance of Asia	Oceania	Latin America	Northern America	Europe	USSR
Vital rates (avg. annual rate per 1,000 population)											
1960-1965											
Births	35.9	42.8	20.3	48.3	35.0	45.8	26.7	41.0	22.8	18.7	22.3
Deaths	16.4	19.7	9.0	23.3	17.9	20.7	10.5	12.2	9.2	10.2	7.2
Natural increase[e]	19.5	23.1	11.3	25.0	17.2	25.1	16.2	28.8	13.6	8.5	15.1
1980-1985 (estimate)											
Births	27.3	31.2	15.5	46.4	18.2	34.9	21.1	31.8	16.0	14.0	18.8
Deaths	10.6	11.0	9.6	16.5	6.8	12.9	8.4	8.2	9.1	10.7	9.3
Natural increase[e]	16.7	20.2	5.9	29.9	11.4	22.0	12.7	23.6	6.9	3.3	9.5
2000-2005 (projected)											
Births	22.5	24.8	13.8	40.4	16.4	23.3	18.1	23.7	13.9	12.6	16.0
Deaths	8.7	8.5	9.8	10.8	7.3	8.9	7.8	6.6	8.9	10.8	9.1
Natural increase[e]	13.8	16.3	4.0	29.6	9.1	14.4	10.3	17.1	5.0	1.8	6.9
Gross reproduction rate[f]											
1980-1985 average	1.73	2.00	0.96	3.16	1.12	2.27	1.32	2.01	0.90	0.93	1.15
2000-2005 (medium proj.)	1.38	1.47	0.99	2.67	0.93	1.37	1.20	1.42	1.01	0.92	1.12
Life expectancy at birth[g]											
1980-1985 average											
Male	57.5	55.5	69.4	48.2	65.9	53.5	65.5	61.8	70.4	70.0	66.5
Female	60.3	57.7	76.9	51.3	70.1	53.8	69.9	66.5	78.1	76.6	75.4
2000-2005 average (projected)											
Male	63.2	61.9	72.3	55.9	70.3	61.3	70.2	66.8	72.8	72.6	70.7
Female	66.4	64.6	79.7	59.4	74.4	62.3	75.1	72.0	80.3	79.5	78.9
Infant mortality rate[h]											
1980-1985 average	81	92	17	115	36	109	39	63	11	16	25
Urban population (% of total)											
1980	39.9	29	71	28.7	28.0	25.4	72	65.3	73.8	71.1	63.2
2000 (medium proj.)	48.2	40	78	42.2	34.2	36.8	73	76.6	78.0	79.0	74.3
Persons per household, 1980	4.29	4.97	3.06	5.10	4.34	5.42	3.47	4.75	2.90	2.98	3.24

NOTE: Figures for subcategories may not add to totals because of rounding

a Development status is based on demographic and other social and economic indicators. Using the United Nations' definition, "less developed" refers to all regions of Africa, Asia (excluding Japan), Latin America, and Oceania (excluding Australia and New Zealand). "More developed" refers to all regions of Europe (including the Union of Soviet Socialist Republics), Northern America, and the countries specivied as being outside the less developed region.

b Comprises China, Hong Kong, Japan, the Democratic People's Republic of Korea, the Republic of Korea, and Mongolia.

c United Nations "medium" variant projection

d Population in the age groups "under 15" and "65 and over" divided by the population "15-64."

e Births minus deaths.

f The gross reproduction rate is the number of daughters born to a woman who survives through the reproductive ages and reproduces at current fertility rates.

g Life expectancy at birth is the average number of years a group of newborn infants would live if they experienced prevailing age-specific mortality rates as they grew older.

h Number of deaths of children under one year of age per 1,000 live births during the year.

i Based on national definitions of "urban."

Sources:
Population data and vital rates: United Nations, Department of International Economic and Social Affairs, *Population and Vital Statistics Report*, Series A, Volume 36, No. 4, (New York, 1984) (for 1984 population); United Nations, *World Population Prospects; Estimates and Projections as Assessed in 1982*, Population Studies, No. 86 (UN Publication No. E.83.XIII.5) 1985.

Persons per household: See Annex Table 5 in United Nations, Department of International Economic and Social Affairs, 1981, *Estimates and Projections of the Number of Households by Country, 1975-2000: Based on the 1978 Assessment of Population Estimates and Projections (medium variant)*, (UN Publication No. ESA/P/WP.73), 1981.

4. Distribution of World Population by Regions (1982)

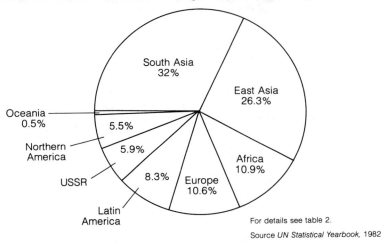

South Asia 32%
East Asia 26.3%
Oceania 0.5%
5.5%
Northern America
5.9%
USSR
8.3%
Latin America
Europe 10.6%
Africa 10.9%

For details see table 2.
Source *UN Statistical Yearbook*, 1982

5. Growth of World Population by Regions
(1975 to 1980)

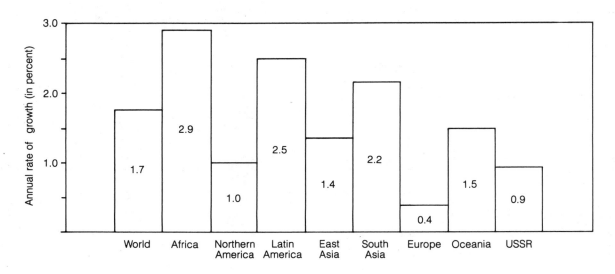

UN Statistical Yearbook, 1982

APPENDIX VI: GNP & GDP

1. Growth rate of real GDP and GDP Per Capita
(% per annum)

Region	GDP				GDP per capita			
	1960-1982	1960-1970	1970-1980	1981-1982	1960-1982	1960-1970	1970-1980	1981-1982
World	4.5	5.1	4.0	0.5	2.5	3.0	2.1	−1.3
Developing countries of which:	5.8	5.6	5.8	0.9	3.1	2.9	3.1	−1.6
America	5.4	5.3	5.4	−1.2	2.6	2.5	2.7	−3.8
Africa	5.0	4.8	5.0	0.8	2.2	2.1	2.1	−2.2
West Asia	7.6	8.0	7.0	2.1	4.6	5.1	4.0	−0.8
South and South-East Asia	5.6	5.1	6.1	3.5	3.1	2.5	3.6	1.0
Developed market-economy countries	3.9	4.8	3.3	−0.2	3.0	3.7	3.1	−1.6
Socialist countries of Eastern Europe	6.0	6.7	5.3	3.1	5.0	5.6	4.4	2.2
Least developed countries	3.3	3.5	3.7	2.0	0.7	0.9	1.0	−0.9

Sources: UNCTAD secretariat computations, based on data from UNSO, and other international sources.

2. Developing Countries: Growth of Real GDP, 1967–86[1,2] (%)

	Average 1967–76[3]	1977	1978	1979	1980	1981	1982	1983	1984	1985	1986
Developing countries	**6.0**	**6.1**	**5.1**	**4.2**	**3.6**	**2.3**	**1.5**	**1.4**	**4.4**	**3.5**	**4.1**
Memorandum: Median growth rate	5.2	5.5	5.6	4.9	3.7	3.2	1.5	1.5	2.9	3.0	3.3
By region											
Africa	4.8	4.4	1.2	2.8	4.5	1.7	0.2	–1.2	2.6	2.2	3.1
Asia	5.2	8.0	9.1	4.3	5.3	5.6	5.0	7.6	8.1	6.8	6.0
Europe	6.0	5.4	5.4	3.8	1.6	2.5	2.2	1.3	3.5	2.9	3.3
Middle East	9.0	7.0	1.7	2.3	–2.1	–1.8	–0.2	—	1.7	—	2.6
Western Hemisphere	5.9	5.3	4.1	6.1	5.3	1.0	–0.9	–3.2	3.1	2.5	3.3
By predominant export											
Fuel exporters	7.9	5.9	2.7	3.3	1.1	0.9	–0.4	–1.5	2.2	1.0	3.0
Non-fuel exporters	5.3	5.9	6.1	4.6	4.6	2.9	2.5	2.9	5.6	4.7	4.6
Primary product exporters	5.5	5.0	3.6	4.8	4.6	1.1	0.2	–0.6	3.5	2.7	3.4
Exporters of manufactures	5.3	8.0	9.2	4.2	4.5	4.8	5.0	7.2	8.5	7.0	6.1
Service and remittance countries	4.1	7.9	5.9	5.7	5.3	3.0	3.1	2.0	3.1	3.9	4.0
By financial criteria											
Capital importing countries	5.5	5.8	5.7	4.7	4.7	3.1	2.0	1.8	5.0	4.2	4.4
Of which, Market borrowers	6.2	5.7	4.6	5.9	4.7	2.3	0.3	–0.9	3.6	2.7	3.7
Of which, Major borrowers	6.8	6.0	4.9	6.4	4.7	1.9	0.4	–1.3	3.6	2.7	3.8
Official borrowers	3.5	5.8	3.8	2.1	2.9	3.3	1.9	2.3	3.2	3.5	4.0
Countries with recent debt-servicing problems	5.4	5.6	3.4	4.9	4.1	1.4	—	–2.2	2.8	2.8	3.3
Countries without debt-servicing problems	5.5	6.3	8.1	4.4	5.4	4.9	3.9	5.6	7.0	5.5	5.3
by miscellaneous criteria											
Small low-income countries	3.2	4.9	3.9	2.9	2.8	2.8	2.1	2.9	3.4	3.9	4.7
Sub-Saharan Africa[4]	3.9	4.0	2.2	2.2	3.2	1.7	0.5	0.7	1.6	3.1	4.0
Middle Eastern oil exporters	10.1	6.4	0.7	1.4	–4.0	–3.2	–1.0	–0.4	1.4	–0.8	2.3
Non-oil Middle Eastern countries	5.1	9.4	6.1	6.2	6.7	5.1	3.9	2.7	3.1	3.5	3.9
By alternative analytical categories											
Oil exporting countries	8.3	6.9	1.3	1.9	–0.9	–1.2	–0.6	–0.6	1.8	0.3	2.7
Non-oil developing countries	5.4	5.8	6.2	4.9	4.9	3.3	2.2	2.1	5.3	4.5	4.5
Net oil exporters	6.2	3.7	6.1	7.6	7.3	6.7	1.1	–2.9	3.9	3.7	4.2
Net oil importers	5.3	6.2	6.2	4.5	4.5	2.8	2.4	3.0	5.6	4.7	4.6
Major exporters of manufactures	6.6	5.7	4.6	6.4	4.4	0.9	0.8	0.3	4.6	2.8	3.8
Low-income countries	3.6	6.7	8.5	2.6	5.6	4.6	5.3	7.5	8.4	7.8	6.1
Other net oil importers	5.1	6.8	5.6	4.0	3.2	3.4	1.0	1.5	3.0	3.3	3.6
Memorandum											
Output of non-oil sector in oil exporting countries	...	9.4	6.0	4.3	5.4	6.9	4.1	1.4	1.9	1.9	2.3

[1] For classification of countries in groups shown here, see note in Appendix III. China is excluded prior to 1978.

[2] Except where otherwise indicated, arithmetic averages of country growth rates weighted by the average U.S. dollar value of GDPs over the preceding three years.

[3] Compound annual rates of change.

[4] Excluding Nigeria and South Africa.

Source: *World Economic Outlook, 1985* (IMF)

3. GDP At Constant Prices

(Index numbers)

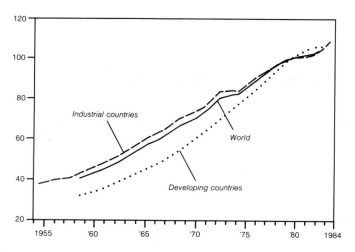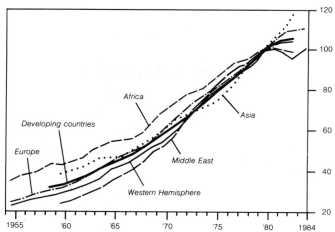

4. World Gross National Product and Population, 1984

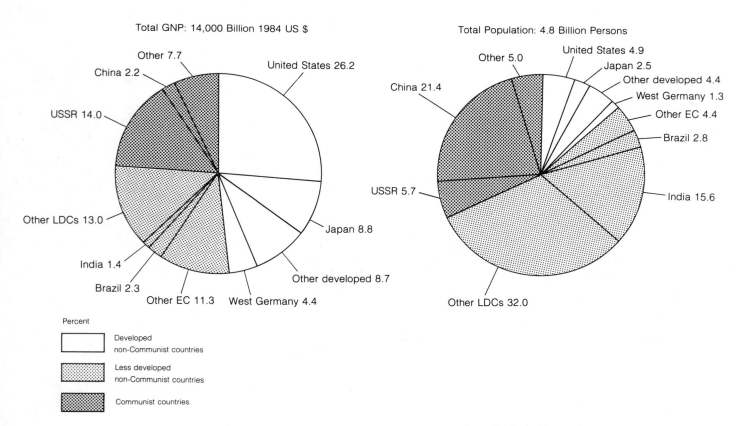

Total GNP: 14,000 Billion 1984 US $

Other 7.7
China 2.2
USSR 14.0
Other LDCs 13.0
India 1.4
Brazil 2.3
Other EC 11.3   West Germany 4.4
Other developed 8.7
Japan 8.8
United States 26.2

Total Population: 4.8 Billion Persons

Other 5.0   United States 4.9
Japan 2.5
Other developed 4.4
West Germany 1.3
Other EC 4.4
Brazil 2.8
India 15.6
China 21.4
USSR 5.7
Other LDCs 32.0

Percent

Developed
non-Communist countries

Less developed
non-Communist countries

Communist countries

Source: *Handbook of Economic Statistics*, 1985 Central Intelligence Agency

5. Real Gross National Product Trends

GNP
Average annual rate
of growth (percent)

Developed Non-Communist Countries

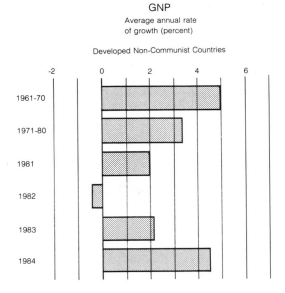

Per Capita GNP
Average annual rate
of growth (percent)

Developed Non-Communist Countries

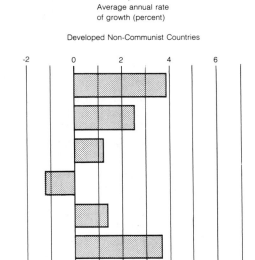

Less Developed Non-Communist Countries

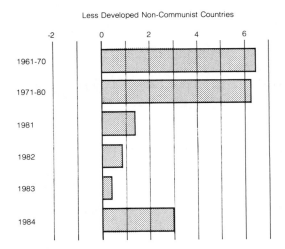

Less Developed Non-Communist Countries

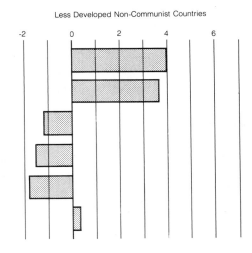

Communist Countries

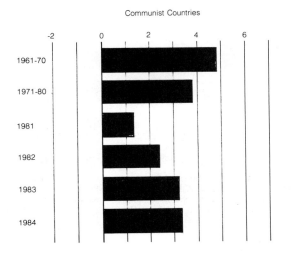

Communist Countries

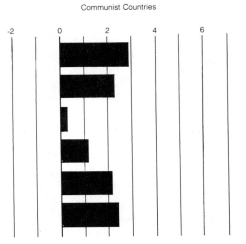

Source: *Handbook of Economic Statistics*, 1985 Central Intelligence Agency

APPENDIX VII: PRODUCTION

1. World Production: Percentage Annual Change, by Country Group, 1976-1983

	1976-1980[a]	1981	1982[b]	1983
World	3.9	1.4	0.2	2
Developed market economies	3.5	1.3	-0.3	2
Centrally planned economies	4.3	2.2	2.6	3.5
Developing countries	5.2	0.7	-0.7	2
Net energy-importing	5.1	1.6	0.9	2.5
Net energy-exporting	5.2	-0.4	-2.6	1
Surplus countries	3.5	-8.3	-7.4	...
Other countries	6.2	4.1	0.1	...

[a] Gross domestic product for market economies; net material product for centrally planned economies.

[b] Preliminary estimates.

Source: Department of International Economic and Social Affairs of the UN Secretariat, based on official national and international sources.

---

2. World Output, 1967-86[1]

(Changes, in percent)

	Average					From Preceding Year					
	1967-76[2]	1977	1978	1979	1980	1981	1982	1983	1984	1985	1986
World	**4.4**	**4.5**	**4.4**	**3.5**	**2.0**	**1.6**	**0.4**	**2.5**	**4.5**	**3.1**	**3.4**
Industrial countries	**3.7**	**3.9**	**4.1**	**3.5**	**1.3**	**1.6**	**-0.2**	**2.6**	**4.9**	**2.8**	**3.1**
United States	2.8	5.5	5.0	2.8	-0.3	2.5	-2.1	3.7	.8	2.6	3.3
Other industrial countries	4.5	2.9	3.5	3.9	2.2	1.1	0.9	2.0	3.5	3.0	2.9
Of which,											
Japan	7.4	5.3	5.1	5.2	4.8	4.0	3.3	3.4	5.8	4.4	4.0
Germany, Fed. Rep. of	3.5	2.8	3.5	4.0	1.9	-0.2	-1.0	1.3	2.6	2.1	3.1
Developing countries	**6.0**	**6.1**	**5.1**	**4.2**	**3.6**	**2.3**	**1.5**	**1.4**	**4.4**	**3.5**	**4.1**
Median growth rate	5.2	5.5	5.6	4.9	3.7	3.2	1.5	1.5	2.9	3.0	3.3
By region											
Africa	4.8	4.4	1.2	2.8	4.5	1.7	0.2	-1.2	2.6	2.2	3.1
Asia	5.2	8.0	9.1	4.3	5.3	5.6	5.0	7.6	8.1	6.8	6.0
Europe	6.0	5.4	5.4	3.8	1.6	2.5	2.2	1.3	3.5	2.9	3.3
Middle East	9.0	7.0	1.7	2.3	-2.1	-1.8	-0.2	—	1.7	—	2.6
Western Hemisphere	5.9	5.3	4.1	6.1	5.3	1.0	-0.9	-3.2	3.1	2.5	3.3
By analytical criteria											
Fuel exporters	7.9	5.9	2.7	3.3	1.1	0.9	-0.4	-1.5	2.2	1.0	3.0
Non-fuel exporters	5.3	5.9	6.1	4.6	4.6	2.9	2.5	2.9	5.6	4.7	4.6
Market borrowers	6.2	5.7	4.6	5.9	4.7	2.3	0.3	-0.9	3.6	2.7	3.7
Official borrowers	3.5	5.8	3.8	2.1	2.9	3.3	1.9	2.3	3.2	3.5	4.0
Other countries[3]	**5.5**	**4.5**	**4.7**	**2.3**	**2.9**	**0.8**	**1.7**	**3.5**	**3.1**	**3.6**	**3.5**

[1] Real GDP (or GNP) for industrial and developing countries and real net material product (NMP) for other countries. Composites for the country groups are averages of percentage changes for individual countries weighted by the average U.S. dollar value of their respective GDPs (GNPs or NMPs where applicable) over the preceding three years. Because of the uncertainty surrounding the valuation of the composite NMP of the other countries, they have been assigned—somewhat arbitrarily—a weight of 15% in the calculation of the growth of world output. Estimates do not include China for the period prior to 1978.

[2] Compound annual rates of change.

[3] The U.S.S.R. and other countries of Eastern Europe that are not members of the Fund.

Source: *World Economic Outlook*, 1985 (IMF)

3. Structure of output (%)

Region	Agriculture[1] 1960	Agriculture[1] 1980	Industry[2] Total 1960	Industry[2] Total 1980	of which Manufactures 1960	of which Manufactures 1980	Services 1960	Services 1980
Developing countries	30.9	17.4	24.8	39.4	15.4	17.8	42.0	43.2
Developed market-economy countries	6.3	3.7	40.8	38.6	30.1	26.4	51.5	57.7
Least developed countries	53.2	49.8	8.8	14.6	4.7	7.8	26.4	35.6

Note: Components may not add to 100 due to rounding.

[1] Including forestry and fishing industries.

[2] Including mining and quarrying, electricity, gas and water, and construction.

Source: UNCTAD secretariat computations, derived from UNSO data on expenditure on GDP.

4. Selected Measures of Production and Consumption for the World, by Development Status and Geographic Region, Recent Data

Category	World total	DEVELOPMENT STATUS[a] Less developed	DEVELOPMENT STATUS[a] More developed	Latin Africa	Northern Asia	Oceania	America	America	Europe	USSR
Population, 1984										
Millions	4,763	3,597	1,166	537	2,778	24.5	397	261	490	276
Distribution (%)	100.0	75.5	24.5	11.3	58.3	0.5	8.3	5.5	10.3	5.8
Per capita GDP, 1980 (US$)[b]	3,310	970	9,890	900	1,331[e]	7,850	2,320	11,340	9,860	u
Increase in real GDP, 1980 over 1970 (%)[b,c]										
Aggregate	43	78	37	66	66[f]	33	79	36	33[g]	u
Per capita	17	43	27	26	35[f]	14	37	22	27[g]	u
Increase in industrial production, 1982 over 1972 (%)[b,c]										
Total	34	40	20	u	38[h]	15	53	16	17[g]	76[i]
Mining	18	9	25	u	6[h]	27	48	13	49[g]	43[i]
Manufacturing	35	67	18	u	52[h]	6	50	15	13[g]	80[i]
Electricity, gas, water	50	133	39	u	74[h]	81	117	25	49[g]	62[i]
Food production index (1974-76 = 100)										
Aggregate										
1978-80 average	110	114	108	107	113	113	115	113	107	105
1980-82 average	114	120	109	112	118	107	122	121	110	100
Per capita										
1978-80 average	103	105	104	95	105	107	104	108	106	101
1980-82	103	106	104	94	106	98	106	114	107	95
Daily food supplies per capita, 1978-80 average										
Calories										
Thousands	2,617	2,328	3,407	2,311	2,326[c]	3,081	2,591	3,624	3,477	3,389[i]
% of needs	110	101	133	94	100[c]	116	109	137	135	132[i]
Protein (grams)	69	59	99	58	59[c]	91	66	106	98	100[i]
Per capita energy consumed, 1982 (kilograms of coal equivalent)	1,825	521	5,595	400	600	5,196	1,129	9,457	4,193	5,768
Annual rate of growth of total labor force (%), 1980-85[d]	1.75	2.10	0.93	2.39	1.89	1.77	2.90	1.21	0.86	0.67

u = unavailable. Used either when no data were available or when available data were considered to be of low quality.

a Development status is based on demographic and other social and economic indicators.

b GDP (gross domestic product) is shown for countries within the respective groupings that have market economies; that is, countries with centrally planned economies are excluded from the data.

c Excludes China, Democratic People's Republic of Korea, Mongolia, and Vietnam.

d Takes account of labor force participation rates.

e Derived from source data by weighting subregions by population size. Excluding Japan and countries with centrally planned economies, the figure for Asia is U.S. $688.

f Excluding Japan, the figures for Asia are 77 and 43 for the percent increase, 1978 over 1968, in aggregate and per capita, respectively.

g Western Europe only.

h Excluding Israel and Japan, the figures for Asia are 33, 16, 83, and 131 for the four listed items, respectively.

i Includes Eastern Europe.

SOURCES:

Population: UN, Department of International Economic and Social Affairs, *Population and Vital Statistics Report*, Series A, Vol. 36, No. 4, 1984.

GDP (gross domestic product): UN, *Yearbook of National Accounts Statistics 1981* (Vol. 2), 1980. Table 1 (per capita) and Table 8C (percent increase).

Industrial production: UN, *Monthly Bulletin of Statistics* 38, no. 2 (1984): special Table A.

Food production and supplies: UN, Food and Agriculture Organization, *Production Yearbook 1982*, Vol. 36 (Rome), Tables 4, 9, 36, annex Table 16.

Energy consumed: UN, Department of International Economic and Social Affairs, *Energy Statistics Yearbook 1982* (New York, 1984), Table 1. (Per capita energy consumed per country weighted by corresponding 1982 population for computation of the following categories: less developed, more developed, Latin America, and Northern America.)

Labor force: International Labour Organisation, *Labour Force Estimates and Projections: 1950-2000: Vol. 5, World Summary*, Second edition (Geneva, 1977), Table 4.

Source: *Population and Family Planning Programs* (1985), by Dorothy L. Norman, 12th edition, Population Council, New York

APPENDIX VIII: AGRICULTURE

1. Agricultural Production, By Commodity

	Developed countries			Developing countries			World		
	1983	1984[a]	Change 1983-84	1983	1984[a]	Change 1983-84	1983	1984[a]	Change 1983-84
	(million tons)		(%)	(million tons)		(%)	(million tons)		(%)
Total cereals[b]	752.6	869.4	15.5	889.8	910.6	2.3	1642.4	1780.0	8.4
Wheat	301.0	312.6	3.9	195.7	199.5	1.9	496.7	512.1	3.1
Rice	22.2	26.1	17.7	427.9	438.4	2.4	450.1	464.5	3.2
Coarse grains	429.4	530.7	23.6	266.1	272.8	2.5	695.5	803.4	15.5
Root crops	203.5	215.4	5.8	351.2	369.8	5.3	554.7	585.2	5.5
Pulses	11.2	11.6	3.4	33.5	33.4	-0.4	44.8	45.0	0.5
Oil-bearing crops[c]									
Oil content	19.3	22.6	17.2	34.3	36.3	5.7	53.6	58.9	9.8
Oil cake content	52.8	62.1	17.7	56.4	60.4	7.0	109.2	122.5	12.2
Sugar, centrifugal (raw)	38.8	40.7	4.8	58.8	57.3	-2.4	97.6	98.0	0.4
Cocoa beans	-	-	-	1.6	1.6	1.6	1.6	1.6	1.6
Coffee	-	-	-	5.6	5.4	-3.4	5.6	5.4	-3.4
Tea	0.3	0.3	4.0	1.8	2.0	7.2	2.1	2.2	6.8
Cotton lint	4.7	6.1	30.4	9.7	11.2	14.9	14.4	17.3	20.0
Tobacco	2.1	2.2	6.7	3.9	4.0	3.3	6.0	6.3	4.5
Total meat	92.3	93.8	1.7	48.0	49.2	2.5	140.3	143.0	1.9
Total milk	381.3	381.9	0.2	113.5	115.7	1.9	494.8	497.6	0.6
Hen eggs	18.4	18.6	0.9	10.5	10.9	4.1	28.9	29.5	2.1

[a] Preliminary.
[b] Including rice in terms of paddy.
[c] Total harvested production.

Source: *The State of Food and Agriculture*, 1984 (FAO)

2. Value of World Agricultural Trade (Crops and Livestock) at Current Prices and Volume, by Region

				Change		Annual rate of change 1979 to 1983	
	1981	1982	1983	1981 to 1982	1982 to 1983	Current prices	Volume[a]
	(000 million $)			(%)			
Developing market economies							
Export	66.0	59.5	61.7	-9.8	3.7	-1.2	3.6
Import	65.9	58.8	57.9	-10.8	-1.5	4.4	5.0
Africa							
Export	8.9	8.3	8.2	-6.7	-1.2	-6.9	1.2
Import	11.0	10.2	9.3	-7.3	-8.8	3.1	6.1
Far East							
Export	19.6	17.5	17.6	-10.7	0.6	-0.4	4.9
Import	17.9	16.1	16.7	-10.1	3.7	4.3	5.8
Latin America							
Export	31.2	27.6	29.9	-11.5	8.3	-0.8	2.9
Import	14.5	11.5	11.8	-20.7	2.6	0.3	-0.7
Near East							
Export	5.8	5.7	5.5	-1.7	-3.5	4.8	5.9
Import	21.8	20.3	19.4	-6.9	-4.4	8.1	6.7
ACPE							
Export	4.4	4.4	4.0	—	-9.1	-0.2	0.8
Import	8.7	8.3	6.9	-4.6	-16.9	-0.3	0.1

2. Value of World Agricultural Trade (Crops and Livestock) at Current Prices and Volume, by Region (continued)

	1981	1982	1983	Change 1981 to 1982	Change 1982 to 1983	Annual rate of change 1979 to 1983 Current prices	Annual rate of change 1979 to 1983 Volume[a]
		(000 million $)		(%)			
All developing countries							
Export	70.4	63.9	65.7	-9.2	2.8	-1.2	3.4
Import	74.7	67.1	64.8	-10.2	-3.4	3.8	4.3
Developed market economies							
Export	152.5	139.1	133.6	-8.8	-4.0	-0.1	2.0
Import	147.1	139.3	137.4	-5.3	-1.4	-2.6	1.8
Eastern Europe and USSR							
Export	9.6	9.1	8.2	-5.2	-9.9	-3.9	-1.0
Import	31.8	27.7	26.2	-12.9	-5.4	1.6	4.2
All developed countries							
Export	162.1	148.2	141.8	-8.6	-4.3	-0.3	2.0
Import	178.9	167.0	163.6	-6.7	-2.0	-1.9	2.1
World							
Export	232.5	212.1	207.5	-8.8	-2.2	-0.6	2.6
Import	253.5	234.1	228.4	-7.7	-2.4	-0.5	2.7
Share of developing countries in world agric. trade		(%)					
Export	30	30	32				
Import	29	29	28				

[a] Obtained by deflating current values of trade with the indices (1974-76 = 100) of export and import unit values of agricultural products. Exports are valued fob and imports cif.

Source: *The State of Food and Agriculture*, 1984 (FAO)

---

3. Annual Changes in World and Regional Food, Agricultural, Crop and Livestock Production

	Food 1982 to 1983	Food 1983 to 1984	Agriculture 1982 to 1983	Agriculture 1983 to 1984	Crops 1982 to 1983	Crops 1983 to 1984	Livestock 1982 to 1983	Livestock 1983 to 1984
				(%)				
Developing market economies	2.5	2.4	2.7	2.4	2.6	2.9	2.3	1.9
Africa	-3.7	3.6	-3.4	3.4	-5.5	4.0	2.3	1.1
Far East	8.2	1.7	7.6	1.9	8.4	1.8	4.4	2.6
Latin America	-0.9	3.1	0.6	2.9	0.2	5.7	—	1.3
Near East	0.2	1.7	0.7	1.7	-1.5	0.8	3.8	2.7
Asian centrally planned economies (ACPE)	6.5	3.1	6.4	4.2	7.2	4.6	5.1	4.7
Developing countries	3.6	2.6	3.8	2.9	4.1	3.5	3.0	2.6
Developed market economies	-6.3	7.6	-6.7	8.1	-12.8	14.3	2.0	-0.1
North America	-16.6	14.4	-17.3	15.8	-25.8	25.4	2.9	-1.2
Southwest Pacific	28.0	-7.3	21.4	-5.3	53.2	-6.5	1.2	-3.6
Western Europe	-1.2	4.5	-1.2	4.6	-6.0	9.4	1.5	0.4
Others	-3.3	7.2	-3.1	6.7	-2.6	6.8	1.6	2.7
Eastern Europe and USSR	3.0	1.9	2.7	2.0	1.2	-0.1	4.4	4.0
Developed countries	-3.2	5.6	-3.5	5.9	-8.2	9.1	2.9	1.5
World	-0.2	4.2	-0.2	4.5	-2.0	6.1	2.9	1.8

Source: *The State of Food and Agriculture*, 1984 (FAO)

APPENDIX IX: FINANCE

1. International Reserves and Import Cover of Developing Countries
(billions of dollars)

		of which:				
Year	Developing countries	Oil exporting countries	Non-oil exporting countries	Major exporters of manufactures	Least developed countries	Memo item DMECs
Total reserves, excluding gold						
1970	15.2	4.6	10.6	3.5	0.7	40.5
1973	39.8	15.0	24.8	13.0	1.4	99.9
1975	82.7	58.7	24.0	11.2	1.7	101.7
1979	146.1	78.7	67.4	31.9	4.1	208.8
1980	157.4	92.1	65.3	27.4	3.8	242.7
1981	151.3	93.1	58.2	29.3	3.4	222.8
1982	141.3	89.9	51.4	28.0	2.7	209.7
1983	138.4	82.1	56.3	24.0	2.7	221.2
Official gold holdings[1]						
1970	3.3	1.4	1.9	0.3	—	34.6
1973	8.8	3.9	4.9	0.7	0.1	90.1
1975	14.3	6.4	7.9	1.2	0.2	148.8
1979	29.4	12.3	17.1	2.6	0.6	253.9
1980	61.8	26.5	35.3	6.1	1.2	503.9
1981	48.0	20.7	27.3	4.7	0.9	379.3
1982	38.5	17.0	21.5	3.3	0.8	309.3
1983	42.9	18.1	24.8	3.7	0.8	347.2
Months of imports covered by total reserves, excluding gold[2]						
1970	3.1	3.8	2.8	2.8	2.4	1.9
1973	3.6	5.0	3.1	4.2	3.5	2.3
1975	5.0	10.0	2.2	2.8	3.0	1.9
1979	4.0	6.6	2.9	3.8	3.6	1.9
1980	3.8	6.1	2.6	2.6	2.9	2.1
1981	3.7	5.8	2.4	2.8	2.6	2.0
1982	3.7	6.0	2.2	2.8	1.6	2.0
1983	3.8	5.9	2.5	2.4	1.3	2.1

Note: International reserves consist of a country's holdings of monetary gold, special drawing rights (SDR) and foreign exchange, as well as its reserve position in the International Monetary Fund (IMF). It should be noted that the figures for total reserves minus gold usually include those of fewer countries than for imports, thus understating the import coverage of reserves.

[1]Holdings of gold in ounces at end of period multiplied by the average daily price of gold per ounce in London during period.

[2]Months of imports covered are defined as total reserves minus gold for the year divided by the average monthly imports of current and following year, except for 1983, where only 1983 imports are used.

Source: Reserves and gold holdings: IMF, *International Financial Statistics*, various issues.
Imports: UNCTAD, *Handbook of International Trade and Development Statistics*.

2. Sources of Financing of the Current-Account Deficit of Developing Countries
(in billions of dollars)

	1970	1975	1980	1981	1982
Non-oil developing countries					
Current-account deficit	9.6	34.0	69.9	79.1	72.4
Use of reserves	-2.1	4.0	-6.8	-7.9	-20.1
Non-debt creating flows[1] (net)	4.5	10.6	18.8	21.8	20.2
Grants	1.6	3.6	9.0	8.5	8.3
Direct foreign investment	2.2	7.0	7.7	11.0	11.5
Long-term financing	5.5	24.3	48.6	50.6	47.7
Official sources	3.4	15.0	25.3	22.2	20.7
Private sources	2.1	9.3	23.3	28.4	27.0
Reserve-related liabilities and other[2]	2.5	-4.9	-4.3	-1.2	-15.6
Least developed countries					
Current-account deficit	0.6	3.6	7.4	8.0	8.0
Use of reserves	—	—	0.5	0.7	1.6
Non-debt creating flows[1] (net)	0.2	1.1	3.4	2.8	2.6
Grants	0.2	1.1	3.3	2.6	2.5
Direct foreign investment	—	—	—	0.1	0.1
Long-term financing	0.2	2.4	3.1	2.5	3.4
Official sources	0.2	2.1	2.3	2.3	3.0
Private sources	—	0.3	0.8	0.2	0.4
Reserve related liabilities and other[2]	0.2	0.1	0.4	2.0	0.4

[1] Including SDR allocations, valuation adjustments and gold monetization.

[2] Comprises use of Fund credit, short-term borrowing and errors and omissions.

Source: UNCTAD secretariat estimates, largely based on data supplied by OECD and IMF.

3. Total Reserves Minus Gold
(In billions of SDRs)

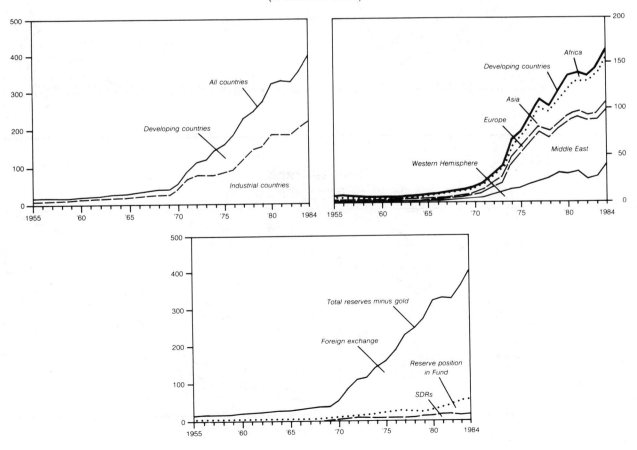

4. Gold Holdings
(In millions of ounces)

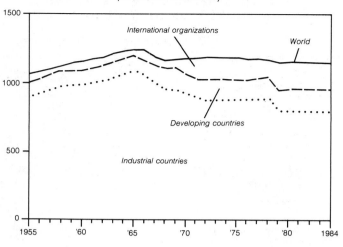

5. Use of Fund Credit
(In billions of SDRs)

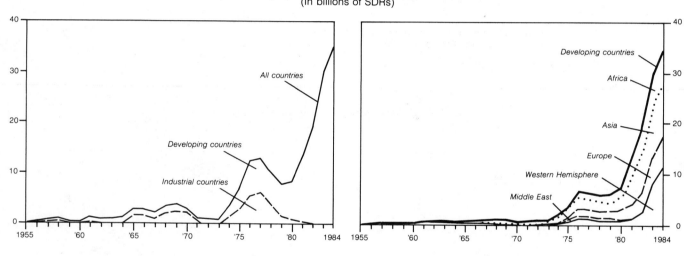

6. Deposit Banks
(In billions of U.S. dollars)

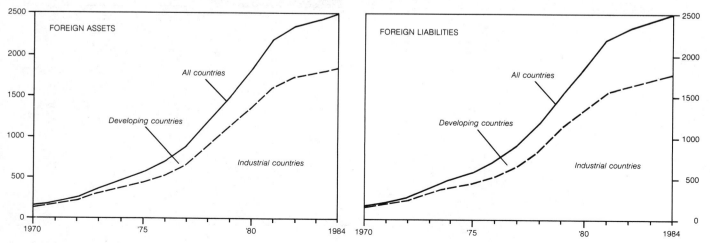

2254 Appendix IX: Finance

7. Money
(Index numbers)

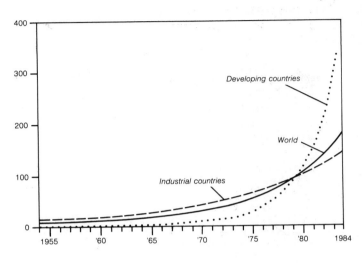

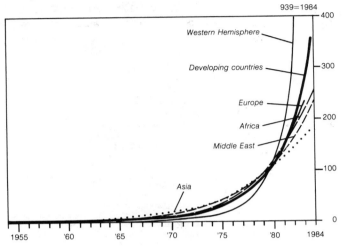

8. Money and Quasi-Money
(Index numbers)

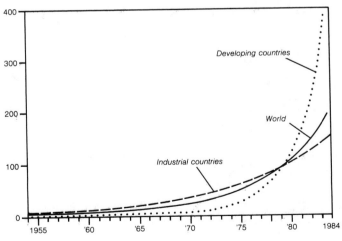

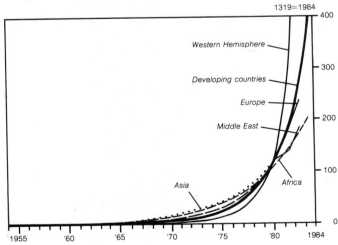

APPENDIX X: DEBT

1. The Total Disbursed Medium- and Long-Term Debt of Developing Countries by Region and Terms of Lending
(billions of dollars)

Year	1975	1980	1982	1983[2]
Developing Countries				
Total disbursed debt	145.3	384.6	486.0	531.8
of which:				
Concessional	51.4	95.8	108.0	118.2
Non-concessional	93.9	288.8	378.0	413.6
Export credits	30.1	86.8	98.8	108.1
Private markets	50.1	157.8	212.9	233.0
Others[1]	13.7	44.2	66.3	72.5
Memo item:				
Offically guaranteed	112.6	307.1	377.9	373.4
Private unguaranteed	32.7	77.5	108.1	158.4
By region:				
America				
Total disbursed debt	62.3	172.2	233.2	255.2
Concessional	7.6	10.9	12.6	13.8
Non-concessional	54.7	161.3	220.6	241.4
Export credits	11.4	27.5	34.5	37.8
Private markets	36.1	113.7	155.6	170.3
Others[1]	7.2	20.1	30.5	33.3
Memo item:				
Offically guaranteed	44.5	127.8	171.8	150.6
Private unguaranteed	17.8	44.4	61.4	104.6
Africa				
Total disbursed debt	28.9	84.8	97.8	107.0
Concessional	13.1	30.5	35.9	39.3
Non-concessional	15.8	54.3	61.9	67.7
Export credits	7.9	29.3	30.1	32.9
Private markets	5.0	15.7	17.9	19.6
Others[1]	2.9	9.3	13.9	15.2
Memo item:				
Offically guaranteed	24.9	74.7	83.0	86.7
Private unguaranteed	4.0	10.1	14.8	20.3
West Asia[2]				
Total disbursed debt	11.9	36.4	38.9	42.6
Concessional	4.7	10.0	11.6	12.7
Non-concessional	7.2	26.4	27.3	29.9
Export credits	3.3	9.9	9.4	10.3
Private markets	2.8	10.2	9.5	10.4
Others[1]	1.1	6.3	8.4	9.2
Memo item:				
Offically guaranteed	7.0	23.6	25.0	28.7
Private unguaranteed	4.9	12.8	13.9	13.9
South and South-East Asia				
Total disbursed debt	42.2	91.2	116.1	127.0
Concessional	26.0	44.4	47.9	52.4
Non-concessional	16.2	46.8	68.2	74.6
Export credits	7.5	20.1	24.8	27.1
Private markets	6.2	18.2	29.9	32.7
Others[1]	2.5	8.5	13.5	14.8
Memo item:				
Offically guaranteed	36.2	81.0	98.1	107.4
Private unguaranteed	6.0	10.2	18.0	19.6

1. The Total Disbursed Medium- and Long-Term Debt of Developing Countries by Region and Terms of Lending (continued)
(billions of dollars)

Year	1975	1980	1982	1983[2]
Least Developed Countries				
Total disbursed debt	8.7	21.5	26.2	28.6
Concessional	6.2	14.6	18.1	19.8
Non-concessional	2.5	6.9	8.1	8.8
Export credits	1.2	3.5	3.2	3.5
Private markets	0.4	0.9	1.4	1.5
Others[1]	0.9	2.5	3.5	3.8
Memo item:				
Offically guaranteed	7.2	18.7	23.3	23.6
Private unguaranteed	1.5	2.8	2.9	5.0
10 Major Borrowers				
Total disbursed debt	81.5	215.9	268.6	293.9
Concessional	13.6	17.9	17.5	19.1
Non-concessional	67.9	198.0	251.1	274.8
Export credits	20.4	52.5	54.5	59.6
Private markets	40.1	122.8	161.3	176.5
Others[1]	7.4	22.7	35.3	38.7
Memo item:				
Offically guaranteed	19.7	57.6	188.8	177.3
Private unguaranteed	61.8	158.3	79.8	116.6

1 Estimated.
2 Including Yugoslavia and Malta.

Source: OECD, *External Debt of Developing Countries, 1983 Survey* (Paris, 1984); *Development Co-operation 1983 Review* (Paris, 1983); *Geographical Distribution of Financial Flows to Developing Countries, 1979-1982* (Paris, 1984); World Bank Debtor Reporting System.

---

2. The Maturity Composition of the Total Disbursed Debt of Developing Countries by Source of Lending
(billions of dollars)

Year	1975	1980	1982	1983
		(billions of dollars)		
Total disbursed debt	183.7	517.5	641.7	670.0
1. Medium and long-term debt[1]	163.7	428.5	528.7	567.0
Concessional	57.7	105.3	118.4	127.3
Non-concessional	106.0	323.2	410.3	439.7
2. Short-term debt[2]	20.0	89.0	113.0	103.0
Memo item:				
Use of IMF credit	1.8	1.6	7.3	11.4
Arrears	..	5.0	18.0	18.0

1 Data for 1980, 1982 and 1983 include estimates for China.

2 Estimated; the data exclude the short-term debt of OPEC countries. Short-term debt is debt with a maturity of less than one year.

Source: OECD, *External Debt of Developing Countries, 1983 Survey;* IMF, *Balance of Payments Yearbook,* various issues; *Recent Multilateral Debt Restructuring with Official and Bank Creditors* (Occasional Paper No. 25, December 1983); *External Indebtedness of Developing Countries* (Occasional Paper No. 3); *World Economic Outlook,* and other data supplied by IMF.

3. Net Long-Term Financial Flows[1] and Net Transfers[2] of Resources to Least Developed Countries
(millions of dollars)

Type of flow	Value in current prices				Average annual growth 1970-1982 (Percentage)	
	1970	1975	1980	1982	Nominal	Real[3]
Least developed countries						
Official flows	874.8	3 511.5	6 717.1	6 777.7	18.6	9.8
Official development assistance:	822.6	3 399.2	6 313.1	6 525.5	18.8	10.0
Bilateral	636.7	2 390.5	4 195.0	4 399.8	17.5	8.8
DAC	630.8	1 814.8	3 365.4	3 448.6	15.2	6.7
OPEC	5.9	575.7	829.6	951.2	52.7	41.4
Multilateral	185.9	1 008.7	2 118.1	2 125.7	22.5	13.4
Other official flows[4]	52.2	112.3	404.0	252.2	14.0	5.6
Exports credits	2.0	-1.3	-1.8	1.4	-2.9	-10.1
Private flows	39.2	322.9	789.6	572.2	25.0	15.8
Direct investment	12.1	53.3	15.2	142.3	22.8	13.7
Export credits[3]	22.7	211.4	872.7	174.1	18.5	9.7
International capital markets (bank lending, bonds)	4.4	58.2	-98.4	255.8	40.2	29.8
Total net flows	914.0	3 834.4	7 506.7	7 349.9	19.0	10.1
less: Interest payments and profit remittances on direct investment by developing countries	126.0	220.5	651.3	536.1	12.8	4.5
Net transfers	787.9	3 613.9	6 855.4	6 813.8	19.7	10.8
Memo item:						
Gross flows	1 005.2	4 230.3	8 222.4	8 278.9	19.2	10.4
Amortization[6]	91.2	395.9	715.7	929.0	21.3	12.3

[1] Gross flows less amortization.

[2] Net flows less interest payments and profit remittances on direct foreign investments by developing countries.

[3] At 1981 constant prices and exchange rates. Nominal values were deflated by the DAC GNP deflator.

[4] Including bilateral and multilateral non-concessional flows and officially supported export credits.

[5] Comprising private guaranteed export credits from DAC member countries.

[6] Estimated.

Source: OECD, *Geographical Distribution of Financial Flows to Developing Countries,* various issues; OECD, *Development Co-operation, 1983 Review;* OECD, *External Debt of Developing Countries, 1983 Survey;* World Bank Debtor Reporting System; IMF, *Balance of Payments Yearbook,* various issues.

---

4. Net Flow of IMF Lending to the Capital-Importing Developing Countries
(billions of dollars)

Year	1970	1973	1975	1979	1980	1981	1982	1983
Low conditionality flows	—	0.1	1.0	0.2	1.3	—	1.4	2.2
Buffer stock financing	—	—	—	—	—	—	0.1	0.3
Compensatory financing	-0.1	0.1	0.2	0.2	0.3	0.6	1.7	2.0
Oil Facility	—	—	0.8	-0.6	-0.7	-0.7	-0.4	-0.1
Trust Fund	—	—	—	0.7	1.6	0.1	—	-0.1
Higher conditionality flows	-0.3	-0.1	0.2	1.0	2.3	5.7	4.2	9.1
Credit tranche drawings	-0.3	-0.1	0.2	0.7	1.5	3.3	1.9	4.2
Extended Facility drawings	—	—	—	0.3	0.7	2.4	2.3	4.9
Total flows	-0.4	-0.1	1.2	1.2	3.6	5.7	5.7	11.3

Source: Department of International Economic and Social Affairs of the UN Secretariat, based on IMF, *International Financial Statistics.*

5. The Outstanding Gross and Net Exposure of Banks[1] to Non-OPEC Developing Countries[2] (billions of dollars)

Year	1977	1980	1982	1983
Medium and long-term credits	64	132	187	216
of which:				
Officially-guaranteed export credits	8	25	32	36
Other bank loans	56	107	155	180
Short-term credits[3]	31	77	104	96
Total gross exposure	95	209	290	312
Deposits (banks' liabilities)	70	100	118	120
Total net bank exposure	25	109	172	192

[1] Commercial banks and other financial institutions, excluding central banks but including participation of non-OPEC banks in international syndics.

[2] The data exclude bonds and other bank assets which do not constitute loans. They also exclude future interest payable but include interest arrears.

[3] Short-term credits are those with original maturity of less than one year.

Source: OECD, *External Debt of Developing Countries, 1983 Survey* (Paris, 1984).

6. Major Debt-Service Ratios and Debt-Service Capacity Indicators of Developing Countries by Region and Analytical Group (percentage)

	1975	1980	1981	1982
Ratio of total debt service to exports of goods and services				
Developing countries	*14.5*	*19.0*	*22.4*	*25.2*
By region:				
America	23.8	33.8	41.9	40.2
Africa	10.6	15.8	20.7	23.8
West Asia	14.7	21.2	21.3	19.8
South and South-East Asia (including Oceania)	8.7	8.3	9.2	12.6
By analytical group:				
Least developed countries	12.3	13.1	17.8	17.6
Major borrowers	18.2	28.9	35.2	33.7
Ratio of interest payments to exports of goods and services				
Developing countries	*5.6*	*8.7*	*10.9*	*13.1*
By region:				
America	10.1	16.0	21.9	23.3
Africa	3.4	6.1	7.9	9.0
West Asia	4.5	9.8	10.1	8.9
South and South-East Asia (including Oceania)	3.2	3.9	4.6	6.4
By analytical group:				
Least developed countries	3.8	5.5	6.5	6.0
Major borrowers	7.2	13.0	18.0	18.8
Ratio of external debt to exports of goods and services				
Developing countries	*105.0*	*107.2*	*123.2*	*136.8*
By region:				
America	142.0	152.5	193.2	185.2
Africa	85.3	104.3	131.2	140.2
West Asia	88.5	133.1	123.1	106.8
South and South-East Asia (including Oceania)	89.4	66.6	68.5	91.5
By analytical group:				
Least developed countries[1]	178.5	253.5	304.9	339.7
Major borrowers	110.2	129.4	149.2	145.6
Ratio of external debt to GDP				
Developing countries	*18.3*	*22.2*	*23.7*	*28.9*
By region:				
America	17.4	21.4	23.2	32.1
Africa	21.5	28.4	32.2	34.2
West Asia	15.7	24.2	24.8	25.9
South and South-East Asia (including Oceania)	18.6	19.1	19.5	22.5
By analytical group:				
Least developed countries	21.2	26.2	35.8	40.0
Major borrowers	21.0	23.6	25.8	31.8
Ratio of total debt service to GDP				
Developing countries	*2.5*	*3.9*	*4.3*	*5.3*
By region:				
America	2.9	4.8	5.0	7.0
Africa	2.7	4.3	5.1	5.5
West Asia	2.6	3.8	4.3	4.8
South and South-East Asia (including Oceania)	1.8	2.4	2.6	3.1

6. Major Debt-Service Ratios and Debt-Service Capacity Indicators of Developing Countries by Region and Analytical Group (continued) (percentage)

	1975	1980	1981	1982
By analytical group:				
Least developed countries[1]	1.5	1.4	2.1	2.1
Major borrowers	3.5	5.2	6.1	7.4
Ratio of interest payments to GDP				
Developing countries	*1.0*	*1.8*	*2.1*	*2.8*
By region:				
America	1.2	2.2	2.6	4.0
Africa	0.9	1.6	1.9	2.1
West Asia	0.8	1.8	2.0	2.2
South and South-East Asia (including Oceania)	0.7	1.1	1.3	1.6
By analytical group:				
Least developed countries[1]	0.4	0.6	0.8	0.7
Major borrowers	1.4	2.4	3.1	4.1

Source: OECD, *External Debt of Developing Countries, 1983 Survey*; IMF, *Balance of Payments Yearbook, 1983* and *Direction of Trade Statistics Yearbook, 1983*; World Bank, *World Debt Tables, 1983-84* and Debtor Reporting System.

7. World Reserves (End of Year) (billions of dollars)

	Reserves minus gold		Official gold holdings		Memo item:
Year	Total	of which: Special Drawing Rights	Volume (billion ounces)	Value[1]	World imports
1970	55.5	3.1	1.1	37.9	328.6
1973	141.0	10.6	1.0	100.0	599.8
1975	186.3	10.2	1.0	163.3	908.9
1979	361.1	16.4	0.9	286.7	1 689.3
1980	410.4	15.1	0.9	570.2	2 054.0
1981	392.0	19.1	0.9	430.8	2 035.3
1982	365.1	19.6	0.9	350.6	1 924.5
1983	380.7	15.1	0.9	385.7	1 908.6

Note: The figures for world imports cover a larger number of countries than those for reserves minus gold and official gold holdings.

[1] Holdings of gold in ounces at end of period multiplied by the average daily price of gold per ounce in London during period.

Sources: Reserves and gold holdings: IMF, *International Financial Statistics*. Imports: UNCTAD, *Handbook of International Trade and Development Statistics*.

8. Change in Export Prices and in Terms of Trade, 1965-84

Country group	1965-73	1973-80	1981	1982	1983[a]	1984[b]
Change in export prices						
Developing countries	6.0	14.7	-2.5	-6.1	-3.7	-1.0
Manufactures	5.1	10.9	-5.0	-1.9	-4.2	-2.8
Food	5.8	8.0	-12.1	-17.4	10.2	7.3
Nonfood	4.0	10.3	-13.5	-8.1	4.8	-3.4
Metals and minerals	1.8	5.8	-10.5	-9.5	0.5	-4.9
Fuels	7.9	27.2	12.5	-3.2	-12.4	-2.4
High-income oil exporters	7.4	24.8	8.3	-2.7	-11.3	-1.6
Industrial countries						
Total	4.7	10.1	-4.6	-4.0	-3.2	-1.5
Manufactures	4.7	10.9	-6.0	-2.1	-4.3	-2.3
Change in terms of trade						
Developing countries	0.5	2.0	0.5	-1.1	-0.6	1.0
Low-income countries	0.4	-1.5	-0.2	-1.5	0.9	4.1
Asia	0.8	-1.6	1.3	-2.2	0.4	3.5
Africa	-0.7	-1.0	-7.2	1.1	4.2	7.8
Middle-income oil exporters	-0.2	-2.3	-5.0	-2.2	3.7	0.4
Middle-income oil exporters	-0.4	9.0	11.7	1.7	-8.5	0.9
High-income oil exporters	2.9	12.3	14.6	2.3	-8.6	-1.0
Industrial countries	-0.5	-3.5	-2.1	2.0	2.1	-0.2

a. Estimated. b. Projected.

9. Growth of Long-Term Debt of Developing Countries, 1970-84
(average annual percentage change)

Country group	1970-73	1973-80	1981	1982	1983[a]	1984[a]
Developing countries						
Debt outstanding and disbursed	18.3	21.3	13.5	11.9	13.5	10.8
Official	15.3	17.6	9.7	10.4	9.8	13.2
Private	21.1	24.0	15.7	12.8	15.6	9.5
Low-income countries						
Debt outstanding and disbursed	12.9	16.0	5.5	8.0	6.3	10.8
Official	12.5	14.1	7.7	10.2	8.2	10.5
Private	16.0	24.9	-2.3	-1.0	-2.2	12.3
Asia						
Debt outstanding and disbursed	11.1	13.2	2.9	8.6	7.8	14.1
Official	11.6	11.2	6.2	10.1	7.4	10.6
Private	4.3	33.2	-12.4	0.1	10.5	36.0
Africa						
Debt outstanding and disbursed	19.7	22.6	10.2	6.9	3.7	4.7
Official	17.3	24.2	10.9	10.6	10.1	10.2
Private	24.4	19.7	8.5	-2.0	-13.5	-14.6
Middle-income oil importers						
Debt outstanding and disbursed	19.7	21.0	14.9	12.9	11.5	10.3
Official	17.8	18.5	12.1	11.0	13.4	15.0
Private	20.8	22.2	16.1	13.7	10.7	8.3
Major exporters of manufactures						
Debt outstanding and disbursed	22.6	20.8	14.7	13.0	12.1	10.2
Official	21.0	18.9	10.5	9.1	12.6	18.8
Private	23.2	21.4	15.9	14.1	12.0	7.9
Other middle-income oil importers						
Debt outstanding and disbursed	13.4	21.5	15.4	12.8	9.9	10.5
Official	14.6	18.0	13.9	13.0	14.3	11.0
Private	11.9	25.8	16.8	12.5	5.8	10.0
Middle-income oil exporters						
Debt outstanding and disbursed	19.6	24.9	14.6	11.8	19.9	11.5
Official	15.5	20.6	7.9	9.4	4.9	12.8
Private	22.6	27.1	17.5	12.7	25.8	11.1

a. The increase in debt outstanding and disbursed and the shift from private to official sources is in part due to the impact of rescheduling.

Source: *World Development Report*, 1985

10. New Commitments to Public and Publicly Guaranteed Borrowers in Developing Countries, 1978-83
(billions of U.S. dollars)

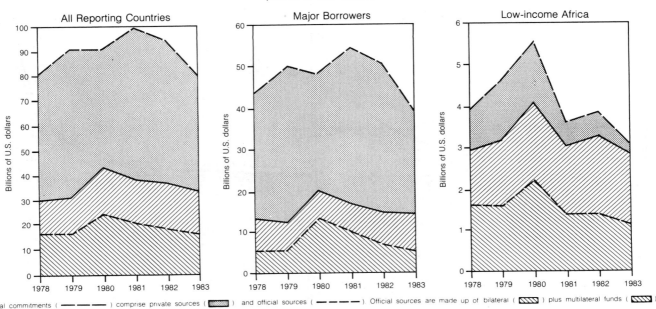

APPENDIX XI: PRICES

1. Wholesale Prices
(Index numbers)

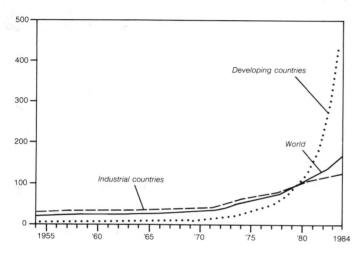

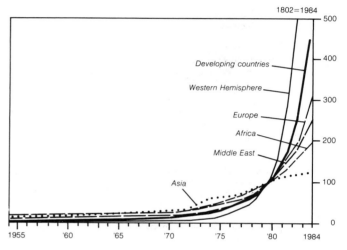

2. Consumer Prices
(Index numbers)

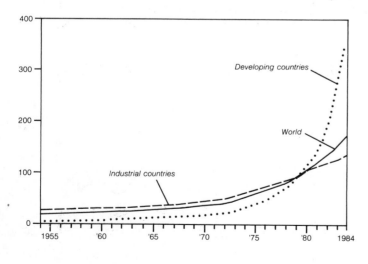

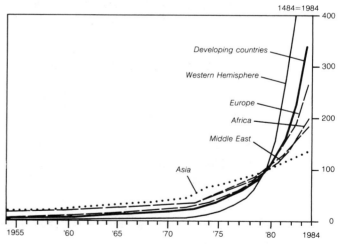

3. Wholesale Prices/Consumer Prices/ GDP Deflator

(World index numbers)

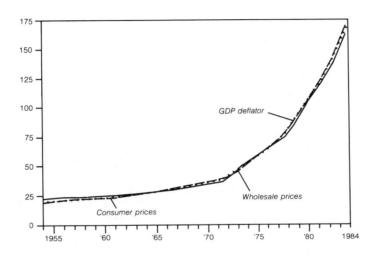

4. Commodity Prices

(Index numbers)

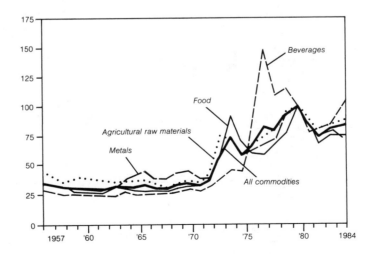

5. Commodity Price Indices, 1970-84

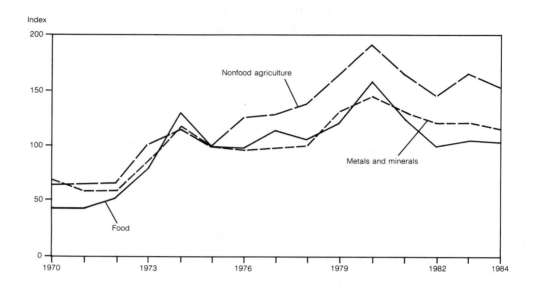

Index

Nonfood agriculture

Metals and minerals

Food

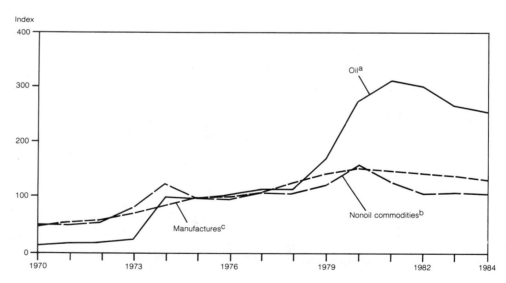

Index

Oil[a]

Manufactures[c]

Nonoil commodities[b]

[a] Average price of internationally traded oil.

[b] Average price of thirty-three primary commodities, weighted by each commodity's share in developing countries' exports.

[c] Average price of industrial countries exports of manufactures to developing countries.

Source *World Bank Annual Report,* 1985

APPENDIX XII: TRADE

1. Export Growth in Developing Countries, 1965-84

(average annual percentage change)

Country group	1965-73	1973-80	1980	1981	1982	1983	1984
All developing countries	5.6	2.0	-2.8	-2.7	4.4	5.6	8.6
Low-income countries	3.0	5.0	5.3	7.3	6.2	3.7	11.1
Asia	2.1	7.2	4.2	13.0	8.1	5.6	12.8
Africa	4.5	-0.8	8.4	-12.3	-1.0	-5.2	2.9
Middle-income oil importers	6.8	6.9	8.3	9.9	4.4	7.0	8.9
Major manufacturing exporters	10.0	9.7	12.6	13.7	4.0	8.0	9.6
Other middle-income oil importers	2.9	1.4	-2.1	-1.0	5.9	3.7	6.7
Middle-income oil exporters	5.3	-2.5	-15.2	-20.9	3.8	3.7	7.3

Note: Growth rates are at constant 1980 prices of merchandise exports.

Source: The World Bank.

---

2. Structure of World Merchandise Trade (%)

Trade structure	Exports						Imports					
	Total		Primary[1]		Manufactures[2]		Total		Primary[1]		Manufactures[2]	
Region	1962	1982	1962	1982	1962	1982	1962	1982	1962	1982	1962	1982
Developing countries of which:	20.6	26.1	36.6	44.9	4.1	10.9	21.8	25.1	16.8	22.5	25.4	28.2
America	7.7	5.7	14.7	11.1	0.5	1.5	7.4	6.1	5.5	6.1	9.2	6.1
Africa	4.0	3.5	7.3	7.8	0.5	0.3	4.4	4.1	3.3	3.2	5.5	5.1
West Asia	3.5	8.6	6.5	17.6	0.4	0.9	2.3	6.4	1.8	4.3	2.7	8.1
South and South-East Asia	5.4	8.2	8.0	8.1	2.7	8.2	7.3	8.5	6.2	8.7	7.9	8.6
Developed market-economy countries	67.1	63.6	51.6	43.6	83.2	80.8	65.9	64.8	70.5	66.5	59.5	62.7
Socialist countries of Eastern Europe	11.2	9.0	10.5	10.1	11.6	7.1	10.8	7.7	10.5	8.6	11.3	7.3
Socialist countries of Asia	1.2	1.2	1.3	1.4	1.1	1.2	1.0	1.1	1.3	1.2	0.6	1.0
World	100.0	100.0	100.0	100.0	100.0	100.0	100.0	100.0	100.0	100.0	100.0	100.0
World (billion current $, f.o.b.)	141.4	1 841.8	71.3	836.8	68.1	975.3	141.4	1 841.8	71.3	836.8	68.1	975.3

[1] Including metals and minerals.
[2] Excluding metals and minerals.

Source: *UNCTAD Statistical Pocketbook*, 1984

3. Developing Countries as a Market for DMECs

Merchandise exports of:			Developed market-economy countries				Annual growth rate of exports, 1962-1982 (percent)		
	Total		Manufactures		Food			Manufac-	
To:	1962	1982	1962	1982	1962	1982	Total	tures	Food
				DMECs					
World (billion $)	87.2	1 094.2	54.4	751.2	13.0	122.2	13.5	14.0	11.8
Percent to:									
Developing countries	23	25	26	28	22	24	13.9	14.5	12.3
				United States					
World (billion $)	21.4	206.0	13.0	135.8	4.4	35.3	12.0	12.5	11.0
Percent to:									
Developing countries	31	35	32	38	34	32	12.7	13.4	10.7
				EEC					
World (billion $)	47.2	583.2	31.2	396.6	5.5	65.9	13.4	13.6	13.2
Percent to:									
Developing countries	20	19	23	22	17	18	13.1	13.3	13.5
				Japan					
World (billion $)	4.9	138.6	3.8	117.3	0.4	1.5	18.2	18.7	7.3
Percent to:									
Developing countries	39	42	41	40	15	57	18.6	18.5	14.7

Source: UNCTAD secretariat computations, based on data from UNSO.

---

4. Trade of Developing Countries by Main Product Categories

Exports (f.o.b.)

	Primary commodities[1]				Manufactures[2]				Total	
	Petroleum[3]		Other		Textiles[4]		Other		SITC 0-9	
Region	1965	1982	1965	1982	1965	1982	1965	1982	1965	1982
Developing countries	31.4	57.0	54.2	20.3	4.9	6.0	6.3	15.8	100.0	100.0
by region:										
America	29.9	45.9	64.6	40.0	0.8	1.6	4.4	12.1	100.0	100.0
Africa	20.2	74.5	71.9	20.3	1.6	0.7	5.9	4.0	100.0	100.0
West Asia	83.1	91.0	14.0	3.1	0.9	0.8	1.9	5.1	100.0	100.0
South and South-East Asia	6.6	22.3	53.5	22.5	15.8	16.1	12.4	36.8	100.0	100.0
Least developed countries[6]	4.9	14.1	86.9	70.8	5.1	5.5	3.0	9.6	100.0	100.0

Imports (f.o.b.)

	Primary commodities[1]				Manufactures[2]				Total	
	Petroleum[3]		Other		Capital goods[5]		Other		SITC 0-9	
Region	1965	1982	1965	1982	1965	1982	1965	1982	1965	1982
Developing countries	8.9	19.4	28.6	19.9	30.8	33.0	28.6	24.5	100.0	100.0
by region:										
America	13.8	28.6	24.7	16.9	32.4	31.9	27.4	21.3	100.0	100.0
Africa	6.1	10.2	25.4	23.9	34.4	38.8	32.3	25.4	100.0	100.0
West Asia	7.9	10.6	29.9	19.9	29.9	38.0	30.3	28.7	100.0	100.0
South and South-East Asia	6.8	24.8	34.4	20.8	28.2	28.9	27.3	24.2	100.0	100.0
Least developed countries	11.5	16.2	23.4	28.5	22.0	25.2	36.5	29.3	100.0	100.0

Note: Primary commodities and manufactures comprise SITC sections 0 to 8. The percentages shown may therefore not add to 100.

[1] Including metals and minerals.
[2] Excluding metals and minerals.
[3] Mineral fuels, lubricants and related materials (SITC section 3).
[4] Textile yarn, fabrics and clothing.
[5] Machines and transport equipment.
[6] Exports of jute products and of diamonds are included in primary commodities.

Source: *UNCTAD Statistical Pocketbook*, 1984

5. World Insurance Premium Volume
(contributions paid)

	Premium volume ($ billion)			World share (percent)		
	1964	1974	1982	1964	1974	1982
World[1]	64.0	194.0	466.0	100.0	100.0	100.0
Developing countries	1.7	6.8	21.8	2.6	3.5	4.7
of which:						
America[2]	0.8	3.5	6.5	1.2	1.8	1.4
Africa[3]	0.2	0.7	3.8	0.3	0.4	0.8
Asia/Oceania[2]	0.7	2.6	11.5	1.1	1.3	2.5
Developed market-economy countries	62.4	187.2	444.2	97.4	96.5	95.3
of which:						
North America	42.3	102.0	237.9	66.1	52.6	51.1
EEC[4]	13.6	51.3	109.4	21.2	26.4	23.5
Japan	2.4	17.4	12.6	3.7	9.0	13.4
Others	4.1	16.5	34.3	6.4	8.6	7.4

Note: Premiums (i.e. income derived from life and non-life insurance business) shown are gross premiums from direct domestic business of local and foreign insurers. Non-life business includes motor marine, fire accident liabilities and miscellaneous.

[1] Excluding socialist countries of Eastern Europe and Asia because of lack of data.

[2] Estimated for 1982.

[3] Estimated for 1964 and 1982.

[4] The EEC totals have been recalculated for the whole period covered by this table to include data for Greece, which joined the community on January 1, 1981, and for Denmark, Ireland and the United Kingdom, which joined the community on January 1, 1973.

Source: *Sigma*, Swiss Reinsurance Company, May 1976, August 1983 and April 1984.

---

6. Summary of Payments Balances on Current Account[1]
(billions of dollars)

	1973	1975	1980	1982
Developing countries				
Merchandise trade balance	12.9	26.7	111.4	17.1
Services and private transfers (net)	-17.0	-28.8	-77.8	-105.0
Investment income and profit remittances (net)	-13.0	-12.1	-32.6	-41.0
Current-account deficit	-4.1	-2.1	33.6	-87.9
Oil exporters				
Merchandise trade balance	17.1	52.9	168.8	67.1
Services and private transfers (net)	-11.8	-21.0	-65.3	-82.6
Investment income and profit remittances (net)	-7.1	-4.0	-8.1	—
Current-account deficit	5.3	31.9	103.5	-15.5
Non-oil developing countries				
Merchandise trade balance	-4.2	-26.2	-57.3	-50.0
Services and private transfers (net)	-5.1	-7.8	-12.5	-22.4
Investment income and profit remittances (net)	-5.9	-8.1	-24.5	-41.6
Current-account deficit	-9.3	-34.0	-69.9	-72.4
of which:				
Major exporters of manufactures				
Merchandise trade balance	-0.1	-8.4	-15.3	-5.1
Services and private transfers (net)	-1.6	-2.6	-11.9	-16.5
Investment income and profit remittances (net)	-2.0	-3.3	-12.2	-23.1
Current-account deficit	-1.7	-11.0	-27.3	-21.6
Least developed countries				
Merchandise trade balance	-1.2	-3.1	-7.7	-8.6
Services and private transfers (net)	-0.4	-0.5	0.3	0.6
Investment income and profit remittances (net)	-0.1	-0.2	-0.2	-0.6
Current-account deficit	-1.6	-3.6	-7.4	-8.0

[1] Trade, services, and private transfers.

Source: *UNCTAD Statistical Pocketbook*, 1984

7. Relative Importance of Trade Among Developing Countries
(percentage)

Share of trade among developing countries	1960	1970	1973	1975	1982
All commodities					
World trade	4.8	3.5	4.0	5.9	7.8
Exports of developing countries	22.3	19.6	21.0	24.6	29.9
Imports of developing countries	20.8	18.9	21.9	25.8	30.4
All commodities (excluding fuels)					
World trade	3.3	2.5	2.8	3.3	4.7
Exports of developing countries	19.4	19.5	21.5	26.9	31.9
Imports of developing countries	14.5	13.4	15.1	13.4	17.3

Source: UNCTAD secretariat computations, based on data from UNSO

---

8. Structure of Intradeveloping and Interdeveloping Country Trade by Region and by Product Group
(percentage)

Commodity — Exports from:	Year	Total exports (less fuels)	Food	Agricultural raw materials and fertilizers	Chemical products	Steel, iron and non-ferrous metals	Machinery and transport equipment	Other manufactures	Total manufactures
America	1960	100	64.6	18.2	3.5	4.4	1.4	7.0	11.9
	1981	100	32.8	8.2	10.0	6.3	21.4	20.8	52.2
Africa	1960	100	52.4	24.4	3.0	6.5	1.6	10.4	15.0
	1981	100	45.4	16.3	12.9	5.3	4.0	16.1	33.1
West Asia	1960	100	38.5	16.0	2.0	—	5.0	31.0	38.0
	1981	100	24.2	7.0	7.3	—	21.7	39.4	68.1
South and South-East Asia	1960	100	36.5	27.1	2.5	1.8	4.6	26.2	33.3
	1981	100	18.7	9.9	5.0	4.9	21.3	37.1	63.4
Total	1960	100	43.2	24.7	2.7	2.9	3.6	20.5	26.9
	1981	100	24.3	9.5	6.8	5.4	20.5	31.6	58.8
of which:									
Intraregional trade	1960	100	44.4	24.7	3.4	2.4	4.4	17.7	25.6
	1981	100	21.8	10.6	8.5	4.8	22.3	30.1	60.9
Interregional trade	1960	100	39.7	24.4	0.9	4.8	1.3	28.2	30.4
	1981	100	28.1	7.7	4.0	6.4	17.3	36.0	57.2
All exports	1960	100	48.8	32.3	1.5	7.1	0.9	9.6	12.0
	1981	100	28.5	13.5	4.8	5.8	14.3	30.8	49.9

Source: *UNCTAD Statistical Pocketbook*, 1984

---

9. Exports
(In billions of U.S. dollars)

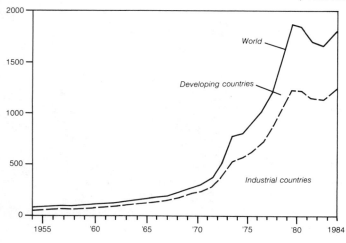

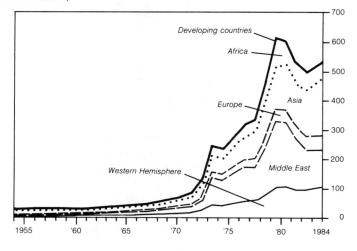

10. Imports

(In billions or U.S. dollars)

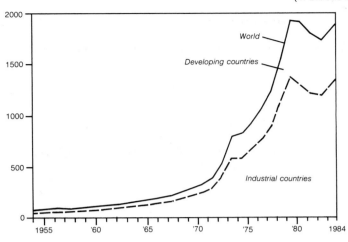

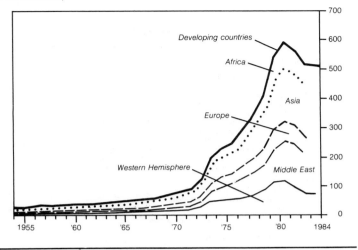

---

11. Developing Countries: Merchandise Trade, 1967-86[1,2]

(Changes, in percent)

	Average 1967-76[3]	From Preceding Year									
		1977	1978	1979	1980	1981	1982	1983	1984	1985	1986
Developing countries											
Value (in U.S. dollar terms)											
Exports	19.7	14.8	7.2	36.3	32.6	-1.0	-12.0	-5.4	8.1	-3.9	7.6
Imports	17.6	18.3	18.5	22.4	28.4	9.1	-7.1	-7.3	1.1	-2.3	7.8
Volume											
Exports	6.0	2.5	4.0	5.5	-4.4	-5.5	-8.0	2.7	8.4	0.3	5.0
Imports	8.4	9.5	6.9	4.7	8.6	7.1	-3.8	-3.4	2.1	-0.1	2.7
Unit value (in U.S. dollar terms)											
Exports	12.9	12.0	3.1	29.3	38.7	4.7	-4.3	-7.9	-0.3	-4.2	2.5
Imports	8.5	8.0	10.8	17.0	18.2	1.9	-3.3	-4.1	-1.0	-2.2	4.9
Terms of trade	4.1	3.7	-6.9	10.5	17.3	2.8	-1.0	-4.0	0.7	-2.0	-2.3
Purchasing power of exports[4]	10.3	6.3	-3.2	16.6	12.1	-2.8	-8.9	-1.4	9.2	-1.8	2.5
Memorandum											
Real GNP growth of trading partners	5.1	4.8	4.5	4.0	2.5	2.1	0.7	2.4	4.4	3.1	3.4
Market prices (in U.S. dollar terms) of primary commodities (excluding petroleum) exported by developing countries	9.0	25.6	-6.5	14.0	8.9	-14.9	-13.7	9.7	3.3	-11.5	0.8
Fuel exporters											
Value (in U.S. dollar terms)											
Exports	26.2	11.0	-0.9	47.0	41.4	-5.2	-19.0	-15.7	2.5	-9.5	3.4
Imports	24.3	23.0	16.8	8.5	28.3	19.9	-3.9	-15.4	-5.8	-8.9	5.7
Volume											
Exports	4.3	1.3	-1.6	2.3	-13.7	-14.9	-16.4	- 4.7	3.4	-5.5	3.1
Imports	15.9	13.6	3.9	-4.8	13.3	20.1	-0.5	-12.7	-4.3	-7.4	—
Unit value (in U.S. dollar terms)											
Exports	21.0	9.6	0.7	43.7	63.8	11.4	-3.1	-11.5	-0.9	-4.2	0.4
Imports	7.2	8.3	12.3	13.9	13.2	-0.1	-3.5	-3.1	-1.6	-1.7	5.7
Terms of trade	12.9	1.2	-10.4	26.2	44.7	11.5	0.4	-8.7	0.7	-2.6	-5.0
Purchasing power of exports[4]	17.7	2.5	-11.8	29.1	24.9	-5.1	-16.1	-13.0	4.1	-8.0	-2.1
Memorandum											
Oil export volume (in billions of barrels)[5]	...	10.8	10.4	10.5	9.1	7.6	6.1	5.6	5.7	5.1	5.3
Average oil export price (in U.S. dollars per barrel)[5]	...	12.8	12.9	18.8	30.7	33.7	32.4	28.4	27.9	26.8	26.5
Annual percentage change	21.7	9.6	0.4	45.9	63.5	9.9	-4.0	-12.2	-2.0	-4.0	-1.0
Real GNP growth of trading partners	5.1	4.7	4.5	4.0	2.4	2.1	0.6	2.3	4.4	3.0	3.3
Export unit value (in U.S. dollar terms) of manufactures	7.5	8.0	14.5	13.9	11.1	-6.0	-2.1	-4.3	-3.4	-2.0	6.0
Non-fuel exporters											
Value (in U.S. dollar terms)											
Exports	14.9	19.1	15.4	27.1	23.7	3.7	-4.7	3.6	12.1	-0.2	10.1
Imports	15.3	15.7	19.4	29.8	28.4	4.3	-8.6	-3.0	4.3	0.4	8.5
Volume											
Exports	6.8	4.0	9.4	8.9	8.9	6.8	0.9	8.9	12.0	4.1	6.1
Imports	6.3	7.5	8.6	9.5	6.6	1.5	-5.5	1.6	5.0	2.9	3.7
Unit value (in U.S. dollar terms)											
Exports	7.6	14.5	5.5	16.7	13.6	-2.9	-5.5	-4.8	—	-4.2	3.7
Imports	8.5	7.5	9.9	18.5	20.4	2.7	-3.3	-4.6	-0.7	-2.4	4.7
Terms of trade	-0.8	6.5	-4.0	-1.5	-5.7	-5.5	-2.3	-0.2	0.8	-1.8	-0.9
Purchasing power of exports[4]	5.9	10.8	5.0	7.2	2.7	1.0	-1.4	8.6	12.9	2.3	5.1

11. Developing Countries: Merchandise Trade, 1967-86[1,2] (continued)

(Changes, in percent)

	Average 1967-76[3]	1977	1978	1979	1980	1981	1982	1983	1984	1985	1986
						From Preceding Year					
Memorandum											
Real GNP growth of trading partners	5.0	4.8	4.5	4.1	2.6	2.1	0.7	2.5	4.4	3.2	3.5
Market price (in U.S. dollar terms) of primary commodities (excluding petroleum) exported by non-fuel exporters	8.8	26.1	-7.1	14.6	9.5	-15.3	-13.8	9.2	3.1	-11.1	1.1
Gross reserves (end of period) as percentage of total imports of goods and services[6]	27.4	25.5	26.7	22.9	17.8	16.4	17.1	19.1	20.6	21.6	21.4

[1] For classification of countries in groups shown here, see note in Appendix III.
[2] Excluding China prior to 1978.
[3] Compound annual rates of change.
[4] Export earnings deflated by import prices.
[5] Of oil exporting countries.
[6] Gold holdings are valued at SDR 35 an ounce.

Source: *World Economic Outlook*, 1985 (IMF)

---

12. Developing Countries: Export Volumes, 1967-86[1,2]

(Changes, in percent)

	Average 1967-76[3]	1977	1978	1979	1980	1981	1982	1983	1984	1985	1986
						From Preceding Year					
Developing countries	6.0	2.5	4.0	5.5	-4.4	-5.5	-8.0	2.7	8.4	0.3	5.0
By region											
Africa	3.6	1.7	3.8	7.8	0.2	-16.3	-5.7	2.7	7.2	5.0	4.2
Asia	10.4	6.2	10.4	9.4	9.2	8.9	1.4	10.8	13.9	3.7	6.9
Europe	8.2	2.3	6.6	2.4	5.0	13.4	1.1	8.2	13.0	4.8	6.0
Middle East	6.4	0.6	-3.3	1.1	-15.9	-17.6	-20.1	-9.7	0.4	-9.3	3.3
Western Hemisphere	0.9	3.9	9.6	9.1	0.2	7.1	-3.0	7.0	8.2	1.1	3.1
By predominant export											
Fuel exporters	4.3	1.3	-1.6	2.3	-13.7	-14.9	-16.4	-4.7	3.4	-5.5	3.1
Non-fuel exporters	6.8	4.0	9.4	8.9	8.9	6.8	0.9	8.9	12.0	4.1	6.1
Primary product exporters	4.0	3.2	9.0	8.5	6.7	3.5	0.2	6.1	10.4	2.9	5.5
Exporters of manufactures	12.3	5.4	9.8	8.4	11.7	10.2	1.6	10.8	13.8	5.0	6.7
Service and remittance countries	3.7	2.7	8.7	15.6	4.7	3.3	—	10.4	7.1	4.4	4.7
By financial criteria											
Capital importing countries	5.6	4.1	7.6	7.8	4.3	2.8	-1.1	7.6	11.2	3.3	5.3
Of which, Market borrowers	6.2	5.6	9.3	8.6	3.7	1.3	-2.5	9.3	11.8	3.6	5.1
Of which, Major borrowers	3.9	10.8	7.3	5.1	3.3	11.3	-3.9	10.1	10.4	-0.2	3.6
Official borrowers	1.7	-3.8	-0.3	4.4	2.4	-2.7	-3.3	1.1	0.3	-0.6	5.5
Countries with recent debt-servicing problems	2.8	2.3	4.7	5.6	1.1	1.0	-2.9	5.5	8.7	3.0	3.8
Countries without debt-servicing problems	8.1	5.7	9.6	9.3	6.5	4.0	—	8.9	12.6	3.4	6.2
By miscellaneous criteria											
Small low-income countries	0.9	-6.2	1.9	4.0	8.2	-2.8	1.3	4.1	0.5	0.6	6.7
Sub-Saharan Africa[4]	2.8	-7.0	0.6	3.1	5.6	-4.3	5.8	—	3.3	0.2	4.4
Middle Eastern oil exporters	6.9	-0.1	-3.2	1.1	-17.3	-19.0	-21.8	-10.5	-0.6	-10.7	3.5
Non-oil Middle Eastern countries	5.0	9.4	-4.3	1.4	5.5	1.4	-1.0	-2.4	8.3	-0.1	2.8
By alternative analytical categories											
Oil exporting countries	4.8	0.6	-2.7	2.3	-15.5	-17.7	-19.6	-6.7	2.8	-7.0	3.3
Non-oil developing countries	6.7	4.5	9.4	8.3	8.7	7.4	1.7	8.6	11.4	3.8	5.7
Net oil exporters	3.1	7.6	9.8	5.4	3.6	6.6	9.6	6.8	8.9	1.0	4.0
Net oil importers	7.3	3.9	9.4	8.8	9.8	7.6	0.2	8.9	11.9	4.4	6.1
Major exporters of manufactures	10.4	7.8	11.8	10.7	12.1	8.7	-2.7	13.3	14.5	5.4	6.2
Low-income countries	2.4	-4.9	4.4	11.8	9.1	6.7	3.7	6.0	7.8	1.4	6.9
Other net oil importers	5.4	1.5	7.9	3.6	5.7	5.7	4.7	1.4	8.3	3.9	5.3

[1] For classification of countries in groups shown here, see note in Appendix III.
[2] Excluding China prior to 1978.
[3] Compound annual rates of change.
[4] Excluding Nigeria and South Africa.

Source: *World Economic Outlook*, 1985 (IMF)

13. Developing Countries: Import Volumes, 1967-86[1,2]

(Changes, in percent)

	Average 1967-76[3]					From Preceding Year					
		1977	1978	1979	1980	1981	1982	1983	1984	1985	1986
Developing countries	8.4	9.5	6.9	4.7	8.6	7.1	-3.8	-3.4	2.1	-0.1	2.7
By region											
Africa	7.3	7.5	3.2	-3.3	9.7	10.3	-6.6	-11.4	2.5	-5.6	-0.3
Asia	7.2	10.1	16.4	13.3	10.3	4.0	-0.1	6.5	5.9	5.2	4.6
Europe	7.4	7.5	0.2	5.8	0.5	2.3	-7.7	2.0	5.9	3.0	5.6
Middle East	15.8	13.0	3.4	-4.4	9.4	16.8	5.9	-2.8	-5.9	-9.1	-2.9
Western Hemisphere	6.5	7.8	5.4	8.0	9.4	2.7	-17.8	-22.6	2.2	1.1	5.0
By predominant export											
Fuel exporters	15.9	13.6	3.9	-4.8	13.3	20.1	-0.5	-12.7	-4.3	-7.4	—
Non-fuel exporters	6.3	7.5	8.6	9.5	6.6	1.5	-5.5	1.6	5.0	2.9	3.7
Primary product exporters	5.2	4.1	3.0	7.2	7.4	-0.3	-9.0	-5.0	1.0	-3.0	1.3
Exporters of manufactures	8.3	9.6	14.7	10.9	5.8	1.8	-4.7	6.8	8.2	7.6	5.8
Service and remittance countries	3.8	12.2	6.0	11.2	7.1	6.7	2.0	2.4	3.7	0.4	0.8
By financial criteria											
Capital importing countries	7.0	8.9	7.6	7.3	7.8	4.6	-6.1	-3.0	4.4	2.3	3.6
Of which, Market borrowers	8.9	8.0	8.1	7.5	9.0	6.9	-6.7	-7.0	3.2	—	4.8
Of which, Major borrowers	11.1	7.7	10.2	7.7	9.0	5.4	-9.1	-14.9	2.2	-1.3	5.8
Official borrowers	3.5	7.6	4.7	1.9	0.6	-1.9	-2.1	1.2	1.3	0.3	-1.2
Countries with recent debt-servicing problems	7.1	9.1	3.0	4.8	4.8	2.6	-13.0	-14.7	1.7	0.8	3.5
Countries without debt-servicing problems	7.1	8.7	10.9	8.9	9.7	5.8	-1.9	3.3	5.6	2.9	3.7
By miscellaneous criteria											
Small low-income countries	1.1	5.8	16.1	-0.3	2.7	-5.7	1.5	-1.6	6.5	4.2	-2.2
Sub-Saharan Africa[4]	3.3	5.1	7.1	-2.1	8.0	-3.2	-4.5	-6.7	1.1	1.0	-1.4
Middle Eastern oil exporters	22.1	13.1	4.1	-7.8	13.3	22.4	7.8	-5.1	-8.7	-12.9	-3.3
Non-oil Middle Eastern countries	7.1	12.9	1.4	4.8	1.0	4.5	0.8	3.6	1.2	-0.3	-1.9
By alternative analytical categories											
Oil exporting countries	19.3	15.5	2.8	-9.1	12.3	22.1	6.6	-11.0	-6.5	-10.3	-1.4
Non-oil developing countries	6.2	7.3	8.7	10.1	7.4	2.6	-7.5	-0.3	5.2	3.2	3.8
Net oil exporters	4.9	5.6	6.8	16.6	12.3	12.5	-13.9	-10.8	7.3	3.0	2.8
Net oil importers	6.4	7.4	9.1	9.1	6.7	0.9	-6.3	1.6	4.9	3.2	4.0
Major exporters of manufactures	10.0	4.2	8.5	11.0	6.5	2.8	-7.1	0.2	6.1	1.1	5.6
Low-income countries	-0.6	9.5	20.8	9.3	12.9	-3.8	-4.7	4.3	10.4	14.8	2.8
Other net oil importers	5.3	12.2	3.8	5.8	3.1	0.6	-6.0	2.6	-0.9	-1.2	1.8

[1] For classification of countries in groups shown here, see note in Appendix III.
[2] Excluding China prior to 1978.
[3] Compound annual rates of change.
[4] Excluding Nigeria and South Africa.

Source: *World Economic Outlook, 1985 (IMF)*

---

14. Direction of trade

A. Exports (f.o.b.)

			Destination			
	Year	DC	DMEC	SCEE	SCA	WORLD
Origin						
			percent			
Developing countries (DC)	1962	22.0	71.5	4.4	0.9	100
	1983	31.5	62.3	3.9	1.2	100
Developed market-economy countries (DMEC)	1962	23.0	73.1	3.1	0.5	100
	1983	23.2	71.2	3.3	1.1	100
Socialist countries of Eastern Europe (SCEE)	1962	13.0	18.2	64.5	4.0	100
	1983	16.6	28.8	51.6	2.8	100
Socialist countries of Asia (SCA)	1962	32.7	14.9	52.4	..	100
	1983	48.9	40.8	8.9	..	100
World	1962	21.8	65.9	10.8	1.0	100
	1983	25.0	64.6	8.1	1.3	100

14. Direction of trade (continued)

B. Imports (f.o.b.)

Destination	Year	DC	DMEC	SCEE	SCA	WORLD
			Origin			
			percent			
Developing countries (DC)	1962	20.7	22.3	8.4	20.4	21.8
	1983	31.8	24.3	12.2	23.2	25.2
Developed market-economy countries (DMEC)	1962	70.8	74.4	19.2	32.6	65.9
	1983	59.4	70.6	26.1	55.3	64.0
Socialist countries of Eastern Europe (SCEE)	1962	6.7	3.1	66.6	46.7	10.8
	1983	6.3	4.2	60.3	20.3	9.5
Socialist countries of Asia (SCA)	1962	1.8	0.3	4.1	..	1.0
	1983	2.5	0.8	1.4	..	1.3
World	1962	100	100	100	100	100
	1983	100	100	100	100	100

Note: Components may not add to 100 due to rounding.

Source: UNCTAD secretariat computations, based on UNSO data. Derived from network of exports by origin and destinations.

---

15. Structure of World Trade by Broad Commodity Groups as Percentages of Total Trade (1970 and 1980)

Developed Countries — 1970

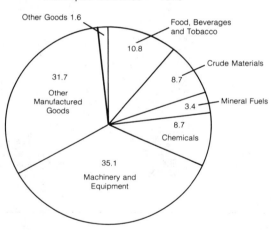

Developing Countries — 1970

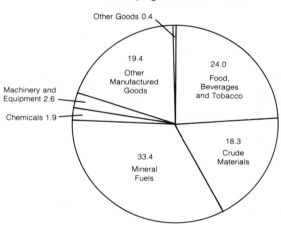

Developed Countries — 1980

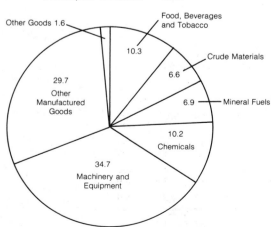

Developing Countries — 1980

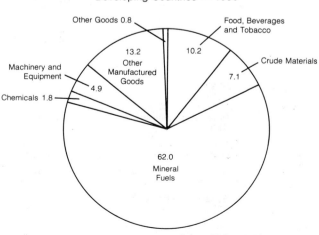

Source: *UN Statistical Yearbook,* 1982

16. Capital-Importing Developing Countries: Ratios of Debt Service to Export Earnings[1], 1978-1982
(Percentage)

	1978	1979	1980	1981	1982[2]
Interest payments	7.6	9.1	10.5	13.3	15.5
Total debt service	37.0	36.4	38.1	48.2	61
Net energy exporters	41.1	34.6	34.1	45.9	63
Net energy importers	34.5	38.1	41.4	50.0	59.5
Twenty largest debtors	41.7	41.1	42.8	54.4	69.5
Others	23.4	22.6	22.6	26.6	33
Memorandum items:					
Debt service on public and publicly guaranteed debt	15.4	15.8	13.8	15.1	20
Total interest payments plus amortization on public and publicly guaranteed debt[3]	17.7	19.2	18.0	21.1	26

[1] Debt-service payments (excluding servicing of IMF credits) as a share of exports of goods and services and net private transfers. Figures are based on a sample of 86 developing countries for which adequate data were available.

[2] Estimates rounded to the nearest half percentage point (no account is taken of any delays in scheduled payments.)

[3] Entails a lower-bound of amortization of all medium- and long-term debt since private, non-guaranteed medium- and long-term debt is excluded.

Source: Department of International Economic and Social Affairs of the United Nations Secretariat, based on World Bank, *Debtor Reporting System*; Bank for International Settlements, *Maturity Distribution of International Bank Lending*; International Monetary Fund, *International Financial Statistics*; and Secretariat estimates.

---

17. World Trade: Annual Rates of Change in Volume and Prices[1], 1971-1984
(Percentage)

	1971-1980	1980	1981	1982[2]	1983[3]	1984[3]
Volume of exports						
World	5.5	2.1	0.8	-1.5	2	4
Developed market economies	6.3	4.2	2.1	-2	2	4
Developing countries	3.0	-4.5	-3.6	-4.5	3.5	5.5
Capital surplus countries	0.8	-17.4	-18.4	-16.5	-	5
Other net energy exporters	0.2	-6.8	-8.4	-3	5	7
Net energy importers	7.2	9.1	9.6	1.5	4	5
Centrally planned economies[4]	6.7	2.4	0.4	4.5	2	2
Volume of imports						
World	5.2	1.0	1.7	-1.5	2	4
Developed market economies	4.6	-1.5	-2.2	-1	2.5	3.5
Developing countries	6.5	8.1	14.7	-3.5	-0.5	5.5
Capital surplus countries	18.0	15.5	30.1	7	5	7
Other net energy exporters	8.7	18.3	22.2	-8	-3	5
Net energy importers	3.5	1.5	5.4	-5.5	-1.5	5
Centrally planned economies[4]	7.4	3.8	0.7	0.5	1.5	2
Unit value of exports						
World	14.0	19.4	-2.7	-4.5	-	...
Developed market economies	11.9	13.4	-4.1	-3.5	2.5	...
Developing countries						
Capital surplus countries	33.6	70.1	11.4	-4.5	14.5	...
Other net energy exporters	26.3	51.8	6.1	-7	-11	...
Net energy importers	11.5	12.2	-3.5	-7	0.5	...
Centrally planned economies[4]	10.2	12.4	0.8	-0.5	2.5	...
Unit value of imports						
World	14.1	21.1	-2.5	-4.5	0.5	...
Developed market economies	14.4	22.4	-2.9	-5	-	...
Developing countries						
Capital surplus countries	13.1	15.0	-3.5	-4	2	...
Other net energy exporters	13.9	17.2	-3.0	-4	1	...
Net energy importers	16.5	25.5	-0.8	-4.5	-1.5	...
Centrally planned economies[4]	9.6	10.8	-0.4	-1.5	5	...

17. World Trade: Annual Rates of Change in Volume and Prices[1], 1971-1984 (continued)
(Percentage)

	1971-1980	1980	1981	1982[2]	1983[3]	1984[3]
Terms of trade						
Developed market economies	-2.1	-7.3	-1.3	1.5	2.5	...
Developing countries						
Capital surplus countries	18.1	47.9	15.3	-1	-16	...
Other net energy exporters	10.9	29.6	9.3	-3	-12	...
Net energy importers	-4.3	-10.6	-2.8	-3	2	...
Centrally planned economies[4]	0.6	1.4	1.2	1	-2.5	...

[1] Rates of change in prices estimated from unit value indices expressed in dollars.

[2] Preliminary estimates, rounded to the nearest half of a percentage point.

[3] Forecasts.

[4] Centrally planned economies of Europe only.

Source: Department of International Economic and Social Affairs of the UN Secretariat, based on IMF, *International Financial Statistics*, and calculations and forecasts made by the Secretariat.

---

18. Net Energy-Importing Developing Countries: Trade Balances in Real and Nominal Terms, and Growth Rates of Real Output and Income, 1977-1982

(Trade balances in billions of dollars; growth rates in percentages)

	1977	1978	1979	1980	1981	1982[1]
Export, f.o.b. (constant 1977 prices)	102.0	113.0	121.7	132.7	145.4	147.7
Imports, c.i.f. (constant 1977 prices)	130.3	140.6	148.2	150.3	158.4	149.8
Real trade balance (constant 1977 prices)	-28.3	-27.6	-26.5	-17.6	-13.0	-2.1
Trade balance in current dollars	-28.4	-39.0	-53.4	-74.9	-76.4	-61.9
Growth rate of real per capita GDP[2]	3.3 (4.1)	2.6 (1.4)	1.3 (0.6)	2.2 (0.4)	-0.6 (-1.4)	-1.1 (-1.7)

[1] Preliminary estimates.

[2] Figures in parentheses refer to growth rates of real per capita GDP adjusted for changes in the terms of trade. Both sets of growth rates are expressed in 1977 prices and exchange rates.

Source: Department of International Economic and Social Affairs of the UN Secretariat, based on IMF, *International Financial Statistics* and other international sources. 7

APPENDIX XIII: ECONOMIC AID

1. US Economic Loans and Grants Extended to the Less Developed Countries[1]

(Million U.S. $)

	1946-84[2]	1975[3]	1980[3]	1981[3]	1982[3]	1983[3]	1984[3]
Total	**143,752**	**4,548**	**7,570**	**7,251**	**8,040**	**8,564**	**8,820**
Africa	**12,171**	**335**	**800**	**922**	**954**	**971**	**1,165**
Ethiopia	408	24	15	5	2	3	10
Ghana	461	8	28	26	17	7	20
Liberia	560	16	24	55	66	63	66
Libya	212	0	0	0	0	0	...
Morocco	1,277	24	27	56	63	54	84
Nigeria	406	9	...	...	...	...	...
Tunisia	985	13	29	40	17	19	18
Zaire	802	5	26	29	24	30	46
Other	7,060	236	651	711	765	795	921
East Asia	**25,570**	**494**	**407**	**326**	**277**	**286**	**308**
Cambodia	913	149	38	14	4	2	3
Indonesia	3,215	90	196	130	91	111	116
Laos	904	26	...	...	...	...	...
Philippines	2,507	68	83	98	107	103	106
South Korea	6,049	37	31	28	...	...	...
China (Taiwan)	2,207	0	...	...	...	...	...
Thailand	877	7	30	31	36	29	42
Other	8,898	117	29	25	39	41	41
Latin America	**16,129**	**520**	**498**	**611**	**840**	**1,161**	**1,217**
Argentina	199	NEGL	...	...	NEGL	...	NEGL
Bolivia	923	26	30	13	20	63	78
Brazil	2,428	15	2	1	1	NEGL	...
Chile	1,181	96	10	12	7	3	2
Colombia	1,383	28	23	6	3	4	8
Dominican Republic	929	12	56	38	82	63	98
Ecuador	493	8	12	18	23	27	29
Guatemala	530	14	13	19	16	30	20
Mexico	362	NEGL	7	10	9	8	8
Panama	466	21	2	11	13	7	12
Peru	1,060	16	53	80	55	94	165
Venezuela	202	2	...	NEGL	NEGL	NEGL	NEGL
Other	5,973	282	290	403	611	862	797
Middle East and South Asia	**50,146**	**1,786**	**2,802**	**2,757**	**2,958**	**2,987**	**3,093**
Afghanistan	537	21	...	...	...	...	...
Bangladesh	1,989	304	157	152	172	172	193
Egypt	10,519	370	1,166	1,130	1,065	1,005	1,104
Greece	1,910	0	...	...	...	...	...
India	11,042	249	222	275	222	210	213
Iran	766	2	...	...	...	...	...
Israel	8,851	353	786	764	806	785	910
Jordan	1,488	99	73	10	15	20	20
Pakistan	5,858	181	59	77	200	279	307
Turkey	3,920	4	198	201	301	286	140
Other	3,266	203	141	148	177	230	206
Europe and Oceania	**2,200**	**95**	**94**	**41**	**48**	**39**	**59**
Spain	1,108	3	7	7	22	12	12
Other	1,092	92	87	34	26	27	47
Interregional	**37,536**	**1,318**	**2,969**	**2,594**	**2,963**	**3,120**	**2,978**

[1] Data are for fiscal years and are for official development assistance, which is concessional.   [2] Data are reported on a net basis, excluding total deobligations.   [3] Data reported are on a gross basis.

Source: *Handbook of Economic Statistics*, 1985 Central Intelligence Agency

2. Communist Economic Aid to Less Developed Countries, Extensions and Drawings

(Million U.S. $)

	Total Extended	Drawn	USSR Extended	Drawn	Eastern Europe Extended	Drawn	China Extended	Drawn
Total	**51,240**	**25,095**	**30,005**	**14,050**	**14,665**	**6,610**	**6,575**	**4,435**
1954-74	19,835	9,210	10,080	5,670	5,830	1,900	3,925	1,640
1975	2,925	985	1,970	500	545	270	410	215
1976	2,285	1,235	1,080	475	995	405	205	360
1977	1,180	1,335	435	545	525	505	220	280
1978	4,820	1,215	3,000	485	1,600	425	220	305
1979	4,625	1,130	3,800	580	645	305	175	245
1980	4,400	1,390	2,605	815	1,325	315	470	260
1981	1,405	1,630	600	860	725	485	80	280
1982	1,645	2,165	1,015	1,190	560	650	70	325
1983	3,950	2,425	3,265	1,435	415	680	270	310
1984	4,180	2,370	2,150	1,495	1,500	660	525	215

APPENDIX XIV: ENERGY

1. Per Capita Consumption and Production of Commercial Energy, by Region (1982)

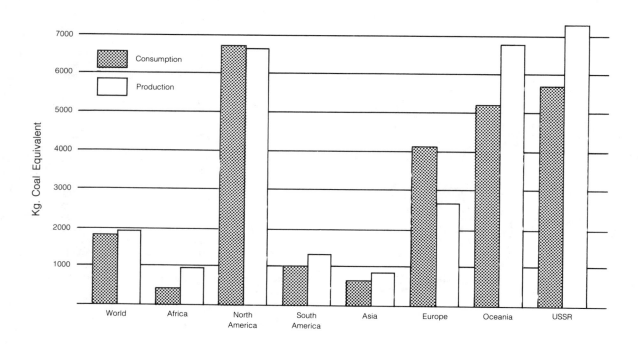

Source: *UN Statistical Yearbook, 1982*

2. Distribution of Primary Energy Production by Regions (1982)

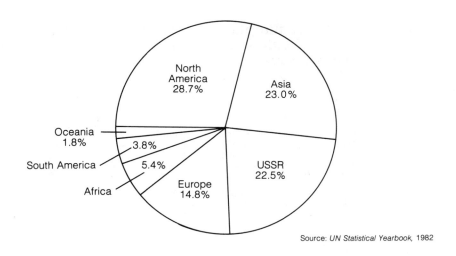

Source: *UN Statistical Yearbook, 1982*

3. Production Trade and Consumption of Commercial Energy – World and Regions

(Quantities in thousand metric tons of coal equivalent and in kilograms per capita)

Primary Energy Production

Regions	Year	Total	Solids	Liquids	Gas	Electricity	Changes in Stocks	Imports	Exports
World	1970	7 044 802	2 147 861	3 432 839	1 310 513	153 588	55 037	2 435 784	2 447 244
	1975	8 086 301	2 304 747	3 980 986	1 576 892	223 677	92 526	2 893 477	2 880 357
	1980	9 257 423	2 618 560	4 499 807	1 837 693	301 363	77 319	3 262 329	3 220 523
	1981	9 048 619	2 628 318	4 247 381	1 852 621	320 398	67 559	2 996 256	2 939 681
	1982	8 936 150	2 712 020	4 036 632	1 853 520	333 978	92 563	2 863 683	2 731 104
Developed Mkt. Econ.	1970	3 010 530	1 012 772	927 857	956 710	113 191	43 067	1 888 201	386 038
	1975	3 049 245	976 470	880 675	1 027 192	164 908	66 146	2 204 462	445 642
	1980	3 395 095	1 141 272	1 030 997	1 016 345	206 480	37 719	2 392 221	633 776
	1981	3 418 928	1 164 463	1 033 375	1 000 301	220 790	9 500	2 158 507	664 936
	1982	3 428 786	1 198 029	1 066 057	933 789	230 910	44 618	2 021 834	678 323
Developing Mkt. Econ.	1970	2 104 087	89 289	1 919 659	76 075	19 064	9 762	418 118	1 846 729
	1975	2 518 122	111 175	2 244 318	132 934	29 696	18 210	493 216	2 123 854
	1980	2 802 632	127 998	2 410 026	216 026	48 582	40 395	621 550	2 159 827
	1981	2 557 399	141 087	2 154 004	211 811	50 497	57 851	604 083	1 858 286
	1982	2 335 420	147 099	1 901 709	233 862	52 749	40 641	606 789	1 615 996
Africa	1970	485 246	52 964	426 598	2 616	3 069	2 594	54 745	422 839
	1975	435 735	61 502	355 759	13 875	4 600	2 437	67 001	349 275
	1980	585 115	98 071	444 904	34 600	7 541	16 603	69 536	416 486
	1981	493 396	109 141	347 040	30 556	6 660	14 257	72 807	319 072
	1982	482 591	106 742	337 597	31 649	6 603	20 525	67 440	301 093
North America	1970	2 376 142	527 762	923 204	869 963	55 214	34 802	522 122	272 805
	1975	2 325 806	539 105	876 671	822 382	87 648	55 269	719 481	287 019
	1980	2 554 551	661 856	988 895	799 215	104 585	21 955	758 239	347 516
	1981	2 554 768	656 337	1 002 256	787 903	108 273	12 796	664 509	372 446
	1982	2 560 279	664 929	1 035 694	745 706	113 951	31 294	575 399	408 047
South America	1970	391 254	6 298	352 772	24 410	7 774	655	45 562	268 822
	1975	314 356	7 742	259 191	33 354	14 069	3 250	78 771	173 294
	1980	344 471	10 102	264 928	44 826	24 617	1 685	96 130	163 537
	1981	346 986	10 774	264 732	46 333	25 147	2 412	89 600	160 251
	1982	341 752	11 784	252 434	50 395	27 138	4 242	85 028	144 007
Asia	1970	1 601 202	394 034	1 148 076	38 681	20 411	11 501	510 116	1 045 561
	1975	2 287 017	500 797	1 674 453	81 396	30 371	8 498	619 468	1 506 176
	1980	2 455 086	609 141	1 681 965	118 846	45 134	12 049	772 577	1 466 743
	1981	2 280 541	623 389	1 490 470	118 771	47 911	38 060	747 944	1 262 361
	1982	2 057 918	655 527	1 228 444	123 267	50 680	13 333	762 632	1 032 982
Europe	1970	911 132	661 503	55 758	145 206	48 664	288	1 250 067	256 665
	1975	1 046 653	634 589	71 329	275 898	64 837	15 128	1 345 770	304 317
	1980	1 261 691	655 253	210 040	310 841	85 557	26 417	1 514 287	447 980
	1981	1 265 361	640 073	225 748	303 006	96 535	−1 901	1 373 259	441 960
	1982	1 318 180	666 584	259 705	291 982	99 908	21 940	1 323 931	438 970

3. Production Trade and Consumption of Commercial Energy – World and Regions (continued)

(Quantities in thousand metric tons of coal equivalent and in kilograms per capita)

Primary Energy Production

Regions	Year	Total	Solids	Liquids	Gas	Electricity	Changes in Stocks	Imports	Exports
Oceania	1970	63 387	46 162	12 469	2 052	2 704	2 796	35 804	17 425
	1975	99 022	59 875	28 752	6 225	4 170	979	28 392	29 038
	1980	118 627	71 735	30 490	12 470	3 931	−2 510	30 948	40 070
	1981	131 875	82 554	30 376	14 505	4 439	1 935	29 458	43 517
	1982	161 957	110 836	30 494	16 328	4 298	228	27 892	58 137
USSR	1970	1 216 439	459 138	513 962	227 585	15 753	2 401	17 036	163 127
	1975	1 577 712	501 137	714 831	343 762	17 982	6 966	34 362	231 237
	1980	1 937 881	512 402	878 586	516 895	29 998	1 120	20 526	338 191
	1981	1 975 692	506 051	886 760	551 548	31 333	...	18 594	340 073
	1982	2 013 473	495 618	892 263	594 193	31 399	...	21 273	347 868

Source: *UN Statistical Yearbook* 1982

APPENDIX XV: MILITARY AID AND ARMS TRANSFERS

1. Value of Imports of Major Weapons by the Third World[1] by Region
(millions of constant (1975) dollars)

Region[2]	1963	1970	1980	1981	1982	Annual growth rate 1963-1982 (percent)
Middle East	393	1 462	4 926	4 287	4 548	13.8
North Africa	34	121	1 441	1 095	1 078	20.0
Far East[3]	310	271	905	576	387	1.2
South Asia	221	300	688	951	881	7.6
South America	72	148	746	916	771	13.3
Sub-Saharan Africa[4]	47	121	806	678	433	12.4
Central America	96	6	240	391	305	6.3
South Africa	155	77	88	20	35	−7.5
Oceania	—	—	1	3	10	—
Total (excluding Vietnam)[5]	1 328	2 506	9 841	8 917	8 448	10.2
Vietnam	56	433	—	—	—	—
TOTAL[6]	1 384	2 939	9 841	8 917	8 448	10.0

[1] Including the value of licenses sold to Third World countries for production of major weapons.

[2] In descending order of average values of exports of weapons around 1980.

[3] Excluding Vietnam.

[4] Excluding South Africa.

[5] Vietnam is included in the Far East after 1975.

[6] Components may not add to totals due to rounding.

Source: *SIPRI Yearbook*, 1983.

2. Value of Exports of Major Weapons to the Third World[1] by Supplier
(millions of constant (1975) dollars)

Supplier[2]	1963	1970	1980	1981	1982	Annual growth rate 1963-1982 (percent)
USSR[3]	429	1 136	4 425	3 172	2 390	9.5
USA[3]	514	1 258	2 983	2 547	2 836	9.4
France[3]	194	203	916	1 047	1 087	9.5
Italy	20	43	367	535	649	20.1
United Kingdom	177	185	318	432	546	6.1
Germany, Federal Republic of	13	1	153	290	119	12.4
China[3]	51[4]	22	75	147	51	—
Netherlands	—	10	108	57	14	—
Canada[3]	13	37	17	42	71	9.3
Sweden	—	—	101	36	21	—
Czechoslovakia	16	31	45	23	7	−4.3
Switzerland	2	2	17	32	32	15.7
Japan	1	—	—	—	—	—
Third World	4	8	269	385	333	26.2
Other industrialized, West	1	3	21	94	292	34.8
Other industrialized, East	—	—	26	78	—	—
TOTAL[3]	1 384	2 939	9 841	8 917	8 448	10.0

Note: Components may not add to totals due to rounding.

[1] Including the value of licenses sold to Third World countries for production of major weapons.

[2] In descending order of average values of exports of weapons around 1980.

[3] Including exports to Vietnam.

[4] 1964.

Source: *SIPRI Yearbook* 1983.

---

3. U.S. Military Deliveries to the Less Developed Countries[a]
(*Million U.S. $*)

	1975-84	1975	1976	1977	1978	1979	1980	1981	1982	1983	1984
Total	72,265	4,412	5,410	7,324	7,546	7,563	5,973	6,965	8,579	10,715	7,778
North Africa and the Middle East	54,548	2,218	4,224	5,609	6,121	6,203	4,324	5,052	6,500	8,685	5,612
Egypt	3,130	0	1	12	57	193	209	207	1,066	1,037	348
Iran	10,180	1,035	1,999	2,555	2,065	2,519	7	0	0	0	0
Israel	8,579	777	1,010	1,091	948	515	853	1,309	1,122	459	495
Jordan	1,721	32	138	112	178	126	277	221	193	344	100
Kuwait	839	13	22	157	191	74	79	67	92	78	66
Lebanon	510	2	5	NEGL	10	11	17	14	39	191	221
Morocco	724	3	20	55	99	142	69	128	64	67	77
North Yemen	309	2	NEGL	22	27	70	72	49	40	17	10
Oman	100	2	1	1	1	1	8	18	34	26	8
Saudi Arabia	27,198	350	1,019	1,594	2,535	2,500	2,640	3,005	3,782	6,092	3,681
Tunisia	275	2	3	6	2	45	11	24	16	26	140
Other	983	NEGL	6	4	8	7	82	10	52	348	466
Sub-Saharan Africa	840	26	63	99	111	38	53	72	160	96	122
Cameroon	35	0	1	8	3	NEGL	3	1	3	4	12
Kenya	141	1	0	1	47	8	4	28	25	21	6
Liberia	23	NEGL	1	NEGL	0	2	1	1	1	10	7
Nigeria	105	4	26	4	10	9	11	11	13	7	10
Somalia	58	0	0	0	0	0	0	0	14	21	23
Sudan	237	0	0	0	32	8	22	23	94	14	44
Zaire	70	1	4	9	12	7	10	7	7	8	5
Other	171	20	31	77	7	4	2	1	3	11	15

3. U.S. Military Deliveries to the Less Developed Countries[a] (continued)
(Million U.S. $)

	1975-84	1975	1976	1977	1978	1979	1980	1981	1982	1983	1984
Latin America	**1,864**	**144**	**219**	**211**	**125**	**122**	**139**	**101**	**239**	**233**	**331**
Argentina	139	10	12	13	24	36	12	11	10	7	4
Brazil	272	46	90	14	12	16	15	15	14	29	21
Chile	146	13	40	57	11	15	10	0	0	0	0
Colombia	88	2	2	8	4	8	5	12	21	12	14
Ecuador	124	2	6	10	24	9	11	8	13	31	10
El Salvador	208	NEGL	1	NEGL	1	NEGL	2	13	59	47	85
Mexico	134	1	2	6	3	2	4	5	76	31	4
Peru	155	9	32	31	18	16	15	10	11	9	4
Venezuela	392	42	13	52	10	14	20	22	30	43	146
Other	206	19	21	20	18	6	45	5	5	24	43
Asia	**13,357**	**1,963**	**756**	**1,200**	**1,068**	**1,082**	**1,329**	**1,504**	**1,390**	**1,525**	**1,540**
India	90	3	10	10	11	11	9	5	6	6	19
Indonesia	435	21	35	37	22	30	117	77	29	41	26
Malaysia	385	32	19	44	66	22	24	58	29	51	40
Pakistan	1,266	14	16	44	53	63	57	89	151	261	518
Philippines	413	30	45	50	54	38	56	33	53	32	22
Singapore	464	13	22	22	14	91	29	75	44	105	49
South Korea	3,797	208	357	272	508	474	497	432	404	331	314
Taiwan	3,031	169	183	194	214	227	269	442	467	510	356
Thailand	1,449	52	69	54	113	98	248	271	171	183	190
Other	2,027	1,421	NEGL	473	13	28	23	22	36	5	6
Europe	**1,656**	**61**	**148**	**205**	**121**	**118**	**128**	**236**	**290**	**176**	**173**
Portugal	279	2	2	4	25	11	20	24	88	33	70
Spain	1,377	59	146	201	96	107	108	212	202	143	103

[a] Fiscal years. Including deliveries under the following programs: (1) Military Assistance Program grants under the various Mutual Security Acts; (2) Foreign Military Sales, which consist of U.S.-financed arms, U.S.-guaranteed private arms credits, and U.S.-approved commercial sales; and (3) Military assistance excess stocks, which involved surplus equipment that has been valued at 33% of the original acquisition value.

Source: *Handbook of Economic Statistics*, 1985 Central Intelligence Agency

---

4. Communist Military Aid to Less Developed Countries, Extensions and Drawings
(Million U.S. $)

	Total		USSR		Eastern Europe		China	
	Extended	Drawn	Extended	Drawn	Extended	Drawn	Extended	Drawn
Total	114,515	92,865	94,470	76,465	12,340	10,450	7,710	5,950
1954-74	21,530	15,450	18,910	13,520	2,010	1,450	605	480
1975	3,860	2,410	3,185	2,035	635	275	40	100
1976	6,640	3,560	6,140	3,110	355	350	145	100
1977	10,370	5,245	9,645	4,815	650	355	75	75
1978	3,485	6,720	2,700	6,075	560	550	225	95
1979	9,775	9,085	8,835	8,340	750	645	195	100
1980	16,450	9,020	14,635	8,125	870	635	945	260
1981	12,025	9,830	6,505	8,105	2,560	1,315	2,965	410
1982	15,135	10,880	11,765	8,065	1,795	1,970	1,575	845
1983	5,075	9,780	2,995	7,130	1,310	1,060	770	1,590
1984	10,165	10,880	9,155	7,135	845	1,845	165	1,900

Source: *Handbook of Economic Statistics*, 1985
Central Intelligence Agency

5. Value of Arms Transfers, Cumulative 1979-1983 by Major Supplier and Recipient Region

(billion current dollars)

Area of circles (suppliers) and squares (recipients) is proportional to cost of arms transferred or received.

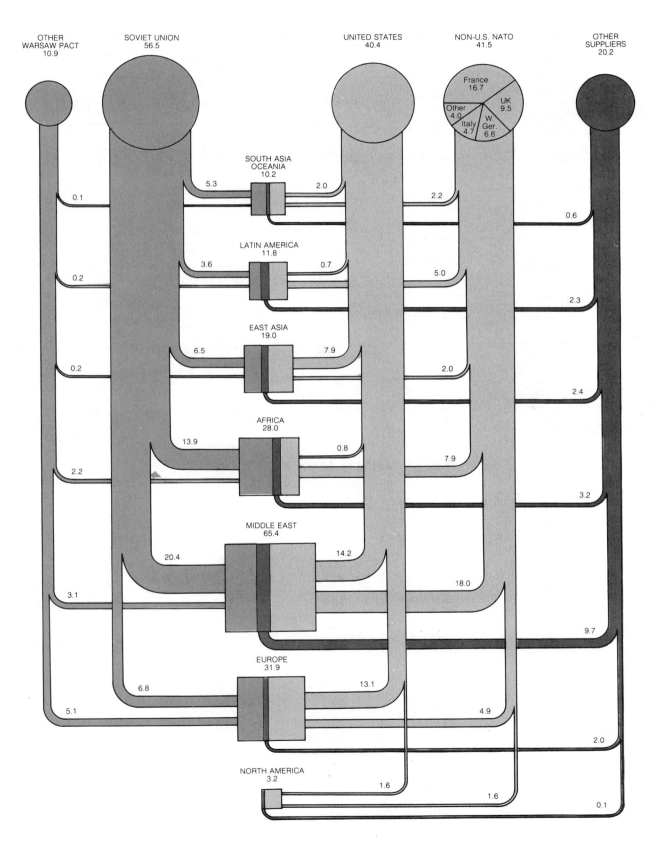

OTHER WARSAW PACT 10.9
SOVIET UNION 56.5
UNITED STATES 40.4
NON-U.S. NATO 41.5
OTHER SUPPLIERS 20.2

France 16.7
Other 4.0
UK 9.5
Italy 4.7
W. Ger. 6.6

SOUTH ASIA OCEANIA 10.2
LATIN AMERICA 11.8
EAST ASIA 19.0
AFRICA 28.0
MIDDLE EAST 65.4
EUROPE 31.9
NORTH AMERICA 3.2

6. Military Expenditures by Region, 1973-1983

In Billions of Constant 1982 Dollars

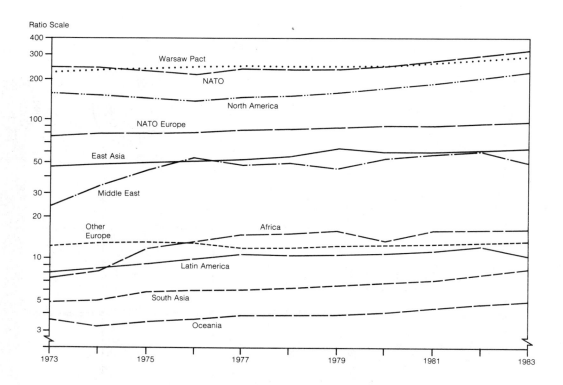

7. Shares of World's Arms Imports, 1983

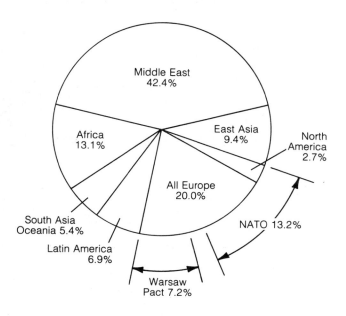

8. World Military Expenditures, 1973-1985

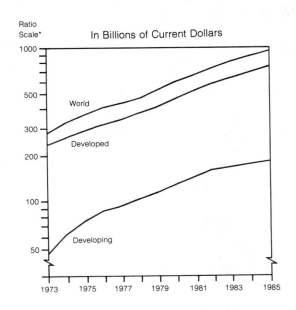

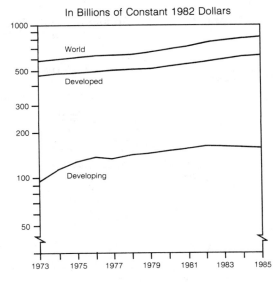

*On a ratio (or semi-log) scale, an equal slope anywhere on the chart means an equal growth rate.

---

9. Arms Exports
(In percent)

	World Share		Real Growth Rate*	
	1973	**1983**	**1973-83**	**1980-83**
World:	100.00	100.0	5.8	1.0
Developed	97.7	88.9	4.7	−1.5
Developing	2.3	11.1	23.4	31.8
Region:				
Africa	0.0	0.2	28.3[a]	104.8
East Asia	1.8	6.3	23.2	38.2
Europe, all	56.3	60.2	7.8	−4.6
NATO Europe	13.8	24.6	12.6	−1.3
Warsaw Pact	42.9	31.8	4.9	−7.6
Other Europe	0.7	4.3	8.8	5.8
Latin America	0.1	0.4	8.9[b]	1.3
Middle East	0.2	0.8	10.7	12.2
North America	40.3	30.4	0.4	9.7
Oceania	0.1	0.1	7.1	−12.5
South Asia	0.0	0.8	18.4	60.8
Organization:				
NATO, all	54.2	55.0	4.4	4.0
Warsaw Pact	42.9	31.8	4.8	−7.6
OPEC	0.0	0.3	9.2	23.1
OECD	54.9	59.1	4.8	4.2

*Average real growth is calculated from data in constant 1982 dollars as a compound rate and fitted to all years.

[a]1975-1983

[b]1974-1983

APPENDIX XVI: EDUCATION

1. Estimated Total Enrollment and Teaching Staff by Level of Education

(% 1970–75 and 1975–83 = Annual average increase in enrollment and teaching staff from 1970 to 1975 and from 1975 to 1983, as percentage)

CONTINENTS, MAJOR AREAS AND GROUPS OF COUNTRIES	YEAR	ENROLLMENT (THOUSANDS)				TEACHING STAFF (THOUSANDS)			
		TOTAL	1ST LEVEL	2ND LEVEL	3RD LEVEL	TOTAL	1ST LEVEL	2ND LEVEL	3RD LEVEL
WORLD TOTAL‡	1970	622 185	433 287	160 719	28 179	25 538	14 329	9 073	2 136
	1975	763 978	517 162	207 197	39 619	32 579	18 184	11 506	2 890
	1980	847 634	558 465	241 984	47 185	37 708	19 929	14 149	3 631
	1982	863 400	568 936	244 251	50 213	39 110	20 809	14 419	3 883
	1983	873 795	572 140	250 143	51 513	39 757	21 007	14 765	3 984
	% 1970–75	4.2	3.6	5.2	7.1	5.0	4.9	4.9	6.2
	% 1975–83	1.7	1.3	2.4	3.3	2.5	1.8	3.2	4.1
AFRICA	1970	38 723	33 360	4 881	483	1 075	816	224	36
	1975	54 168	44 623	8 645	900	1 595	1 177	361	57
	1980	79 566	63 256	14 941	1 368	2 438	1 714	632	93
	1982	88 950	69 439	17 936	1 574	2 841	1 962	765	114
	1983	92 338	71 319	19 339	1 680	2 992	2 050	819	123
	% 1970–75	6.9	6.0	12.1	13.3	8.2	7.6	10.0	9.6
	% 1975–83	6.9	6.0	10.6	8.1	8.2	7.2	10.8	10.1
AMERICA‡	1970	119 422	77 728	30 914	10 780	5 399	2 779	1 845	775
	1975	136 886	88 011	33 225	15 649	6 586	3 640	1 918	1 028
	1980	146 656	94 444	34 396	17 816	7 402	3 755	2 338	1 308
	1982	150 748	96 560	35 488	18 700	7 632	3 855	2 388	1 389
	1983	152 808	97 439	36 357	19 012	7 698	3 845	2 434	1 418
	% 1970–75	2.8	2.5	1.5	7.7	4.1	5.5	0.8	5.8
	% 1975–83	1.4	1.3	1.1	2.5	2.0	0.7	3.0	4.1
ASIA‡	1970	324 457	243 384	74 186	6 886	11 033	6 981	3 483	569
	1975	427 586	311 546	105 762	10 278	15 595	9 717	5 094	785
	1980	477 675	330 607	133 240	13 828	18 745	10 740	6 967	1 038
	1982	480 272	333 408	131 517	15 348	19 426	11 241	7 033	1 151
	1983	485 547	334 325	135 186	16 037	19 806	11 382	7 232	1 192
	% 1970–75	5.7	5.1	7.3	8.3	7.2	6.8	7.9	6.6
	% 1975–83	1.6	0.9	3.1	5.7	3.0	2.0	4.5	5.4
EUROPE (INC USSR)	1970	135 396	76 226	49 364	9 806	7 849	3 658	3 449	742
	1975	140 786	70 408	57 939	12 439	8 564	3 537	4 035	992
	1980	138 962	67 455	57 752	13 756	8 855	3 593	4 100	1 162
	1982	138 613	66 861	57 600	14 152	8 941	3 626	4 115	1 200
	1983	138 238	66 432	57 475	14 331	8 986	3 609	4 158	1 220
	% 1970–75	0.8	–1.6	3.3	4.9	1.8	–0.7	3.2	6.0
	% 1975–83	–0.2	–0.7	–0.1	1.8	0.6	0.3	0.4	2.6
OCEANIA	1970	4 188	2 590	1 374	224	183	96	72	15
	1975	4 553	2 573	1 627	353	238	112	98	28
	1980	4 776	2 704	1 655	417	268	126	112	30
	1982	4 818	2 668	1 710	439	270	124	117	29
	1983	4 864	2 625	1 786	452	276	122	123	31
	% 1970–75	1.7	–0.1	3.4	9.5	5.4	3.1	6.4	13.3
	% 1975–83	0.8	0.3	1.2	3.1	1.9	1.1	2.9	1.3
DEVELOPED COUNTRIES	1970	227 301	126 079	80 099	21 123	12 239	5 624	5 076	1 539
	1975	236 607	119 594	89 792	27 221	13 588	5 841	5 792	1 955
	1980	232 902	115 882	87 226	29 794	14 269	5 873	6 053	2 343
	1982	233 674	115 483	87 546	30 645	14 391	5 904	6 058	2 429
	1983	233 090	114 601	87 523	30 966	14 451	5 871	6 119	2 461
	% 1970–75	0.8	–1.1	2.3	5.2	2.1	0.8	2.7	4.9
	% 1975–83	–0.2	–0.5	–0.3	1.6	0.8	0.1	0.7	2.9
DEVELOPING COUNTRIES‡	1970	394 884	307 208	80 620	7 056	13 299	8 705	3 997	597
	1975	527 371	397 568	117 405	12 398	18 991	12 343	5 714	935
	1980	614 732	442 583	154 758	17 391	23 439	14 056	8 096	1 288
	1982	629 726	453 453	156 705	19 568	24 719	14 905	8 361	1 454
	1983	640 705	457 539	162 620	20 547	25 306	15 136	8 646	1 523
	% 1970–75	6.0	5.3	7.8	11.9	7.4	7.2	7.4	9.4
	% 1975–83	2.5	1.8	4.2	6.5	3.7	2.6	5.3	6.3
AFRICA (EXCLUDING ARAB STATES)	1970	26 948	24 320	2 446	183	717	582	118	17
	1975	38 394	33 315	4 778	300	1 093	867	201	25
	1980	59 395	49 739	9 132	524	1 710	1 304	364	42
	1982	66 572	54 793	11 147	632	2 006	1 507	446	54
	1983	68 989	56 196	12 111	682	2 100	1 568	474	58
	% 1970–75	7.3	6.5	14.3	10.4	8.8	8.3	11.2	8.0
	% 1975–83	7.6	6.8	12.3	10.8	8.5	7.7	11.3	11.1

1. Estimated Total Enrollment and Teaching Staff
by Level of Education (continued)

(% 1970–75 and 1975–83 = Annual average increase in enrollment and teaching staff from 1970 to 1975 and from 1975 to 1983, as percentage)

CONTINENTS, MAJOR AREAS AND GROUPS OF COUNTRIES	YEAR	ENROLLMENT (THOUSANDS)				TEACHING STAFF (THOUSANDS)			
		TOTAL	1ST LEVEL	2ND LEVEL	3RD LEVEL	TOTAL	1ST LEVEL	2ND LEVEL	3RD LEVEL
ASIA (EXCLUDING ARAB STATES)‡	1970	319 661	239 843	73 075	6 742	10 838	6 849	3 426	562
	1975	420 184	306 247	103 931	10 006	15 276	9 510	4 994	772
	1980	467 249	323 513	130 356	13 380	18 280	10 461	6 809	1 010
	1982	468 948	325 787	128 320	14 842	18 889	10 925	6 846	1 119
	1983	473 624	326 314	131 805	14 505	19 229	11 042	7 029	1 158
	% 1970–75	5.6	5.0	7.3	8.2	7.1	6.8	7.8	6.6
	% 1975–83	1.5	0.8	3.0	5.6	2.9	1.9	4.4	5.2
ARAB STATES	1970	16 571	12 581	3 547	444	553	365	163	25
	1975	23 176	16 608	5 697	871	822	517	260	45
	1980	30 597	20 612	8 693	1 292	1 194	690	426	78
	1982	33 701	22 266	9 986	1 449	1 371	772	507	92
	1983	35 272	23 133	10 608	1 530	1 469	822	548	99
	%1970–75	6.9	5.7	9.9	14.4	8.3	7.2	9.8	12.5
	% 1975–83	5.4	4.2	8.1	7.3	7.5	6.0	9.8	10.4
NORTHERN AMERICA	1970	63 137	33 745	20 252	9 140	3 085	1 415	1 055	615
	1975	64 438	31 748	20 687	12 003	3 449	1 618	1 110	722
	1980	59 510	29 640	16 885	12 986	3 647	1 510	1 225	912
	1982	59 553	29 689	16 449	13 415	3 587	1 477	1 163	947
	1983	59 108	29 458	16 129	13 522	3 580	1 466	1 161	952
	% 1970–75	0.4	−1.2	0.4	5.6	2.3	2.7	1.0	3.3
	% 1975–83	−1.1	−0.9	−3.1	1.5	0.5	−1.2	0.6	3.5
LATIN AMERICAN AND THE CARIBBEAN‡	1970	56 285	43 983	10 662	1 640	2 314	1 363	791	160
	1975	72 448	56 264	12 538	3 646	3 137	2 022	809	306
	1980	87 145	64 804	17 511	4 830	3 754	2 245	1 114	396
	1982	91 195	66 871	19 039	5 285	4 045	2 379	1 225	442
	1983	93 700	67 981	20 229	5 490	4 118	2 379	1 273	466
	% 1970–75	5.2	5.0	3.3	17.3	6.3	8.2	0.5	13.8
	% 1975–83	3.3	2.4	6.2	5.2	3.5	2.1	5.8	5.4

APPENDIX XVII: A BASIC BIBLIOGRAPHY OF THE THIRD WORLD (from 1970)

I: General

Abraham, M. Francis, Perspectives of Modernization: Toward a General Theory of Third World Development (Washington, D.C., 1980)

Agarwala, Amar N. and S. P. Singh, Economics of Underdevelopment (New York, 1963)

Alberry, Nicholas, How to Save the World: A Fourth World Guide to the Politics of Scale (North Hollywood, Calif., 1984)

Alpert, Paul, Partnership or Confrontation? Poor Lands & Rich (New York, 1973)

Angelopoulos, Angelo, Third World & the Rich Countries: Prospects for the Year 2000 (New York, 1972)

Asher, Robert E., Development of the Emerging Countries: An Agenda for Research (Washington D.C., 1962)

Austin, Dennis, The Third World: Premises of U.S. Policy (San Francisco, 1978)

Ayoob, Mohadded, Conflict & Intervention in the Third World (New York, 1980)

Bagchi, Amiya K., The Political Economy of Underdevelopment (New York, 1982)

Barlow, Christopher, The Third World (London, 1979)

Bauer, Peter T., Economic Analysis & Policy in Underdeveloped Countries (Durham, N.C., 1957)

Beling, Willard A., & George O. Totten, Developing Nations: A Quest for a Model (New York, 1970)

Bertram, Christoph, Third World Conflict and International Security (Hamden, Conn., 1982)

Bhagwati, Jagdish, Economics of Underdeveloped Countries (New York, 1966)

———, The New International Economic Order: The North-South Debate (Boston, Mass., 1977)

Bosson Rex & Bension Varon, The Mining Industry and the Developing Countries (New York, 1977)

Brand, W., The Struggle for a Higher Standard of Living: The Problem of the Underdeveloped Countries (The Hague, 1958)

Bryant, John, Health & the Developing World (Ithaca, N.Y., 1969)

Butwell, Richard, Foreign Policy & the Developing Nations (Louisville, Ky., 1969)

Cassen, Robert and Richard Jolly, Rich Country Interests and Third World Development (New York, 1982)

Chatterji, Manas, Spatial, Environmental and Resource Policy in the Developing Countries (London, 1984)

Chau, T. N., Population Growth & Costs of Education in Developing Countries (Paris, 1972)

Clinard, Marshall B., and Daniel J. Abbott, Crime in Developing Countries: A Comparative Perspective (New York, 1973)

Cook, W.D. and W.D. Kuhn, Planning Processes in Developing Countries: Techniques and Achievements (New York, 1982)

Cooper, Charles, Science, Technology & Development: Political Economy of Technical Advance in Underdeveloped Countries (Totowa, N.J., 1973)

Crow, Ben, Third World Atlas (London, 1984)

DeSouza, A. R., & P. W. Porter, The Underdevelopment & Modernization of the Third World (New York, 1974)

Dickenson, J.P. and C.G. Clarke, A Geography of the Third World (London, 1983)

Eeinberg, Richard E. and Valerina Kallab, Adjustment Crisis in the Third World (New Brunswick, N.J., 1984)

Elliott, Dave, Imperialism & Underdevelopment (Belfast, Me., 1978)

Fenton, Thomas P. and Mary J. Heffron, Third World Resource Directory (Maryknoll, N.Y., 1984)

Franck, Thomas M., Human Rights in Third World Perspective (Dobbs Ferry, N.Y., 1982)

Gamer, Robert E., Developing Nations: A Comparative Perspective (Boston, 1982)

Gauhar, Altaf, Third World Affairs (Boulder, Colo., 1985)

Gavin, Kitching, Development and Underdevelopment in Historical Perspective (London, 1982)

George, Susan, How the Other Half Dies: The Real Reasons for World Hunger (New York, 1977)

Gheddo, Piero, Why is the Third World Poor? (Maryknoll, N.Y., 1973)

Ghosh, Pradip K., Energy Policy and Third World Development (Westport, Conn., 1984)

———, Urban Development in the Third World (Westport, Conn., 1984)

Girling, J. S., America & the Third World (London, 1980)

Goonatilake, Susantha, Aborted Discovery: Science and Creativity in the Third World (London, 1984)

Grigg, David, Harsh Lands: A Study in Agricultural Development *(New York, 1970)*

Haq, Mahbub L., The Poverty Curtain: Choices for the Third World (New York, 1976)

Harrington, Michael, The Vast Majority (New York, 1977)

Heeger, Gerald, The Politics of Underdevelopment (New York, 1974)

Hermassi, Elbaki, The Third World Reassessed (Berkeley, Calif., 1980)

Hoogvelt, Ankje M. M., The Sociology of Developing Societies (New York, 1977)

————, Third World in Global Development (London, 1982)

Horton, Philip C., The Third World & Press Freedom (New York, 1978)

Howe, Charles W., Managing Renewable Natural Resources in Developing Countries (Boulder, Colo., 1982)

Hugo, Graeme J., Population, Mobility and Wealth Transfers in Indonesia and other Third World Societies (Honolulu, 1983)

Hursh-Cesar, Gerald and Prodipto Roy, Third World Surveys: Survey Research in Developing Countries (Columbia, Mo., 1976)

Hutchinson, Joseph, The Challenge of the Third World (New York, 1975)

Jacobson, Staffan and Jon Sigurdson, Technological Trends and Challenges in Electronic Dominance of the Industrialized World and Responses in the Third World (Croton-on-Hudson, N.Y., 1983)

Jalee, Pierre, Pillage of the Third World (New York, 1968)

Jankowitsch, Odette and Karl P. Sauvant, The Third World Without Superpowers: Basic Documents of the Nonaligned Countries (Dobbs Ferry, N.Y., 1978)

Jayawardena, Kumari, Feminism and Nationalism in the Third World (London, 1985)

Jha, L.K., South-South Debate (Atlantic Highlands, N.J., 1982)

Jones, Gavin, Population Growth & Educational Planning in Developing Nations (New York, 1975)

Jud, Gustav D., Inflation & the Use of Indexing in Developing Countries (New York, 1978)

Kalecki, Michal, Essays on Developing Economies (New York, 1976)

Kamrany, Nake, The New Economics of the Less Developed Countries (Boulder, Col., 1978)

Kautsky, John H., Political Change in Underdeveloped Countries (New York, 1976)

Kollontai, U. M., Industrialization of Developing Countries (New York, 1975)

Kurian, George T., Atlas of the Third World (New York, 1983)

Kursunglu, Behram and Arnold Perlmutter, Energy for Developed and Developing Countries (Lexington, Mass., 1983)

Laswell, Harold D., Values & Development: Appraising Asian Development (Boston, 1977)

Looney, Robert E., Saudi Arabia's Development Potential: Application of an Islamic Growth Model (Lexington, Mass., 1981)

Loup, Jacques, Can the Third World Survive? (Baltimore, 1983)

Lowenthal, Richar, Model or Ally? The Communist Powers & the Developing Countries (New York, 1976)

Macesich, George, The International Monetary Economy and the Third World (New York, 1981)

Madan, B. K., Economic Problems of Underdeveloped Countries in Asia (New York, 1967)

Mandelbaum, K., Industrialization of Backward Areas (New York, 1955)

Marcussen, Henrik and Jens Torp, The Internationalization of Capital (London, 1982)

Marton, Imre, Contribution to a Critique of an Interpretation of Specific Third World Traits (New York, 1978)

Mason, Edward S., Economic Planning in Underdeveloped Areas (New York, 1958)

McDonald, John W., The North-South Dialogue and the United Nations (Washington, D.C. 1982)

Melady, Thomas and Robert Suhartono, Development Lessons for the Future (Maryknoll, N.Y., 1973)

Menon, B. P., Bridges Across the South: Technical Cooperation Among Developing Countries (Elmsford, N.Y., 1980)

Mezerik, Avrahm G., Disarmament: Impacts on Underdeveloped Countries (New York, 1961)

Moavenzadeh, F. and D. Gelner, Transportation, Energy and Economic Development: A Dilemma in the Developing World (New York, 1984)

Morgan, W. B., Agriculture in the Third World: A Spatial Analysis (Boulder, Col., 1978)

Mortimer, Robert A., The Third World Coalition in International Politics (New York, 1980)

Mountjoy, Alan B., The Third World: Problems & Perspectives (New York, 1979)

Murdoch, William W., The Poverty of Nations: The Political Economy of Hunger & Population (Baltimore, Md., 1981)

Murray, Tracy, Trade Preferences for Developing Countries (New York, 1977)

Mushkat, Marion, The Third World and Peace (New York, 1983).

Myrdal, Gunnar, Challenge of World Poverty: A World Poverty Program in Outline (New York, 1970)

Nader, Claire and A. B. Zahlan, Science & Technology in Developing Countries (New York, 1969)

Nair, Bhaskaran, Mass Media and the Transnational Corporation: A Study of Media-Corporate Relationship and its Consequences in the Third World (Athens, Ohio, 1981)

Nash, Manning, Golden Road to Modernity (Chicago, 1973)

Neufeld, Maurice F., Poor Countries & Authoritarian Rule (New York, 1965)

Noguera, Alberto, Third World (New York, 1968)

Offiong, Daniel O., Imperialism and Dependency: Obstacles to African Development (Washington, D.C. 1982)

O'Flynn, Grainne, World Survival: The Third World Struggle (Dublin, 1984)

Okolie, Charles, International Law & the Developing Countries (New York, 1978)

Paige, Jeffrey M., Agrarian Revolution: Social Movements & Exporting Agriculture in the Underdeveloped World (New York, 1978)

Papp, Daniel S., Soviet Perceptions of the Developing World During the 1980s: The Ideological Basis (Lexington, Mass., 1985)

Pincus, John, Economic Aid & International Cost Sharing (Baltimore, Md., 1965)

Plischke, Elmer, Microstates in World Affairs (Washington, D.C., 1977)

Radian, Alex, Resource Mobilization in Poor Countries: Implementing Tax Policies (New Brunswick, N.J., 1980)

Ranis, Gustav, The United States & the Developing Economies (New York, 1973)

Rao, D.V., Dimensions of Backwardness (Atlantic Highlands, N.J., 1981)

Retisma, H.A. and J.M. Kleinpenning, The Third World in Perspective (Totowa, N.J., 1985)

Rhee, Kyu H., Struggle for National Identity in the Third World (Elizabeth, N.J., 1983)

Rhodes, Robert I., Imperialism & Underdevelopment: A Reader (New York, 1971)

Richardson, Neil R., Foreign Policy & Economic Dependence (Austin, Tex., 1978)

Righter, Rosemary, Whose News? Politics, the Press & the Third World (New York, 1978)

Robinson, Joan, Aspects of Development & Underdevelopment (New York, 1979)

Roxborough, Ian, Theories of Underdevelopment (New York, 1979)

Schramm, Wilbur, Mass Media & National Development: The Role of Information in the Developing Countries (Stanford, Calif., 1964)

Sewell, John W., The United States & World Development: Agenda (New York, 1977)

Sfeir-Younis, Alfredo and Daniel W. Bromley, Decision Making in Developing Countries (New York, 1977)

Silverman, Milton and Philip R. Lee, Prescription for Death: The Drugging of the Third World (Berkeley, Calif., 1986)

Singer, H. W., The Strategy of International Development: Essays in the Economics of Backwardness (White Plains, N.Y., 1975)

——, **and Javed A. Ansari,** Rich & Poor Countries (Baltimore, Md., 1977)

Singh, Jyoti, A New International Economic Order: Toward a Fair Redistribution of the World's Resources (New York, 1977)

Singh, K. R., State & Industrilization of Developing Countries (Mystic, Conn., 1969)

Skorov, G. E., Science, Technology & Economic Growth in the Developing Countries (Elmsford, N.Y., 1978)

Smil, V., and W. E. Knowland, Energy in the Developing World (New York, 1980)

Smith, Anthony, The Geopolitics of Information: How Western Culture Dominates the World (New York, 1980)

Stamper, B. Maxwell, Population & Planning in Developing Nations (New York, 1977)

Stavrianos, L.S., Global Rift: The Third World Comes of Age (New York, 1981)

Stevens, Christopher, EEC and the Third World: A Survey (New York, 1983)

Stewart, Francis, Basic Needs in Developing Countries (Baltimore, Md., 1985)

Stockholm International Peace Research Institute, Arms Trade with the Third World (New York, 1975)

Stremlau, John J., Foreign Policy Priorities of Third World States (Boulder, Colo., 1982)

Sussman, Leonard D., Mass News Media & the Third World Challenge (Beverly Hills, Calif., 1977)

Tanzer, Michael, Political Economy of International Oil & the Underdeveloped Countries (Boston, 1970)

Thompson, Carol L., The Current History Encyclopedia of Developing Nations (New York, 1982)

Timmer, C. Peter, The Choice of Technology in Developing Countries: Some Cautionary Tales (Cambridge, Mass., 1975)

Tinker, Irene, Women & World Development (New York, 1976)

Todaro, Michael P., Economic Development in the Third World (New York, 1977)

Tulchin, Joseph S., Habitat, Health and Development: A New Way of Looking at Cities in the Third World. (Boulder, Colo., 1985).

Turner, Louis, Multinational Companies & the Third World (New York, 1973)

Uri, Pierre, Development Without Dependence (New York, 1976)

Vasil, Raj K., Politics in Bi-Racial Societies: The Third World Experience (New Delhi, 1983)

Vogeler, Ingolf, and Anthony De Souza, Dialectics of Third World Development (New York, 1980)

Ward, Barbara, Lopsided World (New York, 1968)

——, Rich Nations & Poor Nations (New York, 1962)

——, Widening Gap: Development in the 1970's (New York, 1971)

Weiss, Thomas G. and Anthony Jennings, More for the Least? Prospects for Poorer Countries in the 1980s (Lexington, Mass., 1982)

World Bank, Assault on World Poverty: Problems of Rural Development, Education & Health (Baltimore, Md., 1975)

——, Landsat Index Atlas of the Developing Countries of the World (Baltimore, Md., 1976)

Worthington, F. Barton, Arid Land Irrigation in Developing Countries: Environmental Problems & Effects (Elmsford, N.Y., 1977)

Wriggins, W. Howard and Gunnar Adler-Karlsson, Reducing Global Inequalities (New York, 1978)

Zimmerman, Louis, Poor Lands, Rich Lands: The Widening Gap (Philadephia, Pa., 1975)

II: Agriculture

Agribusiness Council, Agriculture Initiative in the Third World (Lexington, Mass., 1975)

Brenner, Y. S., Agriculture & the Economic Development of Low Income Countries (The Hague, 1972)

De Vylder, Stephan, Agriculture in Chains: A Case Study of Contradictions and Constraints (London, 1981)

Eicher, Karl K. and John M. Staatz, Agricultural Development in the Third World (Baltimore, Md., 1984)

Ghatak, Subrata and Kenneth A. Ingersent, Agriculture and Economic Development (Baltimore, Md., 1984)

Ghose, Ajit K., Agrarian Reform in Contemporary Developing Countries (New York, 1983)

Graham, G.E. and Ingrid Floering, The Modern Plantations in the Third World (New York, 1984)

Hanson, Haldore and Norman Borlaug, Wheat in the Third World (Boulder, Colo., 1982)

Kiss, Judith, Agricultural Development Strategy in the Developing Countries (New York, 1979)

Molnar, Joseph J. and Howard A. Clonts, Transferring Food Production Technologies to Developing Nations: Economic and Social Dimensions (Boulder, Colo., 1983)

Mukhoti, Bela and Bruce F. Johnston, Agriculture and Employment in Developing Countries (Boulder, Colo., 1985)

Scandizzo, Pasquale L., Agricultural Growth and Factor Production in Developing Countries (New York, 1985)

Tolley, George S., Agricultural Price Policies and the Developing Countries (Baltimore, Md., 1982)

Torun, Benjamin and Vernon R. Young, Protein-Energy Requirements of Developing Countries: Evaluation of New Data (New York, 1981)

Weir, David and Mark Schapiro, The Circle of Poison: Pesticides and People in a Hungry World (San Francisco, Calif., 1981)

III: Commerce

Adams, F. Gerard and Jere R. Behrman, Commodity Exports and Economic Development (Lexington, Mass., 1982)

Akinsanya, Adeoye, Multinationals in a Changing Environment: A Study of Business and Government Relations in the Third World (New York, 1984)

Amsalem, Michel A., Technology Choice in Developing Countries (Cambridge, Mass., 1983)

Balassa, Bela and Associates, The Structure of Protection in Developing Countries (Baltimore, Md., 1971)

Ballance R., The International Economy and Industrial Development, Trade and Investment in the Third World (London, 1982)

Barwell, I., Rural Transport in Developing Countries (Boulder, Colo., 1985)

Cline, William R., Exports of Manufactures from Developing Countries (Washington, D.C. 1984)

Corbo, Vittorio and Anne Kreuger, Export-Oriented Development Strategies: The Success of Five Newly Industrializing Countries (Boulder, Colo., 1985)

Frank, Charles R., Assisting Developing Countries: Problems of Debts, Problem-Sharing, Jobs & Trade (New York, 1972)

Frank, Isaiah, Trade Policy Issues for the Developing Countries in the 1980s (Washington, D.C. 1981)

General Agreement on Tariffs & Trade, Adjustment, Trade & Growth in Developed and Developing Countries (New York, 1979)

Ghosh, Pradip K., International Trade and Third World Development (Wesport, Conn., 1984)

Goodman, Stephen H., Financing & Risk in Developing Countries (New York, 1978)

Havrylyshyn, O and Martin Wolf, Trade Among Developing Countries (Washington, D.C. 1981)

James, Jeffrey, Consumer Choice in the Third World: A Study of the Welfare Effects of Advertising and New Products in a Developing Country (New York, 1983)

Jasperson, Frederick, Adjustment Experience and Growth Prospects of Semi-Industrial Countries (Washington, D.C. 1981)

Kaplinsky, Raphael, Third World Industrialization in the 1980s: Open Economies in a Closing World (London, 1984)

Katz, James E., Arms Production in Developing Countries: An Analysis of Decision Making (Lexington, Mass., 1983)

Kaynak, Erdener, Marketing in the Third World (New York, 1982)

Kindra, Gurprit, Marketing in Developing Countries (New York, 1984)

Kumar, Krishna and Maxwell G. McLeod, Multinationals from Developing Countries (Lexington, Mass., 1981)

Morton, K., and P. Tulloch, Trade & Developing Countries (New York, 1977)

Negandhi, Anant R., and Benjamin S. Prasad, The Frightening Angels: A Study of U.S. Multinationals in Developing Nations (Kent, Ohio., 1975)

OECD, The Development Impact of Barter in Developing Countries (Brussels, 1979)

———— **and Charles Oman,** New Forms of International Investment in Developing Countries (Paris, 1984)

Padolecchia, S. P., Marketing in the Developing World (Totowa, N.J., 1980)

Ramachandran, H., Behavior in Space: Rural Marketing in an Underdeveloped Economy (Bombay, 1982)

Schmitz, Hubert, Technology and Employment Practices in Developing Countries (London, 1985)

Yeats, Alexander J., Trade Barriers Facing Developing Countries (New York, 1979)

IV: Economic Conditions

Afxentiou, Panayiotis C., Patterns of Government Revenue & Expenditure in Developing Countries & Their Relevance to Policy (New York, 1979)

Alvarez, Francisco C., New Horizons for the Third World (New York, 1976)

Anell, Lars and Birgitta Nygren, The Developing Countries & World Economic Order (New York, 1980)

Bairoch, Paul, The Economic Development of the Third World Since 1900 (Berkeley, Calif., 1975)

————, Urban Unemployment in Developing Countries (Geneva, 1976)

Balassa, Bela, Policy Reform in Developing Countries (Elmsford, N.Y., 1977)

————, Adjustment to External Shocks in the Developing Countries (Washington, D.C. 1981)

Barnes, Stanley, Two Hundred Million Hungry Children (London, 1982)

Bauer, P.T., Equality, the Third World and Economic Delusion (Cambridge, Mass., 1983)

Berger, Peter L., Pyramids of Sacrifice: Political Ethics & Social Change (New York, 1975)

Berry, Leonard, & Robert W. Kates, Making the Most of the Least: Alternative Development for Poor Nations (New York, 1980)

Bird, Richard and Oliver Oldman, Readings on Taxation in Developing Countries (Baltimore, Md., 1975)

Bornschier, Volker and Christopher Chase-Dunn, Multinational Corporations and Underdevelopment (New York, 1985)

Bromely, Ray and Chris Jerry, Casual Work & Poverty in Third World Cities (New York, 1979)

Bryant, Coralie and Louise G. White, Managing Development in the Third World (Boulder, Colo., 1982)

Caiden, Naomi and Aaron Wildavsky, Planning & Budgeting in Poor Countries (New York, 1974)

Cheema, B. Shabbir, Reaching the Urban Poor: Project Implementation in Developing Countries (Boulder, Colo., 1985)

————, **and Dennis A. Rondinelli,** Decentralization and Development Policy Implementation in Developing Countries (Beverly Hills, Calif., 1983)

Cleveland, Harlan, Energy Futures of Developing Countries: The Neglected Victims of the Energy Crisis (New York, 1980)

Cline, William R., International Monetary Reform & the Developing Countries (Washington, D.C., 1976)

————, World Inflation and the Developing Countries (Washington, D.C. 1981)

————, **and Sidney Weintraub,** Economic Stabilization in Developing Countries (Washington, D.C. 1981)

Cobbe, James, Government & Mining Companies in Developing Countries (Boulder, Co., 1979)

Cohen, Robin, Peasants & Proletarians: The Struggles of Third World Workers (New York, 1979)

Cole, John The Poor of the Earth (Boulder, Co., 1976)

Cole, J.P., The Development Gaps: Spatial Analysis of World Poverty and Inequality (New York, 1981)

Colman, David and Fred Nixson, Economics of Change in Less Developed Countries (New York, 1985)

Currie, Lauchlin, The Role of Economic Advisors in Developing Countries (Westport, Conn., 1981)

Dasgupta, A. K., Economic Theory & the Developing Countries (New York, 1975)

Dayal, I. and A.K. Dayal, Organization for Management in Developing Countries (Bombay, 1983)

De Kadt, Emanuel, Tourism—Passport to Development? Perspectives on the Social & Cultural Effects of Tourism in Developing Countries (New York, 1979)

Denoon, Donald, Settler Capitalism: The Dynamics of Dependent Development in the Southern Hemisphere (New York, 1983)

De Silva, S.B., The Political Economy of Underdevelopment (London, 1982)

Dube, S.C., Development Perspectives for the 1980s (Atlantic Highlands, N.J. 1982)

Eicher, Karl K. and John M. Staatz, Agricultural Development in the Third World (Baltimore, Md., 1984)

Elyanov, A., Economic Growth and the Market in the Developing Countries (Moscow, 1982)

Enthoven, A. J., Accountancy Systems in Third World Economies (New York, 1977)

Erb, Guy F., and Valeriana Kallab, Beyond Dependency: The Developing World Speaks Out (New York, 1975)

Ernst, Dieter, The New International Division of Labor, Technology and Underdevelopment: Consequences for the Third World (New York, 1982)

Eshag, Eprime, Fiscal and Monetary Policies and Problems in Developing Countries (New York, 1984)

Espiritu, Augusto C. and Reginald H. Green, The International Context of Rural Poverty in the Third World (Croton-on-the-Hudson, N.Y., 1985)

Euh, Yoon-Dae, Commercial Banks & the Creditworthiness of Less Developed Countries (Ann Arbor, Mich., 1979)

Forbes, Dean K., The Geography of Underdevelopment (Baltimore, Md., 1985)

Frank, Charles R., and Richard C. Webb, Income Distribution & Growth in the Less Developed Countries (Washington, D.C., 1977)

Gauhar, Altaf, Third World Strategy: Economic and Political Cohesion in the South (New York, 1983)

Germidis, Dimitri and Charles Michalet, International Banks and Financial Markets in Developing Countries (Paris, 1984)

Ghosh, Pradip K., Development Cooperation and Third World Development (Westport, Conn., 1984)

————, Development Policy and Planning: A Third World Perspective (Westport, Conn., 1984)

————, Economic Integration and Third World Development (Westport, Conn., 1984)

————, Economic Policy and Planning in Third World Development (Westport, Conn., 1984)

———, Health, Food and Nutrition in Third World Development (Westport, Conn., 1984)

———, Industrialization and Development: A Third World Perspective (Westport, Conn., 1984)

———, New International Economic Order: A Third World Perspective (Wesport, Conn., 1984)

———, Third World Development: A Basic Needs Approach (Westport, Conn., 1984)

Gulhati, Ravi and Uday Sekhar, Industrial Strategy for Late Starters: The Experience of Kenya, Tanzania and Zambia (Washington, D.C. 1981)

Gupta K.L., Finance and Economic Growth in Developing Countries (London, 1984)

Hansen, Harald, The Developing Countries and International Shipping (Washington, D.C. 1981)

Harvey, Charles, Analysis of Project Finance in Developing Countries (London, 1981)

Harvey, Charles and Jake Jacobs, Rural Employment & Administration in the Third World (Brookfield, Vt., 1979)

Helleiner, G. K., A World Divided (New York, 1976)

Hong, Wontack and Laurence B. Krause, Trade and Growth of the Advanced Developing Countries (Honolulu, 1981)

International Labor Office, Employment Effects of Multinational Enterprises in Developing Countries (Geneva, 1981)

Jansen, Karel, Monetarism, Economic Crisis and the Third World (London, 1983)

Jones, Gavin W., The Economic Effect of Declining Fertility in Less Developed Countries (New York, 1969)

Jones, Leroy P., Public Enterprise in Less Developed Countries (New York, 1982)

Joshi, Nandini, The Challenge of Poverty: Developing Countries in the New International Order (Mystic, Conn., 1978)

Katz, Jeffrey A., Capital Flows and Developing Country Debt (Washington, D.C. 1979)

Kohr, Leopold, Development Without Aid (New York, 1979)

Krauss, M.B., Development Without Aid: Growth, Poverty and Government (New York, 1982)

Kuklinski, Antoni, Growth Poles & Growth Centers as Instruments of Modernization in Developing Countries (The Hague, 1977)

Kuprianov, A., Developing Countries: Internal Regional Disproportions in Growing Economies (New York, 1976)

Lall, Sanjaya, Developing Countries in the International Economy (New York, 1981)

Lehmann, David, Peasants, Landlords & Governments: Agrarian Reform in the Third World (New York, 1974)

Leipziger, Danny M. and James L. Mudge, Seabed Mineral Resources: The Economic Interests of Developing Countries (Cambridge, Mass., 1976)

Lin. Ching-Yuan, Developing Countries in a Turbulent World (New York, 1981)

Loehr, William and John P. Powelson, Threats to Development: Pitfalls of the NIE (Boulder, Colo., 1982)

Long, Frank, Restrictive Business Practices: Transnational Corporations and Development (Boston, 1981)

Lynch, James and Edward Tasch, Food Production and Public Policy in Developing Countries (New York, 1983)

MacAndrews C. and L.S. Chia, Developing Economies and the Environment: The Southeast Asia Experience (New York, 1982)

MacBean, Alastair and Balasubramanyam, V. N., Meeting the Third World Challenge (New York, 1976)

MacFarlane S. Neil, Superpower Rivalry and Third World Radicalism: The Idea of National Liberation (Baltimore, 1985)

MacKillop, Andrew, Oil Crisis and Economic Adjustment: Case Studies of the Developing Countries (New York, 1984)

Mandi, Peter, Education and Economic Growth in the Developing Countries (London, 1981)

Manirussaman, T., The Security of the Small State in the Third World (Canberra, 1982)

Mathews, R.L., Regional Disparities and Economic Development (Canberra, 1981)

Maxwell, Stanley, Scotland, Multinationals and the Third World (London, 1982)

McHale, John and Magda C. McHale, Basic Human Needs: A Framework for Action (New Brunswick, N.J., 1976)

Mehmet, Ozay, Economic Planning & Social Justice in Developing Countries (New York, 1978)

Mouly, J. and E. Costa, Employment Policies in Developing Countries (London, 1975)

Mountjoy, Alan B., Industrialization & Developing Countries (London, 1982)

Munslow, Barry and Henry Finch, Proletarianism in the Third World (London, 1984)

Nikbakht, Ehsan, Foreign Loans and Economic Performance: The Experience of the Less Developed Countries (New York, 1984)

Nobe, Kenneth C. and R. K. Sampath, Issues in Third World Development (Boulder, Colo., 1984)

OECD, The Employment Problem in Less Developed Countries (Brussels, 1971)

———, External Debt of Developing Countries (Paris, 1984)

———, Geographical Distribution of Financial Flows to Developing Countries (Paris, 1984)

Pitt, David, The Social Dynamics of Development (New York, 1976)

Pyatt, G., Social Accounting for Development Planning (New York, 1978)

Quadeer, M. A., Urbanization in the Third World: A Case Study of Lahore, Pakistan (New York, 1983)

Repetto, Robert, Economic Equality and Fertility in Developing Countries (Baltimore, Md., 1979)

Research Center for Cooperation with Developing Countries, Bibliography on Economic Cooperation among Developing Countries (Boulder, Colo., 1984)

Reynolds, Lloyd G., Economic Growth in the Third World, 1850-1980 (New Haven, Conn., 1985)

Rothstein, Robert L., The Weak in the World of the Strong: The Third World in the International System (New York, 1977)

Safa, Helen I., Toward a Political Economy of Urbanization in Third World Countries (New York, 1982)

Sandford, Stephen, Management of Pastoral Development in the Third World (New York, 1983)

Sauve, Pierre, Private Bank Lending and Developing Country Debt (Toronto, 1984)

Shaner, W. W., Project Planning for Developing Economies (New York, 1979)

Shifer, E., Management Sciences: Developing Countries & National Priorities (New York, 1977)

Sideri S. and S. Johns, Mining for Development in the Third World: Multinationals, State Enterprises and the International Economy (Elmsford, N.Y., 1981)

Simai, M., Developing Countries & International Class Conflicts (New York, 1979)

Sinclair, Stuart W., Urbanization & Labor Markets in Developing Countries (New York, 1978)

——, Third World Economic Handbook (London, 1983)

Sinha, R.K., Fiscal Policy for Developing Countries (Bombay, 1983)

Sorkin, Alan, Health Economics in Developing Nations (Lexington, Mass., 1976)

Stavenhagen, Rodolfo, Between Underdevelopment and Revolution: A Latin American Perspective (Bombay, 1981)

Stewart, Frances and Jeffrey James, The Economics of New Technology in Developing Countries (Boulder, Colo., 1982)

Stockwell, Edward G. and Karen A. Laidlaw, Third World Development: Problems and Prospects (Chicago, Ill., 1981)

Suriyakumaran, C., The Wealth of Poor Nations (New York, 1984)

Taylor, Lance, Macro Models for Developing Countries (New York, 1979)

Thirwall, A. P., Growth and Development: With Special Reference to Developing Economies (London, 1983)

Todaro, Michael P., Economic Development in the Third World (London, 1985)

Tullis, F. LaMond and W. Ladd Hollist, Food, the State and International Political Economy: Dilemmas of Developing Countries (Omaha, Neb., 1985)

Turner, Alan, The Cities of the Poor: Settlement Planning in Developing Countries (New York, 1980)

U Tun Wai, Economic Essays on Developing Countries (Boston, 1981)

Van Schendel, W., Peasant Mobility (The Hague, 1981)

Warren, Bill, Inflation & Wages in Underdeveloped Countries (Totowa, N.J., 1977)

Wells, Louis T., Jr., Third World Multinationals (Cambridge, Mass., 1983)

Wheeler, David, Human Resource Policies: Economic Growth and Demographic Change in Developing Countries (New York, 1984)

Whynes, David K., The Economics of Third World Military Expenditure (Austin, Tex., 1979)

Yusuf, Abdulqawi, Legal Aspects of Trade Preferences for Developing Countries (Boston, 1982)

V: Education

Altbach, Philip, Higher Education in Developing Countries: A Select Bibliography (Cambridge, Mass., 1970)

Berry, Jack, Language & Education in the Third World (The Hague, 1976)

Blaug, Mark, Education and the Employment Problem in Developing Countries (Geneva, 1981)

D'Aeth, Richard, Education & Development in the Third World (Lexington, Mass., 1976)

Ghosh, S. C., Educational Strategies in Developing Countries (Mystic, Conn., 1976)

Kelly, Gail P. and Carolyn M. Elliot, Women's Education in the Third World: Comparative Perspectives (Albany, N.Y., 1982)

Leonor, M. D., Unemployment, Schooling and Training in Developing Countries: Tanzania, Egypt, Philippines and Indonesia (London, 1985)

Lillis, Kevin M., School and Community in Less Developed Areas (London, 1985)

Mandi, Peter, Education and Economic Growth in the Developing Countries (Budapest, 1981)

Phillips, H. M., Basic Education: A World Challenge: Measures & Innovations for Children & Youth in Developing Countries (Paris, 1973)

Rowley, C. D., The Politics of Educational Planning in Developing Countries (Paris, 1972)

Sinclair, M. E., & Kevin Lillis, School & Community in the Third World (Totowa, N.J., 1980)

Smock, Audrey, Women's Education in Developing Countries (New York, 1981)

Watson, Keith, Education in the Third World (London, 1982)

Wells, Stuart, Instructional Technology in Developing Countries (New York, 1976)

VI: Finance

Arya, P. L., Social Accounting for Developing Countries (Columbia, Mo., 1976)

Ballance, R., The International Economy and Industrial Development: Trade and Investment in the Third World (London, 1982)

Bangs, Robert B., Financing Economic Development: Fiscal Policy for Emerging Countries (Chicago, 1968)

Bird, Graham, The International Monetary System & the Less Developed Countries (New York, 1979)

Caiden, Naomi and Aaron Wildavsky, Planning & Budgeting in Poor Countries (New Brunswick, N.J., 1980)

Clarke, W. M., Private Enterprise in Developing Countries (Elmsford, N.Y., 1966)

Coale, A. T., and E. M. Hoover, Population Growth & Economic Development in Low-Income Countries (Princeton, N.J., 1958)

Da Costa, Michael, Finance and Development: The Role of International Commercial Banks in the Third World (Boulder, Colo, 1982)

Das, Dilip K., Migration of Financial Resources to Developing Countries (New York, 1985)

Davey, Kenneth, Financing Regional Government: International Practices and Their Relevance to the Third World (New York, 1983)

Diamond, William, Development Banks (Baltimore, Md., 1957)

Due, John F., Indirect Taxation in Developing Economies (Baltimore, Md., 1970)

Eaton, Jonathan and Mark Gersovitz, Poor-Country Borrowing in Private Financial Markets and the Repudiation Issue (Princeton, N.J., 1981)

Feinberg, Richard E. and Valerina Kallab, Adjustment Crisis in the Third World (New Brunswick, N.J., 1984)

Ghosh, Pradip K., Foreign Aid and Third World Development (Westport, Conn., 1984)

Gutowski, Armin, Financing Problems of Developing Countries (New York, 1985)

International Monetary Fund, Interest Rate Policies in Developing Countries (Washington, D.C. 1983)

———, Foreign Direct Investment in Developing Countries (Washington, D.C. 1985)

Kurdar, Uner, Structure of the United Nations Economic Aid to Underdeveloped Countries (New York, 1969)

Kuz'Min, Stanislav, Developing Countries: Employment & Capital Investment (White Plains, N.Y., 1969)

LaPalombara, Joseph and Stephen Blank, Multinational Corporations & Developing Countries (New York, 1980)

Newlyn, W., The Financing of Economic Development (New York, 1978)

Nunnemkamp, Peter, The International Debt Crisis of the Third World: Cases and Consequences for the World Economy (New York, 1985)

Prakash, Ved, Financing Urban Development in Developing Countries (Paris, 1982)

Prest, A.R., Public Finance in Developing Countries (New York, 1985)

Tavis, Lee A., Multinational Managers and Poverty in the Third World (Notre Dame, Ind., 1984)

Thirwall, A. P., Inflation, Savings & Growth in Developing Countries (New York, 1975)

Valkenier, Elizabeth, The USSR, The Third World and The Global Economy (New York, 1983)

Wolfson, Dirk J., Public Finance & Development Strategy (Baltimore, Md., 1979)

VII: Politics

Al-Mashat, Abdul-Monem M., National Security in the Third World (Boulder, Colo., 1985)

Almond, Gabriel A., and James S. Coleman, Politics of the Developing Areas (Princeton, N.J., 1960)

Barnet, Richard J., Intervention & Revolution: The United States in the Third World (New York, 1969)

Calvez, Jean-Yves, Politics & Society in the Third World (Maryknoll, N.Y., 1973)

Chaliand, Gerard, Revolution in the Third World (New York, 1978)

Chatterjee, Lata and Peter Nijkamp, Urban and Regional Policy Analysis in Developing Countries (London, 1983)

Clapham, Christopher, Foreign Policy Making in Developing States (New York, 1979)

———, Third World Politics: An Introduction (Madison, Wis., 1985)

Clark, Robert P., Power & Policy in the Third World (New York, 1982)

Clawson, Robert W., East-West Rivalry in the Third World (Wilmington, Del., 1985)

Cochrane, Glynn, Policies for Strengthening Local Government in Developing Countries (Washington, D.C. 1983)

Dalton, George, Economic Systems and Society: Capitalism, Communism and the Third World (Boston, 1981)

DeSilva, S. B., The Political Economy of Underdevelopment (Boston, 1984)

Dhanapala, Jayantha, China and the Third World (Bombay, 1984)

Feinberg, Richard E., The Intemperate Zone: The Third World Challenge (New York, 1984)

Frank, Andre G., Crisis in the Third World (New York, 1981)

Gamer, Robert E., The Developing Nations: A Comparative Perspective (Boston, 1976)

Gant, George, Development Administration: Meaning & Application (Madison, Wis., 1979)

Gendzier, Irene L., Managing Political Change: Social Scientists in the Third World (Boulder, Colo., 1984)

Gould, David J., Bureaucratic Corruption in the Third World (Elmsford, N.Y., 1981)

———, **and Jose A., Amaro-Reyes,** The Effects of Corruption on Administrative Performance: Illustrations from Developing Countries (Washington, D.C. 1983)

Grindle, Merilee S., Politics & Policy Implementation in the Third World (Princeton, N.J., 1980)

Gurtov, Melvin and Maghroori, Ray, Roots of Failure: United States Policy in the Third World (Westport, Conn., 1984)

Hachey, Thomas E., and Ralph E. Weber, The Awakening of a Sleeping Giant: Third World Leaders & National Liberation (New York, 1980)

Harkavy, Robert E. and Stephanie G. Neuman, The Lessons of Recent Wars in the Third World: Approaches and Case Studies (Lexington, Mass., 1985)

Harris, Louise G., China's Foreign Policy Toward the Third World (New York, 1985)

Harrison, Paul, Inside the Third World (New York, 1982)

Horowitz, Irving, Beyond Empire and Revolution: Militarization and Consolidation in the Third World (New York, 1982)

Hough, Jerry F., The Struggle for the Third World: Soviet Debates and American Options (Washington, D.C. 1985)

Huntington, Samuel P., and Joan M. Nelson, No Easy Choice: Political Participation in Developing Countries (Cambridge, Mass., 1976)

Jones, Rodney W. and Steven A. Hildreth, Modern Weapons and Third World Powers (Boulder, Colo., 1984)

Kanet, Roger E., The Soviet Union & the Developing Nations (Baltimore, Md., 1974)

Kennedy, Gavin, Military in the Third World (New York, 1975)

Kolodziej, Edward and Robert Harkavy, Security Policies of Developing Countries (Lexington, Mass., 1982)

Korany, Baghat, Foreign Policy Decisions in the Third World (Boulder, Colo., 1985)

Kwiny, Jonathan, Endless Enemies: The Making of an Unfriendly World (New York, 1985)

Laqueur, Walter, The Pattern of Soviet Conduct in the Third World (New York, 1983)

Lea, David A. and D. P. Chaudhri, Rural Development and the State: Contradictions and Dilemmas in Developing Countries (London, 1983)

Lewis, John P. and Valerina Kallab, U.S. Foreign Policy and the Third World Agenda (New York, 1983)

Liska, George, Alliances and the Third World (Ann Arbor, Mich., 1984)

Manning, Hugh, Peacekeeping and Confidence-Building Measures in the Third World (New York, 1985)

Marrell, Kenneth and Robert Duffield, Management, Administration and Organization for the Developing World (West Hartford, Conn., 1985)

Matheson, Neil, The Rules, of the Game of Superpower Military Intervention in the Third World (Lanham, Md., 1982)

Mattalart, Armand, Transnationals and the Third World (Hadley, Mass., 1985)

Maurer, John H. and Richard H. Porth, Military Intervention in the Third World: Threats, Constraints and Options (New York, 1984)

Mawhood, Philip, Local Government for Development: The Experience of Tropical Africa (New York, 1983)

Mehta, Jagat S., Third World Militarization: A Challenge to Third World Diplomacy (Houston, Texas, 1985)

Migdal, Joel S., Peasants, Politics & Revolution: Pressures Toward Political & Social Change in the Third World (Princeton, N.J., 1974)

Moodie, Michael, Sovereignty, Security & Arms (Beverly Hills, Calif., 1979)

Moosbrugger, Bernhard and Gladys A. Weigner, Voice of the Third World: Dom Helder Camara (Philadelphia, Pa., 1972)

Mortimer, Robert A., The Third World Coalition in International Politics (Boulder, Colo., 1984)

Nagai, Michio, Development in the Non-Western World (New York, 1985)

Ohkaw, Kazushi and Gustav Ranis, Japan and the Developing Countries (London, 1985)

Palmer, Monte, Dimensions of Political Development (Chicago, Ill., 1985)

Parodi, Pierre, The Use of Poor Means in Helping the Third World (Weare, N.H., 1970)

Petras, James, Critical Perspectives on Imperialism & Social Class in the Third World (New York, 1979)

Provizer, Norman W., Analyzing the Third World (Cambridge, Mass., 1978)

Ra'anan, Uri, Third World Marxist-Leninist Regimes (Elmsford, N.Y., 1985)

Randall, Vicky and Robin Theobold, Political Change and Underdevelopment: A Critical Introduction to Third World Politics (Durham, N.C., 1985)

Ravenhill, John, Collective Clientism: The Lome Convention and North-South Relations (New York, 1985)

Rubinstein, Alvin Z. and Donald E. Smith, Anti-Americanism in the Third World: Implications for U.S. Foreign Policy (New York, 1985)

Sarkar, Goutam K., Commodities and the Third World (New York, 1983)

Silva-Michelena, Jose A., The Illusion of Democracy in Dependent Nations (Boston, Mass., 1971)

Simai, M., Developing Countries & International Class Conflict (New York, 1979)

Smith, Anthony D., State and Nation in the Third World: The Western State and African Nationalism (New York, 1983)

Somjee, A. H., Political Society in Developing Countries (New York, 1984)

Tachau, Frank, The Developing Nations: What Path to Modernization? (New York, 1972)

Thompson, Kenneth W., American Moral and Political Leadership in the Third World (Lanham, Md., 1985)

Vyasulu, Vinod, The Paradox of Static Change: Lectures on Underdevelopment (Mystic, Conn., 1978)

Webster, A., An Introduction to the Sociology of Development (London, 1984)

Welch, Claude E., Jr., Civilian Right & Military Might: Government Control of the Armed Forces in Developing Countries (Albany, N.Y., 1976)

Wheeler, David, Human Resource Policies, Economic Growth and Demographic Change in Developing Countries (New York, 1984)

White, Gordon, Revolutionary Socialist Development in the Third World (Louisville, Ky., 1983)

Willets, P., Non-Aligned Movement: Formation of a Third World Alliance (New York, 1979)

William, Gwyenth, Third World Political Organization (Totowa, N.J., 1981)

VIII: Social Conditions

American Universities Field Staff, City & Nation in the Developing World (Hanover, N.H., 1968)

Beckford, George L., Persistent Poverty: Underdevelopment in Plantation Regions of the Third World (New York, 1972)

Blacker, Frank, Social Psychology and Developing Countries (New York, 1984)

Brandt Commission, Common Crisis: North-South Cooperation for World Recovery (Cambridge, Mass., 1983)

Bulmer, Martin and Donald P. Warwick, Social Research in Developing Countries: Surveys and Censuses in the Third World (New York, 1983)

Buvinic, Mayra and Margaret A. Layette, Women and Poverty in the Third World (Baltimore, Md., 1983)

Caircross, J., Population and Agriculture in the Developing Countries (Paris, 1981)

Charlton, Sue E., Women in Third World Development (Boulder, Colo., 1984)

Conyers, Diana, An Introduction to Social Planning in the Third World (New York, 1981)

Dakhil, Fahd, Housing Problems in Developing Countries (New York, 1979)

Davies, Miranda, Third World-Second Sex: Women's Struggles and National Liberation (London, 1983)

Demeny, Paul and W. Parker Mauldin, Population Growth and Labor Absorption in the Developing World (New York, 1985)

Desai, A. R., Essays on Modernization of Underdeveloped Societies (New York, 1972)

Dwyer, D. J., People & Housing in Third World Cities (New York, 1979)

Eberstadt, Nick, Fertility Decline in the Less Developed Countries (New York, 1981)

Glaser, William A., The Brain Drain: Emigration & Return (Elmsford, N.Y., 1978)

Goldthorpe, J. E., The Sociology of the Third World (New York, 1975)

Hardman, Margaret and James Midgley, The Social Dimensions of Development: Social Policy and Planning in the Third World (New York, 1982)

Hernandez, Donald J., Success or Failure? Family Planning Programs in the Third World (Westport, Conn., 1984)

Hilhorst, J. G. and M. Klatter, Social Development in the Third World (London, 1985)

Hunter, Guy, Modernizing Peasant Societies (New York, 1969)

Huston, Perdita, Third World Women Speak Out (New York, 1979)

Improving Social Statistics in Developing Countries, UN Study (New York, 1979)

King, Maurice H., Medical Care in Developing Countries (New York, 1981)

Lillis, Kevin M., School and Community in Less Developed Areas (London, 1985)

Livingstone, Arthur, Social Policy in Developing Countries (New York, 1969)

MacPherson, Stewart, Social Policy in the Third World: The Social Dilemmas of Underdevelopment (London, 1982)

McAnany, Emile G., Communication in the Rural Third World (New York, 1980)

Midgley, James, Professional Imperialism: Social World in the Third World (London, 1981)

Murphy, Kathleen J., Macroproject Development in the Third World: An Analysis of Transnational Partnerships (Boulder, Colo., 1982)

Paccione, Michael, Problems and Planning in Third World Cities (New York, 1981)

Payne, Geoffrey K., Urban Housing in the Third World (London, 1977)

Rao, Usha, Women in a Developing Society (Bombay, 1984)

Rogers, Barbara, Domestication of Women: Discrimination in Developing Societies (London, 1981)

Schmitt, D., Dynamics of the Third World: Political & Social Change (Englewood Cliffs, N.J., 1974)

Sinclair, M. E., and Kevin Lillis, School & Community in the Third World (Totowa, N.J., 1980)

Swantz, Marja-Lisa, Women in Development: A Creative Role Denied? (New York, 1985)

Valdes, Alberto, Food Security for Developing Countries (Boulder, Colo., 1981)

Walton, John, Reluctant Rebels: Comparative Studies of Revolution and Underdevelopment (New York, 1984)

Wolpin, Miles D., Militarization, Internal Repression and Social Welfare in the Third World (New York, 1985).

Zelinsky, Wilbur, Geography & A Crowding World: Population Pressures on Physical & Social Resources in the Developing Lands (New York, 1970)

IX: Technical Assistance

Committee for Economic Development, Assisting Development in Low Income Countries (New York, 1969)

Curti, Merle E., and Kendall Birr, Prelude to Point Four: American Technical Missions Overseas, 1838-1938 (Westport, Conn., 1978)

Gordenker, Leon, International Aid & National Decisions (Princeton, N.J., 1976)

Griffith, Alison, Role of American Higher Education in Relation to Developing Areas (Washington, D.C., 1961)

Guth, W., Capital Exports to Less Developed Countries (Boston, 1963)

Hoselitz, Bert F., Progress of Underdeveloped Areas (Chicago, 1952)

Keenleyside, Hugh L., International Aid: A Summary (London, 1967)

Myrdal, Alva, America's Role in International Social Welfare (Boston, 1967)

Nau, Henry R., Technology Transfer & U.S. Foreign Policy (New York, 1976)

O'Kelly, Elizabeth, Aid & Self-Help: A General Guide to Overseas Aid (New York, 1973)

OECD, Choice & Adaptation of Technology in Developing Countries: An Overview of Major Policy Issues (Paris, 1974)

——————, The Evaluation of Technical Assistance (Paris, 1970)

Paddock, William and Elizabeth Paddock, We Don't Know How (Ames, Ia., 1973)

Poats, Rutherford M., Technology for Developing Nations: New Directions for U.S. Technical Assistance (Washington, D.C., 1972)

Ra'Anan, Uri, Arms Transfer to the Third World: Problems & Policies (Boulder, Col., 1978)

Richman, Barry M., and Melvyn R. Copen, International Management & Economic Development (New York, 1972)

Rubinstein, Alvin Z., Soviets in International Organizations: Changing Policies Toward Developing Countries (Princeton, N.J., 1964)

Spitzberg, Irving R., Exchange of Expertise: The Counterpart System in the New International Order (Boulder, Col., 1978)

Storm, William B., Administrative Alternatives in Development Assistance (Cambridge, Mass., 1973)

Sufrin, Sidney C., Technical Assistance: Theory & Guidelines (Syracuse, N.Y., 1966)

INDEX

BAJPAI, K. Shankar—881
BAJRA—888
BAJUN—1036, 1037, 1795
BAKARY, Djibo—1462
BAKELE—700
BAKGATLA—227, 229
BAKHTAR Afghan Airline—39
BAKHTIAR, Shahpur—942, 956
BAKHTIARI—939
BAKI, Boualem—52
BAKIGA—2037, 2039
BAKKUSH, Abdul Hamid—1221
BAKO (Ethnic Group)—666
BAKONGO—68, 476
BAKOY River—1714
BAKR, Ahmed Hasan al—965, 966, 980, 981
BAKWENA—227, 229
BAL, Slaheddine—1990
BALA Chinese—1264
BALAFREJ, Ahmed—1388
BALAGUER, Joaquin—557, 560, 560, 561, 562, 563, 573
BALALI—476
BALANGA, Ndjoli—2177
BALANQUERO—455
BALANTE—1715
BALBIN, Richard—97
BALBOA—1542
BALDE, Capt. Mamadou—786
BALENGUE—652
BALEWA, Alhaji Abubakar Tafawa—1489
BALI—909, 910, 911, 912
BALI, Maj. Gen. Domkat Ya—1476
BALIKESIR—2022
BALKANS—2006
BALLIVIAN, General Hugo—209
BALOPI, Patrick—230
BALOUNDOU-MBO—351
BALSA (Wood)—215, 1446
BALSAM (Medical Gum)—640
BALSAS River—1340
BALTERRA—262
BALTISTAN—1505, 1513
BALTODANO Cantarero, Emilio—1437
BALUCH, Mohyuddin—1510
BALUCHI, Ahmad bin Suwaydan al—32, 42, 954, 1495, 1496, 1501, 1505, 1508, 1513
BALUCHIS—32, 126, 939, 942, 1495, 1507, 1508, 2162
BALUCHISTAN—1506, 1507, 1508, 1512, 1513, 1524, 1525, 1703
BALUCHISTAN Plateau—1506
BALUCHISTAN, University of—1522
BAMA—281
BAMAKA—1304
BAMAKO—1295, 1297, 1299, 1304, 1305, 1306
BAMALETE—227, 229
BAMANGWATO—227, 229
BAMANGWATO Concessions Ltd.—236
BAMBARA—716, 985, 1295, 1297, 1310, 1311, 1715
BAMBARI—379, 381
BAMBOO—150, 774
BAMENDA—349
BAMILEKE—351, 352
BAMINA, Joseph—319, 327
BAMOUM—351, 352
BAMRAULI—896
BANABA—1058
BANANA, Rev. Canaan—2215, 2219
BANANAS—74, 186, 215, 255, 323, 358, 374, 385, 450, 469, 483, 484, 502, 504, 526, 552, 553, 567, 588, 656, 657, 692, 693, 706, 736, 754, 773, 792, 821, 822, 839, 848, 853, 855, 856, 861, 922, 990, 992, 1008, 1009, 1010, 1060, 1062, 1160, 1194,

1235, 1236, 1499, 1540, 1559, 1563, 1576, 1624, 1654, 1673, 1681, 1689, 1725, 1738, 1745, 1754, 1789, 1802, 1803, 1804, 1844, 1859, 1860, 1914, 1935, 1955, 1967, 1968, 2088, 2104, 2140, 2167, 2185, 2191, 2205, 2226
BANANAS Islands—1747
BANARJY, Krishna—877
BANCO di Roma—612
BANDA—379, 380, 1245, 1246, 1247, 1248, 1249, 1250, 1258
BANDA, Hastings—1243, 1247, 1258
BANDA, Kapichira—1247
BANDA, Richard K.—2199
BANDA, Richard Mussa—1247
BANDAMA River—983, 991, 992
BANDAR Abbas—951, 952
BANDAR Pahlavi—951, 952
BANDAR Shahpur—950, 951
BANDARANAIKE., Mrs. Sirimavo—881, 1815, 1819, 1823, 1828, 1829, 1830
BANDARANAIKE, Solomon West Ridgway Dias—1815, 1819, 1829
BANDIRMA—2022
BANDUNG—909, 928, 931, 932
BANDUNG Conference—345
BANDUNG, Institut Teknologi—928
BANERJEE, A.N.—877
BANFORA—281, 289
BANGALA—476
BANGALORE—866, 879, 896, 900
BANGKOK—1101, 1923, 1924, 1926, 1927, 1932, 1934, 1936, 1938, 1939, 1941, 1942, 1943
BANGKOK Post—1942
BANGLA Language—142, 154
BANGLADESH—139-157, 196, 300, 301, 302, 312, 865, 868, 880, 881, 902, 1507, 1513, 1524, 1525, 2058
BANGLADESH Biman (Airline)—152
BANGLADESH Press International—154
BANGLADESH Sangbad Sangasta (News Agency)—154
BANGUI—379, 380, 381, 384, 387, 388, 389, 390
BANGURA, John—1748, 1760
BANGWAKETSI—227, 229
BANGWEULU, Lake—2196, 2207
BANH, Tea—336
BANI-SADR, Abolhassan—942, 956
BANIAS—968, 974, 1892, 1893
BANIRI—380
BANIYAS—976
BANJARMASIN—909
BANJUL—715, 717, 718, 719, 722, 723, 724, 725
BANK of America—423, 501, 2075
BANKING—119, 131, 163, 184, 468, 552, 838, 947, 956, 993, 1024, 1454, 1672, 1681, 1726, 1787, 2088, 2224
BANNY, Jean Konan—986
BANQUE Centrale des Etats de l'Afrique de l'Ouest (BCEAO)—287, 991, 1723, 1954
BANQUE de Paris et des Pays-Bas Gabon—706
BANQUE des Etats de l'Afrique Centrale (BEAC)—355, 384, 401, 706
BANQUE Internationale pour l'Afrique Occidentale—706
BANQUE Internationale pour le Commerce et l'Industrie Gabon—706
BANTI, Teferi—670

BANTON—1614
BANTU—67, 69, 351, 380, 476, 652, 700, 1035, 1173, 1243, 1245, 1649, 1795, 1901, 1904, 2039, 2175, 2195, 2217
BANTU Language—318, 352, 1649
BANYANKORE—2037, 2039
BANYARUANDA—2037, 2039
BANYAT Bantadta—1929
BANYORO—2037, 2039
BANZA, Col. Alexandre—390
BANZER Suarez, General Hugo—207, 216, 223
BAOULE—985
BAPHETLA—1172
BAPHUTHI—1172
BAPPOO, Sheila—1328
BAPTISTS—69, 93, 116, 298, 477, 1003, 1905
BAQDASH, Khaled—1886
BAQJAJI, Dr. Saba—1884
BAQUERO Davila, Col. Angel—596
BARA—1227
BARABANG—1904
BARAGUYU—1904
BARAHONA—569, 570, 571
BARAKAMFITIYE, Damien—320
BARAKAT, Ahmad Qa'id—2147
BARAM River—1262
BARANCIRA, Cyrille—320
BARAQUISIMETO—2107
BARBA—494
BARBALHO, Jáder Fontenelle—249
BARBOT, Clement—844
BARBOUR, Robert E.—1857
BARBUDA—81
BARCELONA—2099, 2108
BARCELOS, Manuel—803
BARCELUS, Annibal—249
BARCLAYS Bank—612, 1008, 1014
BARCO Vargas, Virgilio—437, 442, 443
BARDO—1987
BARGUE—1393
BARIBA—179, 180, 181, 190
BARINAS—2099
BARISAL—139
BARITE—59, 1196
BARKAT, Gourad Hamadou—540
BARKER, E.W.—1766
BARLAVENTO—369
BARLETTA Vallarino, Nicolas Ardito—1533
BARLEY—38, 56, 101, 215, 422, 423, 450, 588, 613, 614, 676, 888, 889, 948, 972, 973, 1025, 1045, 1076, 1096, 1097, 1160, 1215, 1353, 1380, 1517, 1598, 1599, 1702, 1889, 1995, 2017, 2018, 2075, 2152, 2153, 2167
BARLTROP, Roger A.R.—690
BARMOU, Salaou—1460
BARNES, Jr., Harry G.—419
BARO River—664
BAROA—1172
BAROLONG—227, 229
BARQU, Barry Mouss—1950
BARQUISIMETO—2093, 2096, 2099, 2108, 2109
BARR, Justin Dam—284
BARRANCABERMEJA—450
BARRANQUILLA—438, 444, 450, 453, 454, 455, 457
BARRE, Siad—1796, 1797
BARRENTO, Rui—803
BARRI, Nabih—1153
BARRIENTOS, Brig. Gen. (Ret.) César—1571
BARRIENTOS Ortuno, Rene—222
BARRIONUEVO, Hugo—95
BARRIOS de Chamarro, Violeta—1437, 1454

BARROS, Filinto de—803
BARROW, Dean O.—171
BARROW, Errol W.—161, 162, 167
BARROW, Nigel Ansley—161, 162, 167
BARRY-BATTESTI, Ange François—986
BARRY, Dr. Mariama Dielo—786
BARTHE, Obdulio—1574
BARTHOLOMEW, Reginald—1155
BARTLETT Díaz, Manuel—1345
BARTLETT, Edmund—1003
BARTUREN Duenas, Mario—1591
BARWOOD—706
BARZANI, Mustafa al—980
BASHIR, Mohammed el—1031
BASIA—1172
BASOGA—2037, 2039
BASOTHAN—1171, 1182
BASOTHO—1171, 1172, 1173, 1175
BASQUES—413
BASRA—961, 962, 968, 973, 974, 975, 976, 977, 978, 979
BASRA University—978
BASRI, Driss—1373
BASSA—351, 1187
BASSAC—340
BASSARI—1715, 1947, 1948, 1949, 1952
BASSE—715
BASSEIN—295, 296, 306, 307, 308
BASSOUNDI—476
BASU, Jyoti—877, 883
BATA—651, 652, 656, 657, 658, 659
BATA, Dr. Ronald—2042
BATAK—909, 911, 912
BATALOKWA—227, 229
BATANGAS—1612, 1619, 1628
BATAUNG—1172
BATAWANA—227, 229
BATCHI, Stanislas—480
BATEKE—476
BATES, Ronald H.T.—703
BATHEPU—1172
BATHOEN—232
BATISTA y Zaldivar, Fulgencio E.—516, 519, 534
BATLLE Ibanez, Jorge—2073
BATLLE y Barres, Luis—2071, 2081
BATLLE y Ordonnez, Jose—2069, 2073
BATLOKOA—1172
BATNA—52
BATOKO, Ousmane—182
BATOMBA—180
BATORO—2037, 2039
BATRES, Porfirio Morera—496
BATTAMBANG—331
BATTAMBANG, University of—344
BATTERIES—1673
BATUAN—1612
BATUBARA, Cosmas—914
BATUTSI—317
BAUCHI—1478
BAUGH, Dr. Kenneth—1003
BAURE—206
BAUXITE—261, 290, 343, 362, 388, 454, 487, 505, 567, 569, 570, 740, 790, 794, 807, 819, 822, 824, 841, 895, 927, 951, 1010, 1011, 1196, 1238, 1276, 1277, 1403, 1752, 1756, 1757, 1788, 1853, 1858, 1860, 1861, 1862, 1981, 2021
BAUXITE Association, International—794, 823, 1013, 1857
BAWSHAR—1493
BAY Islands—847, 849, 850, 856, 859
BAYA—351
BAYA-MANDJIA—379, 380

1980, 1996, 2019, 2019, 2059, 2060
GASOLINE—75, 103, 150, 187, 216, 257, 288, 306, 324, 424, 451, 527, 568, 589, 641, 737, 774, 793, 840, 857, 891, 924, 949, 973, 994, 1009, 1026, 1046, 1098, 1122, 1161, 1194, 1215, 1237, 1253, 1274, 1303, 1318, 1356, 1381, 1401, 1426, 1447, 1465, 1483, 1518, 1540, 1559, 1577, 1600, 1626, 1655, 1702, 1726, 1755, 1774, 1804, 1824, 1844, 1890, 1915, 1936, 1955, 1980, 1996, 2019, 2046, 2076, 2105, 2127, 2186, 2206
GASSI el Adem—57
GASSI Touil—57
GASTÓN Araoz Levy—208
GASTROINTESTINAL Disorders—237, 471, 572, 645, 743, 778, 860, 1257, 1387, 1405, 1451, 1729, 1759, 1827, 1895, 1983, 2230
GATKUOTH Gwal, Peter—1838
GAY, Dr. Norman—117
GAYA—1465
GAYAN, Anil—1328
GAYOOM, Maumoon Abdul—1285, 1287, 1292
GAZA strip—607, 624, 880
GAZIANTEP—2005
GBANDI—1187
GBAYA—351
GBEDEMAH, K.A.—744
GBENYE, Christophe—2192
GEBA, the Corubal—801
GEGE-NAGO—245
GEISEL, Ernesto—247, 248, 267
GEMAYEL, Amin—1147, 1152, 1153
GEMAYEL, Pierre—1156
GEMSTONES—1826, 2189
GENDA, Ambrose—1748
GENERAL Motors Corp.—423, 424
GENERAL Organization for Assistance to Southern Arabia and the Gulf—1120
GENERAL Petroleum Co.—615
GENERAL Telephone and Electronic International—386
GENEVA—1144
GENEVA Conference on Indochina—345
GENIA, Jack—1554
GEORGE, Henry—551
GEORGETOWN—813, 814, 823, 824, 825, 827, 1262
GEORGIANS—2007
GERMAN–DESCENT Groups—206, 243, 244, 333, 351, 413, 440, 495, 631, 764, 1187, 1590, 2139
GERMAN Language—92, 221, 375, 580, 620, 833, 939, 1362, 1410, 1553, 1581, 1614, 1747, 2008, 2023, 2046, 2069, 2136
GERMAN Evangelical Synod—93
GERMANIA—1569
GERMANY—261, 947, 1190, 1554, 2081, 2136
GERMANY, East—482, 525, 732, 1190, 1403, 1461
GERMANY, West—52, 58, 59, 61, 74, 96, 103, 308, 322, 373, 374, 427, 429, 447, 454, 455, 482, 506, 571, 591, 611, 618, 681, 705, 720, 733, 740, 780, 788, 792, 794, 795, 797, 805, 885, 891, 885, 895, 927, 976, 978, 979, 991, 995, 1046, 1049, 1087, 1099, 1101, 1137, 1196, 1197, 1210, 1303, 1334, 1355, 1371, 1378, 1382, 1384, 1427, 1428, 1466, 1486, 1520, 1522, 1600, 1602, 1628, 1653, 1727, 1740, 1750, 1776, 1799, 1820, 1825,

1841, 1846, 1847, 1887, 1892, 1938, 1956, 1992, 1993, 1999, 2000, 2006, 2013, 2019, 2021, 2022, 2068, 2151, 2154, 2190, 2208
GERVIL-YAMBALA, Lt. Col. Jean-Louis—382
GESSESSE Wolde Kidan, Capt.—671
GESTIDO, Oscar—2071, 2081
GETTY Oil Co.—1702
GEWA—155
GEZIRA Province—1838
GHABBASH, Muhammad—1884
GHAFIRI—1495
GHAGHRA River—867
GHALI, Boutros Boutros—605
GHANA—232, 282, 351, 487, 721, **727-746**, 732, 788, 797, 1194, 1199, 1464, 1750, 1871, 1948, 1952, 1956
GHANA News Agency—1052, 1488
GHANA, University of—741
GHANHALLAH, Ahmed Ould—1312
GHANI, Abdul Aziz Abdul—2157
GHANIM, Dr. Faraj ibn—2164
GHANZI—231
GHAR Yunis University of Benghazi—1219
GHASHMI, Lt. Col. Ahmed Hussein al—2157
GHAYTH, Sa'id al—2056
GHAZALI, Ahmad bin Abdullah al—1495
GHAZALI, Col. Salim bin Abdullah al—1495
GHAZAOUET—59
GHAZOUANI, Rachid—1373
GHIASI, Burhan—33
GHILZAIS—32
GHURBURRUN, Beergoonath—1328
GIA Lam—2129
GIANNATTASIO, Luis—2071, 2081
GIAP, Gen. Vo Nguyen—2128, 2129
GIBARA—529
GIBBS, Oswald M.—752
GIBE—666
GIHENO, John—1554
GILANI, Yusuf Reza—1510
GILANIS (Ethnic Group)—939
GILGIT—1505, 1513, 1521
GILLESPIE, Jr., Charles A.—445
GILLMORE, D.H.—1269
GILMOUR, Dr. Mavis—1003
GIMENEZ Ruiz, Eliseo—1347
GIMIRA—666
GINGER—693, 1008, 1681
GIO—1187
GIRAY, Safa—2011
GIRI, Rudra Prasad—1421
GIRI, Tulsi—1430
GIRON, Maj. Sergio Enrique—596
GISCARD d'Estaing, Valery—390
GISENYI—1647
GISSET, Alphonse—478
GISU—2039
GIZA—599, 621
GIZENGA, Antoine—2192
GLASS—74
GLASSPOLE, Florizel A.—1001, 1003
GLAZE, James—355
GLOVER, Michaël James Kevin—1328
GOA—896
GOAN—1258
GOASCORAN River—847, 848
GOATS–*SEE* chapter headings, subhead Agriculture
GOBA—672
GOBAWEIN—1795
GODAVARI River—867, 894

GODOY Caceres, Hector Garcia—561
GODOY Jiménez, Adán—1571
GOGO—1904
GOGRAS—895
GOH Chok Tong—1766
GOIANIA—242, 243, 249
GOITER—200, 264, 457, 1759
GOLA—1185, 1187, 1747
GOLAN Heights—607, 1879, 1885, 1897
GOLCUK—2022
GOLD—218, 236, 261, 307, 325, 428, 454, 505, 567, 573, 591, 618, 679, 694, 709, 740, 776, 824, 858, 995, 1049, 1101, 1196, 1276, 1359, 1403, 1449, 1485, 1561, 1602, 1603, 1628, 1629, 1700, 1846, 1853, 1862, 2108, 2155, 2168, 2189, 2229
GOLDEN Triangle—1931
GOLDING, Bruce—1003
GOLDSON, Philip—171
GOLFITO—505
GOLKAR—932
GOLOM Yoma, Routouang—397
GOMA, Lameck K. H.—2199
GOMAL University—1522
GOMBADI, Col. Alphonse—382
GOMES, Alberto Lima—803
GOMES, Dr. Ireneu—371
GOMES, Pedro Godinho—803
GÓMEZ Alvarez, Felipe—2097
GOMEZ Castro, Laureano—442
GOMEZ, Laureano—459
GÓMEZ, Maj. Gen. Manuel Antonio Cuervo—560
GÓMEZ Ortega, Adm. Miguel Angel—1345
GOMEZ, Raul—2099
GONAIVES—831, 840, 842, 843
GONDAR—663, 671, 672
GONGA, Othello—1189
GONORRHEA—2049
GONTHIER, Mrs. Giovinella—1736
GONZALE, Carlos Hank—1347
GONZALES, Jose Antonio—1616
GONZALES, Juan Jose Torres—209
GONZALES, Neptali—1616
GONZÁLES Posada, Luis—1591
GONZALEZ Alvear, Gen. Raul—596
GONZÁLEZ Avelar, Miguel—1345
GONZALEZ Blanco, Solomon—1347
GONZÁLEZ Camacho, Ricardo—633
GONZALEZ, Juan Natalicio—1570, 1584
GONZALEZ Lopez, Luis Arturo—765, 780
GONZALEZ, Luis Jose—2099
GONZÁLEZ, Odalier Villalobos—496
GONZALEZ Videla, Gabriel—432
GOODENOUGH Island—1551
GOPALLAWA, William—1829
GOPAYEGHANI, Mohammed Riza—940
GORDON, Marilyn—1976
GORDON, Minita—171
GORGONA Island—437, 457
GORGONILLA Island—437
GOROKA—1551
GOROKOA—1563
GOROWA—1904
GORRIARAN, Enrique—98
GOSHA—1795
GOSHU Wolde, Lt. Col.—671
GOUDJIL, Salah—52
GOULART, Joao—247, 266
GOULED Aptidon, Hassan—545
GOUMBA, Abel—383
GOUN (Ethnic Group)—180

GOURAD Hamadou, Barkad—540, 545
GOURGUE, Gérard—834
GOURMA—282, 283
GOURO—985
GOUROUNSI—282, 283
GOVERNMENT–*SEE* chapter headings, subheads Constitution and Government; Local Government; Parliament; Political Parties
GOVERNMENT Employees–*See* chapter headings, subhead Civil Service
GOWA—2197
GOWON, Lt. Col. Yakubu—1475, 1489
GOYZUETA Weissback, Eduardo—766
GRACIAS de Dios—1453
GRAIN—43, 103, 255, 889, 972, 1074, 1075
GRAN Chaco—1567
GRAN Colombia University—456
GRANADA—1433, 1436, 1441, 1449, 1451
GRANADINO (Wood)—856
GRAND Bahama Island—115, 118, 122
GRAND Bassam Island—988
GRAND Port Range—1325
GRAND Zacate Island—847
GRANDE Comore Island—463, 464
GRANDE Riviere Sud-Est—1325
GRANT, Cedric Hilburn—819
GRAPEFRUIT—553, 1803, 1844, 1860, 1979, 2185
GRAPES—56, 1097, 1160, 1215, 1380, 1702, 1889, 1995, 2017, 2153
GRAPHITE—1238, 1826
GRAU San Martin—534
GRAY, Maj. Yudu S.—1189
GREAT Britain *See* United Kingdom
GREAT Burgan Field—1122
GREAT East African Plateau—315
GREAT Usutu River—1867
GREBO—1187
GREECE—386, 618, 1218, 2013
GREEK Language—323, 1215, 1218, 1989, 2008, 2022, 2027, 2162
GREEK Orthodox Church—116, 540, 1019, 1150, 1151, 1155, 1882
GREEKS–DESCENT Group—351, 540, 601, 665, 667, 1205, 1215, 1228, 1835, 2006, 2007, 2008, 2175, 2197
GREEN, Hamilton—813, 816
GREEN, Muriel—1976
GREENHEART (Wood)—821
GREENIDGE, Carl—816
GREENVILLE—1196
GREGORIAN Church—964, 1150, 1882
GRELOMBE, Lt. Col. Christophe—382
GRENADA—749-758, 750, 755
GRENADINES—749, 750
GRENVILLE—755
GRIFFITH, Clyde—161
GRIFFITH, Edward G.—1679
GRIJALVA River—1340
GROUNDNUTS—74, 186, 234, 255, 288, 305, 323, 341, 359, 385, 401, 402, 484, 676, 706, 719, 721, 736, 792, 806, 807, 889, 922, 992, 1139, 1215, 1236, 1253, 1302, 1317, 1353, 1464, 1482, 1517, 1559, 1576, 1624, 1654, 1681, 1724, 1725, 1752, 1754, 1803, 1844, 1914, 1935, 1955, 2045, 2127, 2185, 2205

T